ROBERT BROWNING: SELECTED POEMS

EDITED BY

John Woolford
Daniel Karlin
Joseph Phelan

Longman
is an imprint of

Harlow, England • London • New York • Boston • San Francisco • Toronto
Sydney • Tokyo • Singapore • Hong Kong • Seoul • Taipei • New Delhi
Cape Town • Madrid • Mexico City • Amsterdam • Munich • Paris • Milan

PEARSON EDUCATION LIMITED

Edinburgh Gate
Harlow CM20 2JE
United Kingdom
Tel: +44 (0)1279 623623
Fax: +44 (0)1279 431059
Website: www.pearsoned.co.uk

First edition published in Great Britain in 2010

© Pearson Education Limited 2010

ISBN: 978-1-4058-4113-9

British Library Cataloguing in Publication Data
A CIP catalogue record for this book can be obtained from the British Library

10 9 8 7 6 5 4 3 2 1
14 13 12 11 10

Set in 10.5/11.5pt Bembo by 35
Printed in Malaysia (CTP-VVP)

The Publisher's policy is to use paper manufactured from sustainable forests.

Contents

Note by the General Editors

Longman Annotated English Poets was launched in 1965 with the publication of Kenneth Allott's edition of *The Poems of Matthew Arnold*. F. W. Bateson wrote that the 'new series is the first designed to provide university students and teachers, and the general reader with complete and fully annotated editions of the major English poets'. That remains the aim of the series, and Bateson's original vision of its policy remains essentially the same. Its 'concern is primarily with the *meaning* of the extant texts in their various contexts'. The two other main principles of the series were that the text should be modernized and the poems printed 'as far as possible in the order in which they were composed'.

These broad principles still govern the series. Its primary purpose is to provide an annotated text giving the reader any necessary contextual information. However, flexibility in the detailed application has proved necessary in the light of experience and the needs of a particular case (and each poet is, by definition, a particular case).

First, proper glossing of a poet's vocabulary has proved essential and not something which can be taken for granted. Second, modernization has presented difficulties, which have been resolved pragmatically, trying to reach a balance between sensitivity to the text in question and attention to the needs of a modern reader. Thus, to modernize Browning's text has a double redundancy: Victorian conventions are very close to modern conventions, and Browning had firm ideas on punctuation. Equally, to impose modern pointing on the ambiguities of Marvell would create a misleading clarity. Third, in the very early days of the series Bateson hoped that editors would be able in many cases to annotate a *textus receptus*. That has not always been possible, and where no accepted text exists or where the text is controversial, editors have been obliged to go back to the originals and create their own text. The series has taken, and will continue to take, the opportunity not only of providing thorough annotations not available elsewhere, but also of making important scholarly textual contributions where necessary. A case in point is the edition of *The Poems of Tennyson* by Christopher Ricks, the Second Edition of which (1987) takes into account a full collation of the Trinity College Manuscripts, not previously available for an edition of this kind. Yet the series' primary purpose remains annotation.

The requirements of a particular author take precedence over principle. It would make little sense to print Herbert's *Temple* in the order of composition even if it could be established. Where Ricks rightly decided that Tennyson's reader needs to be given the circumstances of composition, the attitude to Tennyson and his circle, allusions, and important variants, a necessary consequence was the exclusion of twentieth-century critical responses. Milton, however, is a very different case. John Carey and Alastair Fowler, looking to the needs of their readers, undertook synopses of the main lines of the critical debate over Milton's poetry. Finally, chronological ordering by date of composition will almost always have a greater or lesser degree of speculation or arbitrariness. The evidence is usually partial, and is confused further by the fact that poets do not always write one poem at a time and frequently revise at a later period than that of composition.

John Barnard
Paul Hammond

Introduction

This selection from the poems of Robert Browning is drawn from the Longman *Annotated English Poets* edition, of which three volumes have appeared: vol. I (1826–1840), vol. II (1841–1846) and vol. III (1847–1861). Errors and misprints have been corrected, and there are some new and revised notes. It also includes some items from the forthcoming vol. IV (1862–1871). This selection therefore presents work from the period when nearly all of Browning's best-known poetry was published. This introduction draws in part upon the introduction to the first volume of our edition.

I *Principles of this Selection*

Of Browning's longer single-volume poems we include *Pauline* (1833) and *Pippa Passes* (1842). *Pauline* was his first published poem, and is of interest not only for its curious publication history—it appeared anonymously, only to be immediately withdrawn, reappearing, revised, thirty-five years later in 1868—but also for its place in Browning's poetic development. It constitutes a crucial act of poetic self-definition, in which Browning reflects on and transforms his Romantic inheritance. It is thus, in more than one sense, a manifesto, representing the fraught transition from Romantic to Victorian poetics, a process continued, with some popular success, in *Paracelsus* (1835), but disastrously in *Sordello* (1840), the most catastrophic poetic failure of the nineteenth century. *Pippa Passes* was the first poem published after this *débâcle*, and represents in this selection Browning's early love-affair with the drama. In the period 1837–1855 he published nine plays, of which two—*Strafford* (1837) and *A Blot in the 'Scutcheon* (1843)—were produced, without much success, at Drury Lane Theatre by the actor-manager William Macready; two, *King Victor and King Charles* (1842) and *The Return of the Druses* (1843), were rejected by Macready; one, *Colombe's Birthday* (1843), was accepted by Macready's rival Charles Kean, but not produced by him (though it was eventually staged in 1853); the others, *Pippa Passes*, *Luria* (1846), *A Soul's Tragedy* (1846) and *In a Balcony* (1855), were not offered to any theatre and were probably not intended to be (though some, notably *In a Balcony*, have been produced subsequently). With *Paracelsus* they therefore form contributions to the genre of the unacted drama, founded by Goethe's *Faust* and continued in such English Romantic contributions as Byron's *Manfred* and Shelley's *Prometheus Unbound*. The LAEP policy is to include unacted dramas, but exclude plays written for the stage.

All Browning's plays (except *Strafford*, which was published separately in 1837, and *In a Balcony*, which appeared in *Men and Women*) were published in a series of pamphlets entitled *Bells and Pomegranates* (1841–1846), a venture designed to re-establish Browning's popular standing after *Sordello*. This series also contained Browning's first collections of shorter poems,

Dramatic Lyrics (1842) and *Dramatic Romances and Lyrics* (1845). *Dramatic Lyrics* included the earlier *Porphyria* and *Johannes Agricola* (both published in the *Monthly Repository* in 1836); dramatic lyrics similar to these (such as *Soliloquy of the Spanish Cloister*); and the earliest examples of the genre with which Browning is peculiarly associated, the dramatic monologue (distinguished from the dramatic lyric by the implied presence of a listener or interlocutor). Browning's earliest dramatic monologue, *My Last Duchess* (1842), remains his most celebrated poem, though *The Tomb at St. Praxed's* (*Dramatic Romances and Lyrics*) was the first to be written in blank verse, possibly influenced by Tennyson's *St. Simeon Stylites*, published in 1842. Most of the long or medium-length dramatic monologues that dominate Browning's best-known collections, *Men and Women* (1855) and *Dramatis Personae* (1864), are in blank verse, e.g. *Fra Lippo Lippi, Andrea del Sarto, Bishop Blougram's Apology, Cleon* (all 1855); *Caliban upon Setebos, A Death in the Desert* and *Mr. Sludge, "the Medium"* (all 1864). However, there are notable monologues in various rhyme schemes, e.g. *Two in the Campagna* (1855) and *Dîs Aliter Visum* (1864).

Both *Men and Women* and *Dramatis Personae* also include poems in other genres. These are mainly dramatic lyrics, such as *Childe Roland to the Dark Tower came* (1855) and *Abt Vogler* (1864); but *Men and Women* also includes a one-act play (*In a Balcony*), and other, less easily classifiable works such as the pseudo-medieval 'interlude' *The Heretic's Tragedy*, while *Dramatis Personae* has Browning's only 'sequence' poem, *James Lee*.

Our policy in this selection has been to include works in all the genres to which Browning contributed, and works generally regarded as his most significant and successful. In addition we provide, in appendices, other helpful material: his principal prose work and major aesthetic manifesto, known as the 'Essay on Shelley' (1852); his correspondence with John Ruskin concerning *Men and Women* (1856); and accounts of the collections represented in this volume, *Bells and Pomegranates, Men and Women* and *Dramatis Personae*.

II *Editorial Policy*

Our editorial policy follows that of the *LAEP* edition as a whole. We print the poems in their order of composition, as far as that can be determined, using the texts of their first published editions (obvious misprints are corrected). The following rationale for our choice of the first-edition texts is taken from vol. I:

> It is arguable . . . that an author's earlier intentions may have as great a claim on a modern reader's attention as his final ones. A poem, or any other literary work, on its first publication emerges from, and enters into, a particular historical and biographical context which determines important elements of its identity. This frame of reference is progressively attenuated in subsequent republications, since the historical and biographical context necessarily changes, and while it is clear that alterations to the text may be designed precisely to adapt it to this

changing context, that very process creates a fresh historical identity for the poem and to that extent marks a change in the writer's intention. The context of the publication of *Pauline* in 1833—a young writer's anonymous first attempt—differs sharply from that of its republication, over fifty years later, in the *Poetical Works* of 1888–9—an established public figure's valediction. There can, then, be no 'best text', since each text, as the representative of a different intention, possesses a differing rather than a cumulative value; and if the final text has, as this argument implies, no greater claim to authority than any other, the question becomes, which text presents the most interesting and important realization of its historical contingency? In our view, the answer in Browning's case is the first edition text. A suggestive example is *The Lost Leader*, originally a satire inspired by Wordsworth's assumption of the Poet Laureateship in 1843, but increasingly at odds, as Browning himself clearly felt, with his own growing respect for Wordsworth, especially in the years after the poet's death. Accordingly, the language of the poem modulates from 'Strike our face hard ere we shatter his own' (*1845*: l. 30) to 'Aim at our heart ere we pierce through his own' (*1849*) to 'Menace our heart ere we master his own' (*1863–88*)—moving away from direct physical aggression . . . The rationale of the LAEP series, which aims to present a poet's work in the chronological order of its *composition*, makes our choice of the first published text as copy-text especially appropriate. (I xiii–xiv).

It should be added that across time this policy makes a steadily decreasing amount of difference: Browning revised his early poetry quite heavily in his first collected edition (*1849*), and while he withdrew many of these changes in *1863*, many were allowed to stand. Subsequent poems are much less heavily revised, though exceptions exist (see, for instance, section viii of *James Lee*, pp. 680–4). In most instances, the first edition is fairly close to the final text; and Browning himself, in a comment on Wordsworth's practice, expressed a preference for the originally published text.

III *Annotation*

a) The headnote

The primary rationale of this selection, like that of the complete edition from which it derives, is annotation, and this volume can reasonably claim to be the only fully annotated selection of the poems of Browning yet published. For each poem we give in a headnote:

a) its publication history;
b) its date, where ascertainable, and an account of its process of composition, if obtainable;
c) sources and influences (biographical and historical contexts, the history of ideas, literary sources and parallels)
d) parallels in other Browning poems.

Where necessary, categories are added, as for instance for *Pauline*, which has a section on *Story and structure*. Where we give an account of a poem's critical reception, this is normally restricted (as in the LAEP *Tennyson*) to comments by contemporaries or near-contemporaries: considerations of space make extensive citation of modern criticism impracticable.

b) Textual notes

Textual notes are indicated by a square bracket after the word or phrase, as in *The Tomb at St. Praxed's*:

> 73. *I shall have*] have I not (*1845–88*).

or after the line number if the whole line is concerned, as in *England in Italy*:

> 11.] All the memories plucked at Sorrento (*1849*).

The dates in brackets indicate the edition or editions where the variant reading appears. When a variant appears in a succession of editions, we specify the first and last: (*1849–88*) means that the variant in question appeared in every edition published between 1849 and 1888, whereas (*1849, 1888*) would indicate that the variant appears in these two editions only, and that other editions between these dates correspond to the first-edition reading (or offer different readings, which we record separately). In general, where volumes of selections bear the same date as those of collected editions, the date of the latter is deemed to include that of the former, so that (*1849–63*) indicates a variant found in both the *Poetical Works* and, where applicable, the *Selections from the Poetical Works* of 1863.

The addition in later texts of one or more whole lines is indicated by the caret mark (^), as in this example from *Andrea del Sarto*:

> 199^200.] B. added a line in a copy of his 6-vol. *Poetical Works*, now at the Pierpont Morgan Library . . . The line reads: 'Yes, all I care for if he spoke the truth'.

Where Browning revised a line and then added one or more lines, the original line number is used with no caret mark (the example is from *Bishop Blougram's Apology*):

> 978.] While the great Bishop rolled him out a mind / Long rumpled, till creased consciousness lay smooth. (*1880–88*, except *1888* has 'crumpled').

Besides MSS, proofs, individual volumes, separate editions of poems and volumes annotated by Browning, we have used the following collected and selected editions in our collation (unrevised reprints of these editions are not listed):

Poems, 2 vols, London, Chapman & Hall 1849 ('New Edition')
Poetical Works, 3 vols, London: Chapman & Hall 1863 ('Third Edition')
Selections from Poetical Works, London: Chapman & Hall 1863
Poetical Works, 3 vols, London: Chapman & Hall 1865 ('Fourth Edition')★

A Selection from the Works, London: Edward Moxon 1865 ('Moxon's Miniature Poets')

Poetical Works, 6 vols, London: Smith, Elder 1868

Poetical Works, 6 vols, London: Smith, Elder 1870★

Selections from Poetical Works, London: Smith, Elder 1872 (after the publication of *1880*, re-titled *Selections . . . First Series*)

Poetical Works, 6 vols, London: Smith, Elder 1875★

Selections from Poetical Works, Second Series, London: Smith, Elder 1880

Selections from Poetical Works, 2 vols, London: Smith, Elder 1884 ('New Edition')★

Poetical Works, 16 vols, London: Smith, Elder 1888–9

Poetical Works, 16 vols, London: Smith Elder 1889★

★*1865* is a revised reissue of *1863*; *1870* and *1875* are revised reissues of *1868*; *1884* is a revised reissue of the combined 1872 and 1880 volumes of selections; *1889* is a re-issue of *1888* with revisions to vols i–ix. Since their contents remained unchanged, these reissues are not listed in the textual histories of the poems they contain, though their significant textual variants are, of course, included in those poems' collations. Michael Meredith, following a suggestion by Warner Barnes, has definitively established that the 1870 and 1875 'reissues' of *1868* were actually revised texts: see 'Learning's Crabbed Text: a Reconsideration of the 1868 edition of Browning's Poetical Works', *SBHC* xiii (1985) 97–107.

Volumes of selections which Browning is known to have supervised, and which show significant revision, we count as substantive texts. In a number of instances, their revision anticipates that of subsequent collected editions; occasionally, they appear to have afforded Browning the opportunity to try out a variation, as with *England in Italy*, which in the 1872 *Selections* (and subsequent reissues) was printed in long rather than short lines (see p. 254), a change never implemented in a collected edition. It should be noted that corrected reissues of Browning's 1872 and 1880 volumes of selections have a separate textual history from that of the collected editions, since Browning entered revisions for these reissues on a copy of the preceding selected edition.

In textual notes, short titles for all editions are by date. Short titles for particular poems and individual poems are also by date, indicated in the headnote: thus, in *Pippa Passes*, *1841* refers to the first edition of the poem, and, in *My Last Duchess*, *1842* refers to the date of *Dramatic Lyrics*, the collection in which the poem first appeared. For convenience' sake the edition of 1888–9 is referred to in the notes as *1888*; we take this to be the final collected edition, agreeing with P. Kelley and W. S. Peterson ('Browning's Final Revisions', *BIS* i [1973] 87–118) that the reprinted text of this edition issued as *1889* is not reliable; we have recorded its very few substantive readings, but used it otherwise, along with Browning's own lists of corrections, only as a guide to misprints in *1888*. An exception to the use of dates as short titles relates to periodical publication, where the short title derives from the periodical: thus in *The Tomb at St. Praxed's*, *Hood's* refers to the issue of *Hood's Magazine* in which the poem first appeared. The date of the periodical publication is recorded in the headnote.

In accordance with the policy of LAEP, our edition does not offer a complete textual apparatus. Information about the scale and general character of revisions to particular poems is given in the headnotes; the notes provide a substantial selection of variants from other texts. We record all substantive verbal changes in editions published in Browning's lifetime and which he is known to have supervised. Other variants (e.g. punctuation, minor changes of form or spelling, variation between upper and lower case, misprints in later editions) are not normally recorded, except where there is a significant alteration or clarification of meaning, or where a point of additional interest arises. Where further changes were made to a substantive variant in subsequent editions, we record all such changes, including minor ones, in order to avoid giving an incorrect or misleading history. For reasons of clarity, however, we have not recorded changes in the use of quotation marks before each line in passages of direct or reported speech.

Titles are those under which a poem was first published, except in the case of poems published under collective titles which were subsequently dropped. *My Last Duchess*, for example, was originally published under the title *Italy* in a pair with *Count Gismond*, which appeared as *France*. Since there is no evidence that such pairs were composed together, or in the order in which they appeared, we abandon the collective titles and use the poems' later titles, but print these with an asterisk to indicate that they were not part of the first-edition text. In cases where the first published title differs from the later and more familiar one, we print the original title followed by the later one in square brackets:

The Tomb at St. Praxed's
[The Bishop Orders his Tomb at Saint Praxed's Church]

We give all versions of titles in the Contents and the Index of Titles and First Lines.

c) Explanatory notes

Explanatory notes are indicated by a colon after the word or phrase to be glossed; where the whole line is glossed, the notes directly follows the line number. Thus, in *The Tomb at St. Praxed's*:

71. *block*: this is part of the tomb, not the bath.

or, in *Waring*:

77. Either 'accepting, swallowing our contempt for her' or 'espousing, adopting her attitude of contempt for us'.

Where a long passage involves complex narrative or argument, we have supplied a general note giving an overview, followed by more detailed notes to particular lines or groups of lines.

We annotate the following:

a) proper names;
b) difficult or archaic words, or words used in an unusual or obsolete sense;
c) difficult or convoluted syntax;
d) historical context, biographical or general;
e) comments of contemporaries (such as Elizabeth Barrett's on the poems of *Dramatic Romances and Lyrics*).

d) Short titles and cross-references

Short titles are used for poems included in this volume, in a form which should make them readily identifiable: *Andrea* for *Andrea del Sarto*, *Fra Lippo* for *Fra Lippo Lippi*, etc. Some short titles drop the apostrophe: *Bishop Blougram* for *Bishop Blougram's Apology*, *A Grammarian* for *A Grammarian's Funeral*. The definite article is always dropped, but the treatment of the indefinite article varies: *Patriot* for *The Patriot*, *Lovers' Quarrel* for *A Lovers' Quarrel*, but *An Epistle* for *An Epistle Containing the Strange Medical Experience of Karshish, the Arab Physician*. References to poems in this volume are by simple page number, e.g. 'see *Youth and Art* (p. 700)' or 'see *Apparent Failure* 7–8n. (p. 710)'.

Titles of poems published in vols. I – III of our edition, but not included in this volume, are given in full, except that definite and indefinite articles are omitted: *Flight of the Duchess* for *The Flight of the Duchess*, *Soul's Tragedy* for *A Soul's Tragedy*, etc. References to such poems give their volume and page number, e.g. 'see headnote to *Flight of the Duchess* (II 295)' or 'see *Paracelsus* iii 557n. (I 216)'.

Titles of poems not published in vols. I – III are given in full, with some exceptions (see below). Titles of poems which are also the title of the volume are followed by the date, e.g. *Fifine at the Fair* (1872); titles of individual poems are followed by the title and date of the volume in which they appeared, e.g. *Cherries* (*Ferishtah's Fancies*, 1883). The exceptions are *Ring*, the short title for *The Ring and the Book*, *Prince Hohenstiel-Schwangau* for *Prince Hohenstiel-Schwangau, Saviour of Society*; and *Parleyings* for *Parleyings with Certain People of Importance in Their Day*. In addition, *Ring* is not followed by a date. The individual poems in *Parleyings* appear in the contents page of that volume as 'With Bernard de Mandeville', 'With Christopher Smart', etc., but the preposition is dropped here, as in 'see the opening lines of *Christopher Smart* (*Parleyings*, 1887)'.

Our aim is to provide the modern reader with a route to understanding what a Victorian reader would have brought to poems then as now considered difficult, thereby opening up to the light a remarkable, highly complex and strenuously rewarding body of work.

Acknowledgements

For permission to consult, and quote from, manuscripts of poems, letters, and other materials we wish to thank Sir John Murray and the following institutions: Balliol College, Oxford; Boston Public Library; Brigham Young University; British Library; University of Chicago; Eton College, Windsor; the Syndics of the Fitzwilliam Museum, Cambridge; Isabella Stewart Gardner Museum, Boston; Harry Ransom Humanities Research Center, University of Texas at Austin; Harvard University, Cambridge, MA (Houghton Library, Widener Library); Huntington Library, San Marino, CA; Indiana University Library (Lilly Library); University of Iowa Libraries, Iowa City (Special Collections); Lancaster University (Ruskin Library); University of London (Sterling Library); University of Manchester (John Rylands Library); Massachusetts Historical Society, Boston, MA; Morgan Library, New York (formerly Pierpont Morgan Library); Newberry Library, Chicago; New York Public Library (Henry W. and Albert A. Berg Collection; Astor, Lennox and Tilden Foundations; Carl J. Pforzheimer Library); National Library of New Zealand (Alexander Turnbull Library); Princeton University, NJ (Robert H. Taylor Collection); Pushkin Academy, Leningrad; Somerville College, Oxford; Syracuse University, NY (George Arents Research Library); Texas A & M University; University of Toronto Library; the Trustees of the Victoria and Albert Museum (National Art Library); Wellesley College Library, Wellesley, MA; Yale University Library, New Haven, CN (Beinecke Library and Tinker Collection).

We owe a particular debt of gratitude to the Armstrong Browning Library, Baylor University, Waco, TX, both for permission to quote and for unstinting assistance of other kinds, including the award of Visiting Fellowships to two of the editors. We personally thank Rita Patteson, the current Director; her predecessors Stephen Prickett, Mairi Rennie and Betty Coley; the Curator of Printed Books Cynthia Burgess; Kathleen Williams, and other members of staff at ABL who have helped us so unfailingly.

For institutional support including study leave, research trips, research materials, and assistance with the preparation of the typescript, we thank Boston University, De Montfort University, King's College, Cambridge, King's College London, University of Manchester, University of Sheffield, University College London, and the University of London Central Research Fund. We would also like to thank the British Academy for its generous support.

We acknowledge indispensable assistance not only from the published volumes of *The Brownings' Correspondence*, but personally from its editors, Philip Kelley and Scott Lewis. We likewise acknowledge the fund of knowledge accumulated, and generously shared, by members of the

Browning Society, making special mention of Michael Meredith. We have benefited from the work of previous and current editors of Browning, both collected editions and single volumes, including the Ohio/Baylor edition led by Roma A. King, Jr., the Oxford English Texts edition led by the late Ian Jack, the Penguin Poetry Library edition by the late John Pettigrew and Thomas J. Collins, Richard Altick's edition of *The Ring and the Book* in the same series, and Paul Turner's Oxford University Press edition of *Men and Women*.

Many individual colleagues, friends and family members have given us help and encouragement: Sylvia Adamson, Isobel Armstrong, Rosemary Ashton, Siward Atkins, Janet Bately, Edmund Baxter, Roy Bolton, Roger Brooks, Penny Bulloch, Giovanna Cattini, Berry Chevasco, Dennis Crowley, Christine Dymkowski, Janet Fairweather, Mark Farrell, Philip Ford, the late Wendy Gibb, Greer I. Gilman, Michael Halls, Judith Hawley, Cathy Henderson, Philip Horne, Wendy Hunter, Luba Hussel, Elizabeth Jackson, Patricia Johnson, David Kastan, Sheila Kay, Samantha Matthews, Britta Martens, Karl Miller, Charlotte Mitchell, Laura Morgan, the late Eric Mottram, John North, Leonée Ormond, Pat O'Shea, Kenneth Palmer, Yopie Prins, Richard Proudfoot, the late Philip Radcliffe, Bruce Redford, Christopher Ricks, Adam Roberts, Gill Spraggs, Andrew Stauffer, Guilland Sutherland, John Sutherland, Peter Swaab, Qing-Sheng Tong, Virginia Mason Vaughan, René Weis, Helen Weston, Frances Whistler, John Whitley, Rosemary Whitley, Neil Williams, Sarah Wintle, Angela Woolford, Jack Woolford, and Henry Woudhuysen.

This volume includes work done under the auspices of the first General Editor of the Annotated English Poets series, F. W. Bateson, who gave valuable guidance at the outset of the project; his successors, John Barnard and Paul Hammond, have been equally helpful in their scrutiny and support.

Chronological Table of Robert Browning's Life and Chief Publications

1812   (*7 May*) Born Camberwell, south-east London, son of Robert Browning, clerk in the Bank of England, and Sarah Anna Browning (née Wiedemann). Father, a kindly and eccentric bibliophile, owns large library from which much of B.'s heterogeneous learning derives. Mother a devout Nonconformist, lover of music and gardens.

1814   Birth of sister, Sarianna.

c. 1820   Pupil at the Reverend Thomas Ready's school, Peckham, near Camberwell.

1826   Leaves Ready's school; educated at home for two years. Discovers the work of Shelley, and under his influence becomes for a brief period atheist and vegetarian. Writes a volume of poems (*Incondita*) but subsequently destroys them; two survive in a friend's copy (vol. I, nos. 1 and 2). Makes the acquaintance of his 'literary father', W. J. Fox, Unitarian and Radical, editor of *Monthly Repository*, in which some of B.'s early poems will be published.

1828   (*October*) Enrols in newly founded London University (later University College London) for classes in Latin, Greek, and German.

1829   (*May*) Leaves London University.

c. 1830   Member of 'The Set' or 'The Colloquials', informal literary and debating society; contact with individual members (Alfred Domett, Joseph Arnould) continues until marriage.

1833   (*March*) Publishes *Pauline* anonymously. The poem sells no copies and passes virtually unnoticed; B. conceals his authorship of it from all but close friends until forced by threat of pirated publication to include it in *Poetical Works* of 1868.

1834   (*March–June*) Travels overland to St Petersburg in company of Russian Consul-General.

        (*August*) Meets young French aristocrat, Amédée de Ripert-Monclar, who becomes close friend and stimulates interest in French literature and history; B. and Monclar join newly formed Institut Historique of Paris.

1835   (*August*) Publishes *Paracelsus*, which has critical success and brings B. to notice of London literary society. Important friendships follow with John Forster, editor of the *Examiner*, and with the actor-manager William Charles Macready.

1836   (*January*) *Porphyria* and *Johannes Agricola*, B.'s first dramatic lyrics, published in *Monthly Repository*.

(*April*) First meeting with Thomas Carlyle already a strong influence through his writings.

(*May*) Forster's *Life of Strafford* published; B. had helped Forster to complete the writing of the book. Attends dinner to celebrate success of T. N. Talfourd's tragedy *Ion*, where Wordsworth drinks his health; also meets Walter Savage Landor, a strong contemporary influence. Macready asks B. to 'write him a play'.

1837   (*May*) Publishes first play, *Strafford*, simultaneously produced at Covent Garden with Macready in title role; performed five times.

1838   (*April–July*) Travels to Italy by sea, exploring Venice and the Trevisan region, including 'delicious Asolo', a lifelong love; returns to England overland.

1840   (*March*) Publishes *Sordello*, received with near-universal incomprehension and derision.

1841   (*April*) Publishes *Pippa Passes*, first number of series called *Bells and Pomegranates* (*B & P*), issued in the form of cheap paperbound pamphlets.

1842   (*March*) Publishes play, *King Victor and King Charles* (*B & P* ii), previously rejected for production by Macready. B.'s friend and subsequent benefactor John Kenyon offers to introduce him to Elizabeth Barrett, but she declines for reasons of ill health.

(*July*) Publishes anonymous essay on 18th-century poet and forger Thomas Chatterton in *Foreign Quarterly Review* (see Appendix C, vol. II, p. 475).

(*November*) Publishes *Dramatic Lyrics* (*B & P* iii).

1843   (*January*) Publishes play, *The Return of the Druses* (*B & P* iv), previously rejected for production by Macready.

(*February*) Publishes play, *A Blot in the 'Scutcheon* (*B & P* v), which Macready had reluctantly agreed to produce, and over which he and B. quarrelled; the play is performed without Macready and runs for three nights at Drury Lane to diminishing audiences and enthusiasm.

1844   (*April*) Publishes play, *Colombe's Birthday* (*B & P* vi), previously rejected for production by Charles Kean. B. never again wrote for the stage.

(*July–December*) Travels by sea to Italy (Naples, Rome, Tuscany), returning overland. While B. is abroad, EBB.'s *Poems* published, one of which, *Lady Geraldine's Courtship*, contains flattering allusion to B., who reads it on his return and, with Kenyon's encouragement, determines to write to her.

1845   (*10 January*) Writes first letter to EBB.: beginning of correspondence and, eventually, courtship (clandestine because EBB.'s father opposed any of his children marrying).

(*20 May*) First visit to EBB. in Wimpole Street.

(*November*) Publishes *Dramatic Romances and Lyrics* (*B & P* vii).

1846   (*April*) Publishes two plays, *Luria* and *A Soul's Tragedy* (*B & P* viii, the final number); neither intended for performance.

	(*12 September*) Secret marriage to EBB.; a week later they leave England, travel through France to Pisa.
1847	(*April*) B. and EBB. move to Florence, eventually settling in 'Casa Guidi', which became their permanent residence.
1848–9	Rebellions in several Italian states against Austrian rule; B. and EBB. support Italian nationalism.
1849	(*January*) Publishes *Poems* (2 vols.), changing publisher from Moxon to Chapman & Hall; first collection of previously published work (excluding *Sordello*), with considerable though unevenly distributed revision.
	(*March*) Birth of son, Robert Wiedemann Barrett Browning (nicknamed 'Penini' or 'Pen'). Death of B.'s mother.
	(*Summer*) At Bagni di Lucca, EBB. shows B. her sonnets on their courtship, which he persuades her to publish under the title *Sonnets from the Portuguese*.
1850	(*April*) Publishes *Christmas-Eve and Easter-Day*. EBB. publishes *Poems*, including *Sonnets from the Portuguese*.
1851	EBB. publishes *Casa Guidi Windows*.
	(*June*) B. and EBB. travel to Paris.
	(*July–September*) First visit to England since marriage.
1851–2	(*Winter*) In Paris, B. and EBB. witness Louis Napoleon's *coup d'état* and accession to power, which EBB. supports but B. opposes.
1852	Publishes *Essay on Shelley* as introduction to collection of Shelley's letters; volume withdrawn soon after publication when all but two of the letters turn out to be forgeries.
	(*January*) First meeting with French critic Joseph Milsand; close friendship till Milsand's death in 1886.
	(*July*) Trip to England; B.'s father sued for breach of promise of marriage; after judgment against him, flees to Paris accompanied by B. and settles there with Sarianna. B. revisits England; returns to Italy with EBB. in October.
1855	(*July*) During a visit to London, B. and EBB. attend séance conducted by American medium D. D. Home, which highlights difference of opinion about spiritualism (EBB. a believer, B. a sceptic).
	(*November*) Publishes *Men and Women*; hopes of its being more popular with critics and public are disappointed.
1856	EBB. publishes *Aurora Leigh* to critical and popular acclaim. Death of John Kenyon, whose bequest of £11,000 leaves B. and EBB. financially secure.
1859	Gives refuge to Walter Savage Landor after Landor quarrels with family; looks after Landor until his death in 1864.
1860	EBB. publishes *Poems Before Congress*.
	(*June*) Finds 'Old Yellow Book', basis of *The Ring and the Book*, on market-stall in Florence.
1861	(*29 June*) EBB. dies at Casa Guidi; buried in Protestant cemetery, Florence. A month later, B. leaves Florence with Pen and

settles in London. His usual pattern from now is to spend the 'season' in London, taking long summer holidays in Scotland or abroad (France, Switzerland, and, towards the end of his life, Italy once more, though never Florence).

1862   Publishes EBB.'s *Last Poems.*

1863   Publishes *Poetical Works* (3 vols) including *Sordello*; a revised reissue published in 1865. (*Winter*) Meets Julia Wedgwood; their close friendship broken off by her in 1865.

1864   (*May*) Publishes *Dramatis Personae*; later in the year a second edition is required, for the first time in B.'s career. From this time, B.'s reputation improves steadily after years of comparative neglect and obscurity.

1865   Publishes *A Selection from the Works* ('Moxon's Miniature Poets' series).

1866   (*June*) Death of B.'s father in Paris. Sarianna moves to London and lives with B. until his death.

1867   (*June*) Oxford University awards B. honorary MA; shortly afterwards Balliol College (the Master, Benjamin Jowett, is a friend) makes him an honorary Fellow (B.'s attempt to enter Pen at Balliol is however unsuccessful; he is obliged to go to Christ Church instead).

1868   Publishes *Poetical Works* (6 vols., including *Pauline*), changing publisher from Chapman & Hall to Smith, Elder. Revised reissues published 1870, 1875. Refuses Rectorship of St Andrews University (and again in 1877 and 1884).

1868–9   (*November–February*) Publishes *The Ring and the Book* in four monthly volumes, each containing three books of the poem; widespread critical acclaim. A second edition was published in 1872.

1869   (*March*) Presented, with Carlyle, to Queen Victoria.
         (*September*) Refuses proposal of marriage from Louisa, Lady Ashburton.

1871   (*August*) Publishes *Balaustion's Adventure*, a narrative poem incorporating a 'transcript' (translation) of Euripides' play *Alcestis*; it proves one of his most popular poems, reaching several editions. (*December*) Publishes *Prince Hohenstiel-Schwangau, Saviour of Society*, based on the career of Napoleon III.

1872   Publishes *Selections from the Poetical Works*: after the publication of a second volume in 1880, re-titled *Selections . . . First Series*. Both volumes were many times reissued; a 'New Edition' in 1884 contains some revisions.
         (*June*) Publishes *Fifine at the Fair*. The poem is a failure, and causes a breach with Dante Gabriel Rossetti, who is convinced it contains an attack upon him.

1873   (*May*) Publishes *Red Cotton Night-Cap Country.*

1874   Pen begins career as artist under Jean Arnould Heyermans in Antwerp; later studies sculpture in Rodin's studio in Paris; B.

assiduously promotes his son's work, but Pen's career lapses after marriage (1887).

1875   (*April*) Publishes *Aristophanes' Apology*, which like *Balaustion's Adventure* contains a 'transcript' of a play by Euripides, the *Heracles*. (*November*) Publishes *The Inn Album*.

1876   (*July*) Publishes *Pacchiarotto and How He Worked in Distemper: with Other Poems.*

1877   (*September*) Sudden death of his friend Annie Egerton Smith, on holiday with B. and Sarianna; commemorated in *La Saisiaz*. (*October*) Publishes *The Agamemnon of Aeschylus* (translation).

1878   (*May*) Publishes (in one volume) *La Saisiaz* and *The Two Poets of Croisic*. (*September*) Revisits Asolo for first time since 1838.

1879   (*April*) Publishes *Dramatic Idyls*. (*June*) Cambridge University awards B. the degree of LL.D.

1880   Publishes *Selections from the Poetical Works, Second Series*: see entry for 1872. (*June*) Publishes *Dramatic Idyls, Second Series*.

1881   (*October*) First meeting of Browning Society, founded by F. J. Furnivall and Emily Hickey.

1882   (*June*) Oxford University awards B. the degree of DCL.

1883   (*March*) Publishes *Jocoseria*, which sells well and reaches several editions.

1884   (*April*) Edinburgh University awards B. the degree of LL.D. (*November*) Publishes *Ferishtah's Fancies*, one of the most popular of his later works, reaching several editions.

1885   Declines Presidency of newly formed Shelley Society.

1887   (*January*) Publishes *Parleyings with Certain People of Importance in Their Day*. (*October*) Marriage of Pen Browning and Fannie Coddington (the couple eventually separated; there were no children).

1888–9   Publishes *Poetical Works* (16 vols.).

1889   (*12 December*) Dies in Venice on day of publication of last volume, *Asolando*. (*31 December*) Buried in Poets' Corner, Westminster Abbey.

Abbreviations

B.   Robert Browning

EBB.   Elizabeth Barrett Browning

For books, the place of publication is London unless otherwise specified.

I *Browning's works*

Sections 1, 2 and 3 list only those short titles which consist of dates or initials. References to individual poems included in this volume are either complete (e.g. *My Star, Love in a Life*) or use the first word or phrase of the title, omitting definite articles and apostrophes (e.g. *Pippa* for *Pippa Passes*, *Patriot* for *The Patriot*, *Bishop Blougram* for *Bishop Blougram's Apology*). The full titles of these works can be identified from the Index of Titles and First Lines. References to individual poems not included in this volume, and to titles of books, are usually complete (*Aristophanes' Apology, Halbert and Hob*), with the exception of one major work, *The Ring and the Book*, which is referred to as *Ring*; a few poems with very long titles are likewise referred to by their first word or phrase (e.g. *Very Original Poem* for *Very Original Poem, Written with Even a Greater Endeavour Than Ordinary After Intelligibility, and Hitherto Only Published on the First Leaf of the Author's Son's Account-Book*). The full titles of these works may be found in the alphabetical list of Browning's works published as Appendix B in vol. I.

One case in particular requires mentioning. Browning's 1887 collection *Parleyings with Certain People of Importance in Their Day* contains a number of poems which are headed 'With', the word 'Parleying' being understood: *With Bernard de Mandeville, With George Bubb Dodington, With Christopher Smart*, and so on. We use the short title *Parleyings* for the volume, and the names alone for the individual poems: *Christopher Smart* (*Parleyings*, 1887).

1 *Collected works issued in Browning's lifetime*

1849   *Poems*, 2 vols (Chapman and Hall 1849)

1863   *Poetical Works*, 3 vols (Chapman and Hall 1863) [on title page: 'Third Edition']

1865   *Poetical Works*, 3 vols (Chapman and Hall 1865) [on title page: 'Fourth Edition']

1868   *Poetical Works*, 6 vols (Smith, Elder 1868)

1870   *Poetical Works*, 6 vols (Smith, Elder 1870)

1875   *Poetical Works*, 6 vols (Smith, Elder 1875)

1888   *Poetical Works*, 16 vols (Smith, Elder 1888–9)

1889   *Poetical Works*, 16 vols (Smith, Elder 1889)

Note: *1865* is a revised reissue of *1863*; *1870* and *1875* are revised reissues of *1868*. *1889* is a partially revised reprint of *1888*: before his death B. made corrections to the first ten volumes of *1888* as they appeared. Since their contents remained unchanged, these reissues are not separately listed in the textual history of each poem as it is given in the headnote, though significant variants are included in the notes.

2 *Selections issued in Browning's lifetime*

1863²	*Selections from the Poetical Works* (Chapman and Hall 1863)
1865²	*Selections from the Poetical Works* (Moxon, 1865) ['Moxon's Miniature Poets']
1872	*Selections from the Poetical Works* (Smith, Elder 1872)
1880	*Selections from the Poetical Works*, Second Series (Smith, Elder 1880)
1884	*Selections from the Poetical Works*, 2 vols (Smith, Elder 1884) [on title page of vol. i, 'First Series', on title page of vol. ii, 'Second series']

Note: *1884* is a revised reissue of *1872* and *1880*. As with the reissues of *1863* and *1868*, we do not list *1884* separately in the textual history given in the headnote, but do record its significant variants.

3 *Single volumes and collections of shorter poems issued in Browning's lifetime*

B & P	*Bells and Pomegranates* (see Appendix C., p. 883)
B & P BYU	B.'s copy of the one-volume *Bells and Pomegranates* (Brigham Young University)
B & P Domett	Alfred Domett's copy of *Bells and Pomegranates*, with some MS corrections by B. (Harry Ransom Humanities Research Center, University of Texas, Austin)
CE & ED	*Christmas-Eve and Easter-Day* (Chapman and Hall 1850)
DI¹	*Dramatic Idyls* (Smith, Elder 1879)
DI²	*Dramatic Idyls, Second Series* (Smith, Elder 1880)
DL	*Dramatic Lyrics* (Moxon, 1842) [*Bells and Pomegranates* iii]
DL 1st Proof	Corrected proof sheets of *Dramatic Lyrics* (Widener Library, Harvard)
DL 2nd Proof	Corrected proof sheets of *Dramatic Lyrics* (Widener Library, Harvard)
DP	*Dramatis Personae* (Chapman and Hall 1864)
DP²	*Dramatis Personae*, 2nd edition (Chapman and Hall 1864)
DR & L	*Dramatic Romances and Lyrics* (Moxon, 1845) [*Bells and Pomegranates* vii]
H proof	Proof copy of *Men and Women*, at Huntington Library
H proof²	Copy of first edition of *Men and Women* with proof-readings, at Huntington Library
L & AST	*Luria* and *A Soul's Tragedy* (1846) [*Bells and Pomegranates* viii]
LS & TPC	*La Saisiaz* and *The Two Poets of Croisic* (Smith, Elder 1878)
M & W	*Men and Women*, 2 vols (Chapman and Hall 1855); in textual notes *1855*
1856	*Men and Women* (Boston: Ticknor and Fields 1856) [1st American edition; in one vol.]

Note: for a description of *H proof* and *H proof²*, and a discussion of their significance in the textual history of *M & W*, (see Appendix C, III p. 742-3).

4 *Subsequent editions*

1894   Vol. xvii of 1889, consisting of *Asolando* and notes to the
               poems, ed. E. Berdoe
Centenary   *The Works of Robert Browning*, ed. F. G. Kenyon, 10 vols
               (Smith, Elder 1912)
Florentine   *The Complete Works of Robert Browning*, ed. C. Porter and
               H. A. Clarke, 12 vols (New York: Thomas Y. Crowell 1898)
New Poems   *New Poems by Robert Browning and Elizabeth Barrett
               Browning*, ed. F. G. Kenyon (Smith, Elder, 1914)
Ohio   *The Complete Works of Robert Browning*, gen. ed. Roma A.
               King Jr., Ohio University Press 1969–
Oxford   *The Poetical Works of Robert Browning*, gen. eds I. Jack,
               M. Meredith, Oxford University Press 1983– [Oxford
               English Texts]
Penguin   *Robert Browning: The Poems*, ed. John Pettigrew and
               Thomas J. Collins, 2 vols, Harmondsworth 1981 [Penguin
               English Poets; in USA, publ. by Yale University Press]
Turner   *Men and Women*, ed. Paul Turner (Oxford University Press
               1972)

5 *Browning's Prose Writings*

Chatterton   Review of R. H. Wilde, *Conjectures and Researches
               Concerning the Love Madness and Imprisonment of Torquato
               Tasso*, 2 vols (New York 1842), in *Foreign Quarterly Review*
               xxxix (July 1842) 465–83. [Usually referred to as the 'Essay
               on Chatterton'; see Appendix C in vol. II of the Longman
               Annotated English Poets *Poems of Browning*, p. 475]
Shelley   Introductory Essay in *Letters of Percy Bysshe Shelley*, Moxon
               1852
               [Usually referred to as the 'Essay on Shelley'; see Appendix A
               in this volume, p. 851]

6 *Letters (incl. those of Elizabeth Barrett Browning)*

American Friends   *Browning to his American Friends: Letters between
                        the Brownings, the Storys and James Russell Lowell
                        1841–1890*, ed. G. R. Hudson (1965)
B. to Fields   I. Jack, 'Browning on *Sordello* and *Men and
                        Women*: Unpublished Letters to James T.
                        Fields', *HLQ* xlv, no. 3 (Summer 1982) 185–99
B. to Ruskin   Letter from Browning to Ruskin, in W. G.
                        Collingwood, *Life and Work of John Ruskin*
                        (1893) i 193–202
Correspondence   *The Brownings' Correspondence*, ed. P. Kelley,
                        R. Hudson, S. Lewis and E. Hagan (Winfield,
                        KS 1984–)
Dearest Isa   *Dearest Isa: Robert Browning's Letters to Isabella
                        Blagden*, ed. E. C. McAleer (Austin, TX and
                        Edinburgh 1951)

EBB to Arabella	*The Letters of Elizabeth Barrett Browning to Her Sister Arabella*, 2 vols, ed. S. Lewis (Winfield, KS 2002)
EBB to Boyd	*Elizabeth Barrett to Mr Boyd*, ed. B. P. McCarthy (New Haven 1955)
EBB to Henrietta	*Elizabeth Barrett Browning: Letters to her Sister*, ed. L. Huxley (1929)
EBB to Horne	*Letters of Elizabeth Barrett Browning Addressed to Richard Hengist Horne*, ed. S. R. Townshend Mayer, 2 vols (1877)
EBB to MRM	*The Letters of Elizabeth Barrett Browning to Mary Russell Mitford 1835–1854*, ed. M. B. Raymond and M. R. Sullivan, 3 vols (Winfield, KS 1983)
EBB to Ogilvy	*Elizabeth Barrett Browning's Letters to Mrs David Ogilvy 1849–1861*, ed. P. N. Heydon and P. Kelley (New York 1973)
George Barrett	*Letters of the Brownings to George Barrett*, ed. P. Landis and R. E. Freeman (Urbana, IL 1958)
Invisible Friends	*Invisible Friends: The Correspondence of Elizabeth Barrett Barrett and Benjamin Robert Haydon 1842–1845*, ed. W. B. Pope (Cambridge, MA 1972)
LH	*Letters of Robert Browning collected by Thomas J. Wise*, ed. T. L. Hood (1933)
LK	*The Letters of Robert Browning and Elizabeth Barrett Barrett 1845–1846*, ed. E. Kintner, 2 vols (Cambridge, MA 1969). The volumes are paginated continuously.
Learned Lady	*Learned Lady: Letters from Robert Browning to Mrs Thomas Fitzgerald 1876–1889*, ed. E. C. McAleer (Cambridge, MA 1966)
Letters of EBB	*The Letters of Elizabeth Barrett Browning*, ed. F. G. Kenyon, 2 vols (1897)
Letters of RB and EBB	The Letters of Robert Browning and Elizabeth Barrett Barrett 1845–1846 [ed. R. W. B. Browning], 2 vols (1899)
More Than Friend	*More Than Friend: The Letters of Robert Browning to Katharine de Kay Bronson*, ed. M. Meredith (Waco, TX and Winfield, KS 1985)
New Letters	*New Letters of Robert Browning*, ed. W. C. DeVane and K. L. Knickerbocker (1951)
RB & AD	F. G. Kenyon, *Robert Browning and Alfred Domett* (1906)
RB & JW	*Robert Browning and Julia Wedgwood: A Broken Friendship as Revealed in their Letters*, ed. R. Curle (1937)
Rossetti	A. A. Adrian, 'The Browning–Rossetti Friendship: Some Unpublished Letters', *PMLA* lxxiii (1958) 538–44

Ruskin	D. J. DeLaura, 'Ruskin and the Brownings: Twenty-Five Unpublished Letters', *BJRL* liv (1972) 314–56
Ruskin¹	Letter from John Ruskin to Browning of 2 Dec. 1855, and Browning's reply of 10 Dec. 1855: see Appendix B in this volume, p. 878
Tennyson	*The Brownings to the Tennysons: Letters from Robert Browning and Elizabeth Barrett Browning to Alfred, Emily, and Hallam Tennyson 1852–1889*, ed. T. J. Collins (Waco, TX 1971)
Trumpeter	*Browning's Trumpeter: The Correspondence of Robert Browning and Frederick J. Furnivall 1872– 1889*, ed. W. S. Peterson (Washington, DC 1979)
Twenty-two Letters	*Twenty-two Unpublished Letters of Elizabeth Barrett Browning and Robert Browning Addressed to Henrietta and Arabella Moulton Barrett* [ed. W. R. Benet], New York 1935

Note: the text of letters in *Correspondence* and *EBB to Arabella* has been very lightly normalized: EBB.'s habitual superscript for titles ('M^r.', 'M^{rs}.', 'D^r.') and for contractions ('c^d.', 'sh^d.' etc.) has been standardized as 'Mr.', 'Mrs.', 'Dr.', 'cd.', 'shd.', etc.

II *Periodicals*

BBI	*Baylor University Browning Interests*
BIS	*Browning Institute Studies* [see also *VLC*]
BJRL	*Bulletin of the John Rylands Library*
BNL	*Browning Newsletter*
BNYPL	*Bulletin of the New York Public Library*
BSN	*Browning Society Notes*
EC	*Essays in Criticism*
ELN	*English Language Notes*
ER	*Edinburgh Review*
Hood's	*Hood's Magazine and Comic Miscellany*
HLQ	*Huntington Library Quarterly*
JEGP	*Journal of English and Germanic Philology*
MLN	*Modern Language Notes*
MLQ	*Modern Language Quarterly*
MLR	*Modern Language Review*
MP	*Modern Philology*
MR	*Monthly Repository*
N & Q	*Notes and Queries*
PMLA	*Publications of the Modern Language Association of America*
QR	*Quarterly Review*
RES	*Review of English Studies*
SB	*Studies in Bibliography*
SBC	*Studies in Browning and His Circle*
SEL	*Studies in English Literature 1500–1900*

SP	Studies in Philology
SR	Studies in Romanticism
TLS	Times Literary Supplement
UTQ	University of Toronto Quarterly
VLC	Victorian Literature and Culture [continuation of BIS]
VNL	Victorian Newsletter
VP	Victorian Poetry
VS	Victorian Studies

III Miscellaneous

ABL	Armstrong Browning Library, Baylor University
ABL/JMA	Armstrong Browning Library, Baylor University: Joseph Milsand Archive
Allingham	William Allingham's Diary, ed. G. Grigson (Fontwell 1967)
Baldinucci	Filippo Baldinucci. Notizie de' Professori del Disegno da Cimabue in quà, ed. Giuseppe Piacenza, 21 vols (Torino: Stamperia Reale 1770)
Berg	Henry W. and Albert A. Berg Collection, New York Public Library
Bettenson	H. Bettenson (ed.), Documents of the Christian Church (Oxford 1943, rpt. 1946)
Bibliography	L. N. Broughton, C. S. Northrup, and R. B. Pearsall, Robert Browning: A Bibliography 1830–1950 (Ithaca 1953) [Cornell Studies in English xxxix]
Bibliography²	W. S. Peterson, Robert and Elizabeth Barrett Browning: An Annotated Bibliography 1951–1970 (New York 1974)
Biographie	Biographie Universelle, 50 vols (Paris 1811–22)
BL	British Library
Bronson¹	K. de Kay Bronson, 'Browning in Asolo', Century Magazine lix (Apr. 1900), 920–31; repr. More Than Friend 127–45
Bronson²	K. de Kay Bronson, 'Browning in Venice', Century Magazine lxii (Feb. 1902); repr. More Than Friend 147–65
BSP	Browning Society Papers, 3 vols (1881–90) [vol. i 1881–4, vol. ii 1885–89, vol iii 1889–90]
CH	Browning: the Critical Heritage, ed. B. Litzinger and D. Smalley (1970)
Checklist	P. Kelley and R. Hudson, The Brownings' Correspondence: A Checklist (Arkansas City, KS and New York 1978)
Collections	P. Kelley and B. A. Coley, The Browning Collections: A Reconstruction with Other Memorabilia (Winfield, KS 1984)

Cooke	G. W. Cooke, *A Guidebook to the Poetic and Dramatic Works of Robert Browning* (Boston and New York 1894)
Cruden's Concordance	Alexander Cruden, *Cruden's Complete Concordance to the Old and New Testaments* (1736; rpt. Lutterworth Press 1930)
Cyclopædia	E. Berdoe, *The Browning Cyclopædia* (Swan Sonnenschein 1892)
DeVane *Handbook*	W. C. DeVane, *A Browning Handbook*, 2nd edn (New York: Appleton, Century and Croft 1955)
DeVane *Parleyings*	W. C. DeVane, *Browning's Parleyings: The Autobiography of a Mind* (New Haven 1927)
Domett *Diary*	*The Diary of Alfred Domett*, ed. E. A. Horsman (Oxford: Oxford University Press 1953)
DNB	*Dictionary of National Biography* (2nd edn)
EB	*Encyclopedia Britannica* (1911 edn)
English Poetry	*English Poetry 600–1900 Full-Text Database*, 2nd edn, Chadwyck-Healey 2000
Fantozzi	Federigo Fantozzi, *Nuova Guida ovvero Descrizione Storico-Artistico-Critica della Città e Contorni di Firenze* (Firenze [Florence] 1852).
Foster	Giorgio Vasari, *Lives of the Most Eminent Painters, Sculptors, and Architects*, tr. Mrs. J. Foster, 6 vols (London: Henry G. Bohn 1850–85)
Gaye	Johan Gaye, *Carteggio inedito d'Artisti dei Secoli XIV, XV, XVI*, 3 vols (Florence: Presso Giuseppe Molini 1839–40)
Griffin and Minchin	W. H. Griffin and H. C. Minchin, *The Life of Robert Browning*, 3rd edn (Methuen 1938)
Huntington	Huntington Library, Pasadena
J.	Samuel Johnson, *A Dictionary of the English Language*, 1755
Jameson	Mrs [Anna Brownell] Jameson, *Memoirs of the Early Italian Painters and of the Progress of Painting in Italy*, 2 vols (Charles Knight and Co. 1845)
Le Monnier	Giorgio Vasari, *Le Vite de' Più eccellenti Pittori, Scultori e Architetti*, 13 vols, Firenze: Felice Le Monnier 1846–1857
Lemprière	J. Lemprière, *A Classical Dictionary*, 12th edn (T. Cadell and W. Davies 1823)
Maynard	J. Maynard, *Browning's Youth* (Cambridge, MA: Harvard University Press 1977)
Melchiori	B. Melchiori, *Browning's Poetry of Reticence* (Edinburgh 1968)
Miller	B. Miller, *Robert Browning: A Portrait* (John Murray 1952)

Morgan	Pierpont Morgan Library, New York
Murray	Murray's *Handbook for Travellers in Northern Italy* (1842)
*Murray*²	Murray's *Handbook for Travellers in Central Italy* (1843)
NT	New Testament
OED	*Oxford English Dictionary*
Orr *Handbook*	Mrs [Alexandra Sutherland] Orr, *A Handbook to the Works of Robert Browning*, 7th edn (G. Bell 1896)
Orr *Life*	Mrs [Alexandra Sutherland] Orr, *Life and Letters of Robert Browning* (Smith, Elder, 1891; rev. repr. 1908)
OT	Old Testament
PL	John Milton, *Paradise Lost*
Ruskin *Works*	A. Cook and E. C. Wedderburn, *The Library Edition of the Works of John Ruskin*, 39 vols, (London 1903–13).
Sharp	William Sharp, *Life of Robert Browning* (Walter Scott 1890)
Texas	Harry Ransom Humanities research center, University of Texas at Austin
Thomas	Charles Flint Thomas, *Art and Architecture in the Poetry of Robert Browning* (Troy, NY 1991)
Wanley	Nathaniel Wanley, *The Wonders of the Little World* (1667)
Wellesley MS	Critical notes by EBB. on B.'s poems and plays, 1845–6, in the Special Poetry Collection, Wellesley College Library, Wellesley, Massachusetts
Williams	Raymond Williams, *Keywords* (1976)

Note: Shakespeare's plays and poems are cited from the Riverside Edition, 2nd edn, ed. G. Blakemore Evans et al. (New York 1997). *Paradise Lost* is cited from the Longman Annotated English Poets edition, 2nd edn, ed. Alastair Fowler (Harlow 1998).

1 Pauline:
A Fragment of a Confession

Plus ne suis ce que j'ai été,
Et ne le sçaurois jamais être.
Marot

Text and publication

First publ. March 1833, B.'s first publ. poem, but issued anonymously: 'a loop-hole I have kept for backing out of the thing if necessary', B. wrote to W. J. Fox (*Correspondence* iii 74; for B.'s acquaintance with Fox, see below, p. 21). According to Mrs Orr, B.'s sister Sarianna was in the secret, but not his parents: 'This is why his aunt [Mrs Christiana Silverthorne], hearing that "Robert" had "written a poem," volunteered the sum requisite for its publication' (Orr *Life* 54). In a letter of 15 Jan. 1846, B. told EBB. that even the publishers, Saunders and Otley, did not know his identity (*LK* 389). In a letter to Fanny Haworth of May 1842, B. referred disparagingly to Saunders and Otley: 'they would print Montgomery's execrabilities' (*Correspondence* v 328; i.e. they would print anything for money; however, they later rejected *Paracelsus*). Not repr. separately; not 1849, 1863. Repr. *1868* (when B. first publicly acknowledged his authorship), *1888*. There is no extant MS. Our text is *1833*.

Several copies of *1833* with B.'s comments exist or have been described, the most important being a copy which was annotated by J. S. Mill (who planned a review which never appeared); B. wrote replies to Mill in the same copy, which he subsequently gave to John Forster; it is now in the Forster-Dyce Collection in the Victoria and Albert Museum. We refer to this copy as *Mill*. Early commentators assumed that the 'preface' which B. attached to *Mill* (see below) was addressed to Forster, and was therefore composed later than the replies to Mill's annotations; the latter are presumed to date from 30 Oct. 1833, the date B. entered on the first page of the copy. However, Michael A. Burr ('Browning's Note to Forster', *VP* xii [Winter 1974] 343–9) points out that B.'s final reply to Mill refers to the 'preface', making it unlikely that the latter was written for Forster. In R. H. Shepherd's copy of 1833 (formerly in the Turnbull Library but now missing), B. commented on the number of printer's errors, some of which can be deduced from his corrections in *Mill*; however, since in many cases it is impossible to distinguish between correction and revision, we have emended 1833 only

Motto. 'I am no more that which I have been, and shall never be able to be it'. From Clément Marot (1496–1544), *Epigrammes Diverses* ccxix. Maynard 436 points out the parallel with Byron, *Childe Harold* IV clxxxv: 'I am not now / That which I have been'. This passage strongly influenced the closing movement of *Pauline*: see ll. 831–1031n. Marot's poem continues: 'Mon beau printemps & mon esté / Ont faict le sault par la fenestre, / Amour, tu as esté mon maistre / Ie t'ay servy sur toutes les Dieux; / O si ie pouvois deux fois naistre, / Comme ie te serviroys mieux' [My fair spring and my summer have gone out of the window. Love, you have been my master; I have served you above all gods; Oh, if I could be born a second time, how much better would I serve you!].

where it is obviously defective. It is unlikely that B. borrowed back *Mill* from Forster to use as copy for *1868*: although some of the *Mill* readings appear in *1868–88*, many more do not, incl. the majority of substantive changes (see e.g. ll. 171, 361, 686). A revised copy of *1833* (hereafter *Rylands*) is in the John Rylands Library in Manchester. It cannot be accurately dated, but its systematic substitution of 'thou wast' for 'thou wert' suggests a date in the 1860s, since it was in *1863* that B. regularly introduced this rev. into other works (see e.g. *Paracelsus* v 13n.). Its revs. are mainly of punctuation: many dashes are emended to commas, semi-colons or periods, and commas are usually introduced after 'so' when this word begins a clause, perhaps, as *Oxford* suggests, in response to Mill (see l. 392n.). We have recorded the few substantive variants in *Rylands*, and changes in punctuation which affect the sense. Another copy of *1833*, presented to Frederick Locker [Locker-Lampson] and inscribed 'Corrections made at London, 1867', is in the Lowell Collection of the Library of Harvard University (*Lowell*). These corrections, like those in *Berg* (also presented to Locker-Lampson: see p. 99), are clearly a preliminary draft of revs. for a printed ed. (*1868*): there are directions to the printer such as 'run on to next paragraph'; the changes correspond closely, but not uniformly, to *1868*. The amount of revision in *1868* was relatively light, as B. himself indicated in the preface, though it went on occasion beyond the mere correction of misprints. The revision undertaken for *1888* was more substantial, and much in excess of B.'s own account in the supplementary preface to *1888* (for this, and the *1868* preface, see below, *Contemporary criticism and revision*).

Composition and date

The poem was written some time after 22 Oct. 1832, the date which appears at the end of the poem. According to B., he saw Edmund Kean acting in *Richard III* on that date and 'conceived the childish scheme' of which *Pauline* was the first (and only) product (*Mill*, p. 71; see our final note, p. 69). B. also explained this 'childish scheme' in a handwritten preface (*Mill*, p. 4):

> The following Poem was written in pursuance of a foolish plan which occupied me mightily for a time, and which had for its object the enabling me to assume & realize I know not how many different characters;—meanwhile the world was never to guess that "Brown, Smith, Jones, & Robinson" (as the Spelling-books have it) the respective Authors of this poem, the other novel, such an opera, such a speech &c &c were no other than one and the same individual. The present abortion was the first work of the *Poet* of the batch, who would have been more legitimately *myself* than most of the others; but I surrounded him with all manner of (to my then notion) poetical accessories, and had planned quite a delightful life for him:
> Only this crab remains of the shapely Tree of Life in this Fools paradise of mine.
> RB

A version of this note, using very similar terms, appears in a letter of 9 Aug. 1837 to B.'s friend Amédée de Ripert-Monclar (*Correspondence* iii 265; for Ripert-Monclar see headnote to *Paracelsus*, I 101); it adds the information that after his disillusionment B. 'destroyed "Pauline, Part 2", and some other works written in pursuance of it, and set about a genuine work of my own' (*Paracelsus* or *Sordello*). A version dated 14 Dec. 1838 is rec. in R. H. Shepherd's copy of *1833* (see above; repr. *Trumpeter* 26, *Collections* 217). Maynard challenges B.'s account, arguing: 'What seems actually to have happened is that Kean's acting in Shakespeare began to suggest to him a different kind of art as he was in the midst of writing *Pauline*.

Sarianna [B.'s sister] . . . recalled quite explicitly that it was while he was finishing the poem, not—as he implies—while he was conceiving it, that he was seeing Kean. In her remembrance, he composed the end of the poem in his head on one of several trips he made to Richmond around October 1832' (*Maynard* 222; see also Edmund Gosse, *Robert Browning: Personalia* [1890] 27). In addition to the suggestion that Browning misrepresented the chronology of his composition of the poem, Sarianna's account implies that Browning saw Kean in other roles than that of *Richard III*. Maynard notes that 'In the Harvard Theatre Collection there is a playbill for *Othello* for Oct. 29, 1832. The season ended Nov. 9; along with *Richard III*, *King Lear* and *Macbeth* had also been acted (Sept. 26 and Oct. 3)' (p. 436 n.73). However, Sarianna's account, given in 1902, may not be reliable. The poem was presumably finished by Jan. 1833, the date given at the end of the epigraph (see below, p. 28), and confirmed by B.'s statement, in a letter to W. J. Fox shortly before the poem was publ. in Mar. 1833, that it was written 'some months ago' (*Correspondence* iii 73).

Contemporary criticism and revision

B.'s letter to Fox was intended to secure notice for the poem. Fox replied favourably, and B. sent him twelve copies for distribution to potential reviewers (*Correspondence* iii 74–5). Fox himself reviewed the book warmly (*MR* n.s. vii [Apr. 1833] 252–62), noting B.'s debt to Shelley, comparing him as a young and promising writer with Tennyson, and praising the composition's 'deep stamp of reality': 'though evidently a hasty and imperfect sketch, [it] has truth and life in it, which gave us the thrill, and laid hold of us with the power, the sensation of which has never yet failed us as a test of genius'. Fox's efforts bore fruit in short but generally favourable notices in the *Athenaeum* (6 Apr. 1833, p. 216) and the *Atlas* (14 Apr. 1833, p. 228); three other notices (*Literary Gazette*, 23 March 1833, p. 183, *Tait's Edinburgh Magazine* iii [Aug. 1833] 668, and *Fraser's Magazine* xlii [Dec. 1833] 699–70) were contemptuously dismissive. (The review in *Fraser's* called the author of *Pauline* 'The Mad Poet of the Batch', a phrase which B. may echo in his 'preface' in *Mill*: see above.)

Fox sent a copy of the poem to J. S. Mill; Mill's offer to review it was turned down first by the *Examiner* and then by *Tait's*, whose one-line review had already appeared: '*Paulina* [sic], a piece of pure bewilderment'. Mill thereupon returned his copy to Fox: 'I send Pauline having done all I could, which was to annotate copiously in the margin and sum up on the fly-leaf. On the whole the observations are not flattering to the author—perhaps too strong in the expression to he shown him' (cited in Mary D. Reneau, 'First Editions of Browning's *Pauline*', *BBI*, Second Series [July 1931] 45). Mill's comment implies that his annotations were not intended as the basis for a review, but were made as a substitute for it. His marginal comments are rec. in our notes to the lines to which they refer; his 'summing-up' (not on the flyleaf, as stated, but on the recto and verso of a blank leaf at the end of the book) reads as follows:

> With considerable poetic powers, this writer seems to me possessed with a more intense and morbid self-consciousness than I ever knew in any sane human being—I should think it a *sincere confession* though of a most unloveable state, if the 'Pauline' were not evidently a mere phantom. All about *her* is full of inconsistency—he neither loves her nor fancies he loves her, yet insists upon *talking* love to her—if she *existed* and loved him, he treats her most ungenerously and unfeelingly. All his aspirings and yearnings and regrets point to other things, never to her—then, he *pays her off* towards the end by a piece of flummery,

amounting to the modest request that she will love him and live with him and give herself up to him *without* his loving *her, moyennant quoi* he will think her and call her everything that is handsome and he promises her that she shall find it mighty pleasant. Then he leaves off by saying he knows he shall have changed his mind by tomorrow, & despise 'these intents which seem so fair', but that having been 'thus visited' once no doubt he will again—& is therefore 'in perfect joy' bad luck to him! as the Irish say.

A cento of most beautiful passages might be made from this poem—& the psychological history of himself is powerful and truthful, *truth-like* certainly all but the last stage. *That* he evidently has not yet got into. The self-seeking & self-worshipping state is well described—beyond that, I should think the writer had made, as yet, only the next step; viz. into despising his own state. I even question whether part even of that self-disdain is not *assumed*. He is evidently *dissatisfied*, and feels part of the badness of his state, but he does not write as if it were purged out of him—if he once could muster a hearty hatred of his selfishness, it would *go*—as it is he feels only the *lack* of *good*, not the positive *evil*. He feels not remorse, but only disappointment. A mind in that state can only be regenerated by some new passion, and I know not what to wish for him but that he may meet with a *real* Pauline.

Meanwhile he should not attempt to shew how a person may be *recovered* from this morbid state—for *he* is hardly convalescent, and 'what should we speak of but that which we know?'

Fox did return *Mill* to B., whose reactions to some of Mill's comments are rec. in our notes. He did not respond directly to the 'summing-up', but his comments in later years suggest that he misconstrued Mill's remarks—whether by error or design, and whether at the time or retrospectively, is impossible to determine. He wrote to EBB. in an early letter: 'I know myself—surely—and always have done so—for is there not somewhere the little book I first printed when a boy, with John Mill, the metaphysical head, *his* marginal note that "the writer possesses a deeper self-consciousness than I ever knew in a sane human being"' (26 Feb. 1845, *LK* 28; note the replacement of 'possessed with a more intense and morbid' by 'possesses a deeper'; there is another, similar ref., in a letter of 24 May 1845: see below). According to F. W. Farrar (*Men I Have Known* [New York 1897] 65), B. also claimed that the non-appearance of 'an appreciative review from the pen of the first literary and philosophic critic of his day', and its replacement by 'one insolent epithet from some nameless nobody' in *Tait's*, 'retarded any recognition of me by twenty years' delay'; a claim which, as Lewis F. Haines argues ('Mill and *Pauline*: The "Review" that "Retarded" Browning's Fame', *MLN* lix [June 1944] 410–12), was based on an exaggerated estimate of Mill's status and influence as a critic at that period, as well as some distortion of his opinion of the poem. In later life, B. habitually blamed his slow progress towards public acceptance on the non-appearance of certain reviews or documents (such as Dickens's appreciative letter on *A Blot*, 'suppressed', as B. saw it, by Forster), or the public reticence of influential friends, such as Carlyle, who praised him in private.

'To the best of my belief', B. wrote to T. J. Wise in 1886, 'no single copy of the original edition of *Pauline* found a buyer; the book was undoubtedly "stillborn,"—and that despite the kindly offices of many friends, who did their best to bring about a successful birth' (*LH* 251). In a letter of 27 Mar. 1835 to W. J. Fox, B. blamed this failure on the publishers, Saunders and Otley: 'so much money was paid, so many copies stipulated for,—& from that time to this I have been unable to ascertain whether a dozen have been disposed of or two dozen really printed—but *this* I *did* ascertain, from more quarters than one, that several well-disposed folks actually sought copies & found none—& that so exorbitant a price was affixed to a trifle of a few pages, as to keep it out of the hands of everybody but a critic intending to "show it up"' (*Correspondence* iii 130; the 'exorbitant' price of the first edition, which numbered 67 pages, is not known). B. eventually retrieved the unbound sheets from the publishers (letter to EBB., 15 Jan. 1846, *ibid.* xi 317), and suppressed all trace of his authorship, except among close friends such as Forster and Joseph Arnould (he did not however destroy the copies he retrieved, and several were presented to friends after the appearance of the poem in *1868*: see *Collections* 427). Arnould wrote of it to Alfred Domett in 1847, in terms which may derive from B. himself, as 'a strange, wild (in parts singularly magnificent) poet-biography: his own early life as it presented itself to his own soul viewed poetically: in fact, psychologically speaking, his "Sartor Resartus": it was written and published three years before "Paracelsus," when Shelley was his God' (*RB & AD* 141). However, the poem was mentioned in an article in the *New Quarterly Review* in Jan. 1846 as an example of B.'s precocity in versification, the person who supplied knowledge of its existence being perhaps Thomas Powell, a former friend of B.'s (letter to EBB., 11 Jan. 1846, *Correspondence* xi 308). The article drew the poem to the attention of EBB., who asked to see it; B., however, successfully evaded her request: 'Will you, and must you have "Pauline"? If I could pray you to revoke that decision! For it is altogether foolish and *not* boylike—and I shall, I confess, hate the notion of running over it—yet commented it must be; more than mere correction! I was unluckily *precocious*—but I had rather you saw real infantine efforts . . (verses at six years old,—and drawings still earlier)—than this ambiguous, feverish—Why not wait?' (15 Jan. 1846, *ibid.* 317). EBB. agreed, on condition that she saw the poem '*some day*' (15 Jan. 1846, *ibid.* 319); it is not known whether she did in fact ever see *Pauline*, since it was not included in *1849*, but it is probable that B. did show it to her after their marriage. In 1847, Dante Gabriel Rossetti read the poem 'with warm admiration' in the British Museum and, remarking the 'noticeable analogy in style and feeling to . . . *Paracelsus*', guessed that B. was the author; he wrote to him at Florence asking him to confirm the fact (*Letters of Dante Gabriel Rossetti*, ed. O. Doughty and J. R. Wahl [Oxford 1965] i 32; for B.'s account of this episode, see his letter of *c.* Aug. 1882 to William Sharp, *LH* 220 [wrongly dated *c.* 1883]). B. also mentioned the existence of the poem in a letter of 1848 to R. H. Horne (see I. 4).

There is no indication that B. revised the poem after his alterations in *Mill*, or that he would ever have considered republishing it voluntarily. But in Feb. 1867 he received a letter from R. H. Shepherd requesting permission to publish extracts from the poem, and replied, giving his permission 'if you will strictly confine yourself to "a few extracts"—and will preface these with mention of the fact that the poem was purely dramatic and intended to head a series of "Men & Women" such as I have afterwards introduced to the world under somewhat better auspices,—mentioning this on your own authority, and not in any way alluding to this of mine—and, further, if you will subject the whole of the extracts to my approval—(*not* a single remark upon them,—only the extracts themselves) —in this case, and not otherwise, I give the leave you desire' (cited in William L. Phelps, 'Notes on Browning's *Pauline*', *MLN* xlvii [May 1932] 292–9). Though Shepherd did not go ahead with his project, B. clearly became alarmed at the possibility of an unauthorized edition of the poem appearing, and decided to include it in his forthcoming collection (*1868*). He did so with the following preface:

The poems that follow are printed in the order of their publication. The first piece in the series, I acknowledge and retain with extreme repugnance, indeed purely of necessity; for not long ago I inspected one, and am certain of the existence of other transcripts, intended sooner or later to be published abroad: by forestalling these, I can at least correct some misprints (no syllable is changed) and introduce a boyish work by an exculpatory word. The thing was my earliest attempt at "poetry always dramatic in principle, and so many utter-ances of so many imaginary persons, not mine," which I have since written according to a scheme less extravagant and scale less impracticable than were ventured upon in this crude preliminary sketch—a sketch that, on reviewal, appears not altogether wide of some hint of the characteristic features of that particular *dramatis persona* it would fain have reproduced: good draughtsman-ship, however, and right handling were far beyond the artist at that time.

R.B.

London, December 25, 1867.

The phrase 'poetry always dramatic in principle [etc.]' comes from the supple-mentary 'Advertisement' to *DL*: see Appendix B, II 471. B.'s claim that 'no syllable is changed' is not strictly accurate—and the asterisks which emphasized the status of the text as a 'fragment' in *1833*, disappear in *1868*—but B. made no attempt to revise the poem as a whole. In *1888* B. repr. this preface and then added:

I preserve, in order to supplement it, the foregoing preface. I had thought, when compelled to include in my collected works the poem to which it refers, that the honest course would be to reprint, and leave mere literary errors unaltered. Twenty years' endurance of an eyesore seems more than sufficient: my faults remain duly recorded against me, and I claim permission to somewhat diminish these, so far as style is concerned, in the present and final edition where "Pauline" must needs, first of my performances, confront the reader. I have simply removed solecisms, mended the metre a little, and endeavoured to strengthen the phraseology—experience helping, in some degree, the help-lessness of juvenile haste and heat in their untried adventure long ago.

. . .

R.B.

London: *February 27, 1888.*

The implication that the revs. are merely matters of style is misleading: many of them disembarrass the writer of the 'juvenile haste and heat' of his opinions and feelings, as well as his way of expressing them: see e.g. ll. 193–7n., 387–90n., 410–13n.

Biographical background

The vehemence of B.'s protestations that *Pauline* was a 'dramatic' poem has helped convince most biographers that it is actually autobiographical. However, the hero's situation and personal (as opposed to intellectual) history are evidently imagined. Joseph Arnould may well have been echoing B. himself in calling the poem the story of B.'s 'own early life as it presented itself to his own soul viewed poetically'; the details about the writer's reading, and about the development of his religious and aesthetic ideas, are probably authentic (see below, *Sources*). Vivienne Browning (*My Browning Family Album* [1979] 39f.) argues that B.'s paternal aunt Jemima, who was only two years older than he, is the original of Pauline; there is however no hard evidence for this view, and the figure of Pauline is almost

certainly, as Mill said, 'a mere phantom', at any rate as regards her sexual relationship with the writer. In other respects, there may well be, as Mrs Orr
suggests, a recollection of Eliza Flower, whom B. knew with her sister Sarah
when they were the wards of W. J. Fox in the late 1820s. At that time, Fox was
a well-known Unitarian minister and a leading member of the liberal and
Nonconformist intelligentsia. He later edited the *Monthly Repository*, in which,
after the favourable review of *Pauline*, B. published five early poems; B. wrote
to Fanny Haworth of his 'magnificent and poetical nature' and called him 'my
literary father' (*Correspondence* iii 256). Eliza Flower (1803–46) was a talented
musician and composer (B. later asked her to supply music for the songs in *Pippa*:
see headnote, p. 82). Mrs Orr states that B. 'conceived a warm admiration for
Miss Flower's talents, and a boyish love for herself. She was nine years his senior;
her own affections became probably engaged, and, as time advanced, his feeling
seems to have subsided into one of warm and very loyal friendship . . . he never
even in latest life mentioned her name with indifference' (Orr *Life* 37). B.'s own
account of the relationship is contained in a letter to R. H. Horne of 3 Dec. 1848
requesting Horne's help in retrieving his letters and copies of early poems from
Eliza Flower's executors (*LH* 19–22; see headnote to *The Dance of Death*, I 3–4).

Sources and Influences

In its form, *Pauline* combines the *confession* and the *fragment*. The confession was
originally a religious genre, stemming from the conversion of St Paul (see *Acts*
ix 1–25), in which the autobiographer narrates the life he led previous to his
conversion to the religious security he now enjoys. That life is marked as
unregenerate by sinful conduct and thoughts or by religious doubt, as originally
in St Augustine's *Confessions*, and later in the seventeenth century 'Puritan
confession', the most famous example of which, Bunyan's *Grace Abounding*, was
in Browning's father's library (*Collections* A527–9, p. 47). Eighteenth-century
and Romantic 'confessions' commonly omit or obscure the motif of religious
conversion, as e.g. Rousseau's *Confessions* (1781–8) and De Quincey's *Confessions
of an English Opium-Eater* (1822), where the interest is more purely autobiographical, though the emphasis upon morally dubious conduct persists.
Rousseau may be of particular significance because of Hazlitt's admiration for
the *Confessions* as an epic of egotism and sensibility; cp. his essay *On the Character
of Rousseau* (1817): 'His speculations are the obvious exaggerations of a mind,
giving a loose to its habitual impulses, and moulding all nature to its own
purposes . . . Hence his excessive egotism, which filled all objects with himself,
and would have occupied the universe with his smallest interest . . . Hence his
dissatisfaction with himself and with all around him; for nothing could satisfy
his ardent longings after good, his restless appetite of being. Hence his feelings,
overstrained and exhausted, recoiled upon themselves, and produced his love of
silence and repose, his feverish aspirations after the quiet and solitude of nature'.
In other examples, such as Hazlitt's own *Liber Amoris* and Shelley's *Epipsychidion*,
the story is of a clandestine love-affair, in which the woman may be the
addressee. Elements of all these varieties may be found in *Pauline*, though conversion is present only as a wish (see ll. 986–94); in this respect, and in several
others, *Pauline* clearly owes much to Tennyson's *Supposed Confessions of a
Second-Rate Sensitive Mind not in Unity with Itself* (1830). This poem is however
a soliloquy, and rhetorically much simpler than *Pauline*. B.'s placing of his writer
in the middle of a shifting flux of moods and attitudes, rather than at a stable
point of retrospection, together with the use of an addressee, suggests the
influence of the Romantic 'conversation poem', e.g. Coleridge's *Aeolian Harp* and

Dejection: An Ode; cp. also *The Picture*, which contains a woodland description
having features in common with ll. 732–80. Another source for this style could
be the 'chants de Corinne' with which Mme de Staël's *Corinne* (1809) is
interspersed, and which Corinne herself describes thus: 'I should say that
improvisation is to me like animated conversation. I do not restrict myself
to such and such subjects; I abandon myself to the impression produced by the
interest of those who listen to me'.

The fragment had become a major literary genre during the Romantic
period. Many examples are to be found in Wordsworth and Coleridge, such
as Coleridge's *Kubla Khan* and *Christabel* and Wordsworth's *Nutting* and *A
Night-Piece*; Keats's *Hyperion* is probably the longest. In these poems, however,
the fragmenting involves breaking off (Coleridge, Keats) or starting abruptly
(Wordsworth); the *internal* fragmenting used in *Pauline* is most notably anticipated
in Byron's *The Giaour*, a narrative poem which concludes with a long confessional passage. The posthumous publication of many of Shelley's fragments by
Mary Shelley in 1824, and of some Byron fragments in 1830, may also have
influenced this motif: B.'s first volume of Shelley (a pirated edition of 1826, publ.
by William Benbow) contains, like Mary Shelley's, a whole section entitled
'Fragments', as well as the fragmentary *Triumph of Life*. The pretence that a work
is a fragmented manuscript was a common 18th-century device, e.g. Swift's *Tale
of a Tub* and Mandeville's *Fable of the Bees* (presented to B. by his father in Feb.
1833). These, and Pope's *Dunciad*, also have pseudo-editorial footnotes which may
have influenced B.'s attribution of a footnote to Pauline (see l. 811n.). In the
Romantic period, the technique of a fictitious textual apparatus was used by Shelley
(*Epipsychidion, Julian and Maddalo*) and Scott (*Tales of My Landlord*). With a few
exceptions, B. eschewed both confession and fragment in later works, though the
form of the dramatic monologue owes something to both. B. continued on
occasion to play on the 'documentary' status of his texts: see below, *Parallels in
B*. Later editions of *Pauline* considerably tone down the fragmentariness of 1833,
e.g. in the elimination of asterisks and incomplete lines.

B.'s note at the end of the poem in *Mill* suggests the importance of *Richard III*
in the conception of *Pauline*, though B. implies that Kean himself rather than
Shakespeare was the main influence. The play itself, with its themes of usurpation and despotism, and perhaps the sexual exploitation involved in Richard's
seduction of Lady Anne (I ii), may have influenced some aspects of the writer's
psychomachia. Richard's defiant self-assertion in the face of guilt and defeat
had already made him a proto-Romantic hero in the eyes of Byron and other
writers; B.'s self-identification with him continued at least until his letter to Fox
about *Paracelsus*:

> therefore a certain writer who meditated a notice (it matters not laudatory or
> otherwise) on "Pauline" in the "Examiner," must be benignant or supercilious
> as he may choose, but in no case an idle spectator of my first appearance
> on any stage (having previously only dabbled in private theatricals) and bawl
> "Hats off!" "Down in front!" &c., as soon as I get to the proscenium; and
> he may depend that tho' my "Now is the winter of our discontent" be rather
> awkward, yet there shall be occasional outbreaks of good stuff—that I shall
> warm as I get on, and finally wish "Richmond at the bottom of the seas," &c.
> in the best style imaginable. (*Correspondence* iii 135: B. quotes *Richard III* I i 1
> and misquotes IV iv 463–4)

Equally, the performance imagined in this passage closely resembles B.'s description of the dying Kean's (ll. 669–75), a description corroborated by other

commentators. Thomas Talfourd wrote: 'He whispers when he should shout; creeps and totters when he should spring or rush forward; and is even palpably assisted by his adversary to fight or fall. Yet his last look at Richmond as he stands is fearful'. John Doran, referring to a performance of 1832, commented: 'The sight was pitiable. Genius was not traceable in that bloated face; intellect was all but quenched in those once matchless eyes; and the power seemed gone, despite the will that would recall it. I noted in a diary, that night, the above facts, and, in addition, that by bursts he was as grand as he had ever been' (quoted H. N. Hillebrand, *Life of Edmund Kean* [New York 1933] 320). Richard III had been, in Kean's own words, 'that character which has been the foundation of my fame and fortune', and B. could have read in Thomas Moore's *Letters and Journals of Lord Byron* (2 vols., 1830) Byron's comment on Kean's performance of it in his prime: 'Just returned from seeing Kean in Richard. By Jove, he is a soul! Life—nature—truth—without exaggeration or diminution. Kemble's Hamlet is perfect;—but Hamlet is not Nature. Richard is a man; and Kean is Richard' (i 500). B. almost certainly knew Hazlitt's numerous reviews of performances by Kean (collected in *A View of the English Stage*, 1818), and some details seem to show Hazlitt's influence, in particular the emphasis on power and manipulation: 'Richard should woo, not as a lover, but as an actor—to shew his mental superiority, and power to make others the playthings of his will' was Hazlitt's comment: see e.g. ll. 340–3, 469–88. B.'s opinion of Kean included however an element of revulsion, presumably inspired by Kean's notorious love-affair with one Mrs Cox, which had led to a lawsuit and Kean's public disgrace and private decline; he wrote to EBB. on 24 May 1845: '[I] have known good & wicked men and women, gentle & simple, shaking hands with Edmund Kean and Father Mathew, you and—Ottima!' (*Correspondence* x 234; Ottima's crimes are adultery and murder: see *Pippa* i. Since Father Mathew was a well-known temperance reformer, B. may also have had Kean's alcoholism in mind). B. went on: 'Then, I had a certain faculty of self-consciousness, years, years ago, at which John Mill wondered, and which ought to be improved by this time, if constant use helps at all'—suggesting a continued association between Kean and *Pauline.*

Shelley is invoked in several passages (see ll. 142f., 404f. 1020f.); his poet-biography *Alastor* was clearly important in the formation of B.'s protagonist, and the poem's vocabulary is frequently Shelleyan. However, Shelley's influence should not be overestimated at the expense of other Romantic writers, notably Byron and Coleridge.

Various classical writers are cited, the most important of whom is Plato (see ll. 405–6): the story of a person driven through successive grades of experience by love, or the desire for love, clearly owes something to the *Symposium*. The Swiss nationality of Pauline herself points again to Rousseau's *Confessions*, or more generally to the stress on erotic sensibility in Rousseau's work, as e.g. *La Nouvelle Héloïse*, where the relation between St Preux and Julie has affinities with that between the writer and Pauline. A number of French sources have been suggested by H.-L. Hovelacque (*La Jeunesse de Robert Browning* [Paris 1932]) and reviewed by R. E. Gridley (*The Brownings and France* [1982]). Most involve no more than generalized affinities of character and situation; more useful is Gridley's citation of Balzac's *La Peau de Chagrin* (1831), 'with its romantic egoist Raphael de Valentin seeking redemption through love for his Pauline [and] a long Alpine sojourn and a closing scene with Pauline cradling the head of the hero in his arms' (p. 17). The supernatural powers associated with the ass's skin link Balzac's novel, like *Pauline*, to the Faustianism fashionable in this period. Balzac's specific variation on this theme is to make it a critique of the Will: Valentin's every wish is granted, but each consumes more of the substance of the wild ass's skin whose disappearance will be the moment of his death. The speaker of *Pauline* (not to mention Kean) appears similarly consumed and prematurely aged by his desires. Gridley also draws attention to a possible affinity between B.'s anxiety in the successive prefaces to the poem to distinguish himself from its speaker and the preface to the first edition of *La Peau de Chagrin* in which Balzac discusses the relations between authors and their works, suggesting that there are those, such as himself, 'whose spirit and manner strongly contrast with the form and depth of their works'. Gridley also suggests that Pauline's monitory role owes something to the heroine of Mme de Staël's *Corinne* (1809); for a verbal echo see p. 59.

Parallels in B.

The development of a poet, and his failure in his mission, are themes which dominate B.'s early work, esp. *Paracelsus* (I 98), with the poet Aprile, and *Sordello* (I 350); later figures are painters (Andrea del Sarto [p. 385] and Fra Lippo Lippi [p. 477]), or failures in life rather than art (Childe Roland [p. 384], Prince Hohenstiel-Schwangau [1871]); Cleon (p. 563) is an exception to this pattern. Pauline, the maternal mistress, begins a gallery of similar figures: Michal in *Paracelsus*, Lady Carlisle in *Strafford* (1837), Palma in *Sordello*, Polyxena in *King Victor and King Charles* (1842), and Eulalia in *A Soul's Tragedy* (II 180). The confessional motif reappears in B.'s autobiographical intervention in *Sordello* (iii 577f., I 562–3), where he also addresses a beloved female figure and relates the history of his poetic and moral development. The confession is later refracted into dramatic monologue, in the apologetics of such figures as Bishop Blougram (p. 279), Mr Sludge (p. 771), and Juan in *Fifine at the Fair* (1872). Note also *Confessional* (II 337), *Confessions* (*DP*, 1864), and *A Forgiveness* (*Pacchiarotto*, 1876). Similarly, the 'physical' fragmenting of the text was replaced by dramatic cuttings into and out of a spoken discourse addressed to an interlocutor (see e.g. *My Last Duchess* [p. 197] and *Mr Sludge*, though in *Heretic's Tragedy* [III 219] and *A Death* [p. 714] it is again the poem-as-document which is emphasised). The external commentary introduced by Pauline's note reappears as B.'s introduction to *Holy-Cross Day* (p. 540), in the end-comments in *Bishop Blougram* and *The Statue and the Bust* (III 342), and in later poems as prologues and epilogues which enter into complex relations with the main poem. The kind of elaborate descriptive 'panel' of ll. 732–810 does not reappear until *Gerard de Lairesse* (*Parleyings*, 1887), where it likewise takes the form of a conducted landscape tour, this time with the reader as companion.

Story and structure

The protagonist of *Pauline* is a young poet. He describes his early life as solitary and bookish (ll. 318–35). He was ambitious, though he had not yet found his vocation (ll. 339–43). In his adolescence he underwent a mental crisis, which his solitary life helped him to come through (ll. 344–56). In the aftermath of this crisis, he turned to writing poetry, as one of a number of possible modes of artistic expression (ll. 357–76). His first crude efforts were followed by imitations of 'mighty bards' (ll. 377–93). He then searched for a particular model, and found one in a writer he calls 'sun-treader' (i.e. Shelley: the term 'sun-treader' appears in an earlier invocation, l. 151). In a frenzy of enthusiasm, he adopted Shelley's most radical political programmes: 'Men were to be as gods, and earth as heaven' (ll. 394–428). The disappointment of these visionary hopes (ll. 429–39) was followed by a decision to 'look on real life' (ll. 440–6). However, this too proved disappointing, and he ended by abandoning his faith in, and sympathy with, mankind (ll. 447–61). He now entered a phase of narcissism and cynical detachment, which militated even against his poetic ambitions (ll. 462–544). At the end of this period he experienced some renewal of interest in 'old delights' such as music, and he describes himself as having been 'most happy', although it is clear that his creative faculty was still in abeyance (ll. 563–7). It was at this point that he first met Pauline (ll. 560–3). When he discovered that her love for him was of a higher kind than his for her, he realized the extent of his egotism and the damage it had done to his soul (ll. 577–85). He revealed his state of mind to Pauline, who encouraged him to hope for recovery (ll. 55–75). To help him resume his vocation as a poet, Pauline urged him to write an account of his development up to this point.

Pauline therefore purports to be the fragmentary text of the young man's written confession to Pauline, which she has read and, as she explains in a footnote to l. 811, reluctantly allows to be published. In addition to the narrative passages which have been cited, the young man engages in abstract self-analysis (e.g. ll. 260–317) and invokes and addresses Pauline, the 'sun-treader', and God (e.g. the opening lines, ll. 151–229, 243–51, 729–810, 822–54). The addresses to Pauline are to her as reader and are not to be thought of as the text of a spoken utterance. Mill's objection to the end of the poem (see final note) reflects a misunderstanding of this point.

[Epigraph]

Non dubito, quin titulus libri nostri raritate suâ quamplurimos alliciat ad legendum: inter quos nonnulli obliquae opinionis, mente languidi, multi etiam maligni, et in ingenium nostrum ingrati accedent, qui temerariâ suâ ignorantiâ,
[5] vix conspecto titulo clamabunt: Nos vetita docere, haeresium semina jacere: piis auribus offendiculo, praeclaris ingeniis scandalo esse: . . . . adeò conscientiae suae consulentes, ut nec Apollo, nec Musae omnes, neque Angelus de coelo

Epigraph. Taken from the preface to Heinrich Cornelius Agrippa's *De Occulta Philosophia*, first publ. 1531, included in an anthology which was, with other of Agrippa's works, in Browning's father's library (*Maynard* 210, 434–5; *Collections* A27, p. 5). Agrippa was the most famous alchemist and occultist before Paracelsus. F. A. Pottle (*Shelley and Browning: A Myth and Some Facts* [1923 repr. 1965] 84–90) notes the following omissions:

[*1*]. *nostri raritate*] nostri de Occulta Philosophia, sive de Magia, raritate

[*4–5*]. *ignorantiâ, vix*] ignorantia, Magiae nomen in deteriorem partem accipientes, vix

[*5*]. *vetita docere*] vetitas artes docere

[*7*]. *esse: . . . . adeo*] esse: maleficum esse, superstitiosum esse, daemoniacum esse, Magus qui sim. Quibus si respondeam, Magum apud literatos viros, non maleficum, non superstitiosum, non daemoniacum sonare: sed sapientem, sed sacerdotem, sed prophetam: Sibyllas magas fuisse, proinde de Christo tam apertissime prophetasse: iam vero et Magos ex mirabilibus mundi arcanis, ipsius mundi autorem Christum cognovisse natum, omniumque primos venisse ad illum adorandum, ipsumque Magiae nomen acceptum Philosophis, laudatum a Theologis, etiam ipsi Evangelio non ingratum. Credo ego istos tam pertinacis supercilii censores Sibyllis et sanctis Magis, et vel ipso Evangelio prius sibi interdicturos, quam ipsum magiae nomen recepturi sint in gratiam: adeo

[10] me ab illorum execratione vindicare queant: quibus et ego nunc consulo, ne scripta nostra legant, nec intelligant, nec meminerint: nam noxia sunt, venenosa sunt: Acherontis ostium est in hoc libro, lapides loquitur, caveant, ne cerebrum illis excutiat. Vos autem, qui aequâ mente ad legendum venitis, si tantam prudentiae discretionem [15] adhibueritis, quantam in melle legendo apes, jam securi legite. Puto namque vos et utilitatis haud parùm et voluptatis plurimùm accepturos. Quod si qua repereritis, quae vobis non placeant, mittite illa, nec utimini. NAM ET EGO VOBIS ILLA NON PROBO, SED NARRO. Caetera tamen propterea non [20] respuite. . . . . . . Ideo, si quid liberius dictum sit, ignoscite adolescentiae nostrae, qui minor quam adolescens hoe opus composui.—*H. Cor. Agrippa, De Occult. Phil.*

London, January, 1833.
V.A. XX.

[*20*]. *respuite. . . . . . Ideo*] respuite. Nam et medicorum volumina inspicientibus contingit, cum antidotis et pharmacis simul etiam venena legere. Fateor praeterea magiam ipsam multa supervcua, et ad ostentationem curiosa docere prodigia: simul haec ut vana relinquite, causas tamen illorum ne ignorate. Quae vero ad hominum utilitatem, ad advertendos malos eventus, ad destruendum maleficia, ad curandos morbos, ad exterminanda phantasmata, ad conservandam vitae, honoris, fortunae dexteritatem, sine Dei offensa, sine religionis iniuria fieri possunt: quis illa non tam utilia censeat, quam etiam necessaria? Sed quia admonui vos, multa me narrando potius quam affirmando scripsisse: sic enim opus esse visum fuerat, quo pauciora praeteriremus: multa insuper Platonicorum caeterorumque gentilium Philosophorum placita secuti sumus, ubi instituto nostro scribendi suggerebant argumentum: ideo   *si quid*] si alicubi erratum sit, sive quid

We use the 17th-century translation of the whole passage (repr. Pottle, pp. 87–8), bracketing B.'s omissions; it will be seen that he has chosen to omit all direct refs. to magic. Pottle notes that B.'s 'vetita' (l. [6]), revised from 'vetitas artes', changes 'forbidden arts' to 'forbidden things'.

I do not doubt but the title of our book [of Occult Philosophy, or of Magic,] may by the rarity of it allure many to read it, amongst which, some of a disordered judgment and some that are perverse will come to hear what I have to say, who, by their rash ignorance, may [take the name of Magic in the worse sense and], though scarce having seen the title, cry out that I teach forbidden [Arts], sow the seeds of heresies, offend the pious, and scandalize excellent wits; [that I am a sorcerer, and superstitious and devilish, who indeed am a Magician: to whom I answer, that a Magician doth not, amongst learned men, signify a sorcerer or one that is superstitious or devilish; but a wise man, a priest, a prophet; and that the Sibyls were Magicianesses, and therefore prophecied most clearly of Christ; and that Magicians, as wise men, by the wonderful secrets of the world, knew Christ, the author of the world, to be born, and came first of all to worship him; and that the name of Magic was received by philosophers, commended by divines, and is not unacceptable to the Gospel. I believe that the supercilious censors will object against the Sibyls, holy Magicians and the Gospel itself sooner

> Pauline, mine own, bend o'er me—thy soft breast
> Shall pant to mine—bend o'er me—thy sweet eyes,
> And loosened hair, and breathing lips, and arms
> Drawing me to thee—these build up a screen
> 5   To shut me in with thee, and from all fear,
> So that I might unlock the sleepless brood
> Of fancies from my soul, their lurking place,

than receive the name of Magic into favor.] So conscientious are they that neither Apollo nor all the Muses, nor an angel from heaven can redeem me from their curse. Whom therefore I advise that they read not our writings, nor understand them, nor remember them. For they are pernicious and full of poison; the gate of Acheron is in this book; it speaks stones—let them take heed that it beat not out their brains. But you that come without prejudice to read it, if you have so much discretion of prudence as bees have in gathering honey, read securely, and believe that you shall receive no little profit, and much pleasure; but if you shall find any things that may not please you, let them alone and make no use of them, for I do not approve of them, but declare them to you. But do not refuse other things, [for they that look into the books of physicians do, together with antidotes and medicines, read also of poisons. I confess that Magic teacheth many superfluous things, and curious prodigies for ostentation; leave them as empty things, yet be not ignorant of their causes. But those things which are for the profit of men—for the turning away of evil intents, for the destroying of sorceries, for the curing of diseases, for the exterminating of phantasms, for the preserving of life, honour, or fortune—may be done without offense to God or injury to religion, because they are, as profitable, so necessary. But I have admonished you that I have writ many things rather narratively than affirmatively; for so it seemed needful that we should pass over fewer things, following the judgments of Platonists and other Gentile Philosophers when they did suggest an argument of writing to our purpose.] Therefore if [any error have been committed, or] anything hath been spoken more freely, pardon my youth, for I wrote this being scarce a young man.

Mill wrote above the passage: 'too much pretension in this motto'; he also underlined 'vix conspecto titulo' (l. [5–6]) and wrote in the margin 'why?' (since the phrase applies to Agrippa's title, not B.'s). In *1888* B. added a note in square brackets beneath the passage. 'This introduction would appear less absurdly pretentious did it apply, as was intended, to a completed structure of which the poem was meant for only a beginning and remains a fragment'. For the 'completed structure', see B.'s 'preface' in *Mill* (headnote, p. 2). For other comments added to the printed text in *1868* and *1888*, see headnote, pp. 19–20. B.'s use of 'pretentious' suggests that he was recalling Mill's comment, even at this late date.
5. *fear,*] fear; (*Mill, Lowell-1888*).
6–7. *the sleepless brood / Of fancies*: the writer compares his 'fancies' to the Furies who, in Aeschylus' *Oresteia*, torment Orestes after he murders his mother Clytemnestra. There is an explicit ref. to the Furies at ll. 573–6 and see also l. 624. Another source may be Milton's *Samson Agonistes* 19–22: 'restless thoughts, that like a deadly swarm / Of hornets armed, no sooner found alone. / But rush upon me thronging, and present / Times past, what once I was, and what am now'; cp. also the Marot motto, p. 1.

Nor doubt that each would pass, ne'er to return
To one so watched, so loved, and so secured.
10 But what can guard thee but thy naked love?
Ah, dearest! whoso sucks a poisoned wound
Envenoms his own veins,—thou art so good,
So calm—if thou should'st wear a brow less light
For some wild thought which, but for me, were kept
15 From out thy soul, as from a sacred star.
Yet till I have unlocked them it were vain
To hope to sing; some woe would light on me;
Nature would point at one, whose quivering lip
Was bathed in her enchantments—whose brow burned
20 Beneath the crown, to which her secrets knelt;
Who learned the spell which can call up the dead,
And then departed, smiling like a fiend
Who has deceived God. If such one should seek
Again her altars, and stand robed and crowned
25 Amid the faithful: sad confession first,
Remorse and pardon, and old claims renewed,
Ere I can be—as I shall be no more.

I had been spared this shame, if I had sate
By thee for ever, from the first, in place
30 Of my wild dreams of beauty and of good,
Or with them, as an earnest of their truth.
No thought nor hope, having been shut from thee,
No vague wish unexplained—no wandering aim

10. 'Naked' can mean 'simple', 'unconcealed', 'unadorned', but also 'vulnerable, defenceless' (*OED*); the nature of Pauline's love for the speaker may both expose her to, and protect her from, contamination (see next lines). Cp. *Sordello* ii 211 (I 746) where the phrase 'naked love' refers to a physical body.

17. to sing: i.e. compose poetry; *OED*'s earliest citation is Milton, *Lycidas* (1637) 10–11: 'Who would not sing for Lycidas? He knew / Himself to sing, and build the lofty rhyme'; this sense is common throughout the 18th and 19th centuries.

18. Nature would point at one: Mill underlined this phrase and put a cross in the margin, keyed to a note at the bottom of the page: 'not I think an appropriate image—and it throws considerable obscurity over the meaning of the passage'. *whose quivering lip*: Oxford compares Shelley, *Alastor* 291: 'his quivering lips'.

21. Oxford compares *Sordello* i 7f. (I 394); cp. also *Ring* i 745–59.

27. as I shall be no more: Mill underlined this phrase and put a cross in the margin, with the comment: 'same remark'. *Oxford* takes this to be a repetition of Mill's previous note (see l. 18n.): the (less likely) alternative is that Mill had noticed the similarity between this phrase and the Marot motto.

31. Or with them: 'or if you had been with them [the "wild dreams"]'.

32. nor] or (*1868–88*).

Sent back to bind on Fancy's wings, and seek
35   Some strange fair world, where it might be a law;
But doubting nothing, had been led by thee,
Thro' youth, and saved, as one at length awaked,
Who has slept thro' a peril. Ah! vain, vain!

Thou lovest me—the past is in its grave,
40   Tho' its ghost haunts us—still this much is ours,
To cast away restraint, lest a worse thing
Wait for us in the darkness. Thou lovest me,
And thou art to receive not love, but faith,
For which thou wilt be mine, and smile, and take
45   All shapes, and shames, and veil without a fear
That form which music follows like a slave;
And I look to thee, and I trust in thee,
As in a Northern night one looks alway
Unto the East for morn, and spring and joy.
50   Thou seest then my aimless, hopeless state,
And resting on some few old feelings, won

34. *Fancy's wings*] fancy's wings (*Lowell-1888*). See l. 368n.
36. *But doubting nothing*: Mill underlined this phrase and wrote in the margin: 'not even *poetically* grammatical'. B. added a comma after 'But' in *1888*. Cp. l. 338n.
42. *the darkness*] the dark (*1888*).
44–6. *take . . . slave*: the sense of this difficult passage seems to be that Pauline is to embody the writer's innermost fantasies, which would otherwise prey on him. The 'form' of l. 46, might be hers (her body, or, more broadly, her self), which will disappear in these masquerades; alternatively, it is the creative imagination itself, which Pauline's physical presence will 'veil', i.e. both conceal and suggest. Cp. Jonson's *Epigramme* xxv, *On Sir Voluptuous Beast*, in which 'Beast' degrades 'his faire, and innocent wife': see esp. ll. 5–6: 'And now her (hourely) her owne cucqueane makes, / In varied shapes, which for his lust shee takes'. Cp. also Balzac's *La Peau de Chagrin*, where Valentin transforms in fantasy the humble Pauline into something more desirable: 'Combien de fois n'ai-je pas vêtu de satin les pieds mignons de Pauline, emprisonné sa taille svelte comme un jeune peuplier dans une robe de gaze, jeté sur son sein une légère écharpe en lui faisant fouler les tapis de son hôtel et la conduisant à une voiture élégante; je l'eusse adorée ainsi, je lui donnais une fierté qu'elle n'avait pas, je la dépouillais de toutes ses vertus, de ses grâces naïves, de son délicieux naturel, de son sourire pour la plonger dans le Styx de nos vices' [How often have I clothed Pauline's dainty feet in satin, confined her form, slender as a young poplar, in a robe of gauze, and thrown a light scarf over her breast while making her tread the carpets of her mansion and conducting her to a splendid carriage; I would have adored her so, I gave her a pride she lacked, I stripped her of all her virtues, her naive charms, her delightful naturalness, of her smile, in order to plunge her in the Styx of our vices]. Mill put a note in the margin opposite ll. 45–6: 'qu. meaning?'
50. Cp. *Epilogue* (*Asolando*, 1889) 9: 'Like the aimless, helpless, hopeless, did I drivel[?]' B. was revising *Pauline* for *1888* at the time this poem was written.

Back by thy beauty, would'st that I essay
The task, which was to me what now thou art:
And why should I conceal one weakness more?

55   Thou wilt remember one warm morn, when Winter
       Crept aged from the earth, and Spring's first breath
       Blew soft from the moist hills—the black-thorn boughs,
       So dark in the bare wood, when glistening
       In the sunshine were white with coming buds,
60   Like the bright side of a sorrow—and the banks
       Had violets opening from sleep like eyes—
       I walked with thee, who knew not a deep shame
       Lurked beneath smiles and careless words, which sought
       To hide it—till they wandered and were mute;
65   As we stood listening on a sunny mound
       To the wind murmuring in the damp copse,
       Like heavy breathings of some hidden thing
       Betrayed by sleep—until the feeling rushed
       That I was low indeed, yet not so low
70   As to endure the calmness of thine eyes;
       And so I told thee all, while the cool breast
       I leaned on altered not its quiet beating;
       And long ere words, like a hurt bird's complaint,
       Bade me look up and be what I had been,
75   I felt despair could never live by thee.
       Thou wilt remember:—thou art not more dear
       Than song was once to me; and I ne'er sung
       But as one entering bright halls, where all
       Will rise and shout for him. Sure I must own
80   That I am fallen—having chosen gifts
       Distinct from theirs—that I am sad—and fain

---

53. The task: i.e. of 'singing', as opposed to uttering the 'confession'.
56–7. Cp. Shelley, *Alastor* 11–12: 'spring's voluptuous pantings when she breathes / Her first sweet kisses'.
58. wood,] emended from 'wood;' in *1833*, a correction made by B. in *Mill* and followed in *Lowell-1888*.
61. Cp. *Winter's Tale* IV iv 120–1: 'violets, dim, / But sweeter than the lids of Juno's eyes'.
62. knew] knew'st (*1870–88*).
73. words, like] words like (*Lowell-1888*).   *words*: i.e. Pauline's words.
74. be what I had been: cp. l. 27n.
78–9. In the light of the following lines, presumably a ref. to the various appearances of Satan amongst his followers: see e.g. *PL* i 541–3, x 441–59.

Would give up all to be but where I was;
Not high as I had been, if faithful found—
But low and weak, yet full of hope, and sure
85   Of goodness as of life—that I would lose
All this gay mastery of mind, to sit
Once more with them, trusting in truth and love,
And with an aim—not being what I am.
Oh, Pauline! I am ruined! who believed
90   That tho' my soul had floated from its sphere
Of wide dominion into the dim orb
Of self—that it was strong and free as ever:—
It has conformed itself to that dim orb,
Reflecting all its shades and shapes, and now
95   Must stay where it alone can be adored.
I have felt this in dreams—in dreams in which
I seemed the fate from which I fled; I felt
A strange delight in causing my decay;
I was a fiend, in darkness chained for ever
100 Within some ocean-cave; and ages rolled,
Till thro' the cleft rock, like a moonbeam, came
A white swan to remain with me; and ages
Rolled, yet I tired not of my first joy
In gazing on the peace of its pure wings.

83. *faithful found*: cp. *PL* v 896–7: 'So spake the Seraph Abdiel faithful found, /
Among the faithless, faithful only he'. Cp. ll. 168–9n.
86. *gay mastery of mind*: cp. 'gai saber' ('the gay science'), a Provençal name for
the art of poetry.
88.] In *1833* this line ends the page; there is no line-space after it in *1868–75*, but
there is in *1888*. The likelihood that B. intended a line-space in *1833* is diminished by the fact that at ll. 267, 393, and 619 the page was left a line short to
indicate a space before the next line.
91. *wide*] wild (*1868–88*); *Oxford* suggests a mispr., pointing out that it is not in
Lowell. Cp. l. 612n, and see also l. 238n.
92. *that*] yet (*Mill*).
99–123. The fiend visited by the white swan and the young witch drawing down
a god are inversions of the Andromeda myth: see ll. 656–67.
99–111. Cp. Shelley, *The Revolt of Islam* VII xiif., in which Cythna is imprisoned
in a sea cave and visited by an eagle and a 'Nautilus'; an inverse source might
be the swan which in *Alastor* rises up as the Poet approaches and departs towards
its home (ll. 272–95). Shelley's emphasis on transformations of identity, and on
the passage of time, may have influenced B.'s treatment.
102. *Oxford* points out that the swan is sacred to Apollo; it was a traditional emblem
of poetry from classical times.
103. *my first joy*] my first free joy (*1888*). 'Tired' in *1833* is a dissyllable.

105 And then I said, "It is most fair to me,
    "Yet its soft wings must sure have suffered change
    "From the thick darkness—sure its eyes are dim—
    "Its silver pinions must be cramped and numbed
    "With sleeping ages here; it cannot leave me,
110 "For it would seem, in light, beside its kind,
    "Withered—tho' here to me most beautiful."
    And then I was a young witch, whose blue eyes,
    As she stood naked by the river springs,
    Drew down a god—I watched his radiant form
115 Growing less radiant—and it gladdened me;
    Till one morn, as he sat in the sunshine
    Upon my knees, singing to me of heaven,
    He turned to look at me, ere I could lose
    The grin with which I viewed his perishing.
120 And he shrieked and departed, and sat long
    By his deserted throne—but sunk at last,
    Murmuring, as I kissed his lips and curled
    Around him, "I am still a god—to thee."
    Still I can lay my soul bare in its fall,

112–23. This passage combines several classical and post-classical motifs. There is a clear allusion to stories in Greek mythology about love between gods and mortals; but B. alters the usual balance of power in such relationships in a way which recalls the tradition, in occult literature, that mortals can summon and control spirits. The dethronement of B.'s 'god' echoes that of Hyperion, and inverts the deification of Apollo, in Keats's *Hyperion* (see ll. 114–15n. and l. 120n.); there are several myths involving Apollo's pursuit of river-nymphs (Daphne, Cyrene), and the association is strengthened by B.'s lifelong interest in the figure of Apollo as god of poetry (e.g. *Sordello* i 893–7, I 454). In addition, the 'young witch' who ruins a god or godlike hero recalls other temptresses, e.g. the Sirens, Circe, Eve, Delilah. Cp. also *Fifine at the Fair* (1872) 218–26, referring to Cleopatra, and suggesting that the decline of the 'god-like' Antony under her influence may have been in B.'s mind here, particularly in view of Antony's reconciliation with her after her apparent betrayal of him at Actium (*Antony and Cleopatra* III ix).
114–15. I watched his radiant form / Growing less radiant: cp. Shelley, *Prometheus Unbound* III iv 155–6: 'gentle radiant forms, / From custom's evil taint exempt and pure'; and Keats, *Hyperion* ii 343–5: 'And be ye mindful that Hyperion, / Our brightest brother, still is undisgraced— / Hyperion, lo! his radiance is here!'
120. he shrieked and departed: contrast the (fragmented) end of Keats's *Hyperion* iii 134–6: 'At length / Apollo shriek'd;—and lo! from all his limbs / Celestial'. See ll. 112–23n.
122. Mill wrote underneath this line, which ends the page in *1833*: 'a curious idealisation of self-worship, very fine, though'. The note presumably refers to the whole passage, not just this line.
123.] B. drew a line below this line in *Mill*; there is no line-space in *1868–75*, but there is in *1888*.

125   For all the wandering and all the weakness
      Will be a saddest comment on the song.
      And if, that done, I can be young again,
      I will give up all gained as willingly
      As one gives up a charm which shuts him out
130   From hope, or part, or care, in human kind.
      As life wanes, all its cares, and strife, and toil,
      Seem strangely valueless, while the old trees
      Which grew by our youth's home—the waving mass
      Of climbing plants, heavy with bloom and dew—
135   The morning swallows with their songs like words,—
      All these seem clear and only worth our thoughts.
      So aught connected with my early life—
      My rude songs or my wild imaginings,
      How I look on them—most distinct amid
140   The fever and the stir of after years!

      I ne'er had ventured e'en to hope for this,
      Had not the glow I felt at His award,
      Assured me all was not extinct within.
      Him whom all honor—whose renown springs up

125. For] Since (*1888*).

129–30. Cp. Shelley, preface to *Alastor*, condemning those who 'keep aloof from sympathies with their kind, rejoicing neither in human joy nor mourning with human grief'. This idea is taken up in *Paracelsus* (see esp. pt. ii) and in *Sordello*.

133. our youth's home: the 'our' is general, and does not refer exclusively to the writer's experience.

135. Cp. *Pippa* iv 214–16 (p. 167).

136. clear: underlined by Mill.

137. So] So, (*Lowell-1888*).

138. rude: primitive; see also ll. 258–9.

140. The fever and the stir: cp. Wordsworth, *Tintern Abbey* 52–3: 'the fretful stir / Unprofitable, and the fever of the world', and Keats, *Ode to a Nightingale* 23: 'the weariness, the fever, and the fret'.

141–229. B. here pays homage to Shelley: cp. Arnould's comment that the poem was written 'when Shelley was his God' (see headnote, pp. 5, 9).

142. His award: Mill underlined the phrase, adding in l. margin: 'what does this mean? His opinion of yourself?', and in r. margin: 'only at the fourth reading of the poem I found out what this meant'. B. asterisked the phrase and put a note at the bottom of the page: 'The award of fame to Him. The late acknowledgment of Shelley's genius'. Maynard 209f. argues convincingly that B. had in mind a series of articles in the *Athenaeum* during July and Aug. 1832 by Shelley's friend Thomas Medwin, in which Medwin affirmed Shelley's status as a major poet, and gave a description of his character and opinions which in some respects anticipates B.'s account in *Shelley* (Appendix A, p. 851).

144. Him] His (*Lowell-1888*).

145   Like sunlight which will visit all the world;
       So that e'en they who sneered at him at first,
       Come out to it, as some dark spider crawls
       From his foul nets, which some lit torch invades,
       Yet spinning still new films for his retreat.—
150   Thou didst smile, poet,—but, can *we* forgive?

       Sun-treader—life and light be thine for ever;
       Thou art gone from us—years go by—and spring
       Gladdens, and the young earth is beautiful,
       Yet thy songs come not—other bards arise,
155   But none like thee—they stand—thy majesties,
       Like mighty works which tell some Spirit there
       Hath sat regardless of neglect and scorn,
       Till, its long task completed, it hath risen
       And left us, never to return: and all

145. Cp. *Psalms* xix 6: 'His [the sun's] going forth is from the end of the heaven, and his circuit unto the ends of it: and there is nothing hid from the heat thereof'.
147–9. as some dark spider . . . his retreat: Mill noted: 'a bad simile the spider does not detest or scorn the light'. The comparison of critics or writers to spiders is common in the 18th century; see e.g. Swift's *Battle of the Books.*
150. Thou didst smile, poet: cp. Shelley, *Lines to a Reviewer* 4–5: 'in vain would you assuage / Your frowns upon an unresisting smile'. Cp. also Shelley's preface to *The Revolt of Islam*: 'calumny and misrepresentation, though it may move me to compassion, cannot disturb my peace . . . If certain Critics were as clear-sighted as they are malignant, how great would be the benefit to be derived from their virulent writings! As it is, I fear I shall be malicious enough to be amused with their paltry tricks and lame invectives'. The italics in 'we' and the line-space after the line were removed in *Lowell-1868.*
151. Sun-treader: Oxford cites Aeschylus, *Prometheus Bound* 151: 'toward the flaming dawn, sun-trodden', but mistakenly adds: 'Shelley thus becomes the dawn': the image would be of Shelley as the sun treading on the dawn. Alternatively, the image might be of Shelley treading on, i.e. triumphing over, the sun; 'tread' in Shelley frequently has the sense of 'trample, extinguish', e.g. *Triumph of Life* 382–90. B. may also be recalling Keats's *Hyperion*, in which Apollo supersedes Hyperion as the sun-god and god of poetry, and *Revelation* xix 17: 'And I saw an angel standing in the sun'.
152–71. B. distinguishes between Shelley's real existence, which has terminated with his death (ll. 152–60), and his life in his works, which still continues for B. The phrase 'thou art still for me' (ll. 162, 168) means 'you still really exist', the emphasis falling on 'art'. Cp. ll. 239–41 of Christopher Smart's *Song to David*, a favourite poem of Browning's: 'All nature, without voice or sound, / Replied, O Lord, THOU ART. // Thou art, to give and to confirm [etc.]'.
152–5. Cp. *Sordello* iii 93–102 (I 530).
156–60. Cp. the description of the poet's deathbed in *How It Strikes* (ll. 99–109, p. 444), which in turn echoes Shelley's *Adonais* 262f.
156. Spirit] spirit (*Lowell-1888*).

160   Rush in to peer and praise when all in vain.
       The air seems bright with thy past presence yet,
       But thou art still for me, as thou hast been
       When I have stood with thee, as on a throne
       With all thy dim creations gathered round
165   Like mountains,—and I felt of mould like them,
       And creatures of my own were mixed with them,
       Like things half-lived, catching and giving life.
       But thou art still for me, who have adored,
       Tho' single, panting but to hear thy name,
170   Which I believed a spell to me alone,
       Scarce deeming thou wert as a star to men—
       As one should worship long a sacred spring
       Scarce worth a moth's flitting, which long grasses cross,
       And one small tree embowers droopingly,
175   Joying to see some wandering insect won,
       To live in its few rushes—or some locust
       To pasture on its boughs—or some wild bird
       Stoop for its freshness from the trackless air,
       And then should find it but the fountain-head,
180   Long lost, of some great river—washing towns
       And towers, and seeing old woods which will live
       But by its banks, untrod of human foot,

162–7. Cp. ll. 383–93n.
163–6. Mill wrote 'beautiful' vertically in the margin opposite these lines (possibly with ref. also to ll. 161–2).
165. I felt of mould like them: combining two senses of 'mould': (a) earth regarded as the material of the human body; (b) a pattern by which something is shaped.
166.] And with them creatures of my own were mixed, (*1888*).
168–9. who have adored, / Tho' single: cp. *PL* v 901–3: 'Nor number nor example with him wrought / To swerve from truth, or change his constant mind, / Though single'. The ref. is again to Abdiel, as at l. 83.
171. Scarce] Not (*Mill*).   *wert*] wast (*Rylands, Lowell-1888*).   *a star to men*: cp. the closing lines of Shelley's *Adonais*: 'The soul of Adonais, like a star / Beacons from the abode where the Eternal are'. Note that for Shelley, Keats is a star, not to men generally, but to the voyager who is 'borne darkly, fearfully afar', i.e. Shelley himself. The phrase is applied to Paracelsus in *Paracelsus* i 534 (I 137). The image of the poet as a star is a commonplace of elegy: see e.g. Dryden, *To the Pious Memory of . . . Mrs Anne Killigrew* 165–77. Cp. also B.'s *Popularity* 1–10 (pp. 450–1).
173–80. Mill wrote vertically in the margin: '*most* beautiful'.
177–8. some wild bird . . . the trackless air: the phrase 'trackless air' occurs in Shelley, *The Witch of Atlas* 115; cp. also *Paracelsus* i 567 (I 139): 'I see my way as birds their trackless way'.
180–9. some great river . . . some great country: cp. the description of the Arve in Shelley's *Mont Blanc* 120–6, and Wordsworth, *The River Duddon* (1820) sonnet xxxiii: 'Beneath an ampler sky a region wide / Is opened round him [the Duddon]:—hamlets, towers, and towns, / And blue-topped hills behold him from afar' (ll. 9–11).

Which, when the great sun sinks, lie quivering
In light as some thing lieth half of life
185   Before God's foot—waiting a wondrous change
        —Then girt with rocks which seek to turn or stay
        Its course in vain, for it does ever spread
        Like a sea's arm as it goes rolling on,
        Being the pulse of some great country—so
190   Wert thou to me—and art thou to the world.
        And I, perchance, half feel a strange regret,
        That I am not what I have been to thee:
        Like a girl one has loved long silently,
        In her first loveliness, in some retreat,
195   When first emerged, all gaze and glow to view
        Her fresh eyes, and soft hair, and lips which bleed
        Like a mountain berry. Doubtless it is sweet
        To see her thus adored—but there have been
        Moments, when all the world was in his praise,

184–5. as some thing . . . wondrous change: 'as some thing lies half-way between life and death, waiting for God to bring about the change from mortality to immortality'.

187. Mill underlined 'ever'.

190. Wert] Wast (*Rylands, Lowell-1888*).

192. I am not what I have been to thee: 'I can no longer consider myself your sole admirer'. Cp. the Marot motto, p. 14.

193–200. This simile can apply either to Shelley or to the speaker. The sense is that one or the other has left the retreat in which they were all-sufficient to each other; either Shelley, by being discovered to be worshipped in the outside world, or the speaker, in producing this poem.

193–7.] Like a girl one has silently loved long
            In her first loneliness in some retreat,
            When, late emerged, all gaze and glow to view
            Her fresh eyes and soft hair and lips which bloom
            Like a mountain berry: doubtless it is sweet (*1888*)

193–4. Cp. (noting 'star' and 'spring', ll. 171–2, and 'untrod of human foot', l. 182) Wordsworth, *She dwelt among the untrodden ways*, esp. ll. 1–8: 'She dwelt among the untrodden ways / Beside the springs of Dove, / A Maid whom there were none to praise / And very few to love: // A violet by a mossy stone / Half hidden from the eye! / —Fair as a star, when only one / Is shining in the sky'.

196–7. lips which bleed / Like a mountain berry: OED defines 'bleed' as 'to be red as blood', but cites only this passage; if 'bleed' is taken in its otherwise universal sense, as meaning 'to emit blood', the image here has an unusual rhetorical structure, in which a simile linking two noun-phrases (red lips / red berries) is mediated by a *verb*, 'bleed', which derives *metonymically* from the first noun-phrase (since lips are filled with blood), but applies *metaphorically* to the second (since berries are filled with red juice).

199. Mill underlined the clause 'when all the world was in his praise' and wrote in the margin 'obscurely expressed'. The sense is 'when his [the lover's] praise meant the whole world to her'. In 1888, B. revised to 'our praise'.

200 Sweeter than all the pride of after hours.
Yet, Sun-treader, all hail!—from my heart's heart
I bid thee hail!—e'en in my wildest dreams,
I am proud to feel I would have thrown up all
The wreathes of fame which seemed o'erhanging me,
205 To have seen thee, for a moment, as thou art.

And if thou livest—if thou lovest, spirit!
Remember me, who set this final seal
To wandering thought—that one so pure as thou
Could never die. Remember me, who flung
210 All honor from my soul—yet paused and said,
"There is one spark of love remaining yet,
"For I have nought in common with him—shapes
"Which followed him avoid me, and foul forms
"Seek me, which ne'er could fasten on his mind;
215 "And tho' I feel how low I am to him,
"Yet I aim not even to catch a tone
"Of all the harmonies which he called up,
"So one gleam still remains, altho' the last."
Remember me—who praise thee e'en with tears,
220 For never more shall I walk calm with thee;
Thy sweet imaginings are as an air,
A melody, some wond'rous singer sings,

200. all the pride] any pride (1888).
203.] I proudly feel I would have thrown to dust (1888).
205. To have seen] To see (Lowell, 1888). There is no line-space after this line in 1868–75. Cp. Memorabilia (p. 553).
207–19. The threefold repetition of 'Remember me' (ll. 207, 209, 219) recalls the ghost's injunction to Hamlet in Hamlet I v: see esp. ll. 91–112. Note the inversion by which the writer here asks a 'spirit' to 'remember' him.
207–8. set this final seal / To wandering thought: underlined by Mill, who put a cross in the margin; he wrote at the top of the page: 'The passages where the meaning is so imperfectly expressed as not to be easily understood, will be marked X'. The sense is 'came to this final conclusion'.
211–18. Cp. the similar abnegation of Shelley in Sordello i 60–73 (I 398). Mill put a cross against ll. 213–14 and wrote vertically in the margin (probably referring to the whole passage): 'the obscurity of this is the greater fault as the meaning if I can guess it right is really poetical'.
217.] "Of harmonies he called profusely up; (1888).
218. So] So, (Lowell-1888).
220–9. Mill wrote vertically in the margin: 'beautiful'. Cp. his own simile for the poet in What is Poetry? (1833): 'Who can hear the affecting words . . . and fancy that he sees the singer? That song has always seemed to us like the lament of a prisoner in a solitary cell, ourselves listening, unseen, in the next'.

Which, though it haunt men oft in the still eve,
They dream not to essay; yet it no less,
225   But more is honored. I was thine in shame,
And now when all thy proud renown is out,
I am a watcher, whose eyes have grown dim
With looking for some star—which breaks on him,
Altered, and worn, and weak, and full of tears.

230   Autumn has come—like Spring returned to us,
Won from her girlishness—like one returned
A friend that was a lover—nor forgets
The first warm love, but full of sober thoughts
Of fading years; whose soft mouth quivers yet
235   With the old smile—but yet so changed and still!
And here am I the scoffer, who have probed
Life's vanity, won by a word again
Into my old life—for one little word
Of this sweet friend, who lives in loving me,
240   Lives strangely on my thoughts, and looks, and words,
As fathoms down some nameless ocean thing
Its silent course of quietness and joy.
O dearest, if, indeed, I tell the past,
May'st thou forget it as a sad sick dream;
245   Or if it linger—my lost soul too soon
Sinks to itself, and whispers, we shall be
But closer linked—two creatures whom the earth
Bears singly—with strange feelings, unrevealed

---

225. in shame: in the period when Shelley's genius was not recognized, and he was attacked for atheism and immorality.
227–9. Contrast Keats, *On First Looking into Chapman's Homer*: 'Then felt I like some watcher of the skies / When a new planet swims into his ken'.
236–7. I the scoffer, who have probed / Life's vanity: conflating a number of biblical texts, notably *Ecclesiastes* i 12–14: 'I . . . gave my heart to seek and search out by wisdom concerning all things that are done under heaven . . . and, behold, all is vanity and vexation of spirit'; and *2 Peter* iii 3: 'there shall come in the last days scoffers, walking after their own lusts'. Cp. also *Proverbs* xiv 6: 'A scorner seeketh wisdom and findeth it not'.
238. old] own (*1868–88*); *Oxford* suggests that this is a mispr., pointing out that it is not in *Lowell*. B. however, after *1849*, frequently revises by replacing a word with another of similar sound: see e.g. ll. 91n., 351–5n., 501n. There are many similar examples in *Paracelsus*. *for*] by (*1888*).
241–2. Cp. Tennyson, *The Kraken* (publ. 1830); B. read Tennyson's early poems as they appeared, and with great enthusiasm.
245–51. Possibly referring to Shelley's *Prometheus Unbound*, where Prometheus and Asia, created during the reign of Saturn, resist and reject the world ruled by Jupiter.
247–8. two creatures whom the earth / Bears singly: i.e. each is the only one of its kind.

But to each other; or two lonely things
250   Created by some Power, whose reign is done,
Having no part in God, or his bright world.
I am to sing; whilst ebbing day dies soft,
As a lean scholar dies, worn o'er his book,
And in the heaven stars steal out one by one,
255   As hunted men steal to their mountain watch.
I must not think—lest this new impulse die
In which I trust. I have no confidence,
So I will sing on—fast as fancies come
Rudely—the verse being as the mood it paints.

260   I strip my mind bare—whose first elements
I shall unveil—not as they struggled forth
In infancy, nor as they now exist,
That I am grown above them, and can rule them,
But in that middle stage, when they were full,
265   Yet ere I had disposed them to my will;
And then I shall show how these elements
Produced my present state, and what it is.

I am made up of an intensest life,
Of a most clear idea of consciousness

249. *But*] Save (*1888*).
251. *world.*] emended from 'world,' in *1833*, a correction made by B. in *Mill* and followed in *1868–88*.
250. *Power*] power (*Lowell-1888*).
252. *whilst ebbing day dies soft*: cp. Keats, *Ode to Autumn* 25: 'While barred clouds bloom the soft-dying day'.
259. *Rudely*: 'in a rough-and-ready manner'; cp. l. 138n.
260–7. Mill drew a line through this passage, commenting at the bottom of the page: 'this only says "you shall see what you shall see" & is more prose than poetry'. The scheme proposed here modifies the traditional confessional stance of, e.g., Rousseau, who traces his identity back to its beginnings (see l. 260.), but does not amount to a self-analysis in structural terms of the writer's psychology.
260. *first elements*: 'primary constituents' (not 'earliest in time'). The 'elements' referred to are not the four traditional elements (air, earth, fire, water) of which all matter was held to be composed; note also that the word does not occur at all in *Paracelsus*, and Paracelsus himself was opposed to the theory of the elements. *OED* cites this passage as the first clear application of the word to human psychology.
263. *rule them,*] rule—(*Lowell-1888*).
268–80. This formulation clearly owes a good deal to Coleridge's *Biographia Literaria* (1817), in which Coleridge, following Schelling, argued that self-consciousness is the leading principle or absolute ground of all knowledge. The qualification in ll. 272–6 probably reflects Coleridge's distinction between the 'primary imagination', which is common to all men as their essential self-consciousness, and the 'secondary imagination', which is self-consciousness in action, and exclusive to the poet.

270   Of self—distinct from all its qualities,
        From all affections, passions, feelings, powers;
        And thus far it exists, if tracked, in all,
        But linked in me, to self-supremacy,
        Existing as a centre to all things,
275   Most potent to create, and rule, and call
        Upon all things to minister to it;
        And to a principle of restlessness
        Which would be all, have, see, know, taste, feel, all—
        This is myself; and I should thus have been,
280   Though gifted lower than the meanest soul.

        And of my powers, one springs up to save
        From utter death a soul with such desires
        Confined to clay—which is the only one
        Which marks me—an imagination which
285   Has been an angel to me—coming not
        In fitful visions, but beside me ever,

272. *tracked,*] emended from 'tracked' in *1833*, a correction made by B. in *Mill* and followed in *Lowell, 1888* (though not *1868–75*).   *in all*: 'in all men'.

277–8. The first occurrence of an idea to which B. returns in other (esp. early) poems, e.g. *Paracelsus* ii 199f. (I 165), *Sordello* i 541f. (I 430), and *Cleon* (p. 563); cp. also B. to EBB., 3 May 1845, where he speaks of a 'primitive folly of mine, which I shall never wholly get rid of, of desiring to do nothing when I cannot do all,—seeing nothing, getting, enjoying nothing, where there is no seeing & getting & enjoying *wholly*' (*Correspondence* x 199–200).

280. *meanest*: 'most poorly endowed', or, possibly, 'humblest in station'.

282. *desires*] desire (*Lowell-1888*).

282–3. a soul . . . *clay*: the imprisonment of the soul in the body, a stock idea in Christian thinking, is central in B.'s thought. The particular source here may be Dryden, *Absalom and Achitophel* 156–8: 'A fiery soul, which, working out its way, / Fretted the pigmy body to decay, / And o'er-informed the tenement of clay'. See also ll. 547, 593–4, and *Sordello* iii 27–9 (I 526). It may be significant that Hazlitt used the same quotation to describe Kean's acting (*A View of the English Stage* [1818] 380: see headnote, p. 23). After *Sordello*, B. uses 'clay' in the literal sense of the material for sculpture as well as in the figurative sense of 'flesh', possibly reflecting his own growing interest in clay modelling; there are frequent refs. to the metaphor of the potter (deriving ultimately from *Job* x 9) in the poems of *DP* (e.g. *James Lee* [p. 665] and *Rabbi Ben Ezra* [p. 649]).

283. *which is*] of powers (*1888*).

284. Mill underlined 'imagination' and wrote in the margin: 'not imagination but Imagination[.] The absence of that capital letter obscures the meaning'. B. made the change in *Mill*, but it was not followed in *1868–88*. B. very rarely uses 'imagination' in the sense of 'the faculty responsible for poetry'; he had probably recently read *Biographia Literaria* (see ll. 268–80n.).

285. *an angel to me*] a very angel (*1888*).

And never failing me; so tho' my mind
Forgets not—not a shred of life forgets—
Yet I can take a secret pride in calling
290 The dark past up—to quell it regally.

A mind like this must dissipate itself,
But I have always had one lode-star; now,
As I look back, I see that I have wasted,
Or progressed as I looked toward that star—
295 A need, a trust, a yearning after God,
A feeling I have analysed but late,
But it existed, and was reconciled
With a neglect of all I deemed his laws,
Which yet, when seen in others, I abhorred.
300 I felt as one beloved, and so shut in
From fear—and thence I date my trust in signs
And omens—for I saw God every where;
And I can only lay it to the fruit
Of a sad after-time that I could doubt
305 Even his being—having always felt
His presence—never acting from myself,
Still trusting in a hand that leads me through
All danger; and this feeling still has fought

290. up—to quell] up to quell (*Lowell-1888*). Note the slight change of meaning.
292. A recurring image in B.: see e.g. *Sordello* iii 309f. (I 544), *Two in the Campagna* 55 (p. 548), *My Star* (III 386); see esp. *Fifine at the Fair* (1872) 900–3: 'each soul lives, longs and works / For itself, by itself, because a lodestar lurks, / An other than itself,—in whatsoe'er the niche / Of mistiest heaven it hide'.
293–4. wasted, / Or progressed] halted / Or hastened (*1888*). 'Halted' means 'limped'.
295–9. The idea here is akin to the Calvinist doctrine of 'assurance'; see headnote to *Johannes Agricola*, pp. 74–5.
300–2. Cp. the elaboration of this theme in *Mr. Sludge* 914–85 (pp. 823–6).
303–4. And I . . . after-time: 'I can only attribute it to the events of a sad later period'.
305–8.] Even his being—e'en the while I felt
        His presence, never acted from myself,
        Still trusted in a hand to lead me through
        All danger; and this feeling ever fought (*1888*)
307–8. a hand that leads me through / All danger: the images of the hand of God, and of God leading the righteous man, are biblical commonplaces. Cp. *Paracelsus* v 52 (I 275): 'So doth thy right hand guide us through the world'; B.'s letter to EBB. of 24 May 1845: 'my own way of worldly life is marked out long ago . . . and I am set going with a hand, winker-wise, on each side of my head, and a directing finger before my eyes' (*Correspondence* x 235); *Popularity* 7 (p. 451): 'That loving hand of His which leads you'; and *Ring* i 38–41: 'I found this book . . . when a Hand, / Always above my shoulder, pushed me once'.

Against my weakest reason and resolves.

310   And I can love nothing—and this dull truth
       Has come the last—but sense supplies a love
       Encircling me and mingling with my life.

       These make myself—for I have sought in vain
       To trace how they were formed by circumstance,
315   For I still find them—turning my wild youth
       Where they alone displayed themselves, converting
       All objects to their use—now see their course!

       They came to me in my first dawn of life,
       Which passed alone with wisest ancient books,
320   All halo-girt with fancies of my own,
       And I myself went with the tale—a god,

309. resolves] resolve (*1888*).

310–12. Mill wrote in the margin: 'explain better what this means'. It means that
sensual love, i.e. lust, performs the role which ought to belong to (spiritual)
love.

311. sense: sensuality; cp. *Measure for Measure* I iv 59: 'The wanton stings and motions
of the sense'.

312. Cp. Shelley, *Prometheus Unbound* I i 79–81: 'I saw not, heard not, moved
not, only felt / His presence flow and mingle through my blood / Till it became
his life'.

313–14. The speaker is seeking to identify the essentials of his nature, as distinct
from qualities which are the product of experience. He implicitly rejects, like
Coleridge, the Locke-Hartley *tabula rasa* theory, in which the mind was assumed
to have been born without innate characteristics.

313. myself] underlined by B. in *Mill*, but not *Lowell-1888*. *for I have sought*]
I have long sought (*1888*).

315–16.] Yet ever found them mould my wildest youth / Where they alone
displayed themselves, converted (*1888*).

315. For] And (*Mill*). *turning*: in the double sense of 'changing the course of'
and 'forming the shape of' (i.e. 'turning' as on a lathe). Or possibly, 'turning
over [in my mind] my wild youth etc.'.

318–35. B. draws here on his own childhood experience, though as with
Development (*Asolando*, 1889) we need not interpret this passage as strictly autobiographical. B.'s father was a bibliophile whose library (of over 6,000 volumes)
contained many rare and curious items. B. received comparatively little formal
education. On this subject see *Maynard* 85–91, 241–86.

321–2. a god, / *Wandering after beauty*: the use of the word 'wandering' makes a
ref. to myths such as those of Apollo and Daphne, or Pan and Syrinx, implausible,
since these involve pursuit rather than quest. However, there may be an echo of
Keats's *Hyperion*, in which Apollo (not yet a god) 'wandered forth' towards his
encounter with Mnemosyne.

Wandering after beauty—or a giant,
Standing vast in the sunset—an old hunter,
Talking with gods—or a high-crested chief,
325   Sailing with troops of friends to Tenedos;—
I tell you, nought has ever been so clear
As the place, the time, the fashion of those lives.
I had not seen a work of lofty art,
Nor woman's beauty, nor sweet nature's face,
330   Yet, I say, never morn broke clear as those
On the dim clustered isles in the blue sea:
The deep groves, and white temples, and wet caves—
And nothing ever will surprise me now—
Who stood beside the naked Swift-footed,

322–4. a giant, / Standing vast in the sunset: almost certainly referring to the myth of Atlas, one of the Titans, who, after the Titans' unsuccessful attempt to conquer Olympus, was banished by Zeus to the far west (hence 'in the sunset') where he was condemned to support the heavens on his shoulders.

323–4. an old hunter, / Talking with gods: Penguin suggests Peleus, who took part in the famous hunt for the Calydonian boar, and was favoured, as the most virtuous of mankind, by the gods, who gave him the nereid Thetis in marriage and attended the wedding with gifts. In the context of the following refs. to the Trojan war (ll. 324–5) and, possibly, to Achilles (l. 334), it is suggestive that this wedding was the occasion for the quarrel between Hera, Aphrodite, and Athene which led to the Trojan war, and that Achilles was the son of Peleus and Thetis. *Oxford*'s suggestion of Orion as the 'old hunter' rests on the parallel with *Paracelsus* ii 370–1 (I 176–7), but is otherwise unsupported.

324–5. a high-crested chief . . . Tenedos: one of the leaders of the Greek expedition against Troy, possibly Agamemnon, whose fate in Aeschylus' *Agamemnon* is alluded to later (ll. 567–71); Tenedos, 'a small and fertile island of the Aegean sea, opposite Troy, . . . became famous during the Trojan war, as it was there that the Greeks concealed themselves the more effectually to make the Trojans believe that they were returned home, without finishing the siege' (*Lemprière*). The epithet 'high-crested' is however particularly associated with the Trojan hero, Hector; cp. e.g. Pope's *Iliad* ii: 'The godlike Hector, high above the rest, / Shakes his huge spear, and nods his plumy crest: / In throngs around his native bands appear'.

331. I.e. the islands of the Aegean; cp. Byron's lyric 'The isles of Greece', in *Don Juan* iii, and *Cleon* 1–3 (pp. 565–6): 'the sprinkled isles, / Lily on lily, that o'erlace the sea, / And laugh their pride when the light wave lisps "Greece"'.

334. the naked Swift-footed: the allusion may be to Achilles, the Greek hero in the Trojan war (see above, ll. 323–4n.), to whom Homer applies the epithet 'swift', or Hermes, the messenger of the gods, who, as *Oxford* points out, was sent to fetch Proserpine from the Underworld (see next note). But 'swift-footed' was a cult epithet of Artemis (cp. Callimachus, *Hymn to Artemis*); if the ref. is to her, then her being seen 'naked' carries the connotations of a proscribed act, as in the story of her transformation of Actaeon into a stag for slaughter by his own hounds in retribution for his having glimpsed her bathing.

335   Who bound my forehead with Proserpine's hair.

And strange it is, that I who could so dream,
Should e'er have stooped to aim at aught beneath—
Aught low, or painful, but I never doubted;
So as I grew, I rudely shaped my life
340   To my immediate wants, yet strong beneath
Was a vague sense of powers folded up—
A sense that tho' those shadowy times were past,
Their spirit dwelt in me, and I should rule.

Then came a pause, and long restraint chained down
345   My soul, till it was changed. I lost myself,

335. Proserpine's] B. put an accent on the first 'e' in *Mill* to indicate the metrical
stress. Proserpine (Persephone, or Koré) was the daughter of Demeter, the
goddess of fertility; she was abducted by Hades, the god of the Underworld, and
was restored to her mother at the instigation of Zeus, though only for half of each
year. Proserpine therefore represents a combination of the erotic and the fatal; but
the precise application of the image here is uncertain. Cp. *Balaustion's Adventure*
(1871) 2618–47; note esp. ll. 2618–21: 'Koré,—throned and crowned / The pensive queen o' the twilight, where she dwells / Forever in a muse, but half away
/ From flowery earth she lost and hankers for', and ll. 2623–8: 'the softened eyes
/ Of the lost maidenhood that lingered still / Straying among the flowers in Sicily'.
336. And] emended from 'An'' in *1833*, a correction made by B. in *Mill* and
followed in *Rylands, Lowell-1888*. The contraction appears nowhere else in his work.
338. but I never doubted: Mill underlined this clause and put a cross in the margin
to indicate obscurity; the sense is that the writer, although he has 'stooped' to
inferior aims, 'never doubted' the true nature of his vocation. B. frequently used
'doubt' in this intransitive way. Cp. l. 36n.
339–40. So . . . wants: B'.s choice of phrasing here may echo Richard's first
soliloquy in *Richard III* I i 14–16: 'But I, that am not shap'd for sportive tricks
. . . I, that am rudely stamp'd'. See headnote, pp. 8–9, for the influence of *Richard
III* on the poem. Contrast also *Hamlet* V ii 10–11: 'There's a divinity that shapes
our ends, / Rough-hew them how we will'. 'Rudely' means 'roughly, unevenly,
unskilfully'. See ll. 138, 259, 382.
341. powers] power though (*1888*), making a monosyllable of *1833*'s 'powers'.
342. those shadowy times: Mill underlined this phrase and wrote in the margin:
'what times? your own imaginative times? or the antique times themselves?' The
fact that B. made no immediate response perhaps indicates that he intended either
reading, or both; in *1888* he revised the phrase to 'those shades and times', which
inclines slightly towards Mill's second reading, though not decisively.
343. Oxford compares *Romans* viii 9: 'But ye are not in the flesh, but in the Spirit,
if so be that the Spirit of God dwell in you'. *and I should rule*] with them should
rule (*1868–88*).
344–56. There may be a ref. to a period of B.'s own youth during which he quarrelled with his family over his Shelleyan ideas. However, the theme of guilt and
remorse was a commonplace of Romantic writing (e.g. Byron). See also ll. 398–9.
344–5. chained down / My soul: cp. ll. 504–5, 593.

And were it not that I so loathe that time,
I could recall how first I learned to turn
My mind against itself; and the effects,
In deeds for which remorse were vain, as for
350   The wanderings of delirious dream; yet thence
Came cunning, envy, falsehood, which so long
Have spotted me—at length I was restored,
Yet long the influence remained; and nought
But the still life I led, apart from all,
355   Which left my soul to seek its old delights,
Could e'er have brought me thus far back to peace.
As peace returned, I sought out some pursuit:
And song rose—no new impulse—but the one
With which all others best could be combined.
360   My life has not been that of those whose heaven
Was lampless, save where poesy shone out;
But as a clime, where glittering mountain-tops,
And glancing sea, and forests steeped in light,
Give back reflected the far-flashing sun;
365   For music, (which is earnest of a heaven,

346. *that time*] that loss (*1888*).
351–5.] Came cunning, envy, falsehood, all world's wrong
       That spotted me: at length I cleansed my soul.
       Yet long world's influence remained; and nought
       But the still life I led, apart once more,
       Which left me free to seek soul's old delights, (*1888*)
352. *spotted*: tainted (as with marks of the plague); this sense is common in B.'s
early work. Cp. *Sordello* v 992–5n (I 715).
358–76. In this passage, the writer considers and compares the various arts in which
his imagination might express itself. Poetry (or 'song') is chosen as uniting the
qualities of music and painting. Painting is represented as the less significant form
(cp. *Old Pictures* 49–56, p. 413).
358–9. *the one . . . combined*. cp. *Sordello* ii 440–51 (I 490).
361. *Was . . . shone*] Is . . . shines (*Mill*).
365–7. *For music . . . revealed*: B. is here close to one of the main tenets of German
(as opposed to English) Romantic aesthetics; M. H. Abrams (*The Mirror and the
Lamp* [New York 1958] 93) cites Wackenroder: 'So is it with the mysterious stream
in the depths of the human spirit—speech reckons and names and describes its
changes in a foreign material; music streams it out before us as it is in itself . . .
In the mirror of tones the human heart learns to know itself'. Cp. also Mme de
Staël's *Corinne*: 'when listening to pure and lovely melody we seem nearly to
penetrate the secret of creation, the mystery of life. No words can express this'
(p. 163). B.'s own love of music rivalled that of poetry in his youth (see *Maynard*
140–1) and continued throughout his life. Cp. *Abt Vogler* (p. 759).
365. *earnest of a heaven*: 'earnest' in the sense of 'pledge'; cp. *Ephesians* i 14: 'ye
were sealed with the Holy Spirit of promise, which is an earnest of our inheritance, unto the redemption of God's own possession, unto the praise of his glory'.

Seeing we know emotions strange by it,
Not else to be revealed,) is as a voice,
A low voice calling Fancy, as a friend,
To the green woods in the gay summer time.
370 And she fills all the way with dancing shapes,
Which have made painters pale; and they go on
While stars look at them, and winds call to them,
As they leave life's path for the twilight world,
Where the dead gather. This was not at first,
375 For I scarce knew what I would do. I had
No wish to paint, no yearning—but I sang.

And first I sang, as I in dream have seen
Music wait on a lyrist for some thought,
Yet singing to herself until it came.
380 I turned to those old times and scenes, where all
That's beautiful had birth for me, and made
Rude verses on them all; and then I paused—
I had done nothing, so I sought to know

367. is as a voice] is like a voice (*1888*). Mill put a cross in the margin and wrote:
'do you mean is *to you* as a voice &c.?'
368. Fancy] fancy (*Lowell-1888*); as usually in B., a synonym for imagination.
370. she: Mill underlined this word and wrote in the margin: 'who? Fancy or
Music?' Again, the lack of revision, either in Mill's copy or in later eds., may
imply that B. was prepared to allow the ambiguity.
371. pale: i.e. envious.   *they*: the 'dancing shapes' of l. 370.
372. While] Till (*1888*).
373–4. Mill put a cross in the margin opposite these lines, indicating obscurity,
but did not underline the particular phrase he had in mind. Possibly he found
the phrase 'This was not at first' puzzling; it refers to the writer's active choice
of 'song' over the other arts; he is repeating what he said above (ll. 360–4), that
this choice was not immediately obvious.
376.] An impulse but no yearning—only sang. (*1888*).
377–9. B. may have in mind W. J. Fox's criticism of his early poems: 'Their
faults seem to have lain in the direction of too great splendour of language and
too little wealth of thought; and Mr. Fox . . . confessed afterwards to Mr.
Browning that he had feared these tendencies as his future snare' (Orr *Life* 36–7).
377. seen] emended from 'seen,' in *1833*, a correction made in *Mill* and *Lowell-1888*.
382. Rude: crude, inexpert: see above, ll. 339–40n.
383–93. This passage expresses a recurrent preoccupation in B.'s early work with
imitation as the necessary first stage of a young poet's career. Imitation is rejected
by Paracelsus (see *Paracelsus* i 581f. [I 139f.]), but embraced by Sordello (see *Sordello*
ii 71–84 [I 466–9]); both positions are articulated by the sculptor Jules in *Pippa*
(see ii 68–98, and iv 37–47, pp. 128–9, 159–60). The principle is most clearly
set out in *Chatterton* (see Appendix C, II 476). The passage may be related to
B.'s early collection, *Incondita* (see headnote to *The Dance of Death*, II 3–4).

What mind had yet achieved. No fear was mine
385 As I gazed on the works of mighty bards,
In the first joy at finding my own thoughts
Recorded, and my powers exemplified,
And feeling their aspirings were my own.
And then I first explored passion and mind;
390 And I began afresh; I rather sought
To rival what I wondered at, than form
Creations of my own; so much was light
Lent back by others, yet much was my own.

I paused again—a change was coming on,
395 I was no more a boy—the past was breaking

384–5.] What other minds achieved. No fear outbroke / As on the works of
mighty bards I gazed, (*1888*).
387–90.] Recorded, my own fancies justified,
    And their aspirings but my very own.
    With them I first explored passion and mind,—
    All to begin afresh! I rather sought (*1888*)
388. And] at (*Mill*; *sic* lower case).
392–4.] Creations of my own; if much was light
    Lent by the others, much was yet my own.
    I paused again: a change was coming—came: (*1888*)
392. so: Mill underlined this word and put a cross in the margin; at the bottom
of the page he wrote: 'this writer seems to use "so", according to the colloquial
vulgarism, in the sense of "therefore" or "accordingly"—from which occasionally comes great obscurity & ambiguity—as here'. B. in turn put a cross above
the word 'vulgarism', drew a line from it to another cross in the r. margin, and
wrote: 'The *recurrence* of "so" thus employed is as vulgar as you please: but the
usage itself of "*so* in the sense of accordingly" is perfectly authorized,—take an
instance or two, from Milton. So farewel Hope, & with Hope farewel Fear!
P[aradise]. L[ost]. 4.108[.] So on he fares, and to the border comes Of Eden,
d[itt]o.132. So down they sat and to their viands fell. 5.433. So both ascend In
the visions of God 11.376. So death becomes his final remedy 11.60. So in his
seed all nations shall be blest 12.450. So law appears imperfect 12.300[.] So all
shall turn degenerate 11.806. So violence proceeded, and oppression 11 671 [.]
So send them forth, tho sorrowing yet in peace 11.117'. (B'.s quotations are substantially correct; in the third, 'And to their viands fell' is a new line; in the fifth,
the line ref. should be 61; in the ninth, 'Proceeded, and oppression' is a new
line.) Despite this comprehensive rebuttal, B. added a comma after 'so' in *Mill*,
and *Rylands*, *Lowell* and *1868–75* (*1888* has a different reading: see next note).
Mill's comment seems to have had a listing impact on him, as a reviser if not a
composer, for there are many examples of commas added to 'so' in revs. of later
poems. (The reader is spared 'an instance or two'.)
395–6. the past . . . worked: Mill underlined the first clause, and put a cross in
the margin indicating obscurity. The sense is that the writer's past identity was
giving way to the change which was coming, and that this process resembled a
fever (which would 'break' from sickness to health).

Before the coming, and like fever worked.
I first thought on myself—and here my powers
Burst out. I dreamed not of restraint, but gazed
On all things: schemes and systems went and came,
400   And I was proud (being vainest of the weak),
In wandering o'er them, to seek out some one
To be my own; as one should wander o'er
The white way for a star.

                    ★   ★   ★   ★

On one, whom praise of mine would not offend,
405   Who was as calm as beauty—being such
Unto mankind as thou to me, Pauline,
Believing in them, and devoting all
His soul's strength to their winning back to peace;
Who sent forth hopes and longings for their sake,
410   Clothed in all passion's melodies, which first
Caught me, and set me, as to a sweet task,
To gather every breathing of his songs.
And woven with them there were words,
        which seemed
A key to a new world; the muttering

396–7.] Before the future and like fever worked. / I thought on my new self, and all my powers (*1888*).
398–9. See ll. 344–56n.
401–2.] In wandering o'er thought's world to seek some one / To be my prize, as if you wandered o'er (*1888*).
403.] The white way for a star.
                        And my choice fell
    Not so much on a system as a man—(*Lowell-1888*; *1888* has 'White Way'). For this and all subsequent occurrences, the *1833* asterisks were eliminated in *1868–88*.
403. The white way: the Milky Way.
404–28. Penguin cites Orr *Handbook* 21, where the 'one' is identified as Plato, but phrases such as 'passion's melodies' (l. 410) favour a renewed allusion to Shelley, whose works B. assiduously collected (see l. 412). That B. was aware of Shelley's interest in Plato is indicated by the parallel between l. 414 and l. 435; and note Shelley's contention in the *Defence of Poetry* that 'Plato was essentially a poet—the truth and splendour of his imagery, and the melody of his language, are the most intense that it is possible to conceive'.
404. one] One (*Mill*).   *would not*] shall not (*1888*).
410–13.] Clothed in all passion's melodies: such first
                    Caught me and set me, slave of a sweet task,
                To disentangle, gather sense from song:
                Since, song-inwoven, lurked there words which seemed (*1888*)

415   Of angels, of some thing unguessed by man.
      How my heart beat, as I went on, and found
      Much there I felt my own mind had conceived,
      But there living and burning; soon the whole
      Of his conceptions dawned on me; their praise
420   Is in the tongues of men; men's brows are high
      When his name means a triumph and a pride;
      So my weak hands may well forbear to dim
      What then seemed my bright fate: I threw myself
      To meet it. I was vowed to liberty,
425   Men were to be as gods, and earth as heaven.
      And I—ah! what a life was mine to be,
      My whole soul rose to meet it. Now, Pauline,
      I shall go mad, if I recall that time.

★   ★   ★   ★

      O let me look back, ere I leave for ever
430   The time, which was an hour, that one waits

415–20.] Of angels, something yet unguessed by man.
      How my heart leapt as still I sought and found
      Much there, I felt my own soul had conceived,
      But there living and burning! Soon the orb
      Of his conceptions dawned on me; its praise
      Lives in the tongues of men, men's brows are high (*1888*)

417. there] emended from 'there!' in *1833*, a correction made by B. in *Mill*;
Lowell-1888 have 'there,'.

419–23. their praise . . . bright fate: the writer argues that since Shelley's ideas are
now known and admired, he need not describe his earlier absorption of them.
The *1833* reading contrasts 'tongues' and 'brows' (l. 420), i.e. homage which is
spoken or conceived, with the writer's 'weak hands', an image which combines
the feebleness of a gesture with the ineffectiveness of writing as a means of
expression. The *1888* reading (see next note) eliminates this contrast.

422–3.] So, my weak voice may well forbear to shame / What seemed decreed
my fate: I threw myself (*1888*).

425. Recalling both the serpent's temptation of Eve in *Genesis* iii 5 ('ye shall be
as gods') and the traditional idea of the millennium as heaven on earth. Cp. Pope,
Essay on Man iv 131–66, in which the idea of a 'kingdom of the Just' (l. 133) is
ridiculed: ' "No—shall the good want Health, the good want Pow'r?" / Add
Health and Pow'r, and ev'ry earthly thing; / "Why bounded Pow'r? why
private? why no king?" / Nay, why external for internal giv'n? / Why is not Man
a God, and Earth a Heav'n?' (ll. 158–62).

426. to be] to prove (*1888*).

429–31. Mill drew a vertical line in the margin by the first two of these lines and
wrote 'fine'. The comment probably applies to the whole sentence, and not, as
Oxford suggests, only up to the word 'time' in the second line.

429. ere] emended to agree with *1888* from 'e'er' (*1833–75*); an obvious mispr.

430. that one waits] one fondly waits (*1888*).

For a fair girl, that comes a withered hag.
And I was lonely,—far from woods and fields,
And amid dullest sights, who should be loose
As a stag—yet I was full of joy—who lived
435   With Plato—and who had the key to life.
And I had dimly shaped my first attempt,
And many a thought did I build up on thought,
As the wild bee hangs cell to cell—in vain;
For I must still go on: my mind rests not.

440   'Twas in my plan to look on real life,
Which was all new to me; my theories
Were firm, so I left them, to look upon
Men, and their cares, and hopes, and fears, and joys;
And, as I pondered on them all, I sought
445   How best life's end might be attained—an end
Comprising every joy. I deeply mused.

And suddenly, without heart-wreck, I awoke
As from a dream—I said, 'twas beautiful,
Yet but a dream; and so adieu to it.

432–5. Possibly, as *Maynard* 268 suggests, referring to B.'s own brief and unsatisfactory period of study at the new London University (now University College London), Oct. 1828–May 1829. Cp. Coleridge, *Frost at Midnight* 51–5: 'For I was reared / In the great city, pent 'mid cloisters dim, / And saw nought lovely but the sky and stars. / But thou, my babe! shalt wander like a breeze / By lakes and sandy shores', and Wordsworth, *Tintern Abbey* 67–8: 'when like a roe / I bounded o'er the mountains'.

434. joy] bliss (*1888*).

435. See ll. 404–28n.

439.] For I must still advance, no rest for mind. (*1888*).

440–3. This movement from theoretical to practical knowledge reappears in *Paracelsus*, with Paracelsus' determination to leave Würzburg for a life of travel and discovery (pt. i), and in *Sordello*, in the transition from Sordello's fantasy life at Goito to the 'veritable business of mankind' (i 1000 [I 460]) at Mantua.

441–4.] The life all new to me; my theories
            Were firm, so them I left, to look and learn
            Mankind, its cares, hopes, fears, its woes and joys;
            And, as I pondered on their ways, I sought (*1888*)

444–5. an end / Comprising every joy: see ll. 277–8n, 601–19.

447. Mill wrote in the margin: 'This, to page 36, is finely painted, & evidently from experience'. Page 36 in *1833* consists of ll. 490–506; there is a full stop in l. 506, though no clear break in the argument.

450 As some world-wanderer sees in a far meadow
Strange towers, and walled gardens, thick with trees,
Where singing goes on, and delicious mirth,
And laughing fairy creatures peeping over,
And on the morrow, when he comes to live
455 For ever by those springs, and trees, fruit-flushed,
And fairy bowers—all his search is vain.
Well I remember ★ ★ ★ ★
First went my hopes of perfecting mankind,
And faith in them—then freedom in itself,
460 And virtue in itself—and then my motives' ends,
And powers and loves; and human love went last.
I felt this no decay, because new powers
Rose as old feelings left—wit, mockery,
And happiness; for I had oft been sad,
465 Mistrusting my resolves: but now I cast
Hope joyously away—I laughed and said,
"No more of this"—I must not think; at length
I look'd again to see how all went on.

My powers were greater—as some temple seemed
470 My soul, where nought is changed, and incense rolls
Around the altar—only God is gone,
And some dark spirit sitteth in his seat!
So I passed through the temple; and to me
Knelt troops of shadows; and they cried, "Hail, king!

451−6.] Strange towers and high-walled gardens thick with trees,
Where song takes shelter and delicious mirth
From laughing fairy creatures peeping over,
And on the morrow when he comes to lie
For ever 'neath those garden-trees fruit-flushed
Sung round by fairies, all his search is vain. (1888). We supply a comma
after 1835 'fruit-flushed'.
457.] Not Lowell-1888.
459−61.] Next—faith in them, and then in freedom's self
And virtue's self, then my own motives, ends
And aims and loves, and human loves went last. (1888)
464. And happiness] Light-heartedness (1888).
467. B. extended the speech to 'think' in Mill.
468. how all went on] if all went well (1888).
471−2. Cp. Shelley, Prometheus Unbound II iv 2−3: 'I see a mighty darkness / Filling
the seat of power', referring to Demogorgon, who is about to overthrow Jupiter.
473. So] So, (Lowell-1888).

475   "We serve thee now, and thou shalt serve no more!
       "Call on us, prove us, let us worship thee!"
       And I said, "Are ye strong—let fancy bear me
       "Far from the past."—And I was borne away
       As Arab birds float sleeping in the wind,
480   O'er deserts, towers, and forests, I being calm;
       And I said, "I have nursed up energies,
       "They will prey on me." And a band knelt low,
       And cried, "Lord, we are here, and we will make
       "A way for thee in thine appointed life,—
485   "O look on us!" And I said, "Ye will worship
       "Me; but my heart must worship too." They shouted,
       "Thyself—thou art our king!" So I stood there
       Smiling   ★   ★   ★   ★   ★

       And buoyant and rejoicing was the spirit
490   With which I looked out how to end my days;
       I felt once more myself—my powers were mine;
       I found that youth or health so lifted me,
       That, spite of all life's vanity, no grief
       Came nigh me—I must ever be light-hearted;

477. *strong*—] strong? (*1868–88*). The alteration changes the meaning from 'if you
are strong . . .' to a straight question.
479. Cp. Shelley, *Lines Written in the Bay of Lerici* 4–6: 'Like an albatross asleep,
/ Balanced on her wings of light, / Hovered in the purple night'.
481–2. Under 'nurse' (sense 5), *J.* cites Locke: 'By what fate has vice so thriven
amongst us, and by what hands been nurs'd up into so uncontroul'd dominion?'
The idea, and the use of 'energies' here, recalls Blake, but it is not certain that
B. had encountered his work at this period.
483–4. *we will make / A way for thee*: cp. *Isaiah* xl 3: 'Prepare ye in the wilderness the way of the Lord, make straight in the desert a high way for our God'.
See also *Mark* i 3.
484–6.] "Safe way for thee in thine appointed life!
         But look on us!" And I said "Ye will worship
         Me; should my heart not worship too?" They shouted (*1888*)
484. *thee in . . . life,*—] emended from 'thee—in . . . life' in *1833*, a correction made
in *Mill*; *1868–75* have 'life!'. For the *1888* reading, see prec. note.
488.] Smiling. . . . . (*1868–75*); Smiling—oh, vanity of vanities! (*1888*). There is no
line-space after this line in *1868–88*; in *1868–75* the line comes at the bottom of
a page.
489–93.] For buoyant and rejoicing was the spirit
         With which I looked out how to end my course;
         I felt once more myself, my powers—all mine;
         I knew while youth and health so lifted me
         That, spite of all life's nothingness, no grief (*1888*)
490. *looked out*: inquired.

495   And that this feeling was the only veil
       Betwixt me and despair: so if age came,
       I should be as a wreck linked to a soul
       Yet fluttering, or mind-broken, and aware
       Of my decay. So a long summer morn
500   Found me; and ere noon came, I had resolved
       No age should come on me, ere youth's hopes went,
       For I would wear myself out—like that morn
       Which wasted not a sunbeam—every joy
       I would make mine, and die; and thus I sought
505   To chain my spirit down, which I had fed
       With thoughts of fame. I said, the troubled life
       Of genius seen so bright when working forth
       Some trusted end, seems sad, when all in vain—
       Most sad, when men have parted with all joy
510   For their wild fancy's sake, which waited first,
       As an obedient spirit, when delight

495–7.] And that this knowledge was the only veil
         Betwixt joy and despair: so, if age came,
         I should be left—a wreck linked to a soul (*1888*)
496. so] so, (*Lowell-1888*).
497. be as a] be a mere (*Mill*).
497–8. a soul / Yet fluttering: 'yet' means 'still'. The Greek word for soul, 'psyche', also means 'butterfly', as *Oxford* notes; the butterfly became a traditional emblem for the soul. Cp. *Pippa* ii 216 ^217n. (p. 137).
501. youth's hopes went] youth was spent (*1888*).
500–4. I had resolved . . . and die: see ll. 601–19.
503–10.] Which wasted not a sunbeam; every hour
          I would make mine, and die.
          And thus I sought
          To chain my spirit down which erst I freed
          For flights to fame: I said "The troubled life
          Of genius, seen so gay when working forth
          Some trusted end, grows sad when all proves vain—
          How sad when men have parted with truth's peace
          For falsest fancy's sake, which waited first (*1888*)
506–59. the troubled life . . . still] in quotation marks, *Lowell-1888*, with the exception of the parenthesis in ll. 523–8.
506–10. I said . . . fancy's sake: the sense is that the trials of 'genius' only seem worthwhile when some concrete end is in view, and are otherwise futile, most of all when actual pleasures have been sacrificed in the process, since the 'wild fancy', which at first served its possessor like an obedient spirit, degenerates as soon as it becomes the sole means of securing pleasure. The tone here, and the use of the terms 'joy' and 'fancy', may owe something to Coleridge's *Dejection: An Ode*.
506–7. the troubled life / Of genius: cp. Naddo in *Sordello* i 692–9 (I 440–2).
510. waited: served, attended.

Came not with her alone, but alters soon,
Coming darkened, seldom, hasting to depart,
Leaving a heavy darkness and warm tears.

515   But I shall never lose her; she will live
Brighter for such seclusion—I but catch
A hue, a glance of what I sing, so pain
Is linked with pleasure, for I ne'er may tell
The radiant sights which dazzle me; but now
520   They shall be all my own, and let them fade
Untold—others shall rise as fair, as fast.
And when all's done, the few dim gleams transferred,—
(For a new thought sprung up—that it were well

512. *not with her alone*] without fancy's call (*1888*).
513. *Coming*] Comes (*Lowell-1888*). *hasting*] hastening (*1868–75*); hastens (*1888*).
514.] *1868–88* leave no space after this line.
515–21. Mill marked this passage with a cross, indicating obscurity. The sense is: 'But I shall never lose my "fancy"; it will be all the more powerful for operating in a fitful and fragmentary way. I only catch isolated glimpses of my subject, and therefore pleasure [at its glory] is linked with pain [at the impossibility of expressing it adequately], because I am unable to represent the splendour of my visions. But this very incapacity means that I alone possess my visions, and can keep them to myself; it does not matter if they remain unexpressed, since others just as splendid will rapidly replace them'. The thought here anticipates the analysis of Sordello's creativity in terms of the relation between vision and poetic expression; see e.g. *Sordello* ii 137ff., 601–5 (I 470ff., 500): also below, l. 811n.
515. *her*: the 'wild fancy' of l. 510; and see l. 284n.
516. *Brighter*] Dearer (*1888*). *such seclusion*: referring to the fact that 'fancy', when 'secluded' from other sources of delight, becomes intermittent and transient (see ll. 506–14).
517. *what I sing*: my subject (not 'my singing'). *so*] so, (*Lowell-1888*).
519–20.] Half the bright sights which dazzle me; but now / Mine shall be all the radiance: let them fade (*1888*).
521–2.] B. drew a line between these two lines in *Mill*, but there is no line-space in *1868–88*.
522–30. The sense is that the writer, under the influence of the 'new thought' that writing actual poems would bring him fame and thereby guarantee the survival of some authentic token of his vision (the 'branch from the gold forest'), attempts to write, but only manages to convey a 'few dim gleams' of that vision; this, which constitutes 'success' in the eyes of the world, seems futile to him, either in comparison with the original and inexpressible vision or because of the essential hollowness (or insincerity: see l. 539) of contemporary acclaim.
523–6.] (For a new thought sprang up how well it were,
         Discarding shadowy hope, to weave such lays
         As straight encircle men with praise and love,
         So, I should not die utterly,—should bring (*1888*; 'hope' is a reading which dates from *Lowell*).

To leave all shadowy hopes, and weave such lays
525   As would encircle me with praise and love;
So I should not die utterly—I should bring
One branch from the gold forest, like the knight
Of old tales, witnessing I had been there,)—
And when all's done, how vain seems e'en success,
530   And all the influence poets have o'er men!
'Tis a fine thing that one, weak as myself,
Should sit in his lone room, knowing the words
He utters in his solitude shall move
Men like a swift wind—that tho' he be forgotten,
535   Fair eyes shall glisten when his beauteous dreams
Of love come true in happier frames than his.
Ay, the still night brought thoughts like these, but morn
Came, and the mockery again laughed out
At hollow praises, and smiles, almost sneers;

524. lays: the 'lay' was originally a short poem set to music, associated with the work of the medieval minstrels (cp. its use in *Sordello*, e.g. ii 82, I 468); 'from the 16th to the 18th centuries the word was a mere poetical synonym for "song"' (*OED*), but Romantic writers such as Scott (*Lay of the Last Minstrel*) popularized the term as an archaism for a lyric poem or ballad. Note the satiric use in *Flight of the Duchess* 104 (II 302).

526–8. I should bring . . . there: B. combines two classical stories: that of the golden apples of the Hesperides, which Heracles obtained as one of his twelve labours, and the golden bough in Virgil's *Aeneid* vi 136ff., which gives entry to the Underworld. The word 'knight' suggests that B. is also thinking of later fairytales in which a hero is required to bring back proof that he has been to some magical place.

526. I should not die utterly: Horace *Odes* III xxx 6: 'non omnis moriar'.

530. And all the influence] The vaunted influence (*1888*).

531–44. The first sentence (ll. 531–6) corresponds to the 'new thought' of ll. 523–8, about the value of fame; the remainder (ll. 537–44) corresponds to the realization (in ll. 522, 529–30) that vision cannot be represented in writing.

534–5. he be forgotten, / Fair eyes] dead and gone, / New eyes (*1888*).

537–8. brought . . . Came . . . laughed] brings . . . Comes . . . laughs (*1888*).

539–44.] At hollow praises, smiles allied to sneers;
        And my soul's idol ever whispers me
        To dwell with him and his unhonoured song:
        And I foreknow my spirit, that would press
        First in the struggle, fail again to make
        All bow enslaved, and I again should sink. (*1888*)

539. Praise is 'hollow' when directed at the imperfect work rather than its more perfect conception. See *Sordello* iii 599–614 (I 564–6).

540 And my soul's idol seemed to whisper me
    To dwell with him and his unhonoured name—
    And I well knew my spirit, that would be
    First in the struggle, and again would make
    All bow to it; and I would sink again.

                    ★   ★   ★   ★   ★

545 And then know that this curse will come on us,
    To see our idols perish—we may wither,
    Nor marvel—we are clay; but our low fate
    Should not extend to them, whom trustingly
    We sent before into Time's yawning gulf,
550 To face what e'er may lurk in darkness there—
    To see the painters' glory pass, and feel
    Sweet music move us not as once, or worst,
    To see decaying wits ere the frail body

540–1. 'It seemed better to me to abjure actual writing, which attracted "hollow praises", in favour of the pure imagination which was "unhonoured" [not recognized]' (but note *1888* 'unhonoured *song*'). Cp. *Sordello* iii 32–3 (I 526): 'Better sure be unrevealed / Than part-revealed'; and B. to EBB., 11 Feb. 1845: 'I never wanted a real set of good hearty praisers—and no bad reviewers . . I am quite content with my share. No—what I laughed at in my "gentle audience" is a sad trick the real admirers have of admiring at the wrong place—enough to make an apostle swear!' (*Correspondence* x 71).

542–4. The sense is that the writer knows that his imagination would not yield first place to the inferior faculty which was necessary to the production of poetry, but would insist on its own primacy, and thus cause his efforts to fail—there would therefore be no point in making such efforts.

544. would sink again] should sink again (*Mill, Lowell-1875*); again should sink (*1888*).

546–54. we may wither . . . Decays: i.e. 'it is fitting that we inferior beings should perish, since we are merely mortal; but not that this fate should extend to our admired forbears, whose physical death we had not expected to compromise their works' immortality. It is painful to see a painter's reputation fade, to lose sympathy with a piece of music, or worst of all, to see an artist destroy his reputation by the works of his dotage'. *Maynard* compares *Childe Harold* IV cxxii–cxxiv: 'cure / Is bitterer still, as charm by charm unwinds / Which robed our idols . . . / So we are doubly cursed'. With l. 546 cp. also cxxiv: 'We wither from our youth'. B. has altered Byron's argument, which is that both love and art are futile attempts to express an ideal which cannot exist outside the mind itself.

547. Nor marvel—we] Nor marvel, we (*Lowell*); Nor marvel we (*1868–75*; probably a mispr.); No marvel, we (*1888*).

548. extend to] emended from 'extend' in *1833*, a correction made by B. in *Mill* (but not in *Lowell*) and followed in *1868–88. them,*] those (*1888*).

549–50. Cp. the writer's description of himself at ll. 1026–7.

549. Time's yawning gulf: cp. *Richard III* III vii 128–9: 'the swallowing gulf / Of dark forgetfulness and deep oblivion'.

550. what e'er may] whate'er might (*Lowell-1875*); what dread may (*1888*).

551. see] find (*1888*). *painters'*] painter's (*1870–88*).

Decays. Nought makes me trust in love so really,
555   As the delight of the contented lowness
      With which I gaze on souls I'd keep for ever
      In beauty—I'd be sad to equal them;
      I'd feed their fame e'en from my heart's best blood,
      Withering unseen, that they might flourish still.

                    ★   ★   ★   ★

560   Pauline, my sweet friend, thou dost not forget
      How this mood swayed me, when thou first wert mine,
      When I had set myself to live this life,
      Defying all opinion. Ere thou camest
      I was most happy, sweet, for old delights
565   Had come like birds again; music, my life,
      I nourished more than ever, and old lore
      Loved for itself, and all it shows—the king

554–61.] Decays! Nought makes me trust some love is true,
         But the delight of the contented lowness
         With which I gaze on him I keep for ever
         Above me; I to rise and rival him?
         Feed his fame rather from my heart's best blood,
         Wither unseen that he may flourish still."
         Pauline, my soul's friend, thou dost pity yet
         How this mood swayed me when that soul found thine, (*1888*)

554–9. *Nought . . . still*: the idea that the true love is that of the inferior for the
superior is a common one in B. Cp., e.g., *Sordello* iii 304ff., vi 41–3 (I 544, 718)
and B. to EBB., 10 Aug. 1846: 'There is no love but from beneath, far
beneath,—that is the law of its nature' (*Correspondence* xiii 242).
557. *I'd be sad to equal them*: Mill underlined this clause and put a cross in the
margin, indicating obscurity. The meaning is that if the writer were to 'equal'
his predecessors he would no longer admire them, since he would no longer be
in an inferior position (see prec. note).
561. *wert*] wast (*Rylands, Lowell-1888*)
563–6.] Defying all past glory. Ere thou camest
         I seemed defiant, sweet, for old delights
         Had flocked like birds again; music, my life,
         Nourished me more than ever; then the lore (*1888*)
567–71. *the king . . . doom*: in a letter to T. J. Wise of 5 Nov. 1886 B. explained:
'The "King" is Agamemnon, in the Tragedy of that name by Aeschylus, whose
treading the purple carpets spread before him by his wife, preparatory to his
murder, is a notable passage' (*LH* 256; see also ll. 573–6n.). The *Agamemnon* is
the first play in Aeschylus's trilogy, the *Oresteia*. In *Mill*, B. transcribed in the
margin two lines in Greek from the *Agamemnon*, which he was later to render
in his version of the play (1877): 'So,—since to hear thee, I am brought about
thus,— / I go into the palace—purples treading' (ll. 956–7 in original, ll. 962–3
in B.'s transl.). B. seems to have supplied this gloss, and the two following, on
his own initiative, and not in response to a query by Mill: see also ll. 963–5n.
567. *the king*] the King (*Mill*); that king (*1888*).

Treading the purple calmly to his death,
—While round him, like the clouds of eve, all dusk,
570 The giant shades of fate, silently flitting,
Pile the dim outline of the coming doom,
—And him sitting alone in blood, while friends
Are hunting far in the sunshine; and the boy,
With his white breast and brow and clustering curls
575 Streaked with his mother's blood, and striving hard
To tell his story ere his reason goes.
And when I loved thee, as I've loved so oft,
Thou lovedst me, and I wondered, and looked in
My heart to find some feeling like such love,

572–3. And him . . . sunshine: the ref. is to Ajax, the Greek hero of the Trojan war. 'After the death of Achilles, Ajax and Ulysses disputed their claim to the arms of the dead hero. When they were given to the latter, Ajax was so enraged that he slaughtered a whole flock of sheep, supposing them to be the sons of Atreus, who had given the preference to Ulysses, and stabbed himself with his sword' (*Lemprière*). The 'madness of Ajax' was a traditional subject for Greek tragedy. B. drew a line from 'And' in l. 572, which forms the second line of p. 41 (a right-hand page) of *1833*, downwards and over the facing page (p. 40), at the bottom of which he transcribed in Greek five lines from the *Ajax* of Sophocles, three depicting Ajax' dejection when he realizes what he has done: 'But now, confounded in his abject woe, / Refusing food or drink, he sits there still, / Just where he fell amid the carcases / Of the slain sheep and cattle' (ll. 323–5 in the original), and two his abandonment by his friends: 'Ho Teucer! where is Teucer? Will his raid / End never? And the while I am undone!' (ll. 342–3 in the original).

572. him] Him (*Mill*).

573–6. and the boy . . . reason goes: B. wrote to Wise (see ll. 567–71n.): ' "The boy" is Orestes, as described at the end of the *Choephoroi* by the same Author'. The *Choephoroi* ('Libation Bearers'), the second play in Aeschylus's *Oresteia* trilogy, concerns the return of Orestes to Argos and his murder of his mother, Clytemnestra, in revenge for her murder of Agamemnon. As a punishment for his crime, Orestes is tormented by the Furies, who appear at the end of the play and drive him away. See ll. 6–7n. In *Mill*, B. put a cross in the margin, keyed to a note at the bottom of the page, where he transcribed in Greek two short passages from the play: 'But—since I would have you know—for I know not how 'twill end—methinks I am a charioteer driving my team far outside the course' (ll. 1021–3 in the original); 'But while I still keep my senses, I proclaim to those who hold me dear and declare that not without justice did I slay my mother' (ll. 1026–7 in the original). Mill wrote in the margin opposite these lines: 'striking'; this comment is wrongly ascribed by *Oxford* to the image of Ajax in the prec. lines.

573. boy] Boy (*Mill*).

575. and striving] but striving (*1888*).

577. as I've loved so oft: i.e. lightly, superficially, in contrast to her love for him: see following lines.   *I've loved*] love seemed (*1888*).

578.] Thou lovedst me indeed: I wondering searched (*1888*).

580 Believing I was still what I had been;
     And soon I found all faith had gone from me,
     And the late glow of life—changing like clouds,
     'Twas not the morn-blush widening into day,
     But evening, coloured by the dying sun
585 While darkness is quick hastening:—I will tell
     My state as though 'twere none of mine—despair
     Cannot come near me—thus it is with me.
     Souls alter not, and mine must progress still;
     And this I knew not when I flung away
590 My youth's chief aims. I ne'er supposed the loss
     Of what few I retained; for no resource
     Awaits me—now behold the change of all.
     I cannot chain my soul, it will not rest
     In its clay prison, this most narrow sphere—
595 It has strange powers, and feelings, and desires,

580. *what*] much (*1888*). See the Marot motto and note, p. 1.
581–5.] Too soon I found all faith had gone from me,
          And the late glow of life, like change on clouds,
          Proved not the morn-blush widening into day,
          But eve faint-coloured by the dying sun
          While darkness hastens quickly. I will tell (*1888*)
583. morn-blush: underlined by Mill, though there is no cross in the margin to indicate obscurity; the image is traditional.
585–7. I will tell . . . with me: Mill put a cross in the margin opposite this passage, indicating obscurity, probably in the interpretation of the last clause, which could be (fairly nonsensically) read, 'thus despair is with me'. B.'s addition of a comma after 'near me' (l. 587) in *Mill* may have been intended to ward off this interpretation, but the clause remains ambiguous between 'this [i.e. what follows] is how I am' and 'it is my nature not to despair': hence the *1888* rev. (see next note).
587–92.] Cannot come near us—this it is, my state.
          Souls alter not, and mine must still advance;
          Strange that I knew not, when I flung away
          My youth's chief aims, their loss might lead to loss
          Of what few I retained, and no resource
          Be left me: for behold how changed is all! (*1888*)
588. Cp. l. 439.
593–4. Cp. ll. 282–3n.
594. prison,] emended from 'prison;' in *1833*, a correction made by B. in *Mill* and followed in *Lowell-1888*.
595–600.] It has strange impulse, tendency, desire,
          Which nowise I account for nor explain,
          But cannot stifle, being bound to trust
          All feelings equally, to hear all sides:
          How can my life indulge them? yet they live,
          Referring to some state of life unknown. (*1888*)

Which I cannot account for, nor explain,
But which I stifle not, being bound to trust
All feelings equally—to hear all sides:
Yet I cannot indulge them, and they live,
600   Referring to some state or life unknown. . . .

My selfishness is satiated not,
It wears me like a flame; my hunger for
All pleasure, howsoe'er minute, is pain;
I envy—how I envy him whose mind
605   Turns with its energies to some one end!
To elevate a sect, or a pursuit,
However mean—so my still baffled hopes
Seek out abstractions; I would have but one
Delight on earth, so it were wholly mine;
610   One rapture all my soul could fill—and this
Wild feeling places me in dream afar,
In some wide country, where the eye can see
No end to the far hills and dales bestrewn
With shining towers and dwellings. I grow mad
615   Well-nigh, to know not one abode but holds
Some pleasure—for my soul could grasp them all,
But must remain with this vile form. I look
With hope to age at last, which quenching much,
May let me concentrate the sparks it spares.

599–600. Mill put a cross in the margin opposite this passage, indicating obscurity. The sense is that the writer cannot surrender to his impulses, and therefore they exist in him as anticipations or hints of an unexperienced mode of existence.
603. is pain] grows pain (1888).
604. mind] soul (1888).
605. with its energies] its whole energies (1888).
606.] To elevate an aim, pursue success (1888).
607–8. hopes / Seek out] hope / Seeks out (1888).
608–9. but one / Delight on earth] one joy, / But one in life (1888).
612. wide country] wild country (1868–75); vast country (1888). Oxford suggests that the 1868–75 reading was a mispr., since it is not in Lowell. Cp. l. 91n, and see also l. 238n.
614.] With shining towers and towns, till I grow mad (1888).
616–17.] Some pleasure, while my soul could grasp the world, / But must remain this vile form's slave. I look (1888).
619. the sparks] what sparks (1888).

620   This restlessness of passion meets in me
        A craving after knowledge: the sole proof
        Of a commanding will is in that power
        Repressed; for I beheld it in its dawn,
        That sleepless harpy, with its budding wings,
625   And I considered whether I should yield
        All hopes and fears, to live alone with it,
        Finding a recompence in its wild eyes;
        And when I found that I should perish so,
        I bade its wild eyes close from me for ever;—
630   And I am left alone with my delights,—
        So it lies in me a chained thing—still ready
        To serve me, if I loose its slightest bond—
        I cannot but be proud of my bright slave.

620–33. Remodelling—inverting—the argument put forward by the old man in ch. ix of Balzac's *La Peau de Chagrin*: 'L'homme s'épuise par deux actes instinctivement accomplis qui tarissent les sources de son existence. Deux verbes expriment toutes les formes que prennent ces deux causes de la mort: VOULOIR et POUVOIR. Entre ces deux termes de l'action humaine, il est une autre formule dont s'emparent les sages, et je lui dois le bonheur et ma longévité. *Vouloir* nous brûle et *Pouvoir* nous détruit; mais SAVOIR laisse notre faible organisation dans un perpétuel état de calme. Ainsi le désir ou le vouloir est mort en moi, tué par la pensée; le mouvement ou le pouvoir s'est résolu par le jeu naturel de mes organes' [Man exhausts himself by two actions, instinctively performed, which dry up the springs of his being. Two verbs express all the forms taken by these two causes of death: TO WILL and TO HAVE POWER. Between these two extremes of human action there is another mode which the wise have seized upon, and I owe to it my happiness and my longevity. *To will* consumes us, and *To have power* destroys us; but TO KNOW leaves our feeble organism in a perpetual state of calm. Thus desire or the will is dead in me, killed by thought; motion or power has been dissolved by the natural working of my organs (i.e. ageing)].

622. Of a] Of yet (*1888*). Mill underlined 'that power', put a cross in the margin, indicating obscurity, and commented: 'you should make clearer *what* power'. The ref. is to the 'craving after knowledge' of the prec. line.

624.] The sleepless harpy with just-budding wings (*1888*). The harpies were 'winged monsters, who had the face of a woman, with the body of a vulture, and had their feet and fingers armed with sharp claws. . . . They emitted an infectious smell, and spoiled whatever they touched by their filth and excrements' (*Lemprière*). The harpies traditionally represented rapacious and destructive appetite, and were associated with divine retribution.

625–6.] And I considered whether to forego / All happy ignorant hopes and fears, to live, (*1888*).

630. my delights] old delights (*1888*).

631. So . . . ready] See! . . . prompt (*1888*).

And thus I know this earth is not my sphere,
635   For I cannot so narrow me, but that
I still exceed it; in their elements
My love would pass my reason—but since here
Love must receive its objects from this earth,
While reason will be chainless, the few truths
640   Caught from its wanderings have sufficed to quell
All love below;—then what must be that love
Which, with the object it demands, would quell
Reason, tho' it soared with the seraphim?
No—what I feel may pass all human love,
645   Yet fall far short of what my love should be;
And yet I seem more warped in this than aught,
For here myself stands out more hideously.
I can forget myself in friendship, fame,

634–9.] How should this earth's life prove my only sphere?
    Can I so narrow sense but that in life
    Soul still exceeds it? In their elements
    My love outsoars my reason; but since love
    Perforce receives its object from this earth
    While reason wanders chainless, the few truths (*1888*)

636. *in their elements*: Mill underlined this phrase and put a cross in the margin, indicating obscurity; the sense is: 'in their first principles' (referring to 'love' and 'reason' in the next line) as distinct from 'in their manifestation' (on 'this earth', l. 638); see l. 260.

637–45. In *Mill*, the words 'love' and 'reason' were altered to 'Love' and 'Reason' in ll. 637, 639, 641, and 645; note that 'love' in l. 644 was unchanged. These revs. were not followed in *1868–88*.

637–43. *but since here . . . seraphim?*: 'but since, in this life, love is tied to earthly objects, whereas reason transcends this limitation, the few truths discovered by my reason have made earthly love impossible; how glorious then must be that love which, in company with the object of its devotion, would in turn transcend even the highest flight of reason?' The argument is that, since love is inherently superior to reason, reason's dominance in earthly life reflects the inadequacy of the objects life offers for love, not of love itself. The idea of a hierarchy of objects for love is Platonic (e.g. *Symposium* and *Phaedrus*); for an analogous Platonic hierarchy, see l. 811n. (Pauline's footnote). The argument that the power to conceive something greater than what is already known argues the existence of that greater thing derives from Descartes, who uses it to 'prove' the existence of God (the 'Ontological Proof'). Mill wrote 'self-flattery' vertically in the margin opposite ll. 639–43.

641–3.] Love chained below; then what were love, set free,
    Which, with the object it demands, would pass
    Reason companioning the seraphim? (*1888*)

647–9.] Myself stands out more hideously: of old
    I could forget myself in friendship, fame,
    Liberty, nay, in love of mightier souls; (*1888*; there is no space after l. 649 in *Lowell-1888*).

648–9. Mill wrote in the margin: 'inconsistent with what precedes'.

Or liberty, or love of mighty souls.

★　★　★　★

650　But I begin to know what thing hate is—
　　　To sicken, and to quiver, and grow white,
　　　And I myself have furnished its first prey.
　　　All my sad weaknesses, this wavering will,
　　　This selfishness, this still decaying frame . . .
655　But I must never grieve while I can pass
　　　Far from such thoughts—as now—Andromeda!

653–5.] Hate of the weak and ever-wavering will,
　　　　The selfishness, the still-decaying frame . . .
　　　　But I must never grieve whom wing can waft (*1888*)
654. *this still decaying frame*: 'this ever-decaying body'.
656–67. *Andromeda . . . save her*. Andromeda was the daughter of Cepheus, king
of Ethiopia, and Cassiope; the latter 'boasted herself to be fairer than the
Nereides; upon which, Neptune, at the request of these despised nymphs . . . sent
a huge sea monster to ravage Ethiopia. The wrath of Neptune could be appeased
only by exposing Andromeda, whom Cassiope tenderly loved, to the fury of this
sea monster; and just as she was going to be devoured, Perseus delivered her'
(*Lemprière*). The painting of Andromeda 'is that of Polidoro di [*sic*, for 'da']
Caravaggio [*c.* 1500–1543], of which Mr. Browning possesses an engraving, which
was always before his eyes as he wrote his earlier poems' (Orr *Handbook* 21n.).
The painting, originally a fresco panel, is now in the Museo di Roma; *Maynard*
150–1 argues that B.'s print was the 'eighteenth-century engraving by Volpato in
the Piranesi series', an identification perhaps strengthened by the specific mention
of Volpato as a master of engraving in *A Likeness* 61 (p. 647). B. states his admiration for Caravaggio in a letter to Fanny Haworth of 1841 (*Correspondence* v 188),
and mentions the Andromeda print twice in letters to EBB.: on 26 Feb. 1845:
'my Polidoro's perfect Andromeda' (*Correspondence* x 99) and 15 May 1846: 'my
noble Polidoro' (*ibid.* xii 329). See also *A Likeness* 42–3 (pp. 646–7). B. alludes
to the myth in *Sordello* (see ii 211–12n, I 477) and, in *Francis Furini* (*Parleyings*,
1887), he alludes both to the myth and to a painting of it by Francisco Furini
(*c.* 1600–1649), in a defence of the nude in art, and of art itself: 'Outlining, orb
by orb, Andromeda— / God's best of beauteous and magnificent / Revealed to
earth—the naked female form' (141–3); 'Who proffers help of hand / To weak
Andromeda exposed on strand / At mercy of the monster? Were all true, / Help
were not wanting: "But 'tis false," cry you, / "Mere fancy-work of paint and
brush!" No less, / Were mine the skill, the magic, to impress / Beholders with
a confidence they saw / Life,—veritable flesh and blood in awe / Of just as true
a sea-beast,—would they stare / Simply as now, or cry out, curse and swear, /
Or call the gods to help, or catch up stick / And stone, according as their hearts
were quick / Or sluggish?' (478–90); 'Acquaint you with the body ere your eyes
/ Look upward: this Andromeda of mine— / Gaze on the beauty, Art hangs out
for sign / There's finer entertainment underneath' (517–20). Cp. also the adap-
tations of the myth in *Ring*, discussed by W. C. DeVane, 'The Virgin and the
Dragon', *Yale Review* xxxvii (1947) 33–46, repr. P. Drew (ed.), *Robert Browning:
A Collection of Critical Essays* (1966) 96–109, which traces the Andromeda-motif
in B.'s poetry, and its application to his relationship with Elizabeth Barrett. See
also ll. 99–123n.

And she is with me—years roll, I shall change,
But change can touch her not—so beautiful
With her dark eyes, earnest and still, and hair
660   Lifted and spread by the salt-sweeping breeze;
And one red beam, all the storm leaves in heaven,
Resting upon her eyes and face and hair,
As she awaits the snake on the wet beach,
By the dark rock, and the white wave just breaking
665   At her feet; quite naked and alone,—a thing
You doubt not, nor fear for, secure that God
Will come in thunder from the stars to save her.
Let it pass—I will call another change.
I will be gifted with a wond'rous soul,
670   Yet sunk by error to men's sympathy,
And in the wane of life; yet only so
As to call up their fears, and there shall come
A time requiring youth's best energies;
And strait I fling age, sorrow, sickness off,
675   And I rise triumphing over my decay.

★   ★   ★   ★

659. *dark eyes*] fixed eyes (*1888*).
661. *red beam*] emended from 'red-beam' in *1833*, a correction made by B. in *Mill*
and followed in *Lowell-1888*.
662. *face and hair*] hair, such hair (*1888*).
666–9.] I doubt not, nor fear for, secure some god
        To save will come in thunder from the stars.
        Let it pass! Soul requires another change.
        I will be gifted with a wondrous mind, (*1888*)
668. *I will call another change*: 'I will summon up another image'.
669–75. Referring to the actor Edmund Kean, whose performance in *Richard III* at the end of his career, when he was ravaged by alcoholism and disease, powerfully affected B. See headnote, pp. 8–9.
670. Mill marked this line as obscure; the sense is either 'Yet so degraded by my faults as to excite people's pity', or 'Yet degraded by people's misapprehension of me as pitiable' (not 'mistakenly sympathizing with mankind').
672. *As to call up their fears*: Mill underlined this phrase and put a cross in the margin, indicating obscurity; the sense is that the anxiety aroused by the writer's apparent senility will prove unfounded.
674. *strait*] straight (*1868–75*; for the *1888* reading, see next note.) 'Strait' is a possible, though rare, spelling for 'straight' in the sense of 'straightaway, at once', and no correction is made in either *Mill* or *Lowell*; B. uses it to mean 'narrow, confined' everywhere else in his work except *Sordello* i 915 (I 454) and ii 720 (I 508); in the former case he overrode the printer's correction of 'strait' to 'straight' in proof.
674–5.] And lo, I fling age, sorrow, sickness off, / And rise triumphant, triumph through decay. (*1888*).

And thus it is that I supply the chasm
'Twixt what I am and all that I would be.
But then to know nothing—to hope for nothing—
To seize on life's dull joys from a strange fear,
680 Lest, losing them, all's lost, and nought remains.

★　★　★　★

There's some vile juggle with my reason here—
I feel I but explain to my own loss
These impulses—they live no less the same.
Liberty! what though I despair—my blood
685 Rose not at a slave's name proudlier than now,
And sympathy obscured by sophistries.
Why have not I sought refuge in myself,
But for the woes I saw and could not stay—
And love!—do I not love thee, my Pauline?

★　★　★　★

676–7. Mill marked these lines as obscure; it is hard to see why. B. revised
l. 677, but only in *1888*, and his rev. does not seem to be in response to a sense
of obscurity (see next note).
677. that I would be] I fain would be (*1888*).
678–80. Mill commented in the margin: 'deeply true'. Mill's own nervous
breakdown in 1826, described in his *Autobiography* (1873), gives this note a
special poignancy.
681. 'Something is playing wicked tricks with my powers of reasoning'. Cp. *Macbeth*
V viii 19–20: 'And be these juggling fiends no more believed / That palter with
us in a double sense'. B. uses the word 'juggle' three times in *Paracelsus* (ii 8, 174
and v 177; I 155, 164, 280) and once in *Flute-Music* (*Asolando*, 1889) 152, but
nowhere else; *Oxford* therefore exaggerates in calling it 'a favourite word'.
684–9. A degree of incoherence is clearly intended here, but the general sense is
that, despite his 'despair', the writer still responds to 'impulses' (l. 683) such as
the love of liberty: he has never felt so outraged as now by the idea of slavery,
or by the thought that human sympathy could be rationalized away by specious
arguments. It is this perception of suffering, and of his own inability to prevent
it, that has kept him from self-absorption. As for the love which this human impulse
implies, does he not feel it for Pauline? Note the *1888* revs.
685–8.] Rose never at a slave's name proud as now.
　　　Oh sympathies, obscured by sophistries!—
　　　Why else have I sought refuge in myself,
　　　But from the woes I saw and could not stay? (*1888*)
686. Mill marked this line as obscure; B. first changed the punctuation, putting
three dots at the end in order to suggest the disconnection in the writer's train
of thought (see ll. 684–9n.), and then deleted the whole line, putting a semi-
colon at the end of the prec. line; however, the line was retained in *1868–75*
(note also the *1888* rev.).
689.] No space after this line in *Lowell-1888*. The asterisks would in any case have
disappeared: see l. 403n. and cp. l. 715n.

690   I cherish prejudice, lest I be left
       Utterly loveless—witness this belief
       In poets, tho' sad change has come there too;
       No more I leave myself to follow them:
       Unconsciously I measure me by them.
695   Let me forget it; and I cherish most
       My love of England—how her name—a word
       Of hers in a strange tongue makes my heart beat! . .

                        ★   ★   ★   ★

       Pauline, I could do any thing—not now—
       All's fever—but when calm shall come again—
700   I am prepared—I have made life my own—
       I would not be content with all the change
       One frame should feel—but I have gone in thought
       Thro' all conjuncture—I have lived all life
       When it is most alive—where strangest fate
705   New shapes it past surmise—the tales of men
       Bit by some curse—or in the grasps of doom
       Half-visible and still increasing round,
       Or crowning their wide being's general aim. . . .

                        ★   ★   ★   ★

       These are wild fancies, but I feel, sweet friend,
710   As one breathing his weakness to the ear
       Of pitying angel—dear as a winter flower;
       A slight flower growing alone, and offering

---

690. *prejudice*: 'prepossession; judgment formed beforehand without examination' (*J.*)—the sense is weaker than that of 'unfair bias'.
691. *this belief*] my belief (*1888*).
692. *too;*] emended in agreement with *1868–88* from 'too' in *1833*. Mill has 'too—'.
697. *hers*] emended in agreement with *1888* from 'her's' in *1833–75*.
698–708. Mill drew a line through this passage to indicate that it should be deleted (it was retained in later eds., however). See also ll. 810–21n.
698.] Pauline, could I but break the spell! Not now—(*1888*).
703. *conjuncture*: 'combination of many circumstances or causes'; 'occasion, critical time' (*J.*). B. is fond of this word in his early work (five occurrences before 1844, one thereafter). Cp. esp. *Paracelsus* i 778 (I 148).
705.] New-shapes it past surmise—the throes of men (*1888*).
708. *general aim. . . .*] general aim. (*1888*, which has no space or asterisks after the line).
712–15. Oxford compares *Sordello* ii 290 (I 480); cp. also the Pope's description of Pompilia, *Ring* x 1003–46.

Its frail cup of three leaves to the cold sun,
Yet joyous and confiding, like the triumph
715   Of a child—and why am I not worthy thee?

★   ★   ★   ★

I can live all the life of plants, and gaze
Drowsily on the bees that flit and play,
Or bare my breast for sunbeams which will kill,
Or open in the night of sounds, to look
720   For the dim stars; I can mount with the bird,
Leaping airily his pyramid of leaves
And twisted boughs of some tall mountain tree,
Or rise cheerfully springing to the heavens—
Or like a fish breathe in the morning air
725   In the misty sun-warm water—or with flowers
And trees can smile in light at the sinking sun,
Just as the storm comes—as a girl would look
On a departing lover—most serene.

Pauline, come with me—see how I could build

715.] No space after this line in *Lowell-1888*. Cp. l. 689n.

716–28. Anticipating the account of Sordello's childhood at Goito, *Sordello* i 626ff (I 436ff.). Cp. Balzac's *La Peau de Chagrin*, ch. li, where Raphaël, in refuge from his premature old age and imminent death, is described 'restant des journées entières comme une plante au soleil, comme un lièvre au gîte . . . Ou bien, il se familiarisait avec les phénomènes de la végétation, avec les vicissitudes du ciel, épiant le progrès de toutes les oeuvres, sur la terre, dans les eaux ou les airs . . . Il tenta de s'associer au mouvement intime de cette nature, et de s'identifier assez complètement à sa passive obéissance, pour tomber sous la loi despotique et conservatrice qui régit les existences instinctives' [spending whole days like a plant in the sun, or a hare in its form . . . Or he would familiarise himself with the phenomena of the vegetation, with the changes in the sky, noting the progress of all things, on earth, in the water, or in the air . . . He tried to associate himself with the secret working of this natural world, and to identify so completely with its passive obedience, as to fall under the despotic and preserving law which governs instinctive beings].

724. breathe in] breathe deep (*1888*).

725–6. flowers / And trees] flower / And tree (*1888*).

729–810. This descriptive exploration seems to owe something to Coleridge's *The Picture* (1802), in which a lover similarly descends into a dark, tangled wood, finds a river and a waterfall, and emerges into light again. Like this passage, Coleridge's poem is narrated in the present tense, developing the manner of the 'conversation poems'. Similar passages occur in *Sordello* ii 13–33 (I 462) and *By the Fire-Side* (p. 456). Cp. the analogous account of the progress of a day in terms of landscape 'panels', *Gerard de Lairesse* (*Parleyings*, 1887) 181–362. See also l. 773n.

730   A home for us, out of the world, in thought—
       I am inspired—come with me, Pauline!

       Night, and one single ridge of narrow path
       Between the sullen river and the woods
       Waving and muttering—for the moonless night
735   Has shaped them into images of life,
       Like the upraising of the giant-ghosts,
       Looking on earth to know how their sons fare.
       Thou art so close by me, the roughest swell
       Of wind in the tree-tops hides not the panting
740   Of thy soft breasts; no—we will pass to morning—
       Morning—the rocks, and vallies, and old woods.
       How the sun brightens in the mist, and here,—
       Half in the air, like creatures of the place,
       Trusting the element—living on high boughs
745   That swing in the wind—look at the golden spray,
       Flung from the foam-sheet of the cataract,
       Amid the broken rocks—shall we stay here

729–31. Cp. (noting the landscape descriptions that follow) Keats, *Ode to Psyche*
50–62: 'Yes, I will be thy priest, and build a fane / In some untrodden region
of my mind, / Where branched thoughts, new grown with pleasant pain, / Instead
of pines shall murmur in the wind: / Far, far around shall those dark-clustered
trees / Fledge the wild-ridged mountains steep by steep; / And there by zephyrs,
streams, and birds, and bees, / The moss-lain Dryads shall be lulled to sleep; /
And in the midst of this wide quietness / A rosy sanctuary will I dress / With
the wreathed trellis of a working brain, / With buds, and bells, and stars
without a name, / With all the gardener Fancy e'er could feign'. Cp. also Coleridge.
The Picture 45–54: 'This is my hour of triumph! I can now / With my own
fancies play the merry fool . . . here will I couch my limbs, / Close by this river,
in this silent shade, / As safe and sacred from the step of man / As in invisible
world—unheard, unseen'.
730. world,] emended from 'world;' in *1833*, a correction made by B. in *Mill* and
followed in *Lowell-1888*.
731.] I am uplifted: fly with me, Pauline! (*1888*).
736. giant-ghosts] giant ghosts (*1888*).
737. know] see (*1868–75*). A rare example of both innovation in *1868* and reversion to *1833* in *1888*.
738–40. Cp. *The Picture* 58–64: 'The breeze, that visits me, / Was never Love's
accomplice . . . never half disclosed / The maiden's snowy bosom, scattering thence
/ Eye-poisons for some love-distempered youth'.
745. golden spray] silver spray (*1888*).
746–7. the cataract, / Amid the broken rocks: cp. *The Picture* 138–9: 'a tall weedy
rock / That overbrows the cataract'. *Oxford* compares Shelley, *Alastor* 345–6: 'fled,
like foam / Down the steep cataract of a wintry river'.

With the wild hawks?—no, ere the hot noon come
Dive we down—safe;—see this our new retreat
750 Walled in with a sloped mound of matted shrubs,
Dark, tangled, old and green—still sloping down
To a small pool whose waters lie asleep
Amid the trailing boughs turned water-plants
And tall trees over-arch to keep us in,
755 Breaking the sunbeams into emerald shafts,
And in the dreamy water one small group
Of two or three strange trees are got together,
Wondering at all around—as strange beasts herd
Together far from their own land—all wildness—
760 No turf nor moss, for boughs and plants pave all,
And tongues of bank go shelving in the waters,
Where the pale-throated snake reclines his head,
And old grey stones lie making eddies there;
The wild mice cross them dry-shod—deeper in—
765 Shut thy soft eyes—now look—still deeper in:
This is the very heart of the woods—all round,
Mountain-like, heaped above us; yet even here
One pond of water gleams—far off the river
Sweeps like a sea, barred out from land; but one—
770 One thin clear sheet has over-leaped and wound
Into this silent depth, which gained, it lies
Still, as but let by sufferance; the trees bend
O'er it as wild men watch a sleeping girl,
And thro' their roots long creeping plants stretch out
775 Their twined hair, steeped and sparkling; farther on,
Tall rushes and thick flag-knots have combined
To narrow it; so, at length, a silver thread

---

761. *waters*] lymph (*1888*). *Oxford* compares Shelley, *The Question* 5: 'Along a shelving bank of turf'; and the whole poem, which B. certainly knew, has affinities
with the landscape descriptions here.
764–5. Cp. *The Picture* 120–1: 'O lead, / Lead me to deeper shades and lonelier
glooms'.
766–71. *This is . . . silent depth*: cp. *By the Fire-Side* 36–40 (p. 462): 'A turn, and
we stand in the heart of things; / The woods are round us, heaped and dim; /
From slab to slab how it slips and springs, / The thread of water single and slim,
/ Thro' the ravage some torrent brings!'
768–77. Mill wrote vertically in the margin: 'good descriptive writing'.
773. *as wild men watch a sleeping girl*: cp. Gerard de Lairesse (*Parleyings*, 1887) 262–307.
774. *stretch out*] out-stretch (*1888*).
776. *flag-knots*: clumps of flag, 'a water-plant with bladed leaf and yellow
flower' (*J.*).

It winds, all noiselessly, thro' the deep wood,
Till thro' a cleft way, thro' the moss and stone,
780   It joins its parent-river with a shout.
Up for the glowing day—leave the old woods:
See, they part, like a ruined arch,—the sky!
Nothing but sky appears, so close the roots
And grass of the hill-top level with the air—
785   Blue sunny air, where a great cloud floats, laden
With light, like a dead whale that white birds pick,
Floating away in the sun in some north sea.
Air, air—fresh life-blood—thin and searching air—
The clear, dear breath of God, that loveth us:
790   Where small birds reel and winds take their delight.
Water is beautiful, but not like air.
See, where the solid azure waters lie,
Made as of thickened air, and down below,
The fern-ranks, like a forest spread themselves,
795   As tho' each pore could feel the element;
Where the quick glancing serpent winds his way—
Float with me there, Pauline, but not like air.
Down the hill—stop—a clump of trees, see, set
On a heap of rocks, which look o'er the far plains,
800   And envious climbing shrubs would mount to rest,
And peer from their spread boughs. There they wave,
         looking

780.] There is a space after this line in *1888*.
781–2. Cp. *The Picture* 135–40: 'I pass forth into light . . . How bursts / The landscape on my sight'.
782. *arch,*—] emended from *1833* 'arch,': the correction is in *Mill. Lowell-1888* have 'arch:'.
783. *roots*] emended from 'root' in *1833*, a correction made by B. in both *Mill* and *Lowell-1888*.
784. *level with the air*: cp. *Paracelsus* ii 232n. (I 167); 'level' here is a verb, not an adjective.
785–6. *a great cloud . . . like a dead whale*: adapting *Hamlet* III ii 376–82: '[Hamlet] Do you see yonder cloud . . . like a whale. [Polonius] Very like a whale'.
792–3. Cp. Shelley, *Ode to Naples* 10–11: 'The isle-sustaining ocean-flood, / A plain of light between two heavens of azure'.
796. *quick glancing*] quick-glancing (*1888*). Milton has 'sporting with quick glance' (referring to fish), *PL* vii 405.
797.] (Float with me there, Pauline), but not like air. (*Rylands*); Float with me there, Pauline!—but not like air. (*Lowell-1888*). There is a space after this line in *1888*.
799. *rocks*] rock (*1888*). *plains*] plain (*1868–88*).
800. *And*] So, (*1888*).
801. *boughs. There*] boughs; wide (*1888*).

At the muleteers, who whistle as they go
To the merry chime of their morning bells, and all
The little smoking cots, and fields, and banks,
805 And copses, bright in the sun; my spirit wanders.
Hedge-rows for me—still, living, hedge-rows, where
The bushes close, and clasp above, and keep
Thought in—I am concentrated—I feel;—
But my soul saddens when it looks beyond;
810 I cannot be immortal, nor taste all.
O God! where does this tend—these struggling aims!*

    * Je crains bien que mon pauvre ami ne soit pas toujours parfaitement
compris dans ce qui reste à lire de cet étrange fragment—mais il est moins
propre que tout autre à éclaircir ce qui de sa nature ne peut jamais être
que songe et confusion. D'ailleurs je ne sais trop si en cherchant à mieux
[5] co-ordonner certaines parties l'on ne courrait pas le risque de nuire au
seul mérite auquel une production si singulière peut prétendre—celui de
donner une idée assez précise du genre qu'elle n'a fait qu'ébaucher.—
Ce début sans prétention, ce remuement des passions qui va d'abord en
accroissant et puis s'apaise par degrés, ces élans de l'âme, ce retour soudain
[10] sur soi-même, et par dessus tout, la tournure d'esprit toute particulière
de mon ami rendent les changemens presque impossibles. Les raisons qu'il
fait valoir ailleurs, et d'autres encore plus puissantes, ont fait trouver grâce
à mes yeux pour cet écrit qu'autrement je lui eusse conseillé de jeter au
feu—Je n'en crois pas moins au grand principe de toute composition—
[15] à ce principe de Shakspeare, de Raffaelle, de Beethoven, d'où il suit que
la concentration des idées est due bien plus à leur conception, qu'à leur
exécution . . . j'ai tout lieu de craindre que la première de ces qualités
ne soit encore étrangère à mon ami—et je doute fort qu'un redouble-
ment de travail lui fasse acquérir la seconde. Le mieux serait de brûler
[20] ceci; mais que faire?
    Je crois que dans ce qui suit il fait allusion à un certain examen qu'il
fit autrefois de l'âme ou plutôt de son âme, pour découvrir la suite
des objets auxquels il lui serait possible d'attèndre, et dont chacun une
fois obtenu devait former une espèce de plateau d'où l'on pouvait
[25] apercevoir d'autres buts, d'autres projets, d'autres jouissances qui, à leur
tour, devaient être surmontés. Il en résultait que l'oubli et le sommeil
devaient tout terminer. Cette idée que je ne saisis pas parfaitement lui
est peutêtre aussi inintelligible qu'à moi.
                PAULINE.

---

802. as they go] on their way (*1888*).
803–4.] To the merry chime of morning bells, past all / The little smoking cots,
mid fields and banks (*1888*).
804–6. Cp. Wordsworth, *Tintern Abbey* 11–18: 'These plots of cottage-ground,
these orchard-tufts, / Which at this season, with their unripe fruits, / Are clad
in one green hue, and lose themselves / 'Mid groves and copses. Once again
I see / These hedge-rows, hardly hedge-rows, little lines / Of sportive wood run

wild: these pastoral farms, / Green to the very door; and wreaths of smoke / Sent up, in silence, from among the trees!'

805. wanders.] B. added four dots after the full stop in *Mill*.

806.] Hedgerows for me—those living hedgerows where (*1888*).

808. concentrated: the metre demands a stress on the second syllable—the pronunciation given in *J.*, as *Oxford* notes. The only other examples in B'.s work where this pronunciation is indicated occur in *Prince Hohenstiel* (1871) 785, 815, 1061; early uses favour the modern pronunciation.

809–10. See ll. 277–8n., and cp. *Cleon* 239–50 (p. 580) for a development of the idea that 'life's inadequate to joy'.

810. nor taste all] taste all joy (*1888*, which leaves a space after this line).

810–21. Mill drew a line through this passage and the accompanying note, indicating that he thought they should be deleted (they are retained in later eds., however). See also ll. 698–708n.

811. does this tend] do they tend (*1888*).

811. footnote: (i) [translation]. 'I very much fear that my poor friend will not always be perfectly understood in what remains to be read of this strange fragment—but he is less fitted than anyone else to make clear what of its very nature can never be other than dream and confusion. Besides, I am not sure that in seeking to improve the co-ordination of certain parts one would not run the risk of damaging the only merit to which so peculiar a production can lay claim—that of giving a fairly exact idea of the kind of work of which it is only a sketch.—This unpretentious opening, this stirring of passions which at first increases and then gradually dies down, these motions of the soul, this sudden return upon himself, and, above all, my friend's idiosyncratic cast of mind, make changes virtually impossible. The reasons which he puts forward elsewhere, and others even more compelling, have persuaded me to look favourably on this writing which I would otherwise have advised him to throw in the fire—Not that I believe any the less in the great principle of all composition—the principle of Shakespeare, of Raphael, of Beethoven, according to which concentration of ideas owes a good deal more to their conception than to their execution . . . I have every reason to fear that my friend is a stranger to the first of these qualities—and I strongly doubt whether he could acquire the second even by a redoubling of effort. It would be best to burn this; but what is to be done?

I think that in what follows he alludes to a certain study of the soul, or rather of his own soul, which he made some time ago in order to discover the series of aims which it would be possible for him to accomplish, each one of which, once obtained, was to form a kind of plateau from which other goals, other enterprises, other joys might be perceived, to be surmounted in their turn. The result was that oblivion and sleep were to end all. This idea, which I do not altogether grasp, is perhaps equally unintelligible to him'.

811. footnote (ii) [textual notes]. B. had a good knowledge of French (see *Maynard* 250, 254ff., 302ff.), but there are several grammatical and orthographical errors in the *1833* footnote. Some may be the printer's (though B. made only one grammatical correction in *Mill*, at l. [8], and got it wrong); most were corr. in *Lowell-1875* (one further error was introduced, at l. [10]), and the others in *1888*. There were two misprs. of substance, at ll. [10] and [29]. We have emended the text as follows: [5]. *au*] an (*1833*); [6] *singulière*] singuliere (*1833*); [8]. *qu'ébaucher*] que'ébaucher (*1833*; 'que d'ébaucher', *Mill*); [9]. *s'apaise*] s'appaise (*1833–75*); [9]. *âme*] ame (*1833*); [10] *soi-même, et*] soi-même.—Et (*1833*); *particulière*] parliculière (*1833*; *1868–88* mistakenly correct the prec. word 'toute' to 'tout'); [16]. *due*]

dûe (*1833–75*); [17]. *exécution*] execution (*1833–75*); [19]. *brûler*] bruler (*1833*);
[22]. *plutôt*] plutot (*1833*); *suite*] suité (*1833*); [28]. *inintelligible*] intelligible (*1833*;
B. made the correction in *Mill*, *Rylands* and *Lowell*). The forms 'changemens'
(l. [12], for 'changements') and 'attèndre' (l. [23], for 'atteindre') are correct, though
now archaic.

811. footnote (iii) [annotation]. For possible sources of the technique of 'editorial'
intervention here, see headnote, p. 22. The relation of 'conception' to 'execution'
is one of B.'s most constant preoccupations. The argument here, that primacy
in composition belongs to imagination rather than knowledge of rules, may
owe something to the heroine's praise of Raphael in Mme de Staël's *Corinne*:
'She admired the simple composition of Raphael's pictures . . . All the figures are
turned towards one central object, without the artist's dreaming of grouping them
in attitudes to produce an effect. She considered that this sincerity in imagination . . . is a characteristic of genius, and that any prearrangement for effect is almost
always fatal to enthusiasm' (*Corinne* [Paris 1809] i 144). This argument differs
in emphasis from B.'s later belief that the greatest artists are those whose ideas
are the most powerful, though their actual work may be technically defective,
since the context requires that there should be a *contrast* between the work of
the three artists cited by Pauline and the poem itself. The contrast is between
their achieving 'la concentration des idées' by virtue of their imaginative power,
and his failing to do so, not between their conception and their execution.
For B.'s later position, cp. *Andrea* 103–16, 193–6 (pp. 395–6, 400) where Andrea
imagines Raphael, 'Reaching, that Heaven might so replenish him, / Above and
through his art—for it gives way'; there may be a technical defect in Raphael's
draughtsmanship, but 'its soul is right'. Cp. also *Shelley* 299–312 (Appendix A,
p. 865), where B. speaks of 'an embodiment of verse more closely answering
to and indicative of the process of the informing spirit, (failing as it occasionally
does, in art, only to succeed in highest art)' and praises the 'spheric poetical
faculty of Shelley, as its own self-sufficing central light, radiating equally through
immaturity and accomplishment, through many fragments and occasional completion, reveals it to a competent judgment'; and note that B.'s allusion to Kean's
acting in *Richard III* (see headnote and ll. 669–75, and the subscription which
follows the last line of the poem) involves a parallel contrast between the
'wondrous soul' of the performer and his physical imperfection. The passage is
an early example of B.'s lifelong admiration for Beethoven; in a letter to EBB.
of 15 Aug. 1845 he recalls attending a performance of *Fidelio* 'in the first season
of German Opera', i.e. May 1832 (*Correspondence* xi 29, 31 n. 1), and repeats
his admiration in a letter of 15 May 1846 (*ibid.* xii 329). *Fidelio* is alluded to
in *By the Fire-Side* 101 (p. 466), and Beethoven figures again in *Ring* (*1888*
text, xii 862–7). [9] *élans de l'âme*: the phrase occurs in *Corinne*: 'un sacrifice, quel
qu'il soit, est plus beau, plus difficile, que tous les élans de l'âme et de la pensée' [a sacrifice, of whatever kind, is more beautiful, more difficult, than any motion
of the soul or the intellect] (i 195). [16]. *la concentration des idées*: the sense is ambiguous between 'the intensity of an idea' and 'the distillation of the
elements of artistic conception'; cp. ll. 619, 808 for other occurrences of
'concentrate'. [22–8]. *la suite des objets . . . terminer*: the hierarchy of perception
alluded to here is Platonic in origin (as suggested by the subliminal pun on 'plateau').
Cp. *Sordello* iii 141–5 (I 532); also *Shelley* 197–200: 'that mighty ladder,
of which . . . the world dares no longer doubt that its gradations ascend' and
257–8: 'Did the poet ever attain to a higher platform than where he rested and
exhibited a result?' (Appendix A, pp. 862–3).

What would I have? what is this "sleep," which seems
To bound all? can there be a "waking" point
Of crowning life? The soul would never rule—
815 It would be first in all things—it would have
Its utmost pleasure filled,—but that complete
Commanding for commanding sickens it.
The last point I can trace is, rest beneath
Some better essence than itself—in weakness;
820 This is "myself"—not what I think should be,
And what is that I hunger for but God?
My God, my God! let me for once look on thee
As tho' nought else existed: we alone.
And as creation crumbles, my soul's spark
825 Expands till I can say, "Even from myself
"I need thee, and I feel thee, and I love thee;
"I do not plead my rapture in thy works
"For love of thee—or that I feel as one
"Who cannot die—but there is that in me

812–14. what is . . . crowning life: cp. *Tempest* IV i 156–8: 'We are such stuff / As dreams are made on; and our little life / Is rounded with a sleep'; and Donne, *Divine Meditations* x 13–14: 'One short sleep past, we wake eternally, / And death shall be no more, Death thou shalt die'. Cp. also *Flight of the Duchess* 686–8 (II 326), noting 'crowning' in l. 676.

814. crowning life: consummate life, i.e. life after death; cp. *Revelation* ii 10: 'Be thou faithful unto death, and I will give thee the crown of life'.

814–19. The soul . . . weakness: cp. *Sordello* iii 302–9 (I 544).

816. but that complete: 'but once that is accomplished'.

818–21. Cp. *Sordello* vi 588ff (I 750).

818. point I] emended from 'point that I' in *1833*, a correction made by B. in *Mill* and followed on; in *Lowell-1888*. B. is rarely unmetrical without strong reason; the emphasis in this line seems designed to fall on 'last' rather than 'point'. 'That' may have strayed from l. 816 or more likely l. 821, which has 'that I'.

821.] There is a space after this line in *1888*.

822. My God, my God: cp. (noting l. 853) *Mark* xv 34: 'And at the ninth hour Jesus cried with a loud voice . . . My God, my God, why hast thou forsaken me?'

824. as creation crumbles: cp. *In a Year* 77–80 (p. 273): 'Well, this cold clay clod / Was man's heart. / Crumble it—and what comes next? / Is it God?'

824–5. my soul's spark / Expands: cp. *Ring* xi 2370–2: 'The soul's condensed and, twice itself, expands / To burst thro' life, in alternation due, / Into the other state whate'er it prove'. 'Spark of soul' occurs in *Fifine at the Fair* (1872) 674.

828. or] nor (*Lowell-1888*).

830 "Which turns to thee, which loves, or which should love."

Why have I girt myself with this hell-dress?
Why have I laboured to put out my life?
Is it not in my nature to adore,
And e'en for all my reason do I not
835 Feel him, and thank him, and pray to him?—*Now.*
Can I forego the trust that he loves me?
Do I not feel a love which only ONE. . . . .
O thou pale form, so dimly seen, deep-eyed,
I have denied thee calmly—do I not
840 Pant when I read of thy consummate deeds,
And burn to see thy calm, pure truths out-flash
The brightest gleams of earth's philosophy?
Do I not shake to hear aught question thee? . . . .

If I am erring save me, madden me,
845 Take from me powers, and pleasures—let me die
Ages, so I see thee: I am knit round
As with a charm, by sin and lust and pride,
Yet tho' my wandering dreams have seen all shapes
Of strange delight, oft have I stood by thee—

830.] There is no space after this line in *Lowell-1875.* To 'turn to the Lord' is a biblical commonplace, e.g. *Lamentations* iii 40, *Joel* ii 13, *2 Corinthians* iii 16.
831–1031. With this closing movement of the poem cp. Byron, *Childe Harold* IV clxxxv–clxxxvi: 'My task is done, my song hath ceased, my theme / Has died into an echo; it is fit / The spell should break of this protracted dream. / The torch shall be extinguish'd which hath lit / My midnight lamp—and what is writ, is writ; / Would it were worthier! But I am not now / That which I have been —and my visions flit / Less palpably before me—and the glow / Which in my spirit dwelt, is fluttering, faint, and low. // Farewell! a word that must be, and bath been— / A sound which makes us linger;—yet—farewell! / Ye! who have traced the Pilgrim to the scene / Which is his last, if in your memories dwell / A thought which once was his, if on ye swell / A single recollection, not in vain / He wore his sandal-shoon and scallop-shell; / Farewell! with *him* alone may rest the pain, / If such there were—with you the moral of his strain'. Note the echo of the motto to *Pauline* from Clément Marot: see note, p. 14. This passage may also have influenced the ending of *Sordello* (I 768).
831–6. Mill wrote vertically in the margin: 'why should this follow the description of scenery?'
835. him?—Now.] him—now? (*Lowell, 1888*).
837. which only ONE: 'which only one [i.e. Christ] can inspire'.
840. deeds] power (*1888*).
843.] No space after this line in *1888.*
845–6. let me die / Ages, so I see thee: cp. Marlowe, *Dr Faustus* V ii 179–80: 'Let Faustus live in hell a thousand years, / A hundred thousand, and at last be saved'.

850 Have I been keeping lonely watch with thee,
     In the damp night by weeping Olivet,
     Or leaning on thy bosom, proudly less—
     Or dying with thee on the lonely cross—
     Or witnessing thy bursting from the tomb!

855 A mortal, sin's familiar friend, doth here
     Avow that he will give all earth's reward,
     But to believe and humbly teach the faith,
     In suffering, and poverty, and shame,
     Only believing he is not unloved. . . .

860 And now, my Pauline, I am thine for ever!
     I feel the spirit which has buoyed me up
     Deserting me: and old shades gathering on;
     Yet while its last light waits, I would say much,
     And chiefly, I am glad that I have said
865 That love which I have ever felt for thee,
     But seldom told; our hearts so beat together,
     That speech is mockery, but when dark hours come;
     And I feel sad; and thou, sweet, deem'st it strange
     A sorrow moves me, thou canst not remove,

850–1. See *Mark* xiv 26–42, Christ's vigil before his arrest in the garden of Gethsemane, near Mount Olivet (or the Mount of Olives), during which he rebukes the disciples for falling asleep and being unable to 'watch' with him, and prays to the Father to be spared his coming ordeal.

852. See *John* xiii 23, the Last Supper: 'Now there was leaning on Jesus' bosom one of his disciples, whom Jesus loved'.

854. thy bursting] thine outburst (*1888*). No direct witness to the Resurrection is recorded in the Gospels.

855. friend,] emended in agreement with *1868–88* from 'friend' in *1833*.

859–60. In the space between these lines, Mill wrote: 'strange transition'.

862–5.] Desert me, and old shades are gathering fast;
            Yet while the last light waits, I would say much,
            This chiefly, it is gain that I have said
            Somewhat of love I ever felt for thee (*1888*)

863. while its last light waits: the first appearance in B. of a recurrent motif, the delay of sunset to allow a final revelation: e.g. *Sordello* v 305–12, *Childe Roland* 187–8 (p. 365), *Gerard de Lairesse* (*Parleyings*, 1887) 308–15.

867. is mockery] seemed mockery (*1888*).

868. I feel sad] joy departs (*1888*).

868–9. strange . . . remove,] emended from 'strange; . . . remove.' in *1833*. Neither correction was made by B. in *Mill*, but both appear in *Lowell-1888*, and fit the syntax of ll. 867–70 ('when dark hours come . . . Look on this lay') better than the *1833* punctuation, which, though not nonsensical, destroys the development of the passage.

870 Look on this lay I dedicate to thee,
     Which thro' thee I began, and which I end,
     Collecting the last gleams to strive to tell
     That I am thine, and more than ever now—
     That I am sinking fast—yet tho' I sink,
875 No less I feel that thou hast brought me bliss,
     And that I still may hope to win it back.
     Thou know'st, dear friend, I could not think all calm,
     For wild dreams followed me, and bore me off,
     And all was indistinct. Ere one was caught
880 Another glanced: so dazzled by my wealth,
     Knowing not which to leave nor which to choose,
     For all my thoughts so floated, nought was fixed—
     And then thou said'st a perfect bard was one
     Who shadowed out the stages of all life,
885 And so thou badest me tell this my first stage;—
     'Tis done: and even now I feel all dim the shift
     Of thought. These are my last thoughts; I discern
     Faintly immortal life, and truth, and good.
     And why thou must be mine is, that e'en now,
890 In the dim hush of night—that I have done—
     With fears and sad forebodings: I look thro'

871. and which I end] which thus I end (*1888*).
872–3. Cp. ll. 575–6.
873–9.] How I am thine, and more than ever now
         That I sink fast: yet though I deeplier sink,
         No less song proves one word has brought me bliss,
         Another still may win bliss surely back.
         Thou knowest, dear, I could not think all calm,
         For fancies followed thought and bore me off,
         And left all indistinct; ere one was caught (*1888*)
877–82. Cp. *Paracelsus* ii 522–41 (I 215), and *Two in the Campagna 52–5* (p. 562):
'Must I go / Still like the thistle-ball, no bar, / Onward, whenever light winds
blow, / Fixed by no friendly star?'
880. glanced: 'appeared briefly'; cp. *Sordello* ii 25–6 (I 462).   *so*] so, (*Lowell-1888*).
881–2.] I knew not which to leave nor which to choose, / For all so floated,
nought was fixed and firm. (*1888*)
883–4. Cp. the development of this idea in Aprile's speeches in *Paracelsus* ii.
884–8.] Who chronicled the stages of all life,
         And so thou bad'st me shadow this first stage.
         'T is done, and even now I recognize
         The shift, the change from last to past—discern
         Faintly how life is truth and truth is good. (*1888*)
885. first stage] First Stage (*Mill*).
891.] With fears and sad forebodings,—I look through (*Lowell*); With fears and
sad forebodings, I look through (*1868–75*); Despite the sad forebodings, love looks
through— (*1888*). Note the slight change of meaning in *1868–75*.

And say, "E'en at the last I have her still,
"With her delicious eyes as clear as heaven,
"When rain in a quick shower has beat down mist,
895   "And clouds float white in the sun like broods of swans."
How the blood lies upon her cheek, all spread
As thinned by kisses; only in her lips
It wells and pulses like a living thing,
And her neck looks like marble misted o'er
900   With love-breath, a dear thing to kiss and love,
Standing beneath me—looking out to me,
As I might kill her and be loved for it.

Love me—love me, Pauline, love nought but me;
Leave me not. All these words are wild and weak,
905   Believe them not, Pauline. I stooped so low
But to behold thee purer by my side,
To show thou art my breath—my life—a last
Resource—an extreme want: never believe
Aught better could so look to thee, nor seek
910   Again the world of good thoughts left for me.
There were bright troops of undiscovered suns,
Each equal in their radiant course. There were
Clusters of far fair isles, which ocean kept
For his own joy, and his waves broke on them

---

892. And say] Whispers (*1888*).
892–5.] B. deleted the quotation marks in *Mill* and *Lowell*, and they do not appear
in *1868–1888*.
895. in the sun] above (*1888*).
896–902. Anticipating the description of Porphyria and her lover's account of his
murder of her in *Porphyria* (p. 70).
896. all spread] outspread (*1888*).
899. looks] emended from 'looks,' in *1833*, a correction made by B. in *Mill* and
followed in *Lowell-1888.*
900–5.] With love-breath,—a Pauline from heights above,
          Stooping beneath me, looking up—one look
          As I might kill her and be loved the more.
          So, love me—me, Pauline, and nought but me,
          Never leave loving! Words are wild and weak,
          Believe them not, Pauline! I stained myself (*1888*)
910. me] mine (*1888*).
911–24. There were . . . touch me: Pauline is successively compared to a star, a beautiful island, and a dream, each of which loses its place in the larger scheme to
which it naturally belongs by devoting itself to a particular object (i.e. the writer).
Cp. *Sordello* i 505–21 and notes (I 428–30). Mill placed a cross in the margin
opposite ll. 921–4, indicating obscurity.

915 Without a choice. And there was a dim crowd
     Of visions, each a part of the dim whole.
     And a star left his peers and came with peace
     Upon a storm, and all eyes pined for him.
     And one isle harboured a sea-beaten ship,
920 And the crew wandered in its bowers, and plucked
     Its fruits, and gave up all their hopes for home.
     And one dream came to a pale poet's sleep,
     And he said, "I am singled out by God,
     "No sin must touch me." I am very weak,
925 But what I would express is,—Leave me not,
     Still sit by me—with beating breast, and hair
     Loosened—watching earnest by my side,
     Turning my books, or kissing me when I
     Look up—like summer wind. Be still to me
930 A key to music's mystery, when mind fails,
     A reason, a solution and a clue.
     You see I have thrown off my prescribed rules:
     I hope in myself—and hope, and pant, and love—
     You'll find me better—know me more than when
935 You loved me as I was. Smile not; I have
     Much yet to gladden you—to dawn on you.

     No more of the past—I'll look within no more—
     I have too trusted to my own wild wants—

916. the dim whole] some grand whole (*1888*).
917. a star] one star (*1888*).
919–21. Alluding to the episode of the Lotus-eaters in *Odyssey* ix.
921. fruits] fruit (*1868–75*). *for home*] of home (*1888*).
924–5. I am very weak, / But what I] Words are wild and weak, / But what they
(*1888*); see ll. 900–5n.
927. Loosened—watching] Loosened, be watching (*Lowell-1888*).
930–4.] A help to music's mystery which mind fails
          To fathom, its solution, no mere clue!
          O reason's pedantry, life's rule prescribed!
          I hopeless, I the loveless, hope and love.
          Wiser and better, know me now, not when (*1888*)
932. Mill wrote 'poor' in the margin opposite this line.
936.] Much yet to dawn on you, to gladden you. (*1888*).
936^937] there is no space here in *Lowell-1875*; the line ends a page in *1888*, but
as the page is a line short, a line-space may be indicated.
938–40.] I have too trusted my own lawless wants,
          Too trusted my vain self, vague intuition—
          Draining soul's wine alone in the still night, (*1888*)

Too trusted to myself—to intuition—
940 Draining the wine alone in the still night,
And seeing how—as gathering films arose,
As by an inspiration life seemed bare
And grinning in its vanity, and ends
Hard to be dreamed of, stared at me as fixed,
945 And others suddenly became all foul,
As a fair witch turned an old hag at night.
No more of this—we will go hand in hand,
I will go with thee, even as a child,
Looking no further than thy sweet commands.
950 And thou hast chosen where this life shall be—
The land which gave me thee shall be our home,
Where nature lies all wild amid her lakes
And snow-swathed mountains, and vast pines all girt
With ropes of snow—where nature lies all bare,
955 Suffering none to view her but a race
Most stinted and deformed—like the mute dwarfs
Which wait upon a naked Indian queen.
And there (the time being when the heavens are thick
With storms) I'll sit with thee while thou dost sing
960 Thy native songs, gay as a desert bird
Who crieth as he flies for perfect joy,
Or telling me old stories of dead knights.
Or I will read old lays to thee—how she,

939. *intuition*—] emended from 'intuition.' in *1833*, a correction made by B. in *Mill* and followed in *Lowell-1888*.
943–6.] And grinning in its vanity, while ends
          Foul to be dreamed of, smiled at me as fixed
          And fair, while others changed from fair to foul
          As a young witch turns an old hag at night. (*1888*)
946. Cp. l. 431.
948–9.] I with thee, even as a child—love's slave, / Looking no farther than his liege commands. (*1888*, which leaves a space after this line).
950–7. The allusion is to Switzerland; Rousseau, whose writings are a source for the poem (see headnote, p. 24), was Swiss by birth. B. had not visited Switzerland when he wrote the poem; the comparison of the grandeur of the Swiss landscape with the defects of the Swiss peasantry (through inbreeding) was a Romantic commonplace.
953. *all girt*] begirt (*1888*).
961. *Who . . . he*] Which . . . it (*1888*).
963–5. *how she . . . and live*: an allusion to Sophocles' *Antigone*, in which Antigone, for according burial rites to her brother Polynices against the King's decree, is sentenced to be buried alive, and commits suicide. In *Mill*, below l. 963, which ends the page in *1833*, B. quoted in Greek from Sophocles' play: 'My nature is for mutual love, not hate . . . And now he drags me . . . A bride unwed,

The fair pale sister, went to her chill grave
965   With power to love, and to be loved, and live.
Or we will go together, like twin gods
Of the infernal world, with scented lamp
Over the dead—to call and to awake—
Over the unshaped images which lie
970   Within my mind's cave—only leaving all
That tells of the past doubts. So when spring comes,
And sunshine comes again like an old smile,
And the fresh waters, and awakened birds,
And budding woods await us—I shall be
975   Prepared, and we will go and think again,
And all old loves shall come to us—but changed
As some sweet thought which harsh words veiled before;
Feeling God loves us, and that all that errs
Is a strange dream which death will dissipate;

---

amerced of marriage-song / And marriage-bed and joys of motherhood, / By friends deserted to a living grave' (ll. 523, 916–20). As with the Greek glosses to ll. 567–76, B. seems to have added this gloss on his own initiative; there is no prompting query from Mill.

963. *old lays*] great lays (*1888*). *she*] She (*Mill*).

964. *sister*] Sister (*Mill*).

966–70. *Or we . . . mind's cave*: the main clause is 'we will go together over the unshaped images etc.', the intervening phrases being interpolations. The comparison between the creative process and awaking the dead is common in B.: see esp. *Sordello* i 31–54 (I 396–8) and *Ring* i 707–72. The 'twin gods' refer to Dis and Persephone, god and goddess of Hades; with the 'mind's cave', cp. Shelley, *Mont Blanc*, esp. ll. 34–48, where 'my own, my human mind' contains 'the still cave of the witch Poesy', adapting Plato's image in the *Republic* of the mind as a cave within which the immortal Forms are shadowily reflected.

971. *doubts*] doubt (*1888*).

972. *And sunshine comes*] With sunshine back (*1888*).

974–5. Mill underlined 'I shall be / Prepared' and wrote in the margin: 'he is always talking of being *prepared*—what for?' B. put a cross underneath Mill's note and wrote at the bottom of the page: 'Why, "that's tellings," as schoolboys say'. *Oxford* notes that B. repeats this phrase in a letter to Mrs Story in 1863 (*American Friends* 132).

975–82.] Prepared, and we will question life once more,
    Till its old sense shall come renewed by change,
    Like some clear thought which harsh words veiled before;
    Feeling God loves us, and that all which errs
    Is but a dream which death will dissipate.
    And then what need of longer exile? Seek
    My England, and, again there, calm approach
    All I once fled from, calmly look on those (*1888*)

978. *errs*] emended in agreement with *1868–88* from 'errs,' in *1833*.

979. Cp. Shelley, *Adonais* 344: 'He has awakened from the dream of life'.

980 And then when I am firm we'll seek again
My own land, and again I will approach
My old designs, and calmly look on all
The works of my past weakness, as one views
Some scene where danger met him long before.
985 Ah! that such pleasant life should be but dreamed!

But whate'er come of it—and tho' it fade,
And tho' ere the cold morning all be gone
As it will be;—tho' music wait for me,
And fair eyes and bright wine, laughing like sin,
990 Which steals back softly on a soul half saved;
And I be first to deny all, and despise
This verse, and these intents which seem so fair;
Still this is all my own, this moment's pride,
No less I make an end in perfect joy.
995 E'en in my brightest time, a lurking fear
Possessed me. I well knew my weak resolves,
I felt the witchery that makes mind sleep
Over its treasures—as one half afraid
To make his riches definite—but now
1000 These feelings shall not utterly be lost,
I shall not know again that nameless care,
Lest leaving all undone in youth, some new
And undreamed end reveal itself too late:
For this song shall remain to tell for ever,
1005 That when I lost all hope of such a change,
Suddenly Beauty rose on me again.
No less I make an end in perfect joy,
For I, having thus again been visited,
Shall doubt not many another bliss awaits,
1010 And tho' this weak soul sink, and darkness come,

988–9.] As it may be;—tho' music wait to wile, / And strange eyes and bright wine lure, laugh like sin (*1888*).
991–3.] And I the first deny, decry, despise,
　　　With this avowal, these intents so fair,—
　　　Still be it all my own, this moment's pride! (*1888*)
1006. *Beauty*] beauty (*Lowell-1888*).
1008.] For I, who thus again was visited, (*1888*).
1010–14.] And, though this weak soul sink and darkness whelm,
　　　Some little word shall light it, raise aloft,
　　　To where I clearlier see and better love,
　　　As I again go o'er the tracts of thought
　　　Like one who has a right, and I shall live (*1888*)

Some little word shall light it up again,
And I shall see all clearer and love better;
I shall again go o'er the tracts of thought,
As one who has a right; and I shall live
1015 With poets—calmer—purer still each time,
And beauteous shapes will come to me again,
And unknown secrets will be trusted me,
Which were not mine when wavering—but now
I shall be priest and lover, as of old.

1020 Sun-treader, I believe in God, and truth,
And love; and as one just escaped from death
Would bind himself in bands of friends to feel
He lives indeed—so, I would lean on thee;
Thou must be ever with me—most in gloom
1025 When such shall come—but chiefly when I die,
For I seem dying, as one going in the dark
To fight a giant—and live thou for ever,
And be to all what thou hast been to me—
All in whom this wakes pleasant thoughts of me,
1030 Know my last state is happy—free from doubt,
Or touch of fear. Love me and wish me well!

RICHMOND,
October 22, 1832.

1016. to me again] for me to seize (*1888*).
1018.] Which were denied the waverer once; but now (*1888*).
1019. priest and lover: perhaps recalling Keats, *Ode to Psyche* 50: 'Yes, I will be thy priest'; note that Psyche is an emblem of love. *lover*] prophet (*1888*).
1025. When such shall come] If such must come (*1888*).
1026. seem dying] seem, dying (*Lowell-1888*).
1027. and live] but live (*1888*).
1029-subscription. Mill put a line in the margin opposite ll. 1029–31 and wrote underneath the subscription: 'this transition from speaking to Pauline to writing a letter to the public with *place & date*, is quite horrible'. B. put a cross in the margin opposite the subscription and wrote below Mill's note: 'Kean was acting there: I saw him in Richard III that night, and conceived the childish scheme already mentioned: there is an allusion to Kean, page 47. I don't know whether I had not made up my mind to *act*, as well as to make verses, music, and God knows what.—que de châteaux en Espagne!' For the 'childish scheme', see head-note, p. 15; for the 'allusion to Kean', see ll. 669–75. The French phrase means 'what castles in the air', 'what fantasies'.

2 Porphyria
[Porphyria's Lover]

First publ. *MR* n.s. x (Jan. 1836) 43–4, preceding *Johannes*; the two poems were signed 'Z.' Repr. *B & P* iii (*DL*), 26 Nov. 1842, where *Johannes* now preceded it; the two poems were given the collective title *Madhouse Cells*. Then repr. *1849* (with the title *II.—Madhouse Cell*, and the subtitle *Porphyria's Lover*), *1863* (when it was separated from *Johannes*, called simply *Porphyria's Lover*, and placed in *Romances*), *1865²*, *1868*, *1880* (which, together with its corrected reissue *1884*, is unique in dividing the poem into twelve numbered 5-line stanzas), *1888*. Our text is that of *MR*. Anne Thackeray Ritchie, a close friend of B., claims that the poem was written during B.'s trip to Russia in 1834 (*Records of Tennyson, Ruskin and Browning* [1893] 221); there is however no concrete evidence to support this statement. M. Mason ('Browning and the Dramatic Monologue', *Writers and their Background: Robert Browning*, ed. I. Armstrong, [1974] 255–7) identifies two contemporary sources. The first is a passage from 'Extracts from Gosschen's Diary no. 1' (*Blackwood's Magazine* iii [1818] 596–8), publ. anonymously but now known to be by John Wilson: 'Do you think there was no pleasure in murdering her? I grasped her by that radiant, that golden hair, I bared those snow-white breasts,—I dragged her sweet body towards me, and, as God is my witness, I stabbed, and stabbed her with this dagger, forty times. She never so much as gave one shriek, for she was dead in a moment,—but she would not have shrieked had she endured pang after pang, for she saw my face of wrath turned upon her,—and she knew that my wrath was just, and that I did right to murder her who would have forsaken her lover in his insanity. I laid her down upon a bank of flowers,—that were soon stained with her blood. I saw the dim blue eyes beneath the half-closed lids,—that face so changeful in its living beauty was now fixed as ice, and the balmy breath came from her sweet lips no more. My joy, my happiness, was perfect'. The second source is a passage from *Marcian Colonna* (publ. 1820; III xvi), a poem by B.'s friend Bryan Waller Procter ('Barry Cornwall'):

He sate and watch'd her, as a nurse might do,
And saw the dull film steal across the blue,
And saw and felt her sweet forgiving smile,
That, as she died, parted her lips the while:
Her hand?—its pulse was silent,—her voice gone,
But patience in her smile still faintly shone,
And in her closing eyes a tenderness,
That seem'd as she would still Colonna bless.
She died, and spoke no word: and still he sate
Beside her like an image. Death and Fate
Had done what might he then: The morning sun
Rose upon him: on him?—his task was done.
The murderer and the murder'd—one as pale
As marble shining white beneath the moon,
The other dark as storms, when the winds rail
At the chafed sea,—but not to calm so soon.—
No bitterness, nor hate, nor dread was there;
But love still clinging round a wild despair,

A wintry aspect and a troubled eye,
Mourning o'er youth and beauty born to die.
Dead was she, and her mouth had fallen low,
But still he watch'd her with a steadfast brow:
Unalter'd as a rock he sate, while she
Lay chang'd to clay, and perish'd.

Mason argues convincingly that B.'s poem reflects a contemporary change in psychiatric theory towards a sympathetic and understanding approach to the lunatic; he concludes that Wilson and Procter provided B. with inverse sources, since they treat madness as aberration while B. considers it a logical and coherent extension of character. R. Langbaum, in comparing the poem with *A Forgiveness* (1876), similarly comments that 'extraordinary motives in Browning come not from disordered subconscious urges but, as in Henry James, from the highest moral and intellectual refinement' (*The Poetry of Experience*, [N. Y. 1957; repr. 1972] 88). This reading is supported by B.'s other studies in madness, esp. in *Red Cotton* and *Christopher Smart*. G. O. Marshall, in 'Tennyson's *The Sisters* and *Porphyria's Lover*' (*BNL* i [Fall 1969] 9–11) suggests a partly inverted source in Tennyson's poem, in which a woman lures her dead sister's lover to her house and kills him: see l. 2n., 16–19n. A passage in *Pauline* (ll. 896–902, p. 64) has close affinities with this poem; cp. also B. to EBB., 15 Aug. 1846: 'do you not see that my utmost pride and delight will be to think you are happy, as *you were not*,—in the way you were not: if you chose to come out of a whirl of balls and parties and excursions and visitings—to my side, I should love you as you sate still by me' (*Correspondence* xiii 255). Cp. *Time's Revenges* 31–66 (II 281–2). The poem has been one of B.'s most popular, and is frequently anthologised.

> The rain set early in to-night:
>   The sullen wind was soon awake—
> It tore the elm-tops down for spite,
>   And did its worst to vex the lake:
> 5 I listened, with heart fit to break,
>   When glided in Porphyria: straight
>   She shut the cold out and the storm,
>   And kneeled and made the cheerless grate
>   Blaze up, and all the cottage warm;
> 10 Which done, she rose, and from her form
>   Withdrew the dripping cloak and shawl,
>   And laid her soiled gloves by; untied
>   Her hat and let the damp hair fall,
>   And, last, she sate down by my side

2. Cp. Tennyson, *The Sisters* (1832) l. 3: 'The wind is blowing in turret and tree'.
5. break,] break. (*1863–88*).

15 And called me. When no voice replied,
　　　She put my arm about her waist,
　　　　　And made her smooth white shoulder bare,
　　　And all her yellow hair displaced,
　　　　　And, stooping, made my cheek lie there
20 And spread o'er all her yellow hair,
　　　Murmuring how she loved me—she
　　　　　Too weak, for all her heart's endeavour,
　　　To set its struggling passion free
　　　　　From pride, and vainer ties dissever,
25 And give herself to me for ever:
　　　But passion sometimes would prevail;
　　　　　Nor could to-night's gay feast restrain
　　　A sudden thought of one so pale
　　　　　For love of her—and all in vain;
30 And she was come through wind and rain.
　　　Be sure I looked up at her eyes
　　　　　Proud—very proud—at last I knew
　　　Porphyria worshipped me: surprise
　　　　　Made my heart swell, and still it grew
35 While I debated what to do.
　　　That moment she was mine,—mine, fair,
　　　　　Perfectly pure and good: I found
　　　A thing to do, and all her hair
　　　　　In one long yellow string I wound

16–19. Cp. Tennyson, *The Sisters* (1832) 16–20: 'And after supper, on a bed, / Upon my lap he laid his head: / O the earl was fair to see! // I kissed his eyelids into rest: / His ruddy cheek was on my breast'.

17–20. Cp. *Marcian Colonna* (see headnote) II v: 'Then on her shoulder drooped his feverish head'.

18–20. The sensuous beauty of gold hair is a favourite motif: see e.g. *Sordello* ii 151–60 (I 472), *Song* (II 335), *Andrea* 174–5 (p. 399), *Gold Hair* (DP, 1864). B. wrote to EBB. of his admiration for a painting by Titian of Mary Magdalen with a 'heap of [gold] hair in her hands' (13 Jan. 1845, *Correspondence* x 22); and Mrs Howard, in a diary entry dated 20 Sept. 1869, wrote: 'Aggie [Agnes] Carnegie[,] Edy [Edith Story,] Mrs Story[,] Browning & I went to Lanerton & Aggie let down her golden hair to please Browning as we sat by the waterfall— he said poets ought to be indulged by such sights' (quoted V. Surtees, 'Browning's Last Duchess'. *London Review of Books* viii, no. 17 [9 Oct. 1986] 17).

30. *And*] So, (*1849–88*).

32. *Proud—very proud*—] Proud, very proud; (*1842–49*); Happy and proud; (*1863–88*).

36. *fair,*] emended in agreement with all other eds. from 'fair' in MR.

39–41. Cp. Tennyson, *The Sisters* (1832) 29: 'Three times I stabbed him through and through'.

40 Three times her little throat around
    And strangled her. No pain felt she—
        I am quite sure she felt no pain.
    As a shut bud that holds a bee
        I warily oped her lids—again
45 Laughed the blue eyes without a stain.
    And I untightened next the tress
        About her neck—her cheek once more
    Blushed bright beneath my burning kiss:
        I propped her head up as before,
50 Only, this time *my* shoulder bore
    Her head—which droops upon it still:
        The smiling rosy little head!
    So glad it has its utmost will;
        That all it scorned at once is fled,
55 And I, its love, am gained instead,
    Porphyria's love: she guessed not how
        Her darling, one wish would be heard.
    And thus we sit together now:
        And all night long we have not stirred,—
60 And yet God has not said a word!

43–4. *As a shut bud . . . her lids*: cp. Keats, *Eve of St Agnes* 243: 'As though a rose
should shut, and be a bud again'. In B., cp. *Caliban* 10: 'And now a flower drops
with a bee inside' (p. 625) and *Gerard de Lairesse* (*Parleyings*, 1887) 127–8: 'crisp
buds a struggling bee / Uncrumples, caught by sweet he clambers through'.
44–9. Cp. Tennyson, *The Sisters* (1832) 31–2: 'I curled and combed his comely
head. / He looked so grand when he was dead'.
50. *my*] not italic, *1842, 1868–88*.
52. *head!*] head, (*1842–88*).
55. *instead,*] instead! (*1842–88*).
57. *darling*] darling (*1842–88*).
60. A passage in *Gosschen's Diary* (see headnote) may have influenced B.: 'I cried
unto God, if God there be—Thou madest me a madman! Thou madest me a
murderer! Thou foredoomest me to sin and to hell! . . . I have done thy will,
—I have slain the most blissful of all thy creatures;—and am I a holy and
commissioned priest, or am I an accursed and infidel murderer?'

3 Johannes Agricola
[Johannes Agricola in Meditation]

First publ. *MR* n.s. x (Jan. 1836) 45–6, following *Porphyria*; the two poems were signed 'Z.' Repr. *B & P* iii (*DL*), 26 Nov. 1842, still with *Porphyria* but now preceding it; the poems were given the collective title *Madhouse Cells* and the epigraph was dropped. Then *1849* (with the title *I.—Madhouse Cell*, and the subtitle *Johannes Agricola in Meditation*), *1863* (when it was separated from *Porphyria*, called simply *Johannes Agricola in Meditation*, and placed in *Romances*: see Appendix A, II 464), *1868* (when it was placed in *Men and Women*), *1888*. It is very unusual among the poems of *DL* and *DR & L* in not being included in any volume of selections chosen by B.: it appears in a proof of *1865²* (now at *Texas*) but was deleted before publication. The date of composition is conjectural, but it has features in common with *Paracelsus*, and may have been written at the same time.

DeVane (*Handbook* 124) suggests that it was in Melchior Adam's *Vitae Germanorum Medicorum* (Heidelberg 1720) that B. encountered the name of John Schnitter or Schneider, otherwise Agricola (1494–1566), founder, as the poem's epigraph records, of the Antinomian sect, a name given to it by Luther, who was originally Agricola's patron, but with whom he quarrelled. Agricola denied that the Mosaic law had authority over the true believer, who could be saved by faith alone: he did not however deny the applicability of New Testament moral law. In some of his followers, however, the doctrine assumed the extreme form B. ascribes to Agricola, combining a Calvinist concept of predestination with the belief that no sin or crime can compromise the true believer's right to salvation. The latter concept goes back to the Gnostic elements of the early Church, enters substantially into Calvinism, and thence into extreme English Puritan sects such as the Ranters, of whom Richard Baxter remarked: 'But withal they conjoyned a cursed Doctrine of Libertinism, which brought them to all abominable filthiness of Life. They taught that God regarded not the actions of the outward man, but of the inner heart, and that to the Pure all things are Pure (even things forbidden) and so as allowed by God they . . . committed whoredoms commonly' (*Narrative of his Life and Times* [1696] i 76–7). B.'s Nonconformist background, and his father's extensive library, probably gave him early access to relevant pamphlets from the Puritan period. At several points in the poem Johannes echoes phrases from St Paul, from whom the doctrines of predestination and of salvation by faith as opposed to works principally stem. Antinomianism has often been seen as a logical extreme of Protestant theology, which would broaden the application of B.'s satire. It has been suggested that this satire may have been inversely influenced by the liberal Unitarianism of the *MR*, and of its editor, W. J. Fox, B.'s friend and 'literary father' (see headnote to *Pauline*, p. 21); Unitarianism's emphasis on reason, on tolerance, and on civil and religious liberty contrasts strongly with Johannes' position (at e.g. ll. 41–55). The visionary aspect of the poem may, besides its debt to biblical sources, have been influenced by a passage in Paracelsus' *Archidoxes of Magic*: 'it is to be known, that some have been so spiritually lifted up to God in a dream, that they have seen his glory and the joy of the elect, and the punishments of the damned' (transl. R. Turner [1655] p. 49), and by passages in the Hermetic corpus (see notes). The next entry in the *Dictionary of all Religions*, from which B. took his epigraph, may also have influenced B.'s presentation: 'Antitractes, Christian Hereticks sprung from the

Gnosticks, who taught that Sin deserved rather Reward than Punishment, and accordingly wallowed in all Crimes'. Another possible source for the poem is Burns's *Holy Willie's Prayer*, esp. the first stanza: 'O thou, wha in the Heavens dost dwell, / Wha, as it pleases best thysel', / Sends ane to heaven and ten to hell, / A' for thy glory, / And no for ony guid or ill / They've done afore thee!' Another possible source is *Gosschen's Diary* (see *Porphyria*, headnote, and l. 60n.), in which the murderer invokes the concept of predestination to explain/justify his crime. James Hogg's *Confessions of a Justified Sinner* (1824) deals in the same ideology. There may also be a debt to Shelley who, while vehemently rejecting Christianity, affirmed a strong belief in Necessitarianism in the note to *Queen Mab* vi 198. B.'s interest in extreme religious ideas appears throughout his poetry, and although most of his speakers adopt the opposite doctrine of salvation by works rather than faith, there is a whole series of figures for whom faith, as given by divine revelation, constitutes the foundation of religion: see e.g. *Paracelsus, Abt Vogler* (p. 759), and *Christopher Smart* (*Parleyings*, 1887). *Soliloquy* (p. 201) and *Heretic's Tragedy* (III 219) illustrate the mania which may accompany religious conviction. B. seems to have seen a close association between religious mysticism and what is conventionally called 'insanity': see *Cleon* (p. 563) and *An Epistle* (p. 507); he implied an affinity between *An Epistle* and *Johannes* by juxtaposing the two poems in the *Men and Women* of 1868. Cp. also a passage from a letter of June 1864 to Julia Wedgwood: 'Last night I was talking with a friend who read aloud a passage from Dr. Newman's *Apology* in which he says that "he is as convinced of the existence of God"—an individual, not an external force merely—"as of his own existence:" I believe he deceives himself and that no sane man has ever had, with mathematical exactness, equal conviction on those two points . . . I can see nothing that comes from absolute *contact*, so to speak, between man and God, but everything in all variety from the greater or less distance between the two' (*RB & JW* 33–4).

"ANTINOMIANS, so denominated for rejecting the Law as a thing of no use under the Gospel dispensation: they say, that good works do not further, nor evil works hinder salvation; that the child of God cannot sin, that God never chastiseth
[5]   him, that murder, drunkenness, &c. are sins in the wicked but not in him, that the child of grace being once assured of salvation, afterwards never doubteth . . . that God doth

Epigraph.] not *1842–88*. The *Dictionary* was often ascribed to Defoe. B. modernised spelling and punctuation, made a few changes in wording, and abridged the entry as follows:

[*1*]. *ANTINOMIANS, so*] 'Antinomians, a sort of Christian Hereticks, so (*Dictionary*).

[*4–5*]. *chastisesth him, that*] chastiseth them, nor punisheth any Land for their Sin, that (*Dictionary*).

[*5*]. *murder, drunkenness*] Murder, Adultery, Drunkenness (*Dictionary*).

[*6*]. *him*] them (*Dictionary*).

[*7*]. *doubteth . . . that*] doubteth, that no Man should be troubled in Conscience for Sin; that no Christian should be exhorted to perform the duties of Christianity; that a Hypocrite may have all the Graces that were in *Adam* before his Fall; that Christ is the only Subject of Grace, that no Christian believeth or worketh any Good, but Christ only believeth and worketh; that (*Dictionary*).

not love any man for his holiness, that sanctification is no
evidence of justification, &c. Pontanus, in his Catalogue
[10] of Heresies, says John Agricola was the author of this sect,
A.D. 1535."— *Dictionary of all Religions*, 1704.

    There's Heaven above: and night by night
       I look right through its gorgeous roof—
    No suns and moons though e'er so bright
       Avail to stop me:—splendor-proof
5   I keep the broods of stars aloof:
       For I intend to get to God . . .
       For 'tis to God I speed so fast!
    For in God's breast, my own abode,
       Those shoals of dazzling glory past,
10 I lay my spirit down at last.
    I lie—where I have always lain,
       God smiles—as he has always smiled;—
    Ere suns and moons could wax and wane,

1–7. Cp. *Hermetica*, ed. W. Scott (Oxford 1924) i 155 ('A Discourse of Hermes
to Tat'): 'You see, my son, through how many bodily things in succession we
have to make our way, and through how many troops of demons and courses
of stars we have to make our way that we may press on to the one and only
God'. Also (p. 221): 'Bid [your soul] fly up to heaven, and it will have no need
of wings; nothing can bar its way, neither the fiery heat of the sun, nor the swirl
of the planet-spheres; clearing its way through all, it will fly up till it reaches the
outermost of all corporeal things'.
5. 'I keep aloof (apart) from the brood of stars'.
8. in God's breast: cp. *Luke* xvi 22: 'And it came to pass that the beggar [Lazarus]
died, and was carried by the angels into Abraham's bosom'. See below, ll. 41–50n.
9. glory past] glory, past (*1863*); glory, passed (*1865–88*).
10–11. Perhaps a reminiscence of *Psalms* iv 8: 'I will both lay me down in peace,
and sleep: for thou, Lord, only makest me dwell in safety.'
13–15. Ere suns . . . the heavens: the details are from the account of the Creation
in *Genesis* i, omitting all references to the creation of the earth.
14–20. Cp. *Ephesians* i 3–5: 'Blessed be the God and Father of our Lord Jesus
Christ, who hath blessed us with all spiritual blessings in heavenly places
with Christ: according as he hath chosen us in him before the foundation of
the world, that we should be holy and without blame before him in love:
having predestinated us unto the adoption of children by Jesus Christ to himself,
according to the good pleasure of his will'. See also *Romans* viii 28–30.
14. Ere stars were thundergirt: before the stars were encircled with, or invested with
the attributes of, thunder (the latter sense of 'girt' is common in the *Psalms*).
'Thundergirt' is apparently B.'s coinage. He was fond of compounding words
with 'thunder': *OED* cites 'thunder-free' (*Pippa* ii 47, p. 126) as another coinage.
Often, thunder stands for the will/voice of God; sometimes, it represents an act
of creation, as here. A possible source is Paracelsus's *First Book of Philosophy Written*

Ere stars were thundergirt, or piled
15   The heavens . . . God thought on me his child,
Ordained a life for me—arrayed
    Its circumstances, every one
To the minutest . . . ay, God said
    This head this hand should rest upon
20   Thus,—ere he fashioned star or sun!
And having thus created me,
    Thus rooted me, he bade me grow—
Guiltless for ever, like a tree
    That buds and blooms, nor seeks to know
25   A law by which it prospers so:
But sure that thought and word and deed
    All go to swell his love for me—
Me—made because that love had need
    Of something irrevocably
30   Pledged solely its content to be.
    Yes, yes,—a tree which must ascend—
      No poison-gourd foredoomed to stoop:

---

to the Athenians, transl. H. Pinnell in *Philosophy Reformed and Improved* (1657), a copy of which was in B.'s father's library (see headnote to *Paracelsus*, I 103): 'Thunder comes from the procreations of the Firmament . . . [and] is as it were the harvest of the Stars' (p. 19).

14–15. or piled / The heavens: i.e. 'or the heavens were built'.

17. circumstances,] circumstances (*1865–88*). This rev. was made in the proof of *1865²*, where the poem was originally intended to appear (see headnote).

19. 'This head should rest upon this hand'.

21–40. Cp. *Psalms* i 1–6: 'Blessed is the man that walketh not in the counsel of the ungodly . . . he shall be like a tree planted by the rivers of water, that bringeth forth his fruit in his season; his leaf also shall not wither; and whatsoever he doeth shall prosper . . . but the way of the ungodly shall perish'; note, however, that the righteous man's 'delight is in the law of the Lord' (v.2). Cp. also *Jonah* iv 6–7, where God causes a gourd to grow and wither as an example to Jonah. The tree is a constant image in B.'s work for natural growth and evolution in man; the gourd is also a frequent image, but is not elsewhere used in this way.

25. A] The (*1849–88*).

28. Me—made] Me made (*1842*); Me, made (*1849–88*).

29. irrevocably] irreversibly (*1870–88*).

31–50. Implicit here is St Paul's distinction between faith and works, invariably settled on the side of faith: 'For by grace are ye saved through faith; and that not of yourselves: it is the gift of God: not of works, lest any man should boast' (*Ephesians* ii 8–9); 'Therefore we conclude that a man is justified by faith without the deeds of the law' (*Romans* iii 28). Paul however also says: 'Shall we continue in sin, that grace may abound? God forbid. . . . shall we sin, because we are not under the law, but under grace? God forbid' (*Romans* vi 1–2, 15).

32. stoop:] stoop! (*1842–88*).

I have God's warrant, could I blend
    All hideous sins, as in a cup,—
35 To drink the mingled venoms up,
    Secure my nature will convert
      The draught to blossoming gladness fast:
      While sweet dews turn to the gourd's hurt,
        And bloat, and while they bloat it, blast—
40 As from the first its lot was cast.
    For as I lie, smiled on, full fed
      With unexhausted blessedness,—
    I gaze below on Hell's fierce bed,
      And those its waves of flame oppress,
45 Swarming in ghastly wretchedness,
    Whose life on earth aspired to be
      One altar-smoke,—so pure!—to win
    If not love like God's love to me,
      At least to keep his anger in . . .
50 And all their striving turned to sin!
    Priest, doctor, hermit, monk grown white
      With prayer: the broken hearted nun,
    The martyr, the wan accolyte,
      The incense-swinging child . . . undone
55 Before God fashioned star or sun!
    God—whom I praise . . . how could I praise

41–50. Cp. *Luke* xvi 22–5: 'the rich man also died, and was buried, and in hell
he lift up his eyes, being in torments, and seeth Abraham afar off, and Lazarus
in his bosom. And he cried and said, Father Abraham, have mercy on me, and
send Lazarus, that he may dip the tip of his finger in water, and cool my tongue;
for I am tormented in this flame. But Abraham said, Son, remember that thou
in thy lifetime receivedst thy good things, and likewise Lazarus evil things: but
now he is comforted, and thou art tormented'.
42. blessedness] power to bless (*1842–88*).
47. altar-smoke,—] altar-smoke, (*1842–88*).
50. sin!] sin. (*1863–88*).
51–4. priest . . . child: the offices and rituals described are all Catholic, suggesting
that Johannes, a Protestant, places all Catholics in Hell.
53. accolyte: 'an inferior officer in the church who attended the priests and deacons,
and performed subordinate duties, as lighting and bearing candles etc.' (*OED*).
56–60. Cp. St Paul: 'Now to him that worketh is the reward not reckoned of
grace, but of debt . . . Therefore hath he mercy on whom he will have mercy,
and whom he will he hardeneth. Thou wilt say then unto me, Why doth he yet
find fault? For who hath resisted his will? Nay but, O man, who art thou that
repliest against God? Shall the thing formed say to him that formed it, Why hast
thou made me thus? . . . For who hath known the mind of the Lord? or who
hath been his counsellor? Or who hath first given to him, and it shall be recom-
pensed unto him again?' (*Romans* iv 4, ix 18–20, xi 34–5). Calvin also remarks

If such as I might understand,
Make out, and reckon on his ways,
    And bargain for his love, and stand,
60 Paying a price, at his right hand?

that 'those he dooms to destruction are excluded from access to life by a just and
blameless, but at the same time incomprehensible judgment' (*Institutions* III xxi 1).

4 Pippa Passes

Text and publication

First publ. Apr. 1841, the first number of the *B & P* series (see Appendix C, p. 883). The song 'A king lived long ago' (iii 163–224) had appeared in *MR* n.s. ix (Nov. 1835) 707–8, with the title *The King* and signed 'Z.', B.'s usual signature for contributions to this journal (see I 326). Not repr. separately; repr. *1849, 1863, 1868, 1888*. The Ottima—Sebald scene (i 1–276) was repr. in *1863²*. Four songs from the play were repr. in *1865²*: 'You'll love me yet!' (iii 297–308) and 'Give her but a least excuse to love me!' (ii 195–210), both with the title *Song*

Title.] All other eds. have the subtitle 'a drama'. For the 'Advertisement' containing the dedication of the *B & P* series to Talfourd, see Appendix B, II 472. The 'Advertisement' was dropped in *1849*, which has: 'I dedicate my best intentions, in this poem, most admiringly to the author of "Ion,"—most affectionately to Mr. Serjeant Talfourd. R.B.' Subsequent eds. follow *1849* but delete both occurrences of the word 'most' and add 'London 1841' at the end. The dedication of *Pippa* only, instead of the whole of *B & P*, to Talfourd from *1849* may simply reflect the separation of the series' individual works from *1849*; cp. the similar change in the dedication to Landor of *B & P* viii (*Luria* and *A Soul's Tragedy*) in *1846*, which in *1849* was applied to *Luria* alone. But the further change in the wording of the dedication probably reflects a cooling in B.'s regard for Talfourd. In *1888* the opening section becomes the 'Introduction' and the following sections 'parts', and the word 'Scene.' is supplied before each opening s.d.; other eds. follow *1841*. In *1888* there is also a list of 'Persons' on the verso of the dedication, as follows:

Pippa.
Ottima.
Sebald.
Foreign Students.
Gottlieb.
Schramm.
Jules.
Phene.
Austrian Police.
Bluphocks.
Luigi and his Mother.
Poor Girls.
Monsignor and his Attendants.

The policy behind this list is not obvious. Gottlieb and Schramm, members of the 'foreign students' group, get separate billing, but not the more important Lutwyche, perhaps because his speech-prefix is always '1 Student' (though he is named several times). Nor is the Intendant distinguished from the other 'Attendants' of Monsignor, despite his major role (none of the others speaks). Possibly the list was not compiled by B. himself, but by a publisher's reader/compositor who noticed that *Pippa* was the only play lacking a *dramatis personae*; even so, B. must have passed it in proof.

from Pippa Passes; 'A king lived long ago' (iii 163–224), with the title *Romance from Pippa Passes*, and, immediately following, 'The year's at the spring' (i 215–22), with the title *Song from the Same*. Two songs were repr. in *1872*: 'The year's at the spring' and 'Give her but a least excuse to love me!' Substantive variants from all these texts are given in the notes; because of its special interest, a complete collation is given of 'The year's at the spring', incl. the available extant MSS which B. wrote as autographs. Our text is *1841*; we refer in our notes to the untitled opening section as *Intro*.

B. did not offer the play to the actor-manager William Macready, who had produced *Strafford* (1837), and indeed seems deliberately to have avoided doing so. *Pippa* had been one of three dramas announced as 'nearly ready' when *Sordello* was publ. in 1840 (see below), and Macready had already rejected the other two, *King Victor* and *Return of the Druses* (both publ. after *Pippa*: see Appendix C, p. 883). B. wrote to Macready, enclosing his presentation copy of *Pippa*: 'all things considered, I had rather publish, that is print—this play . . . than take the chance of a stage success that would in the highest degree gratify and benefit me, at the *risk of* "mettre du gêne" [putting constraint] in a friendship which I trust I know how to appreciate, by compelling you once more to say "No", where you would willingly say "Yes"' (*Correspondence* v 37). The play has never been professionally produced, though there have been numerous amateur performances and readings. For B.'s request to Eliza Flower for music for the songs, see below, p. 82; there have been many settings of the songs, notably 'The year's at the spring' (53 listed in *Bibliography*). In 1908, D. W. Griffith made a film based on the play, which is usefully discussed by E. Guiliano and R. C. Keenan in 'Browning Without Words' (*BIS* iv [1976] 125–59) and by F. A. Hilenski in 'D. W. Griffith's Film Version of *Pippa Passes*' (*Literature/Film Quarterly* iv [Winter 1976] 76–82).

Composition and revision

'Mr. Browning was walking alone, in a wood near Dulwich, when the image flashed upon him of someone walking thus alone through life; one apparently too obscure to leave a trace of his or her passage, yet exercising a lasting though unconscious influence at every step of it; and the image shaped itself into the little silk-winder of Asolo, Felippa, or Pippa' (Orr *Life* 55). B.'s letter to Mrs Bronson describing his first visit to Asolo confirms this account; see below, pp. 10–11. The exact date cannot be fixed, but it was some time after B. returned from his 1838 trip to Italy; a likely date would be late summer 1839, when B. had recently completed *Sordello* (note the anticipation of Pippa in *Sordello* vi 849ff., I 768). The work was described as 'nearly ready' in an advertisement at the end of *Sordello* (publ. Mar. 1840). There is no external evidence of the order of composition of the various sections. *Oxford* mistakenly suggests that pt. i must have been written before June 1839, citing a reference to the Ottima—Sebald scene in 'A Familiar Epistle to Robert Browning' by Barry Cornwall (the pseudonym of B.'s friend B. W. Procter), publ. in *English Songs and Other Small Poems* (1851). However, this reference does not occur in the portion of the poem headed 'St. John's Wood, June, 1839', which covers only ll. 1–44; the remainder, in which the reference to Pippa does occur (ll. 149–50), comes in a section headed 'London, 1846–1850'. In a letter of 3 May 1845, B. told EBB.: 'nobody ever sees what I do till it is printed' (*Correspondence* x 201). DeVane conjectures that pt. iii was drafted first, during or shortly after B.'s return from his travels in 1838. In a letter to Julia Wedgwood dated 17 Oct. 1864 (*RB & JW* 102), B. recalls reading the 'revise' (corrected proof) of the poem on 'Good *Saturday*', i.e. 10 Apr., since

Good Friday in 1841 fell on 9 Apr. (see also headnote to *Artemis Prologuizes*, II 106).

B. made a few revs. in *B & P BYU*. The poem was extensively revised for *1849*. EBB. wrote to Mrs Jameson on 4 Feb. 1847: 'Robert is *very* busy with his new edition, & has been throwing so much golden light into "Pippa," that everybody shall see her "pass" properly . . yes, & *surpass*' (*Correspondence* xiv 114). For B.'s own comments on the *1849* revs., see headnote to *Paracelsus*, I 102. The revs. are generally concerned with clarifying, by addition and expansion, supposed obscurities in plot and psychology. The pattern is not uniform. Revision of *Intro* was so heavy (36 new lines and numerous other changes) that B. had to write out a fair copy instead of marking up a printed text: this MS, now at *Texas*, has no substantive differences from *1849*, but a few cancelled readings. The Jules—Phene scene (ii 1–243) was even more heavily revised (*1849* adds 97 lines and deletes 13), perhaps also by means of a new fair copy, though this has not survived. In proportion to its length, the Ottima—Sebald scene (i 1–276) was least affected. Punctuation was consistently overhauled through all eds., in keeping with B.'s usual practice. There were few verbal changes after *1849*. The Ottima—Sebald scene (i 1–276) shows some points of interest in *1863²*. It contains many of the *1863* revs., anticipates a number of *1868* readings, but retains some from *1849* (see e.g. ll. 143^144n.), and has spellings characteristic of *1849*, suggesting that it was produced after *1863* but using *1849* as copy-text. A few readings are unique to *1863²*: for the only substantive one, see l. 91n. In *1863²* the following note, probably not B.'s but presumably approved by him, appears at the beginning of the extract: 'Pippa is a girl from a silk-factory, whose "passing" the various persons of the play, at certain critical moments, in the course of her holiday, becomes, unconsciously to herself, a determining influence on the fortune of each'.

Form

The form of *Pippa Passes*—four entirely separate one-act plays with link-passages and parallel endings—is both its most celebrated and its least documented feature. The consensus is that it is unprecedented, though we have found one particular work which challenges this assumption: see below. A. Symons describes it as containing 'elements of the play and elements of the masque' (*An Introduction to the Study of Browning*, 2nd ed. [1906] 52). These 'elements of the masque' are presumably Pippa's songs. In Elizabethan and Jacobean masques, songs are interspersed with the action, sometimes to mark the appearance of fresh characters; such songs remain, however, subordinate to dance and spectacle. See E. Welsford, *The Court Masque* (1927). Evidence that B. envisaged a musical dimension for the work is to be found in his letter to Eliza Flower of 9 Mar. 1840: 'By the way, you speak of "Pippa"—could we not make some arrangement about it,—the lyrics *want* your music—five or six in all—how say you?' (*Correspondence* iv 256). I. Jack (*Browning's Major Poetry* [Oxford 1973] 64–5) points out that the 'dramatic scene', the form into which each section of *Pippa* falls, was very popular in the 1820s and 1830s; B. probably knew those by 'Barry Cornwall' (B. W. Procter) publ. in 1819–20, some of which have intercalated songs; cp. also Lamb's *Specimens of the English Dramatic Poets* (1808). D. Hair (*Browning's Experiments with Genre* [Toronto 1972] 51) compares Landor's short dramatic pieces (e.g. *Ippolito di Este*), a comparison anticipated by EBB. (see i 4–10n.). The abrupt and discontinuous structure of Goethe's *Faust* may also have influenced B.'s approach.

The particular work, almost certainly known to B., which anticipates in detail the form of *Pippa*, is John Fletcher and Nathan Field's *Four Plays or Moral Representations in One* (?1613–15), not previously cited as a source. This consists of four separate one-act plays (or 'Triumphs'), with a prologue and epilogue, and link-passages. There is a striking thematic parallelism: the four plays are concerned successively with adultery, marriage between social unequals, the killing of a tyrant, and wealth, which are the topics, and in that order, of the sections of *Pippa*. A further parallel is that in *Four Plays* each act concludes with music: a celebratory fanfare ('The Triumph of Honour') or celebratory song ('The Triumph of Time'); or, in 'The Triumph of Love' and 'The Triumph of Death', a dramatically integrated song. The latter are of especial interest because in both the song becomes a means of dramatic reversal or conversion, as in *Pippa*; though derived from the masque (E. M. Waith, in *The Pattern of Tragi-Comedy in Beaumont and Fletcher* [Yale 1952], comments that the playlets of *Four Plays* stand 'somewhere between masques and plays'), this feature goes well beyond the masque's non-dramatic use of song. B. may have been familiar with the 1811 ed. of the Beaumont—Fletcher canon, which included *Four Plays*; the probability that he had read *Four Plays* is enhanced by the fact that it was publ. in 1840 by Moxon, B.'s publisher, in a collection of the Beaumont and Fletcher plays (ed. G. Darley): in fact, it was the format of this and other of Moxon's reissues of Elizabethan and Jacobean plays that supplied the model for *B & P* (see Appendix C, p. 884).

These reissues, assuming that B. had not already encountered the works in their original form in his father's library or in the British Museum, would also have given B. access to other experimental blends of masque and drama, such as Ford and Dekker's *The Sun's Darling*; in 1840, another publisher issued the complete works of Middleton, and B. might have read Middleton and Rowley's *The World Tost at Tennis*, where again a sequence of disparate scenes is modulated by means of songs. Equally, however, a reading of *Four Plays* might have reminded B. of the more ambitious conflations of masque and play in the works of Shakespeare and Jonson, which *Pippa* frequently echoes. However, some features of *Pippa*, such as its dramatic naturalism and integrated structure, remain unprecedented; Welsford remarks of *Four Plays*: 'there is no just cause why these four plays should be joined together' (p. 287).

Time and Place

The date of the action is contemporary, but cannot be precisely determined. The clearest indicator would be the identity of the Austrian Emperor who is the target of the assassination plot in pt. iii. But up to 1865, the corr. reissue of 1863 (see iii 14n.), B. gave no clue to his identity, and even in 1865 it is not certain whether the mention of 'old Franz' refers to a specific individual. Francis II (1768–1835), who became Emperor in 1804, had a pathological fear of liberal or reformist opposition, personally supervised a huge police network, and was responsible, with his chief minister Metternich, for the partition of Italy after the Napoleonic Wars into separate states under Austria's rule, or subject to its influence. This partition, effected by the Treaty of Vienna in 1816, created the Austrian kingdom of Lombardy-Venetia (which included Asolo). However, Francis II died (peacefully) three years before B. went to Italy and five years before the publication of the poem. His successor Ferdinand I (1793–1875), Emperor from 1835 until his abdication in 1848, was a kindly, weak-minded, and ineffectual ruler, with far less interest than Francis in the repression of dissent. In 1830, when he bore the title of King of Hungary, an army officer with a private grudge against him attempted to shoot him. This is the only assassination attempt recorded in the period against a member of the ruling house of Hapsburg.

The action takes place at Asolo, a small village in the 'Trevisan', the district surrounding the town of Treviso in northern Italy. B. called Asolo his 'very own of all Italian cities' (*Bronson*[1] 921) and it is of crucial importance in his career. He first saw it on his 1838 journey, as he wrote to Fanny Haworth on 24 July, after his return: 'I went to Trieste, then Venice—then thro' Treviso & Bassano to the mountains, delicious Asolo' (*Correspondence* iv 68). Asolo was certainly B.'s 'discovery'; it was not a noted tourist spot (*Murray* does not mention it, though it mentions nearby Possagno). A friend later recalled: 'One day Mr. Browning related an incident of a visit to Asolo when Austria was in possession of Venetian territory. He was asked by the chief dignitary of the town, "What have you come here for?" "To see the place." "Do you intend to stay?" "Yes; I hope to remain a few days." "But you have seen the place already; how can you possibly wish to stay longer?" "Because I find it so very beautiful." The Austrian looked at him in puzzled amazement, and then, after a moment's pause, signed the "permit of sojourn" required' (*Bronson*[1] 921). In a letter dated 10 June 1889, B. remembers his first impressions of Asolo: 'When I first found out Asolo I lodged at the main Hotel in the square, an old, large Inn of the most primitive kind. The ceiling of my bedroom was traversed by a huge crack, or rather cleft; "caused by the earthquake last year; the sky was as blue as could be, and we were all praying in the fields, expecting the town to tumble in." On the morning of my arrival I walked up to the Rocca; and, on returning to breakfast, I mentioned it to the landlady, whereon a respectable, middle-aged man, sitting by, said, "You have done what I, born here, never thought of doing." . . . I took long walks every day,—and carried away a lively recollection of the general beauty,—but I did not write a word of "Pippa Passes". The idea struck me when walking in an English wood, and I made use of the Italian memories. I used to dream of seeing Asolo in the distance and making vain attempts to reach it, repeatedly dreamed this for many a year, and when I found myself once more in Italy with my sister [1878], I went there straight from Verona. We found the old inn lying in ruins, a new one about to take its place . . . People told me the number of inhabitants had greatly increased, and things seemed generally more ordinary-life-like . . . When I got my impression Italy was new to me' (*Bronson*[1] 920). With this disillusion, cp. *Prologue* (*Asolando*, 1889).

Besides personal observation, B. could have consulted, in the British Museum, an anonymous pamphlet, *Notizie Istoriche e Geografiche appartenenti alla città di Asolo ed al suo territorio* (Belluno 1780). Prefacing a detailed description of the four 'quarters' of the district is a general eulogy of its beauty and fertility (pp. 5–6), and there are also notes on Asolo's only claim to historical importance, the residence there of Queen Caterina Cornaro of Cyprus (see ii 200n.).

There has been some debate as to whether the day on which the action of the poem takes place, 'New Year's Day', refers to the old date, 25 Mar., rather than the modern 1 Jan. In support of the former are Pippa's song 'The year's at the spring' (i 215–22), and Luigi's mention of the cuckoo (iii 137–9); as against this, Monsignor refers to the 'winter-weather' and implies that it is 'fourteen years and a month, all but three days' since his elder brother's death on 3 Dec. (iv 6, 30–1). Furthermore, in a letter of 8 Jan. 1885 offering belated New Year greetings B. wrote: 'New Year's Day was Pippa's Day, also' (to J. Dunnachie, *ABL MS*). Pippa's itinerary has been traced in J. Korg, *Browning and Italy* (Athens, Ohio, 1983) 41–2.

Sources, and parallels in B.

(1) *The character of Pippa*. B.'s characterization of Pippa draws upon a long and varied tradition of the representation of children as figures of innocence and intuition. The Romantic idealization of childhood in e.g. Rousseau and

Wordsworth (esp. *The Solitary Reaper*, which celebrates the unconscious influence of a girl's singing), emerges strongly in *Pippa*. Marguerite in Goethe's *Faust*, who stands on the borderline between childhood innocence and adult experience, complicates this figure of the child by opening it to sexual and economic exploitation, a theme which Dickens had highlighted in *Oliver Twist* (1837−8) and *The Old Curiosity Shop* (1840). It was at this period, too, that agitation about child labour began to make itself seriously felt.

Pippa's orphan state, and the discovery that she is nobly born, are stock motifs of folktale and romance. The parallel with Shakespeare's romances, esp. *Pericles* and *The Winter's Tale*, is striking, and confirmed by other echoes. The second part ('The Triumph of Love') of Fletcher and Field's *Four Plays* (see *Form*) also involves this motif; so does T. N. Talfourd's *Ion*, where Ion proves to be the son of the tyrant Adrastus. A. E. Dubois ('Robert Browning, Dramatist', *SP* xxxiii [1936] 626−55) extends the parallel, concluding that Pippa is 'a female Ion in a play dedicated to Talfourd'.

Talfourd's *Ion* (1836) concerns the cleansing of Argos from plague by Ion, a foundling, who first persuades the tyrant Adrastus to meet the priests and people, and, when that fails, joins a conspiracy to kill him, knowing that only when Adrastus' line is extinct will Argos be saved. However, during the assassination of Adrastus (not by Ion), Ion learns that he himself is Adrastus' son. He accepts the succession, and publicly kills himself in order to end the curse. Like Ion, Pippa is an orphan; she is likewise involved, though unconsciously, in the redemption of her people; and she similarly proves to be the child of a potentate. Euripides' *Ion*, on which Talfourd drew, also contributed to B.'s conception of Pippa. In Euripides' play, Ion is the secret offspring of Apollo and Creusa, brought up, without his mother's knowledge, as a slave in the temple of Apollo at Delphi. She meanwhile has married Xuthus; because they are childless they have come to Delphi to find out if they will ever have children. The oracle tells Xuthus that the first person he meets will be his son; meeting Ion, he claims him as the child of himself and a former mistress. Learning of this, Creusa conspires to kill Ion to prevent his becoming Xuthus' heir, but the plot fails and the truth is revealed. The conspiracy in *Pippa* iv, in which Pippa is to be lured to prostitution and death in order to prevent her from coming into her rightful inheritance, has strong affinities with this story.

Pippa's role, and in particular the unconscious nature of her influence through song, may owe something to the central episode of conversion in St Augustine's *Confessions*. Augustine describes how, seated in a garden, he was 'weeping in the most bitter contrition of my heart, when lo! I heard from a neighbouring house a voice, as of boy or girl, I know not, chanting, and oft repeating, "Take up and read; Take up and read." Instantly my countenance altered, I began to think most intently, whether children were wont in any kind of play to sing such words: nor could I remember ever to have heard the like. So checking the torrent of my tears, I arose; interpreting it to be no other than a command from God, to open the book, and read the first chapter I should find' (transl. 1848, pp. 169−70). B.'s letter to Fanny Haworth of [?25] Apr. 1839 has some MS music, with the comment, 'What the children were singing last year in Venice, arm over neck' (*Correspondence* iv 138−9). The figure of Pippa strikingly anticipates that of Pompilia in *Ring*.

(2) *Episode 1: Ottima and Sebald* (i 1−276). No specific source has been identified. There are echoes of various Jacobean tragedies, particularly *Macbeth* and Middleton's *The Changeling*. Ottima has some affinity with Vittoria Corrombona, and Sebald with Bracchiano, in Webster's *The White Devil*. Their situation

parallels that of Alice and her lover Mosby in *Arden of Faversham* and, more strikingly, that in Donne's *Elegy* iv.

(3) *Episode 2: Jules and Phene* (i 277 to ii 243; see also iv 39–57).

(a) *The plot of the deceptive marriage.* F. E. Faverty, 'The Source of the Jules—Phene Episode in *Pippa Passes*' (*SP* xxxviii [1941] 97–105), compares Bulwer-Lytton's successful play *The Lady of Lyons*, produced by Macready in 1838. Claude Melnotte, low-born but cultured, is married by deception to the daughter of a wealthy merchant, Pauline, whom two rejected suitors wish to humiliate. Faverty argues that B. may also have consulted Bulwer-Lytton's acknowledged source, a translation by Helen Maria Williams of a French tale (*The History of Perourou*, 1803), because there the rejected suitors are artist-engravers, and six of them (as in B.) gather to witness the dénouement. B. certainly saw Bulwer-Lytton's play, and knew both him and Macready well. Note B.'s reversal of the sex of impostor and victim. Cp. also Victor Hugo's melodrama *Ruy Blas* (1838), where a servant poses as a nobleman at the Spanish court and gains the queen's affection as part of a revenge plot by the servant's master. The theme of 'queen-worship' was a favourite of B.'s: see ii 195–210n. To Faverty's list of the literary sources may be added the Malvolio plot in *Twelfth Night* and the Beatrice—Benedick plot in *Much Ado About Nothing*, conspiracies using forged letters to deceive a man into believing that a woman is in love with him. Faverty also mentions the painter Angelica Kauffmann (1741–1807), who was tricked into marrying an impoverished adventurer. B.'s studies for *Sordello* may have informed him that the troubadour Pierre Vidal (see *Sordello* ii 714–17n., I 508) married a Greek girl (Phene, Jules's bride, is Greek) in the mistaken belief that she was of imperial family. B. may also have known of the practical joke played by Keats's friend Charles Wells on Keats's younger brother Tom, who received love-letters purportedly from a mysterious French lady. B. could have heard the story from a number of Keats's friends, e.g. Leigh Hunt. There is an important parallel with *Ring*, where Guido forges letters between his wife and her 'lover', Caponsacchi.

(b) *The character of Jules the sculptor.* B.'s principal model was Antonio Canova (1757–1822). The action takes place at Possagno, Canova's birthplace and the site of a 'Gipsoteca' (gallery of models and casts) devoted to his work (see i 353–4). Besides direct observation during his trip to Italy in 1838 (he wrote to Fanny Haworth on 24 July 1838, after his return: 'I was disappointed in one thing, Canova' [*Correspondence* iv 67]), and personal contact with Italian intellectuals such as his tutor Angelo Cerutti, B. could have learned about Canova's work and reputation from many sources. Canova's fame was at its height in B.'s boyhood (see e.g. Byron, *Beppo* 368); his studio was an obligatory stop for connoisseurs and collectors on the Grand Tour. Of several accounts which B. might have seen in the British Museum, there are interesting parallels with the anonymous, privately printed *Journal of a Tour in Italy* (now attrib. to the Countess of Clanwilliam, and dated 1836); see e.g. ii 116–17n. The main printed source is *The Works of Antonio Canova, in Sculpture and Modelling, Engraved in Outline by Henry Moses; with Descriptions from the Italian of the Countess Albrizzi, and a Biographical Memoir by Count Cicognara* (3 vols., 1824), whose plates and commentaries cover all the works alluded to in the poem. The following features of Canova's career and personality were major influences on B.'s conception of Jules.

i. Canova's admiration for classical Greek sculpture. This supposedly began in Venice, where he 'found an immense source of knowledge and improvement in the gallery of plaster casts of the Commendatore Farsetti, comprising all the celebrated remains of antiquity, and which, with a noble liberality, was devoted to the use of young students, and the public curiosity' (*Works of Canova* i, p. ii).

Contemporaries frequently stressed the likeness of Canova's work to antique sculpture. But B. may also have noted Canova's opinion that 'The perfect and determinate models of the Greeks . . . and the just prescriptive influence of their conventional modes of art, while they assist and ennoble modern sculpture, preclude it from originality in any of its essential points' (*Works of Canova* iii 7): see below, 'Canova and painting'.

ii. Canova's technical skill. His marbles were noted for their 'softness and delicacy of contour' and 'minute accuracy of expression', while his 'susceptibility and active fancy gave great quickness and energy to his invention, prompting his imagination spontaneously, and without effort, to reach the great and excellent in his designs' (*Works of Canova* i, pp. xiii–xvii). Cp. ii 67–98 and notes.

iii. Canova's relation to his rivals. 'The influence of established practice and professional jealousy created no trifling obstacles to the progress of Canova; these, however, his modest and unpresuming conduct aided greatly to remove, while an air of triumph and superiority would, by wounding the feelings of his rivals, have created additonal opposition' (*Works of Canova* i, p. vii). The Countess of Clanwilliam commented: 'Canova was perfectly conscious of the merit of his performances, but totally unaffected and void of pretension . . . his conversation was always playful, and left a pleasing impression' (*Journal of a Tour in Italy* ii 296–7). Jules displays the exact inverse of this attitude: see i 315–17, 352–70.

iv. Canova's private life. 'More than once during his life, he experienced the passion of love, in a degree corresponding to the susceptibility of his nature . . . On two occasions he was very near to entering into the marriage state, but was, perhaps, deterred by the apprehension of its diverting him from his devotion to his art, which was always his master and engrossing passion: his heart was, however, never entangled by low attachments, but was the seat of the noblest and most elevated sentiments' (*Works of Canova* i, p. xx). Cp. i 371–8 and ii 13–24.

v. Canova and painting. This aspect of Canova's career bears principally on Jules's decision to abandon sculpture for painting, which he explains in a letter to Monsignor (see iv 45–55) as a rejection of the imitation of classical models. B. asserted in many contexts the importance of originality, though in early treatments of this topic (*Pauline* 390–2 [p. 33], *Chatterton* 209–17 [II 484]) he regards a phase of imitation as a natural part of the young artist's development. Jules's letter suggests that such imitation necessarily precedes a supplantation of the models copied: see *Sordello* ii 80–4 (I 468) for an example of this process. In Jules's case the rejection of imitation is accompanied by a change of medium, a change which takes place *after* he breaks his own statues (ii 295–7), since at that point he still intends to continue a sculptor; some time between 'Noon' and 'Night' he decides that his only hope of originality lies in becoming a painter, and writes his letter to Monsignor. The motif of the change of medium appears in *Rudel*, and most prominently in *One Word More* (p. 598), of which it is the subject. See also B.'s letter to Ripert-Monclar of 9 Aug. 1837: 'I cannot remember the time when I did not make verses [. . . but when] subsequently real and strong feeling called for utterance, either Drawing or Music seemed a much fitter vehicle than "verses" ' (*Correspondence* iii 264) and B. to EBB., 11 Mar. 1845: 'I think you like the operation of writing as I should like that of painting, or making music, do you not?' (*Correspondence* x 121). B. was an accomplished musician, and studied sculpture during the 1850s. Monsignor's suggestion that Jules will however 'fail egregiously' in his ambition perhaps reflects the fact that his original, Canova, was a mediocre painter. His partisans claimed that he merely 'found an agreeable relief in the occasional use of the pencil' and denied that he 'thought very highly of his pictures, and that they had withdrawn his attention from more important subjects' (*Works of Canova* i, p. xiv); but Thomas Moore recorded in his journal for 13 Nov. 1819: 'Called at Canova's, and again looked over his treasures. It is strange enough (if the world did not abound with such anomalies) that Canova prides himself more on some wretched daubs he has perpetrated in painting, than on his best sculpture' (*Memoirs*, ed. John Russell [5 vols., 1856] iii 71). B. himself, in a letter of 28 Sept. 1878, noted: 'a wonder of detestability indeed is the paint-performance of the great man!' (*Learned Lady* 93). In the same letter, B. expressed the belief he had come to hold that an artist should aim directly at originality: in reply to a recommendation that his son would improve as a painter by 'imbuing himself with the works of the Great Masters', he wrote: 'Does not all mediocrity come of a beginner's determining to look at nature through the eyes of his predecessors . . . ? I should expect a genuine painter . . . to begin by ascertaining what he likes best to see in nature generally,—then master the means of expressing what he likes and sees,—and, *then only*, ask himself how others have gone through the same process and with what results' (a position which directly repudiates that of Sir Joshua Reynolds, whose *Discourses* [1769–90] constantly insist on the importance of imitation in a painter's development: see e.g. Discourse I, Discourse VI).

Besides Canova, B.'s presentation of Jules may owe something to Michelangelo: Jules's Neo-Platonic philosophy and his arrogant aloofness from social interchange recall similar features in Michelangelo's thought and personality. See ii 67–98n. B. drew on the myth of Pygmalion and Galatea for the actual scene between Jules and Phene (ii 1–243), In Ovid's account (*Metamorphoses* x), Pygmalion's aversion to the debauchery of real women is linked to his love for the beautiful statue he has made: cp. i 371–8, B. may also have known Rousseau's 'scène lyrique' *Pygmalion* (1775), which consists of Pygmalion's monologue in front of his statue of Galatea, before it comes to life. In Rousseau's version, the transformation of the statue into a woman reciprocates Pygmalion's recovery of his sense of his own genius and artistic purpose; a similar reciprocation takes place when Jules discovers a new artistic 'life' as a result of 'vivifying' Phene. Pygmalion's earlier declaration that he has lost all interest in other people may have contributed to the aloofness which his enemies resent in Jules. Both scenes end in an embrace. Another poem on the subject which may have been known to B. is T. L. Beddoes' *Pygmalion*, whose hero has suggestive similarities to Jules: see i 311–14n., 373–8n., ii 67–98n. B. may also have found a ref. to the Pygmalion legend in *Works of Canova*: ' "Pity that this nymph cannot speak," said an English visitor in the studio of Canova, "and that this Hebe does not rise into the skies; if, like Pigmalion's statue, life were added to them, nothing would remain to be desired." "You are mistaken," observed the sculptor, "and would in that case have nothing to be pleased or surprised at. I do not aim in my works at deceiving the beholder; we know they are marble—mute and immobile" ' (iii 26). Cp. also the final scene of *The Winter's Tale* where the 'statue' of Hermione—supposedly the work of the 'rare Italian master, Julio Romano, who, had he himself eternity and could put breath into his work, would beguile Nature of her custom, so perfectly he is her ape' (V ii 97–100)—comes to life. A possible source for the discussion of the relation of art to life is the first of Alciphron's *Letters of Courtesans* (Loeb ed. [1949] 251–2), in which the courtesan Phryne writes to the sculptor Praxiteles: 'Have no fear; for you have wrought a very beautiful work of art, such as nobody, in fact, has ever seen before among all things fashioned by men's hands; you have set up a statue of your own mistress in the sacred precinct. Yes, I stand in the middle of the precinct near your Aphrodite and your Eros too. And do not begrudge me this honour. For it is Praxiteles that people praise when they have gazed at me; and it is because I am a product of your skill that the Thespians do not count me unfit to be placed between gods. One thing only is still lacking to your gift: that you come to me, so that we may lie together in the precinct. Surely we shall bring no defilement to the gods that we ourselves have created. Farewell'. Alciphron is mentioned at i 381. The most important parallels in B., among his numerous works dealing with art and artists, are *Old Pictures* (p. 404) and *James Lee* viii ('Beside the Drawing-Board', p. 680).

(4) *Episode 3: Luigi and his mother* (ii 244 to iii 225).

(a) Historical background for the assassination plot. See p. 83 above. B.'s detailed allusions to political conditions in Lombardy-Venetia (e.g. the presence of Austrian police, employment of spies, censorship, restriction on travel) are glossed in the notes. There was widespread sympathy for Italian nationalism in Britain, stimulated by successive waves of refugees from political repression. (B.'s Italian tutor, Angelo Cerutti, was himself such a refugee.) B.'s interest in the subject is already present in *Sordello*, where the Guelf—Ghibellin struggle parallels the modern struggle against Austria. It is the subject of *Italy in England* (p. 245), and features in *Old Pictures* (p. 404) and *Prince Hohenstiel-Schwangau* (1871); see also *Up at a Villa* 44–6 (III 147) and *De Gustibus* 33–8 (III 27–8). The attempted assassination of a reactionary Italian ruler is the subject of *A Soul's Tragedy* (II 180). For B.'s sympathy with English Radicalism, see iii 163–224n.

(b) Literary sources. B.'s conception of the Austrian Emperor's court, and the kind of assassination plot that Luigi outlines, seem to have been influenced by Elizabethan and Jacobean plays, notably Webster, whose work B. knew well. There are also reminiscences of *Julius Caesar* (the justice of political killing) and of *Coriolanus* (a mother persuading her son against his sense of duty). See also ii 47–9n. The major literary influence comes from Talfourd's *Ion* (see above, p. 85). Luigi's argument with his mother about the morality and expediency of assassination parallels that in *Ion* I ii between Ion and Clemanthe, his betrothed.

(5) *Episode 4: Monsignor and the Intendant* (iv 1–341). The plot to deprive Pippa of her inheritance by seducing her and forcing her into prostitution has clear affinities with *Pericles*. The confrontation between Monsignor and the Intendant is paralleled in B. by that between Ogniben and Chiappino at the end of *A Soul's Tragedy*, and in another way by that between the Pope and an imaginary 'educated man' in bk. x of *Ring*.

Criticism

B. wrote to Monclar on 29 Apr. 1841: 'c'est un effort pour contenter presque tout le monde, et vous savez comme cela réussit ordinairement' [it is an attempt to please practically everybody, and you know what kind of success that normally has] (*Correspondence* v 39). His prediction was accurate: *Pippa Passes* had a mixed reception. As with *Sordello*, most critics objected to the play as obscure, esp. *Intro* and pt. ii, but its central conception was praised: 'The idea of this little drama is, in itself, we think, remarkably beautiful' (*Athenaeum*, 11 Dec. 1841, 952; repr. *Correspondence* v 399). After *1849*, the play became, as one reviewer put it, 'held as set apart and sacred in the mind of any reader' (Moncure Conway in *Victoria Magazine* ii [Feb. 1864] 309); writing in 1890, Edmund Gosse claimed that 'the public was first won to Mr. Browning by *Pippa Passes*' (*Personalia* 55). This process is mirrored in the reaction of EBB. Her first response, in a letter to Mary Russell Mitford (15 July 1841), was that ' "Pippa passes" . . comprehension, I was going to say!' and, while admitting 'the presence of genius' she asked 'Was there any need for so much coarseness?' (*Correspondence* v 75); but in a letter of

20 Jan. 1842 she objected to an adverse review (*ibid*. v 221), and on 19 Oct.
she praised the poem's 'unity & nobleness of conception' (*ibid*. vi 111). An early
letter to B. (17 Feb. 1845) confirmed the change of heart: 'You have taken a great
range—from those high faint notes of the mystics which are beyond personality
. . to dramatic impersonations, gruff with nature, "gr-r- you swine": & when these
are thrown into harmony, as in a manner they are in "Pippa Passes" (which I could
find it in my heart to covet the authorship of, more than any of your works,—)
the combinations of effects must always be striking & noble' (*Correspondence* x 79).
B. told her 'I like "Pippa" better than anything else I have done yet' (26 Feb. 1845,
ibid. 99). However, it seems likely that, as with *Sordello* (see headnote, I 354),
she encouraged B. to remove obscurities by revision, and perhaps to mitigate the
'coarseness' of which she had complained to Miss Mitford. One of B.'s close friends,
Eliza Flower, gave a strongly adverse reaction in a letter to her friend Miss Bromley:
'I send you *Bells and Pomegranates* [i.e. *Pippa*], not because you will like it any
more than I do, but because you won't like it any less than I do. It is just like
his way. This time he has got an exquisite subject, most exquisite, and it seemed
so easy for a poet to handle. Yet here comes one of those fatal ifs, the egoism of
the man, and the pity of it. He cannot metempsychose with his creatures, they are
so many Robert Brownings. Still there are superb parts, and the very last is quite
lovely. But *puppets*, what a false word to use, as if God worked by puppets
as well as Robert Browning!' (quoted in Garnett, *Life of W. J. Fox* [1909] 194;
for the 'puppets', see *Intro* 152).

Synopsis

In the introductory section, Pippa, an orphan girl who works in a silk factory in
Asolo, decides to spend her one day's holiday of the year 'passing' by the four
people whom she regards as the most fortunate in Asolo. Ottima is the wife of Pippa's
employer, the old and wealthy Luca Gaddi, and has a young lover, Sebald. Jules,
a young sculptor, is about to marry the beautiful Phene. Luigi is blessed by the
tranquil love between himself and his mother. The holy Monsignor, visiting Asolo
from Rome after the death of his brother, is happy in the love of God. In four
scenes, interspersed with interludes of 'talk by the way', Pippa passes by each in
turn, unconscious of the fact that their situations are the reverse of happy, and
that each is facing a climactic moment of moral choice. As she passes, she sings
a song which they hear, and which, unknown to her, radically affects the choices
they make. The last of these episodes concerns her own fate. Still unaware of
the effect of her passing, Pippa returns to her room in the final scene of the drama.

New Year's Day at Asolo in the Trevisan. A large,
mean, airy Chamber. A girl, Pippa, from the silk-mills,
springing out of bed.

Day!
Faster and more fast
O'er night's brim day boils at last;

Intro. Opening s.d.] *New Year's . . . Trevisan*: see headnote, pp. 83–4.   *mean*:
shabby.   *the silk-mills*: the silk industry was one of the principal industries of the
region at the time of B.'s first visit to Asolo in 1838.
1–20. Cp. *Ring* vii 1211–26, when Pompilia 'wakes' from her life of misery in
Arezzo. Line 1 is the shortest whole line in B.

Boils, pure gold, o'er the cloud-cup's brim
5   Where spurting and supprest it lay—
For not a froth-flake touched the rim
Of yonder gap in the solid gray
Of eastern cloud an hour away—
But forth one wavelet then another curled,
10 Till the whole sunrise, not to be supprest,
Rose-reddened, and its seething breast
Flickered in bounds, grew gold, then overflowed the
        world.
Day, if I waste a wavelet of thee,
Aught of my twelve-hours' treasure—
15 One of thy gazes, one of thy glances,
(Grants thou art bound to, gifts above measure,)
One of thy choices, one of thy chances,
(Tasks God imposed thee, freaks at thy pleasure,)
Day, if I waste such labour or leisure
20 Shame betide Asolo, mischief to me!
But in turn, Day, treat me not

1–12. Cp. Talfourd's *Ion*, p. 12: 'And lo! the sun is struggling with the gloom, /
Whose masses fill the eastern sky, and tints / Its edges with dull red;—but he
will triumph; bless'd be the omen!' In Euripides' *Ion*, Ion's first speech is similar:
'Lo, yonder the Sun-god is turning earthward his splendour-blazing / Chariot of
light; / And the stars from the firmament flee from his fiery arrows chasing, /
To the sacred night: / And the crests of Parnassus untrodden are flaming and
flushed as with yearning / Of welcome to far-flashing wheels with the glory of
daylight returning/ To mortal sight'.
8. Of eastern] Of the eastern (*1849–88*).
11. Rose-reddened,] Rose, reddened, (*1849–88*).
12^13.] there is a space between these lines in all other eds.
13–20. Cp. *Pauline* 502–4 (p. 39).
13. Day, if I waste] Oh, Day, if I squander (*1849–88*).
14. Aught of] A mite of (*1849–88*).
15–20.] The least of thy gazes or glances,
        (Be they grants thou art bound to, or gifts above measure)
        One of thy choices, or one of thy chances,
        (Be they tasks God imposed thee, or freaks at thy pleasure)
        —My Day, if I squander such labour or leisure,
     Then shame fall on Asolo, mischief on me! (*1849–88*, except no commas
after 'to', 'choices', 'thee', *1868–88*).
20^21.] there is a space between these lines in all other eds.
21–47.] Thy long blue solemn hours serenely flowing,
        Whence earth, we feel, gets steady help and good—
        Thy fitful sunshine minutes, coming, going,
        In which, earth turns from work in gamesome mood—
[5]   All shall be mine! But thou must treat me not
        As the prosperous are treated, those who live

At hand here, and enjoy the higher lot,
In readiness to take what thou wilt give,
And free to let alone what thou refusest;
[10] For, Day, my holiday, if thou ill-usest
Me, who am only Pippa—old-year's sorrow,
Cast off last night, will come again to-morrow—
Whereas, if thou prove gentle, I shall borrow
Sufficient strength of thee for new-year's sorrow.
[15] All other men and women that this earth
Belongs to, who all days alike possess,
Make general plenty cure particular dearth,
Get more joy, one way, if another, less:
Thou art my single day, God lends to leaven
[20] What were all earth else, with a feel of heaven;
Sole light that helps me through the year, thy sun's!
Try, now! Take Asolo's Four Happiest Ones—
And let thy morning rain on that superb
Great haughty Ottima; can rain disturb
[25] Her Sebald's homage? All the while thy rain
Beats fiercest on her shrub-house window-pane,
He will but press the closer, breathe more warm
Against her cheek; how should she mind the storm?
And, morning past, if mid-day shed a gloom
[30] O'er Jules and Phene,—what care bride and groom
Save for their dear selves? 'Tis their marriage-day;
And while they leave church, and go home their way
Hand clasping hand,—within each breast would be
Sunbeams and pleasant weather spite of thee!
[35] Then, for another trial, obscure thy eve
With mist,—will Luigi and his mother grieve—
The Lady and her child, unmatched, forsooth,
She in her age, as Luigi in his youth,
For true content? The cheerful town, warm, close,
[40] And safe, the sooner that thou art morose
Receives them! And yet once again, outbreak
In storm at night on Monsignor, they make
Such stir about,—whom they expect from Rome
To visit Asolo, his brothers' home,
[45] And say here masses proper to release
A soul from pain,—what storm dares hurt his peace?
Calm would he pray, with his own thoughts to ward
Thy thunder off, nor want the angels' guard!
But Pippa—just once such mischance would spoil
[50] Her day that lightens the next twelvemonth's toil
At wearisome silk-winding, coil on coil! (*1849–88*, except l. [4] 'That show,
earth turns', *Texas*, canc.; 'As if earth turned', *1863–88*; l. [6] 'As prosperous
ones', *1888*: one of very few verbal changes in this ed.; l. [11] 'Pippa,—', *1863–88*;
l. [12] 'to-morrow:', *1868–88*; l. [20] 'heaven,—', *1863–88*; l. [22] 'Try', *1865–88*;
l. [32] 'church', *1868–88*; l. [33] 'hand,', *1868–88*; l. [34] 'thee.', *1868–88*; l. [37]
'Madonna and', *Texas*, canc.; The lady *1868–88*; l. [39] 'close', *1865–88*; l. [40]
'morose,', *1863–88*; l. [41] 'them.', *1868–88*; l. [48] 'guard.', *1868–88*).

As happy tribes—so happy tribes! who live
At hand—the common, other creatures' lot—
Ready to take when thou wilt give,
25   Prepared to pass what thou refusest;
Day, 'tis but Pippa thou ill-usest
If thou prove sullen, me, whose old year's sorrow
Who except thee can chase before to-morrow,
Seest thou, my day? Pippa's—who mean to borrow
30   Only of thee strength against new year's sorrow:
For let thy morning scowl on that superb
Great haughty Ottima—can scowl disturb
Her Sebald's homage? And if noon shed gloom
O'er Jules and Phene—what care bride and groom
35   Save for their dear selves? Then, obscure thy eve
With mist—will Luigi and Madonna grieve
—The mother and the child—unmatched, forsooth,
She in her age as Luigi in his youth,
For true content? And once again, outbreak
40   In storm at night on Monsignor they make
Such stir to-day about, who foregoes Rome
To visit Asolo, his brother's home,
And say there masses proper to release
The soul from pain—what storm dares hurt that peace?
45   But Pippa—just one such mischance would spoil,
Bethink thee, utterly next twelvemonth's toil
At wearisome silk-winding, coil on coil!

And here am I letting time slip for nought!
You fool-hardy sunbeam—caught

---

22. 'Tribe' and its cognates are extensively used in B.'s early work, but fade out after the 1850s: note in this connection B.'s revision of this passage.

26–7. *Day, 'tis but . . . sullen*: cp. Wordsworth, *Ode: Intimations of Immortality* 42: 'Oh, evil day! if I were sullen[!]'

48. *am I letting*] I let (*1849–88*).

49–66. Pippa fancifully imagines that a sunbeam has escaped from its pursuers and has taken refuge in her basin, where, believing itself secure, it has fallen asleep. When she splashes water into the basin from her jug ('ewer'), the sunbeam is 'caught': its reflections are thrown up on to the ceiling, where they shift and flicker as the water moves. When the water settles, so does the 'cripple': the sunbeam's reflections fall on Pippa's flower (see below, l. 64n.), which she apostrophizes, comparing its colour to a nipple's, and its fleshiness to that of a turkey's ('Turk bird's') comb. Cp. Virgil, *Aeneid* viii 22: 'Sicut aquae tremulum

50   With a single splash from my ewer!
     You that mocked the best pursuer,
     Was my basin over-deep?
     One splash of water ruins you asleep
     And up, up, fleet your brilliant bits
55   Wheeling and counterwheeling,
     Reeling, crippled beyond healing—
     Grow together on the ceiling,
     That will task your wits!
     Whoever it was first quenched fire hoped to see
60   Morsel after morsel flee
     As merrily,
     As giddily . . . what lights he on—
     Where settles himself the cripple?
     Oh never surely blown, my martagon?
65   New-blown, though!—ruddy as a nipple,
     Plump as the flesh bunch on some Turk bird's poll!
     Be sure if corals, branching 'neath the ripple
     Of ocean, bud there,—fairies watch unroll

---

labris ubi lumen abenis / sole repercussum, aut radiantis imagine Lunae / omnia
pervolitat late loca, iamque sub auras / erigitur, summique ferit laqueraria tecti'
[As water, trembling in a brass bowl, reflects the sun's light or the form of the
shining moon, and so the bright beams flit in all directions, darting up at times
to strike the lofty fretted ceilings]. Montaigne quotes this passage as an image of
the mind at play in his essay 'On Idleness' (*Essays*, bk.I, ch.viii).

49. *You*] Aha, you (*1849–88*).
51. *mocked*] would mock (*1849–88*).
56. *crippled*] broken (*1849–88*).
57. *Grow*] Now grow (*1849–88*).
59.] Whoever quenched fire first, hoped to see (*1849–65*); Whoever it was
quenched fire first, hoped to see (*1868–88*).
61–5.] As merrily, as giddily . . .
        Meantime, what lights my sunbeam on,
        Where settles by degrees the radiant cripple?
        Oh, is it surely blown, my martagon?
        New-blown and ruddy as St. Agnes' nipple, (*1849–88*)
64. *martagon*: 'the Turk's cap lily, *Lilium Martagon* . . . The English name presumably
suggests the ref. to the "Turk bird" [l. 66], and to the "turban-flowers" [l. 69]'
(*Selections from the Early Poems of Robert Browning*, ed. W. H. Griffin [1902] 170).
Line 70 makes it clear that this is the scarlet martagon.
67–70. The details here, and more generally its underwater-world mythology,
may derive from Tennyson's *Poems, Chiefly Lyrical* (1830): see *The Merman*, *The
Mermaid*, *The Sea-Fairies* and *The Kraken*, where 'Unnumbered and enormous polypi
/ Winnow with giant arms the slumbering green' (ll. 9–10).

Such turban flowers . . I say, such lamps disperse
70   Thick red flame thro' that dusk green universe!
Queen of thee, floweret,
Each fleshy blossom
Keep I not, safer
Than leaves that embower it
75   Or shells that embosom,
From weevil and chafer?
Laugh thro' my pane then, solicit the bee,
Gibe him, be sure, and in midst of thy glee
Worship me!

80   Worship whom else? for am I not this Day
Whate'er I please? Who shall I seem to-day?
Morn, Noon, Eve, Night—how must I spend my Day?
Up the hill-side, thro' the morning,
Love me as I love!

69. *turban flowers*: florist's name for the cultivated varieties of *Ranunculus*; more fully *Turk's Turban*. 'Turban' is also the name for certain oceanic molluscs: *OED* cites an occurrence in 1713, and records it as a common name for the genus *Turbo*, or more generally of 'all the whirls, or spires, of a Univalve' (1815). Only occurrence in B.
70. *dusk*: rare as an adj. by B.'s time, but much used by him (12 occurrences; cp. 1 in Tennyson), esp. in his early work.
71–9.] these lines are indented, *1849–65*.
71. *Queen*] I am queen (*1849–88*).
71–2. *floweret, / Each*] floweret; / And each (*1849–88*, except 'floweret!', *1865–88*).
73. *Keep*] Preserve (*1849–88*).
75. Referring to the common practice of using seashells as decorative edgings for flower-borders.
79.] Love thy queen, worship me! (*1849–88*).
81. *Who shall I seem*] What shall I please (*1849–88*).
82.] My morning, noon, eve, night—how spend my day? (*1849–65*); My morn, noon, eve and night—how spend my day? (*1868–88*).
82^83.] Tomorrow I must be Pippa who winds silk,
    The whole year round, to earn just bread and milk:
        But, this one day, I have leave to go,
        And play out my fancy's fullest games;
        I may fancy all day—and it shall be so—
        That I taste of the pleasures, am named by the names
    Of the Happiest Four in our Asolo! (*1849–88*, except that the last five lines are not indented in *1868–88*; *Texas* has 'I am Pippa', canc.).
83–5.] See! Up the Hill-side yonder, through the morning,
    Some one shall love me, as the world calls love:
I am no less than Ottima, take warning!
    The gardens, and the great stone house above, (*1849–88*, except 'hill-side', *1870–88*).

85   I am Ottima, take warning,
     And the gardens, and stone house above,
     And other house for shrubs, all glass in front,
     Are mine, and Sebald steals as he is wont
     To court me, and old Luca yet reposes,
90   And therefore till the shrub-house door uncloses
     I . . . what now? give abundant cause for prate
     Of me (that's Ottima)—too bold of late,
     By far too confident she'll still face down
     The spitefullest of talkers in our town—
95   How we talk in the little town below!

     But love, love, love, there's better love I know!
     This love's only day's first offer—
     Next love shall defy the scoffer:
     For do not bride and bridegroom sally
100 Out of Possagno church at noon?
     Their house looks over Orcana valley—
     Why not be the bride as soon
     As Ottima? I saw, myself, beside,
     Arrive last night that bride—
105 Saw, if you call it seeing her, one flash
     Of the pale snow-pure cheek and blacker tresses
     Than . . . not the black eyelash;
     A wonder she contrives those lids no dresses
     —So strict was she the veil

88. *mine, and Sebald*] mine; where Sebald (*1849–88*).
89. *and old*] while old (*1849–88*).
92.] About me—Ottima, I mean—of late, (*1849–88*).
93. *By far*] Too bold, (*1849–88*).
95^96.] Line 95 ends a page in *1849*; in *1863* and subsequent eds. there is no space, but l. 96 is indented as for a new paragraph.
97. *This love's*] This foolish love was (*1849–88*).
98.] I choose my next love to defy the scoffer: (*1849–88*).
99. *bride and bridegroom*] our Bride and Bridegroom (*1849–88*).
100. *Possagno church*: Possagno church was designed by Canova. See headnote, pp. 86–8.
102. *Why not*] Why should I not (*1849*); Why should not I (*1863–88*), the first of the few verbal changes initiated in *1863*.
103. *I saw, myself,*] For I saw, (*1849–88*).
104. *that bride*] that little bride (*1849–88*).
106. *blacker tresses*] black bright tresses (*1849–88*).
107.] Blacker than all except the black eyelash; (*1849–88*).
108. *A wonder*] I wonder (*1849–88*).

110   Should cover close her pale
        Pure cheeks—a bride to look at and scarce touch,
        Remember Jules!—for are not such
        Used to be tended, flower-like, every feature,
        As if one's breath would fray the lily of a creature?
115   Oh, save that brow its virgin dimness,
        Keep that foot its lady primness,
        Let those ancles never swerve
        From their exquisite reserve,
        Yet have to trip along the streets like me
120   All but naked to the knee!
        How will she ever grant her Jules a bliss
        So startling as her real first infant kiss?
        Oh—no—not envy this!
        Not envy sure, for, if you gave me
125   Leave to take or to refuse
        In earnest, do you think I'd choose
        That sort of new love to enslave me?
        Mine should have lapped me round from the beginning;
        As little fear of losing it as winning—
130   Why look you! when at eve the pair
        Commune inside our turret, what prevents
        My being Luigi?—While that mossy lair
        Of lizards thro' the winter-time, is stirred
        With each to each imparting sweet intents

112. Remember] Scarce touch, remember, (*1849–88*).

114. fray: various senses are applicable, principally 'frighten', 'assault, attack', and (with the flower analogy) 'rub'. Cp. *Aristophanes' Apology* (*1875*) 655, 'Sunshine frays torchlight', and *Magical Nature* (*Pacchiarotto*, *1876*) 7: 'Time may fray the flower-face'. The context might also favour an obsolete sense, 'deflower'.

114^115.] A soft and easy life these ladies lead! / Whiteness in us were wonderful indeed— (*1849–88*, except 'lead:', *1865–88*, 'indeed.', *1863–88*).

115–23.] this passage is indented, *1849–65*.

117. ancles] ankles (*1863*, *1870–88*; *1865* agrees, unusually, with *1841*). Both spellings were current; cp. i 177.

123^124.] Line 123 ends a page in *1849*; in *1863–88* there is a space.

128. beginning;] emended in agreement with all other eds. from 'beginning' in *1841*.

129^130.] Lovers grow cold, men learn to hate their wives, / And only parents' love can last our lives: (*1849–88*, except 'lives.', *1863–88*).

130.] So, look you! when at eve the gentle Pair (*Texas*, canc., except 'Pair', which must have been altered in proof); At eve the son and mother, gentle pair, (*1849–88*, except 'Son and Mother', *1868–88*).

131. turret] Turret (*1849–65*).

135 For this new year, as brooding bird to bird—
    I will be cared about, kept out of harm
    And schemed for, safe in love as with a charm,
    I will be Luigi . . . if I only knew
    What was my father like . . . my mother too!

140 Nay, if you come to that, the greatest love of all
    Is God's: well then, to have God's love befall
    Oneself as in the palace by the dome
    Where Monsignor to-night will bless the home
    Of his dead brother! I, to-night at least,
145 Will be that holy and beloved priest.
    Now wait—even I myself already ought to share
    In that—why else should new year's hymn declare

All service ranks the same with God:

135^136.] (For I observe of late, the evening walk
        Of Luigi and his mother, always ends
        Inside our ruined turret, where they talk,
        Calmer than lovers, yet more kind than friends) (*1849–88*)
136. *I will*] Let me (*1849*); —Let me (*1863–88*).
138–9.] Let me be Luigi! . . . If I only knew / What was my mother's face—my
father, too! (*1849–88*, except 'Luigi! If', *1863–88*).
139^140.] in *1863* and *1865*, l. 139 ends a page; in *1868–88* there is no space, but
in *1888* l. 140 is indented as for a new paragraph.
140–5.] Nay, if you come to that, best love of all
        Is God's; then why not have God's love befall
        Myself as, in the Palace by the Dome,
        Monsignor?—who to-night will bless the home
        Of his dead brother; and God will bless in turn
        That heart which beats, those eyes which mildly burn
        With love for all men: I, to-night at least,
        Would be that holy and beloved priest! (*1849–88*, except 'palace',
'God bless', 'men!', *1870–88*, and 'priest.', *1868–88*).
142. *dome*: cathedral, from Italian 'Duomo'.
146. *even I myself*] even I (*1849–88*).
147.] In God's love: what does New-year's hymn declare? / What other
meaning do these verses bear? (*1849–88*; *Texas* has 'that love', canc.).
148–59. The first stanza of the hymn argues that God's control over the destiny
of each individual makes all such individuals equal in relation to him. The
second stanza (which parallels but does not follow from the first) suggests that,
similarly, no one ought to rank their actions into hierarchies of significance;
each act is equally important. It does not mean that God commands every individual 'deed' of a man's life (despite the biblical echoes of ll. 157–9). Such an
interpretation would contradict all B.'s other statements on this issue, in which
he invariably upholds free will (see e.g. *Prince Hohenstiel-Schwangau* (1871)
111–69, *Christmas-Eve* 288–95, III 59); and his own comment on ll. 152–3 (see
note) suggests that the hymn is more than a dramatic statement and should therefore be reconcilable with his opinion as expressed elsewhere.

If now, as formerly he trod
150   Paradise, God's presence fills
Our earth, and each but as God wills
Can work—God's puppets, best and worst,
Are we; there is no last nor first.

Say not, a small event! Why small?

---

148. Cp. Milton, *Sonnets* xvi ('On his Blindness'): 'who best / Bear his mild yoke,
they serve him best . . . Thousands at his bidding speed / And post o'er land and
ocean without rest: / They also serve who only stand and wait' (10–11, 12–14).
In a letter to EBB. of 18 Jan. 1846 (*Correspondence* xii 2), B. refers to God's
'reasonable service', quoting *Romans* xii 1, a passage which continues, 'For I say
. . . to every man that is among you, not to think of himself more highly than
he ought to think; but to think soberly, according as God hath dealt to every
man the measure of faith. For as we have many members in one body, and all
members have not the same office: so we, being many, are one body in Christ,
and every one members one of another' (vv. 3–5). The concept of service appears
repeatedly in St Paul's epistles: cp. *Ephesians* (vi 5–9) which expands its social
aspect: 'Servants, be obedient to them that are your masters according to the
flesh, with fear and trembling, in singleness of your heart, as unto Christ; not
with eyeservice, as menpleasers; but as the servants of Christ, doing the will of
God from the heart; with good will doing service, as to the Lord, and not to
men: knowing that whatsoever good thing any man doeth, the same shall he
receive of the Lord, whether he be bond or free. And, ye masters, do the same
things unto them, forbearing threatening: knowing that your Master also is in
heaven; neither is there respect of persons with him'. See l. 153n.
149. he] He (*1849–65*). 'When' must be understood before 'he'.
150. God's] His (*1849–65*); his (*1868–88*).
151. and each but] then each but (*Texas*, canc.); each only (*1849–88*).
152–3. God's puppets . . . nor first: *ABL* has a scrap of paper on which is written,
in B.'s early hand, 'whose puppets, best & worst, are *we*' with the comment: 'Better
or worse as we may be with respect to our capabilities, & opportunities for their
exercise, we are one & all, best & worst, but mere *puppets* (in our capacity of
influential agents of the Divine Will—not in any other)'. Above is written,
in the hand of B.'s friend R. H. Horne, 'Robt. Browning's philosophy quoad
Free-will'. For Eliza Flower's comment on this passage, see headnote, p. 90.
Collections records three examples besides this one of B. inscribing the lines for
autographs (E365, E366, E367, p. 429). The last of these is dated 27 Aug. 1889.
153. there is no last nor first: cp. *Luke* xiii 29–30: 'And they shall come from the
east, and from the west, and from the north, and from the south, and shall sit
down in the kingdom of God. And, behold, there are last which shall be first,
and there are first which shall be last'. Cp. also *Mark* ix 35: 'If any man desire
to be first, the same shall be last of all, and servant of all', with *Luke* ix 46–8:
'Then there arose a reasoning among [the disciples], which of them should be
greatest. And Jesus, perceiving the thought of their heart, took a child, and set
him by him, and said unto them, Whosoever shall receive this child in my name
receiveth me: and whosoever shall receive me receiveth him that sent me: for
he that is least among you all, the same shall be great'.
154–7. Say not . . . Than that: cp. *Sordello* vi 496–502n. (I 747).
154.] Say not "a small event!" Why "small?" (*1849–88*, except '"small"?', *1888*).

155   *Costs it more pain this thing ye call*
             A great event should come to pass
             Than that? Untwine me, from the mass
             Of deeds that make up life, one deed
             Power shall fall short in or exceed!
160   And more of it, and more of it—oh, yes!
        So that my passing, and each happiness
        I pass, will be alike important—prove
        That true! oh yes—the brother,
        The bride, the lover, and the mother,—
165   Only to pass whom will remove—
        Whom a mere look at half will cure
        The Past, and help me to endure
        The Coming . . . I am just as great, no doubt,
        As they!
170   A pretty thing to care about
        So mightily—this single holiday!
        Why repine?
        With thee to lead me, Day of mine,
        Down the grass path gray with dew,
175   'Neath the pine-wood, blind with boughs,
        Where the swallow never flew
        As yet, nor cicale dared carouse:
        No, dared carouse!

                                    [*She enters the Street.*

155. this thing] than this, (*1849–75*); 'than' is corrected to 'that' in *1888*.
156. great event] in quotation marks, *1849–88*.
157–9. Untwine me . . . or exceed: cp. *Isaiah* xl 26: 'Lift up your eyes on high, and behold who hath created these things, that bringeth out their host by number: he calleth them all by names by the greatness of his might, for that he is strong in power; not one faileth'.
160. it: either God's love (l. 147) or his power (l. 159).
161–9.] I will pass by, and see their happiness,
            And envy none—being just as great, no doubt,
            Useful to men, and dear to God, as they! (*1849–88*)
162–3. prove / That true: 'let that prove true'.
172–8.] this passage is indented, *1849–65*.
172.] But let the sun shine! Wherefore repine? (*1849–88*).
173. Day] O Day (*1849–88*).
175. 'Neath] Under (*1849–88*).
177. As yet, nor] Nor yet (*1865–88*).   *cicale*] cicala (*1863–88*). In *1863* this spelling, with the *1841* version of the rest of the line, would make the line hard to pronounce because of the change in stress. See also iii 50n. The cicale or cicada, a southern grasshopper, is noted for its shrill chirping sound. Cp. *Sordello* iii 248 (I 540).
178.] Dared carouse! (*1849–63*). This line repeats the sense of the previous one: 'No' is a lyric repetition of 'nor' in the previous line, not a negation of that line's sense.

I.—*Morning. Up the Hill-side. The Shrub House.* Luca's *Wife*
    Ottima, *and her Paramour the German* Sebald.

    Sebald. [*Sings*] *Let the watching lids wink!*
        Day's a-blaze with eyes, think,—
        Deep into the night drink!
    Ottima. Night? What, a Rhineland night, then?
      How these tall

5   Naked geraniums straggle! Push the lattice—
    Behind that frame.—Nay, do I bid you?—Sebald,
    It shakes the dust down on me! Why, of course
    The slide-bolt catches—Well, are you content,
    Or must I find you something else to spoil?

10 Kiss and be friends, my Sebald. Is it full morning?
    Oh, don't speak then!
      Sebald.   Ay, thus it used to be!
    Ever your house was, I remember, shut
    Till mid-day—I observed that, as I strolled
    On mornings thro' the vale here: country girls

15 Were noisy, washing garments in the brook—
    Herds drove the slow white oxen up the hills—
    But no, your house was mute, would ope no eye—
    And wisely—you were plotting one thing there,
    Nature another outside: I looked up—

20 Rough white wood shutters, rusty iron bars,
    Silent as death, blind in a flood of light,

---

i *Opening s.d.*] *Up the Hill-side. The Shrub House*] Up the Hill-side, inside the
Shrub-house (*1849–88*). *Shrub House*: conservatory.
i *1–276*. The whole of this scene was extracted for *1863²*; see headnote, p. 7. We
have included this text in our collation.
i *1–2*. Probably a ref. to the legend of Argus, who, 'as he had an hundred eyes,
of which only two were asleep at one time, Juno set him to watch Io, whom
Jupiter had changed into a heifer; but Mercury, by order of Jupiter, slew him,
by lulling all his eyes asleep with the sound of his lyre' (*Lemprière*).
i *4–10. How these tall . . . my Sebald*: in a letter to Mary Russell Mitford of
17 July 1841, EBB. says of this passage, 'Is'nt that Landor? Is'nt it his very trick
of phrase? Yet M^r. Browning is no imitator' (*Correspondence* v 78).
i *4*.] Night? Such may be your Rhine-land nights, perhaps;
    But this blood-red beam through the shutter's chink,
    —We call such light the morning's: let us see!
    Mind how you grope your way, though! How these tall (*1849–88*, except
'nights perhaps', *1865–88*, 'chink', 'morning', *1868–88*).
i *10. Is it*] Is't (*1870–88*).
i *13. mid-day—I*] mid-day; I (*1863²–88*).
i *16. Herds*] Hinds (*1849–88*). 'Herd' means 'cowherd'; 'hind', 'an agricultural
labourer'.

Oh, I remember!—and the peasants laughed
And said, "The old man sleeps with the young wife!"
This house was his, this chair, this window—his.
25   *Ottima.* Ah, the clear morning! I can see St.
        Mark's:
That black streak is the belfry—stop: Vicenza
Should lie—there's Padua, plain enough, that blue.
Look o'er my shoulder—follow my finger—
        Sebald.   Morning?
It seems to me a night with a sun added:
30   Where's dew? where's freshness? That bruised plant
        I bruised
In getting thro' the lattice yestereve,
Droops as it did. See, here's my elbow's mark
In the dust on the sill.
        Ottima.   Oh shut the lattice, pray!
        Sebald. Let me lean out. I cannot scent blood here
Foul as the morn may be—
35   There, shut the world out!
How do you feel now, Ottima? There—curse
The world, and all outside! Let us throw off
This mask: how do you bear yourself? Let's out
With all of it!
        Ottima.   Best never speak of it.
40   *Sebald.* Best speak again and yet again of it,
Till words cease to be more than words. "His blood,"
For instance—let those two words mean "His blood"
And nothing more. Notice—I'll say them now,
"His blood."
        Ottima.   Assuredly if I repented
The deed—

i *24.* Cp. Donne, *Elegy i* ('Jealousy') 24–5: 'for that [his house] is / His realm,
his castle, and his diocese'. See below, ll. 70–4n.
i *25–7. I can see . . . that blue*: Ottima looks for the three principal cities of the
region, all lying about 50 km from Asolo and visible from it on a clear day.
St Mark's is San Marco, the cathedral church of Venice since 1817; its belfry
(campanile) is 'one of the boldest monuments of ancient Venice' (*Murray*).
i *28–9. Morning . . . with a sun added*: cp. *Macbeth* II iv 6–7, the morning after
the murder of Duncan: 'By the clock 'tis day, / And yet dark night strangles the
travelling lamp'. See also l. 110.
i *33. In the dust on the*] I' the dust o' the] (*1870–88*).
i *38. mask: how*] mask. How (*1863²*).
i *41–4. His blood . . . His blood*: cp. the obsession of Macbeth and Lady Macbeth
with the blood of Duncan after their murder of him. See esp. V i.

45   *Sebald.*   Repent? who should repent, or why?
What puts that in your head? Did I once say
That I repented?
     Ottima.   No—I said the deed—
     Sebald. "The deed" and "the event"—and just
       now it was
     "Our passion's fruit"—the devil take such cant!
50 Say, once and always, Luca was a wittol,
I am his cut-throat, you are—
     Ottima.   Here is the wine—
I brought it when we left the house above—
And glasses too—wine of both sorts. Black? white, then?
     Sebald. But am not I his cut-throat? What are you?
55   *Ottima.* There trudges on his business from the Duomo,
Benet the Capuchin, with his brown hood
And bare feet—always in one place at church,
Close under the stone wall by the south entry;
I used to take him for a brown cold piece
60 Of the wall's self, as out of it he rose
To let me pass—at first, I say, I used—
Now—so has that dumb figure fastened on me—
I rather should account the plastered wall
A piece of him, so chilly does it strike.
This, Sebald?

---

i *47–9. No—I said the deed . . . such cant*: Macbeth and Lady Macbeth habitually refer to Duncan's murder as a 'deed': see esp. II ii 70: '[Macbeth] To know my deed, 'twere best not know myself.'
i *48. and just*] just (*1849–88*).
i *50. wittol*: 'A man who knows the falsehood of his wife, and seems contented; a tame cuckold' (*J*.). A character corresponding to Luca in the first part ('The Triumph of Honour') of *Four Plays* (see headnote, pp. 82–3) is described in the *dramatis personae* as 'a wittol sutler'.
i *51. Here is*] Here's (*1870–88*).
i *53. Black*: red wine, from It. 'vino nero'.
i *55. Duomo*: cathedral. W. H. Griffin (*Selections from the Early Poems of Robert Browning* [1902]) notes: 'the Duomo of S. Maria at Asolo is a Capuchin foundation; the road to it passes immediately below the house B. associates with this scene. The south entry to the church has a little porch with a stone seat beneath it' (p. 144).
i *56. Capuchin*: a friar of the Franciscan order, so called from the characteristic pointed hood; the order's rule stressed poverty and austerity.
i *64. so chilly does it strike*: the referent of 'it' is unclear: either 'that dumb figure' (l. 62) or 'the plastered wall' (l. 63), or, metonymically, both.

65   *Sebald.*   No—the white wine—the white wine!
        Well, Ottima, I promised no new year
        Should rise on us the ancient shameful way,
        Nor does it rise—pour on—To your black eyes!
        Do you remember last damned New Year's day?
70   *Ottima.* You brought those foreign prints.
                We looked at them
        Over the wine and fruit. I had to scheme
        To get him from the fire. Nothing but saying
        His own set wants the proof-mark roused him up
        To hunt them out.
                Sebald.   Faith, he is not alive
        To fondle you before my face.
75   *Ottima.*   Do you
        Fondle me then: who means to take your life
        For that, my Sebald?
                Sebald.   Hark you, Ottima,
        One thing's to guard against. We'll not make much
        One of the other—that is, not make more

i *66–8. I promised no new year . . . Nor does it rise*: the suggestion here of a plan
seems to contradict the apparently unpremeditated character of the murder as
reported at ll. 90–1 and 141–5. There is perhaps a ref. to *Macbeth* I v 58–61:
'[Macbeth] My dearest love, / Duncan comes here to-night. [Lady Macbeth] And
when goes hence? / [Macbeth] To-morrow, as he purposes. [Lady Macbeth] O,
never / Shall sun that morrow see!'
i *70–4. You brought . . . To hunt them out*: this passage and l. 144 come very close
to the scenario of Donne's *Elegy* I 17–24: 'We must not, as we used, flout openly,
/ In scoffing riddles, his deformity; / Nor at his board being together sat, / With
words, nor touch, scarce looks adulterate. / Nor when he swoll'n, and pampered
with great fare, / Sits down, and snorts, caged in his basket chair, / Must we
usurp his own bed any more, / Nor kiss and play in his house, as before'. See
above, l. 24n.
i *73. proof-mark*: a proof in engraving is either a draft or the completed print, and
the various stages of production are given differential marks: as W. M. Ivins remarks,
'For many print collectors these marks play the role played by the wine label for
the man who tells whether a wine is good or bad by reading in a book, not by
testing in a glass' (*How Prints Look* [Boston 1958] 152). 'Proof-mark' might refer
to any of these marks, and therefore any of the stages of production; the
most prized specimens are either an early draft or an early copy from the first
press-run of the finished print. Alternatively, B. might intend a synonym for
'plate-mark', the limit of the impress caused by the printing, whose removal
lowers the value of a print.
i *77–92. Hark you, Ottima . . . forever yours*: the concept of being bound together
by complicity in murder has a general resemblance to the argument put forward
in Middleton's *The Changeling* (1623) III iv 133–41 by De Flores to Beatrice, at
whose instigation he has murdered her betrothed Alsemero.
i *78. One thing's*] One thing (*1868–88*).

80   Parade of warmth, childish officious coil,
      Than yesterday—as if, sweet, I supposed
      Proof upon proof was needed now, now first,
      To show I love you—still love you—love you
      In spite of Luca and what's come to him.
85   —Sure sign we had him ever in our thoughts,
      White sneering old reproachful face and all—
      We'll even quarrel, love, at times, as if
      We still could lose each other—were not tied
      By this—conceive you?
            Ottima.   *Love*—
            Sebald.   Not tied so sure—
90   Because tho' I was wrought upon—have struck
      His insolence back into him—am I
      So surely yours?—therefore, forever yours?
            Ottima. Love, to be wise, (one counsel pays another)
      Should we have—months ago—when first we loved,
95   For instance that May morning we two stole
      Under the green ascent of sycamores—
      If we had come upon a thing like that
      Suddenly—
            Sebald.   "A thing" . . there again—"a thing!"
            Ottima. Then, Venus' body, had we come upon
100   My husband Luca Gaddi's murdered corpse
      Within there, at his couch-foot, covered close—
      Would you have pored upon it? Why persist
      In poring now upon it? For 'tis here—
      As much as there in the deserted house—
105   You cannot rid your eyes of it: for me,
      Now he is dead I hate him worse—I hate—

---

i *80. officious*: combining 'dutiful; active or zealous in doing one's duty' and 'unduly forward in proffering services or taking business upon oneself; meddlesome'. Cp. *My Last Duchess* 27 (p. 199).   *coil*: fuss, ado.

i *81. sweet*] Sweet (*1863, 1865*). Unlike the similar rev. in l. 87, this does not appear in *1863²*.

i *82. was*] were (*1865–88*).

i *83. still love*] yes, still love (*1849–88*).

i *87. love*] Love (*1863–65*).

i *89. Love*—] Love! (*1863–88*).

i *90–1. I was wrought . . . back into him*: see ll. 66–8n.

i *91. am I*] am I, Love, (*1863²*).

i *94. ago—when*] ago, when (*1863²–88*).

i *105. it: for*] it. For (*1863–88*).

Dare you stay here? I would go back and hold
His two dead hands, and say, I hate you worse
Luca, than—
    Sebald. Off, off; take your hands off mine!
110 'Tis the hot evening—off! oh, morning, is it?
    Ottima. There's one thing must be done—you
        know what thing.
Come in and help to carry. We may sleep
Anywhere in the whole wide house to-night.
    Sebald. What would come, think you, if we let him lie
115 Just as he is? Let him lie there until
The angels take him: he is turned by this
Off from his face, beside, as you will see.
    Ottima. This dusty pane might serve for looking-glass.
Three, four—four grey hairs! is it so you said
120 A plait of hair should wave across my neck?
No—this way!
    Sebald.   Ottima, I would give your neck,
Each splendid shoulder, both those breasts of yours,
This were undone! Killing?—Let the world die
So Luca lives again!—Ay, lives to sputter
125 His fulsome dotage on you—yes, and feign
Surprise that I returned at eve to sup,
When all the morning I was loitering here—
Bid me dispatch my business and begone.
I would—
    Ottima. See!
    Sebald.   No, I'll finish. Do you think
130 I fear to speak the bare truth once for all?
All we have talked of is at bottom fine
To suffer—there's a recompense in that:
One must be venturous and fortunate—
What is one young for else? In age we'll sigh

---

i *108–9. I hate you worse / Luca, than—*] in quotation marks, *1868–88.*
i *116. by this*: by this time.
i *123. This*] That this (*1849–88*). *Let the world die*] Kill the world (*1849–88*).
i *124. sputter*: splutter. *OED* records its use as being mainly to express anger rather
than dotage. Ten occurrences in B.; typically, 'you hissed, spat and sputtered' (*Of
Pacchiarotto* [*Pacchiarotto*, 1876] 569).
i *126. returned*] return (*1868–88*).
i *128. dispatch my business*: a Shakespearean phrase; cp. *Love's Labour's Lost* II i
31 and *Antony and Cleopatra* II ii 165–6.
i *132. in that*] in guilt (*1849–88*).

135   O'er the wild, reckless, wicked days flown over:
        But to have eaten Luca's bread—have worn
        His clothes, have felt his money swell my purse—
        Why, I was starving when I used to call
        And teach you music—starving while you pluck'd
        Me flowers to smell!
            Ottima.   My poor lost friend!
140   *Sebald.*   He gave me
        Life—nothing less: what if he did reproach
        My perfidy, and threaten, and do more—
        Had he no right? What was to wonder at?
        Why must you lean across till our cheeks touch'd?
145   Could he do less than make pretence to strike me?
        'Tis not the crime's sake—I'd commit ten crimes
        Greater, to have this crime wiped out—undone!
        And you—O, how feel you? feel you for me?
            Ottima. Well, then—I love you better now than ever—
150   And best (look at me while I speak to you)—
        Best for the crime—nor do I grieve in truth
        This mask, this simulated ignorance,
        This affectation of simplicity
        Falls off our crime; this naked crime of ours
155   May not be looked over—look it down, then!
        Great? let it be great—but the joys it brought
        Pay they or no its price? Come—they or it!
        Speak not! The past, would you give up the past
        Such as it is, pleasure and crime together?

i *135^136.*] Still we have lived! The vice was in its place. (*1849–88*, except 'Still, we', *1863–88*, 'lived: the', *1865–88*).

i *137^138.*] Do lovers in romances sin that way? (*1849–88*).

i *139–40. you pluck'd / Me flowers*] you plucked me / These flowers (*1849–88*).

i *143^144.*] He sate by us at table quietly— (*1849–88*, except 'sat', *1863, 1865–88*, 'quietly:', *1865–88*).

i *144.* See ll. 70–4n.

i *145. to strike me*] to strike (*1865–88*).

i *146. not the*] not for the (*1849–63*).

i *153. simplicity*: used in the sense of 'freedom from artifice, deceit, or duplicity; absence of affectation or artificiality'.

i *155. May not*] May not, now, (*1849–88*). *down, then!*] down! (*1870–88*).

i *157. Pay they or no its price*: cp. *Colombe's Birthday* (1844) ii 98–102.

i *158. past . . . past*] Past . . . Past (*1863–65*).

160   Give up that noon I owned my love for you—
       The garden's silence—even the single bee
       Persisting in his toil, suddenly stopt
       And where he hid you only could surmise
       By some campanula's chalice set a-swing
       As he clung there—"Yes, I love you."
165   *Sebald.*   And I drew
       Back: put far back your face with both my hands
       Lest you should grow too full of me—your face
       So seemed athirst for my whole soul and body!
           Ottima. And when I ventured to receive you here,
       Made you steal hither in the mornings—
170   *Sebald.*   When
       I used to look up 'neath the shrub-house here
       Till the red fire on its glazed windows spread
       Into a yellow haze?
           Ottima.   Ah—my sign was, the sun
       Inflamed the sere side of yon chestnut-tree
       Nipt by the first frost—
175   *Sebald.*   You would always laugh
       At my wet boots—I had to stride thro' grass
       Over my ancles.
           Ottima.   Then our crowning night—
           Sebald. The July night?
           Ottima.   The day of it too, Sebald!

i *160. that noon*: noon was traditionally identified as the hour of the Fall of Man.
i *161–2. the single bee / Persisting in his toil*: cp. *Sordello* vi 619–28n. (I 753).
i *163–5. And where he hid . . . he clung there*: the association of the bee with sexual intercourse is common in B. Cp. *In a Gondola* 56–62 (II 121), *Popularity* 46–50 (p. 454) and *Women and Roses* 28–32 (III 238). The image may owe something to *PL* v 21–5 (Adam addressing Eve, who is waking from her dream of temptation): 'Mark . . . How nature paints her colours, how the bee / Sits on the bloom extracting liquid sweet'.
i *163. hid you*] hid, you (*1863²*). One of the few readings unique to this ed.
i *164. campanula's*] campanula (*1868–88*). Only occurrence in B; but note 'bell-flower', another name for this flower, in *A Toccata* 14 (p. 371).
i *164–5. a-swing / As he clung there*—] a-swing: / Who stammered— (*1863–88*).
i *167–8. your face . . . soul and body*: cp. Marlowe's *Doctor Faustus*: 'Her lips suck forth my soul: see where it flies. / Come, Helen, come, give me my soul again' (V i); and cp. *Confessional* 13–18 (II 338).
i *173. Into*] To (*1849–88*).
i *174. sere*: dry, withered. Cp. *Macbeth* V ii 22–3: 'my way of life / Is fall'n into the sear, the yellow leaf'.
i *177. ancles*] ankles (*1863, 1870–88*; *1865* agrees with *1841*, as at *Intro* 117).

When heaven's pillars seemed o'erbowed with heat,
180　　Its black-blue canopy seemed let descend
Close on us both, to weigh down each to each,
And smother up all life except our life.
So lay we till the storm came.
　　　　Sebald.　　　　　　　　　How it came!
　　　　Ottima. Buried in woods we lay, you recollect;
185　　Swift ran the searching tempest overhead;
And ever and anon some bright white shaft
Burnt thro' the pine-tree roof—here burnt and there,
As if God's messenger thro' the close wood screen
Plunged and replunged his weapon at a venture,
190　　Feeling for guilty thee and me—then broke
The thunder like a whole sea overhead—
　　　　Sebald. Yes.
　　　　Ottima.　　　While I stretched myself upon you, hands
To hands, my mouth to your hot mouth, and shook
All my locks loose, and covered you with them.
You, Sebald, the same you—
195　　*Sebald.*
　　　　Ottima. And as we lay—
　　　　Sebald.　　　　　　Less vehemently—Love me—
Forgive me—take not words—mere words—to heart—
Your breath is worse than wine—breathe slow, speak
　　slow—
Do not lean on me—
　　　　Ottima.　　　　　Sebald, as we lay,

---

i *179. heaven's*] the heaven's (*1849–65*).

i *180. seemed let descend*] suffered descend (*1865–88*).

i *184–91. Buried in woods . . . a whole sea overhead*: the resemblance to *King Lear* III ii has often been noted, esp. ll. 49–51: 'Let the great gods / That keep this dreadful pudder o'er our heads / Find out their enemies now'. Another source is *PL* ix 1080–90, where after his fall Adam laments: 'How shall I behold the face / Henceforth of God or angel, erst with joy / And rapture so oft beheld? Those heavenly shapes / Will dazzle now this earthly, with their blaze / Insufferably bright. O might I here / In solitude live savage, in some glade / Obscured, where highest woods impenetrable / To star or sunlight, spread their umbrage broad / And brown as evening: cover me, ye pines, / Ye cedars, with innumerable boughs / Hide me, where I may never see them more'. In a letter to EBB. about thunderstorms (13 July 1845, *Correspondence* x 305) B. recollected one he had seen at Possagna, the setting for pt. ii of *Pippa*. A similar storm, again associated with retribution, concludes *Caliban* (see ll. 289–91, p. 641).

i *187. Burnt . . . burnt*] Burned . . . burned (*1868–88*).

200   Rising and falling only with our pants,
       Who said, "Let death come now—'tis right to die!
       Right to be punished—nought completes such bliss
       But woe!" Who said that?
            Sebald.   How did we ever rise?
       Was't that we slept? Why did it end?
            Ottima.   I felt
205   You tapering to a point the ruffled ends
       Of my loose locks 'twixt both your humid lips—
       (My hair is fallen now—knot it again).
            Sebald. I kiss you now, dear Ottima, now and now;
       This way? will you forgive me—be once more
       My great queen?
210   *Ottima.*   Bind it thrice about my brow;
       Crown me your queen, your spirit's arbitress,
       Magnificent in sin. Say that!
            Sebald   I crown you
       My great white queen, my spirit's arbitress,
       Magnificent—
215   [*Without*] The year's at the spring,
       And day's at the morn:

i *201. Let death come now—'tis right to die*: cp. *Othello* II i 185–93: 'If after every
tempest come such calms, / May the winds blow till they have wakened death
. . . If it were now to die, / 'Twere now to be most happy; for I fear / My soul
hath her content so absolute / That not another comfort like to this / Succeeds
in unknown fate'.

i *202–3. nought completes such bliss / But woe*: adapting the proverbial 'No weal
without woe'. B. is fond of the 'weal—woe' doublet, replacing 'weal' with 'bliss'
in only one other context (*Apollo and the Fates* 254, where, as here, a love-
relationship is involved). Cp. also Shakespeare, *Sonnets* cxxix: 'lust / Is perjured,
murderous, bloody, full of blame . . . A bliss in proof, and prov'd, a very woe'
(2–3, 11)

i *203–4. How did we . . . we slept?*: cp. Donne, *Break of Day 3*: 'Why should we
rise, because 'tis light?', and *The Good-Morrow* 1–4: 'I wonder, by my troth, what
thou and I / Did till we loved? . . . Snorted we in the seven sleepers' den?'

i *204–5. felt / You tapering to*] felt you, / Fresh tapering to (*1849*); felt you, / Tapering
into (*1863*); felt you / Tapering into (*1863²–1865*); felt you / Taper into (*1868–88*).

i *215–76*. The dramatic structure here closely parallels that of the conclusion of
'The Triumph of Death' in *Four Plays* (see headnote, pp. 82–3), whose protagonist, Lavall, having killed the brother of a woman he is attempting to seduce
and been stabbed himself, sees a 'Spirit' which catalogues his crimes to him, and
'sings and vanishes'.

i *215–22*. For publication details, see headnote, pp. 80–1. No single source has been
suggested for Pippa's first song, but its rhythm and paratactic organization give
it some resemblance to Wordsworth's *Written in March while resting at the foot of
Brothers Water*, which begins: 'The Cock is crowing, / The stream is flowing, /

Morning's at seven;
The hill-side's dew-pearled:
The lark's on the wing,
220   The snail's on the thorn;
God's in his heaven—
All's right with the world!

[Pippa *passes.*

The small birds twitter, / The lake doth glitter, / The green field sleeps in the
sun'. (There is also a more general resemblance to Elizabethan spring-catalogues,
e.g. Surrey's 'The soote season'.) Until recently, this song was heavily anthologized;
it was also taken to 'voice the poet's belief' (W. O. Raymond, *The Infinite Moment*
[2nd ed., Toronto 1965] 160). This view was attacked by E. D. H. Johnson (*The
Alien Vision of Victorian Poetry* [Princeton 1952] 86) on the ground that the song
is dramatically expressive of Pippa's 'naivety and child-like faith'; see also Philip
Drew, *The Poetry of Browning* (1970) 19, 182–3. J. C. Ransom identifies it as an instance
of 'The Concrete Universal' (*Kenyon Review* xvii [1955] 395); A. Hill describes
its structure in ' "Pippa's Song": Two Attempts at Structural Criticism' (*Browning's
Mind and Art*, ed. C. Tracy [1968] 75–81). There is no known precedent for the
song's unusual rhyme-scheme (abcd abcd), but B. may have derived it from
the 'rimas dissolutas' of some troubadour lyrics, in which 'all the different verses
are without a rhyme in their own stanza, but find it in the corresponding verse
of another, or of all other stanzas' (F. Hueffer, *The Troubadours* [1878] 355).
B.'s studies for *Sordello* would have introduced him to this device, which is very
common in, for instance, the verse of Arnaut Daniel. With the context, there
may be an ironic ref. to the Provençal 'Alba', sung by a watchman to warn two
lovers that the day is coming and therefore danger from the jealous husband. B.
frequently inscribed this song for autographs: *Collections* (E 371–6, pp. 429–30)
lists six examples (1858, 1861, 1870 [called 'A Girl's Song'], 1886, 1888, 1889),
the latter being possibly B.'s last autograph inscription. Variants from all of these
MSS except *1888* (whose whereabouts are unknown) are recorded below.
i 215. [*s.d.*] *From without is heard the voice of* PIPPA, *singing*— (*1849–88*, except 'PIPPA
singing', *1868–75*). In *1849–88* the s.d. is placed between l. 214 and l. 215.
The s.d. does not of course appear in selected eds. where the song appears as a
separate item (*1865²*, *1872*), or in autographs, but does appear in *1863²*, which extracts
the whole Ottima—Sebald scene.
i 215. spring,] Spring, (*1861 MS*, *1870 MS*, *1889 MS*); spring (*1870–88*).
i 216. *And day's*] The Day's (*1858 MS*); And Day's (*1861 MS*).   *morn:*] morn;
(*1849–88*, *1870 MS*, *1889 MS*); Morn; (*1861 MS*).
i 217. W. L. Phelps (*Browning and How to Know Him* [1915] 82–3) objects
that 'at seven o'clock on the first of January in Asolo the sun is still below the
horizon'. But it is not necessary to suppose that Pippa's song describes the actual
scene on that day.
i 218. *dew-pearled:*] dew-pearled; (*1861 MS*, *1863–88*, *1870 MS*, *1889 MS*; *1863²* as *1841*).
i 219. *lark's*] bee's (*1858 MS*); Bee's (*1861 MS*).   *wing,*] wing; (*1849–88*, *1870 MS*,
1889 MS).
i 220. *snail's*] Snail's (*1861 MS*).
i 221. *his*] His (*1863–68*, *1872*).   *heaven—*] Heaven, (*1861 MS*); Heaven—(*1889 MS*).
i 222. *world!*] world. (*1858 MS*, *1865²*, *1872*, *1889 MS*).

    Sebald. God's in his heaven! Do you hear that? Who
       spoke?
  You, you spoke!
    Ottima.　　　　Oh—that little ragged girl:
225 She must have rested on the step—we give
  Them but one holiday the whole year round—
  Did you e'er see our silk-mills—their inside?
  There are ten silk-mills now belong to you.
  She stops to pick my double heartsease . . . Sh!
  She does not hear—you call out louder!
230 *Sebald.*　　　　　　　　　　Leave me!
  Go, get your clothes on—dress those shoulders.
    Ottima.　　　　　　　　　Sebald?
    Sebald. Wipe off that paint. I hate you!
    Ottima.　　　　　　　　　Miserable!
    Sebald. My God! and she is emptied of it now!
  Outright now!—how miraculously gone
235 All of the grace—had she not strange grace once?
  Why, the blank cheek hangs listless as it likes,
  No purpose holds the features up together,
  Only the cloven brow and puckered chin
  Stay in their places—and the very hair,
240 That seemed to have a sort of life in it,
  Drops a dead web!
    Ottima.　　　　Speak to me—not of me!
    Sebald. That round great full orbed face, where not
      an angle
  Broke the delicious indolence—all broken!

---

i *223. his*] His (*1863–65*).

i *225–6. we give / Them but*] we give them / But this (*1849–88*).

i *227. e'er*] ever (*1849–88*).

i *229. stops*] stoops (*1849–88*).   *double heartsease*: a cultivated pansy. In 'A Note on the Flowers in *Pippa Passes*' (*VP* xiv [Spring *1976*] 59–63) W. R. Campbell observes that in traditional flower symbolism this plant denotes both *thought* and *willingness to love*. The word itself, as meaning 'ease of mind; blithesomeness' is also significant. See iv 281–303n.

i *230. you call*] call you (*1863–88*).

i *232. Wipe off that paint*: drawing upon the Jacobean—Restoration obsession with cosmetics: cp. *Flight of the Duchess* 825–32n (II 330–1). Note also Perdita's rejection of cultivated flowers in *The Winter's Tale* IV iv 99–103: 'I'll not put / The dibble in earth to set one slip of them; / No more than were I painted I would wish / This youth to say 'twere well'.

i *241. not*] speak not (*1849–63*).

    Ottima. Ungrateful—to me—not of me—perjured
      cheat—
245 A coward too—but ingrate's worse than all:
    Beggar—my slave—a fawning, cringing lie!
    Leave me!—betray me!—I can see your drift—
    A lie that walks, and eats, and drinks!
      Sebald.   My God!
    Those morbid, olive, faultless shoulder-blades—
250 I should have known there was no blood beneath!
      Ottima. You hate me, then? you hate me then?
      Sebald.   To think
    She would succeed in her absurd attempt
    And fascinate with sin! and show herself
    Superior—Guilt from its excess, superior
255 To Innocence. That little peasant's voice
    Has righted all again. Though I be lost,
    I know which is the better, never fear,
    Of vice or virtue, purity or lust,
    Nature, or trick—I see what I have done
260 Entirely now. Oh, I am proud to feel
    Such torments—let the world take credit that
    I, having done my deed, pay too its price!

---

i *244.*] To me—not of me!—ungrateful, perjured cheat— (*1849–65*); To me—
not of me! Ungrateful, perjured cheat! (*1868–88*).
i *246. lie*: not normally used, as here, of a person. Out of 115 occurrences in B.'s
works there is only one other instance of this sense: 'friends, a heap, / Lovers
no lack—a husband in due time, / And every one of them alike a lie!' (*In a
Balcony* 127–9, III 410).
i *249. morbid*: 'of the nature of, indicative of disease'; also 'productive of disease'.
B. may also have had in mind, 'of flesh-tints: painted with "morbidezza"'; for
'morbidezza', *OED* cites Aglionby 1686: 'There is a thing which the Italians
call Morbidezza; The meaning of which word, is to Express the Softness, and
tender Liveliness of Flesh and Blood'. Only occurrence in B.
i *253. with sin! and show*] by sinning; and show (*1849–75*, except 'by sinning, and
show', (*1863²*, *1865–75*); by sinning, show (*1888*).
i *254–5. Guilt from its excess, superior / To Innocence*: the thought here is Byronic;
many of Byron's heroes are, like Sebald, criminals whose crime is viewed
metaphysically rather than judicially. See the excellent discussion in ch. 1 ('The
Dramatic Lyric and the Lyrical Drama') of R. Langbaum's *The Poetry of
Experience* (2nd ed., Chicago 1985). Langbaum draws attention to the final
speech of the eponymous hero of *Manfred*, which may have had some influence
on this passage. *Guilt . . . Innocence*] guilt . . . innocence (*1868–88*).
i *261. take credit*: the usual sense, 'take responsibility', is unlikely: something like
'believe' or 'take note' is more probable. *that*] thence— (*1849–88*).

I hate, hate—curse you! God's in his heaven!
   Ottima.   Me!
   Me! no, no Sebald—not yourself—kill me!
265 Mine is the whole crime—do but kill me—then
   Yourself—then—presently—first hear me speak—
   I always meant to kill myself—wait you!
   Lean on my breast . . not as a breast; don't love me
   The more because you lean on me, my own
270 Heart's Sebald. There—there—both deaths presently!
   Sebald. My brain is drowned now—quite
      drowned: all I feel
   Is . . . is at swift-recurring intervals,
   A hurrying-down within me, as of waters
   Loosened to smother up some ghastly pit—
275 There they go—whirls from a black, fiery sea.
   Ottima. Not me—to him oh God be merciful!

Talk by the way in the mean time. Foreign Students *of
Painting and Sculpture, from Venice, assembled opposite
the house of* Jules, *a young French Statuary.*

  1 *Student.* Attention: my own post is beneath this window, but the pomegranate-clump yonder will hide three or

i *263. his*] His (*1863–65*).   *heaven!*] emended in agreement with all other eds.;
1841 has no punctuation mark.
i *271–5.* A similar vision precedes the death of Lavall in pt. iii of *Four Plays* (see
headnote, pp. 82–3), and cp. the death of Hesperus in T. L. Beddoes, *The Bride's
Tragedy* (1822) V iv 117–19: 'the whole earth's in motion; / I cannot stem the
billows; now they roll: / And what's this deluge? Ah! Infernal flames!'
i *273. hurrying-down*] hurry-down (*1865–88*).
i *274. pit*—] pit: (*1863²–88*).
i *275. There they go*] They—they go (*1868*; possibly a mispr., since *1868* has few
unique readings and this was altered in the first corr. reissue, *1870*).
i *276.*] Not to me, God—to him be merciful! (*1849–65*); *1868–88* as *1841*, except
'him, O God,'.
i *276^277.* [*s.d.*] *Talk by the way in the mean time.*] Talk by the way, while
PIPPA is passing from the Hill-side to Orcana. (*1849–88*, except 'hill-side', *1888*).
Statuary] Statuary, at Possagno (*1865–88*).   The '1 Student', whose name is
Lutwyche (see ll. 305–6n.), is given no nationality in *1841*, but in *1849* is said to
be English. Of the others, Schramm and Gottlieb are clearly German, as are probably the rest (see l. 308n.). Jules's French nationality sets him apart from them:
see also ii 93–4n. The students have come from Venice, which would be their main
centre of study; Jules is living at Possagno because of his special interest in Canova.

four of you with a little squeezing, and Schramm and his
280   pipe must lie flat in the balcony. Four, five—who's a
defaulter? Jules must not be suffered to hurt his bride.
    2 *Student.* The poet's away—never having much meant
to be here, moonstrike him! He was in love with himself,
and had a fair prospect of thriving in his suit, when suddenly
285   a woman fell in love with him too, and out of pure
jealousy, he takes himself off to Trieste, immortal poem and
all—whereto is this prophetical epitaph appended already,
as Bluphocks assured me:—"*The author on the author. Here
so and so, the mammoth, lies, Fouled to death by butterflies.*"
290   His own fault, the simpleton! Instead of cramp couplets,
each like a knife in your entrails, he should write, says

i *281. defaulter? Jules must not . . . bride.*] defaulter? We want everybody, for Jules
must not be suffered to hurt his bride when the jest's found out. (*1849–88*).

i *282–92. The poet's away . . . classically and intelligibly:* the *1849* revs., give the 'poet'
a name, possibly in order to disguise his resemblance to B. himself. Trieste, a city
112 km north-east of Venice across the Adriatic, was the port B. sailed to from
London on his 1838 voyage, during which he first saw Venice and Asolo (see
headnote, p. 83). B. had left 'intending to finish' *Sordello* (*Correspondence* iv 24),
whose form ('cramp couplets') and disastrous critical reception are clearly alluded
to here (see headnote to *Sordello*, I 386 and iii 924n, noting W. S. Landor's
comment that B. ought to 'atticise a little', i.e. learn from the classical Greek
writers). In a letter to William Macready of 9 Aug. 1840, B. commented: 'tomorrow will I betimes break new ground with So & so—an epic in so many books
. . . let it but do me half the good "Sordello" has done' (*Correspondence* iv 295).
It is the neo-classicism attributed to Bluphocks (for whom see ii 243^244n.)
against which Jules eventually rebels: see iv 39–57n. There may also be an allusion
to the literary controversy in Italy between the 'classicisti' and the 'romantici'
which gave rise to 'a thousand grave treatises, and lighter tracts, and satires,
and epigrams' (*European Review* i, no. 2 [July 1824] 259). This controversy had
political overtones: see iii 18n.

i *282–3. The poet's away . . . to be here*] All here! Only our poet's away—never
having much meant to be present (*1949–88*). Cp. Plato's *Phaedo*, where those
assembled to hear Socrates' dying words do not include Plato himself, a joke
repeated at the beginning of the *Timaeus*: 'One, two, three,—but where, my
dear Timaeus, is the fourth of our guests?'

i *283. moonstrike him! He*] moonstrike him! The airs of that fellow, that
Giovacchino! He (*1849–88*).   *moonstrike:* not rec. as a verb in *OED*; derived from
'moonstruck', i.e. lunatic, a traditional satirical epithet for poets (*OED* cites Pope,
Dunciad iv 12).   *He was in love*] He was in violent love (*1849–88*).

i *284–5. suit . . . fell*] suit, so unmolested was it, when suddenly a woman falls
(*1849–88*).

i *288. assured me*] assures me (*1849–88*).

i *288–9. The author . . . the mammoth, lies,*] Here a mammoth-poem lies,—
(*1849–88*).

Bluphocks, both classically and intelligibly.—*Aesculapius, an*
epic. Catalogue of the drugs:—Hebe's plaister—One strip Cools
your lip; Phoebus' emulsion—One bottle Clears your throttle;
295   *Mercury's bolus—One box Cures . . .*

      3 *Student.* Subside, my fine fellow; if the marriage was
over by ten o'clock, Jules will certainly be here in a minute
with his bride.

      2 *Student.* So should the poet's muse have been acceptable,
300   says Bluphocks, and Delia not better known to our dogs than
the boy.

      1 *Student.* To the point, now. Where's Gottlieb? Oh,
listen, Gottlieb—What called down this piece of friendly
vengeance on Jules, of which we now assemble to witness
305   the winding-up. We are all in a tale, observe, when Jules
bursts out on us by and bye: I shall be spokesman, but each
professes himself alike insulted by this strutting stone-

i *292–5. Aesculapius, an epic . . . Cures*: for Aesculapius (the Greek god of
medicine), see *Artemis*. The catalogue of drugs alludes to the catalogue of ships
at the outset of Homer's *Iliad*, and puns on the names or attributes of other Greek
divinities. Hebe was goddess of youth, and cupbearer to the gods: the 'plaister'
(*J.*: 'a glutinous or adhesive salve') is a kiss. Phoebus is Phoebus Apollo, god of
eloquence among other things: the 'emulsion' (liquid medicine) is wine. Mercury
is the Roman name for Hermes, the messenger of the gods; here the play is on
name, not function, since mercury was a treatment for syphilis, or 'the pox'—
this being the suppressed rhyme for 'box'. A bolus is a medicinal substance shaped
for swallowing, larger than an ordinary pill. All these mythological figures appear
in works by Canova.
i *294. throttle*: throat.
i *299–301. So should . . . the boy.*] Good!—Only, so should the poet's muse have
been universally acceptable, says Bluphocks, *et canibus nostris . . .* and Delia not
better known to our literary dogs than the boy—Giovacchino! (*1849–88*, except
'only', *1868–88*, 'the boy Giovacchino!', *1865–88*). Cp. Virgil, *Eclogues* iii 66–7: the
shepherd Menalcas is boasting of the willingness of his lover, the boy Amyntas,
who 'comes to me unsought, so that now Delia [i.e. the moon] is not better
known to my dogs'. The *1849* rev. makes the quotation and its application clearer.
i *302–3. Where's Gottlieb? . . . called down*] Where's Gottlieb, the new-comer? Oh,—
listen, Gottlieb, to what called down (*1849–88*). Gottlieb's name combines the
German words for 'God' and 'love'.
i *305–6. We are all . . . but each*] We are all agreed, all in a tale, observe, when
Jules shall burst out on us in a fury by and bye: I am spokesman—the verses that
are to undeceive Jules bear my name of Lutwyche—but each (*1849–88*, except
'by-and-by:', *1863*, 'by and by:', *1865–88*).
i *307–8. stone-squarer*: one who shapes stone into building-blocks.

squarer, who came singly from Paris to Munich, thence with
a crowd of us to Venice and Possagno here, but proceeds in
310   a day or two alone,—oh! alone, indubitably—to Rome
and Florence. He take up his portion with these dissolute,
brutalized, heartless bunglers! (Is Schramm brutalized? Am
I heartless?)

  Gottlieb. Why, somewhat heartless; for, coxcomb as much
315   as you choose, you will have brushed off—what do folks
style it?—the bloom of his life. Is it too late to alter? These
letters, now, you call his. I can't laugh at them.

  4 *Student.* Because you never read the sham letters of our
inditing which drew forth these.

320   *Gottlieb.* His discovery of the truth will be frightful.

  4 *Student.* That's the joke. But you should have joined us
at the beginning; there's no doubt he loves the girl.

  Gottlieb. See here: "He has been accustomed," he writes,

---

i *308–10. who came . . . indubitably*: cp. T. L. Beddoes, *Pygmalion* 39–45: 'Lonely
Pygmalion: you might see him go / Along the streets where markets thickest
flow / Doubling his gown across his thinking breast / And the men fall aside'.
See also ll. 373–8n. and ii 67–98n.

i *308. singly*] alone (*1865–88*). *Munich, thence*] Munich, and thence (*1849–88*).
Munich is the capital city of Bavaria in southern Germany. There was a
'Glypothek' or gallery of sculpture, 'erected by von Kleuse, for the present King
[Ludwig I], who, while Crown Prince, formed the very interesting and valuable
collection deposited in it' (Murray's *Handbook for Travellers in Southern Germany*
[1837] 31–2). The collection included the Aegina marbles and the 'Tenea
kouros', a figure of Apollo, among the most famous remnants of classical
sculpture. There were also works by Canova, incl. the statue of Psyche mentioned below (l. 357). B. had visited Munich during his 1838 travels.

i *309. Venice and Possagno*: see ll. 276^277n.

i *310. alone,—oh!*] alone again,—oh! (*1849–88*).

i *310–11. Rome and Florence*: neither was on B.'s itinerary in 1838; he first visited
them in 1844.

i *311. He take up*] He, forsooth, take up (*1849–88*).

i *311–13. dissolute, brutalized . . . Am I heartless?*)] dissolute, brutalised, heartless
bunglers!—So he was heard to call us all: now, is Schramm brutalised, I should
like to know? Am I heartless? (*1849–88*, except 'so', *1865–88*, 'brutalized' [both
occurrences], *1863–88*).

i *314–15. for, coxcomb as much as you choose, you*] for, suppose Jules a coxcomb as
much as you choose, still, for this mere coxcombry, you (*1849–88*).

i *314. coxcomb*: 'a fop; a superficial pretender to knowledge or accomplishments' (*J.*).

i *316. the bloom of his life*: the context suggests the sense of 'bloom' given by
J. as 'the blue colour upon plums and grapes newly gathered', esp. taken with
'dew' in l. 335. See ll. 337–8n.

i *316–17. These letters, now*] These love-letters, now (*1849–88*).

i *322. loves the girl.*] loves the girl—loves a model he might hire by the hour!
(*1849–88*).

"to have Canova's women about him, in stone, and the world's
325   women beside him, in flesh, these being as much below,
as those above, his soul's aspiration; but now he is to have"
. . . There you laugh again! You wipe off the very dew of
his youth.

1 *Student.* Schramm (take the pipe out of his mouth,
330   somebody), will Jules lose the bloom of his youth?

Schramm. Nothing worth keeping is ever lost in this
world: look at a blossom—it drops presently and fruits

i *324. Canova's women*: see headnote, pp. 86–7. Canova's sculptures of female
figures (such as the Psyche mentioned below, l. 348) were esp. celebrated.
In 1817 Canova executed a series of busts intended to represent 'ideal female
beauty'.

i *326. he is to have"* . . .] he is to have the real." . . . (*1849*); he is to have the
real." (*1863*); he is to have the reality." (*1865–88*).

i *327. You wipe off*] I say, you wipe off (*1849–88*).

i *330. will Jules lose the bloom of his youth?*: see l. 316n. The 1st student uses the
more traditional trope, where 'bloom' means 'the state of anything improving,
and ripening to a higher perfection' (*J.*). Schramm takes the image in the literal
sense of a blossom.

i *331–42. Nothing worth keeping . . . thus . . .*] Schramm and his opinions may owe
something to Thomas Carlyle, whom B. first met in 1836, and whose work was
a major influence in this period. B. spoke of his liking for Carlyle in a letter to
Fanny Haworth of 16 Dec. 1841 (*Correspondence* v 189), and was impressed both
by his talk (see his letter of 15 May 1843 to Domett, *Correspondence* vii 124) and
by his pipe-smoking—in a letter to EBB. of 28 June 1846 he reports Carlyle
giving an opinion 'between two huge pipe-whiffs' (*ibid.* xiii 90). Schramm's German
nationality may owe something to Carlyle's position as the principal mediator of
German ideas in England at this period. Carlyle certainly advocated the kind of
incessant curiosity about life which Schramm recommends (see, for instance, his
essay 'Boswell's Life of Johnson'). Tennyson's early poem *Nothing Will Die* (1830)
also has affinities with the thought here: 'Nothing will die; / All things will change
/ Through eternity. . . . The world was never made; / It will change but it will
not fade' (14–16, 30–1). Tennyson himself noted of this poem: 'All things are
evolved'. The substance of Schramm's remarks, however, combining a hierarchy
of value with an evolutionary principle, is a commonplace in B. See *Paracelsus* v
627–770 (I 296–304); also *A Forest Thought*, written 1837 (I 342). Note, however, B.'s letter to EBB. (5 May 1846): 'Would it not be perilous in some cases,—
many cases—to contrast the present with the very early Past. The fruit time, even
when there is abundant fruit,—with the dewy springing and blossoming? One
would confess to a regret at the vanishing of that charm, at least, if it were felt
to be somehow vanished out of the present. . . . Now, hear the truth! I never,
God knows, felt the joy of being with you as I felt it YESTERDAY—The fruit
of my happiness has grown under the blossom, lifting it and keeping it as a coronet
—not one feeling is lost, and the new feelings are infinite' (*Correspondence* xii 299).

i *332–3. presently, and fruits succeed; as well affirm*] presently, having done its
service and lasted its time; but fruits succeed, and where would be the blossom's
place could it continue? As well affirm (*1849–88*).

succeed; as well affirm that your eye is no longer in your
body because its earliest favourite is dead and done with,
335   as that any affection is lost to the soul when its first object
is superseded in due course. Has a man done wondering
at women? There follow men, dead and alive, to wonder
at. Has he done wondering at men? There's God to
wonder at: and the faculty of wonder may be at the same
340   time grey enough with respect to its last object, and yet
green sufficiently so far as concerns its novel one:
thus . . .

   1 *Student.* Put Schramm's pipe into his mouth again—There
you see! well, this Jules . . a wretched fribble—oh, I
345   watched his disportings at Possagno the other day! The Model-
Gallery—you know: he marches first resolvedly past great
works by the dozen without vouchsafing an eye: all at once
he stops full at the *Psiche-fanciulla*—cannot pass that old

i *334. favourite is dead*] favourite, whatever it may have first loved to look on, is
dead (*1849–88*).
i *335–6. object . . . man*] object, whatever happened first to satisfy it, is superseded
in due course. Keep but ever looking, whether with the body's eye or the mind's,
and you will soon find something to look on! Has a man (*1849–88*).
i *340. grey*] old and tired (*1849–88*).
i *340. its last object*] its first object (*1849–88*).   *green*] young and fresh (*1849–88*).
i *344. fribble*: a trifling, frivolous person. For the synonym 'fribbler', J. cites *Spectator*
288: 'A fribbler is one who professes rapture for the woman, and dreads her
consent'.
i *345–6. Possagno . . . The Model-Gallery*: the 'Gipsoteca' at Possagno, devoted to
a permanent exhibition of Canova's plaster casts, models, etc. Most of Canova's
'great works' were represented in this form; there were a few marbles and bronzes.
i *345–6. The Model-Gallery*] Canova's gallery (*1849–88*).
i *346. he marches*] there he marches (*1849–88*).
i *348–51. the Psiche-fanciulla . . . at Munich*: 'Psiche-fanciulla' means 'Psyche as a
young girl'—the name of a famous statue by Canova originally executed in 1789
and repeated in 1793; the latter version was in Munich. The 'new place' is not
literal, therefore, but refers to the statue's different versions, the one at Possagno
being a plaster cast (of the head only). Countess Albrizzi gives the following
description of the statue: 'Psyche is here represented by Canova occupied in
holding a butterfly, with the softest touch, between the forefinger and thumb of
her right hand, and placing it gently in the palm of her left: wholly absorbed
in contemplating the beautiful insect, her features wear a smile of tranquil and
celestial sweetness, expressive of the sufficiency of the soul, of which both Psyche
and the butterfly are emblems, to its own proper and entire happiness'. She adds:
'He who long contemplates, however, this beautiful symbol of our immaterial
part, finds a certain cheerless and inquiet feeling arising in his mind, that
sufficiency to its own enjoyment chills the heart, and his mind is led to reflect
on the nature of those unsympathising beings, who having no mutual wants
or pleasures, may enjoy solitary happiness, but never taste that of being dear to
others' (*Works of Canova* i [n.p.]).

acquaintance without a nod of encouragement—"In your
350 new place, beauty? Then behave yourself as well here as at
Munich—I see you!"—Next posts himself deliberately
before the unfinished *Pietà* for half an hour without moving, till up he starts of a sudden and thrusts his very nose
into . . I say into—the group—by which you are informed
355 that precisely the sole point he had not fully mastered in
Canova was a certain method of using the drill in the arti-
culation of the knee-joint—and that, even, has he mastered
at length! Good bye, therefore, to Canova—whose gallery
no longer contains Jules, the predestinated thinker in
360 marble!

      5 *Student.* Tell him about the women—go on to the
women.

      1 *Student.* Why, on that matter he could never be super-
cilious enough. How should we be other than the poor
365 devils you see, with those debasing habits we cherish?
He was not to wallow in that mire, at least: he would love
at the proper time, and meanwhile put up with the *Psiche-
fanciulla.* Now I happened to hear of a young Greek—real
Greek girl at Malamocco, a true Islander, do you see, with

i *351. Next posts*] Next he posts (*1849–88*).

i *352. the unfinished Pietà*: referring to the plaster cast of a 'Pietà' or 'Deposition
from the Cross' (the dead Christ with the Virgin Mary and Mary Magdalen),
made in 1822 but never executed in marble.

i *354. by which you*] by which gesture you (*1849–88*).

i *355–6. mastered in Canova*] mastered in Canova's practice (*1849–88*).

i *357. and that, even*] and that, likewise (*1849–88*).

i *358. therefore, to Canova*] therefore, to poor Canova (*1849–88*).

i *358–9. gallery . . . thinker*] gallery no longer need detain his successor Jules, the
predestinated novel thinker (*1849–88*, except 'needs', *1863–88*).

i *364–8. How should we be other . . . Psiche-fanciulla*: cp. Canova's comment: 'I pity
those young men who think to reconcile a life of amusement with the pursuit of
the arts. Art should be the ruling passion of the sculptor' (*Works of Canova* iii 41).
Cp. also (noting ll. 311–14) T. L. Beddoes, *Pygmalion* 55–63: 'Still, discontent /
Over his sensual kind the sculptor went / Walking his thoughts. Yet Cyprus'
girls be fair . . . and their pleasure / Silent and deep as midnight's starry treasure.
/ Lovely and young, Pygmalion yet loved none. / His soul was bright and lonely
as the sun / Like which he could create'. See also ll. 308–10n. and ii 67–98n.

i *364. other than*] other (he said) than (*1849–88*).

i *366–7. he would love at the proper time*] he would wait, and love only at the proper
time (*1849–88*).

i *369. Malamocco*: a village on the Lido, the littoral strip which lies between the
Lagoon of Venice and the Adriatic. *Ohio* points out that much of the population is of Greek descent. *a true Islander*: the Greek islands are meant—probably
the Cyclades. Venice had been trading with Greece for centuries.

370   Alciphron hair like sea-moss—you know! White and quiet
      as an apparition, and fourteen years old at farthest;
      daughter, so she swears, of that hag Natalia, who helps us
      to models at three *lire* an hour. So first Jules received a scented
      letter—somebody had seen his Tydeus at the Academy, and
375   my picture was nothing to it—bade him persevere—would
      make herself known to him ere long—(Paolina, my little
      friend, transcribes divinely.) Now think of Jules finding
      himself distinguished from the herd of us by such a crea-
      ture! In his very first answer he proposed marrying his
380   monitress; and fancy us over these letters two, three times a
      day to receive and dispatch! I concocted the main of it:
      relations were in the way—secrecy must be observed—

i *370. Alciphron hair like sea-moss—you know*] Alciphron's "hair like sea-moss"
—Schramm knows (*1849–88*). Alciphron was an Athenian sophist and rhetori-
cian of the 2nd century AD, a contemporary of Lucian. He was the author of a
collection of fictitious letters depicting four classes of society: fishermen,
farmers, parasites, and courtesans. These letters were considered models of pure
'Attic' style. The letters concerning courtesans are a source for the scene involving
the 'poor girls' in pt. iii. The phrase 'hair like sea-moss' occurs in a letter from
Glaucippe, a fisherman's daughter, to her mother Charope, and describes a young
man: 'His hair curls more beautifully than sea-moss' (1st Eng. transl. [1791] 146).
i *371. fourteen years old at farthest*: Canova's Psyche is in 'her thirteenth or
fourteenth year' according to the Countess Albrizzi (*Works of Canova* i [n.p.]).
i *372. daughter . . . Natalia*] a daughter of Natalia, so she swears—that hag Natalia
(*1849–88*). *so she swears*: i.e. Natalia swears.
i *373. an hour. So first*] an hour. We selected this girl for the heroine of our jest.
So, first, (*1849–88*, except 'So first,', *1865–88*).
i *374. Tydeus*: in Greek legend, one of the 'Seven against Thebes', wounded by
Menalippus, whom he killed and whose brains he tore out with his teeth before
his own death. His barbarous revenge cost him immortality, which the goddess
Athene had intended to confer on him. No statue of Tydeus by Canova is recorded,
unlike the other mythological figures—see e.g. ll. 295–8n. See also ii 14n.   *the
Academy*: the Accademia, Venice's principal art gallery.
i *375. bade him persevere*] a profound admirer bade him persevere (*1849–88*).
i *376–7. my little friend*] my little friend of the Fenice (*1849–88*); 'the Fenice' [Phoenix]
is a theatre and opera-house in Venice. It had been rebuilt in 1836, two years
before B.'s visit.
i *377. divinely.) Now think*] divinely). And in due time, the mysterious correspondent gave certain hints of her peculiar charms—the pale cheeks, the black hair—
whatever, in short, had struck us in our Malamocco model: we retained her
name, too—Phene, which is by interpretation, sea-eagle. Now, think (*1849–88*,
except 'is, by interpretation,', *1868–88*).
i *380. monitress*: 'one who warns of faults, or informs of duty; one who gives
useful hints' (*J.*).
i *382. relations were in the way*: i.e. the family of the bride would object to the
match.

would he wed her on trust and only speak to her when they
were indissolubly united? St—St!

385   6 *Student.* Both of them! Heaven's love, speak softly!
speak within yourselves!

5 *Student.* Look at the Bridegroom—half his hair in
storm and half in calm—patted down over the left temple,
like a frothy cup one blows on to cool it; and the same old
390   blouse he murders the marble in!

2 *Student.* Not a rich vest like yours, Hannibal Scratchy,
rich that your face may the better set it off.

6 *Student.* And the bride—and the bride—how magnificently pale!

395   *Gottlieb.* She does not also take it for earnest, I hope?

1 *Student.* Oh, Natalia's concern, that is; we settle with
Natalia.

6 *Student.* She does not speak—has evidently let out
no word.

400   *Gottlieb.* How he gazes on her!

1 *Student.* They go in—now, silence!

i *383. would he wed her*] in fine, would he wed her (*1849–88*).
i *384. St—St!*] St—st—Here they come! (*1849–88*).
i *390. blouse he*] blouse that he (*1849–88*).
i *391. Hannibal Scratchy:* i.e. the 16th-century Bolognese painter Annibale
Carracci, to whom '5 Student' (presumably, like Lutwyche, a mediocre painter)
is being ironically compared. Cp. Fielding, *Joseph Andrews* III vi: 'For my own
part, when I have waited behind my lady in a room hung with fine pictures,
while I have been looking at them I have never once thought of their owner,
nor hath any one else, as I have observed; for when it has been asked whose
picture that was, it was never once answered the master's of the house; but
Ammyconni, Paul Varnish, Hannibal Scratchi, or Hogarthi, which I suppose were
the names of the painters'.
i *393–4. And the bride . . . pale!*] And the bride! Yes, sure enough, our Phene!
Should you have known her in her clothes? How magnificently pale! (*1849–88*).
i *399. no word.*] no word. The only thing is, will she equally remember the rest
of her lesson, and repeat correctly all those verses which are to break the secret
to Jules? (*1849–88*).
i *400. gazes on her!*] gazes on her! Pity—pity! (*1849–88*).
i *401. now, silence!*] now, silence! You three,—not nearer the window, mind, than
that pomegranate—just where the little girl, who a few minutes ago passed us
singing, is seated! (*1849–88*, except 'pomegranate:', *1865–88*).

II.—*Noon. Over Orcana. The House of* Jules, *who crosses its threshold with* Phene—*she is silent, on which* Jules *begins*—

Do not die, Phene—I am yours now—you
Are mine now—let fate reach me how she likes
If you'll not die—so never die! Sit here—
My work-room's single seat—I do lean over
5   This length of hair and lustrous front—they turn
Like an entire flower upward—eyes—lips—last
Your chin—no, last your throat turns—'tis their scent
Pulls down my face upon you. Nay, look ever
That one way till I change, grow you—I could
10 Change into you, beloved!
                       Thou by me
And I by thee—this is thy hand in mine—
And side by side we sit—all's true. Thank God!
I have spoken—speak thou!
                    —O, my life to come!
My Tydeus must be carved that's there in clay,
15 And how be carved with you about the chamber?
Where must I place you? When I think that once
This room-full of rough block-work seemed my heaven
Without you! Shall I ever work again—
Get fairly into my old ways again—
20 Bid each conception stand while trait by trait
My hand transfers its lineaments to stone?

ii *Opening s.d. Over Orcana*: overlooking the valley of Orcana from Possagno.
ii *4. I do lean over*] I over-lean (*1849–88*).
ii *5. front*: forehead.
ii *8–10. Nay, look ever . . . beloved*: a Platonic idea (see the *Symposium*), frequently echoed in love poetry: see e.g. Donne, *A Valediction Forbidding Mourning, Love's Infiniteness, The Ecstasy*. Cp. *James Lee* 292–6 (p. 686): 'Strange, if a face, when you thought of me, / Rose like your own face present now, / With eyes as dear in their due degree, / Much such a mouth, and as bright a brow, / Till you saw yourself, while you cried " 'Tis She!" '
ii *9. That*] This (*1849–88*).
ii *10–13. Thou . . . thee . . . thy . . . thou*] You . . . you . . . your . . . you (*1849–88*).
ii *14.* See i 386n. Apparently Jules had exhibited this unfinished work at the Academy; Canova 'thought it very useful to let his designs be seen by the public in their unfinished state' (*Works of Canova* iii 56).
ii *15. And*] Yet (*1849–88*). *chamber*] room (*1865–88*).
ii *17. block-work*: not *OED*. Presumably unfinished work in blocks of stone, drawing on the sense of the verb 'block': 'to sketch out, mark out roughly (work to be finished afterwards)' (*OED* 9).
ii *20–4.* For the artist—model relation in B., cp. *Andrea* (p. 385), *James Lee* viii ('Beside the Drawing-Board' p. 680), and *Beatrice Signorini* (*Asolando*, 1889).

Will they, my fancies, live near you, my truth—
The live truth—passing and repassing me—
Sitting beside me?
                    Now speak!
                                Only, first,
25   Your letters to me—was't not well contrived?
A hiding-place in Psyche's robe—there lie
Next to her skin your letters: which comes foremost?
Good—this that swam down like a first moonbeam
Into my world.
                    Those? Books I told you of.
30   Let your first word to me rejoice them, too,—
This minion of Coluthus, writ in red

ii *22. they, my*] my mere (*1849–88*). *my truth*] their truth (*1865–88*).
ii *25. Your letters to me*—] See, all your letters! (*1849–88*).
ii *26–7.*] Their hiding-place is Psyche's robe; she keeps / Your letters next her
skin: which drops out foremost? (*1849–88*). For Psyche see i 357–60n.; a further
allusion was added in *1849–88* (below, ll. 216^217n.).
ii *28–9. Good . . . my world*: perhaps alluding to the mythological love-affair between
the moon-goddess Artemis and the shepherd Endymion. B. knew Keats's
Endymion, in which the story is told, and Artemis is frequently mentioned in his
work: see e.g. *Artemis Prologuizes* (II 106) and *Pan and Luna* (*Jocoseria*, 1883).
ii *28. Good*—] Ah,— (*1849–88*).
ii *29.*] Into my world!
                    Again those eyes complete
Their melancholy survey, sweet and slow,
Of all my room holds; to return and rest
On me, with pity, yet some wonder too—
As if God bade some spirit plague a world,
And this were the one moment of surprise
And sorrow while she took her station, pausing
O'er what she sees, finds good, and must destroy!
What gaze you at? Those? Books I told you of; (*1849–88*, except in the
fourth line 'too:', *1865–88*).   *Books I told you of:* Canova was 'very solicitous
to instruct and adorn his mind in every respect that could tend to the perfect
education of an artist; he read himself, but more often caused to be read to him,
while at work, the classical Grecian, Roman, and Italian writers' (*Works of Canova*
i xvi).
ii *31. minion of Coluthus*] minion, a Coluthus, (*1849–88*). Cp. the use of 'minion'
to mean a small and delicate person in *Laboratory* 29 (p. 211).
ii *31–2.* 'Coluthus [or Colluthus], a native of Lycopolis in Egypt, in the time of
the Emperor Anastasius, in the beginning of the 6th century, who wrote a poem
on the rape of Helen, in imitation of Homer. The composition remained long
unknown, till it was discovered at Lycopolis [actually at Otranto in Calabria, S.
Italy] in the 15th century, by the learned Cardinal Bessarion [*c.* 1395–1472]'
(*Lemprière*). The Loeb ed. (*Oppian, Colluthus, Tryphiodorus* [1963] 537) lists the
MSS which probably derived from the MS found by Bessarion; they would have

Bistre and azure by Bessarion's scribe—
Read this line . . no, shame—Homer's be the Greek!
My Odyssey in coarse black vivid type
35 With faded yellow blossoms 'twixt page and page;
"He said, and on Antinous directed
A bitter shaft"—then blots a flower the rest!
—Ah, do not mind that—better that will look
When cast in bronze . . an Almaign Kaiser that,
40 Swart-green and gold with truncheon based on hip—
This rather, turn to . . but a check already—
Or you had recognized that here you sit
As I imagined you, Hippolyta

---

been very expensive by B.'s time. B.'s attention may have been drawn to
Colluthus by a number of contemporary eds., incl. one of 1839. Colluthus' poem
is reckoned poor stuff, so there is presumably a deliberate contrast between
the beautiful MS of a bad poem and the popular ed. of a great one (Homer),
mentioned at ll. 33–4. This is B.'s only ref. to Colluthus.

ii *32. Bistre*: a dark-brown pigment made by boiling soot.

ii *33.*] Read this line . . . no, shame—Homer's be the Greek / First breathed me
from the lips of my Greek girl! (*1849–88*, except 3-point ellipsis, *1870–88*).

ii *34. My*] This (*1865–88*).

ii *35.*] With faded yellow blossoms 'twixt page and page, / To mark great places
with due gratitude; (*1849–88*).

ii *36–7.*] the quotation is italicized, *1849–88*. It translates *Odyssey* xxii 8: Odysseus
is beginning the slaughter of Penelope's suitors, foremost of whom was Antinous.
The passage continues: 'Now he [Antinous] was on the point of raising to his
lips a fair goblet, a two-eared cup of gold, and was even now handling it, that
he might drink of the wine, and death was not in his thoughts'.

ii *37. then blots a flower*] a flower blots out (*1849–88*).

ii *37^38.*] Again upon your search? My statues, then! (*1849–88*).

ii *39. Almaign Kaiser*: German emperor. *Ohio* points out that B. could have seen
the monument to the Emperor Maximilian I at Innsbruck on his 1838 travels.
Murray's *Handbook for Travellers in Southern Germany* (1837) describes the 'row of
bronze figures' around the marble sarcophagus, '28 in number, representing some
of "the worthies" of Europe, but principally the most distinguished personages
. . . of the house of Austria . . . they are of colossal size, skilfully executed, and
the elaborate workmanship of the armour and dresses gives them an additional
interest' (p. 214).

ii *40. Swart-green and gold*: dark-green (bronze) with gold-leaf ornament.
truncheon: 'a staff of command' (*J.*).

ii *41–2.*] This, rather, turn to! What, unrecognised? / I thought you would have
seen that here you sit (*1849–88*).

ii *43–4. Hippolyta . . . Numidian horse*: Hippolyta was queen of the Amazons, a
legendary nation of warrior-women. Numidia is the Roman name for the region
of N. Africa roughly equivalent to modern Algeria; B. follows classical authorities
(such as Diodorus Siculus) who place the Amazons in Africa rather than Asia Minor.

Naked upon her bright Numidian horse!
45 —Forget you this then? "carve in bold relief" . . .
So you command me—"carve against I come
A Greek, bay-filleted and thunder-free,
Rising beneath the lifted myrtle-branch,
Whose turn arrives to praise Harmodius."—Praise him!
50 Quite round, a cluster of mere hands and arms
Thrust in all senses, all ways, from all sides,

ii 45.—*Forget*] Recall (*1849–88*). *in bold relief*: see ll. 50–63n.
ii 46. *command me*] commanded (*1849–88*). *against I come*: 'to be ready when I come'.
ii 47–9.] A Greek, in Athens, as our fashion was,
      Feasting, bay-filleted and thunder-free,
      Who rises 'neath the lifted myrtle-branch:
      '*Praise those who slew Hipparchus*,' cry the guests,
      '*While o'er thy head the singer's myrtle waves*
      As erst above our champions': stand up all!'
      See, I have laboured to express your thought! (*1849–88*, except 'myrtle-branch.', *1868–88*, 'champion:', *1865–88*, 'thought.', *1868–88*; in *1868–88* the inset quotation is not in italics). In *B & P BYU* 'Praise him!' in l. 49 is underlined. Harmodius plotted with his friend Aristogiton to kill the Athenian tyrant Hippias, and his younger brother Hipparchus, at the Panathenaea festival in 514 BC. 'The plot miscarried: only Hipparchus was killed . . . After the expulsion of Hippias in 511/10 the deed of Aristogiton and Harmodius received ample recognition, public and private. Bronze statues of them by Antenor were set up . . . Privately, scolia [drinking-songs] were sung claiming them as the men who gave Athens *isonomia* [equal political rights] . . . All this fostered the popular belief that Hipparchus, not Hippias, was the tyrant and that Aristogiton and Harmodius . . . had ended the tyranny; and despite the deliberate refutations of this view by Herodotus and Thucydides, it continued to influence the tradition' (*Oxford Classical Dictionary*, 2nd ed., s.v. Aristogiton). Note the *1849* reading, and see iii 6. B. refers specifically to a famous scolium, almost a national anthem in Athens, which began: 'In a myrtle-branch I will carry my sword, as did Harmodius and Aristogiton, when they slew the tyrant'. The full text is in Athenaeus, *The Deipnosophists* xv 695. B.'s attention may have been drawn to it by a parody in Aristophanes' *Wasps* (1225ff). Plutarch's account of the origin and procedure of scolia is probably B.'s source: 'first the guests would sing the god's song together . . . and next when to each in turn was given the myrtle spray . . . and too the lyre was passed around, the guest who could play the instrument would take it and tune it and sing' (*Moralia: Table-talk* i 1 615). B. adds the detail that the singer is 'bay-filleted', crowned with a wreath of bay-leaves, the bay being sacred to Apollo; he is thus 'thunder-free', since the bay was also traditionally supposed to be immune from lightning. The induction to *Four Plays* (see headnote, pp. 82–3) includes a ref. to the muse's 'thunder-fearless verdant bays'.
ii 50–63. The allusion is to a bas-relief, presumably in marble, a genre in which Canova was renowned, though there is no record of his having undertaken this subject. Indeed the aesthetic is quite alien to Canova's neoclassicism, and closer to the romantic expressionism which Jules, according to his own account, adopts only later (see iv 39–57n.).

Only consenting at the branch's end
They strain towards, serves for frame to a sole face—
(Place your own face)—the Praiser's, who with eyes
55   Sightless, so bend they back to light inside
His brain where visionary forms throng up,
(Gaze—I am your Harmodius dead and gone,)
Sings, minding nor the palpitating arch
Of hands and arms, nor the quick drip of wine
60   From the drenched leaves o'erhead, nor who cast off
Their violet crowns for him to trample on—
Sings, pausing as the patron-ghosts approve,
Devoutly their unconquerable hymn—
But you must say a "well" to that—say "well"
65   Because you gaze—am I fantastic, sweet?
Gaze like my very life's-stuff, marble—marbly
Even to the silence—and before I found

ii *52. consenting*: 'coming together'. B. is drawing on an archaic sense of the verb, 'to agree together'.   *branch's*] emended in agreement with all other eds. from 'branches" in *1841*.

ii *54.*] The Praiser's—in the centre—who with eyes (*1849–88*, except 'Praiser's,', *1863–88*, 'centre:', *1865–88*).

ii *54–6. eyes . . . brain*: the contrast between eyesight and insight is traditional; B. may also be thinking of the 'blind' appearance of 'marbled' eyes in statues. Cp. *Aristophanes' Apology* (*1875*) 5264, where the statue of the blinded bard Thamyris is described as 'Mute marble, blind the eyes and quenched the brain'. Cp. also B.'s definition of the 'subjective poet', in *Shelley*: 'Not what man sees, but what God sees—the *Ideas* of Plato, seeds of creation lying burningly on the Divine Hand—it is toward these that he struggles' (ll. 89–91, p. 858).

ii *57.*] not *1849–88*.

ii *58. nor the*] not that (*1849–88*).

ii *60. the drenched leaves o'erhead*: the leaves of the 'lifted myrtle-branch' (l. 48).

ii *60–1. who cast off / Their violet crowns for him*] crowns cast off, / Violet and parsley crowns (*1849–88*). The violet was a favourite flower in Athens; the city itself was called 'violet-crowned'. Such wreaths (of various flowers: note the *1849* rev.) were worn at ceremonies and festivals.

ii *62. patron-ghosts*: the presiding spirits of Harmodius and Aristogiton.

ii *65. fantastic*: 'fanciful', 'capricious' (*OED*); 'indulgent to one's own imagination' (*J.*).

ii *66. like . . . marble*: cp. *Sordello* i 413–15 (I 422): 'just-tinged marble like Eve's lilied flesh / Beneath her Maker's finger when the fresh / First pulse of life shot brightening the snow'.   *marbly*: cp. *Tomb at St. Praxed's* 75 (p. 241): 'mistresses with great smooth marbly limbs'. See also ll. 93–4n. below.

ii *67. silence—and*] silence! why (*1849*); silence! why, (*1863–88*).

ii *67–98. before I found . . . its track*: this complex passage blends Neo-Platonism with alchemical speculations which recall those of Paracelsus. In ll. 67–79 Jules combines the Neo-Platonic claim that art can forge a 'better nature', a 'golden world' superior to the 'brazen world' of actuality, with the Paracelsian (and

     The real flesh Phene, I inured myself
     To see throughout all nature varied stuff
70   For better nature's birth by means of art:
     With me, each substance tended to one form
     Of beauty—to the human Archetype—
     And every side occurred suggestive germs
     Of that—the tree, the flower—why, take the fruit,
75   Some rosy shape, continuing the peach,
     Curved beewise o'er its bough, as rosy limbs
     Depending nestled in the leaves—and just
     From a cleft rose-peach the whole Dryad sprung!
     But of the stuffs one can be master of,

Kabbalistic) claim that man (the 'Adam Kadmon' of the Kabbala) was God's final creation, and a distillate of all other natural forms. Jules imagines himself as, in effect, in the process of creating man from the inferior matter of nature, re-enacting the divine creative sequence in his art. This passage concerns the *subject-matter* of his art; in ll. 80–98 Jules considers its *materials*, assigning to marble a similar status to that of man in the first passage. Marble resembles the alchemists' 'prima materia', the primordial substance out of which all material forms then emerge. As God created first nature, then man, out of the universal 'prima materia', so Jules creates first 'baser substance' (air, diamond, metal), then human flesh, out of marble. *James Lee* viii ('Beside the Drawing-Board') has many parallels (p. 680); see also *A Death* 609–22 (p. 754) and *Fifine at the Fair* (1872) 756–870. The concept that marble *contains*, in an ideal sense, the form which the sculptor carves derives from Michelangelo's famous statements to that effect, as in his sonnet *Non ha l'ottimo artista alcun concetto*: 'The best of artists hath no thought to show / Which the rough stone in its superfluous shell / Doth not include: to break the marble spell / Is all the hand that serves the brain can do' (transl. J. A. Symons, *The Sonnets of Michael Angelo Buonarrotti* [1904] 17). Cp. also T. L. Beddoes, *Pygmalion* 111–27: 'The magic chisel thrust and gashed and swept / Flying and manifold . . . And as insensibly out of a stick / Dead in the winter-time, the dew-drops quick / And the thin sun-beams and the airy shower / Raise and unwrap a many-leaved flower / And then a fruit . . . he, quiet as the air, / Had shaped a lady wonderfully fair. / Dear to the eyes—a delicate delight / For all her marble symmetry was white / As brow and bosom should be; save some azure / Which waited for a loving lip's erasure / Upon her shoulders to be turned to blush'. See also i 308–10n, 364–8n.

ii *71–2*. Cp. *Paracelsus* v 666–75 (I 298–300).

ii *73. And*] On (*1849–88*).

ii *74. why, take*] or take (*1849–88*).

ii *75–8*. The shape of a peach and the way it hangs on its tree suggest to Jules a 'rosy shape' with 'rosy limbs', which he then identifies with the 'Dryad' (wood-nymph) of classical mythology. Dryads were typical subjects of neo-classical sculpture.

80 How I divined their capabilities
    From the soft-rinded smoothening facile chalk
    That yields your outline to the air's embrace,
    Down to the crisp imperious steel, so sure
    To cut its one confided thought clean out
85 Of all the world: but marble!—'neath my tools
    More pliable than jelly—as it were
    Some clear primordial creature dug from deep
    In the Earth's heart where itself breeds itself
    And whence all baser substance may be worked;
90 Refine it off to air you may—condense it
    Down to the diamond;—is not metal there
    When o'er the sudden specks my chisel trips?
    —Not flesh—as flake off flake I scale, approach,
    Lay bare those blueish veins of blood asleep?
95 Lurks flame in no strange windings where, surprised
    By the swift implement sent home at once,
    Flushes and glowings radiate and hover
    About its track?—
                    Phene? what—why is this?
    Ah, you will die—I knew that you would die!

        Phene *begins, on his having long remained silent.*

ii *80–5.* The chalk is used to sketch the subject, the steel to cut it out from the marble.
ii *81. facile:* easy to use. But B. may also have in mind J.'s sense of 'easily persuaded', since the chalk 'yields' to the persuasion of the air in l. 82.
ii *82. your outline:* 'the outline you [the sculptor] have conceived'.
ii *82^83.*] Half-softened by a halo's pearly gloom; (*1849–88*).
ii *84. its one confided thought:* 'the one thought confided to it'.
ii *85–8.* Cp. *Gerard de Lairesse* (*Parleyings*, 1887) 246–50: 'Why did the chamois stand so fair a mark / Arrested by the novel shape he dreamed / Was bred of liquid marble in the dark / Depths of the mountain's womb that ever teemed / With novel births of wonder?'
ii *87. deep*] depths (*1849–88*).
ii *92. specks*] speck (*1865–88*).
ii *93–4.* The Countess of Clanwilliam (see headnote, p. 86) records Canova's comment on his famous statue of Pauline Borghese as Venus (Villa Borghese, Rome): 'Ce n'est pas du marbre, mais de la chair [It is not marble, but flesh]' (*Journal* ii 295). Note that Canova speaks in French.
ii *94.* Cp. *Tomb at St. Praxed's* 44 (p. 240): 'Blue as a vein o'er the Madonna's breast', and *The Statue and the Bust* 183 (III 355): 'the blood that blues the inside arm'.
ii *98^99.*] That whitening cheek, those still-dilating eyes! (*1849–88*, except 'still dilating', *1888*).

100   Now the end's coming—to be sure it must
       Have ended sometime!—Tush—I will not speak
       Their foolish speech—I cannot bring to mind
       Half—so the whole were best unsaid—what care
       I for Natalia now, or all of them?
105   Oh, you . . what are you?—I do not attempt
       To say the words Natalia bade me learn
       To please your friends, that I may keep myself
       Where your voice lifted me—by letting you
       Proceed . . but can you?—even you perhaps
110   Cannot take up, now you have once let fall,
       The music's life, and me along with it?
       No—or you would . . we'll stay then as we are
       Above the world—
                              Now you sink—for your eyes
            Are altered . . altering—stay—"I love you, love you,"—
115   I could prevent it if I understood

ii *101–2. I will not speak / Their foolish speech*—] why need I speak / Their foolish speech? (*1849–88*).

ii *103–4.*] One half of it, besides; and do not care / For old Natalia now, nor any of them. (*1849–88*, except 'beside', *1865–88*).

ii *105. I do not attempt*] if I do not try (*1849–88*). The alteration in the clause is completed in l. 107.

ii *106. bade*] made (*1849–88*).

ii *107. that I may*] it is to (*1849–88*).

ii *108 your voice*: see ll. 116–17n. *you*] it (*1849–63*); that (*1865–88*).

ii *109. can you*] can it (*1849–88*).

ii *111. it?*] that— (*1849–88*).

ii *113.*] —Above the world.
                    You creature with the eyes!
            If I could look for ever up to them,
            As now you let me,—I believe, all sin,
            All memory of wrong done or suffering borne,
[5]   Would drop down, low and lower, to the earth
            Whence all that's low comes, and there touch and stay
            —Never to overtake the rest of me,
            All that, unspotted, reaches up to you,
            Drawn by those eyes! What rises is myself,
[10]   Not so the shame and suffering; but they sink,
            Are left, I rise above them—Keep me so
            Above the world!
                              But you sink, for your eyes (*1849–88*, except
l. [1] 'Above' *1863–88*; l. [4] 'done, suffering' and l. [10] 'Nor me', *1865–88*;
l. [11] 'them. Keep me so,', *1863–88*).

ii *114. altered . . altering*] altering—altered! (*1849–88*). *love you,"*—] love you"
. . . (*1849–65*); love" . . . (*1868–88*).

ii *115–16. understood / More*] understood: / More (*1863–1888*).

More of your words to me . . was't in the tone
Of the voice, your power?

Stay, stay, I will repeat
Their speech, if that affects you! only change
No more and I shall find it presently—
120 Far back here in the brain yourself filled up:
Natalia said (like Lutwyche) harm would follow
Unless I spoke their lesson to the end,
But harm to me, I thought, not you: and so
I'll speak it,—"Do not die, Phene, I am yours" . .

ii *116–17. the tone / Of the voice*] the tone / Or the words (*1849–88*). The Countess
of Clanwilliam wrote of Canova: 'the tone of his voice was particularly agreeable, and I think it would have been soothing in affliction' (*Journal* ii 296–7).
ii *117. Stay, stay,*] Or stay— (*1849–88*).
ii *118. affects*] contents (*1849–88*).
ii *121.*] Natalia threatened me that harm would follow (*1849–88*, except 'should',
1865–88).   *Lutwyche*: the first mention of the 1st Student's name in *1841*; even
here there is no certain indication (until l. 180) that the two are the same.
B. removed this obscurity in *1849*; see i 305–6n.
ii *123.*] But harm to me, I thought she meant, not you.
　　　　Your friends,—Natalia said they were your friends
　　　　And meant you well,—because, I doubted it,
　　　　Observing (what was very strange to see)
[5]　　　On every face, so different in all else,
　　　　The same smile girls like us are used to bear,
　　　　But never men, men cannot stoop so low;
　　　　Yet your friends, speaking of you, used that smile,
　　　　That hateful smirk of boundless self-conceit
[10]　　Which seems to take possession of this world,
　　　　And make of God their tame confederate,
　　　　Purveyor to their appetites . . you know!
　　　　But no—Natalia said they were your friends,
　　　　And they assented while they smiled the more,
[15]　　And all came round me,—that thin Englishman
　　　　With light, lank hair seemed leader of the rest;
　　　　He held a paper—"What we want," said he,
　　　　Ending some explanation to his friends—
　　　　"Is something slow, involved and mystical,
[20]　　"To hold Jules long in doubt, yet take his taste
　　　　"And lure him on, so that, at innermost,
　　　　"Where he seeks sweetness' soul, he may find—this!
　　　　"—As in the apple's core, the noisome fly:
　　　　"For insects on the rind are seen at once,
[25]　　"And brushed aside as soon, but this is found
　　　　"Only when on the lips or loathing tongue."
　　　　And so he read what I have got by heart— (*1849–88*, except l. [6] 'like me',
l. [10] 'the world', l. [11] 'a tame', *1865–88*; l. [13] 'But no:', *1865*; l. [14] 'assented
though', *1868–88*; l. [16] 'light lank', l. [21] 'on until,', l. [27] 'by heart:', *1865–88*.
ii *124. Phene*] love (*1849–88*).

125   Stop—is not that, or like that, part of what
       You spoke? 'Tis not my fault—that I should lose
       What cost such pains acquiring! is this right?
           The Bard said, do one thing I can—
           Love a man and hate a man

ii *125. Stop*—] No— (*1865–88*).
ii *126–7.*] Yourself began by speaking? Strange to lose / What cost much pains
to learn! Is this more right? (*1849–88, except 'such pains', 1863–88*).
ii *128. The Bard*: Lutwyche, the composer of the verses.
ii *128–79.*]   *I am a painter who cannot paint;*
                  In my life, a devil rather than saint,
                  In my brain, as poor a creature too—
                  No end to all I cannot do!
[5]   *Yet do one thing at least I can—*
                  Love a man, or hate a man
                  Supremely: thus my lore began.
                  Through the Valley of Love I went,
                  In its lovingest spot to abide,
[10]   *And just on the verge where I pitched my tent,*
                  I found Hate dwelling beside.
                  (Let the Bridegroom ask what the painter meant,
                  Of his Bride, of the peerless Bride!)
                  And further, I traversed Hate's grove,
[15]   *In its hatefullest nook to dwell;*
                  But lo, where I flung myself prone, couched Love
                  Where the deepest shadow fell.
                  (The meaning—those black bride's-eyes above,
                  Not the painter's lip should tell!)
[20]   And here," said he, "Jules probably will ask,
                  "You have black eyes, love,—you are, sure enough,
                  "My peerless bride,—so do you tell, indeed,
                  "What needs some explanation—what means this?"
                  —And I am to go on, without a word—
[25]   *So I grew wiser in Love and Hate,*
                  From simple, that I was of late.
                  For once, when I loved, I would enlace
                  Breast, eyelids, hands, feet, form and face
                  Of her I loved, in one embrace—
[30]   *As if by mere love I could love immensely!*
                  And when I hated, I would plunge
                  My sword, and wipe with the first lunge
                  My foe's whole life out, like a sponge—
                  As if by mere hate I could hate intensely!
[35]   *But now I am wiser, know better the fashion*
                  How passion seeks aid from its opposite passion,
                  And if I see cause to love more, or hate more
                  Than ever man loved, ever hated, before—
                  And seek in the Valley of Love,
[40]   *The spot, or the spot in Hate's Grove,*

130   Supremely: thus my lore began.
         Thro' the Valley of Love I went,
         In its lovingest spot to abide;
         And just on the verge where I pitched my tent
         Dwelt Hate beside—
135   (And the bridegroom asked what the bard's smile meant
         Of his bride.)
         Next Hate I traversed, the Grove,
         In its hatefullest nook to dwell—
         And lo, where I flung myself prone,
             couched Love
140   Next cell.
         (For not I, said the bard, but those black bride's eyes above
         Should tell!)

_____

                Where my soul may the sureliest reach
                The essence, nought less, of each,
                The Hate of all Hates, or the Love
                Of all Loves, in its Valley or Grove,—
[45]   I find them the very warders
                Each of the other's borders.
                I love most, when Love is disguised
                In Hate; and when Hate is surprized
                In Love, then I hate most: ask
[50]   How Love smiles through Hate's iron casque,
                Hate grins through Love's rose-braided mask,—
                And how, having hated thee,
                I sought long and painfully
                To wound thee, and not prick
[55]   The skin, but pierce to the quick—
                Ask this, my Jules, and be answered straight
                By thy bride—how the painter Lutwyche can hate! (1849–88, except
l. [2] 'saint;', 1888; l. [3] 'too:', l. [6] 'man or', 1863–88; l. [9] 'the lovingest', l. [15]
'the hatefullest', l. [17] 'Where the shadow threefold fell.', l. [19] 'a painter's',
1865–88; l. [21] 'Love', 1868–88; l. [22] 'so, do you', 1863; 'then do you', 1865–88;
l. [23] 'explanation!', 1868–88; l. [25] 'wise', 1865–88; l. [26] 'simple that',
1868–88; l. [27] 'Once, when', l. [31] 'Once, when', 1870–88; l. [33] 'out like',
1865–88; 'spunge—', 1863–65; l. [36] 'passion:', l. [37] 'love more, hate more',
l. [38] 'hated', l. [40] 'The nest, or the nook in Hate's Grove,', l. [41] 'may surely
reach', l. [43] 'Hates, the Love', l. [44] 'the Valley', l. [47] 'When I love most,
Love is disguised', 1865–88; l. [48] 'surprised', 1863–88; l. [54] 'To reach thy heart,
nor prick', l. [55] 'skin but', 1865–88. In 1868–88 single quotation marks replaced
italics in ll. [21–3]. Cp. B. to EBB. on 'the law by which opposite ideas suggest
opposite, and contrary images come together' (27 Jan. 1845, Correspondence x 44),
repeated in a letter of 3 Sept. 1882 to Mrs Fitzgerald (Learned Lady 152); and cp. Aristophanes' Apology (1875) 2498–501: 'Love smiles "rogue" and "wretch" / When "sweet"
and "dear" seem vapid; Hate adopts / Love's "sweet" and "dear", when "rogue"
and "wretch" fall flat; / Love, Hate—are truths, then, each, in sense not sound'.
ii 137. Next Hate] Next of Hate (B & P BYU).

(Then Lutwyche said you probably would ask,
"You have black eyes, love,—you are sure enough
145   My beautiful bride—do you, as he sings, tell
What needs some exposition—what is this?"
    . . . And I am to go on, without a word,)
            Once when I loved I would enlace
            Breast, eyelids, hands, feet, form and face
150   Of her I loved in one embrace—
            And, when I hated, I would plunge
            My sword, and wipe with the first lunge
            My foe's whole life out like a spunge:
            —But if I would love and hate more
155   Than ever man hated or loved before—
            Would seek in the valley of Love
            The spot, or in Hatred's grove
            The spot where my soul may reach
            The essence, nought less, of each . . .
160   (Here he said, if you interrupted me
With, "There must be some error,—who induced you
To speak this jargon?"—I was to reply
Simply—"Await till . . . until . ." I must say
Last rhyme again—)
165   . . The essence, nought less, of each—
            The Hate of all Hates, or the Love
            Of all Loves in its glen or its grove,
            —I find them the very warders
            Each of the other's borders.
170   So most I love when Love's disguised
            In Hate's garb—'tis when Hate's surprised
            In Love's weed that I hate most; ask
            How Love can smile thro' Hate's barred iron casque,
            Hate grin thro' Love's rose-braided mask,
175   Of thy bride, Giulio!
                              (Then you, "Oh, not mine—

ii *148–50*. Cp. *Love Among the Ruins* 67–72 (p. 538), and *Now* (*Asolando*, 1889)
7–8: 'a moment which gives me at last / You around me for once, you beneath
me, above me'.
ii *151–3*. Cp. *Ring* v 1662–4: 'Then was I rapt away by the impulse, one /
Immeasurable everlasting wave of a need / To abolish that detested life'.
ii *172. weed*: dress; *J*. records as archaic except in the phrase 'widow's weeds'.
ii *173. casque*: 'a helmet; armour for the head: a poetical word' (*J*., citing *Richard
II* I iii 81–2: 'the casque / Of thy adverse pernicious enemy').
ii *175. Giulio*: for the association with 'Julio Romano' in *The Winter's Tale* see
headnote, p. 88; note that the line was deleted in *1849*.

Preserve the real name of the foolish song!"
But I must answer, "Giulio—Jules—'tis Jules!")
    Thus I, Jules, hating thee
    Sought long and painfully . . .

              Jules *interposes.*

180   Lutwyche—who else? But all of them, no doubt,
      Hated me—them at Venice—presently
      For them, however! You I shall not meet—
      If I dreamed, saying that would wake me. Keep
      What's here—this too—we cannot meet again
185   Consider—and the money was but meant
      For two years' travel, which is over now,
      All chance, or hope, or care, or need of it!
      This—and what comes from selling these—my casts
      And books, and medals except . . . let them go
190   Together—so the produce keeps you safe
      Out of Natalia's clutches! If by chance
      (For all's chance here) I should survive the gang
      At Venice, root out all fifteen of them,
      We might meet somewhere since the world is wide.

                 I.
195   [*Without*] Give her but a least excuse to love me!
         When—where—

ii *177. Jules!"*] we supply quotation-marks lacking in *1841.*
ii *181. them*] they (*1849–88*).
ii *182. For them*] Their turn (*1849–88*).
ii *183. that*] this (*1849–88*).
ii *184. this too*] this gold (*1849–63*); the gold (*1865–88*).
ii *186. now,*] emended in agreement with all other eds. from 'now' in *1841.*
ii *195–210.* For publication details, see headnote, p. 81. The opening and closing
s.d.'s are altered in *1849–88*, as with Pippa's first song, i *215–22.* Pippa's second
song is based on a topic common in B., the love of a man for a woman who is
above him in rank (e.g., as here, a subject's love of his queen). B.'s recent work on
Sordello would have informed him that many of the troubadours (e.g. Vidal, Folco
of Marseilles) were humbly born; he may have known of Bernard de Ventadour,
the son of a scullion, who became the troubadour and lover of Agnes of
Montluçon. Cp. *Rudel* (I 770) and *Cristina* (I 774), first publ. with the collective
title *Queen-Worship*; also *Colombe's Birthday* (1844) and *In a Balcony* (III 401). The
idea that misfortune might give the lover his yearned-for opportunity to serve
his mistress figures in *Count Gismond* (II 161), *Glove* (II 360) and *Daniel Bartoli*
(*Parleyings*, 1887). *Collections* records two examples of B. inscribing this song as
an autograph (E369, E370, p. 429). The scene is the subject of an early painting
by D. G. Rossetti, called *Hist, said Kate the queen.*

How—can this arm establish her above me
If fortune fixed my lady there—
—There already, to eternally reprove me?
200   (*Hist, said Kate the queen:*
      —*Only a page who carols unseen*
      Crumbling your hounds their messes!)

2.

She's wronged?—To the rescue of her honor,
My heart!
205   She's poor?—What costs it to be styled a donor?
An earth's to cleave, a sea's to part!
—But that fortune should have thrust all this upon her!
(*Nay, list, bade Kate the queen:*
Only a page that carols unseen,
210   *Fitting your hawks their jesses!*)—

                    [Pippa *passes.*
      Kate? Queen Cornaro doubtless, who renounced

ii *198. fixed my*] fixed her as my (*1849–88*).
ii *200. (Hist,*] ("Hist"—(*1849–65*); ("Hist!"—(*1868–88*). *Kate the queen:* Catherine Cornaro (*1454–1510*), a Venetian noblewoman who became queen of Cyprus on the death of her husband James de Lusignan in 1473, but was deposed by the Venetian republic in 1489. Her compensation was rule over the town of Asolo during her lifetime, and she there created a celebrated court, noteworthy for the presence of Cardinal Bembo, (see headnote to *Tomb at St. Praxed's*, p. 235, and B.'s preface to *Asolando*, 1889). The *1849* revs. give more detail. Mrs Bronson recalls B. saying: 'People always speak of Caterina with compassion because she lost Cyprus; but surely this is a better place, far more beautiful than the distant island, where she was a stranger. I am sure the happiest years of her life were those when she was queen of Asolo' (*Bronson[1]* 922).
ii *201–2.*] But "Oh—" cried the maiden, binding her tresses,
      "'Tis only a page that carols unseen
      "Crumbling your hounds their messes!" (*1849–88,* except ' "Oh"—'.
1863–75, ' "Oh," ', *1872,* ' "Oh!"—', *1888,* 'unseen,', *1868–88.*
ii *203. She's wronged*] Is she wronged (*1849–88*).
ii *205. She's poor*] Is she poor (*1849–88*). *be styled*] become (*1872, 1884*).
ii *206. An*] Merely an (*1849–88*). *earth's . . . sea's*] earth . . . sea (*1865–88*).
ii *208. (Nay, list,*] ("Nay, list,"— (*1849–65*); ("Nay list,"— (*1865[2]*); ("Nay, list!"— (*1868–88*).
ii *209–10.*] And still cried the maiden, binding her tresses,
      "'Tis only a page that carols unseen
      "Fitting your hawks their jesses!") (*1849–88,* except 'unseen,', *1868–88*).
ii *211–13.*]   JULES *resumes.*
      What name was that the little girl sang forth?
      Kate? The Cornaro, doubtless, who renounced
      The crown of Cyprus to be lady here
      At Asolo, where still the peasants keep
[5]   Her memory; and songs tell how many a page

Cyprus to live and die the lady here
At Asolo—and whosoever loves
Must be in some sort god or worshipper,
215   The blessing, or the blest one, queen or page—
I find myself queen here it seems!
                              How strange!
Shall to produce form out of shapelessness
Be art—and, further, to evoke a soul
From form be nothing? This new soul is mine—
220   Now to kill Lutwyche what would that do?—Save
A wretched dauber men will hoot to death
Without me.
                To Ancona—Greece—some isle!

Pined for the grace of one so far above
His power of doing good to, as a queen—
"She never could be wronged, be poor," he sighed,
"For him to help her!"
                              Yes, a bitter thing
[10]   To see our lady above all need of us;
Yet so we look ere we will love; not I,
But the world looks so. If whoever loves (*1849–88*, except ll. [4–5]
'At Asolo, where still her memory stays, / And peasants sing how once a certain
page', *1865–88*; l. [6] 'her so far', *1868–88*; l. [7] 'good to. "She, the queen', *1865*;
'good to. "Kate the Queen', *1868–88*; l. [9] 'Need him', *1865–88*).
ii *215^216*.] Why should we always choose the page's part? / Here is a woman
with utter need of me,— (*1849–88*).
ii *216^217*.] Look at the woman here with the new soul,
Like my own Psyche's,—fresh upon her lips
Alit, the visionary butterfly,
Waiting my word to enter and make bright,
Or flutter off and leave all blank as first.
This body had no soul before, but slept
Or stirred, was beauteous or ungainly, free
From taint or foul with stain, as outward things
Fastened their image on its passiveness:
Now, it will wake, feel, live—or die again! (*1849–88*, except 'Psyche'
for 'Psyche's', *1868–88*).
ii *217. shapelessness*] unshaped stuff (*1849–88*).
ii *218. art*] Art (*1863–88*).
ii *219^220*.] *1849–88* have a space between these lines.
ii *222.*] Without me, from their laughter!—Oh, to hear
God's voice plain as I heard it first, before
They broke in with that laughter! I heard them
Henceforth, not God!
                              To Ancona—Greece—some isle! (*1849–88*, except
'laughter! Oh,', *1863–1865*, 'hooting. Oh,', *1868–88*, 'with their', *1868–88*, 'God.', *1863–88*).
ii *222. Ancona*: a port with 'the best harbour on the Italian shores of the Adriatic'
(*Murray*), and thus a suitable gateway to Greece.

I wanted silence only—there is clay
Every where. One may do whate'er one likes
225   In Art—the only thing is, to be sure
That one does like it—which takes pains to know.
      Scatter all this, my Phene—this mad dream!
Who—what is Lutwyche—what Natalia—
What the whole world except our love—my own
230   Own Phene? But I told you, did I not,
Ere night we travel for your land—some isle
With the sea's silence on it? Stand aside—
I do but break these paltry models up
To begin art afresh. Shall I meet Lutwyche,
235   And save him from my statue's meeting him?
Some unsuspected isle in the far seas!
Like a god going thro' his world I trace
One mountain for a moment in the dusk,
Whole brotherhoods of cedars on its brow—
240   And you are ever by me while I trace
—Are in my arms as now—as now—as now!
Some unsuspected isle in the far seas!
Some unsuspected isle in far off seas!

---

ii *225. be*] make (*1849–88*).
ii *228 Natalia*] Natalia's friends (*1849–88*).
ii *234–5.* On hearing an adverse criticism, Canova dissuaded his friends from replying, 'saying, that it was for him to answer it, but only with his chisel' (*Works of Canova* i xix).
ii *234.*] To begin Art afresh. Meet Lutwyche, I— (*1865–88.   meet:* for a duel.
ii *235 statue's*] statue (*1865–88*).
ii *237. I trace*] there stands (*1849–88*). The rev., together with that in l. 240, suggests that Jules glimpses a holy mountain rather than, as *1841* allows, being himself the 'god'. Cp. *Return of the Druses* (1842), where 'The Cedars' (III 164) and 'the Mountain' (V 393) represent Lebanon: Mt Hermon, holy to the Druses, is conflated in the Bible with Mt Zion, the sacred mountain of Israel. Note (in either reading) the importance of mountains in Romantic definitions of the sublime, e.g. Wordsworth's *Simplon Pass*, Coleridge's *Hymn before Sunrise*, Shelley's *Mont Blanc*.
ii *240. trace*] gaze (*1849–88*).

*Talk by the way in the mean time. Two or three of
the Austrian Police loitering with* Bluphocks,
an English vagabond, just in view of the Turret.

Bluphocks.* *Oh! were but every worm a maggot, Every fly a grig,*
245   *Every bough a christmas faggot, Every tune a jig!* In fact, I
have abjured all religions,—but the last I inclined to was
the Armenian—for I have travelled, do you see, and at
Koenigsberg, Prussia Improper (so styled because there's a
sort of bleak hungry sun there,) you might remark over a
250   venerable house-porch, a certain Chaldee inscription; and
brief as it is, a mere glance at it used absolutely to change

* "He maketh his sun to rise on the evil and on the good, and sendeth rain on
the just and on the unjust".

ii *243^244. [s.d.] way in the mean time*] way, while PIPPA is passing from Orcana
to the Turret (*1849–88*). *Austrian Police*: the Austrian authorities in the time of
Francis I and his chief minister Metternich (see headnote, p. 83, ii 280n., iii 14n.)
maintained an extensive and close surveillance of political opponents. There were
secret as well as civil police; those here appear to be a conflation, since they are
engaged in undercover work but are also the official authority issuing travel visas,
etc. (see ll. 310–12n.). *Bluphocks*: 'the name means *Blue-Fox*, and is a skit on
the *Edinburgh Review*, which is bound in a cover of blue and fox' (*Cyclopedia*).
The source is Furnivall, who may have got this explanation from B. himself; the
Edinburgh was notorious for its ferocious reviews of poetry.
ii *244.*] *Bluphocks.** So, that is your Pippa, the little girl who passed us singing?
Well, your Bishop's Intendant's money shall be honestly earned:—now, don't
make me that sour face because I bring the Bishop's name into the business—
we know he can have nothing to do with such horrors—we know that he is a
saint and all that a Bishop should be, who is a great man besides. *Oh! were
but every* [etc.] (*1849–88*, except: 'business; we', 'horrors: we', lower case for
the second 'Bishop', and 'beside.' for 'besides.', *1865–88*; 'Oh were' *1868–88*).
B.'s footnote comes from Christ's sermon on the mount, *Matthew* v 43–5: 'Ye
have heard that it hath been said, Thou shalt love thy neighbour, and hate
thine enemy. But I say unto you, Love your enemies, bless them that curse you,
do good to them that hate you, and pray for them which despitefully use
you, and persecute you; that ye may be the children of your Father which is in
heaven: for he maketh [etc.]'.
ii *244. grig*: a grasshopper or cricket (*OED* 4; note sense 5: 'a merry grig: an
extravagantly lively person, one who is full of frolic and jest').
ii *245–65. In fact . . . Stolen goods*: Bluphocks here tells a standard kind of
anti-Semitic joke, using 'Armenian', 'Chaldee', and 'Syriac' as code-words for
'Jewish' or 'Hebrew'. Königsberg (l. 249) was the capital of Prussia *Proper*, the
original territory before the expansion of Prussia in 1710; 'Improper' is presumably a joke, perhaps referring to the meagreness of its sunlight or, conversely, to
the impropriety of its having any sun at all. B. had been in this region during his
trip to Russia in 1834.

the mood of every bearded passenger. In they turned, one
and all, the young and lightsome, with no irreverent pause,
the aged and decrepit, with a sensible alacrity,—'twas the
255   Grand Rabbi's abode, in short. I lost no time in learning
Syriac—(vowels, you dogs, follow my stick's end in the mud—
Celarent, Darii, Ferio!) and one morning presented myself
spelling-book in hand, a, b, c,—what was the purport of
this miraculous posy? Some cherished legend of the past,
260   you'll say—*"How Moses hocus-pocust Egypt's land with fly and
locust,"*—or, *"How to Jonah sounded harshish. Get thee up and
go to Tarshish,"*—or, *"How the angel meeting Balaam, Straight
his ass returned a salaam,"*—in no wise! *"Shackabrach—
Boach—somebody or other—Isaach, Re-cei-ver, Pur-cha-ser and*
265   *Ex-chan-ger of—Stolen goods."* So talk to me of obliging
a bishop! I have renounced all bishops save Bishop
Beveridge—mean to live so—and die—*As some Greek dog-*

---

ii *255. I lost*] Struck with curiosity, I lost (*1849–88*). (*vowels*] (these are vowels
(*1849–88*).

ii *257. Celarent, Darii, Ferio*: alluding to the scholastic names (devised as mnemon-
ics) of classical syllogisms. Jacob Korg ('A Reading of *Pippa Passes*', *VP* vi [1968]
5–19) points out that Bluphocks omits the first of the series, 'Barbara'; they have
nothing to do with vowels. There may be an ironic echo of Christ's writing in
the dust (*John* viii 3–8).

ii *258. c,—what*] c,—I picked it out letter by letter, and what (*1849–88*).

ii *259. posy*: inscription.

ii *260–3. How Moses . . . salaam*: Bluphocks refers first to two of the ten plagues
called down on Egypt by Moses (*Exodus* viii 20–32, x 1–19); second, to *Jonah* i
1–3 (but he inverts the story: God commanded Jonah to prophesy to the city of
Nineveh, Tarshish being the city to which Jonah fled); third, to the story of Balaam's
ass, who three times saved her master's life by avoiding the angel who stood in
their path to destroy him: 'And when the ass saw the angel of the Lord, she fell
down under Balaam' (*Numbers* xxii 27). B. himself was fond of such grotesque
rhymes, which he would often compose impromptu in reply to a challenge (see
Penguin ii 970–1).

ii *265–6. obliging a bishop*] the religion of a bishop (*1849–88*).

ii *266–7. Bishop Beveridge*: William Beveridge (1637–1708), scholar and divine,
became Bishop of St Asaph's in 1705. As *Cyclopedia* points out, Bluphocks makes
a double pun on 'bishop'—'a cant word for a mixture of wine, oranges and sugar'
(*J.*)—and on 'Beveridge/beverage'. Note also that Beveridge in 1658 published
a treatise on oriental languages, 'especially Hebrew, Chaldee, Syriac [etc.]' and
one contemporary's attack on his style is reminiscent of Bluphocks himself: 'He
delights in jingle and quibbling, affects a tune and rhyme in all he says, and rests
arguments upon nothing but words and sounds' (quoted *DNB*).

ii *267–8. Greek dog-sage*: referring to the Cynics, Greek philosophers whose name
was popularly derived from the Greek for 'dog'; they 'received this name . . .
from their canine propensity to criticise the lives and actions of men' (*Lemprière*).

*sage, dead and merry, Hellward bound in Charon's ferry—With
food for both worlds, under and upper, Lupine-seed and Hecate's*
270   *supper, And never an obolus . .* (it might be got in somehow)
*Tho' Cerberus should gobble us—To pay the Stygian ferry—*or
you might say, *Never an obol To pay for the coble.* . . . Though
thanks to you, or this Intendant thro' you, or this Bishop
thro' his Intendant—I possess a burning pocket-full of
275   zwanzigers.

    1 *Policeman.* I have been noticing a house yonder this long
while—not a shutter unclosed since morning.

    Policeman. Old Luca Gaddi's, that owns the silk-mills
here: he dozes by the hour—wakes up, sighs deeply, says he
280   should like to be Prince Metternich, and then dozes again
after having bidden young Sebald, the foreigner, set his wife
to playing draughts: never molest such a household, they mean
well.

ii *268. dead and merry*: Bluphocks's version of Sophocles: 'Call no man happy until
he is dead'.

ii *268–71. Hellward . . . Stygian ferry*: 'Charon, a god of hell, conducted the souls
of the dead in a boat over the rivers Styx and Acheron to the infernal regions,
for one obolus [see 1. 273n.] . . . As all the dead were obliged to pay a small piece
of money for their admission, it was always usual, among the ancients, to
place under the tongue of the deceased, a piece of money for Charon'
(*Lemprière*). 'Lupine-seed' is the food of the 'upper' world (*OED* cites Pliny (transl.
Holland), ii 143: 'There is not a thing more light of digestion . . . than white Lupines,
if they be eaten dry'); 'Hecate's supper' was a traditional monthly offering at the
shrines of Hecate, goddess of the underworld. Cerberus was the monstrous
three-headed dog who guarded the gates of hell. The dead were usually
provided with a honey-cake as the traditional 'sop to Cerberus'.

ii *268. Charon's ferry*] Charon's wherry (*B & P Domett, 1849–88*). The *1841*
reading is possibly, but not certainly, a mispr. in view of 'ferry' in l. 27.

ii *270. obolus*: the smallest denomination of coin in classical Greece.

ii *270–5.*] (*it might be . . . zwanzigers.*] (Though thanks to you, or this
Intendant through you, or this Bishop through his Intendant—I possess a burning pocketful of *zwanzigers*) . . . *To pay the Stygian ferry!* (*1849–88*). *coble*: small
fishing boat.

ii *275. zwanzigers*: an Austrian silver coin, worth about £1 at today's values.

ii *276. I have been*] There is the girl, then; go and deserve them the moment you
have pointed out to us Signior Luigi and his mother. (*To the rest*) I have been
(*1849–88*).

ii *280. Prince Metternich*: Klemens, Prince von Metternich (1773–1859), conservative Austrian statesman and opponent of Italian nationalism: see *Italy in England*
19, 121–3 (pp. 246, 250).

Bluphocks. Only tell me who this little Pippa is I must have
285   to do with—one could make something of that name.
Pippa—that is, short for Felippa—*Panurge consults Hertrippa*
—*Believ'st thou, King Agrippa?* Something might be done with
that name.

2 *Policeman.* Your head and a ripe musk-melon would not
290   be dear at half a *zwanziger*! Leave this fool, and look out—
the afternoon's over or nearly so.

3 *Policeman.* Where in this passport of Signior Luigi does
the principal instruct you to watch him so narrowly?
There? what's there beside a simple signature? That English
295   fool's busy watching.

2 *Policeman.* Flourish all round—"put all possible
obstacles in his way;" oblong dot at the end—"Detain
him till further advices reach you;" scratch at bottom—
"send him back on pretence of some informality in the
300   above." Ink-spirt on right-hand side, (which is the case here)—
"Arrest him at once," why and wherefore, I don't concern myself, but my instructions amount to this: if Signior
Luigi leaves home to-night for Vienna, well and good—

ii *284–5. Only . . . with—one*] Only, cannot you tell me something of this little
Pippa, I must have to do with?—one (*1849–88*, except 'with? One', *1863–88*).
ii *286. Felippa—Panurge*] Felippa—rhyming to—*Panurge* (*1849–88*, except 'to
Panurge', *1863–88*).
ii *286–7. Panurge . . . Agrippa*: in Rabelais, *Gargantua and Pantagruel* (bk. III
ch. xxv) Pantagruel's companion Panurge consults 'Herr Trippa' on his prospects
for marriage, and is told he will be a cuckold. 'Herr Trippa' is a parody of an occult
philosopher, and by association 'Agrippa' suggests Cornelius Agrippa (see *Pauline*,
epigraph, I 26). 'King Agrippa' refers, however, to the episode in *Acts* xxvi 27–8
where the Apostle Paul confronts King Herod Agrippa: 'King Agrippa, believest
thou the prophets? I know thou believest. Then Agrippa said unto Paul, "Almost
thou persuadest me to be a Christian"'.
ii *289. Your head*] Put into rhyme that your head (*1849–88*). *musk-melon*:
originally denoting a particular variety of melon; then became one of the names
of the common melon, *Cucumis melo*.
ii *293. the principal*] our principal (*1849*); our Principal (*1863–88*).
ii *302–9. my instructions . . . at once*: the police suspect Luigi of belonging to
an Italian nationalist conspiracy, and of obtaining a passport for use by a known
dissident who would be prohibited from travelling. By using the passport
himself, Luigi will disarm this suspicion; by staying in Asolo he will confirm
it. The police do not realize that Luigi is about to set off on a mission to
assassinate the Austrian Emperor, and that his departure would, after all, confirm
his 'guilt' (though not as a member of a conspiracy, since he has devised the plot
himself).

the passport deposed with us for our *visa* is really for his
305   own use, they have misinformed the Office, and he means
        well; but, let him stay over to-night—there has been the
        pretence we suspect—the accounts of his corresponding
        and holding intelligence with the Carbonari are correct
        —we arrest him at once—to-morrow comes Venice—and
310   presently, Spielberg. Bluphocks makes the signal sure enough!

ii *304–5. the passport . . . his own use: Murray* points out that in Lombardy-
Venetia, 'as in every other part of the Austrian dominions, no person can, under
any pretence, cross the frontier without a passport signed by an Austrian minister. . . . On quitting Milan, or Venice, the passport must be *visé* by the Police'
(p. 125). Restrictions on travel were commonly imposed on political dissidents.
ii *308. the Carbonari*: the most famous of the Italian secret societies dedicated
to reform or revolution; they take their name from the French 'charbonniers', a
confraternity of charcoal-burners. An offshoot of freemasonry, they came to
prominence in the Napoleonic period; they were, in fact, mainly active in
southern Italy, and had lost ground, after the collapse of the 1830–1 insurrec-
tions, to movements such as Mazzini's Giovine Italia. Perhaps the name is meant
generically. The Austrians certainly had an exaggerated fear of such societies, and
repressed them ruthlessly.
ii *309–10. to-morrow . . . Spielberg*: many Italian patriots arrested in this period were
confined before trial in the prison of the 'Plombi' in Venice (see *Sordello* iii 850n.,
I 585) and afterwards transported to the prison of Spielberg in Moravia. This was
the case of Silvio Pellico (see iii 18n.).
ii *310. sure enough!*] sure enough! That is he, entering the turret with his mother,
no doubt. (*1849–88*).

III.—*Evening. Inside the Turret.* Luigi *and his Mother entering.*

Mother. If there blew wind you'd hear a long sigh, easing

The utmost heaviness of music's heart.
   Luigi. Here in the archway?
   Mother.   Oh no, no—in further.
Where the echo is made—on the ridge.
   Luigi.   Here surely then!
5 How plain the tap of my heel as I leaped up:
   Aristogeiton! "ristogeiton"—plain
   Was't not? Lucius Junius! The very ghost of a voice—
   Whose flesh is caught and kept by those withered
      wall-flowers,
   Or by the elvish group with thin bleached hair
10 Who lean out of their topmost fortress—look
   And listen, mountain men and women, to what
   We say—chins under each grave earthy face:
   Up and show faces all of you!—"All of you!"

iii *Opening s.d. Inside the Turret.*] Inside the Turret on the Hill above Asolo. (*1865–88*).
See ii 243^244n.
iii *1–14.* Mrs Bronson records a visit by B. to la Rocca in 1889: 'He remembered
an echo he had discovered within the fortress walls fifty years before . . . and so
anxious was he to re-find it that he would scarcely be persuaded to wait until
the fatigue of his journey from England should be dispelled before seeking to
hear it again . . . Once within the Rocca fortress we could find no echo . . .
"I should have thought an echo could never fade," he said rather sadly; but she
was there, after all, his nymph Echo, only she proved for some reason coy on
that occasion.' (*Bronson¹* 928). Echo-scenes are fairly common in Elizabethan and
Jacobean drama (e.g. Webster, *The Duchess of Malfi* V iii).
iii *6–12.*] Hark—"*Lucius Junius!*" The very ghost of a voice,
          Whose body is caught and kept by . . . what are those?
          Mere withered wall-flowers, waving overhead?
          They seem an elvish group with thin bleached hair
[5]   Who lean out of their topmost fortress—looking
          And listening, mountain men, to what we say,
          Hands under chin of each grave earthy face: (*1849–88*, except l. [1], no
italics, 'voice', *1868–88*, l. [3] 'wallflowers,', *1863–88*; l. [5] 'That lean', ll. [5–6]
'look / and listen', l. [7], 'Hand', *1865–88*, 'face.', *1888*).
iii *6. Aristogeiton*: see ii 47–9n.
iii *7. Lucius Junius*: Lucius Junius Brutus, legendary founder of the Roman
republic in the 6th century BC. He was known as 'Brutus' (stupid) because he feigned
insanity during the tyrannical rule of the Tarquins, whose expulsion he instigated;
Luigi's omission of the name may relate to doubts concerning his own sanity: see
ll. 31–6 below. Brutus is mentioned in *Sordello* (iv 956, I 648) and *A Soul's Tragedy*
(ii 39, II 199).
iii *13. "All of you!"*] in italics, *1849–65*.

That's the king with the scarlet comb: come down!—
"Come down."

15   *Mother.* Do not kill that Man, my Luigi—do not
Go to the City! putting crime aside,
Half of these ills of Italy are feigned—
Your Pellicos and writers for effect
Write for effect.
    Luigi.   Hush! say A writes, and B.
20   *Mother.* These A's and B's write for effect I say.
Then evil is in its nature loud, while good
Is silent—you hear each petty injury—
None of his daily virtues; he is old,
Quiet, and kind, and densely stupid—why
Do A and B not kill him themselves?

iii *14.*] That's the king's dwarf with the scarlet comb; now hark— (*1849–63*);
That's the king dwarf with the scarlet comb; old Franz, (*1865–88*). The ref. to
'old Franz' in *1865–88* has generally been taken to refer to the Austrian Emperor
Francis I: see headnote, p. 83.
iii *14^15.*] Come down and meet your fate! Hark—"*meet your fate!*" (*1849–88*,
except no italics, *1868–88*; 'fate? Hark—', *1870–88*).
iii *15. Do not kill that Man*] Let him not meet it (*1849–88*).
iii *18.* Silvio Pellico (1789–1854), poet and dramatist, a major contributor to the
journal *Il Conciliatore*, and, through his friend Pietro Maroncelli, an associate of
the Carbonari (see ii 316n). He was arrested in 1820 during a period of severe
Austrian repression. Imprisoned in the 'Piombi' at Venice, Pellico was condemned
to death; the sentence was commuted to twenty years' 'carcere duro' (harsh imprisonment). He was sent in 1822 to Spielberg prison in Moravia (see ii 316–17n.)
and released in 1830. In 1832 he published *Le mie prigioni* (*My Prisons*), an account
of his ordeal which made him famous, and Spielberg infamous, thoughout
Europe. B. may also have been aware of Pellico's support for the 'romantici',
and its political implications. After the suppression of *Il Conciliatore*, Pellico commented: '*romantic* was recognised as a synonym for *liberal*, and nobody dared to
call himself a classicist, except for the ultras and spies' (quoted in Stuart Woolf,
A History of Italy 1700–1860 [1979] 249). See i 282–92n. B. could have read about
Pellico in *Biographie*, where he would have found that Pellico's father was man-
ager of a silk-mill at Pinerolo in N. Italy, and that he had a brother called Luigi.
iii *22–4. you hear . . . stupid*: the portrait fits the age, but not the character, of
the Emperor Francis II; vice versa for his successor Ferdinand I (see headnote,
p. 83). Cp. the contrast (drawn by the Devil) between the aged George III's
domestic virtues and reactionary politics in Byron's *Vision of Judgment:* ' "He ever
warr'd with freedom and the free: / Nations as men, home subjects, foreign foes,
/ So that they utter'd the word 'Liberty!' / Found George the Third their first
opponent. . . . I grant his household abstinence; I grant / His neutral virtues, which
most monarchs want' (ll. 353–60).
iii *23.*] None of his virtues; he is old beside, (*1865–88*).

25   *Luigi.*   They teach
        Others to kill him—me—and if I fail
        Others to succeed; now if A tried and failed
        I could not do that: mine's the *lesser* task.
        Mother, they visit night by night . . .
            Mother.   You Luigi?
30   Ah will you let me tell you what you are?
            Luigi. Why not? Oh the one thing you fear to hint
        You may assure yourself I say and say
        Often to myself; at times—nay, now—as now
        We sit, I think my mind is touched—suspect
35   All is not sound—but is not knowing that
        What constitutes one sane or otherwise?
        I know I am thus—so all is right again!
        I laugh at myself as thro' the town I walk
        And see the world merry as if no Italy
40   Were suffering—then I ponder—I am rich,
        Young, healthy, happy, why should this fact trouble me . . .
        More than it troubles these? But it does trouble me!
        No—trouble's a bad word—for as I walk
        There's springing and melody and giddiness,
45   And old quaint turns and passages of my youth—
        Dreams long forgotten, little in themselves—
        Return to me—whatever may recreate me,
        And earth seems in a truce with me, and heaven
        Accords with me, all things suspend their strife,
50   The very cicales laugh "There goes he and there—
        "Feast him, the time is short—he is on his way
        "For the world's sake—feast him this once, our friend!"
        And in return for all this, I can trip
        Cheerfully up the scaffold-steps: I go
        This evening, mother.

iii *28. do*] teach (*1849–88*).   *lesser*] not italic, *1849–88*.
iii *33.*] Ever to myself; at times—nay, even now (*1849–88*, except 'myself! At',
1868–88).
iii *39. the world*] men (*1849–88*).
iii *41. healthy, happy,*] healthy; (*1849–88*). Unless *1841* is misprinted, a rare case
of an unmetrical line in B.
iii *42. trouble me!*] trouble! (*1863–65*); trouble. (*1868–88*); 'me!' is emended in
agreement with *1849* from 'me' in *1841*.
iii *47. recreate*] amuse (*1849–88*).
iii *50. cicales laugh*] cicalas laugh (*1849*); cicale laugh (*1863*); cicala laughs (*1865–88*).
B. had constant difficulty with this word: see *Intro.* 177n.

55   *Mother.*   But mistrust yourself—
        Mistrust the judgment you pronounce on him.
            Luigi. Oh, there I feel—am sure that I am right.
            Mother. Mistrust your judgment then of the mere means
        Of this wild enterprise: say you are right,—
60   How should one in your state e'er bring to pass
        What would require a cool head, a cold heart,
        And a calm hand? you never will escape.
            Luigi. Escape—to wish that even would spoil all!
        The dying is best part of it—I have
65   Enjoyed these fifteen years of mine too much
        To leave myself excuse for longer life—
        Was not life pressed down, running o'er with joy,
        That I might finish with it ere my fellows
        Who sparelier feasted make a longer stay?
70   I was put at the board head, helped to all
        At first: I rise up happy and content.
        God must be glad one loves his world so much—
        I can give news of earth to all the dead
        Who ask me:—last year's sunsets and great stars
75   That had a right to come first and see ebb
        The crimson wave that drifts the sun away—
        Those crescent moons with notched and burning rims
        That strengthened into sharp fire and there stood
        Impatient of the azure—and that day
80   In March a double rainbow stopped the storm—
        May's warm, slow, yellow moonlit summer nights—
        Gone are they—but I have them in my soul!

---

iii *59. Of*] *To* (*1868–88*).
iii *63–5.*] Escape—to even wish that would spoil all!
                The dying is best part of it. Too much
                Have I enjoyed these fifteen years of mine (*1849–88*, except 'Escape?
                to', *1865*, 'Escape? To', *1868–88*).
iii *67.* Cp. *Luke* vi 38: 'Give, and it shall be given unto you; good measure, pressed
down, and shaken together, and running over, shall men give into your bosom'.
iii *73–4. I can give . . . ask me*: more usually a courtesy of living visitors to the
underworld, such as Odysseus, Aeneas, Dante.
iii *74–80.* W. Sharp asserted 'it was from the Dulwich wood that, one afternoon
in March, he saw a storm glorified by a double rainbow of extraordinary beauty'
(*Life of Robert Browning* [1890] 104).
iii *75. That*] Which (*1849–88*).
iii *81.* Cp. *May and Death* 7–8 (III 363): 'the warm / Moon-births and the long
evening-ends'.

    Mother. (He will not go!)
    Luigi.   You smile at me—I know
    Voluptuousness, grotesqueness, ghastliness
85   Environ my devotedness as quaintly
    As round about some antique altar wreathe
    The rose festoons, goats' horns, and oxen's skulls.
        Mother. See now—you reach the city—you must cross
    His threshold—how?
        Luigi.   Oh, that's if we conspire!
90   Then come the pains in plenty you foresee
    —Who guess not how the qualities required
    For such an office—qualities I have—
    Would little stead us otherwise employed,
    Yet prove of rarest merit here—here only.
95   Every one knows for what his excellences
    Will serve, but no one ever will consider
    For what his worst defects might serve; and yet
    Have you not seen me range our coppice yonder
    In search of a distorted ash?—it happens
100 The wry spoilt branch's a natural perfect bow:
    Fancy the thrice sage, thrice precautioned man
    Arriving at the city on my errand!
    No, no—I have a handsome dress packed up—
    White satin here to set off my black hair—
105 In I shall march—for you may watch your life out
    Behind thick walls—binding friends to betray you;
    More than one man spoils every thing—March straight—
    Only no clumsy knife to fumble for—
    Take the great gate, and walk (not saunter) on
110 Thro' guards and guards—I have rehearsed it all
    Inside the Turret here a hundred times—

---

iii *83. I know*] 'Tis true,— (*1849–88*).
iii *90.*] Then would come pains in plenty, as you guess— (*1849–88*).
iii *91. —Who*] But (*1849–88*). *required*] most fit (*1863–88*).
iii *93. us*] me (*1849–63*); me, (*1865–88*).
iii *94. here—here only.*] only here (*1865–88*).
iii *95–7. excellences . . . defects*] excellence . . . defect (*1849–88*).
iii *99–100. it happens / The wry spoilt branch's*] I find / The wry spoilt branch (*1868–88*).
iii *102. city*] palace (*1849–88*).
iii *103–18.* The court here is closer to the Renaissance than to the 19th century, esp. with the presence of a powerful 'favourite' (l. 115).
iii *106. binding friends*] make friends there (*1849–88*).
iii *108.* Luigi will strangle the Emperor. Cp. *Italy in England* 121–3 (p. 250).

Don't ask the way of whom you meet, observe,
But where they cluster thickliest is the door
Of doors: they'll let you pass . . they'll never blab
115   Each to the other, he knows not the favourite,
Whence he is bound and what's his business now—
Walk in—straight up to him—you have no knife—
Be prompt, how should he scream? Then, out with you!
Italy, Italy, my Italy!
120   You're free, you're free—Oh mother, I believed
They got about me—Andrea from his exile,
Pier from his dungeon, Gaultier from his grave!
    Mother. Well you shall go. If patriotism were not
The easiest virtue for a selfish man
125   To acquire! he loves himself—and then, the world—
If he must love beyond, but nought between:
As a short-sighted man sees nought midway
His body and the sun above. But you
Are my adored Luigi—ever obedient
130   To my least wish, and running o'er with love—
I could not call you cruel or unkind!
Once more, your ground for killing him!—then go!
    Luigi. Now do you ask me, or make sport of me?
How first the Austrians got these provinces—
135   (If that is all, I'll satisfy you soon)
. . . Never by warfare but by treaty, for
That treaty whereby . . .
    Mother.   Well?
    Luigi.   (Sure he's arrived—
The tell-tale cuckoo—spring's his confidant,
And he lets out her April purposes!)

iii *119.* Cp. *De Gustibus* 39 (III 28): 'Italy, my Italy!'
iii *120. I believed*] I could dream (*1849–88*).
iii *121–2. Andrea . . . Pier . . . Gaultier*: imaginary figures, in contrast to Pellico (l. 18).
iii *123. If patriotism were not*] Yet seems this patriotism (*1849–88*).
iii *125. then*] next (*1849–88*).
iii *133. ask*] try (*1868–88*).
iii *134–7. How first . . . whereby*: the provinces are Lombardy and Venetia, which Austria acquired by the Treaty of Vienna (1815). But the Austrians were already in military control of northern Italy.
iii *136.*] . . . Never by conquest but by cunning, for (*1849–88*, except '—Never', *1863–88*).

140   Or . . better go at once to modern times—
     He has . . they have . . in fact I understand
     But can't re-state the matter; that's my boast;
     Others could reason it out to you, and prove
     Things they have made me feel.
        Mother.   Why go to-night?
145   Morn's for adventure. Jupiter is now
     A morning-star. . . . I cannot hear you, Luigi!
        Luigi. "I am the bright and morning-star," God saith—
     And, "such an one I give the morning-star!"
     The gift of the morning-star—have I God's gift
     Of the morning-star?
150   *Mother.*   Chiara will love to see
     That Jupiter an evening-star next June.
        Luigi. True, mother. Well for those who live June over.
     Great noontides—thunder storms—all glaring pomps
     Which triumph at the heels of June the God
155   Leading his revel thro' our leafy world.
     Yes, Chiara will be here—
        Mother.   In June—remember
     Yourself appointed that month for her coming—
        Luigi. Was that low noise the echo?
        Mother.   The night-wind.
     She must be grown—with her blue eyes upturned
160   As if life were one long and sweet surprise—
     In June she comes.

---

iii *140. times*] time (*1865–88*).

iii *147–8.* The first quotation is from *Revelation* xxii 16: 'I Jesus have sent mine angel to testify unto you these things in the churches. I am the root and the off-spring of David, and the bright and morning star'. The second is from *Revelation* ii 26–8: 'And he that overcometh, and keepeth my works unto the end, to him will I give power over the nations . . . And I will give him the morning star.' See also iv 219n.

iii *147. God saith*] saith God (*1868–88*).

iii *148. "such*] "to such (*1849–88*).

iii *150. Chiara*: lit., 'bright'.

iii *152. June over*] through June (*1849–88*).

iii *154. June the God*] sovereign June (*1849*); the god June (*1863*); June the god (*1865–88*).

iii *155.*] Leading his glorious revel thro' our world. (*1849*). With the prec. line, this is a rare example of a return to the *1841* reading after *1849* or *1863*.

iii *161. are*] were (*1849–88*).

Luigi.   We are to see together
The Titian at Treviso—there again!

[*Without*] A king lived long ago,
In the morning of the world,
165 When earth was nigher heaven than now:
And the king's locks curled
Disparting o'er a forehead full
As the milk-white space 'twixt horn and horn
Of some sacrificial bull—
170 Only calm as a babe new-born:
For he was got to a sleepy mood,
So safe from all decrepitude,
Age with its bane so sure gone by,

---

iii *162. The Titian at Treviso*: a fresco of the Annunciation, in the chapel of that name in the Cathedral at Treviso; in the diary of his 1838 trip B. records visiting Treviso on 17 June (*Correspondence* iv, p. xiii).

iii *163–224.*] For publication details, see headnote, p. 80. Variants from the MR text are not rec. here; see I 326. The opening and closing s.d.'s are altered in *1849–88* as for Pippa's first song (i 215–22). There are no s. d.'s in *1865²*; *1863–88* have no intermediate s. d.'s at ll. 178 and 204; in *1849* these read '[From without.]'. The poem's original appearance in *MR* had signalled B.'s affiliation to the political radicalism of that journal's editor, W. J. Fox (see headnote to *Paracelsus*, I 107). In *MR* the poem comes immediately after an article by Fox 'On Organic Reforms' which attacks both conservatives and moderate reformers from a radical and republican perspective: 'The old slavish devotion to a particular family, the unquestioning loyalty which was claimed by and vowed to the Stuarts, is, I know, transferred by many to the forms of our Government, and the ancient privileges of certain classes of society. It is not much the better for the transfer. . . . Irresponsible power may be one of the "branches" of the constitution; but what then, if it bear bitter fruit, and overshadow the land pestiferously? Nay, even should "unquestionable danger to the Monarchy" be logically predicated of any arrangements which are essential to the nation's rights, security, prosperity, and improvement, then must such danger be incurred, unless we are prepared to revert to "the monstrous faith of millions made for one." ' In this light B.'s poem, with its mythical setting and idealized portrait of a just monarch, suggests an ironic contrast with present-day rulers, a contrast which Luigi implicitly grasps in *1841* and explicitly states in *1849–88* (see below, ll. 224–5n.). Cp. Pope's evocation of a primitive social order in which 'each Patriarch sate, / King, priest, and parent of his growing state; / On him, their second Providence, they hung, / Their law his eye, their oracle his tongue' (*Essay on Man* iii 215–18); and note that Pope, following Locke, sees this as a state antecedent and opposed to that of absolute monarchy, 'Th' enormous faith of many made for one' (l. 242; note Fox's misquotation of this line in the passage just cited). Pope himself glossed this section of the *Essay*: 'Origin of True Religion and Government from the Principle of Love: and of Superstition and Tyranny from that of Fear'.

iii *173. Age*] From age (*1849–88*).

(The Gods so loved him while he dreamed,)
175   That, having lived thus long, there seemed
        No need the king should ever die.

        Luigi. No need that sort of king should ever die.

        [*Without*] Among the rocks his city was:
        Before his palace, in the sun,
180   He sate to see his people pass,
        And judge them every one
        From its threshold of smooth stone.
        They haled him many a valley-thief
        Caught in the sheep-pens—robber-chief,
185   Swarthy and shameless—beggar-cheat—
        Spy-prowler—or some pirate found
        On the sea-sand left aground;
        Sometimes there clung about his feet
        With bleeding lip and burning cheek
190   A woman, bitterest wrong to speak
        Of one with sullen, thickset brows:
        Sometimes from out the prison-house
        The angry priests a pale wretch brought,
        Who through some chink had pushed and pressed,
195   Knees and elbows, belly and breast,
        Worm-like into the temple,—caught
        He was by the very God,
        Who ever in the darkness strode
        Backward and forward, keeping watch
200   O'er his brazen bowls, such rogues to catch:
        These, all and every one,
        The king judged, sitting in the sun.

        Luigi. That king should still judge sitting in the sun.

        [*Without*] His councillors, on left and right,
205   Looked anxious up,—but no surprise

iii *186. some pirate*] rough pirate (*1849–88*).
iii *188. Sometimes*] And sometimes (*1849–88*).
iii *192. Sometimes from out*] And sometimes from (*1849–88*).
iii *195. Knees*] On knees (*1849–88*).
iii *197.*] At last there by the very God, (*1849–63*; *1865–88* as *1841*, except 'god',
the *MR* reading).
iii *201. These*] And these (*1849–63*).

Disturbed the king's old smiling eyes,
Where the very blue had turned to white.
A python passed one day
The silent streets—until he came,
210 With forky tongue and eyes on flame,
Where the old king judged alway;
But when he saw the sweepy hair,
Girt with a crown of berries rare
The God will hardly give to wear
215 To the maiden who singeth, dancing bare
In the altar-smoke by the pine-torch lights,
At his wondrous forest rites,—
But which the God's self granted him
For setting free each felon limb
220 Because of earthly murder done
Faded till other hope was none;—
Seeing this, he did not dare
Approach that threshold in the sun,
Assault the old king smiling there.

[Pippa *passes.*

225 *Luigi.* Farewell, farewell—how could I stay?
Farewell!

---

iii *208.*] 'Tis said, a Python scared one day (*1849–88*, except 'python', *1865²*).
iii *209.*] The breathless city, till he came (*1849–88*).
iii *213–17.* The details suggest that the God is Bacchus (Dionysus) whose festivals were celebrated with orgiastic dancing; *Lemprière* notes that 'According to Pliny, he was the first [god] who ever wore a crown'.
iii *214. The God*] Which the God (*1849–88*, except 'god' *1865²–88*).
iii *218–21.*] not *1849–88*.
iii *222. Seeing*] Beholding (*1849–63*).
iii *224–5.*] Assault the old king smiling there.
        Such grace had kings when the world begun!

(PIPPA *passes.*)
        Luigi. And such grace have they, now that the world ends!
        The Python in the city, on the throne,
[5]   And brave men, God would crown for slaying him,
        Lurk in bye-corners lest they fall his prey!
        Are crowns yet to be won, in this late trial,
        Which weakness makes me hesitate to reach?
        'Tis God's voice calls, how could I stay? Farewell! (*1849–88*, except l. [4], 'Python at', *1865–88*; l. [7] 'won', *1865–88*, 'late time', *1863–88*, l. [9], 'calls: how', *1865–88*).
iii *225^226. [s. d.]* Talk by the way, while PIPPA is passing from the Turret to the Bishop's brother's House, close to the Duomo S. Maria. Poor Girls sitting on the steps. (*1849–88*, except 'Brother's', *1865–88*).

Talk by the way in the mean time. Poor Girls *sitting on the steps of*
   Monsignor's *brother's house, close to the Duomo S. Maria.*
     1 *Girl.* There goes a swallow to Venice—the stout sea-farer!
Let us all wish; you wish first.
     2 *Girl.*   I? This sunset
To finish.
     3 *Girl.* That old . . . somebody I know,
To give me the same treat he gave last week—
230   Feeding me on his knee with fig-peckers,
Lampreys, and red Breganze-wine, and mumbling
The while some folly about how well I fare—
Since had he not himself been late this morning
Detained at—never mind where—had he not . .
235   Eh, baggage, had I not!—
     2 *Girl.*   How she can lie!
     3 *Girl.* Look there—by the nails—
     2 *Girl.*   What makes your fingers red?
     3 *Girl.* Dipping them into wine to write bad words with
On the bright table—how he laughed!
     1 *Girl.*   My turn:
Spring's come and summer's coming: I would wear
240   A long loose gown—down to the feet and hands—
With plaits here, close about the throat, all day:
And all night lie, the cool long nights, in bed—
And have new milk to drink—apples to eat,
Deuzans and junetings, leather-coats . . ah, I should say

iii *226^227*.] Seeing those birds fly, makes one wish for wings. (*1849–88*).
iii *228–44*. The contrast between rich food and a simple rural diet reappears in
the *Prologue* to *Ferishtah's Fancies* (1884). See also l. 286n.
iii *228^229*.] Greyer and older than my grandfather, (*1849–88*).
iii *230. fig-peckers*: It. 'beccafico'; small migratory birds of the genus Sylvia, eaten
as dainties in the autumn, when they have fattened on figs and grapes.
iii *231. Lampreys*: eel-like fish. A citation dated 1720 in *OED* suggests an
aphrodisiac effect. Not mentioned by B. outside this poem.   *Breganze-wine*: wine
from Breganze, a town 30 km west of Asolo.
iii *232^233*.] To be let eat my supper quietly—(*1849–88*, except 'quietly:',
1863–88, 'Let sit and', *1868–88*).
iii *235. Eh, . . . not!*] in quotation marks, *1849–88*.
iii *244. Deuzans and junetings, leather-coats*: 'Three kinds of apple. *Deuzan* (fr. *deux
ans*) was so called as it was supposed to keep for two years. *Juneting* [is] the
earliest apple of the year[.] *Leather-coat*, the golden russet, is so named from
the leathery brown skin' (W. H. Griffin, *Selections from the Early Poems of Robert
Browning* [1902] 154–5).

This is away in the fields—miles!
245   3 *Girl.*   Say at once
You'd be at home—she'd always be at home!
Now comes the story of the farm among
The cherry orchards, and how April snowed
White blossoms on her as she ran: why fool,
250 They've rubbed the chalk-mark out how tall you were,
Twisted your starling's neck, broken his cage,
Made a dunghill of your garden—
    1 *Girl.*   They destroy
My garden since I left them? well—perhaps!
I would have done so—so I hope they have!
255 A fig-tree curled out of our cottage wall—
They called it mine, I have forgotten why,
It must have been there long ere I was born,
Criq—criq—I think I hear the wasps o'erhead
Pricking the papers strung to flutter there
260 And keep off birds in fruit-time—coarse long papers
And the wasps eat them, prick them through and
through.
    3 *Girl.* How her mouth twitches! where was I before
She broke in with her wishes and long gowns
And wasps—would I be such a fool!—Oh, here!
265 This is my way—I answer every one
Who asks me why I make so much of him—
(Say, you love him—he'll not be gulled, he'll say)
"He that seduced me when I was a girl
Thus high—had eyes like yours, or hair like yours,
270 Brown, red, white,"—as the case may be—that pleases!
(See how that beetle burnishes in the path—
There sparkles he along the dust—and there—
Your journey to that maize-tuft's spoilt at least!

---

iii *248–9.* Cp. Wordsworth, *The Green Linnet* 1–2: 'Beneath these fruit-tree boughs
that shed / Their snow-white blossoms on my head', and see *Home-Thoughts,
from Abroad* 11–13 (p. 253).
iii 250.] They've rubbed out the chalk-mark of how tall you were, (*1849–63;
1865–88* as *1841*, except 'out, how').
iii *255.* The fig-tree recalls Biblical imagery of peace and plenty, as in *1 Kings* iv
25: 'And Judah and Israel dwelt safely, every man under his vine and under his
fig-tree'. Cp. *Jochanan Hakkadosh* (*Jocoseria,* 1883) 263–5, where Jochanan 'sits /
Under his vine and fig-tree mid the wealth / Of garden-sights and sounds'.
iii 267.] (If you say, you love him—straight "he'll not be gulled") (*1849–88,* except
'"you love him"—', *1868–88,* 'gulled!"', *1863–88*).
iii *273. maize-tuft's*] maize-tuft (*1865–88*).

    1 *Girl.* When I was young they said if you killed one
275 Of those sunshiny beetles, that his friend
    Up there would shine no more that day or next.
       3 *Girl.* When you were young? Nor are you young,
    that's true!
    How your plump arms, that were, have dropped away!
    Why I can span them! Cecco beats you still?
280 No matter so you keep your curious hair.
    I wish they'd find a way to dye our hair
    Your colour—any lighter tint, indeed,
    Than black—the men say they are sick of black,
    Black eyes, black hair!
      2 *Girl.*   Sick of yours, like enough,
285 Do you pretend you ever tasted lampreys
    And ortolans? Giovita, of the palace,
    Engaged (but there's no trusting him) to slice me
    Polenta with a knife that had cut up
    An ortolan.
      3 *Girl.*   Why—there! is not that Pippa
290 We are to talk to, under the window, quick
    Where the lights are?
      1 *Girl.* No—or she would sing
    —For the Intendant said . . .
      3 Girl.   Oh, you sing first—
    Then, if she listens and comes close . . I'll tell you,
    Sing that song the young English noble made,
295 Who took you for the purest of the pure
    And meant to leave the world for you—what fun!
      2 *Girl.* [*Sings*]

iii *276. or*] nor (*1849–88*).

iii *277–91.*] in *1841* the order of speakers is given as '2 Girl . . . 3 Girl . . . 2 Girl'.
This makes nonsense of the dialogue, since '3 Girl' is made to contradict her
claim to have been fed on dainties by her rich admirer (ll. 228–31). B. corrected
the error in *B & P Domett*, and we have emended accordingly; in *1849–88* he
introduced a new character, '4 Girl', to speak ll. 284–9, leaving '2 Girl' to speak
ll. 289–91 as she does in the unemended *1841* text.

iii *280. curious*: unusual; also perhaps 'such as interests the curioso or connoisseur'
(*OED* 17).

iii *286. ortolans*: 'The Ortolan is a small singing-bird . . . common in France,
Italy and other parts of Europe. It is the epicure's prime morceau' (*OED*, 1837).
The *Prologue* to *Ferishtah's Fancies* (1884) gives an Italian recipe for cooking the bird.

iii *288. Polenta*: 'A large flat thin cake made of the meal of maize or ground
chestnuts; it is a favourite food of the Italian peasantry' (W. H. Griffin, *Selections
from the Early Poems of Robert Browning* [1902], note to l. 244).

iii *291. No—or*] That she? No, or (*1868–88*).

You'll love me yet!—and I can tarry
Your love's protracted growing:
June reared that bunch of flowers you carry
300   From seeds of April's sowing.

I plant a heartfull now—some seed
At least is sure to strike
And yield—what you'll not care, indeed,
To pluck, but, may be like

305   To look upon . . my whole remains,
A grave's one violet:
Your look?—that pays a thousand pains.
What's death?—You'll love me yet!

3 Girl. [*To* Pippa *who approaches*] Oh, you may come
310   closer—we shall not eat you!

iii *297–308.* For publication details, see headnote, p. 81. This is the only song
not sung by Pippa herself. In *1863–88* the shorter lines are indented.
iii *297–8.* Cp. Marvell, *To his Coy Mistress*, esp. ll. 11–12: 'My vegetable Love
should grow / Vaster than Empires, and more slow.'
iii *303–5.*] And yield—what you'll not pluck indeed,
          Not love, but, may be, like!

          You'll look at least on love's remains, (*1849–88*, except 'like.',
1868–88).
iii *310. eat you!*] eat you! Why, you seem the very person that the great rich
handsome Englishman has fallen so violently in love with! I'll tell you all about
it. (*1849–88*).

IV.—*Night. The Palace by the Duomo.* Monsignor,
dismissing his Attendants.

    Monsignor. Thanks, friends, many thanks. I desire life now
chiefly that I may recompense every one of you. Most I know
something of already. *Benedicto benedicatur* . . ugh . . ugh! Where
was I? Oh, as you were remarking, Ugo, the weather is mild,
5 very unlike winter-weather,—but I am a Sicilian, you
know, and shiver in your Julys here: To be sure, when 'twas
full summer at Messina, as we priests used to cross in procession the great square on Assumption Day, you might see
our thickest yellow tapers twist suddenly in two, each like
10 a falling star, or sink down on themselves in a gore of wax.
But go, my friends, but go! [*To the* Intendant] Not you, Ugo!
[*The others leave the apartment, where a table with refreshments
is prepared.*] I have long wanted to converse with you, Ugo!
    Intendant. Uguccio—

iv *Opening s.d.*] *The Palace*] Inside the Palace (*1865–88*).   *Palace*: transl. of It. 'palazzo',
a 'large, stately dwelling'.   *Monsignor*: 'an ecclesiastical title attached to an office
or distinction ordinarily bestowed by the Pope. It is also used in some countries
. . . as a regular style for archbishops and bishops' (*Oxford Dictionary of the
Christian Church*, 2nd ed.). Its use here suggests the Bishop's closeness to the Pope.
his Attendants: i.e. his brother's servants.
iv *1–2. I desire life now chiefly*] I chiefly desire life now (*1849–88*).
iv *2. recompense*: in the (hidden) sense of 'punish, pay back'.
iv *3. already.*] already. What, a repast prepared? (*1849–88*).
iv *3. Benedicto benedicatur*: lit., 'it is blessed in being blessed', a standard Catholic
grace before meals.
iv *3. ugh . . . ugh*: the sound of a cough, as in e.g. Jonson's *Volpone*.
iv *6–10. To be sure . . . a gore of wax*: referring to the feast celebrating the ascent
of the Virgin Mary into heaven, held on 13 Aug. in Catholic countries. Cp. *England
in Italy* 250ff. (pp. 267–8) and *Up at a Villa* 51–2 (III 148). Murray's *Handbook
for Travellers in Southern Italy* says: 'The great feast of the Virgin in Messina is in
August, to commemorate her Assumption [. . . It] occupies three days (from the
13th to the 15th) . . . at night the city is illuminated, and all Messina is in the
streets. In the evening of the 14th the Cathedral is also lighted up with more
than 8000 wax tapers, and makes a brilliant spectacle' (pp. 501–2).
iv *7. Messina*: Sicilian city, situated opposite the Italian mainland; an archiepis-
copal see and capital of Messina province.
iv *8. the great square*: the Piazza del Duomo, 'the finest in Messina, having on the
E. the Cathedral with its quaint facade and its modern campanile' (Murray's *Handbook
for Travellers in Southern Italy* 477).
iv *9. tapers*: ecclesiastical candles.
iv *13. s.d.*] [The others leave the apartment.] (*1849–88*).
iv *13–16 converse with you, Ugo . . . Fossombruno*: the Intendant objects to Monsignor's abbreviation of his name, but Monsignor affects to take him to mean
that he does not know it, or the details of his career.

15   *Monsignor* . . . 'guccio Stefani, man! of Ascoli, Fermo,
        and Fossombruno:—what I do need instructing about are
        these accounts of your administration of my poor brother's
        affairs. Ugh! I shall never get through a third part of your
        accounts: take some of these dainties before we attempt it,
20   however: are you bashful to that degree? For me, a crust
        and water suffice.
            Intendant. Do you choose this especial night to question me?
            Monsignor. This night, Ugo. You have managed my
        late brother's affairs since the death of our elder brother—
25   fourteen years and a month, all but three days. The 3rd of
        December, I find him . . .
            Intendant. If you have so intimate an acquaintance with
        your brother's affairs, you will be tender of turning so far
        back—they will hardly bear looking into so far back.
30   *Monsignor.* Ay, ay, ugh, ugh,—nothing but disappointments
        here below! I remark a considerable payment made to your-
        self on this 3rd of December. Talk of disappointments!
        There was a young fellow here, Jules, a foreign sculptor, I
        did my utmost to advance, that the church might be a gainer
35   by us both: he was going on hopefully enough, and of a
        sudden he notifies to me some marvellous change that has
        happened in his notions of art; here's his letter,—"He never
        had a clearly conceived Ideal within his brain till to-day.
        Yet since his hand could manage a chisel he has practised

iv *15–6. Ascoli, Fermo, and Fossombruno*: all the towns, here and ll. 89, 91, in which
the Intendant is said to have lived are in central Italy, in the Papal States. All are
also the seats of bishops or archbishops.
iv *19–21. these dainties* . . . *For me, a crust and water suffice*: Monsignor may have in
mind *Psalms* cxli 4: 'Incline not my heart to any evil thing, to practise wicked
works with men that work iniquity: and let me not eat of their dainties'. See
also *Luke* xiv 12, and cp. the self-denying frugality of the Pope in *Ring* i 320–1.
iv *23. This night*: in the light of many echoes of the Gospels in this episode, perhaps a ref. to *Luke* xii 19–20: 'And I will say to my soul, Soul, thou hast much
goods laid up for many years; take thine ease, eat, drink, and be merry. But God
said unto him, Thou fool, this night thy soul shall be required of thee: then whose
shall those things be, which thou hast provided?'
iv *25. The 3rd*] On the 3rd (*1849–63*); On the Third (*1865–88*).
iv *32. on this 3rd*] on this Third (*1865–88*).
iv *32–56. Talk of disappointments* . . . *eh, Ugo*: there is no hint in the former episode
that Jules has been patronized by Monsignor. The relationship parallels that between
Caponsacchi and his Bishop in *Ring*: see vi 264–331, 349–89, 463–78. Nor was
there any hint that Jules intends to abandon sculpture (see ii 233–5 for evidence
to the contrary). See also headnote, p. 87.

40   expressing other men's Ideals—and in the very perfection
      he has attained to he foresees an ultimate failure—his
      unconscious hand will pursue its prescribed course of old
      years, and will reproduce with a fatal expertness the ancient
      types, let the novel one appear never so palpably to his spirit:
45   there is but one method of escape—confiding the virgin type
      to as chaste a hand, he will paint, not carve, its character-
      istics,"—strike out, I dare say, a school like Correggio: how
      think you, Ugo?
           Intendant. Is Correggio a painter?
50   *Monsignor.* Foolish Jules! and yet, after all, why foolish?
      He may—probably will, fall egregiously: but if there should
      arise a new painter, will it not be in some such way—a poet,
      now, or a musician, spirits who have conceived and perfected

---

iv 46. *he will paint*] he will turn painter instead of sculptor, and paint (*1849–88*).
iv 47. *strike out . . . Correggio*: Antonio Allegri (1494–1534), called Correggio after
his birthplace, was described by Vasari in terms which support the parallel drawn
by Monsignor: 'Correggio was the first in Lombardy who commenced the execution of works in the modern manner, and it is thought that if he had travelled
beyond the limits of his native Lombardy and visited Rome, he would have performed wonders . . . Be this as it may, his works, being what they are, although
he had never seen those of antiquity, nor was even acquainted with the best works
of the modern masters; it necessarily follows that if he had studied these works he
would have materially improved his own' (*Lives of the Painters*, transl. Mrs J. Foster
[1850] 403–4). The painter Annibale Caracci (1560–1609) put the case less
negatively: 'the thoughts and conceptions of Correggio were his own, evidently
drawn from his own mind, and invented by himself, guided only by the original
idea. The others all rest on something not their own; some on models, some on
statues and paintings' (quoted in the anonymous *Sketches of the Lives of Correggio
and Parmigianino* [1823] pp. v-vi). By B.'s time, however, this view was controversial: A. Mengs argued that an artist as great as Correggio must have
'studied the works and maxims of the ancients and of the best masters' (*Mengs on
Painting* [1796] ii 57). So Monsignor is taking one side in a controversy that cen-
trally reflects Jules's dilemma. The sense in which Correggio began 'a school'
is equally controversial. Vasari claimed that 'the Lombards were induced by his
example to open their eyes: the result of his painting has seen more than one fine
genius belonging to that country subsequently following his steps' (p. 410). Mengs
cites the Caracci as having 'formed their style of design upon that of Correggio'
(ii 47) but adds that, like Raphael, he was 'little imitated' (ii 171). The author of
Sketches notes that 'he seems to have instructed few or no regular scholars'
(p. 199), but also that 'he shone forth as the founder of a new school of painting' (p. 70). Canova's career was viewed in a similar fashion: 'The age was prepared
in some measure to hail a reformer, but seemed incapable by its own energies of
producing one. Canova at this crisis appeared, than whom, perhaps, no illustrious
name ever owed less to external circumstances, in the cultivation of talents' (*Works
of Canova* iii 5). It is also noted that Canova had no pupils as such.
iv 52. *a poet*] by a poet (*1849–88*).

an Ideal through some other channel, transferring it to this,
55   and escaping our conventional roads by pure ignorance of
them, eh, Ugo? If you have no appetite, talk at least, Ugo!

Intendant. Sir, I can submit no longer to this course of
yours: first, you select the group of which I formed one,—
next you thin it gradually,—always retaining me with your
60   smile,—and so do you proceed till you have fairly got me
alone with you between four stone walls: and now then?
Let this farce, this chatter end now—what is it you want
with me?

Monsignor. Ugo . . .

65   *Intendant.* From the instant you arrived I felt your smile
on me as you questioned me about this and the other
article in those papers—why, your brother should have
given me this manor, that liberty,—and your nod at the
end meant,—what?

70   *Monsignor.* Possibly that I wished for no loud talk here—
if once you set me coughing, Ugo!

Intendant. I have your brother's hand and seal to all I possess: now ask me what for! what service I did him—ask me!

Monsignor. I had better not—I should rip up old disgraces—
75   let out my poor brother's weaknesses. By the way, Maffeo
of Forli, (which, I forgot to observe, is your true name)
was the interdict taken off you for robbing that church at
Cesena?

Intendant. No, nor needs be—for when I murdered your
80   brother's friend, Pasquale for him . . .

Monsignor. Ah, he employed you in that matter, did he?
Well, I must let you keep, as you say, this manor and that
liberty, for fear the world should find out my relations were

---

iv *68. this manor, that liberty*] this villa, that *podere* (*1849–88*); replacing the English
terms, here and on subsequent occurrences, by their Italian equivalents. A
'liberty' is a person's domain or property.

iv *74. I had better not*] I would better not (*1863–88*).

iv *76–8.* Forli and Cesena lie close together and about 190 km north of the
complex of towns mentioned at ll. 18–19.

iv *77. interdict*: in Catholic Church law, an instruction debarring particular persons from taking the sacraments. Since the Intendant's crimes were committed
in the Papal States, which are under Church jurisdiction, it is possible that his
presence in Asolo is a result of flight from that jurisdiction.   *taken off*] ever taken
off (*1849–88*).

iv *81. that matter*] that business (*1849–88*).

iv *82–3. this manor and that liberty*] this villa and that *podere* (*1849–88*).

of so indifferent a stamp: Maffeo, my family is the oldest in
85   Messina, and century after century have my progenitors gone
on polluting themselves with every wickedness under
Heaven: my own father . . . rest his soul!—I have, I know,
a chapel to support that it may: my dear two dead brothers
were,—what you know tolerably well: I, the youngest,
90   might have rivalled them in vice, if not in wealth, but from
my boyhood I came out from among them, and so am not
partaker of their plagues. My glory springs from another
source, or if from this, by contrast only,—for I, the bishop,
am the brother of your employers, Ugo. I hope to repair
95   some of their wrong, however; so far as my brother's ill-
gotten treasure reverts to me, I can stop the consequences
of his crime, and not one *soldo* shall escape me. Maffeo, the
sword we quiet men spurn away, you shrewd knaves
pick up and commit murders with; what opportunities the
100   virtuous forego, the villanous seize. Because, to pleasure myself,
apart from other considerations, my food would be millet-
cake, my dress sackcloth, and my couch straw, am I therefore to let the off-scouring of the earth seduce the ignorant
by appropriating a pomp these will be sure to think lessens

iv *88. may: my dear*] may rest: my dear (*1849–88*).

iv *91–2. I came out . . . their plagues*: cp. *Revelation* xviii 4: 'And I heard another
voice from heaven, saying, Come out of her [Babylon] my people, that ye be
not partakers of her sins, and that ye receive not of her plagues'.

iv *95. so far as my brother's*] so far as my brothers' (*1870–88*; probably, as *Oxford*
suggests, a mispr., since 'his' in l. 112 is unchanged).

iv *97. not one soldo shall escape me*: cp. *Luke* xii 58–9: 'When thou goest with
thine adversary to the magistrate, as thou art in the way, give diligence that thou
mayest be delivered from him; lest he hale thee to the judge, and the judge deliver
thee to the officer, and the officer cast thee into prison. I tell thee, thou shalt
not depart thence, till thou hast paid the very last mite'.   *soldo*: a coin valued at
one-twentieth of a lire, i.e. of very small value.

iv *100. villanous*: the standard spelling until the late 19th century, unchanged
in all eds.

iv *102. sackcloth*: the traditional garb of repentance: cp. e.g. *Daniel* ix 3: 'And
I set my face unto the Lord God, to seek by prayer and supplications, with
fasting, and sackcloth, and ashes'.

iv *102–6. am I therefore . . . associated with it*: cp. *Luke* xvi 15: 'And he said unto
them, Ye are they which justify yourselves before men; but God knoweth your
hearts: for that which is highly esteemed among men is abomination in the sight
of God'.

iv *103. to let . . . ignorant*] to let you, the off-scouring of the earth, seduce the
poor and ignorant, (*1849–88*, except 'ignorant', *1865–88*).

105 the abominations so unaccountably and exclusively associated with it? Must I let manors and liberties go to you,
a murderer and thief, that you may beget by means of them
other murderers and thieves? No . . . if my cough would but
allow me to speak!

110   *Intendant.* What am I to expect? you are going to punish
me?

    Monsignor. Must punish you, Maffeo. I cannot afford to
cast away a chance. I have whole centuries of sin to redeem,
and only a month or two of life to do it in! How should
115 I dare to say . . .

    Intendant. "Forgive us our trespasses."

    Monsignor. My friend, it is because I avow myself a very
worm, sinful beyond measure, that I reject a line of conduct you would applaud, perhaps: shall I proceed, as it were,
120 a-pardoning?—I?—who have no symptom of reason to
assume that aught less than my strenuousest efforts will keep
myself out of mortal sin, much less, keep others out. No—
I do trespass, but will not double that by allowing you to
trespass.

125   *Intendant.* And suppose the manors are not your brother's
to give, or yours to take? Oh, you are hasty enough just
now!

iv *106–8. Must I let . . . murderers and thieves*: the sense is that the Intendant's bad
example will mislead others, not that he will literally father wicked children.

iv *106. manors and liberties*] villas and *poderes* (1849); villas and *poderi* (1863–88).

iv *107. a murderer and thief*: cp. *Job* xxiv 14: 'The murderer rising with the light
killeth the poor and needy, and in the night is as a thief'.

iv *112–4. I cannot afford . . . do it in*: cp. the Pope in *Ring* x 337–45, who also
sees his condemnation of Guido as potentially his last act.

iv *116. "Forgive us our trespasses"*: from the Lord's Prayer. *Matthew* has 'And
forgive us our debts, as we forgive our debtors' (vii 12); *Luke* has 'sins' (xi 4).
Matthew goes on: 'For if ye forgive men their trespasses, your heavenly father will
also forgive you: But if ye forgive not men their trespasses, neither will your
father forgive your trespasses' (vii 15). In *Matthew*, this quotation comes, like many
others in this episode, from the Sermon on the Mount.

iv *117–18. I avow . . . measure*: cp. *Psalms* xxii 6: 'But I am a worm, and no man;
a reproach of men, and despised of the people', and the Apocryphal *Prayer of
Manasses*: 'thou hast promised repentance to them that have sinned; thou hast
not appointed repentance to the just, which have not sinned, but to me, for
I have sinned above the number of the sands of the sea; I have sinned, O Lord,
I have sinned'.

iv *125. suppose the manors*] suppose the villas (1849–88).

iv *126. or yours*] nor yours (1849–88).

Monsignor. 1, 2—No. 3!—ay, can you read the substance
of a letter, No. 3, I have received from Rome? It is on the
130   ground I there mention of the suspicion I have that a
certain child of my late elder brother, who would have
succeeded to his estates, was murdered in infancy by you,
Maffeo, at the instigation of my late brother—that the
pontiff enjoins on me not merely the bringing that Maffeo
135   to condign punishment, but the taking all pains, as
guardian of that infant's heritage for the church, to recover
it parcel by parcel, howsoever, whensoever, and wheresoever. While you are now gnawing those fingers, the
police are engaged in sealing up your papers, Maffeo, and
140   the mere raising my voice brings my people from the next
room to dispose of yourself. But I want you to confess
quietly, and save me raising my voice. Why, man, do I not
know the old story? The heir between the succeeding
heir, and that heir's ruffianly instrument, and their complot's
145   effect, and the life of fear and bribes, and ominous
smiling silence? Did you throttle or stab my brother's infant?
Come, now!

Intendant. So old a story, and tell it no better? When did
such an instrument ever produce such an effect? Either the
150   child smiles in his face, or, most likely, he is not fool
enough to put himself in the employer's power so thoroughly—the child is always ready to produce—as you say—
howsoever, wheresoever, and whensoever.

Monsignor. Liar!

155   *Intendant.* Strike me? Ah, so might a father chastise! I shall
sleep soundly to-night at least, though the gallows await me

---

iv *129–30. on the ground I there mention*] precisely on the ground there mentioned,
(*1849–88*).

iv *133. my late brother*] my late younger brother (*1870–88*).

iv *135. condign punishment*: appropriate punishment. By B.'s time 'condign' was
used only in this phrase.

iv *136. that infant's heritage*] the infant's heritage (*1865–88*).

iv *144. and that heir's*] and this heir's (*1868–88*).

iv *144. complot's*: a 'complot' is a plot or conspiracy.

iv *155. so might a father chastise*: the combination of 'father' and 'chastise' recalls *1
Kings* xii 11: 'And now whereas my father did lade you with a heavy yoke,
I will add to your yoke: my father hath chastised you with whips, but I will
chastise you with scorpions'. However, the Intendant seems to be making an ironic
comment on the Bishop's fatherly care for him, along the lines of *Proverbs*
xix 18: 'Chasten thy son while there is hope, and let not thy soul spare for his
crying'; a third possibility is suggested by *Jeremiah* xxxi 18–20: 'I have surely heard
Ephraim bemoaning himself thus; Thou hast chastised me . . . Is Ephraim my dear
son? is he a pleasant child? . . . I will surely have mercy upon him, saith the Lord'.

to-morrow; for what a life did I lead? Carlo of Cesena reminds
me of his connivance every time I pay his annuity (which
happens commonly thrice a year). If I remonstrate, he will
160 confess all to the good bishop—you!
    Monsignor. I see thro' the trick, caitiff! I would you spoke
truth for once; all shall be sifted, however—seven times sifted.
    Intendant. And how my absurd riches encumbered me!
I dared not lay claim to above half my possessions. Let me
165 but once unbosom myself, glorify Heaven, and die!
    Sir, you are no brutal, dastardly idiot like your brother
I frightened to death . . . let us understand one another. Sir,
I will make away with her for you—the girl—here close at
hand; not the stupid obvious kind of killing; do not
170 speak—know nothing of her or me. I see her every day—
saw her this morning—of course there is no killing; but at
Rome the courtesans perish off every three years, and I can
entice her thither—have, indeed, begun operations already
—there's a certain lusty, blue-eyed, florid-complexioned,
175 English knave I employ occasionally.—You assent, I perceive—no, that's not it—assent I do not say—but you will
let me convert my present havings and holdings into
cash, and give time to cross the Alps? 'Tis but a little
black-eyed, pretty singing Felippa, gay silk-winding girl.
180 I have kept her out of harm's way up to this present; for
I always intended to make your life a plague to you with
her! 'Tis as well settled once and forever: some women
I have procured will pass Bluphocks, my handsome
scoundrel, off for somebody, and once Pippa entangled!—
185 you conceive?
    Monsignor. Why, if she sings, one might . . .

iv *158. annuity*: lit., 'a yearly grant of income'; here, a euphemism for blackmail
payments.
iv *162. seven times sifted*: a biblical intensifier; cp. *Leviticus* xxvi 18: 'I shall punish
you seven times more'; cp. *Sordello* i 434 (I 422): 'Gold seven times globed'.
iv *167–73. Sir, I will . . . entice her thither*: cp. the episode in *Pericles* IV vi in which
Marina is sold to a brothel in Mytilene by those who have rescued her from
attempted murder.
iv *170. her or me.*] her or me! (*1849–63*); her nor of me! (*1865–88*).
iv *175. I employ*] I and the Police employ (*1849–88*).
iv *178. give time*] give me time (*1849–88*).
iv *178. cross the Alps*: the Intendant wants to escape from Austrian jurisdiction;
his destination is either France or Switzerland.
iv *185. you conceive?*] you conceive? Through her singing? Is it a bargain? (*1849–88*).
iv *186.*] not *1849–88*.

[*Without*] Over-head the tree-tops meet—
Flowers and grass spring 'neath one's feet—
What are the voices of birds
190   —Ay, and beasts, too—but words—our words,
Only so much more sweet?
That knowledge with my life begun!
But I had so near made out the sun—
Could count your stars, the Seven and One!
195   Like the fingers of my hand—
Nay, could all but understand
How and wherefore the moon ranges—
And just when out of her soft fifty changes
No unfamiliar face might overlook me—
200   Suddenly God took me.

                                        [Pippa *passes*.

        Monsignor [*Springing up*] My people—one and all—all—
within there! Gag this villain—tie him hand and foot: he

---

iv *187*] the s.d.'s are altered in *1849–88* as with Pippa's first song, i 215–22.

iv *187*. Cp. *Round Us the Wild Creatures* (*Ferishtah's Fancies*, 1884) 1–2: 'Round us the wild creatures, overhead the trees, / Underfoot the moss-tracks,—life and love with these!'

iv *188^189*.] There was nought above me, and nought below, / My childhood had not learned to know! (*1849–88*, except 'know:', *1863–88*; 'me, nought', *1865–88*).

iv *189*. *What*] For, what (*1849–88*).

iv *190*. *and beasts, too*—] and of beasts,—(*1849–88*).

iv *192*. *That knowledge*] The knowledge of that (*1849–88*). Cp. Wordsworth, *My heart leaps up* 1–6: 'My heart leaps up when I behold / A rainbow in the sky: / So was it when my life began; / So is it now I am a man; / So be it when I shall grow old, / Or let me die!'

iv *194*. *Could count*] And counted (*1849–88*).   *the Seven and One*: lit., the constellation of the Pleiades or Seven Sisters, and one of the other major stars, perhaps Aldebaran or Fomalhaut (the latter is mentioned in *Sordello* iii 416 (I 550); but B. probably also alludes to the 'seven stars' held in the right hand of Christ, *Revelation* i 16, and to Christ himself as the 'bright and morning star', *Revelation* xxii 16: see above, iii 147–8n. Cp. also, noting the next lines, *Psalms* viii 3: 'When I consider thy heavens, the work of thy fingers, the moon and the stars, which thou hast ordained'.

iv *196*. *Nay, could*] Nay, I could (*1849–88*).

iv *197*.] Wherefore through heaven the white moon ranges (*1849–88*).

iv *198*. *fifty*: often used by B. with the indefinite sense of 'a large number': cp. *Sordello* v 182 (I 670): 'For one thrust forward, fifty such fall back!' But cp. the link between the moon as image of EBB. and the fifty poems of *M & W* in *One Word More* (p. 598).

iv *200*. *took me*.] took me! (*1849–88*).

dares—I know not half he dares—but remove him—quick!
Miserere mei, Domine! quick, I say!

———————

Pippa's *Chamber again. She enters it.*

205 The bee with his comb,
     The mouse at her dray,
     The grub in its tomb
     Wile winter away;
     But the fire-fly and hedge-shrew and lobworm, I pray,
210 Where be they?
     Ha, ha, thanks my Zanze—
     "Feed on lampreys, quaff Breganze"—
     The summer of life's so easy to spend!
     But winter hastens at summer's end,
215 And fire-fly, hedge-shrew, lob-worm, pray,
     Where be they?
     No bidding you then to . . what did Zanze say?
     "Pare your nails pearlwise, get your small feet shoes
     "More like . . (what said she?)—and less like canoes—"
220 Pert as a sparrow . . . would I be those pert

———————

iv *204. Miserere mei, Domine*: 'Have mercy on me, Lord'. From *Psalms* li, a Penitential Psalm: 'Have mercy upon me, O God, according to thy lovingkindness: according to the multitude of thy tender mercies blot out my transgressions'. A standard prayer in the Catholic Church. *OED* cites Blount, 1656: '*Miserere* . . . is commonly that Psalm, which the Judge gives to such guilty persons as have the benefit of Clergy allowed by the Law'.

iv *205–10*. Adapting Aesop's fable of the grasshopper and the ant. Croxall's translation (known to B.) concludes: 'they who drink, sing and dance in Summer, must starve in Winter'. Croxall's moral, like Pippa's, relates the fable to youth, as either misspent or prudent.

iv *206. dray*: lit., a squirrel's nest; not applied to mice in any *OED* citation.

iv *207. its*] his (*1888*).

iv *216.*] How fare they? (*1849–88*).

iv *217.*] Ha, ha, best thanks for your counsel, my Zanze— (*1849–88*, except 'ha, thanks', *1865–88*; 'Zanze!', *1868–88*).

iv *212. "Feed on*] "Feast upon (*1849–88*). *quaff Breganze"*—] quaff the Breganize"— (*1849–75*). See iii 231n.

iv *213. life's*] life (*1865–88*). *spend!*] spend, (*1849–88*; see next note).

iv *213^214.*] And care for to-morrow so soon put away! (*1849–88*).

iv *216.*] How fare they? (*1849–88*).

iv *220. Pert as a sparrow . . .*] How pert that girl was!— (*1849–88*). The sparrow was Venus' bird and associated with lust. Cp. *Youth and Art* 3n. (p. 702).

Impudent staring wretches! it had done me,
However, surely no such mighty hurt
To learn his name who passed that jest upon me.—
No foreigner, that I can recollect,
225   Came, as she says, a month since to inspect
Our silk-mills—none with blue eyes and thick rings
Of English-coloured hair, at all events.
Well—if old Luca keeps his good intents
We shall do better—see what next year brings—
230   I may buy shoes, my Zanze, not appear
So destitute, perhaps, next year!
Bluf—something—I had caught the uncouth name
But for Monsignor's people's sudden clatter
Above us—bound to spoil such idle chatter,
235   The pious man, the man devoid of blame,
The . . . ah, but—ah, but, all the same
No mere mortal has a right
To carry that exalted air;
Best people are not angels quite—
240   While—not worst people's doings scare
The devils; so there's that regard to spare!
Mere counsel to myself, mind! for
I have just been Monsignor!

---

v *221. wretches*] women (*1849–88*).

iv *227. English-coloured hair*] raw-silk-coloured hair (*1849–88*).

iv *230. not appear*] nor appear (*B & P BYU*).

iv *231.*] More destitute than you, perhaps, next year! (*1849–88*, except 'you perhaps', *1865–88*).

iv *234. chatter*] chatter (*1849–88*); see next note.

iv *234^235.*] As ours; it were, indeed, a serious matter / If silly talk like ours should put to shame (*1849–88*, except 'ours:', *1868–88*; 'It were indeed', *1865–88*).

iv *235.* Cp. *Ephesians* i 4: 'holy and without blame'.

iv *239.* Conflating two proverbs: 'the best of men are but men at best' and 'men are not angels'. *Oxford Dictionary of Proverbs* cites T. Cooper, 1589: 'They [bishops] are men, and no Angels . . . He is an Angel that never falleth, hee is no man'; also *Henry VIII* V ii 45–9 (spoken to Archbishop Cranmer): 'we all are men, / In our own natures frail, and capable / Of our flesh; few are angels; out of which frailty / And want of wisdom, you, that best should teach us, / Have misdemean'd yourself'. Cp. also *Psalms* viii 5: 'For thou hast made him [man] a little lower than the angels'.

iv *240. not worst people's*] not the worst of people's (*1849–88*).

iv *241. devils*] devil (*1863–88*). *regard*] proud look (*1849–88*).

iv *242. Mere*] Which is mere (*1849–88*). This line is indented, *1868–88*.

iv *243. Monsignor*] the holy Monsignor (*1849–88*).

And I was you too, mother,
245   And you too, Luigi!—how that Luigi started
        Out of the Turret—doubtlessly departed
        On some love-errand or another—
        And I was Jules the sculptor's bride,
        And I was Ottima beside,
250   And now what am I?—tired of fooling!
        Day for folly, night for schooling—
        New year's day is over—over!
        Even my lily's asleep, I vow:
        Wake up—here's a friend I pluckt you.
255   See—call this a heart's-ease now!
        Something rare, let me instruct you,
        Is this—with petals triply swollen,
        Three times spotted, thrice the pollen,
        While the leaves and parts that witness
260   The old proportions and their fitness
        Here remain, unchanged unmoved now—
        Call this pampered thing improved now!
        Suppose there's a king of the flowers
        And a girl-show held in his bowers—
265   "Look ye, buds, this growth of ours,"
        Says he, "Zanze from the Brenta,
        I have made her gorge polenta
        Till both cheeks are near as bouncing

iv *244. mother*] Luigi's gentle mother (*1849–88*).
iv *247. love-errand*] good errand (*1849–88*).   *another—*] another, (*1849–88*); see next note.
iv *247^248.*] For he past just now in a traveller's trim,
                    And the sullen company that prowled
                    About his path, I noticed, scowled
                    As if they lost a prey in him. (*1849–88*, except 'pass'd', *1863–65*; 'passed', *1868–88*).
iiv *252. over—over!*] over and spent, (*1849–88*); see next note.
iv *252^253.*] Ill or well, I must be content! (*1849–88*, except 'content.', *1865–88*). The next line is indented as for a new para., *1868–88*.
iv *254. I pluckt you.*] I've pluckt you! (*1849–88*, except 'plucked', *1868–88*).
iv *255–277.* With Pippa's criticism of the over-cultivated flower, and the parallel between flowers and girls which follows, cp. Perdita in *Winter's Tale* IV iv 79ff.
iv *255. See—call this*] See—call this flower (*1849–63*); Call this flower (*1865–88*). *heart's-ease*: pansy. See i 229n.
iv *256. Something*] And something (*1849–63*).
iv *260. The old*] Old (*1865–88*).
iv *261. Call*] So call (*1849*); So, call (*1863*).
iv *267. polenta*: see iii 288n.

As her . . . name there's no pronouncing!
270   See this heightened colour too—
For she swilled Breganze wine
Till her nose turned deep carmine—
'Twas but white when wild she grew!
And only by this Zanze's eyes
275   Of which we could not change the size,
The magnitude of what's achieved
Elsewhere may be perceived!"

Oh what a drear, dark close to my poor day!
How could that red sun drop in that black cloud!
280   Ah, Pippa, morning's rule is moved away,
Dispensed with, never more to be allowed.
Day's turn's over—now's the night's—
Oh Lark be day's apostle
To mavis, merle and throstle,
285   Bid them their betters jostle
From day and its delights!
But at night, brother Howlet, over the woods
Toll the world to thy chantry—
Sing to the bats' sleek sisterhoods
290   Full complines with gallantry—
Then, owls and bats, cowls and twats,

iv *269. As her . . . pronouncing*: her breasts.
iv *276. what's achieved*] all achieved (*1865–88*).
iv *277. Elsewhere*] Otherwise (*1849–88*).
iv *282.*] Day's turn is over—now arrives the night's— (*1849–88*, except 'over:', *1863–65*; 'over,', *1868–88*; 'night's.', *1863–88*).
iv *283–6.* Cp. *Luke* xiv 15–24, the parable of the rich man who 'bids' many guests to his 'great supper'; when they do not come he commands his servants to 'bring in hither the poor' instead.
iv *284.* The 'mavis' is the song-thrush, the 'merle' the blackbird. The 'throstle' is another name for the song-thrush.
iv *287. brother*: monk.   *Howlet*: owl.   *over*] far over (*1849–63*).
iv *288. chantry*: a chapel where mass is sung for the souls of the dead.
iv *290. complines*: in the Roman Catholic liturgy, the last service of the day, completing the services of the canonical hours.   *gallantry*] emended in agreement with *1863–88* from 'galantry', *1841–49*. Although *OED* has a couple of instances of 'galantry', none is recorded after the 17th century.
iv *291.*] Then, owls and bats, / Cowls and twats, (*1870–88*).   *twats*: B. wrote to Furnivall: 'In the Royalist rhymes entitled "Vanity of Vanities, or Sir Harry Vane's Picture"—wherein Vane is charged with being a Jesuit—occur these lines "'Tis said they will give him a Cardinal's hat: / They sooner will give him an old nun's twat!" The ballad is partly quoted in the Appendix to Forster's *Life of Vane*, but the above lines are left out—I remember them, however, and the word struck

Monks and nuns, in a cloister's moods,
Adjourn to the oak-stump pantry!

> [*After she has begun to undress herself.*

Now one thing I should like to really know:
295   How near I ever might approach all these
I only fancied being this long day—
. . . Approach, I mean, so as to touch them—so
As to . . in some way . . move them—if you please,
Do good or evil to them some slight way.
300   For instance, if I wind
Silk to-morrow, silk may bind

> [*Sitting on the bedside.*

And broider Ottima's cloak's hem—
Ah, me and my important passing them
This morning's hymn half promised when I rose!
305   True in some sense or other, I suppose.

> [*As she lies down.*

God bless me tho' I cannot pray tonight.
No doubt, some way or other, hymns say right.
All service is the same with God—
Whose puppets, best and worst,
310   *Are we . . . . . .*

> [*She sleeps.*

---

me as a distinctive part of a nun's attire that might fitly pair off with the cowl
appropriated to a monk' (*Trumpeter* 135). B.'s surmise is famously wrong; the word
means 'cunt'. B. slightly misquotes the lines, which in the original broadside
ballad to which he refers read: 'They talkt of his having a Cardinalls Hat, / They'd
send him as soon an Old Nuns Twat'. The ballad is undated; in two copies in
the Bodleian Library, Oxford (Wood 416 [32, 91]) the date is conjectured as 1659
or 1661–2. It was also repr., as *Oxford* points out, in *Rump, or an Exact Collection
of the Choycest Poems and Songs Relating to the Late Times* (2 pts., 1662) ii 108–11.
Forster's version, considerably abridged, appears in Appendix C of his *Life of
Sir Henry Vane* (*Lives of Eminent British Statesmen* iv [1838] 398–400).
iv *294. to really*] really to (*1849–88*).
iv *301. silk*] my silk (*1849–88*).
iv *302. broider*] border (*1868–88*).
iv *303. Ah, me*] Ah me, (*1865–88*).   *passing them*] part with them (*1849–88*).
iv *305. suppose.*] suppose, (*1849–63*); see next note.
iv *305^306.*] Though I passed by them all, and felt no sign. (*1849–63*). This is a
rare example of a whole line being added in one ed. and deleted later.
iv *306.*] God bless me! I can pray no more to-night. (*1849–88*).
iv *308–10.* The last three lines echo the 'new year's hymn', *Intro* 148–59.
iv *308. is*] ranks (*1865–88*).
iv *309. Whose*] With God, whose (*1849–88*).
iv *310*] Are we: there is no last nor first.—(*1849–88*, except 'first.', *1863–88*).

5 The Pied Piper of Hamelin
A Child's Story
(Written for, and inscribed to, W. M. the Younger)

First publ. *B & P* iii (*DL*), 26 Nov. 1842; repr. *1849, 1863, 1863², 1868, 1888*. Our text is *1842*. The poem was written for Willie, the son of the actor-manager William Macready, during the period when he and B. were close friends and colleagues. The child was in bed with a bad cough in the spring of 1842. 'He had a talent for drawing, and asked me to give him some little thing to illustrate; so, I made a bit of a poem out of an old account of the Pope's legate at the Council of Trent—which he made such clever drawings for, that I tried a more picturesque subject, the Piper' (*Trumpeter* 27). For the first poem, see *The Cardinal and the Dog* (II 114). Two letters from Willie Macready, thanking B. for his poems and offering his illustrations, can be found in *Correspondence* v 329–31, 350–1. The second letter, which refers to *The Pied Piper*, is dated 12 May 1842. B.'s sister Sarianna's account adds some detail: 'At first, there was no thought of publishing them, but I copied the Pied Piper and showed it to Alfred Domett who was so much pleased with it that he persuaded Robert to include it in the following number of Bells and Pomegranates' (*Correspondence* v 330). Kelley and Hudson argue that Domett's departure for New Zealand on 30 Apr. makes this account 'suspect', and it does imply a somewhat protracted illness for Willie Macready; however, Sarianna's account is too circumstantial to be dismissed, though B.'s decision to publish the poem was prompted by Moxon, his publisher, who needed additional copy for *DL* to fill up the pamphlet; it is not in *DL 1st proof*, appearing first in *DL 2nd proof.*

The primary source, according to B., was a story in *Wanley* from which B. also obtained the story of *Cardinal*. In B.'s copy of *Wanley*, now in *ABL*, a note on the fly-leaf cites the passage. *Wanley*'s account is as follows:

At *Hammel*, a town in the Dutchy of *Brunswick*, in the year of Christ 1284. upon the 26. day of *June*, the Town being grievously troubled with Rats and Mice, there came to them a Piper, who promised upon a certain rate to free them from them all; it was agreed, he went from street to street, and playing upon his Pipe, drew after him out of the Town all that kind of Vermine, and then demanding his wages was denied it. Whereupon he began another tune, and there followed him one hundred and thirty Boys to a Hill called *Koppen*, situate on the North by the Road, where they perished, and were never seen after. This Piper was called the pyed Piper, because his cloaths were of several colours. This story is writ and religiously kept by them in their Annals at *Hammel*, read in their Books, and painted in their Windows and Churches, of which I am a witness by my own sight. Their elder Magistrats, for the confirmation of the truth of this, are wont to write in conjunction in their publick books, such a year of Christ, and such a year of the Transmigration of the children, &c. It's also observed in the memory of it, that in the street he passed out of, no Piper be admitted to this day. The street is called *Burgelosestrasse*; if a Bride be in that street, till she is gone out of it there is no dancing to be suffered. *Wier. de praestig. Daemon.* I. 1, c. 16 p. 47. *Schot. phys. curios.* I. 3. c. 24. p. 519. *Howels Ep.* vol. i. #. 6., *epist. 59. p. 241.*

B. seems to have told Frederick Furnivall for his *Bibliography* (*BSP* i 159) that he used no other sources than Wanley and the sources cited there (J. Wier, *De Praestigiis Daemonium* [1564]; G. Schott, *Physica Curiosa* [1662]; J. Howell, *Epistolae Ho-Elianae* [1645]). Howell differs from Wanley in having the children, not merely 'boys', taken into the Hill rather than killed; for other details, see notes. B. denied that he at that time consulted Richard Verstegen's *Restitution of Decayed Intelligence in Antiquities* (1605), but A. Dickson ('Browning's Source for *The Pied Piper of Hamelin*', *SP* xxiii [July 1926] 327–32) convincingly argues that some details in the poem come so close to Verstegen as to make it likely that B. was mistaken. Verstegen's account is as follows:

There came into the town of *Hamel* in the countrey of *Brunswyc* an od kynd of compagnion, who for the fantastical cote which hee wore being wrought with sundry colours, was called the pyed piper; for a pyper hee was, besides his other qualities. This fellow forsooth offred the townsmen for a certain somme of money to rid the town of all the rattes that were in it (for at that tyme the burgers were with that vermin greatly annoyed)[.] The accord in fyne beeing made; the pyed piper with a shril pype went pyping through the streets, and foorthwith the rattes came all running out of the howses in great numbers after him; all which hee led vnto the riuer of *Weaser* and therein drowned them. This donne, and no one rat more perceaued to be left in the town; he afterward came to demaund his reward according to his bargain, but beeing told that the bargain was not made with him in good earnest, to wit, with an opinion that euer hee could bee able to do such a feat: they cared not what they accorded vnto, when they imagyned it could neuer bee deserued, and so neuer to bee demaunded: but neuerthelesse seeing hee had donne such an vnlykely thing in deed, they were content to giue him a good reward; & so offred him far lesse then hee lookt for: but hee therewith discontented, said he would haue his ful recompence according to his bargain, but they vtterly denying to giue it him, hee threatened them with reuenge; they bad him do his wurst, wherevpon he betakes him again to his pype, & going through the streets as before, was followed of a number of boyes out at one of the gates of the citie, and coming to a litle hil, there opened in the syde thereof a wyde hole, into the which himself and all the children beeing in number one hundreth & thirty, did enter; and beeing entred, the hil closed vp again, and became as before. A boy that beeing lame & came somwhat lagging behynd the rest, seeing this that hapned, returned presently back & told what hee had seen; foorthwith began great lamentation among the parents for their children, and men were sent out with all dilligence, both by land & by water to enquyre yf ought could bee heard of them, but with all the enquyrie they could possibly vse, nothing more then is aforesaid could of them bee vnderstood. In memorie whereof it was then ordayned, that from thence-foorth no drum, pype or other instrument, should be sounded in the street leading to the gate through which they passed; nor no osterie to bee there holden. And it was also established, that from that tyme forward in all publyke wrytings that should bee made in that town, after the date therein set down of the yeare of our Lord, the date of the yeare of the going foorth of their children should bee added, the which they haue accordingly euer since continued. And this great wonder hapned on the 22. day of Iuly, in the yeare of our Lord one thousand three hundreth seauentie, and six.

The occasion now why this matter came vnto my remembrance in speaking of *Transiluania*, was, for that some do reporte that there are diuers found

among the Saxons in *Transiluania* that haue lyke surnames vnto diuers of the
burgers of *Hamel*, and wil seem thereby to inferr, that this iugler or pyed pyper,
might by negromancie haue transported them thether, but this carieth little
apparence of truthe; because it would haue bin almost as great a wonder vnto
the Saxons of *Transiluania* to haue had so many strange children brought among
them, they knew not how, as it was to those of *Hamel* to lose them: & they
could not but haue kept memorie of so strange a thing, yf in deed any such
thing had there hapned.

DeVane (*Handbook* 127–31) notes that various intermediate sources transmit
Verstegen's account, and that a portion was repr. in Chambers' *Book of Days*, a
book which B.'s father 'almost certainly' owned. *Oxford* plausibly suggests a further source, in which several details coincide with Verstegen, the entry on 'Hamelen'
in Jeremy Collier's *Great Historical, Geographical, Genealogical and Poetical
Dictionary*, the second edition of which (2 vols., 1701) B. told Furnivall he read
'right through' as a boy, and which his father gave him 'many years after' (*Trumpeter*
101). Collier describes Hamelin as 'Watered by the River *Weser*' and states:

> It is famous for the wonderful Accident said to have happened here *July* 22.
> 1376; for being incredibly troubled with Rats, a Musician (whom they call'd
> the *Py'd-Piper*) offer'd to destroy 'em for a certain Summ which was agreed
> upon. Then the Piper tuning his Pipes, all the Rats in the Town danced after
> him as he cross'd the River, and were drowned. This done, he demanded
> his Pay, but was denied. Whereupon striking up a new Fit of Mirth, all the
> children of the Town (Male and Female) were so much charmed therewith,
> that they followed him to a neighbouring Hill, which opening, swallowed all up
> but one that lagged behind, and, according to some, they were seen again
> in Transilvania. In memory of this Tragedy, it was Ordered, That in all publick
> Writings, after the date of our Saviours Nativity, this of their Childrens
> being swallowed up, should be added.

B.'s father wrote three versions of a poem on the Piper; the earliest of these was
begun at the same time as B.'s poem, but, according to B.'s father's MS note,
abandoned when he realized that his son 'had written on this subject'; there was
therefore no connection between them. (Later, however, he did complete his
poem, in two versions, repr. *Oxford* iii 522–42; in both, the Piper is represented
as a diabolical agent, in sharp contrast to B.'s interpretation: we therefore
cannot agree with Mr Philip Kelley's suggestion to us that, by analogy with B.'s
father's transcript of *Cardinal* (see II 114), these texts may be copies of B.'s
own early drafts.) See also *Flight of the Duchess* 545–51n. (II 420). A. Kincaid and
P. Blayney, in 'A Book of Browning's and his *Essay on Chatterton*', *BSN* ii (Dec.
1972) 11–25, point out that B. may well have been working on *Chatterton* at the
same time as he wrote *Pied Piper*, and suggest that the theme of the artist exploited
and abandoned by ungrateful patrons is common to the two works. Annotations
in a copy of *Walpoliana* that B. consulted while writing *Chatterton* (see headnote,
II 476) suggest that he saw the relation between Chatterton and Walpole in this way,
esp. in connection with Walpole's notorious stinginess as a patron: 'an artist has
pencils, and an author has pens, and the public must reward them *as it happens*'
(p. 24; B.'s italics).

The poem is written in the irregular, jocular style, full of absurd rhymes,
typical of Samuel Butler's *Hudibras* and the comic poetry of Southey, Hood, and
Barham. An analogy between magicianship and the poet's visionary power is
common in B.'s work: see e.g. the epigraph to *Pauline* (pp. 11–12), *Paracelsus*,

and *Ring* i 742ff. With the Piper's success in ridding the town of its vermin, contrast the comic failure of the artist-reformer Pacchiarotto in *Of Pacchiarotto* (1876).

I.

Hamelin Town's in Brunswick,
  By famous Hanover city;
The river Weser, deep and wide,
Washes its wall on the southern side;
5 A pleasanter spot you never spied;
  But, when begins my ditty,
Almost five hundred years ago,
To see the townsfolk suffer so
  From vermin, was a pity.

II.

10   Rats!
They fought the dogs, and killed the cats,
  And bit the babies in the cradles,
And eat the cheeses out of the vats,
  And licked the soup from the cooks' own ladles,
15 Split open the kegs of salted sprats,
Made nests inside men's Sunday hats,
And even spoiled the women's chats,
  By drowning their speaking
  With shrieking and squeaking
20 In fifty different sharps and flats.

III.

At last the people in a body
  To the Town Hall came flocking:
'Tis clear, cried they, our Mayor's a noddy;
  And as for our Corporation—shocking
25 To think we buy gowns lined with ermine
For dolts that can't or won't determine

---

1. Hamelin is in Hanover, not Brunswick; Verstegen has this error.
4. southern: actually western.
7. This dates the story in the 14th century, closer to Verstegen's and Collier's 1376 than Wanley's 1284: see ll. 267–8n.
9. was] 'twas (*1849–88*).
13. eat] ate (*1849–88*). 'Eat' is the old form of the past tense, not an error.
21–7. In Howell's account the piper 'covenanted with the chief Burgers'.
23–30.] the people's speech is in quotation marks, *1849–88*; subsequent speeches are also marked.

What's like to rid us of our vermin!
Rouse up, Sirs! Give your brains a racking
To find the remedy we're lacking,
30   Or, sure as fate, we'll send you packing!
     At this the Mayor and Corporation
     Quaked with a mighty consternation.

IV.

An hour they sate in council,
     At length the Mayor broke silence:
35   For a guilder I'd my ermine gown sell;
     I wish I were a mile hence!
It's easy to bid one rack one's brain—
I'm sure my poor head aches again,
I've scratched it so, and all in vain.
40   Oh for a trap, a trap, a trap!
Just as he said this, what should hap
At the chamber door but a gentle tap?
Bless us, cried the Mayor, what's that?
(With the Corporation as he sate,
45   Looking little though wondrous fat)
Only a scraping of shoes on the mat?
Anything like the sound of a rat
Makes my heart go pit-a-pat!

V.

Come in!—the Mayor cried, looking bigger:
50   And in did come the strangest figure!
His queer long coat from heel to head
Was half of yellow and half of red;
And he himself was tall and thin,
With sharp blue eyes, each like a pin,

27. *like*] best (*1849–88*).
27^28.] You hope, because you're old and obese, / To find in the furry civic robe ease? (*1849–88*).
35. *guilder*: a small gold coin, originally in use in the Netherlands and parts of Germany; later, a Dutch silver coin.
38. *again,*] emended in agreement with *1865–88* from 'again' in *1842–63*.
45. *fat)*] fat; (*1849–88*); see next note.
45^46.] Nor brighter was his eye, nor moister
          Than a too-long-opened oyster,
        Save when at noon his paunch grew mutinous
        For a plate of turtle green and glutinous) (*1849–88*)

55 And light loose hair, yet swarthy skin,
No tuft on cheek nor beard on chin,
But lips where smiles went out and in—
There was no guessing his kith and kin!
And nobody could enough admire
60 The tall man and his quaint attire:
Quoth one: It's as my great-grandsire,
Starting up at the Trump of Doom's tone,
Had walked this way from his painted tomb-stone!

VI.

He advanced to the council-table:
65 And, Please your honours, said he, I'm able,
By means of a secret charm, to draw
All creatures living beneath the sun,
That creep, or swim, or fly, or run,
After me so as you never saw!
70 And I chiefly use my charm
On creatures that do people harm,
The mole, and toad, and newt, and viper;
And people call me the Pied Piper.
(And here they noticed round his neck
75 A scarf of red and yellow stripe,
To match with his coat of the self same cheque;
And at the scarf's end hung a pipe;
And his fingers, they noticed, were ever straying
As if impatient to be playing
80 Upon this pipe, as low it dangled
Over his vesture so old-fangled.)
Yet, said he, poor piper as I am,
In Tartary I freed the Cham,
Last June, from his huge swarms of gnats;
85 I eased in Asia the Nizam
Of a monstrous brood of vampyre-bats:
And, as for what your brain bewilders,
If I can rid your town of rats
Will you give me a thousand guilders?
90 One? fifty thousand!—was the exclamation
Of the astonished Mayor and Corporation.

73. *Piper.*] emended in agreement with all other eds. from 'Piper' in *1842*.

VII.

Into the street the Piper stept,
   Smiling first a little smile,
As if he knew what magic slept
95   In his quiet pipe the while;
Then, like a musical adept,
To blow the pipe his lips he wrinkled,
And green and blue his sharp eyes twinkled
Like a candle flame where salt is sprinkled;
100 And ere three shrill notes the pipe uttered,
You heard as if an army muttered;
And the muttering grew to a grumbling;
And the grumbling grew to a mighty rumbling;
And out of the houses the rats came tumbling.
105 Great rats, small rats, lean rats, brawny rats,
Brown rats, black rats, grey rats, tawny rats,
Grave old plodders, gay young friskers,
   Fathers, mothers, uncles, cousins,
Cocking tails and pricking whiskers,
110   Families by tens and dozens,
Brothers, sisters, husbands, wives—
Followed the Piper for their lives.
From street to street he piped advancing,
And step for step they followed dancing,
115 Until they came to the river Weser
Wherein all plunged and perished
   —Save one who, stout as Julius Caesar,
Swam across and lived to carry
(As he the manuscript he cherished)
120 To Rat-land home his commentary,
Which was, At the first shrill notes of the pipe,
I heard a sound as of scraping tripe,
And putting apples, wondrous ripe,
Into a cider-press's gripe:
125 And a moving away of pickle-tub-boards,
And a leaving ajar of conserve-cupboards,

---

116. *perished*] perished! (*1863–88, except 1863², as 1842*).
117. When Caesar's ship was captured at Alexandria, he swam ashore carrying
the MS of his historical memoir, *De Gallico Belli*; such texts were known as
'commentarii'. *Oxford* notes that Willie Macready probably knew the story, 'since
selections from Caesar are often read by beginners at Latin'.

And a drawing the corks of train-oil-flasks,
And a breaking the hoops of butter-casks;
And it seemed as if a voice
130 (Sweeter than by harp or by psaltery
Is breathed) called out, Oh rats, rejoice!
The world is grown one vast drysaltery!
So munch on, crunch on, take your nuncheon,
Breakfast, supper, dinner, luncheon!
135 And just as one bulky sugar puncheon,
Ready staved, like a great sun shone
Glorious scarce an inch before me,
Just as methought it said, Come, bore me!
—I found the Weser rolling o'er me.

VIII.

140 You should have heard the Hamelin people
Ringing the bells till they rocked the steeple;
Go, cried the Mayor, and get long poles!
Poke out the nests and block up the holes!
Consult with carpenters and builders,
145 And leave in our town not even a trace
Of the rats!—when suddenly up the face
Of the Piper perked in the market-place,
With a, First, if you please, my thousand guilders!

IX.

A thousand guilders! The Mayor looked blue;
150 So did the Corporation too.
For council dinners made rare havock
With Claret, Moselle, Vin-de-Grave, Hock;
And half the money would replenish
Their cellar's biggest butt with Rhenish.

127. *train-oil*: oil obtained from whale blubber.
130. *Sweeter*] Sweeter far (*1849–88*).   *by . . . by*] by . . . bý (*1849–65*); bý . . . bý
(*1870–1888*). Note that *1868* returns, unusually, to the first-edition reading.
psaltery: an ancient and medieval stringed instrument.
132. *drysaltery*: a shop dealing in chemicals, oils, sauces, tinned meats, etc.
133. *nuncheon*: a light refreshment taken between meals. Cp. Samuel Butler's *Hudibras*:
'They took their Breakfasts or their Nuncheons' (I i 344).
135. *one*] a (*1849–88*).   *puncheon*: a large cask for liquids, fish, etc.
136. *Ready*] All ready (*1849–88*).   *staved*: broken into staves.
151. *havock*] havoc (*1863–88*).
152. All names of French and German wines ('Grave' in error for 'Graves').
154. *Rhenish*: a general term for Rhine wine.

155   To pay this sum to a wandering fellow
       With a gipsy coat of red and yellow!
       Beside, quoth the Mayor with a knowing wink,
       Our business was done at the river's brink;
       We saw with our eyes the vermin sink,
160   And what's dead can't come to life, I think.
       So, friend, we're not the folks to shrink
       From the duty of giving you something for drink,
       And a matter of money to put in your poke;
       But, as for the guilders, what we spoke
165   Of them, as you very well know, was in joke.
       Beside, our losses have made us thrifty;
       A thousand guilders! Come, take fifty!

                    X.
       The Piper's face fell, and he cried,
       No trifling! I can't wait, beside!
170   I've promised to visit by dinner time
       Bagdat, and accept the prime
       Of the Head Cook's pottage, all he's rich in,
       For having left, in the Caliph's kitchen,
       Of a nest of scorpions no survivor—
175   With him I proved no bargain-driver,
       With you, don't think I'll bate a stiver!
       And folks who put me in a passion
       May find me pipe after another fashion.

                    XI.
       How? cried the Mayor, d'ye think I'll brook
180   Being worse treated than a Cook?
       Insulted by a lazy ribald
       With idle pipe and vesture piebald?
       You threaten us, fellow? Do your worst,
       Blow your pipe there till you burst!

---

163. poke: purse or pocket.
166. Beside] Besides *(1849–88)*.
167. Howell has 'the Burgers put him off with slightings, and neglect, offring him
som small matter'.
176. stiver: a small coin, worth about a twentieth of a Dutch guilder.
178. after] to *(1849–65)*.
179. I'll] I *(1865–88)*.

XII.

185 Once more he stept into the street;
     And to his lips agáin
Laid his long pipe of smooth straight cane;
     And ere he blew three notes (such sweet
Soft notes as yet musician's cunning
190   Never gave th'enraptured air)
There was a rustling, that seem'd like a bustling
Of merry crowds justling at pitching and hustling,
Small feet were pattering, wooden shoes clattering,
Little hands clapping, and little tongues chattering,
195 And, like fowls in a farm-yard when barley is scattering,
Out came the children running.
All the little boys and girls,
With rosy cheeks and flaxen curls,
And sparkling eyes and teeth like pearls,
200 Tripping and skipping, ran merrily after
The wonderful music with shouting and laughter.

XIII.

The Mayor was dumb, and the Council stood
As if they were changed into blocks of wood,
Unable to move a step, or cry
205 To the children merrily skipping by—
Could only follow with the eye
That joyous crowd at the Piper's back.
But how the Mayor was on the rack,
And the wretched Council's bosoms beat,
210 As the Piper turned from the High Street
To where the Weser rolled its waters
Right in the way of their sons and daughters!
However he turned from South to West,
And to Coppelburg Hill his steps addressed,
215 And after him the children pressed;
Great was the joy in every breast.
He never can cross that mighty top!
He's forced to let the piping drop,

---

190. th'] the (*1849–88*).
192. 'Pitch-and-hustle' is a children's game in which coins are thrown at a mark, the player who comes closest taking the lot.
206. Could] And could (*1849–65*);—Could (*1868–88*).
213–14. from South . . . addressed: the hill is actually east of Hamelin.

And we shall see our children stop!
When, lo, as they reached the mountain's side,
220 A wondrous portal opened wide,
As if a cavern was suddenly hollowed;
And the Piper advanced and the children follow'd,
And when all were in to the very last,
The door in the mountain side shut fast.
225 Did I say, all? No! One was lame,
And could not dance the whole of the way;
And in after years, if you would blame
His sadness, he was used to say,—
It's dull in our town since my playmates left!
230 I can't forget that I'm bereft
Of all the pleasant sights they see,
Which the Piper also promised me;
For he led us, he said, to a joyous land,
Joining the town and just at hand,
235 Where waters gushed and fruit-trees grew,
And flowers put forth a fairer hue,
And every thing was strange and new;
The sparrows were brighter than peacocks here,
And their dogs outran our fallow deer,
240 And honey-bees had lost their stings,
And horses were born with eagles' wings;
And just as I felt assured
My lame foot would be speedily cured,
The music stopped and I stood still,
245 And found myself outside the Hill,
Left alone against my will,
To go now limping as before,
And never hear of that country more!

XIV.

Alas, alas for Hamelin!
250   There came into many a burgher's pate
        A text which says, that Heaven's Gate

---

219. *mountain's side*] mountain-side (*1865–88*).
224. *mountain side*] mountain-side (*1863, 1865–88*).
230–41. This vision is in none of the sources.
234. *Joining*: adjoining.
242. *felt*] became (*1849–88*).
251–3. Cp. *Matthew* xix 24: 'And I say unto you again, It is easier for a camel to go through a needle's eye, than for a rich man to enter into the kingdom of God'.

Opes to the Rich at as easy a rate
As the needle's eye takes a camel in!
The Mayor sent East, West, North, and South
255   To offer the Piper by word of mouth,
           Wherever it was men's lot to find him,
       Silver and gold to his heart's content,
       If he'd only return the way he went,
           And bring the children behind him.
260   But when they saw 'twas a lost endeavour,
       And Piper and dancers were gone for ever,
       They made a decree that lawyers never
           Should think their records dated duly
       If, after the day of the month and year,
265   These words did not as well appear,
           "And so long after what happened here
               "On the Twenty-second of July,
       "Thirteen hundred and Seventy-six:"
       And the better in memory to fix
270   The place of the Children's last retreat,
       They called it, The Pied Piper's Street—
       Where any one playing on pipe or tabor
       Was sure for the future to lose his labour.
       Nor suffered they Hostelry or Tavern
275   To shock with mirth a street so solemn;
       But opposite the place of the cavern
           They wrote the story on a column,
       And on the Great Church Window painted

263–81. All sources append these details, though variously. For Wanley, Verstegen, and Collier, see headnote. Howell has: 'in that Town, they date their Bills and Bonds, and other Instruments in Law, to this day from the yeer of the going out of their children: Besides, ther is a great piller of stone at the foot of the said Hill, whereon this story is ingraven'.

267. July] Júly (*1849–68*). The stress on the first syllable is the older form (so in J.).

267–8. B. follows Verstegen and Collier; Wanley has the accepted date, 1284. In a letter of 1884 (the six hundredth anniversary of the legend) B. stuck charmingly to his guns: 'I am obliged by . . . the suggestion of the young lady that the date of my little poem should be altered. But there is equal if not superior authority for the date as I give it,—one being probably as imaginary as the other: and since no important point of doctrine is affected by letting it continue,—while there would follow (as you observe) some trouble in un-rhyming and re-rhyming, I hope you will permit me to remain "masterly inactive" in the matter' (to unidentified correspondent, 19 Nov. 1884, *ABL MS*).

275. shock] spoil (*DL 1st proof*, canc.).

278–80. This window was not in fact introduced until 1572.

The same, to make the world acquainted
280   How their children were stolen away;
And there it stands to this very day.
And I must not omit to say
That in Transylvania there's a tribe
Of alien people that ascribe
285   The outlandish ways and dress
On which their neighbours lay such stress
To their fathers and mothers having risen
Out of some subterraneous prison
Into which they were trepanned
290   Long time ago in a mighty band
Out of Hamelin town in Brunswick land,
But how or why they don't understand.

XV.

So, Willy, let you and me be wipers
Of scores out with all men—especially pipers:
295   And, whether they rid us from rats or from mice,
If we've promised them aught, let us keep our promise.

---

289. *trepanned*: caught in a trap, ensnared, beguiled.

293. *Willy*: i.e. Willie Macready (see headnote).

295–6. In his copy of *1863*, now in the Tennyson Centre in Lincoln, Tennyson marked up *Pied Piper* for reading aloud to his sons, rewriting these lines: 'But don't count too much on what he said or Charlie meant— / For what each means is 'Return *me* for Parliament'.

295. *from . . . from*] from . . . frớm (*1849–63*); frớm . . . frớm (*1865–88*).

296. *promise*] B. underlined 'mise' in *DL 1st proof*. In a letter of 7 Nov. 1881 (in the possession of Mr Michael Meredith; cited in *Oxford*) B. denied that he intended the moral of the poem as a 'sly hit' at Willie Macready's father. 'I certainly had a difference with him on quite another matter—but long after the "Pied Piper" was written'. For this 'difference', see headnote to *Lines to Helen Faucit* (II 173).

6 Waring

First publ. *B & P* iii (*DL*), 26 Nov. 1842; repr. *1849, 1863, 1865², 1868, 1872, 1888*.
Our text is *1842*. The date of composition was probably the early summer of
1842, in the aftermath of the emigration to New Zealand at the end of April of
B.'s close friend Alfred Domett. Domett (1811–87) was a member of B.'s 'set',
the 'Colloquials', contributed occasional poems to periodicals, and had published
two volumes: *Poems* (1833), and *Venice* (1839), a long poem which B. mentions
admiringly (*Correspondence* v 328). For further details of Domett's life, and his relations with B. when he eventually returned from New Zealand in 1872, see *RB
& AD*, Domett *Diary*, and *Maynard*. In a letter of May 1842 B. expressed indignation over Domett's failure to find a commercial publisher for *Venice*: 'not even
his earnest handsome face . . . not his sincere voice & gentlemanly bearing, could
tempt Moxon to look at a line of it' (*Correspondence* v 328). It is likely that B.
telescoped this disappointment and Domett's emigration, making one the motive
of the other. In *DL 2nd proof*, the words 'Alfred Domett, or' are written over
the title. In the words of another 'Colloquial', Joseph Arnould (letter to Domett,
c. May 1843), ' "Waring" delighted us all very much for we recognized in it a
fancy portrait of a very dear friend' (*Correspondence* vii 391). In 1875 a correspondent
asked B. if he had had in mind a real person called Waring; B. wrote: 'I assure
you I never heard of the Gentleman you mention: and, if you consider, I should
be little likely to address the subject of such a poem publicly by his name. I had
in my mind some characteristics of an old friend who, after thirty years' absence,
is returned alive and well' (to Newton Bennett, 5 Dec. 1875, *ABL MS*). Several
details do not fit, e.g. the date of Domett's departure, that of 'Waring' being in
winter (l. 14), and in any event the poem's fanciful and burlesque elements
hinder a straightforward biographical reading; J. F. McCarthy ('Browning's
"Waring": The Real Subject of the "Fancy Portrait" ', *VP* ix [1971] 371–82) seems
nearer the mark in describing the poem as 'an ironic treatment of the early
Browning's favorite theme—the dilemma of the non-communicating artist-
prophet'. It has been suggested that some details of 'Waring's' character and appearance were drawn from those of R. H. Horne, author of the 'farthing epic' *Orion*
and a close friend of B.'s at this period. Horne had led an adventurous life abroad
before entering English literary life in the 1830s; he later emigrated to Australia.
The poem accurately portrays B.'s mixed feelings about London literary society
in the period; he wrote to Domett on 22 May 1842 of its 'creeping magnetic
assimilating influence nothing can block out' (*Correspondence* v 355), and again on
13 July: 'There is much, everything to be done in England just now—& I have
certain plans which shall either fill or succeed, but not lie dormant.—But all my
heart's interest goes to your tree-planting life . . Yet I don't know' (*ibid.* vi 33).
For other refs. to Domett in B.'s poetry, see *Time's Revenges* 1–30 (II 279–81),
and *Guardian Angel* 36–7, 54–5 (III 18, 19): 'Guercino drew this angel I saw teach
/ (Alfred, dear friend)—that little child to pray . . . Where are you, dear old friend?
/ How rolls the Wairoa at your world's far end?' The name 'Waring' itself is
that of a 'king's messenger' whom B. met during his trip to Russia in 1834 (*Griffin
and Minchin* 63); see l. 109ff. A possible literary influence is Dryden's *Ode to the
Pious Memory of the Accomplisht Young Lady Mrs Anne Killigrew, Excellent in the two
Sister-Arts of Poesie and Painting* (1686); note the allusion to painting at ll. 146–52.
Dryden stresses the corruption of the age in contrast to the purity and integrity
of Killigrew's art; cp. ll. 192–200. There is a verbal parallel at ll. 254–5. The

idea of escape from social constrictions into Romantic vagabondage is strong in Byron, notably *Childe Harold*; in B.'s works of the period, cp. *Colombe's Birthday* (1844), *Flight of the Duchess* (II 295), *Glove* (II 360); cp. also the ending of *Bishop Blougram* (pp. 338–9), and contrast *How It Strikes* (p. 435).

I.

i.

What's become of Waring
Since he gave us all the slip,
Chose land-travel or seafaring,
Boots and chest, or staff and scrip,
5   Rather than pace up and down
Any longer London-town?

ii.

Who'd have guessed it from his lip,
Or his brow's accustomed bearing,
On the night he thus took ship,
10   Or started landward, little caring
For us, it seems, who supped together,
(Friends of his too, I remember)
And walked home thro' the merry weather,
Snowiest in all December;
15   I left his arm that night myself
For what's-his-name's, the new prose-poet,
That wrote the book there, on the shelf—
How, forsooth, was I to know it
If Waring meant to glide away
20   Like a ghost at break of day!
Never looked he half so gay!

iii.

He was prouder than the Devil:
How he must have cursed our revel!
Ay, and many other meetings,
25   Indoor visits, outdoor greetings,
As up and down he paced this London,

4. *staff and scrip*: traditional emblems of pilgrimage ('scrip' means wallet or satchel), both literal and figurative: cp. Raleigh. *The Passionate Man's Pilgrimage* 2–3: 'My staff of faith . . . My scrip of joy'.
14. *Snowiest*] The snowiest (*1849–88*).
17. *That*] Who (*1865–88*).

With no work done, but great works undone,
Where scarce twenty knew his name.
Why not, then, have earlier spoken,
30 Written, bustled? Who's to blame
If your silence kept unbroken?
True, but there were sundry jottings,
Stray-leaves, fragments, blurrs and blottings,
Certain first steps were achieved
35 Already which—(is that your meaning?)
Had well borne out whoe'er believed
In more to come: but who goes gleaning
Hedge-side chance-blades, while full-sheaved
Stand cornfields by him? Pride, o'erweening
40 Pride alone, puts forth such claims
O'er the day's distinguished names.

iv.
Meantime, how much I loved him,
I find out now I've lost him:
I, who cared not if I moved him,
45 —Could so carelessly accost him,
Never shall get free
Of his ghostly company,
And eyes that just a little wink
As deep I go into the merit
50 Of this and that distinguished spirit—
His cheeks' raised colour, soon to sink,
As long I dwell on some stupendous
And tremendous (God defend us!)
Monstr'-inform'-ingens-horrend-ous

32–4. sundry jottings . . . first-steps: for Domett's writing in this period, see headnote.
38. chance-blades: blades of grass which have been sown by chance; the prefix 'chance-' occurs several times in B., usually attached to a verb, e.g. 'chance-sown plant' (*Paracelsus* v 686, I 300), 'chance-sown cleft-nursed seed' (*Ring* x 1036), and 'chance-rooted' (*Inapprehensiveness* [*Asolando*, 1889] 9).
44. moved: annoyed, irritated.
45. —Could] Who could (*1849–88*).
46. Never] Henceforth never (*1849–88*).
48. And] His (*1849–88*).
53. God] Heaven (*1849–88*).
54. A burlesque of Virgil, *Aeneid* iii 658: 'Monstrum horrendum, informe, ingens' [a horrid monster, mis-shapen, huge]. There may be a hint of self-parody of *Sordello*; see also *Pippa* i 282–92n. (p. 115).

55   Demoniaco-seraphic
      Penman's latest piece of graphic.
      Nay, my very wrist grows warm
      With his dragging weight of arm!
      E'en so, swimmingly appears,
60   Thro' one's after-supper musings,
      Some lost Lady of old years,
      With her beauteous vain endeavour,
      And goodness unrepaid as ever;
      The face, accustomed to refusings,
65   We, puppies that we were . . . Oh never
      Surely, nice of conscience, scrupled
      Being aught like false, forsooth, to?
      Telling aught but honest truth to?
      What a sin had we centupled
70   Its possessor's grace and sweetness!
      No! she heard in its completeness
      Truth, for truth's a weighty matter,
      And, truth at issue, we can't flatter!
      Well, 'tis done with: she's exempt
75   From damning us thro' such a sally;
      And so she glides, as down a valley,
      Taking up with her contempt,
      Past our reach; and in, the flowers
      Shut her unregarded hours.

                              V.

80   Oh, could I have him back once more,
      This Waring, but one half-day more!

55. The accent falls on the third syllable, the 'i' of 'Demoniaco', pronounced 'eye'.
59–79. The speaker feels the ghostly presence of Waring as he would that of a
woman whom he and others had formerly treated with arrogant 'frankness', being
proud of their forthrightness about her lack of beauty, and not valuing her real
qualities; she is now dead, and 'exempt', therefore, from 'damning them' by really
telling the truth about them, as they had made a show of doing about her. In
the same way, Waring is now past being affected by his friend's former misprision.
59–61. Cp. *Dubiety* (*Asolando*, 1889), in which the speaker, 'ensconce[d] / In luxury's sofa-lap of leather' (ll. 3–4), muses on the past, and remembers 'when a
woman leant / To feel for my brow where her kiss might fall' (ll. 22–3).
73. *And, truth*] And truth (*1863–1888*, except *1872, 1884* as *1842*).
77. Either 'accepting, swallowing our contempt for her' or 'espousing, adopting
her attitude of contempt for us'.
78–9. *and in . . . hours*: 'the flowers [of the grave] enclose her sad history of neglect';
cp. the use of 'shut in' in the final lines of *Love Among the Ruins* (p. 539).
81. *This Waring*: a typical Carlylean phrasing.

Back, with the quiet face of yore,
So hungry for acknowledgment
Like mine! I'd fool him to his bent!
85 Feed, should not he, to heart's content?
I'd say, "to only have conceived
"Your great works, tho' they never progress,
"Surpasses all we've yet achieved!"
I'd lie so, I should be believed.
90 I'd make such havoc of the claims
Of the day's distinguished names
To feast him with, as feasts an ogress
Her sharp-toothed golden-crowned child!
Or, as one feasts a creature rarely
95 Captured here, unreconciled
To capture; and completely gives
Its pettish humours licence, barely
Requiring that it lives.

---

84. I'd fool him to his bent: from *Hamlet* III ii 408: 'They fool me to the top of my bent'. See also ll. 185−6n.

86−8. Cp., among many other expressions of this idea in B.'s work, *A Grammarian* 97ff. (p. 595).

86−7. conceived / Your great works, tho' they never progress,] conceived / Your great works, tho' they ne'er make progess, (*1849−65*); conceived, / Planned your great works, apart from progress, (*1868−88*).

88. all we've yet] little works (*1868−88*).

90−8. Cp. B. to Domett, 13 July 1842 (*Correspondence* vi 33): 'Sir L. Bulwer has published a set of sing-songs—I read two, or one, in a Review—& thought them abominable. Mr Taylor's affected unreal putting-together, called "Edwin the Fair," is the flattest of fallen. . . . Dickens is back, and busy in "doing" America for his next numbers—sad work'. See also ll. 199−200n.

92−3. as feasts an ogress . . . child!: taken, with characteristic variations, from one of Charles Perrault's fairy-stories, 'Little Thumb' ('Le Petit Poucet', originally publ. in *Histoires et contes du temps passé*, Paris 1697) in which Little Thumb and his six brothers come to an ogre's house; his wife takes pity on them and attempts to conceal them, but the ogre discovers their hiding-place: 'Here is good game, which comes very luckily to entertain three Ogres of my acquaintance, who are to pay me a visit in a day or two . . . The Ogre had seven daughters, all little children, and these young Ogresses . . . had little grey eyes quite round, hooked noses, wide mouths and very long sharp teeth, standing at a good distance from each other. They were not as yet over and above mischievous; but they promised very fair for it; for they already bit little children, that they might suck their blood. They had been put to bed early, with every one a crown of gold upon her head' (transl. R. Samber, 1729).

93.] Her feverish sharp-toothed gold-crowned child (*1868−88*).

94−8. Cp. the description of Goito as a 'captured creature in a pound' (*Sordello* i 384ff., I 420).

vi.

Ichabod, Ichabod,
100 The glory is departed!
Travels Waring East away?
Who, of knowledge, by hearsay,
Reports a man upstarted
Somewhere as a God,
105 Hordes grown European-hearted,
Millions of the wild made tame
On a sudden at his fame?
In Vishnu-land what Avatar?
Or, North in Moscow, toward the Czar,
110 Who, with the gentlest of footfalls
Over the Kremlin's pavement, bright
With serpentine and siennite,
Steps, with five other Generals,
Who simultaneously take snuff,
115 That each may have pretext enough
To kerchiefwise unfurl his sash
Which, softness' self, is yet the stuff
To hold fast where a steel chain snaps,
And leave the grand white neck no gash?
120 In Moscow, Waring, to those rough
Cold natures borne, perhaps,

99–100. Cp. *1 Samuel* iv 21; the daughter-in-law of Eli, the high priest, gives birth at a time of calamity: 'And she named the child Ichabod, saying, The glory is departed from Israel'.

103. upstarted: 'who has sprung up'.

108. 'Vishnu-land' is India. B. refers to the cycles of creation over which the god Vishnu rules in Hindu religious myth. 'To each cycle of creation there corresponds an "avatar", literally a "descent", of the god Vishnu. These avatars theoretically number ten, but the wealth of popular imagination has greatly increased the number' ('Mythology of Hinduism', *Larousse Encyclopedia of Mythology*).

109–10.] Or who, in Moscow, toward the Czar, / With the demurest of footfalls (*1849–88*, except 'who in' *1865–88*).

112. Serpentine is an ornamental stone with markings resembling those of a serpent's skin; siennite (syenite) is a crystalline rock allied to granite.

114. Who] That (*1849–88*).

115. That each may] For each to (*1849–88*).

116. To] And (*1865–88*). *unfurl*] unfold (*1863–88*).

120–33. This sentence lacks a main verb, unless 'is' is understood before 'borne' in l. 121.

120. In Moscow, Waring] Waring, in Moscow (*1849–88*, except 'Waring in', *1865–88*).

121. Cold natures] Cold northern natures (*1849–88*).

Like the lambwhite maiden, (clear
Thro' the circle of mute kings,
Unable to repress the tear,
125   Each as his sceptre down he flings),
To the Dome at Taurica,
Where now a priestess, she alway
Mingles her tender grave Hellenic speech
With theirs, tuned to the hailstone-beaten beach,
130   As pours some pigeon, from the myrrhy lands
Rapt by the whirlblast to fierce Scythian strands
Where breed the swallows, her melodious cry
Amid their barbarous twitter!
In Russia? Never! Spain were fitter!
135   Ay, most likely 'tis in Spain
That we and Waring meet again—
Now, while he turns down that cool narrow lane
Into the blackness, out of grave Madrid
All fire and shine—abrupt as when there's slid
140   Its stiff gold blazing pall
From some black coffin-lid.
Or, best of all,
I love to think
The leaving us was just a feint;
145   Back here to London did he slink;

122–33. The 'lambwhite maiden' is Iphigenia, for whose sacrifice by her father
Agamemnon, at the outset of the expedition against Troy, the other Greek
leaders reluctantly voted (by throwing their sceptres to the ground), in order to
ensure a favourable wind; however, in one version of the legend she was
spirited away by Artemis to her temple at Tauris, in Scythia (Asia Minor), where
she became priestess; she was eventually rescued by her brother Orestes. In Euripides'
Iphigenia at Tauris, which B. greatly admired, Iphigenia laments her enforced
isolation among barbarians who do not speak her language. B. treats a similar
legend, the rescue of Hippolytus, in a poem written in the same period, *Artemis*.
122. *maiden, (clear*] maiden clear (*1849–88*; the closing bracket was removed in
l. 125).
123. *Thro'*] From (*1849–88*).
126. *the Dome*] Dian's fane (*1849–88*); i.e. 'temple'. 'Dian' (Diana) is the Latin
name for Artemis.
127. *a priestess*] a captive priestess (*1849–88*).
130. *the myrrhy lands*: Arabia, or 'the East' generally, the source of myrrh; B.'s use
is the first rec. in *OED*.
131. *whirlblast*: a Cumbrian dialect word for a whirlwind or hurricane, popularized
by Wordsworth, after whom *OED* cites Coleridge and Shelley.
134. *Spain were fitter*: B. had not visited Spain.
145. *slink*: the implication of stealth is usually, but not always, pejorative.

And now works on without a wink
Of sleep, and we are on the brink
Of something great in fresco-paint:
Some garret's ceiling, walls and floor,
150   Up and down and o'er and o'er
He splashes, as none splashed before
Since great Caldara Polidore:
Then down he creeps and out he steals
Only when the night conceals
155   His face—in Kent 'tis cherry-time,
Or, hops are picking; or, at prime
Of March, he steals as when, too happy,
Years ago when he was young,
Some mild eve when woods were sappy,
160   And the early moths had sprung
To life from many a trembling sheath
Woven the warm boughs beneath,
While small birds said to themselves
What should soon be actual song,
165   And young gnats, by tens and twelves,
Made as if they were the throng
That crowd around and carry aloft
The sound they have nursed, so sweet and pure,
Out of a myriad noises soft,
170   Into a tone that can endure
Amid the noise of a July noon,
When all God's creatures crave their boon,
All at once and all in tune,
And get it, happy as Waring then,
175   Having first within his ken
What a man might do with men,

152. *great Caldara Polidore*: Polidoro Caldara da Caravaggio (*c.* 1492–1543), a painter
B. greatly admired (see *Pauline* 656–67n., p. 49).
152 ^153.] Or Music means this land of ours
          Some favour yet, to pity won
          By Purcell from his Rosy Bowers,—
          "Give me my so long promised son,
          "Let Waring end what I begun!" (*1849–88*)
Henry Purcell (1659–95) was working on a setting of 'From Rosy Bowers' at
his death.
153–82. In *Sordello* i, Sordello goes through a similar formative process in which
the mastery of the imagination excuses him from any practical creative work.
157. *he steals as when*] he wanders as (*1849–88*).
159. *were sappy*] grew sappy (*1849–88*).

And far too glad, in the even-glow,
To mix with the world he meant to take
Into his hand, he told you, so—
180   And out of it his world to make,
To contract and to expand
As he shut or oped his hand.
Oh, Waring, what's to really be?
A clear stage and a crowd to see!
185   Some Garrick—say—out shall not he
The heart of Hamlet's mystery pluck?
Or, where most unclean beasts are rife,
Some Junius—am I right?—shall tuck
His sleeve, and out with flaying-knife!
190   Some Chatterton shall have the luck
Of calling Rowley into life!
Some one shall somehow run a muck
With this old world, for want of strife
Sound asleep: contrive, contrive
195   To rouse us, Waring! Who's alive?
Our men scarce seem in earnest now:
Distinguished names, but 'tis, somehow,

178. the world] your world (*1849–88*).
185–6. David Garrick (1717–79), the great actor and friend of Samuel Johnson, was especially celebrated in the role of Hamlet; l. 186 is an adaptation of Hamlet's words to Guildenstern (III ii 389): 'you would pluck out the heart of my mystery'. This comes from the same portion of the play as the allusion in l. 84 above. Cp. also *Bishop Blougram* 946–7 (p. 355), and note that Gigadibs in that poem ends by emigrating.
187. unclean beasts: alluding to the Old Testament prohibition of the eating of certain animals; here used metaphorically to mean corrupt politicians.
188. Junius: pseudonym (borrowed from the Roman satirist) of the famous 18th-century Whig pamphleteer who castigated corruption in government, and whose real identity is still at issue. Books relating to the controversy over his identity were in the library of B.'s father, who also wrote a short essay on the subject (*Collections* J 83, p. 533).
190–1. Thomas Chatterton (1752–70) passed off some of his own poetry as the work of a medieval priest called Rowley. B. defended him in *Chatterton*, written in the same period as *Waring* (see Appendix C, II 475).
192–203. Cp. Wordsworth's two sonnets *London, 1802* and *Written in London, September, 1802*, and Shelley's *Sonnet: England in 1819*.
193–4. this old world, for want of strife / Sound asleep: cp. B. to Domett, 15 May 1843 (*Correspondence* vii 124): 'What shall I tell you?—that we are dead asleep in literary things and in great want of a "rousing word" (as the old puritans phrase it) from New Zealand or any place *out* of this snoring dormitory'. This is clearly a case of the poem influencing the letter, but see also the letters of 22 May and 13 July 1842 quoted above, and next note.

As if they played at being names
Still more distinguished, like the games
200   Of children. Turn our sport to earnest
With a visage of the sternest!
Bring the real times back, confessed
Still better than the very best!

                              II.

                              i.
"When I last saw Waring . . ."
205   (How all turned to him who spoke—
You saw Waring? Truth or joke?
In land-travel, or sea-faring?)

                              ii.
"We were sailing by Triest,
"Where a day or two we harboured:
210   "A sunset was in the West,
"When, looking over the vessel's side,
"One of our company espied
"A sudden speck to larboard.
"And, as a sea-duck flies and swims
215   "At once, so came the light craft up,
"With its sole lateen sail that trims
"And turns (the water round its rims
"Dancing as round a sinking cup)
"And by us like a fish it curled,
220   "And drew itself up close beside,
"Its great sail on the instant furled,

199–200. like the games / Of children: cp. B. to Domett, 13 July 1842
(*Correspondence* vi 33): 'our poems &c are poor child's play'.
200–3. Turn our sport . . . the very best: Carlyle is indicated here. See headnote to
Flight of the Duchess, II 297.
203. the] our (*1849–88*).
208. Triest: the modern spelling is Trieste; B. had visited this Adriatic port on his
1838 trip.
213. to larboard: to the port side.
214–15. And . . . At once: cp. Pope, *Dunciad* ii 63–4: 'As when a dabchick
waddles through the copse / On feet and wings, and flies, and wades, and hops'.
214. sea-duck: the eider duck.
216. lateen sail: a triangular sail suspended by a long yard at an angle of 45 degrees
to the mast; lateen-rigged boats such as feluccas were common in the
Mediterranean.

"And o'er its planks, a shrill voice cried,
"(A neck as bronzed as a Lascar's)
" 'Buy wine of us, you English Brig?
225   " 'Or fruit, tobacco and cigars?
" 'A Pilot for you to Triest?
" 'Without one, look you ne'er so big,
" 'They'll never let you up the bay!
" 'We natives should know best.'
230   "I turned, and 'just those fellows' way,'
"Our captain said, 'The 'long-shore thieves
" 'Are laughing at us in their sleeves.'

                        iii.
"In truth, the boy leaned laughing back;
"And one, half-hidden by his side
235   "Under the furled sail, soon I spied,
"With great grass hat, and kerchief black,
"Who looked up, with his kingly throat,
"Said somewhat while the other shook
"His hair back from his eyes to look
240   "Their longest at us; and the boat,
"I know not how, turned sharply round,
"Laying her whole side on the sea
"As a leaping fish does; from the lee
"Into the weather cut somehow
245   "Her sparkling path beneath our bow;
"And so went off, as with a bound,
"Into the rose and golden half
"Of the sky, to overtake the sun,
"And reach the shore like the sea-calf
250   "Its singing cave; yet I caught one
"Glance ere away the boat quite passed,
"And neither time nor toil could mar

---

222. *planks*] thwarts (*1868–88*); 'thwarts' are rowing-benches.
223. *Lascar's*: Lascars were East Indian sailors.
227. *look you ne'er so big*: 'no matter how important a pose you strike'.
231. *'long-shore*: from 'along shore', i.e. employed or active on the shoreline; often derogatory, as here (*OED* cites Marryat, 1837: 'half-bred, long-shore chap').
240. *and*] then (*1849–88*).
247. *rose*] rosy (*1863–88*).
248. *Of the*] O' the (*1870–88*).
249. *sea-calf*: the common seal.

"Those features: so I saw the last
"Of Waring!"—You? Oh, never star
255   Was lost here, but it rose afar!
       Look East, where whole new thousands are!
       In Vishnu-land what Avatar?

254–5. Cp. Dryden, *Ode to . . . Mrs Anne Killigrew* (see headnote): 'But look aloft, and if thou ken'st from far / Among the *Pleiads* a new-kindl'd star, / If any sparkles, than the rest, more bright, / 'Tis she that shines in that propitious light'; also Shelley, *Adonais* 494–5: 'The soul of Adonais, like a star, / Beacons from the abode where the Eternal are'.

7 My Last Duchess
Ferrara

First publ. *B & P* iii (*DL*), 26 Nov. 1842, with *Count Gismond* (II 161), which followed it, under the collective title *Italy and France*; the title was *Italy*. Repr. *1849* (when it was separated from *Count Gismond* and given its present title and subtitle), *1863, 1863², 1868, 1872, 1888*. Our text is *1842*. The date of composition is conjectural, but there are links with *Flight of the Duchess* (II 295) and *Chatterton* (II 475), which would place the poem in the late summer of 1842.

The poem, like *Sordello*, is written in heroic couplets; it may have been during his researches into the history of Ferrara and the Este family for *Sordello* that B. came across the figure of Alfonso II (1533–98), fifth Duke of Ferrara and last of the Este line, whom L. S. Friedland ('Ferrara and *My Last Duchess*', *SP* xxxiii [1936] 656–84) claims as the original of B.'s Duke. Alfonso married the 14-year-old Lucrezia de' Medici in 1558; she died in 1561, and there were suspicions (almost certainly groundless) that she had been poisoned. Four years later Alfonso married Barbara, daughter of the Emperor Ferdinand I of Austria. It was the Emperor's son, Ferdinand, Count of Tyrol, who, after his father's death in 1564, negotiated the marriage through his envoy, Nikolaus Madruz, a native of Innsbruck (see ll. 49n., 54–6n.). DeVane (*Handbook* 108) succinctly describes Alfonso's character: 'he was cold and egotistical, vengeful and extremely possessive; and a patron of the arts, painting, music, and literature'. In particular, he was the patron of the poet Torquato Tasso, about whom B. would have read in the biography of Tasso which he 'reviewed' in July 1842 as a preliminary to his essay on Chatterton (see Appendix C, II 475). It should be emphasized, however, that B. did not name the Duke, and that the location, Ferrara, was first indicated in a subtitle in *1849*: Friedland's source is convincing, but not definitive in terms of the poem's interpretation. Shakespeare's Leontes (*The Winter's Tale*) has also been proposed as a source for the Duke, though DeVane (*Handbook* 109) objects that Leontes' sexual jealousy differs from the Duke's possessive egotism. Even so, the play's final scene, in which the 'statue' of Hermione comes to life, may be an inverse source for the poem. In Feb. 1889, B. himself, when he was asked whether the Duchess '[was] in fact shallow and easily and equally well pleased with any favour: or did the Duke so describe her as a supercilious cover to real and well justified jealousy', replied: 'As an excuse—mainly to himself—for taking revenge on one who had unwittingly wounded his absurdly pretentious vanity, by failing to recognize his superiority in even the most trifling matters' (*New Poems* 175). See also l. 6n. For B.'s personal attitude to this topic, see his account to EBB., in a letter of 18 Jan. 1846, of his 'nightmare dreams' of 'the infliction of tyranny on the unresisting', and the story of a former friend's ill treatment of his wife (*Correspondence* xii 1–2). A source for the portrait of the Duchess has been suggested by C. E. Carrington (*TLS* 6 Nov. 1969, p. 1288): the portrait of a young woman, item no. 254 in the Dulwich collection with which B. was familiar from boyhood. The portrait is assigned to the school of Susterman (1506–60), a Flemish painter who worked in Florence. There are portraits of Lucrezia, though none in Ferrara. But as with the character of the Duke, the historical identification of the portrait is not a necessary feature of its presence in the poem, and it may be taken

as being, to all intents and purposes, imaginary (see also l. 3n., and headnote to
Pictor, p. 226).

The poem's setting relates it to other Renaissance character studies in B., such
as *Tomb at St. Praxed's* (p. 232) and *Andrea* (p. 385); the Duke in *Flight of the
Duchess* (II 295) seems a bathetic parody of the one here. The figure of Guido in
Ring is the most complex and extended study of the type; the Duchess may be
a prototype of Pompilia. Cp. also *A Forgiveness*. B.'s interest in the mysterious
expressiveness of portraits is most fully developed in *A Likeness* (p. 642). The
collective title under which the poem was first published reflects B.'s interest in
national characteristics and in categories generally during this period, and also his
lifelong practice of pairing poems with or against each other.

> That's my last Duchess painted on the wall,
> Looking as if she were alive; I call
> That piece a wonder, now: Frà Pandolf's hands
> Worked busily a day, and there she stands.
> 5   Will't please you sit and look at her? I said
> "Frà Pandolf" by design, for never read
> Strangers like you that pictured countenance,
> The depth and passion of its earnest glance,
> But to myself they turned (since none puts by
> 10 The curtain I have drawn for you, but I)
> And seemed as they would ask me, if they durst,
> How such a glance came there; so not the first
> Are you to turn and ask thus. Sir, 'twas not
> Her husband's presence only, called that spot
> 15 Of joy into the Duchess' cheek: perhaps
> Frà Pandolf chanced to say "Her mantle laps

1. *painted on the wall*: either a framed portrait or, more likely, a fresco; this phrase,
and the speed of Frà Pandolf's work (see l. 4), favour the latter, 'piece' in l. 3
the former; either might be concealed by the 'curtain' of l. 10. B. N. Pipes Jr.
('The Portrait of "My Last Duchess"', *VS* iii [1959–60] 381–6) points out that
Alfonso II (see headnote) ordered a number of portrait frescoes in 1559, the year
in which his bride Lucrezia came to Ferrara, though they were too decayed by
B.'s day to indicate whether a portrait of Lucrezia was among them.
3. Frà Pandolf is an imaginary painter, though B. may have taken the name from
that of the painter Giovanni Antonio Pandolfi, who, as Friedland points out (see
headnote), was employed by the Este family to paint a portrait of Alfonso II's
sister Lucrezia in 1570 (nine years after the death of Lucrezia de' Medici,
Alfonso's first wife); the name occurs in Pilkington's *Dictionary of Painters* (1805),
a standard reference work which B. knew well. 'Frà' means 'brother', i.e. the
painter is a monk; cp. such real Italian Renaissance painters as Fra Angelico and
Fra Bartolommeo, as well as B.'s own *Fra Lippo Lippi* (p. 477).
6. *by design*: B. was asked 'By what design?' and replied 'To have some occasion
for telling the story, and illustrating part of it' (*New Poems* 175). For another reply
from the same letter of Feb. 1889, see headnote, and see also ll. 45–6n.

"Over my Lady's wrist too much," or "Paint
"Must never hope to reproduce the faint
"Half-flush that dies along her throat;" such stuff
20 Was courtesy, she thought, and cause enough
For calling up that spot of joy. She had
A heart . . how shall I say? . . too soon made glad,
Too easily impressed; she liked whate'er
She looked on, and her looks went everywhere.
25 Sir, 'twas all one! My favor at her breast,
The dropping of the daylight in the West,
The bough of cherries some officious fool
Broke in the orchard for her, the white mule
She rode with round the terrace—all and each
30 Would draw from her alike the forward speech,
Or blush, at least. She thanked men,—good; but thanked
Somehow . . I know not how . . as if she ranked
My gift of a nine hundred years old name
With anybody's gift. Who'd stoop to blame
35 This sort of trifling? Even had you skill
In speech—(which I have not)—could make your will
Quite clear to such an one, and say "Just this
"Or that in you disgusts me; here you miss,
"Or there exceed the mark"—and if she let
40 Herself be lessoned so, nor plainly set
Her wits to yours, forsooth, and made excuse,
—E'en then would be some stooping, and I chuse

17–19. "Paint . . . throat;": cp. *Ring* xi 1554–6: 'slur / The line o' the painter just
where paint leaves off / And life begins'.
21–43. *She had . . . Never to stoop*: cp. the Duke in *Flight of the Duchess*, who tries
to 'lesson' his wife in this way; see ll. 309–31 (II 310–11).
23–4. *she liked . . . everywhere*: cp. *Andrea* 29–32 (p. 392).
25. *Sir*: the first indication of the envoy's identity; the Duke addresses him politely,
but as an inferior. *favor*: reversing the usual application of the term to a token
(such as a scarf or ribbon) given by a lady to her chosen lover.
25–9. *My favor . . . terrace*: Pipes (see l. 1n.) suggests that the Duke borrows
these details from the painting, where they form part of Frà Pandolf's pictorial
reading of the Duchess's character; alternatively, they might spring to the Duke's
mind by their evocation of a common response in the Duchess.
27. *officious*: the sense, still current in B.'s time, of 'attentive, obliging' is overlaid
here by the contemptuous sense of 'importunate, meddling'. Cp. *Pippa* i 80 (p. 105).
30. *forward*] approving (*1849–88*). Like 'officious' (l. 27), 'forward' could have both
good and bad senses in B.'s time: 'warm, earnest' or 'immodest, presumptuous'.
33. a *nine hundred years old name*: the Este family (see headnote) traced their
ancestry even further back than this: see *Sordello* i 291ff (I 414ff.).

Never to stoop. Oh, Sir, she smiled, no doubt,
Whene'er I passed her; but who passed without
45   Much the same smile? This grew; I gave commands;
Then all smiles stopped together. There she stands
As if alive. Will't please you rise? We'll meet
The company below then. I repeat,
The Count your Master's known munificence
50   Is ample warrant that no just pretence
Of mine for dowry will be disallowed;
Though his fair daughter's self, as I avowed
At starting, is my object. Nay, we'll go
Together down, Sir! Notice Neptune, tho',
55   Taming a sea-horse, thought a rarity,
Which Claus of Innsbruck cast in bronze for me.

45−6. I gave commands; / Then all smiles stopped together: in response to questions
about the fate of the Duchess, B. 'replied meditatively, "Yes, I meant that the
commands were that she be put to death." And then, after a pause, he added,
with a characteristic dash of expression, and as if the thought had just started up
in his mind, "Or he might have had her shut up in a convent"' (H. Corson, *An
Introduction to the Study of Robert Browning's Poetry* [3rd ed., Boston 1903] p. viii).
49. The identification of the Duke's prospective father-in-law as a 'Count' supports the connection of the Duke with Alfonso II (see headnote), although Alfonso's
second wife was a sister, not daughter, of the Count of Tyrol. See also next note.
54−6. Notice . . . for me: the statue and sculptor, like the portrait and painter, are
imaginary; the classical subject is typical of the period, during which Innsbruck
(which B. visited in 1838) was a famous centre of bronze-casting. Innsbruck was
also the capital of Tyrol, and Nikolaus Madruz, the Count of Tyrol's envoy to
Alfonso II in the negotiations over his second marriage, was a native of that city.
See prec. note and headnote.

8 Soliloquy of the Spanish Cloister

First publ. *B & P* iii (*DL*), 26 Nov. 1842, with *Incident of the French Camp* (II 3), which preceded it, under the collective title *Camp and Cloister*, with the title 'Cloister (*Spanish*)'. Repr. *1849* (when it was separated from *Incident* and given its present title), *1863*, *1863²*, *1868*, *1880*, *1888*. In *1863* the poem was listed on the contents page as no. III of *Garden-Fancies*, but, though it immediately follows that poem in the text, it retains its separate identity. The contents page may be misprinted, or may contain the trace of a change which B. thought better of; the contents page of *1865*, the revised reissue of *1863*, lists the poem separately. The date of composition is unknown. J. U. Rundle (*N & Q* cxcvi [1951] 252) suggests a debt to Burns's *Holy Willie's Prayer*. G. Bornstein, in *Poetic Remaking: The Art of Browning, Yeats and Pound* (Pennsylvania 1988, p. 23) suggests that the poem 'may glance at the debate over religious ritual stirred by the Oxford Movement': see headnote to *Tomb at St Praxed's* (pp. 233–4). The setting is contemporary, but articulates a traditional Protestant attack on monastic life as a breeding-ground for petty feuds and religious hypocrisy; cp. the 'old monk' in *Sordello* i 299–308 (I 414). False or perverted religious feeling, whether Protestant or Catholic, is a recurring topic of B.'s work; cp., in this period, *Johannes Agricola* (p. 74) and *Tomb at St. Praxed's* (p. 232). Spanish Catholicism in particular is further attacked in *Confessional* (II 337).

I.

Gr-r-r—there go, my heart's abhorrence!
    Water your damned flower-pots, do!
If hate killed men, Brother Lawrence,
    God's blood, would not mine kill you!
5   What? your myrtle-bush wants trimming?
    Oh, that rose has prior claims—
Needs its leaden vase filled brimming?
    Hell dry you up with its flames!

II.

At the meal we sit together:
10   *Salve tibi!* I must hear
Wise talk of the kind of weather,
    Sort of season, time of year:
Not a plenteous cork-crop: scarcely
    Dare we hope oak-galls, I doubt:

---

10. Salve tibi: a Latin greeting, lit. 'hail to thee'.
14. oak-galls: growths produced by gall-flies on various species of oak; used in the manufacture of ink. See also *Sordello* iii 42n. (I 529) and *Caliban* 51 (p. 628).

15   *What's the Latin name for "parsley"?*
               What's the Greek name for Swine's Snout?

                              III.
               Phew! We'll have our platter burnished,
                  Laid with care on our own shelf!
               With a fire-new spoon we're furnished,
20   And a goblet for ourself,
               Rinsed like something sacrificial
                  Ere 'tis fit to touch our chaps—
               Marked with L. for our initial!
                  (He, he! There his lily snaps!)

                              IV.
25   *Saint*, forsooth! While brown Dolores
                  Squats outside the Convent bank,
               With Sanchicha, telling stories,
                  Steeping tresses in the tank,
               Blue-black, lustrous, thick like horsehairs,
30   —Can't I see his dead eye grow
               Bright, as 'twere a Barbary corsair's?
                  That is, if he'd let it show.

                              V.
               When he finishes refection,
                  Knife and fork across he lays
35   Never, to my recollection,
                  As do I, in Jesu's praise.
               I, the Trinity illustrate,
                  Drinking watered orange-pulp;

16. *Swine's Snout*: the dandelion (punningly insulting Brother Lawrence's appearance). The phrase 'swine's snout' also occurs in *Proverbs* xi 22.
17. *Phew*] Whew (*1849–88*).
22. *chaps*: jaws or cheeks.
24. R. A. Day (*Explicator* xxiv, no. 4 [Dec. 1965] item 33) points out that the lily is a traditional emblem of chastity, and that this line is immediately followed by the erotic images of the following stanza.
30–1. *grow / Bright, as*] glow / Bright, as (*1849, 1863²*); glow, / Bright as (*1863, 1865–88*).
32.] (That is, if he'd let it show!) (*1849–88*).
33. *refection*: a light meal.
34–5. *across he lays / Never,*] he never lays / Cross-wise, (*1849–88*).
37–40. The speaker's 'three sips' symbolize his adherence to the doctrine of the Trinity, rejected by the 4th-century theologian Arius (the 'Arian' heresy).

In three sips the Arian frustrate;
40   While he drains his at one gulp!

VI.

Oh, those melons! If he's able
          We're to have a feast; so nice!
One goes to the Abbot's table,
          All of us get each a slice.
45   How go on your flowers? None double?
          Not one fruit-sort can you spy?
Strange!—And I, too, at such trouble,
          Keep 'em close-nipped on the sly!

VII.

There's a great text in Galatians,
50   Once you trip on it, entails
Twenty-nine distinct damnations,
          One sure, if another fails.
If I trip him just a-dying,
          Sure of Heaven as sure can be,
55   Spin him round and send him flying
          Off to Hell a Manichee?

42. *feast;*] feast! (*1870–88*, except 'feast:', *1884*, a rare example of a reading unique to this ed.).
48. *Keep 'em*] Keep them (*1863–88*, except *1863²*, as *1842*).
49–56. No passage in *Galatians* can be made to fit the context satisfactorily. B. later wrote admitting that the reference was inaccurate, adding that he 'was not careful to be correct' (letter of Apr. 1888 in *SBC* ii, no. 1 [1974] 62). An ingenious, but not wholly convincing, attempt has been made by R. B. Pearsall ('Browning's Texts in Galatians and Deuteronomy', *MLQ* xiii [1952] 256–8) to transfer the 'twenty-nine distinct damnations' to the litany of curses in *Deuteronomy* xxviii 16–44, a passage connected with *Galatians* iii 10. As *Oxford* remarks, the general tenor of *Galatians*, with its attack on formal religious observance, fits the poem; cp. also the contrast between flesh and spirit in v 19–23: 'Now the works of the flesh are manifest, which are these; Adultery, fornication, uncleanness, lasciviousness, idolatry, witchcraft, hatred, variance, emulations, wrath, strife, seditions, heresies, envyings, murders, drunkenness, revellings, and such like . . . But the fruit of the Spirit is love, joy, peace, longsuffering, gentleness, goodness, faith, meekness, temperance: against such there is no law'. With the speaker's fantasy of 'tripping' Brother Lawrence, cp. Hamlet's notion of killing Claudius when he is 'about some act / That has no relish of salvation in't; / Then trip him, that his heels may kick at heaven, / And that his soul may be as damn'd and black / As hell, whereto it goes' (III iii 91–5).
56. *Manichee*: a follower of the Manichaean heresy; a dualist, holding that good and evil are independent and equally balanced forces in the cosmos, rather than, as Christian orthodoxy maintains, both being the work of God. See M. K. Starkman, 'The Manichee in the Cloister: A Reading of Browning's "Soliloquy of the Spanish Cloister"', *MLN* lxxv (1960), 399–405.

VIII.

Or, my scrofulous French novel,
    On grey paper with blunt type!
Simply glance at it, you grovel
60   Hand and foot in Belial's gripe.
If I double down its pages
    At the woeful sixteenth print,
When he gathers his greengages,
    Ope a sieve and slip it in't?

IX.

65 Or, the Devil!—one might venture
        Pledge one's soul yet slily leave

57. French novels in general were a byword for immorality, but the speaker may mean something explicitly pornographic (see l. 62n.). 'Scrofulous' (from scrofula, the disfiguring disease also known as the 'king's evil') implies sexual license; *OED* cites Swift, *Argument against abolishing Christianity* (1708): 'the scrophulous and consumptive productions furnished by our men of wit and pleasure'. Contrast the 'jolly chapter of Rabelais' enjoyed by the speaker of *Sibrandus Schafnaburgensis* (l. 32, p. 217), and the 'little edition of Rabelais' adorning the bachelor's apartment in *A Likeness* (l. 24, p. 645).

60. *Belial's gripe*: cp. *PL* i 490–2: 'Belial came last, than whom a Spirit more lewd / Fell not from heaven, or more gross to love / Vice for itself'.

62. *the woeful sixteenth print*: the illustrations to French novels were considered one of their most licentious features; Starkman (see l. 56n.) cites *Manon Lescaut*; other examples include works by the Marquis de Sade, whose illustrations were 'woeful' both in the obscenity of their content and the execrable standard of their draughtsmanship.

64. *sieve*: a basket, used chiefly for market produce.

65–6.] Or, there's Satan!—one might venture / Pledge one's soul to him, yet leave (*1849–88*).

65–70. *Or, the Devil . . . so proud of*: the speaker would trick the devil into persecuting Brother Lawrence, by pretending to pledge the devil his (the speaker's) soul, but leaving a 'flaw' in the contract which would allow him to escape damnation, a flaw which the devil would not notice until after he had fulfilled his side of the bargain. The apparent triviality of asking the devil to do no more than 'blast' (wither) a plant has led some commentators to argue that the 'rose-acacia' is a symbol of Brother Lawrence himself. See L. D. Fryxell and V. H. Adair in *Explicator* xxii, no. 4 (Dec. 1963) item 24. Adair makes the useful point that the 'rose-acacia' appears in *Flora's Dictionary* (1832) as a symbol of friendship, but her speculation about its theological application (rose = Lawrence, from Latin 'laurus' = Greek 'rhododendron', a rose-tree; acacia = Arian heretic, follower of Acacius, Bishop of Caesarea) seems far-fetched. Other commentators have defended the literal sense as both appropriate to the speaker's pettiness and indicated by the use of 'that', which would suggest that the speaker has just noticed Brother Lawrence tending to this particular shrub. See e.g. R. G. Malbone in *VP* iv (1966) 218–21. By this reading, the 'we' of l. 70 would be a further example of the speaker's sarcastic identification with Lawrence, as in st. iii,

Such a flaw in the indenture
　　As he'd miss till, past retrieve,
Blasted lay that rose-acacia
70　　　We're so proud of! *Hy, Zy, Hine* . . .
St, there's Vespers! *Plena gratiâ*
　　　Ave, Virgo! Gr-r-r—you swine!

---

rather than the collective voice of the monastery, as in st. vi. In our view, the 'rose-acacia' is both a literal plant and a symbol of everything that the speaker hates about Brother Lawrence; his asking the devil to destroy it has, therefore, a metaphorical as well as a literal force, but a sense of incongruity at the triviality for which the speaker is prepared to risk his soul remains appropriate. Cp. Burns, *Holy Willie's Prayer* 78–9: 'Curse thou his basket and his store, / Kail and potatoes', and see headnote to *Johannes Agricola* (p. 75) for another ref. to this poem.

69. rose-acacia: a tree with rose-coloured flowers, *Robina hipsida*.

70. Hy, Zy, Hine: only two of the astonishingly numerous and frequently bizarre accounts of this phrase carry any conviction, those of G. Pitts ('Browning's "Soliloquy of the Spanish Cloister": *Hy, Zy, Hine*', *N & Q* xiii [1966] 339–40) and J. F. Loucks ('"Hy, Zy, Hine" and Peter of Abano', *VP* xii [1974] 165–9). Pitts argues that B. derived it from a medieval liturgical parody, the Mass of the Ass; Loucks, that B. adapted the phrase from a string of nonsense words in a medieval manual of magic formulae, the *Heptameron*, or *Elementa Magica*, ascribed to Pietro of Abano (*c.* 1250–*c.* 1316). B. was certainly familiar with Abano's work from his reading in the occult (see headnote to *Paracelsus*, I 105); cp. his translation of a quatrain ascribed to Abano (II 371) and the late poem *Pietro of Abano* (*DI*², 1880). S. H. Aiken ('"*Hy, Zy, Hine*" and Browning's Medieval Sources for "Soliloquy of the Spanish Cloister"', *VP* xvii [1979] 377–85), while admitting that B.'s spelling of the phrase may have been influenced by the Abano source, supports Pitts' argument by drawing attention to the availability of the Mass of the Ass in learned and popular writings of the period, esp. William Hone's *Ancient Mysteries Described* (1823). Hone notes that the mock-ceremony begins before vespers and parodies vesper anthems; he also mentions the survival of such customs in contemporary Spain. Aiken's argument is persuasive except that it gives the speaker no motive for uttering the phrase other than a general inclination to mock Brother Lawrence; Loucks's interpretation, that the phrase is the beginning of a magic formula which will raise the devil with whom the speaker proposes (whether in earnest or no) to make his pact, fits the context better.

71–2. Plena gratiâ / Ave, Virgo: 'full of grace, hail, Virgin'. Two problems arise in connection with this phrase: the first, that its Latin, besides being in an odd order, represents a hybrid of two prayers, the 'Hail Mary' and the 'Litany to the Blessed Virgin'; and second, that neither of these two was the conventional opening of vespers in the 19th century. It is unlikely either that the speaker would deliberately mock the ritual, or that he, of all people, would make a mistake; according to C. T. Phipps, SJ (*VP* vii [1969] 158–9), the error is B.'s, and 'resulted from equating the vesper bell with the evening *Angelus*. The thrice-daily *Angelus* bell is a signal for an antiphonal prayer honoring the Incarnation . . . which includes most of the words of the present-day form of the *Ave Maria*'. As for the words themselves, and their order, it is probable that B. altered them to fit the rhyme and rhythm of the stanza. Cp. *Ring* vi 438ff. for another passage in which the Latin liturgy is interjected with a speaker's profane comments.

9 The Lost Leader

First publ. *B & P* vii (*DR & L*), 6 Nov. 1845; repr. *1849, 1863, 1868, 1872, 1888.*
Our text is *1845.*

That the 'lost leader' was Wordsworth was confirmed by B. in later correspondence, most emphatically in a letter to Ruskin of 1 Feb. 1856: 'Don't tell
that I thought of—who else but Wordsworth?' (*A Letter from Robert Browning
to John Ruskin* [Waco 1958] n.p.). B. had met Wordsworth in 1835, after the
publication of *Paracelsus* introduced him to the literary world, but the acquaintance did not develop. The poem may have been composed in reponse to
Wordsworth's first appearance at Court as Poet Laureate (25 Apr. 1845), when
B. wrote sardonically to EBB. of the ridiculous figure which Wordsworth cut in
Samuel Rogers' ill-fitting court costume (28 May 1845, *Correspondence* x 246);
EBB. first saw the poem in proof, calling it in her letter to B. of 21–22 Oct.
1845 one of 'the new poems' (*ibid.* xi 133–4; her comments rec. in the notes are
from *Wellesley MS*). However, B. might have withheld the poem until the last
moment because EBB. did not share his hostility to Wordsworth (see below).
On balance we prefer a date closer to the award of the Laureateship itself
(Apr. 1843). In a fragment from a letter to R. H. Horne (now in the Berg
Collection of the New York Public Library; *Collections* E511, p. 445, though not
there identified in connection with Horne), B. responds to Horne's request for
a suitable epigraph for the essay on Wordsworth and Leigh Hunt in Horne's *A
New Spirit of the Age* (1844) by quoting, for Wordsworth, *PL* x 441–54 (omitting
l. 444), followed by a comment: 'He, thro' the midst unmarked, / In show
plebeian angel militant / Of lowest order, passed: and from the door / [Of that
Plutonian hall, invisible] / Ascended his high throne which, under state / Of
richest texture spread, at the upper end / Was placed in regal lustre. Down awhile
/ He sat, and round about him saw unseen. / At last, as from a cloud, his
fulgent head / And shape star-bright appeared, or brighter, *clad / With what per-
missive glory since his Fall / Was left him, or false glitter.* All amazed / At that so
sudden blaze, the *Stygian throng / Bent their aspect.* (As Jeffrey does in the reprint
of his review of the Excursion: this is too good a bit, I fear: take the kinder side
of the matter and give him some or all of your own fine sonnet)'. Unsurprisingly,
Horne did not use this passage, though he did adopt several of B.'s suggestions
for other writers (see *Correspondence* viii 202–5). Since *A New Spirit of the Age* was
published in March 1844, a date for the Berg letter of autumn/winter 1843 seems
probable, and we date the poem to this period.

The 'handful of silver' of l. 1 may be a ref. to Wordsworth's acceptance of
a government appointment in 1813, and the 'ribband' of l. 2 to the (effectively
unpaid) Laureateship, though B. later denied believing that such mercenary considerations influenced Wordsworth's conduct (see below). The fact that B. did
not show the poem to EBB. until *DR & L* was in proof may reflect his awareness that her opinion of Wordsworth was more sympathetic than his: in her
letter of 30 May 1845, though she agreed with his ridicule of Wordsworth's
conduct in going to Court, she dissociated herself from 'the sighing kept up by
people about that acceptance of the Laureateship . . . Not that the Laureateship
honored *him*, but that he honored it; & that, so honoring it, he preserves a symbol instructive to the masses, who are children & to be taught by symbols now
as formerly . . . And wont the court laurel (such as it is) be all the worthier
of *you* for Wordsworth's having worn it first?' (*Correspondence* x 247). After the

publication of the poem, however, B. made further savagely satirical remarks about Wordsworth's character in a letter to EBB. of 15 Feb. 1846 (*ibid.* xii 73–4), and the poem makes it clear that, contrary to her, he saw the Laureateship as a symbolic climax to Wordsworth's defection from the liberal cause. B. shared the opinion of the second generation of Romantic writers (Shelley, Byron, Keats, Hazlitt, Leigh Hunt) that the first (Wordsworth, Coleridge, Southey: the 'Lake School') had committed political apostasy in their conversion to conservatism; hence his remark to EBB. that 'I always retained my first feeling for Byron in many respects . . . while Heaven knows that I could not get up enthusiasm enough to cross the room if at the other end of it all Wordsworth, Coleridge & Southey were condensed into the little china bottle yonder, after the Rosicrucian fashion' (22 Aug. 1846, *ibid.* xiii 280). In later life, however, B. played down his hostility. He wrote in 1875 to the Rev. A. Grosart: 'I *did* in my hasty youth presume to use the great and venerable personality of Wordsworth as a sort of painter's model; one from which this or the other particular feature may be selected and turned to account: had I intended more, above all, such a boldness as portraying the entire man, I should not have talked about "handfuls of silver and bits of ribbon". These never influenced the change of politics in the great poet; whose defection, nevertheless, accompanied as it was by a regular face-about of his special party, was to my juvenile apprehension, and even mature consideration, an event to deplore . . . so, though I dare not deny the original of my little poem, I altogether refuse to have it considered as the "very effigies" of such a moral and intellectual superiority' (*LH* 166–7).

B. was interested, esp. during this period, in political apostasy: *Strafford* (1837) and *A Soul's Tragedy* (II 180) both have close parallels; see also *Italy in England* (p. 245), and, later, *Prince Hohenstiel-Schwangau* (1871); for non-political parallels, cp. *Pictor* (p. 226) and *Andrea* (p. 385).

I.

Just for a handful of silver he left us,
    Just for a ribband to stick in his coat—
Got the one gift of which fortune bereft us,
    Lost all the others she lets us devote;
5   They, with the gold to give, doled him out silver,
    So much was their's who so little allowed:
How all our copper had gone for his service!
    Rags—were they purple his heart had been proud!
We that had loved him so, followed him, honoured him,
10   Lived in his mild and magnificent eye,
Learned his great language, caught his clear accents,
    Made him our pattern to live and to die!

1. A ref. to Judas's betraying Christ for thirty pieces of silver.

3. Got] Found (*1849–88*).

4. devote: 'to dedicate; to consecrate; to appropriate by vow' (*J.*). Cp. *Leviticus* xxvii 28 (quoted in *J.*): 'No devoted thing, that a man shall devote unto the Lord of all that he hath . . . shall be sold or redeemed: every devoted thing is most holy unto the Lord'.

Shakespeare was of us, Milton was for us,
   Burns, Shelley, were with us,—they watch from their
     graves!
15 He alone breaks from the van and the freemen,
   He alone sinks to the rear and the slaves!

II.

We shall march prospering,—not thro' his presence;
   Songs may excite us,—not from his lyre;
   Deeds will be done,—while he boasts his quiescence,
20   Still bidding crouch whom the rest bade aspire:
   Blot out his name, then,—record one lost soul more,
    One task unaccepted, one footpath untrod,
  One more devils'-triumph and sorrow to angels,
    One wrong more to man, one more insult to God!
25 Life's night begins: let him never come back to us!
   There would be doubt, hesitation and pain,
   Forced praise on our part—the glimmer of twilight,
    Never glad confident morning again!
  Best fight on well, for we taught him,—come gallantly,
30   Strike our face hard ere we shatter his own;
  Then let him get the new knowledge and wait us,
    Pardoned in Heaven, the first by the throne!

13–14. B. commented: 'Shakespeare was *of* us—not *for* us, like Him of the Defensio [Milton]; nor abreast with our political sympathies like the other two: I wish he had been more than *of* us' (letter to Ruskin: see headnote). B. owned a copy of Milton's anti-Royalist polemic *Pro Populo Anglicano Defensio* [Defence of the People of England], 1651 (*Collections* A1621).

13. When the poem was in proof, EBB. noted 'Burns was with us' without comment; she discussed the proofs of *DR & L* with B. on 21 Oct. 1845.

18. excite] inspirit (*1849–88*).

22.] One task more declined, one more footpath untrod, (*1849–88*).

23. devils'-triumph] triumph for devils (*1849–88*, except 'devil's triumph', *1872, 1884*).

24. EBB. made a note of this line when the poem was in proof, with 'done' canc. after 'wrong' and replaced by 'more'; it is not certain whether the canc. reading was authorial or EBB.'s slip.

29. come] strike (*1849–88*).

30.] Aim at our heart ere we pierce through his own; (*1849*); Menace our heart ere we master his own; (*1863–88*).

31. get] receive (*1849–88*).   *new knowledge*: cp. *Colossians* iii 9–10: 'ye have put off the old man with his deeds; and have put on the new man, which is renewed in knowledge after the image of him that created him'.

32. Pardoned in Heaven: EBB. jotted this phrase down when the poem was in proof, without comment. Cp. *Hebrews* viii 1: 'We have such an high priest [Jesus], who is set on the right hand of the throne of the Majesty in the heavens'.

10 The Laboratory
Ancien Régime

First publ. *Hood's Magazine* i (June 1844) 513–14, during the crisis caused by the illness of its editor, Thomas Hood. Repr. *B & P* vii (*DR & L*), 6 Nov. 1845, paired with *Confessional* (II 337) under the collective title *France and Spain*, and with the stanzas numbered; then *1849* (when the collective title was dropped, though the poem still appeared alongside *Confessional*), *1863, 1863², 1868, 1872, 1888*. Our text is *Hood's*.

B. knew Thomas Hood (1799–1845), the comic poet and essayist (though best known today for a serious poem, *Song of the Shirt*), and admired his work, suggesting to R. H. Horne that the entry on Hood in *A New Spirit of the Age* (1844) should have for its motto a passage from Jonson's *Cynthia's Revels*: 'Act freely, carelessly, and capriciously; as if our veins ran with quicksilver; and not utter a phrase but what shall come forth steeped in the very brine of conceit, and sparkle like salt in fire' (*Correspondence* viii 202). All Hood's friends were approached for contributions to his magazine during his last illness: see T. L. Hood, *Memorials of Thomas Hood* (1860) ii 200. B. was approached for a contribution by F. O. Ward, acting editor of *Hood's*, and responded on 22 May 1844: 'I will this minute set about transcribing the best of whatever I can find in my desk likely to suit you—and will send it in the course of the day . . . morning, I hope' (*Correspondence* viii 318). It is probable that *Laboratory* alone was initially sent: a second letter, headed 'Friday Mg.', and conjecturally dated 24 May 1844 in *Correspondence*, encloses another poem or poems (probably *Claret and Tokay*), and adds: 'Do as you like about putting in, or out, the one you have already. Take counsel with yourself, too, about the line I have noted: nor forget to send proofs & copy' (*ibid.*, p. 319). Hood died on 3 May 1845.

The date of composition is unknown; 1843–4 seems likely (see below). The speaker has been identified with Marie-Madeleine de Brinvilliers (*c.* 1630–76), a notorious poisoner during the reign of Louis XIV, an identification supported by the subtitle. She obtained poison from her lover, Sainte-Croix, and murdered her father and her two brothers; in an experimental spirit, she was also alleged to have poisoned her maid and large numbers of poor women. The death of Sainte-Croix, in his laboratory, poisoned by his own poison when his glass mask slipped, brought about her exposure, and later her trial, torture, and execution. Her story is in *Biographie*; B. may also have read it in Alexandre Dumas' *Crimes Célèbres* (London 1843). A review of *Crimes Célèbres* in the *Foreign Quarterly Review* (xxx [1842] 26–60) devoted three pages to Brinvilliers. A poem entitled *Brinvilliers*, by B.'s father, is in the Library of Northwestern University (*Collections* J 63, p. 531). No source gives Brinvilliers' motive as jealousy, but this idea may have been partly suggested by the contrast between her small stature and delicate features, as described by Dumas and transcribed by his reviewer, and the more robust beauty of the heroine of the next case cited by the reviewer, the Marchioness de Ganges (see ll. 23–4n.), who was poisoned by her brothers-in-law. The 'old man' may have been inspired either by the Italian Exili, a famous poisoner whom Sainte-Croix met in the Bastille, and who taught him his trade, or by the apothecary Glazer, who was later Sainte-Croix's accomplice, working for him in a small secret laboratory. The detail of the laboratory in the poem corresponds to descriptions of this laboratory, and of the secret closet which, as Dumas reports, was discovered in 1814 in the castle where Brinvilliers poisoned her father. Another source, suggested to us by Mr Michael Meredith, is a chapter entitled 'The Laboratory' in Harrison Ainsworth's *Crichton* (1837), which begins with an elaborate description of the laboratory of Cosmo Ruggieri, an old astrologer: 'On the floor near to the furnaces is strewn all the heterogeneous lumber proper to the retreat of an adept; to wit, earths, metals, "vitriol, sal-tartar, argaile, alkali," gums, oils, retorts, alembics, "crosslets, crucibles and curcurbites." Nor must we omit a slab of black marble, on which are deposited certain drugs and small phials, together with a vizard of glass, a circumstance testifying to the subtle and deadly nature of the tinctures sometimes extracted by the inmates of the chamber' (ii 138–9). Ruggieri and Catherine de' Medici then confer over the life and possible death by poison of Crichton, who is her enemy. For another important borrowing from Ainsworth, see headnote to *How They Brought the Good News*, p. 221. The poem illustrates B.'s interest in the psychology of murder; cp. *Porphyria* (p. 70), *My Last Duchess* (p. 197), *A Forgiveness* (*Pacchiarotto*, 1876), and most fully, *Ring*. EBB., who first saw the poem with B.'s other contributions to *Hood's*, commented in her letter of 21 July 1845: 'the Laboratory is hideous as you meant to make it:— only I object a little to your tendency .. which is almost a habit .. & is very observable in this poem I think, .. of making lines difficult for the reader to read .. see the opening lines of this poem. Not that music is required everywhere, nor in *them* certainly, but that the uncertainty of rhythm throws the reader's mind off the rail .. & interrupts his progress with you & your influence with him. Where we have not direct pleasure from rhythm, & where no peculiar impression is to be produced by the changes in it, we sh^d be encouraged by the poet to *forget it altogether*—should we not?' (*Correspondence* x 315–16). See also l. 1n. All EBB.'s other comments on the poem recorded in the notes derive from *Wellesley MS*, unless otherwise stated.

> Now I have tied thy glass mask on tightly,
> May gaze thro' these faint smokes curling whitely,
> As thou pliest thy trade in this devil's-smithy,
> Which is the poison to poison her, prithee?
>
> 5 He is with her; and they know that I know
> Where they are—what they do: they believe my tears flow
> While they laugh—laugh at me—at me fled to the drear
> Empty church to pray God in for them!—I am here.
>
> Grind away, moisten and mash up thy paste,
> 10 Pound at thy powder—am I in haste?
> Better sit thus, and observe thy strange things,
> Then go where men wait me, and dance at the king's.
>
> That in the mortar—call you a gum?
> Ah, the brave tree whence such gold oozings come!

1.] Now that I, tying thy glass mask tightly, (*1845–885*). The rev., prompted by EBB. (see headnote), left at least one other reader still dissatisfied: W. L. Phelps (*Robert Browning* [1931] 200) records that 'Tennyson passed a severe judgment on the first line . . . saying that it lacked smoothness, that it was a very difficult mouthful'.
10. *am I in haste?*] I am not in haste! (*1849–88*).
13. *call you*] you call it (*1845–88*). EBB. queried 'call you' in proof.

15 And yon soft phial, the exquisite blue,
     Sure to taste sweetly—is that poison too?

     Had I but all of them, thee and thy treasures—
     What a wild crowd of invisible pleasures—
     To carry pure death in an earring, a casket,
20 A signet, a fan-mount, a filagree-basket!

     Soon, at the king's, but a lozenge to give,
     And Pauline should have just thirty minutes to live!
     To light a pstille, and Elise, with her head,
     And her breast, and her arms, and her hands, should
        drop dead!

25 Quick—is it finished? The colour's too grim;
     Why not like the phial's, enticing and dim?
     Let it brighten her drink, let her turn it and stir,
     And try it and taste, ere she fix and prefer!

     What a drop! She's not little—no minion like me;
30 That's why she ensnared him: this never will free

15. *yon*] yonder (*1845–88*). EBB. jotted down 'yonder' in proof, either suggesting or recording this rev.

19–20. Brinvilliers's poisons were administered in food, but Sainte-Croix was a connoisseur who wished to rediscover the secret of the kind of poisons mentioned here.

19. an] emended in agreement with other eds. from 'a' in *Hood's*.

20. filagree: or filigree: jewel-work in threads and beads of gold or silver.

21. but a] a mere (*1849–88*).

23–4. Cp. (with ll. 29–32) a passage describing the Marchioness de Ganges quoted by the reviewer of Dumas's *Crimes Célèbres* immediately after his summary of the Brinvilliers case (see headnote): 'This brilliancy of her face was set off by the decided blackness of her hair . . . The roundness of her face, produced by an *embonpoint bien ménagé*, presented all the vigour and freshness of health. To complete her charms, the Graces seemed to direct her looks, the movement of her lips, and of her head; her figure corresponded to the beauty of her face; indeed, her arms, her hands, her carriage, and her deportment, left nothing to desire if we would have the most agreeable image of a beautiful person'.

23. To] But to (*1849–88*).

26. not like] not soft like (*1849–88*).

29. minion: a small, delicate creature; hence insignificant. The context requires this sense, which is not in *OED*; it is close to 'minim', one of whose senses is 'a creature of the least size or importance', and which B. later used to describe an insect in *Red Cotton Night-Cap Country* (1873) iv 169: 'Look how the marvel of a minim crawls!' The connotations of 'minion', all originally positive ('darling', 'beloved', 'favourite'), are now all negative ('pampered creature', 'servile courtier'): the word could thus encapsulate the speaker's sense of the loss of her lover's favour. Cp. the use of the word in *Pippa* ii 31 (p. 124).

The soul from those strong, great eyes: say, "No!"
To that pulse's magnificent come-and-go.

For only last night, as they whispered, I brought
My own eyes to bear on her so, that I thought,
35   Could I keep them one half minute fixed, she'd fall
Shrivelled: she fell not; yet this does it all!

Not that I bid you spare her pain!
Let death be felt and the proof remain;
Brand, burn up, bite into its grace—
40   He is sure to remember her dying face!

Is it done? Take my mask off! Be not morose!
It kills her, and this prevents seeing it close—
The delicate droplet, my whole fortune's fee—
If it hurts her, beside, can it ever hurt me?

45   Now, take all my jewels, gorge gold to your fill,
You may kiss me, old man, on my mouth, if you will!
But brush this dust off me, lest horror there springs
Ere I know it—next moment I dance at the king's.

31. EBB. quoted this line and commented: 'Will you read this line with the context, & see if the rhythm is not perplexed in it?'   *strong, great*] masculine (*1845, 1863–88*). It is very unusual for B. to restore his original reading in a later text (here, *1849*) and then re-revise it.

35. she'd fall] she would fall (*1845–88*). EBB. suggested the rev. in her original notes on the poem; she jotted down 'she would fall' in proof, either repeating her suggestion or noting its adoption.

37–40. Lionel Stevenson (*UTQ* xxi [1952] 243–4) compares Racine, *Andromache* IV iv, where the intended victim is a faithless lover: 'Quel plaisir de venger moi-même mon injure, / De retirer mon bras teint du sang du parjure, / Et pour rendre sa peine et mes plaisirs plus grands, / De cacher ma rivale à ses regards mourants!' [What pleasure to take revenge myself for the wrong done to me, to withdraw my arm stained with the perjured man's blood, and, to increase his pain and my pleasures, to prevent him from looking his last on my rival!]. Cp. also the final lines of Tennyson's *The Lady of Shalott* (1842 text): 'But Lancelot mused a little space; / He said, "She has a lovely face; / God in his mercy lend her grace, / The Lady of Shalott."'

37. EBB. quoted the line and commented: 'And the rhythm here! Is it well done that it should change?'   *pain*] the pain (*1845–88*).

41–2. The speaker insists, despite the old man's objection that it is dangerous, on removing her mask for a closer view of the poison.

41. Be] Nay, be (*1845–88*).

47. EBB. quoted this line, underlining its last three words, and commented: 'The last words are clogged, I think .. & the expression seems forced'.   *there springs*] it brings (*1845–88*).

11 Garden Fancies

First publ. *Hood's Magazine* ii (July 1844) 45–8; for B.'s contributions to *Hood's*, see p. 209. A letter of ?24 June 1844 from B. to F. O. Ward, the acting editor of *Hood's* (*Correspondence* ix 30), shows that Ward, and Hood himself, suggested revs. in proof, but the lines to which they refer must have been further changed, since the fragmentary phrases which B. quotes fit neither *Garden Fancies* nor any other poem of the period. Repr. *B & P* vii (*DR & L*), 6 Nov. 1845, with both sections given stanza numbers; then *1849, 1863, 1868, 1880, 1888*. Our text is *Hood's*. *Garden Fancies* is the only one of B.'s collective titles for paired poems (e.g. *Italy and France* for *My Last Duchess* and *Count Gismond*) which survived *1849*. With his letter of ?18 July 1845 (*Correspondence* x 312–13), B. sent EBB. all the poems he had publ. in *Hood's*, for criticism before publication in *DR & L*; her comment on *Sibrandus* 46 (*Wellesley MS*; all her comments recorded in the notes are from this text, unless otherwise stated) makes it clear that he showed her his own MS, not the printed texts.

For B.'s love of plants and small wild creatures, see *Pauline* 716–28 (p. 53), *Sordello* vi 619–28n. (I 752–4), and *Flight of the Duchess* 726–30n. (II 327). *Miller* 155 links the poem with Shelley's *The Sensitive Plant*; cp. esp. the description of the 'ruling Grace' of the garden, 'A Lady, the wonder of her kind', e.g. ii 29–32: 'I doubt not the flowers of that garden sweet / Rejoiced in the sound of her gentle feet; / I doubt not they felt the spirit that came / From her glowing fingers through all their frame', and ll. 37–40: 'She lifted their heads with her tender hands, / And sustained them with rods and osier-bands; / If the flowers had been her own infants, she / Could never have nursed them more tenderly'. (For other parallels, see notes.) If, as Miller suggests, the garden is that of B.'s mother, *Sibrandus*, by contrast, may be seen as a humorous tribute to B.'s father's large library, which contained many antiquarian volumes. In one of these, *Wanley* (also a source for *Pied Piper* [p. 172] and *The Cardinal and the Dog* [II 114], B. found the name Sibrandus of Aschaffenburg, a town in Bavaria (hence 'Schafnaburgensis'). E. Cook (*Browning's Lyrics* [Toronto 1974] 79) cites Rabelais, *Gargantua* I i: a mouldy, vermin-eaten book containing Gargantua's genealogy is found in a tomb with the inscription 'Hic bibitur' [Here be drinking]. For a further source in Rabelais, see ll. 17–72n. DeVane (*Handbook* 169) suggests that the incident is authentic, though B. told EBB.: 'I have no little insight to the feelings of furniture, and treat books and prints with a reasonable consideration' (26 Feb. 1845, *Correspondence* x 99). In a letter to Mrs Fitzgerald of 4 Dec. 1886, B. wrote that he was 'beginning to somewhat arrange my books—such a chaotic mass, in real want of a good clearing fire! For how can I part with old tomes annotated by my Father, and yet how can nine out of ten of them do other than cumber the shelves like the dead weight they *are*? Oh that *helluo librorum* [devourer of books] my father, best of men, most indefatigable of book-digesters!' (*Learned Lady* 193). Cp. the attack on pedantry in *Paracelsus*; also *Master Hugues* (III 388), *A Grammarian* (p. 586), and *Transcendentalism* (III 641). The poem was 'a great favourite' with EBB.: 'it is so new, & full of a creeping crawling grotesque life'.

I. The Flower's Name

Here's the garden she walked across,
    Arm in my arm, such a short while since:
Hark, now I push its wicket, the moss
    Hinders the hinges and makes them wince!
5 She must have reached this shrub ere she turned,
    As back with that murmur the wicket swung;
For she laid the poor snail, my chance foot spurned,
    To feed and forget it the leaves among.

Down this side of the gravel-walk
10   She went while her robe's edge brushed the box:
And here she paused in her gracious talk
    To point me a moth on the milk-white flox.
Roses, ranged in valiant row,
    Think will I never she passed you by!
15 She loves noble roses, I know;
    But this—so surely this met her eye!

This flower she stopped at, finger on lip;
    Stooped over, in doubt, settling its claim,
Till she gave me, with pride to make no slip,
20   Its soft meandering Spanish name:

11.i *1–3*. Cp. Shelley, *The Sensitive Plant* i 49–50: 'sinuous paths of lawn and of moss, / Which led through the garden along and across'. The rhyme recurs in *Sibrandus* 33–5.

i *10. box*: an evergreen shrub, used as a hedge or border.

i *12*. Cp. (noting ll. 35–6) Shelley, *The Sensitive Plant* ii 50–2: 'soft moths that kiss / The sweet lips of the flowers, and harm not, did she / Make her attendant angels be', cited also for *In a Gondola* 49–55 (II 121).

i *14. Think will I never*] I will never think (*1849–88*).

i *15. loves*] loves you (*1849–88*).

i *16*.] But yonder, see, where the rock-plants lie! (*1845–88*). EBB. quoted the *Hood's* reading and commented: 'Is it hypercritical to complain of this "eye". I seldom like the singular "eye"—and then, when it is a Spanish eye!—The line is not a great favorite of mine altogether—and the poem *is*—& you see the least speck on a Venice glass: and if it is "*my fancy*", at least I speak it off my mind & have done with it. The beauty & melody we never shall have done with . . none of us'.

i *18. settling*] as settling (*1845–88*).

i *20*. In her letter of 21 July 1845 (*Correspondence* x 315), EBB. praised 'that beautiful & musical use of the word "meandering," which I never remember having seen used in relation to *sound* before. It does to mate with your "*simmering* quiet" in Sordello' (referring to i 910, I 454).

What a name! Was it love, or praise?
　　Speech half-asleep, or song half-awake?
I must learn Spanish one of these days,
　　Only for that slow sweet name's sake.

25　Roses, if I live and do well,
　　I may bring her, one of these days,
To fix you fast with as fine a spell,
　　Fit you each with his Spanish phrase!
But do not detain me now; for she lingers
30　　There, like sunshine over the ground,
And ever I see her soft white fingers
　　Searching after the bud she found.

Flower, you Spaniard, look you grow not,
　　Stay as you are and be loved for ever!
35　Bud, if I kiss you, 'tis that you blow not,
　　Mind the pink shut mouth opens never!
For while it pouts thus, her fingers wrestle,
　　Twinkling the audacious leaves between,
Till round they turn and down they nestle—
40　　Is not the dear mark still to be seen?
Where I find her not, beauties vanish;
　　Whither I follow her, beauties flee;
Is there no method to tell her in Spanish
　　June's twice June since she breathed it with me?
45　Come, bud, show me the least of her traces,

i _22_. In her letter of 21–22 Oct. 1845 (_Correspondence_ xi 134), EBB. used this
line to describe the rhythm of _Flight of the Duchess_ (see l. 512n., II 318), and see
also _Sibrandus_ 52n.

i _23–4_. In 1834 B. wrote to Amédée de Ripert-Monclar (see headnote to _Paracelsus_,
I 101) that he had 'learned Spanish enough [to] be able to read "the majestic
Tongue which Calderon along the desert flung!—"' (_Correspondence_ iii 111;
B quotes Shelley, _Letter to Maria Gisborne_ 180–1). In 1878 he wrote to
Mrs Fitzgerald: 'a few weeks since, I took it into my head to learn Spanish . . .
Of the pronunciation I know nothing but what the grammar attempts to teach
. . . Of course, like everybody, I had amused myself years ago by stumbling along
a few passages, by means of Latin and Italian' (_Learned Lady_ 55–6).

i _33. look_] look that (_1845–88_). EBB. suggested the change.

i _35–6_. Cp. Keats, _Eve of St Agnes_ 243: 'As though a rose should shut, and be
a bud again'. Cp. B.'s _A Face_ 4–10 (III 233–4).

i _36. Mind the pink shut_] Mind that the pink (_1845_); Mind, the shut pink
(_1849–88_). EBB. had commented: 'A clogged line—is it not? Difficult to read'.

i _37. it pouts thus_] thus it pouts (_1845–65_); it pouts (_1868–88_).

Tread in my lady's lightest foot-fall
—Ah, you may flout and turn up your faces!
Roses, are you so fair after all?

II. Sibrandus Schafnaburgensis

Plague take all pedants, say I!
    He who wrote what I hold in my hand,
Centuries back was so good as to die,
    Leaving this rubbish to bother the land;
5 This, that was a book in its time,
    Printed on paper and bound in leather,
Last month in the white of a matin-prime
    Just when the birds sang all together.

Into the garden I brought it to read;
10   And under these arbutes and laurustine

i 46. *Tread in*] Treasure (*1845–88*).
i 47. *flout*: jeer.
i 48. *are you . . . all?*] you are not . . . all. (*1845–88*, except 'all!', *1849–88*). EBB.
quoted the line, commenting: 'And I just ask whether to put it in the affirmative thus // "Roses, ye are not so fair after all." // does not satisfy the ear &
mind better. It is only *asking*, you know'.

ii *1*. In Richard Henry Wilde's *Conjectures and Researches concerning . . . Tasso* (1842),
the book which he was ostensibly reviewing when he wrote *Chatterton* (see Appendix
C, II 474), B. could have read: 'At the time of his departure for Modena, he
[Tasso] jokes with *Scalabrino*, crying, "plague on the pedants!"' (i 154).   *pedants*]
your pedants (*1849–88*).
ii *4. bother*] cumber (*1849–88*).
ii *7–8*. In the sense intended here, 'white' means 'propitious, favourable' or 'highly
prized, precious'; for its use as a noun in this construction, *OED* cites only Keats,
Endymion iii 402: 'I loved her to the very white of truth'. 'Matin-prime' means,
first, 'the best part of the morning' (or 'the beginning of the morning': l. 8 could
refer to the dawn chorus), but matins and prime are both early-morning
religious services, and l. 8 suggests that B. may be recalling *OED* sense 2a: 'chiefly
of birds . . . to sing their morning song' (as in Milton, *L'Allegro* 114: 'Ere the first
cock his matin rings'), and, by extension, *Job* xxxviii 4–7, where God speaks of
the time 'when I laid the foundations of the earth' and 'the morning stars sang
together'. Cp. *Fifine at the Fair* (1872) 855: 'fresh morning-prime'.
ii *10. these arbutes*] the arbute (*1845–49*). EBB. quoted the *Hood's* reading and
commented: 'Are these pluralities quite correct? You know best .. & I doubt, at
worst'. She suggested the revised reading as 'a more *consistent* course .. but I do
not attempt even to decide'. The 'arbutes' belong to the genus *Arbutus*, evergreen shrubs and trees; the name was commonly applied to the strawberry-tree.
For the form 'arbute', *OED* cites Dryden's translation of Virgil's *Georgics* (ii 96).
laurustine: laurustinus, an evergreen winter-flowering shrub.

Read it, so help me grace in my need,
    From title-page to closing line.
Chapter on chapter did I count,
    As a curious traveller counts Stonehenge;
15   Added up the mortal amount;
    And then proceeded to my revenge.

Yonder's a plum-tree, with a crevice
    An owl would build in, were he but sage;
For a lap of moss, like a fine pont-levis
20   In a castle of the middle age,
Joins to a lip of gum, pure amber;
    When he'd be private, there might he spend
Hours alone in his lady's chamber:
    Into this crevice I dropped our friend.

25   Splash, went he, as under he ducked,
    —I knew at the bottom rain-drippings stagnate:
Next a handful of blossoms I plucked
    To bury him with, my book-shelf's magnate:
Then I went in-doors, brought out a loaf,
30   Half a cheese, and a bottle of Chablis;
Lay on the grass and forgot the oaf
    Over a jolly chapter of Rabelais.

ii *11. so help me grace*: this oath appears in 'Ode to the Ladies of England' by the satirist 'Peter Pindar' (John Wolcot, 1738–1819), in the context of reading: 'So help me, Grace! I ever meant to *please*—/ Ev'n *now* would I ask pardon on my knees*: / If aught I've sinn'd, the stanza must not *live*—/ Bring me the knife— I'll cut the wanton page, / Which puts my lovely readers in a rage: / But hark! they cry, "Barbarian, we forgive"' (ll. 88–92).

ii *14.* Cp. B.'s comparison of poetry to a 'Druid stone-circle' in his reply to Ruskin's criticism of *Men and Women* (Appendix B, p. 881). It is not known when (or whether) B. had visited Stonehenge.

ii *15. mortal*: 'long and tedious' (*OED* 8c, citing Edward Bulwer-Lytton's introduction to his novel *Zanoni* [1842]: 'And so on for 940 mortal pages in foolscap!').

ii *19. pont-levis*: drawbridge.

ii *26.*] At the bottom, I knew, rain-drippings stagnate; (*1870–88*).

ii *32. Rabelais*: François Rabelais (*c.* 1483–1553), the great Renaissance physician, humanist scholar, and writer; the 'jolly chapter' is doubtless from his comic masterpiece *Gargantua and Pantagruel*. Rabelais's name in the period was synonymous with bawdy; cp. *A Likeness* (p. 645) where 'the little edition of Rabelais' (l. 24) figures in the description of a bachelor's lodgings. In 1879 B. was invited to join the Rabelais Club, and sent a gracious refusal: 'I have a huge love for Rabelais, and hope to die even as did his Raminagrobis,—but, what

Now, this morning, betwixt the moss
     And gum that locked our friend in limbo,
35   A spider had spun his web across,
     And sate in the midst with arms a-kimbo:
So I took pity, for learning's sake,
     And, *de profundis, accentibus laetis,*
Cantate, quoth I, as I got a rake,
40   And up I fished his delectable treatise.

Here you have it, dry in the sun,
     With all the binding all of a blister,
And great blue spots where the ink has run,
     And reddish streaks that wink and glister
45   O'er the page so beautifully yellow—
     Oh, the droppings have played their tricks!
Did he guess how toadstools grew, this fellow?
     Here's one stuck in his chapter six!

How did he like it when the live creatures
50   Tickled and toused and browsed him all over,
And worm, slug, eft, with serious features,

Johnson calls a "clubbable person"—I am *not*,—and why should I pretend to be one?' (to W. H. Pollock, 28 June 1879, *ABL MS*). The death of the free-thinking poet Raminagrobis is described in *Gargantua and Pantagruel* (bk. III, ch. xxi). Cp. H. Ainsworth, *Crichton* (1837; see headnote to *Laboratory*, p. 210) I xli: 'jolly old Rabelais'.

ii *34. limbo*: combining the senses of 'prison' and 'a condition of neglect or oblivion'. K. Allott (*Browning: Selected Poems* [Oxford 1967] 203), noting ll. 38–9 and ll. 71–2, suggests an allusion to the Christian limbo.

ii *35–6*. In a letter of *c.* June 1843 to R. H. Horne, B. wrote that he had two skulls in his writing room, 'each on its bracket by the window . . . a huge field-spider [has] woven his platform-web from the under-jaw of one of these sculls [sic] to the window-sill . . . the spider's self is on the watch, with each great *arm* wide out in a tooth-socket' (*Correspondence* vii 184).

ii *38–9*. The Latin means 'sing from the depths in joyful accents'; cp. the opening of *Psalms* cxxx, in the Vulgate *De profundis clamavi*: 'Out of the depths have I cried unto thee, O Lord'.

ii *46. the droppings have*] well have the droppings (*1845–88*). EBB. quoted the line and commented: ' "Oh, well have the droppings" you had written—& better written, I think'. This indicates that she was working from B.'s MS, though not whether it was the printer's copy for *Hood's*.

ii *50. toused*: rumpled, pulled about. Only occurrence in B.

ii *51. eft*: newt, species of lizard. B. wrote enthusiastically to EBB. about the 'English water-eft' (4 Jan. 1846, *Correspondence* xi 277), and told an anecdote in the same letter which displayed his knowledge of newts (see l. 55).

Came in, each one, for his right of trover;
　　When the water-beetle with great blind deaf face
　　Made of her eggs the stately deposit,
55　And the newt borrowed so much of the preface
　　As tiled in the top of his black wife's closet.

All that life, and fun, and romping,
　　All that frisking, and twisting, and coupling,
　　While slowly our poor friend's leaves were swamping,
60　Clasps cracking, and covers suppling!
　　As if you had carried sour John Knox
　　To the play at Paris, Vienna, or Munich,
　　Fastened him into a front-row box,
　　And danced off the Ballet in trowsers and tunic.

65　Come, old martyr! what, torment enough is it?
　　Back to my room shall you take your sweet self!
　　Good bye, mother-beetle; husband-eft, *sufficit!*
　　See the snug niche I have made on my shelf.
　　A's book shall prop you up, B's shall cover you,
70　Here's C to be grave with, or D to be gay,
　　And with E on each side, and F right over you,
　　Dry-rot at ease till the judgment-day!

ii 52. *right of trover:* a mock-solemn form of 'finders keepers', derived from
one of the senses of 'treasure-trove'; technically, 'trover' is an action to recover
illegally-held property. EBB. commented that B. had 'right of trover' to the 'novel
effects of rhythm' in *Flight of the Duchess* (21–22 Oct. 1845); see *Flower's Name*
22n.
ii 55. *so*] just so (*1849–88*).
ii 60. *Clasps*] And clasps were (*1845–88*). EBB. quoted the *Hood's* reading and
commented: 'Or query .. "While clasps were crackling & covers suppling."
A good deal is to be said for the abrupt expression of the "text" . . . but the
other is safer .. & less trusting the reader. You will judge'.
ii 61–4. After praising the poem (see headnote), EBB. added: 'Ah but . . . do
you know besides, . . . it is almost reproachable in you to hold up John Knox
to derision in this way!' Knox (*c.* 1514–72) was the foremost leader of the
Reformation in Scotland, and a type of stern Calvinist morality. Extreme
Protestants had a particular aversion to drama and dance as immoral activities,
and to theatres as immoral places; theatres in foreign (and Catholic) cities would
of course be even worse.
ii 62. *play*] play-house (*1845–88*).
ii 64. *in*] with (*1845–88*). *trowsers*] trousers (*1845–88*); the *Hood's* spelling is the
earlier form and was still allowed, though becoming rare.
ii 67. *sufficit:* enough (Latin).

12 "How They Brought the Good News from Ghent to Aix"

First publ. *B & P* vii (*DR & L*), 6 Nov. 1845, the opening poem of the pamphlet; repr. *1849, 1863, 1868, 1872, 1888*. Our text is *1845*. B. was often asked for details of the composition and background; the following is a conflation of his replies (see esp. *LH* 215–16; *NL* 300; *BSP* i 49; *Pall Mall Gazette*, 31 Dec. 1889). He drafted the poem in Aug. 1844, while 'on board ship off Tangiers' in transit 'from Sicily to Naples', 'after I had been at sea long enough to appreciate even the fancy of a gallop on a certain good horse "York," then in my stable at home'. 'The poem was written . . . in a gay moment on the inside of the cover of the one book I had with me,—Bartoli's "Simboli" ': i.e. his teacher Angelo Cerutti's 1830 ed. of Daniello Bartoli's *De' Simboli Trasportati al Morale* (Rome 1677). B. later carefully erased the text (the book is in the library of Balliol College, Oxford; see also headnote to *Home-Thoughts, from the Sea*, II 246). A fair copy MS of the poem, signed and dated Paris 4 Feb. 1856, is in the Morgan Library (no significant variants from *1849–88*), and several autographs of passages from the poem are extant; in one, of ll. 1–6, dated 1 June 1882 (now in the Huntington Library), l. 5 is incomplete and B. wrote in the margin '(forgotten!)'; see also l. 53n. In 1889 B. recorded from memory the opening lines on an Edison wax cylinder, substituting 'saddle' for 'stirrup' in l. 1, missing out l. 3 and faltering at l. 4:

> I sprang to the saddle, and Joris, and he;
> I galloped, Dirck galloped, we galloped all three;
> 'Speed!' echoed the wall to us galloping through;
> The gate shuts behind us, the lights sink to rest . . .

At this point B. stops, saying: 'I'm incredibly sorry that I can't remember me own verses' (see M. Hancher and J. Moore, 'The Sound of a Voice that is Still', *BNL* iv and v [1970]; we give our own version of B.'s words). Note that the phrase 'The gate shuts' is closer to B.'s MS, as quoted by EBB., than to the published text (see ll. 2–6n.).

There is no historical foundation for the poem, 'merely [a] general impression of the characteristic warfare and besieging which abounds in the Annals of Flanders'. Aix is besieged and about to surrender, and the 'good news' that unexpected help is on its way is brought from Ghent by a route 'hitherto impracticable' but 'discovered to be open for once'. In one place, B. claims that he 'had no map, and wrote swiftly . . . the places mentioned were remembered or guessed at loosely enough'; but elsewhere he states that the story of the siege and the 'impracticable' route could account 'for some difficulties in the time and space occupied by the ride in one night'. B. passed through Flanders in 1834 on his way to Russia, and in 1838 and 1844 on his return from Italy. J. Platt (*N & Q* 8th series, xii [1897] 345) points out the 'medley of languages' in the place-names; but his conclusion that B. 'had never personally explored the route' is not necessarily

---

Title. The only title in B. in the form of a quotation not of literary or proverbial origin.   *Ghent*: the English form; Flemish Gent, French Gand, capital of East Flanders province in what is now Belgium.   *Aix*: short for French Aix-la-Chapelle, Flemish Aken, now Aachen in the state of North-Rhine Westphalia, Germany. All intervening places are in Belgium.

correct; some of the forms may have been adopted for metrical reasons, and, like many Victorians, B. was cavalier about linguistic consistency. In a letter to the Rev. V. D. Davis of Dec. 1881, B. expressed vexation at the repeated inquiries. He commented that 'attention was meant to be concentrated' on the ride itself and, after giving his usual summary, concluded: 'A film or two, even so slight as the above, may sufficiently support a tolerably big spider-web of a story—where there is ability and good will enough to look most at the main fabric in the middle' (*TLS*, 8 Feb. 1952, p. 109). When she saw the poem in manuscript, EBB. wrote: 'You have finely distanced the rider in Rookwood here—not that I sh^d think of saying so, if we had not talked of him before' (*Wellesley MS*: all her comments recorded in the notes derive from this text, unless otherwise stated). The ref. is to Harrison Ainsworth's account of Dick Turpin's ride to York, in his novel *Rookwood* (1834; iii 253–355), a famous set piece in the popular genre of the 'ride'. *Rookwood* also contains an inset lyric, 'Black Bess', Turpin's tribute to his horse, in the same metre as *How They Brought the Good News*, and with some shared details. See ll. 17n., 22–30n., 47–8n., and 58n. (we are grateful to Mr Michael Meredith for drawing our attention to the importance of this source). Cp. also Byron's *The Destruction of Sennacherib* and Scott's ballad *Lochinvar*: both are in couplets, again in the same metre as B.'s poem, and Scott uses a six-line stanza. Other 'rides' in B. include *My Wife Gertrude* (*Cavalier Tunes* iii, I 348), *Through the Metidja* (II 155), *Last Ride Together* (III 285), and *Muléykeh* (*DI*², 1880); the messenger bearing news of deliverance reappears in *Saul* 313–18 (III 520) and *Pheidippides* (*DI*, 1879). EBB. further commented: 'You hear the very trampling & breathing of the horses all through—& the sentiment is left in its right place through all the physical force-display. Then the difficult management of the *three* horses, of the *three* individualities, . . & Roland carrying the interest with him triumphantly! I know you must be fond of this poem: & nobody can forget it who has looked at it once'.

I.

I sprang to the stirrup, and Joris, and He;
I galloped, Dirck galloped, we galloped all Three;
"Good speed!" cried the watch, as the gate-bolts undrew;
"Speed!" echoed the wall to us galloping through;

1. Cp. Scott, Lochinvar 40: 'So light to the saddle before her he sprung'.   *Joris*: B. may have taken the name from David Joris, the 16th-century Flemish Anabaptist leader.   *He*] he (*1849–88*). Referring to Dirck, l. 2.
2–6. EBB. quoted:

> I *galloped*, Dirck *galloped*, we *galloped* all three—
> Good speed cried the watch as the eastgate undrew—
> Good speed from the wall, to us *galloping* through . . .
> The gate, shut the porter, the lights sank to rest,
> And into the midnight we *galloped* abreast.

The italics are her own; she commented: 'By the way, how the word "galloping" is a good galloping word! & how you felt it & took the effect up & dilated it by repeating it over & over in your first stanza, . . doubling, folding one upon another, the hoof-treads'. The changes in the published version were presumably not suggested by her.
2. Three] three (*1849–88*).

5   Behind shut the postern, the lights sank to rest,
     And into the midnight we galloped abreast.

II.

Not a word to each other; we kept the great pace
Neck by neck, stride for stride, never changing our place;
I turned in my saddle and made its girth tight,
10   Then shortened each stirrup, and set the pique right,
Rebuckled the cheek-strap, chained slacker the bit,
Nor galloped less steadily Roland a whit.

III.

'Twas moonset at starting; but while we drew near
Lokeren, the cocks crew and twilight dawned clear;
15   At Boom, a great yellow star came out to see;
At Düffeld, 'twas morning as plain as could be;
And from Mecheln church-steeple we heard the
       half-chime,
So Joris broke silence with, "Yet there is time!"

5. *postern*: a back- or side-gate (i.e. the riders are not leaving by the main gate);
cp. *Flight of the Duchess* 800 (II 330).
8. *for*] by (*1849–88*).
10. *set the pique right*: in a letter of 1884, B. wrote: 'I certainly had and have
the impression that the old-fashioned projection in front of the military
saddle on the Continent was called the "pique"—and, when of a smaller size,
the "demi-pique": I might as well have styled it simply the "peak". In a large
loose-sitting saddle, the "pique" might, by shifting it to one side, show that the
trim wanted adjustment—"setting right," opposite the withers of the horse. Such
was my impression,—how far justified I cannot immediately say, the question
never before having occurred to me' (to Messrs Blackie & Son, 20 Feb. 1884,
ABL MS).
14. EBB. quoted 'Lokeren, the cocks crew & twilight seemed clear', and commented: 'I doubt about "twilight seeming clear". Is it a happy expression? But
I only *doubt*, you know'. Twilight can refer to either morning or evening.
     Lokeren: a town 18 km east-north-east of Ghent; Platt (see headnote) points
out that it is wrongly accented on the second syllable instead of the first.
15. *Boom*: a town 25 km east of Lokeren.
16. *Düffeld*: now Duffel, a town 10 km east of Boom.
17. *Mecheln*: Flemish Mechelen, French Malines; Platt (see headnote) queries the
use of the German form. A town 7 km south-south-west of Duffel.   *church-steeple*:
the cathedral of St Rumboldus at Mechelen has a tall steeple and a 49-bell
carillon. Cp. *Rookwood* iii 292: 'as Turpin rode through the deserted streets of
Huntingdon, he heard the eleventh hour given from the iron tongue of Saint
Mary's spire'.

IV.

At Aerschot, up leaped of a sudden the sun,
20 And against him the cattle stood black every one,
To stare thro' the mist at us galloping past,
And I saw my stout galloper Roland at last,
With resolute shoulders, each butting away
The haze as some bluff river headland its spray.

V.

25 And his low head and crest, just one sharp ear bent back
For my voice, and the other pricked out on his track;
And one eye's black intelligence,—ever that glance
O'er its white edge at me, his own master, askance!
And the thick heavy spume-flakes which aye and anon
30 His fierce lips shook upwards in galloping on.

VI.

By Hasselt, Dirck groaned; and cried Joris, "Stay spur!
"Your Roos galloped bravely, the fault's not in her,
"We'll remember at Aix"—for one heard the quick wheeze

19–30. EBB. admired this passage: 'The leaping up of the sun . . . & the cattle standing black against him, & staring through the mist at the riders, . . all that, . . I do not call it *picture*, because it is so much better . . it is the very sun & mist & cattle themselves. And I like the description of Roland, . . I like *him* . . seeing him, . . with one sharp ear bent back & the other pricked out! it is so livingly the horse—even to me who know nothing of horses in the ordinary way of sitting down & trying to remember what I know, but who recognize this for a real horse galloping'.

19. Aerschot: properly Aarschot, the second syllable pronounced 'scot' (Platt; see headnote); a town 25 km south-east of Duffel.

20. him: the sun; cp. *Morning* [*Parting at Morning*] 3–4n. (II 359).

22–30. This passage was clearly influenced by sts. iii–iv of Ainsworth's 'Black Bess': 'Look! look! how that eyeball glows bright as a brand! / That neck proudly arches, those nostrils expand! / Mark! that wide-flowing mane! of which each silky tress / Might adorn prouder beauties—though none like Black Bess. // Mark! that skin sleek as velvet, and dusky as night, / With its jet undisfigured by one lock of white; / That throat branched with veins, prompt to charge or caress, / Now is she not beautiful—bonny Black Bess?' (iii 241).

22. stout: of a horse: characterized by endurance or staying power, contrasted with 'speedy'.

29–30. Cp. (noting l. 24) Byron, *The Destruction of Sennacherib* 15–16: 'And the foam of his gasping lay white on the turf, / And cold as the spray of the rock-beating surf'.

29. spume-flakes: cp. *Childe Roland* 114 (p. 360): 'bespate with flakes and spumes'.

31. Hasselt: a town 35 km east-south-east of Aarschot.

Of her chest, saw the stretched neck and staggering knees,
35   And sunk tail, and horrible heave of the flank,
As down on her haunches she shuddered and sank.

VII.

So left were we galloping, Joris and I,
Past Looz and past Tongres, no cloud in the sky;
The broad sun above laughed a pitiless laugh,
40   'Neath our feet broke the brittle bright stubble like chaff;
Till over by Dalhem a dome-spire sprang white,
And "Gallop," gasped Joris, "for Aix is in sight!

VIII.

"How they'll greet us"—and all in a moment his roan
Rolled neck and croup over, lay dead as a stone;
45   And there was my Roland to bear the whole weight
Of the news which alone could save Aix from her fate,
With his nostrils like pits full of blood to the brim,
And with circles of red for his eye-sockets' rim.

IX.

Then I cast loose my buffcoat, each holster let fall,
50   Shook off both my jack-boots, let go belt and all,
Stood up in the stirrup, leaned, patted his ear,
Called my Roland his pet-name, my horse without peer;
Clapped my hands, laughed and sang, any noise, bad or good,
Till at length into Aix Roland galloped and stood.

---

37. *left were we*] we were left (*1849–88*).
38. *Looz*: the French form; Flemish Loon, now Borgloon, 15 km south of Hasselt.
     Tongres: again the French form; Flemish Tongeren, 7 km south-east of Borgloon.
41. *Dalhem*: a village so called lies 20 km south-east of Tongeren, but it is another
30 km east-north-east of Aachen, which is meant to be 'in sight'.   *dome-spire*:
Charlemagne's famous Palace Chapel at Aachen has a high dome.
42. *sight!*] emended in agreement with *1872, 1884* from 'sight!"'', all other eds.
(since Joris clearly speaks the next sentence).
44. *neck and croup*: cp. the expression 'neck and crop', 'bodily, completely'. The
'croup' is a horse's rump or hindquarters: cp. Scott, *Lochinvar* 39: 'So light to the
croup the fair lady he swung'. B. has 'neck by croup' in *Muléykeh* (*DI²*) 94.
47–8. Cp. *Rookwood* iii 318: 'her eyeballs were dilated, and glowed like flaming
carbuncles; while her widely distended nostril seemed . . . to snort forth smoke'.
49. *buffcoat*: a stout coat of buff leather; used again, with 'jackboots' (see next
line), in *Flight of the Duchess* 253 (II 307).
53. In an undated autograph of the last two stanzas of the poem, now in the Berg
Collection of the New York Public Library, 'any' is replaced by 'every'.

X.

55 And all I remember is, friends flocking round
    As I sate with his head 'twixt my knees on the ground,
    And no voice but was praising this Roland of mine,
    As I poured down his throat our last measure of wine,
    Which (the burgesses voted by common consent)
60 Was no more than his due who brought good news
        from Ghent.

55–60. EBB. had 'One query at the last stanza'. She quoted the line 'That they saved to have drunk our Duke's health in, but grieved', and commented: 'You mean to say . . "would have grieved" . . do you not? The construction seems a little imperfect'. It is possible, though not certain, that this line came in the place of l. 59; in any case the rhyme-word for 'grieved' has been lost. In a letter to B. of 12–14 Nov. 1845 (after publication), EBB. praised 'that touch of natural feeling at the end, to prove that it was not in brutal carelessness that the poor horse was driven through all that suffering . . Yes, & how that one touch of softness acts back upon the energy & resolution & exalts both, instead of weakening anything, as might have been expected by the vulgar of writers or critics' (*Correspondence* xi 167).

58. Conflating two incidents from *Rookwood*, one the report of a publican: ' "I know he gave his mare more ale than he took for himself" ' (iii 276), the other describing how Turpin gave his horse a restorative potion: 'Raising her head upon his shoulder, Dick poured the contents of the bottle down the throat of his mare' (iii 333).

13 Pictor Ignotus
Florence, 15—

First publ. *B & P* vii (*DR & L*), 6 Nov. 1845; repr. *1849, 1863, 1865², 1868, 1872, 1888*. The Latin title means lit. 'painter unknown', used for anonymous works; 'ignotus' can also mean 'of low birth' and (as past participle of 'ignosco') 'forgiven', 'overlooked'. The date of composition is unknown, but a time during or shortly after B.'s second trip to Italy (Aug.–Dec. 1844) is likely. DeVane (*Handbook* 155) argues that it was 'certainly conceived, and possibly written, during Browning's visit to Florence, which may have been early in November, 1844'. Rome, however, which B. visited during his 1844 trip, is also an important presence in the poem; B. would have seen there the work of Raphael, to whom Pictor contrasts himself (see ll. 1–2).

Elvan Kintner (*LK* 129n. 1) suggests that it was to this poem that B. referred in a letter to EBB. of ?18 July 1845 (*Correspondence* x 312–13) in which he describes

> a poem you are to see—written some time ago—which advises nobody who thinks nobly of the Soul, to give, if he or she can help, such a good argument to the materialist as the owning that any great choice of that Soul, which it is born to make and which—(in its determining, as it must, the whole future course and impulses of that soul)—which must endure for ever (even tho' the object that induced the choice should disappear) —owning, I say, that such a choice may be scientifically determined and produced, at any operator's pleasure, by a definite number of ingredients, so much youth, so much beauty, so much talent &c &c with the same certainty and precision that another kind of operator will construct you an artificial volcano with so much steel filings and flower of sulphur and what not: there is more in the soul than rises to the surface and meets the eye; whatever does *that*, is for the world's immediate uses; and were this world *all*, all in us would be producible and available for use, as it *is* with the body now—but with the soul, what is to be developed *afterward* is the main thing, and instinctively asserts its rights—so that when you hate (or love) you shall not be able to explain "why" ("You" is the ordinary enough creature of my poem—*he* might not be so able.)

Pictor's 'great choice', according to this theory, would be his decision to retire to a monastery instead of pursuing the commercial career that his 'talent' might seem to warrant; and this decision results from a hatred of the world which reflects Pictor's instinctive longing to transcend it, though he himself is unable to understand his action in those terms, and represents it as misanthropy, or dislike of commercialism. The question of the value or otherwise of popularity to a poet was discussed by B. and EBB. during their early correspondence, and *Pictor* may have been written in the context of their debate: see EBB. to B., 3 Feb. 1845, and B.'s reply, 11 Feb. 1845 (*Correspondence* x 52, 70–1).

A historical original for the painter has been suggested by J. B. Bullen ('Browning's "Pictor Ignotus" and Vasari's "Life of Fra Bartolommeo di San Marco"', *RES* xxiii [1972] 313–19). Bullen argues that it was from Vasari's *Vite de' Pittori* (Florence 1550) and A. F. Rio's *De la Poésie Chrétienne* (Paris 1836) that B. learned of Bartolommeo (*c.* 1475–1517), who painted predominantly religious subjects, and who, under the influence of Savanarola, entered the

Dominican Order in 1499 and abandoned painting altogether for four years, a decision Vasari attributes in part to personal timidity. Bullen points out that Fra Bartolommeo's surname was unknown, and that he was commonly called simply 'il Frate' (the Friar); following earlier commentators, he identifies the 'youth' of l. 1 with Raphael, and goes on to suggest a reference to the period (mentioned by Vasari and Rio) when Bartolommeo visited Rome and painted with him. Cp. Anna Jameson, *Memoirs of the Early Italian Painters* (first publ. 1843): '[Bartolommeo] might have been *the* Raphael, had not Fortune been determined in favour of the other'. See also headnote to *Lines on Correggio*, II 454. M. H. Bright ('Browning's Celebrated Pictor Ignotus', *ELN* xiii [1976] 192–4) objects to the identification both on circumstantial grounds (Fra Bartolommeo did paint on canvas and in the houses of rich men, whereas Pictor paints frescoes in churches; Bartolommeo did sell his pictures; he was not a monotonous anti-realist but was praised for the animation of his figures, etc.), and on the interpretative ground that the poem hinges on the fact that the painter has not achieved, and will not achieve, recognition, either during his lifetime or after death, a state of affairs which emphatically did not apply to Fra Bartolommeo. For further exchanges between Bullen and Bright, see *ELN* xiii (1976) 206–15; we accept Bright's view that Bartolommeo is not the literal subject of the poem; but it is plausible to claim that B. drew on some details of his career.

Many *DR & L* poems, such as *Lost Leader* (p. 206), *Lost Mistress* (II 293), *Time's Revenges* (II 279), also deal with loss, renunciation, and defection, but by placing *Pictor*, in *1863*, in *Men, and Women*, B. elected to stress its place in his theory of the development of Renaissance art. EBB. commented: 'This poem is so fine, . . so full of power, . . as to claim every possible attention to the working of it. It begins greatly, grandly, & ends so—the winding up winds up the soul in it. The versification too is noble . . . & altogether it classes with your finest poems of the length—does it not, in your own mind? I cannot tell you how much it impresses mine' (*Wellesley MS*: all her comments recorded in the notes derive from this text, unless otherwise stated). William Stigand, summing up B.'s career towards the close of his review of *DP* (*ER* cxx [Oct. 1864] 537–65; repr. *CH* 230–60), suggested an analogy between B.'s own attitude to popular success, and Pictor's: 'Mr. Browning has always chosen . . . to remain apart from the beaten track of the ordinary world; and we can imagine him sharing in the feelings of his own "Pictor Ignotus" who . . . thus expresses his contempt for the vulgar crowd—[quotes ll. 46–57]. So Mr. Browning has chosen his portion, and the popularity which he has despised will in all probability never be thrust upon him.'

> I could have painted pictures like that youth's
>   Ye praise so. How my soul springs up! No bar
> Stayed me—ah, thought which saddens while it soothes!
>   Never did fate forbid me, star by star,
> 5   To outburst on your night with all my gift
>   Of fires from God: nor would this flesh have shrunk
> From seconding that soul, with eyes uplift

6–7. this . . . that] my . . . my (*1849–88*).
7–10. uplift . . . sunk . . . Sent: these verbs are all past participles modifying 'eyes'.

And wide to Heaven, or, straight like thunder, sunk
To the centre of an instant, or around
10   Sent calmly and inquisitive to scan
The license and the limit, space and bound,
Allowed to Truth made visible in Man.
And, like that youth ye praise so, all I saw,
Over the canvass could my hand have flung,
15   Each face obedient to its passion's law,
Each passion clear proclaimed without a tongue;
Whether Hope rose at once in all the blood,
A-tiptoe for the blessing of embrace,
Or Rapture drooped the eyes as when her brood
20   Pull down the nesting dove's heart to its place,
Or Confidence lit swift the forehead up,
And locked the mouth fast, like a castle braved,—
Men, women, children, hath it spilt, my cup?
What did ye give me that I have not saved?
25   Nor will I say I have not dreamed (how well!)
Of going—I, in each new picture,—forth,

8–9. EBB. quoted: 'like a thunder sunk / To the centre of an instant', and commented: 'Is there not something obscure in the expression? And it is all so fine here, that you should let the reader stand up as straight as he can, to look round'.

10. Sent] Turned (*1849–88*).

15–16. Cp. *Fifine* (1872) 1719–26: 'the infinitude / Of passions, loves and hates, man pampers till his mood / Becomes himself, the whole sole face we name him by, / Nor want denotement else, if age or youth supply / The rest of him: old, young,—classed creature: in the main / A love, a hate, a hope, a fear, each soul a-strain / Some one way through the flesh—the face, the evidence / O' the soul at work inside'.

19–20. EBB. quoted these lines (with 'rapture' for 'Rapture' and 'her eyes' for 'the eyes') and commented: 'A most exquisite image, & perfect in the expression of it I think'. Cp. *A Forest Thought* 52 (I 344), 'the brood-song of the cushat-dove'.

23. Men, women, children] O Human faces (*1849–88*, except 'human', *1863–88*.

23–4. The 'cup' is a frequent biblical image of God's bounty: the speaker's use of it contrasts with *Psalms* xxiii 5: 'thou hast anointed my head with oil; my cup runneth over'.

26–35. These lines, together with ll. 57–68, suggest a contrast, not simply between secular and religious art, but between easel painting (portable and therefore saleable) and fresco (stationary: the usual medium of ecclesiastical art). *Murray²* claims: 'in the sixteenth century, it may be doubted whether any *cabinet pictures*, that is to say, moveable pictures, intended merely to hang upon the wall and be looked at as ornaments . . . ever existed' (p. 428).

And making new hearts beat and bosoms swell,
    As still to Pope and Kaiser, South and North,
Bound for the calmly satisfied great State,
30   Or glad aspiring little burgh, it went,
Flowers cast upon the car which bore the freight
    Through old streets named afresh from its event,
—Of reaching thus my home, where Age should greet
    My face, and Youth, the star as yet distinct
35   Above his hair, lie learning at my feet,—
    Oh, thus to live, I and my pictures, linked
With love about, and praise, till life should end,
    And then not go to Heaven but linger here,
Here on my earth, its every man my friend,—
40   Oh, that grows frightful, 'tis so wildly dear!

27. EBB. quoted 'Ever new hearts made beat & bosoms swell', and commented:
'The construction seems to me to be entangled a little by this line, . . & the
reader pauses before he clears the meaning to himself. Why not clear it for him
by writing the line thus . . for instance . . ? "New hearts being made to beat, &
breasts to swell" or something better which will strike you. Will you consider?'
    And] As, (*1849–88*).
28.] To Pope or Kaiser, East, West, South or North, (*1849–88*, except 'South,
or', *1870–88*). For 'Kaiser' see *Sordello* i 78–9n., 131n. (I 399, 403).
32. DeVane (*Handbook* 156) suggests a reference to the Borgo Allegri in Rome,
so named after a Madonna by Cimabue was carried along it.   *its event*] the event
(*1865–88*). The *1845* reading involves an unusual sense of 'event', as meaning
something like 'appearance, apparition'.
33.] Till it reached home, where learned Age should greet (*1849–88*, except 'age',
1868–88). EBB. quoted 'And thus to reach my home, where Age sh^d greet', and
commented: 'Should you not write it . . "Of reaching thus my home" &c, the
construction taking you back to what he dreamed of. First he dreamed "of going"—
& then "of reaching" his home &c'.   *home*: the picture's 'home', where it is to
be hung (not the painter's literal home).
34. as yet] not yet (*1849–88*). With the *1845* text, cp. Wordsworth's *Ode: Intimations
of Immortality*, where 'The Soul that rises with us, our life's Star' fades for 'The
Youth, who daily farther from the east / Must travel' (ll. 59, 72–3); note also
ll. 122–3: 'Thou little Child, yet glorious in the might / Of heaven-born freedom'.
With the revised reading, cp. *Soul's Tragedy* ii 634–41n. (II 217). Cp. also *In a
Balcony* 688–9 (III 439): 'I am not bid create, they see no star / Transfiguring
my brow'.
36. pictures] picture (*1849–88*).
38. EBB. quoted 'And then not go to Heaven &c', adding: 'Fine, all this!'
39. its] earth's (*1849–88*).
40.] The thought grew frightful, 'twas so wildly dear! (*1849–88*).

But a voice changed it! Glimpses of such sights
　　Have scared me, like the revels thro' a door
Of some strange House of Idols at its rites;
　　This world seemed not the world it was before!
45　Mixed with my loving ones there trooped—for what?
　　Who summoned those cold faces which begun
To press on me and judge me? As asquat
　　And shrinking from the soldiery a nun,
They drew me forth, and spite of me . . enough!
50　　These buy and sell our pictures, take and give,
Count them for garniture and household-stuff,
　　And where they live needs must our pictures live,
And see their faces, listen to their prate,
　　Partakers of their daily pettiness,
55　Discussed of,—"This I love or this I hate,
　　"This likes me more and this affects me less!"

41–56. Mrs Jameson (see headnote) cites one description of Bartolommeo as 'a monk in the retirement of his cloister, shut out from the taunts and criticisms of the world'. Bullen (see headnote) argues that the 'voice' is that of Savanorola, whose preaching caused Fra Bartolommeo to destroy all his studies of nudes, and probably influenced his temporary abandonment of painting. According to Vasari, Bartolommeo was 'a man of little courage, or rather, very timid and retiring', and on the occasion of an attack upon a convent where he was staying, 'began to be in great fear, and made a vow that if he escaped he would assume the religious habit'. But the parallel cannot be pressed too far: there is no evidence that Bartolommeo's withdrawal expressed a distaste for commercialism, and B. presumably meant Pictor's 'voice' to be understood metaphorically rather than literally, since without an explicit identification with Bartolommeo the reference to Savanorola could not be appreciated.

41. *it!*] it. (*1865²*, *1868–88*).

45.] Mixed with my loving trusting ones there trooped (*1849–88*, except 'ones,' *1870–88*).

46. *which*] that (*1849–88*).

47. *As asquat*] Tho' I stooped (*1849–88*, except 'Though', *1863–88*).

48. *And shrinking*] Shrinking, as (*1849–88*).

50. EBB. quoted 'These men may buy us, sell us, &c.', and commented: 'meaning pictures, by "*us*". But the reader cannot see it until afterwards, & gets confused. Is it not so? And moreover I do think that by a touch or two you might give a clearer effect to the previous verses about the "jibing" &c'. These 'previous verses' were altered, beyond reconstruction.

52. *needs must our pictures*] our pictures needs must (*1849–63*).

55–6. Contrast B. to EBB., 24 May 1845: 'I do myself justice, and dare call things by their names to myself, and say boldly, this I love, this I hate, this I would do, this I would not do, under all kinds of circumstances' (*Correspondence* x 234–5).

Wherefore I chose my portion. If at whiles
   My heart sinks as monotonous I paint
These endless cloisters and eternal aisles
60   With the same series, Virgin, Babe, and Saint,
With the same cold, calm, beautiful regard,
   At least no merchant traffics in my heart;
The sanctuary's gloom at least shall ward
   Vain tongues from where my pictures stand apart;
65   Only prayer breaks the silence of the shrine
   While, blackening in the daily candle smoke,
They moulder on the damp wall's travertine,
   'Mid echoes the light footstep never woke.
So die, my pictures; surely, gently die!
70   Oh youth men praise so, holds their praise its worth?
Blown harshly, keeps the trump its golden cry?
   Tastes sweet the water with such specks of earth?

57–61. If at whiles . . . regard: *Murray*[2], speaking of ecclesiastical painters in fresco, comments: 'From the fixed types of sacred subjects, transmitted from the earlier ages, no artist could dare to depart' (p. 428). Speaking of Bartolommeo, Rio (see headnote) mentions that accusations of 'powerlessness to draw the nude' were perhaps intended to tempt him to 'transgress the narrow circle of religious representations to which he had scrupulously confined himself' (p. 285).

57. chose] choose (*1865*[2]).

58. paint] emended in agreement with all other eds. from 'paint,' in *1845*.

60. Virgin, Babe, and Saint: Fra Bartolommeo (see headnote), along with Raphael, 'evolved a new treatment . . . of the theme of the Madonna and Child with the Infant S. John in a Landscape' (*Oxford Companion to Art*). See however ll. 26–35n. Cp. Lippo's impatience, 'A-painting for the great man, saints and saints / And saints again' (*Fra Lippo* 48–9, p. 487).

63–9. Cp. *Old Pictures* 185–93 (pp. 423–4), where the 'ghosts' of the early Florentine painters 'stand . . . Watching each fresco flaked and rasped, / Blocked up, knocked out, or whitewashed o'er / —No getting again what the church has grasped! / The works on the wall must take their chance, / "Works never conceded to England's thick clime!" / (I hope they prefer their inheritance / Of a bucketful of Italian quick-lime.)'

67. travertine: a hard, white stone, used for building in Italy; cp. *Tomb at St. Praxed's* 66n. (p. 241).

71. trump: trumpet. Fama (fame) 'was worshipped by the ancients as a powerful goddess, and generally represented blowing a trumpet' (*Lemprière*). Cp. Chaucer, *House of Fame* iii, where the goddess summons her trumpeter, Eolus, to proclaim either infamy with his 'blake trumpe of bras' (l. 545) or honour with his 'trumpe of gold' (l. 687).

14 The Tomb at St Praxed's
[The Bishop Orders His Tomb at Saint Praxed's Church]
Rome, 15—

Text and publication

First publ. *Hood's Magazine* iii (March 1845) 237–9; for B.'s contributions to *Hood's*, see p. 209. Repr. *B & P* vii (*DR & L*), Nov. 1845, *1849* (with the later title), *1863*, *1868*, *1872*, *1888*.

Date and composition

K. I. D. Maslen, citing a source for ideas and images in the poem from 1840 (for details see below) suggests that 'as with many of Browning's later poems, the idea had been with him for some years'; but the composition of the poem itself probably belongs to the winter of 1844–5. B. saw the church of Santa Prassede in Rome during his second trip to Italy in the autumn of 1844. Shortly after his return, in a letter to EBB. of 27 Jan. 1845 (*Correspondence* x 43), he mentioned 'three or four half-done-with' poems; he sent the poem to F. O. Ward, acting editor of *Hood's*, on 18 Feb.: 'I send you *one* poem as long as the *two* I promised— (about 4 pages, I think) and I pick it out as being a pet of mine, and just the thing for the time—what with the Oxford business, and Camden society and other embroilments' (*ibid.* 83). DeVane's assumption (*Handbook* 166) that B. conceived the poem during his 1844 visit is challenged by *Penguin*, which argues that the phrase 'I pick it out' in B.'s letter to Ward, together with the ref. to the Tractarian controversy ('the Oxford business'), which had been in progress for many years, could imply an earlier date. An error taken from *Murray²* (see ll. 48–9n.) could mean either that B. used this guidebook before he went to Italy in 1844, or that he used it after his return to refresh his memory. However, DeVane makes the point that B. would probably have sent the poem to *Hood's* before Feb. 1845 had he written it earlier. We concur with this view, and would add that another inaccuracy in B.'s description of the church supports the later date. Santa Prassede has a domed apse, whereas in the poem it is said to have a full dome; this would accord well with an imperfect recollection.

B. sent the poem to EBB. along with his other 'sins of commission with Hood' in a letter of ?18 July 1845 (*Correspondence* x 313). The evidence of *Wellesley MS* suggests that she gave him a batch of notes on all the *Hood's* poems at a meeting on 22 Sept. She criticized the phrasing of ll. 17–18, but suggested no other revs. in her notes or in her letter commenting on the proofs of *DR & L* (21–22 Oct. 1845, *ibid.* xi 133–4). She may, of course, have made suggestions verbally to B.

Sources and influences; parallels in B.

'Praxed' is the anglicized form of 'Prassede'; B. would have found 'Praxed' in *Murray²*, which says that the church was 'founded on the site of a small oratory built here by Pius I A.D. 160 as a place of security to which the early Christians might retire during the persecutions' (p. 367). As the daughter of a senator, Pudens (mentioned in *2 Timothy* iv 21), Prassede had great wealth which she used to help other Christians during the persecutions. An 18th-century painting in the church shows her having a vision of the martyrdom of her fellow-Christians. Commentators have perceived some irony in the contrast between her and the Bishop; this is supported by the presence in the church of a slab of granite on which Prassede was reputed to sleep. B.'s knowledge of Church history makes it unlikely that he committed the error which has been attributed to him (at l. 95) of mistaking Prassede's gender; his visit to the church makes such an error practically inconceivable.

B.'s choice of the church of Santa Prassede as the setting for the poem has been much misunderstood. Mrs Orr (*Handbook* 247) states, probably on B.'s authority: 'The Bishop's tomb is entirely fictitious; but something which is made to stand for it is now shown to credulous sightseers in St. Praxed's Church'. Since the Bishop's sons have obviously no intention of complying with his grandiose design, no exact model of the tomb could possibly exist; if anything, an inferior tomb should be looked for. The church in fact contains two funerary monuments of Cardinals of Santa Prassede. The first, of Cardinal Anchero Pantaleone of Troyes, dating from 1287, is small, modestly decorated, with an inscription which does not mention the Cardinal's name. The second, of Cardinal Cetti (who was also Bishop of Sabina), dating from 1474, is much larger and more lavish, decorated 'with portraits of himself, St. Peter and St. Paul, and statues of S. Prassede and S. Pudenzia' (*Murray*² 382). Murray implies that the two monuments are within sight of each other, though in fact they are not; but whether B. was relying on Murray or on his own memory, the conjunction of these two monuments could have suggested the idea of rivalry. This possibility is strengthened by the fact that there are no other similar monuments in the church. J. W. Binns ('Real Sources for the Bishop's Tomb in the Church of St. Praxed', *SBC* xii [1984] 160–66) points out that the 'statue' of S. Prassede is in fact a bas-relief and that other details such as the 'tripod' and 'vase' also appear on the tomb (see ll. 56, 58; and see also l. 60n.). Competition for the best location for one's tomb was common in the period in which the poem is set: the best position was thought to be in the choir, near the altar (see ll. 20–4, and L. M. Thompson, 'The Placement of the Bishop's Tomb in St. Praxed's Church', *SBC* xi [1983] 74–5).

The Bishop compares a detail of his projected tomb with one belonging to the monument to St Ignatius Loyola, founder of the Jesuit order and one of the chief architects of the Counter-Reformation, in the Gesù church in Rome (see ll. 48–9). Scholars have pointed out that the date of the monument (1690) is incompatible with the date of the poem. This anachronism is however presumably a deliberate mistake drawing attention to an argument in the poem, articulated through the development of funerary sculpture, about the history and contemporary state of the Roman Catholic Church. According to this argument, the poem's setting in the 16th century places it at a mid-point between the decline of the Renaissance Church into corruption and materialism, with the consequent devastation of the Reformation, and its resurgence in the 17th century, the period of the Counter-Reformation. This mid-point is represented by the Bishop's visionary tomb, which both sums up the sensuality and paganism of the High Renaissance, and anticipates the militant splendour of the Baroque. Browning's satire in the poem would therefore hit simultaneously at the old, unregenerate Catholic Church, and at its Counter-Reformation successor; the allusion to Loyola would be apt because the Jesuits were devoted to the Papacy and had helped to restore its power and prestige. But this same satire could also be applied to the Anglican Church: hence B.'s claim that it was 'just the thing for the time, what with the Oxford business'. The Tractarian (or 'Oxford') movement in England was a kind of 'Counter-Reformaton' within the Church of England, which sought to bring it closer to Catholic doctrine and practice (some of its leading figures, such as Newman and Pugin, did in fact become Catholics, Newman in 1845, the year of the poem's publication). The poem could be seen as a Dissenter's view of this controversy, in which the Anglican Church is both paralleled to the Roman Catholic Church in its internal divisions, and ideologically associated with it despite surface differences.

B.'s mention of the 'Camden society' in his letter to Ward leads to another set of possible sources. R. A. Greenberg, in an excellent article ('Ruskin, Pugin, and the Contemporary Context of *The Bishop Orders His Tomb*', *PMLA* lxxxiv [1960] 1588–94), points out that there were two Camden Societies at this time, both internally divided between Catholic and Protestant interpretations of the antiquarian and historical research in which they were engaged, and both taking part in the Tractarian controversy. He notes that these divisions were at their fiercest in both societies in late 1844. Greenberg quotes extensively from ch. i of Pugin's *Contrasts* (2nd ed., 1842) as a parallel to B.'s reflections on what Pugin calls 'the revived paganism'. Pugin's hostility, as a devout Catholic, to the mingling of Christian and pagan motifs in every aspect of ecclesiastical architecture (including 'monuments for the dead') may be gauged from the following passages: 'The inverted torch, the club of Hercules, the owl of Minerva, and the cinerary urn, are carved . . . on the tombs of popes, bishops, kings, ecclesiastics . . . frequently accompanied by pagan divinities, in pagan nudity'; 'When I see a man professedly a Christian, who, neglecting the mysteries of the faith, the saints of the Church, and the glories of religion, surrounds himself with the obscene and impious fables of mythology, and the false divinities of the heathen, I may presume, without violation of charity, that although he is nominally a son of Christian Rome, his heart and affections are devoted to that city in the days of its Paganism'.

K. I. D. Maslen ('Browning and Macaulay', *N & Q* n. s. xxvii [1980] 525–7) suggests that 'the germs, and indeed the main ingredients of the poem are to be found already gathered in a review by Macaulay in the *Edinburgh Review* for October 1840 of Leopold von Ranke's *Ecclesiastical and political history of the Popes of Rome*, translated by Sarah Austin'. Maslen quotes persuasively from Macaulay's review: 'During the generation which preceded the Reformation, that court [of Rome] had been a scandal to the Christian name. Its annals are black with treason, murder, and incest. Even its more respectable members were utterly unfit to be ministers of religion. . . . Their years glided by in a soft dream of sensual and intellectual voluptuousness. Choice cookery, delicious wines, lovely women, hounds, falcons, horses, newly-discovered manuscripts of the classics, sonnets and burlesque romances in the sweetest Tuscan . . . plate from the hand of Benvenuto, designs for palaces by Michael Angelo, frescoes by Raphael, busts, mosaics, and gems just dug up from among the ruins of ancient temples and villas;—these things were their delight and even the serious business of their lives . . . it was felt that the Church could not be safely confided to chiefs whose highest praise was, that they were good judges of Latin compositions, of paintings, of statues, whose severest studies had a Pagan character'.

G. Monteiro (*VP* viii [1970] 209–18) gives an interesting though occasionally strained account of biblical sources. P. A. Cundiff, in 'Browning's Old Bishop' (*VP* ix [1971] 452–3), suggests a verbal and structural parallel with *Job*, ch. vii; note T. Scott's translation of vv. 5–7, in *The Book of Job in English Verse* (1773): 'Behold my putrid frame; it was not cast / A substance through whole centuries to last' (p. 48), which comes close to the central motif of the poem. The iconography of the Bishop's projected tomb is usefully discussed in *Melchiori* 20−39.

There is no single original for the Bishop himself. J. D. Rea's derivation of certain details from Ireneo Affo's *Vita de Vespasiano Gonzaga* ('My Last Duchess', *SP* xxix [1932] 120−1) is disputed by L. S. Friedland ('Ferrara and *My Last Duchess*', *SP* xxxiii [1936] 657, 665), but Rea's argument retains some conviction. He finds a 'Gandolfo' who is a priest in the *Vita* (though Friedland argues it is a common Italian name); more important, he cites a passage from Gonzaga's will which describes him as 'lying in bed in a certain state chamber of the prefect's palace': cp. 'As here I lie / In this state-chamber' (ll. 10−11). In the will itself, Gonzaga orders his daughter to construct him a sumptuous tomb, and mentions 'the stones necessary to adorn the aforesaid tomb, which I have had brought from Rome'. The rare form 'elucescebat' (see l. 99) also occurs in the *Vita*. Dr M. Halls has suggested to us a resemblance between the Bishop and Cardinal Pietro Bembo (1470−1547): advocacy of Cicero's Latin style, sexual profligacy before ordination, and interest in pagan antiquity and classical scholarship are in common between them. B. may have known W. P. Greswell, *Memoirs of Politianus* (1805), which contains all these details. Greswell mentions Bembo's 'connection with a beautiful female' with whom he had three sons and a daughter, but stresses that this affair came before his ordination (cp. ll. 3−7). He notes that 'Bembo is charged with carrying his affected imitation of the style of Cicero to so ridiculous an extreme as professedly to avoid perusal of his Bible and breviary, for fear of spoiling his latinity'. Bembo founded a society no member of which might use a non-Ciceronian word, and engaged in a protracted controversy with Pico Gianfrancesco as to the value of the Ciceronian style (cp. ll. 77−9, 98−100). Bembo was also accused of denying the doctrine of a future state. B. certainly knew of Bembo, two of whose works were in his library (*Collections* A192 and A193, p. 18). In a letter to EBB. of 28 June 1846, he quotes Carlyle's opinion of Bembo as the type of Italian scholar who neglected to 'examine the new problems of the Reformation &c—trim the balance at intervals, and throw overboard the accumulation of falsehood', and instead devoted themselves to 'verse making, painting, music-scoring' (*Correspondence* xiii 90). B. mentions Bembo in two later works (*Ring* vi 1666, and the preface to *Asolando*), referring both times to his literary dilettantism. B. may well have used Bembo as a model for the Bishop, but the poem is not a portrait of Bembo; cp. the use of Fra Bartolommeo in *Pictor* (headnote, pp. 226−7). The Bishop has affinities with the Intendant in *Pippa* iv (p. 158), who has also robbed a church and amassed many villas, and with the Duke of *My Last Duchess* (p. 197).

Two important literary sources have been suggested by H. M. Richmond in 'Personal Identity and Literary Persona: A Study in Historical Psychology', *PMLA* xc (1975) 209−19, who describes the poem as 'a clever superimposition of the theatrical death-bed episodes from Izaak Walton's *Life of Donne*, on analogous but purely pagan and frivolous material excerpted from the role-playing of Trimalchio in the *Satyricon* of Petronius' (p. 219). The latter ref. is to *Satyricon* lxxi, part of the 'Cena Trimalchionis' (Trimalchio's Feast), in which the wealthy sensualist Trimalchio gives a lavish supper to his cronies and hangers-on: towards the end of the supper he becomes maudlin and reads out his will to the assembled company. He then turns to his friend Habinnas with some instructions concerning his tomb:

> Are you building my monument the way I told you? I particularly want you
> to keep a place at the foot of my statue and put a picture of my pup there, as

well as paintings of wreaths, scent-bottles, and the contents of Petraites, and thanks to you I'll be able to live on after I'm dead . . . After all, it's a big mistake to have nice houses just for when you're alive and not worry about the one we have to live in for much longer. And that's why I want this written up before anything else:

THIS MONUMENT DOES NOT GO TO THE HEIR

But I'll make sure in my will that I don't get done down once I'm dead . . . Propped up on a lot of cushions, he stretched out along the edge of the couch and said: 'Pretend I'm dead and say something nice'.

(transl. J. Sullivan [Harmondsworth 1965])

B. owned a copy of the *Satyricon* (*Collections* A1841, p. 157). Richmond's other source is the account of Donne's last days in Izaak Walton's *Life*:

It is observed, that a desire of glory or commendation is rooted in the very nature of man; and, that those of the severest and most mortified lives . . . have not been able to kill this desire of glory . . . and, we want not sacred examples to justifie the desire of having our memory to out-live our lives; which I mention, because Dr. *Donne* . . . easily yielded at this very time to have a Monument made for him . . . Dr. *Donne* sent for a Carver to make him in wood the figure of an *Urn* . . . and, to bring with it a board of the height of his body. These being got, then without delay a choice Painter was to be in a readiness to draw his picture, which was taken as followeth.—Several Charcole-fires being first made in his large Study, he brought with him into that place his winding-sheet in his hand; and, having put off all his cloaths, had this sheet put on him . . . as dead bodies are usually fitted to be shrowded and put into the grave. Upon this *Urn* he thus stood with his eyes shut, and with so much of the sheet turned aside as might shew his lean, pale, death-like face; which was purposely turned toward the East, from whence he expected the second coming of his and our Saviour. Thus he was drawn at his just height; and when the picture was fully finished, he caused it to be set by his bed-side, where it continued, and became his hourly object till his death: and, was then given to his dearest friend and Executor Dr. *King*, who caused him to be thus carved in one entire piece of white Marble, as it now stands in the Cathedral Church of St. Pauls; and by Dr. *Donne's* own appointment, these words were to be affixed to it as his Epitaph: [quotes Latin epitaph]. Upon Monday following, he took his last leave of his beloved Study; and, being sensible of his hourly decay, retired himself to his bed-chamber: and, that week sent at several times for many of his most considerable friends, with whom he took a solemn and deliberate farewell; commending to their considerations some sentences useful for the regulation of their lives, and then dismist them, as good *Jacob* did his sons, with a spiritual benediction.

(*The Lives of Dr. John Donne, Sir Henry Wotton* [etc.],
1670, repr. 1969, 74–7)

The biblical allusion in Walton's last sentence is to *Genesis* xlix; in vv. 29–30 Jacob instructs his sons on his place of burial.

B. himself drew attention to the strain of anti-Catholicism in the poem (see above), but his attitude to the Catholic Church was flexible, ranging from uncompromising hostility (*Confessional* [II 337], *Holy-Cross Day* [p. 540]) to the interest and limited tolerance of *CE & ED* (III 34). *Sordello, Bishop Blougram* (p. 279), and *Ring* show B.'s attitude at its most complex.

Criticism

The poem was, for B., 'a pet of my own', and EBB. praised it as 'of course the finest & most powerful' of the *Hood's* poems (21 July 1845, *Correspondence* x 315); in her critical notes, she wrote: 'This is a wonderful poem I think—& classes with those works of yours which show most power . . most unquestionable genius in the high sense. You force your reader to sympathize positively in his glory in being buried!' (*Wellesley MS*). Ruskin quoted ll. 10–81 (with a few omissions) in *Modern Painters* iv (1856; *Works*, ed. Cook and Wedderburn [1913] vi 448), as an example of B.'s 'unerring' historical sense, 'always vital, right, and profound', and in particular B.'s understanding of 'the kind of admiration with which a southern artist regarded the *stone* he worked in; and the pride which populace or priest took in the possession of precious mountain substance, worked into the pavements of their cathedrals, and the shafts of their tombs'. Ruskin concluded: 'I know of no other piece of modern English, prose or poetry, in which there is so much told, as in these lines, of the Renaissance spirit,—its worldliness, inconsistency, pride, hypocrisy, ignorance of itself, love of art, of luxury, and of good Latin. It is nearly all that I have said of the central Renaissance in thirty pages of the *Stones of Venice*, put into as many lines, Browning's also being the antecedent work'. B. was vexed that Ruskin's praise was not more widely circulated by Chapman, his publisher at this period (*New Letters* 93), but it undoubtedly enhanced his literary reputation in the 1860s.

Vanity, saith the Preacher, vanity!
Draw round my bed: is Anselm keeping back?
Nephews—sons mine . . . ah God, I know not! Well—
She, men would have to be your mother once,
5 Old Gandolf envied me, so fair she was!
What's done is done, and she is dead beside,

---

1. From *Ecclesiastes* i 2: 'Vanity of vanities, saith the Preacher; vanity of vanities, all is vanity'. 'Vanity' here means 'futility', 'worthlessness', 'emptiness'. This is the first of several biblical tags which emphasize the transience and futility of life: see ll. 51–2n., 101n. *Melchiori* 29 points out that the verse also recurs in the final chapter of *Ecclesiastes* (xii 8), and cites the preceding verse: 'Then shall the dust return to the earth as it was: and the spirit shall return unto God who gave it'.

2–3. S. A. Brooke (*The Poetry of Robert Browning* [1902] 283) compares this scene to the deathbed of St John in *A Death*: see ll. 29–34, 71–4 (pp. 727, 729). Rabbi Ben Ezra, in his 'Song of Death' in *Holy-Cross Day*, 'Called sons and sons' sons to his side' (l. 68, p. 549).

3. It was not uncommon for a powerful (and nominally celibate) Roman Catholic priest in this period to pass off his own children as nephews or nieces (hence the term 'nepotism'). B.'s library included a volume (by G. Leti) called *Il Nipotismo di Roma, or The History of the Pope's Nephews* (1669): *Collections* A1442, p. 123. Cp. *Ring* iii 1475–6 and xi 1088, 1097–98, and the 'Prior's niece' in *Fra Lippo Lippi* 170–1 (p. 494), where the fiction conceals a mistress rather than a child.

6. Cp. *Macbeth* III ii 12 ('What's done is done') and Marlowe, *Jew of Malta* IV i: 'Thou hast committed— / Fornication: but that was in another country, and besides, the wench is dead'.

And long ago, and I am Bishop since,
And as she died so must we die ourselves,
And thence ye may perceive the world's a dream.
10   Life, how and what is it? As here I lie
In this state-chamber, dying by degrees,
Hours and long hours in the dead night, I ask
"Do I live, am I dead?" Peace, peace seems all:
St. Praxed's ever was the church for peace;
15   And so, about this tomb of mine. I fought
With tooth and nail to save my niche, ye know:
—Old Gandolf came me in, despite my care,
For a shrewd snatch out of the corner south
To grace his carrion with, God curse the same!
20   Yet still my niche is not so cramp'd but thence
One sees the pulpit o' the epistle-side,
And somewhat of the choir, those silent seats,
And up into the aery dome where live
The angels, and a sunbeam's sure to lurk:

---

7. And long ago] Dead long ago (*1845–88*).

10. Life, how and what is it?: cp. Shelley, *Triumph of Life* 544: 'Then, what is life? I cried', and its biblical source, *James* iv 14: 'For what is your life? It is even a vapour, that appeareth for a little time, and then vanisheth away'. Also Mrs Barbauld, *Life*, a poem known to B. (a transcription of it exists in his hand: see *Collections* E547, p. 448): 'Life! I know not what thou art, / But know that thou and I must part; / And when, or how, or where we met / I own to me's a secret yet'. A poem entitled *What is Life?* appeared in Coleridge's *Literary Remains* i 60.

15–16. Melchiori 27–8, following a suggestion in DeVane (*Parleyings* 57), cites a passage from Daniello Bartoli, *De' Simboli Trasportati al Morale*, a book B. knew well. The living who seek refuge in the Theatre of Pompey are crowded out by the profusion of statuary: 'there is no room for them because all the niches are full; how many of them, full of the statues of men: how few of men! . . . All the niches are full, and there is no room left for you: look elsewhere, and take refuge where you may'.

17–19.]—Old Gandolf cozened me, despite my care;
         Shrewd was that snatch from out the corner South
         He graced his carrion with, God curse the same! (*1845–88*)

EBB. had objected to the phrasing of l. 17: 'Is that "came me in" a correct expression . . or rather, does it *express* . . *does* it not make the meaning hard to get at?' (*Wellesley MS*). It is in fact a fencing term, meaning 'to make a pass or home-thrust, to get within an opponent's guard'. *OED* cites *2 Henry IV* III ii 283: 'He would about, and about, and come you in, and come you in'.

21. o' the] on the (*1872, 1884*). *epistle-side*: the south side of the church, from which the epistle (an extract from one of the Apostles' letters) is read.

23. the aery dome: S. Prassede in fact has a domed apse: see headnote. B. may have had in mind the Gesù church (see ll. 48–9n.), which does have a dome.

25   And I shall fill my slab of basalt there,
      And 'neath my tabernacle take my rest
      With those nine columns round me, two and two,
      The odd one at my feet where Anselm stands:
      Peachblossom-marble all, the rare, the ripe
30   As fresh-pour'd red wine of a mighty pulse
      —Old Gandolf with his paltry onion-stone,
      Put me where I may look at him! True peach,
      Rosy and flawless: how I earn'd the prize!
      Draw close: that conflagration of my church
35   —What then? So much was sav'd if aught were miss'd!
      My sons, ye would not be my death? Go dig
      The white-grape vineyard where the oil-press stood,
      Drop water gently till the surface sinks,
      And if ye find . . Ah, God I know not, I! . . .
40   Bedded in store of rotten figleaves soft,
      And corded up in a tight olive-frail,
      Some lump, ah God, of *lapis lazuli*,
      Big as a Jew's head cut off at the nape,

25. The Bishop means that his statue will lie outstretched on the basalt lid of his tomb. Basalt is a stone like marble, whose colour can be green or brownish-black.
26. *tabernacle*: here, a sculpted canopy supported by the 'columns' of l. 27. The word has strong religious associations: in Judaism it is the tent which contains the Ark of the Covenant; in Christian (esp. Catholic) tradition, it is a receptacle for the vessel containing the consecrated Host.
27. *two and two*: Melchiori 33 notes the phrase 'Pilasters of the Corinthian order, two and two together' in Gerard de Lairesse's *Art of Painting* (1778 ed.), one of B.'s favourite books.
31. *onion-stone*: an inferior kind of marble, as B. explained to Ruskin: 'the grey *cipollino*—good for pillars and the like, bad for finer work, thro' its being laid coat upon coat, onion-wise,—don't I *explain* by translating the word, and do you like it a whit more?' ('A Letter from Robert Browning to John Ruskin', *BBI* xvii [Waco 1958], n. p.). Ruskin accepted B.'s definition, glossing the word, together with 'antique-black' (l. 54), in his published comments on the poem (see head-note): '"Nero Antico" is more familiar to our ears: but Browning does right in translating it; as afterwards "cipollino" into "onion-stone". Our stupid habit of using foreign words without translation is continually losing us half the force of the foreign language. How many travellers hearing the term "cipollino" perceive the intended sense of a stone splitting into concentric rings, like an onion?'
38. *sinks*] sink (*1865–88*).
41. *olive-frail*: a frail is 'a basket made of rushes' (*J.*).
42. *lapis lazuli*: J. cites John Hill's *General Natural History* (1748): 'The lapis lazuli, or azure stone, is a copper ore, very compact and hard, so as to take a high polish . . . It is found in detached lumps, of an elegant blue colour, variegated with clouds of white, and veins of a shining gold colour'. See ll. 48–9n.
43–4. The Bishop's imagery draws on traditional subjects of religious art: the beheading of John the Baptist, and pictures of the Virgin Mary.

    Blue as a vein o'er the Madonna's breast . . .
45 Sons, all have I bequeath'd you, villas, all,
    That brave Frascati villa with its bath,
    So let the blue lump poise between my knees,
    Like God the Father's globe on both his hands
    Ye worship in the Jesu church so gay,
50 For Gandolf shall not choose but see and burst!
    Swift as a weaver's shuttle fleet our years:
    Man goeth to the grave, and where is he?
    Did I say basalt for my slab, sons? Black—
    'Twas ever antique-black I meant! How else
55 Shall ye contrast my frieze to come beneath?
    The bas-relief in bronze ye promis'd me,
    Those Pans and Nymphs ye wot of, and perchance
    Some tripod, thyrsus, with a vase or so,
    The Saviour at his sermon on the mount,

46. That brave Frascati villa: the slopes above Frascati, a town 21 km south-east of Rome, were a favourite site for villas in Roman times; Cicero owned a small property in the area, and Lucullus a villa famed for its luxury. This classical association was part of the attraction when the site came to be built over again from the mid-16th century—notably by several of the great Roman cardinals. These Renaissance villas were of unparalleled architectural and decorative splendour: see C. L. Franck, *The Villas of Frascati* (1966). *brave*: fine, splendid.

   bath: this could be the bath mentioned in l. 70, but the Bishop possibly refers to an apartment for bathing, a feature of both classical and Renaissance villas. Franck (pp. 11–12) points out that 'the hills of Tusculum have no natural resources of water . . . Hence the endeavours of the cardinals eager to build again at Frascati had to be directed, almost in the first place, to the construction of pipelines . . . all but the very rich had to drop out of this contest'. This may be why the Bishop singles out Frascati from among his villas, and the bath as its principal luxury.

48–9. The Gesù church in Rome contains the tomb of St Ignatius Loyola, founder of the Jesuit order. It is to this monument that the Bishop refers—anachronistically, since it was not built till 1690. Its enormous, sumptuous and elaborate structure is topped by a lapis lazuli globe such as the Bishop describes, which, however, is held not by God but by a *putto*. This mistake occurs in *Murray²*: 'The globe held by the Almighty is to said to be the largest lump of lapis lazuli in existence' (p. 367). The 'bas-relief in bronze' (l. 56) also derives from the Loyola monument.

51–2. Cp. *Job* vii 6: 'My days were swifter than a weaver's shuttle', and xiv 10: 'But man dieth and wasteth away: yea, man giveth up the ghost, and where is he?'

54. antique-black: 'nero antico', a black marble found in Roman ruins, thus giving it added prestige in the Bishop's eyes. See l. 31n.

58. tripod: 'a seat with three feet, such as that from which the priestess of Apollo [at Delphi] delivered oracles' (*J.*). *thyrsus*: a staff or spear tipped with an ornament like a pine-cone, and sometimes wreathed with ivy and vine-branches; borne by Dionysus (Bacchus) and his votaries.

60 St. Praxed in a glory, and one Pan
    Ready to twitch the nymph's last garment off,
    And Moses with the tables . . . but I know
    Ye mark me not! What do they whisper thee,
    Child of my bowels, Anselm? Ah, ye hope
65 To revel down my villas while I gasp
    Brick'd o'er with beggar's mouldy travertine
    Which Gandolf from his tomb-top chuckles at!
    Nay, boys, ye love me—all of jasper then!
    'Tis jasper ye stand pledged to, lest I grieve
70 My bath must needs be left behind, alas!
    One block, pure green as a pistachio nut,
    There's plenty jasper somewhere in the world—
    And I shall have St. Praxed's ear to pray
    Horses for ye, and brown Greek manuscripts,
75 And mistresses with great smooth marbly limbs
    —That's if ye carve my epitaph aright,
    Choice Latin, picked phrase, Tully's every word,

60. St. Praxed in a glory: a 'glory' is a halo; Binns (see headnote, p. 233) points out that 'Around the head of the statue' of St. Praxed in the bas-relief on the Cetti tomb in St. Praxed's Church 'is a shelled vault in the form of a halo' (p. 161).

64. Child of my bowels: cp. *2 Samuel* xvi 11: 'Behold, my son, which came forth of my bowels, seeketh my life'. The speaker is David, lamenting the rebellion of Absalom, his favourite son.

66. Brick'd o'er: implying that there will be no statue on the tombtop. *beggar's mouldy travertine*: travertine is a hard, white stone, used for ordinary building in Italy. Cp. *Pictor* 67n. (p. 231), 'moulder on the damp wall's travertine'.

68. jasper: 'a hard stone of a bright beautiful green colour, sometimes clouded with white, found in masses of various sizes and shapes. It is capable of a very elegant polish' (*J.*). Like lapis lazuli (see l. 42n.), jasper is not a building material (but see next note). Both form part of the fabric of the New Jerusalem in *Revelation* xxi 11–12, 18–20.

70. bath: Melchiori 27 suggests that the Bishop's jasper bath derives from 'the great green jasper bath of the Emperor Constantine, which stands in the Baptistery of the Church of San Giovanni in Laterano, Rome'. Cp. *Bishop Blougram* 112 (p. 292): 'slabbed marble, what a bath it makes!'

73. I shall have] have I not (*1845–88*).

77–9. 'Tully' was the common English Renaissance version of the name of Marcus Tullius Cicero (106–43 BC), the great lawyer and orator of Republican Rome, whom the apostles of the 'revived paganism' (see headnote) held to be the ideal Latin stylist. 'Ulpian' refers to Domitius Ulpianus, a lawyer and scholar who died 228 AD during the reign of the Emperor Alexander Severus. See ll. 99–100n. F. J. Chierenza (*Explicator* xix [1961] item 22) argues that the Bishop is remembering his instructions to the craftsmen ('my masters') who carved Gandolf's tomb to give him an epitaph in inferior Latin. 'My masters' certainly

No gaudy ware like Gandolf's second line
—Tully, my masters? Ulpian serves his need!
80   And then how I shall lie through centuries
And hear the blessed mutter of the mass,
And see God made and eaten all day long,
And feel the steady candle-flame, and taste
Good strong thick stupifying incense-smoke!
85   For as I lie here, hours of the dead night,
Dying in state and by such slow degrees,
I fold my arms as if they clasp'd a crook,
And stretch my feet forth straight as stone can point,
And let the bed-clothes for a mortcloth drop
90   Into great laps and folds of sculptors'-work:
And as yon tapers dwindle, and strange thoughts
Grow, with a certain humming in my ears,
About the life before this life I lived,
And this life too, Popes, Cardinals and Priests,
95   St. Praxed at his sermon on the mount,
Your tall pale mother with her talking eyes,
And new-found agate urns as fresh as day,

---

appears frequently in Shakespeare as a form of address to social inferiors, or as
a form of condescension. But the connection between this line and ll. 99–100
seems to indicate that the Bishop is expressing his contempt of Gandolf's own
taste, esp. in view of B.'s comment that the phrasing of Gandolf's epitaph was
chosen 'to provoke the bile of my Bishop'.

81–4. EBB. thought this 'a grand passage' (*Wellesley MS*). Line 82 refers to the
Catholic doctrine of the 'real presence' of the body of Christ in the communion
wafer. A. C. Dooley, in 'An Echo of Wesley in *The Bishop Orders His Tomb*',
SBC xiii (1980) 54–5, compares John Wesley, *An Earnest Appeal to Men of Reason
and Religion* (1743): 'Is it now in your power to see, or hear, or taste, or feel God?'

87. crook: the Bishop's crozier, symbol of his pastoral office, which would be carved
as part of his funerary statue.

89. mortcloth: funeral pall.

93. this life I liv'd] I lived this life (*1863–88*).

95. B. commented: 'the blunder about the sermon is the result of the dying
man's haziness; he would not reveal himself as he does but for that' (*Select Poems
of Robert Browning*, ed. W. J. Rolfe and H. E. Hersey [New York 1886] 195).
There are actually two blunders: the confusion of St Praxed with Christ, and the
mistake about the Saint's gender. It is not certain which one B. means, but he
would have known that both were blunders: see headnote, and cp. *Flight of the
Duchess* 884n. (II 333).

97. new-found agate urns: urns (normally funerary) from the classical period,
recently unearthed. Agate, a variety of chalcedony, with colours in separate bands
or blended in clouds, is an unlikely material for such urns, which were usually
of earthenware or metal. Cp. *Ring* i 2–5.

And marble's language, Latin pure, discreet,
—Aha, ELUCESCEBAT, quoth our friend?
100 No Tully, said I, Ulpian at the best!
Evil and brief hath been my pilgrimage.
All *lapis*, all, sons! Else I give the Pope
My villas: will ye ever eat my heart?
Ever your eyes were as a lizard's quick,
105 They glitter like your mother's for my soul,
Or to the tripod ye would tie a lynx
That in his struggle throws the thyrsus down,

99–100. The Bishop's invocation of 'marble's language' reminds him of the word 'elucescebat', which occurs in Gandolf's epitaph. The Bishop claims that the word is 'No Tully', that is, not used by Cicero, but 'Ulpian at the best', and therefore inferior Latin. The Bishop is right. Dr J. Fairweather has pointed out to us that the *Thesaurus Linguae Latinae* (Leipzig 1953) v 2 records the earliest use of 'elucesce-bat' in the sense of 'to shine, be notable' in the writings of St. Jerome, who died AD 420, nearly two centuries *after* Ulpian, who died in 228. Gandolf had confused the word with 'elucere', which *is* in Cicero (*De Oratorio* 255) and would be considered the canonical form. In 1886, F. Hitchman wrote to B. asking where he had found the word, and commenting that it occurred in the epitaph of his ancestor Humphrey Henchman (1592–1675), Bishop of London (whereabouts of this letter unknown; see *Checklist* 328). B. replied that this 'curious fact' was 'quite unknown' to him: 'I wanted a word "infimae latinitatis" [in the lowest style of Latin] to provoke the bile of my Bishop, and took the one you know—simply because a classical writer would use "eluceo": and I charged it upon "Ulpian" at a venture. This is one of perhaps fifty instances that have occurred to me in the course of my literary experience—of how fancies have already been forestalled by facts' (3 Nov. 1886, *ABL MS*).
101. Cp. *Genesis* xlvii 9: 'few and evil have been the days of the years of my life'.
105^ 106.] Or ye would heighten my impoverished frieze,
          Piece out its starved design, and fill my vase
          With grapes, and add a vizor and a Term, (*1845–88*)
106–7. Melchiori 29–36 suggests that the details here derive from an emblem, 'Sweete Repose Disturbed by Lewdness', in Lairesse, *Art of Painting*, one of B.'s favourite books (see also l. 27n.). The point is strengthened by the lines added in *1845* (see prec. note). A group of satyrs find some 'almost naked' nymphs asleep; they hang the nymphs' hunting equipment on the genitals of a 'Priapus term', 'sticking their *thyrses* in the ground round about it, and adorning them with vizors'; they scatter the nymphs' clothes in the branches of a tree, below which they set two panthers to prevent the nymphs from retrieving them, together with wine and grapes. The satyrs taunt the nymphs when they awaken, until the appearance of Diana puts them to flight: 'the *term* of *Priapus* fell to the ground, and the panther at the tree endeavoured to get loose'. Melchiori points out the affinity of this scene with ll. 60–1, and suggests a further connection with *Pan and Luna* (*DI²*, 1880).
106. Or] And (*1845–88*).

To comfort me on my entablature
Whereon I am to lie till I must ask
110   "Do I live, am I dead?" There, leave me, there!
For ye have stabb'd me with ingratitude
To death—ye wish it—God, ye wish it! Stone—
Gritstone, a-crumble! Clammy squares which sweat
As if the corpse they keep were oozing through—
115   And no more *lapis* to delight the world!
Well, go! I bless ye. Fewer tapers there,
But in a row: and, going, turn your backs
—Ay, like departing altar-ministrants,
And leave me in my church, the church for peace,
120   That I may watch at leisure if he leers—
Old Gandolf, at me, from his onion-stone,
As still he envied me, so fair she was!

108. entablature: the slab, whether of 'basalt' (l. 25) or 'antique-black' (ll. 53–4) on which the Bishop's effigy is to lie.
111. Cp. *Julius Caesar* III ii 176, 183–6: 'the well-beloved Brutus stabb'd . . . This was the most unkindest cut of all; / For when the noble Caesar saw him stab, / Ingratitude, more strong than traitors' arms / Quite vanquish'd him'. There was a tradition that Brutus was Caesar's son.
113. Gritstone: coarse sandstone.
117–18. turn your backs . . . altar-ministrants: the Bishop tells his sons to back away from him, as though he himself were the Christ above the altar, whom the priest's acolytes, under the old rites, must always face during a service.

15 Italy in England
[The Italian in England]

First publ. *B & P* vii (*DR & L*), 6 Nov. 1845; repr. *1849* (when the title was changed in accordance with B.'s practice of removing overt references to national stereotypes), *1863*, *1868*, *1872*, *1888*. Our text is *1845*.

EBB. saw a draft in Aug. 1845. However, the date of composition is probably earlier; the subject would have been on B.'s mind after his long tour of Italy (Aug.-Dec. 1844). The poem may have been one of the 'three or four half-done-with "Bells"' which B. mentions in a letter to EBB. of 27 Jan. 1845 (*Correspondence* x 43); we would date it to the early spring of that year.

The poem is set during the 'Risorgimento', the nineteenth-century movement of agitation and struggle for Italian unity and independence which concluded in 1870. Britain harboured many Italian political exiles, among them B.'s friend and teacher Angelo Cerutti (see *Maynard* 304–6), and by the time of the poem's publication B. had met (probably through their common acquaintance Thomas Carlyle) one of the most prominent Risorgimento leaders, Giuseppe Mazzini (1805–1872), who had been living in England since 1837. F.G. Kenyon (*Centenary* iii, p. xxxiv) first suggested as a possible source for the poem the 1844 uprising in Calabria led, with Mazzini's encouragement, by Attilio and Emilio Bandiera, which ended with their betrayal and execution. However, this episode does not much resemble the Italian speaker's story in B.'s poem, and Maurizio Masetti ('Lost in Translation: "The Italian in England"', *BSN* xxxii [2007] 17–26) argues that Mazzini's own history offers a closer parallel: 'Like Mazzini the narrator has spent much of his life in exile. Like Mazzini, too, he has been betrayed by a friend. In the character of Charles—the perjured traitor—there are reminiscences of Raimondo Doria, the man who enrolled Mazzini in the Carboneria [secret society] and later sold him to the Austrians' (Masetti, p. 22). B. sent Mazzini a copy of *B & P* vii on publication, and Mazzini thanked him in terms which stress the poem's value as propaganda: 'Ho letto, riletto, e fatto leggere a miei amici l' "Italy in England." Non parlo della poesia: sono da lungo tempo vostro ammiratore sincero; ma parlo ora del sentimento che l'ha ispirata. Vi è bisogno assoluto di far nota qui in Inghilterra la nostra condizione e la nostra causa; e uomini come voi sono i migliori per diffondere la simpatia che cerchiamo' ([13 Nov. 1845], *Correspondence* xi 169). [I have read, re-read, and read out to my friends 'Italy in England.' I am not now talking about the poetry—I have been your sincere admirer for a long time—but about the sentiment that inspired it. There is an absolute need to make our condition and our cause known here in England; and men like you can best help spread the sympathy that we are looking for.] In return, Mazzini sent B. a copy of a pamphlet he had recently written on the Bandiera brothers (*Ricordi dei Fratelli Bandiera* [Paris, 1844]; see *Collections* A1577). Mazzini produced his own translation of B.'s poem, which he sent to his mother by 9 Dec. 1845 (Masetti, p. 21); the translation itself, however, is now lost.

For a direct treatment of Italian nationalism in the 1840s, cp. *Pippa* iii (p. 144f.); in the 1850s, *Old Pictures* 249–88 (pp. 429–34) and *De Gustibus* 33–8 (III 27–8); in the aftermath of unification, *Prince Hohenstiel-Schwangau* (1871). Cp. also *Sordello*, *A Soul's Tragedy* (II 180) and *Luria* (II 374), where contemporary Italian politics are alluded to by analogy with past history. The relationship between the speaker and the peasant woman who helps him anticipates that between Pompilia and Caponsacchi in *Ring*.

EBB. commented: 'A serene, noble poem this is—an heroic repose in it—but nothing to imagine queries out of . . . I like the simplicity of the greatehearted-ness of it, (though perhaps half Saxon in character)' (*Wellesley MS*). See also l. 122n., and her letter to B. of 12–14 Nov. 1845 (*Correspondence* xi 167).

> That second time they hunted me
> From hill to plain, from shore to sea,
> And Austria, hounding far and wide
> Her blood-hounds thro' the country-side,
> 5   Breathed hot and instant on my trace,
> I made six days a hiding-place
> Of that dry green old aqueduct
> Where I and Charles, when boys, have plucked
> The fire-flies from the roof above,
> 10   Bright creeping thro' the moss they love.
> —How long it seems since Charles was lost!
> Six days the soldiers crossed and crossed
> The country in my very sight;
> And when that peril ceased at night,
> 15   The sky broke out in red dismay
> With signal-fires; well, there I lay
> Close covered o'er in my recess,
> Up to the neck in ferns and cress,
> Thinking on Metternich our friend,
> 20   And Charles's miserable end,
> And much beside, two days; the third,
> Hunger o'ercame me when I heard

2–5. The setting is an area between Padua and the Adriatic coast, in the then kingdom of Lombardy-Venetia, part of the Hapsburg Empire since 1815. Cp. *Pippa* iii 134–7n. (p. 149).

3. hounding: inciting, urging on (*OED* 3).

5. instant: 'pressing', 'importunate'; also 'impending, imminent'. Cp. *Balaustion's Adventure* (1871) 541: 'the abrupt Fate's footstep instant now'.   *trace,*] trace,— (*1849–88*), allowing the syntax of ll. 1–6 to be read as three self-contained clauses ('they hunted me', 'Austria . . . Breathed', and 'I made . . . a hiding-place'), whereas *1845* has one main clause ('I made . . . a hiding-place') to which the others are subordinate.

11. lost: equivocating between 'dead' and 'lost to the cause'; Charles's miserable end' (l. 20) is similarly ambivalent; l. 116 decides the question.

19. Metternich our friend: ironic; the Austrian statesman Klemens, Prince von Metternich (1773–1859), a chief architect of the reactionary post-Napoleonic political order in Europe, opposed Italian unity as part of a wider anti-reformist policy. See *Pippa* ii 280 (p. 141).

The peasants from the village go
To work among the maize; you know,
25 With us, in Lombardy, they bring
Provisions packed on mules, a string
With little bells that cheer their task,
And casks, and boughs on every cask
To keep the sun's heat from the wine;
30 These I let pass in jingling line,
And, close on them, dear noisy crew,
The peasants from the village, too;
For at the very rear would troop
Their wives and sisters in a group
35 To help, I knew; when these had passed,
I threw my glove to strike the last,
Taking the chance: she did not start,
Much less cry out, but stooped apart
One instant, rapidly glanced round,
40 And saw me beckon from the ground:
A wild bush grows and hides my crypt;
She picked my glove up while she stripped
A branch off, then rejoined the rest
With that; my glove lay in her breast:
45 Then I drew breath: they disappeared:
It was for Italy I feared.

An hour, and she returned alone
Exactly where my glove was thrown.
Meanwhile came many thoughts; on me
50 Rested the hopes of Italy;
I had devised a certain tale
Which, when 'twas told her, could not fail
Persuade a peasant of its truth;
This hiding was a freak of youth;

---

41. *crypt*: fig., a recess or secret hiding-place; B. Brown (*VP* vi [1968] 179–83)
connects the more usual sense of a burial vault with l. 7, and comments:
'Ironically, the "crypt" proved not to be a tomb, but a womb of new life; the
aqueduct, which seemed to be dried up, proved to be a sort of spiritual baptismal
font'. Cp. *Sordello* i 410, 438 ('font' linked to 'crypt'), and vi 630 ('that cold
font-tomb') (I 422, 754).
54–5.] I meant to call a freak of youth / This hiding, and give hopes of pay,
(*1849–88*).

55   I meant to give her hopes of pay,
        And no temptation to betray.
        But when I saw that woman's face,
        Its calm simplicity of grace,
        Our Italy's own attitude
60   In which she walked thus far, and stood,
        Planting each naked foot so firm,
        To crush the snake and spare the worm—
        At first sight of her eyes, I said,
        "I am that person on whose head
65   "They fix the price because I hate
        "The Austrians over us: the State
        "Will give you gold—oh, gold so much,
        "If you betray me to their clutch!
        "And be your death, for aught I know,
70   "If once they find you saved their foe.
        "Now, you must bring me food and drink,
        "And also paper, pen, and ink,
        "And carry safe what I shall write
        "To Padua, which you'll reach at night
75   "Before the Duomo shuts; go in,
        "And wait till Tenebrae begin;
        "Walk to the Third Confessional,
        "Between the pillar and the wall,
        "And kneeling whisper *whence comes peace?*
80   "Say it a second time; then cease;
        "And if the voice inside returns,
        "*From Christ and Freedom; what concerns*

61–2. Brown (sec l. 41n.) compares God's curse on the serpent, *Genesis* iii 15:
'I will put enmity between thee and the woman, and between thy seed and
her seed; it shall bruise thy head, and thou shalt bruise his heel'. Cp. also
Ring v 1667–8: 'I was mad, / Blind, stamped on all, the earth-worms with the
asp'.
64. *person on*] man upon (*1849–88*).
75. *the Duomo*: the Cathedral.
76. *Tenebrae*: 'the office of matins and lauds for the three last days in Holy Week.
Fifteen lighted candles are placed on a triangular stand, and at the conclusion of
each psalm one is put out, till a single candle is left at the top of the triangle.
The extinction of the other candles is said to figure the growing darkness of the
world at the time of the Crucifixion. The last candle (which is not extinguished,
but hidden behind the altar for a few moments) represents Christ over whom
Death could not prevail' (*Cyclopaedia* 226). Brown (see l. 41n.) suggests a metaphor of rebirth in the setting of the action at Eastertide.

"*The cause of Peace?*—for answer, slip
"My letter where you placed your lip;
85   "Then come back happy we have done
"Our mother service—I, the son,
"As you the daughter of our land!"

Three mornings more, she took her stand
In the same place, with the same eyes:
90   I was no surer of sun-rise
Than of her coming: we conferred
Of her own prospects, and I heard
She had a lover—stout and tall,
She said—then let her eyelids fall,
95   "He could do much"—as if some doubt
Entered her heart,—then, passing out,
"She could not speak for others—who
"Had other thoughts; herself she knew:"
And so she brought me drink and food.
100   After four days the scouts pursued
Another path: at last arrived
The help my Paduan friends contrived
To furnish me: she brought the news:
For the first time I could not choose
105   But kiss her hand and lay my own
Upon her head—"This faith was shown
"To Italy, our mother;—she
"Uses my hand and blesses thee!"
She followed down to the sea-shore;
110   I left and never saw her more.

How very long since I have thought
Concerning—much less wished for—aught
Beside the good of Italy
For which I live and mean to die!
115   In love I never was; and since

83–4. slip . . . lip: i.e. slip the letter through the curtain or grate between the
penitent's stall and the confessor's. Contrast the implied sympathy of the Italian
priest here for the revolutionary cause with the reactionary stance of the Spanish
priest in *Confessional* (II 337).
93. stout: strong in body; also brave, resolute.
115. In love I never was] I never was in love (*1849–88*).

Charles proved false, nothing could convince
My inmost heart I had a friend;
However, if I pleased to spend
Real wishes on myself—say, Three—
120   I know at least what one should be;
I would grasp Metternich until
I felt his red wet throat distil
In blood thro' these two hands: and next,
—Nor much for that am I perplexed—
125   Charles, perjured traitor, for his part,
Should die slow of a broken heart
Under his new employers—last
—Ah, there, what should one wish? For fast
Do I grow old and out of strength;
130   If I resolved to seek at length
My father's house again, how scared
They all would look, and unprepared!
My brothers live in Austria's pay
—Disowned me long ago, men say;
135   And all my early mates who used
To praise me so—perhaps induced
More than one early step of mine—
Are turning wise; while part opine
"Freedom grows License," part suspect
140   "Haste breeds Delay," and recollect
They always said such premature
Beginnings never could endure:
So, with a sullen "All's for best,"
The land seems settling to its rest.
145   I think, then, I should wish to stand
This evening in that dear, lost land,
Over the sea the thousand miles,
And know if yet that woman smiles
With the calm smile—some little farm

116–17. *nothing could convince . . . had a friend;*] what shall now convince . . . have
a friend? (*1868–88*).
122. EBB. quoted 'I felt his throat, & had my will', and commented: 'is not "had
my will" a little wrong—*I would what I would*—? There is a weakness in the expression . . is there not?' (*Wellesley MS*).
128. *one*] I (*1849–88*).
138–9. *part . . . part*] some . . . some (*1849–88*).

150   She lives in there, no doubt—what harm
       If I sate on the door-side bench,
       And, while her spindle made a trench
       Fantastically in the dust,
       Inquired of all her fortunes—just
155   Her children's ages and their names,
       And what may be the husband's aims
       For each of them—I'd talk this out,
       And sit there, for an hour about,
       Then kiss her hand once more, and lay
160   Mine on her head, and go my way.

       So much for idle wishing—how
       It steals the time! To business now!

16 Home-Thoughts, from Abroad

First publ. *B & P* vii (*DR & L*), 6 Nov. 1845, as the first of three numbered sections with the collective title *Home-Thoughts, from Abroad*. The second section consisted of *Here's to Nelson's memory*, later incl. in *Nationality in Drinks* (see II 248); the third consisted of the lines later called *Home-Thoughts, from the Sea* (II 246). The title *Home-Thoughts, from Abroad* was given exclusively to the first section when it was repr. in *1849*; it was then repr. *1863, 1865², 1868, 1872, 1888*. Our text is *1845*. A fair-copy MS, with some variants, is in the Morgan Library (*Collections* E170, p. 410); it may be the one given to EBB. at a meeting on 3 Oct. 1845, in response to her request, in a letter to B. of 1 Oct., for an autograph for Mary Hunter, the daughter of the Rev. George Barrett Hunter (*Correspondence* xi 107). B. responded: 'Now I will write you the verses .. some easy ones out of a paper-full meant to go between poem & poem in my next number, and break the shock of collision' (2 Oct., *ibid.* 108). This implies that the poem had been written some time before; a likely date on internal grounds would be the spring of 1845, supported by refs. in B.'s letters to EBB., e.g. 26 Feb. 1845, headed 'Wednesday morning—Spring!' and continuing: 'Real warm Spring, dear Miss Barrett, and the birds know it' (*ibid.* x 97). Another topic in the letters of this period concerned England's relation to Italy (see headnote to *England in Italy*, p. 255).

When she saw the poem, EBB. wrote on 4 Oct. (*Correspondence* xi 109–10):

> Your spring-song is full of beauty as you know very well—& "that's the wise thrush," so characteristic of you (& of the thrush too) that I was sorely tempted to ask you to write it "twice over," . . & not send the first copy to Mary Hunter notwithstanding my promise to her. And now when you come to print these fragments, would it not be well if you were to stoop to the vulgarism of prefixing some word of introduction, as other people do, you know, . . a title . . a name? You perplex your readers often by casting yourself on their intelligence in these things—and although it is true that readers in general are stupid & cant understand, it is still more true that they are lazy & wont understand . . & they dont catch your point of sight at first unless you think it worth while to push them by the shoulders & force them into the right place. Now these fragments . . you mean to print them with a line between . . & not one word at the top of it . . now dont you? And then people will read
> "Oh, to be in England"
> & say to themselves . . . "Why who is this? . . . who's out of England?" Which is an extreme case of course,—but you will see what I mean . . & often I have observed how some of the very most beautiful of your lyrics have suffered just from your disdain of the usual tactics of writers in this one respect.

B. replied: 'Thank you, thank you. I will devise titles—I quite see what you say, now you do say it' (6 Oct., *ibid.* 111). In her letter of 21–22 Oct. (*ibid.* 134), EBB. further suggested numbering the sections, advice which B. also took DeVane (*Handbook* 163) suggests that the *DR & L* title may have been influenced by that of J. H. Newman's pamphlet *Home Thoughts Abroad* (1836); in her letter

---

Title.] no comma in *1884* (the corr. reissue of *1872* and *1880*).

of 1 Oct. requesting the autograph, EBB. mentioned Shelley's *Letters from Abroad* (*Correspondence* xi 106). B.'s contrast between England and 'Abroad' inverts that drawn between England and Italy in Byron's *Beppo* 321–92 ('With all its sinful doings, I must say, / That Italy's a pleasant place to me'), thereby echoing the preference in Wordsworth's *I Travelled Among Unknown Men*: 'I travelled among unknown men, / In lands beyond the sea; / Nor, England! did I know till then / What love I bore to thee' (1–4). For another comparison in B. between Italy and England, in which Italy is preferred, see *De Gustibus* (III 25).

> Oh, to be in England
> Now that April's there,
> And who wakes in England
> Sees, some morning, unaware,
> 5 That the lowest boughs and the brush-wood sheaf
> Round the elm-tree bole are in tiny leaf,
> While the chaffinch sings on the orchard bough
> In England—now!
>
>   And after April, when May follows,
> 10 And the whitethroat builds, and all the swallows—
> Hark! where my blossomed pear-tree in the hedge
> Leans to the field and scatters on the clover
> Blossoms and dewdrops—at the bent spray's edge—
> That's the wise thrush; he sings each song twice over
> 15 Lest you should think he never could recapture
> The first fine careless rapture!
> And though the fields are rough with hoary dew,
> All will be gay when noontide wakes anew
> The buttercups, the little children's dower,
> 20 —Far brighter than this gaudy melon-flower!

1–4.] printed as two lines in *1872, 1884*.
1. In his letter of 6 Oct. 1845, referring to EBB.'s projected trip to Italy, B. made one of his very rare self-quotations: 'Oh to be in Pisa. Now that E. B. B. is there!' (*Correspondence* xi 111).
3. *who*] whoever (*1849–88*).
7. *orchard*] fruit tree (*Morgan MS*).
8. *England—now*] England now (*Morgan MS*).
11–13. See *Pippa* iii 248–9n. (p. 155).
11. *my*] the (*Morgan MS*).
17. *are*] look (*1849–88*).   *hoary*: white; lit., the colour of an old man's hair.
19. *dower*: gift, endowment; lit., dowry.

17 England in Italy
[The Englishman in Italy]
Piano di Sorrento

First publ. *B & P* vii (*DR & L*), 6 Nov. 1845; repr. *1849* with changed title, *1863* (when it was placed in *Romances*), *1865²*, *1868*, *1872* (with a change in line-length— see below), *1888*. Our text is *1845*. EBB. saw an unfinished draft in the summer of 1845, when the subtitle was 'Autumn at Sorrento'; all her comments recorded in the notes derive from *Wellesley MS*, unless otherwise stated. The poem is written in the same five-stress metre, divided into long and short lines, as the unfinished *Saul* (see II 286). In the completed *Saul* (III 491), B. amalgamated the long and short lines into single long lines, and in *1872* (and its corrected reissue, *1884*) he did the same with *England*, adjusting the punctuation and capitalization accordingly. Cp. the similar experiment with a long line in *Cristina* (see headnote, I 774). The first six lines read:

> Fortù, Fortù, my beloved one, sit here by my side,
> On my knees put up both little feet! I was sure, if I tried,
> I could make you laugh spite of Scirocco. Now, open your eyes,
> Let me keep you amused, till he vanish in black from the skies,
> With telling my memories over, as you tell your beads;
> All the Plain saw me gather, I garland—the flowers or the weeds.

The poem was written after B.'s return from his second trip to Italy (Aug.–Dec. 1844). There is an allusion to the 'isles of the syren' (see l. 199n.) in a letter to EBB. dated 15 Apr. 1845 (*Correspondence* x 166); the bulk of the source material in the letters to EBB. comes at the end of Apr. and the beginning of May (see below), and the poem was probably begun then. EBB. first saw it on 6 Aug., and gave B. her criticisms on 12 Aug.; he replied the same day that she was 'too indulgent by far' to 'treat these roughnesses as if they were advanced so many a stage' (*ibid.* xi 26); EBB. replied on 13 Aug. that she understood 'that it is *unfinished*, & in a rough state round the edges' (*ibid.* 27). In her letter of 21–22 Oct., when she had seen the poem in proof, EBB. remarked on B.'s additions: 'The end you have put to "England in Italy" gives unity to the whole . . just what the poem wanted. Also you have given some nobler lines to the middle than met me there before' (*ibid.* 134). The ending refers to debates in Parliament about the Corn-Laws; it was probably written in Sept. 1845, when these debates were at their height. The added lines in the 'middle' of the poem cannot be distinguished.

B. visited the Sorrento peninsula in 1844; the 'Piano' (Plain) extends eastward across the peninsula from the town of Sorrento itself, which lies on the north coast, 25 km south of Naples. Sorrento is said to derive its name from the sirens (see ll. 200–8n.). The speaker of the poem is lodging, as B. may have done, with a local peasant family; probably on the south-eastern coast, as there is regular contact with towns on the Gulf of Salerno (see ll. 53, 69). Orr (*Handbook* 287 n. 1) states, probably on B.'s authority, that every detail is 'given from personal observation'. However, B. may also have consulted a guidebook, *Notes*

Subtitle. Piano di Sorrento: the Plain of Sorrento.

on Naples . . . by a Traveller (1838), which he owned and later lent to EBB. (see *LK* 721 n.4). This describes the Piano di Sorrento as 'one sea of ever-living leaf and fruit . . . *such* flowers and *such* plants . . . you are enabled to see from any part of its slope, as from a theatre, the whole of the marvellous scenery of the gulf spread out before you' (p. 99). *Notes on Naples* has B.'s spelling of 'scirocco' (see l. 5n.), and an account of a climbing excursion similar to that described in ll. 133–228: 'Among vineyards and olive-grounds, the fruit shaken by the wind dropping on us as we passed, and orchards, where grows the sorbo, the most beautiful fruit-tree in the world, and where the red pomegranate bends to the ground with its own richness; among these we wound our tortuous way, through rocky gully and up green ravine, mounting to surmount the mountain chain that crowns the siren shore' (pp. 125–6). There is also a description of the Piedigrotta fête, which mocks Catholic ritual in the same way that B. does both in the poem (see ll. 246–85) and in an important letter to EBB. which forms part of the background to the composition of the poem. This background may be traced in a series of letters between B. and EBB. from late Mar. to early May 1845 (*Correspondence* x 132–205) centred upon Hans Christian Andersen's novel *The Improvisatore*, recently translated by Mary Howitt (2 vols., 1845). EBB. recommended it warmly (17 Apr.), and B. spoke of seeing journal extracts 'full of truth & beauty' (30 Apr.). Their discussion of Andersen's book became linked to exchanges about the artistic advantages of travel, and the alleged incapacity of Italian writers to describe Italian landscape, A review of *The Improvisatore* in the *Athenaeum* (8 Mar., p. 236), which B. almost certainly saw, quoted lengthy passages and commented: 'It is strange that we know of no descriptions of Italy equal to those which travellers have given us . . . To these must Andersen's pages henceforth be added'. On 30 Apr., B. wrote to EBB.: 'That a Dane should write so, confirms me in an old belief—that Italy is stuff for the use of the North, and no more . . . strange that those great wide black eyes should stare nothing out of the earth that lies before them!' (*Correspondence* x 184). On 3 May, in the course of elaborating this argument, he gives descriptions of his own, closely paralleled in the poem (see ll. 133–71n.), and cites lines from Shelley's *Marenghi* which are a specific source for ll. 138–40. He also criticizes Catholic ritual and superstition in a manner close to ll. 246–85 in the poem: 'does not all Naples-bay and half Sicily, shore and inland, come flocking once a year to the Piedigrotta fête only to see the blessed King's Volanti, or livery servants all in their best, as tho' heaven opened? and would not I engage to bring the whole of the Piano (of Sorrento) on its knees to a red dressing gown properly spangled over, before the priest that spread it out on a pole had even begun his story of how Noah's son Shem, the founder of Sorrento, threw it off to swim thither, as the world knows he did? Oh, it makes one's soul angry, so enough of it' (*ibid.* 200–1). For a detailed discussion, see D. Karlin, 'The Sources of *The Englishman in Italy*', *BSN* xiv, no. 3 (Winter 1984–5) 23–43. In a letter to Isa Blagden of 19 May 1866 (when he had left Italy after EBB.'s death but was writing *Ring*, set in Italy) B. again comments on the Italians, and his own relation to them: 'I agree with you, & always did, as to the uninterestingness of the Italians individually, as thinking, originating souls: I never read a line in a modern Italian book that was of use to me,— never saw a flash of poetry come out of an Italian *word*: in art, in action, *yes*,—not in the region of ideas: I always said, they *are* poetry, don't and can't *make* poetry— & you know what I mean by *that*,—nothing relating to rhymes and melody and *lo stile* [style]: but as a nation, politically, they are most interesting to me . . . my liking for Italy was always a selfish one,—I felt alone with my own soul there: here, there are fifties and hundreds, even of my acquaintance, who do habitually

walk up & down in the lands of thought I live in,—never mind whether they
go up to the ends of it, or even look over them,—*in* that territory, they are,—
and I never saw footprint of an Italian there yet' (*Dearest Isa* 238–9).

DeVane (*Handbook* 159) suggests Shelley's *Stanzas written in Dejection, near Naples*
as an inverse source, but a likelier one is *Lines written among the Euganean Hills*,
and cp. also *Ode to the West Wind*. The Romantic period saw the development
of what may be called the versified travelogue (as distinct from the 18th-century
'loco-descriptive' poem), most notably Byron's *Childe Harold*; Samuel Rogers' *Italy*
(1822–34), a uniformly solemn production, may have stimulated the very different tone of *England*. The climb up a mountain which leads to a revelatory vision
is a familiar Romantic (esp. Wordsworthian) topic, with strong biblical connotations: Moses at Pisgah (*Deuteronomy* xxxiv 1–4), Christ's transfiguration (*Mark*
ix 2–10); B. reworked it in a later poem, *La Saisiaz* (1878), and cp. *A
Grammarian* (p. 586). For the contrast between the (warm, sensual) life of Italy
and the (cold, pettifogging) life of England, cp. Byron, in particular *Beppo*
321–92. In B.'s work, the unfinished *Saul* (II 286) is closest to the poem in tone,
outlook, and structure. Among treatments of Italian scenery and contemporary
life, cp. *Pippa*, *De Gustibus* (III 25), *By the Fire-Side* (p. 456), *Up at a Villa* (III
143), *Love Among the Ruins* (p. 528), *Two in the Campagna* (p. 556), and *Prologue*
(*Asolando*, 1889). For B.'s reaction to the contemporary Catholic Church, cp.
esp. *Christmas-Eve* (III 46), *Bishop Blougram* (p. 279), and, later, *Red Cotton Night-
Cap Country* (1873). Some details of the storm in ll. 117–28 reappear in *Caliban*
284–91 (pp. 640–1).

EBB. responded enthusiastically to the specific descriptions in the poem (see
e.g. ll. 54–64n.); in her concluding comments, she (perhaps only half-seriously)
objected to the narrative frame: 'I think it will strike you when you come to
finish this unfinished poem, that all the rushing & hurrying life of the descriptions of it, tossed in one upon another like the grape-bunches in the early part,
& not "kept under" by ever so much breathless effort on the poet's part [ll. 73–80],
. . can be very little adapted to send anybody to sleep . . even if there were no
regular dinner in the middle of it all [ll. 101–15]. Do consider. For giving the
sense of Italy, it is worth a whole library of travel-books'. W. S. Landor echoed
the passage about the sirens (ll. 197–228) in his poem *To Robert Browning*, written
after receiving a presentation copy of *DR & L*, and published in the *Morning
Chronicle*, 22 Nov. 1845. The poem ends: 'warmer climes / Give brighter
plumage, stronger wing: the breeze / Of Alpine heights thou playest with, borne
on / Beyond Sorrento and Amalfi, where / The Siren waits thee, singing song
for song'. This poem profoundly affected both B. and EBB., and, as Kintner says,
'came to sound like prophecy to the two poets when they were planning their
marriage and escape to Italy . . . the Siren became a recurrent image in these
letters from here on' (*LK* 273 n.7).

> Fortù, Fortù, my loved one,
>   Sit by my side,
> On my knees put up both little feet!
>   I was sure, if I tried,

1. *Fortù*: a diminutive of Fortuna or Fortunata.   *loved one*] beloved one (*1849–88*).
2. *Sit by*] Sit here by (*1849–88*).
4. *was*] am (*1884*). A very rare example of a reading unique to this ed.

5   I could make you laugh spite of Scirocco:
        Now, open your eyes—
    Let me keep you amused till he vanish
        In black from the skies,
    With telling my memories over
10   As you tell your beads;
    All the Plain saw me gather, I garland
        —Flowers prove they, or weeds.

    'Twas time, for your long hot dry Autumn
        Had net-worked with brown
15 The white skin of each grape on the bunches,
        Marked like a quail's crown,
    Those creatures you make such account of,
        Whose heads,—specked with white
    Over brown like a great spider's back,
20   As I told you last night,—
    Your mother bites off for her supper;
        Red-ripe as could be,
    Pomegranates were chapping and splitting
        In halves on the tree:

5. *Scirocco*: more usually 'sirocco': 'a warm wind which blows most frequently in the spring and autumn when depressions in the Sahara and western Mediterranean move eastward . . . It can blow for days or weeks on end and is always dry . . . it often precedes a fresh cyclonic storm in the western Mediterranean' (*Oxford Illustrated Encyclopedia*). B. conflates the sirocco itself with its stormy aftermath. *Notes on Naples* 89 has B.'s spelling. In the diary of his 1838 trip to Italy, B. recorded 'Fresh wind. Scirocco' on 26 May in the Adriatic (*Correspondence* iv, p. xii).
7–8. EBB. quoted 'While I talk you asleep till he's o'er / With his black in the skies', and commented: 'I don't like "he's o'er" much, or at all perhaps. There is something to me weak & un-scirocco-like in the two contractions. Would "till he carries / His black from the skies—" be more *active*'.
9–10. Cp. *By the Fire-Side* 148–50 (p. 470): 'Let us now forget and then recall, / Break the rosary in a pearly rain, / And gather what we let fall!'
11–12. 'I put together all the experiences, good or bad, that I had in the Plain'.
11.] All the memories plucked at Sorrento (*1849*).
12.] —The flowers, or the weeds. (*1849–88*).
13. *'Twas time,*] Time for rain! (*1849–88*). EBB. quoted ''Twas time, for your long dry autumn', and commented: 'I just doubt if "and dry" might not improve the rhythm—doubt. Only if the emphasis is properly administered to "long", nothing of course is wanted—only, again, it is trusting to the reader!'
18. *specked with white*] speckled with white (*1870*); speckled white (*1875–88*). B. may have adapted a mispr. in *1870*, the first corr. reissue of *1868*; *1870* provided the copy-text for *1875*.

25   And 'twixt the loose walls of great flintstone,
          Or in the thick dust
     On the path, or straight out of the rock side,
          Wherever could thrust
     Some starved sprig of bold hardy rock-flower
30   Its yellow face up,
     For the prize were great butterflies fighting,
          Some five for one cup:
     So I guessed, ere I got up this morning,
          What change was in store,
35   By the quick rustle-down of the quail-nets
          Which woke me before
     I could open my shutter, made fast
          With a bough and a stone,
     And look thro' the twisted dead vine-twigs,
40   Sole lattice that's known;
     Sharp rang the rings down the bird-poles
          While, busy beneath,
     Your priest and his brother were working,
          The rain in their teeth.
45   And out upon all the flat house-roofs
          Where split figs lay drying,
     The girls took the frails under cover:
          Nor use seemed in trying
     To get out the boats and go fishing,
50   For under the cliff
     Fierce the black water frothed o'er the blind-rock—

25. *'twixt*] betwixt (*1849–88*).
29. *starved*] burnt (*1849–88*).
32. *Some five*] Five foes (*1865²*). Cp. *Two in the Campagna* 16–18 (p. 559).
34. EBB. quoted 'What was in store', and commented: 'Surely "what change"
or "what fate" or some additional word sh^d assist the rhythm in this place.
The line is brokenly short'.
35. *quail-nets*: 'nets spread to catch quails as they fly to or from the other side of
the Mediterranean. They are slung by rings on to poles, and stand sufficiently
high for the quails to fly into them' (Orr *Handbook* 287 n. 1).
40. i.e. the only form of lattice known to the peasants with whom the speaker
is lodging.
41.] Quick and sharp rang the rings down the net-poles, (*1849–88*).
43. *were working*] tugged at them (*1849–88*).
47. *frails*: large baskets made of rushes. Cp. *Tomb at St. Praxed's* 41 (p. 239).
51. *blind-rock*: a concealed rock, lying just below the surface (see ll. 214–16).

No seeing our skiff
Arrive about noon from Amalfi,
　　—Our fisher arrive,
55　And pitch down his basket before us,
　　All trembling alive
With pink and grey jellies, your sea-fruit,
　　—Touch the strange lumps,
And mouths gape there, eyes open, all manner
60　　Of horns and of humps,
Which only the fisher looks grave at,
　　While round him like imps
Cling screaming the children as naked
　　And brown as his shrimps,
65　Himself too as bare to the middle
　　—You see round his neck
The string and its brass coin suspended,
　　That saves him from wreck.
But to-day not a boat reached Salerno,
70　　So back to a man
Came our friends, with whose help in the vineyards
　　Grape-harvest began:

52−4. i.e. 'there is no chance of seeing the fisherman arrive about noon [as usual] from Amalfi in his skiff'. 'No seeing' governs both 'our skiff / Arrive' and 'Our fisher arrive'.

53. Amalfi: a town on the north coast of the Gulf of Salerno, about 19km west-south-west of Salerno itself (see l. 69n.).

54−64. EBB. quoted l. 58 and commented: 'I do like all this living description . . living description which never lived before in poetry . . & now will live always. These fishes have suffered no earth-change, though they lie here so grotesquely plain between rhyme & rhyme. And the grave fisher too! & the children "brown as his shrimps"!' In a letter to John Kenyon (undated, but before July 1845 and probably before B. began corresponding with EBB.), B. wrote of an unidentified 'novel' which he was sending to Kenyon: 'Let it figure among your books (at the house-top) as one sees from time to time in the shop of a Bondstreet Fishmonger some thorny queer lump-fish suspended as a show over all the good quiet ordinary turbots and salmon—not that such a prodigy is to be eaten by any means, but to show *what* the "vast sea's entrail" can produce on occasion' (*ABL MS*).

57. sea-fruit: seafood; translating It. 'frutti di mare'. Not *OED*.

58. —Touch] You touch (*1849−88*).

66. EBB. suggested 'And you see round his neck', 'for rhythm. The line stops you: & you need not stop, when you are looking at him, to "see round his neck"'. This was one of the rare occasions on which B. did not follow her advice.

69. Salerno: a major port lying west of the mouth of the Irno river in the Gulf of Salerno, 54 km east-south-east of Naples.

In the vat half-way up in our house-side
 Like blood the juice spins
75 While your brother all bare-legged is dancing
 Till breathless he grins
Dead-beaten, in effort on effort
 To keep the grapes under,
For still when he seems all but master
80 In pours the fresh plunder
From girls who keep coming and going
 With basket on shoulder,
And eyes shut against the rain's driving,
 Your girls that are older,—
85 For under the hedges of aloe,
 And where, on its bed
Of the orchard's black mould, the love-apple
 Lies pulpy and red,
All the young ones are kneeling and filling
90 Their laps with the snails
Tempted out by the first rainy weather,—
 Your best of regales,
As to-night will be proved to my sorrow,
 When, supping in state,
95 We shall feast our grape-gleaners—two dozen,
 Three over one plate,—
Maccaroni so tempting to swallow
 In slippery strings,
And gourds fried in great purple slices,
100 That colour of kings,—

73–8. EBB. commented: 'The treading of the grapes is admirable painting—that "breathless he grins", so true to life—& the effort to "keep the grapes under"! —all, admirable'.

74. spins: gushes or spirts (*OED* 8).

77. Dead-beaten: usually 'dead-beat': *OED* does not record B.'s form, which was perhaps adopted to allow a secondary sense, 'completely defeated' (by the grapes).

79. For still] Since still (*1849–88*).

86–7. on its bed / Of the orchard's black mould, the love-apple: i.e. the tomato on its bed of richly manured earth ('orchard' is a transferred sense from 'love-*apple*'). The cultivation of the 'love-apple' by 'lavishing manure' recurs in a complex figure in *Fifine* (1872) 1325ff.

91. the] this (*1863–88*).

92. regales: choice articles of food, dainties.

97–100. Maccaroni . . . strings . . . kings] With lasagne . . . ropes . . . popes (*1849–88*).

Meantime, see the grape-bunch they've brought you,—
    The rain-water slips
O'er the heavy blue bloom on each globe
    Which the wasp to your lips
105   Still follows with fretful persistence—
    Nay, taste while awake,
This half of a curd-white smooth cheese-ball,
    That peels, flake by flake,
Like an onion's, each smoother and whiter—
110   Next sip this weak wine
From the thin green glass flask, with its stopper,
    A leaf of the vine,—
And end with the prickly-pear's red flesh
    That leaves thro' its juice
115   The stony black seeds on your pearl-teeth
    . . . Scirocco is loose!
Hark! the quick pelt of the olives
    Which, thick in one's track,
Tempt the stranger to pick up and bite them
120   Tho' not yet half black!
And how their old twisted trunks shudder!
    The medlars let fall
Their hard fruit—the brittle great fig-trees
    Snap off, figs and all,
125   For here comes the whóle of the tempest!
    No refuge but creep

---

103. heavy] leaden (*B & P BYU*).

109. onion's] onion (*1863–88*).

113–15. Cp. Andersen's *Improvisatore* (see headnote) i 114: 'delicious green water-melons which . . . shewed the purple-red flesh with the black seeds', quoted in both the *Athenaeum* and the *Spectator*.

116–125. Cp. B.'s description of 'la bora' in a letter to EBB. of 13 July 1845, esp. (with ll. 123–4): 'you see the acacia heads snap off, now one, then another' (*Correspondence* x 305–6). Cp. also *Caliban* 284–91 (pp. 640–1).

117. the quick pelt] the quick, whistling pelt (*1849–88*, except 'quick whistling', *1868–88*).

121.] How the old twisted olive trunks shudder! (*1849–88*, except 'shudder,', *1865²*, *1868–88*).

122. medlars: probably *Mespilus germanica*, whose fruit is eaten only when decayed; note 'hard fruit' in l. 123. The poem's location might also suggest *Crataegus azaro-lus*, the 'Neapolitan Medlar'.

123. fruit—the] fruit, and the (*1849–88*).

126–8. Cp. *Sordello* iii 758–9 (I 578): 'So sleep upon my shoulder, child, nor mind / Their foolish talk'.

Back again to my side and my shoulder,
    And listen or sleep.

O how will your country show next week,
130   When all the vine-boughs
Have been stripped of their foliage to pasture
    The mules and the cows?
Last eve I rode over the mountains—
    Your brother, my guide,
135 Soon left me to feast on the myrtles
    That offered, each side,
Their fruit-balls, black, glossy and luscious,
    Or strip from the sorbs
A treasure, so rosy and wondrous,
140   Of hairy gold orbs!
But my mule picked his sure, sober path out,
    Just stopping to neigh
When he recognised down in the valley
    His mates on their way
145 With the faggots, and barrels of water;
    And soon we emerged
From the plain where the woods could scarce follow,
    And still as we urged
Our way, the woods wondered, and left us,
150   As up still we trudged

---

127. EBB. quoted 'Back to my side', and commented: 'Is not some word, some dissyllable, (as if you were to write "Back again" &c,) wanted for rhythm,—reading it with the preceding line?'
128^129.] there is no division at this point in *1865²*.
133–71. Cp. B. to EBB., 3 May 1845: 'and which of you eternal triflers was it called yourself "Shelley" and so told me years ago that in the mountains it was a feast "when one should find those globes of deep red gold—which in the woods the strawberry-tree doth bear, suspended in their emerald atmosphere," so that when my Mule walked into a sorb-tree, not to tumble sheer over Monte Calvano, and I felt the fruit against my face, the little ragged bare-legged guide fairly laughed at my knowing them so well' (*Correspondence* x 200). The quotation is from Shelley's *Marenghi* 72–5. But B. had mistaken the 'strawberry-tree' for the sorb; it is actually the arbutus (see next note).
139–40.] A treasure, or, rosy and wondrous, / Those hairy gold orbs! (*1868–88*). Presumably B. made the change after realizing that his description of the sorb, derived from Shelley's 'strawberry-tree' (see prec. note), actually applied to the arbutus. But the original description is not inaccurate, since the sorb does have reddish-yellow fruits.
149–50. left us, / As up] left us. / Up, up (*1872, 1884*).

Though the wild path grew wilder each instant,
    And place was e'en grudged
'Mid the rock-chasms, and piles of loose stones
    Like the loose broken teeth
155 Of some monster, which climbed there to die
    From the ocean beneath—
Place was grudged to the silver-grey fume-weed
    That clung to the path,
And dark rosemary, ever a-dying,
160   Which, 'spite the wind's wrath,
So loves the salt rock's face to seaward,—
    And lentisks as staunch
To the stone where they root and bear berries,
    And—what shows a branch
165 Coral-coloured, transparent, with circlets
    Of pale seagreen leaves—
Over all trod my mule with the caution
    Of gleaners o'er sheaves:
Foot after foot like a lady—
170   So round after round,
He climbed to the top of Calvano;
    And God's own profound
Was above me, and round me the mountains,
    And under, the sea,

---

152. place was e'en grudged: to the 'fume-weed' of l. 157, where the phrase is repeated because of the intervening image.

157. fume-weed: fumitory (*Fumaria officinalis*), a weed which grows close to the ground; apparently B.'s coinage (not *OED*), from the Latin derivation of fumitory, 'fumus terrae' (smoke of the earth).

160. Which] That (*1849–88*).

161. rock's face] rock-face (*1865²*).

162–3. The lentisk is the mastic tree, an evergreen shrub. Cp. *Sordello* iv 798–807 (I 640).

169. Foot] Still, foot (*1849–88*). *Foot after foot*: cp. Wordsworth, *Strange fits of passion* 21–2: 'My horse moved on; hoof after hoof / He raised, and never stopped'.

170. So] Still (*1872, 1884*); Till (*1888*).

171. Calvano: a contraction of Vico Alvano, in the southern part of the Piano. It is 642 metres high and commands a sweeping view, north across the plain and south over the Mediterranean, including the Galli islets (see l. 199n.). B. told Furnivall he was unsure of the name, which he had 'heard . . . in Sorrento . . . but the names are greatly changed in the dialect there' (*BSP* i [*1881*] 170).

172–4. Cp. Shelley, *The Triumph of Life* 27–8: 'the deep / Was at my feet, and Heaven above my head'.

172. profound: used in the same sense of 'sky, firmament' in *La Saisiaz* 19.

175   And with me, my heart to bear witness
           What was and shall be!
       Oh heaven, and the terrible crystal!
           No rampart excludes
       The eye from the life to be lived
180   In the blue solitudes!
       Oh, those mountains, their infinite movement!
           Still moving with you—
       For ever some new head and breast of them
           Thrusts into view
185   To observe the intruder—you see it
           If quickly you turn
       And, before they escape you, surprise them—
           They grudge you should learn
       How the soft plains they look on, lean over,
190   And love, they pretend,
       —Cower beneath them—the flat sea-pine crouches,
           The wild fruit-trees bend,
       E'en the myrtle-leaves curl, shrink and shut—
           All is silent and grave—
195   'Tis a sensual and timorous beauty—
           How fair, but a slave!
       So I turned to the sea,— and there slumbered
           As greenly as ever

175. with me] within me (*1849–88*).
177. Oh heaven,] Oh, heaven (*1863–65, 1868–88*); Oh heaven (*1865²*).   *terrible crystal*: cp. *Ezekiel* i 22: 'And the likeness of the firmament . . . was as the colour of the terrible crystal'. Cp. *Saul* (1855) 99–101, *Sordello* iii 440, *Prince Hohenstiel* 1334, and *Aristophanes* 45: 'Above all crowding, crystal silentness'.
179. The] Your (*1849–88*).
181–7. EBB. admired this passage as 'finely true'.
183. EBB. quoted 'For some', and suggested 'With ever some'.
189–91. EBB. quoted 'How the soft plains they look on & love so / As they would pretend / Lower beneath them', and commented: 'I do not see the construction. The "lower" put here as a verb? & if correctly, is it clearly, so, put?' In the margin B. wrote 'Cower', and explained in his letter of 12 Aug. 1845: 'So you can decypher my *utterest* hieroglyphic? Now droop the eyes while I triumph: the plains *Cower, Cower* beneath the mountains their masters' (*Correspondence* xi 26). The changes were presumably not suggested by her. See also l. 272n.
191. flat] black (*1872, 1884*).
194. EBB. quoted 'All's silent & grave', and suggested the present reading: 'The rhythm gains by it, I think'.
196.] How fair! but a slave. (*1865–88*).
198. EBB. quoted 'Greenly as ever', and commented: 'Would not "*As* greenly as ever" take the rhythm on better?'

Those isles of the syren, your Galli;
200   No ages can sever
The Three—nor enable their sister
To join them,—half way
On the voyage, she looked at Ulysses—
No farther to-day,
205   Tho' the small one, just launched in the wave,
Watches breast-high and steady
From under the rock, her bold sister
Swum half-way already.
O when shall we sail there together
210   And see from the sides
Quite new rocks show their faces—new haunts
Where the syren abides?

199. Li Galli (The Cocks) are three rocky little islets (la Castelluccia, la Rotonda, and il Gallo Lungo), off the south-eastern coast of the Sorrento peninsula. They are known also as the Syrenusae, from their association with the Homeric sirens, though this title is not unique to them (see next note). In his letter to EBB. of 15 Apr. 1845, B. made a little sketch of 'the green little Syrenusae where I have sate and heard the quails sing' (*Correspondence* x 166). See ll. 223–4n.

200. EBB. quoted 'Years cannot sever', and suggested 'And years' or 'For years'.

200–8. In a letter of 12 May 1846, B. told EBB., 'there are *three* siren's isles, you know' (*Correspondence* xii 320), but despite this he refers to five islets here. The furthest from the coastline are the Galli, the 'Three' of l. 201, which form a distinct group. 'Their sister' is the islet of Vetara, roughly midway between the Galli and the coast; and the 'small one' of l. 205 is the islet of Isca, close inshore—'just launched in the wave'. All these are 'isles of the syren': see N. Douglas, *Siren Land* (1957) 29. Vetara, swimming to join the Galli, had got half-way there when she 'looked at Ulysses', and has got no further; though this still seems impressive to Isca watching from the safety of the shallows. It is not clear what variant of the myth of Ulysses and the sirens B. is alluding to. The sirens are said to have thrown themselves into the sea after failing to lure Ulysses from his ship with their singing, either out of shame and vexation or in order to follow him; and to have been metamorphosed into islets, their original home being a headland on the peninsula, where they later had a famous sanctuary (Strabo, *Geography* I ii 12). Possibly B. refers to their respective positions when the metamorphosis occurred. But he goes on to combine the idea of the islets being the sirens themselves with that of their being the sirens' home (ll. 209–12), and further on he interprets their song as the 'birds' quiet singing' (ll. 222–8).

205. EBB. quoted 'Though the one breast-high in the water' and suggested 'bosom-high', 'for rhythm'. In proof she jotted down 'in the water / Watches' without comment. B. transferred 'breast-high' to l. 206 (whose original version cannot be recovered) and altered the rhythm of l. 205 in accordance with EBB.'s suggestion.

209. O when] Fortù, (*1849–88*). EBB. quoted 'When' and suggested that B. restore 'O', which he had erased, 'for rhythm & expression'.

Oh, to sail round and round them, close over
 The rocks, tho' unseen,
215 That ruffle the grey glassy water
 To glorious green,—
Then scramble from splinter to splinter,
 Reach land and explore
On the largest, the strange square black turret
220 With never a door—
Just a loop that admits the quick lizards;
 —To stand there and hear
The birds' quiet singing, that tells us
 What life is, so clear;
225 The secret they sang to Ulysses,
 When ages ago
He heard and he knew this life's secret
 I hear and I know!

---

213. Oh, to sail] Shall we sail (*1849–88*). EBB. quoted 'Oh to sail round them, close over', and commented: 'The line is broken I think. Should it not either be "And oh, to sail round them", or "Oh, to sail round & round them"'.

215. EBB. quoted 'That ruffle the grey sea-water', and suggested 'ocean-water', 'for rhythm'. She added: 'All beautiful description'.

219–20. A cistern remains of a tower built on il Gallo Lungo (see l. 199n.) in 1330 by King Robert of Naples. See *Sordello* vi 779–85n. (I 763)

219. EBB. quoted 'The square black tower on the largest', and commented: 'Did you write "*built* on the largest"—because [of] the eternal rhythm!' In proof, she jotted down 'The strange square black turret on the largest / Built with never a door', without comment.

221. that admits] to admit (*1849–88*).

222. —To] Then, (*1849–88*).

223–4. B. may refer to the singing of quails (see l. 199n.). N. Douglas (*Siren Land* 30) says that on one of the Galli 'the laminated strata are broken to form a melodious sea-cave . . . the haunt of countless . . . swifts who raise their families in the shelving rock'. The sirens were winged or bird-bodied women; the Muses plucked their wings after defeating them in a singing contest.

225–8. Cp. Sir Thomas Browne, *Hydriotaphia, or Urne Buriall* (1658), whose final chapter opens: 'What song the Syrens sang, or what name Achilles assumed when he hid himself among women, though puzzling questions, are not beyond all conjecture'; B. quotes this in his letter to EBB. of 8 Apr. 1846 (*Correspondence* xii 226). In fact Ulysses recounts the song at the court of Alcinous (*Odyssey* xii). The sirens wooed him in flattering terms, promising him knowledge of all that happened on earth, in heaven, and in the underworld. For the speaker's visionary assertion in l. 228, cp. *Saul* 312 (III 519).

Ah see! O'er Calvano the sun breaks:
230   He strikes the great gloom
And flutters it over his summit
    In airy gold fume!
All is over. Look out, see the gypsy,
    Our tinker and smith,
235   Has arrived, set up bellows and forge,
    And down-squatted forthwith
To his hammering under the wall there;
    One eye keeps aloof
The urchins that itch to be putting
240   His jews'-harps to proof,
While the other thro' locks of curled wire
    Is watching how sleek
Shines the hog, come to share in the windfalls
    —An abbot's own cheek!
245   All is over! wake up and come out now,
    And down let us go,
And see all the fine things set in order
    At church for the show
Of the Sacrament, set forth this evening;
250   To-morrow's the Feast
Of the Rosary's virgin, by no means
    Of virgins the least—

---

229. Ah, see! The sun breaks o'er Calvano— (*1849–88*, except 'Calvano;',
1863–70, 1875, 1888; 'Calvano.', *1872, 1884*).
230. EBB. quoted 'Strikes the great gloom', and commented: 'For clearness, the
personal pronoun is wanted, I fancy. What "strikes?"'
231. *over his*] o'er the mount's (*1849–88*).
233–44. Cp. the Gypsies in *Flight of the Duchess* 350–89 (II 312–13).
240. *jews'-harps*] jews'-harp (*1872, 1884*).
241. *locks of curled wire*: the Gypsy's wiry hair.
243. *windfalls*] windfall (*1863–88*).
244. Chew, abbot's own cheek! (*1872, 1884, 1888*; a rare example of *1888*
agreeing with a rev. introduced in a vol. of selections, not a collected ed.). Cp.
Holy-Cross Day 19–24 (pp. 545–6).
245. EBB. quoted 'And now come out, you best one' and suggested: 'And now
come out, come out, you best one'.
247.] And see the fine things got in order (*1849–88*).
248–9. *the show / Of the Sacrament*: the ceremonial display of the Host.
250–1. *the Feast / Of the Rosary's virgin*: the Feast of Our Lady of the Rosary,
initially commemorating the Christian victory over the Turks at Lepanto, 7 Oct.
1571. In 1716, after another victory over the Turks in Hungary, Pope Clement
XI directed its observance throughout Christendom every 7 Oct.

As we'll hear in the off-hand discourse
    Which (all nature, no art)
255 The Dominican brother these three weeks
    Was getting by heart.
Not a post nor a pillar but's dizened
    With red and blue papers;
All the roof waves with ribbons, each altar's
260 A-blaze with long tapers;
But the great masterpiece is the scaffold
    Rigged glorious to hold
All the fiddlers and fifers and drummers,
    And trumpeters bold,
265 Not afraid of Bellini nor Auber,
    Who, when the priest's hoarse,
Will strike us up something that's brisk
    For the feast's second course.
And then will the flaxen-wigged Image
270 Be carried in pomp
Thro' the plain, while in gallant procession
    The priests mean to stomp.
And all round the glad church stand old bottles
    With gunpowder stopped,

253–6. Cp. (noting the context of anti-Catholic satire) Marvell, *Upon Appleton House* 93–6: 'And oft she spent the summer suns / Discoursing with the subtle nuns. / Whence in these words one to her weaved / (As 'twere by chance) thoughts long conceived'.

253. we'll] you'll (*1849–88*).

255. Dominican brother: members of the Dominican order were chiefly responsible for spreading the use of the rosary as a devotional exercise.

257.] Not a pillar nor post but is dizened (*1863–88*). *dizened*: adorned.

259. altar's] altar (*1849–88*).

265. Bellini: Vincenzo Bellini (1801–35), Italian composer, best known for the operas *Norma* and *I Puritani*. *Auber*: Daniel-François-Esprit Auber (1782–1871), French composer of light operas, including *Fra Diavolo* (1830).

272. EBB. quoted 'The priests mean to stamp', and commented: 'But is this word "stamp", & is it the rhyme to "pomp". I object to that rhyme—*I*!!' B. wrote 'stomp' in the margin, and explained to EBB. in his letter of 12 Aug. 1845: 'the priests stomp over the clay ridges, (a palpable plagiarism from two lines of a legend that delighted my infancy, and now instruct my maturer years in pretty nearly all they boast of the semi-mythologic era referred to—"In London town, when reigned King Lud, His lords went stomping thro' the mud"—would all historic records were half as picturesque!)' (*Correspondence* xi 26). OED records B.'s use as being only 'to obtain a rime'.

273. And all] All (*1868–88*). *stand*] lie (*1849–88*).

275   Which will be, when the Image re-enters,
          Religiously popped.
      And at night from the crest of Calvano
          Great bonfires will hang,
      On the plain will the trumpets join chorus,
280   And more poppers bang!
      At all events, come—to the garden,
          As far as the wall,
      See me tap with a hoe on the plaster
          Till out there shall fall
285   A scorpion with wide angry nippers!

          . . . "Such trifles" you say?
      Fortù, in my England at home,
          Men meet gravely to-day
      And debate, if abolishing Corn-laws
290   Be righteous and wise
      —If 'tis proper Scirocco should vanish
          In black from the skies!

286–92. B. alludes to the bitter debates in Parliament over the repeal of the Corn-Laws, which imposed heavy duty on the import of foreign grain. The controversy was at a peak of intensity in Sept. 1845, after the renewed failure of the potato crop in Ireland, and the consequent famine. B.'s refs. to the Corn-Laws in his letters are uniformly hostile. Cp. Byron, *Beppo* 375–7: 'I like a parliamentary debate, / Particularly when 'tis not too late; // I like the taxes, when they're not too many'.

290. Be] Is (1849).

291–2. 'It would be as absurd to debate gravely the obvious benefit of the storm ending, as it is to debate the repeal of the Corn-Laws.' Some reviewers misconstrued the passage into the opposite sense, based on the reading, 'if [abolishing Corn-laws] were proper, then Scirocco would vanish [i.e. an event against the natural order, the permanent extinction of the sirocco, would occur]'; B.'s revisions if anything progressively encouraged this error (see l. 291n.), but 'should' confirms the overall syntax.

291. 'tis] 'twere (1863–88). *proper Scirocco]* proper, Scirocco (1849–88).

18 In a Year

First publ. *M & W*, 10 Nov. 1855; repr. *1863*, *1863²*, *1868*, *1872* (the only ed. in which it is not paired with *In Three Days* [III 5]), *1888*. Our text is *1855*.

This is one of a small number of poems in *M & W* written in the voice of a woman; cp. *Any Wife to Any Husband* (III 647), *Woman's Last Word* (III 273), and *Another Way of Love* (III 677). Although each of these poems deals with unhappiness within a relationship, perhaps the closest parallel is with *Another Way*, which also attempts to articulate the feelings of a woman whose lover (or husband: see below) has turned against her; cp. also *James Lee* (p. 665).

The dramatic situation of the poem arises from the conversation reported in the fifth stanza (ll. 33–40). The man demanded an expression of complete love from the woman, one that matched his own feeling for her. Line 33 ('Speak, I love thee best') elliptically fuses his statement 'I love thee best' with his demand that she respond by saying it back to him. The woman, however, does *not* love the man as he loves her, and made the mistake of confessing as much. Line 35 means that the man would have to trust that his feeling would, in time, create a reciprocal feeling in her. She went on to plead with him that he should not blame her, but rather bear the burden for both of them (since true, faithful love leads to salvation, and since he is the only one of them who has it, if he fails they will both fail). In stanzas 6–7, the woman explains that she was so overwhelmed by the man's supreme gift of love, although she could not return it, that she gave him everything else she could ('wealth and ease, / Beauty, youth'). Moreover, the man himself had not, at first, demanded her love, but had seemed content with exchanging the 'gold' of his love for the 'dust' of her beauty and wealth.

The consequence of the woman's honesty was disastrous; the man turned against her, and nothing she could do to repair the damage was of any use. It is at this point that the the the poem begins, with the woman bitterly rueing the man's alienation and recalling how happy they had been before she made the mistake of telling him the truth.

B. glossed this ending, as *Oxford* points out, in a letter to Edward Irenaeus Stevenson, published in *The Independent* of 27 Jan. 1887, and also reported in *The Critic* of 29 Jan. 1887, p. 54: 'Mr. Browning says, in reply to the question whether the speaker in "In a Year" be wife or mistress, and the person referred to actually dead or only recreant: "The little poem was meant to express the feeling of a woman towards a hopelessly alienated lover—husband, if you will. The summing-up of the account between much endeavor and as constant a resistance to it, leaves the result a mere 'clay-cold clod' in the shape of a heart—to be 'left' finally and altogether; when 'what comes *next*?'—as something must."'

The metre is trochaic (omitting the final unstressed syllable) in a line pattern of 3:2:4:2 beats, making two quatrains per stanza; the rhyme scheme, however (abcadbcd), runs over this metrical pattern, creating one of B.'s most unusual effects. No precedent has been found for this stanza, and B. never reused it; the closest parallel is with *Saint Martin's Summer* (*Pacchiarotto*, 1876), also a poem about a broken relationship.

The poem follows *In Three Days* in all eds. except *1872*, marking B.'s fondness for paired poems: see headnote to *Love in a Life* (III 1).

There are a number of verbal resemblances between this poem and EBB.'s *Bianca Among the Nightingales* (1861), which tells the story of an Italian woman who follows her lover Giulio to England, where he has been lured by an English girl. The poem's speaker calls her rival a 'worthless woman; mere cold clay / As all false things are: but so fair, / She takes the breath of men away / Who gaze upon her unaware' (ll. 100–3), and criticizes her 'white and pink' complexion; cp. ll. 77, 70.

1

Never any more
  While I live,
Need I hope to see his face
  As before.
5 Once his love grown chill,
  Mine may strive—
Bitterly we re-embrace,
  Single still.

2

Was it something said,
10   Something done,
Vexed him? was it touch of hand,
  Turn of head?
Strange! that very way
  Love begun.
15 I as little understand
  Love's decay.

3

When I sewed or drew,
  I recall
How he looked as if I sang,
20   —Sweetly too.
If I spoke a word,
  First of all
Up his cheek the color sprang,
  Then he heard.

7–8. Reversing the motif of reunion in *In Three Days* 5–7 (III 6).
8. *single still*: still essentially separate from each other.
14. *love begun*: elliptical: 'had love begun'.
19–23. *sang . . . sprang*] sung . . . sprung (*1863–88*).
23. The rush of colour to the man's cheek is a sign of his emotional response to the woman's voice, before he makes out the words; cp. *Waring* 51 (p. 187).

4

25   Sitting by my side,
          At my feet,
      So he breathed the air I breathed,
          Satisfied!
      I, too, at love's brim
30   Touched the sweet:
      I would die if death bequeathed
          Sweet to him.

5

      "Speak, I love thee best!"
          He exclaimed,
35   "Let thy love my own foretell,—"
          I confessed:
      "Clasp my heart on thine
          Now unblamed,
      Since upon thy soul as well
40   Hangeth mine!"

6

      Was it wrong to own,
          Being truth?
      Why should all the giving prove
          His alone?
45   I had wealth and ease,
          Beauty, youth—
      Since my lover gave me love,
          I gave these.

7

      That was all I meant,
50   —To be just.

27–8. 'As long as he breathed the air I breathed, he was satisfied.'

27. the air] but air (*1868–88*).

29. brim: edge.

30. the sweet: 'That which is pleasant to the mind or feelings; something that affords enjoyment or gratifies desire; (a) pleasure, (a) delight; the pleasant part *of* something.' (*OED*) Cp. *La Saisiaz* (1878) 309–10: 'Must the rose sigh "Pluck—I perish!" must the eve weep "Gaze—I fade!" / —Every sweet warn " 'Ware my bitter!" every shine bid "Wait my shade?" '

41. own: admit.

45–6. Implying that the man does not possess these attributes.

And the passion I had raised
   To content.
Since he chose to change
   Gold for dust,
55 If I gave him what he praised
   Was it strange?

      8
Would he loved me yet,
   On and on,
While I found some way undreamed
60   —Paid my debt!
Gave more life and more,
   Till, all gone,
He should smile "She never seemed
   Mine before.

      9
65 "What—she felt the while,
   Must I think?
Love's so different with us men,"
   He should smile.
"Dying for my sake—
70   White and pink!
Can't we touch these bubbles then
   But they break?"

     10
Dear, the pang is brief.
   Do thy part,
75 Have thy pleasure. How perplext
   Grows belief!
Well, this cold clay clod
   Was man's heart.
Crumble it—and what comes next?
80   Is it God?

---

53. *change*: exchange.
67. On the differences between men's and women's views of love, see headnote
to *Any Wife to Any Husband* (III 647).
71. *bubbles*: attractive but fragile things; cp. *Lovers' Quarrel* 86 (p. 381).
77–80. For B.'s paraphrase of the meaning of these lines, see headnote.
79. *Crumble it*—] Crumble it, (*1865–88*).

19 Evelyn Hope

First publ. *M & W*, 10 Nov. 1855; repr. *1863, 1863², 1868, 1888.* Our text is *1855.*
B. inscribed lines 1–2 of the poem as the first entry in an album he gave to Mary
Buchanan, daughter of the poet Robert Buchanan, in 1876 (*Collections,* E121).
The Massachusetts Historical Society has a copy of the last stanza in B.'s hand
(*Collections,* E120), almost certainly written out as an autograph, although for whom
is not known. It is on a small sheet of notepaper, signed but not dated; it has no
verbal variants, but the punctuation variants suggest that it was written out after
the revisions for *1868* but before those for *1888.* It does not, however, correspond
to any printed text: for example, it contains a reading from *1870* at l. 50, but at
l. 54 agrees with *1855–63.*

There is no direct evidence of the date of composition, but phrases similar to
revisions B. was making in *Pippa Passes* for his 1849 *Poems* (see ll. 7–8n., 15n.,
18–20n.) may indicate a relatively early date, between 1848 and 1850. A similar
date is suggested by EBB.'s interest in the question of the survival of love into
the next life, which she discusses frequently in her letters dating from the
late 1840s in the context of her interest in Swedenborgianism. There were a
number of Swedenborgians in the Brownings' circle, e.g. Charles Augustus Tulk
(see *Lovers' Quarrel* 1n. [p. 377]), who expressed his desire to rejoin his wife in
the 'new world' in a conversation reported by EBB. in a letter of 10–11 May
1848: '"Tell me," he asked . . . "if Mr. Browning were to go from you, wouldn't
you desire to rejoin him?—I want to go to my wife—There's no other tie in
life like that tie. What exists between parent & child, is comparatively nothing—
merely temporal—Conjugal love is the one eternal bond which God has set his
seal on." Swedenborg saw in the vision that true husbands and wives were seen
as one body in the spiritual life,—the two making one angel' (*EBB to Arabella*
i 176; see also *Two in the Campagna* [p. 556], and *An Epistle* [p. 507]). The
speaker's understanding of the afterlife in *Evelyn Hope* may be couched in
Swedenborgian terms; see ll. 29–32n. and l. 35n. An alternative source is suggested by ll. 39–40, where the phrase 'new life', together with the suggestion
that the speaker will be in Evelyn Hope's hands, and not vice versa, recalls Dante's
Vita Nuova, the early death of Beatrice which seals Dante's devotion to her, and
Beatrice's role as Dante's guide in the *Paradiso.* In a letter to Julia Wedgwood of
19 Aug. 1864 B. cited a passage from Dante's *Convivio* which he applied to his
own relationship to EBB.: '"Thus I believe, thus I affirm, thus I am certain it
is, that from this life I shall pass to another better, there, where that Lady lives,
of whom my soul was enamoured"' (*RB & JW* 64); a verse translation of the
same passage appears in *La Saisiaz* (1878) 213–15.

In 'The Philosophy of Composition' (1846) Edgar Allan Poe writes: 'When
it most closely allies itself to beauty: the death . . . of a beautiful woman is, unquestionably, the most poetical topic in the world—and equally is it beyond doubt
that the lips best suited for such a topic are those of a bereaved lover.' Both B.

Title. Evelyn Hope: the name 'Evelyn' seems to have become fashionable for women
in the mid-nineteenth century; the heroine of *Rank and Beauty* (1856), one of
the 'Silly Novels by Lady Novelists' criticized by George Eliot, is called Evelyn
Wyndham.

and EBB. were admirers of Poe's work; see *Mesmerism* (III 475). The poem contains some verbal resemblances to the opening stanza of the second part of the poem 'Flowers' (1833) by B.'s friend Alfred Domett: 'Sweet is the dazzling whiteness / Of the Maiden's brow; / Sweet is the azure brightness / Of her meek eyes' glow; / Her lip's geranium-red—the flush / Of her modest, mantling blush' (cp. ll. 16, 38). For B.'s friendship with Domett during the 1830s and 1840s, see headnote to *Waring* (pp. 185–6). The mention of the geranium may be significant; although the precision of the 'language of flowers' in Victorian England has been overestimated, most flower books identified the scarlet geranium as an emblem of folly or stupidity; see J. J. Grandville, *Les fleurs animées* (1847), and Beverly Seaton, *The Language of Flowers* (1995), pp. 178–9. On the use of flower symbolism, and especially of analogies between women and flowers, in nineteenth-century poetry see headnote to *Women and Roses* (III 235).

The topic of love between persons of unequal age appears in other poems by B., but is not consistently treated as either justifiable or indefensible. The speaker of this poem, who defends his love for Evelyn Hope despite being 'thrice as old' as her (l. 21), is not as obvious a prey to wishful thinking as the Queen in *In a Balcony* (see esp. ii 141–94, III 428–30); in *Dis Aliter Visum* (p. 688) a young woman rebukes an older man for *not* proposing to her; Guido's marriage to Pompilia in *Ring*, however, in which the age difference is the same as in *Evelyn Hope*, is unequivocally condemned. B. would have been aware of the traditional satirical view of old men's sexual desire for younger women (reaching back to Greek comedy, and including celebrated treatments of the theme such as Chaucer's *The Merchant's Tale*), as well as contemporary versions such as Dickens's *Dombey and Son* (1846–48), in which Mr Dombey marries (disastrously) the much younger Edith Granger. The preferred Victorian resolution was that proposed by Dickens in a later novel, *Bleak House* (1852–53), in which Mr Jarndyce nobly renounces his love for Esther Summerson in favour of her younger suitor Alan Woodcourt. The speaker's attitude here, it should be said, is very much not that of renunciation; the metaphysical, indeed mystical dimension of the poem does not exclude sexual desire, explicitly voiced at l. 32.

I

Beautiful Evelyn Hope is dead!
  Sit and watch by her side an hour.
That is her book-shelf, this her bed;
  She plucked that piece of geranium-flower,
5 Beginning to die too, in the glass.
  Little has yet been changed, I think—

1. *dead!*] emended from *1855* which has no punctuation, in agreement with *H proof*, *1856*, *1863–88*. In the list of 'Errata' he supplied to his American publisher, James T. Fields, B. requests a full stop, not an exclamation mark (*B to Fields* 192), but this does not accord with the proof reading and was not implemented in *1856* or any subsequent edition.
2. Alluding to the custom of 'watching' of the body between death and burial in order to pray for the soul of the deceased.

The shutters are shut, no light may pass
    Save two long rays thro' the hinge's chink.

               2
Sixteen years old when she died!
10   Perhaps she had scarcely heard my name—
It was not her time to love: beside,
    Her life had many a hope and aim,
Duties enough and little cares,
    And now was quiet, now astir—
15 Till God's hand beckoned unawares,
    And the sweet white brow is all of her.

               3
Is it too late then, Evelyn Hope?
    What, your soul was pure and true,
The good stars met in your horoscope,
20   Made you of spirit, fire and dew—
And just because I was thrice as old,

7–8. Cp. lines added in *1849* to *Pippa Passes* i 4 (p. 101): 'But this blood-red beam through the shutter's chink, / —We call such light, the morning's'. Note that line 5 then mentions geraniums.

7. *no light*] nor light (*H proof*, but not *H proof*²).

15. Cp. (noting the connection in ll. 7–8) Pippa's fourth song in *Pippa Passes* (iv 187–200, p. 166), which ends 'Suddenly God took me' In *1849* B. added two lines at 188^189 which make clear that the song concerns the death of a child: 'There was nought above me, and nought below, / My childhood had not learned to know!' See also ll. 18–20n. *unawares*: suddenly, unexpectedly; cp. *Home-Thoughts, from Abroad* 4 (p. 253).

16. 'The sweet white brow now sums up her whole being'; 'the brow is the only remaining feature which tells of her as she was when she was alive'. The brow does not (immediately) lose its expressive power like the eyes or the mouth. On the possible reminiscence of Domett's poetry in this line, see headnote. Cp. also the belief attributed to B. by the Dowager Countess of Jersey: 'he had the rather curious idea that the soul's last sojourn was just between the eyebrows. He said that he had seen several people die, and that the last movement was there. I cannot think that a quiver of the forehead proves it' (*Fifty-One Years of Victorian Life* [1922] 87). The remark is undated, but probably comes from the 1870s. For another quotation from this book, see *Old Pictures* 175–6n. (p. 422).

18–20. The signs of the zodiac are traditionally divided into four groups named after the 'elements' of air, fire, water and earth; the speaker takes issue with the suggestion that Evelyn's 'horoscope' would reveal no constellations associated with 'earth'. Pippa's fourth song (see l. 15n.) mentions 'stars, the Seven and One' in a context which may have mystical meaning: see iv 194n. (p. 166).

21. *thrice as old*: for this motif in B., see headnote.

And our paths in the world diverged so wide,
Each was nought to each, must I be told?
We were fellow mortals, nought beside?

4

25 No, indeed! for God above
Is great to grant, as mighty to make,
And creates the love to reward the love,—
I claim you still, for my own love's sake!
Delayed it may be for more lives yet,
30   Through worlds I shall traverse, not a few—
Much is to learn and much to forget
Ere the time be come for taking you.

5

But the time will come,—at last it will,
When, Evelyn Hope, what meant, I shall say,
35 In the lower earth, in the years long still,
That body and soul so pure and gay?

25–8. Cp. the moment in *A Soul's Tragedy* when Chiappino forces Eulalia
to confirm that, despite his lifelong passion for her, she has never loved him:
'That's sad—say what I might, / There was no helping being sure this while /
You loved me—love like mine must have return, / I thought—no river starts
but to some sea!' (i 233–6, II 191).

29–32. An apparent allusion to the doctrine of 'metempsychosis', or the
transmigration of souls; in his essay 'Swedenborg; or, the Mystic' (1844),
Emerson suggests that Swedenborgianism adheres to a doctrine of 'subjective'
metempsychosis: 'All things in the universe arrange themselves to each person
anew, according to his ruling love. Man is such as his affection and thought are.
Man is man by virtue of willing, not by virtue of knowing and understanding.
As he is, so he sees. The marriages of the world are broken up. Interiors associate all in the spiritual world.' See also headnote, and cp. *Old Pictures* 161–76n.
(p. 422), and *By the Fire-Side* (p. 456). The speaker's wording recalls Wordsworth's
version of this doctrine in 'Ode: Intimations of Immortality', l. 58: 'Our birth is
but a sleep and a forgetting'.

31. learn and much] learn, much (*1870–88*).

35. lower earth: either 'in this world' (from the perspective of a new and higher
one), or an allusion to Swedenborgian doctrine (see headnote) as explained in
Arcana Coelestia, transl. Elliott (1853–57), 4728: 'The lower earth is directly below
the feet, and is a region that does not extend to any great distance all around.
There the majority stay after death before being raised up into heaven.' During
this period their souls undergo 'vastation' or purification until they are ready to
be admitted to heaven.   *in the years long still*: during the years between death and
admission to the 'new life' (see headnote).

Why your hair was amber, I shall divine,
　　And your mouth of your own geranium's red—
And what you would do with me, in fine,
40　　In the new life come in the old one's stead.

6

I have lived, I shall say, so much since then,
　　Given up myself so many times,
Gained me the gains of various men,
　　Ransacked the ages, spoiled the climes;
45　Yet one thing, one, in my soul's full scope,
　　Either I missed or itself missed me—
And I want and find you, Evelyn Hope!
　　What is the issue? let us see!

7

I loved you, Evelyn, all the while;
50　　My heart seemed full as it could hold—
There was place and to spare for the frank young smile
　　And the red young mouth and the hair's young gold.
So, hush,—I will give you this leaf to keep—
　　See, I shut it inside the sweet cold hand.
55　There, that is our secret! go to sleep;
　　You will wake, and remember, and understand.

---

44. *spoiled the climes*: plundered or 'despoiled' all the 'climes' or regions of the earth; cp. *Sordello* v 623–4 (I 699): 'they ranged / The spoils of every clime at Venice'.

48. *issue*: outcome, result.

49. *while;*] while (*H proof, 1888*); while! (*Mass. Hist. Soc. MS, 1863–68, 1872*). The agreement between *1888* and *H proof* is fortuitous, since although the reading in *H proof* may not be a misprint, that in *1888* certainly is one: it was corrected in *1889* and features in both the lists of corrections which B. compiled for that text. The syntax of *H proof* makes sense with 'that' understood after 'while', but this cannot be said of *1888* because of the revision in the next line.

50. *hold—*] hold? (*Mass. Hist. Soc. MS, 1870–88*); hold; (*1872*). This is a relatively rare instance of *1872* not agreeing with the corrected version of *1868*, and introducing a variant of its own.

52. *hair's young gold*: gold hair is a recurring motif in B.'s poetry; see *Porphyria* 18–20n. (p. 72).

53. *this leaf*: the leaves of various plants (e.g. laurel, acanthus) have traditional associations with the afterlife, but none has been previously mentioned; '*this leaf*' may therefore mean the 'leaf' or sheet of paper on which the poem itself is written.

54. *hand.*] hand! (*1868–88*). This variant does not appear in *Mass. Hist. Soc. MS*.

55. *secret! go to sleep;*] secret: go to sleep! (*1868–88*).

20 Bishop Blougram's Apology

Text and publication
First publ. *M & W*, 10 Nov. 1855; repr. *1863*, *1863²*, *1868*, *1880*, *1888*. Our text
is *1855*.

Composition and date
The poem seems to have been conceived in 1850–51; it is clearly linked to
the controversy surrounding the 'Papal Aggression' (see below, *Background*), and
includes references to two people (A. W. N. Pugin [l. 6] and Count D'Orsay
[l. 53]) who died in 1852. The apparent allusion to the Crimean War (which
broke out in 1854) at l. 938, and the possible allusion to the projected edition of
Balzac's novels advertised in 1855 and published in 1856 (l. 108n.), would suggest that B. was still working on the poem in 1854–55.

Background and context
Like many of the other speakers of B.'s lengthy 'casuistical' monologues (such
as Sludge and Prince Hohenstiel-Schwangau), Blougram is based on a particular
individual: Cardinal Nicholas Wiseman, Roman Catholic Archbishop of Westminster (1802–1865).

   In a conversation at the house of John Forster in 1865, B. took issue with
Sir Charles Gavan Duffy's suggestion that his poetry 'habitually disparaged' the
Roman Catholic Church:

> Browning replied that the allusions to the Catholic Church, which I complained
> of, were mainly attributable to local circumstances. He had lived in Italy, and
> he took his illustrations of life from the facts which fell under his notice there;
> had he lived in England he would probably have taken them from the Church
> of which Forster was so enamoured [i.e. the Church of England]. I said I had
> always assumed that one of his illustrations from the Catholic Church which
> was English and certainly unfriendly, Bishop Blogram [sic] was intended to sug-
> gest Cardinal Wiseman. Yes, he said, Bishop Blogram was certainly intended
> for the English Cardinal, but he was not treated ungenerously.
>
> (*My Life in Two Hemispheres* [2 vols, 1898], ii 261)

Again, in a letter to F. J. Furnivall of 1881 B. wrote that '[the] most curious
notice [he] ever had was from Cardinal Wiseman on Blougram—i.e. himself'
(*LH* 195). The review in question was not, however, by Wiseman, but by Richard
Simpson; see Esther Roades Houghton, *VN* xxxiii [1968] 46. Simpson calls the
poem 'impertinent and satirical', and notes that it is 'probably supposed by ninety-
nine readers out of a hundred to be a squib on Cardinal Wiseman':

> [It] is scandalous in Mr. Browning *first* to show so plainly *whom* he means,
> when he describes an English Catholic bishop, once bishop *in partibus*, now a
> member of 'our novel hierarchy', one who 'plays the part of Pandulph', one
> too, who, though an Englishman, was born in a foreign land; and *then* to go

Title. 'Apology' here means justification or explanation of a course of action;
cp. John Henry Newman's *Apologia pro Vita Sua* (1864). Most of the examples
cited in *OED* are taken from the realm of Christian doctrine.

on sketching a fancy portrait which is abominably untrue, and to draw this
person not only as an arch-hypocrite, but also as the frankest of fools.

    ('Browning's Men and Women', *The Rambler* n.s. v [1856] 61)

The suggestion put forward by C. R. Tracy (*MLR* xxxiv [July 1939] 422–5)
and seconded by R. C. Schweik (*MLN* lxxi [1956] 416–18) that Blougram is a
composite figure based partly on Wiseman and partly on John Henry Newman
is incompatible with the fact that Blougram mentions Newman by name, and
with the extent of B.'s knowledge of the subject (see *Sources*, and ll. 703–4n.).
It should also be noted that the Brownings knew of Cardinal Wiseman well before
his role in the Papal Aggression (see below); they met his mother Xaviera Wiseman
in Fano in 1848 (*Correspondence* xv 123, 128; see also *Guardian-Angel*, III 13).

    Cardinal Wiseman was the central figure in the controversy over the 'Papal
Aggression' which erupted during 1850. Before 1850 the Roman Catholic
Church in England and Wales was organized on a missionary basis, with priests
directly answerable to 'Vicars-Apostolic' appointed by Rome. Plans to replace
this with some form of 'territorial organization' into parishes and dioceses were
discussed soon after the election of Pius IX as Pope in 1846, but due to Pius's
own difficulties in Rome were not enacted until Sept. 1850, at which time Nicholas
Wiseman was appointed Cardinal and invited to become Archbishop of the newly
created Diocese of Westminster. Wiseman responded to these appointments by
issuing a Pastoral letter on 7 Oct. 1850 'from out of the Flaminian Gate' in Rome
which seemed to imply that Roman Catholic territorial organization was more
than merely spiritual, and involved some revival of Roman Catholic jurisdiction
over England: 'We govern . . . and shall continue to govern, the counties of
Middlesex, Hertford, and Essex, as ordinary thereof, and those of Surrey, Sussex,
Kent, Berkshire, and Hampshire, with the islands annexed, as administrator
with ordinary jurisdiction' (cited in E. R. Norman, *Anti-Catholicism in Victorian
England* [1968] 56). This Pastoral was reprinted in a number of newspapers, and
provoked indignation from almost all of them; on 22 Oct. 1850 *The Times* printed
a leader on the subject: 'If this appointment [of Wiseman as Archbishop of
Westminster] be not intended as a clumsy joke, we confess we can only regard
it as one of the grossest acts of folly and impertinence which the court of Rome
has ventured to commit since the crown and people of England threw off its
yoke.' Popular anti-Catholic feeling manifested itself in a 'monster procession'
in London on 5 Nov. 1850 which 'centered about a huge effigy of Wiseman . . .
escorted by men dressed as monks and nuns . . . Many parishes throughout
England held services commemorating the day, and effigies of Pius and Wiseman
often replaced the usual straw guys' (D. G. Paz, *Popular Anti-Catholicism in Mid-
Victorian England* [Stanford 1992] 10). The situation was inflamed still further
by the intervention of the Prime Minister, Lord John Russell, who published
a letter to the Bishop of Durham in *The Times* on 7 Nov. 1850 in which he
regretted what the Bishop had called 'the late aggression of the Pope upon our
Protestantism' and linked it to the Romanizing tendencies of certain sections
of the Church of England (Norman, *Anti-Catholicism* 159; see headnote to *CE*,
p. 43). By Dec. 1850 the uproar had reached the Brownings in Italy, as EBB.
makes clear in one of her letters to Arabella:

    Is Papa furious about the Pope—he cares about the Pope surely ... more (to
    tell you the truth) than I do. Robert rages & blazes,—but the political embers
    are gone to ashes in me. It's too late in the world, I hold, for the Church of
    Rome to make way anywhere . . . Then what is called the 'papal aggression,'
    which never was meant for an insult but is purely the result of a *mistake* on

the part of the Papacy (as to the weakening of the protestant feeling in England)
.. a mistake produced by Tractarian representations here & at home .. it will
teach a wholesome lesson, & bring the new movement in the English Church
to a crisis—I apprehend no evil whatever from it.

(16–19 Dec. 1850; EBB to Arabella i 362)

The British government committed itself to legislation on the matter, and after
much acrimonious debate a statute was created on 30 July 1851 declaring the
titles illegal. Thereafter Catholic Bishops themselves refrained from using the titles
(although they were freely used by their congregations) until the statute in question was repealed twenty years later. B.'s poem pointedly refuses to accord Blougram
the disputed titles.

The association with Wiseman is strengthened by allusions to Blougram's taste
for luxury and display in both ecclesiastical and domestic life. Lytton Strachey, for
example, portrays Wiseman as an innocent bon-vivant, not at all a 'subtle and worldly-
wise ecclesiastic' like Blougram, but like him in 'his love of a good table. Some
of Newman's disciples were astonished and grieved to find that he sat down to four
courses of fish during Lent. "I am sorry to say," remarked one of them afterwards,
"that there is a lobster salad side to the Cardinal"' (*Eminent Victorians* [1918] 58).

Speculation about the original of 'Gigadibs', the journalist to whom Bishop
Blougram offers his 'apology', has been less conclusive. Various possibilities have
been suggested, including the journalist George Augustus Sala, Francis Mahony
('Father Prout'), the former Jesuit priest who regularly visited the Brownings in
Italy, and B.'s friend Richard Hengist Horne. Julia Markus makes a case for Mahony
based on his writing for *The Globe* and on Wiseman's acknowledgement of the
strength and coherence of his attacks, but the evidence is inconclusive ('"Bishop
Blougram's Apology" and the Literary Men', *VS* xxi [1977–78] 171–95). Horne
is a slightly more convincing candidate; he wrote for Dickens's periodical
Household Words between 1850 and 1852 (see ll. 949–52n.), produced a biography of Napoleon (see ll. 53, 436), and took an interest in German theories of
drama, writing an introduction to A. W. von Schlegel's *Lectures on Tragedy* (see
ll. 946–7, and cp. headnote to *Old Pictures*, pp. 406–7). Moreover, he emigrated
to Australia in 1852. He did not, however, write for the Tory *Blackwood's Magazine*.
Frank Allen (*A Critical Edition of Robert Browning's 'Bishop Blougram's Apology'*
[Salzburg 1976]), in contrast, suggests that the character is a representative figure,
whose Dickensian name is designed to combine a reference to 'gigs' or carriages,
which had become the embodiment of bourgeois respectability in Carlyle's
writing, with an allusion to 'dibs', a nineteenth-century slang term for money.

Setting
B. offers a number of indications as to the date and location of Blougram's
dinner with Gigadibs; some of these are more precise than others, but taken together
they suggest that Blougram is entertaining Gigadibs at his residence, after conducting a service in a church designed or decorated by the chief exponent of
the 'Gothic Revival', A. W. N. Pugin (1812–52), on the midsummer Feast of
Corpus Christi (see l. 34n.). It has generally been assumed that the poem is set
in London, and that the Pugin 'masterpiece' is St George's, Southwark, which
was founded in 1840 and was the principal Roman Catholic church in London
before the building of Westminster Cathedral in 1903. Wiseman 'assisted at the
solemn opening' of this church on 4 July 1848 in his capacity as temporary Vicar
Apostolic of the London District; the event was said to have excited great
interest in London, and was widely reported in the press; see Wilfrid Ward, *The*

Life and Times of Cardinal Wiseman (2 vols, 1897), i 503–4. Although Wiseman was never assigned to St George's, the popular representations of him in the press, on which B. seems to have drawn extensively in assembling his portrait (see *Sources*), sometimes depicted him in that setting; Markus (pp. 176–7) draws attention to a caricature in *Punch* (14 Dec. 1850) purporting to defend Wiseman from the charge that he has been 'receiving Catholic visitors and neophytes in state in the dining-room attached to St. George's Chapel. It was said of him, that "he threw himself comfortably back into an arm-chair, and that he exacted more than the extreme rigour of royal etiquette."' Markus adds, '*Punch* does not accept this '"malignity" . . . we can believe him with paternal affection receiving "young friends, entire strangers to him, to dinner"'.

A further complication stems from the history of Wiseman's relations with Pugin. Wiseman became Rector of Oscott College near Birmingham in 1840; both the chapel and the other college buildings had been decorated and embellished by Pugin in the 1840s. Under Wiseman's rectorship, Oscott became a centre for English Catholic intellectual and cultural life. Ceremonies in the splendid chapel of St Mary were carried out with great care and were accompanied by fine music. Wiseman was initially a patron and promoter of Pugin, but they parted company on the question of liturgy. Pugin wished to build Gothic Revival churches for the celebration of an archaeologically correct Gothic liturgy and was therefore stubbornly unwilling to make accommodations for the post-Tridentine liturgy or for any of the Italianate devotions, such as the Forty Hours, which had become increasingly popular in England, especially amongst the poor. Wiseman preferred the Gothic to the neo-classical style, but was unwilling to follow Pugin in making it an article of faith. Wiseman came to regard Pugin as a real obstacle to the evangelization of England. By the time the poem is presumed to take place (in the early 1850s) Pugin was dead or near death, and Blougram's condescension towards him has a touch of cruelty.

Sources and Influences

B. seems to have drawn heavily for his account of Blougram's beliefs on reviews and accounts of the Papal Aggression in periodicals. Julia Markus ('Literary Men') notes similarities between the caricatures of Wiseman in *Punch* and the portrait of Blougram in the poem, and suggests that articles in *The Globe* written by Thackeray, Mahony and others may well have suggested some of the language and imagery of the poem (see ll. 3n., 13n., 99n., 377n.). Markus (p. 174) also argues that some of the details in the poem are taken from Wiseman's own article on 'The Hierarchy' (*Dublin Review* [Dec. 1850] 507–30); see l. 212n. R. C. Schweik (see *Background*) points out a number of similarities between the poem and a review of George Borrow's novel *Lavengro* in *Blackwood's Magazine* lxix (1851) 322: see below ll. 377n., 424–6n.

Blougram compares himself (l. 519) to Pandulph, the Papal Legate in Shakespeare's *King John*. The possible significance of *King John* as a source for the poem was first suggested by Allen (see *Background*), and there are intriguing parallels between Pandulph and Blougram. Pandulph's main aim in *King John* is to re-establish the Pope's authority in England by enforcing his choice of Stephen Langton as Archbishop of Canterbury (III i 62–70); in order to achieve this end he is willing to prolong war between England and France, and indeed to countenance the possibility of political assassination. He is also a master of the art of 'casuistry', the name used in Catholic theology for the ability to reconcile competing moral imperatives; at one point he produces a *tour de force* of casuistical reasoning to persuade the French King Philip that he has not only the right but the duty to break his promise to King John when the interests of the church are at stake:

> The better act of purposes mistook
> Is to mistake again; though indirect,
> Yet indirection thereby grows direct,
> And falsehood falsehood cures, as fire cools fire,
> Within the scorched veins of one new-burn'd.
> It is religion that doth make vows kept,
> But thou hast sworn against religion
> By what thou swear'st against the thing thou swear'st,
> And mak'st an oath the surety for thy truth
> Against an oath.
>
> (III i 274–83)

There is, moreover, a significant correlation between this play and the periodic outbreaks of anti-Catholic feeling in post-Reformation England. The play itself dates from the last decade of the sixteenth century, when Britain was at war with Catholic Spain; the Jacobite rebellions of the early eighteenth century prompted Colley Cibber to update it as *Papal Tyranny in the Reign of King John* in 1737; and the 'Puseyite' movement in the Church of England during the 1830s and 1840s produced renewed attention to its anti-Catholic dimension. As Joseph Candido points out in his history of the reception and criticism of the play, the publication of Charles Knight's 'extremely popular Pictorial Edition of [Shakespeare's] plays' between 1838 and 1843 helped to 'establish the scholarly agenda' for the play throughout the rest of the nineteenth century by reviving 'an issue that had essentially lain dormant since Cibber's *Papal Tyranny*: the question of Shakespeare's religious attitudes as reflected in *King John* . . . Knight (without crediting Cibber) rather polemically cites John's statement against the selling of indulgences . . . as strong evidence of Shakespeare's aversion to Roman Catholicism' (*Shakespeare: The Critical Tradition: King John* [1996] 11). B. owned a copy of Knight's eight-volume *Pictorial Shakespeare* (*Browning Collections* A2072), and drew on it for his vignette of Shakespeare's life in this poem; see l. 511n. *King John* was revived by Charles Kean (whom B. knew) in the aftermath of the Papal Aggression, and his production, which ran for 60 nights from 9 Feb. 1852, seems to have become something of a focus for popular anti-Catholic sentiment; a review in *The Times* of 10 Feb. 1852 noted that King John's 'determination to check Papal aggression met with all the *accustomed* cheers, the "Italian priest" coming in for his due share of vociferous defiance from boxes, pit and gallery' (cp. *King John* III i 73–80; italics in original).

   Blougram refers to the contemporary German Idealist philosophers F. W. J. Schelling (1775–1854) and J. G. Fichte (1762–1814), both of whom attempted to bring the insights of Kantian philosophy to bear on questions connected with religion and morality (see ll. 411n., 744n.). As *Oxford* notes, B. denied any knowledge of Schelling's work in a letter to Furnivall of 1882: 'I take the opportunity of saying, once for all, that I never read a line, original or translated, by Kant, Schelling, or Hegel in my whole life' (*Trumpeter* 51); the mention of his name in *Bishop Blougram* might have been prompted by his recent death. There is, however, some evidence that B. was acquainted with Fichte's work. In a letter of 19 Dec. 1847 Joseph Arnould urges B. to read 'the German transcendental writers . . . especially *Fichte*': 'I have been reading them with that engrossing, rapt, concentrated attention which no book can command except one which speaks to the very soul of the reader: formalized in Fichte's books I find what has long

been hovering vaguely before my own mind as truth: especially on Religion
& Christianity. DO READ THEM' (*Correspondence* xiv 349). There is no evidence
that B. took up Arnould's offer to send him some of the volumes he had been
reading, but another attempt to acquaint him with the German philosopher's
doctrines was made by Walter Richard Cassels a few years later; recounting a
visit to the Brownings in a letter to David Holt of 26 Jan.–1 Feb. 1853, he describes
a discussion between the three of them about Swedenborg and Fichte:

> Mrs. B. was speaking very well of Swedenborg, whose doctrines she said were
> extending tremendously. She said she did not know him at all deeply, but admired
> a good deal of what she did. For instance, his theory of correspondencies. I
> cut him up, and said I greatly preferred Fichte's 'Divine Idea', which was another
> form of the same view. She did not know Fichte, but afterwards, when, talking
> of Emerson and the spiritualists, I expounded his doctrine, they did not agree
> —she not being able to receive anything which did not give a distinct Ego to
> the Divine Spirit. She could not see how this was quite allowed by Fichte.
> However, as Browning said, the half of all these things arose from one man
> choosing to call things by a different name: thus, one man named an animal
> horse, another equus, another Hippos, another Cavallo, but all meant the same.
> (*Cornhill Magazine* lvi [Jan. 1924] 103)

Cp. ll. 993–5. The discussion was renewed in Sept. 1854, when Cassels again
attempted to persuade EBB. of Fichte's superiority to Swedenborg (*ibid.* 106–11).

Parallels in B.

This is one of three poems based on real people whom B. mistrusted and even
despised; the others are *Mr. Sludge, 'the Medium'* (p. 771) and *Prince Hohenstiel-
Schwangau* (1871), portraits of the spiritualist Daniel Dunglas Home and the Emperor
Napoleon III respectively. In general terms the poem belongs with other
'apologetic' monologues (see note on title) in which contemporary or historical
figures attempt to justify their conduct; in *M & W Fra Lippo* (p. 477) and *Andrea*
(p. 385); in *DP A Death in the Desert* (p. 714), which offers a counter-example
to *Mr. Sludge* in that its speaker, St John, is not morally disreputable. The 'coda'
of the poem (ll. 979–1013), in which B. seems to offer an authorial judgement
on the speaker's moral and intellectual self-justification, is paralleled in a small
number of other poems, including *The Statue and the Bust* 214 ff. (III 357), *Gold
Hair* (*DP*, 1864) 126 ff., and *Cenciaja* (*Pacchiarotto*, 1876) 296 ff. The Victorian Catholic
Bishop Blougram makes a pair with the Renaissance Bishop in *The Tomb at St
Praxed's* (p. 232), a poem which also draws on contemporary anti-Catholic polemic;
but his closest parallel is the figure of the worldly-wise Papal Legate Ogniben in
A Soul's Tragedy (II 180).

> No more wine? Then we'll push back chairs and talk.
> A final glass for me, tho'; cool, i'faith!

1–2. Wine was mostly drunk after dinner in the period (see S. Freeman, *Mutton
and Oysters: The Victorians and their Food* [1989] 102). It is not clear what wine is
on the table, nor whether this is indeed the Bishop's 'final glass'. At ll. 132–3 the
Bishop urges Gigadibs to 'Try the cooler jug' (which suggests that he has
changed his mind and decided to have another drink after all) and to 'Put back
the other'; at l. 535 the Bishop pours himself a glass of 'claret'; and at l. 918 he

We ought to have our Abbey back, you see.
It's different, preaching in basilicas,
5   And doing duty in some masterpiece
Like this of brother Pugin's, bless his heart!
I doubt if they're half baked, those chalk rosettes,
Ciphers and stucco-twiddlings everywhere;

---

pours 'this last glass' for his guest. The Bishop relishes the coolness because of
the 'hot long ceremony' he has conducted during the day (l. 10); for the Keatsian
resonance of his choice of claret, see l. 535n. The references to wine throughout the poem are an ironic reminder of its place in the Catholic ritual of the Eucharist;
see l. 34n. *i'faith*: a mild oath; Blougram's use of it here and l. 38 (where he puts
it in Gigadibs' mouth) suggests that he is aware of its 'deeper' resonance.

3. Westminster Abbey, built before the Reformation, was a monastic foundation,
finally dissolved by Elizabeth I in 1559, after which it became one of the principal churches of the Anglican communion. The Bishop's playful suggestion that
the Abbey should revert to its original Catholic status is paralleled in the anti-
Catholic literature of the time; Markus (see *Background*) cites a *Punch* cartoon of
23 Nov. 1850 showing Pius IX and Cardinal Wiseman attempting to break into
a church and using the Catholic hierarchy as 'the thin end of the wedge' (p. 173).

4–6. Blougram is suggesting that there is a big difference between preaching
in a grand setting (like a basilica, or indeed Westminster Abbey), and having
to 'do duty' in a modern and very recently completed neo-Gothic church.
On the setting of the poem, and the identity of the 'masterpiece' by Pugin,
see headnote. The 'basilicas' in question are churches designed in pre-Christian
or neo-classical form, i.e. not cruciform but rectangular with a raised central
section; several Roman Catholic churches in London, such as St Patrick's, Soho
Square, St Mary Moorfields, and one of the surviving 'embassy chapels', St Mary
of the Assumption, Warwick Street, were basilican in style. Blougram is, however,
thinking primarily of the Roman basilicas with which he would have been familiar during his long residence in Rome, as his biographer Ward (see *Setting*) points
out in accounting for his uneasy relations with Pugin: 'Wiseman's arrival at Oscott
was naturally looked on with anxiety and suspicion by Pugin. A man who had
lived in basilicas for twenty-two years could scarcely be free from Paganism' (i 358).

7. half baked: the pun expresses disdain for the inferior materials and workmanship which supposedly characterize Pugin's decorative style; Blougram either does
not know of, or deliberately ignores, Pugin's frequent quarrels with the Catholic
authorities over the dilution of his plans for splendid new Catholic chapels in
favour of cheaper but more affordable places of worship: 'They actually propose
deal and plaster . . . [before] long they will advocate a *new service*, suited to these
conventicles—a sort of *Catholicised Methodism*' (from the *Weekly Register* 6 Oct.
1849; cited in Owen Chadwick, *The Victorian Church* [2 vols., 1971] i 273).

7–8. chalk rosettes, / Ciphers and stucco-twiddlings: a chalk rosette is an 'ornament
resembling a rose in form, painted, sculptured, or moulded upon, attached to, or
incised in a wall or other surface' (*OED*); ciphers are monograms and emblems
let into the architectural decor, especially dear to Pugin who loved to revive and
invent ciphers and apply them liberally; stucco is a fine plaster from which architectural mouldings could be made. The sense is that the decorative scheme is
fussy and over-elaborate.

It's just like breathing in a lime-kiln: eh?
10   These hot long ceremonies of our church
Cost us a little—oh, they pay the price,
You take me—amply pay it! Now, we'll talk.

So, you despise me, Mr. Gigadibs.
No deprecation,—nay, I beg you, sir!
15   Beside 'tis our engagement: don't you know,
I promised, if you'd watch a dinner out,
We'd see truth dawn together?—truth that peeps
Over the glass's edge when dinner's done,
And body gets its sop and holds its noise

---

9. lime-kiln: 'A kiln in which lime is made by calcining limestone' (*OED*); proverbi-
ally, an unpleasantly hot and smelly place: 'Thou mightst as well say I love to
walk by the Counter-gate, which is as hateful to me as the reek of a lime-kill
[sic]' (*The Merry Wives of Windsor*, III iii 77–9). Blougram is also alluding to the
fact that the church has only recently been completed.

10. Cp. the Bishop of St Praxed's, who plans to enjoy 'the blessed mutter of the
mass' for all eternity (*Tomb at St. Praxed's* 80–4, p. 242).

11. they pay the price: Blougram may be referring here to the 'long hot ceremonies'
of the church, which are worth enduring because of the privileges which the
Bishop's rank confers; or to the congregation, who keep him in state despite his
disdain for them.

12^13.] no line space in *1863²*.

13. You despise me: Markus (see *Background*) points out that *Punch* of 7 Dec. 1850
carried a caricature of Cardinal Wiseman with the caption: 'I like to be despised'
(p. 177).   *Mr. Gigadibs.* On this name and the suggestions made about his identity see *Background*.

16. watch a dinner out: the word 'watch' has strong biblical associations; cp. esp.
the 'agony in the garden' in which Jesus asks Peter and two other disciples to
'watch with [him]' in Gethsemane, but they fall asleep: 'And he cometh unto
the disciples, and findeth them asleep, and saith unto Peter, What, could ye not
watch with me one hour? Watch and pray, that ye enter not into temptation:
the spirit indeed is willing, but the flesh is weak' (*Matthew* xxvi 40–1). The word
is also associated with the Second Coming of Christ: 'Watch ye therefore: for ye
know not when the master of the house cometh, at even, or at midnight, or at
the cockcrowing, or in the morning' (*Mark* xiii 35). Blougram (or Browning)
may also be slyly recalling a phrase used by St Paul, 'let us watch and be sober'
(*1 Thessalonians* v 6). Blougram's invitation of Gigadibs to dinner also has a biblical
resonance, which is picked up at the very end of the poem: see l. 1013n.

17–20. truth that peeps . . . free a little: 'when the body's appetites are satisfied, the
soul has a chance to express itself'.

18. the glass's edge] the glasses' edge (*1888*).

19. body gets its sop: a 'sop' is a piece of bread dipped in wine or some other
liquid, but has come to mean 'Any thing given to pacify: from the *sop* given to
Cerberus' (*J.*); see *Aeneid* vi 417.

20   And leaves soul free a little. Now's the time—
       'Tis break of day! You do despise me then.
       And if I say, "despise me,"—never fear—
       I know you do not in a certain sense—
       Not in my arm-chair for example: here,

25   I well imagine you respect my place
       (Status, *entourage*, worldly circumstance)
       Quite to its value—very much indeed
       —Are up to the protesting eyes of you
       In pride at being seated here for once—

30   You'll turn it to such capital account!
       When somebody, through years and years to come,
       Hints of the bishop,—names me—that's enough—
       "Blougram? I knew him"—(into it you slide)
       "Dined with him once, a Corpus Christi Day,

35   All alone, we two—he's a clever man—
       And after dinner,—why, the wine you know,—
       Oh, there was wine, and good!—what with the wine . . .
       'Faith, we began upon all sorts of talk!
       He's no bad fellow, Blougram—he had seen

40   Something of mine he relished—some review—
       He's quite above their humbug in his heart,

21. 'Tis break of day] Truth's break of day (*1889*). The revision, which appears in B.'s lists of corrections for *1889*, makes clear that the 'break of day' is not literal: the Bishop means that truth is about to dawn as predicted in l. 17.

26. entourage: either the Bishop's (luxurious) physical surroundings, or his (numerous) attendants; the word had only recently been naturalized from the French (*OED*'s first citation is from De Quincey, and dated 1832).

28. protesting: perhaps with a pun on 'Protestant'; although no religion is ascribed to Gigadibs, the likelihood is that he belongs at least nominally to the Church of England.

30. capital: to turn something to account is to realize its financial value; Blougram is punning on the slang sense of the word 'capital' (meaning 'excellent' or 'first-rate') to hint at Gigadibs's financial interest in the interview as a journalist, a point he returns to at the end of his monologue (ll. 954–62).

34. a Corpus Christi Day: the feast commemorating Christ's institution of the Eucharist (the communion rite) at the Last Supper; a moveable feast in the church calendar, falling on the first Thursday after Trinity Sunday, i.e. around mid-summer. Cp. *Sordello* iii 740: 'God's day, the great June Corpus Domini' (I 576). B. often notes the names of church feast-days, e.g. 'Assumption Day' (*Pippa* iv 8, p. 158) and 'the Feast / Of the Rosary's virgin' (*England in Italy* 250–1, p. 267). Allen (see headnote, *Background*) suggests that this date highlights 'the ironic contrast between the Eucharist and Blougram's dinner' (p. 126).

38. 'Faith: short for 'in faith'; cp. l. 2n.

41. their humbug: i.e. the beliefs of the Roman Catholic Church.

Half-said as much, indeed—the thing's his trade—
I warrant, Blougram's sceptical at times—
How otherwise? I liked him, I confess!"
45 *Che ch'é,* my dear sir, as we say at Rome,
Don't you protest now! It's fair give and take;
You have had your turn and spoken your home-truths—
The hand's mine now, and here you follow suit.

Thus much conceded, still the first fact stays—
50 You do despise me; your ideal of life
Is not the bishop's—you would not be I—
You would like better to be Goethe, now,
Or Buonaparte—or, bless me, lower still,
Count D'Orsay,—so you did what you preferred,
55 Spoke as you thought, and, as you cannot help,
Believed or disbelieved, no matter what,
So long as on that point, whate'er it was,

---

45. Che ch'é] Che che (*1868–88* [in italic]). B. uses this expression, with the first
ed. spelling, in a postscript to EBB.'s letter of 15 July 1848 to Anna Jameson,
although there he describes it as a Tuscan rather than Roman expression
(*Correspondence* xv 114). According to the editors of *Correspondence*, the expression
means 'whatever', but here it seems to mean something more like 'come, come!'
It is normally written 'chechè', which is closer to B.'s revised version.
47. home-truths: searching or pointed observations.
48. The hand . . . follow suit: the metaphor of card-playing, which returns at the
end of the poem (see ll. 983–8) might be seen as revealing something about
Blougram's personal morality. It was not thought 'respectable' for clergymen to
play cards, esp. for money; cp. Mr Farebrother, in George Eliot's *Middlemarch*
(publ. 1871–2 but set in the 1830s), who supplements his stipend by whist, but
gives it up as soon as he gets a better living. B. himself thoroughly disliked card-
playing: 'Robert says laughingly that perhaps it is the old Puritanism which brews
in his blood against the very sign & symbol of any sort of gambling . . . The Drama
was a different thing—it conquered: but he never touched cards .. shrank from
them by a sort of instinct, even in Russia where everybody plays his course through
society' (12 Apr. 1847, *Correspondence* xiv 169). The poet who is glimpsed
'Playing a decent cribbage with his maid' in *How It Strikes* 83 (p. 443) is presumably not gambling. At the beginning of *The Inn Album* (1875) the principal
characters are playing cards for stakes which ruin one of them; in *Clive* (*DI²*,
1880), Clive is involved in a duel caused by his accusation that his antagonist is
cheating at cards.
52–4. Goethe . . . Buonaparte . . . Count D'Orsay: Goethe's reputation in Britain was
at its height during the 1840s. Blougram may be using Napoleon's surname
'Buonaparte' to distinguish him from Napoleon III, nephew of the first
Napoleon and Emperor of France at the time of the poem's first publication.
A long passage on Napoleon's career appears further on in the poem (ll. 436–85).
Alfred, Count D'Orsay (1801–52) was a noted 'dandy' of the 1820s and 1830s

You loosed your mind, were whole and sole yourself.
—That, my ideal never can include,
60 Upon that element of truth and worth
Never be based! for say they make me Pope
(They can't—suppose it for our argument)
Why, there I'm at my tether's end—I've reached
My height, and not a height which pleases you.
65 An unbelieving Pope won't do, you say.
It's like those eerie stories nurses tell,
Of how some actor played Death on a stage
With pasteboard crown, sham orb, and tinselled dart,
And called himself the monarch of the world,
70 Then going in the tire-room afterward
Because the play was done, to shift himself,

---

who scandalized society by marrying the daughter of the Earl of Blessington while remaining her mother's lover; Blougram's 'bless me' may (as Allen [see headnote, *Background*] notes) represent a submerged allusion to Lady Blessington. B. seems to have taken a dim view of D'Orsay and his lifestyle; when D'Orsay became godfather to one of Charles Dickens's children (the other godfather was Alfred Tennyson), B. wrote to EBB. 'And what, *what* do you suppose Tennyson's business to have been at Dickens'—what caused all the dining and repining? He has been sponsor to Dickens' child *in company with Count D'Orsay*, and accordingly the *novus homo* glories in the praenomina .. Alfred D'Orsay Tennyson Dickens! Ah, Charlie, if this don't prove to posterity that you might have been a Tennyson and were a D'Orsay .. why, excellent labour will have been lost! You observe, "Alfred" is common to both the godfather and the—devil father, as I take the Count to be' (7 May 1846, *Correspondence* xii 308).
58. loosed your mind: 'spoke your mind'; also 'set your mind free from dogmatic constraint'.   *whole and sole*: the first of nine occurrences of this tag in B.; the next, in *Mr. Sludge* is also the closest to the Bishop's asociation of it with identity: 'Myself am whole and sole reality' (l. 909, p. 823).   *yourself.*] yourself! (*H proof*).
62. They can't: the Bishop means 'it's not likely'; there is no technical reason why he should not become Pope, although there had in fact been no non-Italian Pope since 1523.
67.] Of how some actor on a stage played Death, (*1888*).
68. crown . . . orb . . . dart: traditional attributes of the figure of Death in emblems and popular drama: the crown and orb signifying his universal dominion, and the 'dart' or spear his power to kill. *Ohio* compares the figure of Death in *PL*, who 'shook a dreadful dart; what seemed his head / The likeness of a kingly crown had on' (ii 672–3).
70. Then going] Who going (*H proof*).   *tire-room*: dressing-room; cp. *The Boy and the Angel* 47–62n. (II 237), where the 'actor' is the Pope himself.
71. to shift himself: lit., to change his clothes, with a pun on the sense of a transformation of identity.

Got touched upon the sleeve familiarly
The moment he had shut the closet door
By Death himself. Thus God might touch a Pope
75   At unawares, ask what his baubles mean,
And whose part he presumed to play just now?
Best be yourself, imperial, plain and true!

So, drawing comfortable breath again,
You weigh and find whatever more or less
80   I boast of my ideal realised
Is nothing in the balance when opposed
To your ideal, your grand simple life,
Of which you will not realise one jot.
I am much, you are nothing; you would be all,
85   I would be merely much—you beat me there.

No, friend, you do not beat me,—hearken why.
The common problem, yours, mine, every one's,
Is not to fancy what were fair in life
Provided it could be,—but, finding first
90   What may be, then find how to make it fair
Up to our means—a very different thing!
No abstract intellectual plan of life
Quite irrespective of life's plainest laws,
But one, a man, who is man and nothing more,
95   May lead within a world which (by your leave)

74. *himself. Thus God*] himself: so God (*H proof*).

75. *at unawares*: unexpectedly; B. often uses the word in this sense (cp. *Home-Thoughts, from Abroad*, p. 253).

80. *my ideal realised*: the need to 'realise' the ideal was a common theme of much of Carlyle's writing during the 1840s; see e.g. *Past and Present*, ch iv, 'Abbot Hugo': 'For, alas, the Ideal always has to grow in the Real, and to seek out its bed and board there, often in a very sorry way'. One chapter in *The French Revolution* (1837) is (ironically) entitled 'Realised Ideals'. Blougram suggests that Gigadibs has yet to reach the stage of maturity at which he recognizes this necessity.

84–5. A contrasting viewpoint is put forward in *A Grammarian* 113–24 (pp. 595–6); the 'high man' who tries (but fails) to accomplish everything is praised in comparison to the 'low man' who is content with accomplishing a limited objective.

84. *you would be all*: cp. *Pauline* 277–8 (p. 26).

86. *hearken why.*] listen why: (*H proof*).

95–6. *a world . . . Fool's-paradise*: Markus (see headnote, *Background*) notes another similarity to *Punch*, this time from 7 Dec. 1850: 'N. Wiseman speaks of the

Is Rome or London—not Fool's-paradise.
Embellish Rome, idealise away,
Make Paradise of London if you can,
You're welcome, nay, you're wise.

A simile!
100　We mortals cross the ocean of this world
Each in his average cabin of a life—
The best's not big, the worst yields elbow-room.
Now for our six months' voyage—how prepare?
You come on shipboard with a landsman's list
105　Of things he calls convenient—so they are!
An India screen is pretty furniture,
A piano-forte is a fine resource,

"little Paradise" that, under the influence of his church, might be all around Westminster Abbey. There can remain no doubt of the fact upon every just and reflecting mind that has beheld the perfect Eden that lies all about St. Peter's in Rome' (p. 179). Cp. also Wordsworth, 'French Revolution', ll. 36–40: 'Not in Utopia, subterranean fields, / Or some secreted island, Heaven knows where! / But in the very world, which is the world / Of all of us,—the place where in the end / We find our happiness, or not at all!' This poem, first publ. in Coleridge's *The Friend* (1809), had been extracted from *The Prelude*, which was not publ. until 1850. B. almost certainly read it in both places. Rome appears at the end of bk. iv of *Sordello* as an ideal of civilization: see the passage beginning 'Rome's the Cause!' (iv 985–1000; I 650–2); Sordello's idealism is brought down to earth in bk. v, although not by the kind of cynicism which Blougram manifests here; rather Sordello learns that the ideal cannot be accomplished all at once, but only through a long historical evolution. With the phrase 'Fool's-paradise', cp. B.'s handwritten note on J. S. Mill's copy of *Pauline* (p. 2).

99. nay, you're wise: the emphatic placing of this word, combined with the double occurrence of 'man' in l. 94, suggests an allusion to the name of Blougram's original, 'Wiseman'. *A simile!* Blougram's extended analogy between life and a voyage is both traditional and topical. Markus (see headnote, *Background*) highlights the possible relevance of yet another cartoon in *Punch*; the edition of 4 Jan. 1851 contained a sketch entitled 'Proposal for a Happy New Year' which shows Wiseman about to embark on a voyage from Westminster to Melipotamus (the town of which he was formerly the nominal Bishop; see ll. 972–3n.). In his article on 'The Hierarchy' (see headnote, *Sources*) Wiseman compares the Catholic Church to 'the Ark, that floats, though tossed upon the billows' (p. 509).

106. India screen: cp. the scene at Hampton Court in Pope's *The Rape of the Lock*: 'One speaks the glory of the *British Queen*, / And one describes a charming *Indian Screen*' (iii 13–14).

107. fine] great (*H proof*, but not *H proof²*).

> All Balzac's novels occupy one shelf,
> The new edition fifty volumes long;
110 And little Greek books with the funny type
> They get up well at Leipsic fill the next—
> Go on! slabbed marble, what a bath it makes!
> And Parma's pride, the Jerome, let us add!
> 'Twere pleasant could Correggio's fleeting glow
115 Hang full in face of one where'er one roams,
> Since he more than the others brings with him
> Italy's self,—the marvellous Modenese!
> Yet 'twas not on your list before, perhaps.
> —Alas! friend, here's the agent . . . is't the name?
120 The captain, or whoever's master here—
> You see him screw his face up; what's his cry

108–9. B. shared with EBB. a high opinion of Balzac: he wrote to her on 27 Apr. 1846: 'I entirely agree with you in your estimate of the comparative value of French & English Romance-writers. I bade the completest adieu to the latter on my first introduction to Balzac, whom I greatly admire for his faculty, whatever he may choose to do with it' (*Correspondence* xii 281). A few years later, after their marriage, EBB. was imagining the possibility of buying a complete set of Balzac's work: 'When Robert & I are ambitious, we talk of buying Balzac in full some day, to put him up in our bookcase from the convent—if the carved-wood angels, infants & serpents shd. not finish mouldering away in horror at the touch of him' (4 July 1848, *Correspondence* xv 99). C. R. Tracy speculates that the fifty-five volume edition of Balzac's novels published by the Librairie Nouvelle, Paris, which began to appear in 1856, might have been advertised in 1855; see *TLS* 24 Jan 1935 (xxxiv 48), and headnote, *Composition*.

110–11. A number of Greek texts in the Brownings' library were published in 'Lipsiae' (Leipzig) by Tauchnitz; see e.g. *Collections*, A0011 (Aeschylus, 1805) and A0142 (Babrius, 1845). The 'funny type' refers to the Greek italic font used by Tauchnitz.

112. Cp. the bath of jasper to which the Bishop of St Praxed's refers lovingly in *Tomb at St Praxed's* (l. 70n., p. 241).

113–17. The painting in question is the Virgin with Saint Jerome and Mary Magdalene (also known as 'Il Giorno' or 'Day') by Correggio, an altarpiece donated to the Church of Sant'Antonio Abate in Parma. For earlier references to Correggio in B., see *Pippa Passes* iv 55–6n. (p. 160) and *Lines on Correggio* (II 454–5); see also *A Face* (III 230). Later references appear in *Ring* iv 888–9, *Inn Album* (1875) 393, and *Francis Furini* (*Parleyings*, 1887) 171–6. For other references to pictorial representations of St Jerome see *Old Pictures* 207n. (p. 425) and *Fra Lippo* 73–4n. (p. 489).

117. Modenese: Correggio's real name was Antonio Allegri; his nickname came from the name of his home town near Modena in Italy.

118. Yet 'twas] Yet was (*1868–88*).

119–20. Blougram's hesitation may be affected, as a sign of contempt for nautical jargon; this would also account for the looseness of his usage at l. 125.

Ere you set foot on shipboard? "Six feet square!"
If you won't understand what six feet mean,
Compute and purchase stores accordingly—
125 And if in pique because he overhauls
Your Jerome, piano and bath, you come on board
Bare—why you cut a figure at the first
While sympathetic landsmen see you off;
Not afterwards, when, long ere half seas o'er,
130 You peep up from your utterly naked boards
Into some snug and well-appointed berth
Like mine, for instance (try the cooler jug—
Put back the other, but don't jog the ice)
And mortified you mutter "Well and good—
135 He sits enjoying his sea-furniture—
'Tis stout and proper, and there's store of it,
Though I've the better notion, all agree,
Of fitting rooms up! hang the carpenter,
Neat ship-shape fixings and contrivances—
140 I would have brought my Jerome, frame and all!"
And meantime you bring nothing: never mind—
You've proved your artist-nature: what you don't,
You might bring, so despise me, as I say.

Now come, let's backward to the starting place.

---

122. Six feet square: cabins on transatlantic steamers were notoriously cramped: see, e.g., Dickens's description in ch. i of *American Notes* (1842), which contrasts his delusive anticipation of the size and comforts of the 'state-room' with the reality; Dickens compares the 'chaste and pretty, not to say gorgeous little bowers, sketched by a masterly hand, in the highly varnished lithographic plan hanging up in the agent's counting-house' with the 'utterly impracticable, thoroughly hopeless, and profoundly preposterous box' which he actually gets.

125. he overhauls] they overhaul (*H proof*). The general sense is clear: the passenger is forbidden to take his luxurious furniture on board, and it is all removed. 'Overhauls' is glossed by *Turner* and *Penguin* to mean 'hauls overboard' but this sense is not attested in *OED* or anywhere else that we can discover. The closest sense in *OED* is 'to pull asunder for the purpose of examining in detail'. See ll. 119–20n., and note Blougram's later use of the term in l. 156.

126. piano and bath] piano, bath (*1888*).

129. Not afterwards] Not afterward (*1868–88*). *half-seas o'er*] half-seas over (*1863–88*); i.e. halfway through the voyage (the colloquial sense of 'half-drunk' is now commoner, but the literal meaning was still current in B.'s day).

134. And] Then (*H proof*).

137. Though] Still, (*H proof*).

145   See my way: we're two college friends, suppose—
      Prepare together for our voyage, then,
      Each note and check the other in his work,—
      Here's mine, a bishop's outfit; criticise!
      What's wrong? why won't you be a bishop too?

150   Why, first, you don't believe, you don't and can't,
      (Not statedly, that is, and fixedly
      And absolutely and exclusively)
      In any revelation called divine.
      No dogmas nail your faith—and what remains
155   But say so, like the honest man you are?
      First, therefore, overhaul theology!
      Nay, I too, not a fool, you please to think,
      Must find believing every whit as hard,
      And if I do not frankly say as much,
160   The ugly consequence is clear enough.

         Now, wait, my friend: well, I do not believe—
      If you'll accept no faith that is not fixed,
      Absolute and exclusive, as you say.
      (You're wrong—I mean to prove it in due time)
165   Meanwhile, I know where difficulties lie
      I could not, cannot solve, nor ever shall,
      So give up hope accordingly to solve—
      (To you, and over the wine). Our dogmas then
      With both of us, tho' in unlike degree,
170   Missing full credence—overboard with them!
      I mean to meet you on your own premise—

154. nail your faith: possibly a submerged allusion to the crucifixion.
156. overhaul: examine (and discard); see l. 125n.
160. The ugly consequence: that Blougram, not being a fool, must be a fraud because he claims to believe in things that enlightened people like him can no longer believe in.
164.] no parentheses in *H proof* and *1868–88*, a rare example of a reading in *H proof* agreeing with eds. after *1855.   to prove it*] to show you (*H proof*).
168. (To you, and over the wine): Blougram is confiding the thought expressed in ll. 165–7—that he 'gives up' on certain 'difficulties'—to Gigadibs on this private occasion, but would never acknowledge it in public. For another example of Blougram's calculated confidence in 'betraying' himself to Gigadibs, see ll. 920–32.
169. With both] In both (*H proof*).

Good, there go mine in company with yours!

And now what are we? unbelievers both,
Calm and complete, determinately fixed
175   To-day, to-morrow, and for ever, pray?
You'll guarantee me that? Not so, I think.
In no-wise! all we've gained is, that belief,
As unbelief before, shakes us by fits,
Confounds us like its predecessor. Where's
180   The gain? how can we guard our unbelief,
Make it bear fruit to us?—the problem here.
Just when we are safest, there's a sunset-touch,
A fancy from a flower-bell, some one's death,
A chorus-ending from Euripides,—
185   And that's enough for fifty hopes and fears
As old and new at once as Nature's self,
To rap and knock and enter in our soul,

177–8. Oxford compares Donne's *Holy Sonnets* xix 12–13: 'So my devout fits come
and go away / Like a fantastic ague.'

182–3. Oxford cites Isaac Williams's *The Gospel Narrative of Our Lord's Passion har-
monised* (1841): 'The sound of distant music or a plaintive note, a passing word,
or the momentary scent of a flower, or the sound of a bell, or the retiring of the
day, or the falling leaf of autumn . . . all these will touch a chord' (p. 434). Williams
(1802–65) was one of the leading poets of the Tractarian movement. He came
to public attention in 1841 when his nomination as Professor of Poetry at Oxford
(in succession to John Keble) encountered opposition from those hostile to the
Tractarians. The similarity between Williams's words and Blougram's may be meant
to indicate the similar outlook of Tractarians and Roman Catholics.

184. Florentine notes that five of Euripides' plays end with near-identical choruses;
the version in *Alcestis* is translated by B. in *Balaustion's Adventure* (1872) 2392–6:
'Manifold are thy shapings, Providence! / Many a hopeless matter Gods arrange.
/ What we expected never came to pass: / What we did not expect, Gods brought
to bear; / So have things gone, this whole experience through!'

185. fifty hopes and fears: B.'s usual term for 'a large number': see *Pippa Passes* iv
198n. (p. 166).

187. rap and knock: The phenomenon of 'spirit-rapping'—conjuring up spirits who
manifested themselves by knocking or 'rapping' on a table—was highly topical
during the early 1850s, and became a point of contention in the Browning household. EBB. describes an experiment in which the Brownings participated in Nov.
1853: '[On] somebody soliciting "raps", we had raps—There was a sound like a
cricket chirping, from the table—"Will the spirits give three raps more?" *Three
came*' (*EBB to Arabella* ii 38). Blougram is mocking the appeal of 'spiritualism' to
a largely secular public. Cp. *Lovers' Quarrel* 43–9n. (p. 379), and headnote to
Mesmerism (III 475); B.'s major treatment of the topic came after EBB.'s death,
in *Mr Sludge* (p. 771).   *our soul*] one's soul (*H proof*, but not *H proof²*).

Take hands and dance there, a fantastic ring,
Round the ancient idol, on his base again,—
190   The grand Perhaps! we look on helplessly,—
There the old misgivings, crooked questions are—
This good God,—what he could do, if he would,
Would, if he could—then must have done long since:
If so, when, where, and how? some way must be,—
195   Once feel about, and soon or late you hit
Some sense, in which it might be, after all.
Why not, "The Way, the Truth, the Life?"

                                    —That way
Over the mountain, which who stands upon
Is apt to doubt if it's indeed a road;
200   While if he views it from the waste itself,
Up goes the line there, plain from base to brow,
Not vague, mistakeable! what's a break or two
Seen from the unbroken desert either side?

188–9. Cp. *Fifine at the Fair* (1872) 2032–140, referring to the survival of pagan cults among the peasants of Brittany, centred on a 'huge stone pillar'; see esp. ll. 2127–30: 'Ask our grandames how they used / To dance around it, till the Curé disabused / Their ignorance'. Blougram, with conscious irony, identifies the religious yearning of the avowed sceptic with a primitive or archetypal form of religious belief; he is also showing his knowledge of modern developments in religious anthropology (cp. his account of the 'French book' which demystifies the origin of chastity, ll. 824–33n.).

190–7. Cp. *Cleon* 323–35 (pp. 583–4).

190. grand Perhaps!] grand Perhaps: (*H proof*). Cp. Carlyle, 'Burns' (1828): 'His religion, at best, is an anxious wish; like that of Rabelais, "a great Perhaps"'; cp. also *Any Wife to Any Husband* 46–7n. (III 650). The phrase was attributed to Rabelais on his death-bed: 'je vais quérir un grand peut-être' [I am going to seek a great perhaps]. EBB. frequently uses the phrase 'the grand peutêtre' in her correspondence; see e.g. her letters to John Kenyon of 8 Nov. 1844 (*Correspondence* ix 219–21), and to B. of 12 July 1846 (*Correspondence* xiii 150–1).

195.] Once feel for it, and soon you hit upon (*H proof*).

197. See *John* xiv 5–6: 'Thomas saith unto him, Lord, we know not whither thou goest; and how can we know the way? Jesus saith unto him, I am the way, the truth, and the life: no man cometh unto the Father but by me.' Blougram goes on to develop the metaphor of 'the way' as the journey of life, familiar in Christian allegory, most famously Bunyan's *Pilgrim's Progress*, where the specific image of a path over a hill or mountain occurs in several places (e.g. the Hill Difficulty); cp. also George Herbert's *The Pilgrimage*.

199. if it's indeed a road] if it's a road at all, (*H proof*); if it be indeed a road; (*1863–68*); if it be meant for a road; (*1888*).

200. if he views] if he view (*1865–68*).

And then (to bring in fresh philosophy)
205   What if the breaks themselves should prove at last
The most consummate of contrivances
To train a man's eye, teach him what is faith,—
And so we stumble at truth's very test?
What have we gained then by our unbelief
210   But a life of doubt diversified by faith,
For one of faith diversified by doubt.
We called the chess-board white,—we call it black.

"Well," you rejoin, "the end's no worse, at least,
We've reason for both colours on the board.
215   Why not confess, then, where I drop the faith
And you the doubt, that I'm as right as you?"

Because, friend, in the next place, this being so,
And both things even,—faith and unbelief
Left to a man's choice,—we'll proceed a step,
220   Returning to our image, which I like.

A man's choice, yes—but a cabin-passenger's—
The man made for the special life of the world—
Do you forget him? I remember though!
Consult our ship's conditions and you find

209–10. What have we gained . . . But a life] All we have gained . . . Is a life (*1863–88*).
211.] not *H proof*, which has a dash after 'faith' in l. 210.
212. chess-board: Markus (see headnote, *Background*) notes that a similar image is used by Wiseman in his article on 'The Hierarchy' (p. 528; see headnote, *Sources*) in relation to the role of *The Times* in generating anti-Catholic sentiment: 'Who that has followed its chequered career, seeing it now on the white, now on the black upon the board, sometimes shifted by the easy glide of queen or rook, now jerked equivocally by a knightly move, has not long known, that in every case it is playing a game, and is only intent on winning?'
213–14. at least, / We've reason] at least / We've reason (*1863*); at least; / We've reason (*1865–88*). The latter revision suggests that *1863* may be a mispr., but it does make sense; cp. the analogous case of ll. 241–2.
215. where I drop] when I drop (*H proof*, but not *H proof²*).
216. And you the doubt] Which you retain (*H proof*).
216^217.] Line 216 ends the page in *1863* and *1888*; all other eds. have a line space.
222. of the world] o' the world (*1880–1888*).
224–8. Consult . . . ground: 'if you examine all the conditions of existence, you will find that only one choice of life (that of belief) fits them all; whereas *your* choice (of unbelief) makes a chaos of those conditions, in which your own way of life would be confounded'.
224. Consult our ship's] Consult the ship's (*H proof*, but not *H proof²*).

225   One and but one choice suitable to all,
       The choice that you unluckily prefer
       Turning things topsy-turvy—they or it
       Going to the ground. Belief or unbelief
       Bears upon life, determines its whole course,
230   Begins at its beginning. See the world
       Such as it is,—you made it not, nor I;
       I mean to take it as it is,—and you
       Not so you'll take it,—though you get nought else.
       I know the special kind of life I like,
235   What suits the most my idiosyncrasy,
       Brings out the best of me and bears me fruit
       In power, peace, pleasantness, and length of days.
       I find that positive belief does this
       For me, and unbelief, no whit of this.
240   —For you, it does, however—that we'll try!
       'Tis clear, I cannot lead my life, at least
       Induce the world to let me peaceably,
       Without declaring at the outset, "Friends,
       I absolutely and peremptorily
245   Believe!"—I say faith is my waking life.
       One sleeps, indeed, and dreams at intervals,

---

237. Cp. *Proverbs* iii 13–17: 'Happy is the man that findeth wisdom . . . Length
of days is in her right hand; and in her left hand riches and honour. Her ways
are ways of pleasantness, and all her paths are peace.'
240. *try*: test.
241–2. at least / *Induce*] at least, / Induce (*H proof, 1863–88*). See ll. 213–14.
246–8. The privileging of waking life over dreams is characteristic of B. in certain
contexts. In general, B.'s sceptical positivism increases through his career: in
Pauline there are still strong elements of the Romantic equation of dream with
imagination, but a different attitude is already present in *Sordello*: 'Sordello's dream-
performances that will / Never be more than dreamed' (iii 607–8, I 566); and
in one of his last poems, *Development* (*Asolando*, 1889) B. cites himself as a habitual sceptic: 'But then "No dream's worth waking"—Browning says' (l. 84). Other
occurrences include *The Statue and the Bust* 153–5 (III 353), *Easter-Day* 478–83
(III 120–1), *Ring* ix 1106 ('to keep wide awake is our best dream'), *Prince Hohenstiel-
Schwangau* (1871) 2146–7 ('My reverie concludes, as dreaming should, / With
daybreak') and, importantly, *Fifine at the Fair* (1872), whose speaker, Don Juan,
prefaces his narration of a long dream with the proviso: 'A poet never dreams:
/ We prose-folk always do . . . What ghosts do poets see? / What dæmons fear?
what man or thing misapprehend?' (ll. 1529–45). At the end of the dream-vision
he says: 'Enough o' the dream! You see how poetry turns prose. / Announcing
wonder-work, I dwindle at the close / Down to mere commonplace old facts
which everybody knows. / So dreaming disappoints!' (ll. 2208–11). See also *Gerard
de Lairesse* (*Parleyings*, 1887) 111–15: 'I who myself contentedly abide / Awake,

We know, but waking's the main point with us,
And my provision's for life's waking part.
Accordingly, I use heart, head and hands
250 All day, I build, scheme, study and make friends;
And when night overtakes me, down I lie,
Sleep, dream a little, and get done with it,
The sooner the better, to begin afresh.
What's midnight's doubt before the dayspring's faith?
255 You, the philosopher, that disbelieve,
That recognise the night, give dreams their weight—
To be consistent you should keep your bed,
Abstain from healthy acts that prove you a man,
For fear you drowse perhaps at unawares!
260 And certainly at night you'll sleep and dream,
Live through the day and bustle as you please.
And so you live to sleep as I to wake,
To unbelieve as I to still believe?
Well, and the common sense of the world calls you
265 Bed-ridden,—and its good things come to me.
Its estimation, which is half the fight,
That's the first cabin-comfort I secure—

nor want the wings of dream,—who tramp / Earth's common surface, rough,
smooth, dry or damp, / —I understand alternatives, no less / —Conceive your
soul's leap, Gerard de Lairesse!'
248. *And my provision's*] So my provision's (*H proof*, but not *H proof²*).
254. *midnight's doubt*] midnight doubt (*1868–88*). *the dayspring's faith*: the word
'dayspring' occurs in *Job* xxxviii 12, and in *Luke* i 76–9: 'And thou, child, shalt
be called the prophet of the Highest: for thou shalt go before the face of the
Lord to prepare his ways; to give knowledge of salvation unto his people by the
remission of their sins, through the tender mercy of our God; whereby the dayspring
from on high hath visited us, to give light to them that sit in darkness and in
the shadow of death, to guide our feet into the way of peace.' B. uses it again
in *Saul* 278 (III 517) and *Shah Abbas (Ferishtah's Fancies*, 1884) 110.
255. *philosopher*: Blougram associates philosophy with scepticism and impractical-
ity; the first recalls the French 'philosophes' of the Enlightenment (e.g. Voltaire
and Diderot), the second the 'philosophic radicals' whom J. S. Mill characterizes
as 'those who in politics observe the common practice of philosophers—that is,
who, when they are discussing means, begin by considering the end' (*Westminster
Review* xxvii [1837] 67).
258. *prove you a man*] prove you man (*1868–88*).
264. *of the world*] o' the world (*1870–88*).
267. *the first cabin-comfort*] the first-cabin comfort (*1865–88*). The later reading is
probably a misprint, and is emended in *Oxford*; since B. allowed it to stand, there
is a chance that he intended the sense of 'a first-class cabin's comfort', but if so
it is odd that he should have left 'next' in l. 268 unchanged.

The next . . . but you perceive with half an eye!
Come, come, it's best believing, if we can—
You can't but own that.

270   Next, concede again—
If once we choose belief, on all accounts
We can't be too decisive in our faith,
Conclusive and exclusive in its terms,
To suit the world which gives us the good things.
275   In every man's career are certain points
Whereon he dares not be indifferent;
The world detects him clearly, if he is,
As baffled at the game, and losing life.
He may care little or he may care much
280   For riches, honour, pleasure, work, repose,
Since various theories of life and life's
Success are extant which might easily
Comport with either estimate of these,
And whoso chooses wealth or poverty,
285   Labour or quiet, is not judged a fool
Because his fellows would choose otherwise.
We let him choose upon his own account
So long as he's consistent with his choice.
But certain points, left wholly to himself,
290   When once a man has arbitrated on,
We say he must succed there or go hang.
Thus, he should wed the woman he loves most
Or needs most, whatsoe'er the love or need—
For he can't wed twice. Then, he must avouch

---

268. *you perceive with half an eye*: 'you catch my drift', 'I don't need to labour the point'.
269. *if we can*] if we may (*1863–88*).
276. *he dares not*] he dare not (*1865*), a rare example of a substantive variant unique to this text; see next line.
277. *if he is*] if he dares (*1863–65*); if he dare (*1868–88*).
286. *his fellows*] his fellow (*1868–88*).
291. *or go hang*] or be lost (*H proof*).
294. *he can't wed twice*: Blougram is stating Catholic doctrine rather than English law at this point; divorce (although difficult until reform began in 1857) was possible under English civil and religious law. But even widowed Catholics could remarry.   *avouch*: to claim as one's own.

295 Or follow, at the least, sufficiently,
The form of faith his conscience holds the best,
Whate'er the process of conviction was.
For nothing can compensate his mistake
On such a point, the man himself being judge—
300 He cannot wed twice, nor twice lose his soul.

Well now—there's one great form of Christian faith
I happen to be born in—which to teach
Was given me as I grew up, on all hands,
As best and readiest means of living by;
305 The same on examination being proved
The most pronounced, moreover, fixed, precise
And absolute form of faith in the whole world—
Accordingly, most potent of all forms
For working on the world. Observe, my friend,
310 Such as you know me, I am free to say,
In these hard latter days which hamper one,
Myself, by no immoderate exercise
Of intellect and learning, and the tact
To let external forces work for me,
315 Bid the street's stones be bread and they are bread,
Bid Peter's creed, or, rather, Hildebrand's,
Exalt me o'er my fellows in the world
And make my life an ease and joy and pride,
It does so,—which for me's a great point gained,
320 Who have a soul and body that exact
A comfortable care in many ways.

300^301.] Line 300 ends the page in *1863*; all other eds. have a line space.
301–2. *one great form . . . born in*: Wiseman was born a Catholic, in contrast to his
fellow Cardinals, Newman and Manning, both converts from Anglicanism: cp.
Ring i 444–6: 'Go get you manned by Manning and new-manned / By Newman
and, mayhap, wise-manned to boot / By Wiseman'.
313. *and the tact*] but the tact (*1888*).
315. B. mischievously makes Blougram cite Satan's temptation of Jesus in the wilderness: 'If thou be the Son of God, command that these stones be made bread.'
Jesus refuses to perform the miracle, saying, 'Man shall not live by bread alone,
but by every word that proceeds out of the mouth of God' (*Matthew* iv 3–4).
316. The Papacy claimed descent in 'apostolic succession' from St Peter as the
first Bishop of Rome; Blougram traces its modern authority to the reforming zeal
of the medieval papacy, exemplified by Gregory VII, whose secular name was
Hildebrand; see *Sordello* i 308n. (I 415) and v 154n. (I 668–9).
318.] And let them make my life an ease and joy, (*H proof*).

There's power in me and will to dominate
Which I must exercise, they hurt me else:
In many ways I need mankind's respect,
325   Obedience, and the love that's born of fear:
While at the same time, there's a taste I have,
A toy of soul, a titillating thing,
Refuses to digest these dainties crude.
The naked life is gross till clothed upon:
330   I must take what men offer, with a grace
As though I would not, could I help it, take!
A uniform to wear though over-rich—
Something imposed on me, no choice of mine;
No fancy-dress worn for pure fashion's sake
335   And despicable therefore! now men kneel
And kiss my hand—of course the Church's hand.
Thus I am made, thus life is best for me,
And thus that it should be I have procured;
And thus it could not be another way,
I venture to imagine.

340   You'll reply—
So far my choice, no doubt, is a success;
But were I made of better elements,
With nobler instincts, purer tastes, like you,
I hardly would account the thing success
Though it do all for me I say.

345   But, friend,
We speak of what is—not of what might be,

323. *they hurt me*] it hurts me (*H proof*).
328. *Refuses*: i.e. 'which refuses'.   *crude*: raw. Blougram wants the satisfaction of his appetites to be disguised as the impersonal trappings of office.
329. The image recalls Carlyle's satiric 'Clothes-Philosophy' in *Sartor Resartus* (1837).
332. *A uniform*] An uniform (*H proof*, but not *H proof²*).   *to wear*] I wear (*1863–88*).
334. *pure fashion's sake*] pure fancy's sake (*1863–88*).
335. *men kneel*] folks kneel (*1870, 1880*); folk kneel (*1888*).
335–6. *men kneel / and kiss my hand*: the Brownings saw Wiseman passing through Florence (where he dined as an honoured guest of the Grand Duke) in 1850, and EBB. was greatly amused by the devotion he inspired: 'You can't think how many English paid their devoirs to Cardinal Wiseman as he passed through Florence . . . One lady was on her knees, kissing his feet' (*EBB to Arabella* i 362).
338. 'And I have procured (i.e. arranged matters) that it should be thus'.
344–5. *I hardly . . . I say*] You hardly . . . you say (*H proof*).
345. *Though it do*] Though it did (*1863–88*).

And how 'twere better if 'twere otherwise.
I am the man you see here plain enough—
Grant I'm a beast, why beasts must lead beasts' lives!
350 Suppose I own at once to tail and claws—
The tailless man exceeds me; but being tailed
I'll lash out lion-fashion, and leave apes
To dock their stump and dress their haunches up.
My business is not to remake myself,
355 But make the absolute best of what God made.
Or—our first simile—though you proved me doomed
To a viler berth still, to the steerage-hole,
The sheep-pen or the pig-stye, I should strive
To make what use of each were possible;
360 And as this cabin gets upholstery,
That hutch should rustle with sufficient straw.

But, friend, I don't acknowledge quite so fast
I fail of all your manhood's lofty tastes
Enumerated so complacently,
365 On the mere ground that you forsooth can find
In this particular life I choose to lead
No fit provision for them. Can you not?
Say you, my fault is I address myself
To grosser estimators than I need,
370 And that's no way of holding up the soul—
Which, nobler, needs men's praise perhaps, yet knows

349. Cp. *Easter Day* 33 (III 101) and *Fra Lippo* 80 (p. 489).
356. *though you proved*] though you prove (*1888*).
351–3. *being tailed . . . haunches up*: 'since I have appetites I will not try to disguise them, like an ape pretending to be a man'. The image of the ape comes from one of Aesop's fables, a favourite work of B.'s since childhood.
352. *I'll lash out*] I'll lash mine (*H proof*).   *lion-fashion*] lion's-fashion (*H proof*, but not *H proof²*).
353. *haunches*] buttocks (*H proof*).
357. *steerage-hole*: the lower forward deck of a ship, where the cheapest berths for transatlantic voyages were located, associated with the poorest emigrants; in Dickens's *Martin Chuzzlewit* (1843), Martin causes consternation to his 'genteel' American hosts by confessing that, 'to observe strict economy I took my passage in the steerage' (ch. xvii).
365. *forsooth can find*] forsooth can see (*H proof*).
369. *than I need,*] than I need? (*1863–65*); than should judge? (*1868–88*).
371. *yet knows*] but knows (*H proof*).

One wise man's verdict outweighs all the fools',—
Would like the two, but, forced to choose, takes that?
I pine among my million imbeciles
375 (You think) aware some dozen men of sense
Eye me and know me, whether I believe
In the last winking Virgin, as I vow,
And am a fool, or disbelieve in her
And am a knave,—approve in neither case,
380 Withhold their voices though I look their way:
Like Verdi when, at his worst opera's end

372. Oxford compares Plato, *Gorgias* 490A: 'One wise man is worth more than ten thousand fools.' Allen (see headnote, *Background*) compares *Hamlet* III ii 24–8: 'Now this overdone, or come tardy off, though it make the unskilful laugh, cannot but make the judicious grieve, the censure of the which one must in your allowance o'erweigh a whole theatre of others.'

373. takes that?: i.e. the 'wise man's verdict' rather than the fools'.

374. million imbeciles: Gigadibs's (or Blougram's) contemptuous description of his Catholic congregation.

377. the last winking Virgin: reports that pictures of the Virgin Mary had miraculously moved their eyes circulated in the period; Markus (headnote, *Background*) suggests that this is a reference to the contemporary 'miracle of Rimini', in which 'an image of the Virgin Mary painted on canvas began to lower its eyes during the mass' (pp. 177–8; see ll. 699–712 and 724–30). The phrase 'winking Virgin' is used by Thackeray in a satirical sketch of Wiseman's life in *The Globe* of 28 Nov. 1850 (cited Markus, p. 177); a similar formulation is also used in William Edmondstone Aytoun's review of George Borrow's *Lavengro* in *Blackwood's* lxix (1851) 322–37: cp. l. 728n. C. R. Tracy (*MLR* xxxiv [1939] 423) has suggested that B. may have encountered an exchange of letters between John Henry Newman and the Anglican Bishop of Norwich in *The Times* of 22 October 1851 in which the latter cites Newman as asserting: 'I think it impossible to withstand the evidence which is brought for the liquefaction of the blood of St Januarius at Naples, and for the motion of the eyes of the pictures of the Madonna in the Roman States.' See ll. 702–3n.

381–6. Blougram's analogy draws on the rivalry between Giuseppe Verdi (1813–1901) and Gioacchino Rossini (1792–1868); Rossini is one of the 'dozen men of sense' who withhold their approval despite the plaudits of the 'million imbeciles'. B. met Rossini in 1849; in an unpubl. letter to H. F. Chorley, dated 9 Dec. 1849 (*MS* at *ABL*), EBB. comments: 'we have both been pleased by his falling upon an introduction to Rossini at Bortolini's studio, which has led to various shakes of the hand & goodnatured smiles on the part of the only man of genius in Italy, & may lead perhaps to fuller intercourse'. The judgement that Rossini was 'the only man of genius in Italy' is likely to have been B.'s; when he and EBB. attended performances of Verdi's *Attila* and *Ernani* in Venice in June 1851, there was a difference of opinion. EBB. commented that 'Robert criticis[ed] the music .. I in my ignorance thinking it beautiful because so dramatic. Verdi is the idol of Italy just now, as to music' (*EBB to Arabella* i 380). The subsequent decline in Rossini's reputation is exemplified in 1893 by Bernard Shaw in connection

(The thing they gave at Florence,—what's its name?)
While the mad houseful's plaudits near out-bang
His orchestra of salt-box, tongs and bones,
385 He looks through all the roaring and the wreaths
Where sits Rossini patient in his stall.

Nay, friend, I meet you with an answer here—
For even your prime men who appraise their kind
Are men still, catch a thing within a thing,
390 See more in a truth than the truth's simple self,
Confuse themselves. You see lads walk the street
Sixty the minute; what's to note in that?

with this very passage: 'even Browning thought it safe to represent [Verdi] as an
empty blusterer shrinking amid a torrent of vulgar applause from the grave eye
of—of—of—well, of ROSSINI! (poor Browning!)' (D. H. Laurence, ed. *Shaw's
Music* [1981] ii 855–6). Blougram's judgement may suggest political and aesthetic
conservatism; Verdi was closely identified with the cause of Italian unification
and independence from Austria (the 'Risorgimento'): see headnotes to *Italy in
England*, p. 245, and *Old Pictures*, p. 408.
382. The thing they gave at Florence: the only opera of Verdi's that was premiered
in Florence before 1855 was *Macbeth*, which was performed at the Teatro della
Pergola on 14 Mar. 1847.
384. salt-box: salt-boxes were commonly used as percussion instruments in burlesque performances and street-music, dating from the mid-18th century (e.g. George
Alexander Stevens, *The Choice Spirits' Feast* [1754] 44–5: 'Salt-Box Bang, and Jews-
Harp Twang, / With Hurdy Gurdy Grunting'); B. would have recently come
across Wordsworth's description of Bartholomew Fair in bk. vii of *The Prelude*
(1850), 'with buffoons against buffoons / Grimacing, writhing, screaming,—him
who grinds / The hurdy-gurdy, at the fiddle weaves, / Rattles the salt-box, thumps
the kettle-drum' (ll. 698–701). *tongs and bones*: as requested by Bottom in
Midsummer Night's Dream: '[Titania]: 'What, wilt thou hear some music, my sweet
love? [Bottom] I have a reasonable good ear in music. Let's have the tongs and
the bones' (IV i 27–9). As with the salt-box, these are popular street instruments;
Blougram is not of course implying that Verdi's orchestra actually used such
instruments, but that his music was vulgar and coarse in its effects.
387. an answer here] an answer there (*H proof*).
388–91. For even . . . themselves: Blougram means that even those who are capable
of judging between true and sham values are susceptible to the attraction of ambivalence: as he goes on to explain, his religious position is not unequivocally that
of 'fool' or 'knave', which preserves him from the kind of judgement which Rossini
passes on Verdi.
388. For even] That even (*1863–88*).
389. a thing within a thing] a wheel within a wheel (*1863–88*). With the revised
reading, *Oxford* compares *Ezekiel* i 16.
392. note in that?] note in such? (*H proof*).

You see one lad o'erstride a chimney-stack;
Him you must watch—he's sure to fall, yet stands!
395   Our interest's on the dangerous edge of things.
The honest thief, the tender murderer,
The superstitious atheist, demireps
That love and save their souls in new French books—
We watch while these in equilibrium keep
400   The giddy line midway: one step aside,
They're classed and done with. I, then, keep the line
Before your sages,—just the men to shrink
From the gross weights, coarse scales, and labels broad
You offer their refinement. Fool or knave?
405   Why needs a bishop be a fool or knave
When there's a thousand diamond weights between?
So I enlist them. Your picked Twelve, you'll find,
Profess themselves indignant, scandalised
At thus being held unable to explain
410   How a superior man who disbelieves

393. one lad o'erstride] one lad stand on (*H proof*). The reference is probably to a steeplejack rather than a chimney-sweep.

395–8. The reference to 'demireps / That love and save their souls' may be specifically to *La Dame aux camélias* (1848) by Alexandre Dumas the younger; this immensely popular novel was dramatized in 1852, in a production which the Brownings saw in Paris (*Letters of EBB*, ii 66 and 106), and on which EBB. commented: 'Even Robert, who gives himself out for *blasé* on dramatic matters, couldn't keep the tears from rolling down his cheeks' (p. 66). *La Dame aux camélias* was also the basis of Verdi's opera *La Traviata*, first performed in 1853. The 'honest thief' and 'tender murderer' may belong more to English literary history; Blougram's sarcasm is reminiscent of Thackeray's attack on the fashionable 'Newgate novel' of the 1830s (Harrison Ainsworth, Edward Bulwer-Lytton, and others, including the Dickens of *Oliver Twist*). But there are also examples in French fiction by Balzac, Victor Hugo, Eugène Sue and others, all of whom were avidly read by EBB.

397–8. demireps / That love and save their souls] demirep / That loves and saves her soul (*1868–88*).

397. demireps: women of dubious reputation; *OED* cites Fielding's *Tom Jones* (1749): 'He had yet no knowledge of that character which is vulgarly called a demi-rep; that is to say, a woman who intrigues with every man she likes, under the name and appearance of virtue' (bk. xv, ch. 9). By B.'s time the term was virtually synonymous with 'courtesan'.

406. diamond weights: i.e. carats, the measure of weight used in jewellery, equivalent to a tiny fraction of an ounce.

407. Your picked Twelve] Your picked twelve (*1868–88*); the 'dozen men of sense' of l. 375, although the phrase here also glances at the twelve disciples of Christ and the twelve members of a jury. Cp. *Sludge* 377–8 (p. 799).

May not believe as well: that's Schelling's way!
It's through my coming in the tail of time,
Nicking the minute with a happy tact.
Had I been born three hundred years ago
415   They'd say, "What's strange? Blougram of course
           believes;"
And, seventy years since, "disbelieves of course."
But now, "He may believe; and yet, and yet
How can he?"—All eyes turn with interest.
Whereas, step off the line on either side—
420   You, for example, clever to a fault,
The rough and ready man that write apace,
Read somewhat seldomer, think perhaps even less—
You disbelieve! Who wonders and who cares?
Lord So-and-So—his coat bedropt with wax,

411. Schelling's way!] Schelling's way— (*H proof*). Blougram suggests that the ability to negotiate between contrary positions is characteristic of the philosophy of Schelling. For B.'s probable knowledge of Schelling's philosophy, see head-note, *Sources*.

412. my coming] one's coming (*H proof*, but not *H proof²*).   *the tail of time*: i.e. in latter days; Blougram's concept of belatedness may be seen in one sense as tra-ditional (the Christian belief that most of the time allotted to human history had already expired) and in another as highly modern (the critical self-consciousness which Carlyle and Matthew Arnold regarded as characteristic of the age). See also the headnote to *Cleon* (p. 612).

414. three hundred years ago: according to Blougram, in the mid-16th century there would have been no question of a bishop being an atheist; B.'s own Renaissance bishop, in *Tomb at St. Praxed's* (p. 232), sees no contradiction between his adher-ence to Christianity and his pagan sensualism. Note however that in *Ring*, which is set in the Rome of 1697, B. has the anti-hero Guido scoff at the notion that anyone really subscribes to the doctrines of Christianity (see, e.g., xi 557–80).

415. Blougram] the man (*H proof*).

416. seventy years since: if it were not for 'tail of time' (see l. 412n.) this might be taken as a forecast of the future: 'seventy years from now no one will believe in Christianity any more'; but if the allusion is to the past, it refers to the intel-lectual fashion for free-thinking and religious scepticism in the late 18th century, stimulated by the writings of Hume, Voltaire, and Gibbon. Cp. the subtitle to Sir Walter Scott's *Waverley*: ''Tis Sixty Years Since'.

421. man that write] man who write (*1868–88*).

422. Read . . . think] Think . . . read (*H proof*).

424. bedropt with wax: from carrying candles in Catholic church services and reli-gious processions; cp. Fra Lippo Lippi's description of the gentlemen 'processional and fine' from whom he begs candle-droppings (ll. 117–21, p. 491), and Guido Franceschini's chagrin at being rewarded by his cardinal-patron with 'The unburnt end o' the very candle, Sirs, / Purfled with paint so prettily round and round, / He carried in such state last Peter's-day' (*Ring* v 317–19).

425   All Peter's chains about his waist, his back
       Brave with the needlework of Noodledom,
       Believes! Again, who wonders and who cares?
       But I, the man of sense and learning too,
       The able to think yet act, the this, the that,
430   I, to believe at this late time of day!
       Enough; you see, I need not fear contempt.

       —Except it's yours! admire me as these may,
       You don't. But what at least do you admire?
       Present your own perfections, your ideal,
435   Your pattern man for a minute—oh, make haste!
       Is it Napoleon you would have us grow?
       Concede the means; allow his head and hand,
       (A large concession, clever as you are)
       Good!—In our common primal element

424–6. The church of San Pietro in Vincoli (in Latin 'ad Vincula', i.e. 'in Chains')
in Rome is a basilica (see l. 4), originally built in the 5th century to house the
relic of the two chains with which St Peter was bound in Jerusalem (*Acts* xii 6);
when these chains were delivered to Pope Leo I they fused miraculously with
those which had bound St Peter in Rome. Markus (headnote, *Background*) suggests an allusion to Lord Fielding, a convert whose devotion to his new faith was
highlighted by Mahony (Father Prout) in *The Globe* of 29 Jan. 1851: ' "Lord Fielding
is making his round of devotional pilgrimages here. Yesterday he visited the church
of St. Peter *ad vincula*, and at his request the chains of the Apostle were placed
on his neck" ' (cited p. 192). Cp. also W. E. Aytoun's review of George Borrow's
Lavengro in *Blackwood's* (see *Sources*): 'Pious young noblemen, whose perversion
is only of a few weeks' standing, have already laid in such a stock of exuberant
faith, that all Europe rings with the fame of their pilgrimages; and the chain in
the church of St Peter ad Vincula has already been suspended around more than
one English neck, in token of the entire submission of the proselytes to the spiritual yoke of Rome' (*Blackwood's* lxix [1851] 322). Note also that the Chapel Royal
of St Peter ad Vincula is the parish church of the Tower of London.
426. *needlework of Noodledom*: the 'needlework' would be an ornamented livery
connected with a sacred office; Blougram associates the supporters of traditional
Catholic belief and forms of worship with 'Noodledom', the social compound
of silly, unthinking, or superstitious believers; cp. *Two Poets of Croisic* (1878) 854–5:
' "Ninnies stock Noodledom, but folk more sage / Resist contagious folly, never
fear!" ' 'Noodle' and its variants had been popular terms of abuse since the Regency
period, and the 'House of Noodles' was a slang term for the House of Lords.
431^432.] no line space in *1868*.
432. *Except*: unless.
433. *But what*] But whom (*1863–88*).
434. *your own perfections*] your own perfection (*1868–88*).
435. *a minute*] a moment (*1863²*), a rare example of a substantive variant unique
to this ed.

440   Of unbelief (we can't believe, you know—
       We're still at that admission, recollect)
       Where do you find—apart from, towering-o'er
       The secondary temporary aims
       Which satisfy the gross tastes you despise—
445   Where do you find his star?—his crazy trust
       God knows through what or in what? it's alive
       And shines and leads him and that's all we want.
       Have we aught in our sober night shall point
       Such ends as his were, and direct the means
450   Of working out our purpose straight as his,
       Nor bring a moment's trouble on success
       With after-care to justify the same?
       —Be a Napoleon and yet disbelieve!
       Why, the man's mad, friend, take his light away.
455   What's the vague good of the world for which you'd
          dare
       With comfort to yourself blow millions up?
       We neither of us see it! we do see
       The blown-up millions—spatter of their brains

441. *at that admission*] at that concession (*H proof*).
442. *towering-o'er*] towering o'er (*1863–88*, except *1863²*, which agrees with *1855*); the reading is in *H proof*, and B. is fond of compound words.
444. *the gross tastes*] the gross taste (*1868–88*).
445. *his star:* his guiding destiny; combining the sense that Napoleon had been born under a particular astrological sign with the concept of a personal inspiration leading to great deeds or achievements. Cp. the 'star' or 'orb' for which Palma yearns in *Sordello* (iii 309–22, I 544). For a different use of the 'star' image, and for its general importance in B.'s work, see headnote to *My Star* (III 386).
446–7. *it's alive / And shines*] it's alive, / It shines (*H proof; H proof²* has the punctuation variant in l. 446, but not the verbal variant in l. 447).
450. *straight as his*] straight as he (*H proof*).
451–2. Blougram suggests that one's 'success' would be compromised by any retrospective anxiety to justify the means used to achieve it, an anxiety from which Napoleon was free.
454. *take his light away:* with 'if' understood, i.e. if you discount Napoleon's guiding 'star', the only explanation for his conduct would be madness.
455–75. The argument here anticipates that deployed by Prince Hohenstiel-Schwangau (a fictitious portrait of Napoleon III, nephew of Napoleon) to justify his career of compromise. *Prince Hohenstiel-Schwangau* was publ. in 1871, after Napoleon III's abdication; at the time of writing of *Bishop Blougram*, Napoleon III had taken power in a *coup d'état* witnessed by the Brownings during a period of residence in Paris in 1851, and made himself Emperor in 1852. Cp. headnote to *Lovers' Quarrel* (p. 376).
455. *of the world*] o' the world (*1888*).   *you'd dare*] you dare (*1868–88*).

And writhing of their bowels and so forth,
460 In that bewildering entanglement
Of horrible eventualities
Past calculation to the end of time!
Can I mistake for some clear word of God
(Which were my ample warrant for it all)
465 His puff of hazy instincts, idle talk,
"The state, that's I," quack-nonsense about kings,
And (when one beats the man to his last hold)
The vague idea of setting things to rights,
Policing people efficaciously,
470 More to their profit, most of all to his own;
The whole to end that dismallest of ends
By an Austrian marriage, cant to us the church,
And resurrection of the old *régime*.

463. some clear word of God: the notion that a person can be directly inspired by God is common in B. in both positive and negative forms. Paracelsus satirizes the facile readiness of religious people to claim knowledge of God's will, as if it were 'character'd / On the heaven's vault', whereas the truth is that God's purpose is inscrutable, and human 'doubts are many and faith is weak' (iii 511–24, I 214–15); Caponsacchi's reliance on divine inspiration to justify his unorthox behaviour is a matter of debate in *Ring*, impugned by sceptics but half-endorsed by the Pope (see *Ring* x 1912–42).

464. ample warrant: a phrase used by the Duke in *My Last Duchess* (l. 50, II 160).

465. hazy instincts] hazy instinct (*1865–88*).

466. The state, that's I: 'L'État c'est moi', said not by Napoleon but (allegedly) by his equally autocratic predecessor Louis XIV before the Parlement de Paris, 13 Apr. 1655. The mistake is almost certainly Blougram's and not B.'s. "*The state*] "The State (*1863–88*). *about kings*] about Fate (*H proof*); about crowns (*1863–88*, except *1863²* which agrees with *1855*).

467. hold: stronghold, refuge.

468. The vague idea] A vague idea (*1863–88*).

470. to his own;] to his, (*H proof*).

471. to end: with 'in' understood, i.e. after all Napoleon's talk of radical change, he reverted to traditional monarchical and clerical ideas (see next note).

472. After his divorce from Josephine in 1809, Napoleon married the Archduchess Marie-Louise, daughter of the Emperor of Austria, thus allying himself with the Habsburgs, the pre-eminent European dynasty. Napoleon's rapprochement with the Catholic Church (in contrast to the strong anti-clericalism of the French Revolution) was symbolized by the presence of Pope Pius VII at his coronation as Emperor in 1804; Blougram's sarcastic phrase 'cant to us the Church' implies that he thought Napoleon's motives less than spiritual.
us the church] us the Church (*1863–88*).

473. Alluding to Napoleon's re-establishment of the hereditary principle for the monarchy, and his creation of an aristocratic order, although Blougram is not quite correct in saying that the latter was equivalent to the pre-Revolutionary nobility; the legitimacy of Napoleonic titles remained a matter of dispute in France.

Would I, who hope to live a dozen years,
475   Fight Austerlitz for reasons such and such?
No: for, concede me but the merest chance
Doubt may be wrong—there's judgment, life to come!
With just that chance, I dare not. Doubt proves right?
This present life is all? you offer me
480   Its dozen noisy years with not a chance
That wedding an Arch-Duchess, wearing lace,
And getting called by divers new-coined names,
Will drive off ugly thoughts and let me dine,
Sleep, read and chat in quiet as I like!
Therefore, I will not.

485   Take another case;
Fit up the cabin yet another way.
What say you to the poet's? shall we write
Hamlets, Othellos—make the world our own,

475. Austerlitz: battle in which Napoleon defeated the Austrians and Russians on 2 Dec. 1805; there were nearly 7,000 French, and over 12,000 allied casualties.
477. life to come!] life to come—(*H proof*).
479. life is all?] life is all—(*H proof*),
480.] Its dozen years with not a chance at all (*H proof*). *with not a chance*] without a chance (*1863–88*).
481. an Arch-Duchess] an arch-duchess (*1865–88*).
482. divers new-coined names] half a dozen names (*H proof*); Napoleon was successively First Consul (1798), Consul for Life (1802), and Emperor (1804).
487. to the poet's?] to the poets? (*1865–88*).
487–8. shall we write / Hamlets, Othellos: cp. B. to EBB., 6 May 1846, remembering an incident from 1837: 'But of all accusations in the world .. what do you say to my having been asked if I was not the author of Romeo & Juliet, and Othello? A man actually asked me that, as I sate in Covent Garden Pit to see the second representation of "Strafford"—I supposed he had been *set on* by somebody .. but the simple face looked too quiet for that impertinence—I was muffled up in a cloak, too,—so I said "no—so far as I am aware". (His question was, "is not THIS Mr Browning the author of &c &c") After the play, all was made clear by somebody in Macready's dressing room—two burlesques on Shakespeare *were* in the course of performance at some minor theatre by a Mr Brown, or Brownley, or something Brown-like—and to these my friend had alluded. So is begot, so nourished "*il mondan rumore*"—I, author of Othello!' (*Correspondence* xii 305). The phrase 'il mondan romore' [*sic*, 'worldly fame'] appears in Dante's *Purgatorio* xi 100; for another allusion to this passage, see *Old Pictures* 180n. (p. 423).
488. Hamlets, Othellos] Hamlet, Othello (*H proof*).

Without a risk to run of either sort?
490 I can't!—to put the strongest reason first.
"But try," you urge, "the trying shall suffice:
The aim, if reached or not, makes great the life.
Try to be Shakspeare, leave the rest to fate!"
Spare my self-knowledge—there's no fooling me!
495 If I prefer remaining my poor self,
I say so not in self-dispraise but praise.
If I'm a Shakspeare, let the well alone—
Why should I try to be what now I am?
If I'm no Shakspeare, as too probable,—
500 His power and consciousness and self-delight
And all we want in common, shall I find—
Trying for ever? while on points of taste
Wherewith, to speak it humbly, he and I
Are dowered alike—I'll ask you, I or he,
505 Which in our two lives realises most?
Much, he imagined—somewhat, I possess.
He had the imagination; stick to that!
Let him say "In the face of my soul's works
Your world is worthless and I touch it not
510 Lest I should wrong them"—I withdraw my plea.
But does he say so? look upon his life!

---

493. Shakspeare] Shakespeare (*1863–88*); also ll. 497, 499, 521, 528, 539. The *1855* spelling was common in the period: it occurs in Hazlitt's essay cited below.

495–6. Cp. Hazlitt, 'On Personal Identity' (*The Plain Speaker*, 1826): 'In thinking of those one might wish to have been, many people will exclaim, "Surely, you would like to have been Shakspeare?" Would Garrick have consented to the change? No, nor should he.' See also ll. 528–32n.

497. let the well alone: 'let what is well alone'.

499. no Shakspeare] not Shakspeare (*H proof*, but not *H proof²*).

501. all we want in common: i.e. everything that you (Gigadibs) and I share the lack of (in comparison with Shakespeare).

504. dowered: endowed or gifted with.

505. realises: in *J.*'s sense of 'bring into being or act', i.e. converting the taste for something into the possession of it. For the Carlylean echo of 'realised ideals', see l. 8on.

510. I withdraw my plea] I should yield my cause (*H proof*); I'll withdraw my plea (*1863–88*).

511. look upon his life: B. owned a copy of Charles Knight's *Pictorial Edition of the Works of Shakspere* (see headnote, *Sources*), the last volume of which consists of a biography of Shakespeare, upon which B. drew for the details of Shakespeare's life (see ll. 514n., 550n., 551n.).

Himself, who only can, gives judgment there.
He leaves his towers and gorgeous palaces
To build the trimmest house in Stratford town;
515   Saves money, spends it, owns the worth of things,
Guilio Romano's pictures, Dowland's lute;
Enjoys a show, respects the puppets, too,
And none more, had he seen its entry once,
Than "Pandulph, of fair Milan cardinal."
520   Why then should I who play that personage,
The very Pandulph Shakspeare's fancy made,
Be told that had the poet chanced to start
From where I stand now (some degree like mine
Being just the goal he ran his race to reach)
525   He would have run the whole race back, forsooth,
And left being Pandulph, to begin write plays?
Ah, the earth's best can be but the earth's best!

513. towers and gorgeous palaces: from Prospero's speech in *The Tempest*: 'The cloud-capp'd tow'rs, the gorgeous palaces, / The solemn temples, the great globe itself, / Yea, all which it inherit, shall dissolve' (IV i 152–4).

514. the trimmest house: New Place, Shakespeare's house in Stratford, purchased in 1597. According to Knight, Shakespeare '[invested] the gains of his profession in the purchase of property at Stratford' between 1597 and 1605: 'he improved his worldly advantages with that rare good sense which formed so striking a feature in the whole character of his mind' (viii 477, 481–2).

515. owns: acknowledges (not possesses, in contrast to Blougram).

516. Giulio Romano's pictures: Giulio Romano (?1499–1546) was a pupil of Raphael who became one of the foremost painters and architects of the Mannerist school. Shakespeare praises him, not as a painter but as a sculptor, in *The Winter's Tale* as 'that rare Italian master' (V ii 97); he may have influenced the character of Jules in *Pippa* (see headnote, p. 88).   *Dowland's lute*: John Dowland (1562–1626) was the greatest lutanist of his day. Poem viii of *The Passionate Pilgrim* (1599), a collection which used to be ascribed to Shakespeare, contains the lines: 'Dowland to thee is dear, whose heavenly touch / Upon the lute doth ravish human sense'; this poem is actually by Richard Barnfield (1574–1627). Blougram's allusions may have a hint of salaciousness: Giulio Romano was forced to flee from Rome after designing pornographic prints, and some of the verses in *The Passionate Pilgrim* would have been thought obscene in B.'s day. Cp. ll. 907–8n.

517. Enjoys a show] Would see a show (*H proof*).

518–19. And none more . . . Than "Pandulph] None more than . . . "I, Pandulph (*H proof*). On the significance of Pandulph and the play in which he appears, *King John*, see headnote, *Sources*.

520. I who play] one who plays (*H proof*).

521. Shakspeare's fancy made] Shakspeare made so fine (*H proof*).

522–4. Cp. the metaphor in *Old Pictures*: 'When mankind ran and reached the goal / This much had the earth to show *in fructu*' (ll. 83–4, p. 415).

       Did Shakspeare live, he could but sit at home
       And get himself in dreams the Vatican,
530   Greek busts, Venetian paintings, Roman walls,
       And English books, none equal to his own,
       Which I read, bound in gold, (he never did).
       —Terni and Naples' bay and Gothard's top—
       Eh, friend? I could not fancy one of these—
535   But, as I pour this claret, there they are—
       I've gained them—crossed St. Gothard last July
       With ten mules to the carriage and a bed
       Slung inside; is my hap the worse for that?
       We want the same things, Shakspeare and myself,
540   And what I want, I have: he, gifted more,

528–32. Cp. another passage from Hazlitt's essay 'On Personal Identity' (see ll. 495–6n.): 'By becoming Shakspeare in reality we cut ourselves out of reading Milton, Pope, Dryden, and a thousand more—all of whom we have in our possession, enjoy and *are*, by turns, in the best part of them, their thoughts, without any metamorphosis or miracle at all.' Blougram's argument vulgarizes Hazlitt by replacing the pleasure of reading literature produced after Shakespeare's time with the enjoyment of material wealth (including the reading of luxury editions of Shakespeare's own work). There is also an analogy with Cleon's praise of his own belatedness (ll. 64–72, p. 572).

530. Venetian paintings] Venetian painting (*H proof*).

532. I read . . . (he never did)] I have . . . (he never had) (*H proof*).

533. Well-known European beauty-spots, which Blougram will have visited either in his official capacity or as a wealthy tourist. *Terni*: a town in Umbria, still at this period part of the Papal States, which the Brownings visited in Nov. 1853. *Naples' bay*: B. had visited Naples in 1844 and would also have known the poems by Byron and Shelley ('Ode to Naples') in which the bay is celebrated; Naples is the home of Monsignor in *Pippa Passes* iv (pp. 158–67). *Gothard's top*: the alpine pass of Mont St Gothard (between Switzerland and Italy); the Brownings travelled from Venice to Lucerne via this pass in June 1851: '[We] talk of seeing Como, and of passing into Switzerland by St Goatherd [sic] rather than the Splugen. People tell us that we shall see more of the glory of the Swiss lakes that way' (*EBB to Arabella* i 378).

533. —Terni and Naples' bay] Terni's fall, Naples' bay (*1868–88*).

535. as I pour this claret: see ll. 1–2n. Claret was not definitively identified with red wine from Bordeaux at this period; *OED* cites a history of wine publ. in 1836 to the effect that in England claret 'is a mixture of Bordeaux with Benicarlo, or with some full wine of France'. The fact that the worldly and successful Bishop mentions Keats's favourite drink in the context of a disparaging reflection on the rewards of a literary life points to an analogy with the closing lines of *Popularity*, in which 'claret crowns [the] cup' of one of the true poet's derivative successors (l. 62n., p. 455).

536. I've gained them] I've seen them (*H proof*, but not *H proof²*).

538. hap: fate, lot in life.

Could fancy he too had it when he liked,
But not so thoroughly that if fate allowed
He would not have it also in my sense.
We play one game. I send the ball aloft
545   No less adroitly that of fifty strokes
Scarce five go o'er the wall so wide and high
Which sends them back to me: I wish and get.
He struck balls higher and with better skill,
But at a poor fence level with his head,
550   And hit—his Stratford house, a coat of arms,
Successful dealings in his grain and wool,—
While I receive heaven's incense in my nose
And style myself the cousin of Queen Bess.

541. Could fancy he too] Can fancy that he (*H proof*).   *had it*] had them (*1888*).
542–3. That is, Shakespeare's imaginative possession of material things would not
have been so satisfying as to prevent him from taking real possession of them if
he had had the chance.
542. that if fate] that when fate (*H proof,* but not *H proof²*).   *allowed*] allows (*H proof*).
543. have it also] have them also (*1888*).
544–54. The 'game' is not a recognized sport, although it clearly relates to fives or
racquets, the ancestors of squash. Blougram's point is that, although a less skilful
player at the game of life than Shakespeare (cp. l. 540), he plays for more substantial rewards and so can afford to be profligate with his efforts. The argument
resembles that of *A Grammarian* (e.g. ll. 113–20, pp. 595–6). As Blougram goes on
to emphasize, he and Shakespeare can only be thought to 'play one game' on
the assumption that 'this life's all', i.e. that worldly success is the chief good of life.
546. Scarce] Not (*H proof*).
550. his Stratford house . . . a coat of arms: B.'s information comes from Knight's
Pictorial Edition (see headnote, *Sources*); for the Stratford house, see above, l. 514n.
According to Knight, John Shakspere [sic], the playwright's father, was granted
a coat of arms in 1568 or 1569, 'which shield or coat of arms was confirmed by
William Dethick, Garter, principal King of Arms, in 1596' (viii 6).
551. grain and wool: Knight mentions a 'plea of debt' entered by Shakespeare in
1604 'against Philip Rogers, for the sum of thirty-five shillings and ten-pence,
for corn delivered', and concludes that 'William Shakspere [sic], at the very period
when his dramas were calling forth the rapturous applause of the new Sovereign
and his Court, and when he himself, as it would seem, was ambitious of a courtly
office, did not disdain to pursue the humble though honourable occupation of
a farmer in Stratford, and to exercise his just rights of property in connexion with
that occupation' (viii 479).
552. Cp. *Tomb at St. Praxed's* 83–4: 'And feel the steady candle-flame, and taste
/ Good strong thick stupifying incense-smoke!' (p. 242).
553. Ohio suggests that Blougram would have been able to 'style himself' the
'cousin' of Queen Bess [Queen Elizabeth I] 'because he would have represented
a fellow-sovereign, the Pope.' Cp. *OED* sense 5 a: 'Used by a sovereign in addressing or formally naming another sovereign'.

Ask him, if this life's all, who wins the game?

555   Believe—and our whole argument breaks up.
Enthusiasm's the best thing, I repeat;
Only, we can't command it; fire and life
Are all, dead matter's nothing, we agree:
And be it a mad dream or God's very breath,
560   The fact's the same,—belief's fire once in us,
Makes of all else mere stuff to show itself.
We penetrate our life with such a glow
As fire lends wood and iron—this turns steel,
That burns to ash—all's one, fire proves its power
565   For good or ill, since men call flare success.
But paint a fire, it will not therefore burn.
Light one in me, I'll find it food enough!
Why, to be Luther—that's a life to lead,
Incomparably better than my own.
570   He comes, reclaims God's earth for God, he says,
Sets up God's rule again by simple means,
Re-opens a shut book, and all is done.
He flared out in the flaring of mankind;
Such Luther's luck was—how shall such be mine?
575   If he suceeded, nothing's left to do:

559–65. The 'fire' of belief may be divinely inspired and therefore creative, or delusory and therefore destructive, but either way its power is demonstrated (and, Blougram adds, people don't distinguish between 'good' and 'bad' outcomes, since what they value is the 'flare', i.e. the excitement and energy which come from the display of power).

561. show itself.] show itself: (*H proof, 1863–88*). Although not of great significance in itself, this variant is a rare example of a return to the proof reading in eds. after *1855*.

562. We penetrate] You penetrate (*H proof*, but not *H proof²*); It penetrates (*1863²*). This is a rare example of a substantive variant unique to *1863²*; it comes in a reading over which B. clearly hesitated in proof.

564. proves its power] proves itself (*H proof*).

568–9. Blougram is being especially 'daring' and heterodox in expressing admiration for the instigator of the Protestant Reformation (but see below, ll. 920–32). For B.'s lifelong admiration for Martin Luther, see *Paracelsus* iii 994–7 (I 236); also *Twins* (III 656).

570–2. Blougram gives a summary of the programme of the Reformation, namely to deny the secular authority of the Church, to reform ecclesiastical hierarchy and abolish the mediating power of the priest, and to base faith on the Bible ('a shut book') translated into the vernacular.

573. He flared out in] He could enjoy (*H proof*); the sense is that Luther embodied the spirit of the age.

And if he did not altogether—well,
Strauss is the next advance. All Strauss should be
I might be also. But to what result?
He looks upon no future: Luther did.
580 What can I gain on the denying side?
Ice makes no conflagration. State the facts,
Read the text right, emancipate the world—
The emancipated world enjoys itself
With scarce a thank-you—Blougram told it first
585 It could not owe a farthing,—not to him
More than St. Paul! 'twould press its pay, you think?
Then add there's still that plaguey hundredth chance
Strauss may be wrong. And so a risk is run—
For what gain? not for Luther's, who secured
590 A real heaven in his heart throughout his life,
Supposing death a little altered things!

577. *Strauss*: David Friedrich Strauss (1808–74), author of *Das Leben Jesu* (*The Life of Jesus*), one of the leading texts of the 'Higher Criticism' of the Bible, which denied the supernatural element in Christianity and exposed contradictions in the gospel accounts; it had been translated by George Eliot in 1846. For details of B.'s knowledge of Strauss's work, see headnotes to *CE & ED* (III 43–4) and *A Death* (pp. 719–21).
579. Cp. the despair ascribed to the 'Second Speaker' of the *Epilogue* to *DP* (1864), named in later eds. as another of the foremost exponents of the 'Higher Criticism' of the Bible, Ernest Renan.
581–6. Blougram argues that if he adopted and promoted an enlightened, rational attitude to religion, he would be undermining his worldly position: if he informed people that they did not need the Church to mediate between themselves and God, they would have no reason to fund the Church (and his expensive lifestyle).
584. *With scarce*] With just (*H proof*, but not *H proof²*).   *Blougram*] since I (*H proof*; *H proof²* has 'Since I').
585. *not to him*] not to me (*H proof*).
591. I.e., '[even] supposing death a little altered things'. Blougram suggests a prudential calculation about the value of belief as opposed to rational scepticism: whether there is an afterlife or not, it is better to believe (or profess to believe) in one. Luther really believed, and his inner life was enriched by his belief; Blougram professes belief, and his material life is enriched. If death means oblivion, both Luther and Blougram will have had the benefit of their belief, whereas someone like Strauss will have made his life desolate for nothing. This argument recalls 'le pari de Pascal' ('Pascal's wager'), put forward in the *Pensées* (1670). 'If God exists, then it is clearly better [to believe in Him]: infinitely better, given the prospect of eternal bliss for believers, and eternal damnation for non-believers. If God does not exist, we lose nothing . . . So belief is the dominant strategy. It can win, and cannot lose. The wager is "infini-rien": infinity to nothing' (*Oxford Dictionary of Philosophy*). The entry cites a comment by Coleridge which B. may well have known, and which is pertinent to Blougram's sectarian advocacy of Roman Catholicism and to his self-centredness: 'He who begins by loving Christianity

"Ay, but since really I lack faith," you cry,
"I run the same risk really on all sides,
In cool indifference as bold unbelief.
595   As well be Strauss as swing 'twixt Paul and him.
It's not worth having, such imperfect faith,
Nor more available to do faith's work
Than unbelief like yours. Whole faith, or none!"

Softly, my friend! I must dispute that point.
600   Once own the use of faith, I'll find you faith.
We're back on Christian ground. You call for faith:
I show you doubt, to prove that faith exists.
The more of doubt, the stronger faith, I say,
If faith o'ercomes doubt. How I know it does?
605   By life and man's free will, God gave for that!
To mould life as we choose it, shows our choice:
That's our one act, the previous work's His own.

---

better than Truth, will proceed by loving his own sect or Church better than
Christianity, and in the end loving himself better than all.'
592–8. The personal pronouns are centred on Blougram rather than Gigadibs,
i.e. 'I' refers to Blougram while 'you' and 'yours' refer to Gigadibs. The inverted
commas are somewhat misleading: what looks like a direct quotation is in fact
indirect speech. B. evidently concluded that the syntax was awkward, as the revisions in *1863–88* show.
592–3. I lack . . . I run] you lack . . . You run (*1863–88*).
595. Paul: St Paul; here used as an emblem of 'belief' in opposition to the scepticism of Strauss.
596.] Myself, for instance, have imperfect faith, (*H proof*).
597. Nor more] No more (*H proof*, but not *H proof²*, *1868–88*), a rare example of
a return to a proof reading in eds. after 1855.
598. like yours] like mine (*1863–88*).
603–4. Cp. Tennyson, *In Memoriam* (1850) xcvi 9–21: 'Perplext in faith, but
pure in deeds, / At last he beat his music out. / There lives more faith in
honest doubt, / Believe me, than in half the creeds. // He fought his doubts
and gather'd strength, / He would not make his judgment blind, / He faced the
spectres of the mind / And laid them: thus he came at length // To find a stronger
faith his own; / And power was with him in the night, / Which makes the darkness and the light, / And dwells not in the light alone, // But in the darkness
and the cloud'. The Brownings read *In Memoriam* together soon after its publication in 1850: 'We have been reading together Tennyson's "In Memoriam" in
the evenings. Most beautiful and pathetic. I read aloud, Robert looking over the
page—and we talked and admired and criticised every separate stanza' (16–19 Dec.
1850; *EBB to Arabella* i 360).
606–7. Cp. *Prince Hohenstiel-Schwangau* (1871) 120–5: 'I,—not He,— / Live, think,
do human work here—no machine, / His will moves, but a being by myself, /
His, and not He who made me for a work, / Watches my working, judges its
effect, / But does not interpose'.

You criticise the soil? it reared this tree—
This broad life and whatever fruit it bears!
610 What matter though I doubt at every pore,
Head-doubts, heart-doubts, doubts at my fingers' ends,
Doubts in the trivial work of every day,
Doubts at the very bases of my soul
In the grand moments when she probes herself—
615 If finally I have a life to show,
The thing I did, brought out in evidence
Against the thing done to me underground
By Hell and all its brood, for aught I know?
I say, whence sprang this? shows it faith or doubt?
620 All's doubt in me; where's break of faith in this?
It is the idea, the feeling and the love
God means mankind should strive for and show forth,
Whatever be the process to that end,—
And not historic knowledge, logic sound,
625 And metaphysical acumen, sure!
"What think ye of Christ," friend? when all's done and
    said,
You like this Christianity or not?
It may be false, but will you wish it true?
Has it your vote to be so if it can?

608–19. Cp. *Matthew* vii 16–20: 'Ye shall know them by their fruits. Do men gather grapes of thorns, or figs of thistles? Even so every good tree bringeth forth good fruit; but a corrupt tree bringeth forth evil fruit. . . . Every tree that bringeth not forth good fruit is hewn down, and cast into the fire. Wherefore by their fruits ye shall know them.' Blougram argues that what matters in life is the result of belief in God, not the 'process' by which this has been brought about; his struggle against 'Hell and all its brood' remains hidden from view.

620. 'In me' means 'inside me', i.e. the internal struggle in Blougram's mind or soul; 'this' refers to his actual life, 'the thing I did' (l. 616).

621–5. Cp. Wordsworth, 'Tintern Abbey', ll. 77–84: 'The sounding cataract / Haunted me like a passion: the tall rock / The mountain, and the deep and gloomy wood, / Their colours and their forms, were then to me / An appetite: a feeling and a love, / That had no need of a remoter charm, / By thought supplied, or any interest / Unborrowed from the eye.' Blougram argues that 'the feeling and the love' implied by Christianity are more important than defensible intellectual arguments in its favour.

625. *acumen*: the stress must fall on the second syllable to make the line metrical.

626. Cp. *Matthew* xxii 41–2: 'While the Pharisees were gathered together, Jesus asked them, saying, What think ye of Christ?'

627. *You like*] Like you (*1863–88*).

630   Trust you an instinct silenced long ago
       That will break silence and enjoin you love
       What mortified philosophy is hoarse,
       And all in vain, with bidding you despise?
       If you desire faith—then you've faith enough.
635   What else seeks God—nay, what else seek ourselves?
       You form a notion of me, we'll suppose,
       On hearsay; it's a favourable one:
       "But still" (you add), "there was no such good man,
       Because of contradictions in the facts.
640   One proves, for instance, he was born in Rome,
       This Blougram—yet throughout the tales of him
       I see he figures as an Englishman."
       Well, the two things are reconcileable.
       But would I rather you discovered that,
645   Subjoining—"Still, what matter though they be?
       Blougram concerns me nought, born here or there."

       Pure faith indeed—you know not what you ask!
       Naked belief in God the Omnipotent,
       Omniscient, Omnipresent, sears too much
650   The sense of conscious creatures to be borne.

---

630. an instinct silenced long ago: instinctive or unquestioning religious faith has been suppressed in the face of scientific rationalism ('long ago' is a relative term, referring here to the life of a typical modern individual, not to a particular historical period).
632. What: 'That which', i.e. Christianity.   *mortified philosophy*: the primary sense is that philosophy is shamed and humiliated by its failure to eradicate faith; but the term also borrows ironically from the Christian vocabulary of asceticism and self-denial (the 'mortification of the flesh'): philosophy is cold, austere, and life-denying in contrast to the 'fire' of faith. For an extended treatment of this opposition, see *Christmas-Eve* 649 ff. (III 73–5)
635. What else seeks God: 'What else does God seek'.
638–43. A pastiche of the Straussian method of analysis, which demonstrates (for example) that Jesus was almost certainly born in Nazareth, not Bethlehem, and suggests that the sequence of events described in the Bible is an unhistorical attempt to comply with mythological precepts about the Messiah's lineage and place of birth. Blougram argues that such apparent discrepancies are 'reconcileable', but that they are less important than the imaginary speaker's general attitude. There may also be an allusion here to Wiseman's origins: he was born in Spain of Irish parents.
639. contradictions] contradiction (*1868–88*).
647–61. Compare Karshish's account of Lazarus in *An Epistle* 126 ff. (pp. 518–19). Lazarus does not go mad, but is certainly unbalanced by his premature attainment of complete religious certainty.

It were the seeing him, no flesh shall dare.
Some think, Creation's meant to show him forth:
I say, it's meant to hide him all it can,
And that's what all the blessed Evil's for.
655 Its use in time is to environ us,
Our breath, our drop of dew, with shield enough
Against that sight till we can bear its stress.
Under a vertical sun, the exposed brain
And lidless eye and disemprisoned heart
660 Less certainly would wither up at once
Than mind, confronted with the truth of Him.
But time and earth case-harden us to live;

---

651. Cp. God's words to Moses in *Exodus* xxxiii 20: 'Thou canst not see my face: for there shall no man see me, and live.' There is also an allusion to the myth of Semele, who asked her lover Zeus to reveal himself to her in his divine form, and was destroyed as a result; the story is in Ovid, *Metamorphoses* iii 254–321. Sir John Hanmer, whose poems B. knew and admired, has the following couplet in 'Proteus', ll. 88–9: 'The world would gaze on Reason face to face, / Then burns like Semele in Jove's embrace' (*Fra Cipolla and Other Poems*, 1839).

652. Alluding both to ancient belief (e.g. *Psalms* xix 1: 'The heavens declare the glory of God; and the firmament sheweth his handywork') and to the modern doctrine of 'natural theology', which held that the existence and beneficence of God could be inferred from the design of the universe and the natural world without the need for a special revelation.

654. blessed Evil's: Blougram's mild expletive produces a startling oxymoron, but one which also articulates the doctrine that evil has no independent existence, but is part of God's providential design.

656. Our breath, our drop of dew: traditional images for human life, and also for the soul, as in *Fra Lippo* 184–6 (p. 495) and *An Epistle* 6 (p. 511); B. may have had in mind Marvell's poem 'On a Drop of Dew', in which the human soul is compared to 'the Orient Dew, / Shed from the Bosom of the Morn' (1–2).

658–61. One's mind would be even more certain to be destroyed by direct contact with God than one's organs (brain, eye, heart) would be if exposed without a layer of skin to the full glare of the sun. Cp. EBB.'s poetic drama 'The Seraphim' (1837): 'Or, brother, what if on thine eyes / In vision bare should rise / The life-fount whence his hand did gather / With solitary force / Our immortalities! / Straightway how thine own would wither, / Falter like a human breath, / By gazing on its source!' (i 88–96). B. may also have recalled EBB.'s sonnet 'Grief' (1844): 'Full desertness, / In souls as countries, lieth silent-bare / Under the blanching, vertical eye-glare / Of the absolute Heavens' (ll. 5–8).

659.] The lidless eye, the disemprisoned heart, (*H proof*). *disemprisoned*: freed (from the 'cage' of the ribs).

661. Than mind] Than we (*H proof*).

662. time and earth] Time and Earth (*H proof*). *case-harden us*: harden us on the surface, develop a tough shell (enabling us to bear life). Cp. *Fifine at the Fair* (1872) 1777–8: 'we must learn to live / Case-hardened at all points, not bare and

> The feeblest sense is trusted most; the child
> Feels God a moment, ichors o'er the place,
665 Plays on and grows to be a man like us.
> With me, faith means perpetual unbelief
> Kept quiet like the snake 'neath Michael's foot
> Who stands calm just because he feels it writhe.
> Or, if that's too ambitious,—here's my box—
670 I need the excitation of a pinch
> Threatening the torpor of the inside-nose
> Nigh on the imminent sneeze that never comes.
> "Leave it in peace" advise the simple folk—
> Make it aware of peace by itching-fits,
675 Say I—let doubt occasion still more faith!

> You'll say, once all believed, man, woman, child,
> In that dear middle-age these noodles praise.

---

sensitive'; the phrase is used more harshly by Paracelsus: 'men have oft grown old among their books / And died, case-harden'd in their ignorance' (i 757–8, I 147).

664. *ichors o'er the place*: 'covers the wound with a healing balm (of forgetfulness or indifference)'; this sense of 'ichor', and its use as a verb, is B.'s invention (not rec. in *OED*); in classical myth, 'ichor' referred to the blood of the gods. Blougram may be implying that God himself supplies the means by which the 'wound' of direct contact with him is alleviated. The notion that children have a special faculty for apprehending the divine has Platonic, Christian, and Romantic associations, active here in the form of a glancing allusion to Wordsworth's 'Ode: Intimations of Immortality from Recollections in Early Childhood'.

667. The Archangel Michael is traditionally represented in art as trampling on Satan in the form of a serpent, an image from *Revelation* xii 7–9: 'And there was war in heaven: Michael and his angels fought against the dragon; and the dragon fought and his angels, and prevailed not . . . And the great dragon was cast out, that old serpent, called the devil, and Satan, which deceiveth the whole world'. *Florentine* suggests that B. might have had Raphael's *St Michael and the Dragon* in mind (both versions of which are in the Louvre); *Thomas* in contrast argues that two paintings mentioned by Mrs Jameson in her *Sacred and Legendary Art* are closer to B.'s description: a St Michael by Innocenza da Imola in the Brera Gallery in Milan, and another by a Flemish artist in the Pinakothek (i 422).

669. *box*: snuff-box; in a letter to Julia Wedgwood of 31 Oct. 1864, B. wrote: 'there happens to be a spice in me of the snuff-taker's vice, love of sub-irritation,—mild pugnaciousness' (*RB & JW* 108).

675.] Say I—give still occasion for more faith! (*H proof*).

676. *You'll say, once*] Why, once we (*H proof*).

677. The 'noodles' are the supporters of 'Young England' and other such groups whose medievalism embraced art, politics, and social policy: cp. l. 426n.

How you'd exult if I could put you back
Six hundred years, blot out cosmogony,
680   Geology, ethnology, what not,
(Greek endings with the little passing-bell
That signifies some faith's about to die)
And set you square with Genesis again,—
When such a traveller told you his last news,
685   He saw the ark a-top of Ararat
But did not climb there since 'twas getting dusk
And robber-bands infest the mountain's foot!
How should you feel, I ask, in such an age,
How act? As other people felt and did;
690   With soul more blank than this decanter's knob,
Believe—and yet lie, kill, rob, fornicate
Full in belief's face, like the beast you'd be!

No, when the fight begins within himself
A man's worth something. God stoops o'er his head,

678–83. Blougram refers to advances in science and thought leading to religious scepticism, and in particular challenges to biblical 'cosmogony' (the account of creation). The most revolutionary of these changes before Darwin (whose *Origin of Species* had not been publ. when the poem was written) concerned geology and the age of the earth, which called into question the traditional chronology of *Genesis*: Blougram is probably thinking of such works as Charles Lyell's *Principles of Geology* (1839) and Robert Chambers's *Vestiges of the Natural History of Creation* (1844); cp. *Saul* 110n. (III 505). Ethnology or anthropology, another of the growth sciences of the period, also implicitly challenged orthodox Christianity by emphasizing common features in the belief systems of different peoples.

681. *Greek endings with*] Greek endings, each (*1868–88*). Words ending in 'ology' derive from the Greek λογια (logia, meaning 'discourse'); the spread of modern, and implicitly anti-Christian, modes of knowledge is linked to the enquiring and sceptical spirit of classical Greek thought. The Bishop is right to imply that these terms are of recent date: *OED* records the first use of 'geology' as 'the science which has for its object the investigation of the earth's crust' in James Hutton's *Theory of the Earth* (1795), and of 'ethnology' in James Prichard's *Natural History of Man* (1843). The three-syllabled 'endings' of the words punningly signify the 'end' of religious faith. In her letter to Eliza Ogilvy of 5 Aug. 1852, EBB. writes: 'I send you a note upon babies, feeling instinctively that babyology will be more welcome to you just now than most other of the *ologies*' (*EBB to Ogilvy* 82).

passing-bell: the church peal rung for the death of a parishioner.
684. *such a traveller*: 'some traveller or other'.
685. Noah's ark is said in *Genesis* viii 3–4 to have grounded on 'the mountains of Ararat' (in modern Turkey) after the waters of the Flood receded.
690. *this decanter's knob*: another reminder of the setting in which this monologue takes place; the knob is 'blank' because made of glass.

695   Satan looks up between his feet—both tug—
        He's left, himself, in the middle: the soul wakes
        And grows. Prolong that battle through his life!
        Never leave growing till the life to come!
        Here, we've got callous to the Virgin's winks
700   That used to puzzle people wholesomely—
        Men have outgrown the shame of being fools.
        What are the laws of Nature, not to bend
        If the Church bid them, brother Newman asks.
        Up with the Immaculate Conception, then—
705   On to the rack with faith—is my advice!
        Will not that hurry us upon our knees
        Knocking our breasts, "It can't be—yet it shall!
        Who am I, the worm, to argue with my Pope?

696. *in the middle*] i' the middle (*1870–88*).
699–700. See l. 377n.
702–3. In the exchange of letters with the Bishop of Norwich printed in *The Times* (see l. 377n.), Newman attempts to defend himself from the charge of credulity by arguing that the miracles of Scripture have increased the 'antecedent probability' of an interruption of the laws of nature, and so added credibility to the disputed miracles of the early church: 'Protestants find a difficulty in even listening to evidence adduced for ecclesiastical miracles. I have none. Why? Because the admitted fact of the scripture miracles has taken away whatever *prima facie* unlikelihood attaches to them as a violation of the laws of nature.'
702. *laws of Nature*] laws of nature (*1868–88*).
704. *Up with*] Out with (*H proof*, but not *H proof²*). *Immaculate Conception*: the belief that the Virgin Mary was conceived without the taint of original sin was a favourite notion of Pius IX's, and became official Catholic doctrine by means of the bull *Ineffabilis Deus*, issued on 8 Dec. 1854. The author of the article on 'The Papal Aggression Bill' in *Blackwood's* lxix (1851) uses the prospect of this addition to doctrine as a way of exposing the fraudulence of the notion of Papal Infallibility: 'The Virgin Mary was, as the infallible present Pope decrees, born without sin; she was miraculously, immaculately conceived; and hence, what follows? Awful to contemplate is this most recently received dogma. She has an altar to her by the side of that to God the Father. The Roman Catholic Church is no longer Trinitarian—it is Quaternian' (p. 586; cp. l. 708n.). The clear understanding of the doctrine here makes unlikely the suggestion in *Turner* and J. Britton (*Explicator* xvii [1959], Item 50) that 'since the context requires something conflicting with "the laws of Nature" (not merely of theology), RB may have confused this doctrine with that of the Virgin Birth'.
705. *the rack*: an instrument of torture in which an individual is stretched, primarily associated in the English mind with the Inquisition.
708. The dogma of 'Papal Infallibility' (according to which the Pope cannot err when he pronounces *ex cathedra* on matters of doctrine) was formally promulgated at the First Vatican Council in 1870, but the concept was already current, and controversial (see l. 704n.); Blougram would be aware of debates within the

      Low things confound the high things!" and so forth.
710   That's better than acquitting God with grace
      As some folks do. He's tried—no case is proved,
      Philosophy is lenient—He may go!

      You'll say—the old system's not so obsolete
      But men believe still: ay, but who and where?
715   King Bomba's lazzaroni foster yet
      The sacred flame, so Antonelli writes;
      But even of these, what ragamuffin-saint
      Believes God watches him continually,
      As he believes in fire that it will burn,
720   Or rain that it will drench him? Break fire's law,
      Sin against rain, although the penalty
      Be just a singe or soaking? No, he smiles;
      Those laws are laws that can enforce themselves.

      The sum of all is—yes, my doubt is great,
725   My faith's the greater—then my faith's enough.
      I have read much, thought much, experienced much,
      Yet would die rather than avow my fear

Catholic Church on the issue, among others to do with the Pope's authority. Cp. *Ring* x 150–1: 'Which of the judgments was infallible? / Which of my predecessors spoke for God?' Vol. IV of *Ring*, which contains bk. x, was publ. in Feb. 1869, two months after the opening of the Council. Cp. also B.'s skit, 'The Dogma Triumphant: Epigram on the Voluntary Imprisonment of the Pope as Proving His Infallibility', which alludes to the fact that the Council was ended in July 1870 by the outbreak of the Franco-Prussian War and the subsequent Italian occupation of the city by King Victor Emmanuel (*Penguin* ii 957).

709. Cp. *Job* v 11 where God is said 'to set up on high those that be low'.

711. As some folks do. He's] As folks do now—He's (*H proof*); As folks do now He's (*H proof²*); As some folk do. He's (*1888*). The lack of punctuation after 'now' in *H proof²* is probably an error, though the sense 'now that He's tried' is grammatically possible.

715–16. Ferdinand II of Naples (1810–59) was known as 'Re Bomba' ('King Bomb') because of his use of bombardment to suppress an uprising in Sicily in 1848. EBB. refers to him as 'that wretch the King of Naples' in a letter of Feb. 1852 (*EBB to Arabella* i 458). See *De Gustibus* 35–8n. (III 28). *lazzaroni*: a name given to the poor and the criminal classes of Naples by their Spanish rulers, from the Spanish word 'Lazaro' meaning Lazarus (the beggar in *Luke* xvi 20).

716. Antonelli: Cardinal Giacomo Antonelli (1806–76), secretary of state to Pope Pius IX, an enthusiastic supporter of the temporal power of the Papacy.

722. No, he smiles;] "No," he smiles; (*1868–88*).

723. Those . . . themselves.] "Those . . . themselves." (*1868–88*).

725. the greater] still greater (*1863–88*).

The Naples' liquefaction may be false,
When set to happen by the palace-clock
730   According to the clouds or dinner-time.
I hear you recommend, I might at least
Eliminate, decrassify my faith
Since I adopt it; keeping what I must
And leaving what I can—such points as this!
735   I won't—that is, I can't throw one away.
Supposing there's no truth in what I said
About the need of trials to man's faith,
Still, when you bid me purify the same,
To such a process I discern no end,
740   Clearing off one excrescence to see two;
There's ever a next in size, now grown as big,
That meets the knife—I cut and cut again!
First cut the Liquefaction, what comes last
But Fichte's clever cut at God himself?
745   Experimentalize on sacred things?
I trust nor hand nor eye nor heart nor brain
To stop betimes: they all get drunk alike.
The first step, I am master not to take.

You'd find the cutting-process to your taste

728. the Naples' liquefaction: the miraculous liquefaction of the solidified blood of St Januarius, the patron saint of Naples, is supposed to take place when a silver bust believed to contain the head of the saint is placed near it. See l. 377n.
731. recommend] interpose (*H proof*).
732. eliminate: in the sense of 'purify, rid of waste matter'; B.'s use of the verb in a transitive mode is unusual, probably influenced by the transitive 'decrassify', which means 'to divest of what is crass, gross, or material' (*OED*, which cites this as the first occurrence).
744. Perhaps a reference to the controversy which followed the publication of Fichte's 1798 essay 'On the Foundation of our Belief in a Divine Government of the Universe'. Fichte's suggestion that 'the concept of God as a particular substance is impossible and contradictory' resulted in accusations of atheism and the loss of his post at the University of Jena; see J. Heywood Thomas, 'Fichte and Schelling', *Nineteenth-Century Religious Thought in the West* [3 vols., Cambridge 1985] i 44. This is B.'s only mention of Fichte in his poetry; for his knowledge of Fichte's work see headnote, *Sources*. The assumption that German critical philosophy was essentially irreligious was widespread in the nineteenth century: see for instance *Prince Hohenstiel-Schwangau* (1871) 1149–50, where a 'pastor' is abjured not to 'burn Kant's self / Because Kant understands some books too well'.
749–51. Blougram imputes to Gigadibs the idea that the process of applying logic to sacred matters is preferable to allowing lies to proliferate.

750 As much as leaving growths of lies unpruned,
     Nor see more danger in it, you retort.
     Your taste's worth mine; but my taste proves more wise
     When we consider that the steadfast hold
     On the extreme end of the chain of faith
755 Gives all the advantage, makes the difference,
     With the rough purblind mass we seek to rule.
     We are their lords, or they are free of us
     Just as we tighten or relax that hold.
     So, other matters equal, we'll revert
760 To the first problem—which if solved my way
     And thrown into the balance turns the scale—
     How we may lead a comfortable life,
     How suit our luggage to the cabin's size.

     Of course you are remarking all this time
765 How narrowly and grossly I view life,
     Respect the creature-comforts, care to rule
     The masses, and regard complacently
     "The cabin," in our old phrase! Well, I do.
     I act for, talk for, live for this world now,
770 As this world calls for action, life and talk—
     No prejudice to what next world may prove,
     Whose new laws and requirements my best pledge

752–8. Blougram acknowledges that superstition is necessary if the mass of people are to be kept in subjection to the Church. This was an argument often attributed by Protestant reformers to the Catholic Church, although it could also be deployed in attacks by rationalists on religion in general. Blougram's vocabulary suggests a link between spiritual authority and reactionary political principles: see headnote to *Old Pictures* (p. 404).
754. *On the extreme*] Of the extreme (*H proof*, but not *H proof²*).
769–74. For an earlier version of this argument, see *Sordello* vi 381 ff. (I 738). Blougram's analogy between one's behaviour in this life and the next assumes that the laws of both derive from the same source, and that God will therefore be pleased that a person has obeyed worldly laws on earth because they can be relied upon to obey divine ones in the afterlife. This assumption is categorically denied in the New Testament: 'No man can serve two masters: for either he will hate the one, and love the other; or else he will hold to the one, and despise the other. Ye cannot serve God and mammon. Therefore I say unto you, Take no thought for your life, what ye shall eat, or what ye shall drink; nor yet for your body, what ye shall put on' (*Matthew* vi 24–5).

To observe then, is that I observe these now,
Doing hereafter what I do meanwhile.
775   Let us concede (gratuitously though)
Next life relieves the soul of body, yields
Pure spiritual enjoyments: well, my friend,
Why lose this life in the meantime, since its use
May be to make the next life more intense?

780   Do you know, I have often had a dream
(Work it up in your next month's article)
Of man's poor spirit in its progress still
Losing true life for ever and a day
Through ever trying to be and ever being
785   In the evolution of successive spheres,
Before its actual sphere and place of life,
Halfway into the next, which having reached,
It shoots with corresponding foolery
Halfway into the next still, on and off!
790   As when a traveller, bound from north to south,
Scouts fur in Russia—what's its use in France?
In France spurns flannel—where's its need in Spain?
In Spain drops cloth—too cumbrous for Algiers!
Linen goes next, and last the skin itself,
795   A superfluity at Timbuctoo.
When, through his journey, was the fool at ease?
I'm at ease now, friend—worldly in this world

775–7. *Let us concede . . . enjoyments*: in orthodox Christian theology (both Catholic and Protestant) the resurrection of the body at the Last Judgement is an article of faith, although the nature of this 'spiritual body' was much debated. The relevant passage in the New Testament is *1 Corinthians* xv.

779. *the next life*] the contrast (*H proof*, but not *H proof²*).

780–9. Blougram's argument that people are foolish to spoil their enjoyment of each stage of life's journey by anticipating the next does not take into account the idea that such dissatisfaction is a necessary part of the process itself, providing the motive for change and growth: see *Fifine at the Fair* (1872) 2265–9: 'For bodies sprouted legs, through a desire to run: / While hands, when fain to filch, got fingers one by one, / And nature, that's ourself, accommodative brings / To bear that, tired of legs which walk, we now bud wings, / Since of a mind to fly'.

783. *true life*] its life (*H proof*); it's life (*H proof²*).

787. *Halfway*] emended from 'half way' in 1855; 1856 and 1863² have 'half-way' (in 1863² this word is also hyphenated in l. 789); all other eds. have 'Halfway'.

790–5. Cp. the imaginary journey to Russia and Spain undertaken in *Waring* I vi (pp. 190–4).

I take and like its way of life; I think
My brothers who administer the means
800   Live better for my comfort—that's good too;
And God, if he pronounce upon it all,
Approves my service, which is better still.
If He keep silence,—why for you or me
Or that brute-beast pulled-up in to-day's "Times,"
805   What odds is't, save to ourselves, what life we lead?

You meet me at this issue—you declare,
All special pleading done with, truth is truth,
And justifies itself by undreamed ways.
You don't fear but it's better, if we doubt,
810   To say so, acting up to our truth perceived
However feebly. Do then,—act away!
'Tis there I'm on the watch for you! How one acts
Is, both of us agree, our chief concern:
And how you'll act is what I fain would see
815   If, like the candid person you appear,
You dare to make the most of your life's scheme
As I of mine, live up to its full law
Since there's no higher law that counterchecks.
Put natural religion to the test
820   You've just demolished the revealed with—quick,
Down to the root of all that checks your will,
All prohibition to lie, kill, and thieve
Or even to be an atheistic priest!
Suppose a pricking to incontinence—

799. *administer*: provide. The reference is to the laity whose contributions
support the Church.
801. *upon it all*] upon such life (*1868–88*).
804. The Brownings read *The Times* regularly during their residence abroad;
see 377n., 703–4n., and cp. *Lovers' Quarrel* 29 (p. 378).
815. *candid*: sincere.   *you appear*] that you are (*H proof*).
819. *natural religion*: a form of belief which does not depend on supernatural
revelation, but can be evolved from human experience and knowledge of
the world. Christianity is a 'revealed' religion in that the Incarnation constitutes
a miraculous divine intervention in human history which reveals God's nature
and purpose. See headnote to *Caliban*, pp. 619–21.
824. *a pricking to incontinence*: a lustful urge.
824–33. R. E. Neil Dodge (*TLS* xxxiv [21 Mar. 1935] 176) suggests that
Blougram has in mind Balzac's *Physiologie du Mariage*, and in particular the following passage from 'Méditation xvii, Théorie du lit': 'Quelque poètes voudront

825 Philosophers deduce you chastity
    Or shame, from just the fact that at the first
    Whoso embraced a woman in the plain,
    Threw club down, and forewent his brains beside,
    So stood a ready victim in the reach
830 Of any brother-savage club in hand—
    Hence saw the use of going out of sight
    In wood or cave to prosecute his loves—
    I read this in a French book t'other day.
    Does law so analyzed coerce you much?
835 Oh, men spin clouds of fuzz where matters end,
    But you who reach where the first thread begins,
    You'll soon cut that!—which means you can, but won't
    Through certain instincts, blind, unreasoned-out,
    You dare not set aside, you can't tell why,
840 But there they are, and so you let them rule.
    Then, friend, you seem as much a slave as I,
    A liar, conscious coward and hypocrite,
    Without the good the slave expects to get,
    Suppose he has a master after all!

voir dans la pudeur, dans les prétendus mystères de l'amour, une cause à la
réunion des époux dans un même lit; mais il est reconnu que si l'homme a
primitivement cherché l'ombre des cavernes, la mousse des ravins, le toit silicieux
des antres pour protéger ses plaisirs, c'est parce que l'amour le livre sans défense
à ses ennemis' [Some poets will want to see in 'pudeur' ('chastity' or 'shame')
and the supposed mysteries of [sexual] love the origin of the fact that husbands
and wives sleep in the same bed; but it is recognized that if man originally sought
shady caves, mossy ravines, and flint-roofed dens to protect his pleasures, he did
so because sexual intercourse renders him defenceless to his enemies]. Dodge's
suggestion is more plausible than C. R. Tracy's identification of Stendhal's *De
l'Amour* as the likely source (*ibid.* [24 Jan. 1935] 48).
827. in the plain] in the field (*1865–88*).
828. Threw club down] Used both arms (*H proof*).
829. in the reach] in the sight (*H proof*).
831. saw the use] saw the good (*H proof*, but not *H proof²*).
832. prosecute his loves] set about the same (*H proof*).
834. coerce: constrain, inhibit (a sense close to the Latin root *coercere*, to restrain or
confine).
838. certain instincts: cp. the comment on 'certain hell-deep instincts' which
Blougram himself ignores in his argument (ll. 989–95).
841–4. Having realized that the moral arguments derived from 'natural religion'
are specious, Gigadibs will (Blougram argues) continue to be a 'slave' to them
nonetheless out of mere cowardice.
844. Suppose] In case (*1868–88*).

845 You own your instincts—why what else do I,
Who want, am made for, and must have a God
Ere I can be aught, do aught?—no mere name
Want, but the true thing with what proves its truth,
To wit, a relation from that thing to me,
850 Touching from head to foot—which touch I feel,
And with it take the rest, this life of ours!
I live my life here; yours you dare not live.

Not as I state it, who (you please subjoin)
Disfigure such a life and call it names,
855 While, in your mind, remains another way
For simple men: knowledge and power have rights,
But ignorance and weakness have rights too.
There needs no crucial effort to find truth
If here or there or anywhere about—
860 We ought to turn each side, try hard and see,
And if we can't, be glad we've earned at least
The right, by one laborious proof the more,
To graze in peace earth's pleasant pasturage.
Men are not gods, but, properly, are brutes.
865 Something we may see, all we cannot see—
What need of lying? I say, I see all,
And swear to each detail the most minute
In what I think a man's face—you, mere cloud:
I swear I hear him speak and see him wink,
870 For fear, if once I drop the emphasis,
Mankind may doubt if there's a cloud at all.
You take the simpler life—ready to see,

852. *you dare not*] you cannot live (*H proof*).
855. *in your mind*] to your mind (*1865–88*).
862. *the more,*] the more. (*H proof*), a change dictated by the transposition of the following lines.
863–4.] transposed in *H proof*; line 863 ends with a colon.
864.] Men are not Gods, but, if you like, are brutes (*H proof*); Men are not angels, neither are they brutes. (*1863–88*, except 'brutes:' *1865–88*). *properly*: 'strictly speaking', i.e. according to 'natural religion'; Blougram continues to argue on Gigadibs's terms. The notion that human beings are simply a more highly developed kind of animal runs counter to Christian belief in man being made in the image of God (*Genesis* i 26–7).
868. *a man's face*] a Pan's face (*1863–88*).
871. *if there's a cloud*] there's any cloud (*1863–88*).
872. *the simpler life*] the simple life (*1868–88*).

Willing to see—for no cloud's worth a face—
And leaving quiet what no strength can move,
875   And which, who bids you move? who has the right?
I bid you; but you are God's sheep, not mine—
"*Pastor est tui Dominus.*" You find
In these the pleasant pastures of this life
Much you may eat without the least offence,
880   Much you don't eat because your maw objects,
Much you would eat but that your fellow-flock
Open great eyes at you and even butt,
And thereupon you like your friends so much
You cannot please yourself, offending them—
885   Though when they seem exorbitantly sheep,
You weigh your pleasure with their butts and kicks
And strike the balance. Sometimes certain fears
Restrain you—real checks since you find them so—
Sometimes you please yourself and nothing checks;
890   And thus you graze through life with not one lie,
And like it best.

But do you, in truth's name?
If so, you beat—which means—you are not I—
Who needs must make earth mine and feed my fill
Not simply unbutted at, unbickered with,

---

875. who has] who with (*H proof*).
877. Pastor est tui Dominus: 'the Lord is your shepherd', adapting the first line of Psalm xxiii, 'The Lord is my shepherd'; *Turner* (p. 346) suggests that the Latin is B.'s own translation, since it does not correspond to that of the Vulgate, the traditional Latin text.
878.] In this the pleasant pasture of our life (*1865–88*).   *pleasant pastures*: cp. *Psalms* xxiii 2: 'He maketh me to lie down in green pastures' (and see prec. note); cp. also *Psalms* xvi 6: 'The lines are fallen unto me in pleasant places; yea, I have a goodly heritage.'
882–3. even butt, / And thereupon] even butt— / Well, in the main (*H proof*).
883. so much] so well (*1863–88*, except *1863²*, which agrees with *1855*). This revision is in the list sent by B. to James T. Fields (see Appendix C, p. 889).
885.] Though sometimes, when they seem to exact too much, (*H proof*).
886. their butts and kicks] their kicks and butts (*H proof*); their butts and bleats (*1863–88*).
888. Restrain you—real checks] Will stay you—real fears, (*H proof*).
889. you please yourself] you sate yourself (*1863²*), a rare example of a substantive variant unique to this ed.
893. Who needs must . . . and feed] Who cannot . . . so, feed (*H proof*).

895 But motioned to the velvet of the sward
    By those obsequious wethers' very selves.
    Look at me, sir; my age is double yours.
    At yours, I knew beforehand, so enjoyed,
    What now I should be—as, permit the word,
900 I pretty well imagine your whole range
    And stretch of tether twenty years to come.
    We both have minds and bodies much alike.
    In truth's name, don't you want my bishopric,
    My daily bread, my influence and my state?
905 You're young, I'm old, you must be old one day;
    Will you find then, as I do hour by hour,
    Women their lovers kneel to, that cut curls
    From your fat lap-dog's ears to grace a brooch—
    Dukes, that petition just to kiss your ring—
910 With much beside you know or may conceive?
    Suppose we die to-night: well, here am I,
    Such were my gains, life bore this fruit to me,
    While writing all the same my articles
    On music, poetry, the fictile vase

896. those obsequious wethers'] the obsequious short horns' (*H proof*). The Bishop's contempt for his flock is emphasized by the revision: a 'wether' is a castrated ram.

899. as, permit] while, permit (*H proof*).

904. daily bread: From the Lord's Prayer (*Matthew* vi 11): 'Give us this day our daily bread.'

907–8. Blougram implies that his priestly power and status make him attractive to beautiful women; since they cannot acknowledge this directly, they find other ways of showing their feelings. Instead of asking for a lock of his hair as a love token, they take one from his lapdog. It is not certain whether Blougram intends this particular example to be taken seriously, or as a burlesque of popular anti-Catholic prejudice. The latter is made more likely by the knowing allusion in l. 910.

909. Dukes, that] Dukes who (*H proof*).   *your ring*] my ring (*H proof*, but not *H proof²*).

914–15. the fictile vase / Found at Albano: 'fictile' means 'moulded into form by art', so the sense here is that the vase has been made as an art object, not for utility; according to George Dennis in the introduction to his *The Cities and Cemeteries of Etruria* (2 vols., 1848): 'Pliny states that in his time fictile vases, by which he probably means those that were painted, fetched more money than the celebrated Murrhine vases, the cost of which he records ... and which are supposed to have been of porcelain' (vol. i, p. lxxxv n.). Dennis also discusses 'the curious urns of Albano, which are imitations of rude huts formed of boughs and covered with skins' (vol. i, p. lxvi n.). Albano is a town in the Lazio region of Italy, near Rome; the Alban hills are frequently mentioned in classical poetry.

915   Found at Albano, or Anacreon's Greek.
       But you—the highest honour in your life,
       The thing you'll crown yourself with, all your days,
       Is—dining here and drinking this last glass
       I pour you out in sign of amity
920   Before we part for ever. Of your power
       And social influence, worldly worth in short,
       Judge what's my estimation by the fact—
       I do not condescend to enjoin, beseech,
       Hint secresy on one of all these words!
925   You're shrewd and know that should you publish it
       The world would brand the lie—my enemies first,
       Who'd sneer—"the bishop's an arch-hypocrite,
       And knave perhaps, but not so frank a fool."
       Whereas I should not dare for both my ears
930   Breathe one such syllable, smile one such smile,
       Before my chaplain who reflects myself—
       My shade's so much more potent than your flesh.
       What's your reward, self-abnegating friend?
       Stood you confessed of those exceptional
935   And privileged great natures that dwarf mine—
       A zealot with a mad ideal in reach,
       A poet just about to print his ode,
       A statesman with a scheme to stop this war,
       An artist whose religion is his art,
940   I should have nothing to object! such men
       Carry the fire, all things grow warm to them,

---

915. *Albano, or*] Albano, chess, or (*1863*); Albano, chess, (*1865–88*). *Anacreon's Greek*: five editions of Anacreon are listed in *Collections*, one of which belonged to B.'s father (A0061); Mrs Orr notes as an example of Robert Browning Sr's familiarity with classical literature that 'he was wont, in later life, to soothe his little boy to sleep by humming to him an ode of Anacreon' (Orr *Life* 12). Anacreon's epicurean subject matter makes him an ironically apt choice for Blougram.
925. *publish it*] publish one (*1863–88*).
927. *Who'd sneer—"the bishop's*] emended in agreement with *1865–88* from ' "Who'd sneer—the bishop's'. It is rare for B. to have missed such an obvious error not only in proof but in publ. texts; see also l. 963.   *sneer*] laugh (*H proof*).
931. *my chaplain*] the chaplain (*1868–88*).
934. *Stood you confessed of*: 'If you were admitted to possess'.
935. *that dwarf mine*] dwarfing mine (*H proof*).
938. *this war*: the Crimean War, which began in Mar. 1854; B. was said by EBB. to be in 'a frenzy of excitement' about the siege of Sebastopol which began in October 1854 (*EBB to Arabella* ii 103).

Their drugget's worth my purple, they beat me.
But you,—you're just as little those as I—
You, Gigadibs, who, thirty years of age,
945   Write stately for Blackwood's Magazine,
Believe you see two points in Hamlet's soul
Unseized by the Germans yet—which view you'll
       print—
Meantime the best you have to show being still
That lively lightsome article we took
950   Almost for the true Dickens,—what's the name?
"The Slum and Cellar—or Whitechapel life
Limned after dark!" it made me laugh, I know,

---

942. drugget . . . purple: 'drugget' is a coarse woollen cloth; purple is the imperial and papal colour (as in *Sordello* i 78–9: 'The Second Friedrich wore / The purple' (I 398–400); see also *Protus* 10n. [III 637]).   *they beat me*] these beat me (*H proof*, but not *H proof²*).

943. as little those] as little these (*H proof*).

945. stately: regularly.   *Blackwood's Magazine*: this periodical began life in 1817; it was generally conservative in politics and tone, and consisted of a mixture of fiction, reviews and articles on cultural life and current affairs. Under the editorship of John Blackwood (1845–79) the magazine managed to attract many of the leading writers of the day; EBB. published some poems in it during the late 1840s, but became annoyed with its refusal to publish her poem 'A Meditation in Tuscany' (which later became the first part of *Casa Guidi Windows*); see l. 953n.

946–7. Believe . . . yet: Blougram suggests that Gigadibs is picking up the crumbs of German scholarship, at its apogee in this period; cp. Mr Casaubon, in George Eliot's *Middlemarch* (1870, but set forty years before), whose scholarship is fatally flawed through his ignorance of German. German critics had been active in Shakespeare studies, and *Hamlet* was a particular favourite, in part because of Goethe's use of it in *Wilhelm Meister*, which involves an extended analysis of 'Hamlet's soul'. B.'s own study of German involved looking at Tieck and Schlegel's translation of Shakespeare (*Maynard* 277). *Turner* (p. 346) cites a recent four-volume commentary on Shakespeare publ. 1840–50 by the German critic Gervinus.

947. which view] which views (*H proof*).

949–52. Blougram is referring not to Dickens's fiction but to his journalism, and in particular to such pieces as 'A Walk in a Workhouse' (*Household Words*, 25 May 1850). Whitechapel workhouse was one of the places Dickens visited on his 'night walks'; see John Forster, *The Life of Charles Dickens* (1872; Everyman ed., 1980) ii 131. The Brownings were not at this stage friendly with Dickens, although they became so when they lived 'nearly opposite' one another in Paris during the winter of 1855–56.

950. what's the name?] what's its name? (*1863–88*).

951. Whitechapel: an area of London's East End, synonymous with urban deprivation and crime for much of the nineteenth century.

952. Limned: painted, described.

And pleased a month and brought you in ten pounds.
—Success I recognise and compliment,
955   And therefore give you, if you please, three words
(The card and pencil-scratch is quite enough)
Which whether here, in Dublin, or New York,
Will get you, prompt as at my eyebrow's wink,
Such terms as never you aspired to get
960   In all our own reviews and some not ours.
Go write your lively sketches—be the first
"Blougram, or The Eccentric Confidence"—
Or better simply say, "The Outward-bound."
Why, men as soon would throw it in my teeth
965   As copy and quote the infamy chalked broad
About me on the church-door opposite.
You will not wait for that experience though,
I fancy, howsoever you decide,
To discontinue—not detesting, not
970   Defaming, but at least—despising me!

Over his wine so smiled and talked his hour
Sylvester Blougram, styled *in partibus*

---

953. ten pounds: cp. the payment EBB. received—'five and twenty guineas!'—for a 'few lyrics and sonnets' published in *Blackwood's* in 1846–47 (*EBB to Arabella* i 294). At ll. 959–60 Blougram implies that the payment to Gigadibs is relatively meagre.

956.] The simple card and pencil-scratch's enough (*H proof*).

957. Wiseman founded *The Dublin Review*, a Catholic journal, in 1836; New York by the date of the poem had a large Irish immigrant population.

960. our own reviews: i.e. journals either controlled by the Catholic Church or sympathetic to it, such as *The Dublin Review*.

963. "The Outward-bound": alluding to the metaphor of the sea voyage through which Blougram has articulated his thoughts; see also ll. 1006–7.

964. would throw] will throw (*H proof*, but not *H proof²*).

965. the infamy . . . opposite: presumably an insult aimed at Blougram; Wiseman notes the existence of such expressions of popular anti-Catholic sentiment in 'The Hierarchy' (see headnote, *Sources*).

970. Defaming] Degrading (*H proof*).

971. At this point in the poem an authorial voice takes over; see headnote, *Parallels*.

972. Sylvester: Allen (headnote, *Background*) notes that the middle name of Father Prout was Sylvester.

972–3. styled . . . nec non: the commentator's garbled version of the phrase 'Episcopus in partibus infidelium', 'Bishop in the lands of the unbelievers'.

Episcopus, nec non—(the deuce knows what
It's changed to by our novel hierarchy)
975 With Gigadibs the literary man,
Who played with spoons, explored his plate's design,
And ranged the olive stones about its edge,
While the great bishop rolled him out his mind.

For Blougram, he believed, say, half he spoke.
980 The other portion, as he shaped it thus
For argumentatory purposes,
He felt his foe was foolish to dispute.
Some arbitrary accidental thoughts
That crossed his mind, amusing because new,
985 He chose to represent as fixtures there,
Invariable convictions (such they seemed
Beside his interlocutor's loose cards

Wiseman became 'Bishop of Melipotamus [in Crete] *in partibus infidelium*' in
June 1840, and retained this title until the establishment of the 'novel hierarchy'
in 1850; thereafter he became Archbishop of Westminster and Cardinal. The poem's
reversion to Blougram's earlier title may be a reflection of the legal position in
1855, by which time the title 'Archbishop of Westminster' had been declared
unlawful (see headnote).

974. by our novel] by the novel (*H proof*, but not *H proof²*).

977. And ranged the] Arranged its (*H proof*, but not *H proof²*).

978.] While the great bishop rolled him out a mind / Long rumpled, till creased
consciousness lay smooth. (*1880, 1888*, except *1888* has 'crumpled'). It is exceptionally rare for a revision involving the addition of a whole line to appear first
in a volume of selections, but cp. *Andrea del Sarto* 199^200n. (p. 400).

979–95. The difficulty in elucidating this passage is deliberate on B.'s part, since
he does not specify which 'half' of his speech Blougram believed, or say which
statements were 'arbitrary accidental thoughts' and which the (distorted) expression of 'certain hell-deep instincts'. It is particularly hard to see why Blougram
should feel that Gigadibs was 'foolish to dispute' the half of his speech which he
did *not* believe, but merely put forward for the sake of the argument. What seems
clear is that Blougram has constructed an argument designed to confound this
particular opponent, and uses whatever materials come to hand, relying on
the weight of his intellectual and social eminence. These materials include some
'arbitrary accidental thoughts' and some 'hell-deep instincts', which he himself
does not fully articulate because he does not identify their true origin (see below,
ll. 989–95.).

979. say, half] say half (*H proof²*, but not *H proof*), a very rare example of a unique
reading in *H proof²*; see Appendix C, III 742–3. *he spoke*] he said (*H proof*).

986–8. Cp. l. 48n.

Flung daily down, and not the same way twice)
While certain hell-deep instincts, man's weak tongue
990 Is never bold to utter in their truth
Because styled hell-deep ('tis an old mistake
To place hell at the bottom of the earth)
He ignored these,—not having in readiness
Their nomenclature and philosophy:
995 He said true things, but called them by wrong names.
"On the whole," he thought, "I justify myself
On every point where cavillers like this
Oppugn my life: he tries one kind of fence—
I close—he's worsted, that's enough for him;
1000 He's on the ground! if the ground should break away
I take my stand on, there's a firmer yet
Beneath it, both of us may sink and reach.
His ground was over mine and broke the first.
So let him sit with me this many a year!"

1005   He did not sit five minutes. Just a week
Sufficed his sudden healthy vehemence.

990. Is never bold] Shall never dare (*H proof*).

991–2. Markus (p. 183; see *Background*) suggests an allusion to the anti-Copernican view of cosmology put forward by Dr Cullen, the Primate of Ireland, in an obscure Roman journal, and given publicity in *The Globe* by Father Prout thanks to B.: 'How did the *Globe* discover the obscure and incriminating article? "On the original suggestion of a Florentine reader of the 'review', a distinguished English Writer, ROBERT BROWNING, Esq. (who reads everything)"' (28 June 1851).

991.] Till one demonstrate it an old mistake (*H proof*, which consequently lacks the parenthesis at the end of the next line).

996–1004.] Blougram's speech is not in quotation marks in *H proof.*

997. cavillers: a 'caviller' is '[a] man fond of making objections; an unfair adversary; a captious disputant' (*J.*).

998. oppugn: 'To oppose; to attack; to resist' (*J.*).

998–1000. he tries . . . on the ground! the metaphor is taken from wrestling: Gigadibs's attempt at 'fence' (or self-defence) is ineffective when Blougram 'closes' with him and he ends up 'on the ground' in consequence.

999. close: '[to] grapple with in wrestling' (*J.*).

1000. if the ground] if ground (*1870–88*).

1004. So let him] So, let him (*1868–88*).

1005–13. Gigadibs enacts or realizes (ironically) the 'outward-bound' metaphor of sea voyage employed by Blougram; his decision to emigrate to Australia reflects that country's recent change in status from penal colony to settler colony. B.'s close friend Alfred Domett had emigrated to New Zealand in 1842 (see headnote to *Waring*, p. 185); B. wrote to Domett, 13 Dec. 1842: 'We all talk of you,

(Something had struck him in the "Outward-bound"
Another way than Blougram's purpose was)
And having bought, not cabin-furniture
1010   But settler's-implements (enough for three)
And started for Australia—there, I hope,
By this time he has tested his first plough,
And studied his last chapter of St. John.

wish you well, and wonder all manner of ways. Arnould & his wife came here last week, and we spoke irreverently of your ploughing, hopefully of your harvest, & so on, just as if you were not in the thick of it, and victorious over it, too, by this time' (*Correspondence* vi 221). The motif of emigration to the colonies was a frequent one in writing of this time; cp. Elizabeth Gaskell, *Mary Barton* (1848), Charles Dickens, *David Copperfield* (1849–50), and Arthur Hugh Clough, *The Bothie of Toper-na-Fuosich* (1848), a poem which the Brownings read and enjoyed, in which the hero Philip Hewson escapes from his difficulties by emigrating to New Zealand with his wife Elspie: 'They are married, and gone to New Zealand. / Five hundred pounds in pocket, with books, and two or three pictures, / Tool-box, plough, and the rest, they rounded the sphere to New Zealand. / There he hewed, and dug; subdued the earth and his spirit' (ix 222–5).

1005. five minutes. Just] five minutes; for (*H proof*).

1012. Peter Ebbs suggests an allusion to *Luke* ix 62: 'No man, having put his hand to the plough, and looking back, is fit for the kingdom of God'; see 'Tipping the Scales: Contextual Clues in "Bishop Blougram's Apology"', *SBC* xxiv (2001) 65.

1013. John xxi begins with Jesus, after his resurrection, appearing to his disciples on the seashore while they are fishing, and relates the miracle of the great haul of fish which they catch at his instigation. When they come to land, Jesus says to them: 'Come and dine. And none of the disciples durst ask him, Who art thou? knowing that it was the Lord. Jesus then cometh, and taketh bread, and giveth them, and fish likewise' (vv. 12–13). This frugal meal contrasts with Blougram's luxurious dinner (see ll. 16–19). As *Florentine* notes, Jesus then repeatedly enjoins Peter to 'Feed my sheep!' (vv. 15–17) and prophesies his martyrdom (vv. 18–19); contrast Blougram's scornful reference to the 'obsequious wethers' of his flock (l. 896) and his emphasis on his own material comfort. The contrast with Peter would be esp. pointed because of his importance to the Catholic Church and the Papacy. B. may be turning the tables on Wiseman, who makes mocking reference to this verse in his account of the Bishop of Oxford's attempt to formulate a response to the 'Papal Aggression': 'The bishop is presiding over his clergy: he has himself composed an ecclesiastical document; he himself proposes it; and actually an amendment is carried against him, and he is compelled to admit the amendment. This is the most curious commentary we have ever seen on "Feed my sheep"' ('The Hierarchy', p. 519; see headnote, *Sources*, and l. 212n.).

21 The Patriot

AN OLD STORY

First publ. *M & W*, 10 Nov. 1855; repr. *1863*, *1865²*, *1868*, *1880*, *1888*. Our text is *1855*. In *H proof* the title is 'The Old Story' and there is no subtitle, although the running title changes from 'The Old Story' on p. 192 (erroneously numbered 208) to 'The Patriot' on p. 193, the first page of signature O. In *1855* the table of contents gives the title as 'The Patriot.—An Old Story' but the poem itself has the title and subtitle as here.

The Brownings visited Brescia briefly in June 1851. The city was the site of a heroic but doomed attempt to stem the tide of Austrian military success during the nationalist uprisings of 1848–49; the 'ten days of Brescia' (23 Mar.–1 Apr. 1849) became part of nationalist folklore. There is, however, no evidence that the poem was composed at this time, and the link with the city of Brescia was eliminated from 1863 onwards (see l. 26n.). The poem's reflections on the rapidity with which a hero's fortunes can be transformed might have been prompted by the entry of Louis Napoleon into Paris on 16 Oct. 1852, an event witnessed by the Brownings and described at length by EBB. in a letter to her sister Arabella: 'Yesterday was a grand day with us . . . we saw the great spectacle of Louis Napoleon passing on after his entrance into Paris—Nothing so magnificent was ever seen before. All the military & civil pomp of France had gone out to meet him, & from end to end of the broad beautiful boulevard, as far as our eyes could go, and miles beyond, floated down under that limpid sky & cloudless sun the multitudes of the people—it was wonderful. He rode on horseback *quite alone*—that is, with a considerable space between those who preceded & those who followed, & with no one at his side. As the people shouted he bowed to right & left, & those who were cursing him stopped suddenly to call him at least a brave man' (17 Oct. 1852, *EBB to Arabella* i 504). On the Brownings' differing attitudes to Louis Napoleon, see *Lovers' Quarrel* (p. 376).

The term 'patriot' acquired pejorative overtones during the eighteenth century, and came to be applied not only to 'one whose ruling passion is the love of his country' but also to 'a factious disturber of the government' (*J.*). These overtones were strengthened during the period of the French Revolution, when 'patriot' became more or less synonymous with 'Jacobin'; see (e.g.) Wordsworth, *The Prelude* (1850) ix 121–4: 'I gradually withdrew / Into a noisier world, and thus ere long / Became a patriot; and my heart was all / Given to the people, and my love was theirs'.

B. could have found archetypes for his doomed 'patriot' in a number of Renaissance plays, most obviously Shakespeare's *Coriolanus* and Ben Jonson's *Sejanus*. There are affinities between the fate of the poem's speaker and that of Spenser's 'mightie Prince' in his translation of Du Bellay's *The Ruines of Time*:

Subtitle. In the sense of 'a familiar or well-worn story'; note title in *H proof* (see headnote).

It is not long, since these two eyes beheld
A mightie Prince, of most renowmed race,
Whom *England* high in count of honour held,
And greatest ones did sue to gaine his grace
Of greatest ones he greatest in his place,
Sate in the bosome of his Soueraine,
And *Right and loyall* did his word maintaine.

I saw him die, I saw him die, as one
Of the meane people, and brought forth on beare.
I saw him die, and no man left to mone
His dolefull fate, that late him loued deare.
. . . He now is dead, and all is with him dead,
Saue what in heauens storehouse he vplaid.
                    (ll. 183–93, 211–12)

For other echoes of this work, see headnote to *Love Among the Ruins* (p. 528)
and *Lovers' Quarrel* 86n. (p. 381). The suggestion that the poem's narrative is based
on the story of Arnold of Brescia (d. 1155), a cleric who opposed the temporal
power of the clergy and was condemned to death at the instigation of Pope Adrian
IV, was denied by B. himself according to DeVane (*Handbook* 239), but he
gives no source. Arnold of Brescia became, however, an important icon for the
Italian national movement; effigies of Arnold and of Savonarola were carried in
Mazzini's funeral procession. A play on the subject of Arnold by Giovanni Battista
Niccolini (1782–1861), drawing explicit parallels between Arnold's period and the
Italy of the early nineteenth century, appeared in 1843, and was translated into
English in 1847 by Theodosia Garrow, later Theodosia Trollope, a friend of EBB.'s
and neighbour of the Brownings in Tuscany. The crux of the drama is popular
support for Arnold, which ebbs and flows throughout, but the symmetrical
reversal of B.'s poem is not anticipated. Arnold is presented as a champion of the
people, like Rienzi and Sordello (see *Sordello* [I 369–70]).

   B.'s poem suggests that the patriot's fault is excessive ambition for his people;
the image of his leap at the sun (ll. 11–12) aligns him with other overreaching
heroes such as Paracelsus, Sordello, and Djabal in *The Return of the Druses* (1842);
cp. also the downfall of the populist leader Chiappino in *A Soul's Tragedy*
(II 180), and the emblematic division of that work into the 'poetry' and 'prose'
of its hero's life. The fickleness and ingratitude of a liberated people is another
recurring motif in B.'s work; see e.g. *One Word More* 73–108n. (p. 606). *The
Patriot* represents another example of B.'s interest in 'impossible' renditions of
speech, since its speaker is about to die, and the transmission of his monologue
is hard to explain naturalistically. Cp. *Childe Roland* (p. 348) and (a slightly different case) *Red Cotton Night-Cap Country* (1873), where the thoughts of 'M. Léonce
Miranda' just prior to his solitary suicide are recorded.

1

It was roses, roses, all the way,
   With myrtle mixed in my path like mad.
The house-roofs seemed to heave and sway,
   The church-spires flamed, such flags they had,
5 A year ago on this very day!

2

The air broke into a mist with bells,
   The old walls rocked with the crowds and cries.
Had I said, "Good folks, mere noise repels—
   But give me your sun from yonder skies!"
10 They had answered, "And afterward, what else?"

3

Alack, it was I who leaped at the sun,
   To give it my loving friends to keep.

1–2. The patriot's entry echoes that of Christ into Jerusalem, and is followed by a similar reversal of public acclaim into ignominy and death. Cp. *Two Poets of Croisic* (1878) 391–2: 'a crown of bay / Circled his brows, with rose and myrtle mixed'.
1. roses all the way: The line 'Strowing with fragrant Roses all the way' appears in Mary Pix's *The Conquest of Spain* (1705; Act II p. 21). The phrase 'roses all the way' is used by a number of poets after B., who is presumably their source.
2. myrtle: the flower of Venus, often made into wreaths or sprays during classical antiquity to symbolize 'love, peace, honour etc.' (*OED* sense 3). *like mad*: previous uses of this phrase occur mainly in comic and/or vernacular or dialect writing.
3–7. Cp. EBB.'s description of the procession to the Grand Duke's palace in the first part of *Casa Guidi Windows* (1851): 'the stones seemed breaking into thanks / And rattling up the sky, such sounds in proof / Arose; the very house-walls seemed to bend; / The very windows, up from door to roof, / Flashed out a rapture of bright heads' (i 516–20).
8–10. Cp. *In a Balcony* i 63–6 (III 407): 'Name your own reward! . . . Put out an arm and touch and take the sun'.
8. "Good folks] "Good folk (*1863–88*). *mere noise*: this phrase appears in John Hookham Frere's *Prospectus and Specimen of an intended National Work . . . relating to King Arthur and his Round Table* (1817), in a context bearing affinities with *Patriot*: 'From realm to realm he ran—and never staid; / Kingdoms and crowns he won—and gave away: / It seem'd as if his labours were repaid / By the mere noise and movement of the fray: / No conquests nor acquirements had he made: / His chief delight was on some festive day / To ride triumphant, prodigal, and proud, / And shower his wealth amidst the shouting crowd' (i 153–60).
11–12. Cp. the image of the grasshoppers whose 'passionate life . . . spends itself in leaps all day / To reach the sun' (*Easter Day* 309–11, III 113); there may also be an allusion to the myth of Icarus (Ovid, *Metamorphoses* viii 183–235).

Nought man could do, have I left undone,
And you see my harvest, what I reap
15 This very day, now a year is run.

4

There's nobody on the house-tops now—
Just a palsied few at the windows set—
For the best of the sight is, all allow,
At the Shambles' Gate—or, better yet,
20 By the very scaffold's foot, I trow.

5

I go in the rain, and, more than needs,
A rope cuts both my wrists behind,
And I think, by the feel, my forehead bleeds,
For they fling, whoever has a mind,
25 Stones at me for my year's misdeeds.

13–15. Cp. *Isaiah* xvii 11: 'In the day shalt thou make thy plant to grow, and in the morning shalt thou make thy seed to flourish: but the harvest shall be a heap in the day of grief and of desperate sorrow.'

13. do, have I left] do, surely, I left (*H proof*). *undone,*] emended from *1855* 'undone', in agreement with *H proof* and *1856* (which was printed from advance proofs); *1863–88* have 'undone:'.

16–25. Cp. the description of Guido's execution in *Ring* xii 118–208.

16–17. now— / Just] now / Save (*H proof*). See next note.

17. a palsied] the palsied (*H proof*, but not *H proof²*). See prec. note; this is a rare example of *H proof²* recording one substantive variant in a line, but not another. *palsied*: B. probably uses the word primarily to mean 'old', following Shakespeare's 'palsied-Eld' (*Measure for Measure* III i 36). Cp. (among several uses) *King Victor and King Charles* (1842) II 309–10: 'crowns should slip from palsied brows to heads / Young as this head', and *Childe Roland* 154 (p. 363).

18. the best of the sight: the best view of the execution.

19. Shambles' Gate: A 'shambles' was originally a meat market; the 'Shambles' Gate' would therefore have been the place where meat was bought and sold; the term is being applied metaphorically here to the gate that leads to the speaker's place of execution.

20. I trow: I believe (archaic).

21. more than needs: 'more than is necessary' (to restrain me).

24–5. Cp. Jesus's response to the Pharisees when they brought him the woman taken in adultery: 'He that is without sin among you, let him first cast a stone at her' (*John* viii 7).

6

Thus I entered Brescia, and thus I go!
   In such triumphs, people have dropped down dead.
   "Thou, paid by the World,—what dost thou owe
      Me?" God might have questioned: but now instead
30 'Tis God shall requite! I am safer so.

26–30. The speaker means that if he had died a year ago, at the height of his
triumph, he would have been 'paid by the World' and left owing a debt to God;
now the situation is reversed. B. has in mind the Sermon on the Mount in which
Jesus warns: 'Take heed that ye do not your alms before men, to be seen of them:
otherwise ye have no reward of your Father which is in heaven. Therefore when
thou doest thine alms, do not sound a trumpet before thee, as the hypocrites do
in the synagogues and in the streets, that they may have glory of men. Verily I
say unto you, They have their reward' (*Matthew* vi 1–2). Cp. the similar endings
of *Porphyria* (p. 73), *Johannes Agricola* (p. 79), *Mesmerism* (III 486) and *In a Year*
(p. 273).
26.] So I entered this Brescia and quit it so! (*H proof*); Thus I entered, and thus
I go! (*1863–88*). For Brescia, see headnote. Cp. Arthur Hugh Clough's poem
Peschiera, published in *Putnam's Magazine* in May 1854: 'Yet not in vain, although
in vain / O men of Brescia, on the day / Of love past hope, I heard you say /
Your welcome to the noble pain' (ll. 13–16).
27. *In such triumphs, people*] In such triumphs some people (*H proof*); In triumphs,
people (*1863–88*). Cp. the late poem *Imperante Augusto Natus Est* (*Asolando*, 1889),
in which the emperor Augustus is compelled to pose as a beggar one day a year
to atone for his good fortune; see esp. ll. 144–51.
28. *"Thou, paid*] "Paid (*1863–88*).
29. *Me?"*] Me!" (*H proof*, but not *H proof²*). *might have questioned*] might question (*1863–88*).
30. *'Tis God shall requite!*] It is God who requites: (*H proof*); 'Tis God shall
repay! (*1863–65*); 'Tis God shall repay: (*1868–88*). Both 'requite' and 'repay' have
biblical connotations of vengeance as well as reward: 'the spoiler is come upon
her, even upon Babylon, and her mighty men are taken, every one of their bows
is broken: for the Lord God of recompences shall surely requite' (*Jeremiah* li 56);
'Vengeance is mine; I will repay, saith the Lord' (*Romans* xii 19).

22 Respectability

First publ. *M & W*, 10 Nov. 1855; repr. *1863, 1868, 1880, 1888*. Our text is *1855*.
  This poem is clearly linked to the Brownings' period of residence in Paris between Sept. 1851 and July 1852; the closing lines allude to an event which B. witnessed, the reception of Charles Montalembert (1810–70) into the Académie Française by his political opponent François Guizot (1787–1874) on 5 Feb. 1852. In a letter to George Barrett dated 4 Feb. 1852, B. notes that 'people are waiting curiously for the sort of reception Montalembert will have to-morrow at the Institute, where he "reads himself in"—those who, as liberals, hate him most (for his ultra-montane bigotry, "legitimate" opinions & so forth) will see it their duty to applaud him to the echo, on the ground of his having broken with the government on its promulgation of the spoliation measures—just as if he had not done his utmost to help that government when it most needed help—and now that, in consequence, it can act as it pleases, Montalembert cries out on it & expects sympathy! None of mine shall he have when I hear him tomorrow, as I hope to do' (*George Barrett* 170). B.'s recollection of the event was still vivid years later, as he makes clear by quoting a phrase from Guizot's reception speech in a letter of 19 Sept. 1880 to Eliza Fitzgerald:

> I shall be greatly interested in reading Guizot's Memoirs when you lend them to me on my return. No doubt he had strong affections and they were answerably rewarded: but I confess to a thorough dislike of the man—whose great powers nobody could dispute . . . Again, the strenuous protestant (I heard him say proudly in a speech "Protestant comme mes pères"[)]—he was a vehement opposer of any attempt on the part of the Italians to get rid of the Pope's catholic rule.
>
> (*Learned Lady* 92)

  The poem might have been prompted by the Brownings' proximity to two of the leading literary figures of 1850s Paris, George Sand and Pierre-Jean de Béranger. EBB.'s admiration for George Sand is expressed in a number of her poems, and, having procured a letter of introduction from Giuseppe Mazzini, the Brownings visited her on 15 Feb. 1852. The French novelist was almost as famous for her unconventional lifestyle as she was for her literary productions, but although B. later claimed to have felt that 'his studied courtesy towards her was felt by her as a rebuke to the latitude which she granted to other men' (Orr *Life* 171), he visited her seven times during the next month or so (*EBB to Arabella* i 480). Pierre-Jean de Béranger (1780–1857) was an immensely popular *chansonnier* whose lyrical addresses to his mistress 'Lisette' were well known in England. B. saw him 'in his white hat, wandering along the asphalte' in Feb. 1852, and although he was too 'modest' to introduce himself, he claimed on another occasion to have told Pen to run up to him and touch him, so that he would later be able to claim that he had touched such a man (Orr *Life* 167, 356). Béranger's reputation for libertinism in verse was matched by aspects of his personal life; even in his old age he never married his long-term partner Judith Frère.
  'Respectability', meaning the 'state, quality, or condition of being respectable in point of character or social standing', entered the language during the late eighteenth century, although it quickly seems to have acquired what the *OED* calls 'a somewhat derogatory implication of affectation or spuriousness'. By the mid-nineteenth century it was routinely used in a derogatory sense; cp. e.g. Thomas

Carlyle's review of Lockhart's *Life of Scott*, in which he links 'ambition, money-getting, respectability of gig or no gig' with the desire for outward signs of society's recognition and esteem, and the description of the parlour in B.'s *The Inn Album* (1875) as the embodiment of 'Vulgar flat smooth respectability' (l. 43). There are similar defences of conventionally 'immoral' conduct in *The Statue and the Bust* (ll. 226–50, III 357–9), *Dîs Aliter Visum* (p. 688), and *Fifine at the Fair* (1872); the last two are also associated with France.

1

Dear, had the world in its caprice
    Deigned to proclaim "I know you both,
    Have recognised your plighted troth,
Am sponsor for you—live in peace!"—
5 How many precious months and years
    Of youth had passed, that speed so fast,
    Before we found it out at last,
The world, and what it fears?

2

How much of priceless life were spent
10   With men that every virtue decks,
    And women models of their sex,
Society's true ornament,—
Ere we dared wander, nights like this,
    Thro' wind and rain, and watch the Seine,
15   And feel the Boulevart break again
To warmth and light and bliss?

3

I know! the world proscribes not love;
    Allows my finger to caress
    Your lip's contour and downiness,

---

3. plighted troth: a reference to the wedding service in the *Book of Common Prayer*, in which the bride and groom conclude their vows with the words 'and thereto I plight thee my troth'.

9. were spent: would have been spent.

10. 'With men bedecked with every virtue'.

15. And feel] And bid (*H proof*, but not *H proof*[2]).   *Boulevart*: an alternative spelling of 'boulevard' in the mid-nineteenth century.

17. proscribes not love: does not forbid sexual love (on condition, as the following lines make clear, that it take the respectable form of marriage).

19. your lip's] your lips' (*1868–88*).

20   Provided it supply a glove.
     The world's good word!—the Institute!
       Guizot receives Montalembert!
       Eh? down the court three lampions flare—
     Put forward your best foot!

20. The approval of the world has the effect of diminishing the sensual pleasure felt by the lovers. Gloves are often associated with the relations between men and women in B.'s poetry; see esp. *The Glove* (II 360) and *Any Wife to Any Husband* 37 (p. 650).

21.] And then, rewards—the Institute! (*H proof*). The Institut de France was created in 1795 to bring together five 'Académies', including the Académie Française; from 1805 onwards the Académie was based in the Palais de l'Institut de France.

23. lampions: festive lights hung for the occasion (not street lamps). *OED*'s earliest citation is from Thackeray, *Vanity Fair* (1847–48).

24. 'Put your best foot forward' (present yourself in your best light). Cp. *The Inn Album* (1875) 844–5: 'I put / Bold face on, best foot forward'.

23 "Childe Roland to the Dark Tower came"
(See Edgar's Song in "LEAR")

Text and publication

First publ. *M & W*, 10 Nov. 1855; repr. *1863, 1865²* (without stanza numbers), *1868, 1872, 1888*. Our text is *1855*.

Composition and date

If B.'s account of the poem's composition is to be trusted, *Childe Roland* was written immediately after *Women and Roses* in early Jan. 1853: 'The next day "Childe Roland" came upon me as a kind of dream. I had to write it, then and there, and I finished it the same day, I believe. But it was simply that I had to do it. I did not know then what I meant beyond that, and I'm sure I don't know now. But I am very fond of it' (Lilian Whiting, *The Brownings: their Life and Art* [1911] 261; see headnote to *Women and Roses*, III 235). He told a very similar story to Daniel Sargent Curtis late in his life: 'Asked Mr. Browning if there were any sous-entendu [subtext] in his poem of Childe Roland?— "Not the least. I wrote it on the 2d January, having begun the year with the intention of writing a lyric poem every day that year . . . The first I wrote was 'Women and Roses,' about a rose-tree which some American lady had sent to my wife as a New Year's gift. I wrote half of Childe Roland, and finished it the next day. Then somebody or something put it out of my head, and I relapsed into my old desultory way"' (Daniel Sargent Curtis, 'Robert Browning, 1879 to 1885', in *More than Friend* 170). The Brownings were living in Florence at this time, so the suggestion that the poem was written in Paris (Orr *Life* 362; *Cyclopedia* 103; DeVane *Handbook* 229) is incompatible with this version of events, notwithstanding B.'s assertion in a letter of 29 Apr. 1866 (commenting on a picture based on the poem by Alfred William Hunt) that *Childe Roland* was written 'at Paris' (*New Letters* 173; see also *Non-literary sources*).

Sources and influences

As early as 1925 DeVane observed that critics have 'ransacked ballad, fairy tale and legend to find the origin' of the poem ('The Landscape of Browning's Childe Roland,' *PMLA* xl [1925] 426). Like Coleridge's *Kubla Khan*, with which it has often been compared, the poem claims to be the imperfectly remembered record of a dream, and as such it has been analysed by critics for traces of the raw material from which the poet drew his conscious ideas. It is, however, important to make a clear distinction between those texts to which the poem explicitly refers, and those which B. may have drawn on unconsciously in constructing the story of his imaginary knight's quest.

Title. A 'Childe' is 'a youth of gentle birth'; the word is 'applied to a young noble awaiting knighthood' in a number of medieval ballads and romances (*OED*). Byron adopted the term for *Childe Harold's Pilgrimage.*
Subtitle. Edgar's] the Fool's (*H proof*). See headnote, *Sources* (i) *King Lear.*

(i) *King Lear*

As the poem's subtitle makes clear, its title comes from 'Edgar's song in "Lear"':
'Childe Rowland to the dark tower came, / His word was still, "fie, foh, and
fum, / I smell the blood of a British man"' (III iv 182–4). Edgar is still at this
stage disguised as Poor Tom, and is attempting, along with Gloucester, to
persuade Lear to take shelter for the night rather than stay out on the heath.
Some general similarities between Edgar's situation and that of the speaker in B.'s
poem have been highlighted; Mario D'Avanzo, for instance, notes that both poem
and play use landscape as an emblem of the speaker's psychological state, and suggests that 'the triumph of love, fidelity and virtue' in B.'s poem is 'mirrored in
Edgar's "pilgrimage" (V iii 197) to truth and in his victory for justice and good'
(*SEL* xvii [1977], 705).

Edgar's song may in turn derive from 'the romance of Child Roland', one of
the stories recorded in *Illustrations of Northern Antiquities* (ed. Henry Weber, R.
Jamieson and W[alter] S[cott], 1814), pp. 397–403. In this collection Jamieson
gives a prose paraphrase, with some verse excerpts, of 'Rosmer Haf-Mand,
or the Mer-man Rosmer', as narrated to him 'by a country tailor then at work
in my father's house', which turns out to be 'the Romance of Child Rowland'
(p. 403). Rowland, the youngest sibling in King Arthur's family, goes on a quest
to Elfland to find his sister, Burd Ellen, who has been stolen by the elves, and
his two elder brothers, who have been captured trying to rescue her. Jamieson
notes the presence in this ballad of the 'fee, faw, fum' motif, and adds: 'When
on a former occasion, in "Popular Ballads and Songs," vol. ii. p. 282, the present writer laid before the public a translation of the first ballad of "Rosmer," he
expressed an opinion that this was the identical romance quoted by Edgar in "King
Lear," which in Shakespeare's time was well-known in England, and is still
preserved, in however mutilated a state, in Scotland' (p. 397). There are several
parallels between the story and B.'s poem. The 'Warluck Merlin' tells Rowland
that he 'should kill every person he met after entering the land of Fairy, and
should neither eat nor drink of what was offered him in that country, whatever
his hunger or thirst might be; for if he tasted or touched in Elfland, he must
remain in the power of the Elves, and never see *middle eard* again' (p. 399). When
Rowland arrives at the place where his sister is held captive, the King of
Elfland emerges from its 'folding doors' and sings: 'With "*fi, fi, fo*, and *fum!* / I
smell the blood of a Christian man! / Be he dead, be he living, wi' my brand /
I'll clash his harns frae his harn-pan!"' At this, the 'undaunted' Child Rowland
exclaims, 'Strike, then, Bogle of Hell, if thou darest!', and '[draws] the good
claymore [Excalibar,] that never struck in vain' (pp. 402–3).

(ii) *The Bible*

Although a large number of potential sources have been identified for the poem,
the only other text to which it alludes directly is the Bible. 'Tophet', mentioned
at l. 143 in the phrase 'Tophet's tool', was a 'place of burning' lying to the south
of Jerusalem in which 'the carcases and other filthiness from the city' were destroyed;
it is frequently used in the Bible as an emblem of hell (e.g. *2 Kings* xxiii 10; *Isaiah*
xxx 33). The allusion to 'Apollyon' (l. 160) invokes one of B.'s habitual points
of reference, *Revelation*, and more specifically the terrifying locusts unleashed by
the star which falls from heaven to earth in ch. ix: 'And in those days shall men
seek death, and shall not find it; and shall desire to die, and death shall flee from
them. And the shapes of the locusts were like unto horses prepared unto battle
. . . And they had a king over them, which is the angel of the bottomless pit
. . . in the Greek tongue hath his name Apollyon' (ix 6–11). There is also a

reference to the Last Judgement, graphically described in *Revelation*, at ll. 65–6. In 'Biblical Influence in Childe Roland', Leslie M. Thompson suggests some thematic similarities between the poem and passages of the New Testament comparing the Christian to a soldier; see *Papers on Language and Literature* iii (1967), 339–53.

(iii) *Pilgrim's Progress*

The 'foul fiend' mentioned by Edgar in *Lear* (III iv 51–62) is linked to Apollyon in Bunyan's *Pilgrim's Progress*, whose hero is, of course, also engaged on a journey or quest through a hostile landscape largely composed of valleys. Christian meets a fearsome monster called Apollyon in the Valley of Humiliation and eventually overcomes him through faith in Christ. There are, as *Melchiori* notes, some verbal parallels between this passage in *Pilgrim's Progress* and the poem (see below ll. 160–1n.). Bunyan's text also illustrates the use of 'Tophet' as a synonym for Hell: 'Then said *Evangelist*, Why not willing to die? since this life is attended with so many evils? The Man answered, Because I fear that this burden that is upon my back, will sink me lower than the Grave; and I shall fall into *Tophet*' (Oxford 1966, p. 9).

(iv) *Fairy Tales*

Taking his cue from B.'s account of the poem's composition, Harold Golder suggests that there is a dreamlike association between Edgar's song and *Childe Roland*, with the words of the song triggering a whole series of associations with material that B. had known since childhood ('Browning's *Childe Roland*', *PMLA* xxxix [1924] 963–78). He points out that the 'doggerel' words in Edgar's song occur in *Hop-o'-my-thumb*, *Jack and the Beanstalk*, and *Jack the Giant Killer*, texts to which B. alludes elsewhere; see e.g. *Ring* i 136–7. There are, moreover, similarities between these stories and the narrative of *Childe Roland*. At the end of *Jack the Giant-Killer*, the hero is guided to a castle by a white-headed man, 'where a host of lost adventurers, who had previously essayed the conquest of the tower, lie imprisoned. On arriving before the gates, Jack finds a golden trumpet hanging suspended by a silver chain, under which is written: "Whoever can this trumpet blow, / Soon shall the giant overthrow, / And break the black enchantment straight, / So all shall be in happy state"' (Golder, 966). B.'s tendency towards creative reintepretation of this fairy-tale material is indicated in *Lovers' Quarrel* 131–3 (p. 383), where 'the valiant Thumb' is transformed into a hero; as Golder puts it, 'B. . . . has obviously confused these tales with others in which the main character is a fighting hero' (p. 965). Cp. also the closing lines of *Pauline*, whose protagonist declares: 'I seem dying, as one going in the dark / To fight a giant' (ll. 1026–7, p. 69).

(v) *Romance and Chivalry*

B. undoubtedly knew the *Chanson de Roland*, and he may have known of 'the publication in 1837 of the earliest, most complete and most literate manuscript that gained the attention of modern readers' (Howard S. Robertson, ed., *The Song of Roland* [1972], p. vii). Roland is a vassal of the Emperor Charlemagne, who is left behind in Spain with a small force, which is attacked by a much larger Saracen army and utterly destroyed; towards the end of the battle he repeatedly blows his horn to summon Charlemagne's main force to his assistance, but they arrive only in time to avenge his death. Roland became one of the main heroes of the chivalric tradition, featuring in a number of Middle English romances, and his exploits were alluded to in many nineteenth-century texts. These mainly relate to his relationship with his friend Oliver and his blowing of his horn at Roncevaux. Contemporary references to Roland tend to treat him as an exemplar of medieval romance chivalry; see for instance bk. v of *Aurora Leigh*, where EBB. considers the duty of contemporary poets: 'Their sole work is to represent the age, / Their age, not Charlemagne's,—this live, throbbing age, / That brawls, cheats, maddens, calculates, aspires, / And spends more passion, more heroic heat, / Betwixt the mirrors of its drawing-rooms, / Than Roland with his knights at Roncesvalles' (ll. 202–7). Roland is the name of the speaker's horse in *How They Brought the Good News* (p. 220).

Golder points out resemblances to other stories of chivalry and romance. Perhaps the most significant of these is Spenser's *Faerie Queene*; the 'hoary cripple' who guides Roland towards the dark tower in B.'s poem is compared with Archimago, the sorcerer who attempts to beguile the Red Cross Knight from his quest: 'At length they chaunst to meet upon the way / An aged Sire, in long blacke weedes yclad, / His feete all bare, his beard all hoarie gray' (I i st. 29). He also notes similarities to Richard Johnson's *Renowned History of the Seven Champions of Christendom*, especially the story of St George, and to *Palmerin of England*, a Spanish romance translated into English by Robert Southey at the beginning of the nineteenth century. Similarities have also been noted to sections of Malory's *Morte D'Arthur*, inc. the story of Balin (Linda Hughes, *SBHC* ix [1981] 42–50) and the Tale of Sir Gareth of Orkney (Lionel Stevenson, 'Pertinacious Victorian Poets', *University of Toronto Quarterly* xxi [1952], 239–40).

(vi) *Dante*
Ruth Elizabeth Sullivan ('B.'s *Childe Roland* and Dante's *Inferno*', *VP* v [1967] 296–302), notes some general similarities between the setting and landscape of the poem and that of Dante's *Inferno*, and suggests a specific comparison between the 'engine' mentioned in ll. 140–4 and the punishment meted out by Satan to Judas, Brutus and Cassius in hell: 'Da ogni bocca dirompea co' denti / un peccatore, a guisa di maciulla, / sì che tre ne facea così dolenti' [At every mouth his teeth a sinner champ'd, / Bruised as with ponderous engine; so that three / Were in this guise tormented.] (299; *Inferno* xxxiv, 55–7). The horn of Orlando [Roland] is mentioned in Canto xxxi of the poem, as Dante and Virgil enter the deepest circles of hell: 'Quiv'era men che notte e men che giorno / sì che 'l viso m'andava innanzi poco; / ma io senti' sonare un alto corno, / tanto ch'avrebbe ogne tuon fatto fioco, / che, contra sé la sua via seguitando, / dirizzò li occhi miei tutti ad un loco. / Dopo la dolorosa rotta, quando / Carlo Magno perdé la santa gesta, / non sonò sì terribilmente Orlando. / Poco portäi in là volta la testa, / che me parve veder molte alte torri[.] (ll. 10–20) [There / Was less than day and less than night, that far / Mine eye advanced not: but I heard a horn / Sounded so loud, the peal it rang had made / The thunder feeble. Following its course / The adverse way, my strained eyes were bent / On that one spot. So terrible a blast / Orlando blew not, when that dismal rout / O'er threw the host of Charlemain, and quench'd / His saintly warfare. Thitherward not long / My head was raised, when many a lofty tower / Methought I spied.] Cp. D. S. S. Parsons, 'Childe Roland and the Fool', *University of Windsor Review* iv.1 (1968) 24–30.

(vii) *Gerard de Lairesse*
In his *PMLA* article and again (more briefly) in *Handbook*, DeVane suggests that the poem's unusual focus on landscape ultimately derives from ch. 17 of de Lairesse's *The Art of Painting in All its Branches* (1778), entitled 'Of Things Deformed and Broken, Falsely Called Painter-like'. This was clearly a favourite book of B.'s as a child; he noted on the fly-leaf that he 'read this book more often and with greater delight ... than any other' when he was a child ('Landscape of *Childe*

Roland', 428); and he returned to de Lairesse in the late *Parleyings* (1887). The chapter traces an imaginary 'walk' designed to show the difference between the 'painter-like' and the 'unpainter-like' in landscape. Verbal resemblances are noted at ll. 51–2 and 154 below.

(viii) *Contemporary Sources*

Tennyson's 'The Vision of Sin' (1842) takes the form of a dream vision in which a 'gray and gap-toothed man as lean as death' rides across 'a withered heath' and joins a ghoulish company at a 'ruined inn' determined to pursue a life of degraded hedonism. The final section of the poem is especially reminiscent of *Childe Roland*:

> The voice grew faint: there came a further change:
> Once more uprose the mystic mountain-range:
> Below were men and horses pierced with worms,
> And slowly quickening into lower forms;
> By shards and scurf of salt, and scum of dross,
> Old plash of rains, and refuse patched with moss
>
> (ll. 207–12)

The idea of writing a poem around a line of Shakespeare may also have been prompted by Tennyson's example in poems such as *Mariana*.

Melchiori draws attention to the possible influence of Edgar Allan Poe's short story *Metzengerstein* on the portrait of the horse at ll.76–84, and on the atmosphere of the poem as a whole (pp. 208–13); C. Alphonso Smith (*Poet Lore* xi [1899] 626–8) compares the poem to the opening sentences of Poe's *The Fall of the House of Usher*. Other suggested influences include Shelley's *Julian and Maddalo* (Richard Dellamora, *Journal of Pre-Raphaelite Studies* ii [1981] 36–52) and Wordsworth's *Peter Bell*, which contains a night journey across a psychologically inflected landscape, a 'gaunt' ass with 'staring bones', and a drowned man in a river (see ll. 121–6n., and also Thomas Harrison, 'B.'s Childe Roland and Wordsworth', *Tennessee Studies in Literature* vi [1961] 1–23). EBB.'s *The Cry of the Children* (1844) is presented as a possible influence by David Erdman, 'Browning's Industrial Nightmare', *Philological Quarterly* xxxvi [1957] 417–35, but verbal parallels between the two poems are slight, and Erdman's attempts to place *Childe Roland* in its contemporary historical context are undermined by his acceptance of DeVane's (almost certainly erroneous) assertion that the poem was written in Paris (see *Composition*). B. himself rejected Irene Hardy's suggestion that the poem might have been inspired by Scott's 'The Bridal of Triermain'; see *Poet Lore* xxiv (1913) 53–8.

(ix) *Non-literary sources*

In a footnote, Orr comments that the 'picturesque materials' which went into the poem included 'a tower which Mr. Browning once saw in the Carrara mountains, a painting which caught his eye years later in Paris; and the figure of a horse in the tapestry in his own drawing-room' (Orr *Handbook* 274). Her authority for this may derive from B. himself, who mentioned the tower in Massa-Carrara in a letter to A. W. Hunt (DeVane *Handbook* 229). *Thomas* investigates the various tapestries known to have been in the drawing-room at Casa Guidi, and concludes that none of them was likely to have served as the model for the horse in the poem, although he does not rule out the possibility that other tapestries owned by B. might eventually come to light (p. 61). He also investigates the whereabouts of the tower, and suggests the Malaspina Castle in Massa as its possible prototype (p. 424).

Parallels in B.

Miller (p. 12) places Childe Roland with Paracelsus in B.'s 'great gallery of brilliant tainted characters'; she draws attention to a passage from *Paracelsus* (iii 718–24, I 223) in which the hero laments the failure of his quest for knowledge, using a chivalric metaphor: 'I have address'd a frock of heavy mail, / Yet may not join the troop of sacred knights . . . Best follow, dreaming that ere night arrive / I shall o'ertake the company, and ride / Glittering as they!' *Melchiori* (pp. 124–5) notes another strong parallel with *Paracelsus* ii 289–313, a passage in which Paracelsus overhears Aprile singing of the 'wan troop' of poets who have betrayed their gifts; they urge the 'Lost one' to join them, for although they had hoped that he would 'speak / The message which our lips, too weak, / Refused to utter', he has failed like them. *Melchiori* refers not to the first edition text (1835) but to the text which B. had recently and extensively revised for his collected *Poems* of 1849 (where 'The message' read 'God's message'): see the notes in our edition, I 169–70. The apocalyptic tone recalls the vision of the Last Judgement in *Easter Day*, which also anticipates its narrative in its description of a knight who fails his task at the last moment (ll. 483–8, III 121). *Melchiori* also points out a similar moment in *A Blot in the 'Scutcheon* (1843) III i 8–11: 'And the dim turret I have fled from, fronts / Again my step; the very river put / Its arm about me and conducted me / To this detested spot' (p. 138). Both *Melchiori* and Daniel Karlin (*Browning's Hatreds*, Oxford 1993) note the resemblance of the 'Dark Tower' to the 'strange square black turret' on the largest of the 'isles of the syren' which the speaker of *England in Italy* proposes to explore (see ll. 217–21, p. 266); for the recurrence of such structures in B., see *Sordello* vi 779–85n. (I 763). *Melchiori* also notes a similarity to *Ring* vii 867–70, in which Pompilia's mother is compared to a 'plashy pool'. The speaker's anticipation of imminent death (whether fulfilled or not) recalls *Pauline* 1026 ff. (p. 69); cp. also *Prospice* (*DP*, 1864).

Criticism

Some of the difficulties of interpretation offered by this poem are summarized by Orr. After her account of the poem's apparent action, she adds: 'So far, the picture is consistent; but if we look below its surface discrepancies appear. The Tower is much nearer and more accessible than Childe Roland has thought; a sinister-looking man of whom he asked the way, and who, he believed, was deceiving him, has really put him on the right track; and as he describes the country through which he passes, it becomes clear that half its horrors are created by his own heated imagination, or by some undefined influence in the place itself. We are left in doubt whether those who have found failure in this quest, have not done so through the very act of attainment in it, and when, dauntless, Childe Roland sounds his slughorn and announces that he has come, we should not know, but that he lives to tell the tale, whether in doing this he incurs, or is escaping, the general doom' (*Handbook* 273–4). Orr's summary raises the central problem of the object of the quest. Line 176 would seem to suggest that the Dark Tower is itself the object, but the fact that Roland takes the cripple's direction *despite* knowing that 'all agree' he is pointing the way to the Dark Tower (ll. 10–15) implies that he has asked the way to somewhere else; drawing on the poem's possible allusion to Bunyan (see *Sources* and ll. 160–1n.), *Melchiori* nominates the 'Celestial City'. Golder attempts to resolve this difficulty by claiming that the words 'all agree' 'are not Roland's words . . . but the cripple's, which Roland quotes indirectly and ironically' (Golder, op. cit., 968n.).

In the remarks about the poem's composition recorded by Lilian Whiting, B. stated that he 'was conscious of no allegorical intention in writing' the poem; to another enquirer he replied that the poem was 'only a fantasy'. Berdoe records a similarly emphatic statement to this effect by Furnivall at a meeting of the *Browning Society*: '"he had asked Browning if it was an allegory, and in answer had, on three separate occasions, received an emphatic 'no'; that it was simply a dramatic creation called forth by a line of Shakespeare's"' (*Cyclopaedia* 103). B. was, however, willing to give qualified assent to J. W. Chadwick's suggestion that the meaning of the poem could be summed up in the words of *Matthew* x 22: 'he that endureth to the end shall be saved' (*Cyclopaedia* 104; DeVane *Handbook* 229, 231). The poem's Biblical allusions and its similarities to Christianized versions of the quest romance such as *The Faerie Queene* and *Pilgrim's Progress* have led some critics to see it as a representation of the journey of the soul towards salvation deeply rooted in the language and conventions of evangelical Protestantism (see e.g. Donald Hair, *Robert Browning's Language*, Toronto 1999). Others read the poem in biographical or even psychoanalytical terms as an out-pouring of some of B.'s deepest fears about himself and his creativity (e.g. Karlin, *Browning's Hatreds*). *Melchiori*'s suggestion that Childe Roland's predecessors and the 'wan troop' of *Paracelsus* might be B.'s poetic precursors (see *Parallels*) is developed by Harold Bloom in his various essays on the poem; see e.g. *A Map of Misreading* (Oxford 1975), ch. 6.

I

My first thought was, he lied in every word,
   That hoary cripple, with malicious eye
   Askance to watch the working of his lie
On mine, and mouth scarce able to afford
5   Suppression of the glee that pursed and scored
   Its edge at one more victim gained thereby.

2

What else should he be set for, with his staff?
   What, save to waylay with his lies, ensnare

---

2. *hoary*: 'White or grey with age' (*J.*).

3. *the working*] the lurking (*H proof*, but not *H proof²*); clearly a compositor's misprint, although its provenance is puzzling; it is unlikely to be the result of a misreading of B.'s MS, and may be an example of the compositor making a 'poetic' error, since 'lurking' fits the context if not the grammar.

4. *mine*: 'my eye', with the sense that the cripple, with his 'malicious eye', is observing Roland's (psychological) reaction; but the syntax, supported by the proximity of 'his lie', allows for a darker reading, in which 'mine' means 'my lie', i.e. the cripple is lying in response to a question which he knows or believes to be itself a lie, and is watching to see what Roland will (physically) do. Even if this is not the 'right' reading it fits the poem's atmosphere of ambivalence and its theme of self-division.

7. *be set*] bet set (*H proof*). This mispr. is underlined and noted in ink, probably by the printer's reader, in the margin of *H proof*, and is one of the few misprs. in *H proof* which are also recorded in *H proof²*.   *with his staff?*] on his staff? (*H proof*).

All travellers that might find him posted there,
10 And ask the road? I guessed what skull-like laugh
Would break, what crutch 'gin write my epitaph
For pastime in the dusty thoroughfare,

3

If at his counsel I should turn aside
Into that ominous tract which, all agree,
15 Hides the Dark Tower. Yet acquiescingly
I did turn as he pointed; neither pride
Nor hope rekindling at the end descried,
So much as gladness that some end should be.

4

For, what with my whole world-wide wandering,
20 What with my search drawn out thro' years, my hope
Dwindled into a ghost not fit to cope
With that obstreperous joy success would bring,—
I hardly tried now to rebuke the spring
My heart made, finding failure in its scope.

5

25 As when a sick man very near to death
Seems dead indeed, and feels begin and end
The tears and takes the farewell of each friend,
And hears one bid the other go, draw breath
Freelier outside, ("since all is o'er," he saith,
30 "And the blow fall'n no grieving can amend")

9. *that might*] who might (*1865–88*).
11. *what crutch*] whose crutch (*H proof*).
14. *all agree*: on this possible inconsistency in the action of the poem, see *Criticism*.
17. *descried*: 'to descry' is defined by *J.* as '[to] discover; to perceive by the eye; to see any thing distant or obscure'.
18. *should be*] might be (*1863–88*).
22. *obstreperous*: 'Loud; clamorous; noisy; turbulent; vociferous' (*J.*).
25–36. The resemblance between these lines and the opening of Donne's 'A Valediction: Forbidding Mourning' was pointed out by Livingston Lowes, *NQ* [1953] 491–2; Christopher Ricks (*NQ* [1967] 374) compares Tennyson, *The Princess* vii 136–9.
30. *the blow fall'n*] the blow fallen (*1863–88*). The metrical contraction of '—en' words is unusual for B., especially at this period; for another example, see below, l. 166.

6

While some discuss if near the other graves
　　Be room enough for this, and when a day
　　Suits best for carrying the corpse away,
With care about the banners, scarves and staves,—
35　And still the man hears all, and only craves
　　He may not shame such tender love and stay.

7

Thus, I had so long suffered in this quest,
　　Heard failure prophesied so oft, been writ
　　So many times among "The Band"—to wit,
40　The knights who to the Dark Tower's search addressed
　　Their steps—that just to fail as they, seemed best,
　　And all the doubt was now—should I be fit.

8

So, quiet as despair, I turned from him,
　　That hateful cripple, out of his highway
45　Into the path he pointed. All the day
　　Had been a dreary one at best, and dim
　　Was settling to its close, yet shot one grim
　　Red leer to see the plain catch its estray.

34. banners, scarves and staves: staves is a plural of 'staff' (*J.*), a pole from which a flag is flown. Cp. Byron, *Siege of Corinth* 256–7: 'The winds were pillow'd on the waves; / The banners droop'd along their staves'.

44. out of his highway: in Bunyan's *Pilgrim's Progress* (see headnote, *Sources*) Christian is warned not to leave 'the King's [i.e. God's] highway', but does so on the advice of Mr Worldly-Wiseman; as a result he falls into the hands of Giant Despair and is imprisoned in Doubting Castle. But the image here is characteristically complicated by its being 'his [the cripple's] highway'; by l. 52 it has become 'the safe road'. Highway is accented on the second syllable, as often in Renaissance verse; cp. e.g. Chapman's 1616 translation of Homer's *Iliad* (vi 33–4): 'he would a traueller pray / To be his guest; his friendly house, stood in the brode high way' (ll. 33–4).

45–8. With this description of the sunset, cp. Keats, 'There is a charm in footing slow across a silent plain', l. 17: 'Blood-red the Sun may set behind black mountain peaks'; and Shelley, *Julian and Maddalo* 53–4: 'Meanwhile the sun paused ere it should alight, / Over the horizon of the mountains'. Cp. also Lairesse, *Art of Painting* (see headnote, *Sources*): 'The sun, now on the point of setting, darted his refulgent rays between some heavy clouds' (p. 261). This moment is repeated at ll. 182–4.

48. estray: 'A creature wandered beyond its limits; a stray' (*J.*). Melchiori (p. 212) points out that this unusual word is also used in Poe's story *Metzengerstein*, a possible source for the horse described in ll. 76–84.

9

For mark! no sooner was I fairly found
50   Pledged to the plain, after a pace or two,
        Than pausing to throw backward a last view
To the safe road, 'twas gone! grey plain all round!
Nothing but plain to the horizon's bound.
        I might go on; nought else remained to do.

10

55   So on I went. I think I never saw
        Such starved ignoble nature; nothing throve:
        For flowers—as well expect a cedar grove!
But cockle, spurge, according to their law
Might propagate their kind, with none to awe,
60   You'd think: a burr had been a treasure-trove.

11

No! penury, inertness, and grimace,
        In some strange sort, were the land's portion. "See
        Or shut your eyes"—said Nature peevishly—
"It nothing skills: I cannot help my case:
65   The Judgment's fire alone can cure this place,
        Calcine its clods and set my prisoners free."

51–2. DeVane compares Lairesse's description of an 'unpainter-like' landscape as 'without roads or ways' ('Landscape of *Childe Roland*', p. 429; see headnote, *Sources*).
52. *To*] O'er (*1865–88*).
57. *a cedar grove*: the cedar has biblical associations of nobility and religious devotion; cedar wood was used in the building of Solomon's temple. But the phrase 'cedar grove' does not appear in the Bible; the word 'grove' itself is consistently associated with pagan idolatry.
58. *cockle*: 'A weed that grows in corn' (*J.*).   *spurge*: 'A plant violently purgative' (*J.*).
60. *burr*: 'A rough head of a plant, which sticks to the hair or cloaths' (*J.*); cp. *Twins* 4, and headnote to that poem (III 657).
62–6.] no quotation marks in *H proof*.
64. *"It nothing skills"*: 'it doesn't help; it makes no difference'.
65.] 'Tis the Last Judgment's fire must cure this place, (*1863–88*). There is no exact parallel in *Revelation*, or elsewhere in the Bible, for this concept of fire as a purifying agent with regard to the earth itself; the closest parallel is *Revelation* xx 9–15, in which fire from heaven destroys God's enemies, an event that immediately precedes the Last Judgement and the vision of the New Jerusalem in ch. xxi.
66. *Calcine*: to burn (something) to powder, from 'calx', the Latin word for quicklime, but used in English as an alchemical term denoting a powder produced by thoroughly burning a mineral or metal and reducing it to its purest state. *OED*

12

If there pushed any ragged thistle-stalk
    Above its mates, the head was chopped—the bents
    Were jealous else. What made those holes and rents
70   In the dock's harsh swarth leaves—bruised as to baulk
All hope of greenness? 'tis a brute must walk
    Pashing their life out, with a brute's intents.

13

As for the grass, it grew as scant as hair
    In leprosy—thin dry blades pricked the mud
75   Which underneath looked kneaded up with blood.
One stiff blind horse, his every bone a-stare,
    Stood stupified, however he came there—
    Thrust out past service from the devil's stud!

---

cites works by authors B. certainly knew, e.g. Ben Jonson and Sit Thomas Browne.
Cp. *Easter Day* 631n. (III 126).   *set my prisoners free*: seeds, locked in the earth,
require heat to trigger their fertilization; but here no natural heat will suffice.
67–9. If there pushed . . . jealous else: the grass is like a democracy in which each
blade is 'jealous' of the advancement of any other; in this, as in other respects,
the poem revises some of the political imagery of *Sordello*, e.g. the contrast between
the 'real pines' in Taurello Salinguerra's garden and the 'throng / Of shrubs . . .
a nameless common sort' (iv 211–13, I 606). For another echo of Taurello's
garden, see *By the Fire-Side* 23n. (p. 460).
68. the head was chopped: this action implies human agency, yet none is visible, as
in the case of the horse at l. 77; another mark of the hallucinatory strangeness of
the landscape.   *the bents*: a 'bent' is 'A stalk of grass, called bent-grass' (*J.*).
70–1. swarth leaves— . . . hope of greenness?] swarth leaves? . . . hope of greenness—
(*H proof*). On the spelling of 'baulk' see *An Epistle* 190n. (p. 521).
70. dock's harsh swarth leaves: a dock is a plant or weed (*J.*); cp. *Sordello* iv 23
(I 594): 'Docks, quitchgrass, loathly mallows no man plants', part of the landscape of the devastated city of Ferrara.
72. pashing: from 'to pash', '[to] strike; to crush; to push against; to dash with
violence' (*J.*).
73–4. as scant as hair / In leprosy: loss of hair from eyebrows, eyelashes and other
parts of the body is one of the symptoms of leprosy; cp. *An Epistle* 58–9n. (p. 514).
76–84. The suffering horse is unusual in B. for being associated with wickedness;
such images (especially of cab-horses) were common in the period, but were more
often used to evoke pity and indignation. Roland's final judgement is especially
striking in its Calvinist 'logic', which distances him from B.'s own theology, and
from his personal opposition to cruelty towards animals. Cp. *How It Strikes* 31–2n.
(p. 440).
78. A 'stud' is 'A collection of breeding horses and mares' (*J.*). 'Past service' means
that the horse, a stallion, is impotent and can no longer 'serve' the devil's mares.

14

Alive? he might be dead for all I know,
80   With that red gaunt and colloped neck a-strain,
        And shut eyes underneath the rusty mane.
    Seldom went such grotesqueness with such woe:
    I never saw a brute I hated so—
        He must be wicked to deserve such pain.

15

85   I shut my eyes and turned them on my heart.
        As a man calls for wine before he fights,
        I asked one draught of earlier, happier sights
    Ere fitly I could hope to play my part.
    Think first, fight afterwards—the soldier's art:
90   One taste of the old times sets all to rights!

16

    Not it! I fancied Cuthbert's reddening face
        Beneath its garniture of curly gold,
        Dear fellow, till I almost felt him fold
    An arm in mine to fix me to the place,
95   That way he used. Alas! one night's disgrace!
        Out went my heart's new fire and left it cold.

17

    Giles, then, the soul of honour—there he stands
        Frank as ten years ago when knighted first.
    What honest men should dare (he said) he durst.

---

79. *for all*] for aught (*1863–88*).
80. *colloped*: derived from 'collop', 'a piece of any animal' (*J.*); the sense may be that the horse's vertebrae protrude and give its neck the effect of being articulated in pieces, like meat prepared for cooking; cp. *Aristophanes' Apology* (1875) 5314: 'Collops of hare with roast spinks rare!'
90. *old times*] old time (*1863–88*).
91–7. Cuthbert . . . Giles: names of fictitious knights.
97–102. cp. *The Patriot* (p. 340), and see headnote, *Criticism.*
98. *Frank*: there may be a pun on 'Frank' as a proper noun, used in the Levant to designate a native of northern Europe, especially a crusading knight; B. uses this term extensively and often ironically in *The Return of the Druses* (1843), his play about the duplicitous actions of the 'Knights-Hospitallers of Rhodes' on an imaginary 'islet of the Southern Sporades'.
99. *Oxford* suggests an allusion here to *Macbeth* I vii 46–7: 'I dare do all that may become a man; / Who dares do more is none'.   *honest men*] honest man (*1868–88*).

100   Good—but the scene shifts—faugh! what hangman's hands
       Pin to his breast a parchment? his own bands
         Read it. Poor traitor, spit upon and curst!

                              18
       Better this present than a past like that—
         Back therefore to my darkening path again.
105   No sound, no sight as far as eye could strain.
       Will the night send a howlet or a bat?
       I asked: when something on the dismal flat
         Came to arrest my thoughts and change their train.

                              19
       A sudden little river crossed my path
110   As unexpected as a serpent comes.
         No sluggish tide congenial to the glooms—
       This, as it frothed by, might have been a bath
       For the fiend's glowing hoof—to see the wrath
         Of its black eddy bespate with flakes and spumes.

                              20
115   So petty yet so spiteful! all along,
         Low scrubby alders kneeled down over it;
         Drenched willows flung them headlong in a fit

---

100. faugh! an exclamation of disgust. *hangman's hands*] hangman hands
(*1868–88*). Cp. *Macbeth* II ii 25.

104–21. This passage may owe something to one in Lairesse's *Art of Painting*
(see headnote, *Sources*): 'I found myself again at the lake before-mentioned;
which lay near a shattered tomb, with the corpse half tumbled out. The head
and arm rested on a large root of a tree lying near it; the lid was almost off, and
just on the totter, and a snake, from underneath, was creeping into the tomb.
A sight frightful enough' (p. 261).

106. 'Howlet' is 'the vulgar name for an owl' (*J.*). Cp. *Pippa Passes* iv 287–90
(p. 170): 'But at night, brother Howlet, over the woods / Toll the world to thy
chantry— / Sing to the bats' sleek sisterhoods / Full complines with gallantry'.
Pippa introduces this scene by remarking: 'Oh, what a drear, dark close to my
poor day! / How could that red sun drop in that black cloud!' (ll. 279–80).

114. bespate: not in *J.*; *OED* cites this as the only post-medieval use of this
variant of 'bespit' ('spat upon'), but it is more plausible to see it as a variant of
'bespattered', which B. has put in this form because it calls up the image of a
river 'in spate'. *spumes*: *J.* defines 'spume' as 'Foam; froth'.

117–20. Roland's image is typically dense (or confused): the willows (probably
the variety known as 'weeping willow') are compared to women throwing
themselves into the river because they have been 'wronged' (their leaning

Of mute despair, a suicidal throng:
The river which had done them all the wrong,
120   Whate'er that was, rolled by, deterred no whit.

21

Which, while I forded,—good saints, how I feared
    To set my foot upon a dead man's cheek,
    Each step, or feel the spear I thrust to seek
For hollows, tangled in his hair or beard!
125   —It may have been a water-rat I speared,
    But, ugh! it sounded like a baby's shriek.

22

Glad was I when I reached the other bank.
    Now for a better country. Vain presage!
    Who were the strugglers, what war did they wage
130   Whose savage trample thus could pad the dank
Soil to a plash? toads in a poisoned tank,
    Or wild cats in a red-hot iron cage—

23

The fight must so have seemed in that fell cirque.
    What kept them there, with all the plain to choose?

---

attitude reinforces the idea that they are 'fallen women'); at the same time, the river is the lover who has 'done them all the wrong'. B. may have been remembering the scene of Ophelia's death ('There is a willow grows aslant a brook', *Hamlet* IV vii 166), and he would have known many Victorian evocations of women drowning or thinking of drowning themselves, e.g. in Thomas Hood's famous poem 'The Bridge of Sighs' (1844), and in novels by Dickens (*Oliver Twist*, 1839; *David Copperfield*, 1850). Cp. also Cowper, *The Task* i 268–9: 'We pass a gulph in which the willows dip / Their pendent boughs, stooping as if to drink'. *121–6*: cp. Wordsworth, *Peter Bell*, 573–5: 'He touches here—he touches there— / And now among the dead man's hair / His sapling Peter has entwined'. *Oxford* also compares Shelley, *The Revolt of Islam*, 2466–8.

128. a better country: a biblical phrase, associated with salvation: 'But now they desire a better country, that is, an heavenly' (*Hebrews* xi 16). *presage*: 'Prognostick; presension of futurity' (*J.*); note that B. follows J. in placing the emphasis on the last syllable.

131. plash: 'A small lake of water or puddle' (*J.*).

133. cirque: a cirque is a 'space or area for sports, with seats round for the spectators' (*J.*). The association here is with the Roman 'circus' where gladiatorial combats were held.

134. kept them] penned them (*1863–88*).

135   No foot-print leading to that horrid mews,
       None out of it: mad brewage set to work
       Their brains, no doubt, like galley-slaves the Turk
       Pits for his pastime, Christians against Jews.

                          24
       And more than that—a furlong on—why, there!
140   What bad use was that engine for, that wheel,
          Or brake, not wheel—that harrow fit to reel
       Men's bodies out like silk? with all the air
       Of Tophet's tool, on earth left unaware,
          Or brought to sharpen its rusty teeth of steel.

                          25
145   Then came a bit of stubbed ground, once a wood,
          Next a marsh, it would seem, and now mere earth
          Desperate and done with; (so a fool finds mirth,
       Makes a thing and then mars it, till his mood

135. mews: derived (somewhat obscurely) from the sense in *J.*: 'A cage; an inclosure; a place where any thing is confined' (*J.*).

136. brewage: 'Mixture of various things' (*J.*).

137–8. Turkish cruelty was proverbial; note their appearance as victims of Christian cruelty in *Heretic's Tragedy* 50 (III 224). Cp. *Red Cotton Night-Cap Country* (1873) 3651–3: 'One galley-slave, whom curse and blow compel / To labour on, ply oar—beside his chain, / Encumbered with a corpse-companion now'. The idea of 'partners enforced and loth' also features in *Bad Dreams II* (*Asolando*, 1889) 21–5.

140. engine: 'A military machine' (*J.*); here an instrument of torture. David Erdman (see headnote, *Sources*) suggests an allusion to the silk factories mentioned in *Pippa Passes* (e.g. *Intro* 47, p. 93), a suggestion supported by the simile in l. 142. But there is also an (inverted) allusion to the 'engine' whose gradual, collective construction is an emblem of human progress in *Sordello* iii 811–35 (I 582), and whose component parts are also, as here, a mystery ('Remark this tooth's spring, wonder what that valve's / Fall bodes' [ll. 820–1]).

141. harrow: B. seems to have in mind here something like the 'back harrow', defined in *OED* as 'a harrow of which the teeth are fixed on radiating arms, so as to revolve horizontally'.

143. Tophet's tool: for Tophet, see headnote, *Sources*.

145. stubbed: 'Of trees: Cut down to a stub; cut off near the ground; also, deprived of branches or pollarded' (*OED*).

148. Makes a thing and then mars it: cp. *Caliban upon Setebos* 97 (p. 630), and *Prince Hohenstiel-Schwangau* (1871) 371.

Changes and off he goes!) within a rood
150   Bog, clay and rubble, sand and stark black dearth.

26

Now blotches rankling, coloured gay and grim,
   Now patches where some leanness of the soil's
   Broke into moss or substances like boils;
Then came some palsied oak, a cleft in him
155   Like a distorted mouth that splits its rim
   Gaping at death, and dies while it recoils.

27

And just as far as ever from the end!
   Nought in the distance but the evening, nought
   To point my footstep further! At the thought,
160   A great black bird, Apollyon's bosom-friend,
   Sailed past, nor beat his wide wing dragon-penned
   That brushed my cap—perchance the guide I sought.

---

149. rood] rood—(*1863–88*); 'a measure of sixteen feet and a half in long measure' (*J.*).

150. Possibly influenced by a sentence in Lairesse's *Art of Painting* (see headnote, *Sources*): 'His whole port-folio was full of such-like painter-like trumpery; such as muddy water, decayed and broken stones, pieces of wood, barren shrubs and bushes, rough grounds, toads, snakes, &c.' (p. 259). Cp. also *PL* ii 621: 'Rocks, caves, lakes, fens, bogs, dens, and shades of death'. *rubble, sand*] rubble stones (*H proof*).

151. rankling: from rankle, '[to] fester; to breed corruption; to be inflamed in body or mind' (*J.*).

152. where some leanness] raw where leanness (*1865²*), a rare example of a substantive variant unique to this edition; see also below, l. 159.

154. DeVane ('Landscape of Browning's *Childe Roland*', p. 430; see headnote, *Sources*) compares a description by Lairesse of oaks 'which had been thunder-struck; the stem cleft from top to bottom'.

157. the end!] the end. (*1872*); the end, (*H proof, 1884*). It is rare to find variants unique to *1872* and even rarer to find them revised in reissues of this edition. The full stop in *1872* may be a mispr.; the comma in *1884* is more likely to be authorial, with B. noticing the error and correcting it without having another text to hand (and just possibly with a memory of the original proof reading almost thirty years previously!). See also ll. 166n., 174n.

160–1. Apollyon is the 'angel of the bottomless pit' in *Revelation* ix 11; his 'wide wing dragon-penned' (lit. 'feathered like a dragon's', although the sense is probably 'shaped', since dragons are usually depicted with wings like those of a bat) probably derives, as *Melchiori* suggests, from his appearance in Bunyan's *Pilgrim's Progress*: 'now the Monster was hideous to behold, he was cloathed with scales like a Fish; (and they are his pride) he had Wings like a Dragon, feet like a Bear, and out of his belly came Fire and Smoak' (p. 128).

28

For looking up, aware I somehow grew,
　　'Spite of the dusk, the plain had given place
165　　All round to mountains—with such name to grace
Mere ugly heights and heaps now stol'n in view.
How thus they had surprised me,—solve it, you!
How to get from them was no plainer case.

29

Yet half I seemed to recognise some trick
170　Of mischief happened to me, God knows when—
In a bad dream perhaps. Here ended, then,
Progress this way. When, in the very nick
Of giving up, one time more, came a click
As when a trap shuts—you're inside the den!

30

175　Burningly it came on me all at once,
　　This was the place! those two hills on the right
　　Crouched like two bulls locked horn in horn in fight—
While to the left, a tall scalped mountain . . . Dunce,

---

165. *with such name to grace*: 'if I might grace with such a name . . .'
166. *stol'n*] stolen (*H proof*, but not *H proof²*, *1863–88*). The '—en' contraction is
rare in B. (see above, l. 30n.), as is the return to a proof reading in eds. after
1855; see l. 157.
167. *me,—solve it, you!*] me, tell who knew, (*H proof*).
168. *get from them*] get through them (*H proof*, but not *H proof²*).　*no plainer case*]
no clearer case (*1863–88*).
174. *the den!*] the den (*1872*); the den. (*1884*). *1872* is clearly misprinted (contrast
the less obvious case in l. 157); it seems likely that B. made the correction without recourse to another text, and he did not retain it because the next printing,
1888, would not have been set from *1884*, a volume of selections, but from the
Poetical Works of 1868 or one of its reissues. See also l. 177.
177. *Crouched*] Couched (*1884*). Variants unique to *1884* are even rarer than ones
unique to *1872*; this may be a mispr., although it makes sense and the proximity of the line to l. 174, in which B. corrected an obvious mispr. in *1872*, makes
it more likely that his eye fell on this line and that he introduced a variant which
he did not recall, or about which he changed his mind, when he read proof for
the next appearance of the poem, in *1888* (the text of which would not, of course,
have been set from a volume of selections: see l. 174n.). See also next note.
177–8. *in fight— / While*] in fight; / While (*1863–88*, except *1884*, which has 'in
fight, / While,'. The occurrence of these variants in punctuation unique to *1884*
strengthens the argument that 'Couched' in l. 177 is authorial.

Fool, to be dozing at the very nonce,
180   After a life spent training for the sight!

31

What in the midst lay but the Tower itself?
    The round squat turret, blind as the fool's heart,
    Built of brown stone, without a counterpart
In the whole world. The tempest's mocking elf
185   Points to the shipman thus the unseen shelf
    He strikes on, only when the timbers start.

32

Not see? because of night perhaps?—Why, day
    Came back again for that! before it left,
    The dying sunset kindled through a cleft:
190   The hills, like giants at a hunting, lay—
    Chin upon hand, to see the game at bay,—
    "Now stab and end the creature—to the heft!"

179. Fool, to be dozing] *Fool, to be caught blind* (*H proof*, but not *H proof²*); Dotard,
a-dozing (*1865–88*). B. may have noticed the phrase 'fool's heart' only 3 lines
later.   *nonce*: not in *J*. in this sense; only in the phrase 'for the nonce', meaning
'for the purpose'.
180.] With my life spent in training for the sight! (*H proof*).
181–4. What in the midst . . . the whole world: for possible sources for the description of the tower, and other such structures in B., see headnote.
182. blind as the fool's heart: cp. *Psalms* xiv 1: 'The fool hath said in his heart,
There is no God.' 'Blind' in the architectural sense means 'windowless', but also
carries biblical connotations of spiritual darkness in both OT and NT; note esp.
Matthew xxiii 16–17: 'Woe unto you, ye blind guides . . . Ye fools and blind'.
184. The tempest's mocking elf: an elf is 'A wandering spirit, supposed to be seen
in wild unfrequented places; a fairy' or 'a devil' (*J*.). There may be an echo of
Ariel in *The Tempest*: he creates (at Prospero's bidding) the false 'effects' of the
storm which opens the play, and can be seen as a 'mocking elf' in his relation
to other characters such as Caliban, Stephano and Trinculo. B. may also recall
the phrase 'deceiving elf' from Keats's 'Ode to a Nightingale' (l. 74).
186. when the timbers start: i.e. when the ship has already collided with the 'unseen
shelf'. Cp. *James Lee* 48–53 (p. 670): 'Did a woman ever—would I knew!— /
Watch the man / With whom began / Love's voyage full-sail,—(now, gnash
your teeth!) / When planks start, open hell beneath / Unawares?' *Oxford* suggests a possible indebtedness to George Anson's *A Voyage round the World* (1748),
a copy of which was in B.'s library (*Collections*, A0067): 'a but-end or plank might
start, and we might go down immediately' (III ii 317).
192. heft: 'Handle' (*J*.).

33

Not hear? when noise was everywhere? it tolled
   Increasing like a bell. Names in my ears,
195   Of all the lost adventurers my peers,—
How such a one was strong, and such was bold,
And such was fortunate, yet each of old
   Lost, lost! one moment knelled the woe of years.

34

There they stood, ranged along the hill-sides—met
200   To view the last of me, a living frame
   For one more picture! in a sheet of flame
I saw them and I knew them all. And yet
Dauntless the slug-horn to my lips I set
   And blew. *"Childe Roland to the Dark Tower came."*

195. Cp. the dying Aprile's vision, at the end of bk. ii of *Paracelsus*, of the 'phantoms [and] powers' whom he recognizes as the spirits of his fellow-poets (ll. 594–9, I 188); see also *How It Strikes* 99–103 (p. 444). Cp. also (noting 'I knew them all' in l. 202) EBB.'s *A Vision of Poets* (1844), which B. greatly admired: 'The poet knew them . . . these were poets true, / Who died for Beauty as martyrs do / For truth' (ll. 286, 289–91). These are all positive images of precursors; again, *Childe Roland* suggests a nightmarish inversion.

196. a one] an one (1856). Verbal variants unique to the first American ed. are extremely rare; this one is probably, though not certainly, a misprint.

202–4. Turner compares Malory, *Morte D'Arthur*: 'And also there was fast by a sycamore tree, and there hung an horn, the greatest that ever they saw . . . and this Knight of the Red Laundes had hanged it up there, that if there came any errant-knight, he must blow that horn, and then he will make him ready and come to him to do battle.'

203. Dauntless: in the 'Romance of Child Rowland' (see headnote, *Sources*), Rowland is said to be 'undaunted' by the Elf-king's challenge. *slug-horn*: B. follows Chatterton in using this word incorrectly to mean a trumpet of some kind: 'Some caught a slug-horn, and an onset wound, / King Harold heard the charge, and wondered at the sound' (*The Battle of Hastings* ii 99–100). For the etymology of this word see W. Maddan, *Poetry Review* ii (1913) 308: 'The word is a poor attempt to represent two Gaelic words: sluagh, a host or army, and gairm, a call or outcry . . . Slogan is also a softened equivalent and better known.'

24 A Toccata of Galuppi's

Text and publication
First publ. *M & W*, 10 Nov. 1855; repr. *1863, 1863², 1868, 1872, 1888*. Our text
is *1855*. In both the earliest and latest text, *H proof* and *1888*, the turnovers are
further to the left, so that l. 2, for example, instead of reading:

> I can hardly misconceive you; it would prove me deaf
> > and blind;

reads, in *H proof*:

> I can hardly misconceive you; it would prove me deaf
> > and blind;

See also headnote to *Up at a Villa*, III 144.

Composition and date
The last words of the poem appear at the top of the MS leaf which contains the
draft of *A Woman's Last Word* (see Appendix C, p. 888), in the form 'I feel chilly
& grown old', underneath which is the date 'Florence, Jan 15, '53.' As Michael
Meredith argues (*BSN* xxvi [May 2000] 51) the notebook from which this leaf
was torn probably contained drafts of poems on which B. was working, and the
composition of *A Toccata* may therefore be dated with reasonable confidence to
Jan. 1853. Its genesis, however, as with many of B.'s poems, may be earlier: there
is a suggestive passage in a letter of EBB.'s written during the Brownings' stay
in Venice in May–June 1851, when they rented rooms in a Palazzo on the Grand
Canal. Although it was EBB.'s first visit to the city, B. had stayed there before
in 1838 during the writing of *Sordello*. Writing to her sister Arabella EBB. describes
her rapture at being in a city she had dreamt of visiting: 'I could be content
to live out my life here. I never saw a place which I could be so glad to live
a life in. It fitted my desires in a moment . . . Robert & I were sitting outside
the caffè in the piazza of St Mark last night at nearly ten, taking our coffee &
listening to music, & watching the soundless crowd drift backwards & forwards
through that grand square, as if swept by the airs they were listening to. I say
"soundless"—for the absence of carriage or horse removed all ordinary noises.
You heard nothing but the music. It was a phantom-sight altogether' (16 May
1851, *EBB to Arabella* i 376).

Sources and contexts
A letter from B. to EBB. of 7 Mar. 1846 suggests that one of the key associations of ideas in the poem, the playing of 'old music' with a feeling of melancholy, pre-dates the composition of the poem by several years: 'For music, I made
myself melancholy just now with some "Concertos for the Harpsichord by
Mr Handel"—brought home by my father the day before yesterday:—what were
light, modern things once!' (*Correspondence* xii 137; see also *Last Ride Together* 83–7n.,
III 289–90). Baldassare Galuppi (1706–85) was a Venetian composer and keyboard
player, famous in his day; he worked in London and at the court of Catherine II
in Russia. He was a versatile musician, producing comic operas with Goldoni and
sacred music in his position as choirmaster at St Mark's Cathedral. The toccata
is defined by the *New Grove Dictionary of Music and Musicians* as originally 'a purely
decorative, improvisatory keyboard piece' related to the fugue. In a letter to
Henry G. Spaulding dated 30 June 1887 (also cited in *Master Hugues*, p. 389),

B. claims that he once possessed 'two huge manuscript volumes almost exclusively made up of [Galuppi's] "Toccata-pieces"—apparently a slighter form of the Sonata to be "touched" lightly off' (*PMLA* lxii [1947] 1099). In the light of B.'s claim, noted by *Oxford*, that he 'had only a general fancy of the character of Galuppi's music floating in [his] head' and not a 'particular piece' when he wrote the poem (see *Checklist* 80:34), it is probably futile to attempt to identify the 'toccata' in question. Charles van den Borren, however, tentatively puts forward the D minor Sonata contained in 'the eight MS. pieces for harpsichord by Galuppi in the Library of the Brussels Conservatoire' as a possible candidate ('Round About "A Toccata of Galuppi's"', *The Musical Times* lxiv [1923] 314).

In another letter to Arabella from Venice EBB. makes fun of the city's reputation for 'dissipation': 'You have heard perhaps that dissipation is the way of a Venice life—Robert & I have therefore been dissipated, not to disgrace the poets who came before us—In this month I have been twice to the opera & the play' (5–6 June 1851, *EBB to Arabella* i 379). In referring to 'the poets who came before us' EBB. clearly has Byron in mind; in the same letter she mentions 'the *Lido*, where poor Lord Byron used to ride, and . . . the Armenian convent where he studied Armenian' (*ibid.* 380). Byron's poetry (and his legendary personal exploits) consolidated the city's long-standing reputation for hedonism in the eyes of its British visitors; see e.g. the portrait of Venetian husbands in *Beppo* 142–4: 'When weary of the matrimonial tether / His head for such a wife no mortal bothers, / But takes at once another, or another's'. The poem's confrontation between the moralizing Anglo-Saxon consciousness of the speaker and the imagined sensuality of Venice is prefigured in Alfred Domett's *Venice* (1839). Domett, a close friend of B. at the time of the poem's publication (see headnotes to *Waring*, p. 185 and *Guardian-Angel*, III 13), attempts to read a moral lesson into the decline of the '[fair] Magdalene of faded Cities! gay / And guilty once as sad, yet lovely now! (ii 11–12):

> To hide thy crimes, thou hast but to display
>   That sorrowful sweet brow!
>   It tasks the mind, though stern it be
>   To dwell on them, yet gaze on thee!
>   Before thy beautiful distress,
>   Before thy death-struck loveliness,
>   We feel awhile our indignation fly,
> Our loathing all forgot in lively sympathy!
>
>   (ii 13–20)

Domett's poem also sees music as both an emblem and a poignant reminder of Venice's former glories:

> A queenly beauty in a slow decline,
>   Too visibly thou witherest day by day;
>   No hectic mimicry of health is thine
>   To decorate decay!
>   For thee,—whose very voice so long
>   Was Music, all thy converse song,
>   No sounds of wail need Woe invent,
>   Thy silence is thy best lament!
>   And hushed are all thy chaunts—and all the daughters
> Of Music are laid low by thy deserted waters!
>
>   (i 81–90)

A similarly fraught encounter with the city is enacted in Ruskin's *The Stones of Venice*, the second and third volumes of which appeared in 1853; the Brownings had known Ruskin personally since the early 1850s, and corresponded with him regularly throughout this decade; see *Guardian-Angel* (III 14) and *Old Pictures* (p. 404).

Metre

Daniel Karlin argues that there are two consistent and equally plausible ways of reading the poem. It can either be read as a catalectic trochaic octameter (like Tennyson's 'Locksley Hall'), consisting of eight trochaic feet with the final unstressed syllable omitted in each line; or it can be read as a four-beat line, with the initial stress on the third syllable of each line. Karlin suggests that this second rhythm imparts a 'subversive levity' to the lines, and therefore complicates and undermines the speaker's confidence in his own reading of Galuppi's music (Introduction to *Robert Browning*, ed. A. Roberts [Oxford, 1997], pp. xxv–xxvii). It should be noted, however, that B. himself describes the metre of the poem as 'purely Trochaic' in a letter to Furnivall, and glosses the first line accordingly (15 Sept. 1881; *Trumpeter* 24).

Criticism and Parallels in B.

B. seems to have been a talented amateur musician; he learned cello and violin as well as keyboard instruments in his youth, playing the piano in particular to a high standard, and receiving lessons in composition from John Relfe. He 'emerged from this long program of musical education with the ability to set songs to music and to speak with some authority on musical matters' (*Maynard* 140). This knowledge of the technicalities of music on B.'s part has led some critics to suggest precise correspondences between the toccata and the form of the poem; see e.g. Marc R. Plamondon, ' "What do you mean by your mountainous fugues?", *VP* xxvii (1999) 309–31 and Stephen H. Ford, 'The Musical Form of Robert Browning's "A Toccata of Galuppi's" ', *SBC* xiv (1986) 22–4. The emotional response evoked by music is a frequent topic of B.'s poetry; cp. *Master Hugues* (III 388), *Abt Vogler* (p. 759), and *Charles Avison* (*Parleyings*, 1887). There are also many other poems and sections of poems dealing with Venice: see e.g. *Sordello* iii 656 ff (I 570), *Fifine at the Fair* (1872) 1683 ff., and the late sonnet *Goldoni* (1883; *Penguin* ii 963). The parallel with *Fifine at the Fair* is esp. important because the speaker, Don Juan, has his vision of Venice while playing Schumann's *Carnaval* on the piano.

I

Oh, Galuppi, Baldassaro, this is very sad to find!
I can hardly misconceive you; it would prove me deaf and
blind;
But although I give you credit, 'tis with such a heavy mind!

1. Oh,] Oh! (*H proof*, but not *H proof²*).   *Galuppi, Baldassaro*: note the slight misspelling of the composer's Christian name.
2. misconceive: combining the senses of 'misunderstand you' and 'imagine you wrongly'.   *it would*] that would (*H proof*, but not *H proof²*, *1863²*). See l. 11 for another example of this rare agreement between *H proof* and *1863²*.
3. although I] if I must (*H proof*, but not *H proof²*).   *give you credit*] take your meaning (*1863–88*).

2

Here you come with your old music, and here's all the
good it brings.
5   What, they lived once thus at Venice, where the
merchants were the kings,
Where St. Mark's is, where the Doges used to wed the
sea with rings?

3

Ay, because the sea's the street there; and 'tis arched by
. . . what you call
. . . Shylock's bridge with houses on it, where they kept
the carnival:
I was never out of England—it's as if I saw it all!

4

10   Did young people take their pleasure when the sea was
warm in May?

5–9. The speaker, who was 'never out of England' (l. 9), constructs an imaginary
Venice from the emotional atmosphere of Galuppi's music and his imperfect
recollection of literary representations of the city; cp. Byron, *Childe Harold* iv 154–9:
'I lov'd her from my boyhood— she to me / Was as a fairy-city of the heart, /
Rising like water-columns from the sea, / Of joy the sojourn, and of wealth
the mart; / And Otway, Radcliffe, Schiller, Shakespeare's art, / Had stamp'd her
image in me'.

5. Alluding both to the great commercial power of Venice in former times, and
to its method of government, according to which the city's ruling council (one
of whose members was elected Doge) was drawn mainly from the merchant class.

6. The Basilica of St Mark is the cathedral church of Venice; for the annual
ceremony in which the Doge threw a golden ring into the sea to symbolize the
'marriage' of the city to the source of its wealth and power, see Byron, *Childe
Harold* iv 91–4: 'The spouseless Adriatic mourns her lord; / And, annual marriage now no more renewed, / The Bucentaur lies rotting unrestored, /
Neglected garment of her widowhood!'   *St. Mark's*] Saint Mark's (*1888*).

7–9. Cp. EBB.'s comment in a letter to Thomas Westwood of 12 Dec. 1850:
'You know it's a more than doubtful point whether Shakespeare ever saw Italy
out of a vision, yet he and a crowd of inferior writers have written about Venice
and vineyards as if born to the manner of them' (*Letters of EBB* i 470).

8. *Shylock's bridge*: the Rialto, 'where merchants most do congregate' (*Merchant
of Venice* I iii 49). The Rialto bridge spans the Grand Canal; its arcades still contain shops, but not houses.   *carnival:*] emended in agreement with *H proof*,
1863–88 from 'carnival!' in *1855*; the exclamation mark was probably 'borrowed'
by the printer from the end of the next line.

9. *saw it all!*] saw it all. (*1868–88*).

Balls and masks begun at midnight, burning ever to
mid-day,
When they made up fresh adventures for the morrow, do
you say?

5
Was a lady such a lady, cheeks so round and lips so red,—
On her neck the small face buoyant, like a bell-flower on
its bed,
15   O'er the breast's superb abundance where a man might
base his head?

6
Well (and it was graceful of them) they'd break talk off
and afford
—She, to bite her mask's black velvet, he to finger on his
sword,
While you sat and played Toccatas, stately at the
clavichord?

7
What? Those lesser thirds so plaintive, sixths diminished,
sigh on sigh,

11. *masks*: either masked balls (for which Venice was famous) or masques, i.e.
musical entertainments; cp. Byron's description of Venice as '[the] revel of the
earth, the masque of Italy!' (*Childe Harold* iv 27).   *begun*] began (*H proof*, but not
H proof², *1863²*).
12. *When*] Then (*H proof*, but not *H proof²*).
14. *bell-flower*: the campanula; cp. *Pippa* i 164 (p. 108).
16. *graceful*: 'gracious' (in that the revellers are taking time to listen to Galuppi's
music); also in the sense that their attitudes and gestures are 'graceful' in themselves.   *afford*: 'time' is understood.
18. *clavichord*: an early (fifteenth century) keyboard instrument which produces a
(small) sound by striking a string with a thin piece of metal when a key is depressed.
It was in common use, mainly as an instrument to practise on, until the early
nineteenth century, but had never been much used for public music, being
too quiet.
19–25. *Those lesser thirds . . . answer*: in these lines the speaker uses a number of
technical terms to describe the structure of the music he is listening to, prompting
debate amongst B.'s critics about their accuracy. 'Lesser thirds' are minor thirds;
Stefan Hawlin notes that B.'s music teacher, John Relfe, published a book in
which he 'described the different effects of major and minor in these terms:
the major keys were "Masculine, Majestic or Sprightly", and the minor keys
"Effeminate, Plaintive or Pathetic"' (from Relfe's *The Elements of Harmony*
[1801]; cited *RES* n.s. xli [1990] 504).

20   Told them something? Those suspensions, those
                              solutions—"Must we die?"
      Those commiserating sevenths—"Life might last! we can
                              but try!"

                              8
      "Were you happy?"—"Yes."—"And are you still as
                              happy?"—"Yes—And you?"
      —"Then more kisses"—"Did *I* stop them, when a
                              million seemed so few?"
      Hark—the dominant's persistence, till it must be answered
                              to!

                              9
25   So an octave struck the answer. Oh, they praised you,
                              I dare say!

19. sixths diminished: 'All intervals, perfect or imperfect, major or minor, may also
be "augmented" or "diminished" . . . any minor or perfect interval reduced
chromatically by a semitone at either end becomes diminished . . . C to Ab, a
minor sixth, becomes a diminished sixth in either of the forms C to Abb or C#
to Ab' (*New Oxford Companion to Music*). Charles van den Borren (headnote, *Sources*)
points out that 'this interval [was] of a purely theoretic nature in the system of
harpsichord tempering . . . in practice from the second quarter of the 18th century' ('Round About "A Toccata of Galuppi's"', p. 315).
20. Those suspensions, those solutions: a suspension is '[a] form of discord arising
from the holding over of a note in one chord as a momentary part of the chord
which follows, it then resolving by falling a degree to a note which forms a real
part of the second chord'. 'Solution' is a way of describing the second part of
this process (*New Oxford Companion to Music*).
20–3. The question of who is speaking at this point in the poem was put to B.
by his friend Domett: 'He repeated the passage; said the words were the lovers',
uttered at the time, as the music was going on. I said I thought, "*Must* I stop
them" would perhaps have been clearer in that case, as the kisses were, or had
been presumably going on just as the exclamation was made. But he maintained
that the expression was best as written' (*Diary* 48).
21. commiserating sevenths: a seventh has traditionally been regarded as a mildly discordant interval; the speaker is trying to give an impression of the emotion evoked
by it in his choice of adjective.
22. are you still as happy?"] are you happy?" (*H proof*).
23. more kisses"] more kisses!" (*1863–88*).
24. the dominant's persistence: the 'dominant' chord is based on the fifth note of
the octave in any particular key; it is often sounded as a prelude to the tonic
(forming a 'perfect cadence'). B.'s speaker here puns on the term to refer not
just to the musical 'dominant', but also to the dominant atmosphere of the piece
(which must be 'answered to' by the listeners).
25. an octave struck the answer: resolving the tension created by the sounding of
the 'dominant' and enabling the listeners to resume their normal life.

"Brave Galuppi! that was music! good alike at grave and
gay!
I can always leave off talking, when I hear a master play."

10

Then they left you for their pleasure: till in due time, one
by one,
Some with lives that came to nothing, some with deeds as
well undone,
30   Death came tacitly and took them where they never see
the sun.

11

But when I sit down to reason,—think to take my stand
nor swerve
Till I triumph o'er a secret wrung from nature's close
reserve,
In you come with your cold music, till I creep thro' every
nerve,

12

Yes, you, like a ghostly cricket, creaking where a house
was burned—
35   "Dust and ashes, dead and done with, Venice spent what
Venice earned!

---

26. *grave and gay*: on this and similar pairings in B. see *Love Among the Ruins* 7n.
(p. 534).
30. *Death came tacitly*] Death stepped tacitly (*1868–88*). Death is silent in itself,
and (by a transferred epithet) silences its victims.
31–2. Cp. Paracelsus's description of the painful process of his scientific discoveries, e.g. i 804–6 (I 150).
31. *think to take*] say I'll take (*H proof*).
31–2. *nor swerve / Till I triumph*] nor swerve, / When I triumph (*H proof*, but not
H proof²); nor swerve, / While I triumph (*1863–88*).
35–9. Galuppi's music has conjured up the sensuous, exotic world of Venice; now,
however, the speaker finds in it a message of disenchantment, which also undermines his belief that he, with his earnest scientific bent, is different in kind from
the frivolous, pleasure-seeking Venetians.
35. *Dust and ashes*: this phrase occurs in *Genesis* xviii 27 and in *Job* xxx 19; cp.
also 'The Order for the Burial of the Dead' from the *Book of Common Prayer*:
'earth to earth, ashes to ashes, dust to dust'. *dead and done with*: a cliché used
by B. on a few occasions; cp. *Pippa Passes* i 334 (p. 119) and *Master Hugues* 8
(III 390).

The soul, doubtless, is immortal—where a soul can be
discerned.

13
"Yours for instance, you know physics, something of
geology,
Mathematics are your pastime; souls shall rise in their
degree;
Butterflies may dread extinction,—you'll not die, it
cannot be!

14
40   "As for Venice and its people, merely born to bloom and
drop,
Here on earth they bore their fruitage, mirth and folly
were the crop.
What of soul was left, I wonder, when the kissing had to
stop?

36. *where a soul*] if a soul (*H proof*).
38–9. souls . . . cannot be! the primary sense is of a hierarchy of human souls,
some of whom resemble butterflies and are therefore doomed to 'extinction', others
of whom have a more earnest nature and higher expectations; Galuppi's music
seems to urge this upon the speaker (when presumably it is his own thought),
while simultaneously mocking it and him. Ironically, in view of the contrast being
drawn here, the butterfly is a traditional emblem of the soul; cp. the lines which
B. added to one of Jules's speeches in *Pippa* ii 216^217 (p. 137). There may also
be an allusion to the larger hierarchy of creation, beginning with inorganic nature
and rising through organic and animal life to man, which Paracelsus expounds
in his deathbed speech (see v 668–706n., I 298–9) and which Cleon also
articulates (see l. 202n., p. 578).
39. extinction: individual death; B. may, however, also have had in mind the sense
of the extinction of whole species, esp. given the mention of 'geology' in l. 37.
Charles Lyell's *Principles of Geology* (1830–3) and Robert Chambers's *Vestiges of
Creation* (1844) had both drawn attention to the fossil record of extinct species.
Cp. *Saul* 110n. (III 505).
40. its people] her people (*1868–88*).   *bloom*] blow (*H proof*).
41. mirth and folly: both terms are used frequently in the Bible; see e.g. *Proverbs*
xiv 13: 'Even in laughter the heart is sorrowful; and the end of that mirth is
heaviness' and xv 21: 'Folly is joy to him that is destitute of wisdom: but a man
of understanding walketh uprightly.'

15

"Dust and ashes!" So you creak it, and I want the heart
to scold.
Dear dead women, with such hair, too—what's become
of all the gold
45 Used to hang and brush their bosoms? I feel chilly and
grown old.

43–5. The last stanza is the only one in the poem which remained unchanged
from the proof stage to the final state of the text in *1888*.
43. *I want the heart to scold*: either 'I want (lack) the heart to criticise you (Galuppi)
for your cynicism', or 'I lack the heart to criticise the doomed Venetians for their
misguided lifestyle'.
44–5. *all the gold . . . bosoms*: yellow hair, esp. when it is let down, has strong
erotic connotations in B.: cp., among others, the description of Palma in *Sordello*
i 948–51 (I 456), *Porphyria* 18–20 (p. 72), and *Love Among the Ruins* 55 (p. 537).

25 A Lovers' Quarrel

First publ. *M & W*, 10 Nov. 1855; repr. *1863, 1865², 1868, 1872, 1888.* Our text is *1855.*

   The 'emperor' who has 'taken a bride / To his gruesome side' (ll. 29–35) is clearly Napoleon III, whose *coup d'état* of Dec. 1851 the Brownings witnessed during one of their periods of residence in Paris. He was proclaimed Emperor (after a plebiscite) on 2 Dec. 1852, and married Eugenia de Montijo, Countess of Téba, on 29 Jan. 1853. Looking forward to the marriage on Saturday 22 Jan. 1853, *The Times* commented on the personal attractions of the Emperor's fiancée: 'The Countess of Téba possesses considerable personal attractions, but more in the style of English than of Spanish beauty. Her complexion is transparently fair, her features regular and yet full of expression.' An editorial on the Monday following the marriage, however, saw the magnificence and expense of the wedding ceremony as symptoms of France's political instability: 'The French revolution, and the powers which it has called into being, have continued for so many years to masquerade in one guise or another—now ghastly and now gay, sometimes burlesque and sometimes magnificent—that we have ceased to feel surprise at any aspect these Protean Governments may assume. Among the more stable sovereignties of Europe there is a greater sobriety of display, a more cautious use of the public money, and less disposition to catch the eye of a few thousand spectators by a species of exhibition which may be thought puerile or theatrical' (cp. ll. 29–30). In a letter of 2 Mar. 1853, EBB. wrote: 'What do I think of Napoleon's marriage? Well—*I like it*' (*EBB to Arabella* i 545); later she relates gossip she has heard about the occasion: 'let me tell you that the "unfortunate Eugenie" fainted twice just before the marriage, when the "coiffeur" was engaged on her hair' (*ibid.* 546; cp. l. 35). These events might well have produced a 'quarrel' in the Brownings' household given their profound disagreements about Napoleon III; see headnote to *Woman's Last Word*, III 273.

   Although these allusions would seem to date the poem to early 1853, a period during which B. produced a number of the shorter poems in *M & W* (see headnote to *Women and Roses*, III 235, and cp. ll. 43–9n. below), it may have its origins in the very earliest days of the Brownings' marriage, and more particularly the cold winter of 1846–47 which Robert and Elizabeth spent in Pisa in relative isolation from the outside world: see Daniel Karlin, *EC* xxxiii (1989) 47–64. This suggestion is supported by the fact that there are a number of verbal similarities between the poem and the courtship correspondence: 'where is the proper, rationally-to-be-expected, "*lovers' quarrel?*" *Here*, as you will find! "Iræ amantium"' (B. to EBB., 9 Nov. 1845, *Correspondence* xi 159); 'Of such are "Lovers quarrels" for the most part. The growth of power on one side .. & the struggle against it, by means legal & illegal, on the other' (EBB. to B., 4 July 1846, *ibid.* xiii 116). The idea of their quarrelling to add some variety to their married life together seems to have been suggested by Arabella, to whom EBB. wrote on 8 Feb. 1847: 'So you are of opinion that Robert & I shd. quarrel rather, to break up the monotony? How we shd. ever quarrel, is impossible for me to conceive of— though I have had my pardon begged several times for mysterious offences beyond my apprehension. Seriously, how shd. we quarrel, when I am always in the right,

---

Title: cp. Terence, *Woman of Andros*, 555: 'Amantium iræ amoris integratio est' ('Lovers' quarrels are love's renewals').

& *he knows it?*' (*Correspondence* xiv 124). There were, however, 'tremendous combats' between them during this period over the trial of Alexandre Dumas; he was sued in early 1847 'for violation of contract by . . . several . . . periodicals for not providing feuilletons he had agreed to write' (see *Correspondence* xiv 185n.).

There are clear parallels between this poem and B.'s other poems of married love and discord; besides *Woman's Last Word*, cp. *Any Wife to Any Husband* (III 647) and *Andrea* (p. 385); the main contrast is with *By the Fire-Side* (p. 456). Cp. also *James Lee* (p. 665).

1

Oh, what a dawn of day!
How the March sun feels like May!
    All is blue again
    After last night's rain,
5   And the South dries the hawthorn-spray.
    Only, my Love's away!
I'd as lief that the blue were grey.

2

Runnels, which rillets swell,
Must be dancing down the dell
10   With a foamy head
      On the beryl bed
Paven smooth as a hermit's cell;
    Each with a tale to tell,
Could my Love but attend as well.

3

15 Dearest, three months ago!
When we lived blocked-up with snow,—
    When the wind would edge
    In and in his wedge,

1. dawn of day: Cp. Blake, 'I rose up at the dawn of day': 'I have Mental Joy & Mental Health / And Mental Friends & Mental wealth / I've a Wife I love & that loves me' (ll. 9–11). B. wrote to EBB. of Blake's 'power and glory' (9 July 1845, *Correspondence* xiii 140); EBB. reports that he spoke to Charles Augustus Tulk about 'Coleridge & Blake, subjects interesting to each' (*c.* 7 Feb. 1848, *Correspondence* xv 11); and he may have seen some of the Blake manuscripts owned by D. G. Rossetti during the 1850s. *Oxford* compares Tennyson, 'The Death of the Old Year' (1832), l. 11.
5. the South: the south wind.
7. as lief: as soon (archaic in B.'s day).
10. foamy] foaming (*1868–88*).
11.] O'er each beryl bed (*H proof*, but not *H proof²*).   *beryl*: a yellowish semi-precious stone; mentioned several times in the Bible (e.g. *Revelation* xxi 20).
17. wind] cold (*H proof*, but not *H proof²*).

In, as far as the point could go—
20   Not to our ingle, though,
Where we loved each the other so!

4

Laughs with so little cause!
We devised games out of straws.
          We would try and trace
25   One another's face
In the ash, as an artist draws;
          Free on each other's flaws,
How we chattered like two church daws!

5

What's in the "Times?"—a scold
30   At the emperor deep and cold;
          He has taken a bride
          To his gruesome side,
That's as fair as himself is bold:
          There they sit ermine-stoled,
35   And she powders her hair with gold.

6

Fancy the Pampas' sheen!
Miles and miles of gold and green

---

23. games out of straws: either 'games using straws' (to draw with) or 'games out of trifles'. Cp. ll. 111–12.

29–35. See headnote.

36. the Pampas' sheen: *The Times* for 3 Apr. 1853 contains an advertisement for *The Narrative of a Journey Round the World* by F[rederick] Gerstaecker, which begins: 'Starting from Bremen for California, the author of this narrative proceeded to Rio, and thence to Buenos Ayres [sic], where he exchanged the wild seas for the yet wilder Pampas, and made his way on horseback to Valparaiso across the Cordilleras—a winter passage full of difficulty and danger.' B.'s friend William Wetmore Story's poem *The Gaucho* (1848) contains a description of the Pampas: 'Ne'er a tide but the fleeting seasons / Sweeps o'er the inland sea of grass; / Roaring herds, like clouds of thunder, / Over its lonely levels pass. / Jaguars yell; and, striding, hiding, / Ostriches rush—for they fear the knife— / Over the prairies of Buenos Ayres, / Let him who pursues me look out for his life!' (ll. 9–16). B. had read Story's 1847 volume (*American Friends* 37). In his *Notes on Gilfillan's Literary Portraits* De Quincey disagrees with the suggestion that Shelley might not have proclaimed himself an atheist had he been pitied rather than reproached in his youth: 'Like a wild horse of the Pampas, he would have thrown up his heels, and *whinnied* his disdain of any man coming to catch *him* with a bribe of oats' (*Tait's Edinburgh Magazine* xii [1845] 761).

Where the sun-flowers blow
In a solid glow,
40 And to break now and then the screen—
Black neck and eyeballs keen,
Up a wild horse leaps between!

7
Try, will our table turn?
Lay your hands there light, and yearn
45   Till the yearning slips
Thro' the finger tips
In a fire which a few discern,
And a very few feel burn,
And the rest, they may live and learn!

8
50 Then we would up and pace,
For a change, about the place,
Each with arm o'er neck.
'Tis our quarter-deck,
We are seamen in woeful case.
55   Help in the ocean-space!
Or, if no help, we'll embrace.

9
See, how she looks now, drest
In a sledging-cap and vest.
'Tis a huge fur cloak—

---

40. *now and then*] once a while (*H proof*).

43–9. EBB. participated in a number of séances during which tables seemed to turn of their own volition, but B. remained sceptical: 'my poor Robert is in a glorious minority, trying hard to keep his ground as a denier, & well-nigh carried off his feet . . . Robert has his mind open, he maintains, & is ready to believe what he shall see & hear himself . . . We tried the table-experiment the other day .. Mr. Tennyson, Mr. Lytton, Robert & I .. & *failed*. We tried only for twenty minutes though—& Robert was laughing all the time .. which was wrong .. because there ought to be concentration of thought' (30 Apr.–1 May 1853, *EBB to Arabella* i 572). See headnote to *Mesmerism* (III 475) and the 'mesmeriser Snow' (l. 72), and headnote to *Mr Sludge* (p. 773).

50–6. With the use of shipwreck imagery here cp. *James Lee* ii (pp. 668–70).

53. *quarter-deck*: '[the] short upper deck' (*J.*).

55. *ocean-space*: apparently B.'s coinage.

58. *vest*: defined in *J.* as 'an outer garment'.

60   Like a reindeer's yoke
      Falls the lappet along the breast:
                  Sleeves for her arms to rest,
      Or to hang, as my Love likes best.

                        10
      Teach me to flirt a fan
65   As the Spanish ladies can,
                  Or I tint your lip
                  With a burnt stick's tip
      And you turn into such a man!
                  Just the two spots that span
70   Half the bill of the young male swan.

                        11
      Dearest, three months ago
      When the mesmeriser Snow
                  With his hand's first sweep
                  Put the earth to sleep,
75   'Twas a time when the heart could show
                  All—how was earth to know,
      'Neath the mute hand's to-and-fro!

                        12
      Dearest, three months ago
      When we loved each other so,
80   Lived and loved the same
                  Till an evening came
      When a shaft from the Devil's bow
                  Pierced to our ingle-glow,
      And the friends were friend and foe!

---

61. lappet: '[the] parts of a head dress that hang loose' (*J.*).

76–7. I.e. the heart 'could show / All' because the earth, hidden by the 'mute hand's to-and-fro' which covers the earth with snow, will never know about it.

82. the Devil's bow: according to Clarence H. Miller, 'the devil's bows and arrows were well known' in medieval art and literature; he adduces evidence from Chaucer's *Friar's Tale*, St Jerome's *Commentaries*, and the Bible itself, esp. *Ephesians* vi 16: see 'The Devil's Bow and Arrows: Another Clue to the Identity of the Yeoman in Chaucer's *Friar's Tale*', *The Chaucer Review* xxx (1995) 211–14.

83. ingle-glow: the glow from the hearth fire (not listed as a compound in *OED*).

13

85   Not from the heart beneath—
'Twas a bubble born of breath,
      Neither sneer nor vaunt,
      Nor reproach nor taunt.
See a word, how it severeth!
90   Oh, power of life and death
In the tongue, as the Preacher saith!

14

Woman, and will you cast
For a word, quite off at last,
      Me, your own, your you,—
95   Since, as Truth is true,
I was you all the happy past—
      Me do you leave aghast
With the memories we amassed?

15

Love, if you knew the light
100 That your soul casts in my sight,
      How I look to you
      For the pure and true,
And the beauteous and the right,—
      Bear with a moment's spite
105 When a mere mote threats the white!

86. bubble born of breath: cp. Spenser, *The Ruines of Time* 50–1: 'Why then doth flesh, a bubble glas of breath, / Hunt after honour and advancement vaine'; see also headnote to *Love Among the Ruins* (p. 573). Cp. also the translation of Psalm xc by Francis Quarles: 'His breath's a *bubble*, and his daies a *Span*. / Tis glorious misery to be borne a Man'.

89. Cp. the commentary on *Matthew* xvii 5 in the Geneva Bible (1560): 'The article or the word, That, severeth Christ from other children.'

90–1. Cp. *Proverbs* xviii 21: 'Death and life are in the power of the tongue: and they that love it shall eat the fruit thereof.'

94. your you] your You (*1863–88*).

95. Truth] truth (*1863–88*).

96. I was you] I was You (*1863–88*). *past*] Past (*1863–65*).

104–5. Cp. *Matthew* vii 3–5.

16

What of a hasty word?
Is the fleshly heart not stirred
        By a worm's pin-prick
        Where its roots are quick?
110 See the eye, by a fly's-foot blurred—
        Ear, when a straw is heard
Scratch the brain's coat of curd!

17

Foul be the world or fair,
More or less, how can I care?
115   'Tis the world the same
        For my praise or blame,
And endurance is easy there.
        Wrong in the one thing rare—
Oh, it is hard to bear!

18

120 Here's the spring back or close,
When the almond-blossom blows;
        We shall have the word
        In that minor third
There is none but the cuckoo knows—
125   Heaps of the guelder-rose!
I must bear with it, I suppose.

106–12. Cp. *By the Fire-Side* 191–5 (p. 472).

107. fleshly heart: cp. *Ezekiel* xxxvi 26: 'A new heart also will I give you, and a new spirit will I put within you: and I will take away the stony heart out of your flesh, and I will give you an heart of flesh.' Cp. also Fulke Greville, *Caelica,* sonnet xcviii, ll. 1–2: 'Eternal Truth, almighty, infinite, / Only exilèd from man's fleshly heart'.

109. quick: alive.

113. Cp. *Macbeth* (I i 11–12): 'Fair is foul, and foul is fair: / Hover through the fog and filthy air'.

122.] omitted 'through a blunder of the printer's' in early copies of *1863;* 'he cancelled the sheet before many copies had been issued' (B. to the Revd Walter G. Wilkinson, 21 May 1864; see Nathaniel A. Hart, *N & Q* [June 1974] 213–15).

123–4. that minor third / There is none but the cuckoo knows: the interval of a descending minor third has often been used by musicians to imitate the sound of the cuckoo (e.g. in Beethoven's Sixth or 'Pastoral' Symphony).

123. that] a (*1868–88*).

125. guelder-rose: also known as the snowball-tree, *Viburnum Opulus,* bearing globular bunches of white flowers (*OED*); cp. *Aurora Leigh* ii 44–5.

19

Could but November come,
Were the noisy birds struck dumb
    At the warning slash
130   Of his driver's-lash—
I would laugh like the valiant Thumb
    Facing the castle glum
And the giant's fee-faw-fum!

20

Then, were the world well stript
135 Of the gear wherein equipped
    We can stand apart,
    Heart dispense with heart
In the sun, with the flowers unnipped,—
    Oh, the world's hangings ripped,
140 We were both in a bare-walled crypt!

21

Each in the crypt would cry
"But one freezes here! and why?
    When a heart as chill
    At my own would thrill
145 Back to life, and its fires out-fly?
    Heart, shall we live or die?
The rest, . . . settle it by and by!"

131–3. On B.'s use of this fairy-tale material see headnote to *Childe Roland* (p. 350).
134–40. The sense is that in 'November' (whether literal or metaphorical, as in 'life's November', *By the Fire-Side* 5) the world would be 'stript' of the qualities which enable people to 'stand apart' from each other, i.e. consider themselves self-sufficient; the lovers would thus find themselves without any resource save each other. It would be as though they were dead and needed each other's warmth to come back to life.
140. bare-walled crypt: cp. *By the Fire-Side* 196–7n. (p. 472).
143. heart as chill] heart, as chill, (*1865–88*). This is the only variant introduced in *1865.*
145. its fires out-fly: 'its fires would flare up'. B. is fond of the 'out-' prefix, e.g. 'out-staggering' (*Sordello* i 74 [I 398]), 'out-bang' (*Bishop Blougram* 383 [p. 305]), 'Out-Homering' (*Prince Hohenstiel-Schwangau* [1871] 2081).
147. settle it] settle (*1870–88*).

22

So, she'd efface the score,
And forgive me as before.
150   Just at twelve o'clock
        I shall hear her knock
In the worst of a storm's uproar—
        I shall pull her through the door—
I shall have her for evermore!

150. *Just at*] It is (*1863–88*).

26 Andrea del Sarto

(CALLED "THE FAULTLESS PAINTER")

Text and publication

First publ. *M & W*, 10 Nov. 1855; repr. *1863*, *1863²*, *1868*, *1872*, *1888*. Our text is *1855*.

Composition and date

B. seems to have known about Andrea del Sarto's work from an early age; *Oxford* notes that there were two Holy Families by Andrea in Dulwich Picture Gallery, and in 1834 B. wrote a comic poem 'On Andrea del Sarto's "Jupiter and Leda"' as part of his *Cockney Anthology* (I 94–5). Several pictures by Andrea were on display in the gallery of the Palazzo Pitti during B.'s time, including one in the 'Stanza di Giove' [Jove Room] listed in *Fantozzi* as 'Ritratto di Andrea del Sarto e sua moglie, *di esso Andrea*' [Portrait of Andrea del Sarto and his wife, *by Andrea himself*] (634). (The picture is not now thought to be by Andrea; see S. J. Freedberg, *Andrea del Sarto: Catalogue Raisonné* [Cambridge, MA 1963], p. 223; and *Thomas* i 21.) The poem seems to have originated in a request made by the Brownings' friend John Kenyon in March 1853 for a copy of this picture of the painter and his wife. B. replied on 17 Mar. 1853:

> Now of the 'Andrea' you would have copied—I have made the proper enquiries. I know the picture well and esteem it just as you do. It should be well copied. The business of copying is carried on with remarkable rascality here. Such an one, for instance, is in vogue: do you order a picture of *him*? It is, nine-tenths of it, painted by one of his dozen assistants—& the final touch put in by himself—which, as that touch is like to be an inventive one, might better be wanting. I think I find a man as fit as any who will do the whole conscientiously & well—a Roman & able to *draw*. But I think he asks too much—for he considers two heads as two pictures, and wants 100 dollars for them.

> (MS at Wellesley College)

See also Julia Markus, *SBC* i.2 [Fall 1973], 52–3; and cp. *Old Pictures* (p. 404). According to several accounts, B. was unable to get a satisfactory copy made at an acceptable price, and so sent Kenyon the poem instead (Mrs Andrew Crosse, 'John Kenyon and his Friends', *Temple Bar* lxxxviii [1890] 489; *Griffin and Minchin* 200; *Trumpeter* 40). B. later confirmed (in a letter to an unidentified correspondent of 11 Feb. 1878) that this picture was his principal source of inspiration for the poem: 'The poem to which you refer is in accordance with the account of the relations of Andrea and his wife as given in the Life of the

---

Title. del Sarto: son of a tailor; see headnote. Andrea's lack of manliness associates him with the proverbial 'nine tailors make one man'; see Buckingham et al., *The Rehearsal* (1672), Act 3, scene i: 'But pr'ythee, *Tom Thimble*, why wilt thou needs marry? If nine Taylors make but one man; and one woman cannot be satisfi'd with nine men: what work art thou cutting out here for thy self, trow we?' *Subtitle.*] The "Faultless." (*H proof*, but not *H proof²*).

former by Vasari: there is a dissent from the judgment of Vasari in the Life by Baldinucci. But my best warrant for what I wrote is in the wonderful portraits of Andrea and his wife—half-lengths in one picture, still on the walls of the Pitti Palace' (MS at *ABL*).

Julia Markus speculates that Andrea and his wife may have been modelled on the American artist William Page and his second wife Sarah Dougherty Page; she points out some similarities between Andrea's theories of painting and those of Page, and adds that Mrs Page, who was uninterested in her husband's work, eventually left him for another man after having been notoriously unfaithful during their marriage (see *BIS* ii [1974] 1–24). B. clearly knew about Sarah Dougherty's conduct (see l. 221n.) Another resemblance, not noted by Markus, is the fact that Andrea refers to a passage in *Revelation* from which Page derived his theories about the proportions of the human body; see ll. 260–1n., and cp. *Cleon* 55–6n. (p. 619).

In comparison with other poems of the same length and importance in *M & W*, this poem was lightly revised both at the proof stage and in subsequent printed eds.

Sources and influences

Andrea del Sarto was born in Florence on 16 July 1486. He was the son of a tailor (hence 'del Sarto') called Agnolo di Francesco, but his real surname is not known for certain; Vasari suggests Vannucchi, but a recent scholar has argued that it may have been Lanfranchi (John Shearman, *Andrea del Sarto* [Oxford 1965] 2). In 1517 he married a widow, Lucrezia del Fede, who had a daughter from her previous marriage to Carlo Recanati. At some point during 1518–19 he accepted an invitation to work for François I (1494–1547), the King of France; Andrea seems to have stayed at Fontainebleau for about a year before returning to Florence. Soon after his return he visited Rome in connection with a commission to decorate the Villa Medici at Poggio a Caiano. Giorgio Vasari, who later wrote the *Lives of the Painters*, was briefly apprenticed to Andrea around 1525. In May 1527 the ruling Medici family was expelled from Florence, leading to three years of warfare and great hardship for the people of the city. The capitulation of the Republic in 1530 was followed by an outbreak of plague which claimed the life of Andrea in September of that year. The poem is probably set during 1525 (see l. 104n.).

Interest in Andrea del Sarto's work was stimulated in the early nineteenth century by his status as one of the leading painters of the Florentine Renaissance, and also by his association with François I, the great French monarch and patron of the arts. The idea of the Renaissance as an important cultural and historical event emerged during the first half of the nineteenth century, principally in the work of French scholars; Burckhardt's *The Civilisation of the Renaissance in Italy* (1860) represents the most complete exposition of the idea. This Renaissance was characterized by the rediscovery of the art of classical antiquity, the development of secular forms of art patronage, and an emphasis on the original genius of the greatest artists of the period. In B.'s poem Andrea measures himself against the generally recognized triumvirate of great Renaissance artists—Leonardo da Vinci, Michelangelo Buonarroti, and Raffaello Sanzio (Raphael). The development of the idea of the Renaissance was connected with the cult of François I, since François had acted as patron to a number of important Florentine painters during this period, most notably Leonardo da Vinci, and amassed a collection of their work. This collection was moved to the Louvre in 1793, and two paintings by Andrea were on view there as early as 1804. 'By the early 1820s,' according to Janet

Cox-Rearick, 'François was enjoying a great vogue in Paris, with a street, a square, and an entire quartier named after him' ('Imagining the Renaissance: The nineteenth-century cult of François I as patron of art', *Renaissance Quarterly* i [1997] 207–50). The revival of interest in François generated many early-nineteenth century paintings, with the subject of the king's relations with the various Italian artists he invited to Fontainebleau a favourite theme; the apocryphal story that Leonardo da Vinci died in the king's arms was regularly depicted, and Benvenuto Cellini, the artist whose *atelier* the king is supposed to have visited, was the subject of an opera by Berlioz.

B. seems to have consulted the following sources in developing his portrait of Andrea: (i) Giorgio Vasari, *Le Vite de' Più eccellenti Pittori, Scultori e Architetti*. Firenze: Felice Le Monnier, vol. viii (1852), pp. 250–307 [*Le Monnier*]; (ii) Filippo Baldinucci, *Notizie de' Professori del Disegno da Cimabue in quà*. Ed. Giuseppe Piacenza. 1728; rpt, Torino: Nella Stamperia Reale, 1770, vol. ii, pp. 419–41 [*Baldinucci*]; (iii) Anna Jameson, *Memoirs of the Early Italian Painters, and of the Progress of Painting in Italy* (1845), vol. ii, pp. 73–81 [*Jameson*]; (iv) Alfred de Musset, *André del Sarto* (1833; acted in Nov. 1848 and in 1850) [*Musset*].

B. also owned a copy of Luigi Biadi's *Notizie Inedite della Vita d'Andrea del Sarto* (Firenze 1829) but this is unlikely to have been a source as it is inscribed '[to] Robert Browning, with best wishes for this day and all days, from J. Dykes Campbell': Campbell was secretary of the Browning Society, and this gift presumably dates from the 1880s. It is, however, mentioned by Mrs Foster in a footnote to her translation of the *Life* of Andrea: 'There is much discord among the authorities as to the period of Andrea's birth; Della Valle and most of the later writers give it as above [i.e. 1488]; Biadi only, *Notizie Inedite della Vita d'Andrea del Sarto*, Florence, 1829, is of a different opinion, and will have it to have taken place ten years earlier' (*Foster* iii 180n.). *Foster* is itself also a possible source; some of the readings from the first ed. of Vasari's 'Life' of Andrea are reprinted in her translation, which appeared a year before the relevant volume of *Le Monnier*.

(i) *Le Monnier*

The Brownings moved into 'an ancient college built by Vasari' on their arrival in Pisa in 1846, and by Feb. 1847 were (in EBB.'s words) 'ploughing through' Vasari. EBB. thought the *Lives* 'a dull book', but B. seems to have found it more stimulating; in a letter of 13 Apr. 1853 to Julia Martin EBB. says that B. is 'as fond of digging at Vasari as I am at the Mystics, & goes to and from him as constantly, making him a "betwixt and between" to other writers' (MS at Wellesley College). Although *Collections* lists three editions of Vasari, it is overwhelmingly likely that the edition used by the Brownings was the 13-volume edition published between 1846 and 1857 in Florence by Felice Le Monnier (see headnote to *Fra Lippo*, pp. 477–80). Volume viii of *Le Monnier*, which includes the chapter on Andrea, was first published in 1852. It incorporates material from the first edition of the *Life* (1550) which Vasari later suppressed, probably due to the fact that it severely criticizes Andrea's widow Lucrezia who was still alive at the time of its publication:

[Lo] eccellentissimo pittore Andrea del Sarto fiorentino, il quale obbligatissimo alla natura per uno ingegno raro nella pittura, se avesse atteso a una vita più civile e onorata, e non trascurato sè e i suoi prossimi, per lo appetito d'una sua donna che lo tenne sempre et povero et basso, sarebbe stato del continuo in Francia, dove egli fu chiamato da quel Re, che adorava l'opere sue et

stimavalo assai; et lo arebbe rimunerato grandemente; dove per satisfare al deside-
rio de l'appetito di lei et di lui, tornò et visse sempre bassamente; et non fu
delle fatiche sue mai, se non poveramente, sovvenuto; et da lei, ch'altro di ben
non vedeva, nella fine vicino alla morte fu abandonato.

(Le Monnier viii 250n.)

[If the most excellent Florentine painter Andrea del Sarto, who had nature to
thank for having given him a rare gift in the art of painting, had achieved a
more civilized and honourable way of life, and not neglected himself and his
family for the desire of a wife who always kept him poor and in a low social
condition, he would have stayed in France, where he had been summoned by
that king who loved his work and held him in great esteem, and who would
have rewarded him handsomely; whereas to satisfy both of their cravings, he
returned and lived in a state of poverty; and was never properly rewarded for
his labours; and was abandoned by her in whom he could see nothing but
good when close to his death.]

Vasari describes Andrea as a 'timid soul' with a 'humble and simple nature' (*Le
Monnier* viii 251), and accuses Lucrezia of mistreating his pupils (including Vasari
himself) and of using his infatuation with her to alienate his affections from his
own family: 'datogli il tossico delle amorose lusinghe, egli ne più qua ne più la
faceva, ch'essa voleva; et abbandonato del tutto que' miseri e poveri vecchi, tolse
ad aiutare le sorelle et il padre di lei in cambio di quegli' (*Le Monnier* viii 262).
[Having received the poison of her amorous enticements, he no longer did anything but her bidding, and having completely abandoned his own poor and unfortunate parents took it upon himself to support her sisters and her father instead.]
This task of supporting his wife and her family eventually wears him down, and
friends advise him to leave his wife 'in qualche luogo sicuro' [in some safe place]
in order to develop his artistic career. He goes to France to work at the court
of François I and wins the favour of the king, but receives letters from his wife
imploring him to come home. François gives Andrea money to buy 'pictures and
sculptures of great value' (*Foster* iii 206), but despite swearing on the Bible that
he will return to France he never does, spending the money on the construction
of his house and on enjoyment, and working slavishly to support Lucrezia and
her family.

There are substantial similarities between Vasari's first edition text and B.'s
poem, but there are also significant differences between them. Like B., Vasari
emphasizes the 'faultless' quality of Andrea's pictures, both in the Preface to
Part 3 of the *Lives* and in the *Life* of Andrea itself. He also, however, somewhat
inconsistently claims that Andrea 'continually improved in everything' connected
with his art, adding: 'had he lived longer, his art would have continued to improve
in the same way'. The poem follows Vasari in describing Andrea as 'jealous' of
Lucrezia, but goes beyond the source in its explicit suggestion of infidelity; her
crime for Vasari is exploitation of Andrea's talent in the interests of herself and
her family.

(ii) *Baldinucci*

In the letter of 1878 cited above (*Composition and date*) B. states that there is a
'dissent' from Vasari's judgment in Filippo Baldinucci's *Notizie de' Professori del
Disegno da Cimabue in quà*. There is, however, substantial agreement between *Le
Monnier* and *Baldinucci* on several matters; Baldinucci in fact uses the first edition
of the *Lives* as his primary source. *Baldinucci* notes, for example, that Andrea was
a 'very timid person with little spirit' who charged little or nothing for his

pictures, and berates him for returning from France: 'sarebbe . . . arrivato a gradi onoratissimi, e ricchissimo diventato, s'egli fosse stato più uomo di quel, ch'e fu.' [he would have been greatly honoured and become very rich if he had been more of a man than he was.] Like *Le Monnier*, *Baldinucci* emphasizes the 'faultlessness' of Andrea's work: 'si può dire . . . che nell'infinite opere, che e' fece, non sia che sappia trovare un errore'. [It might be said that, in all the great number of works he produced, it would be impossible to find an error.] *Baldinucci*'s editor Piacenza adds: 'Inoltre nel disegno fu cosi corretto, che venne communemente chiamato Andrea senza errori' (ii 441n.) [Moreover in his drawing he was so correct that he came to be commonly called 'Andrea without mistakes'.]

(iii) *Jameson*

Anna Jameson was a personal friend of the Brownings and B. certainly read her account of Andrea's life in her *Memoirs of the Early Italian Painters* (1845). Mrs Jameson repeats the idea that Andrea 'was called in his own time "Andrea senza errori," that is, Andrea *the Faultless*' (ii 73); note that B. uses the same term to translate 'senza errori' in the poem. Following Vasari, she describes Andrea as 'miserable, unfortunate, and contemned' thanks to his marriage to a woman 'of infamous character', after which 'he never had a quiet heart, or home, or conscience' (ii 73–4). The idea of Lucrezia's infidelity may originate with Mrs Jameson: Lucrezia's 'avarice and infidelity' are said to have blighted Andrea's life (ii 79). Mrs Jameson criticizes Andrea's work for its 'want of any real elevation of sentiment and expression', and amplifies Vasari's suggestion that he routinely used his wife as a model:

> In general his Madonnas are not pleasing; they have, with great beauty, a certain vulgarity of expression, and in his groups he almost always places the Virgin on the ground, either kneeling or sitting. His only model for all his females was his wife; and even when he did not paint from her, she so possessed his thoughts that unconsciously he repeated the same features in every face he drew, whether Virgin, or saint, or goddess.
>
> (*Jameson* ii 80)

(iv) *Musset*

Alfred de Musset's play *André del Sarto* was first published in the *Revue des Deux Mondes* of 1 Apr. 1833; it was not originally intended for performance, but was eventually staged (without success) at the Comédie Française on 21 Nov. 1848. It was then revived, in a much shortened and slightly bowdlerized version, at the Odéon on 21 Oct. 1851 (not 1850 as has previously been thought; see Simon Jeune, *De Musset: Théâtre Complet* [Paris 1990] 871) and this time enjoyed a run of thirty-seven performances. The Brownings lived in Paris from Sept. 1851 to June 1852, so it is possible that they might have seen the play during this time. The original version of Musset's play opens with Cordiani, a pupil of Andrea's, descending from Lucrezia's balcony at four o'clock in the morning, and this sets the tone for the melodrama to follow. Lucrezia agonizes over her infidelity, Cordiani inadvertently kills an innocent man, and the play ends with the death of Andrea and the flight of Lucrezia and Cordiani to start a new life together. (In the 1851 version, Cordiani also dies in order to prevent the triumph of vice.) There are a number of parallels between the play and the poem, some of which are noted in *Melchiori* 199–204. Both, for example, stress Lucrezia's infidelity, something hinted at (but not overtly stated) in Vasari and Baldinucci. Again, Musset's Andrea, like B.'s, is a world-weary and disappointed figure, conscious of his own belatedness, as he makes clear in the opening scene of Act I:

La nature veut toujours être nouvelle, c'est vrai; mais elle reste toujours la même. Es-tu de ceux qui souhaiteraient qu'elle changeât la couleur de sa robe, et que les bois se colorassent en bleu ou en rouge? Ce n'est pas ainsi qu'elle entend; à côté d'une fleur fanée naît une fleur tout semblable . . . Que les arts tâchent de faire comme elle, puisqu'ils ne sont rien qu'en l'imitant. [Nature desires perpetual novelty, it is true, but is always the same. Are you one of those who would like her to change the colour of her dress, or to colour the woods red or blue? She does not work like that; beside a faded flower grows another one exactly the same . . . Let the arts try to do the same as her, because they are worthless unless they imitate her.]

Another similarity between the play and B.'s poem is Andrea's tendency to blame himself for what others might see as his wife's shortcomings. In Act I, scene ii, reflecting on the ignominious end to his year in France, he blames himself and exonerates his wife: 'Ah! voilà ce que c'est que de manquer de caractère! Que faisait-elle de mal en me demandant ce qui lui plaisait? Et moi je le lui donnais, parcequ'elle le demandait, rien de plus: faiblesse maudite! pas une réflexion' [Ah! That's what it means to lack character! What did she do wrong in asking me to do what pleased her? And I did it for her, because she asked for it, that's all. Cursed weakness! Without thinking]. Andrea's confession to the French envoy Montjoie that he has stolen the money entrusted to him by François I for the purchase of paintings, which is echoed at l. 145, was, however, cut from the acting version.

Parallels in B.

Andrea's justification of the technical defects of his great contemporaries—'Ah, but a man's reach should exceed his grasp, / Or what's a Heaven for?' (ll. 96–7)—represents B.'s best known formulation of the idea of the aesthetic superiority of imperfection. This notion is often linked with the contrast between Christian and Pagan art forms in the early nineteenth century; see, for example, August Wilhelm von Schlegel, *Lectures on Dramatic Art and Poetry* (1809; transl. 1846) 27: 'The Grecian executed what it proposed in the utmost perfection; but the modern can only do justice to its endeavours after what is infinite by approximation; and, from a certain appearance of imperfection, is in greater danger of not being duly appreciated'; and cp. *Old Pictures*, esp. ll. 83–160n. (p. 415). Andrea's commitment to technical perfection makes him a version of the 'objective' or mimetic poet; see the explanation of the difference between 'subjective' and 'objective' poets in *Shelley* 11–112 (Appendix A, pp. 621–5), and the contrast between Sordello and Eglamor in bk. ii of *Sordello*. The relations between artist, model, patron and artefact are dealt with in a number of B.'s poems, most notably *My Last Duchess* (p. 197), *Pictor Ignotus* (p. 226), *A Likeness* (p. 642), and *Beatrice Signorini* (*Asolando*, 1889). Andrea's situation has similarities to that of Jules the sculptor in *Pippa* ii. Like Andrea, Jules sees marriage as an impediment to the achievement of his artistic ambitions (ii 18–24; pp. 123–4). Jules, though, makes a conscious decision to idealize the object of his affections, while Andrea finds himself tied to Lucrezia in spite of his knowledge of her failings. Unhappy marriages and infidelity are frequent topics in B.'s poetry from the time of *M & W* onwards: see for example *Woman's Last Word* (III 273), *Any Wife to Any Husband* (III 647), *The Statue and the Bust* (III 342) and *A Forgiveness* (*Pacchiarotto*, 1876). *Ring* also centres on the story of a possibly adulterous relationship between Pompilia Franceschini and Giuseppe Caponsacchi. François I also features in *The Glove* (II 360) and Fontainebleau is the setting for *Cristina and Monaldeschi* (*Jocoseria*, 1883).

But do not let us quarrel any more,
No, my Lucrezia; bear with me for once:
Sit down and all shall happen as you wish.
You turn your face, but does it bring your heart?
5   I'll work then for your friend's friend, never fear,
Treat his own subject after his own way,
Fix his own time, accept too his own price
And shut the money into this small hand
When next it takes mine. Will it? tenderly?
10 Oh, I'll content him,—but to-morrow, Love!
I often am much wearier than you think,
This evening more than usual, and it seems
As if—forgive now—should you let me sit
Here by the window with your hand in mine
15 And look a half hour forth on Fiesole,
Both of one mind, as married people use,
Quietly, quietly, the evening through,
I might get up to-morrow to my work
Cheerful and fresh as ever. Let us try.
20 To-morrow how you shall be glad for this!
Your soft hand is a woman of itself,
And mine the man's bared breast she curls inside.

---

2. *Lucrezia*: *Le Monnier* gives her full name as Lucrezia di Baccio del Fede. For accounts of her character and behaviour as Andrea's wife, see headnote.

5. *friend's friend*: obviously the person to whom Lucrezia's 'Cousin' is indebted: see l. 233n. Andrea's willingness to work for little or no financial reward is emphasized by Vasari, who notes how Fra Mariano dal Canto alla Macine persuaded him to paint scenes from the life of St Filippo Benizzi in the cloisters of SS. Annunziata for a nominal fee. Details of these frescoes are given in *Fantozzi*, 407–8.

10. *Love!*] love! (*1868*). Variants unique to *1868* are rare; this one is not accidental, since it is repeated at ll. 58 and 119. See also ll. 210, 266.

15. *Fiesole*: a hilltop town north-east of Florence, frequently mentioned by the Brownings in their correspondence and relished by them for its historical associations, as in EBB.'s letter of 22–23 Dec. 1847 to her sister Arabella: ' "But what is there to see?" asked Capt. Reynolds—Milton's Fiesole, the Fiesole of the Romans, the Fiesole of the Etruscans, and "what to see"?' (*Correspondence* xiv 352). On 'Milton's Fiesole' see *PL* i 289. In another letter to Arabella (*c.* 7 Feb. 1848, *ibid.* xv 9) EBB. says that B. has decided that port is good for her, and 'one might as well talk to the mountain above Fiesole as talk to him about my leaving it off', an expression she uses on several other occasions. The metre would suggest a trisyllabic pronunciation (Fi-so-le) in line with Milton's spelling ('Fesole').

16. *as married people use*: 'as married people are accustomed to do'.

Don't count the time lost, either; you must serve
For each of the five pictures we require—
25   It saves a model. So! keep looking so—
My serpentining beauty, rounds on rounds!
—How could you ever prick those perfect ears,
Even to put the pearl there! oh, so sweet—
My face, my moon, my everybody's moon,
30   Which everybody looks on and calls his,
And, I suppose, is looked on by in turn,
While she looks—no one's: very dear, no less!
You smile? why, there's my picture ready made.
There's what we painters call our harmony!
35   A common greyness silvers everything,—
All in a twilight, you and I alike
—You, at the point of your first pride in me
(That's gone you know),—but I, at every point;
My youth, my hope, my art, being all toned down
40   To yonder sober pleasant Fiesole.

23–5. *Don't count . . . model*: Vasari attributes Andrea's use of his wife as a model
to infatuation rather than the desire to save money; see *Melchiori* 205–6, and cp.
Jameson (headnote, *Sources*).
23. *lost, either*] lost, neither (*1865–88*).
26. *serpentining*: associating Lucrezia with Eve, the archetype of female weakness;
her golden hair (see l. 174) recalls Milton's Eve, although in *PL* Eve's 'unadorned
golden tresses' are 'dishevelled' and 'in wanton ringlets waved' (iv 305–6);
Lucrezia's elaborate hairdo is that of a fashionable Florentine beauty. Real serpents are associated with hair in depictions of Bacchus's followers, the Maenads:
cp., e.g., Christopher Smart's transl. of Horace (*Odes* II xix 19–20): 'You . . .
bind in serpentine knot unhurt your handmaid's hair'; this volume was in B.'s
library (*Collections* A2147). 'Serpentining' is usually a topographical term (denoting the course of a path, stream, etc.); B.'s more 'sensational' usage appears in
Christmas-Eve 428 (III 64) and *Aristophanes' Apology* (1875) 5595 (the 'serpentining
blood' of the murdered Agamemnon).
29–32. Cp. the moon imagery in *One Word More* 144 ff. (pp. 611–15), also associated with Florence and with the private and public 'faces' of a beloved woman.
Cp. also *My Last Duchess* 23–4 (p. 199). *Oxford* notes a parallel in Ventidius's
words to Antony in Dryden's *All for Love* IV i 300–1: 'Your Cleopatra; / Dolabella's
Cleopatra; every man's Cleopatra'.
32. *While she looks*: 'while she seems' (changing the sense of 'looks' from active
to passive).
34. *harmony*: as *Oxford* points out, this word is used by Mrs Foster in her translation of Vasari (*Foster* iii 192, 236).
36–8. Andrea sees both himself and Lucrezia as 'twilight' figures, but in opposed
senses. Twilight can refer either to the period before dawn or nightfall; Andrea
juxtaposes a fantasy of Lucrezia in the early days of her love for him with his
own actual condition, steeped in the melancholy 'greyness' of evening.
39. *my hope*] my hopes (*H proof*, but not *H proof²*).

There's the bell clinking from the chapel-top;
That length of convent-wall across the way
Holds the trees safer, huddled more inside;
The last monk leaves the garden; days decrease
45 And autumn grows, autumn in everything.
Eh? the whole seems to fall into a shape
As if I saw alike my work and self
And all that I was born to be and do,
A twilight-piece. Love, we are in God's hand.
50 How strange now, looks the life he makes us lead!
So free we seem, so fettered fast we are:
I feel he laid the fetter: let it lie!
This chamber for example—turn your head—
All that's behind us! you don't understand
55 Nor care to understand about my art,
But you can hear at least when people speak;
And that cartoon, the second from the door

41–5. Contrast the much more positive image of the convent near Casa Guidi in *Ring* i 484–7: 'Whence came the clear voice of the cloistered ones / Chanting a chant made for midsummer nights— / I know not what particular praise of God, / It always came and went with June'. Thomas suggests that the convent in question is that of the Servites adjoining the Church of the Santissima Annunziata in which Andrea is buried (*Thomas* 23).

45. *autumn in everything*: There is a corresponding feeling of belatedness in Alfred de Musset's *André del Sarto*, act II, scene i (see headnote, *Sources*): 'Rome et Venise sont encore florissantes. Notre patrie n'est plus rien. Je lutte en vain contre les ténèbres, le flambeau sacré s'éteint dans ma main.' [Rome and Venice are still flourishing. Our country (i.e. Florence) is now finished. I fight in vain against the shadows; the sacred flame dies in my hands.]

49. *a twilight-piece*: this is, as *Oxford* notes, similar to the expression 'night-piece', commonly used for a 'picture representing a scene or landscape at night' (*OED*). 'Twilight' is a traditional image for life's decline: cp. Shakespeare, *Sonnets* lxxiii 5–6: 'In me thou seest the twilight of such day / As after sunset fadeth in the west'. Contrast the sense of 'twilight' as the approach of day in *How They Brought the Good News*: 'the cocks crew and twilight dawned clear' (l. 14, p. 222); cp. also the last line of *Fra Lippo*: 'There's the grey beginning' (p. 506).

49–52. *we are in God's hand . . . let it lie!* cp. Ecclesiastes ix 1: 'For all this I considered in my heart even to declare all this, that the righteous, and the wise, and their works, are in the hand of God; no man knoweth either love or hatred by all that is before them.' Trust in God's providence turns, in Andrea's formulation, to passive fatalism and a denial of free will.

54. *All that's behind us*: i.e. all the pictures in the 'chamber', Andrea's studio. This could also refer obliquely to all the evidence of their life together.

57. *cartoon*: 'a drawing on stout paper, made as a design for a painting of the same size' (*OED*). None of Andrea's cartoons for his frescoes survives (Shearman, *Andrea*, p. 151).

—It is the thing, Love! so such things should be—
Behold Madonna, I am bold to say.
60 I can do with my pencil what I know,
What I see, what at bottom of my heart
I wish for, if I ever wish so deep—
Do easily, too—when I say perfectly
I do not boast, perhaps: yourself are judge
65 Who listened to the Legate's talk last week,
And just as much they used to say in France.
At any rate, 'tis easy, all of it,
No sketches first, no studies, that's long past—
I do what many dream of all their lives
70 —Dream? strive to do, and agonise to do,
And fail in doing. I could count twenty such
On twice your fingers, and not leave this town,
Who strive—you don't know how the others strive
To paint a little thing like that you smeared
75 Carelessly passing with your robes afloat,
Yet do much less, so much less, some one says,

58. *the thing, Love!*] the thing, love! (*1868*).

59. *Behold Madonna,*] Behold Madonna!—(*1868–88*). For Andrea's reputation as a religious painter, esp. of the Virgin, see headnote; cp. also ll. 176–8. Note also though Mrs Jameson's denial that his pictures conveyed any 'devotional feeling' (*Jameson* ii 73).

65. Referring presumably to a Papal Legate, that is to say, a diplomatic representative of the Pope in his capacity as temporal ruler of the Papal states; cp. Ogniben in *A Soul's Tragedy* (II 180), and see also headnote to *Bishop Blougram* (p. 279).

66. *in France*: for Andrea's career in France, see headnote, *Sources*; his passing allusion here is developed in ll. 148–71.

68. *No sketches first, no studies*: Vasari stresses the fact that Andrea used 'sketches' in an unorthodox way: 'Quando egli disegnava le cose di naturale per metterle in opera, faceva certi schizzi cosi abbozzati, bastandogli vedere quello che faceva il naturale; quando poi gli metteva in opera, gli conduceva a perfezione: onde i disegni gli servivano piu per memoria di quello che aveva visto, che per copiare a punto da quelli le sue pitture' (*Le Monnier* viii 294). [When he drew things from life in order to put them in one of his works, he made some hasty ill-formed sketches, it being enough for him to see what the original was doing. When he then set about his work he perfected it; the drawings therefore served more as an aide-mémoire than as something from which he could then copy his pictures.]

72. *On twice your fingers*: this might suggest that Lucrezia is innumerate (or illiterate), or at least has little education.

76–7. For the identity of the 'some one', see ll. 182–92.

76. *some one says*] Someone says (*1863*, but not *1863²*, which agrees with *1855*; *1868–88*); Some one says (*1865*).

(I know his name, no matter) so much less!
Well, less is more, Lucrezia! I am judged.
There burns a truer light of God in them,
80   In their vexed, beating, stuffed and stopped-up brain,
Heart, or whate'er else, than goes on to prompt
This low-pulsed forthright craftsman's hand of mine.
Their works drop groundward, but themselves, I know,
Reach many a time a heaven that's shut to me,
85   Enter and take their place there sure enough,
Though they come back and cannot tell the world.
My works are nearer heaven, but I sit here.
The sudden blood of these men! at a word—
Praise them, it boils, or blame them, it boils too.
90   I, painting from myself and to myself,
Know what I do, am unmoved by men's blame
Or their praise either. Somebody remarks
Morello's outline there is wrongly traced,
His hue mistaken—what of that? or else,
95   Rightly traced and well ordered—what of that?
Ah, but a man's reach should exceed his grasp,
Or what's a Heaven for? all is silver-grey
Placid and perfect with my art—the worse!
I know both what I want and what might gain—
100 And yet how profitless to know, to sigh
"Had I been two, another and myself,
Our head would have o'erlooked the world!" No doubt.
Yonder's a work, now, of that famous youth
The Urbinate who died five years ago.

78. *less is more*] it is more (*H proof*).
83–6. *themselves, I know . . . shut to me*: cp. Lazarus in *An Epistle*, esp. ll. 178–210 (pp. 521–2).
93. *Morello's outline*: the mountain of Morello to the north of Florence. Cp. *Aurora Leigh* vii 520.
95^96.] Speak as they please, what does the mountain care? (*1863–88*). A rare example of a whole line added after *1855*; for another example see *Bishop Blougram* 978^979 (p. 337).
96–7. *Ah . . . Heaven for?* this famous dictum encapsulates the 'doctrine of the imperfect': see headnote, *Parallels*.
97. *a Heaven*] a heaven (*1868–88*).
104. *the Urbinate*: Raffaello Sanzio (Raphael), 1483–1520 (named at l. 118) who came from Urbino in Tuscany; his career was principally in Rome, and he is referred to as 'the Roman' in l. 177. The editors of *Le Monnier* argue in a footnote that Vasari's reference to Raphael's 'disciples' implies that Raphael was dead

105   ('Tis copied, George Vasari sent it me.)
      Well, I can fancy how he did it all,
      Pouring his soul, with kings and popes to see,
      Reaching, that Heaven might so replenish him,
      Above and through his art—for it gives way;
110   That arm is wrongly put—and there again—
      A fault to pardon in the drawing's lines,
      Its body, so to speak! its soul is right,
      He means right—that, a child may understand.
      Still, what an arm! and I could alter it.
115   But all the play, the insight and the stretch—
      Out of me! out of me! And wherefore out?
      Had you enjoined them on me, given me soul,
      We might have risen to Rafael, I and you.
      Nay, Love, you did give all I asked, I think—
120   More than I merit, yes, by many times.
      But had you—oh, with the same perfect brow,
      And perfect eyes, and more than perfect mouth,
      And the low voice my soul hears, as a bird

---

by the time Andrea went to Rome to see his works and those of Michelangelo (viii 293n.). This would date the monologue to 1525, the year in which Andrea painted the 'Madonna del Sacco' praised by Mrs Jameson.

105. In his 'Life' of Andrea, Giorgio ['George'] Vasari mentions that, as a young artist in the employment of Ottaviano de' Medici, he saw Andrea carrying out Ottaviano's order to copy Raphael's painting *Leo X with Two Cardinals*; *Le Monnier* viii 282. As Markus notes (see headnote, *Composition*), there is no suggestion in the poem that Andrea himself has copied Raphael's work.

106–7. Andrea refers again to the 'popes and kings' who were Raphael's patrons at l. 191.

119. Nay, Love] Nay, love (*1868*).

121–2. perfect brow . . . perfect eyes . . . perfect mouth: cp. Tennyson, *Maud* i 80–3: 'Perfectly beautiful: let it be granted her: where is the fault? / All that I saw (for her eyes were downcast, not to be seen) / Faultily faultless, icily regular, splendidly null, / Dead perfection, no more'. The poem was published on 28 July 1855, almost certainly too late to have influenced B.'s phrasing; Tennyson read the poem to B., EBB., Arabella Barrett and Dante Gabriel Rossetti on Thursday 27 Sept. 1855, an event commemorated by Rossetti in a sketch. According to Tennyson both B. and EBB. were 'great admirers of poor little "Maud"' (*EBB to Arabella* ii 175–6n.).

123. the low voice: this phrase is also associated with illicit passion in B.'s play *A Blot in the 'Scutcheon* (1843) ii 266–8: Mildred is described as having no equal in the history of the Treshams: 'no loosener / O' the lattice, practised in the stealthy tread, / The low voice and the noiseless come-and-go!'

123–4. as a bird . . . snare: 'my soul is entranced by your voice as a bird is by the pipe of the bird-catcher (fowler) who lures it into a snare'.

The fowler's pipe, and follows to the snare—
125 Had you, with these the same, but brought a mind!
Some women do so. Had the mouth there urged
"God and the glory! never care for gain.
The present by the future, what is that?
Live for fame, side by side with Angelo—
130 Rafael is waiting. Up to God all three!"
I might have done it for you. So it seems—
Perhaps not. All is as God over-rules.
Beside, incentives come from the soul's self;
The rest avail not. Why do I need you?
135 What wife had Rafael, or has Angelo?
In this world, who can do a thing, will not—
And who would do it, cannot, I perceive:
Yet the will's somewhat—somewhat, too, the power—
And thus we half-men struggle. At the end,
140 God, I conclude, compensates, punishes.
'Tis safer for me, if the award be strict,
That I am something underrated here,
Poor this long while, despised, to speak the truth.
I dared not, do you know, leave home all day,
145 For fear of chancing on the Paris lords.
The best is when they pass and look aside;
But they speak sometimes; I must bear it all.

129. *with Angelo*—] with Agnolo! (*1868–88*). The spelling 'Michelagnolo' is used by Mrs Foster in her 1852 tr. of Vasari's Lives (*Foster* iv pp. 227–370), and by B. in a letter to John Kenyon of 17 Mar. 1853 (see *Old Pictures*, p. 405). Michelangelo is often bracketed with Raphael and Leonardo da Vinci as joint archetypes of the great painter: see headnote.

135. *or has Angelo?*] or has Agnolo? (*1868–88*). Raphael did eventually marry, but Michelangelo never did.

139–43. One of a number of reflections on the relation between worldly success and heavenly reward in B.; see e.g. *Old Pictures* 161–76 (p. 422).

142–3. Vasari's comments (see headnote) would seem to imply that Andrea's contemporaries 'despised' him for not making the most of his talent either personally or financially.

145. *the Paris lords*: Andrea's fear of the 'Paris lords' is prompted by his failure to keep his promise to return to France with pictures and statues for which the king had provided him with money; in the original version of Musset's *André del Sarto* (see headnote, *Sources*) Andrea is accosted by a 'Paris lord' called Montjoie and openly admits to him that he has stolen the king's money: 'J'ai volé votre maitre, Monsieur. L'argent qu'il m'a confié est dissipé' [I have robbed your master, Sir. The money he gave to me has been frittered away] (III ii). This scene was omitted from the version staged in Paris during 1851–2.

Well may they speak! That Francis, that first time,
And that long festal year at Fontainebleau!
150 I surely then could sometimes leave the ground,
Put on the glory, Rafael's daily wear,
In that humane great monarch's golden look,—
One finger in his beard or twisted curl
Over his mouth's good mark that made the smile,
155 One arm about my shoulder, round my neck,
The jingle of his gold chain in my ear,
I painting proudly with his breath on me,
All his court round him, seeing with his eyes,
Such frank French eyes, and such a fire of souls
160 Profuse, my hand kept plying by those hearts,—
And, best of all, this, this, this face beyond,
This in the back-ground, waiting on my work,
To crown the issue with a last reward!
A good time, was it not, my kingly days?
165 And had you not grown restless—but I know—

148. That Francis: François I; for the cult of François I as patron of the arts see headnote.

149. Fontainebleau: as Cox-Rearick (see headnote, *Sources*) notes: '[Beginning] in 1528 the king [François I] enlarged an old royal hunting lodge at Fontainebleau. It then became the privileged centre from which his patronage of art radiated, thereby changing the course of French culture.' *Melchiori* compares Musset's *André del Sarto* II i, in which Andrea describes his year at Fontainebleau as 'une année de richesse et de bonheur' [a year of riches and of happiness].

153. twisted curl: of his moustache.

154. mouth's good mark: the sense is clear enough although the wording is hard to follow: Francis's mouth is a 'good mark', i.e. a pleasing feature of his face, either made so by his smile or one which habitually made itself pleasant by smiling.

155. my shoulder . . . my neck] your shoulder . . . your neck (*H proof*).

156. my ear] your ear (*H proof*).

157. I painting] emended in agreement with *1863–88* from 'You painting' in *H proof* and *1855. H proof²* has a note: 'This should have been printed "I." It was evidently overlooked when the other changes were made. L. S. L.' (i.e. the book dealer Luther S. Livingston: see Appendix C, III 742). The correction is made in the list of 'Errata' B. sent to his American publisher James T. Fields (*B to Fields* 192). See also l. 165.

161–2. this, this, this face beyond . . . in the back-ground: perhaps pointing to the multiple portraits of Lucrezia in the studio (see note to ll. 23–5 above); Lucrezia had remained in Florence during Andrea's trip to France.

164. kingly: a pun: both 'days spent with the king' and 'days of my glory'.

165. had you not grown restless: a reference to Lucrezia's letters urging Andrea to return to Florence; see also l. 171 below and headnote. *had you not*] had I not

'Tis done and past; 'twas right, my instinct said;
Too live the life grew, golden and not grey—
And I'm the weak-eyed bat no sun should tempt
Out of the grange whose four walls make his world.
170 How could it end in any other way?
You called me, and I came home to your heart.
The triumph was to have ended there—then if
I reached it ere the triumph, what is lost?
Let my hands frame your face in your hair's gold,
175 You beautiful Lucrezia that are mine!
"Rafael did this, Andrea painted that—
The Roman's is the better when you pray,
But still the other's Virgin was his wife—"
Men will excuse me. I am glad to judge
180 Both pictures in your presence; clearer grows
My better fortune, I resolve to think.
For, do you know, Lucrezia, as God lives,
Said one day Angelo, his very self,
To Rafael . . . I have known it all these years . . .
185 (When the young man was flaming out his thoughts
Upon a palace-wall for Rome to see,
Too lifted up in heart because of it)
"Friend, there's a certain sorry little scrub

(corrected by B. in *H proof*, the only such correction for this poem; *H proof*[2]
underlines 'you' and has a note at the bottom of the page which has been erased
and is too faint to read; it might be something like 'is this misprinted?'). See also
l. 157.
172.] The triumph was to reach and stay there; since (*1888*). *H proof* has 'if then'
for 'then if'.
177. *The Roman's*: i.e. Raphael's; see l. 104n.
183–92. 'Narra il Bocchi, nelle *Bellezze di Firenze*, che Michelangelo ragionando
con Raffaello sul valore de' rari artefici, gli dicesse: "Egli ha in Firenze un omacetto
(volendo significare Andrea) il quale se in grandi affari, come in te avviene, fosse
adoperato, ti farebbe sudar la fronte' (*Le Monnier* viii 293n; also cited by Allan
C. Dooley, *MP* lxxxi [1983–4] 41). B.'s words, esp. in l. 192 with its reference
to sweat, are closer to the Italian original than to Mrs Foster's translation:
'The estimation in which the powers of Andrea were held by Michael Angelo
likewise, may be inferred from a remark of that master to Raphael, which we
find cited in Bocchi, *Bellezze di Firenze*. "There is a bit of a mannikin in Florence,"
observes Michael Angelo, "who, if he had chanced to be employed in great under-
takings as you have happened to be, would compel you to look well about you"'
(*Foster* ii 232).
183. *one day Angelo*] one day Agnolo (*1868–88*).

          Goes up and down our Florence, none cares how,
190   Who, were he set to plan and execute
          As you are pricked on by your popes and kings,
          Would bring the sweat into that brow of yours!"
          To Rafael's!—And indeed the arm is wrong.
          I hardly dare—yet, only you to see,
195   Give the chalk here—quick, thus the line should go!
          Ay, but the soul! he's Rafael! rub it out!
          Still, all I care for, if he spoke the truth,
          (What he? why, who but Michael Angelo?
          Do you forget already words like those?)
200   If really there was such a chance, so lost,
          Is, whether you're—not grateful—but more pleased.
          Well, let me think so. And you smile indeed!
          This hour has been an hour! Another smile?
          If you would sit thus by me every night
205   I should work better, do you comprehend?
          I mean that I should earn more, give you more.
          See, it is settled dusk now; there's a star;
          Morello's gone, the watch-lights shew the wall,
          The cue-owls speak the name we call them by.
210   Come from the window, Love,—come in, at last,

---

191. As you are pricked on] As you, pricked forward (*H proof*); As you are, pricked on (*1863–88*), making it clear that 'As you are' refers to 'set to plan and execute' in l. 190.
198. What he? In response to an unrecorded question from Lucrezia, suggesting that she is not really paying attention to Andrea's impassioned apology.   *Michael Angelo*] Michel Agnolo (*1868–88*); see l.129n.
199^200.] B. added a line in a copy of vol. v of his 6-vol. *Poetical Works*, now at the Pierpont Morgan Library. The volume is dated *1872* (a reissue of *1870*, itself a corrected reprint of *1868*: see Abbreviations, p. xxvii, and Editorial Note to vol. II, p. vii). The line reads: 'Yes, all I care for if he spoke the truth,'; it was not adopted either in *1875* (a second corrected reprint of *1868*) or *1888*.
205–6. Lucrezia's avarice is insisted on by Vasari; see headnote.
206. I mean that I] Lucrezia—I (*H proof*).
208. watch-lights: this may mean either 'lights carried by watchmen' or 'lamps lit at regular intervals along the city walls'; *OED* cites this line in support of the former, but has no other examples.
209. cue-owls: 'a name applied to the Scops-owl (*Scops Giu*), common on the shores of the Mediterannean' (*OED*). Its song is described as 'a clear metallic ringing *ki-ou*—whence the Italian names *chiù, ciù*'. Cp. *Aurora Leigh* viii 32.
210. window, Love] window, love (*1863²*, *1868–88*). In previous instances (ll. 10, 58, 119) only *1868* had this variant; see also l. 266, where the pattern is different again. This is also a rare example of *1863²* agreeing neither with *1855* nor *1863*.

Inside the melancholy little house
We built to be so gay with. God is just.
King Francis may forgive me. Oft at nights
When I look up from painting, eyes tired out,
215   The walls become illumined, brick from brick
Distinct, instead of mortar fierce bright gold,
That gold of his I did cement them with!
Let us but love each other. Must you go?
That Cousin here again? he waits outside?
220   Must see you—you, and not with me? Those loans!
More gaming debts to pay? you smiled for that?
Well, let smiles buy me! have you more to spend?
While hand and eye and something of a heart
Are left me, work's my ware, and what's it worth?
225   I'll pay my fancy. Only let me sit
The grey remainder of the evening out,
Idle, you call it, and muse perfectly

211–12. According to *Thomas*, the 'melancholy little house' is the one Andrea built for himself and Lucrezia at 22 Via Gino Capponi with the money obtained from France (p. 29).

213–7. Vasari states that Andrea dreamt of obtaining Francis's forgiveness for deserting him and for stealing his money: 'Mentre le cose succedevano in questa maniera, ricordandosi alcuna volta Andrea delle cose di Francia, sospirava di cuore; e se avesse pensato trovar perdono del fallo commesso, non ha dubbio che egli vi sarebbe tornato' (*Le Monnier* viii 277). [While things were going on in this way, Andrea sighed from his heart every now and then, remembering his time in France; and if he had been able to obtain forgiveness for the fault he had committed, there is no doubt that he would have gone back there.] Andrea imagines that the mortar of the house he has built with Francis's money has been transformed into 'fierce bright gold'.

218–21. Melchiori compares Musset's *André del Sarto* I iii: 'Réponds-moi, qui t'amène à cette heure? As-tu une querelle? faut-il servir de second? As-tu perdu au jeu? Veux-tu ma bourse? *Il lui prend la main.*' [Answer me, who brings you at this hour? Are you involved in a dispute? Must I serve as your second? Have you lost money gambling? Would you like my purse? *He takes her hand.*]

219. That Cousin: this detail is not in Vasari; in Musset's play Lucrezia's lover is one of Andrea's pupils. 'Cousin' was 'an understood Renaissance term for a married woman's lover' (W. F. McNeir, *NQ* cci [1956] 500).

221. more gaming debts to pay? Vasari repeatedly emphasizes Lucrezia's use of Andrea's money to assist her own family: see headnote. There may, as Markus (see headnote, *Composition*) points out, also be an allusion to Sarah Dougherty's desertion of her husband William Page; B. wrote to the Storys on 27 Dec. 1854: 'I fear Page is deeply involved in debts of her contracting' (*BIS* ii 11).

How I could paint were I but back in France,
One picture, just one more—the Virgin's face,
230   Not your's this time! I want you at my side
To hear them—that is, Michael Angelo—
Judge all I do and tell you of its worth.
Will you? To-morrow, satisfy your friend.
I take the subjects for his corridor,
235   Finish the portrait out of hand—there, there,
And throw him in another thing or two
If he demurs; the whole should prove enough
To pay for this same Cousin's freak. Beside,
What's better and what's all I care about,
240   Get you the thirteen scudi for the ruff
Love, does that please you? Ah, but what does he,
The Cousin! what does he to please you more?

I am grown peaceful as old age to-night.
I regret little, I would change still less.
245   Since there my past life lies, why alter it?
The very wrong to Francis! it is true
I took his coin, was tempted and complied,
And built this house and sinned, and all is said.
My father and my mother died of want.
250   Well, had I riches of my own? you see
How one gets rich! Let each one bear his lot.
They were born poor, lived poor, and poor they died:

230. Not your's] Not yours (*1863²*, *1888*). The possessive form 'your's' was allowable in the mid-19th century but is rare in B.
231. Michael Angelo] Michel Agnolo (*1868–88*).
233. your friend: perhaps the person to whom the cousin owes money; Andrea
suggests that he will pay for the cousin's 'freak' [escapade] with a number of
pictures for the man's corridor and a portrait of him.
240. scudi: the scudo was a silver coin, worth about four shillings; thirteen scudi
would have been a considerable sum to spend on an item such as a ruff.
243–5. B. inscribed these lines on the fly-leaf of a presentation copy of *Selections*
(dated 1882, a reprint of *1872*) and wrote underneath: 'From Lippo Lippi. Robert
Browning. Dec. 20, '84.' The volume is now at ABL (*Browning Collections*, C550,
E11). The two poems follow each other in *Selections*, but *Fra Lippo* comes first,
so there is no possibility that B. was misled by the running title for the second
poem coming on the same page as the closing passage of the first. In any case
the misattribution is intriguing, given that Lippi and Andrea are so opposed in
temperament.
249–52. For Andrea's treatment of his parents, see headnote, p. 388.

And I have laboured somewhat in my time
And not been paid profusely. Some good son
255 Paint my two hundred pictures—let him try!
No doubt, there's something strikes a balance. Yes,
You loved me quite enough, it seems to-night.
This must suffice me here. What would one have?
In heaven, perhaps, new chances, one more chance—
260 Four great walls in the New Jerusalem
Meted on each side by the angel's reed
For Leonard, Rafael, Angelo and me
To cover—the three first without a wife,
While I have mine! So—still they overcome
265 Because there's still Lucrezia,—as I choose.

Again the Cousin's whistle! Go, my Love.

255. my two hundred pictures: S. J. Freedberg's *Catalogue Raisonné* of Andrea's works
(*Andrea del Sarto*, 2 vols., Cambridge, MA, 1963) lists ninety extant works, commenting that 'a great many others have no doubt perished'; this estimate is accepted
as authoritative by Antonio Natali, *Andrea del Sarto* (New York 1998).
260–1. Alluding to *Revelation* xxi 15–17: 'And he that talked with me had a golden
reed to measure the city, and the gates thereof, and the wall thereof. And the
city lieth foursquare, and the length is as large as the breadth: and he measured
the city with the reed, twelve thousand furlongs. The length and the breadth
and the height of it are equal. And he measured the wall thereof, an hundred
and forty and four cubits, according to the measure of a man, that is, of the angel.'
The last verse of this extract became the basis of William Page's theory about
the proportions of the human body which B. utilized in *Cleon*; see headnote to
that poem, *Composition* (p. 612).
262. Leonard: Leonardo da Vinci (1452–1519); for this triumvirate see headnote.
Angelo and me] Agnolo and me (*1868–88*).
266. my Love] my love (*1863²*, *1868*). In previous instances (ll. 10, 58, 119) only
1868 had this variant; see also l. 210, where the pattern is different again.

27 Old Pictures in Florence

Text and publication
First publ. *M & W*, 10 Nov. 1855; repr. *1863, 1868, 1880, 1888.* Our text is *1855.*
  The title in *H proof* is 'Opus Magistri Jocti' [A Work of Master Giotto]: see below, *Composition. H proof* also has corrections in B.'s hand, but only one of these (l. 261) appears in *1855* and they were clearly not intended as directions to the printer; the evidence of l. 274 suggests in fact that they were added to the proof after the publication of *1855*, perhaps when B. presented the proofs to Leighton (see Appendix C, p. 888). In a letter to Dante Gabriel Rossetti of 29 Oct. 1855 B. wrote: 'I perceive some blunders in my poems, which I shall not, I think, draw attention to, but quietly correct hereafter. But it happens unluckily that the worst of them occur just in a thing I would have you like if it might be—so, please alter the following in your copy, before you begin it, won't you?' (*LH* 42). There follow a series of corrections to vol. ii of *1855*, almost all to *Old Pictures.* Most also appear on the list of 'Errata' which B. sent to his American publisher James T. Fields (*B to Fields* 192–4). All but one anticipate the readings of *1863*; B.'s term 'blunders' suggests that they were misprints, but some are clearly revisions, as B. makes clear in a letter of 31 Oct. to his publisher Edward Chapman, in which he refers to 'a few errors, and a passage or two susceptible of improvement' (*New Letters* 82).

Composition and date
As soon as the Brownings arrived in Italy to begin their married life together, B. started to indulge his passion for early Italian art. His enthusiasm and expertise are attested to by a number of contemporaries, most notably Dante Gabriel Rossetti, who claimed in a letter of 25 Nov. 1855 that he 'found Browning's knowledge of early Italian Art beyond that of anyone I ever met—*encyclopaedically* beyond that of Ruskin himself' (William E. Fredeman ed., *The Correspondence of Dante Gabriel Rossetti* ii [Cambridge 2002] 55:58). EBB.'s letters contain numerous stories of B.'s artistic discoveries, such as the occasion when he found the fragments of an altarpiece by Ghirlandaio in a corn-merchant's shop just outside Florence:

> The pictures [at Casa Guidi] are a few, which, Robert, who understands a good deal about Art in general & Florentine art in particular, has picked up at different times & places, for a few shillings each . . . [In] the early part of the winter, he bought two companion pictures of angels .. gave four & six-pence for the two .. painted on panel . . . He heard, where he procured them, that they had been sawn off the sides of a great picture representing the Madonna, in a church at Arezzo—the priest was reported to have said that the Madonna

Title.] Opus Magistri Jocti (*H proof*). The meaning of the phrase is 'A Work of Master Giotto's'. In one of the notes to her translation of Vasari's chapter on Giotto, Mrs Foster points out that his picture of the Stigmatæ, originally in S. Francesco in Pisa, had been moved 'to the principal chapel of the Campo Santo [cemetery], where it was seen by Morrona, who discovered the name of Giotto on it, much injured by restorations. It is now at Paris, in the Louvre, whither it was transported by Napoleon; the name of the painter is on the cornice, in letters of gold, thus: "OPUS JOCTI FLORENTINI"' (*Foster* i 100–1n.).

cd. take care of the altar alone, .. saying which, he had sawn off the angels &
sold them. Well—Robert sent to Arezzo to try to get the Madonna for a few
shillings more—he thought the priest cd. not resist a few more shillings. The
answer was, the holy man had gone to Rome, & nothing cd. be done until
his return. So we thought no more about it.—A few days since, Robert fell
upon some pictures in a corn shop outside the walls, & was much struck by
one called the 'Eterno padre' . . . On putting them into the light of our new
drawingroom, the whole glory of the discovery became apparent . . . Robert
cried out .. 'How curious! the hands are painted precisely in the manner of the
angels from Arezzo, in the next room—I will go and fetch them & prove it
to you.' In a moment he came back with the angels, and burst into fresh exclamations. Arabel, our angels had been sawn off that very picture . . . Robert is in
a state of rapture at the discovery—Whenever we can afford it, we shall have
the pictures fastened together, and a frame to unite them. It is a fine picture
of Ghirlandaio, of whom I think there is only one specimen in the Florentine
gallery. But this is not all—Robert went directly to Mr Kirkup the artist and
antiquarian, who has a fine collection himself, & great experience & acumen
in matters of art . . . After recognising and praising the Ghirlandaio, he said
that Robert had done admirably in respect to the other pictures—that the
crucifixion, if not Giotto, was Giottesque, of his time, and an unique specimen
or nearly so, being painted upon linen .. it was very valuable, .. and that the
Christ with the open gospel, a deep, solemn, moving picture, he believed to
be a Cimabue, and worth five hundred guineas.

(?3 May 1850; *EBB to Arabella* i 314–5)

A picture similar to the 'Eterno padre' described can be seen above the mantel-
piece in Mignaty's picture of the drawing room at Casa Guidi.

The poem's use of a narrator who shares this passion for collecting the works
of neglected ancient masters, and the allusions to EBB.'s poem *Casa Guidi Windows*
(see *Sources and Contexts*, and l. 260n.), have led some critics to suggest that the
poem may have been written around 1850–51 (see e.g. David De Laura, *PMLA*
xcv [1980] 367–88; *SBC* viii.2 [1980] 7–16; and Jacob Korg, *Browning and Italy*
[Athens, OH 1983] 98–106). There are, however, a number of features which
link it to early 1853. The Brownings returned to Florence in Nov. 1852 after a
lengthy period in Paris: 'dead & dull we must confess our poor poor Florence
to be—trodden flat too under the heel of Austria . . . the people are down, down
.. and loathing those who keep them down. It is certainly a very sad spectacle,
and I don't wonder that Robert should feel saddened by it—it saddens me. Such
hatred, such internal revolt & protestation as we hear on all sides—the Austrians
are detested' (13–15 Nov. 1852; *EBB to Arabella* i 518). The political coda to the
poem may be a reflection of the poet's particularly hostile attitude towards the
Austrians at this time. Moreover, in a letter of 17 Mar. 1853 to John Kenyon, at
Wellesley College, B. narrates the story of the discovery of a lost 'tablet' (a small
painting on a wooden panel) by Giotto (see ll. 233–40); Metzger, the art
dealer, 'has discovered the precious little picture by Giotto, of which Vasari says
so much, and how he heard Michelagnolo admire it to heart's content—"the
death of the Virgin"—missing from S. Spirito in Vasari's time, and supposed to
be recovered in England—that is, a picture was engraved as this of Giotto's which
was by Fra Angelico—the most purely unlike of men!' (also cited in Julia
Markus, ' "Old Pictures in Florence" Through *Casa Guidi Windows*', *BIS* vi [1978]
54–5.) An illustration of the tablet, now in the Gemäldegalerie of the Staatliche
Museum, Berlin, is in our volume III as Plate 5. Cp. l. 4n. We therefore date

the inception of the poem to Mar.–Apr. 1853, although as in other instances B. may have continued to work on the poem until shortly before publication.

Sources and contexts

(i) *Artistic*
B.'s knowledge of early Italian art undoubtedly derived in large part from his reading of Vasari; see headnotes to *Andrea* (p. 387) and *Fra Lippo* (p. 477). In Vasari's life of Stefano, a follower of Giotto, whom B. mentions in the poem (see ll. 69–72n.), there is a paragraph which anticipates the poem's argument about the importance of innovation in the arts:

> [Stefano] contributed more than any other, Giotto excepted, to the ameliora-tion of art: his powers of invention were richer and more varied, his colour-ing was more harmonious, and his tints were more softly blended; while, more than all, in care and diligence he surpassed all other artists. And with respect to his foreshortening, although he is defective on this point, as I have said, because of the great difficulties to be encountered, yet, more gratitude is due to him who is the first to investigate and conquer the worst obstacles in any pursuit, than to those who do but follow on the path previously made clear, even though it be with a better and more carefully regulated march. Thus, we have certainly great obligations to Stefano, for he who, walking in darkness, encourages others by showing them the way, confers the benefit of making known the dangerous points, and warning from the false road, enables those who come after to arrive in time at the desired goal.
>
> (*Foster* i 137–8)

Old Pictures also makes extensive use of the opposition between Greek or Pagan and Christian art which became a commonplace of nineteenth-century art criticism; one of the most influential versions of this idea was put forward in A. W. von Schlegel's *Lectures on Dramatic Art and Literature*:

> Among the Greeks human nature was in itself all-sufficient; it was conscious of no defects, and aspired to no higher perfection than that which it could actually attain by the exercise of its own energies. We, however, are taught by superior wisdom that man, through a grievous transgression, forfeited the place for which he was originally destined; and that the sole destination of his earthly existence is to struggle to regain his lost position, which, if left to his own strength, he can never accomplish. The old religion of the senses sought no higher possession than outward and perishable blessings; and immortality, so far as it was believed, stood shadow-like in the obscure distance, a faint dream of this sunny waking life. The very reverse of all this is the case with the Christian view: every thing finite and mortal is lost in the contemplation of infinity; life has become shadow and darkness, and the first day of our real existence dawns in the world beyond the grave . . . The Grecian ideal of human nature was perfect unison and proportion between all the powers,—a natural harmony. The moderns, on the contrary, have arrived at the consciousness of an internal discord which renders such an ideal impossible; and hence the endeavour of their poetry is to reconcile these two worlds between which we find ourselves divided, and to blend them indissolubly together. The impressions of the senses are to be hallowed, as it were, by a mysterious connexion with higher feelings; and the soul, on the other hand, embodies its forebodings, or indescribable intuitions of infinity, in types and symbols borrowed from the visible world . . . In Grecian art and poetry we find an original and

unconscious unity of form and matter; in the modern, so far as it has remained true to its own spirit, we observe a keen struggle to unite the two, as being naturally in opposition to each other. The Grecian executed what it proposed in the utmost perfection; but the modern can only do justice to its endeavours after what is infinite by approximation; and, from a greater appearance of imperfection, is in greater danger of not being duly appreciated.

(A. W. von Schlegel, *A Course of Lectures on Dramatic Art and Literature*, tr. John Black [1846], 26–7)

For B.'s knowledge of Schlegel see letter of 30 Jan. 1880 to the Revd J. D. Williams; *BIS* iv (1976) 14. Schlegel's arguments helped rehabilitate the imperfections or defects of early Christian art, and so facilitated the rediscovery of medieval and early Renaissance art celebrated in the poem.

Similar sentiments can be found in the work of A. W. N. Pugin (see *Bishop Blougram* 4–6n., p. 285) and A. F. Rio, whose *De la poésie chrétienne* B. notes as an influence on Mrs Jameson in a letter to EBB. of 11 Sept. 1845 (*Correspondence* xi 70). Rio was in fact a personal acquaintance of Anna Jameson, having spent the years 1836–41 in London. She, in turn, was a close friend of EBB., and accompanied the Brownings on their wedding journey to Italy (see headnote to *A Pretty Woman*, III 20). Mrs Jameson's writings on Italian art history make extensive use of the distinction between Christian and Pagan art, and De Laura (in his *SBC* article; see above) notes the congruity between her views and those expressed by the speaker in the poem: 'If . . . we are to consider painting as purely religious, we must go back to the infancy of modern art, when the expression of sentiment was all in all, and the expression of life in action nothing;—when, reversing the aim of Greek art, the limbs and form were defective, while character, as it is shown in physiognomy, was delicately felt, and truly rendered' (Mrs Jameson, *Memoirs and Essays Illustrative of Art, Literature and Social Morals* [1846] 6). B. would certainly have known Ruskin's argument, in vol. ii of *The Stones of Venice* (publ. July 1853), that Greek architecture was essentially enslaving, where medieval Christian art was democratic. In fact, the poem may be read in the context of some of the ideas and attitudes that Ruskin was engaged in popularizing in the early 1850s in *Modern Painters* and later in *The Stones of Venice*. All the artists mentioned in *Old Pictures* are referred to repeatedly by Ruskin, in terms of high commendation, at the expense of later artists, including Raphael: the label 'Pre-Raphaelite' adopted by the group of artists centred round Dante Gabriel Rossetti in the early 1850s reflects a widespread reaction against the 'academic' style favoured by the Royal Academy, a style dominated by heavy chiaroscuro, in contrast to the pure colours of earlier art. Rossetti (like Ruskin) was already a friend of B.'s at this time, and B. almost certainly read Ruskin's pamphlet *Pre-Raphaelitism* (1851), in part an extended defence of the Pre-Raphaelite aesthetic.

The critical revaluation of medieval art prompted by the work of Schlegel, Rio, Ruskin and others was not, however, universal, least of all in Italy itself; and the poem laments the fact that many frescoes had been allowed to deteriorate or even whitewashed over (ll. 185–92n.). Korg (see headnote, *Composition*) notes that the Bargello Chapel, 'decorated with frescoes by Giotto showing scenes from *Inferno* and *Paradiso*, had been divided horizontally to make two rooms, the walls . . . whitewashed, and the upper portion . . . used as a prison' (p. 105). Korg also points out that B.'s friend Seymour Kirkup, who verified his Ghirlandaio find, led the campaign to restore the frescoes. There was, in addition, a theoretical challenge to the notion of the supremacy of Christian art in Matthew

Arnold's Preface to his 1853 *Poems*. Arnold argues that Greek artists are superior to their modern successors precisely because of their attention to the overall design of their work: 'They regarded the whole; we regard the parts. With them, the action predominated over the expression of it; with us, the expression predominates over the action' (R. H. Super ed., *Complete Prose Works of Matthew Arnold* [Ann Arbor, 1960], i 5). The poem's discussion of the relative merits of perfection and imperfection may be an attempt to restate the case for Christian art in the face of Arnold's attempt at a neo-classical revival (see l. 146n.; and cp. headnote to *Cleon* [p. 563]).

(ii) *Political*
The speaker ends the poem by prophesying the end of Austrian rule in Tuscany and the establishment of an Italian Republic with Florence as its capital (ll. 249–88). During 1848 and 1849 uprisings throughout Italy had led to the establishment of a number of republics, including a restored Roman Republic under a triumvirate including Giuseppe Mazzini (1805–72), whom B. had met and corresponded with during Mazzini's period of exile in London (see headnote to *Italy in England* [p. 245]). These risings were, however, defeated, and Austrian rule was restored in Tuscany, which was occupied by Austrian troops until 1855. In the aftermath of these defeats there were ideological conflicts between the partisans of Italian nationalism, and Mazzini's advocacy of direct action and unswerving commitment to republican and democratic politics placed him in conflict with those who looked to foreign powers (especially France) to effect Italy's liberation. In spite of her husband's friendship with Mazzini, EBB. became disillusioned with him in direct proportion to her increasing faith in Napoleon III as the potential saviour of Italy; her poetic meditation on the events of these years, *Casa Guidi Windows* (1851), characterizes Mazzini as an 'extreme theorist' who will 'stand apart' from the broadly based national movement of the future (ii 573, 568; see also l. 260n. below). B. in contrast seems to have maintained a sympathetic interest in Mazzini's politics: he owned a number of Mazzini's publications, and lent Charles Eliot Norton a copy of his pamphlet *Foi et Avenir* [Faith and the Future] in Nov. 1850 (*Letters of Charles Eliot Norton* [Boston 1913] i 72). The speaker of the poem uses explicitly Mazzinian language in his description of the future Italian republic (see l. 285n.). The association between Giotto's Campanile (bell-tower) and the splendour of Republican Florence is emphasized in *Fantozzi* (p. 320): 'La Repubblica fiorentina, sempre magnifica e splendida nelle opere di pubblica utilità e decoro, ne ordinò la fondazione [del campanile] al celebre Giotto nel 1334' [The Florentine Republic, always splendidly ostentatious in works of public utility and display, commanded the construction of the bell-tower from the celebrated Giotto in 1334]. See also l. 264n.

Parallels in B.
The most important precursor to the poem in terms of its artistic subject is *Pictor Ignotus* (p. 226) whose speaker is an obscure early painter (probably Florentine although this is not specifically stated), and whose paintings suffer the fate of those described in *Old Pictures*: see ll. 41–8n. Note, however, that *Pictor* is the study of an artist who colludes in his paintings' fate, whereas B. suggests in this poem that the spirits of the old masters are injured and indignant at their neglect. The poem is one of a number in *M & W* on the subject of painting. Like *Fra Lippo* (p. 477), *Old Pictures* contains an account of the development of art; but, unlike *Fra Lippo*, this poem sees art as developing not by imitation of reality, but through a recognition of the limitations of a perfect representation of the world.

The 'doctrine of the imperfect' is a recurring motif of B.'s work: it shapes the evolutionary politics (and aesthetics) of *Sordello* (see e.g. iii 811–28, I 582), and is a major constitutive principle of the dramatic monologue form which B. developed in the 1840s, in which partial or one-sided perspectives replace authorial omniscience or the claim to offer a complete vision. Imperfection also has an important influence on B.'s theology: cp. *CE & ED* (III 34) and *Saul* (III 491). In other poems the theme is handled with an ironic or ambivalent edge, notably in *A Grammarian* (p. 586); in *Cleon* (p. 563) and *Two in the Campagna* (p. 556) it has a tragic dimension, although *Cleon* also exposes what B. thought of as the limitations of the Greek world-view, its inability to recognize what the Fates (made drunk by wine) proclaim in one of B.'s last works: 'Manhood—the actual? Nay, praise the potential! / (Bound upon bound, foot it around!) / What *is*? No, what *may* be—sing! that's Man's essential!' (*Apollo and the Fates: A Prologue* [*Parleyings*, 1887] 211–14). As this example indicates, the theme remains a constant preoccupation for B. throughout his career.

Contemporary Italian politics is an occasional theme of B.'s work—see headnote to *Pippa Passes* (p. 89), and *Italy in England* (p. 245)—but a perennial one of EBB.'s, especially during the last decade of her life. Julia Markus (see above, *Composition*) suggests that *Old Pictures* should be read as a kind of riposte to EBB.'s *Casa Guidi Windows*. B. returned to the theme in *Prince Hohenstiel-Schwangau* (1871), whose speaker, a thinly disguised portrait of Napoleon III, attempts to justify his policy towards Italy; this poem, too, may be said to answer EBB.'s *Poems Before Congress* (1860).

I

The morn when first it thunders in March,
   The eel in the pond gives a leap, they say.
As I leaned and looked over the aloed arch

1–2. We have not found a source for this weather proverb, which opens the poem with a signal of spring; the speaker goes on (ll. 3–16) to say that, although there was no thunderstorm on the morning he looked out over Florence, the sight of Giotto's bell-tower 'more than startle[d]' him. The eel's leap is a natural response to the coming of spring; the speaker's feelings are a more complex response to the political, artistic, and personal regeneration for which he yearns. Cp. (noting 'water-gold' in l. 7) the moment in *Flight of the Duchess* which forms a symbolic prelude to the Duchess's escape: 'Well, early in autumn, at first winter-warning, / When the stag had to break with his foot, of a morning, / A drinking-hole out of the fresh tender ice / That covered the pond till the sun, in a trice, / Loosening it, let out a ripple of gold, / And another and another, and faster and faster, / Till, dimpling to blindness, the wide water rolled' (ll. 216–22, II 305–6). *3. aloed arch*: an archway covered with aloes, whose tenacious climbing is mentioned in *Sordello* iv 753–4, 800–5 (I 638, 640). Leaning out of a window or balcony is used as an image of creativity in *Ring* i 469–96, in which B. describes how he 'fused [his] live soul' with the 'inert stuff' of the Old Yellow Book; note however that this scene takes place at Casa Guidi, i.e. within Florence rather than in the hills above it.

Of the villa-gate, this warm March day,
5   No flash snapt, no dumb thunder rolled
      In the valley beneath, where, white and wide,
      Washed by the morning's water-gold,
      Florence lay out on the mountain-side.

2

      River and bridge and street and square
10   Lay mine, as much at my beck and call,
      Through the live translucent bath of air,
      As the sights in a magic crystal ball.
      And of all I saw and of all I praised,
      The most to praise and the best to see,
15   Was the startling bell-tower Giotto raised:
      But why did it more than startle me?

3

      Giotto, how, with that soul of yours,
      Could you play me false who loved you so?

4. *villa-gate*: the Brownings did not live in a villa, but their friend Robert Bulwer Lytton ('Owen Meredith') rented the Villa Brichieri at Bellosguardo, overlooking Florence, in 1853; see headnote to *Up at a Villa* (III 143). This is the villa later rented by the Brownings' close friend Isa Blagden. *this warm March day*: almost certainly March 1853; see headnote, *Composition*.

7. *Washed by*] And washed by (*1863–88*). Cp., noting 'bath of air' in l. 11, the landscape of 'England's best' in *The Inn Album* i 50–2: 'He leans into a living glory-bath / Of air and light where seems to float and move / The wooded watered country'; and *Ring* i 685–6: 'the renovating wash / O' the water'. *Oxford* suggests that the painterly sense of 'washed' might also be implied. *the morning's*] the morning (*1868–88*). *water-gold*: pale sunlight (not in *OED*, and not hyphenated in subsequent editions).

12. *magic crystal ball*: one of the instruments of fortune-telling and mediumship; cp. *Mr. Sludge* 181–4 (pp. 789–90): 'So, David holds the circle, rules the roast, / Narrates the vision, peeps in the glass ball, / Sets to the spirit-writing, hears the raps, / As the case may be.' In her Norton edition of *Aurora Leigh* (New York and London 1996) Margaret Reynolds notes that the Brownings saw a crystal ball belonging to Lord Stanhope at a lunch given by Euphrasia Fanny Haworth in July 1852 (vi 169–70n., p. 187). For EBB.'s interest in spiritualism and associated phenomena see headnotes to *Mesmerism* (III 475) and *Mr Sludge* (pp. 772–3).

15. Giotto di Bondone (1267–1337), a crucial figure in the history of Florentine art, designed the bell-tower (It. *Campanile*) in Florence, but his design was never completed; according to *Fantozzi* it was left at around three-quarters of the projected height by his successors. This unfinished bell-tower is a key motif of the poem; see ll. 273–88 below.

17–24. Anticipating the section of the poem (l. 193 ff.) in which B. fancifully rebukes the early Florentine painters for ignoring him and allowing their works to be

Some slights if a certain heart endures
20   It feels, I would have your fellows know!
'Faith—I perceive not why I should care
   To break a silence that suits them best,
But the thing grows somewhat hard to bear
   When I find a Giotto join the rest.

4

25 On the arch where olives overhead
   Print the blue sky with twig and leaf,
(That sharp-curled leaf they never shed)
   'Twixt the aloes I used to lean in chief,
And mark through the winter afternoons,
30   By a gift God grants me now and then,
In the mild decline of those suns like moons,
   Who walked in Florence, besides her men.

5

They might chirp and chaffer, come and go
   For pleasure or profit, her men alive—
35 My business was hardly with them, I trow,
   But with empty cells of the human hive;

---

acquired by collectors who do not appreciate them; here, the crowning insult is that Giotto has joined this 'conspiracy'.

19. Some slights] There be slights (*H proof* but not *H proof²*).

20. It feels] Yet it feels (*H proof, 1863–88*); this is a rare example of B. reverting to a reading in *H proof*.

21. 'Faith—I perceive] I' faith, I perceive (*1863–88*). ''Faith' is a contraction of a mild oath or expletive, 'in faith', here meaning 'truly'.

22. a silence that suits them best: the pronoun refers to Giotto's 'fellows' or contemporaries, with the suggestion that they are best left in 'silence' or obscurity.

25–8. The syntax runs: 'I used to lean in chief [habitually] 'twixt the aloes on the arch [of the gate]'.

27. leaf they never] leaf which they never (*1863–88*).

32. who walked in Florence: i.e. the ghosts of the early Florentine painters, who are 'walking' the city; they are not at peace because of the mistreatment of their work described in the next two stanzas.

33. chaffer: to haggle or barter.

35. I trow: I believe (archaic).

36. the human hive: the comparison between human society and a beehive is a traditional one; cp. *Christmas-Eve* 560–1 (III 69–70). One of B.'s favourite books when he was a young man was Bernard de Mandeville's *Fable of the Bees* (1714), which forms the subject of the first of the *Parleyings* (1887).

—With the chapter-room, the cloister-porch,
   The church's apsis, aisle or nave,
Its crypt, one fingers along with a torch—
40   Its face, set full for the sun to shave.

6

Wherever a fresco peels and drops,
   Wherever an outline weakens and wanes
Till the latest life in the painting stops,
   Stands One whom each fainter pulse-tick pains!
45   One, wishful each scrap should clutch its brick,
   Each tinge not wholly escape the plaster,
—A lion who dies of an ass's kick,
   The wronged great soul of an ancient Master.

37–8. The first line refers to monastic, the second to ecclesiastical architecture: a 'chapter-room' is a room where the 'chapter', or order of monks would assemble on formal occasions; the 'apsis' (more usually 'apse') of a church is a recess at the end of the aisle or nave. B.'s very unusual spelling occurs in Mrs Jameson's *Legends of the Madonna* (1852); Jameson was a close friend of the Brownings during their early years in Italy (see headnote).

39. *crypt*: cp. B.'s first letter to EBB. giving his response to missing the possibility of meeting her: 'I feel as at some untoward passage in my travels—as if I had been close, so close, to some world's-wonder in chapel or crypt, .. only a screen to push and I might have entered' (10 Jan. 1845, *Correspondence* x 17).

41–8. Cp. Dickens on the Cathedral of Parma: 'The decayed and mutilated paintings with which this church is covered, have, to my thinking, a remarkably mournful and depressing influence. It is miserable to see great works of art—something of the Souls of Painters—perishing and fading away, like human forms' (*Pictures from Italy* [1846; ed. D. Paroissien, 1973] 105). Cp. also *Pictor Ignotus*, esp. ll. 63–9 (p. 231): 'The sanctuary's gloom at least shall ward / Vain tongues from where my pictures stand apart; / Only prayer breaks the silence of the shrine / While, blackening in the daily candle smoke, / They moulder on the dark wall's travertine, / 'Mid echoes the light footsteps never woke. / So die, my pictures; surely, gently die!' Ruskin notes in a letter to *The Times* of 7 Jan. 1847: 'I had seen in Venice the noblest works of Veronese painted over with flake-white with a brush fit for tarring ships; I had seen in Florence Angelico's highest inspiration rotted and seared into fragments of old wood, burnt into blisters, or blotted into glutinous maps of mildew' (*Works* xii 398).

45. *its brick*] the brick (*1863–88*).

47. Alluding to Aesop's fable in which the wounded lion feels the ass's kick as the final indignity before his death; B. knew this story from Samuel Croxall's version of Aesop: 'His mother used to read Croxall's Fables to his little sister and him. The story contained in them of a lion who was kicked to death by an ass affected him so painfully that he could no longer endure the sight of the book; and as he dared not destroy it, he buried it between the stuffing and the wood-work of an old dining-room chair, where it stood for lost, at all events for the

7

For oh, this world and the wrong it does!
50   They are safe in heaven with their backs to it,
The Michaels and Rafaels, you hum and buzz
    Round the works of, you of the little wit!
Do their eyes contract to the earth's old scope,
    Now that they see God face to face,
55   And have all attained to be poets, I hope?
    'Tis their holiday now, in any case.

8

Much they reck of your praise and you!
    But the wronged great souls—can they be quit
Of a world where all their work is to do,
60   Where you style them, you of the little wit,

---

time being' (Orr *Life* 26–7). The asses here are the church authorities who neglect the masterpieces of early religious painting; cp. ll. 185–92 and see headnote. B. may have connected the neglect of the early painters with that of his own work through this image: he had almost certainly read James Russell Lowell's sympathetic review essay, 'Browning's Plays and Poems', in *North American Review* lxvi (Apr. 1848), in which Lowell remarks: 'there is scarce any truly living book which does not bear the print of that hoof which Pindar would have Olympicized into the spurner of dying lions' (p. 359).

49–64. The speaker's fanciful conception is that great painters such as Michelangelo and Raphael no longer need the care and attention that their works receive, since the recognition they gained on earth has freed them from concern with these works or with earthly reputation; they are enjoying a transcendent immortality, whereas the neglected early painters are condemned to haunt the sites of their work, hoping for a similar recognition and release.

51. Michaels and Rafaels: Michelangelo Buonarroti (1475–1564) and Raffaello Sanzio (1483–1520), two of the triumvirate of Italian High Renaissance Art (the third, Leonardo da Vinci, is mentioned at l. 64).

54. see God face to face: cp. *1 Corinthians* xiii 12: 'For now we see through a glass, darkly; but then face to face: now I know in part; but then shall I know even as also I am known.'

55. The speaker implies that poetry is the highest of the arts; cp. the speaker's claims for music in ll. 43–50 of *Abt Vogler* (p. 766). Michelangelo was in fact a poet as well as an artist; a number of his sonnets were translated into English by Wordsworth. B. also refers to the tradition that Raphael wrote 'a century of sonnets' in *One Word More* 5 (p. 602).

57. reck of: care for.

59. all their work is] their work is all (*1863–88*); B. noted this reading on *H proof* and in the lists he sent to D. G. Rossetti and James T. Fields: see headnote, *Text*. On balance we think this is a revision rather than a correction, and have not emended *1855*.

Old Master this and Early the other,
    Not dreaming that Old and New are fellows,
That a younger succeeds to an elder brother,
    Da Vincis derive in good time from Dellos.

9

65   And here where your praise would yield returns
    And a handsome word or two give help,
Here, after your kind, the mastiff girns
    And the puppy pack of poodles yelp.
What, not a word for Stefano there
70   —Of brow once prominent and starry,
Called Nature's ape and the world's despair
    For his peerless painting (see Vasari)?

---

61. Old Master this . . . Early the Other: unknown artists are occasionally referred to as 'Master' (e.g. 'Master of the Barberini Panels'). 'Early' is a way of indicating an artist's place in the history of the form.

62–4. Cp. the account of the development of poetry and society in *Sordello* v 80 ff., esp. l. 105: 'An elder poet's in the younger's place' (I 662). Artists like Leonardo da Vinci (1452–1519) are said to 'derive' from more obscure figures such as Dello di Niccolo Delli (*c.* 1404–71), who made a living by painting decorative scenes onto chests and other items of furniture. As *Foster* points out, Dello 'is probably the diminutive of Leonardello' (i 327).

63. That a younger] A younger (*1863–88*); B. noted this reading on H proof and in the lists he sent to D. G. Rossetti and James T. Fields: see headnote, *Text*. On balance we think this is a revision rather than a correction, and have not emended *1855*.

65. would yield] might yield (*1863–88*).

67. Here,] Why, (*H proof*).

67–8. mastiff . . . poodles: scornful images for art critics and historians who disparage early Italian painting: the 'mastiff' would represent a 'heavyweight' art critic, and the 'puppy-pack of poodles' his younger followers and imitators. B. regularly resorted to animal imagery to characterize critics, whether of art or literature; cp. his response to the hostile reviews of *M & W* cited in Appendix C, p. 893.

67. girns: snarl, show one's teeth.

69–72. Vasari describes the Florentine painter Stefano (1301?–50?), a 'disciple' of Giotto, as 'an artist of such excellence, that he not only surpassed all those who had preceded him in the art, but left even his master, Giotto himself, far behind' (*Foster* i 133). Vasari goes on to describe some of his paintings, commenting in particular on their early use of foreshortening and perspective, and adds that his 'brother artists' called him ' "the ape of nature" ' ['scimia [sic] della natura'] because of his skill (*ibid.* 135). See also headnote, *Sources*.

70. Cp. *Pictor Ignotus* 34–5 (p. 229), and *In a Balcony* iii 83–4 (III 439); in nineteenth-century physiognomy a prominent brow was considered a sign of high intelligence, but B. also intends an allusion to a more mystic or occult sign of greatness, like the aura of a saint.

10

There he stands now. Study, my friends,
    What a man's work comes to! so he plans it,
75   Performs it, perfects it, makes amends
    For the toiling and moiling, and then *sic transit!*
Happier the thrifty blind-folk labour,
    With upturned eye while the hand is busy,
Not sidling a glance at the coin of their neighbour!
80   'Tis looking downward makes one dizzy.

11

If you knew their work you would deal your dole.
    May I take upon me to instruct you?
When Greek Art ran and reached the goal,
    Thus much had the world to boast *in fructu—*

73. There he stands now] There stands the Master (*1863–88*).

76. toiling and moiling: an expression meaning 'to work hard, to drudge'; cp. *Doctor—*
in *DI²* (*1880*) 34: 'A lawyer wins repute—Having to toil and moil'.   *then sic transit!*] emended from 'there's its transit!' in *1855*; B. corrected this evident misprint
on *H proof* and in the lists he sent to D. G. Rossetti and James T. Fields: see
headnote, *Text*. The allusion is to a phrase used in the ceremony for the coronation of a new Pope; three bundles of tow are burned in front of him, and the
Master of Ceremonies says: 'Sancte Pater sic transit gloria mundi' ['Holy Father,
thus passes away the glory of this world'].

77–80. The 'blind-folk' symbolize those artists who are indifferent to earthly reward
and their status relative to others (their 'upturned eye' is fixed on heaven), in
contrast to painters such as Stefano who are self-conscious about the value of
their work and envious of their neighbours' accomplishments. *Oxford* suggests
that the image derives from schools for the blind (the first of which in London
dates from *1799*). Cp. B.'s insistence that 'a poet's affair is with God, to whom
he is accountable, and of whom is his reward: look elsewhere, and you find
misery enough' (letter to Ruskin: see Appendix B, p. 882), and (noting the 'upturned
eye') *How It Strikes* 66–8 (p. 442).

80. downward makes] downward that makes (*1863–88*, except *1880* which agrees
with *1855*). It is rare for a reading in a volume of selections to revert to the
original.

81.] in quotation marks, *1863–88*.   *deal your dole*: continuing the metaphor of alms-giving associated with the 'blind-folk'; a 'dole' is a portion or charitable gift.

83–160. For the possible sources of the contrast between Christian and Pagan art
developed in this 'allocution' (l. 159) see headnote, *Sources*.

84. in fructu: cp. *Deuteronomy* xxx 9: 'And the Lord thy God will make thee
plenteous in every work of thine hand, in the fruit of thy body, and in the fruit
of thy cattle, and in the fruit of thy land, for good'; in the Latin (Vulgate)
version the phrase 'in the fruit of' is 'in fructu'.

85 The truth of Man, as by God first spoken,
        Which the actual generations garble,
    Was re-uttered,—and Soul (which Limbs betoken)
        And Limbs (Soul informs) were made new in marble.

                        12
        So you saw yourself as you wished you were,
90   As you might have been, as you cannot be;
        And bringing your own shortcomings there,
            You grew content in your poor degree
        With your little power, by those statues' godhead,
            And your little scope, by their eyes' full sway,
95   And your little grace, by their grace embodied,
            And your little date, by their forms that stay.

                        13
        You would fain be kinglier, say than I am?
        Even so, you would not sit like Theseus.

85–96. The triumph of classical Greek art (principally, as the following lines make clear, its sculpture) was to rediscover the perfection of God's original creation of the human form, giving ideal images, in imperishable marble, of the unity of flesh and spirit which is obscured in the 'actual generations' of the human race. Lawrence Poston (*SBC* iii.2 [1975] 124–5) suggests the influence of a passage in Hazlitt's essay 'On Poetry in General' from his *Lectures on the English Poets* (1818), contrasting Raphael's cartoons on the Scriptures with Greek art: 'It is for want of some such resting place for the imagination that the Greek statues are little else than specious forms. They are marble to the touch and to the heart. They have not an informing principle within them. In their faultless excellence they appear sufficient to themselves. By their beauty they are raised above the frailties of passion or suffering. By their beauty they are deified. But they are not objects of religious faith to us, and their forms are a reproach to common humanity. They seem to have no sympathy with us, and not to want our admiration.' Cp. the description of the statues in the grounds of Taurello Salinguerra's palace at Ferrara in *Sordello* iv 141–69 (I 602–4), and *In a Balcony* 253–9 (III 416).
88. were made new] made new (*1863–88*).
91.] Earth here, rebuked by Olympus there: (*1863–88*); B. noted this reading on *H proof* and in the lists he sent to D. G. Rossetti and James T. Fields: see headnote, *Text*. This (along with the consequent reading in the next line) is clearly a revision rather than a correction, and we have not emended *1855*.
92. You grew] And grew (*1863–88*); B. noted this reading on *H proof* and in the lists he sent to D. G. Rossetti and James T. Fields: see prec. note.
94. scope . . . eyes: punning on the origin of 'scope' in the Greek 'skopos' ('watcher').
96. date: lifespan.
98. sit like Theseus: Theseus was a legendary King of Athens; according to *Thomas*, B. is thinking here of the carving of the seated Theseus on the east pediment of

<blockquote>

You'd fain be a model? the Son of Priam

100   Has yet the advantage in arms' and knees' use.

You're wroth—can you slay your snake like Apollo?

You're grieved—still Niobe's the grander!

You live—there's the Racer's frieze to follow—

You die—there's the dying Alexander.

</blockquote>

---

the Parthenon, now in the British Museum (see pp. 186–7 for an illustration). The statue was described by Charles Knight in his *Guide Cards to the Antiquities in the British Museum* (1840) as combining 'ideal beauty with the truth of nature' and as 'unquestionably finished in the very perfection of art'.

99. You'd fain be] You'd prove (*1868–88*).   *model*: a type of physical beauty.   *Son of Priam*: Paris was the son of Priam, King of Troy; Thomas suggests that B. is referring to the Paris of the Aeginetan Sculptures, now in the Glyptothek in Munich (*Thomas* p. 186). The statue in question depicts Paris in a kneeling position firing an arrow, with his 'arms' and 'knees' prominent.

101. wroth: angry (archaic).   *Apollo*: Apollo slew the Python at Delphi with an arrow, a feat commemorated in the institution of the Pythian games; variants of this legend are found in *Sordello* (i 928, I 456) and in *Pippa Passes* (Pippa's third song, 'A king lived long ago', pp. 151–3). The Apollo Belvedere in the Vatican's Museo Pio-Clementino depicts Apollo in the immediate aftermath of this feat; cp. Byron's description of it in *Childe Harold*, iv, st. 161. In *1880* B. added the following note at the end of the poem, on page 210, which has only the last stanza: 'The space left here tempts me to a word on the line about Apollo the snakeslayer, which my friend Professor Colvin condemns, believing that the god of the Belvedere grasps no bow, but the Ægis, as described in the 15th Iliad'. Sidney Colvin (1845–1928) was at the time Slade Professor of Fine Art at Cambridge; his friendship with B. dates from the early 1870s. B. counters Colvin's theory, correlating the text of the *Iliad* with the physical gestures of the statue, and concluding: 'The conjecture of Flaxman that the statue was suggested by the bronze Apollo Alexikakos of Kalamis, mentioned by Pausanias, remains probable,—though the "hardness" which Cicero considers to distinguish the artist's workmanship from that of Muron is not by any means apparent in our marble copy, if it be one.' The pagination of *1884* (rev. reissue of *1880*) differs from that of *1880*; the poem finishes near the bottom of page 165, and the note consequently runs across to the following page, making nonsense of B.'s comment about there being space to fit it in. *1884* also revises 'bronze Apollo' to 'bronze Apollon'; the whole episode marks B.'s increasingly high opinion of himself as a classical scholar in the 1870s and 1880s, in the wake of his translations of Aeschylus and Euripides.

102. Niobe boasted that her seven sons and seven daughters were more beautiful than Venus's children Apollo and Artemis, who retaliated by slaying them with arrows. Niobe wept so copiously that she was transformed into a fountain (see Ovid, *Metamorphoses*, bk vi). A statue of her mourning the death of her children is in the Uffizi. Cp. *Casa Guidi Windows* i 30–5.

103. the Racers' frieze: the Parthenon Frieze in the British Museum depicts a horse race.

104. the dying Alexander: there is a bust of the dying Alexander the Great in the Uffizi in Florence.

14

105   So, testing your weakness by their strength,
             Your meagre charms by their rounded beauty,
       Measured by Art in your breadth and length,
             You learn—to submit is the worsted's duty.
       —When I say "you" 'tis the common soul,
110   The collective, I mean—the race of Man
       That receives life in parts to live in a whole,
             And grow here according to God's own plan.

15

       Growth came when, looking your last on them all,
             You turned your eyes inwardly one fine day
115   And cried with a start—What if we so small
             Are greater, ay, greater the while than they!
       Are they perfect of lineament, perfect of stature?
             In both, of such lower types are we
       Precisely because of our wider nature;
120   For time, theirs—ours, for eternity.

---

108. The 'lesson' of Greek art is one of resignation: the living, 'worsted' in the contest between the ideal image of art and the imperfection of actual existence, accept the limitations of life. The moral debility of this attitude is suggested by the conclusion of *The Statue and the Bust* (III 358–9), in which the two lovers substitute images of themselves for the selfhood they have failed to achieve.   *the worsted's duty*] a mortal's duty (*1863–88*).

109–12. With this view of the 'collective' nature of human progress, and the place of art in 'God's own plan', cp. part v of *Paracelsus* (esp. ll. 729–824, I 302–6) and bk. v of *Sordello*: cp. esp. ll. 95–6: 'collective man / Outstrips the individual!' (I 662). Cp. also *By the Fire-Side* 246–50 (p. 475).

110. The collective: either 'the collective soul' (in apposition to 'common'), or a noun for the mass of humanity; the latter usage belongs to 'the new Democratic consciousness of [the early nineteenth century]', with examples in *OED* from Cobbett and Carlyle (*Williams* 60). Cp. *In a Balcony* iii 96–7n. (III 440).

112. God's own plan] God's clear plan (*1863–88*).

113–20. For the contrast between Christian and Pagan art and the 'doctrine of imperfection' in this and other poems by B., see headnote, *Sources and Parallels in B.*

116.] Be greater and grander the while than they! (*1863–88*, except that from *1870* the line ends 'than they?'; in *H proof* the original version of the line also ended with a question mark).

117–18. perfect of stature? / In both] perfect of stature, / And in both (*H proof*). The question postponed here in *H proof* is relocated to l. 120: see next note.

120. for eternity.] for eternity? (*H proof*).

16

To-day's brief passion limits their range,
    It seethes with the morrow for us and more.
They are perfect—how else? they shall never change:
    We are faulty—why not? we have time in store.
125   The Artificer's hand is not arrested
    With us—we are rough-hewn, no-wise polished:
They stand for our copy, and, once invested
    With all they can teach, we shall see them abolished.

17

'Tis a life-long toil till our lump be leaven—
130   The better! what's come to perfection perishes.
Things learned on earth, we shall practise in heaven.
    Works done least rapidly, Art most cherishes.
Thyself shall afford the example, Giotto!

121–2. In classical art the present moment is all that matters, whereas for modern art the present 'seethes with' the prospect of change and growth. This sense of 'seethes' as 'To be in a state of inward agitation, turmoil, or "ferment" ' (*OED* 5) anticipates the image of the 'leaven' in l. 129.
125–6. Echoing the wording, although not the thought, of *Hamlet* V ii 210–11: 'There's a divinity that shapes our ends / Rough-hew them how we will'. Cp. the image of God as a potter in *Rabbi Ben Ezra* 151f. (p. 660).
127. They stand . . . copy: they provide us with a model for imitation.   *They stand*] They are set (*H proof* but not *H proof²*).
129. Cp. *Galatians* v 9: 'A little leaven leaveneth the whole lump.'
130. what's come to perfection perishes: cp. Ruskin's argument in 'The Nature of Gothic' (*The Stones of Venice* ii [1853]: see headnote, *Sources*): '*the demand for perfection is always a sign of a misunderstanding of the ends of art* . . . The building of the bird and the bee need not express anything like this [desire for change]. It is perfect and unchanging. But just because we are something better than birds or bees, our building must confess that we have not reached the perfection we can imagine, and cannot rest in the condition we have attained' (*Works* x 202, 214).
131. Things learned] Things half-learned (*H proof* but not *H proof²*).   *in heaven*] in Heaven (*1863–65*).
132. least rapidly] less rapidly (*1884*). Substantive variants unique to this ed. are very rare; this one is probably, but not certainly, a misprint.
133–6. The anecdote in question is in Vasari's *Life* of Giotto. Pope Benedict IX sent a 'courtier' to assess whether or not Giotto should be asked to paint some pictures in St Peter's: 'He declared the purpose of the pope, and the manner in which that pontiff desired to avail himself of his assistance, and, finally, requested to have a drawing, that he might send it to his holiness. Giotto, who was very courteous, took a sheet of paper, and a pencil dipped in a red colour; then, resting his elbow on his side, to form a sort of compass, with one turn of the hand he drew a circle, so perfect and exact that it was a marvel to behold. This done, he turned, smiling to the courtier, saying, "Here is your drawing" ' (*Foster* i 102–3). The circle is an ancient symbol of perfection, and eternity. B. would have known

Thy one work, not to decrease or diminish,
135   Done at a stroke, was just (was it not?) "O!"
Thy great Campanile is still to finish.

18

Is it true, we are now, and shall be hereafter,
And what—is depending on life's one minute?
Hails heavenly cheer or infernal laughter
140   Our first step out of the gulf or in it?
And Man, this step within his endeavour,
His face, have no more play and action
Than joy which is crystallized for ever,
Or grief, an eternal petrifaction!

19

145   On which I conclude, that the early painters,
To cries of "Greek Art and what more wish you?"—

---

that the introduction of the concept of mathematical zero was Arabic and post-classical. For the 'great Campanile' see l. 15n.

133. shall afford] shalt afford (*1868–88*).

136. Thy great] While thy great (*H proof* but not *H proof*²).

137–44. Since human life is a state of uncertainty, poised between salvation and damnation, art should reflect the 'play and action' of this condition, and not the eternal fixity of the next world. For the 'Christian aesthetic' of this argument, see headnote, *Sources*; and cp. *Bishop Blougram* 693–8 (p. 324).

137. Is it true, we] Is it true that we (*1863–88*).

138.] But what and where depend on life's minute? (*1863–88*).

141. And Man, this step] Shall Man, such step (*1863–88*).

142. His face, have] Has his face, do you think, (*H proof*); Man's face, have (*1863–88*); B. noted the latter reading on *H proof* and in the lists he sent to D. G. Rossetti and James T. Fields: see headnote, *Text*. On balance we think this is a revision rather than a correction, and have not emended *1855*.

143–4. Than joy . . . Or grief] Than a joy . . . Or a grief (*H proof* but not *H proof*²).

145–52. The 'early painters'' resolve to represent human life in all its complexity and inwardness, although this may mean distorting the outward form; such distortion has a positive value here, as a sign of spiritual life, in contrast to its negative value in *Fra Lippo* (see esp. ll. 179–220, pp. 495–7). Cp. *CE & ED* 649–92n. (III 73–5).

146. Cp. Ruskin, 'Nature of Gothic' (see l. 130n.): 'The Greek could stay in his triglyph furrow, and be at peace; but the work of the Gothic heart is fretwork still, and it can neither rest in, nor from, its labour, but must pass on, sleeplessly, until its love of change shall be pacified for ever in the change that must come alike on them that wake and them that sleep' (*Works* x 214). *To cries*] To the cry (*H proof* but not *H proof*²).

Replied, "Become now self-acquainters,
    And paint man, man,—whatever the issue!
Make new hopes shine through the flesh they fray,
150   New fears aggrandise the rags and tatters.
So bring the invisible full into play,
    Let the visible go to the dogs—what matters?"

20

Give these, I say, full honour and glory
    For daring so much, before they well did it.
155   The first of the new, in our race's story,
    Beats the last of the old, 'tis no idle quiddit.
The worthies began a revolution
    Which if on the earth we intend to acknowledge
Honour them now—(ends my allocution)
160   Nor confer our degree when the folks leave college.

147. "Become] "To become (*H proof* [but not *H proof*²], *1863–88*).

148. And paint] To paint (*H proof* but not *H proof*²).

149. Make new hopes] emended from 'Make the hopes' in *1855*. The original reading in *H proof* was 'Make the new hopes'; B. changed it to 'Make new hopes' on *H proof* and noted this reading in the lists he sent to D. G. Rossetti and James T. Fields (see headnote, *Text*). All other eds. have 'Make new hopes', and we have emended accordingly, although there is a case for reverting to the original reading in *H proof*; see below, l. 259n.

149–50. flesh they fray . . . rags and tatters: alluding to the ascetic practices and lifestyles of the early church.

151. So bring] So we bring (*H proof* but not *H proof*²); To bring (*1863–88*).

153.] Give these, I exhort you, their guerdon and glory (*1863–88*); B. noted this reading (with 'I exhort' for 'I exhort you') on *H proof* and in the lists he sent to D. G. Rossetti and James T. Fields: see headnote, *Text*. It is clearly a revision rather than a correction, and we have not emended *1855*.

154. well did it: did it well.

155–6. On the source of this idea in Vasari's *Life* of Stefano, see headnote, *Sources*.

156. quiddit: a rare form of 'quiddity', meaning quibble or nicety of argument.

157–60. Returning to the argument that the 'worthies' or unrecognized painters need acknowledgement in this world and not after graduation to the next life.

157. revolution: anticipating the political argument at the end of the poem; see headnote, *Sources*.

158. Which if on the earth we] Which if we on the earth (*H proof*); Which if on earth you (*1863–88*). B. deleted 'we' in *H proof* but made no other change, leaving the line ungrammatical; in the lists he sent to D. G. Rossetti and James T. Fields he noted the reading 'Which if on earth' (keeping 'we' however). There is no clear case for emending *1855*.

159. Honour them now—] Let us honour them now—(*H proof*). Why, honour them now—(*1863–65*); Why, honour them now! (*1868–88*).

160. our degree] your degree (*1863–88*). *when folks*] when folk (*1888*).

21

There's a fancy some lean to and others hate—
    That, when this life is ended, begins
New work for the soul in another state,
    Where it strives and gets weary, loses and wins—
165   Where the strong and the weak, this world's congeries,
        Repeat in large what they practised in small,
    Through life after life in unlimited series;
        Only the scale's to be changed, that's all.

22

Yet I hardly know. When a soul has seen
170   By the means of Evil that Good is best,
    And through earth and its noise, what is heaven's
        serene,—
    When its faith in the same has stood the test—
    Why, the child grown man, you burn the rod,
        The uses of labour are surely done.
175   There remaineth a rest for the people of God,
        And I have had troubles enough for one.

161–76. Contrasting two different attitudes towards the purpose of life. The first (ll. 161–8) suggests that the struggles of this life are repeated in magnified form in the next; the second (ll. 169–76) that earthly life is a probation or test designed to teach certain lessons, and that once these lessons are learned no further 'labour' is required. There are parallels to both these attitudes elsewhere in B.'s work, occasionally (as here) in the same poem: cp. the image of the 'engine' in *Sordello* iii 811–28 (I 582), in which death transfers the 'task' of life 'To be set up anew elsewhere, begin / A task indeed but with a clearer clime / Than the murk lodgment of our building-time'; and the late poem *Rephan* (*Asolando*, 1889), in which the speaker is impelled by existence in a 'faultlessly exact' and unchanging world to seek '[hopes], fears, loves, hates' on earth.

165. congeries: a disordered mass or heap (pronounced to rhyme with 'series' below, although the orthodox pronunciation would place the emphasis on the first syllable).

172. its faith] our faith (*1868–88*).

173. Conflating the well-known saying 'Spare the rod and spoil the child' (*Proverbs* xiii 24; cp. Samuel Butler, *Hudibras*, II i 843) with St Paul's injunction to 'put away childish things' on attaining manhood (*1 Corinthians* xiii 11).

175–6. According to the Dowager Countess of Jersey, B. told her that 'he had embodied his feelings in the "Old Pictures in Florence" in the lines ending "I have had troubles enough for one"' (*Fifty-One Years of Victorian Life* [1922] 87). The remark is undated but probably comes from the 1870s. For another quotation from this book, see *Evelyn Hope* 16n. (p. 276).

175. Quoting *Hebrews* iv 9: 'There remaineth therefore a rest to the people of God'.

23

But at any rate I have loved the season
    Of Art's spring-birth so dim and dewy,
My sculptor is Nicolo the Pisan;
180   My painter—who but Cimabue?
Nor ever was man of them all indeed,
    From these to Ghiberti and Ghirlandajo,
Could say that he missed my critic-meed.
    So now to my special grievance—heigh ho!

24

185   Their ghosts now stand, as I said before,
    Watching each fresco flaked and rasped,

179. My sculptor] And my sculptor (*H proof* but not *H proof*²).   *Nicolo the Pisan*: Nicola Pisano, born *c.* 1220, one of the most important figures in the history of sculpture; he is said by Vasari to have 'liberated' both sculpture and architecture 'from the rude and tasteless old Greek manner' (*Foster* i 60). His most famous work is the pulpit of the Baptistery of S. Giovanni at Pisa, which the Brownings would certainly have seen during their period of residence in the city. He is mentioned in *Sordello* i 575 (I 434), although there the relation between Greek and Gothic art is different; B. spells his first name as 'Nicolo' there too.

180. My painter] And my painter (*H proof* but not *H proof*²); And painter (*1863* only).   *Cimabue*: Cenni di Pepi, called Cimabue (*c.* 1240–*c.* 1302), is the first artist to be commemorated in Vasari's *Lives*. He was, according to Vasari, 'the first cause of the restoration of the art of painting' in Italy (*Foster* i 44), but, as Dante notes in *Purgatorio* (xi 94–6) his fame was eclipsed by his great successor Giotto: 'Credette Cimabue nella pintura / tener lo campo, e ora ha Giotto il grido, / sì che la fama di colui è scura' [It used to be thought that Cimabue held the field in painting, but now the cry is for Giotto, so that the fame of the former is obscured]. Cp. *Pictor Ignotus* 32n. (p. 229).

182. Ghiberti: Lorenzo di Bartolo (Ghiberti) (1378–1455), Florentine sculptor and painter, famous for his bronze doors for the Baptistery of Florence.   *Ghirlandajo*: Domenico Bigordi (1449–94; see l. 201n.) was called 'Ghirlandaio' ('garland maker') because he came from a family which was famous for its skill in making ladies' headdresses. For the story of B.'s discovery of the broken-up pieces of a Ghirlandaio altarpiece see headnote.

183. my critic-meed: the reward of my attention to his work.

184. heigh ho!: a conventional exclamation, here a sigh; in common with many Victorian poets B. found it in Elizabethan song and drama, e.g. Amiens's song in *As You Like It* II vii.

185–92. For the scandal of the Catholic Church's neglect of its art treasures, see headnote, *Sources*. David De Laura (*SBC* 9; see headnote, *Sources*) suggests an allusion to a passage in Anna Jameson's *Visits and Sketches at Home and Abroad* (1837): 'It has been said that fresco-painting is unfitted for our climate, damp and sea-coal fires being equally injurious; but the new method of warming all large

Blocked up, knocked out, or whitewashed o'er
        —No getting again what the church has grasped!
The works on the wall must take their chance,
190   "Works never conceded to England's thick clime!"
(I hope they prefer their inheritance
        Of a bucketful of Italian quick-lime.)

                                25
When they go at length, with such a shaking
        Of heads o'er the old delusions, sadly
195   Each master his way through the black streets taking,
        Where many a lost work breathes though badly—
Why don't they bethink them of who has merited?
        Why not reveal, while their pictures dree
Such doom, that a captive's to be out-ferreted?
200   Why do they never remember me?

---

buildings, either by steam or heated air, obviates, at least, this objection.' Cp. also Coleridge's comments in his 1818 lectures on Shakespeare: 'And in truth, deeply, O! far more than words can express, as I venerate the Last Judgment and the Prophets of Michel Angelo Buonarotti,—yet the very pain which I repeatedly felt as I lost myself in gazing upon them, the painful consideration that their having been painted in *fresco* was the sole cause that they had not been abandoned to all the accidents of a dangerous transportation to a distant capital . . . forced upon my mind the reflection: how grateful the human race ought to be that the works of Euclid, Newton, Plato, Milton, Shakespere [sic], are not subjected to similar contingencies,—that they and their fellows, and the great, tho' inferior, peerage of undying intellect, are *secured*' (*Lectures and Notes on Shakespere*, ed. T. Ashe [1897], pp. 209–10).

185. now stand] would stand (*H proof* but not *H proof²*); still stand (*1868–88*).

190. This statement is made by an imaginary opponent of the acquisition of Italian art by foreigners (like the speaker); the point is that frescoes by their nature are linked to the buildings in which they are painted.

194. the old delusions] the old delusion (*1865–88*).

198–9. dree / Such doom: 'endure such a fate' (Scottish dialect, here used with burlesque intent).

198. Why not reveal] Why won't they reveal (*H proof*).

199.] Such doom, that a captive might be out-ferreted? (*1865*); Such doom, how a captive might be out-ferreted? (*1868–88*); meaning that a work by one of the neglected early painters may be going cheap (either from a church or art dealer in Florence: see headnote, p. 404); the speaker humorously imagines that the artists themselves ought to inform him as to the whereabouts of such treasures.

200. Why do they] Why is it they (*H proof, 1863–88*).

26

Not that I expect the great Bigordi
    Nor Sandro to hear me, chivalric, bellicose;
Nor wronged Lippino—and not a word I
    Say of a scrap of Fra Angelico's.
205   But are you too fine, Taddeo Gaddi,
    To grant me a taste of your intonaco—
Some Jerome that seeks the heaven with a sad eye?
    No churlish saint, Lorenzo Monaco?

27

Could not the ghost with the close red cap,
210   My Pollajolo, the twice a craftsman,

201. Bigordi: according to *Foster* (i 200), the family name of Domenico called 'Ghirlandaio'; see above l. 182n.

202. Sandro: Botticelli (1444/5–1510) was born Alessandro ('Sandro') di Mariano Filipepi. *chivalric, bellicose*: there is very little in Vasari's brief *Life* of Botticelli to justify either of these epithets; he is instead described as 'whimsical', 'eccentric', and given to profligacy.

203. Nor wronged Lippino] Nor the wronged Lippino (*1863–88*). Filippino Lippi (*c.* 1457–1504), son of Fra Lippo Lippi and Lucrezia Buti (see headnote to *Fra Lippo*, p. 456). Orr suggests that he is '"wronged" because others were credited with some of his best work' (*Handbook* 210), including the frescoes in the Brancacci Chapel of the Carmine, where his father was a monk. Vasari argues that he had to work hard to remove 'the stain'—presumably of illegitimacy—'left to him by his father' (*Foster* ii 282).

204. Fra Angelico's: Guido di Pietro, Fra Giovanni Angelico da Fiesole (1387–1455); see *Fra Lippo* 235–6n. (p. 498). He was exalted as an 'inspired saint' by Ruskin in *Modern Painters* ii (1846), a work B. knew and which may account for his modesty here (in which there may also be a hint of irony).

205. Taddeo Gaddi: Florentine painter (*c.* 1300–66); see l. 207n. Gaddi is blamed by Fantozzi for scaling down Giotto's original plans for the Campanile (*Fantozzi* 321).

206. intonaco: the final coating of plaster spread upon a wall or other surface, esp. for fresco painting (*OED*); pronounced with accent on second syllable.

207. Jerome: the most severely ascetic and self-denying of the saints of the early church (*c.* 341–420), St Jerome was a popular subject for religious painting in the Renaissance, as Fra Lippo Lippi sardonically notes (ll. 73–4; p. 489); on the representation of Jerome in Renaissance art see Malcolm Andrews, *Landscape and Western Art* (Oxford 1999), ch. ii. In his *Life* of Gaddi, Vasari mentions a depiction of St Jerome 'robed in the vestments of a cardinal' by Gaddi in Santa Maria Novella. *the heaven*] the Heaven (*1863–65*), a rare example of capitalization being introduced in an edition after *1855*.

208. No churlish] Not a churlish (*H proof* [but not *H proof²*], *1863–88*). *Lorenzo Monaco*: Lorenzo Monaco ('Lawrence the Monk') (*c.* 1370–*c.* 1422) was a member of the Camaldolese Order; see *Fra Lippo* 235–6n (p. 498).

209–10. Antonio Pollaiuolo (*c.* 1432–98) is depicted wearing a fez in Filippino Lippi's fresco 'St. Peter and St. Paul before the Proconsul', which B. would have

Save me a sample, give me the hap
 Of a muscular Christ that shows the draughtsman?
No Virgin by him, the somewhat petty,
 Of finical touch and tempera crumbly—
215   Could not Alesso Baldovinetti
 Contribute so much, I ask him humbly?

28
Margheritone of Arezzo,
 With the grave-clothes garb and swaddling barret,

---

seen in the Brancacci Chapel, Florence; a reproduction is included in *Le Monnier* (*Thomas* 435). He is said to be 'twice a craftsman' either as a tribute to his technical skill, or (as *Ohio* suggests) in recognition of the fact that he learned two trades, having originally trained as a goldsmith.

211. give me the hap: give me the lucky find.

212. muscular Christ: the 'Christ at the Column', owned by the Brownings (see *Collections* Plate 16), currently at Harewood House. There is some disagreement amongst modern scholars about whether or not it is the work of Pollaiuolo. *shows the draughtsman*: illustrates the artist's technical skill. Vasari notes that Pollaiuolo 'treated his nude figures in a manner which approaches more nearly to that of the moderns than was usual with the artists who had preceded him' and 'dissected many human bodies to study the anatomy'; he was 'the first who investigated the action of the muscles in this manner, that he might afterwards give them their due place and effect in his works' (*Foster* ii 227).

213–16. Alesso Baldovinetti (1425–1499), a painter and mosaic-maker. His 'finical touch' is emphasized by Vasari: 'Alesso was extremely careful and exact in his works, and of all the minutiæ which mother nature is capable of presenting, he took pains to be the close imitator' (*Foster* ii 66). He also attempted to invent a new method of fresco painting with the aim of '[defending] his work from the effects of damp'; but it was a failure, with the result that 'the work has in several places peeled off' (*ibid.*). Leonée Ormond identifies the 'Virgin' in question as the 'Virgin and Child' given to D. G. Rossetti by B.

214. tempera: distemper, a method of painting in which the colours are thickened with other substances before being applied to a dry surface (*OED*).

217–20. Margarito of Arezzo flourished *c.* 1262. *Turner* (p. 358) suggests that the details of the description that follows are taken from the portrait of Margheritone by Spinello Aretino, reproduced at the beginning of his *Life* in *Le Monnier*. Cp. EBB.'s *Casa Guidi Windows* i 379–90: 'If old Margheritone trembled, swooned, / And died despairing at the open sill / Of other men's achievements (who achieved, / By loving art beyond the master!) he / Was old Margheritone, and conceived / Never, at first youth and most ecstacy, / A Virgin like that dream of one, which heaved / The death-sigh from his heart. If wistfully / Margheritone sickened at the smell / Of Cimabue's laurel, let him go!—/ For Cimabue stood up very well / In spite of Giotto's—'.

218. barret: a small flat cap, It. *biretta*, often worn by Roman Catholic clerics (*OED*).

(Why purse up mouth and beak in a pet so,
220   You bald, saturnine, poll-clawed parrot?)
No poor glimmering Crucifixion,
    Where in the foreground kneels the donor?
If such remain, as in my conviction,
    The hoarding does you but little honour.

29

225   They pass: for them the panels may thrill,
    The tempera grow alive and tinglish—
Rot or are left to the mercies still
    Of dealers and stealers, Jews and the English!
Seeing mere money's worth in their prize,
230   Who sell it to some one calm as Zeno

219. in a pet so: 'in such a fit of petulance'.
220. saturnine: gloomy; pronounced here with the accent on the second syllable.
poll-clawed parrot: the epithet refers to Margheritone's bald head ('poll') which is seamed or scarred, but the phrase as a whole also recalls 'poll-parrot', often used as a comic insult: *OED* cites the humorist Douglas Jerrold (1851), a friend of B.'s: 'You've no more manners than a poll-parrot'; cp. also Grandfather Smallweed addressing his wife in ch. xxxiii of Dickens's *Bleak House* (1852–35): 'Sit down, you dancing, prancing, shambling, scrambling poll-parrot!' See also *2 Henry IV* II iv 258–9, where the Prince mocks Falstaff: 'Look, whether the withered elder hath not his poll clawed like a parrot'.
221. No poor] Not a poor (*1863–88*).
223. If such remain] If such still remain (H proof but not H proof²).
224. The hoarding] The hoarding it (*1863–88*).
225. They: the painters, last seen taking their way through the streets (l. 195).
227. Rot or are left] Works rot or are left (H proof); Their pictures are left (*1863–88*). B.'s note on H proof has 'The pictures'; the lists he sent to D. G. Rossetti and James T. Fields both agree with this note (see headnote, *Text*). This reading is clearly a revision, not a correction, and we have not emended *1855*.
228. The Jews are the dealers, the English the stealers (the English reputation for cultural pillage was well established by this date). *the English!*] the English, (*1863–68, 1888*); the English (*1870, 1880*). The lack of punctuation in *1870* and *1880* (which was probably set from a copy of *1870*) may be a misprint but it makes sense taken with the next line.
229. Seeing]—Who see (H proof); Who, seeing (*1863–88*).
230–2. The sense is that modern collectors are unmoved by the early painters whose work seems to them primitive ('naked art') but go into ecstasies over the sophisticated but lifeless productions of the modern school.
230. Who sell it] And sell it (H proof but not H proof²); Will sell it (*1863–88*).
calm as Zeno: Zeno of Citium in Cyprus (*c.* 333–262 BC) was the founder of the Stoic school of philosophy which preached equanimity in the face of the vicissitudes of life (hence his 'calm' demeanour).

At naked Art, and in ecstacies
     Before some clay-cold, vile Carlino!

30
     No matter for these! But Giotto, you,
        Have you allowed, as the town-tongues babble it,
235 Never! it shall not be counted true—
        That a certain precious little tablet
     Which Buonarroti eyed like a lover,—
        Buried so long in oblivion's womb,

231. At naked Art] At the naked Art (*H proof*); At naked High Art (*1863–88*).
ecstacies] ecstasies (*1863–88*); the *1855* spelling was allowable in the period.
232. clay-cold: cp. Ruskin, *Modern Painters* I (1846): '[Stansfield's] picture of
the Doge's palace at Venice was quite clay-cold and untrue' (*Works* iii 228).   *Carlino*:
Carlo Dolci (1616–86), a baroque Florentine artist. B.'s low opinion of him was
shared by Ruskin: 'Three penstrokes of Raffaele are a greater and a better
picture than the most finished work that ever Carlo Dolci polished into inanity'
(*Works* iii 91). Cp. *Shelley* (Appendix A, p. 874), where B. has to account for
Shelley's admiration of Dolci.
233–40. The speaker laments that an unworthy collector has unearthed a lost
masterpiece by Giotto. The story of this lost work is in Vasari: 'A chapel and four
pictures were painted by Giotto, for the fraternity of the Umiliati d'Ognissanti,
in Florence . . . there was a small picture in distemper, in the transept of the church
belonging to the Umiliati, which had been painted by Giotto with infinite care.
The subject was the death of the Virgin, with the Apostles around her, and with
the figure of Christ, who receives her soul into his arms. This work has been
greatly prized by artists, and was above all valued by Michael Angelo Buonarroti,
who declared, as we have said before, that nothing in painting could be nearer
to the life than this was . . . [the painting] has since been carried away from the
church.' Mrs Foster adds in a footnote: 'This picture reappeared at a later period,
and after various vicissitudes became the property of Mr. N. Ottley, where I [Schorn]
saw it in 1826' (*Foster* i 113; see headnote, *Composition*). B. had forgotten some
of these details by the time he explained the lines in a letter to Hiram Corson
of 28 Dec. 1886: '[the] "little tablet" was a famous "Last Supper," mentioned by
Vasari, and gone astray long ago from the Church of S. Spirito: it turned up,
according to report, in some obscure corner, while I was in Florence, and was
at once acquired by a stranger. I saw it,—genuine or no, a work of great beauty'
(Corson, *Introduction to the Study of Browning's Poetry* [Boston, 1891], facsimile between
pp. ii and iii). See headnote, *Composition*, and cp. ll. 241–2.
235. Never!] Oh, never! (*H proof, 1863–88*).
236. tablet: a small wooden panel; most paintings were done on wood before the
adoption of canvas in the fifteenth century.
237: Buonarroti: Michelangelo's surname, used (and misspelled) by B. in *Easter Day*
799 (p. 133).
238. Buried] Was buried (*1863–88*).

Was left for another than I to discover,—
240   Turns up at last, and to whom?—to whom?

31

I, that have haunted the dim San Spirito,
    (Or was it rather the Ognissanti?)
Stood on the altar-steps, patient and weary too!
    Nay, I shall have it yet, *detur amanti!*
245   My Koh-i-noor—or (if that's a platitude)
        Jewel of Giamschid, the Persian Sofi's eye!
So, in anticipative gratitude,
        What if I take up my hope and prophesy?

32

When the hour is ripe, and a certain dotard
250   Pitched, no parcel that needs invoicing,
To the worse side of the Mont St. Gothard,
        Have, to begin by way of rejoicing,

239. Was left] And left (*1863–88*).
241. San Spirito: the church of Santo Spirito (the Holy Spirit), begun by Brunelleschi in the early fifteenth century and completed in 1481.
242. the Ognissanti: It. 'All Saints'; begun in 1251, rebuilt in baroque style in 1627.
243.] Patient on altar-steps planting a weary toe! (*1863–88*, except *1868–88* which have 'altar-step').
244. detur amanti: 'let it be given to the one who loves it' (Latin).
245. Koh-i-noor: the arrival of the 'Koh-i-noor' ('Mountain of Light'), reputed to be the world's largest diamond, aboard the steam-ship *Medea* at Portsmouth was reported in *The Times* for Monday 1 July 1850; its history as a trophy of the rulers of India made it, for *The Times*, a 'fitting symbol' of British supremacy in India. It was displayed at the Great Exhibition of 1851.
246. Jewel of Giamschid: cp. Byron, *The Giaour*. 'Her eye's dark charm 'twere vain to tell . . . Soul beam'd forth in every spark / That darted from beneath the lid, / Bright as the Jewel of Giamschid' (ll. 473, 477–9). Byron explains in a footnote that he is referring to '[the] celebrated fabulous ruby of Sultan Giamschid'.
247. So, in] And in (*H proof*).
249–51. The sense is 'when the Austrians are finally thrown out of Italy': the 'certain dotard' is named in l. 255 as Count Radetzky, aged 89 in 1855, the commander of the Austrian forces which defeated the uprising of Piedmont-Sardinia at the battle of Novara in 1849. The 'worse side' of the St Gothard pass over the Alps would be the Swiss side, i.e. outside Italy.
250. Pitched] Is pitched (*1863–88*).
251. worse side] worser side (*H proof* but not *H proof²*).   *Mont St. Gothard*] Mont Saint Gothard (*1863–88*, except *1870* and *1880* which agree with *1855*).
252. Have, to begin] We'll, have to begin (*H proof*); We shall begin (*1863–88*); the revs. clarify the sense of 'Have' in *1855* as 'Let's have' or 'We should have'.
rejoicing,] rejoicing; (*1863–88*).

None of that shooting the sky (blank cartridge),
No civic guards, all plumes and lacquer,
255   Hunting Radetsky's soul like a partridge
Over Morello with squib and cracker.

33

We'll shoot this time better game and bag 'em hot—
No display at the stone of Dante,
But a sober kind of Witan-agemot
260   ("Casa Guidi," quod videas ante)

253–6. A satirical glance at the celebrations which followed the grant of a formal constitution by Leopold II of Tuscany in 1848; B. suggests that the volleys of shots fired into the air ('blank cartridge') are in fact an attempt to hunt the departing soul of Radetzky as if it were a partridge. In a letter of March 1849 EBB. refers to 'the stupid habit of expressing joy & triumph here [in Florence] by firing into the air .. gunpowder without balls! so stupid!' (*EBB to Arabella* i 229). Julia Markus notes a similar sentiment in the *Tuscan Athenaeum* of 18 Dec. 1847: 'we almost dread to think what it may become, when the Civica actually fire with real Gunpowder!' (Markus, *BIS* vi [1978] 50–1).

253. None of that] None of our (*H proof*).

254. No civic guards] As when civic guards (*H proof*); Nor a civic guard (*1863–88*).

255. Hunting] We hunted (*H proof*).

256. Over Morello] Over Mount Morello (*H proof*). Monte Morello overlooks Florence; cp. *Andrea* 93 (p. 302). *squib and cracker*: both forms of small firework.

257. We'll shoot this time] This time we'll shoot (*1863–88*). *game*: continuing the metaphor of patridge-shooting begun in l. 253.

258. No display] No stupid display (*H proof*); No mere display (*1863–88*). *the stone of Dante*: the stone reputed to have been Dante's favourite seat; see Wordsworth, *Memorials of a Tour in Italy* xix 1–5: 'Under the shadow of a stately Pile / The dome of Florence, pensive and alone, / Nor giving heed to aught that passed the while, / I stood, and gazed upon a marble stone, / The laurelled Dante's favourite seat'. The Florentines' 'display' at the Stone of Dante in 1848 is described in *Casa Guidi Windows* i 601–60.

259. a sober kind of] emended in agreement with *H proof* from 'a kind of' in *1855*; *1863–88* have 'a kind of sober'. The latter reading is in the lists B. sent to D. G. Rossetti and James T. Fields (see headnote, *Text*), but in this instance, in contrast to l. 149, we prefer to restore the reading which B. evidently intended for *1855*; unlike the earlier instance, the reading B. gives in the Rossetti and Fields lists is not supported by a note on *H proof*. *Witan-agemot*] Witanagemot (*1868–88*); the Anglo-Saxon parliament or council of wise men; like EBB. in *Casa Guidi Windows*, the speaker is implying that Italy needs to follow the English model in order to develop effective forms of popular representation. The use of a hyphen in the middle of the word is common in most of its variant spellings.

260. ("Casa Guidi,"] Ex: "Casa Guidi," (*1863–88*). Casa Guidi was the name of the Brownings' home in Florence. *quod videas ante*] in italic, *1863–88*; B. requested this change in the list he sent to James T. Fields, but it does not appear in the list he sent to D. G. Rossetti (see headnote, *Text*); on balance we do not think there is a case for emending *1855*. The Latin phrase means 'for which, see above'; EBB.'s *Casa Guidi Windows* had been published in 1851.

To ponder Freedom restored to Florence,
How Art may return that departed with her.
Go, hated house, go each trace of the Loraine's!
And bring us the days of Orgagna hither.

34
265 How we shall prologuise, how we shall perorate,
Say fit things upon art and history—

261. *To ponder Freedom*] To ponder now Freedom's (*H proof*); Shall ponder, once
Freedom (*1863–88*). B.'s note on *H proof* agrees with the *1855* reading, the only
one which does so. The lists B. sent to D. G. Rossetti and James T. Fields (see
headnote, *Text*) both have 'to ponder, Freedom'. There is no case for emending *1855*.
263. *Go, hated*] With the hated (*H proof* but not *H proof*²). The 'hated house' is
that of the Hapsburg François de Lorraine [sic], to whom the Grand Duchy of
Tuscany had been given by the Treaty of Vienna in 1735 as compensation for
the loss of his own duchy (Lorraine) to the dispossessed King of Poland. The
Grand Duke of Tuscany at the time of the poem's composition was Leopold II.
264. *Orgagna hither.*] Orgagna hither! (*1863–88*). Andrea di Cione (*c.* 1315–1368),
a Florentine painter, sculptor, architect and poet was nicknamed 'Orcagna' or
'Orgagna'. He lived during the heroic period of the Florentine Republic, and
was, like Dante, involved in the construction of the Duomo or Cathedral at Florence.
He is particularly associated with the Florentine Republic because he initiated
the reconstruction of the Loggia dell'Orgagna (or Loggia de'Lanzi): 'L'oggetto di
questa fabbrica . . . fu di avere un luogo pubblico difeso dalle pioggie, per dare
il possesso alla suprema magistratura della Repubblica fiorentina . . . finchè la patria
di Dante, del Boccaccio, di Giotto, la maestra di gentile idioma e d'altissime idee,
sarà visitata dagli stranieri, essi pure volgeranno lo sguardo a questo portico, nel
quale il cittadino artista un cosi augusto seggio inalzava ai magistrati della sua
Repubblica' [The aim of this building . . . was to have a sheltered public place
for the supreme magistrature of Florence to use . . . for as long as the homeland
of Dante, Boccaccio and Giotto, the mistress of beautiful forms and sublime ideas,
is visited by foreigners, they will turn their gaze on this grand entrance, in which
the citizen-artist has erected such an august seat for the magistrates of his Republic]
(*Fantozzi* 30–2). In *Modern Painters* (3rd ed., 1846) Ruskin places Orcagna alongside Giotto, Fra Angelico and Perugino as artists whose work will never be widely
popular because of its rarefied intellectual and moral qualities (*Works* ii 82). *Thomas*
(p. 437) notes that Mazzini delivered a speech calling on the Florentines to join
Rome in its struggle for Italian freedom from Orcagna's Loggia on 5 Mar. 1849.
265. *prologuise*] prologuize (*1863–68, 1880*); prologize (*1888*). Note the spelling of
the title *Artemis Prologuizes* in its first edition (*DL*, 1842; see II 106); this was
altered to 'Prologizes' in *1863*, the same ed. in which 'prologuize' was introduced
here. It means 'to deliver a prologue' (i.e. at the opposite end of the speech from
the 'peroration' or closing passage).
266. *Say fit things*] Say proper things (*H proof*); Utter fit things (*1863–88*).

Set truth at blood-heat and the false at a zero rate,
  Make of the want of the age no mystery!
Contrast the fructuous and sterile eras,
270   Show, monarchy its uncouth cub licks
Out of the bear's shape to the chimæra's—
Pure Art's birth being still the republic's!

35
Then one shall propose (in a speech, curt Tuscan,
  Sober, expurgate, spare of an "*issimo,*")

267. Set truth] Set the true (*H proof*); Feel truth (*1863–88*).   *the false at a*] falsehood at (*1865–88*).
268. I.e. 'Make clear what modern life requires'.   *Make*] And make (*H proof,
1863–65*).
269–72. The view of history here, and the vocabulary, are influenced by Carlyle,
although B. goes against Carlyle's political bias towards the 'hero' or 'great man';
the 'fructuous' (fruitful, truly civilized) eras are those of republican government
in contrast to the 'sterility' of monarchical or absolute regimes.
269. Contrast] Contrasting (*1863* only).
270–1. The earliest instance of the popular legend that the bear gives birth to
unformed cubs, which it then licks into shape, is in Pliny the Elder's *Naturalis
Historia* (AD 77) viii 54; B. plays on this by imagining that works of art produced
under a monarchy are distorted from their natural shape into deformed mon-
strosities (or 'chimæras').
271. to the chimæra's] into Chimæra's (*1865–88*).
272. Pure Art's birth being] While pure Art's birth was (*H proof* but not *H proof²*);
While Pure Art's birth is (*1863–88*). Cp. R. H. Stoddard's account of a conversation which took place between Bayard Taylor and the Brownings in London
in September 1851: 'The Brownings expressed great satisfaction with their
American reputation, and the conversation taking a turn that led to American
Art Mrs. Browning expressed the belief that a Republican form of government
was unfavourable to the Fine Arts. Mr. Taylor dissented to this opinion, and a
general historical discussion ensued, which was carried on for some time with
the greatest spirit, husband and wife taking directly opposite views' (*Life, Letters
and Essays of Elizabeth Barrett Browning*, 2 vols. [New York 1877], vol. i, p. xxvi).
273–88. For the association of the Campanile with the cause of Italian liberation
see headnote, and cp. *Casa Guidi Windows* i 68–72: 'What word will men say,—
here where Giotto planted / His campanile, like an unperplexed / Fine question
Heavenward, touching the things granted / A noble people who, being greatly
vexed / In act, in aspiration keep undaunted?'
273. (in a speech, curt Tuscan,] in a speech (curt Tuscan, (*1863–88*). Tuscan is the
dialect from which modern Italian developed.
274.] Expurgate and sober, with scarcely an "*issimo,*") (*1863–88*). B.'s note on *H
proof* alters 'an "*issimo*"' to '"altissimo"', which makes less sense than what it
replaces; B. probably meant to correct the misprint in l. 276, and this in turn
suggests that he was copying these readings into *H proof*: see headnote, *Text*. The
suffix 'issimo' is used to intensify adjectives in Italian.

275   Ending our half-told tale of Cambuscan,
      Turning the Bell-tower's alt to altissimo.
    And fine as the beak of a young beccaccia
      The Campanile, the Duomo's fit ally,
    Soars up in gold its full fifty braccia,
280   Completing Florence, as Florence, Italy.

36

    Shall I be alive that morning the scaffold
      Is broken away, and the long-pent fire
    Like the golden hope of the world unbaffled
      Springs from its sleep, and up goes the spire—
285   As, "God and the People" plain for its motto,

275. Ending] To finish (*H proof* but not *H proof²*); To end now (*1863–88*). *half-told tale of Cambuscan*: the Squire in Chaucer's *Canterbury Tales* tells the story of Cambuscan, the legendary King of Sarra in Tartary, but does not finish it; Milton refers to Chaucer as 'him that left half told / The story of Cambuscan bold' in *Il Penseroso* (ll. 109–10).

276. Turning the Bell-tower's] Turn the Bell-tower's (*H proof* but not *H proof²*); And turn the Bell-tower's (*1863–68*); And turn the bell-tower's (*1870–88*). *alt to altissimo*] emended in agreement with *1863–88* from 'altaltissimo' in *1855*; *H proof* has 'alto to altissimo'. In the lists B. sent to Rossetti and James T. Fields the *1855* misprint is corrected to the present reading, and B. probably intended to correct it on *H proof*, but mistook the line: see l. 274n. and headnote, *Text.* The misprint in *1855* may have resulted from the compositor setting 'alto to altissimo' in error (repeating the 'to' would be an easy mistake to make); B. may then have corrected 'alto' to 'alt', whereupon the compositor compounded his first error by a second. The phrase 'alt to altissimo' means 'high' to 'very high'.

277. beccaccia: woodcock (It.).

278–9. The Campanile . . . Soars] Shall the Campanile . . . Soar (*H proof*); The Campanile . . . Shall soar (*1863–88*).

278. Duomo: lit. 'dome', the Italian term for cathedral.

279. its full fifty] full fifty (*1863–88*). *braccia*: an old Italian unit of length (used, e.g., by Vasari), named after the Italian for 'arms' (pl. 'le braccia'); approximately the distance between the elbow and the wrist.

280. Florence became the first capital of the reunited Italy between 1865 and the final incorporation of the Papal States in 1871 (when Rome became the capital).

281.] So said, so done. That morning the scaffold (*H proof*).

283. unbaffled: freed from an obstacle or difficulty; *OED* also cites Edward Bulwer Lytton, *The Disowned* (1829): 'There seemed to dwell the first flow and life of youth, undimmed by a single fear and unbaffled in a single hope.'

284–5. the spire— / As, "God] the spire— / When with "God (*H proof*); the spire / While, "God (*1863–88*, except *1870* and *1888* which have no comma after 'While').

285. "God and the People": a translation of Giuseppe Mazzini's slogan 'Dio e popolo'; see headnote, p. 408, and cp. EBB.'s remark in a letter of 28 Apr. 1852: 'Mazzini writes "God & the people" on a banner, & thinks this enough both for theology & politics' (*EBB to Arabella* i 487).

Thence the new tricolor flaps at the sky?
Foreseeing the day that vindicates Giotto
And Florence together, the first am I!

---

286. tricolor: the emblem of Republicanism, modelled on the French tricolor; the speaker is clearly imagining the united Italy of the future as a republic rather than a monarchy (cp. ll. 270–1n.).

287.] Why, to hail him, the vindicated Giotto (*H proof*); At least to foresee that glory of Giotto (*1863–88*). The phrase 'At least' implies that the speaker's prophecy of a united and 'completed' Italy is meant to be some kind of recompense for his failure to acquire the art treasures described earlier in the poem.

288. And Florence together] Thanking God for it all, (*H proof*).

28 How It Strikes a Contemporary

Text and publication

First publ. *M & W*, 10 Nov. 1855; repr. *1863, 1863², 1868, 1872, 1888*. Our text is *1855*.

Composition and date

Although there is no definite evidence of the date of composition, some commentators, following *Cooke*, have suggested that the poem's reflections on the role of the poet might be linked to *Shelley*, which B. was writing towards the end of 1851 (see Appendix A, p. 851). There is, however, a letter written by B. to his friend Joseph Milsand, dated 16 June 1853, which discusses the role of the poet in England in terms similar to those used in the poem:

> In your letter you bid me tell you something about the way of life of our literary men!—we have none in your sense of the word. Ours are not your ways: it is the worse for us in many respects, if perhaps the better in some few. We have no analogies, in any of our characters that I know, with A. de Musset, George Sand, A. Dumas—and the rest. The whole life is led differently, you all tend to influence politically, I think—with us, it would be absurd for the man who writes articles in the 'Times' which are condensed into telegraphic messages from Kingdom to Kingdom, to try & obtain, on the strength of them, the secretaryship to the poorest embassy there. So a man learns his decreed place and curbs his desires accordingly—if he does not, nobody sympathises with him. So with us, those who are without a real vocation for literature as its own reward, keep very clear of it—the others take their love & labour into the quietest corner and live there as they like—and when people live so,— that is, not as others like & prescribe,—they generally lead praiseworthy lives.

B. continues by taking the example of 'Tennyson's brother'—Frederick Tennyson (1807–98), whom B. had recently met in Italy—as the type of the English poet:

> [His] poetry, of which I have read a quantity—is all *about to become* the very thing, and never quite *is*. He wants the dramatic power of his brother entirely—writes wholly *subjectively*: that purely veracious, earnest and simple mind of his cannot be other than itself for a moment. But, as I say, how you would like the entire truthfulness, and faith!—which I don't remember having ever seen so prominent & characteristic of a man to the exclusion of other qualities. He is of great & various culture, deep sympathies, and the regular English temperament that is provided to neutralise all such good things,—the extreme sensitiveness & shyness which are the island soul's disease, as consumption is the body's. He will stand aside all his life and see others act—yet he could not himself act, even as well, without an effort of which he is quite incapable. Now, would you be glad at seeing such an one, sufficient to himself under such restrictions, by reason of his *true* deep passion for nature—or vexed that such a solace prevents his necessity for working? Ought a man to rest here if he can?

> (ABL/JMA)

The date of mid-1853 suggested by this and similar letters to Milsand (see *Popularity*, p. 446) would be consistent with other evidence that B. wrote most of the *M &*

W poems during 1853–54 (see Appendix C, p. 889). It is, perhaps, significant in this respect that Milsand, who was sent a proof copy of vol. i of *M & W* in Sept. 1855, copied out sections of this poem (as well as a complete version of *By the Fire-Side*), accompanying his transcription with some jottings on the different kinds of English poet: 'Tennyson c'est l'homme de l'imagination . . . Browning c'est l'intelligence. Wordsworth le sentiment et le sens moral. Byron les desirs' [Tennyson is the man of imagination . . . Browning is the intellect. Wordsworth feeling and the moral sense. Byron the desires] (*ABL/JMA*).

Sources and contexts

Like *Childe Roland* (p. 348) and perhaps also *Love Among the Ruins* (p. 528), the material for this poem seems to have been drawn from various aspects of B.'s reading. *Cooke* (pp. 444–5) was the first to point out the resemblance between the title of the poem and Jane Taylor's *How it Strikes a Stranger*; there was a copy of the volume in which this brief moral fable appears, *The Contributions of Q. Q. to a Periodical Work: With Some Pieces Not Before Published* (1824), in B.'s library (*Collections* A2258). The opening of Taylor's story has obvious similarities to the opening of B.'s poem: 'In a remote period of antiquity, when the supernatural and the marvellous obtained a readier credence than now, it was fabled that a stranger of extraordinary appearance was observed pacing the streets of one of the magnificent cities of the East, remarking with an eye of intelligent curiosity every surrounding object.' B. mentions the 'noble woman and imaginative writer, Jane Taylor of Norwich' [sic, for Ongar] in a footnote to *Rephan* (*Asolando*, 1889).

The setting of the poem in Valladolid seems to derive from B.'s acquaintance with Lesage's picaresque novel *Gil Blas* (1715–35). In a letter to EBB. of 16 Sept. 1845, B. claims that he ' "did" an Elementary French book' for his French master (*Correspondence* xi 83), which was favourably reviewed alongside his own *Paracelsus*; the book in question has been identified as an abbreviated version of *Gil Blas*, entitled *Le Gil Blas de la Jeunesse*; see Lionel Stevenson, *MLN* (May 1927) 299–305. *Miller* (p. 22) notes that the chapter of *Gil Blas* entitled 'Histoire de dona Mencia de Mosquera' includes a 'corregidor de Valladolid', and another character of Valladolid called 'Sédillo', 'whose housekeeper is called Jacinte'. Thomas Noon Talfourd's play *The Castilian*, published in 1853, mentions Valladolid; B. was an admirer of Talfourd's work, having dedicated *Pippa* to him as 'the author of *Ion*', on which *Pippa* itself may have been partly modelled (see headnote, p. 85).

Another element in the poem may be derived from B.'s sight of the elderly songwriter Pierre-Jean de Béranger in Paris in 1852 'wandering along the asphalte' (see headnote to *Respectability*, p. 227). Despite being repeatedly pressed to do so, Béranger refused to participate in the provisional government which followed the revolution of 1848, resigning as soon as he had been elected (against his will) to the National Assembly. He was famous for the simplicity of his lifestyle, but also (following the *coup d'état* of December 1851 which brought Napoleon III to power) an object of suspicion to some because of his Bonapartist leanings.

Setting

John Coates (*SBC* xi, no. 1 [1983] 41–6) argues that the poem is set in early seventeenth-century Spain, the period in which *Gil Blas* is set and during which Miguel de Cervantes lived. He suggests that the reference to the 'new shop a-building' (l. 22) and the destruction of the last vestiges of Moorish architecture in the town (ll. 18–19) date it to the years 1601–06, when the Duke of Lerma, 'Philip III's favourite . . . decided to transfer the capital of Spain from Madrid to

Valladolid . . . This absurd and extravagant decision involved a mass of new building around the old city to house courtiers and shopkeepers who made their living from the court' (p. 42). This was also the period immediately preceding the final expulsion of the Moors from Spain in 1609. Coates adds that Cervantes moved to Valladolid in 1604, and published *Don Quixote* while living there in 1605; he suggests that B. might have derived some of the ideas for the appearance of the poet and the location of his house from the biographies of Cervantes available to him (see ll. 50–3n., 78–80n.). B.'s strong and enduring interest in *Don Quixote* makes this a plausible suggestion (see headnote to *Sordello*, I 366–7), and an early reviewer of *M & W*, Richard Simpson, also suggested Cervantes as a possible prototype (*The Rambler* n.s. v [1856] 54–71). On the other hand, there are features which do not correspond to early seventeenth-century Spain, e.g. references to coffee (l. 25), to 'bold-print posters' (l. 29) and to cribbage (l. 83), all of them of later date; there had been no 'Jewry' (l. 74) in any Spanish city since the Jews were expelled in 1492 (they did not begin to return until 1868). Arguably these touches of local colour were borrowed from B.'s observation of contemporary Italy (e.g. the Ghetto in Rome—cp. *Holy-Cross Day*, p. 540); it would not be untypical of B. to have to have compounded his Valladolid out of different materials, both historical and topographical.

Parallels in B. and Criticism

This is one of a number of poems in which B. reflects on his own art and on the role of the poet; cp. *Transcendentalism* (III 641), *Popularity* (p. 446), and *Memorabilia* (p. 553). The difficulty and obscurity of the poetic vocation are discussed again in the brief lyric '"Touch him ne'er so lightly"' which concludes DI^2 (1880); cp. also the *Epilogue* to *Pacchiarotto* (1876) and *At the Mermaid* from the same volume. In this last poem 'Shakespeare' makes thinly-veiled reference to Wordsworth (ll. 57–64), whose '[tale] adorned and pointed moral' enabled him to be crowned 'king', and disclaims all such ambition for himself. There may be a similar although less derogatory allusion in *How it Strikes*, which recalls in its portrait of the poet B.'s descriptions of Wordsworth in his 'court-habiliments'; see ll. 5–8n. The poet's death, surrounded by a 'relieving guard' and his fellow immortals (ll. 99–103), echoes the death of Aprile in *Paracelsus*, surrounded by a vision of 'White brows, lit up with glory; poets all!' (ii 599, I 188), a scene repeated less benignly at the climax of *Childe Roland* (ll. 193–204, p. 366); all these are ultimately indebted to the scene in Shelley's *Adonais* (ll. 262–315) in which the deathbed of Adonais (Keats) is visited by spirits who represent his poetic peers, among them Byron and Shelley himself. The assertion that the poet is '[the] town's true master if the town but knew!' (l. 40) is reminiscent of Shelley's assertion that poets are the 'unacknowledged legislators of the world' (*Defence of Poetry*); B. was of course deeply familiar with Shelley's poetry, but recent work on *Shelley* might have prompted a renewed acquaintance with it. The poet of *How It Strikes*, however, does not correspond exactly to either the 'subjective' or the 'objective' poet of B.'s essay: his close observation of character and social behaviour resembles the 'objective' poet's realism, while his relation to 'our Lord the King' (see ll. 66–71) resembles the 'subjective' poet's role as a kind of intermediary between human and divine realms. B.'s comment to Ruskin that '[a] poet's affair is with God' (see Appendix B, p. 882) clearly bears on the poet's relationship to the King (see esp. ll. 23–40); B.'s use of upper-case in pronominal references to 'our Lord the King' suggests that the King is God, although this is not consistent in editions before *1868*, when lower-case becomes uniform. The relationship may have an equivocal side, with the poet acting as a spy or informer on his fellow men:

note, in this connection, Sludge's story of a 'hunchback cobbler' in Rome who unobtrusively observes his neighbours and reports on their doings to the government (ll. 518–43, pp. 805–6).

Spain features much less frequently in B.'s poetry than France or Italy, and usually in connection with fervent Catholicism; cp. *Soliloquy of the Spanish Cloister* (p. 201) and *Confessional* (II 337). Coates, however, argues that the poem's setting in seventeenth-century Spain reinforces the Shelleyan understanding of the role of the poet; the only thing that is now remembered about the period in question is

> the sheer quality of the writers' response to the experience of the age and its neglect by a ruling group of singular mediocrity and folly. The favourite, the Duke of Lerma, or the Duke of Bejar, who ignored the dedication of *Don Quixote* . . . are dim figures whose doings, seemingly important at the time, are hard even for professional historians to lend substance to now. Browning could hardly have chosen a better example of the poet as witness and 'unacknowledged legislator' (p. 44).

Susan Hardy Aiken (*VP* xiii.2 [1975] 99–109), basing her argument in part on a speculative dating of the poem to 1851–52, notes the poem's emphasis on clothing as an indication of status and links it to Carlyle's discussion of the nature of heroism in both *Sartor Resartus* (1837) and *On Heroes and Hero-Worship* (1840); Carlyle describes Shakespeare as a 'poet-hero' 'sent to take note' of the world, and to give 'long-enduring record of it'. The speaker of the poem is, according to Aiken, a version of Carlyle's 'valet', who 'expects his heroes to advance in royal stage-trappings, with measured step, train borne behind him, trumpets sounding before him . . . The Valet does not know a Hero when he sees him!' (p. 107). Carlyle admired the poem: 'That old "*corregidor*" is a diamond— *unequalled* since something else of yours I saw' (letter of 4 Dec. 1855, publ. *Cornhill Magazine* [May 1915] 663).

> I only knew one poet in my life:
> And this, or something like it, was his way.
>
>   You saw go up and down Valladolid,
>   A man of mark, to know next time you saw.
> 5 His very serviceable suit of black

---

3. go up and down: like Satan in *Job* i 7; cp. *ED* 98n. (III 104).   *Valladolid*: on the possible significance of the poem's Spanish setting, see headnote.

4. 'A man of striking appearance, whom you would recognize the next time you saw him.' The primary sense is that the poet's dress and demeanour make him stand out from the crowd; but 'man of mark' also carries the connotation of a noteworthy or significant person, esp. in the public sense; cp., e.g., Trollope, *Framley Parsonage* (1861), ch. xxiii: 'Mr. Plantagenet Palliser was the Duke of Omnium's heir—heir to that nobleman's title and to his enormous wealth; and, therefore, was a man of mark in the world.' The poet, however, is a 'man of mark' not because of his wealth and position, but because of his divine vocation.

Was courtly once and conscientious still,
And many might have worn it, though none did:
The cloak that somewhat shone and shewed the threads
Had purpose, and the ruff, significance.
10 He walked and tapped the pavement with his cane,
Scenting the world, looking it full in face,
An old dog, bald and blindish, at his heels.
They turned up, now, the alley by the church,
That leads no whither; now, they breathed themselves
15 On the main promenade just at the wrong time.
You'd come upon his scrutinising hat,
Making a peaked shade blacker than itself
Against the single window spared some house
Intact yet with its mouldered Moorish work,—

6. courtly: fit to be worn at court; elegant.   *conscientious still*: 'still doing its duty'; as with the cloak and ruff in ll. 8–9 and the 'scrutinising hat' in l. 16, the suit's appearance is described in terms applicable to the wearer. With the speaker's good-natured condescension here, contrast B.'s satirical remarks to EBB. on Wordsworth's presentation to Queen Victoria in 1845 in borrowed and ill-fitting 'court-habiliments' (28 May 1845, *Correspondence* x 246).
9. ruff: the fashion for wearing ruffs is associated primarily with the late sixteenth and early seventeenth centuries; this reinforces the idea that the poet is set in early seventeenth-century Spain. The most widely disseminated portrait of Cervantes shows him wearing a ruff.
10. See headnote, *Sources*, for the possible reminiscence of B.'s sight of Béranger here.
12. Possibly alluding to EBB.'s adored and adoring spaniel, Flush, who was growing old in the 1850s. Flush had long been reconciled to B. (whom he had bitten twice in Wimpole Street) and there are frequent mentions in EBB.'s letters to his accompanying B. on walks around Florence. Since the summer of 1847 his beautiful curls were shorn because of the 'summer plague of fleas' in Florence (*Correspondence* xiv 341).
14. breathed themselves: took exercise.
15. the wrong time: i.e. at an unfashionable hour; in Spanish and other southern European cities the fashionable time for strolling on the 'main promenade' is usually early evening. See also l. 115n.
16. scrutinising hat: Aiken (see headnote, *Parallels*) suggests a reminiscence of Carlyle's description of Teufelsdröckh in *Sartor Resartus* (1837), his 'philosophical figure . . . with its steeple hat', 'pacing and repacing . . . that foolish street'.
18–19. On the extensive rebuilding occasioned by the relocation of the capital to Valladolid, see Coates (headnote, *Setting*). The destruction of the Moorish buildings may also (as Coates suggests) be intended to symbolize the final expulsion of the 'Moriscoes' (descendants of the Moors) from Spain in 1609. Cp. the 'Moorish front' which Luria designs for the cathedral in Florence, *Luria* i 121–31 (II 385). For a more modern source for the new building, see l. 22n.

20   Or else surprise the ferrel of his stick
        Trying the mortar's temper 'tween the chinks
        Of some new shop a-building, French and fine.
        He stood and watched the cobbler at his trade,
        The man who slices lemons into drink,
25   The coffee-roaster's brazier, and the boys
        That volunteer to help him turn its winch.
        He glanced o'er books on stalls with half an eye,
        And fly-leaf ballads on the vendor's string,
        And broad-edge bold-print posters by the wall.
30   He took such cognisance of men and things,
        If any beat a horse, you felt he saw;
        If any cursed a woman, he took note;
        Yet stared at nobody,—they stared at him,

20. ferrel: alternative spelling of 'ferrule', the protective ring at the end of the stick; in *1863* only, 'ferule'.

22. Coates (headnote, *Setting*) notes that French fashions and tradesmen were widespread during the rebuilding of Valladolid in the early seventeenth century. The association of 'French' with modern luxury shopping was also common in B.'s time, esp. in the mid-1850s when central Paris was being remodelled under the direction of Baron Haussmann.

23–40. For the parallel with *Mr. Sludge*, see headnote. With the scenes of street life here, cp. *Fra Lippo* 112–26 (p. 491) and (noting especially ll. 27–8) *Ring* i 38 ff.

25. the coffee-roaster's brazier: an anachronism if the poem is set in the early seventeenth century; coffee was very new to Europe in 1600.

26. its winch] his winch (*H proof*, but not *H proof*²).

27. glanced o'er] took in (*H proof*).

28. And] The (*H proof*). *fly-leaf*: used loosely for 'fly-sheet'; a 'flying sheet' is a short pamphlet or other printed work for street sale. The ballads here are hung on a string through the centre fold.

31–2. These two images of cruelty to animals (esp. horses) and insult to women appear together in a letter to EBB. of 18 Jan. 1846, prompted by her account of her father's domestic tyranny: 'I never *used* to dream unless indisposed . . . and *those* nightmare dreams have invariably been of *one* sort—I stand by (powerless to interpose by a word even) and see the infliction of tyranny on the unresisting —man or beast (generally the last)—I wake just in time not to die: let no one try this kind of experiment on me or mine! Tho' I have observed that by a felicitous arrangement, the man with the whip puts it into use with an old horse commonly: I once knew a . . . fellow, [who] . . . at a dinner party at which I was present, insulted his wife . . . brought the tears into her eyes and sent her from the room' (*Correspondence* xii 1). B. goes on to describe his indignant reaction to the latter incident.

33. Yet stared . . . they stared] He looked . . . they looked (*H proof*); Yet stared . . . you stared (*1868–88*).

And found, less to their pleasure than surprise,
35 He seemed to know them and expect as much.
So, next time that a neighbour's tongue was loosed,
It marked the shameful and notorious fact,
We had among us, not so much a spy,
As a recording chief-inquisitor,
40 The town's true master if the town but knew!
We merely kept a Governor for form,
While this man walked about and took account
Of all thought, said, and acted, then went home,
And wrote it fully to our Lord the King
45 Who has an itch to know things, He knows why,
And reads them in His bed-room of a night.
Oh, you might smile! there wanted not a touch,
A tang of . . . well, it was not wholly ease
As back into your mind the man's look came—
50 Stricken in years a little,—such a brow
His eyes had to live under!—clear as flint
On either side the formidable nose
Curved, cut, and coloured, like an eagle's claw.
Had he to do with A.'s surprising fate?
55 When altogether old B. disappeared
And young C. got his mistress,—was't our friend,

34–5. *their pleasure . . . them*] your pleasure . . . you (*1863–68*).

36. *loosed*: loosened (and elsewhere in B; cp. *Bishop Blougram* 58 [p. 289]).

39. *chief-inquisitor*. The most famous Chief Inquisitor of Spain, Tomás Torquemada, was born at Valladolid in 1420; B. may recall William Godwin's novel *St Leon* (1799), whose hero escapes from the Inquisition in Valladolid. For the Inquisition in B.'s work, see headnote to *Heretic's Tragedy* (III 219).

40. *but knew! / We merely kept*] but knew, / Which kept (*H proof*); but knew, / We kept (*H proof²*).

45. *He knows*: on the use of upper case for the divine pronoun in the poem, see headnote, *Parallels*.

47–8. *a touch, / A tang*: cp. *An Epistle* 67 (p. 515).

48. *it was not wholly ease*] 'twas not of easiness (*H proof*).

50–3. For the possible allusion to Carlyle and/or Cervantes here, see headnote. Cp. also the late poem *Imperante Augusto Natus Est* (*Asolando*, 1889) 120–2, in which the Emperor Augustus disguises himself as a beggar but is recognized by his countenance of authority: 'That unkempt careless hair—brown, yellowish,— / Those sparkling eyes beneath their eyebrows' ridge / (Each meets each, and the hawk-nose rules between)'.

52. *On either side the*] On either side o' the (*1872*); a rare example of a substantive variant unique to this text.

54–6. Cp. the use of initials by the revolutionary Luigi in *Pippa* iii 19–25 (p. 145).

His letter to the King, that did it all?
What paid the bloodless man for so much pains?
Our Lord the King has favourites manifold,
60   And shifts his ministry some once a month;
Our city gets new Governors at whiles,—
But never word or sign, that I could hear,
Notified to this man about the streets
The King's approval of those letters conned
65   The last thing duly at the dead of night.
Did the man love his office? frowned our Lord,
Exhorting when none heard—"Beseech me not!
Too far above my people,—beneath Me!
I set the watch,—how should the people know?
70   Forget them, keep Me all the more in mind!"
Was some such understanding 'twixt the Two?

I found no truth in one report at least—
That if you tracked him to his home, down lanes

58. bloodless: dispassionate. B.'s speakers invariably use this term pejoratively, to imply sexual and emotional frigidity: Guido in *Ring* xi 1416 ('All the poor bloodless creature never felt', of a eunuch), *Balaustion's Adventure* (1871) 1372 ('Stands forth a statue, bloodless, hard, cold bronze', of an old man), and *Fifine at the Fair* (1872) 173 ('sexless and bloodless sprite', of a woman). Cp. also *Pippa* i 249–50 (p. 113).

63. to this man] to the man (*H proof*, but not *H proof²*); see also l. 66n.

66. Did the man] Did this man (*H proof*, but not *H proof²*).

67. Exhorting] Reproving (*H proof*, but not *H proof²*).

69. The image of the watchman appointed by God is biblical: see e.g. *Isaiah* xxi 6.

71^72.] line 71 ends the page in *1855*, but the line space is confirmed by *1856* and other eds.

72–7. Cp. B.'s letter to EBB., 9 July 1845: 'tho' on other grounds I should be all so proud of being known for your friend by everybody, yet there's no denying the deep delight of playing the Eastern Jew's part here in this London—they go about, you know by travel-books, with the tokens of extreme destitution & misery, and steal by blind ways & bye-paths to some blank dreary house, one obscure door in it—which being well shut behind them, they grope on thro' a dark corridor or so, and then, a blaze follows the lifting a curtain or the like, for they are in a palace-hall with fountains and lights and marble and gold,—of which the envious are never to dream!' (*Correspondence* x 296). B. accompanied Mazzini on a visit to 'the house of a Jew-Merchant of Italian extraction' in London during 1845, according to Jane Carlyle (see letter of 18 Sept. 1845 to Thomas Carlyle; Clyde de L. Ryals, ed., *The Collected Letters of Thomas and Jane Welsh Carlyle* xix [1993] 202).

Beyond the Jewry, and as clean to pace,
75 You found he ate his supper in a room
Blazing with lights, four Titians on the wall,
And twenty naked girls to change his plate!
Poor man, he lived another kind of life
In that new, stuccoed, third house by the bridge,
80 Fresh-painted, rather smart than otherwise!
The whole street might o'erlook him as he sat,
Leg crossing leg, one foot on the dog's back,
Playing a decent cribbage with his maid
(Jacynth, you're sure her name was) o'er the cheese
85 And fruit, three red halves of starved winter-pears,
Or treat of radishes in April! nine—
Ten, struck the church clock, straight to bed went he.

My father, like the man of sense he was,
Would point him out to me a dozen times;

74. Beyond the Jewry] Beyond the Ghetto (*H proof*, but not *H proof²*). The sense of the line is that, although the streets leading to the poet's supposed residence lie beyond the Jewish quarter, they are just as filthy as if they were inside it ('as clean to pace' is ironic). The ghetto was usually overcrowded and insanitary; popular prejudice converted effect into cause with the image of the 'dirty Jew'. On the issue of there being a 'Jewry' in Valladolid, see headnote, *Setting*.

76. four Titians on the wall: B. alludes several times to Titian as the type of the sensual painter; see e.g. *Any Wife to Any Husband* 77–8 (III 652), *Ring* xi 2017–19: 'Give me my gorge of colour, glut of gold / In a glory round the Virgin made for me! / Titian's the man, not Monk Angelico', and *Filippo Baldinucci on the Privilege of Burial* (*Pacchiarotto*, 1876) 417–22 (describing a painting of Leda and the swan). B. would have known that Titian painted a series of erotic subjects drawn from classical mythology for King Philip II of Spain.

78–80. Coates (headnote, *Sources*) suggests that this description might be based on Cervantes' house in Valladolid, which was similarly modest.

79.] In that third, stuccoed, new house, by the bridge, (*H proof*); In that new stuccoed third house by the bridge, (*1868–88*).

80. rather smart than otherwise!] more genteel than otherwise; (*H proof*).

83. decent cribbage: both 'a tolerable standard of cribbage' and 'a respectable pastime' (as opposed to the narrator's fantasy of the 'twenty naked girls'). The game of cribbage is claimed by John Aubrey (in his *Brief Lives*) to have been invented by the Cavalier poet Sir John Suckling (1609–42); see headnote, *Setting*.

84. Jacynth: for the possible source of this name in *Gil Blas*, see headnote; the Duchess's maid in *Flight of the Duchess* (II 295) is called Jacynth.

85. And fruit] And wine (*H proof*, but not *H proof²*).

87. straight to bed] and to bed (*H proof*).

88–98. The allusions work at both the literal and metaphorical levels. The speaker's father knows that the poet is only metaphorically the 'Corregidor' (the town's magistrate); the speaker confuses the actual Corregidor with the town crier, but the latter also functions as a metaphor for an inferior type of popular poet.

90   "St-St," he'd whisper, "the Corregidor!"
      I had been used to think that personage
      Was one with lacquered breeches, lustrous belt,
      And feathers like a forest in his hat,
      Who blew a trumpet and proclaimed the news,
95   Announced the bull-fights, gave each church its turn,
      And memorized the miracle in vogue!
      He had a great observance from us boys—
      I was in error; that was not the man.

      I'd like now, yet had haply been afraid,
100   To have just looked, when this man came to die,
      And seen who lined the clean gay garret's sides
      And stood about the neat low truckle-bed,
      With the heavenly manner of relieving guard.
      Here had been, mark, the general-in-chief,
105   Thro' a whole campaign of the world's life and death,
      Doing the King's work all the dim day long,
      In his old coat, and up to his knees in mud,
      Smoked like a herring, dining on a crust,—
      And now the day was won, relieved at once!

90. Corregidor: magistrate; for the possible source of B.'s use of this term, see headnote.
96. memorized: memorialized, celebrated. *the miracle in vogue:* although the speaker is himself a Catholic, he pokes fun at the excesses of popular superstition; cp. *Up at a Villa* 51–2 (III 148) and *Bishop Blougram* 728n. (p. 326).
98. I was in error] We were in error (*1863–88*).
99–103. For the possible allusion to Shelley's *Adonais,* and parallels with *Paracelsus* and *Childe Roland,* see headnote.
100. when this man] when that man (*H proof,* but not *H proof²*).
101. garret's sides] garret sides (*1868–1872*); garret-sides (*1888*). The 'garret' or attic-room was the traditional dwelling of the impoverished poet or artist; cp. *Time's Revenges* 30 (II 281) and *Youth and Art* (p. 700). Several of Béranger's poems concern the life of the artist in the humble 'grenier'.
102. truckle-bed: 'a bed that runs on wheels under a higher bed' (*J.*). *J.* cites Samuel Butler's *Hudibras,* which B. knew well: 'If he that is in battle slain, / Be in the bed of honour lain; / He that is beaten may be said, / To lie in honour's truckle-bed' (I iii 1047–50).
105. Thro' a whole campaign] A whole campaign (*H proof*).
107. up to his knees] up to knees (*1868–88*).
108. Smoked like a herring: presumably because of the heat and bustle of the poorer part of town (cp. ll. 23–40n.); but there may also be a reminiscence here of William Allingham's poem *Cant* (1850): 'When the altar-fire he's stirring / To roast and stew, / As if for cure of souls, like herring, / The smoke would do' (ll. 5–8).

110 No further show or need for that old coat,
    You are sure, for one thing! Bless us, all the while
    How sprucely we are dressed out, you and I!
    A second, and the angels alter that.
    Well, I could never write a verse,—could you?
115 Let's to the Prado and make the most of time.

110–13. Cp. *1 Corinthians* xv 51–3: 'We shall not all sleep, but we shall be changed, in a moment, in the twinkling of an eye, at the last trump: for the trumpet shall sound, and the dead shall be raised incorruptible, and we shall be changed'. The 'old coat' is in this sense a metaphor for the mortal body; but cp. also *Revelation* iii 5: 'He that overcometh, the same shall be clothed in white raiment; and I will not blot his name out of the book of life'.
115. Prado: according to Thackeray, in a footnote to l. 15 of 'The Excellent New Ballad of Mr. Peel at Toledo', the Prado is 'the Hyde Park of Madrid, where the nobility drive about in their tertulias, and the idlers pass their time in dancing the Muchacha, etc., and amusing themselves with "cigars" and "guitars"'. Other towns also had their 'Prado'; scene xi of W. E. Aytoun's *Firmilian; or, The Student of Badajoz* (1854) ends with the 'First Gentleman' saying to the second: 'Let us go / Towards the Prado'.

29 Popularity

Text and publication
First publ. *M & W*, 10 Nov. 1855; repr. *1863*, *1865²*, *1868*, *1880*, *1888*. Our text
is *1855*.

Composition and date
The direct allusion to Keats at the end of the poem, and the strong likelihood
that he was the model for the 'true poet' of the poem, suggest a date following
the publication in 1848 of Richard Monckton Milnes's *Life, Letters, and Literary
Remains of John Keats*, important for the establishment of Keats's fame beyond
a devoted circle of admirers (who included B.: see below). The subject of his
own popularity was on B.'s mind throughout the 1840s, but was sharpened by
the relative ill success of *CE & ED* in 1850; in the same year his friend and rival
Tennyson published *In Memoriam* and became Poet Laureate, and EBB.'s poetry
continued to outsell his own. A date between 1850 and 1854 seems likely; the
poem may be close to the letter in which B. told his friend Joseph Milsand that
he was writing lyrics as 'a sort of first step towards popularity' (24 Feb. 1853;
first publ. in *Revue Germanique* xii [1921] 253).

Background and contexts

(i) *Keats*
The 'true poet' (l. 1) is a generic figure, but B. clearly has in mind the exemplary case of John Keats (1795–1821). Keats himself spoke of 'the attack made
on me in "Blackwood's Magazine" and the "Quarterly Review"' in a letter to
George and Georgiana Keats of Oct. 1818, first published by Milnes, with
the comment: 'This is a mere matter of moment: I think I shall be among the
English Poets after my death.' Keats features prominently in a discussion, early
in the courtship correspondence, of the issue of popularity as against posthumous
esteem for poets. In a letter of 3 Feb. 1845 EBB. writes: 'It appears to me that
poets who, like Keats, are highly susceptible to criticism, must be jealous, in their
own persons, of the future honour of their works. Because if a work is worthy,
honour must follow it—though the worker should not live to see that following or overtaking' (*Correspondence* x 52). In his letter of 11 Feb. 1845 B.
responded: 'for Keats and Tennyson to "go softly all their days" for a gruff word
or two is quite inexplicable to me' (*Correspondence* x 71). But in a later letter
to Julia Wedgwood of 18 Feb. 1865 B. wrote more sympathetically about
Keats's response to criticism, and linked his unpopularity with his own long-
standing admiration:

> I believe Keats *did* have death accelerated, if not induced, by that criticism.
> He did not put finger in eye, nor bully—but certainly felt strongly, what we
> feel strongly: don't believe a man of average sensibility is ever insulted by a
> blackguard without suffering enough: despise it? yes,—but you feel the slap in
> the face, too: and, in this case, to feel anything unduly was to spill the fast-
> lessening life: 'the seeds of death were in him already', say the foolish
> people:—why quicken them under a melon-glass then? Next, his personal
> discomforts were infinitely increased—that is, his death was hastened—by poverty
> . . . this came, or was not hindered coming, by the criticism which stopped
> the sale of his books.—what poor fraction *could* have fallen to his share, when,

at least six years after his death, I sent to his publisher and got a copy of each first edition?—no second having been called for even then . . .

(RB & JW 128–9, corr. from MS at *ABL)*

Cp. also Domett *Diary* 194 (entry for 2 June 1877) recording B.'s account of a conversation between Keats and the painter Joseph Severn, who looked after him in his last illness, and whom B. subsequently met in Florence:

> [Severn] found Keats, who was diligently studying Italian, deep in Ariosto: 'Fine—isn't it?' said Severn. 'Yes', answered Keats sadly; and then, tapping his own forehead, 'but there's something here that could equal it, if they would give me but a chance.' I [Domett] said, 'And I believe he would have done it, had he lived'. 'Aye', said Browning, 'and beaten it too!' and then expressed as high an opinion of Keats's extraordinary powers of imagination and especially of poetic diction as the several allusions to Keats in his own poetry shew he has always held.

Keats's singular quality is again emphasized in *One Word More* 165 (p. 613). In the opening lines of *Two Poets of Croisic* (1877) the speaker, sitting by his fireside, plays 'an old nurse-taught game' in which the sparks represent 'the flights / From earth to heaven of hero, sage and bard', with the difference that their fates are still undecided, so that, by a kind of wish-fulfilment, 'New long bright life' may be awarded to 'some prematurely lost / Child of disaster': the example given is 'Octogenarian Keats' (ll. 17–32). Cp. also *Christopher Smart (Parleyings*, 1887) in which Smart is praised as the only poet 'out of throngs between / Milton and Keats' who 'pierced the screen / 'Twixt thing and word, lit language straight from soul' (ll. 111–14). B. was personally acquainted with several of Keats's friends, including Milnes and Leigh Hunt as well as Severn. In EBB.'s *A Vision of Poets* (1844) the poet complains that poets 'are scorned / By men they sing for, till inurned' (ll. 59–60): the first example is 'English Keats' (l. 84).

In a letter to EBB., B. contrasted two attitudes to lack of popular acclaim: Blake's, of indifference, and Haydon's, of anger:

> —That letter [Haydon's] about the glory of being a painter 'if only for the neglect' is most touching and admirable ... *there* is the serene spot attained, the solid siren's isle amid the sea; and while *there*, he was safe and well ... but he would put out to sea again, after a breathing time, I suppose: though even a shorter strip of land was enough to maintain Blake, for one instance, in power and glory thro' the poor, fleeting 'sixty years'—then comes the rest from cartooning and exhibiting—But, there is no standing, one foot on land and one on the waves, now with the high aim in view, now with the low aim . . .

(Correspondence xiii 140)

See also below *(Hobbs, Nobbs, Stokes and Nokes)* for the account by Edmund Gosse of the poem which B. planned, but never executed, on a similar subject. In a letter to B. of 9 Sept. 1845 EBB. wrote: 'you are *not* looking well at all . . . you should & must care to consider how unavailing it will be for you to hold those golden keys of the future with a more resolute hand than your contemporaries, should you suffer yourself to be struck down by the gate' *(Correspondence* xi 66). In the same letter she mentions a letter from Mrs Carlyle (current whereabouts unknown) containing 'as ingenious "a case" against poor Keats, as could well be drawn'. The conjunction could have influenced B.'s conception of *Popularity.*

B. may have known John Clare's essay, 'Popularity in Authorship' *(European Magazine* n.s. i [1825–6] 300–2), in which Clare makes the case that 'popularity is not the forerunner of fame's eternity'.

(ii) *The star*

Lines 1–15 of the poem depict the 'true poet' as a star, whose brilliance is recognized by the speaker but not by 'this dark world'. The speaker goes on to suggest that this lack of recognition is providential: God is keeping the poet's 'light' in reserve, in order to illuminate future ages. R. D. Altick (*VP* i [1963] 65–6) points out that Milnes reprints a sonnet sent to Keats by an admirer which begins: 'Star of high promise! Not to this dark age / Do thy mild light and loveliness belong' and foresees his future fame: 'Yet thy clear beam shall shine through ages strong, / To ripest times a light and heritage' (*Life, Letters, and Literary Remains of John Keats*, i 254; see headnote, *Composition*). But note the lines from the end of *Paracelsus* cited below (*B. and popularity*), which make it clear that B. had long had such an image in mind. Cp. also the concluding lines of *Adonais*, Shelley's elegy for Keats: 'The soul of Adonais, like a star / Beacons from the abode where the eternal are.' The image of God's hand which 'locks [the poet] safe' may have been suggested to B. by Henry Vaughan's 'They are all gone into the world of light!' (1655): 'If a star were confined into a tomb / Her captive flames must needs burn there; / But when the hand that locked her up, gives room, / She'll shine through all the sphere' (ll. 29–32). B. often uses the image of God's hand as a guiding or controlling force, e.g. *Ring* i 40–1, where 'a Hand / Always above my shoulder, pushed [him] once' to find the Old Yellow Book. See also l. 6n.

(iii) *The murex*

The central portion of the poem (ll. 21–50) consists of an extended simile comparing the 'true poet' to a fisherman of 'Tyre the Old' (i.e. the city famous in biblical and classical history) who has landed a 'netful' of 'Tyrian shells', the source of a precious dye, enough to colour the curtains of the throne room of Solomon's royal palace. The shell is the murex (l. 64): 'Any of various predatory gastropod molluscs of the genus *Murex* or the family Muricidae, found in tropical and temperate seas, which are distinguished by spiny shells and from some of which the crimson dye called Tyrian purple was formerly obtained' (*OED*). B. calls the colour of this 'dye of dyes' (l. 27) 'blue', perhaps, as *Turner* suggests, 'for reasons of rhythm, [or] perhaps because of Keats's sonnet to blue eyes, beginning: "Blue! 'Tis the life of heaven"' (p. 376). Line 21 declares that the history of the 'dye of dyes' is common knowledge; although this is not quite true, B. 'fished the murex up' from 18th-century sources which were less obscure in his time than in ours. One such is *The Fleece* (1757), a long poem on the wool trade by the aptly named John Dyer; Dyer mentions the murex twice (ll. 204–11, 591–9), in both passages emphasizing that it was the foundation of Tyre's wealth; in the second he ascribes the origin of the trade to a legendary Tyrian figure, Melcartus: 'when o'er the mouth / Of his attendant sheep-dog he beheld / The wounded murex strike a purple stain, / The purple stain on fleecy woofs he spread, / Which lur'd the eye, adorning many a nymph, / And drew the pomp of trade to rising Tyre'. The connection with Solomon is made in a poem by Matthew Prior, *Solomon on the Vanity of the World* (1718); in bk. ii Solomon describes how, in his vain quest for pleasure, he plundered the resources of the earth to adorn his palace: 'A thousand Maidens ply the purple Loom, / To weave the Bed, and deck the Regal Room; / 'Till Tyre confesses her exhausted Store, / That on her Coast the *Murex* is no more' (ll. 41–4). The fame of the murex in classical antiquity is glossed by Thomas Warton in a note to his 1753 translation of Virgil's Fourth Eclogue, a passage in which Virgil prophesies a golden age of natural, not manufactured luxury: 'No wool shall glow with alien colours gay, / The ram himself rich fleeces shall display / Of native purple' (ll. 47–9); Warton comments on the word 'purple' that 'Murex was a shell fish set about with spikes, from whence the Tyrian colour was obtained'. Finally, Christopher Smart (one of B.'s favourite poets) praises the murex 'who is good and of a precious tincture'—although he does so in *Jubilate Agno*, a poem B. could not have known since it was only released from God's clenched Hand in 1939.

(iv) *Hobbs, Nobbs, Stokes and Nokes*

The concluding lines of the poem (50–65) concern both the difference in talent between the 'true poet' and his followers and imitators, and the difference in the way they are treated by 'the world'. Clearly, the dye must be extracted from the live whelks before it can furnish Solomon's cedar-house, but what does this process signify and who undertakes it? For the poem to make sense, ll. 51–5, although their diction and tone are ambivalent and uneasy (esp. given the revision to l. 52 which replaces 'art' with 'cunning') must refer to what the *true poet* does—the long, slow business of transforming original ideas and perceptions into something which can be published (there is perhaps a pun on 'refines to proof' in l. 53). While this process is going on, 'the world stands aloof'—in other words, the true poet gets no recognition or material reward for his work. Instead, inferior poets exploit the new discoveries he has made, and make their fortune on the back of his labour. B.'s conflicted feelings about the economic aspect of literature, which lead him both to embrace and recoil from the energetic industrial process he describes in ll. 51–4, belong to a wider pattern of response in the period to the growth of literacy and the literary market; at the same time, the passage reflects an older, more traditional and satirical view of the pettiness and greed of hack writers who make a living by feebly imitating their betters—the view of Pope's *Dunciad*, or Byron's *English Bards and Scotch Reviewers*. The question of whether the artist who has actually produced 'the extract, flasked and fine, / And priced, and saleable at last' ought to benefit materially from its sale remained a vexed one for B. to the end of his life: see Edmund Gosse's account of the poem B. projected in the summer of 1889, about a young artist who indignantly abjures painting because he fails to win the prize he deserves: 'Mr. Browning . . . finally suggested the non-obvious or inverted moral of the whole, in which the act of spirited defiance was shown to be, really, an act of tame renunciation, the poverty of the artist's spirit being proved in his eagerness to snatch, even though it was by honest merit, a benefit simply material' (*Robert Browning: Personalia* [1890] 85–7).

(v) *B. and popularity*

B.'s divided feelings about popular success go back to the very beginnings of his career, and do not spring from his own experience as a published author. The artist's necessary obscurity, or neglect, or even rejection, as the condition of future glory, is already stated in *Paracelsus*, whose hero's dying words anticipate the star-image in *Popularity*: see v 882–9 (I 308). At the time these lines were written (1835), B. had published only one (anonymous) poem, *Pauline*, and could not really have based his whole attitude to popularity on the failure of that work. Similarly, although the much more wounding failure of *Sordello* is often held to be a watershed in his feelings about his own prospective fame, *Sordello* itself begins with a passage in which B. disavows popularity in favour of the judgement of his (dead) peers (i 35 ff., I 396), and ends with a polemical defence of his difficult verse: 'any nose / May ravage with impunity a rose—/ Rifle a musk-pod and 'twill ache like yours' (vi 877–9, I 768). The 'musk-pod' prefigures the 'murex' in *Popularity* as a symbol of originality and authenticity. The sources of B.'s attitude are rather to be found in literary and intellectual history than in his own experience; cp. e.g. Milton's *Lycidas* on the true reward of the poet who 'meditate[s] the thankless Muse':

> Fame is no plant that grows on mortal soil,
> Nor in the glistering foil
> Set off to th'world, nor in broad rumour lies,
> But lives and spreads aloft by those pure eyes,
> And perfect witness of all-judging Jove;
> As he pronounces lastly on each deed,
> Of so much fame in Heaven expect thy meed.
>   (ll. 78–84)

(These lines are virtually summarized by B. in his statement to Ruskin: 'A poet's affair is with God, to whom he is accountable and of whom is his reward'; see Appendix B, p. 647.) The Romantic conception of 'genius' contributed to this attitude, as did Carlyle's conception of the poet as hero; by B.'s time the link between the artist and the embattled prophet was a critical commonplace, which he deploys both in *Sordello* (iii 778–806, I 580–2) and in *One Word More* (ll. 73–99, pp. 606–8). The poet of *How It Strikes* (p. 435) is the mildest example of this fate, suffering merely from obscurity and respectable poverty.

Yet B. also clearly yearned for popularity, and took steps throughout his career to achieve it, e.g. by publishing his work during the 1840s in the cheap format of *Bells and Pomegranates* (see Appendix C, p. 883), or aiming *CE & ED* at the Christmas-book market created by Dickens (see headnote, III 34), or issuing *Ring* in monthly parts like a serial novel. In *Ring* itself there is a familiar snarl at the start: 'Well, British Public, ye who like me not, / (God love you!)' (i 410–11), but a more placatory tone at the end: 'So, British Public, who may like me yet, / (Marry and amen!)' (xii 835–6). B. had to come to terms with his growing fame in the 1870s, and had to resolve the paradox he expressed in another passage from his letter to Ruskin: 'I shall never change my point of sight, or feel other than disconcerted and apprehensive when the public, critics and all, begin to understand and approve me' (Appendix B, p. 882).

I

Stand still, true poet that you are,
    I know you; let me try and draw you.
Some night you'll fail us. When afar
    You rise, remember one man saw you,
5 Knew you, and named a star.

---

1. Cp. the opening lines of *Transcendentalism* (III 644) and *Dîs Aliter Visum* (p. 688).
3–4. *When afar / You rise*: when your fame is established in the future.
4. *remember*: cp. *Pauline* 206–7 (p. 23), addressed to Shelley: 'And if thou livest— if thou lovest, spirit! / Remember me'; with the imagining of a future in which the present will be remembered as the past, which is repeated at ll. 13–15, cp. *By the Fire-Side* 1–20 (pp. 459–60).

2

My star, God's glow-worm! Why extend
　　That loving hand of His which leads you,
Yet locks you safe from end to end
　　Of this dark world, unless He needs you—
10　Just saves your light to spend?

3

His clenched Hand shall unclose at last
　　I know, and let out all the beauty.
My poet holds the future fast,
　　Accepts the coming ages' duty,
15　Their present for this past.

4

That day, the earth's feast-master's brow
　　Shall clear, to God the chalice raising;
"Others give best at first, but Thou

6. *My star, God's glow-worm*: God's power is so great that he can hold a star in his hand as though it were no bigger than a glow-worm. 'My Star' is the title of one of the *M & W* poems (III 386).

9. *this dark world*: the best-known of the many instances of this phrase is in l. 2 of Milton's Sonnet XIX ('When I consider how my light is spent'), but there are also two in Shelley.

11. *His clenched Hand*] That clenched Hand (*H proof*, but not *H proof²*).

12, 14. On the 'duty / beauty' rhyme, see *Guardian Angel* 33–5n. (III 18), but note that 'duty' here does not mean 'obligation' but 'homage, reverence'.

13. Cp. EBB. to B., 17 Feb. 1845: 'I felt sure that as a poet you fronted the future' (*Correspondence* x 79). Cp. also EBB., 'A Lay of the Early Rose', ll. 121–4, where a poet speaks of 'Vaunting to come before / Our own age evermore, / In a loneness, in a loneness, / And the nobler for that oneness'.

16–20. In *John* ii, Jesus performs his first miracle at a marriage in Cana, turning water into wine: 'When the ruler of the feast had tasted the water that was made wine, and knew not whence it was . . . the governor of the feast called the bridegroom, and saith unto him, Every man at the beginning doth set forth good wine; and when men have well drunk, then that which is worse: but thou hast kept the good wine until now' (vv. 9–10). The speaker imagines God's release of the poet's 'light' as a gift which will astonish the world by its belatedness, it being a commonplace that the 'golden age' of poetry lay in the past. The term 'feast-master', which here replaces the biblical 'ruler' or 'governor of the feast', occurs in Alexander Brome's 'An Essay of the Contempt of Greatnesse' (*Songs and Other Poems*, 1661), although not with the same meaning, since it refers to God himself: '*God's* this feast-*Master*, who of every kind / With *store* of *various* blessings has supply'd / Our various *wants*, and *vast desires*' (ll. 171–3). B. reuses the term in *Aristophanes' Apology* (1875) 1348.

For ever set'st our table praising,—
20   Keep'st the good wine till now."

                            5
Meantime, I'll draw you as you stand,
     With few or none to watch and wonder.
I'll say—a fisher (on the sand
     By Tyre the Old) his ocean-plunder,
25   A netful, brought to land.

                            6
Who has not heard how Tyrian shells
     Enclosed the blue, that dye of dyes
Whereof one drop worked miracles,
     And coloured like Astarte's eyes
30   Raw silk the merchant sells?

                            7
And each bystander of them all
     Could criticise, and quote tradition

23–65. The process of 'drawing' the 'true poet' becomes the construction of an elaborate extended simile concerning him, with the usual markers of a simile ('like', 'as') omitted. On Tyre, the 'dye of dyes', and Solomon's 'cedar-house', see headnote, *Murex*. Cp. *Sordello* iii 11–16 (I 524–6) where the process is the reverse of the one described here: as a precious garment loses its dye in the ocean, 'so the stain / O' the world forsakes Sordello'.

23–5. The syntax in *1855* may be read in two ways: either it forms a narrative: 'I'll say that a fisher . . . brought his ocean-plunder to land', or it forms a picture: 'I'll say that you resemble a fisher . . . with his ocean-plunder which has been brought to land'. The latter is supported by the revision in l. 24 (see next note) and is more suited to the metaphor of drawing; it is as though the speaker is 'posing' his model.

24. *Tyre the Old*: Phoenician city, founded in the fifth millenium BC, eventually conquered by Alexander the Great in 332 BC, subsequently falling under Roman rule in 64 BC. For its dye manufacture, see headnote, *Murex*.   *his ocean-plunder*] with ocean-plunder (*1863–88*).

29. *Astarte's eyes*: Astarte (also known as Astarat and Astoreth) was the Phoenician goddess of fertility and reproduction and the principal deity of the port city of Sidon. As Astarte she was worshipped as far west as Carthage, Sicily, Sardinia and Cyprus. She was also the sister and co-consort of Baal, sharing this role with their sister Anath. King Solomon built a temple to her as Ashtoreth, near Jerusalem, for which God punished him (*1 Kings* xi).

How depths of blue sublimed some pall,
   To get which, pricked a king's ambition;
35 Worth sceptre, crown and ball.

8

Yet there's the dye,—in that rough mesh,
   The sea has only just o'er-whispered!
Live whelks, the lip's-beard dripping fresh,
   As if they still the water's lisp heard
40 Through foam the rock-weeds thresh.

9

Enough to furnish Solomon
   Such hangings for his cedar-house,
That when gold-robed he took the throne

---

33. sublimed: made sublime.   *pall*: the technical term for the royal robe, used in coronations; *OED* cites a book on monarchical ritual of 1847: 'This now called "Royal Robe" is the ancient pallium; the "open pall" as it is called in the orders of Charles II and James II.' But B. is drawing on a complex set of associations, beginning with the original sense of 'fine or rich cloth (as a material); esp. as used for the robes of persons of high rank'. The word has a special association with purple: in Old English it was a synonym for 'purple (cloth)'; Spenser uses the idiom 'purple and pall' as one of his poetic archaisms in *The Shepherd's Calendar* (1579; 'July', l. 173), and in *The Faerie Queene* uses 'pall' in the sense of 'garment': 'In a long purple pall, whose skirt with gold / Was fretted all about, she was arrayed' (II ix 37–8). The sense of 'pall' as 'a cloth, usually of black, purple, or white velvet, spread over a coffin, hearse, or tomb' is also present, since a king might well be imagined as making extravagantly luxurious provision for his funeral; the word had recently been used in this sense by Tennyson in *Ode on the Death of the Duke of Wellington* (1852; l. 6).

35. All items in royal regalia: the ball is the orb.

38. whelks: poetic licence: technically the murex is not a whelk. The phrase 'Tyrrhene whelks' occurs in *Sordello* (see ll. 23–65n.). See also l. 51n.   *the lip's-beard*] each lip's beard (*1863–88*).

41. B. names King Solomon nineteen times in his poetry, usually in connection with his regality and his building of the Temple. Cp. esp. *Abt Vogler* 3–8 (pp. 762–3) and the late poem *Solomon and Balkis* (*Jocoseria*, 1883).

42. cedar-house: cedar was an important component of the temple built by Solomon for the Lord: 'So he built the house, and finished it; and covered the house with beams and boards of cedar' (*1 Kings* vi 9).

43. the throne: 'Moreover the king made a great throne of ivory, and overlaid it with the best gold' (*1 Kings* x 18).

In that abyss of blue, the Spouse
45   Might swear his presence shone

10

Most like the centre-spike of gold
    Which burns deep in the blue-bell's womb,
What time, with ardours manifold,
    The bee goes singing to her groom,
50   Drunken and overbold.

11

Mere conchs! not fit for warp or woof!
    Till art comes,—comes to pound and squeeze
And clarify,—refines to proof
    The liquor filtered by degrees,
55   While the world stands aloof.

12

And there's the extract, flasked and fine,
    And priced, and saleable at last!
And Hobbs, Nobbs, Stokes and Nokes combine

44. the Spouse: in the *Song of Songs*, traditionally attributed to Solomon, the beloved is often addressed as 'my spouse'.
46–50. Solomon, wearing a golden robe, sits on his throne surrounded by blue 'hangings': he is compared to the yellow anther of a bluebell, and this image in turn is associated with an erotic symbol, the bee which gathers pollen. The 'spouse' is attracted to Solomon as the bee is attracted to the plant: the bluebell is her 'groom' (contrast *Women and Roses* 28–32 [III 238], where the bee is male and the flower female).
48. What time: i.e. 'while': an archaism.
51. The train of thought dropped at l. 40 resumes here.   *conchs*: combining *OED* senses 1 and 2: a 'conch' can be a shellfish, or (noting the force of 'mere'), the shell of such a shellfish.   *not fit for warp or woof*: not fit for being used with textiles (the 'warp' and 'woof' are the vertical and horizontal threads on a weaving loom).
52. Till art comes,—comes] Till cunning comes (*1863*); Till cunning come (*1865–88*). *1863* may be misprinted, since it has 'refine' in the next line.
53. refines to proof: the sense is, 'distills to its essence': 'proof' refers to the alcoholic strength of the 'liquor' to which the dye is being compared.   *refines*] refine (*1863–88*).
58. B. was fond of these generic names: cp. his letter of 23 Mar. 1840 to Domett in which he attempts to explain the difficulty of *Sordello* by reference to his habit of writing for imaginary 'lovers' (of his verse) rather than real people: 'whence it happens that precisely when "lovers" one and all bow themselves out at the book's conclusion . . . enter (according to an old stage direction) two fishermen

To paint the future from the past,
60   Put blue into their line.

                        13

Hobbs hints blue,—straight he turtle eats.
  Nobbs prints blue,—claret crowns his cup.
Nokes outdares Stokes in azure feats,—
  Both gorge. Who fished the murex up?
65   What porridge had John Keats?

---

to the one angel, Stokes and Nokes to the author of "Venice" [i.e. Domett himself] (who *should* have been there *comme de droit*, had I known him earlier)—and [Stokes and Nokes] ask, reasonably enough, why the publication is not confined to the aforesaid brilliant folks, and what do hard boards and soft paper solicit if not *their* intelligence, such as it may be? I wish I had thought of this before— meantime I am busy on some plays (those advertised) that shall be plain enough if my pains are not thrown away—and in lieu of Sir Philip [Sidney] & his like, Stokes may assure himself that I see *him*—(first row of the pit, under the second Oboe, hat between legs, play-bill on a spike, and a "comforter" round his throat "because of the draught from the stage"—) and unless *he* leaves off sucking his orange at the pathetic morsels of my play—I hold them naught' (*Correspondence* iv 261–2). *Turner* (p. 377) suggests a reference to poets of the 'Spasmodic' school (P. J. Bailey, A. Smith, S. Dobell etc.): see J. Thale, *JEGP* liv (1955) 348–54; C. C. Watkins, *JEGP* lvii (1958) 57–9.

59. I.e. to use the dead artist's discoveries to secure a name for themselves.

60. Altick draws attention to the 'capacious pun' on the word 'line': '(a) "line" in the artist's sense" ("Let me try and draw you"); (b) "line" of verse; (c) "line" as a commercial term ("priced and saleable at last!"); and (d) "line" as "lineage" ' ('Memo to the Next Annotator of Browning', *VP* i, no. 1 [1963] 66).

61. *he turtle eats*: associated with luxury: turtle soup was a cherished Victorian delicacy: in Dickens's *Hard Times* (1854) the harsh employer Bounderby interprets any complaint on the part of his workforce as expressing the desire to 'eat turtle soup and venison with a golden spoon': cp. *Pied Piper* 45^46n. (p. 176).

62. *claret crowns his cup*: 'crowns' in the sense of 'fill to overflowing, or till the foam rises like a crown above the brim' (*OED*); the image is apt for Keats's love of claret, attested in letters and poems; his letter to Fanny Keats of 1 May 1819 ('a little claret-wine cool out of a cellar a mile deep') is close to the famous lines from 'Ode to a Nightingale' where fullness (and purple) feature: 'O, for a draught of vintage! that hath been / Cool'd a long age in the deep-delvèd earth . . . O for a beaker full of the warm South, / Full of the true, the blushful Hippocrene, / With beaded bubbles winking at the brim, / And purple-stainèd mouth' (ll. 11–12, 15–18).

63. *azure*: blue, with particular reference to the blue of the heavens.

64. *murex*: see headnote, *Background* (iii).

65. *porridge*: in his letter to his brother George of Oct. 1818, first publ. by Milnes (p. 152; see headnote, *Composition*) Keats remarks: 'I fed upon beef all the way, not being able to eat the thick porridge which the ladies managed to manage, with large, awkward, horn-spoons into the bargain.'

30 By the Fire-Side

Text and publication
First publ. *M & W*, 10 Nov. 1855; repr. *1863, 1865², 1868, 1872, 1888*. Our text is *1855*.

Composition, date and setting

Mrs Orr (*Life* 196–7) implies that the poem was written, or at least conceived, during the Brownings' visit to Bagni di Lucca in July–Oct. 1853, when, as EBB. wrote to Mary Russell Mitford, 'we mean to buy our holiday by doing some work' (*EBB to MRM* iii 388). Orr states that 'Mr. Browning's share of the work referred to was *In a Balcony*; also some of the *Men and Women*; the scene of the declaration in *By the Fireside* [sic] was laid in a little adjacent mountain-gorge to which he walked or rode'. William Wetmore Story, who was staying with his family nearby, records a 'constant & delightful intercourse' with the Brownings, 'interchanging long eve[nin]gs together two or three times a week & driving & walking together whenever we can meet . . . Both are busily engaged in writing. He on a new volume of lyrical poems & she on a tale or novel in verse' (*American Friends* 277). See also Appendix C, p. 890. Drawing on William Wetmore Story's letters, DeVane (*Handbook* 221–2) suggests that the ruined chapel of the poem stands beside the mountain path to Prato Fiorito; and, more recently, M. B. M. Calcraft has attempted to identify the chapel itself as the 'Oratorio della Madonna delle Grazie', alongside the river Refubbri near Bagni di Lucca (' "A Place to Stand and Love in": By the Refubbri Chapel with the Brownings', *BSN* xvi.1 (Spring 1986) 12–22; see *Thomas* figs. 235–6 for illustrations). Calcraft disputes DeVane's dating of the poem, linking it not to 1853 when the Brownings visited Bagni di Lucca in company, but to the more private visit undertaken during 1849 in the immediate aftermath of the death of B.'s mother and the birth of Pen. Jean Stirling Lindsay, in contrast, suggests that the poem is based not on an actual visit to Bagni di Lucca, but on a visit to Lago di Orta planned but never undertaken by the Brownings in 1847, and compares its descriptions of Alpine scenery with those to be found in Murray's *Handbook for Travellers in Switzerland, and the Alps of Savoy and Piedmont* (*SP* xxxix [1942] 571–9); see l. 43n.

The internal evidence of the poem, and in particular the complexity of its rhetorical structure, would appear to favour a later date: like *Women and Roses* (III 235) and unlike the earlier *England in Italy* (p. 254) which it otherwise resembles, it utilizes a structure of three tenses: the *present* situation of the speaker is in 'middle life' (ll. 101–50, 256–65), from which he projects himself imaginatively *forward* into old age (ll. 1–25), the better to evaluate a crucial experience in the *past* (ll. 26–100, 151–265). This process is complicated by his use of the historic present for all three layers: he addresses his future children as 'my friends'; and he communes with his 'perfect wife' as though they still both stood in the place and at the time he is recalling. This complex rhetorical structure makes it difficult to ascertain who is being addressed at certain moments; at l. 27 (for instance) it is not clear if the speaker is talking to his wife or merely imagining doing so. B. for his part sought to pre-empt inquiry into the circumstances of the poem's composition with the assertion that 'all but the personality [of the speaker and addressee] is fictitious—that is, the portraiture only is intended to be like—the circumstances are a mere imaginary framework' (letter to Revd James Graham, 6 April 1888; cited in G. David, 'Four New Browning Letters', *SBC* ii, no. 1 [Spring 1974] 62).

Sources and contexts

In spite of B.'s disclaimer the poem has generally been seen as one of his most directly personal utterances, and finds many parallels in the poets' correspondence. In a series of letters in the autumn of 1845 B. and EBB. exchanged ideas about marriage and what they each expected from it; cp., e.g., B.'s letter of 23 Oct. 1845: 'do you really think that before I found you, I was going about the world seeking whom I might devour,—that is, be devoured by, in the shape of a wife .. do you suppose I ever dreamed of marrying?—what would it mean for me, with my life I am hardened in,—considering the rational chances,—how the land is used to furnish its contingent of Shakespeare's-women . . . what do you meet at every turn, if you are hunting about in the dusk to catch my good, but *yourself?*' (*Correspondence* xi 135). See also ll. 141–5n. In a letter of 11 Jan. 1846 B. looks forward to his future with EBB.: 'now I most think of you in the dark hours that must come—I shall grow old with you, and die with you . . . Hear this said *now before* the few years, and believe in it *now, for then*, dearest!' (*Correspondence* xi 306–8). After the marriage, EBB. wrote to her sisters: 'Always he will have it, that our attachment was "predestinated from the beginning,": & that no two persons could have one soul between them so much as we' (21–4 Nov. 1846, *Correspondence* xiv 51); again on 7 Jan. 1847 she confided: 'What makes *him* perfectly happy is to draw his chair next mine & to let the time slip away' (*Correspondence* xiv 94). A letter from B. to Richard Hengist Horne of 3 Dec. 1848 describes the two poets '[sitting] here over the log-fire hearing wild news go in & out' (*Correspondence* xv 169). This impression of personal significance is reinforced by a number of possible allusions to EBB.'s poetry. The speaker's comparison of himself to a tree might 'answer' EBB.'s representation of B. as a 'strong tree' in *Sonnets from the Portuguese* xxix, and her representation of herself as a 'sere leaf' in 'The Weakest Thing'. This metaphor in turn seems to derive from an image in Felicia Hemans's 1826 poem 'The Forest Sanctuary' (I xi), as do some of the other details in this poem. Its hero, a Spaniard fleeing religious persecution, elopes with and marries a woman called Leonor, much to the displeasure of her father, who feels that she has 'cast darkness . . . on the clear renown' of her family's 'ancestral heritage of fame' (II xxix; see below l. 101n.). Both the Brownings were admirers of Felicia Hemans's work; her son presented EBB. with a copy of Mrs Hemans's *Commonplace Book* on 25 May 1854 (*Collections* A1166).

Married love was a popular topic in mid-Victorian poetry, as evidenced by the success of the first volume of Coventry Patmore's *The Angel in the House* in 1854 (on which see *A Face*, III 230). In Tennyson's 'The Miller's Daughter' (1842 ed.) there is a similar combination of intimate domestic talk and impassioned reminiscence; the poem's speaker invites his wife to revisit the millpond which had been the scene of their courtship: 'So sweet it seems with thee to walk, / And once again to woo thee mine— / It seems in after-dinner talk / Across the walnuts and the wine' (ll. 29–32); later passages anticipate the vocabulary and emotional tone of B.'s poem: ll. 215–18: 'Look through mine eyes with thine. True wife, / Round my true heart thine arms entwine / My other dearer life in life, / Look through my very soul with thine!' and ll. 235–8: 'But that God bless thee, dear—who wrought / Two spirits to one equal mind— / With blessings beyond hope or thought, / With blessings which no words can find'. A verbal similarity to Arthur Munby's 'Communion' (1852) is noted at l. 74. Munby's poem contrasts the love of the natural world, which is '[loving] and fair, but— blind!' with the stronger and more lasting desire for '[communion] with a human soul'. Donne's Platonic approach to heterosexual love, in particular in 'The Extasie', is another possible source, as is Shelley's version of this in *Epipsychidion* and other works. The Brownings were interested in the writings of Swedenborg in the 1850s, and his *Conjugial Love* may have influenced the poem's love philosophy (cp. head-note to *Evelyn Hope*, p. 274).

With the poem's setting (a remembered climb in wooded mountain scenery) and theme of intense emotional companionship, cp. Matthew Arnold's 'Resignation' (1849), where the couple are the poet and his sister (addressed as 'Fausta'); see, e.g., ll. 50–9:

> The valley-pastures, one by one,
> Are threaded, quiet in the sun;
> And now beyond the rude stone bridge
> Slopes gracious up the western ridge.
> Its woody border, and the last
> Of its dark upland farms is past—
> Cool farms, with open-lying stores,
> Under their burnish'd sycamores;
> All past! And through the trees we glide,
> Emerging on the green hill-side.

Ten years later they repeat the excursion, arriving at the same vantage-point: 'Here sit we, and again unroll, / Though slowly, the familiar whole' (ll. 94–5). Like B.'s poem, Arnold's contains detailed images of the remembered (and revisited) landscape, linked to thoughts about the persistence of identity and feeling:

> The loose dark stones on the green way
> Lie strewn, it seems, where then they lay;
> On this mild bank above the stream,
> (You crush them!) the blue gentians gleam.
> Still this wild brook, the rushes cool,
> The sailing foam, the shining pool!
> These are not changed; and we, you say,
> Are scarce more changed, in truth, they say.
>
> (ll. 100–7)

The mood of rapture in *By the Fire-Side* strongly contrasts with the 'resignation' which Arnold enjoins; B.'s poem may belong to the 'dialogue' with Arnold conducted in the 1850s (see headnote to *Cleon*, p. 563).

Parallels in B.

The title 'By the Fire-Side' is that of the second section of *James Lee* (p. 668), where it signifies not an ideal communion of souls but marital breakdown. Both *James Lee* and another poem from *DP*, *Dîs Aliter Visum* (p. 688), invert many elements of *By the Fire-Side*, including the gender of the speaker, who in the latter poem remembers a moment of (male) emotional cowardice. These poems date from after EBB.'s death, but failed marriages and the inability to achieve a desired complete union are not absent from *M & W*: see esp. *Two in the Campagna* (p. 556).

The action of the poem turns on the 'moment, one and infinite' (l. 181) which is one of B.'s most constant themes, with a particular importance in his love poems. In poems before *M & W*, cp. *Cristina* 33–40 (I 776); in *M & W*, cp. esp. the concluding stanza of *Last Ride* (III 285). Among post-*M & W* poems, cp. *Now* (*Asolando*, 1889), which begins 'Out of your whole life give but a moment!' and describes that moment as one 'which gives me at last / You around me for once, you beneath me, above me' (ll. 7–8) and as 'The moment eternal—just that and no more / When ecstasy's utmost we clutch at the core' (ll. 12–13); cp. also *A Pearl, a Girl* from the same volume. The metaphysics of this concept are expounded in *Prince Hohenstiel-Schwangau* (1871) 589–98: 'I suppose Heaven is, through Eternity, / The equalizing, ever and anon, / In momentary rapture, great with small, / Omniscience with intelligency, God / With man,—the thunder-glow from pole to pole / Abolishing, a blissful moment-space, / Great cloud alike and small cloud, in one fire— / As sure to ebb as sure again to flow / When the new receptivity deserves / The new completion. There's the Heaven for me.'

I

How well I know what I mean to do
     When the long dark Autumn evenings come,
And where, my soul, is thy pleasant hue?
     With the music of all thy voices, dumb
5   In life's November too!

2

I shall be found by the fire, suppose,
     O'er a great wise book as beseemeth age,   .
While the shutters flap as the cross-wind blows,
     And I turn the page, and I turn the page,
10   Not verse now, only prose!

---

3. Present for future: 'where, my soul, will thy pleasant hue be?' Cp. Disraeli, *Tancred* (1847), bk ii, ch xii: '"Because you have a soul," continued Tancred, with animation, "still of a celestial hue. They are rare in the nineteenth century. Nobody now thinks about heaven. They never dream of angels. All their existence is concentred in steam-boats and railways."'

4. of all thy voices] of thy voices (*H proof*).

5. life's November: with the exact phrase, 'life's November', cp. Bernard Barton, *The Twelve Months of Human Life* (1824) 139–44: 'And thus, in human life's November, / When sixty years and six are by, / 'Tis time that man should oft remember / "The hour approaches he must die!" / True, he may linger to four-score, / But death is waiting at the door!' With the concept, cp. *Macbeth* V iii 22–3: 'my way of life / Is fall'n into the sear, the yellow leaf'; and cp. also *Lovers' Quarrel* 134–40n. (p. 383). The events recorded in the poem are attributed to November too (see l. 55), so some kind of probably informal anniversary celebration might be involved.

7. a great wise book: cp. (noting 'Greek' in l. 12) *Development* (*Asolando*, 1889) 105–15, where the poet describes himself in old age reading Aristotle's *Ethics*.

7–8. as beseemeth age, / While] as beseemeth age; / How (*H proof*, but not *H proof²*).

8. cross-wind: usually a contrary, thwarting wind, as in *PL* iii 487–8: 'A violent cross wind from either Coast / Blows them transverse ten thousand Leagues awry'. Here it is not quite clear what the wind is contrary to; the sense is perhaps 'a vexatious wind', in that it makes the shutters flap.

10. Cp. Tennyson, 'The Miller's Daughter' (1842 ed.), ll. 191–4: 'So, if I waste words now, in truth / You must blame love. His early rage / Had force to make

3

Till the young ones whisper, finger on lip,
    "There he is at it, deep in Greek—
Now or never, then, out we slip
    To cut from the hazels by the creek
15 A mainmast for our ship."

4

I shall be at it indeed, my friends!
    Greek puts already on either side
Such a branch-work forth, as soon extends
    To a vista opening far and wide,
20 And I pass out where it ends.

5

The outside-frame like your hazel-trees—
    But the inside-archway narrows fast,
And a rarer sort succeeds to these,
    And we slope to Italy at last
25 And youth, by green degrees.

---

me rhyme in youth, / And makes me talk too much in age.' See ll. 52–3n., and headnote, *Sources*.

12–15.] no quotation marks in *H proof*.

13. Now or never, then,] Now then or never, (*H proof*, but not *H proof²*). *1863–65* revert to the word order in *H proof*, but with changed punctuation: 'Now, then, or never'; *1868–88* agree with *H proof*. This is a very rare example of B. returning in two stages to a reading which originates in proof.

17–20. By poring over the 'great wise book', the speaker gives the 'young ones' the slip (they believe him to be 'deep in Greek' while he is in fact daydreaming about his past); at the same time, the act of reading itself is the means by which he re-enters the landscape of memory. The children are off to play at exploration and adventure among the 'hazels by the creek'; the speaker imagines the physical and mental properties of reading Greek (the turning of pages, the shapes of the letters) forming an imaginative 'branch-work', like a pergola along which he makes his way towards the place he wishes to reach.

21. outside-frame: apparently B.'s coinage.

22. inside-archway: another of B.'s coinages. Cp. Tennyson, 'Ulysses': 'I am a part of all that I have met; / Yet all experience is an arch wherethrough / Gleams that untravelled world, whose margin fades / For ever and for ever when I move' (ll. 18–21). *narrows*] widens (*1865²*, *1868–88*).

23. rarer sort: i.e. a rarer sort of trees; cp. the description of the 'trees / Of rarer leaf' in Salinguerra's garden in Ferrara, *Sordello* iv 125–6 (I 600–2).

24–5. slope . . . by green degrees: lit., to descend in stages, as though memory were a path leading downward; note the original meaning of 'degree' as one of

6

I follow wherever I am led,
    Knowing so well the leader's hand—
Oh, woman-country, wooed, not wed,
    Loved all the more by earth's male-lands,
30 Laid to their hearts instead!

7

Look at the ruined chapel again
    Half way up in the Alpine gorge.
Is that a tower, I point you plain,
    Or is it a mill or an iron forge
35 Breaks solitude in vain?

---

a flight of steps; perhaps also influenced by the traditional way in which English travellers entered Italy by crossing the Alps; but B. may also be playing on a more recent, colloquial sense of 'slope', imported from America, as 'to amble off' or even 'to sneak off', since he is giving his 'friends' the slip. With the 'green degrees' cp. also Pope's translation of *Odyssey* vi 353–4: 'Around the grove a mead with lively green / Falls by degrees, and forms a beauteous scene'. There is also an affinity with the 'concrete abstractions' of Metaphysical poetry, as in Marvell, 'The Garden': 'Annihilating all that's made / To a green thought in a green shade' (ll. 47–8); B. may also have in mind the sense of 'green' as fresh and youthful.
27. the leader's hand: either his wife's, or the hand of a personification of Italy (see next note). On the question of addressees in the poem see headnote. The image inverts the motif of Orpheus leading his beloved wife Eurydice out of Hades, a theme B. treated in *Eurydice to Orpheus* (*DP*, from 1868); see also ll. 100–5.
28–30. B.'s personification of Italy as a beautiful and much loved woman, reiterated in *De Gustibus* (III 25), contrasts with the dominant iconography of Italian nationalism, which portrayed the 'woman-country' as the victim of foreign violation: see e.g. Byron's loose translation of Vincenzo Da Filicaia's sonnet 'Italia, O Italia' in canto iv of *Childe Harold*: 'Oh God! that thou wert in thy nakedness / Less lovely or more powerful, and could'st claim / Thy right, and awe the robbers back, who press / To shed thy blood, and drink the tears of thy distress' (ll. 375–9). Cp. EBB.'s rejection of such images at the beginning of *Casa Guidi Windows*: 'Of such songs enough, / Too many of such complaints!' (i 40–1).
31–5. For the actual landscapes on which B. may be drawing in the poem, see headnote.
31. ruined chapel: cp. Murray's *Handbook for Travellers in Switzerland* (1846): 'Behind the town of Orta a hill rises, on which there is a sanctuary, dedicated to St Francis of Assisi: over it are distributed 22 chapels or oratories' (p. 271).
32. Alpine gorge: Calcraft (see headnote, *Composition*) points out that the mountains near Carrara are known as the Alpi Apuane; but cp. l. 43n.
33. a tower, I] a tower which I (*H proof*); a tower I (*H proof*²).

8

A turn, and we stand in the heart of things;
 The woods are round us, heaped and dim;
From slab to slab how it slips and springs,
 The thread of water single and slim,
40 Thro' the ravage some torrent brings!

9

Does it feed the little lake below?
 That speck of white just on its marge
Is Pella; see, in the evening glow
 How sharp the silver spear-heads charge
45 When Alp meets Heaven in snow.

10

On our other side is the straight-up rock;
 And a path is kept 'twixt the gorge and it
By boulder-stones where lichens mock
 The marks on a moth, and small ferns fit
50 Their teeth to the polished block.

11

Oh, the sense of the yellow mountain flowers,
 And the thorny balls, each three in one,

36–40. Cp. *Pauline* 729–81on. (p. 54). Cp. also Murray, *Handbook*, p. 271: 'A steep path leads up the mountain side to Arola, amidst the richest vegetation.'
42. That speck] And the speck (*H proof*, but not *H proof²*).
43. Pella: the small town of Pella is on the shores of Lago di Orta, in the province of Novara (Piemonte); glimpsed from the mountains it might look like a 'speck of white'. As Jean Lindsay points out, B. might have obtained his information about this location from Murray's *Handbook*; see headnote.
46–55. Cp. the climb up mount Calvano in *England in Italy* 170–96 (pp. 263–4).
48–9. lichens mock / The marks on a moth: i.e. the pattern formed by the lichens on the rocks resembles (parodies) the marks on a moth's wings.
51. Cp. EBB., *Lessons from the Gorse*: 'Mountain gorses, ever golden . . . / Do ye teach us to be strong, / Howsoever pricked and holden / Like your thorny blooms, and so / Trodden on by rain and snow / Up the hill-side of this life, as bleak as where ye grow?' (ll. 1, 3–7).
52–3. B. probably refers to the fruit of the sweet chestnut (*Castanea sativa*) whose prickly outer casing often contains three nuts. Cp. Tennyson, 'The Miller's Daughter' (1842 ed.): 'Or from the bridge I leaned to hear / The milldam rushing down with noise . . . / Or those three chestnuts near, that hung / In masses thick with milky cones' (ll. 49–50, 55–6). See l. 10n.
52. And the thorny] And thorny (*1868– 88*).

The chestnuts throw on our path in showers,
　　For the drop of the woodland fruit's begun
55　These early November hours—

12

That crimson the creeper's leaf across
　　Like a splash of blood, intense, abrupt,
O'er a shield, else gold from rim to boss,
　　And lay it for show on the fairy-cupped
60　Elf-needled mat of moss,

13

By the rose-flesh mushrooms, undivulged
　　Last evening—nay, in to-day's first dew
Yon sudden coral nipple bulged
　　Where a freaked, fawn-coloured, flaky crew
65　Of toad-stools peep indulged.

53. *on our path in showers,*] in this path of ours (*H proof*).
56. 'That' is a relative pronoun referring to the 'early November hours': i.e. autumn is turning the foliage red.
58. *boss*: 'the part rising in the midst of any thing' (*J.*); here, the rounded knob at the centre of a shield, although the word can also refer to protuberances in plants. Cp. *Instans Tyrannus* 65 (III 263).
59–64. *fairy-cupped . . . Elf-needled . . . rose-flesh . . . fawn-coloured*: one of the densest clusters of compound epithets in B.; cp. *Pretty Woman* 1 (III 201), *Caliban* 40 (p. 627), and see B. W. A. Massey, *Browning's Vocabulary: Compound Epithets* (Poznau 1933).
59. *for show*] to show (*H proof*, but not *H proof²*). *fairy-cupped*: the 'mat of moss' (l. 60) is dotted with 'fairy-cups', either the cowslip (*Primula veris*) or harebell (*Campanula rotundifolia*); *OED* cites this line for the former definition: the word is B.'s coinage.
60. *elf-needled*: the moss is so finely textured that it might have been stitched by elves. References to elves and fairies are rare in B. (in contrast to, e.g., Tennyson or Christina Rossetti). B.'s coinage.
61. *By*: by the side of. *rose-flesh*: cp. *De Gustibus* 34 (III 27): 'green-flesh melons'.
63. *coral nipple*: i.e. the mushroom's coral-pink cap; the Apennines are famous for their wild mushrooms.
64. *freaked*: streaked, variegated; cp. Milton, *Lycidas* 144 ('the pansy freaked with jet') and James Thomson, *Winter* (1726) 814 ('freak'd with many a mingled hue'). *flaky*: the toadstools have a rough, irregular surface; B. probably has in mind *J.*'s second definition of 'flaky' as 'lying in layers or strata', not the first, 'loosely hanging together'.

14

And yonder, at foot of the fronting ridge
 That takes the turn to a range beyond,
Is the chapel reached by the one-arched bridge
 Where the water is stopped in a stagnant pond
70 Danced over by the midge.

15

The chapel and bridge are of stone alike,
 Blackish grey and mostly wet;
Cut hemp-stalks steep in the narrow dyke.
 See here again, how the lichens fret
75 And the roots of the ivy strike!

16

Poor little place, where its one priest comes
 On a festa-day, if he comes at all,
To the dozen folk from their scattered homes,
 Gathered within that precinct small
80 By the dozen ways one roams

68. the chapel reached by the one-arched bridge: the ruined chapel at Refubbri (see headnote) is reached via a one-arched bridge. Cp. *Ring* xi 9: 'The one-arched brown brick bridge'. In a letter to Isa Blagden of 19 July 1867, B. remarked: 'I would gladly ride with Annette [Bracken] once more up to the little old ruined chapel, by the bridge,—she may remember,—where we took shelter in a thunderstorm' (*Dearest Isa* 274).

73. Hemp (*Cannabis sativa*) is a plant used for making cheap clothing and ropes; the stalks here have been cut by the 'hemp-dressers' (l. 82) and left to 'steep' (soak) in the channel which leads to the 'stagnant pond'. See also *Up at a Villa* 34 (III 146).

74. lichens fret: lit., 'corrode, eat away' (*J.*). Cp. Arthur Munby, 'Communion': 'Old shaggy gnarls the lichen frets— / Steep banks of mountain lanes— / Moss-cushion'd arms of rivulets— / The hush of woodland rains' (ll. 97–100, and see headnote).

77. festa-day: the day of a religious festival; cp. *Ring* vii 967. Every Italian village has its patron saint and a day dedicated to festivities in his or her honour.

80–1. one roams / To drop] one roams— / Who drops (*H proof*); one roams— / To drop (*1863–88*). In *H proof* 'Who drops' (and 'Or [who] climbs' in l. 82) are in apposition to 'one roams', hence the dash; B. may then have decided that the *1855* construction 'one roams [in order] to drop' was awkward or unclear, and restored the dash so that 'To drop . . . or [to] climb' become examples of 'the dozen ways one roams'.

17

To drop from the charcoal-burners' huts,
　　Or climb from the hemp-dressers' low shed,
Leave the grange where the woodman stores his nuts,
　　Or the wattled cote where the fowlers spread
85　Their gear on the rock's bare juts.

18

It has some pretension too, this front,
　　With its bit of fresco half-moon-wise
Set over the porch, art's early wont—
　　'Tis John in the Desert, I surmise,
90　But has borne the weather's brunt—

19

Not from the fault of the builder, though,
　　For a pent-house properly projects
Where three carved beams make a certain show,
　　Dating—good thought of our architect's—
95　'Five, six, nine, he lets you know.

20

And all day long a bird sings there,
　　And a stray sheep drinks at the pond at times:
The place is silent and aware;

81–2. Cp. B's letter to George Barrett from Bagni di Lucca (16–18 July 1853): 'Then, we are quiet—for there's nothing civilized beyond us, on *this* side, but a few charcoal-burners' huts, the river & the woods' (*George Barrett* 195).
82. *Or climb*] Or climbs (*H proof*).
83. *Leave the grange*] Or the grange (*H proof*).
84. *wattled cote*: small shed made of interwoven canes; cp. Milton's *Comus* 343 and Arnold's 'Scholar-Gipsy', l. 2, where it means a sheep-fold. *fowlers*: bird hunters; their 'gear' (l. 85) is probably nets and poles, as in *England in Italy* 35 (p. 258).
86. *this front*: the facade of the chapel.
88. *o'er the porch*] over the porch (*H proof*). *art's early wont*: in the manner of early Renaissance church architecture (but see l. 95n.).
89. *John in the Desert*: John the Baptist, who preaches in the 'wilderness' (*Matthew* iii 1), a common subject in Renaissance painting.
90. Cp. the description of the damage suffered by early Italian art in *Old Pictures* 41–8, 185–92 (pp. 412, 423–4).
92. *pent-house*: a sloping roof over the porch.
95. The date '1569' does not quite fit the phrase 'art's early wont' in l. 88, which indicates (as in *Old Pictures*, 57–64, pp. 413–14) Italian art of the 'Quattrocento' or 15th century.
98. *aware*: 'Vigilant; in a state of alarm; attentive' (*J.*).

It has had its scenes, its joys and crimes,
100   But that is its own affair.

21

My perfect wife, my Leonor,
      Oh, heart my own, oh, eyes, mine too,
Whom else could I dare look backward for,
      With whom beside should I dare pursue
105   The path grey heads abhor?

22

For it leads to a crag's sheer edge with them;
      Youth, flowery all the way, there stops—
Not they; age threatens and they contemn,

99. *its joys*] and joys (*H proof*, but not *H proof²*).

101–10. A further possible allusion to the myth of Orpheus leading his wife Eurydice out of Hades (see l. 27n. and next note): he was warned not to look back at her as they went, but could not help doing so. Here, the husband looks 'backward' in time for his wife, with whom he remembers journeying from youth to age; it is this journey of memory which most old people cannot bear to undertake, because it leads to the end of youth and, by implication, love as well, but which in the speaker's case has led to his salvation.

101. *Leonor*: the name of the wife in Felicia Hemans's 'The Forest Sanctuary' (see headnote): 'And thou, my Leonor! that unrepining, / If sad in soul, didst quit all else for me, / When stars—the stars that earliest rise—are shining, / How their soft glance unseals each thought of thee! / For on our flight they smiled; their dewy rays, / Through the last olives, lit thy tearful gaze / Back to the home we never more might see; / So passed we on, like earth's first exiles, turning / Fond looks where hung the sword above their Eden burning' (II xxx). Leonora is also the name of the heroine of Beethoven's opera *Fidelio*, who, disguised as the title character, rescues her husband from imprisonment; the opera's subtitle is 'Die Eheliche Liebe' (Married Love). B. mentions the opera admiringly in a letter to EBB. of 15 Aug 1845 (*Correspondence* xi 29).

102. Cp. Donne, 'The Extasie', ll. 33–6: 'But as all several souls contain / Mixture of things, they know not what, / Love, these mix'd souls doth mix again, / And makes both one, each this and that'. See also *Lovers' Quarrel* 92–4 (p. 381) and *Two in the Campagna* 41–5 (p. 561). *Oh, heart my own, oh, eyes,*] Oh, heart my own, oh eyes, (*1865, 1865²*); Oh heart, my own, oh eyes, (*1868–88*). Cp. *Love Among the Ruins* 79n. (p. 539).

103. *could I dare look*] could I look (*H proof*).

107. *Youth, flowery all the way*: the association of youth, love, and a flowery path is traditional; cp. e.g. Samuel Daniel, *Delia* li 5–6: 'Ah sport (sweet Maide) in season of these yeares, / And learne to gather flowers before they wither: / And where the sweetest blossomes first appeares, / Let loue and youth conduct thy pleasures thither'.

108. *contemn*: 'To despise; to scorn; to slight; to disregard; to neglect; to defy' (*J.*).

Till they reach the gulf wherein youth drops,
110 One inch from our life's safe hem!

23

With me, youth led—I will speak now,
No longer watch you as you sit
Reading by fire-light, that great brow
And the spirit-small hand propping it
115 Mutely—my heart knows how—

24

When, if I think but deep enough,
You are wont to answer, prompt as rhyme;
And you, too, find without a rebuff
The response your soul seeks many a time
120 Piercing its fine flesh-stuff—

109. *the gulf . . . life's safe hem*: cp. Murray, *Handbook*: 'the path leads down through pastoral scenes . . . then changes almost suddenly to the deep gloom of a ravine.' With the image of the 'gulf', cp. *Old Pictures* 137–40 (p. 420). Cp. also *Ring*, in which the Pope twice describes Guido's desperate attempt to save his life, first in bk. i, by 'pressing up so close / Only to set a blood-smutch on our robe' (ll. 324–5), and again in bk. x: 'I sit and see / Another poor weak trembling human wretch / Pushed by his fellows, who pretend the right, / Up to the gulf which, where I gaze, begins / From this world to the next,—gives way and way, / Just on the edge over the awful dark: / With nothing to arrest him but my feet' (ll. 170–6). In *Christmas-Eve* (III 34) the speaker is transported around the world by clutching the 'hem' of Christ's garment.

111. *With me, youth led*—: the *aposiopesis* is total: we are not directly told what youth led to in the speaker's case. *I will speak now*: for the debate about whether the speaker means 'speak aloud', see headnote.

113–14. Cp. the description of EBB. in George Stillman Hillard's *Six Months in Italy* (2 vols., 1853) i 140: 'I have never seen a human frame which seemed so nearly a transparent veil for a celestial and immortal spirit'.

115. *Mutely*—] Mutely, (*1863–88*); the rev. reading makes clear that it qualifies 'speak' (l. 111), implying a form of unspoken or telepathic communication.

116–20. Mesmerism, telepathy and spiritualism were all popular and related topics in the 1850s. B.'s interest in mesmerism (involving telepathic communication) can be traced in his revisions to *Sordello*, drafted around this time (see headnote, I 358). The belief that lovers in particular could communicate wordlessly is suggested in many poems of Donne (e.g. *The Extasie*; see 102n., 127–30n.). Cp. *Mesmerism* (III 475), where telepathic communication is also posited.

118. *without a rebuff*] without rebuff (*1865–88*).

119. *The response*] Response (*1868–88*).

25

My own, confirm me! If I tread
    This path back, is it not in pride
To think how little I dreamed it led
    To an age so blest that by its side
125 Youth seems the waste instead!

26

My own, see where the years conduct!
    At first, 'twas something our two souls
Should mix as mists do: each is sucked
    Into each now; on, the new stream rolls,
130 Whatever rocks obstruct.

27

Think, when our one soul understands
    The great Word which makes all things new—
When earth breaks up and Heaven expands—
    How will the change strike me and you
135 In the House not made with hands?

---

123. how little I dreamed] how blind I was, (*H proof*).
127–30. At first their souls mingled as thoroughly as two mists, but over time they have condensed into a single substance. With this stanza cp. Donne, 'The Extasie', esp. ll. 41–4: 'When love, with one another so / Interinanimates two soules, / That abler soule, which thence doth flow, / Defects of loneliness controls.' See also *Confessional* 17–18n. (II 338) and *Any Wife to Any Husband* 50 (III 650).
129. Into each] In each (*1868–88*).
131. our one soul: cp. Donne, 'A Valediction, Forbidding Mourning', l. 21: 'Our two souls therefore, which are one', and Shelley, *Epipsychidion*: 'We shall become the same, we shall be one / Spirit within two frames' (ll. 573–4); 'Let us become the overhanging day, / The living soul of this Elysian isle— / Conscious, inseparable, one' (ll. 538–40). Cp. also EBB., 'Inclusions' (1850): 'Oh, must thou have my soul, Dear, commingled with thy soul?— / Red grows the cheek, and warm the hand; the part is in the whole: / Nor hands nor cheeks keep separate, when soul is joined with soul' (ll. 7–9).
132–3. Conflating two biblical sources: *John* i 1: 'In the beginning was the Word', and *Revelation* xxi 5: 'Behold, I make all things new'. Cp. also *Any Wife to Any Husband* 18 (III 649).
135. See *2 Corinthians* v 1: 'For we know that if our earthly house of this tabernacle were dissolved, we have a building of God, an house not made with hands, eternal in the heavens'. Cp. *Abt Vogler* 66 (p. 767).

28

Oh, I must feel your brain prompt mine,
   Your heart anticipate my heart,
You must be just before, in fine,
   See and make me see, for your part,
140   New depths of the Divine!

29

But who could have expected this,
   When we two drew together first
Just for the obvious human bliss,
   To satisfy life's daily thirst
145   With a thing men seldom miss?

30

Come back with me to the first of all,
   Let us lean and love it over again—

136–40. The stance here echoes that frequently adopted by B. in his letters to EBB.: 'I should like to breathe and move and live by your allowance and pleasure' (23 Apr 1846, *Correspondence* xii 272); 'I wish your will to be mine, to originate mine' (4 June 1846; *ibid.* xiii 22). Cp. the relation between Eglamor, the eternally secondary artist, and the genius whom he admires, in *Sordello* vi 793–814 (I 764–6); and contrast *Two in the Campagna* 36–50 (pp. 561–2).

138. Cp. *Love in a Life* 13 (III 2): 'Still the same chance! She goes out as I enter'.

139. See and make me see: cp., in *Sordello*, the description of the highest kind of artist, the 'Makers-see' who 'impart the gift of seeing to the rest' (iii 842, I 584).

141–5. Cp. EBB.'s letter of 21–4 Dec. 1845: 'People used to say to me, "You expect too much—you are too romantic"—And my answer always was that "I could not expect too much when I expected nothing at all"' (*Correspondence* xi 258). Later in the same letter she expressed her horror of conventional marriage: 'To see the marriages which are made everyday! worse than solitudes & more desolate!' (*ibid.* 259). But B. was prepared to defend what the poem calls 'the obvious human bliss', i.e. marriage as a social partnership rather than a mode of transcendent passion: 'if you look on the world *altogether*, and accept the small natures, in their usual proportion, with the greater .. things do not look *quite* so bad; because, the conduct which *is* atrocious in those higher cases, of proposal and acceptance, *may* be no more than the claims of the occasion justify . . . in certain other cases where the thing sought for and granted is avowedly less by a million degrees . . . He who honestly wants his wife to sit at the head of the table and carve .. that is be his *help-meat* (not "help mete for him"[)]—he shall assuredly find a girl of his degree who wants the table to sit at' (25 Dec. 1845, *ibid.* 262–3). For another quotation from this letter, see below, l. 234n., and see also headnote.

141. But who] And who (H *proof* but not H *proof*²).

146–50. Cp. the 'rosary' of memory in *England in Italy* 7–10: 'Let me keep you amused . . . with telling my memories over / As you tell your beads' (p. 257).

Let us now forget and then recall,
   Break the rosary in a pearly rain,
150 And gather what we let fall!

31
What did I say?—that a small bird sings
   All day long, save when a brown pair
Of hawks from the wood float with wide wings
   Strained to a bell: 'gainst the noon-day glare
155 You count the streaks and rings.

32
But at afternoon or almost eve
   'Tis better; then the silence grows
To that degree, you half believe
   It must get rid of what it knows,
160 Its bosom does so heave.

33
Hither we walked, then, side by side,
   Arm in arm and cheek to cheek,
And still I questioned or replied,
   While my heart, convulsed to really speak,
165 Lay choking in its pride.

34
Silent the crumbling bridge we cross,
   And pity and praise the chapel sweet,
And care about the fresco's loss,
   And wish for our souls a like retreat,
170 And wonder at the moss.

---

148. and then recall] and now recall (*1863–88*).

150. And gather] And pick up (*H proof*).

151–5. Cp. l. 96, although the hawks were not mentioned there; cp. *Woman's Last Word* 5–8 (III 274), where there are two birds and one hawk. Cp. also *Misconceptions* (III 680).

154. Strained to a bell: presumably, to the shape of a bell, with the hawks gliding.

155. streaks and rings: markings on the hawks' plumage.

158–60. The place needs to unburden itself of its secrets; cp. ll. 99–100.

161–5. Cp. the couple in *Dîs Aliter Visum* 101–10 (p. 696).

168. the fresco's loss: cp. *Old Pictures* 185–92 (pp. 423–4).

35

Stoop and kneel on the settle under—
  Look through the window's grated square:
Nothing to see! for fear of plunder,
  The cross is down and the altar bare,
175 As if thieves don't fear thunder.

36

We stoop and look in through the grate,
  See the little porch and rustic door,
Read duly the dead builder's date,
  Then cross the bridge we crossed before,
180 Take the path again—but wait!

37

Oh moment, one and infinite!
  The water slips o'er stock and stone;
The West is tender, hardly bright.
  How grey at once is the evening grown—
185 One star, the chrysolite!

38

We two stood there with never a third,
  But each by each, as each knew well.

171. settle: 'A seat; a bench; something to sit on' (*J.*).

175. The thieves might be expected to be superstitiously fearful that God would strike them dead if they stole from a church; but the church authorities are taking no chances.

179. we crossed] that we crossed (*1888*).

181. For the importance of this concept in B., see headnote, *Parallels.   Oh moment, one*] Oh, moment one (*H proof*); Oh moment one (*1872*).

182. stock and stone: see *Love Among the Ruins* 30n. (p. 535).

183–5. Cp. *Andrea* 35, 207 (pp. 392, 400). Perhaps derived from Keats, *Ode to a Nightingale* 35: 'Tender is the night'.

183. The West] emended in agreement with *H proof* and all other eds from 'The west' in *1855*; such agreement between proof and subsequent printed eds is rare, as is the restoration of upper case in eds after 1855.

185. one star: cp. *PL* viii 519–20: 'bid haste the evening star / On his hill top, to light the bridal lamp', and *Two in the Campagna* 52–5 (p. 562).   *the chrysolite!*] its chrysolite! (*1870–88*); a green semi-precious stone, the 'garnish' of the seventh foundation of the New Jerusalem (*Revelation* xxi 20); cp. *Othello* V ii 146–9.

186. with never a third: as Turner points out (p. 323), the courtship correspondence contains references to a fictional 'third person' who views the lovers' relationship from the outside; see letters of 31 Aug. 1845 (*Correspondence* xi 54); and the three letters dated 26 Feb 1846 (*Correspondence* xii 105–10). Cp. ll. 228–30.

The sights we saw and the sounds we heard,
  The lights and the shades made up a spell
190 Till the trouble grew and stirred.

39

Oh, the little more, and how much it is!
  And the little less, and what worlds away!
How a sound shall quicken content to bliss,
  Or a breath suspend the blood's best play,
195 And life be a proof of this!

40

Had she willed it, still had stood the screen
  So slight, so sure, 'twixt my love and her.
I could fix her face with a guard between,
  And find her soul as when friends confer,
200 Friends—lovers that might have been.

41

For my heart had a touch of the woodland time,
  Wanting to sleep now over its best.

191–5. Cp. *Lovers' Quarrel* 106–12 (p. 382). *Oxford* notes a possible source in *Tristram Shandy*, vol. ii, ch. 6: 'Just heaven! how does the *Poco più* and the *Poco meno* of the Italian artists;—the insensible MORE or LESS, determine the precise line of beauty in the sentence, as well as in the statue!'

196–7. Cp. B.'s very first letter to EBB., lamenting the fact that he had missed seeing her on a previous occasion: 'I feel as at some untoward passage in my travels—as if I had been close, so close, to some world's-wonder in chapel or crypt, only a screen to push and I might have entered, but there was some slight .. so it now seems .. slight and just-sufficient bar to admission, and the half-opened door shut, and I went home my thousands of miles, and the sight was never to be!' (10 Jan. 1845; *Correspondence* x 17) Cp. *Pauline* 4–5: 'a screen / To shut me in with thee, and from all fear' (p. 13), *Lovers' Quarrel* 140 (p. 383), and the image in Henry Alford's 'An Answer to a Question': 'When the thing thou lovest puts a screen / Thy heart and thy heart's Christ between' (ll. 3–4). Mary Russell Mitford gave EBB. a copy of Alford's *Poems and Poetical Fragments* (1833) in which this poem appeared (*Correspondence* iv 16).

196. willed it] willed so (*H proof*).

198. fix: see *Cristina* l. 8n. (I 775).

201–10. The speaker suggests that he might have allowed the 'screen' to remain between himself and his wife because his heart was like a tree in winter with just one leaf left on it; had he been in his prime he could have withstood many such tests. This metaphor might answer EBB.'s representation of herself as a 'wild vine' wrapping itself around a 'strong tree' (*Sonnets from the Portuguese* xxix); see

Shake the whole tree in the summer-prime,
　　But bring to the last leaf no such test.
205　"Hold the last fast!" says the rhyme.

42

For a chance to make your little much,
　　To gain a lover and lose a friend,
Venture the tree and a myriad such,
　　When nothing you mar but the year can mend!
210　But a last leaf—fear to touch.

43

Yet should it unfasten itself and fall
　　Eddying down till it find your face
At some slight wind—(best chance of all!)
　　Be your heart henceforth its dwelling-place
215　You trembled to forestal!

---

headnote. This passage also recalls EBB.'s 'The Weakest Thing' (*Poems*, 1850): 'Which is the weakest thing of all . . . / The wind, a little leaf above, / Though sere, resisteth? / What time that yellow leaf was green, / My days were gladder . . . / Ah me! a *leaf* with sighs can wring/ My lips asunder?' (ll. 1, 7–10, 13–14).
202. now over its best: now its best (time) was over.
204. bring to the last leaf] bring the last leaf to (*H proof*).
205. says the rhyme.] runs the rhyme. (*1863–88*, except *1865* which has no full stop at the end of the line; taken by itself this looks like a mispr., but it makes sense taken with the rev. in the following line). We have not found this proverbial 'rhyme', but the phrase 'Hold fast' occurs several times in the Bible, once in proverbial form in *1 Thessalonians* v 21: 'Prove all things; hold fast that which is good', and once with an internal rhyme in *Revelation* iii 11: 'hold that fast which thou hast'. Cp. also Richard Crashaw's 'In the Glorious Assumption of our Blessed Lady. The Hymn': 'Thy pretious name shall be / Thy self to us; & we / With holy care will keep it by us. / We to the last / Will hold it fast / And no *Assumption* shall deny us' (ll. 46–51). Note, however, the difference between B.'s 'the last [thing]' and Crashaw's 'to the last [moment of time]'.
206. much,] much. (*1865*), joining this line syntactically to l. 205, instead of initiating a new sentence.
208–9.] Tug though you venture a myriad such; / Nothing you mar but the year can mend: (*H proof*).
211–15. Fortunately the leaf flutters down of its own accord and lands on 'Leonor', making its home in her heart in a way she had 'trembled' to 'forestal'.
212. Eddying down] Eddying it down (*H proof*).

44

Worth how well, those dark grey eyes,
— That hair so dark and dear, how worth
That a man should strive and agonise,
And taste a very hell on earth
220 For the hope of such a prize!

45

Oh, you might have turned and tried a man,
Set him a space to weary and wear,
And prove which suited more your plan,
His best of hope or his worst despair,
225 Yet end as he began.

46

But you spared me this, like the heart you are,
And filled my empty heart at a word.
If you join two lives, there is oft a scar,
They are one and one, with a shadowy third;
230 One near one is too far.

47

A moment after, and hands unseen
Were hanging the night around us fast.
But we knew that a bar was broken between

216–30. Had 'Leonor' decided to 'test' the speaker, then she would have been worth the most intense 'striving' and 'agonising'; but, aware of his vulnerability, she has 'spared' him the 'trial' which might have cost him too much, and 'filled his empty heart at a word'. With this notion of a woman's 'test' of a man's love, cp. *In a Balcony* iii 172–5n. (III 445).

219. a very hell] a veriest hell (*1870–88*).

221. Oh, you might] You might (*1868–88*).

222. Set him a space] Set him such a space (*H proof*, but not *H proof²*).

225. The test is that the man's feelings should remain the same at the end of his ordeal as at the beginning: he must avoid becoming either too confident through 'hope' or too cast down by 'despair'.

226. the heart you are: it is unusual to find 'heart' used as a term of endearment without a preceding adjective (e.g. 'dear' or 'sweet'); see *OED* sense 14a.

227. filled my] filled up my (*H proof*, but not *H proof²*).

228–30. Cp. *Two in the Campagna* 39–40n. (p. 561).

228. If you join two lives] If two lives join (*1865–88*).

230. One near one] One beside one (*H proof*).

Life and life; we were mixed at last
235   In spite of the mortal screen.

48

The forests had done it; there they stood—
    We caught for a second the powers at play:
They had mingled us so, for once and for good,
    Their work was done—we might go or stay,
240   They relapsed to their ancient mood.

49

How the world is made for each of us!
    How all we perceive and know in it
Tends to some moment's product thus,
    When a soul declares itself—to wit,
245   By its fruit—the thing it does!

50

Be Hate that fruit or Love that fruit,
    It forwards the General Deed of Man,
And each of the Many helps to recruit
    The life of the race by a general plan,
250   Each living his own, to boot.

234. Cp. B.'s letter to EBB. of 25 Dec. 1845 (another passage from which is cited at ll. 141–5n.): 'My dear Christmas gift of a letter! I will write back a few lines . . . just that I may forever .. certainly during our mortal "forever"—mix my love for you, and, as you suffer me to say, your love for me .. dearest! .. these shall be mixed with the other loves of the day and live therein' (*Correspondence* xi 261).
236–40. On the possible literary sources for the forest in the poem see headnote.
237. *for a second*] for a moment (*1865–88*).
238. *so, for*] here for (*H proof*, but not *H proof²*). *for once and for good*: combining 'for once and all' and 'for good' as meaning both 'forever' and 'for the good of both'. *and for good*] and good (*1868–88*).
242. *all we perceive*] all we see (*H proof*, but not *H proof²*).
244–5. Cp. *Matthew* vii 16–17: 'Ye shall know them by their fruits . . . every good tree bringeth forth good fruit; but a corrupt tree bringeth forth evil fruit.'
246. *Hate . . . Love*] hate . . . love (*1865²*, *1868–88*).
247. *It forwards*] It goes to (*H proof*, but not *H proof²*). *General Deed of Man*] general deed of man (*1868–88*).
248.] And each of the millions helps recruit (*H proof*). *1868–88* have 'many'. *recruit*: 'To repair any thing wasted by new supplies' (*J.*).
250. *Each living*] Each man with (*H proof*). *to boot*: as well; i.e. each individual lives his own life as well as participating in 'the life of the race'.

51

I am named and known by that hour's feat,
    There took my station and degree.
So grew my own small life complete
    As nature obtained her best of me—
255   One born to love you, sweet!

52

And to watch you sink by the fire-side now
    Back again, as you mutely sit
Musing by fire-light, that great brow
    And the spirit-small hand propping it
260   Yonder, my heart knows how!

53

So the earth has gained by one man more,
    And the gain of earth must be Heaven's gain too,
And the whole is well worth thinking o'er
    When the autumn comes: which I mean to do
265   One day, as I said before.

251. named and known: a legal phrase used (e.g.) in adoption documents.   *that hour's*] that moment's (*1865–88*).

252–3. There . . . So] So . . . There (*H proof*).

256–60. A reprise, with variations, of ll. 111–15.

261.] So, earth has gained by one man the more (*1870–88*).

263–5. Cp. the poem's opening lines.

264. the autumn] autumn (*1865–88*).

31 Fra Lippo Lippi

Text and publication

First publ. *M & W*, 10 Nov. 1855; repr. *1863, 1863², 1868, 1872, 1888*. Our text is *1855*. In common with most of the long poems in *M & W*, the text was only lightly revised in subsequent eds.

Composition and date

In a letter of May 1850, EBB. states that the drawing room at Casa Guidi contains 'specimens of Gaddi, Lippi .. [and] the like' which B. had managed to buy cheaply thanks to his extensive knowledge of early Italian art (*EBB to Arabella* i 314; see also headnote to *Andrea*, p. 385). These picture-buying expeditions form the background to *Andrea* and *Old Pictures* (pp. 404–5), both of which can probably be dated to early 1853. It is, then, plausible to suggest that *Fra Lippo* also belongs to this period. *Sharp*, on the other hand, dates the poem to the winter of 1853–54 in Rome, a suggestion supported by an unpublished letter from B. to Edward Sartoris (for whom, and his wife Adelaide, see headnote to *Two in the Campagna*, p. 556) of 24 Aug. 1854: 'Are you repenting by this time your first commission to me? The Carrier only makes a transit once a week, he says—& then, I was delayed by somebody's promise of getting me a one-volume with good print to boot: but after all, Le Monnier's in three portable tomes seems to suit your requirement best, I think, and you will receive it tomorrow accordingly. I send too Mrs Sartoris' orris-root & the books wh. I hoped to bring myself—but there is no visit to your Bagni for us, I am sorry to say: both of you must come & see Florence and us, and make us the best amends' (*ABL MS*). The requests by Mr and Mrs Sartoris, for Le Monnier (possibly his ed. of Vasari) and 'orris-root' respectively, might plausibly have been prompted by the sight of B.'s poem; see *Sources* and l. 351n.

Sources

B. clearly had some first-hand knowledge of the work of Filippo Lippi (*c.* 1406–1469), but most of the information in the poem derives from the following printed sources: (i) Giorgio Vasari, *Le Vite de' Più eccellenti Pittori, Scultori e Architetti.* Firenze: Felice Le Monnier, 1846–57, vol. iv (1848), pp. 114–30 [*Le Monnier*]; (ii) Filippo Baldinucci, *Notizie de' Professori del Disegno da Cimabue in quà.* Ed Giuseppe Piacenza. 1728; rpt. Torino: Nella Stamperia Reale, 1770, vol. i, pp. 556–64 [*Baldinucci*]; (iii) Johan Gaye, *Carteggio inedito d'Artisti dei Secoli XIV, XV, XVI* (Florence 1839–40), 3 vols. [*Gaye*]; (iv) Mrs Jameson, *Memoirs of the Early Italian Painters and of the Progress of Painting in Italy* (1845), vol. i [*Jameson*]; (v) W. S. Landor, 'Fra Lippo Lippi and Pope Eugenius the Fourth' (1846) in *The Works of Walter Savage Landor.* London 1853, vol. 2, pp. 81–90; (vi) John Ruskin, *Modern Painters* (vols. i–ii, 1843–46) and *The Stones of Venice* (1851–53).

(i) Le Monnier

B. was reading Vasari soon after his arrival in Pisa (see headnote to *Andrea*, p. 385), and the poem is largely based on the portrait of Lippi that emerges from Vasari's account. A long letter to John Ruskin (15 Dec. 1879; MS at Ruskin Library, Lancaster University) indicates the precise extent of B.'s indebtedness to Vasari in this poem (editorial comment and translations in square brackets):

19 Warwick Crescent, W.

Dec. 15. '79.

My dear Mr Ruskin,

I have to beg your pardon for some delay in fulfilling my promise concerning certain points in the life & character of Lippo Lippi: it came of my being unable to get at my books. But I find that, out of Vasari alone, I can produce the authority you require. I shall abridge, annotate and transcribe the various passages to save you the trouble of reference.

1. Fra Filippo di Tommaso Lippi, per la morte di suo padre restò povero fanciullino d'anni due senza alcuna custodia, essendosi ancora morta la madre non molto dopo averlo partorito. Rimaso dunque costui in governo d'una Mona Lapaccia sua zia, poiché l'ebbe allevato con suo agio [*for* disagio] grandissimo, quando non potette più sostenerlo [*for* sostentarlo], essendo egli già di ott'anni, lo fece frate nel convento del Carmine,' (at the back of which, in the 'Canto alla Cuculia della contrada detta Ardiglione,' he was born—probably in 1412.) [Fra Filippo di Tommaso Lippi was made a poor orphan with no one to look after him at the age of two thanks to the death of his father, his mother having died soon after giving birth to him. He was placed therefore under the guardianship of his aunt 'Mona Lapaccia' who after bringing him up with great difficulty, made him a friar at the Carmine convent at the age of eight when she could no longer support him.]

2. Animosamente si cavò l'abito d'età d'anni diciasette'. [He boldly threw off the monk's habit at the age of seventeen.] (This is a mistake: in the Picture for Sant'Ambrogio, painted in 1447,—he retains not only 'l'abito' but the shaved head: and there is other evidence that he called himself a monk all his life.)

3. Dicesi ch'era tanto venereo che, vedendo donne che gli piacessero, se le poteva avere, ogni sua facoltà donato le arebbe. Ed era tanto perduto dietro a questo appetito, che all'opre prese da lui, quando era in questo umore, poco o nulla attendeva. Onde una volta, fra l'altre, Cosimo de'Medici, facendogli fare un'opera in casa sua, lo rinchiuse, perchè a perder tempo non andasse. Ma egli, statoci già due giorni, spinto da furore amoroso, anzi bestiale, una sera, con un paio di forbici fece alcune liste de'lenzuoli del letto, e da una finestra calatosi, attese per molti giorni a'suoi piaceri'. (Two pictures from the Medici Palace (now Riccardi) are now in our own Gallery: one (The Annunciation) contains the device of Cosimo and Lorenzo,—Three feathers within a Ring.) [He is said to have been so lustful that, when he saw a woman he liked, he would have given all his possessions to have her. And he was given up to this craving to such an extent that little or nothing was expected of the works undertaken by him when he was in this mood. On one of these occasions Cosimo de' Medici, who had ordered him to undertake some work, confined him in his house in order to prevent him from wasting time in this way. But Lippo one evening, having already been there two days, and prompted by lustful, almost bestial desires, cut the bed sheets into strips with a pair of scissors and descended from a window, freeing himself to pursue his pleasures for several days.]

4. Essendogli poi dalle Monache di Sta Margherita (in Prato) data a fare la tavola dell'altar maggiore, gli venne veduta una figliuola di Francesco Buti la quale o in serbanza o per monaca era quivi condotta. Filippo, dato d'occhio alla Lucrezia, tanto operò che ottenne di farne un ritratto per metterlo in una figura di Nostra Donna: e fece poi tanto che egli sviò la Lucrezia dalle monache, e la menò via'. (In a letter by Giovanni de'Medici to Bartolommeo Serragli, May, 1458, he says 'we laughed a bit at the prank of Brother Philip'.)

Di che le monache molto per tal caso furono svergonate [*for* "svergognate"],
e suo padre non fu mai più allegro, e fece ogni opera per riaverla, ma ella non
volle mai ritornare, anzi starsi con Filippo, il quale n'ebbe un figliuol maschio,—
Filippino'. [Having been commissioned to paint a picture for the High Altar
by the nuns of Santa Margherita in Prato, he happened to see one of the daughters of Francesco Buti, who had been brought there either as a ward or as a
novice. Filippo, seeing Lucrezia, managed to obtain permission to do a drawing
of her to put in a picture of Our Lady: and then managed to spirit her away from
the nuns. . . . The nuns were ashamed at this, and Lucrezia's father was never
happy again, and did everything he could to get her back, but she never wanted
to return, and stayed with Filippo, with whom she had a son, Filippino.]

5. Fu tanto per le sue buone qualità stimato, che molte cose, che di biasimo
erano alla vita sua, furono ricoperte mediante il grado di tanta virtù. Fu Fra
Filippo molto amico delle persone allegre, e sempre lietamente visse. Delle fatiche
sue visse onoratamente: e straordinariamente spese nelle cose d'amore, delle
quali del continuo, mentre che visse, fino alla morte si dilettò. Perciocchè dicono
che, essendo egli tanto inclinato a questi suoi beati amori, alcuni parenti *della
donna da lui amata* lo fecero avvelenare. (October 8, 1469) (i.e. 'the lady he
was *then* attached to,' not necessarily Lucrezia.) Dolse la morte sua a molti amici,
e particolarmente a Cosimo de'Medici ed a Papa Eugenio, il quale in vita sua
volle dispensarlo che potesse avere per sua donna legittima la Lucrezia di F.
Buti; la quale, per potere far di sé e dell'appetito suo come gli paresse, non si
volse curare di avere'. (Both these were dead—the Pope five years before Fra
Filippo: the story may be true no less.) [He was admired so much for his good
qualities that many of the blameworthy things in his life were covered over
by his good qualities. Fra Filippo was very friendly with lively people, and
always lived joyously. He lived honourably on the fruits of his own labour,
and spent extraordinary amounts of money on his amorous affairs, in which
he delighted right up to the time of his death. For which reason some say that
some relatives *of the woman he loved* poisoned him . . . His death grieved many
friends, especially Cosimo de' Medici and Pope Eugenius, who had wanted
during his lifetime to grant him a dispensation from the monastic life so that
he could make Lucrezia his legitimate wife. But Lippo, in order to remain free
to do as he liked, did not bother with this.]

There, Dear Mr Ruskin, you have, I hope, my justification for what my
little poem alleges of Brother Philip,—who, in the midst of his irregularities,
was decorous enough in his picture preachments. In the convent of St.
Domenic, in Prato, Saint Vincent is painted reading from the book he holds—
'Timete Deum, quia venit hora judicii ejus!' ['Fear God . . . for the hour of
his judgment is come' (*Revelation* xiv 7); the painting, *Nativity with St George
and St Vincent Ferrer*, is now in the Galleria Communale di Palazzo Pretorio,
Prato] From a passage, however in Vasari, I conclude he was the first on
record to treat sacred subjects indecorously: for, having painted a picture
of the Coronation of the Virgin for a church in Arezzo, "dal messer Carlo
Marsuppino (who had ordered the work) gli fu detto, 'che egli avvertisse alle
mani che dipingeva, perchè molto le sue cose erano biasimate:' per il che Fra
Filippo, nel dipingere da indi innanzi, la maggior parte o con panni o con altra
invenzione ricoperse, per fuggire il predetto biasimo." [It was said to him by
Mr Carlo Marsuppino, 'that he was warned to take care what he painted, because
many of his productions were censured'; for which reason Fra Filippo covered
most of his figures with draperies or other devices from that time onwards in
order to escape this censure.]

I may have tired you—but the tiresomeness of referring to Vasari, Baldinucci and the rest is spared perhaps: and I gladly seize the occasion of saying how happy I was to see you again, the other day, after an absence too prolonged by far.

Ever truly yours,
Robert Browning.

For Ruskin's reply to this letter, see below, *Criticism*. Although we do not have Ruskin's list of questions, it is reasonably obvious which parts of the poem B. is referring to in each section: (1) explains the account of Lippi's childhood in ll. 81–91; (2) deals with the general question of whether or not Lippi ever formally abandoned the monastic life; (3) highlights Lippi's unmonastic love life; ll. 15–18 and 61–6 indicate that the action of the poem takes place during the nocturnal escape from Cosimo de' Medici's house described in Vasari's anecdote (although B., or possibly Lippi himself, exaggerates the length of time Lippi was shut up in Cosimo's house; see l. 47n.); (4) and (5) both refer to details of Lippi's life after the time described in the poem; the lines in (5) referring to Lippi's profligacy are echoed in the poem (e.g. ll. 27–31).

B.'s corrections of Vasari in (2) and (5) are taken from the notes to *Le Monnier*. B.'s dependence on the authority of this edition led to scholarly controversy when he decided to adopt its suggestion that Masaccio ('Hulking Tom') was the pupil and not the teacher of Lippi (see ll. 273–80). He might also have been encouraged in this belief by the fact that many of the frescoes in the Brancacci chapel of the Carmine were painted by Masaccio and by Filippino, Lippi's son; see *Fantozzi* 706, and ll. 266–7n. In a letter to Edward Dowden of 13 Oct. 1866 B. slightly misquotes one of the scholarly footnotes from *Le Monnier* to justify his version, and calls Vasari's *Life* of Lippi 'a tissue of errors' (see Johnstone Parr, 'Browning's Fra Lippo Lippi, Baldinucci, and the Milanesi edition of Vasari', *ELN* iii [1966], 197–201). He also defends his position by referring to 'the competent authority of the editor of the last Florentine edition of Vasari' in the first of two letters to the *Pall Mall Gazette* on the subject prompted by an adverse notice in the *Revue des Deux Mondes*; see *Pall Mall Gazette* 6 Feb. and 16 Mar. 1870. More recent scholarship has established the date of Masaccio's death as 1428, making it impossible for him to have been Lippi's pupil. Lippi's description of the altarpiece he intends to paint for Sant' Ambrogio in Florence bears strong similarities to the description of the painting in the footnotes to *Le Monnier* (iv 117); see ll. 347–77n.

Many of the notes from *Le Monnier* edition were incorporated into Mrs Foster's English translation of Vasari (1851), and it is possible that B. might also have used this text. She too, for instance, rejects Vasari's assertion about Lippi's ecclesiastical status, citing Masselli: 'If Filippo, as Della Valle affirms, left his convent after a few months of noviciate, without being professed, how does it happen that he is always called Fra Filippo through his whole life? He painted his own portrait with the tonsure, and his death is registered in the necrology of the Carmelites as that of a member, under the name *Frater Philippus*. From all these things it is to be supposed that he was certainly professed, if not in full orders' (*Foster* ii 75n.). See also section iii below.

(ii) *Baldinucci*

In the letter to Dowden cited above B. states: 'I suppose Lippo to have been born—as Baldinucci says—about 1400'. Filippo Baldinucci's account of Lippi's life is substantially based on that of Vasari but he too accuses the earlier writer of 'notibile errori' [notable errors], esp. in connection with Lippi's date of birth.

After examining the evidence Baldinucci concludes 'che [Lippi] fosse contemporaneo in tutto, e per tutto del . . . Masaccio, che egli imparasse l'arte da lui, e che fosse il suo natale circa all'anno 1400' [that (Lippi) was contemporary in every way with . . . Masaccio, that he learned his art from him, and that his birth took place around the year 1400] (i 557; also cited DeVane *Handbook* 217). Baldinucci does not, then, argue that Lippi was Masaccio's teacher, as B. does in his poem; throughout his account he refers to Lippi as 'della scuola di Masaccio', and reports that 'egli prese tanto la maniera di Masaccio, che, dopo la morte di lui, dicevasi comunemente per ischerzo, lo spirito di Masaccio esser entrato in Fra Filippo' [He adopted the manner of Masaccio to such an extent that, after Masaccio's death, it was commonly said as a joke that his spirit had entered into Fra Filippo] (i 559). Johnstone Parr has argued (*ELN* iii (1966) 197–201) that Baldinucci was not a source for the poem on the grounds that B. did not acquire any information from Baldinucci that he could not have obtained elsewhere, but there seems no good reason to dispute B.'s own assertion that he read Baldinucci as well as Vasari.

(iii) *Gaye*

In the second of his letters to the *Pall Mall Gazette* (see above, section i) B. refers in support of his opinion to 'the whole result of modern criticism, from Gaye and Rumohr downwards'. Rumohr would appear to be Carl Friedrich Ludwig von Rumohr, a German art critic of the early nineteenth century. None of his works is translated into English, but he indirectly affected British thinkers of the time through his influence on A. F. Rio's *De la poésie chrétienne*, which B. certainly knew (see headnote to *Old Pictures*, p. 314). Gaye can plausibly be identified as Johan Gaye, author of *Carteggio inedito d'artisti dei secoli XIV, XV, XVI (1326–1672)*, published in Florence in 1839–40. (Neither Rumohr nor Gaye makes an appearance in *Collections*.) Gaye's book (also not translated into English) consists of transcriptions of previously unpublished letters written by various Florentine artists of the fourteenth, fifteenth and sixteenth centuries. The first volume (1839) contains two letters by Lippo to members of the Medici family, complaining about lack of payment for work done. The first of these letters, dating from 1439, supports B.'s assertion that Lippi remained a monk into adult life; he describes himself as 'uno de piu poveri Frati, che sia in Firenze' (i 141) [one of the poorest monks in the whole of Florence]. Gaye argues that the letters contradict, or at least throw into doubt, Vasari's unflattering portrait of Lippo's character: 'Il rozzo si, ma sincero modo di esprimersi del pittore, non mostra punto quella leggerezza di carattere, di cui lo taccia il Vasari. Lo troviamo carico di famiglia, oppresso da domestiche angustie' [The painter's rough but honest way of expressing himself does not exhibit in the least that lightness of character with which Vasari taxes him. We see him burdened by his family, oppressed by domestic anxieties]. There is nothing in the poem that can be attributed to the influence of Gaye alone. Both Gaye and Rumohr are cited as authorities on a number of occasions in *Foster*; B.'s comment in the fourth section of his letter to Ruskin (see *Le Monnier*) is taken from Gaye, as cited by Mrs Foster: 'It is supposed that the carrying off of Lucrezia is the event to which Giovanni de' Medici refers, where, in a letter to Bartolommeo Serragli, written from Florence, on the 27th of May, 1458, he uses the following words: "And so we laughed a good while at the error of Fra Filippo"' (*Foster* ii 80n.). Gaye also features as an authority in *Fantozzi* (e.g. p. 706).

(iv) *Jameson*

Anna Jameson was a close friend of the Brownings (see headnotes to *Andrea del Sarto*, p. 389, and *Pretty Woman*, III 20), so B. would have been aware of her chapter on Lippi in *Memoirs of the Early Italian Painters*. Lippi and Angelico da Fiesole ('Fra Angelico') are said to be 'the very antipodes of each other' and are seen as responsible for 'the very opposite impulses . . . prevailing through the rest of the century at Florence and elsewhere' (i 110). Adopting the language of German art criticism, Mrs Jameson calls Lippi a '*Naturalist* . . . intent on studying and imitating the various effects of nature in colour and in light and shade, without any other aspiration than the representation of beauty for its own sake' (i 110), while Angelico is characterized as one of the '*Idealists* or *Mystics*' for whom 'the cultivation of art [is] a sacred vocation—the representation of beauty a means, not an end' (i 111). She follows Vasari (and the prevailing tradition) in making Lippi a pupil of Masaccio, and ends by stating that Lippi's 'talent was degraded by [his] immorality' (i 113); he was the first 'who desecrated [sacred] subjects by introducing the portraits of women who happened to be the objects of his preference at the moment' (i 114). The possible influence of Mrs Jameson's chapter on B.'s poem has been noted in general terms by Johnstone Parr (for whom see above, *Le Monnier*) in *ELN* v (1967–68) 277–83. The main point of similarity is the suggestion that Lippi exemplifies the new 'naturalist' current in painting; the contrast with Fra Angelico also appears in the poem (see ll. 233–7).

(v) *Landor*

Given B.'s esteem for and personal acquaintance with Landor (see *Variation on Lines of Landor*, III 704), it is overwhelmingly likely that he read Landor's imaginary dialogue between Lippi and Pope Eugenius IV. Landor follows Vasari (and disagrees with B.) in having Lippi give up his religious vocation: Pope Eugenius IV says to him 'I am informed by my son Cosimo de' Medici . . . of thy throwing off the habit of a friar' (p. 81). Landor's Pope is a lecherous, prying buffoon, anxious for details of Lippi's sexual conquests while pretending to condemn them; after hearing Lippi say that his sins are of an 'amorous' nature, the Pope continues: 'Well, well! I can guess, within a trifle, what that leads unto. I very much disapprove of it, whatever it may be. And then? and then? Prythee go on: I am inflamed with a miraculous zeal to cleanse thee'. Landor dwells at length on the episode, briefly mentioned in Vasari and ignored by B., of Lippi's capture and enslavement by Turkish pirates.

(vi) *Ruskin*

For B.'s citing of evidence concerning Lippi's life to Ruskin, see above. John Ruskin was a major influence on the British conception of the history of art in the 1850s, and an important aspect of his polemic was recommendation of early Renaissance painting, in particular Giotto, Fra Angelico and Lorenzo (all mentioned in the poem). His ranking of Italian artists in *Modern Painters* was as follows:

> Thus, Angelico, intensely loving all spiritual beauty, will be of the highest rank; and Paul Veronese and Correggio, intensely loving physical and corporeal beauty, of the second rank; and Albert Dürer, Rubens, and in general the Northern artists, apparently insensible to beauty, and caring only for truth, whether shapely or not, of the third rank; and Teniers and Salvator, Caravaggio, and other such worshippers of the depraved, of no rank, or as we said before, of a certain order in the abyss.
>
> (*Works* v 56).

In *The Stones of Venice* ii (1853), however, the first two categories are inverted, moving 'Naturalists' above 'Purists', a viewpoint corresponding to Lippi's in B.'s poem. Ruskin and B. were good friends during this period, and the Brownings read Ruskin's work avidly (see headnote to *Guardian Angel*, III 14).

Contexts

Fra Lippo is another product of B.'s profound interest in and knowledge of medieval and early Renaissance art (on which see headnote to *Old Pictures*, pp. 404–8). There are, moreover, contemporary resonances to some of Lippi's arguments. His plea for freedom of expression in art—a plea reinforced by some of the poem's bawdier moments—parallels the Victorian debate on the limits of propriety in literary and artistic representation. In his Preface to *Pendennis* (1850), Thackeray complains that since 'the author of "Tom Jones" was buried, no writer of fiction among us has been permitted to depict to his utmost power a MAN. We must drape him, and give him a certain conventional simper. Society will not tolerate the Natural in our Art.' The Brownings saw a good deal of Thackeray and his family during their period of residence in Rome. Such 'draping' was even more obligatory in the visual arts; *The Times* for 8 May 1854 reports details of a protest against the exhibition of naked classical statuary at the Crystal Palace which prompted the directors to order 'plaster foliage' to cover up the offending parts. Lippi's experiences as an orphan in the Carmelite monastery implicitly invoke some of the debates on the treatment of the poor and destitute in Victorian Britain; see (e.g.) Carlyle's *Past and Present* (1843), in which the charitable arrangements of a medieval monastery are favourably compared to the social provisions of Victorian England.

Parallels in B.

Fra Lippo takes its place as one of B's 'painter' poems on the subject of art and artists (cp. in this volume, *Pictor Ignotus*, p. 226; *Andrea*, p. 385, and *Old Pictures*, p. 404). Each of these poems is based on an understanding of the history of art as a development from stylized medieval hagiography ('saints and saints / And saints again', as Lippi puts it in ll. 48–9) to the imitation of real life, although the value of this movement is assessed differently in each case. This narrative, which underpins the emerging concept of the Renaissance, is articulated most clearly in *Old Pictures* (see pp. 415–21). The Quattrocento Italian spoken by Lippi is rendered in the poem as Elizabethan or Shakespearean English ('Zooks', 'By your leave'); cp. *My Last Duchess* (p. 197) and *The Tomb at St. Praxed's* (p. 232). The use of Shakespearean English also invokes the familiar context of Shakespeare's Italy, with its animation and physicality.

In *Johannes Agricola* (p. 74) B. attempts to give an insight into the mind of the religious fanatic who despises this world and longs for the next. *Fra Lippo*, with its emphasis on the importance of attending to this world rather than the next, can be seen as the inverse of this poem. These contrasting outlooks are, moreover, linked to Protestantism and Roman Catholicism respectively in B.'s poetry; B.'s Catholic clergy are almost invariably venal, self-serving, and seething with poorly repressed human passion: cp. *Soliloquy of the Spanish Cloister* (p. 201) and *Tomb at St. Praxed's* (p. 232), and see ll. 8–11n.

Criticism

On 16 Dec. 1879 Ruskin replied to the letter from B. which we quote above (*Sources*) in terms which dissent from B.'s view of Lippi in the poem (unpublished MS at Eton College):

> Dear Browning,
> It is wonderfully pretty and good of you to write all that out for me: but truly, it is for cause: for this question is a most vital and central one with me. That very picture of St Vincent and St Michael at the Nativity, at Prato—I am going to put a copy of in my Sheffield Museum—as the very Morning Star and queen

of all Italian sacred painting.—and it will be . . . full of Lucifer and Vashti with
a vengeance, if Vasari and you are right—I simply mean it to be physically
impossible—as it would be for a ~~coal~~ chimneysweep to bring me a bagfull of
pure snow—for a man such as you read him to have painted any one thing
he ever did—I hold the Madonnas of Angelico to be mere dainty grisettes,
and Raphael's, household muses—compared to the solemn purity of Lippi's;
and I would rather have painted Lippi's Annunciation than Giotto's—so you
see what a pretty quarrel we have on hand! . . .

 Ever affectionately and gratefully yrs,
 J Ruskin

 I am poor brother Lippo, by your leave!
 You need not clap your torches to my face.
 Zooks, what's to blame? you think you see a monk!
 What, it's past midnight, and you go the rounds,
5 And here you catch me at an alley's end
 Where sportive ladies leave their doors ajar.
 The Carmine's my cloister: hunt it up,
 Do,—harry out, if you must show your zeal,
 Whatever rat, there, haps on his wrong hole,
10 And nip each softling of a wee white mouse,
 Weke, weke, that's crept to keep him company!

1–2. Lippi has been stopped by the city watch; he first addresses the men who
are physically holding him, and then (at l. 12) their officer, to whom he speaks
the remainder of his monologue.

1. by your leave! used as an apology for taking a liberty, in Shakespeare often a
kiss (e.g. *Merchant of Venice* III ii 139), but also used more aggressively, as when
Bassianus seizes hold of Lavinia in *Titus Andronicus* I i 276: 'Lord Titus, by your
leave, this maid is mine'. The tinge of archaism in the phrase is confirmed by
OED's citation of Dickens's historical novel, *Barnaby Rudge*, set in the 18th century: 'The solitary passenger was startled by the chairmen's cry of "By your leave
there!" as two came trotting past him' (ch. xvi).

2. clap: thrust (into).

3. Zooks: contraction of 'gadzooks', from 'God's hooks' (= the nails of the cross);
'An exclamation or minced oath, expressing vexation, surprise, or other emotion' (*OED*).

6. sportive ladies: sportive: 'gay; merry; frolick; wanton; playful; ludicrous' (*J.*);
here the phrase is a euphemism for prostitutes.

7. Carmine: the Church of Santa Maria del Carmine in Florence; see letter to
Ruskin (headnote, *Sources*) for B.'s source in Vasari. The Carmelite Order of monks
was founded around 1200; they are a mendicant and contemplative order.

8–11. Lippi suggests that the watch would be better employed at the monastery
looking for each 'softling'—'effeminate or viciously nice person' (*J.*) —who has
crept into the 'wrong hole'; with this possible suggestion of homosexual practices in the Catholic Church cp. *Holy-Cross Day* 20n., 21–2n. (p. 546).

11. Cp. *Titus Andronicus* IV ii 146–7: 'Weeke weeke! / So cries a pig prepared
to the spit'.

Aha, you know your betters? Then, you'll take
Your hand away that's fiddling on my throat,
And please to know me likewise. Who am I?
15   Why, one, sir, who is lodging with a friend
Three streets off—he's a certain . . . how d'ye call?
Master—a . . . Cosimo of the Medici,
In the house that caps the corner. Boh! you were best!
Remember and tell me, the day you're hanged,
20   How you affected such a gullet's-gripe!
But you, sir, it concerns you that your knaves
Pick up a manner nor discredit you.
Zooks, are we pilchards, that they sweep the streets
And count fair prize what comes into their net?
25   He's Judas to a tittle, that man is!

12–18. The watchmen acknowledge the arrival of their officer, and Lippi implies that he is of equivalent social rank; the officer then asks him who he is, and Lippi reveals that he has a powerful patron, whereupon the man holding him lets him go.

17. Cosimo of the Medici: the first Cosimo de' Medici, Cosimo il Vecchio [Cosimo the Elder] (1389–1464); see headnote, *Sources* for B.'s letter to Ruskin detailing the incident in Vasari. As *Oxford* notes, Vasari states that the altarpiece of Sant' Ambrogio projected by Lippi towards the end of the poem (ll. 344–77) was the piece that first brought Lippi to Cosimo de' Medici's attention: 'lavorò alle Donne di S. Ambruogio all'altare maggiore una bellissima tavola, la quale molto grato lo fece a Cosimo de' Medici, che per questa cagione divenne suo amicissimo' ['he made for the nuns of Sant'Ambrogio a most beautiful altarpiece for the high altar, which greatly pleased Cosimo de' Medici, who for this reason became his [Lippi's] great friend'].

18. In the house] I' the house (*1870–88*).   *the house that caps the corner*: the verb 'to cap' is defined by *J.* as 'to cover on the top'; hence a ref. to the imposing size of the Medici Palace, situated at the corner of what is now Via Cavour and Via de' Gori.   *Boh!* An Italian exclamation of disdain or disgust.   *you were best!* 'you'd better!'

20. affected: 'liked, enjoyed'; since the watchman enjoys gripping people round the neck ['a gullet's gripe'], it would be poetic justice for him to be hanged.

21–2. 'It is of importance to you, as an officer and a man of rank, that your subordinates learn to behave properly and do not discredit you.'

21. your knaves: combining the sense of 'servant' or 'subordinate' with that of 'petty rascal, scoundrel'; the first sense was already obsolete in *J.*

23–4. The watch are rounding people up for unimportant offences, like fishermen using a net with small meshes, so that even a pilchard cannot escape; Lippi implies that they should be catching bigger prey. The metaphor derives from one of Aesop's fables, 'The Fisherman and the Large and Small Fish' (*Complete Fables*, transl. Olivia and Robert Temple, Penguin 1998, p. 22).

25. He's Judas to a tittle! 'he would make an excellent model for Judas in one of my paintings', with the implication that the man's character suits his appearance.

Just such a face! why, sir, you make amends.
Lord, I'm not angry! Bid your hangdogs go
Drink out this quarter-florin to the health
Of the munificent House that harbours me
30 (And many more beside, lads! more beside!)
And all's come square again. I'd like his face—
His, elbowing on his comrade in the door
With the pike and lantern,—for the slave that holds
John Baptist's head a-dangle by the hair
35 With one hand ("look you, now," as who should say)
And his weapon in the other, yet unwiped!
It's not your chance to have a bit of chalk,
A wood-coal or the like? or you should see!

There is in fact no image of Judas in Lippi's extant work. The traditional subjects of paintings in which Judas features were the Last Supper and the Betrayal
(or Arrest) of Christ; Lippi is not known to have painted either subject. Cp. B.'s
remarks to Richard Hengist Horne about his poetic drama *Judas Iscariot: a Miracle
Play*, published in a volume with other poems in 1848: 'Yes, I saw your "Judas"
advertised, and reviewed in the Athenæum,—one of the best subjects, it strikes
me, possible for poet—the one extract I read was admirable,—and the plot &
purpose admirable. I shall have a great read of it, whenever the lucky day comes.
I wish I could have referred you to a pamphlet of the last century called something like "Remarks on the life <or character?> of Judas,"—with striking things,
as I seem to remember them' (3 Dec. 1848, *Correspondence* xv 168).
26. you make amends: Lippi is responding to a conciliatory gesture on the part of
the officer.
27. Bid your hangdogs] Have your hangdogs (*H proof*, but not *H proof²*). A hang-
dog is '[a] despicable or degraded fellow fit only to hang a dog, or to be hanged
like a dog' (*OED*).
28. quarter-florin: A florin is the English name for the gold coins issued in Florence.
29. munificent House] munificent house (*H proof*, but not *H proof²*).
30. many more besides: Lippi informs the watch that Cosimo's house harbours many
more people besides him, and thereby reminds them of his patron's power.
Alternatively, he is hinting at possible future 'quarter-florins'.
31–6. I'd like . . . unwiped! the story of the beheading of John the Baptist at the
behest of Herodias's daughter is told in *Mark* vi 17–29. See ll. 196–7n. Lippi
painted frescoes on the theme of the Feast of Herod in the Duomo [Cathedral]
at Prato, near Florence, including a 'Decapitation of John the Baptist' in the
chancel of the same church. In this fresco a servant is depicted in exactly the
pose described by Lippi, with John's head held by the hair in one hand and his
unwiped sword in the other; see *Thomas* 97, 99.
31. all's come square: 'all's come right, everything's settled satisfactorily', with the
implication that money has changed hands, since to 'square' someone meant to
buy them off (*Penguin Dictionary of Historical Slang*, ed. E. Partridge).
38. wood-coal: a piece of charcoal. *or you should*] and you should (*H proof*, but
not *H proof²*).

Yes, I'm the painter, since you style me so.
40 What, brother Lippo's doings, up and down,
You know them and they take you? like enough!
I saw the proper twinkle in your eye—
'Tell you I liked your looks at very first.
Let's sit and set things straight now, hip to haunch.
45 Here's spring come, and the nights one makes up bands
To roam the town and sing out carnival,
And I've been three weeks shut within my mew,
A-painting for the great man, saints and saints
And saints again. I could not paint all night—
50 Ouf! I leaned out of window for fresh air.
There came a hurry of feet and little feet,

39. since you style me so: 'since you are kind enough to call me by that name'
(Lippi is affecting modesty at his being recognized).
40. brother Lippo's doings] works about the city (*H proof*).
41. they take you: 'they catch your fancy' (*OED* 10, citing Ben Jonson, *Epicoene,
or The Silent Woman* I i 86–7: 'such sweet neglect more taketh me / Than all
th'adulteries of art').
43. 'Tell: the apostrophe indicates the omission of the pronoun; see *An Epistle*
101n. (p. 517).
44. hip to haunch: 'side by side', 'close together'; cp. *Holy-Cross Day* 25: 'Aaron's
asleep—shove hip to haunch' (p. 546).
45–6. Carnival is the traditional period of revelry permitted in Roman Catholic
countries before the austerities of Lent; see headnote to *Toccata* (p. 368).
46. sing out carnival] sing at carnival (*H proof*, but not *H proof²*).
47. three weeks: according to the source in Vasari mentioned by B. in his letter
to Ruskin (see headnote, *Sources*), Lippi escaped from Cosimo's house after two
days; Lippi may be exaggerating in order to gain the sympathy of the officer and
his men.   *mew*: 'a cage; an inclosure; a place where any thing is confined' (*J.*).
Cp. *Childe Roland* 135 (p. 362).
48–9. saints and saints / And saints again: the picture is convincingly identified
in *Thomas* as 'Seven Saints, Sacred Conversation', which belonged to the
picture-dealer Metzger in the Borgo Ognissanti in Florence until it was acquired
by the National Gallery in London in 1861 (pp. 425–6; For B.'s knowledge of
art-dealers in Florence, see headnote to *Old Pictures*, pp. 404–5). B. mentions
this fact in one of his annotations to Vasari in his letter to Ruskin (see headnote,
Sources), and in a letter to Furnivall he remarks: 'By the bye, that picture of Lippi's,
mentioned by Mr. Radford,—with the saints in a row—has,—either that or its
companion, "*the Annunciation*", also in the National Gallery,—the Arms of
the Medici above the figures,—and in all likelihood both pictures were painted
during Lippi's stay, enforced or otherwise, in the Medici Palace' (9 Jan. 1883;
Trumpeter 63). Contrast the painter in *Pictor Ignotus* 57–62, who although painting
the same tedious series of religious subjects is not doing so for a patron (p. 231).
51. feet and little feet: i.e. male and female revellers. cp. *Paracelsus* v 186 (I 280):
'I am come back . . . to love you, and to kiss your little feet, / Soft as an ermine's
winter coat!'

A sweep of lute-strings, laughs, and whiffs of song,—
Flower o' the broom,
Take away love, and our earth is a tomb!
55   *Flower o' the quince,*
I let Lisa go, and what good's in life since?
Flower o' the thyme—and so on. Round they went.
Scarce had they turned the corner when a titter,
Like the skipping of rabbits by moonlight,—three slim
         shapes—
60   And a face that looked up . . . zooks, sir, flesh and blood,
That's all I'm made of! Into shreds it went,
Curtain and counterpane and coverlet,
All the bed furniture—a dozen knots,
There was a ladder! down I let myself,
65   Hands and feet, scrambling somehow, and so dropped,
And after them. I came up with the fun
Hard by St. Laurence, hail fellow, well met,—
Flower o' the rose,

52. *lute-strings*: the lute is the traditional instrument for Renaissance love-songs and serenades; cp. *Serenade* 20n. (III 488).   *whiffs*: 'a whiff or slight blast of wind' (*OED*); the application to song seems to be B.'s invention.

53–7. The first of several imitations in the poem of the 'Stornello' ['Starling'], a traditional and popular Italian verse form of two or three lines (with regional variations) 'generally amorous or satirical in nature . . . [and normally including] the invocation of a flower' (Salvatore Battaglia, *Grande Dizionario della Lingua Italiana*, 1961). See also ll. 68–9; 238–9; 248–9. Francesco Dall'Ongaro (1808–73), the poet and patriot who translated EBB.'s *A Court Lady* into Italian and later became her 'great friend' (*EBB to Arabella* ii 487), attempted to incorporate forms of this kind into his work, and issued a volume of *Stornelli* which achieved popularity during the Risorgimento; Garibaldi is reputed to have chanted one on leaving Montevideo to return to Italy. His poems have little formal resemblance to Lippi's, however, and are political or satirical in nature.

56. *what good's in life*] what good in life (*1868–88*).

61–6. *Into shreds . . . after them*: One of the incidents derived directly from Vasari; see letter to Ruskin (headnote, *Sources*).

66. *I came up with the fun*: 'I caught up with the revellers'.

67. *St. Laurence*] Saint Laurence (*1863–88*, except *1872* which has 'Saint Lawrence'). The church of San Lorenzo was closely connected with the Medici family and was rebuilt by Brunelleschi during the period in question; see also 323n.   *hail fellow, well met*: used here adverbially to describe Lippi's easy, over-familiar demeanour on approaching the group; cp. Lydia Melford's description of the Pump-Room in Bath, in Smollett's *Humphrey Clinker* (1771): 'You see the highest quality and the lowest trades-folk jostling each other, without ceremony, hail-fellow well met' (ch. iv, letter 1); and Leigh Hunt, *Men, Women, & Books* (1847), vol. i., p. 91: 'Palavering rascals, who come, hail-fellow-well-met'.

68–9. Another 'stornello'; see ll. 53–7n.

If I've been merry, what matter who knows?
70   And so as I was stealing back again
     To get to bed and have a bit of sleep
     Ere I rise up to-morrow and go work
     On Jerome knocking at his poor old breast
     With his great round stone to subdue the flesh,
75   You snap me of the sudden. Ah, I see!
     Though your eye twinkles still, you shake your head—
     Mine's shaved,—a monk, you say—the sting's in that!
     If Master Cosimo announced himself,
     Mum's the word naturally; but a monk!
80   Come, what am I a beast for? tell us, now!
     I was a baby when my mother died
     And father died and left me in the street.
     I starved there, God knows how, a year or two
     On fig-skins, melon-parings, rinds and shucks,
85   Refuse and rubbish. One fine frosty day
     My stomach being empty as your hat,
     The wind doubled me up and down I went.
     Old Aunt Lapaccia trussed me with one hand,

73–4. St Jerome (*c.*345–420), one of the most important figures in the early Church, translated and wrote commentaries on the Bible and was celebrated for his asceticism. Cosimo de' Medici founded a monastery and church for the order of 'Hieronymites' near the Villa Medici at Fiesole. Lippi painted at least five St Jeromes, but the picture in question must be the small one of Jerome in penance which (according to Vasari) he painted for Cosimo de' Medici; the editors of *Le Monnier* claim to have found this painting, wrongly attributed to Masolino da Panicale, in the Galleria delle Belle Arti in Florence (p. 118). Cp. *Old Pictures* 207n. (p. 425).

75. snap: 'catch', with the implication of a predator 'snapping up' its prey.

77. Mine's shaved: i.e. Lippi has the monk's tonsure, whereby the crown of the head is shaved; see headnote, *Sources* for the debate over whether Lippi was in fact still a monk at this period.

79. Mum's the word: 'say nothing'; cp. *2 Henry VI,* I ii 89: 'Seal up your lips and give no word but mum'.

80. what am I a beast for? a number of senses are possible: 'why do I behave like a beast?'; 'why do you see me as a beast?' (given the fact that Lippi is defending himself against the suggestion that his behaviour is all the worse because he is a monk); or possibly 'why was I made a beast if not to behave like this?' Cp. *Easter Day* 33 (III 101) and *Bishop Blougram* 349 (p. 303).

81–91. This account of Lippi's origins is very closely based on Vasari; see letter to Ruskin in headnote, *Sources.*

84. shucks: husks or shells.

88. trussed: 'To tie in a bundle, or stow away closely in a receptacle; to bundle, pack' (*OED*).

(Its fellow was a stinger as I knew)
90   And so along the wall, over the bridge,
       By the straight cut to the convent. Six words, there,
       While I stood munching my first bread that month:
       "So, boy, you're minded," quoth the good fat father
       Wiping his own mouth, 'twas refection-time,—
95   "To quit this very miserable world?
       Will you renounce" . . . The mouthful of bread? thought I;
       By no means! Brief, they made a monk of me;
       I did renounce the world, its pride and greed,
       Palace, farm, villa, shop and banking-house,
100 Trash, such as these poor devils of Medici
       Have given their hearts to—all at eight years old.
       Well, sir, I found in time, you may be sure,
       'Twas not for nothing—the good bellyful,
       The warm serge and the rope that goes all round,
105 And day-long blessed idleness beside!
       "Let's see what the urchin's fit for"—that came next.
       Not overmuch their way, I must confess.
       Such a to-do! they tried me with their books.

89. *Its fellow was a stinger*: her other hand was capable of inflicting a sharp slap.
90–1. And so . . . convent: Santa Maria del Carmine is south of the Arno
('Oltrarno'); these lines suggest that Mona Lapaccia dragged Lippi to it across one
of the city's bridges, probably the Ponte alla Carraia. Santa Maria del Carmine is
very close to Casa Guidi, so B. would have been familiar with the geography of
this area.
91. Six words: B. often uses 'six' for a small quantity; cp. (e.g.) *The Statue and the
Bust* 219: 'Six steps out of the chapel yonder' (III 357).
94. refection-time: mealtime in the monastery.
95–6. To quit . . . renounce: cp. the rite of Infant Baptism in *The Book of Common
Prayer*: 'Dost thou . . . renounce the devil and all his works, the vain pomp and
glory of the world, with all covetous desires of the same, and the carnal desires
of the flesh[?]'
100–1.] Trash, such poor devils as these Medici / Give their hearts to—and all
at eight years old. (*H proof*).
103. 'Twas not for nothing: i.e. the renunciation of 'the world' had brought some
compensation in the form of adequate nourishment.
104. serge: the monk's habit of coarse woollen cloth girdled by a rope. The type
of clothing to be worn by each Order was dictated by ecclesiastical law; the
Carmelites adopted a white cloak in 1287, and so became known as the White
Friars (see below l. 145n.).
105. The image of monastic life as an excuse for physical and mental laziness was
a commonplace of anti-Catholic satire in B.'s time, although its roots go back
before the Reformation in (e.g.) the tales of Chaucer and Boccaccio.
108. tried: both 'attempted to interest' and 'annoyed'.

Lord, they'd have taught me Latin in pure waste!
110 *Flower o' the clove,*
All the Latin I construe is, "amo" I love!
But, mind you, when a boy starves in the streets
Eight years together, as my fortune was,
Watching folk's faces to know who will fling
115 The bit of half-stripped grape-bunch he desires,
And who will curse or kick him for his pains—
Which gentleman processional and fine,
Holding a candle to the Sacrament
Will wink and let him lift a plate and catch
120 The droppings of the wax to sell again,
Or holla for the Eight and have him whipped,—
How say I?—nay, which dog bites, which lets drop
His bone from the heap of offal in the street!
—The soul and sense of him grow sharp alike,
125 He learns the look of things, and none the less
For admonitions from the hunger-pinch.
I had a store of such remarks, be sure,

109.] Lord, Latin they'd have taught me in pure waste. (*H proof*; *H proof²* has the verbal variant but does not record the punctuation variant).
110–11. Another of the 'stornelli'; see ll. 53–7n.
111. construe: pronounced with the stress on the first syllable: cónstrue.
115. he desires] that he eyes (*H proof*).
117–20. Candles are usually carried in Roman Catholic religious processions; cp. *Up at a Villa* 51–2 (III 148–9). In this procession the 'Sacrament' (the communion host), housed in a tabernacle, is accompanied by prominent citizens of the town holding large wax tapers; Lippi is imagining one of these 'processional' gentlemen allowing him to collect and resell his used candle wax. The association of Catholicism and thrift here may owe something to lines from one of Donne's satires which are cited below, l. 148n.
117. processional] processioning (*H proof*).
121. the Eight: the magistrates of Florence.
124–6. Lippi suggests that his artistic talent for the representation of human emotion derives from his early experiences, and in particular the harsh lesson of the 'hunger-pinch' he felt when he misread people's feelings and characters. B. makes no mention of his having received any artistic training (of the kind he offers to his own pupil at ll. 273–80), sacrificing verisimilitude in order to emphasize Lippi's natural gift, honed by his experiences in the streets of Florence.
124. —The soul] Why, soul (*1863–88*).
125. and none the less] minds none the less (*1863²*). Verbal variants unique to *1863²* are rare; another example close by, at l. 131, suggests that B. may have been glancing over the proofs and made a couple of changes which he later forgot.
126. For admonitions] For admonition (*1868–88*).
127. remarks: perceptions, observations.

Which, after I found leisure, turned to use:
I drew men's faces on my copy-books,
130   Scrawled them within the antiphonary's marge,
Joined legs and arms to the long music-notes,
Found nose and eyes and chin for A.s and B.s,
And made a string of pictures of the world
Betwixt the ins and outs of verb and noun,
135   On the wall, the bench, the door. The monks looked
       black.
"Nay," quoth the Prior, "turn him out, d'ye say?
In no wise. Lose a crow and catch a lark.
What if at last we get our man of parts,
We Carmelites, like those Camaldolese

128. Which, after] Which, now that (*H proof*).

129–41. 'Questo putto . . . essendo tenuto con gli altri in noviziato e sotto la dis-
ciplina del maestro della grammatica, pur per vedere quello che sapesse fare; in
cambio di studiare, non faceva mai altro che imbrattare con fantocci i libri suoi
e degli altri: onde il priore si risolvette a dargli ogni comodità ed agio d'imparare
a dipingere' (*Le Monnier* 115) [This boy . . . being a novice like the others and
like them subject to the discipline of the master of grammar, if only to see what
he was capable of doing, instead of studying never did anything but cover his
books and those of the other boys with caricatures. The Prior therefore resolved
to give him every opportunity to learn how to paint].

130. Scrawled them within] Scrawled them on (*H proof*, but not *H proof²*).
antiphonary's marge: antiphons are 'short melodies sung before and after a psalm';
W. M. Johnston (ed.), *Encyclopaedia of Monasticism* (Chicago 2000) i 10. An antiphonary is a book containing a number of antiphons.

131. the long music-notes: i.e. probably breves and semi-breves, which indicate
a note held over a long interval, although there may be a pun on a 'long', an
even longer note not used in modern notation; B.'s knowledge of Renaissance
scoring may be a little inaccurate, however, since breves and semi-breves were
the standard notation, and Lippi would not have distinguished them as '*long* music-
notes'.   *long*] square (*1863²*). The 'long' was written as a 'square'.

132. Oxford points out that '[since] chant notation is black, not hollow, the "A's
and B's" . . . are not musical notes, but letters of the alphabet'; cp. l. 134.   *nose
and eyes*] eyes and nose (*H proof*).

135. The monks looked black] The monks were mazed (*H proof*).

137. Lose a crow and catch a lark: this looks proverbial, but we have not been able
to discover any sources. The sense is obviously something like, 'it's a stroke of
luck to lose something ordinary and get something valuable in its place'; the Prior
is saying that although Lippi may not turn out to be a run-of-the-mill monk, he
will be worth keeping.

138. parts: talents.

139–40. Camaldolese / And Preaching Friars: the Camaldolese Order, a strongly ascetic
Benedictine Order, was founded in the early eleventh century by St Romuald;
the Dominicans were known as the 'preaching friars' as this activity was central
to their ministry. See also ll. 235–6n.

140 And Preaching Friars, to do our church up fine
And put the front on it that ought to be!"
And hereupon they bade me daub away.
Thank you! my head being crammed, their walls a blank,
Never was such prompt disemburdening.
145 First, every sort of monk, the black and white,
I drew them, fat and lean: then, folks at church,
From good old gossips waiting to confess
Their cribs of barrel-droppings, candle-ends,—
To the breathless fellow at the altar-foot,
150 Fresh from his murder, safe and sitting there
With the little children round him in a row
Of admiration, half for his beard and half
For that white anger of his victim's son
Shaking a fist at him with one fierce arm,

140. to do our church] shall do our church (*H proof*).

141. The primary meaning is that the façade of the order's church will at last be given the ornamentation it deserves (although as *Thomas* points out, the façade of Santa Maria del Carmine, the Carmelite church, remains unfinished [p. 106]); cp. the 'Moorish front' which Luria designs for the Cathedral in Florence (*Luria* i 124–5, II 385). 'Front' also suggests the church's self-presentation, its prestige in the wider world.

142. they bade me] he bade me (*1868–88*).

143. being crammed] was crammed (*H proof*).

145. black and white: Dominicans ('Black Friars') and Carmelites ('White Friars').

146. fat and lean] good and bad (*H proof*). *folks at church*] folk at church (*1888*).

147. gossips: a 'gossip' is 'A person, mostly a woman, of light and trifling character, esp. one who delights in idle talk; a newsmonger, a tattler' (*OED*); cp. *Ring* ii 513.

148. cribs: 'trivial thefts' (of minute quantities of wine or food, etc.). Oxford (with acknowledgement to Michael Meredith) points out the resemblance to Donne's 'Satire II': 'For as a thrifty wench scrapes kitchen-stuff, / And barrelling the droppings and the snuff / Of wasting candles, which in thirty year / (Relic-like kept) perchance buys wedding gear' (ll. 81–4). See also above, ll. 117–20n. B.'s great admiration for Donne, unusual in the mid-nineteenth century, makes this connection even more likely.

149–62. The murderer in Lippi's imaginary drama has claimed the right of sanctuary by entering the church, and cannot be arrested or harmed. The tradition that the church represented a place of 'sanctuary' within which those suspected of crimes could take refuge dates from the early church (it was recognized under the Code of Theodosius in 399) and continued in Catholic countries until the eighteenth century.

151. in a row] in a ring (*H proof*).

153. white anger: pallor is associated with extreme anger or hatred in B.; cp. *Light Woman* 25 (III 610).

155   Signing himself with the other because of Christ
       (Whose sad face on the cross sees only this
       After the passion of a thousand years)
       Till some poor girl, her apron o'er her head
       Which the intense eyes looked through, came at eve
160   On tip-toe, said a word, dropped in a loaf,
       Her pair of ear-rings and a bunch of flowers
       The brute took growling, prayed, and then was gone.
       I painted all, then cried, " 'tis ask and have—
       Choose, for more's ready!"—laid the ladder flat,
165   And showed my covered bit of cloister-wall.
       The monks closed in a circle and praised loud
       Till checked, (taught what to see and not to see,
       Being simple bodies) "that's the very man!
       Look at the boy who stoops to pat the dog!
170   That woman's like the Prior's niece who comes
       To care about his asthma: it's the life!"

155. *Signing himself . . . because of Christ*: making the sign of the cross out of superstitious fear, because there is a statue or painting of the crucified cross above the
altar. Bishop Blougram ridicules the supposed incongruity of religious faith with
brutal criminality (ll. 688–92, p. 323).
156. *only this*] only that (*H proof*).
157. *passion*: suffering (Latin *patior*, to suffer or endure); another name for the
Crucifixion was the Passion of Christ.
158. *poor girl*: possibly a euphemism for prostitute; cp. *Pippas* iii 225^226, p. 153),
and see l. 162n.   *her apron o'er her head*: as she is bringing food to the murderer,
the 'poor girl' is anxious to conceal her identity.
160. *dropped in a loaf*] threw in a loaf (*H proof*).
162.] (The brute took growling) and so was gone. (*1868–88*, except that *1888* has
a comma after the closing bracket). *Oxford* suggests that the 'brute' is 'the priest
taking Confession', but this cannot be right; it refers to the murderer in the anecdote taking food during his period of refuge in the church. The scene transplants
to Florence a stereotype of Victorian popular fiction, the devotion of a prostitute to her abusive lover and pimp, of which the most famous example is the
relationship between Bill Sikes and Nancy in *Oliver Twist*.
163. *I painted all, then cried*] I got all ready, cried (*H proof*).
164. *more's ready*] my head's full (*H proof*).
167. *checked, (taught*] checked, taught (*H proof, 1868–88*); checked—taught (*1863²*);
checked,—taught (*1863–65*). B. evidently had trouble getting the punctuation of
this line to his satisfaction; see also next line.
168. *simple bodies)*] bodies: (*H proof*); bodies,—(*1863–88*).
170–1. *the Prior's niece . . . asthma*: as Turner points out, this is a euphemism for
the Prior's mistress. His sexual licence resembles that of the Bishop of St Praxed's
(p. 232) and the Bishop in *Holy-Cross Day* (pp. 545–7).

But there my triumph's straw-fire flared and funked—
Their betters took their turn to see and say:
The Prior and the learned pulled a face
175 And stopped all that in no time. "How? what's here?
Quite from the mark of painting, bless us all!
Faces, arms, legs and bodies like the true
As much as pea and pea! it's devil's-game!
Your business is not to catch men with show,
180 With homage to the perishable clay,
But lift them over it, ignore it all,
Make them forget there's such a thing as flesh.
Your business is to paint the souls of men—
Man's soul, and it's a fire, smoke . . no it's not . .
185 It's vapour done up like a new-born babe—
(In that shape when you die it leaves your mouth)
It's . . well, what matters talking, it's the soul!
Give us no more of body than shows soul.
Here's Giotto, with his Saint a-praising God!
190 That sets you praising,—why not stop with him?
Why put all thoughts of praise out of our heads
With wonder at lines, colours, and what not?

172. straw-fire flared and funked: 'blazed and then went out'; a 'straw fire' was prover-bial, although for smokiness rather than brevity. Cp. Tennyson, *Morte d'Arthur* 273–4: 'our last light, that long / Had winked and threatened darkness, flared and fell'.

173.] Their betters had to see and say instead: (*H proof*).

176. the mark of painting: 'the correct standard of painting'.

179. to catch men] to maze men (*H proof*, but not *H proof²*).

180. With homage] Mere homage (*H proof*). *perishable clay*: a biblical metaphor for the human body: see e.g. *Isaiah* lxiv 8: 'But now, O Lord, thou art our father; we are the clay, and thou our potter; and we all are the work of thy hand.' Cp. *Rabbi Ben Ezra* 150 ff. (p. 660).

184–7. Lippi satirizes the proliferation and confusion of medieval theories about the soul, which extends back to antiquity; cp. *An Epistle* 1–12 (pp. 511–12), and *Cleon* 57–9 (p. 570).

184. it's a fire, smoke] it's a vapour (*H proof*).

186.] In that shape when they die it leaves their mouth, (*H proof*).

188. than shows soul] than shows that (*H proof*).

189. For Giotto see headnote to *Old Pictures* (pp. 404 ff.). It seems unlikely that an allusion to any particular painting is intended. *a-praising God!*] a-praising there, (*H proof*); a-praising God, (*1863–88*).

190. sets you praising] sets us praising (*1868–88*). The revision emphasizes the con-trast between Lippi's naturalism and the conventionalism of his fellow monks; the original reading allows him to admire Giotto.

191. out of our heads] out of our head (*1868–88*).

Paint the soul, never mind the legs and arms!
Rub all out, try at it a second time.
195 Oh, that white smallish female with the breasts,
She's just my niece . . . Herodias, I would say,—
Who went and danced and got men's heads cut off—
Have it all out!" Now, is this sense, I ask?
A fine way to paint soul, by painting body
200 So ill, the eye can't stop there, must go further
And can't fare worse! Thus, yellow does for white
When what you put for yellow's simply black,
And any sort of meaning looks intense
When all beside itself means and looks nought.
205 Why can't a painter lift each foot in turn,
Left foot and right foot, go a double step,
Make his flesh liker and his soul more like,
Both in their order? Take the prettiest face,
The Prior's niece . . . patron-saint—is it so pretty
210 You can't discover if it means hope, fear,
Sorrow or joy? won't beauty go with these?
Suppose I've made her eyes all right and blue,

195. white smallish female: in Lippi's fresco of *The Feast of Herod* at Prato (see ll. 31–6n.), Salome is depicted in a luminous white dress against a predominantly dark background.

196–7. Herodias . . . cut off: it was not Herodias who danced for Herod, but her daughter Salome, who was instructed by Herodias to ask for the head of John the Baptist as her reward (*Matthew* xiv 3–11). As Turner (p. 319) points out, the slip may be intended to show the Prior's ignorance (cp. *Tomb at St. Praxed's* 95, p. 242), or may derive from Vasari, who refers to Lippi's depiction of 'la destrezza di Herodias' [the dexterity of Herodias].

198. is this sense] is that sense (H *proof*, but not H *proof²*). The term comprises both 'good sense' and 'sensuality'.

200–1. must go further / And can't fare worse! inverting the proverbial expression: 'You could go farther and fare worse'; see e.g. *Martin Chuzzlewit* (1844), ch. xvii: ' "You will have to go farther." "And to fare worse?" said Martin, pursuing the old adage.'

205–8. Lippi's analogy is intended to suggest that soul and flesh are like the left foot and the right foot, which are both equally necessary: cp. *Aurora Leigh* i 1095–9: 'Vincent Carrington, / Whom men judge hardly as bee-bonneted, / Because he holds that, paint a body well, / You paint a soul by implication, like / The grand first Master.'

209. Lippi's hesitation here might be a deliberately playful stumbling over his words, or a sign of his anxiety lest his admiration for the Prior's 'niece' be reported back to the monastery; see ll. 170–1n.

212–14. The 'breath of life' derives from *Genesis* ii 7: 'And the Lord God formed man of the dust of the ground, and breathed into his nostrils the breath of life;

Can't I take breath and try to add life's flash,
And then add soul and heighten them threefold?
215 Or say there's beauty with no soul at all—
(I never saw it—put the case the same—)
If you get simple beauty and nought else,
You get about the best thing God invents,—
That's somewhat. And you'll find the soul you have missed,
220 Within yourself when you return Him thanks!
"Rub all out!" well, well, there's my life, in short,
And so the thing has gone on ever since.
I'm grown a man no doubt, I've broken bounds—
You should not take a fellow eight years old
225 And make him swear to never kiss the girls—
I'm my own master, paint now as I please—
Having a friend, you see, in the Corner-house!
Lord, it's fast holding by the rings in front—
Those great rings serve more purposes than just
230 To plant a flag in, or tie up a horse!
And yet the old schooling sticks—the old grave eyes
Are peeping o'er my shoulder as I work,
The heads shake still—"It's Art's decline, my son!
You're not of the true painters, great and old:

and man became a living soul.' *Genesis* does not distinguish between the 'flash'
which signifies 'life' (physical animation) and the 'soul'. With the 'threefold'
structure, cp. *A Death* 82–104 (pp. 729–30).
215–20. Lippi suggests that even beauty without soul has a spiritual dimension,
since it produces a reflex of gratitude to God in the viewer.
216.] I never saw that—put the case, the same—(*H proof*).
219–20.] Is not that somewhat? And the soul you have missed, / Find in yourself
when you return him thanks! (*H proof*; *H proof²* does not record the question
mark in l. 219).
221–2. in short, / And so] in short: / That way (*H proof*).
227. a friend: Cosimo de' Medici (see l. 17n.); Lippi may mean personal friendship
with Cosimo (who is said by Vasari to have been one of Lippi's 'amici': see headnote, p. 479), though 'friend' can also mean a 'patron, or supporter' (*OED* 5a).
you see, in the Corner-house!] you see—the Corner-house—(*H proof*). See l. 18n.
228–30. Lippi imagines himself holding on to the iron rings bolted to the front
of the Medici palace as a metaphor for the protection he receives from his patron.
229. than just] than one, (*H proof*).
232. Are peeping] Still peeping (*H proof*, but not *H proof²*).
233. The heads shake still] The shaking heads (*H proof*).

235   Brother Angelico's the man, you'll find:
        Brother Lorenzo stands his single peer.
        Fag on at flesh, you'll never make the third!"
        Flower o' the pine,
        You keep your mistr . . . manners, and I'll stick to mine!
240   I'm not the third, then: bless us, they must know!
        Don't you think they're the likeliest to know,
        They, with their Latin? so I swallow my rage,
        Clench my teeth, suck my lips in tight, and paint
        To please them—sometimes do, and sometimes don't,
245   For, doing most, there's pretty sure to come
        A turn—some warm eve finds me at my saints—
        A laugh, a cry, the business of the world—
        (Flower o' the peach,
        Death for us all, and his own life for each!)
250   And my whole soul revolves, the cup runs o'er,
        The world and life's too big to pass for a dream,

235–6. Brother Angelico . . . Brother Lorenzo: Guido di Pietro, known as Fra Angelico (1387–1455) was a member of the 'Observant' branch of the Dominican Order based at the Monastery of San Marco in Florence; Piero di Giovanni, known as Lorenzo Monaco ('Lawrence the Monk') (*c.*1370–*c.*1422) was a member of the Camaldolese Order based in the Monastery of Santa Maria degli Angeli in Piazza Brunelleschi (see above ll. 139–40n.).

236. Brother Lorenzo stands] Brother Lorenzo, that's (*H proof*, but not *H proof²*).

237. Fag on at flesh: 'continue to devote your efforts to painting the human body' (rather than, by implicit contrast with Angelico and Lorenzo, the soul). *you'll never make the third*: cp. *Andrea* 258–64 (p. 403), in which the painter imagines himself as the fourth artist along with 'Leonard, Rafael, [and] Angelo'; and *Aristophanes' Apology* (1875) 5134–40, in which Aristophanes dismisses the possibility of a master of 'tragicomic verse' who will combine the genius of himself and Euripides (i.e. Shakespeare) as an 'imaginary Third'.

238–9. Another 'stornello'; see ll. 53–7n.

248–9. See ll. 53–7n.

250. the cup runs o'er] the cup runs over (*H proof, 1863–88*, except *1863²* which agrees with *1855*). See also l. 291. The phrase 'my cup runneth over' comes from *Psalms* xxiii 5, but refers there to pleasure, not frustration; cp. also *Psalms* lxxiii 10, referring to divine punishment: 'waters of a full cup are wrung out to them', and *Matthew* xxvi 39, the cup which Jesus prays to be spared in the garden of Gethsemane.

251. Denying one of the tenets (or, as Lippi sees it, clichés) of Christian *contemptus mundi*, as expressed by the Bishop in *Tomb at St. Praxed's*: 'And as she died so must we die ourselves, / And thence ye may perceive the world's a dream' (ll. 8–9, p. 238). The specific image of life, or the world, as a dream is not biblical (the closest parallel is with *Job* xx 8, on the fate of the wicked: 'He shall fly away as a dream, and shall not be found'), but the thought itself is close to many biblical texts on the brevity and 'vanity' of earthly existence, and on the need to

And I do these wild things in sheer despite,
And play the fooleries you catch me at,
In pure rage! the old mill-horse, out at grass
255   After hard years, throws up his stiff heels so,
Although the miller does not preach to him
The only good of grass is to make chaff.
What would men have? Do they like grass or no—
May they or mayn't they? all I want's the thing
260   Settled for ever one way: as it is,
You tell too many lies and hurt yourself.
You don't like what you only like too much,
You do like what, if given you at your word,
You find abundantly detestable.
265   For me, I think I speak as I was taught—
I always see the Garden and God there
A-making man's wife—and, my lesson learned,
The value and significance of flesh,

---

reject the 'world', e.g., *1 John* ii 15–17: 'Love not the world, neither the things that are in the world. . . . For all that is in the world, the lust of the flesh, and the lust of the eyes, and the pride of life, is not of the Father, but is of the world. And the world passeth away, and the lust thereof; but he that doeth the will of God abideth for ever.' B. may also have been influenced by literary instances, e.g. Prospero's famous lines in *The Tempest*: 'We are such stuff / As dreams are made on, and our little life / Is rounded with a sleep' (IV i 156–8), or Shelley's *Adonais*: 'He hath awakened from the dream of life' (l. 344). Cp. also Longfellow's 'A Psalm of Life', publ. 1839 and widely known: 'Tell me not, in mournful numbers, / Life is but an empty dream! / For the soul is dead that slumbers / And things are not what they seem' (ll. 1–4). B. may also have had in mind Calderon's play *Life is a Dream* (1636).

254–7. the old mill-horse . . . make chaff: contrast the horse in *Childe Roland* 76–84 (pp. 358–9).

255. chaff: the refuse of winnowed grain; frequently used in the Bible (and therefore in the monks' 'preaching') in connection with the wrath of God: see e.g. *Isaiah* v 24: 'Therefore as the fire devoureth the stubble, and the flame consumeth the chaff, so their root shall shall be as rottenness, and their blossom shall go up as dust: because they have cast away the law of the LORD of hosts, and despised the word of the Holy One of Israel.'

261. too many] so many (*H proof*).

264. You find] Is found (*H proof*, but not *H proof²*).

266–7. I always see . . . man's wife: *Genesis* ii 8–25. Thomas (p. 118) points out that the Brancacci Chapel of Santa Maria del Carmine, Lippi's monastery, contains two early fifteenth-century depictions of a naked Adam and Eve by Masolino and Masaccio respectively, although B.'s erroneous belief that Lippi was Masaccio's master and not his pupil rules the latter out as a possible source for Lippi's 'lesson' on '[the] value and significance of flesh'; cp. ll. 273–80n.

267.] A-making man his wife—my lesson learned, (*H proof*).

I can't unlearn ten minutes afterward.
270   You understand me: I'm a beast, I know.
But see, now—why, I see as certainly
As that the morning-star's about to shine,
What will hap some day. We've a youngster here
Comes to our convent, studies what I do,
275 Slouches and stares and lets no atom drop—
His name is Guidi—he'll not mind the monks—
They call him Hulking Tom, he lets them talk—
He picks my practice up—he'll paint apace,
I hope so—though I never live so long,
280 I know what's sure to follow. You be judge!
You speak no Latin more than I, belike—
However, you're my man, you've seen the world
—The beauty and the wonder and the power,
The shapes of things, their colours, lights and shades,
285 Changes, surprises,—and God made it all!
—For what? do you feel thankful, ay or no,
For this fair town's face, yonder river's line,
The mountain round it and the sky above,
Much more the figures of man, woman, child,
290 These are the frame to? What's it all about?
To be passed o'er, despised? or dwelt upon,
Wondered at? oh, this last of course, you say.
But why not do as well as say,—paint these
Just as they are, careless what comes of it?
295 God's works—paint anyone, and count it crime
To let a truth slip. Don't object, "His works
Are here already—nature is complete:

269^270.] All eds. have a line-space except *1863²*, which agrees with *1855*.
270. *I'm a beast*: cp. l. 80n.
271. *why, I see*] why, I know (*H proof*).
273–80. *We've a youngster . . . follow*: for B.'s erroneous suggestion that Tommaso di Giovanni di Guidi, known as Masaccio (1401–28) was Lippi's pupil rather than his teacher see headnote, *Sources*.
273. *We've a youngster*] There's a youngster (*H proof*, but not *H proof²*).
277. *Hulking Tom*: B.'s attempted translation of 'Masaccio'; the suffix '-accio' in Italian means unpleasant or awkward.
282.] You've seen the world however, you're my man. (*H proof*).
287–8. The river is the Arno; Florence is surrounded by hills. Cp. the ecstatic view of Florence in the opening lines of *Old Pictures* (pp. 409–10).
291. *passed o'er*] passed over (*H proof*, *1863–88*, except *1863²*, which agrees with *1855*). See also l. 250.

Suppose you reproduce her—(which you can't)
There's no advantage! you must beat her, then."
300 For, don't you mark, we're made so that we love
First when we see them painted, things we have passed
Perhaps a hundred times nor cared to see;
And so they are better, painted—better to us,
Which is the same thing. Art was given for that—
305 God uses us to help each other so,
Lending our minds out. Have you noticed, now,
Your cullion's hanging face? A bit of chalk,
And trust me but you should, though! How much more,
If I drew higher things with the same truth!
310 That were to take the Prior's pulpit-place,
Interpret God to all of you! oh, oh,
It makes me mad to see what men shall do
And we in our graves! This world's no blot for us,
Nor blank—it means intensely, and means good:
315 To find its meaning is my meat and drink.
"Ay, but you don't so instigate to prayer"
Strikes in the Prior! "when your meaning's plain
It does not say to folks—remember matins—

298. *reproduce her*] reproduced her (*H proof*, but not *H proof²*).

300–2. This argument is based on chapter 4 of Aristotle's *Poetics*: 'The instinct for imitation is inherent in man from his earliest days . . . Also inborn in all of us is the instinct to enjoy works of imitation. What happens in actual experience is evidence of this; for we enjoy looking at the most accurate representations of things which in themselves we find painful to see, such as the forms of the lowest animals and of corpses' (transl. T. S. Dorsch, Harmondsworth 1988).

306. *Lending our minds out*: 'allowing us to understand how the world looks to others'.

307. *cullion's*: a cullion is 'A base, despicable, or vile fellow; a rascal' (*OED*); derived from an old French word for testicle. *hanging face*: the primary sense here is 'the face of someone who will end up being hanged'; see ll. 19–20.

312. *men shall do*] men will do (*H proof*, but not *H proof²*).

313–14. *blot . . . blank*: cp. the Prologue to *Jocoseria* (1883): 'Wanting is—what? / Summer redundant, / Blueness abundant, / —Where is the blot? / Beamy the world, yet a blank all the same, / —Framework which waits for a picture to frame: / What of the leafage, what of the flower? / Roses embowering with naught they embower!' (ll. 1–8)

313. *no blot for us*] no trap for us (*H proof*).

315. *meat and drink*: 'a source of pleasure to me'; cp. *As You Like It* V i 10: 'It is meat and drink to me to see a clown'.

318. *matins*: despite its etymological derivation from Matuta, the Roman Goddess of the dawn, this term signifies the 'Night Office' of the Roman Catholic liturgy, and consists of the chanting of a selection of Psalms and the reading of lessons.

Or, mind you fast next Friday." Why, for this
320   What need of art at all? A skull and bones,
Two bits of stick nailed cross-wise, or, what's best,
A bell to chime the hour with, does as well.
I painted a St. Laurence six months since
At Prato, splashed the fresco in fine style.
325   "How looks my painting, now the scaffold's down?"
I ask a brother: "Hugely," he returns—
"Already not one phiz of your three slaves
That turn the Deacon off his toasted side,
But's scratched and prodded to our heart's content,
330   The pious people have so eased their own
When coming to say prayers there in a rage.

319. fast next Friday: fasting on Fridays is enjoined on Catholics at certain periods of the year, most notably Lent and Advent.

323–4. Unlike Lippi's *Coronation of the Virgin* (see ll. 344–77n.) this work is a fiction: B. almost certainly knew that Lippi never painted a 'Martyrdom of St. Laurence', the saint who was martyred in Rome during the persecution of Christians by the Emperor Valerian in 258 AD, traditionally by being roasted on a gridiron. Lippi's only major treatment of St Laurence is a dignified image of him 'Enthroned with Saints and Donors' (the 'Alessandri altarpiece', placed in the church at Vincigliata near Fiesole and now in the Metropolitan Museum of Art in New York). As *Thomas* points out (p. 121), B. would have seen a painting by Mario Balassi and Carlo Dolci of the martyrdom of St Laurence in the cathedral at Prato (which he and EBB. visited in 1853); he would also have seen Bronzino's painting of this subject in the church of San Lorenzo in Florence (which Lippi mentions at l. 67). Both represent St. Laurence at the moment when, according to legend, he taunted the Prefect of Rome who had ordered his torture: 'Turn me over, for this side is done' (see below, l. 328). St. Laurence does appear, carrying his gridiron, in *The Coronation of the Virgin*, in the row of saints in the foreground, though he is not mentioned in Lippi's description of this group (ll. 353–9).

323. a St Laurence] a Saint Laurence (*1868–88*).

327. phiz: a humorous term for the face derived from an abbreviation of 'physiognomy'.

328. That turn] That turned (*H proof*); Who turn (*1868–88*).   *the Deacon*: the rank below Bishop and priest; St Laurence was one of the seven deacons at Rome in the pontificate of Sixtus II (AD 257–8).

329–32. There are, as *Thomas* notes, similarities between this description and an incident associated with Andrea del Castagno's *Christ on the Column* as described in Mrs Foster's translation of Vasari: 'The picture is, in fine, of such merit, that were it not for the carelessness which has permitted it to be scratched and injured by children and simple folks, who have maltreated the head, arms, and almost the entire persons of the Jews, as though they would thereby avenge the injuries inflicted on the Saviour, this work would, without doubt, be the most beautiful of all that Andrea executed' (*Thomas* 428).

330. their own: i.e. their own hearts.

331. When coming] With coming (*1868–88*).

We get on fast to see the bricks beneath.
Expect another job this time next year,
For pity and religion grow i' the crowd—
335 Your painting serves its purpose!" Hang the fools!

—That is—you'll not mistake an idle word
Spoke in a huff by a poor monk, God wot,
Tasting the air this spicy night which turns
The unaccustomed head like Chianti wine!
340 Oh, the church knows! don't misreport me, now!
It's natural a poor monk out of bounds
Should have his apt word to excuse himself:
And hearken how I plot to make amends.
I have bethought me: I shall paint a piece
345 ... There's for you! Give me six months, then go, see
Something in Sant' Ambrogio's ... (bless the nuns!
They want a cast of my office) I shall paint

336–40. Lippi is suddenly anxious that his words will be reported to the church authorities and that he will be accused of heresy, a charge against which even his powerful Medici patron might find it difficult to protect him; cp. l. 209n.

343. And hearken] But hearken (*H proof*, but not *H proof²*).

344–77. The painting which Lippi projects here, *The Coronation of the Virgin*, is reproduced in vol. III of our edition (Plate 6); see l. 17n. Cp. the description given in the footnotes to *Le Monnier* (iv 117): 'In essa, con certa novità d'inven-zione, espresse Nostra Donna incoronata, con attorno in belle movenze molti Angeli leggiadramente vestiti e acconciati, e vari santi, tra' quali San Giovan Batista, Sant' Eustachio, San Martino e San Giobbe. A piè di essi, in mezze figure, è il ritratto del pittore di profilo, colla testa rasa, e dinanzi un Angioletto che sostiene una fascia dove è scritto: *Is perfecit opus*' [In this picture, with a certain imagina-tive novelty, [Lippi] depicts the Coronation of Our Lady, placing around her several angels gracefully dressed and arranged in pleasing attitudes, and various saints, amongst whom are St John the Baptist, Saint Eustace, Saint Martin and Saint Job. At the foot of these, in the midst of the figures, is a portrait of the artist in profile, his head shaved, and in front of him an angel holding a plaque upon which is written: *Is perfecit opus*]. As *Thomas* points out, however, Lippi's picture does not (and could not) contain the infant Jesus (p. 124). Vasari erro-neously identifies Lippi's self-portrait in the painting, an error which B. followed even though he probably knew it was an error: see ll. 360–4n.

345. There's for you! 'I've thought of it!'; or 'here's some more money!'

346. Sant' Ambrogio's ... (bless] Saint Ambrogio's: bless (*H proof*; *H proof²* only records the removal of the parenthesis); Sant' Ambrogio's! Bless (*1863–88*, except *1863* which agrees with *H proof*).

347. They want a cast of my office: 'they want to see a specimen of my work'; Lippi clearly intends a bawdy pun ('they want what I've got'); besides the allusion to popular stories of sexual misbehaviour between monks and nuns, there is the fact

God in the midst, Madonna and her babe,
Ringed by a bowery, flowery angel-brood,
350   Lilies and vestments and white faces, sweet
As puff on puff of grated orris-root
When ladies crowd to church at midsummer.
And then in the front, of course a saint or two—
Saint John, because he saves the Florentines,
355   Saint Ambrose, who puts down in black and white
The convent's friends and gives them a long day.
And Job, I must have him there past mistake,
The man of Uz, (and Us without the z,
Painters who need his patience.) Well, all these
360   Secured at their devotions, up shall come

that Lippi's mistress Lucrezia Buti was probably a novice when he seduced her (see headnote, *Sources* (i) *Le Monnier*). For the sense of 'cast' as a specimen or 'taste', see *J.* and *OED* sense 9. *of my office*)] of my office. (*H proof*, *1863–68*); o' my office. (*1870–88*).

351. orris-root: 'The rhizome of three species of Iris (*I. florentina, I. germanica, I. pallida*), which has a fragrant odour like that of violets; it is used powdered as a perfume and in medicine' (*OED*). Orris-root was used as a perfume for linen undergarments until personal hygiene became fashionable; hence the excessive use of it by the 'ladies' crowding to church at the hottest time of the year. Ruskin objected to the term, to B.'s surprise (see Appendix B, pp. 880, 882).

353. in the front] i' the front (*1870–88*).

354. Saint John] St. John (*1872*). *because he saves the Florentines*: John the Baptist is one of the patron saints of Florence.

355–6. Alluding to the practice of making votive offerings to a church whose patron saint will then record the donors' names in God's 'book of life' (thus ensuring their salvation: see *Revelation* 20: 12), and also intercede for them to enjoy a long life on earth. St Ambrose (339–397), Bishop of Milan, was one of the most important Fathers of the Christian church: 'he encouraged monasticism, recommending the Virgin Mary as the patron and model of nuns' (*Oxford Dictionary of Saints*). *Penguin* suggests that Lippi may be confusing this Ambrose with the theologian and scholar Ambrogio Traversari (1386–1439), but this seems very unlikely, not least because such a recently deceased person could not have been canonized; Traversari has in fact never been officially canonized.

355. Saint Ambrose] Sant' Ambrose (*H proof*, but not *H proof²*); St. Ambrose (*1872*).

357–9. And Job . . . patience: 'There was a man in the land of Uz, whose name was Job' (*Job* i 1). Job's patience in adversity is proverbial.

357. I must have him there] I mean to set him there (*H proof*).

358. of Uz, (and Us] of Uz and Us (*H proof*).

359.] Who need his patience—I at least. Well, these (*H proof*).

360. at their devotions] at their devotion (*1865–88*), the only verbal rev. to this poem which originates in *1865*. *up shall come*] up there comes (*H proof*).

360–4. up shall come . . . I'm the man! B., apparently following Vasari (see ll. 344–77n.), identifies the figure who emerges into the picture space in this way, in the right

Out of a corner when you least expect,
As one by a dark stair into a great light,
Music and talking, who but Lippo! I!—
Mazed, motionless and moon-struck—I'm the man!
365 Back I shrink—what is this I see and hear?
I, caught up with my monk's things by mistake,
My old serge gown and rope that goes all round,
I, in this presence, this pure company!
Where's a hole, where's a corner for escape?
370 Then steps a sweet angelic slip of a thing
Forward, puts out a soft palm—"Not so fast!"
—Addresses the celestial presence, "nay—
He made you and devised you, after all,
Though he's none of you! Could Saint John there, draw—
375 His camel-hair make up a painting-brush?
We come to brother Lippo for all that,
Iste perfecit opus!" So, all smile—

foreground facing the angel with the scroll, as Lippi's self-portrait, whereas it represents the donor who commissioned the altarpiece, Francesco Maringhi. But in his letter to Ruskin B. specifically identifies Lippi in this painting as a tonsured monk (he 'retains not only "l'abito" but the shaved head'; see headnote, *Sources*), and Maringhi, although balding, is not tonsured and is not wearing a monk's habit (he was a Canon of San Lorenzo and Rector of Sant' Ambrogio, but not a monk). The actual figure who represents Lippi is the younger of the two monks in the left foreground of the painting, leaning his chin on his hand; Job is looking directly at him (see ll. 357–9). It is likely that B. used poetic licence in repositioning Lippi in the painting, because he wanted the phrase 'iste perfecit opus' to apply to the artist, not the donor (see l. 377n.).

362. light,] emended in agreement with *H proof* and all other eds from 'light' in 1855, although the idea of Lippo emerging into an atmosphere of 'light music' has its charm. There is in fact no music in Lippi's painting.

364. Mazed: to maze is 'To bewilder, perplex, confuse' (*OED*).   *moon-struck*: 'distracted or dazed as the result of some mental obsession, esp. a romantic infatuation' (*OED*).

367. My old serge gown: on Lippi's monastic clothing see l. 104n.

375. camel-hair: A punning reference, linking John the Baptist's traditional garment (*Matthew* iii 1–4) with the material used to make artists' brushes. The figure of John the Baptist in Lippi's painting is wearing a rough shirt of a similar material.

377. Iste perfecit opus: 'This very man made the work' or 'This very man caused the work to be done'; in the painting these words flatter the donor, not the artist (see ll. 360–4n.). In the painting the scroll reads 'Is' not 'Iste'; B. may have thought the 'te' was concealed by the fold in the scroll. 'Iste' is a stronger, more emphatic designation than 'is', which simply means 'he'.

I shuffle sideways with my blushing face
Under the cover of a hundred wings
380   Thrown like a spread of kirtles when you're gay
And play hot cockles, all the doors being shut,
Till, wholly unexpected, in there pops
The hothead husband! Thus I scuttle off
To some safe bench behind, not letting go
385   The palm of her, the little lily thing
That spoke the good word for me in the nick,
Like the Prior's niece . . . Saint Lucy, I would say.
And so all's saved for me, and for the church
A pretty picture gained. Go, six months hence!
390   Your hand, sir, and good bye: no lights, no lights!
The street's hushed, and I know my own way back—
Don't fear me! There's the grey beginning. Zooks!

380. spread of kirtles: 'a skirt or outer petticoat' (*OED*). *gay*: this word was associated with immorality, and more specifically prostitution, during the mid-nineteenth century; see *OED* senses 2a and 2b, and l. 381n.

381. hot cockles: a traditional game played by a group of people in a ring; one of the players kneels in front of the others with his or her head in somebody's lap, then places a hand palm uppermost in the small of their back and cries out 'hot cockles hot'. Another of the players then hits them on the hand, and attempts to sit down again before being detected. The phrase is used as a sexual euphemism in a number of Restoration plays; see e.g. Farquhar's *Sir Harry Wildair* (1701), Act I: 'I went to Sir *Harry* all the way to *Rome*; and where d'ye think I found him? . . . Why, in the middle of a Monastery amongst a Hundred and fifty Nuns, playing at Hot-cockles'.

383. husband! Thus] husband—So (*H proof*).

386. That spoke] That said (*H proof*, but not *H proof²*). *in the nick*] i' the nick (*H proof*).

387. Saint Lucy: a virgin and martyr of the early church (*c*.283–303) who died rather than be forced into prostitution; Lippi's comparison of the Prior's 'niece' to Saint Lucy may be designed to counteract the suggestion that she is really the Prior's mistress. Cp. the similar hesitation at l. 209.

392. the grey beginning: i.e. the first glimmers of dawn, with obvious symbolic resonance; see headnote, *Parallels in B*. B.'s edition of Chaucer has an epigraph in his hand, dated 5 July 1873, consisting of a passage of Greek from Aristophanes' *Birds* which may be translated: 'The dawn is at hand, the dawn is breaking, and this star is one of its precursors'; and a phrase in the introduction describing Chaucer as 'Loadstarre of the English language' is marked, possibly by him. Cp. also the vision of daybreak at the end of EBB.'s *Aurora Leigh* (ix 950–7).

32 An Epistle

CONTAINING THE
STRANGE MEDICAL EXPERIENCE OF
KARSHISH, THE ARAB PHYSICIAN

Text, publication and revision
First publ. *M & W*, 10 Nov. 1855; repr. *1863, 1863², 1868, 1872, 1888*. Our text is *1855*. Revision after *1855* was generally light, although B. made more substantive changes than usual in the two volumes of selections in which the poem appeared (*1863²* and *1872*), perhaps indicating his continuing regard for it.

Composition
Sharp claims that part of this poem was written in Rome during 1853–54, although he does not say whether B. began or completed the poem at this time. DeVane connects the poem with B.'s speculations on religious matters in *Christmas-Eve* (III 34), which was written 1849–50, but agrees with *Sharp* in suggesting that it was written in Rome, placing it amongst the group of poems on subjects connected with Roman history (*Protus* [III 635], *Holy-Cross Day* [p. 540]) prompted by B.'s residence in the city.

Sources and influences
The story is based on *John* xi 1–46. Lazarus, the brother of Mary and Martha, falls sick and his sisters send for Jesus, who arrives (possibly by design) too late. 'Then when Jesus came, he found that he had lain in the grave four days already.' Jesus tells Martha 'Thy brother shall rise again', and when she mistakes this for a reference to 'the resurrection at the last day', Jesus utters his famous declaration: 'I am the resurrection, and the life: he that believeth in me, though he were dead, yet shall he live: And whosoever liveth and believeth in me shall never die.' When Mary and a number of Jewish mourners come to meet Jesus, Mary says to him 'Lord, if thou hadst been here, my brother had not died':

> When Jesus therefore saw her weeping, and the Jews also weeping which came with her, he groaned in the spirit, and was troubled,
> And said, Where have ye laid him? They said unto him, Lord, come and see.
> Jesus wept.
> Then said the Jews, Behold how he loved him!
> And some of them said, Could not this man, which opened the eyes of the blind, have caused that even this man should not have died?
> Jesus therefore again groaning in himself cometh to the grave. It was a cave, and a stone lay upon it.

Title. THE STRANGE MEDICAL EXPERIENCE OF KARSHISH] THE MEDICAL EXPERIENCE OF BEN KARSHISH (*H proof*, but not *H proof²*). The appearance of 'Ben' in the original title may help to explain B.'s confusion between 'Karshish' and 'Karshook' in *One Word More* (see l. 136, p. 611).

Jesus said, Take ye away the stone. Martha, the sister of him that was dead, saith unto him, Lord, by this time he stinketh: for he hath been dead four days.

Jesus saith unto her, Said I not unto thee, that, if thou wouldest believe, thou shouldest see the glory of God?

Then they took away the stone from the place where the dead was laid. And Jesus lifted up his eyes, and said, Father, I thank thee that thou hast heard me.

And I knew that thou hearest me always: but because of the people which stand by I said it, that they may believe that thou hast sent me.

And when he had thus spoken, he cried with a loud voice, Lazarus, come forth.

And he that was dead came forth, bound hand and foot with graveclothes: and his face was bound about with a napkin. Jesus saith unto them, Loose him, and let him go.

Then many of the Jews which came to Mary, and had seen the things which Jesus did, believed on him.

But some of them went their ways to the Pharisees, and told them what things Jesus had done.

This event is recounted in the poem from the point of view of an imaginary 'Arab physician', as EBB. explains in letters to her two sisters (see below, *Criticism*). Karshish is travelling in Palestine around AD 69 (see below, and ll. 26–8n.). He makes no mention of Martha and Mary, and has none of the circumstantial detail as to the place of burial, Jesus's behaviour, or the divided response of the other witnesses. When Karshish meets Lazarus he is an isolated figure in Bethany, apparently regarded as crazy, and not part of an early Christian community; indeed Karshish seems unaware that Jesus, whom he calls a 'Nazarene physician', has any kind of following. The fact that Lazarus did not die suddenly, but after a period of sickness, allows Karshish to interpret events from the medical rather than the spiritual point of view; on the other hand he clearly grasps the potential theological force of Lazarus's testimony, both as regards its implications for a belief in life after death—a belief which Lazarus holds with an unnatural certainty—and for the doctrine of God as the 'all-Loving' (l. 305). The double emphasis in John's Gospel on Jesus's human feelings of love, and on God as the principle of Love itself, made it B.'s favourite Gospel, and the one which most influenced both his theology and his poetics.

There were a number of attempts during the nineteenth century to explain the absence of the Lazarus story from the other three Gospels (*Matthew, Mark,* and *Luke,* the so-called 'synoptic' Gospels), with some biblical scholars arguing (as D. F. Strauss notes) that its inclusion in the synoptic Gospels would have been dangerous to Lazarus and his family, 'the former of whom, according to *John* xii 10, was persecuted by the Jewish hierarchy on account of the miracle which had been performed in him; a caution for which there was no necessity at the later period at which John wrote his gospel' (*Life of Jesus,* transl. Marian Evans [1846; rpt, 1892], p. 492). Strauss himself dismisses this suggestion, but B.'s poem lends it some support by alluding to the unsettled political circumstances of first-century Palestine. The action of the poem takes place at a particularly dangerous moment, during the Roman subjugation of the Jewish rebellion of AD 67–70; this may also help to explain Karshish's suspicion of the Syrian 'run-a-gate' (l. 49) to whom he gives his message. (B.'s awareness of the critical issues surrounding John's Gospel is discussed in more detail in the headnote to *A Death in the Desert,* pp. 718–24). Karshish's attitude towards miracles resembles that of

Matthew Arnold's Empedocles—both see them as tricks or subterfuges designed to appeal to ordinary people of limited understanding (see ll. 257–9n)—and in this respect he reminds the reader that the miracles of Jesus took place in a comparatively 'modern' era; cp. Thomas Arnold's critique of Strauss for putting forward 'the idea of men writing mythic histories between the time of Livy and Tacitus, and of St. Paul mistaking such for realities!' (A. P. Stanley, *The Life and Correspondence of Thomas Arnold, D.D.* [1890] 291).

B. may have been prompted to make Karshish an Arab by the role of Arab writers in preserving and transmitting the heritage of classical Greek and Roman medicine during the Middle Ages; cp. *Paracelsus* iii 959–60n. (I 234–5). Karshish's interest in leprosy, epilepsy and his method of classifying fevers are all consistent with surviving evidence of the understanding of these conditions in antiquity (see Vivian Nutton, *Ancient Medicine* [2005] and ll. 42–3n., 50–1n., 58–9n., 83n.).

The subject of the raising of Lazarus was treated in a number of mid-nineteenth-century poems. Like B., Tennyson (*In Memoriam* xxxi) emphasizes the inability or unwillingness of both Lazarus and the Gospel writer to give any details about Lazarus's experience between his death and resurrection: 'Behold a man raised up by Christ! / The rest remaineth unreveal'd; / He told it not; or something seal'd / The lips of that evangelist'. Cp. also William Lisle Bowles, *St. John in Patmos* ii 443–7: 'I spurred my horse; we passed the sepulchre / Of Lazarus, restored from the dark grave, / So those who own the faith of Christ affirm, / With eyeballs ghastly glaring in the light, / At the loud voice of Him who cried, Come forth!' EBB. uses an image that may be indebted to this poem in *Aurora Leigh* (1856): 'My father, who through love had suddenly / Thrown off the old conventions, broken loose / From chin-bands of the soul, like Lazarus, / Yet had no time to learn to talk and walk / Or grow anew familiar with the sun' (i 176–80). A possible reminiscence of Felicia Hemans's sonnet 'The Sisters of Bethany after the Death of Lazarus' is noted at l. 305.

The form of the poem, and especially the title word 'epistle', link to the epistles of the New Testament, especially those of St Paul (see l. 1n.). Karshish's rational, empirical stance (although mitigated by his adherence to an occult master: see ll. 167–8n.) sets him, like Cleon, in opposition to Paul, although from the standpoint of humility rather than overweening intellectual pride. His attitude also makes him resemble the corresponding member of a learned society of B.'s own day; and the poem may be read in the context of the extensive travel literature relating to the Holy Land in this period by British, French, and American authors. The Brownings owned Lamartine's *Souvenirs . . . pendant un Voyage en Orient* (1832–33; *Collections*, A1381), and B. may have come across Harriet Martineau's *Eastern Life, Present and Past* (1848), which EBB. mentions in letters before its publication (*Letters of EBB* i 352, 355). Martineau's book includes a visit to Bethany and a visit to the supposed tomb of Lazarus (pt. iii, ch. 4; see also l. 32n.); a more general reflection in chapter 1 is also pertinent. Here Martineau inveighs against those who travel to the Holy Land seeking for literal traces of Christian history instead of attempting to evoke the spirit of the Gospel narratives; true travellers possess 'the power of setting themselves back to the time when Christ lived and spoke, so as to see and hear him as if he spoke and lived at this day'.

Parallels in B.

As already indicated, the poem's main 'partner' is *Cleon*. Like the Greek philosopher, the Arab physician finds it hard to accept Christian doctrine, and both resort to calling its adherents mad; but Karshish has been powerfully moved by his direct encounter with Lazarus, whereas Cleon has heard only second-hand accounts of Paul's preaching. B. returned much later to the theme of a non-Christian perspective on the New Testament in *Imperante Augusto Natus Est* (*Asolando*, 1889). Arab characters and subjects appear in several poems and plays; see (e.g.) *Through the Metidja to Abd-el-Kadr* (II 155–6), *Return of the Druses* (1842) and *Muléykeh* (*DI²*, 1880). Lazarus's experience in the poem highlights the incompatibility of human and divine knowledge, a common theme in B.'s work. Cp., e.g., *Sordello* i 523–66 (I 430–2), in which the inability of the 'subjective' poet to '[thrust] in time eternity's concern' is lamented, and *Bishop Blougram* 648–50 (pp. 320–1). See also B.'s letter to Julia Wedgwood of 27 June 1864 in which he questions the sincerity of Newman's claim that he is certain of the existence of God: 'I can see nothing that comes from absolute *contact*, so to speak, between man and God, but everything in all variety from the greater or less distance between the two' (*RB & JW* 34). B. links this incompatibility to his own poetic method in his letter to Ruskin replying to Ruskin's criticism of the obscurity of some of the poems in *Men and Women*: see Appendix B, p. 881. Ruskin in fact exempted *Karshish* from his general criticism of the collection, a fact EBB. was quick to notice and take advantage of (see next section).

Criticism

B. and EBB. were surprised by the reaction of EBB.'s younger sister Henrietta to the poem, as EBB. wrote to her older sister Arabella on 22 Nov. 1855: 'what do you think she has taken into her head .. that his poem about Lazarus is written with irreverent and even blasphemous intentions against our Lord. Can you conceive of the poem striking any human being so? Here is a Gentile of that day giving his own impression of Lazarus!. The phenomenon of the raising of Lazarus is looked on *from without*? Can any one say rationally that the poem is not for the honor of the Lord? It seems to me wonderful that a dramatic intention should be so mistaken. People in general praise the poem as "sublime in conception," which to my mind it is' (*EBB to Arabella* ii 190). To Henrietta herself, EBB. wrote on 6 Dec.: 'no want of reverence, much less blasphemy, was intended by that poem, the object of which is in the highest degree reverential and Christian. It is one of my great favourites—(and we have this morning a letter from Mr. Ruskin, author of the Stones of Venice, a most Christian man, calling it his favourite,) and among all the criticisms we have heard, private and public, such an idea as yours seems to have occurred to no one. The Arabian physician considers the case of Lazarus as "a case"— represents it as such a man would, who had never heard of Christ before, or conceived of the miracle. It is a view *from without* of the raising from the dead, &c—and shows how this must have impressed the thinkers of the day, who came upon it with wondering, unbelieving eyes, for the first time. The way in which Lazarus is described as living his life after his acquaintance with the life beyond death, strikes me as entirely sublime, I confess' (*EBB to Henrietta* 235–6). For this letter from Ruskin, see prec. section. Note, however, that the long review-essay in the *Edinburgh Review* of October 1864 (a piece which particularly exasperated B. at the time) took up just this point: 'The subject is treated with all Mr. Browning's usual subtlety, quaintness, and ingenuity; but it seems to us irreverent in the highest degree to attempt to describe, through Karshish, the demeanour and mode of thought of Lazarus after his three days' experience of the mysterious realms of death.'

Karshish, the picker-up of learning's crumbs,
The not-incurious in God's handiwork
(This man's-flesh He hath admirably made,
Blown like a bubble, kneaded like a paste,
5   To coop up and keep down on earth a space
That puff of vapour from his mouth, man's soul)
—To Abib, all-sagacious in our art,
Breeder in me of what poor skill I boast,
Like me inquisitive how pricks and cracks
10 Befall the flesh through too much stress and strain,
Whereby the wily vapour fain would slip

1–20. The grammatical structure is 'Karshish [l. 1] sends greeting [l. 16] to Abib [l. 7]'; this elaborate rhetorical device may be designed to imitate the openings of St Paul's epistles in the New Testament; see for example *Romans* i 1–7; and cp. the opening of *Cleon* (p. 563).

1. Karshish: The name 'Karshish' means 'one who gathers' in Arabic (M. Wright, *TLS* 1 May 1953, p. 285).   *the picker-up of learning's crumbs*: cp. *Mark* vii 24–30, where Jesus at first refuses to heal the daughter of a non-Jewish woman, but then relents: 'Jesus said unto her, Let the children first be filled: for it is not meet to take the children's bread, and to cast it unto the dogs. And she answered and said unto him, Yes, Lord: yet the dogs eat of the children's crumbs.' The story is also in *Matthew* xv 21–8. Cp. also the story of Dives and Lazarus (not the Lazarus of the poem) in *Luke* xvi 19–31, where the beggar Lazarus desires 'to be fed with the crumbs which fell from the rich man's table'.

2–6. Characteristically 'Oriental' imagery: cp. *Psalms* xix 1: 'The heavens declare the glory of God; and the firmament sheweth his handywork'; *Genesis* ii 7: 'And the Lord God formed man of the dust of the ground, and breathed into his nostrils the breath of life; and man became a living soul'; *Job* xxxiv 19–20: 'they are all the work of his hands. In a moment shall they die'; *James* iv 14: 'For what is your life? It is even a vapour, that appeareth for a little time, and then vanisheth away.' To these biblical references may be added an allusion to the myth of Prometheus creating man out of clay: cp. Dryden's translation of Ovid, *Metamorphoses* i 101–6, which *J.* cites under 'paste': '[With] particles of heav'nly fire / The God of Nature did his soul inspire . . . Which wise Prometheus temper'd into paste, / And, mixt with living streams, the godlike image cast'. Cp., in B., *Lovers' Quarrel* 86n. (p. 381), *Fra Lippo* 184–7 (p. 495) and *Caliban* 75–97 (pp. 629–30).

7–15. Karshish's deferential manner here and at l. 220 may be an elaborately courteous compliment, since at ll. 169–73 he implies that both he and Abib were tutored by an older sage; cp., however, the relations between Festus, Paracelsus, and Trithemius in *Paracelsus* i 238–52 (I 125): both Festus and Paracelsus are pupils of Trithemius, but Festus is also Paracelsus's elder and mentor.

11–12. Cp. Marvell, 'On a Drop of Dew', where the soul is compared to a dew-drop which yearns to return to its source, 'the clear Fountain of Eternal Day', and (noting 'slip') Wordsworth, 'To H. C., Six Years Old', ll. 27–33: 'Thou art a dew-drop, which the morn brings forth ... [and which] Slips in a moment out of life'. Cp. also *Bishop Blougram* 656n. (p. 321).

Back and rejoin its source before the term,—
And aptest in contrivance, under God,
To baffle it by deftly stopping such:—
15   The vagrant Scholar to his Sage at home
Sends greeting (health and knowledge, fame with peace)
Three samples of true snake-stone—rarer still,
One of the other sort, the melon-shaped,
(But fitter, pounded fine, for charms than drugs)
20   And writeth now the twenty-second time.

My journeyings were brought to Jericho,
Thus I resume. Who studious in our art
Shall count a little labour unrepaid?
I have shed sweat enough, left flesh and bone
25   On many a flinty furlong of this land.
Also the country-side is all on fire
With rumours of a marching hitherward—
Some say Vespasian cometh, some, his son.
A black lynx snarled and pricked a tufted ear;
30   Lust of my blood inflamed his yellow balls:
I cried and threw my staff and he was gone.
Twice have the robbers stripped and beaten me,

---

12. before the term: i.e. before the natural end of human life (seventy years, or eighty at most, according to the Bible: *Psalms* xc 10).

13. aptest in contrivance: 'most skilful at contriving (remedies or cures)'.

14. it: the 'wily vapour'.   *stopping such*: blocking up the 'pricks and cracks'.

15. The vagrant Scholar. Arnold's 'The Scholar-Gipsy' was published in 1853. B.'s Karshish may be an antithetical reply to Arnold's pensive and withdrawing figure; for another such possible reply, see *James Lee* 212–21 (p. 678).

17–18. true snake-stone: snake-stone is a name given to any porous stone (or compound) supposed to cure snake-bite, either by absorbing the venom or as an antidote.

21–34. Jericho . . . Jerusalem: Karshish journeys from Jericho towards Jerusalem, reversing the direction of the man who falls among thieves in the parable of the good Samaritan (*Luke* x 30–7), but suffering the same fate (see l. 32n.).

26–8. Vespasian (Titus Flavius Vespasianus, AD 9–79, Emperor AD 69–79) commanded the Roman forces against the Jewish rebellion in 67–68, and subdued most of Judaea apart from Jerusalem itself, which was captured by his son Titus in 70. The allusion to a coming siege at ll. 146–7 indicates that the action of the poem takes place around AD 69; see also l. 109n.

29. Black lynx: 'the Syrian lynx is distinguished by black ears' (*Florentine*).

30. balls: eyeballs.

32. The Good Samaritan rescues a man who 'fell among thieves, which stripped him of his raiment, and wounded him, and departed, leaving him half dead' (*Luke* x 30). Harriet Martineau (see headnote, *Sources*), following her visit to Bethany,

And once a town declared me for a spy,
But at the end, I reach Jerusalem,
35   Since this poor covert where I pass the night,
This Bethany, lies scarce the distance thence
A man with plague-sores at the third degree
Runs till be drops down dead. Thou laughest here!
'Sooth, it elates me, thus reposed and safe,
40   To void the stuffing of my travel-scrip
And share with thee whatever Jewry yields.
A viscid choler is observable
In tertians, I was nearly bold to say,
And falling-sickness hath a happier cure
45   Than our school wots of: there's a spider here
Weaves no web, watches on the ledge of tombs,
Sprinkled with mottles on an ash-grey back;

---

comments on the dangers of the Jerusalem–Jericho road and cites the case of Sir Frederick Henniker who was 'stripped and left for dead by robbers in 1820'.
35. covert: shelter.
36. Bethany: the town in which Lazarus and his sisters live. *thence*: i.e. from Jerusalem.
39. 'Sooth: 'in sooth', i.e. 'in truth', 'indeed'.
40. 'To empty my travel-bag of its contents'.
41. Jewry: apparently both the people and the land. For another meaning of the term, see *How It Strikes* 74 (p. 443).
42–3. A viscid choler: 'viscid' is defined in *J.* as 'glutinous' or 'tenacious', and 'choler' as 'bile' or '[the] humour, which, by its super-abundance, is supposed to produce irascibility'. *tertians*: a tertian is defined in *J.* as 'an ague intermitting but one day, so that there are two fits in three days'; cp. Byron, *Don Juan* i 271. Nutton (see headnote, *Sources*) points out that '[the] largest group of conditions mentioned in our ancient medical texts is that of fevers, *puretoi* or *febres*, a broad term deriving from the feeling of fiery heat . . . the most common taxonomy depended on their periodicity, whether the high temperature was constant or waned and then returned after one, two, three or more days' (p. 32). This is the only occurrence of the word in B.'s poetry.
43. I was nearly bold to say: Karshish doubts whether he should go into details because the messenger who is to deliver his letter may be untrustworthy: see headnote, and cp. ll. 48–9, 61–4, 297–300.
44. falling-sickness: epilepsy, which is what Karshish diagnoses in Lazarus (l. 80). The term was already archaic in B.'s day, and belongs to 16th/17th-century English (cp. e.g. *Julius Caesar* I ii 256). Epilepsy was often regarded as having a divine origin in classical antiquity; this, and the fact that it has a 'happier cure', suggests a play on the idea of 'felix culpa', the 'fortunate fall': in this sense, 'falling-sickness' is original sin, the sickness caused by the Fall of Man.
45–8. a spider . . . drop them: as *Florentine* states: 'It was long a prevalent idea that the spider in various forms possessed some occult power of healing, and men administered it internally or applied it externally as a cure for many diseases.'

Take five and drop them . . . but who knows his mind,
The Syrian run-a-gate I trust this to?
50 His service payeth me a sublimate
Blown up his nose to help the ailing eye.
Best wait: I reach Jerusalem at morn,
There set in order my experiences,
Gather what most deserves and give thee all—
55 Or I might add, Judea's gum-tragacanth
Scales off in purer flakes, shines clearer-grained,
Cracks 'twixt the pestle and the porphyry,
In fine exceeds our produce. Scalp-disease

49. run-a-gate: the primary sense is 'vagabond', with the implication that the Syrian might be a fugitive or deserter; *OED* cites a 1737 translation of Josephus's *History of the Jewish War*: 'two thousand Syrian runagates' as well as 'the runagate Jews' (this is the same war, waged by Vespasian, to which Karshish refers at l. 28). Note also that the word was originally a variant form of 'renegade'; *OED* cites Nashe, *Martin Marprelate* (1589): 'Lucian the Atheist, was neuer so irreligious; nor euer Iulian the runnagate so blasphemous'. Finally, although this is less likely, B. may have connected the unreliable messenger with St Paul's servant Onesimus, who is the subject of the Epistle to Philemon; *OED* cites a 1612 commentary in which it is asserted that 'Paul hauing converted Onesimus a runnagate servant . . . sent him to Philemon againe'.

50–1. Nutton (headnote, *Sources*) states that '[eye] diseases are . . . well represented in ancient art, and were sufficiently common to justify their own speciality' (31). Karshish's healing of the Syrian's 'ailing eye' is a medical counterpart to Jesus's curing of two blind men on his way from Jericho to Jerusalem; see *Matthew* xx 29–34.

50. sublimate: sublimation is a chemical process in which a solid is heated to a vapour, then cooled; the residue, often in crystalline form, is the 'sublimate'. The composition of Karshish's 'sublimate', which is here probably, as *Oxford* suggests, a powder meant to be inhaled, is not specified; the term was also a synonym for 'mercury sublimate' or mercuric chloride, a powerful poison (*OED* cites Ben Jonson, *Epicoene, or The Silent Woman*: 'Take a little sublimate and go out of the world like a rat' [II ii]), but one which could also be used medicinally.

55. gum-tragacanth: a gum obtained from several species of *Astragalus*, a low-growing spiny shrub native to the Near East, used in medicine mainly as a vehicle for drugs; *OED* cites it (as simply 'tragacanth') in Holland's translation of Pliny, which B. certainly knew, and in a context where its value is emphasized: 'A pound of Tragacanth is worth thirteen deniers Romane'.

57. porphyry: i.e. the mortar (made of a hard polished substance such as porphyry) in which the 'gum-tragacanth' would be pounded.

58–9. Scalp-disease . . . leprosy: according to Nutton (headnote, *Sources*) there is good evidence that leprosy had entered the Mediterranean world by 250 BC; she also notes that the Hebrew word *za'arath*, translated as 'leprosy' in the Authorized Version, might well refer to a 'scaly disease' like psoriasis rather than leprosy itself. The frequent mentions of this disease in the Bible, and the story of Christ's meeting with the ten lepers on the way to Jerusalem (*Luke* xvii 11–19) 'gave this disease a special prominence in Christian literature' (p. 30).

Confounds me, crossing so with leprosy—
60   Thou hadst admired one sort I gained at Zoar—
But zeal outruns discretion. Here I end.

Yet stay: my Syrian blinketh gratefully,
Protesteth his devotion is my price—
Suppose I write what harms not, though he steal?
65   I half resolve to tell thee, yet I blush,
What set me off a-writing first of all.
An itch I had, a sting to write, a tang!
For, be it this town's barrenness—or else
The Man had something in the look of him—
70   His case has struck me far more than 'tis worth.
So, pardon if—(lest presently I lose
In the great press of novelty at hand
The care and pains this somehow stole from me)
I bid thee take the thing while fresh in mind,
75   Almost in sight—for, wilt thou have the truth?
The very man is gone from me but now,
Whose ailment is the subject of discourse.
Thus then, and let thy better wit help all.

'Tis but a case of mania—subinduced
80   By epilepsy, at the turning-point
Of trance prolonged unduly some three days,

---

60. *Zoar*. Lot's place of refuge; the only one of the five 'cities of the plain' not to be destroyed; *Genesis* xix 22–4.

62. *blinketh gratefully*: proving that his 'ailing eye' is healed.

67. Cp. *How It Strikes* 47–8 (p. 441).

65. *yet I blush*] though I blush (*H proof*).

70. *'tis worth*] it's worth (*H proof*).

79–101. For the story of Lazarus as related in *John*, see headnote, pp. 507–8. Karshish's account resembles the 'rationalistic' accounts of the gospel miracles proposed by various critics during the early nineteenth century, some of whom suggested that Jesus effected the 'resurrection' after realizing that Lazarus was not dead but merely ill. Strauss paraphrases one such critic, Paulus, thus: '[From] the messenger whom the sisters had sent with news of their brother's illness, Jesus had obtained accurate information of the circumstances of the disease; and the answer which he gave to the messenger, *This sickness is not unto death* (v. 4), is said to express, merely as an inference which he had drawn from the report of the messenger, his conviction that the disease was not fatal' (*Life of Jesus* 481).

79. *subinduced*: produced as a by-product; *OED* cites this as the only use of the word in this sense.

80. *epilepsy*: see l. 44n.

When by the exhibition of some drug
Or spell, exorcisation, stroke of art
Unknown to me and which 'twere well to know,
85   The evil thing out-breaking all at once
Left the man whole and sound of body indeed,—
But, flinging, so to speak, life's gates too wide,
Making a clear house of it too suddenly,
The first conceit that entered pleased to write
90   Whatever it was minded on the wall
So plainly at that vantage, as it were,
(First come, first served) that nothing subsequent
Attaineth to erase the fancy-scrawls
Which the returned and new-established soul
95   Hath gotten now so thoroughly by heart
That henceforth she will read or these or none.

82. exhibition: a medical term meaning 'application' (*OED* 2.4).

83. exorcisation: casting out of an evil spirit; Nutton (headnote, *Sources*) notes that prayers and incantations were often used to 'cure' epilepsy in antiquity. Karshish's willingness to countenance the possibility of both 'exhibition' and 'exorcisation' of the condition parallels the attitude of the author of *The Sacred Disease*, a text formerly attributed to Hippocrates, who 'is prepared to allow sacrifice, prayer and supplication to the gods' despite being convinced by his investigations into 'epilepsy and mania' that 'these conditions have a purely natural cause'.

84. 'twere well to know] were fit to know (*H proof*, but not *H proof²*).

85–96. Cp. *Luke* xi 24–6: 'When the unclean spirit is gone out of a man, he walketh through dry places, seeking rest; and finding none, he saith, I will return unto my house whence I came out. And when he cometh, he findeth it swept and garnished. Then goeth he, and taketh to him seven other spirits more wicked than himself; and they enter in, and dwell there: and the last state of that man is worse than the first.'

85.] The evil thing, out-breaking, all at once, (*1872*).

87–8. Cp. *Transcendentalism* 45 (III 646).

89–90. inscribe . . . on the wall: cp. *Daniel* v, in which a disembodied hand writes mysterious words on the wall of Belshazzar's palace, prophesying the end of his kingdom.

89. conceit: idea.   *pleased to write*] might inscribe (*1863–88*).

91. at that vantage: 'having that advantage'.

92. First come, first served: proverbial.

93. the fancy-scrawls] her fancy-scrawls (*H proof*, but not *H proof²*); those fancy-scrawls (*1863–88*).

94. Which the returned] And the returned (*H proof*, but not *H proof²*); The just-returned (*1863–88*).

95. Hath gotten] Hath got them (*H proof*, but not *H proof²*).

96. or these or none: 'either these or none'.   *or these*] or those (*1863²*), possibly a misprint, as substantive variants unique to this ed. are rare; but see also ll. 133, 137.

And first—the man's own firm conviction rests
That he was dead (in fact they buried him)
That he was dead and then restored to life
100 By a Nazarene physician of his tribe:
—'Sayeth, the same bade "Rise," and he did rise.
"Such cases are diurnal," thou wilt cry.
Not so this figment!—not, that such a fume,
Instead of giving way to time and health,
105 Should eat itself into the life of life,
As saffron tingeth flesh, blood, bones and all!
For see, how he takes up the after-life.
The man—it is one Lazarus a Jew,
Sanguine, proportioned, fifty years of age,
110 The body's habit wholly laudable,
As much, indeed, beyond the common health
As he were made and put aside to shew.
Think, could we penetrate by any drug

98. (in fact they buried him): an emphasis derived from the gospel account: see headnote.

100. Nazarene: from Nazareth, Jesus's home town (*Matthew* ii 23).

101. 'Sayeth: the apostrophe stands for an elided pronoun: 'He sayeth'. The purpose here is colloquial, as in *Fra Lippo* 43 (p. 487); B.'s most extensive use of elided pronouns is in *Caliban upon Setebos* (p. 616).

102. diurnal: daily.

103. fume: 'Idle conceit; vain imagination' (*J.*). Cp. *PL* viii 188–97 'But apt the mind or fancy is to rove / Uncheck'd, and of her roving is no end, / 'Till warn'd, or by experience taught, she learn, / That not to know at large of things remote / From use, obscure and subtle, but to know / That which before us lies in daily life, / Is the prime wisdom; what is more, is fume / Or emptiness, or fond impertinence, / And renders us in things that most concern / Unpractis'd, unprepar'd, and still to seek'.

105. life of life: cp. Shelley, 'Hymn to the Spirit of Nature', ll. 1–2: 'Life of Life! thy lips enkindle / With their love the breath between them'; the phrase is used by Matthew Arnold in *Empedocles on Etna* ii 357, which may have influenced another poem set in the early Christian period, *Cleon* (see headnote, pp. 563–4).

107. after-life: Karshish means the life which Lazarus led after his cure, but the phrase also suggests that this life is like life after death.

109. Sanguine: cheerful or confident, from the idea that this was characteristic of people '[abounding] with blood more than any other humour' (*J.*); on the poem's medical vocabulary see headnote. *fifty years of age:* there is an apparent inconsistency here: the poem is set around AD 69 (see headnote), in which case Lazarus, who was brought back from the dead by Jesus in AD 33, should be around sixty-five years of age. It might, however, be the case that Lazarus is understood to have retained his youthful appearance due to his experience (see l. 117).

112. As: as if.

And bathe the wearied soul and worried flesh,
115   And bring it clear and fair, by three days sleep!
Whence has the man the balm that brightens all?
This grown man eyes the world now like a child.
Some elders of his tribe, I should premise,
Led in their friend, obedient as a sheep,
120   To bear my inquisition. While they spoke,
Now sharply, now with sorrow,—told the case,—
He listened not except I spoke to him,
But folded his two hands and let them talk,
Watching the flies that buzzed: and yet no fool.
125   And that's a sample how his years must go.
Look if a beggar, in fixed middle-life,
Should find a treasure, can he use the same
With straightened habits and with tastes starved small,
And take at once to his impoverished brain
130   The sudden element that changes things,
—That sets the undreamed-of rapture at his hand,
And puts the cheap old joy in the scorned dust?
Is he not such an one as moves to mirth—
Warily parsimonious, when's no need,
135   Wasteful as drunkenness at undue times?
All prudent counsel as to what befits
The golden mean, is lost on such an one.
The man's fantastic will is the man's law.

117. Cp. *Matthew* xviii 3: 'Verily I say unto you, Except ye be converted, and become as little children, ye shall not enter into the kingdom of heaven.'

128. straightened] straitened (*1863–88*, except *1863²* which agrees with *1855*). *habits and with tastes*] habitude and tastes (*1872*), a rare example of a substantive variant unique to this ed.

133. such an one] such a one (*1863²*); less likely to be a mispr. than 'those' in l. 96, because it is repeated at l. 137.

134. when's no need] when no need (*1863–88*). Radical contractions such as this ('when's' = 'when there is') are very rare in B. and disappear entirely from *1863*.

137. golden mean: Aristotle's idea that 'moral virtue . . . is a mean between two vices, one of excess and the other of deficiency'; the story of the rich beggar illustrates his inability to shake off the habit of 'illiberality' (*analeutheria*) in spite of his good fortune (*Nicomachean Ethics*, transl. J. A. K. Thomson [1986], pp. 104, 108). Cp. also Wordsworth, *Ecclesiastical Sonnets* III xi: 'As if a church, though sprung from heaven, must owe / To opposites and fierce extremes her life,— / Not to the golden mean, and quiet flow / Of truths that soften hatred, temper strife' (11–14). *such an one*] such a one (*1863²*).

So here—we'll call the treasure knowledge, say—
140 Increased beyond the fleshly faculty—
Heaven opened to a soul while yet on earth,
Earth forced on a soul's use while seeing Heaven.
The man is witless of the size, the sum,
The value in proportion of all things,
145 Or whether it be little or be much.
Discourse to him of prodigious armaments
Assembled to besiege his city now,
And of the passing of a mule with gourds—
'Tis one! Then take it on the other side,
150 Speak of some trifling fact—he will gaze rapt
With stupor at its very littleness—
(Far as I see) as if in that indeed
He caught prodigious import, whole results;
And so will turn to us the bystanders
155 In ever the same stupor (note this point)
That we too see not with his opened eyes!
Wonder and doubt come wrongly into play,
Preposterously, at cross purposes.
Should his child sicken unto death,—why, look

139–42. For B.'s preoccupation with the incompatibility between divine and human knowledge, see headnote.
139. we'll call] we call (*1865–88*).
146–7. See ll. 26–8n.
146. Discourse to him: i.e. 'If you speak to him'.
148. gourds: the hollowed rinds of large cucumber-like plants often used to carry water.
149. 'Tis one! 'It is all the same.'
150–6. Cp. the extended treatment of this idea in *Mr Sludge* 1068–1122 (pp. 829–32).
151. With stupor at] With stupor from (*H proof*, but not *H proof²*).
156. Cp. Jesus to the disciples: 'Having eyes, see ye not?' (*Mark* viii 18). Cp. also Paul's blinding on the road to Damascus and subsequent conversion: 'And Saul arose from the earth; and when his eyes were opened, he saw no man . . . And immediately there fell from his eyes as it had been scales: and he received sight forthwith, and arose, and was baptized' (*Acts* ix 8–18). *opened eyes!*] opened eyes— (*H proof*); altered eyes. (*1863–88*, except *1863²* which agrees with *1855*). The dash in *H proof* goes with 'brought' in l. 157.
157. come wrongly] brought wrongly (*H proof*), a reading which makes this and the following line in apposition to the main sentence beginning at l. 149.
159–83. Lazarus is unconcerned at the mere prospect of his child's death (since that would lead to eternal life, of which Lazarus is assured), but he is afraid at even the most trifling sign that his child might be damned and go to hell. Cp. the reaction of Charles Tulk, a Swedenborgian friend of the Brownings, to the death of his daughter: 'Mr. Tulk's most singular letter on his daughter's death,

160 For scarce abatement of his cheerfulness,
Or pretermission of his daily craft—
While a word, gesture, glance, from that same child
At play or in the school or laid asleep,
Will start him to an agony of fear,
165 Exasperation, just as like! demand
The reason why—"'tis but a word", object—
"A gesture"—he regards thee as our lord
Who lived there in the pyramid alone,
Looked at us, dost thou mind, when being young
170 We both would unadvisedly recite
Some charm's beginning, from that book of his,
Able to bid the sun throb wide and burst
All into stars, as suns grown old are wont.
Thou and the child have each a veil alike
175 Thrown o'er your heads from under which ye both
Stretch your blind hands and trifle with a match
Over a mine of Greek fire, did ye know!

which his sister read to me at the time, was worth hearing read. With great tenderness for his "dear blessed Louisa" ... he expressed the most absolute satisfaction in the event, free from a single drawback—"It was altogether impossible for him even for the sake of what was called decency by the world, to pretend to feel regret on account of the consummated happiness of his child— He had not felt so well for years! He seemed to be running over in his heart with thoughts of felicity"' (19–22 Jan. 1849, *EBB to Arabella* i 220–1).

161. pretermission: interruption. *his daily*] the daily (*H proof* [but not *H proof²*], *1868–88*), a rare example of a return to a proof reading in eds. after *1855*.

164. Will start him] Will startle him (*1863–88*). *OED* last records the transitive sense of 'start' ('To cause to start or flinch; to startle') in *1871*; it also cites instances in Shakespeare, e.g. *All's Well That Ends Well*: 'You boggle shrewdly, every feather starts you' (V iii 232). B.'s usage is influenced by the intransitive sense 'To undergo a sudden involuntary movement of the body, resulting from surprise, fright, sudden pain, etc.'; *OED* again cites Shakespeare, *Henry VIII*: 'My lord, we have / Stood here observing him; some strange commotion / Is in his brain: he bites his lip, and starts' (III ii 112–14).

167–8. our lord ... alone: the sage who taught both Karshish and Abib; he seems to have been a practitioner of the occult as well as a physician.

171. beginning, from] beginning in (*H proof*, but not *H proof²*).

174.] Thou and this man's child have a veil alike (*H proof*, but not *H proof²*, which records only 'this man's' but not the deletion of 'each'). 'Thou' refers back to 'thee' in l. 167; Karshish is projecting how Lazarus might explain his apparently irrational behaviour to an onlooker.

177. a mine of Greek fire: a tunnel under a fortification which is filled with explosive; 'Greek fire' is inaccurate for this purpose, however, since it refers to a weapon invented by the Greeks of Constantinople to set fire to ships. Here, a metaphor for hellfire.

He holds on firmly to some thread of life—
(It is the life to lead perforcedly)
180 Which runs across some vast distracting orb
Of glory on either side that meagre thread,
Which, conscious of, he must not enter yet—
The spiritual life around the earthly life!
The law of that is known to him as this—
185 His heart and brain move there, his feet stay here.
So is the man perplext with impulses
Sudden to start off crosswise, not straight on,
Proclaiming what is Right and Wrong across—
And not along—this black thread through the blaze—
190 "It should be" baulked by "here it cannot be."
And oft the man's soul springs into his face
As if he saw again and heard again

178–90. Lazarus's knowledge of the reality of the spiritual world tempts him
to apply its absolute values prematurely to the normal conditions of human life.
The image is of him holding onto a 'thread' which guides him along the path of
ordinary life; he is impelled to 'start off crosswise', to judge things not according
to what normal people can see, but according to his supernatural awareness of
the 'vast distracting orb / Of glory on either side' (ll. 180–1). For B.'s belief in
progressive spiritual growth as opposed to transcendent revelation, see his letter
to Julia Wedgwood, 27 June 1864: 'you should *live*, step by step, *up* to the proper
place where the pin-point of light is visible: nothing is to be overleaped, the joy
no more than the sorrow, and then, your part done, God's may follow, and will,
I trust' (*RB & JW* 36); for another passage from this letter, see headnote, *Parallels*.
Although Lazarus did not seek the transcendent knowledge he has gained, he
cannot disavow it.

178. With the image of the 'thread of life', cp. *Sordello* iii 697–700 (I 574).

179.] (Perforcedly it is the life to lead) (*H proof*). 'Perforcedly' may be a new
coinage based on the Italian 'per forza' ('necessarily' or 'of course'); this is the
only instance cited in *OED*.

183.] The universal life, the earthly life, (*H proof*).

184. as this: meaning both that Lazarus is as aware of the spiritual life as he is of
the earthly, and that he experiences the spiritual life in the same way as the earthly,
that is with the same concreteness; with the latter sense, cp. St John's argument
in *A Death* 267–99 (pp. 738–9).

190. baulked] emended from 'balked' in *1855* and all other eds.; this correction
appears in the list of 'Errata' B. sent to James T. Fields, his American publisher
(*B to Fields* 192); note, however, that he did not implement the change in *1863*.
'Baulk' was not changed by the printers in *Childe Roland* 70 (p. 358) or *Master
Hugues* 15 (III 391). It clearly remained B.'s preferred spelling: 'No Briton's to
be baulked!' appears in *Apparent Failure* 18 (p. 710).

191–3. Cp. *A Death in the Desert* 58–66 (p. 728), where St John is similarly aroused
by a recollection of Jesus's words, also to do with resurrection.

His sage that bade him "Rise" and he did rise.
Something—a word, a tick of the blood within
195 Admonishes—then back he sinks at once
To ashes, that was very fire before,
In sedulous recurrence to his trade
Whereby he earneth him the daily bread—
And studiously the humbler for that pride,
200 Professedly the faultier that he knows
God's secret, while he holds the thread of life.
Indeed the especial marking of the man
Is prone submission to the Heavenly will—
Seeing it, what it is, and why it is.
205 'Sayeth, he will wait patient to the last
For that same death which will restore his being
To equilibrium, body loosening soul
Divorced even now by premature full growth:
He will live, nay, it pleaseth him to live
210 So long as God please, and just how God please.
He even seeketh not to please God more
(Which meaneth, otherwise) than as God please.
Hence I perceive not he affects to preach
The doctrine of his sect whate'er it be—

194. tick of the blood: pulse; cp. *Old Pictures* 44 (p. 412).   *of the blood*] o' the blood (*1870–88*).

195–6. then back . . . fire before: cp. *A Death in the Desert* 105–8 (p. 730).

196. that was] who was (*1868–88*).

197–8. Cp. *The Boy and the Angel* 3–4 (II 235).

198. the daily bread: cp. 'The Lord's Prayer': 'Give us this day our daily bread' (*Matthew* vi 11).

199. And studiously] Most studiously (*H proof*, but not *H proof²*).

205. 'Sayeth: see l. 101 above and note.

206. which will restore] which must restore (*1863–88*).

209–12. The terminology here is strongly Pauline, but Lazarus does not obey Paul's injunction to despise earthly life in order to 'please God', e.g. *Romans* viii 6–9: 'For to be carnally minded is death; but to be spiritually minded is life and peace. Because the carnal mind is enmity against God: for it is not subject to the law of God, neither indeed can be. So then they that are in the flesh cannot please God. But ye are not in the flesh, but in the Spirit, if so be that the Spirit of God dwell in you.' Although the 'Spirit' does dwell in Lazarus, he is enjoined to accept earthly conditions; cp. the development of this argument in *Rabbi Ben Ezra* 67–72 (p. 656).

213–15. With Karshish's incredulity at the claims made by Christianity, here and at ll. 249–51, 260–2, cp. the concluding lines of *Cleon* (pp. 584–5).

213. affects: aims at, endeavours to (sense 3 in *J.*), as opposed to the sense in l. 228.

215 Make proselytes as madmen thirst to do.
How can he give his neighbour the real ground,
His own conviction? ardent as he is—
Call his great truth a lie, why still the old
"Be it as God please" reassureth him.
220 I probed the sore as thy disciple should—
"How, beast," said I, "this stolid carelessness
Sufficeth thee, when Rome is on her march
To stamp out like a little spark thy town,
Thy tribe, thy crazy tale and thee at once?"
225 He merely looked with his large eyes on me.
The man is apathetic, you deduce?
Contrariwise he loves both old and young,
Able and weak—affects the very brutes
And birds—how say I? flowers of the field—
230 As a wise workman recognises tools
In a master's workshop, loving what they make.
Thus is the man as harmless as a lamb:
Only impatient, let him do his best,
At ignorance and carelessness and sin—

---

215. proselytes: converts.
221. carelessness: lack of care, indifference; see also l. 234n.
222–4. when Rome . . . at once: see ll. 26–8n.
226. apathetic: passionless, in a state of detachment from either joy or suffering. In this sense, apathy is a philosophy associated with the Stoics: *OED* cites Pope, *Essay on Man* ii 101–3: 'In lazy Apathy let Stoics boast / Their Virtue fix'd; 'tis fix'd as in a frost, / Contracted all, retiring to the breast'.
228. affects: is fond of, pleased with, loves (sense 5 in *J*.); see l. 213n.   *the very brutes*] the very beasts (*H proof*).
229. flowers of the field: cp. *Psalms* ciii 15: 'As for man, his days are as grass: as a flower of the field, so he flourisheth.'
230–1. The 'tools' are the processes of divine creation by which God, the 'master workman', makes the world of nature and man; Lazarus, whose revelation has given him a privileged insight into these processes, knows that the visible world expresses its divine origin. This extends the 18th century 'argument from design' in which God's existence and benevolence were deduced from the coherence and beauty of the natural order. For a more sceptical treatment of such 'natural theology', see *Caliban upon Setebos* (p. 616), and cp. l. 306n.
232. The lamb is a traditional image of Christ, the 'Lamb of God' (*John* i 29 and *Revelation*); with 'harmless', cp. (noting ll. 218–19) *Philippians* ii 13–15: 'For it is God which worketh in you both to will and to do of his good pleasure. Do all things without murmurings and disputings, that ye may be blameless and harmless, the sons of God, without rebuke, in the midst of a crooked and perverse nation, among whom ye shine as lights in the world.'
234. carelessness: either 'indifference' (as in l. 221) or frivolity (as in the 'careless women' rebuked in *Isaiah* xxxii 9–11).

235   An indignation which is promptly curbed.
      As when in certain travels I have feigned
      To be an ignoramus in our art
      According to some preconceived design,
      And happed to hear the land's practitioners
240   Steeped in conceit sublimed by ignorance,
      Prattle fantastically on disease,
      Its cause and cure—and I must hold my peace!

        Thou wilt object—why have I not ere this
      Sought out the sage himself, the Nazarene
245   Who wrought this cure, enquiring at the source,
      Conferring with the frankness that befits?
      Alas ! it grieveth me, the learned leech
      Perished in a tumult many years ago,
      Accused,—our learning's fate,—of wizardry,
250   Rebellion, to the setting up a rule
      And creed prodigious as described to me.
      His death which happened when the earthquake fell

---

235. promptly curbed] curbed by fear (*H proof*).

236. certain travels] certain travel (*1868–88*).

237. To be] Myself (*1863²*), a rare example of a substantive variant unique to this ed.

239. And happed] And happened (*1872*), a rare example of a substantive variant unique to this ed.

240. sublimed: made sublime (ironic); always used by B. in this sense: cp. *Sordello* ii 649 (I 504), *Popularity* 33 (p. 453).

241. fantastically: irrationally, with a sense of capriciousness or absurdity (*J.*).

243. ere this] ere thus (*H proof*, a mispr. not rec. in *H proof²*).

247–59. Karshish's version of the events of the Crucifixion, in contrast to the Gospel narratives, sees Christ as no different from other sages who have fallen victim to the irrational expectations of their followers; cp. the career of Paracelsus and the speaker of *Patriot* (p. 214), among many examples in B.'s work. For the idea that Christ was a mere man, see headnote to *A Death*, pp. 717–18.

247. leech: physician; the sense was already archaic in B.'s time, but occurs frequently in poetry. An even more archaic sense is of Christ as healer: *OED* cites Chaucer, *Summoner's Tale* 184: 'Hye God, that is oure lyves leche'.

249–51. In all Gospel accounts, Jesus is accused of blasphemy; in *Luke* only, of rebellion; in none, of 'wizardry'. See also ll. 213–15n.

250. a rule] a crown, (*H proof*).

251. prodigious: combining the senses of 'unnatural, abnormal' and 'amazing'.

252. the earthquake: caused by the Crucifixion, according to *Matthew* xxvii 51. Like the story of Lazarus itself this event appears in just one of the gospels, and is not corroborated by contemporary evidence from non-Christian writers. Karshish's suggestion that it was the earthquake that marked the passing of his 'sage'

(Prefiguring, as soon appeared, the loss
To occult learning in our lord the sage
255 That lived there in the pyramid alone)
Was wrought by the mad people—that's their wont—
On vain recourse, as I conjecture it,
To his tried virtue, for miraculous help—
How could he stop the earthquake? That's their way!
260 The other imputations must be lies:
But take one—though I loathe to give it thee,
In mere respect to any good man's fame!
(And after all our patient Lazarus
Is stark mad—should we count on what he says?
265 Perhaps not—though in writing to a leech
'Tis well to keep back nothing of a case.)
This man so cured regards the curer then,
As—God forgive me—who but God himself,
Creater and Sustainer of the world,
270 That came and dwelt in flesh on it awhile!
—'Sayeth that such an One was born and lived,

---

underlines Strauss's point that such stories represent 'a poetical or mythical embellishment of the death of a distinguished man; as, for example, on the death of Caesar, Virgil is not content with eclipsing the sun, but also makes the Alps tremble with unwonted commotion' (*Life of Jesus* 693).

255. That lived] Who lived (*1863–88*).

256. the mad people: cp. *Sordello* iv 703 (I 636).

257–9. Karshish suggests that the people may have executed their 'wizard' for his failure to stop the earthquake; with this view of miracles as a concession to the limited understanding of the multitude cp. B.'s play *Return of the Druses* (1842) iv 63–7; see also Arnold, *Empedocles on Etna* I ii 102–11.

258. virtue: healing power (cp. *Mark* v 30, where Jesus is touched and 'immediately know[s] in himself that virtue had gone out of him').

261. But take one] Take but this one (*H proof*).

262. respect to] respect for (*1868–88*).

265. though in writing] yet in writing (*H proof*, but not *H proof²*).

269–70. Cp. *John* i 3, 10, 14: 'All things were made by him; and without him was not anything made that was made . . . He was in the world, and the world was made by him, and the world knew him not . . . And the Word was made flesh, and dwelt among us.' The notion that God sustains the world he has created is present in the Bible (e.g. *Nehemiah* ix 6: 'thou hast made . . . the earth, and all things that are therein . . . and thou preservest them all') but B. may be alluding here to the philosophical debate about God's active presence being necessary for the continuation of the material universe.

269. Sustainer] sustainer (*1865–88*).

271. 'Sayeth: See l. 101n.   *such an One*] such a One (*1863²*); such an one (*H proof, 1868–88*).

Taught, healed the sick, broke bread at his own house,
Then died, with Lazarus by, for aught I know,
And yet was . . . what I said nor choose repeat,
275   And must have so avouched himself, in fact,
In hearing of this very Lazarus
Who saith—but why all this of what he saith?
Why write of trivial matters, things of price
Calling at every moment for remark?
280   I noticed on the margin of a pool
Blue-flowering borage, the Aleppo sort,
Aboundeth, very nitrous. It is strange!

Thy pardon for this long and tedious case,
Which, now that I review it, needs must seem
285   Unduly dwelt on, prolixly set forth.
Nor I myself discern in what is writ
Good cause for the peculiar interest
And awe indeed this man has touched me with.
Perhaps the journey's end, the weariness
290   Had wrought upon me first. I met him thus—
I crossed a ridge of short sharp broken hills
Like an old lion's cheek-teeth. Out there came

272. *his own*: Lazarus's.
273. Lazarus is not mentioned in the Gospel accounts of the Crucifixion.
275–6. Jesus suggests (rather than declares) his divinity in a dialogue with his disciples in *Matthew* xvi 13–20; he also instructs them 'that they should tell no man that he was Jesus the Christ' (the episode also appears in *Mark* and *Luke*). In *John* x 30 ff., Jesus delares 'I and my Father are one' and is accused of blasphemy by the Jews: 'because that thou, being a man, makest thyself God'. The following chapter in *John* contains the story of Lazarus, whose sister says to Jesus: 'I believe that thou art the Christ, the Son of God, which should come into the world' (xi 27). See also *John* v 17 ff.
276–7. *this very Lazarus / Who saith*] this very Lazarus. / He saith (*H proof*; *H proof²* does not record the full stop at the end of l. 276).
279. *for remark?*] for record! (*H proof*).
280. *a pool*] a lake (*H proof*).
281. *Blue-flowering borage*: Borage was commonly 'used in medicinal cordials' (*J.*), hence Karshish's interest in it; it was (and still is) believed to have originated in Aleppo in Syria. 'According to Pliny, this flower has a stimulating effect upon the spirits' (Glazebrook, *Selections from the Poems of Robert Browning* [1909] 134).
282. *nitrous*: 'The natrum or *nitre* of the ancients, is a genuine, native, and pure salt . . . About Smyrna and Ephesus, and through a great part of Asia Minor, this salt is extremely frequent on the surface of the earth' (*J.*, citing John Hill's *History of Fossils*, 1748).
291–2. *I crossed . . . cheek-teeth*: cp. *England in Italy* 151–6 (p. 263).

A moon made like a face with certain spots
Multiform, manifold, and menacing:
295   Then a wind rose behind me. So we met
In this old sleepy town at unaware,
The man and I. I send thee what is writ.
Regard it as a chance, a matter risked
To this ambiguous Syrian—he may lose,
300   Or steal, or give it thee with equal good.
Jerusalem's repose shall make amends
For time this letter wastes, thy time and mine,
Till when, once more thy pardon and farewell!

The very God! think, Abib; dost thou think?
305   So, the All-Great, were the All-Loving too—
So, through the thunder comes a human voice
Saying, "O heart I made, a heart beats here!
Face, my hands fashioned, see it in myself.
Thou hast no power nor may'st conceive of mine,
310   But love I gave thee, with Myself to love,
And thou must love me who have died for thee!"
The madman saith He said so: it is strange.

293–4. The idea of the man in the moon can be found in most traditions; according to the Revd Timothy Harley's *Moon Lore* (1885), spots or marks on the moon were interpreted in Jewish tradition as the outline of a man placed there by Moses for gathering sticks on the sabbath (p. 21). This notion underlies the Christian tradition associating moonspots with Cain carrying his bundle of sticks as an offering to the Lord; see Dante, *Paradiso* ii 46–51.

304–11. With this understanding of the doctrine of the Incarnation, cp. *Ring* x 1347–71.

305. Cp. Felicia Hemans's sonnet 'The Sisters of Bethany after the Death of Lazarus' in which God is described as 'the All Seeing and All Just'.

306. *through the thunder:* thunder was habitually regarded as a divine phenomenon in the ancient world; fear of thunder is a sign of Caliban's primitive 'natural theology': 'His thunder follows! Fool to gibe at Him!' (*Caliban upon Setebos* 291, p. 641), while in another poem from *DP*, *Mr. Sludge*, it is argued that such 'evidence' of God's power has been superseded in the modern world: 'Lightning, forsooth? No word more upon that!' (l. 1123, p. 832). *the thunder comes*] the thunder came (*H proof*, but not *H proof*²).

307. *"O heart*] "Oh, heart (*H proof*, but not *H proof*²).

33 Love Among the Ruins

Text, publication and revision

First publ. *M & W*, 10 Nov. 1855; repr. *1863, 1863², 1868, 1872, 1888*. Our text is *1855*. A fair copy MS with some corrections and revisions is at Harvard (Houghton MS Lowell 4). It is undated, but evidently earlier than *1855* and was not the printer's copy. The title is 'Sicilian Pastoral'; apart from this (important) difference, there are few substantive variants from *1855*, but because manuscript evidence from the period of *M & W* is so scarce we record all variants except trivial copying errors. A facsimile of the MS was printed in the catalogue of the sale at the American Art Association, New York, 10 April 1922 (lot 35); see also J. Maynard, 'Browning's "Sicilian Pastoral"', *Harvard Library Bulletin* xx (1972) 436–43. MS divides the poem into seven sections of twelve lines, with a gap after the sixth line; *1868–88* revert to the 12-line section but close up the gap. MS does not indent short lines. There was no verbal revision to the poem in eds. after *1855*, a fact which makes it unique for a poem of its length in *M & W*.

Composition and date

DeVane's assertion (*Handbook* 212) that '*Love Among the Ruins* was written in an apartment in the Champs Elysées in Paris, on January 3, 1852,' can be discounted; the resolution to write 'something each day' belongs to January 1853 (see *Women and Roses*, III 235; see also Johnstone Parr, *PQ* xxxii [1953] 443–6). *Sharp's* suggestion that the poem is another product of the Brownings' residence in Rome during the winter of 1853–54 is much more plausible; *Love Among the Ruins* has marked affinities with *Two in the Campagna*, which almost certainly belongs to the Spring of 1854, when B. regularly went on picnic excursions to the Campagna with a group of friends (see p. 556).

Setting and sources

Literary treatments of the rise and fall of empires are found in both classical and biblical traditions. The cyclical nature of the topic is illustrated by two famous passages by Ovid, both of which B. would have known well: the first, from the *Fasti* (v 93–4), has a landscape like that of *Love Among the Ruins*, but set in the past, *before* the rise of the imperial city: 'hic, ubi nunc Roma est, orbis caput, arbor et herbae / et paucae pecudes et casa rara fuit' [On the spot where now stands Rome, the capital of the world, there were trees, and grass, and a few sheep, and here and there a cottage (transl. Sir J. G. Frazer, *Loeb* ed., 1931)]; the other, from the *Heroides* (i 53–6) has, like B.'s poem, a woman waiting for her lover, but the woman is Penelope, mournfully reflecting on Ulysses' non-arrival, even though so much time has passed: 'iam seges est, ubi Troia fuit, resecandaque falce / luxuriat Phrygio sanguine pinguis humus; / semisepulta birum curvis feriuntur aratris / ossa, ruinosas occulit herba domos' [Now are fields of corn where Troy once was, and soil made fertile with Phrygian blood waves rich with harvest ready for the sickle; the half-buried bones of her heroes are struck by the curvèd share, and herbage hides from sight her ruined palaces] (transl. G. Showerman, *Loeb* ed., 1914).

In her survey of the numerous suggestions that have been made about the setting and sources of the poem, Ann Farkas concludes that 'a classically educated and well-read person like B. would have formed a stereotype of the ancient city shaped by the common features which had attracted the attention of centuries of writers and travellers—vast, faintly Greek in plan and architectural details, once immensely and impressively stone-walled, with views across a plain, now desolate except for remnants of a tower, and covered by grassy meadows' ('Digging Among the Ruins', *VP* xxix [1991] 36). Many of the generic features of the poem can be plausibly linked to multiple literary sources, from classical antiquity and more recent periods. Marilyn Sirugo (*SBC* iv [1976]), for instance, following up the hint provided by the *MS* title *Sicilian Pastoral*, suggests a similarity with the account of the life of Nicias in Plutarch's *Lives*: 'In the account of Nicias' life, Plutarch describes the "multitude" of Syracusans, the "city gates" and "bridges", the "plains," a "temple of Jupiter Olympius," the "wealth" of "gold and silver," and "a wall" drawn in a circle around the city' (p. 43). She also highlights possible sources in books owned by B.: Daniel Bartoli's *De' simboli trasportati al morale* (*Collections* A167–8; see headnote to *How They Brought the Good News*, p. 220) which 'devotes a chapter (III vii) to Agathocles, a tyrant of Syracuse', and the sections of Sir Walter Ralegh's *History of the World* (*Collections* A1926) dealing with ancient Sicilian history. C. R. Tracy (*PMLA* lxi [1946] 600–1]) points to letter cxvii from Goldsmith's *The Citizen of the World* as a possible source:

> There will come a time when this temporary solitude may be made continual, and the city itself, like its inhabitants, fade away, and leave a desart in its room.
>
> What cities, as great as this, have once triumph'd in existence, had their victories as great, joy as just, and as unbounded, and with short-sighted presumption, promised themselves immortality. Posterity can hardly trace the situation of some. The sorrowful traveller wanders over the awful ruins of others, and as he beholds, he learns wisdom, and feels the transience of every sublunary possession.
>
> Here, he cries, stood their citadel, now grown over with weeds; there their senate-house, but now the haunt of every noxious reptile; temples and theatres stood here, now only an undistinguished heap of ruin. They are fallen, for luxury and avarice first made them feeble. The rewards of state were conferred on amusing, and not on useful members of society. Their riches and opulence invited the invaders, who, though at first repulsed, returned again, conquered by perseverance, and at last swept the defendants into undistinguish'd destruction.

Other suggestions include Volney's *Les Ruines ou Méditations sur les révolutions des empires* (1791; transl. 1795 and generally known in English as *The Ruins of Empire*), Goethe's *Italian Journey*, the fourth Canto of Byron's *Childe Harold*, and Shelley's *Ozymandias*.

Notwithstanding the generic character of much of the description in the poem, however, there are four groups of sources which seem to have a stronger claim than others: (i) Sicilian and pastoral sources; (ii) sources connected with the Roman Campagna; (iii) sources connected with the ruined city of Palmyra; (iv) sources in the Bible.

(i) *Sicilian and pastoral sources.* Following the emergence of the MS of the poem entitled *Sicilian Pastoral*, a number of sources in or about Sicily have been suggested. Acragas (Latin Agrigentum), an ancient city in the south-west of the island, was once ruled by the infamous tyrant Phalaris and celebrated for its wealth and luxury. Acragas was also the home of Empedocles (see headnote to *Cleon*, pp. 563–4), who remarked that its citizens built as if they were to live for ever, and lived as if they expected to die tomorrow. Sirugo's suggestions that the city is Syracuse (noted above) are given added plausibility by the fact that the story of the defeat of the Athenians at Syracuse in 415 BC forms the backdrop to *Balaustion's Adventure* (1871). Against these various theories, however, is the fact that B. never visited Sicily. It is, however, possible that the MS title might have been intended to refer to the poem's generic rather than geographical affiliations, as an example of the kind of poetry written by (e.g.) the Greek Sicilian poet Theocritus, to whom EBB. alludes in the first of the *Sonnets from the Portuguese*. Maynard (see *Text*) notes that Spenser's *The Ruines of Time* and his version of Du Bellay's *The Ruines of Rome*, suggested as possible sources by R. K. R. Thornton (*NQ* ccxiii [1968] 178–9) have significant affinities with the genre of pastoral. B.'s specific knowledge of these poems is indicated in a letter of 1 June 1889 to the Revd J. D. Williams; see *BIS* iv (1976) 1–56. Thornton goes on to suggest that the unusual metre of B.'s poem might have been suggested by *Ruines of Rome* 39–40: 'Ne ought save Tyber hastning to his fall / Remaines of all'; see also ll. 19–20n., 55–6n., 75–6n. (For another possible metrical source, see below.)

(ii) *The Roman Campagna*. The poem is said by *Sharp* to have been written in Rome (see *Composition and date*), and for this reason several commentators have assumed that the setting is the Roman Campagna. A flourishing independent territory during the early Roman Empire, Latium (the modern 'Campagna') became depopulated after 300 BC, and by the nineteenth century formed a 'magnificent desert which stretches on every side of Rome' (Fanny Kemble, *Further Records, 1843–83* [New York 1891] 160; for B.'s association with Fanny Kemble during the winter of 1853–54 see headnote to *Two in the Campagna*, p. 556). Several Etruscan cities located there are candidates for the 'city great and gay', in particular Tarquinii and Veii. Their sites were commonly visited by travellers (both tourists and scholars of antiquity): B. may have read, e.g., Mrs Hamilton Gray's *Tour of the Sepulchres of Etruria in 1839*, which contains many passages such as the following: 'We looked for traces of buildings, but we could distinguish not even a vestige of masonry . . . The site of one of the mightiest cities of ancient Europe can scarcely be discovered; her works of piety and ornament, her solemn temples, her solid aqueducts, her magnificent theatres and forum, the trophies of her glory, her triumphal arches, and stately colonnades, all crumbled in the dust' (2nd ed. [1841], 177–8); 'Well does Mother Earth cover up her children on that green hill, for not the slightest sign of the hand or foot of a man is to be seen upon her surface' (80); 'It [Veii] was in size equal to Athens, and larger and finer than Rome, the walls being four miles in extent. It was full of the ornaments of a rich, civilized, and luxurious people, and was famous for its chariot games' (115). A very similar response is found in George Dennis, *The Cities and Cemeteries of Etruria* (2 vols., 1848): 'Who can behold unmoved her present desolation? Where stood temple and tower, palace and forum, where shone the glories of art and the lavishments of wealth and luxury, nature now displays, as in mockery, her summer tribute of golden corn' (i 386). Parr (see *Composition*) notes some verbal similarities to the descriptions of the Campagna in Murray's *Handbook for Travellers in Central Italy* (1853). Murray emphasizes 'the grand effects produced by the magnificent aqueducts which span the Campagna with their colossal arches . . . On the right of the road are the ruins of Bovillae . . . Among the ruins are portions of the circus, the theatre, and the ancient walls . . . Looking back . . . Rome is seen with its domes and towers and obelisks, rising in solitary grandeur amidst the ruins of the desolate Campagna, like an oasis in the desert.'

(iii) *Palmyra.* A third possibility locates the poem in the ruins of the fabulously wealthy Syrian city of Palmyra, destroyed by the Roman Emperor Aurelian in AD 273. The rediscovery of the ruins of this city, as represented in the engravings of Robert Wood's *The Ruins of Palmyra* (1753), became enormously influential in the late eighteenth century, and contributed towards the neo-classicism of the period. Noting the extensive 'review of the various publications of Shelley's youth' which B. undertook in late 1851 in preparation for writing *Shelley* (see Appendix A, p. 851), Philip Raisor (*VP* xiv.2 [1976] 142−9) argues for the influence on the poem of the sections of *Queen Mab* dealing with Palmyra:

'Behold,' the Fairy cried,
    'Palmyra's ruined palaces!
Behold where grandeur frowned!
Behold where pleasure smiled!
What now remains?—the memory
    Of senselessness and shame.
    What is immortal there?
    Nothing—it stands to tell
    A melancholy tale, to give
    An awful warning; soon
Oblivion will steal silently
    The remnant of its fame.
    Monarchs and conquerors there
Proud o'er prostrate millions trod—
The earthquakes of the human race;
Like them, forgotten when the ruin
    That marks their shock is past.

    'Beside the eternal Nile
    The Pyramids have risen.
Nile shall pursue his changeless way;
    Those Pyramids shall fall.
Yea! not a stone shall stand to tell
    The spot whereon they stood;
Their very site shall be forgotten,
    As is their builder's name!

    'Behold yon sterile spot,
Where now the wandering Arab's tent
    Flaps in the desert blast!
There once old Salem's haughty fane
Reared high to heaven its thousand golden domes,
    And in the blushing face of day
    Exposed its shameful glory

(ii 109−40)

See also ll. 37–44n., 67−72n. The Brownings had, moreover, recently been reminded of the ruins of Palmyra by their friend William Ware (1797−1852), whose *Letters of Lucius M. Piso from Palmyra, to his friend Marcus Curtius, at Rome* (1837), later renamed *Zenobia; or, the Fall of Palmyra* they had read: see EBB. to Mary Russell Mitford, 4 July 1848 (*Correspondence* xv 99). Ware's story is set during the last days of the city, and begins (pp. 23–5) with an enraptured description of its glories:

I urged forward my steed, and in a moment the most wonderful prospect I ever beheld—no, I cannot even except Rome—burst upon my sight. Flanked by hills of considerable elevation on the East, the city filled the whole plain below as far as the eye could reach, both toward the North and the South. This immense plain was all one vast and boundless city. It seemed to me to be larger than Rome. Yet I knew very well that it could not be—that it was not. And it was some time before I understood the true character of the scene before me, so as to separate the city from the country, and the country from the city, which here wonderfully interpenetrate each other and so confound and deceive the observer. For the city proper is so studded with groups of lofty palm trees, shooting up amongst its temples and palaces, and on the other hand, the plain of the immediate vicinity is so thickly adorned with magnificent structures of the purest marble, that it is not easy, nay it is impossible at the distance at which I contemplated the whole, to distinguish the line which divided the one from the other. It was all city and all country, all country and all city . . . There was a central point, however, which chiefly fixed my attention, where the vast Temple of the Sun stretched upward its thousand columns of polished marble to the heavens . . . On each side of this, the central point, there rose upward slender pyramids—pointed obelisks—domes of the most graceful proportions, columns, arches and lofty towers, for number and for form, beyond my power to describe.

The hero of the story, a Roman citizen, comes under the influence of a Christian, and begins to feel the shortcomings of Roman society and its animating passions of ambition and glory. At the end of the story (p. 257), looking over the ruins of the newly desolated city, he begins to feel that Christianity might provide an answer to these shortcomings:

The silence of death and of ruin rests over this once and but so lately populous city. As I stood upon a high point which overlooked a large extent of it, I could discern no signs of life . . . O, miserable condition of humanity! Why is it that to man have been given passions which he cannot tame, and which sink him below the brute! Why is it that a few ambitious are permitted by the Great Ruler, in the selfish pursuit of their own aggrandizement, to scatter in ruin, desolation, and death, whole kingdoms—making misery and destruction the steps by which they mount up to their seats of pride! O, gentle doctrine of Christ! doctrine of love and of peace, when shall it be that I and all mankind shall know thy truth, and the world smile with a new happiness under thy life-giving reign!

As a story set at a moment of transition between Paganism and Christianity, Ware's story might also have influenced the form of *Cleon* (p. 563) and *An Epistle* (p. 507).

(iv) *The Bible*. The ruin motif features frequently in the Old Testament, as in these examples:

Isaiah xvii 1–2: 'Behold, Damascus is taken away from being a city, and it shall be a ruinous heap. The cities of Aroer are forsaken: they shall be for flocks, which shall lie down, and none shall make them afraid.'

Isaiah xxxii 13–14: 'Upon the land of my people shall come up thorns and briers; yea, upon all the houses of joy in the joyous city: because the palaces shall be forsken; the multitude of the city shall be left; the forts and towers shall be for dens for ever, a joy of wild asses, a pasture of flocks'.

Zephaniah ii 13–15: 'And he will stretch out his hand against the north, and destroy Assyria; and will make Nineveh a desolation, and dry like a wilderness. And flocks shall lie down in the midst of her, all the beasts of the nations . . . This is the rejoicing city that dwelt carelessly, that said in her heart, I am, and there is none beside me: how is she become a desolation, a place for beasts to lie down in!'

Cp. also *Isaiah* xiii 19–22; *Jeremiah* xvii 25–7 (which mentions 'kings and princes . . . riding in chariots and on horses') and xxxiii 12–13; *Nahum* ii 3–4.

Metre

For the possible influence of Spenser's translation of Du Bellay's *Ruines of Rome*, see above. However, no exact sustained precedent for the poem's alternating pattern of long and short lines has been found. Daniel Karlin (*BSN* x, no.2 [Aug. 1980] 10–11) suggests that B. may have come across Francis Davison's metrical version of Psalm xxiii, reprinted in *Select Poetry, Chiefly Devotional, of the Reign of Queen Elizabeth*, ed. Edward Farr (Cambridge: Parker Society, 1845), which renders a pastoral scene in long and short lines: 'God, who the universe doth hold / In his fold / Is my shepherd kind and heedful,— / Is my shepherd, and doth keepe / Me his sheepe / Still supplied with all things needfull.' Like Browning's poem, this alternates fundamentally trochaic lines with three-syllable lines consisting of a single anapaestic or cretic foot. Another psalm translated by Davison in the same metre, Psalm cxxxvii, appears in the Parker Society volume; this psalm concerns the exile of the Jews, the destruction of the Temple, and the anticipated fall of Babylon.

Parallels in B.

The most obvious parallel is with the strikingly similar *Two in the Campagna* (p. 556) which also deals with the theme of love in a landscape associated with the ruins of an ancient civilization. The theme of the glorious city which falls into ruins is treated from a different perspective in *Abt Vogler* (p. 759), and (again associated with music) in the vision of Venice in *Fifine at the Fair* (1872); the Venetian connection also suggests a parallel with the lost world of aristocratic pleasure evoked in *Toccata* (p. 367). B.'s interest in landscapes with vestiges of ruins goes back to the landscape of Asolo in *Sordello*: see vi 774–89n. (I 762). Cp. also *Bad Dreams III* (*Asolando*, 1889).

I

Where the quiet-coloured end of evening smiles
Miles and miles

1. quiet-coloured] quiet-colored (*MS*), B.'s preferred spelling in this period (see *Text*, p. xi); another example occurs at l. 49.   *evening*] even (*MS*).
1–2. smiles / Miles and miles: with 'for' understood after 'smiles'.   *smiles . . . miles*] smiles, . . . miles, (*MS*, *1870*, *1872*).
1–6. Cp. the opening of Gray's *Elegy Written in a Country Churchyard*, which has details and phrases in common with the poem ('parting day', 'The lowing herd wind slowly', 'drowsy tinklings lull the distant folds'). Twilight is also the setting for *Andrea* (p. 385), which opened the second volume of *M & W*.

On the solitary pastures where our sheep
Half-asleep
5 Tinkle homeward thro' the twilight, stray or stop
As they crop—

2

Was the site once of a city great and gay,
(So they say)
Of our country's very capital, its prince
10   Ages since
Held his court in, gathered councils, wielding far
Peace or war.

3

Now—the country does not even boast a tree,
As you see,
15 To distinguish slopes of verdure, certain rills
From the hills
Intersect and give a name to, (else they run
Into one)

7. *city*] City (*MS*, corr. from 'city'); on the possible identity of this city, see
headnote.   *great and gay*: B. is fond of 'gay' as an adjective (123 occurrences),
and of combinations such as this: cp. 'grave and gay' (*A Toccata* 26, p. 373) and
'fresh and gay' (*Women and Roses* 8, III 236), the latter also appearing in
Fifine at the Fair (1872) 1390; among later poems cp. esp. 'grand and gay', *Ned
Bratts* (*DI*, 1879) 233.
8.] So they say; (*MS*).
9–12. Sirugo (headnote, *Sources*) suggests that this passage might have been
suggested by Ralegh's description of the exploits of Dionysius I, king of
Syracuse.
9. *Of our country's*: i.e. 'was the site of our country's very capital'; the phrase is
in apposition to 'of a city great and gay'.   *Of*] Was (*MS*).   *its prince*] the prince
(*MS first reading*).
11. *gathered councils, wielding far*] had his councils, sent afar (*MS*).
13. Parr (see headnote) cites Murray's *Handbook*, describing the road over the
Campagna which B. traversed in the winter of 1853–54: 'Its bare and desolate
clay hills are generally destitute of a single tree' (p. 217).
15. *slopes of verdure, certain rills*: with 'which' understood between the two
phrases.
17–18. *(else they run / Into one)*] else they run / Into one—(*MS, H proof*).

4

Where the domed and daring palace shot its spires
20   Up like fires
O'er the hundred-gated circuit of a wall
       Bounding all,
Made of marble, men might march on nor be prest,
       Twelve abreast.

5

25 And such plenty and perfection, see, of grass
       Never was!
Such a carpet as, this summer-time, o'erspreads
       And embeds
Every vestige of the city, guessed alone,
30   Stock or stone—

6

Where a multitude of men breathed joy and woe
       Long ago;
Lust of glory pricked their hearts up, dread of shame
       Struck them tame;
35 And that glory and that shame alike, the gold
       Bought and sold.

19–20. Cp. Spenser's version of Bellay's *Ruines of Rome* (see headnote): 'Great Babylon her haughtie walls will praise, / And sharped steeples high shot vp in ayre' (ll. 15–16). Cp., in B., *Old Pictures* 281–4 (pp. 433–4) and *Abt Vogler* 21–4 (p. 764).

21. hundred-gated: Thebes in Egypt was known as 'Hecatompylos' on account of its hundred gates; Babylon also had one hundred gates.

23. marble, men . . . prest,] marble men . . . prest (*MS*).

25–30. Cp. *Two in the Campagna* 21–5 (pp. 559–60).

26.] Never was, (*MS*).

27. summer-time] summertime (*MS*).

29. guessed alone: i.e. whose presence can only be guessed at.

30. 'Stock and stone' is a traditional phrase for natural objects in a landscape (so used in *By the Fire-Side* 182, p. 471) but here also alludes to the worship of idols: cp. *Jeremiah* iii 9, in which Judah 'defiled the land, and committed adultery with stones and with stocks', an allusion picked up by Milton in 'On the Late Massacre in Piedmont', l. 4 ('When all our fathers worshiped stocks and stones'). The phrase is used here in apposition with 'vestige of the city'.

31–6. The sense is that the 'multitude of men' were apparently inspired by the desire for 'glory' and kept under control by 'dread of shame'; but these chivalric values are then themselves undermined by the assertion that money was in fact society's determining value, since the soldiers could be '[bought] and sold'.

34. Struck] Kept (*MS first reading*).   *tame;*] tame, (*MS, H proof*).

7

Now,—the single little turret that remains
    On the plains,
By the caper overrooted, by the gourd
40   Overscored,
While the patching houseleek's head of blossom winks
    Through the chinks—

8

Marks the basement whence a tower in ancient time
    Sprang sublime,
45 And a burning ring all round, the chariots traced
    As they raced,
And the monarch and his minions and his dames
    Viewed the games.

9

And I know, while thus the quiet-coloured eve
50   Smiles to leave
To their folding, all our many-tinkling fleece

37–44. Raisor (headnote, *Sources*) compares Shelley, *Queen Mab*, ii 189–92: 'There, now, the mossy columnstone, / Indented by time's unrelaxing grasp, / Which once appeared to brave / All, save its country's ruin'.

37. the single little turret: for the recurrence of this motif in B., see *Sordello* vi 779–85n. (I 763) and headnote to *Childe Roland*, p. 353.

38. On the plains: Farkas (headnote, Sources) suggests a reminiscence of Sodom and Gomorrah, the 'cities of the plain' (*Genesis* xiii 12).

39–40.] Which the caper roots a-top of, by the gourd / Oversoared, (*MS*).

39. caper: a small, spiny shrub (*Capparis spinosa*), with conspicuous white or lilac flowers. 'This plant grows in the South of France, in Spain and in Italy, upon old walls and buildings' (*J.*). *gourd*: a climbing or trailing plant of the pumpkin family, with white or yellow flowers.

41. While] Where (*MS*; 'While' was the first reading). *patching houseleek's*: the houseleek is a succulent plant with yellow or pink flowers, whose largest species, *Sempervivum tectorum*, was formerly planted on roofs to seal leaks and ward off lightning.

43. Marks] Was (*MS*). *basement*: base, foundation (not in *J.*; *OED*'s earliest citation is 1793).

46. raced,] raced (*MS*).

47. monarch] monarch, (*MS*). *minions*: courtiers, favourites. B. uses the word in *Sordello* i 643 (I 438), and (in another sense) in *Laboratory* 29 (p. 211). See also *Pippa Passes* ii 31 (p. 124), *Abt Vogler* 17 (p. 764), *Ixion* (*Jocoseria*, 1883) 72.

49. quiet-coloured] quiet-colored (*MS*).

51. folding,] folding (*MS*); the sheep are being returned to their 'fold'. *many-tinkling*] many tinkling (*1870, 1872*). *fleece*: synecdoche for 'sheep', as in *As You Like It* II iv 79.

> In such peace,
> And the slopes and rills in undistinguished grey
> Melt away—

10

55 That a girl with eager eyes and yellow hair
>> Waits me there
> In the turret, whence the charioteers caught soul
>> For the goal,
> When the king looked, where she looks now, breathless,
>> dumb
60 >> Till I come.

11

> But he looked upon the city, every side,
>> Far and wide,
> All the mountains topped with temples, all the glades'
>> Colonnades,

53. undistinguished grey: cp. Robert Southey, 'Night' (1798), ll. 10–11: 'A dim obscurity o'ermantles all, / An undistinguished greyness.'

55–6. Cp. Spenser, *The Ruines of Time*, 8–12: 'There on the other side I did behold / A Woman sitting sorrowfullie wailing, / Rending her yeolow locks, like wyrie golde, / About her shoulders careleslie down trailing, / And streames of teares from her faire eyes forth railing'. The woman with yellow hair in Spenser's poem, however, seems to embody rather than counteract the dominant notion of 'ruin'.

56. there] there, (*MS*).

57. turret,] turret (*MS*).

57–8. caught soul / For the goal: 'were fired with enthusiasm to try to win the race'. The rhyme 'soul / goal' often occurs in B. in contexts which suggest an achievement undercut by irony, e.g. *Sordello* vi 640–4 (I 754): 'Taurello passed / With foe and friend for an outstripping soul / Nine days at least: then, fairly reached the goal, / He, by one effort, blotted the great hope / Out of his mind'; cp. *Easter Day* 895–6 (III 137) and *Last Ride* 94–5 (III 290); also *Dís Aliter Visum* 73–5: 'Thus girls give body and soul / At first word, think they gain the goal, / When 'tis the starting-place they climb!' (p. 694).

59. dumb] dumb, (*MS*).

61.] But the city he looked out on, every side, (*MS*). *he*: the king.

63–4. The image is of nature subordinated to human art: the mountains are 'topped with temples', and the forest glades are lined with sculptured pillars, replacing the natural 'colonnades' of the trees (*OED* cites Cowper, *The Task* i 252: 'Not distant far, a length of Colonnade . . . These chesnuts rang'd in corresponding lines'). Cp. also Aprile's description in *Paracelsus* ii 406–9 (I 179) of the paintings he dreamed of accomplishing: 'Bronze labyrinths, palace, pyramid, and crypt, / Baths, galleries, courts, temples, and terraces, / Marts, theatres, and wharfs—all fill'd with men! / Men everywhere!' Cp. also the image of the mountain 'citied to the top, / Crowded with culture' in *A Grammarian* 15–16, (pp. 590–1).

65   All the causeys, bridges, aqueducts,—and then,
           All the men!

                                    12
        When I do come, she will speak not, she will stand,
           Either hand
        On my shoulder, give her eyes the first embrace
70   Of my face,
        Ere we rush, ere we extinguish sight and speech
           Each on each.

                                    13
        In one year they sent a million fighters forth
           South and north,
75   And they built their gods a brazen pillar high
           As the sky,
        Yet reserved a thousand chariots in full force—
           Gold, of course.

---

65. *causeys*: causeways; B.'s is the older and, according to *J*., the correct form.
67–72. For the motifs here of silence, gazing, and blissful oblivion, cp. among
others *Pippa Passes* i 192–4 (p. 109), *Night* [*Meeting at Night*] 11–12 (II 358), *By
the Fire-Side* 181 ff. (p. 471), *Women and Roses* 28–34 (III 238), and the concluding
lines of *Now* (*Asolando*, 1889): 'When ecstasy's utmost we clutch at the core /
While cheeks burn, arms open, eyes shut and lips meet!' Raisor (headnote, *Sources*)
compares the description of Ianthe in *Queen Mab*: 'She looked around in wonder
and beheld / Henry, who kneeled in silence by her couch, / Watching her sleep
with looks of speechless love' (ix 236–8).
68–9. *Either . . . shoulder*,] —Either . . . shoulder— (*MS first reading*).
72.] Each on each! (*MS*).
75–6. Cp. Spenser, *The Ruines of Time* 407–13: 'In vaine doo earthly Princes then,
in vaine / Seeke with Pyramides, to heauen aspired: / Or huge Colosses, built
with costlie paine; / Or brasen Pillours, never to be fired, / Or Shrines, made
of the mettall most desired; / To make their memories for euer liue: / For how
can one mortall immortalitie giue?' Farkas (headnote, *Sources*) suggests that both
images have their origins in the pillars of bronze erected by Solomon outside his
sanctuary in the Temple at Jerusalem (see *1 Kings* vii 15–22).
75. *brazen*: both 'made of bronze' and 'ostentatious or impudent'; Thornton (see
headnote, *Sources*) suggests a reminiscence of *Ruines of Rome*, 659–61: 'an Arke
of purest golde / Upon a brazen pillour standing hie, / Which th'ashes seem'd
of some great Prince to hold'.
77–8.] And yet mustered five-score chariots in full force / —Gold, of course.
(*MS*). *H proof* (but not *H proof* [2]) has 'And reserved'. Farkas (see headnote, *Sources*)
suggests that B. is remembering literary and artistic representations of gold chariots at this point, citing Guido Reni's 'Golden Chariot of Apollo' in the Palazzo
Rospigliosi and Ovid's description of the Sun God's chariot in *Metamorphoses*

14

Oh, heart! oh, blood that freezes, blood that burns!
80   Earth's returns
For whole centuries of folly, noise and sin!
          Shut them in,
With their triumphs and their glories and the rest.
          Love is best!

---

ii 107–10. Sirugo (headnote, *Sources*) suggests a possible additional reference to Syracusan gold coins, 'such as the decadrachms struck in 480 BC, which showed on the reverse a triumphal chariot above a fleeing lion, symbol of conquered Africa' (p. 46).

79–81. The heart's twin impulses of fear and desire refer back to the 'lust of glory' and 'dread of shame' on which the lost empire was founded (ll. 31–4); the speaker points to the obliteration of that empire as the natural outcome of 'centuries of . . . sin'. Line 79 is self-contained; ll. 80–1 elliptically gesture towards the landscape with its ruins.

79. In *MS* 'blood' is written over an illegible, shorter word. Cp. *By the Fire-Side* 102n. (p. 466).   *freezes*] tingles (*MS del.*; 'freezes' was the first reading). Cp. Scott, *Lay of the Last Minstrel*, xxvi, 13–14: 'His blood did freeze, his brain did burn, / 'Twas fear'd his mind would ne'er return'.

81. *sin!*] sin— (*MS*).

83. *their triumphs*] their grandeurs (*MS*).   *and the rest.*] and the rest— (*MS, H proof*); and the rest! (*1868–88*).

84.] *This* is best! (*MS*); This is best! (*H proof*); Love is best. (*1868–88*). B. seems to have popularized this phrase; several later poets pick it up, and Francis Turner Palgrave quotes it in the last lines of his elegy 'In Memory of Robert Browning': 'And *Blest are the dead in the Lord*; / *For they rest from their labours*, I heard; / With a *Love is best!*—and the life now at rest / Was summ'd in that one brief word' (*Amenophis and Other Poems Sacred and Secular*, 1892).

34 Holy-Cross Day

ON WHICH THE JEWS WERE FORCED
TO ATTEND AN ANNUAL CHRISTIAN
SERMON IN ROME

Text and publication

First publ. *M & W*, 10 Nov. 1855; repr. *1863, 1863², 1868, 1880, 1888*. Our text
is *1855*.

Composition and date

According to *Sharp*, the poem was composed during the Brownings' period of
residence in Rome in the winter and spring of 1853–54; this suggestion is given
added credibility by the Roman subject of the poem. There is, however, evidence that B. was still revising the poem just a month or so before its publication; see ll. 113–14n.

Sources and contexts

In his book *Six Months in Italy* (1853; rpt. 1856) B.'s American friend George
Stillman Hillard notes the existence of a Papal Bull dating from 1584 which obliged
Jews to attend a Christian sermon once a week, and adds: 'This burden is not
yet wholly removed from them; and to this day, several times in the course of
a year, a Jewish congregation is gathered in the church of S. Angelo in Pescheria,
and constrained to listen to a homily from a Dominican friar, to whom, unless
his zeal have eaten up his good feelings and his good taste, the ceremony must
be as painful as to his hearers' (p. 305). The church of Sant' Angelo in Peschiera
is on the edge of the Roman 'ghetto', the area in which Jews were forced to
live after the accession of Paul IV in 1555. Hillard describes Paul IV as a 'dark
and fervid bigot' and indicates some of the humiliations heaped on the Jews
during his Papacy: 'He compelled them to wear a visible badge of separation,
which for men was a yellow hat, and for women a yellow veil or handkerchief.
Jewish physicians were forbidden to prescribe for Christian patients, and Jewish
families were not allowed to employ Christian servants . . . Since that time, the
Jews in Rome have been restricted to a particular quarter, which is called the
Ghetto. It is a cluster of narrow and crooked streets, bounded on one side by
the Tiber, and situated near the island where the river makes a sudden bend
. . . It is entered by eight gates, which, until the accession of the present Pontiff
[Pius IX], were closed from Ave Maria till sunrise' (p. 303).

According to Giacomo Blustein, *Storia degli ebrei in Roma* (Roma 1921):
'In the early days of the [compulsory sermon] no less than a third of the community had to attend the sermons every week according to the decree; this was
reduced by Pope Gregory XIII to 150 people, but then grew to 300. As the traveller Abraham Levi mentions in 1724, no fewer than 300 men and 200 women
had therefore to listen to the sermon (which lasted two hours) every Saturday,
while the pontifical authorities later contented themselves with 100 men and
50 women' (p. 173; our transl.). He adds: 'Many used to go there with their ears
already sealed with wax so as not to have to listen to the attacks that were made
on their religion and the formal invitations they were given to relinquish it. As
soon as anyone started to fall asleep, or even failed to pay sufficient attention,

the overseer warned him with a blow from a stick: at which point a hubbub—perhaps somewhat forced—would arise, in order to make the preacher pause and therefore lose the thread of his subtle reasonings' (*ibid.* 174). This account is corroborated by an entry in Evelyn's *Diary* for 7 Jan. 1645: 'A Sermon was preach'd to the Jewes at Ponte Sisto, who are constrain'd to sit, till the houre is don; but it is with so much malice in their countenances spitting, humming, coughing and motion, that it is almost impossible they should heare a word, nor are there any converted except it be very rarely' (Melchiori, 'Browning and the Bible', *Review of English Literature* vii [1966] 23).

'Holy Cross Day', also known as The Feast of the Exaltation of the Cross, is celebrated on 14 Sept.; it is supposed to commemorate the recovery of the true Cross from the Persians by the Emperor Heraclius in AD 629, but the date in question actually refers to an earlier feast for the dedication of the basilica built by the Emperor Constantine on the site of the Holy Sepulchre in Jerusalem in AD 335. Holy Cross Day has no recorded connection with the practice described in the poem; B.'s imaginary sermon seems to be set during Lent (see ll. 51–4n.).

Rowena Fowler ('Browning's Jews', *VP* xxxv (1997), 245–65) places the poem in the context of the 'conversionist' attitude to Judaism which was part of the evangelical heritage of both the Brownings. The name of the Rabbi whose 'Song of Death' closes the poem (ll. 69–120) may be significant in this respect. This figure has usually been identified with the renowned scholar and teacher Abraham Ben Meir Ibn Ezra (AD 1092–1167), but B. would also have been aware of the fictional Juan Josafat Ben-Ezra, a converted Jew created by the Jesuit priest Manuel Lacunza in his book *La venida del Mesías en gloria y majestad* [The Coming of Messiah in Glory and Majesty]. This book was translated into English by the Revd Edward Irving in 1827 (*The Coming of Messiah in Glory and Majesty. By Juan Josafat Ben-Ezra, A Converted Jew. Translated from the Spanish, with a Preliminary Discourse, by the Rev. Edward Irving, A.M.* 2 vols.) and was clearly well known to EBB.; in a letter to Susanna Thorold she states: 'Irving's "Orations" I have read, & also his preface to "Ben Ezra," giving much admiration to his fervour & elevation, & richness of poetic imagery—but I heard him preach only once, when I was very young' (3 Dec. 1848, *Correspondence* xv 178). In his Preface (vol. i, pp. v–vi), Irving suggests that amongst the signs of the Second Coming will be a renewal of messianic fervour amongst the Jews, and their restoration to the biblical land of Israel:

When the Lord shall have finished the taking of witness against the Gentiles . . . he will begin to prepare another ark of testimony, or rather to make the whole earth an ark of testimony; and to that end will turn his Holy Spirit unto his ancient people the Jews, and bring unto them those days of refreshing spoken of by all the holy prophets since the world began: in the which work of conveying to them his Spirit by the preaching of the word, he may, and it is likely will use the election according to grace, who still are faithful among the Gentiles; though I believe it will chiefly be by the sending of Elias, who is promised before the dreadful and terrible day of the Lord, and by other mighty and miraculous signs . . . [this preaching will accomplish] in the Jewish church . . . that refining and passing through the fire which is spoken of immediately on their restoration. (Mal. iii. 3. Zech. xiii. 9.) Which Antichristian spirit among the Gentiles, and enraged infidel spirit among the Jews, may amalgamate with one another, to produce a spurious restoration of the nations to their own land, and occasion that great warfare in the neighbourhood of Jerusalem, when Antichrist shall fall, and his powers be broken in the battle of Armaggeddon.

> But the faithful among the Jews now brought to believe on him whom they
> have pierced, shall in the meantime be prepared by much sorrow, and distress,
> and supplication, for the coming of the Lord to settle and establish them surely
> and for ever in their own land . . . in this way the Lord will be preparing for
> himself an ark of testimony in the Jewish nation, through whom to make the
> whole world one great and universal ark of faithful testimony.

Irving also points out that the book was banned by the Catholic authorities, a
fact which increases its value for him as a testament to the survival of the 'truth'
of Christian doctrine in the face of persecution. His faith in its value is unshaken
by his discovery that it was written by a Jesuit priest, not least because he remains
'sceptical' that the character of the converted Jew is 'assumed' (pp. xix–xx).

B.'s interest in theories of this kind is indicated by his admiration for Dunbar
Isidore Heath's *The Future Human Kingdom of Christ* (1852). Heath takes what
EBB. calls the 'dense material view of the personal reign at Jerusalem' which involves
the restoration of Israel as a temporal kingdom (2 Mar. 1853, *EBB to Arabella* i
543). His argument combines conversionism with Zionism, suggesting that the
revived nation of Israel will recognize Christ as its saviour and be 'nationally'
saved in first place amongst the nations of the earth: 'If the Jews were gathered
into the land they still claim as their own, and they were to incur in consequence
a formidable military attack from European powers; if the Jews were on the very
point of being put down, and some sign of the Son of Man should appear, what
more probable, humanly speaking, and merely taking Europe and the Jews as we
now find them,—than that the Jews should nationally accept Christ, that nine
European newspapers out of ten should scoff at the "sign," that individuals should
accept it, and that the sudden taking away of these individuals should then be
the beginning of a moral action upon the remaining nations'; cp. ll. 109–20n.

In spite of the similarities between these theories and the ending of the poem,
B. later denied any 'conversionist' intention in a letter to Furnivall: 'in *Holy Cross
Day*, Ben Ezra is not supposed to acknowledge Christ as the Messiah because he
resorts to the obvious argument "even on your own showing, and accepting for
a moment the authority of your accepted Lawgiver, you are condemned by His
precepts—let alone ours"' (17 Feb. 1888, *Trumpeter* 151).

The 'Diary by the Bishop's Secretary' is fictional; note that it is a pastiche of
Elizabethan English prose, not (as it should logically be) Italian. This, and other
features of the first half of the poem, such as its 'vulgar' vocabulary and grotesque
rhymes, may owe something to the *Ingoldsby Legends*: see headnote to *Heretic's
Tragedy*, III 219.

Parallels in B.

A number of B.'s poems are on Jewish subjects; cp. *Ben Karshook* (III 659).
Rabbi Ben Ezra (see above, *Sources*) is given his own poem in *DP* (p. 649);
Jewish resistance to Christian persecution is the subject of *Filippo Baldinucci
on the Privilege of Burial* (*Pacchiarotto*, 1876). The proto-Zionism of the closing
stanzas is, as Fowler notes, anticipated in bk. v of *Paracelsus*: 'See how bright
St. Saviour's spire / Flames in the sunset; all its figures quaint / Gay in the glancing light; you might conceive them / A troop of yellow-vested, white-hair'd
Jews / Bound for their own land where redemption dawns!' (ll. 324–7 in the
first-edition text; the last line was added in B.'s revisions to the poem made in
1847: see II 285). Fowler also notes a parallel with the (pre-Christian) Roman
persecution of the Jews in the second century AD mentioned in *Jochanan
Hakkadosh* 176 (*Jocoseria*, 1883).

["Now was come about Holy-Cross Day, and now must
my lord preach his first sermon to the Jews: as it was of
old cared for in the merciful bowels of the Church, that,
so to speak, a crumb at least from her conspicuous table
5 here in Rome, should be, though but once yearly, cast
to the famishing dogs, under-trampled and bespitten-upon
beneath the feet of the guests. And a moving sight in
truth, this, of so many of the besotted, blind, restive and
ready-to-perish Hebrews! now paternally brought—nay,
10 (for He saith, "Compel them to come in") haled, as it

Epigraph. [*3.*] *cared for in*] cared for by (*1863²*).
Epigraph [*3*] *merciful bowels*: bowels are (as *Cruden's Concordance* puts it) 'used often
in Scripture for the seat of pity or kindness'; see e.g. *Jeremiah* iv 19.
Epigraph [*4*] *a crumb at least from her conspicuous table*: cp. *Matthew* xv 22–7: 'And
behold, a woman of Canaan came out of the same coasts, and cried unto him,
saying, Have mercy on me, O Lord, thou Son of David; my daughter is
grievously vexed with a devil. But he answered her not a word. And his disciples came and besought him, saying, Send her away, for she crieth after us. But
he answered and said, I am not sent but unto the lost sheep of the house of Israel.
Then came she and worshipped him, saying, Lord, help me. But he answered
and said, It is not meet to take the children's bread, and to cast it to dogs.
And she said, Truth, Lord: yet the dogs eat of the crumbs which fall from their
masters' table.' The passage is used ironically here; the Jews are placed in the
position of the woman of Canaan, but where she sought Jesus's help, they are
being forced to pick up the 'crumbs' from the Christians' table.
Epigraph [*6*] *famishing dogs, under-trampled and bespitten-upon*: cp. Shylock in *The
Merchant of Venice*: 'You call me misbeliever, cut-throat dog, / And spat upon
my Jewish gaberdine . . . You, that did void your rheum upon my beard, / And
foot me as you spurn a stranger cur / Over your threshold' (I iii 111–12, 117–19).
For another parallel with this scene, see l. 20n.
Epigraph [*8.*] *besotted, blind, restive*] besotted blind restif (*1868–88*).
Epigraph [*9*] *ready-to-perish Hebrews*: cp. *Deuteronomy* xxvi 5: 'A Syrian ready to
perish was my father, and he went down into Egypt, and sojourned there with
a few, and became there a nation, great, mighty, and populous'; as Melchiori
(headnote, *Sources*) notes, this allusion conceals 'behind the belittling adjective
. . . a reference to the two great hopes of the Jewish people; the promised land,
and that they shall be honoured "high above all nations"' (p. 26).
Epigraph [*9*] *paternally*] maternally (*1863–88*).
Epigraph [*10*] *for He saith, "Compel them to come in"*: in *Luke* xiv Jesus tells the
story of a man who invites his neighbours to a great supper. When they refuse
to come he calls instead for 'the poor, and the maimed, and the halt, and the
blind': 'Go out into the highways and hedges, and compel them to come in,
that my house may be filled' (vv. 21, 23). The Secretary interprets the parable
as implying that compulsion is justified in order to allow people to 'partake of
the heavenly grace'.
Epigraph [*10*] *haled*: hauled.

were, by the head and hair, and against their obstinate
hearts, to partake of the heavenly grace. What awakening,
what striving with tears, what working of a yeasty
conscience! Nor was my lord wanting to himself on so
15   apt an occasion; witness the abundance of conversions
which did incontinently reward him: though not to my
lord be altogether the glory.'—*Diary by the Bishop's Secretary,*
1600.]

Though what the Jews really said, on thus being driven
20   to church, was rather to this effect:

                                   I
Fee, faw, fum! bubble and squeak!
Blessedest Thursday's the fat of the week.
Rumble and tumble, sleek and rough,

Epigraph [11–12] obstinate hearts . . . awakening: Oxford cites *Deuteronomy* ii 30: 'the
Lord thy God hardened his spirit, and made his heart obstinate'. The language
used is (anachronistically) redolent of evangelical Christianity.
Epigraph [13–14] working of a yeasty conscience: either 'working of an underdevel-
oped conscience' or 'working of a conscience just planted in them'; cp. Charles
Kingsley's novel *Yeast* (1848) and *Galatians* v 9: 'A little leaven leaveneth the whole
lump', a text B. cites in *Old Pictures* 129 (p. 419).
Epigraph [16] incontinently: immediately.
Epigraph [16–17] though not to my lord be altogether the glory: cp. 1 *Corinthians* x 31:
'whatsoever ye do, do all to the glory of God', and the motto of the Knights Templar:
'Non nobis Domine, non nobis, sed nomine tua da gloriam', the Latin version
of Psalm cxv: 'Not unto us Oh Lord, not unto us, but to Thy name give glory'.
Epigraph [19] Though what the Jews] What the Jews (*H proof* [but not *H proof²*],
1865–88). It is rare for a variant after 1855 to revert to the proof reading.

1. *Fee, faw, fum*: cp. *Lovers' Quarrel* 131–3 (p. 383); also *Ring* v 585. The phrase
is used here as a playful way of undermining the pretensions of a tyrant; cp. Southey's
satire on Napoleon's retreat from Moscow: 'And Counsellor Brougham was all
in a fume / At the thought of the march to Moscow: / The Russians, he said,
they were undone, / And the great Fee-Faw-Fum / Would presently come /
With a hop, step, and jump unto London' ('The March to Moscow', ll. 36–41).
On the use of similar fairy-tale material in B.'s poetry see headnote to *Childe
Roland* (p. 350). *bubble and squeak*: a dish of meat and cabbages fried together;
presumably the kind of thing eaten on Thursdays (see l. 2 and note).
2. *Blessedest*: a translation of the Italian 'santissimo'. *the fat of the week*: Giovedi
Grasso (fat Thursday), the last Thursday before Lent, but by extension, because
Friday is a weekly fast-day, any Thursday (as a day of gluttony).
3. *Rumble and tumble*: cp. *Pied Piper of Hamelin* 103–4 (p. 178); Melchiori (see
headnote, *Sources*) points out that the description of the Jews here resembles the
description of the rats in the earlier work.

Stinking and savoury, smug and gruff,
5   Take the church-road, for the bell's due chime
Gives us the summons—'tis sermon-time.

2

Boh, here's Barnabas! Job, that's you?
Up stumps Solomon—bustling too?
Shame, man! greedy beyond your years
10   To handsel the bishop's shaving-shears?
Fair play's a jewel! leave friends in the lurch?
Stand on a line ere you start for the church.

3

Higgledy piggledy, packed we lie,
Rats in a hamper, swine in a stye,
15   Wasps in a bottle, frogs in a sieve,
Worms in a carcase, fleas in a sleeve.
Hist! square shoulders, settle your thumbs
And buzz for the bishop—here he comes.

4

Bow, wow, wow—a bone for the dog!

---

4. *smug*: 'Nice; spruce' (*J.*)   *gruff*: 'sour of aspect, harsh of manners' (*J.*).

8–12. The implication is that Solomon is eager to get to the church ahead of the others, since he will then have an opportunity of becoming one of the converts, and thus secure for himself an easy livelihood (see ll. 34–6). But this idea of a 'race' for the church (from the 'line' of l. 12) is inconsistent with the later statement that the converts have already been chosen by lot (ll. 31–6).

10. handsel: 'To use or do anything the first time' (*J.*); any converts would be expected to shave off their hair, which some orthodox Jews allow to grow long. See ll. 39–40n.

11. Fair play's a jewel: *OED* notes that this phrase is used by Sir Walter Scott in *Redgauntlet* (1824), ch. xx.

13–16. Melchiori (headnote, *Sources*) cites a nursery rhyme beginning 'Higgledy-piggledy / Here we lie, / Picked and plucked / And put in a pie' (p. 30). The rhyme is a charade whose two elements 'cur' and 'rants' give 'currants'. Fowler (headnote, *Sources*) compares Gratiano's observation in *The Merchant of Venice* that Shylock is enough to make one believe '[that] souls of animals infuse themselves / Into the trunks of men.' (IV i 132–3).

17–18. Cp. *Christmas-Eve* 807–14 (III 79), where, however, the 'Professor' at Göttingen is not a contemptible figure like the Bishop, and in his case the audience's reactions are sincere; the Jews here are only pretending to be attentive. 'Hist!' in l. 17 has the effect of 'Hark!' or 'Look out!'

19. 'The dog is barking—give him something to shut him up' (the Jews wish they could stop the Bishop's tedious speech). Cp. (noting the rhyme word in the

20 I liken his Grace to an acorned hog.
    What, a boy at his side, with the bloom of a lass,
    To help and handle my lord's hour-glass!
    Didst ever behold so lithe a chine?
    His cheek hath laps like a fresh-singed swine.

                          5
25 Aaron's asleep—shove hip to haunch,
    Or somebody deal him a dig in the paunch!
    Look at the purse with the tassel and knob,
    And the gown with the angel and thingumbob.
    What's he at, quotha? reading his text!
30 Now you've his curtsey—and what comes next?

                          6
    See to our converts—you doomed black dozen—
    No stealing away—nor cog nor cozen!
    You five that were thieves, deserve it fairly;
    You seven that were beggars, will live less sparely.

---

next line) the nursery rhyme beginning: 'Bow-wow, says the dog, / Mew, mew, says the cat, / Grunt, grunt, goes the hog'; again the implication is one of scornful belittlement of the ceremony.

20. acorned hog: a pig fed with acorns; the speaker's derogatory description alludes to Jewish dietary laws which forbid the eating of pigs; see l. 24. Rowena Fowler points out that '[the] sexual connotations of [this phrase] . . . are brought to the fore in the juxtaposition with Shakespeare's Iachimo who "Like a full-acorn'd boar . . . Cried 'O!' and mounted" (*Cymbeline*, II v 16–17)'; *SP* xcv (1998) 333–50. Cp. also Shylock in *The Merchant of Venice*, refusing to dine with Bassanio: 'Yes, to smell pork; to eat of the habitation which your prophet the Nazarene conjured the devil into' (I iii 33–5).

21–2. With this suggestion of homosexuality in the Catholic Church cp. *Fra Lippo* 8–11n. (p. 484).

22. my lord's hour-glass: presumably to time the sermon (with an indecent innuendo).

23. so lithe a chine: 'chine' is an archaism for 'spine'.

27–30. The speaker feigns ignorance of Catholic ritual. The 'purse with the tassel and knob' is the receptacle handed round the congregation during the collection. The bishop's 'reading [of] his text' is probably the reading from the Gospels, after which he will genuflect (or 'curtsey') in reverence. EBB. uses 'curtsey' in this sense in a letter to Arabella of 15–17 Apr. 1848 (*Correspondence* xv 59).

31–6. The speaker implies that the Jews have agreed amongst themselves who will be 'converted' by the sermon; and also perhaps that the leaders have manipulated the draw (l. 35) to rid themselves of undesirable elements.

32. cog nor cozen: both words are archaic terms meaning 'cheat, deceive'.

34. sparely.] emended in agreement with *H proof*; *1855* has no punctuation; *1863–88* have a semi-colon.

35   You took your turn and dipped in the hat,
    Got fortune—and fortune gets you; mind that!

7
    Give your first groan—compunction's at work;
    And soft! from a Jew you mount to a Turk.
    Lo, Micah,—the self-same beard on chin
40   He was four times already converted in!
    Here's a knife, clip quick—it's a sign of grace—
    Or he ruins us all with his hanging-face.

8
    Whom now is the bishop a-leering at?
    I know a point where his text falls pat.
45   I'll tell him to-morrow, a word just now
    Went to my heart and made me vow
    I meddle no more with the worst of trades—
    Let somebody else pay his serenades.

9
    Groan all together now, whee—hee—hee!
50   It's a-work, it's a-work, ah, woe is me!
    It began, when a herd of us, picked and placed,

---

37. Give your first groan: an imaginary instruction to the 'converts'; *Oxford* compares *Romans* viii 23: 'even we ourselves groan within ourselves, waiting for the adoption, to wit, the redemption of our bodies'. *compunction*: 'pricking or stinging of conscience' (*OED*), a traditional Christian term for the feeling of remorse at one's sins.

38. from a Jew you mount to a Turk: i.e. you rise up the scale of the heathen from a Jew to a Muslim (from a Christian point of view). Cp. *Childe Roland* 137–8 (p. 362).

39–40. implying that some of the Jews have already been 'converted' several times.

41. The practice of shaving the Jews as a sign of conversion, referred to at ll. 9–10 above; *Oxford* compares *Numbers* vi 5, and *Judges* xiii 5.

42. hanging-face: cp. *Fra Lippo* 307 (p. 501).

47. I meddle . . . of trades—] To meddle . . . of trades! (*1880*). *the worst of trades*: usury in money-lending, a traditional Jewish role in Christian societies. The bishop is presumably preaching hypocritically against this practice. Given what he is going to use the money for (see next line), the speaker may also mean that he is not going to act as a pandar.

48. The speaker implies that he has lent the bishop money in the past to pay for his sexual dissipations (euphemistically referred to as his 'serenades').

51–4. Under the heading ' "Corse" degli ebrei durante il Carnevale' [' "Races" of the Jews during Carnival'], Blustein (see headnote, *Sources*) cites a contemporary observer writing in 1583: 'On Monday, as usual, eight naked Jews ran to obtain

Were spurred through the Corso, stripped to the waist;
Jew-brutes, with sweat and blood well spent
To usher in worthily Christian Lent.

10

55   It grew, when the hangman entered our bounds,
Yelled, pricked us out to this church like hounds.
It got to a pitch, when the hand indeed
Which gutted my purse, would throttle my creed.
And it overflows, when, to even the odd,
60   Men I helped to their sins, help me to their God.

11

But now, while the scapegoats leave our flock,
And the rest sit silent and count the clock,
Since forced to muse the appointed time
On these precious facts and truths sublime,—

---

a prize, favoured by the rain, the wind and the cold as the infidels deserved; and
after these two-legged beasts, ran others with four legs' (p. 138). This custom
pre-dated the persecutions of the sixteenth century; it is mentioned as early as
1466.

53. sweat and blood: cp. *Luke* xxii 44: 'And being in an agony he [Jesus] prayed
more earnestly: and his sweat was as it were great drops of blood falling down
to the ground.'

54. Carnival precedes Lent, the month during which Christians are supposed to
do penance in preparation for Easter.

55. It: i.e. the feeling which is 'a-work' in the Jews, and which eventually 'overflows'
(l. 59) in 'Ben Ezra's Song of Death' (l. 66).

55. the hangman: as *Oxford* notes, the public hangman might be engaged in other
works of punishment or persecution (e.g. the burning of books); but the use of
this term would have a particular resonance for Jews because of the biblical story
of Esther, in which the wicked Haman tries to have Mordecai hanged, but ends
up being hanged himself.   *our bounds*: the area of the 'ghetto' within which Jews
were forced to live; see headnote.

56. pricked: urged forward, goaded.   *this church*] his church (*1863–88*, except *1863²*)
which agrees with *1855*).

58. gutted: emptied.

60. Cp. ll. 47–8n.

61. scapegoats: cp. *Leviticus* xvi 8–10: 'Aaron shall cast lots upon the two goats;
one lot for the Lord, and the other lot for the scapegoat. And Aaron shall
bring the goat upon which the Lord's lot fell, and offer him for a sin offering.
But the goat, on which the lot fell to be the scapegoat, shall be presented alive
before the Lord, to make an atonement with him, and to let him go for a scapegoat into the wilderness.' The converts play the role of the 'scapegoats' in this
exercise.

65   Let us fitly employ it, under our breath,
     In saying Ben Ezra's Song of Death.

                        12

     For Rabbi Ben Ezra, the night he died,
     Called sons and sons' sons to his side,
     And spoke, "This world has been harsh and strange,
70   Something is wrong, there needeth a change.
     But what, or where? at the last, or first?
     In one point only we sinned, at worst.

                        13

     "The Lord will have mercy on Jacob yet,
     And again in his border see Israel set.
75   When Judah beholds Jerusalem,
     The stranger-seed shall be joined to them:
     To Jacob's House shall the Gentiles cleave.
     So the Prophet saith and his sons believe.

                        14

     "Ay, the children of the chosen race
80   Shall carry and bring them to their place:
     In the land of the Lord shall lead the same,
     Bondsmen and handmaids. Who shall blame,
     When the slaves enslave, the oppressed ones o'er
     The oppressor triumph for evermore?

---

66. Ben Ezra's Song of Death: This seems to be B.'s invention; for the identity of 'Ben Ezra' see headnote, *Sources*.

67–120. With Ben Ezra's deathbed homily, contrast *Tomb at St. Praxed's* (p. 232), whose dying speaker is a corrupt Renaissance bishop very like the one represented in this poem.

72. In one point only we sinned: by failing to acknowledge Jesus as the Messiah: see ll. 91–6.

73–82. A close paraphrase of the prophecy in *Isaiah* xiv 1–2, which envisages the Jews returning to the Promised Land from exile and '[ruling] over their oppressors'.

74. On this suggestion of the restoration of Israel as a temporal realm see headnote, *Sources*. Melchiori (headnote, *Sources*) notes that the term 'border' is not in Isaiah, and suggests that B. might have interwoven this passage with a similar one in *Jeremiah*: 'And there is hope in thine end, saith the Lord, that thy children shall come again to their own border' (xxxi 17).

15

85   "God spoke, and gave us the word to keep:
     Bade never fold the hands nor sleep
     'Mid a faithless world,—at watch and ward,
     Till the Christ at the end relieve our guard.
     By his servant Moses the watch was set:
90   Though near upon cock-crow—we keep it yet.

16

     "Thou! if thou wast He, who at mid-watch came,
     By the starlight naming a dubious Name!
     And if we were too heavy with sleep—too rash
     With fear—O thou, if that martyr-gash
95   Fell on thee coming to take thine own,
     And we gave the Cross, when we owed the Throne—

17

     "Thou art the Judge. We are bruised thus.
     But, the judgment over, join sides with us!
     Thine too is the cause! and not more thine
100 Than ours, is the work of these dogs and swine,

85–90. This passage uses a number of phrases from *Mark* xiii 32–7.

88. the Christ: the Messiah, literally 'the anointed one'; Rowena Fowler (head-note, *Sources*) notes that 'no professing Jew would use the name of Christ in a messianic sense', as Ezra seems to do here. Ben Ezra's words may, however, be sung by the Jews at this point because the sermon they were forced to attend was 'usually an exposition of some passage from the Old Testament, and especially those relating to the Messiah, from the Christian point of view' (Hillard, *Six Months in Italy*, II 51; cited DeVane, *Handbook* 260).   *Till the Christ*] Till Christ (*1863–88*, except *1863²* which agrees with *1855*).

89. By his servant Moses the watch was set: Melchiori (headnote, *Sources*) suggests that this is a reminiscence of *Malachi* iv 4–5: 'Remember ye the law of Moses my servant, which I commanded unto him in Horeb for all Israel, with the statutes and judgements. Behold I will send you Elijah the prophet.' Jesus is repeatedly compared to, and occasionally identified with, Elijah (or 'Elias'); see, e.g., *Mark* vi 15, *Luke* ix 19. He is not, however, accepted as the promised saviour by the Jews in the poem (who 'keep [their watch] yet').

91–108. Ben Ezra, addressing Jesus, concedes that he might indeed have been the Messiah, despite coming at an unexpected time ('at mid-watch . . . by the starlight') and not identifying himself clearly enough ('naming a dubious Name'). However, Ben Ezra goes on, even if the Jews mistook Christ's real nature, they themselves are now persecuted as he was, and are therefore his natural allies.

93. And if we were] And if, (*1863–88*, except *1863²* which agrees with *1855*).

100. dogs and swine: Ben Ezra describes the Christians, who profess to follow Christ's teachings in theory but deny them in practice, in the terms used by the diarist to abuse the Jews themselves.

Whose life laughs through and spits at their creed,
Who maintain thee in word, and defy thee in deed!

18

"We withstood Christ then? be mindful how
At least we withstand Barabbas now!
105 Was our outrage sore? but the worst we spared,
To have called these—Christians,—had we dared!
Let defiance to them, pay mistrust of thee,
And Rome makes amends for Calvary!

19

"By the torture, prolonged from age to age,
110 By the infamy, Israel's heritage,
By the Ghetto's plague, by the garb's disgrace,
By the badge of shame, by the felon's place,
By the branding-tool, the bloody whip,
And the summons to Christian fellowship,

---

103. withstood: stood against; denied; cp. *Any Wife to Any Husband* 8–9 (III 648).
104. Barabbas was the murderer released at the request of the Jews instead of Jesus (*Mark* xv 6–14); he is now the symbol of the Christian persecutors themselves.
106. 'To have called our present persecutors Christians would have been a real "outrage" against the Messiah.'
107. defiance to them] defiance of them (*1863²*).
108. 'Let our present defiance of the Roman Catholic Church make amends for our part in the crucifixion.'
109–120. Ben Ezra invokes the sufferings of the Jewish people as evidence of their determination to 'wrest Christ's name from the Devil's crew' and carry it back with them to the Promised Land. On the possible 'conversionist' background to this notion, see headnote, *Sources*.
111–12. On the indignities inflicted on the Jews of Rome, see headnote.
113–14.] Each heavier to us as these braggarts waxed, / Each lighter whenever their power relaxed—(*H proof*.) B. wrote and then cancelled an alternative version of these lines on the envelope of a letter from Bryan Waller Procter dated 2 Oct. 1855 (MS at University of Chicago): 'By the branding iron, the hangman's whip / And the summons to Christian fellowship.' 'Iron' has subsequently been altered to 'tool'. This is closer to *1855* than *H proof*; the change from 'hangman's whip' to 'bloody whip' may have been prompted by the earlier appearance of the figure of the hangman (at l. 55). (We are grateful to Philip Kelley for this information.) Although *Holy-Cross Day* is, overall, one of the most lightly revised poems in *M & W*, this local instance is one of the most radical changes made to the text in proof. (The next revision, at l. 115, comes in with pleasing aptness.)

20

115   "We boast our proofs, that at least the Jew
       Would wrest Christ's name from the Devil's crew.
       Thy face took never so deep a shade
       But we fought them in it, God our aid!
       A trophy to bear, as we march, a band
120   South, east, and on to the Pleasant Land!"

> [*The present Pope abolished this bad business of the*
> *sermon.—R.B.*]

115. our proofs] our proof (*1863–88*, except *1863²* which agrees with *1855*).

116. Would wrest] Could wrest (*1863²*). *from the Devil's crew*: Melchiori (head-note, *Sources*) suggests an allusion to I *Corinthians* x 20–1, placing the Christians in the position assigned by St Paul to the 'Gentiles': 'But I say, that the things which the Gentiles sacrifice, they sacrifice to devils, and not to God: and I would not that ye should have fellowship with devils.'

117–18. 'No matter how badly they obscured or distorted your image, we continued to fight them in your name, with the help of God.'

119. a band] Thy band (*1863–65*); thy band (*1868–88*).

120. Cp. *Jeremiah* iii 18–19; Ben Ezra clearly thinks of the 'Pleasant Land' as the biblical land of Israel, which lies 'South' and 'East' of Rome.

Author's note. The present Pope] The late Pope (*1880*); Pope Gregory XVI (*1888*). *this bad business of the sermon.*] this bad business. (*H proof*); this bad business of the Sermon. (*1888*). The 'present Pope' in 1855, and the 'late Pope' in 1880, was Pius IX, who abolished both 'the insults against [the Jews], normal in the annual comedies of the Carnival', and 'the sermons to convert them' on his assumption of the Papacy (Owen Chadwick, *A History of the Popes 1830–1914* [Oxford 1998] 129–30). B. seems, however, to have been informed subsequently that it was in fact Pius's predecessor Pope Gregory XVI who eliminated this practice, and modified his note accordingly.

35 Memorabilia

First publ. *M & W*, 10 Nov. 1855, the concluding poem of the first volume; repr. *1863*, *1865²*, *1868*, *1872*, *1888*. Our text is *1855*. The title of the poem appears in the Contents page of *H proof*, but the leaf on which it should appear is blank; *H proof²* also notes 'This leaf is blank in proof copy.' *Oxford* suggests that the poem was added at the last minute to fill up the blank page, but there is no concrete evidence that this was the case.

There are two plausible datings for this poem: late 1851, the period during which B. was writing *Shelley* (see Appendix A, p. 851); or 1853–54 (in Rome), the period to which *Sharp* assigns the poem. On the basis of the evidence that the majority of the *M & W* poems were written in 1853–54, and the use of the relatively new term 'memorabilia' (see below), the later date is to be preferred.

B.'s early devotion to Shelley has been well documented: see *Pauline* 141–229 and notes (pp. 19–24), and the headnotes to *Sordello* (I 367) and *Shelley* (pp. 852–3). In a conversation with W. G. Kingsland, B. claimed that the poem had been prompted by an incident which took place 'in the shop of Hodgson, the well-known London bookseller': '[A] stranger came in, who, in the course of conversation with the bookseller, spoke of something that Shelley had once said to him. Suddenly the stranger paused, and burst into laughter as he observed me staring at him with blanched face . . . I still vividly remember how strangely the presence of a man who had seen and spoken with Shelley affected me' (W. G. Kingsland, 'Some Browning Memories', *Contemporary Review* cii [1912] 206–7). Leigh's *New Picture of London* (1819) lists under 'Booksellers who chiefly sell Modern Publications' a Hodgson in Upper Wimpole Street; this shop is mentioned frequently in the courtship correspondence, and B. chose it as the meeting place for the poets' departure to Italy after their marriage (*Correspondence* xiii 379).

This was not, however, B.'s only acquaintance with someone who 'saw Shelley plain'; in June 1847 EBB. describes a visit to the 'ex consul of Venice & his family, Mr & Mrs Hoppner . . the Hoppners mentioned & written to in Lord Byron's letters & I think Shelley's . . . There was . . . a good deal of talk about poor Shelley & his wife, and how they passed three weeks, with the Hoppners once at Venice, & how on their arrival they ate nothing except water gruel & boiled cabbages & cherries, because it was a principle of Shelley's not to touch animal food, & how Mrs Hoppner did, as she said, "seduce" him into taking roast beef & puddings' (*EBB to Arabella* i 100).

OED suggests that 'the currency of the word [memorabilia] in English may be due to its use as the Latin title of Xenophon's 'Recollections (Ἀπομνημονεύματα) of Socrates'; EBB. owned a copy of a 1741 edition, *Memorabilium Socratis Dictorum, libri IV* (*Collections* A2507). *OED*'s first citation is from 1806–07. In its primary signification the word means 'Memorable or noteworthy thoughts, observations, writings, etc.', but B.'s poem also seems to refer to the other sense listed in *OED*: 'Objects kept or collected because of their historical interest or the memories they evoke of events, people, places, etc., with which they have been associated; souvenirs, mementos.' This latter sense is identified as an American usage, whose earliest citation is 1855. Many of B.'s friends in Rome were American, and he might have picked up the word from them. B. collected some memorabilia of his own, in this sense, e.g. pressed flowers from Keats's and Shelley's graves (1859; *Collections* H566); and cp. *La Saisiaz* (1878),

579–80: 'Turn thence! Is it Diodati joins the glimmer of the lake? / There I plucked a leaf, one week since,—ivy, plucked for Byron's sake'. He admitted in an early letter to EBB. that he had 'always retained [his] first feeling for Byron in many respects .. the interest in the places he had visited, in relics of him', and 'would at any time have gone to Finchley to see a curl of his hair or one of his gloves' (22 Aug. 1846: *Correspondence* xiii 280).

The metaphor of the moulted eagle's feather in the fourth stanza has been the focus of much of the critical discussion of the poem. Shelley mentions eagles frequently in his poetry, often in connection with his contemporaries; the Byron character in *Julian and Maddalo* is described as an 'eagle spirit' (l. 51), and Keats in *Adonais* is compared to 'the eagle, who like thee could scale / Heaven, and could nourish in the sun's domain / Her mighty youth with morning' (ll. 147–9). The image also, of course, applies to Shelley himself, the 'sun-treader' of *Pauline* (l. 151, p. 20). Shen Yao ('A Note on Browning's "Eagle-feather", *SBC* v, no. 2 [Fall 1977] 7–16) argues that the image recalls Keats as well as Shelley; he points out a number of uses of the motif of the 'moulted feather' in Keats's work, and highlights similarities to the poem's language and images in other poems of B.'s, most strikingly *Light Woman* 13–24 (III 609) and *Prince Hohenstiel-Schwangau* (1871) 764. See also headnote to *Popularity* (p. 446).

Oxford notes a poem by Sarah Flower for W. J. Fox which makes the link between the feather and the pen: 'His pen it hath come / From the wing of an eagle, / And tells of its home' (p. 257).

I

Ah, did you once see Shelley plain,
        And did he stop and speak to you?
    And did you speak to him again?
        How strange it seems, and new!

2

5   But you were living before that,
        And you are living after,
    And the memory I started at—
        My starting moves your laughter!

1. *plain*: 'clearly, manifestly'; for this adverbial use of the adjective in respect of perception, *OED* cites Spenser *Faerie Queene* I i 16: 'Ay wont in desert darknes to remaine, / Where plain none might her see, nor she see any plaine'.
3. *again*: 'in reply'.
6. *And you*] And also you (*1865²*, *1868–88*).
7. *started at*: was startled by.

3

I crossed a moor with a name of its own

10 And a use in the world no doubt,

Yet a hand's-breath of it shines alone

'Mid the blank miles round about—

4

For there I picked up on the heather

And there I put inside my breast

15 A moulted feather, an eagle-feather—

Well, I forget the rest.

9–16. The 'moor' is an image of the life of the person whom the speaker meets, and who is of interest only because of his encounter with Shelley; the speaker picks up this recollection like a stray 'eagle-feather', disparaging the importance of the rest of the man's life. For the image of the 'eagle-feather', see headnote.

10. *And a use*] And a certain use (*1868–88*).

11. *hand's-breadth*: cp. *In Three Days* 11 (III 6).

15. *an eagle-feather*—] an eagle-feather! (*1865², 1868–88*).

36 Two in the Campagna

Text and publication

First publ. *M & W*, 10 Nov. 1855; repr. *1863, 1863², 1868, 1872, 1888.* Our text is *1855.* This, and *Another Way of Love*, are the only poems in *M & W* for which there are no variants in *H proof.*

Composition and date

Sharp, who identifies *Two in the Campagna* as one of the poems written in Rome, states: 'I have been told that the poem entitled "Two in the Campagna" was as actually personal as . . . "Guardian Angel"' (p. 259); and, like *Guardian Angel*, it seems to be based quite closely on incidents from B.'s own life. Excursions of the kind described in the poem were undertaken frequently from March 1854 onwards, as EBB. indicates in a letter of 10 May 1854 to Mary Russell Mitford: 'The pleasantest days in Rome we have spent with the Kembles—the two sisters .. who are charming & excellent, both of them, in different ways—& certainly they have given us some exquisite hours on the campagna, upon picnic excursions .. they, & certain of their friends' (*EBB to MRM* iii 409). A letter written by EBB. the day before their departure from Rome notes that 'Robert has been present at *fourteen* Kemble picnics—and I at some five or six' (*EBB to Arabella* ii 80). The 'Kembles' were Frances Anne ('Fanny') Butler (née Kemble), the famous actress and writer, who had married and then divorced Georgia plantation owner Pierce Butler, and her sister, the singer Mrs Adelaide Sartoris. 'Fanny and Adelaide had known Robert Browning for years, having met him often at the houses of Bryan Procter and Henry Chorley. His wife was a newer acquaintance, though the sisters had heard many times of her romantic elopement with her husband to Italy' (Ann Blainey, *Fanny and Adelaide* [Chicago 2001] 255). A strong friendship formed between Fanny and the Brownings during their residence in Rome, with Fanny visiting them alone in their apartment on a number of occasions. (For Fanny Kemble's possible influence on B.'s poetry, see headnote to *Light Woman*, III 608.)

Betty Miller suggests that the poem might have an even more precise connection to this period, seeing its origins in an incident evoked by B. in a letter to Mrs Fitzgerald of 15 July 1882, in which he comments with some asperity on the fact that Fanny Kemble had only just begun to appreciate his poetry: 'none of the kind things she says now can move me like a word of hers in the Campagna "You are the only man I ever knew who behaved like a Christian to his wife"—and this simply because, on an excursion, that wife [was] unable to follow the party [on a walk]' (*Learned Lady* 142 and 143 n.8). Despite Kemble's tribute, Miller reads *Two in the Campagna* as indicating a certain estrangement in the relationship between B. and EBB., and a 'desperate longing for the unimpaired communion of happier days' (*Miller* 182–3). Mrs Orr in contrast (*Life* 199–200), vehemently denies any suggestion of a 'personal' dimension to *Two in the Campagna*:

> We are told . . . in Mr. Sharp's 'Life,' that a personal character no less actual than that of the *Guardian Angel* has been claimed for it. The writer, with characteristic delicacy, evades all discussion of the question; but he concedes a good deal in his manner of doing so. The poem, he says, conveys a sense of that necessary isolation of the individual soul which resists the fusing power of the deepest love; and its meaning cannot be personally—because it is universally—

true. I do not think Mr. Browning meant to emphasize this aspect of the mystery of individual life, though the poem, in a certain sense, expresses it. We have no reason to believe that he ever accepted it as constant; and in no case could he have intended to refer its conditions to himself. He was often isolated by the processes of his mind; but there was in him no barrier to that larger emotional sympathy which we think of as sympathy of the soul. If this poem were true, *One Word More* would be false, quite otherwise than in that approach to exaggeration which is incidental to the poetic form. The true keynote of *Two in the Campagna* is the pain of perpetual change, and of the conscious, though unexplained, predestination to it. Mr. Browning could have still less in common with such a state, since one of the qualities for which he was most conspicuous was the enormous power of anchorage which his affections possessed . . . I make no deduction from this statement when I admit that the last and most emphatic words of the poem in question [ll. 58–60] did probably come from the poet's heart, as they also found a deep echo in that of his wife, who much loved them.

In the letter to Mrs Fitzgerald cited above, B. goes on to note that Fanny Kemble hardly mentions him in her *Memoirs*, and adds: 'Hardly one anecdote but was old in my memory,—many, relating to herself, might be supplemented to advantage if you wished to have the right and complete knowledge of the matter. I met her much oftener than is set down, in those days—but she hardly noticed me; though I always liked her extremely . . . I first became intimate with her in Rome some twenty five years ago—and then she liked me, I know,—as a generally sympathetic person, not without poetic sympathies' (*Learned Lady* 142). See also ll. 36–8n.

Sources and contexts

Some characteristic features of literary representations of the Roman Campagna are examined in the headnote to *Love Among the Ruins* (p. 530). There are a number of verbal resemblances in *Two in the Campagna* to passages in Shelley's *Epipsychidion*, his famous defence of freedom in love; Shelley's poet compares his two loves to 'married lights, which from the towers / Of Heaven look forth' (ll. 355–6; cp. l. 30), and describes the Ionian island on which he plans to set up his utopian community of lovers as 'Washed by the soft blue Oceans of young air' (l. 460; cp. l. 24). This island has a ruined tower, in which 'all the antique and learnèd imagery' has been replaced by 'Parasite flowers' which 'illume with dewy gems / The lampless halls' (ll. 502–3; cp. ll. 12–13). People who conform to 'the code / Of modern morals' by loving only once are compared to 'poor slaves' who 'travel to their home among the dead / By the broad highway of the world, and so / With one chained friend, perhaps a jealous foe, / The dreariest and the longest journey go' (ll. 153–4, 155–9). There are also echoes of Arthur Hugh Clough's *Natura Naturans* ['creating nature']; the Brownings read the collection in which this appears (*Ambarvalia*) in December 1849 (*Letters of EBB* i 429). The poem in question describes an awakening of desire between two people sitting next to one another in a railway carriage, and sees this awakening as part of '[the] Power which e'en in stones and earths / By blind elections felt, in forms / Organic breeds to myriad births' (ll. 42–4): 'Such sweet preluding sense of old / Led on in Eden's sinless place / The hour when bodies human first / Combined the primal prime embrace, / Such genial heat the blissful seat / In man and woman owned unblamed, / When, naked both, its garden paths / They walked unconscious, unashamed' (ll. 73–80; cp. l. 28).

The poem's principal theme—the yearning for complete communion between lovers—is also apparent in *By the Fire-Side* (p. 456), where (as Mrs Orr points out) the conclusion is the opposite to the one drawn here at ll. 41–5. Plato's *Symposium*, with its notion that love represents 'the desire and pursuit of the whole', clearly lies behind such passages, as it does the ending of Shelley's *Epipsychidion*: 'We shall become the same, we shall be one / Spirit within two frames, oh! wherefore two? / One passion in twin-hearts, which grows and grew, / Till like two meteors of expanding flame, / Those spheres instinct with it become the same, / Touch, mingle, are transfigured; ever still / Burning, yet ever inconsumable: / In one another's substance finding food, / Like flames too pure and light and unimbued / To nourish their bright lives with baser prey, / Which point to Heaven and cannot pass away: / One hope within two wills, one will beneath / Two overshadowing minds, one life, one death, / One Heaven, one Hell, one immortality, / And one annihilation' (ll. 573–87). Another famous literary expression of this desire comes in Donne's *The Ecstasie*, a poem whose opening has many affinities with *Two in the Campagna*: 'Where, like a pillow on a bed, / A pregnant bank swelled up, to rest / The violet's reclining head, / Sat we two, one another's best; // Our hands were firmly cemented / With a fast balm, whence there did spring, / Our eye-beams twisted, and did thread / Our eyes, upon one double string . . .' and which confidently affirms what B.'s poem sorrowfully denies: 'When love, with one another so / Interinanimates two souls, / That abler soul, which thence doth flow, / Defects of loneliness controls' (ll. 41–4).

Parallels in B.

Besides the parallels already cited with *Love Among the Ruins* and *By the Fire-Side*, cp. *James Lee* vi (p. 678) which contains a lament for the inability of human beings to 'draw one beauty into our hearts' core, / And keep it changeless' (ll. 214–15) in a stanza form very similar to that of *Two in the Campagna*. Unsuccessful or unachieved relationships are a perennial theme in B., e.g. *In a Year* (p. 270), *The Statue and the Bust* (III 342), and *Youth and Art* (p. 700). John Maynard compares *A Serenade at the Villa* (III 487): both present 'a lover speaking to his mistress in a particular realistic setting' (*BSN* vi.1 [1976] 4).

I

I wonder do you feel to-day
    As I have felt, since, hand in hand,
We sat down on the grass, to stray
    In spirit better through the land,
5   This morn of Rome and May?

2

For me, I touched a thought, I know,
    Has tantalised me many times,

5. *May*: B.'s birth month: see *May and Death* 1n. (III 363).
6–10. Cp. the opening lines of 'A Reverie' (*Poems*, 1833) by B.'s close friend Alfred Domett: 'As thus I sate in musing mood, / With nought to break my solitude, / Mingling and mangling bits of rhymes / And changing each a thousand times; / Now catching at a straggling thought / And shifting it about, when caught, / To see in what form it would look / The best . . .'

(Like turns of thread the spiders throw
Mocking across our path) for rhymes
10 To catch at and let go.

3

Help me to hold it: first it left
The yellowing fennel, run to seed
There, branching from the brickwork's cleft,
Some old tomb's ruin: yonder weed
15 Took up the floating weft,

4

Where one small orange cup amassed
Five beetles,—blind and green they grope
Among the honey-meal,—and last
Everywhere on the grassy slope
20 I traced it. Hold it fast!

5

The champaign with its endless fleece
Of feathery grasses everywhere!

8–9. Cp. *Sordello* i 663–71 (I 440–1). *Oxford* compares a speech by Tresham in B.'s play *A Blot in the 'Scutcheon* (1843) ii 196–204; he is addressing his sister Mildred, whose guilty secret he has just discovered: 'Each day, each hour throws forth its silk-slight film / Between the being tied to you by birth, / And you, until those slender threads compose / A web that shrouds her daily life of hopes / And fears and fancies, all her life, from yours—/ So close you live and yet so far apart! / And must I rend this web, tear up, break down / The sweet and palpitating mystery / That makes her sacred?'

11–20. The 'thought' attaches itself to images of fecundity in apparently waste or unproductive places.

12–13. With this image of the plant growing in a cleft of rock or brickwork cp. *England in Italy* 25–32 (p. 258) and the Pope's description of Pompilia in *Ring* x 1041–6.

14. *Some old tomb's ruin*: one of many such structures in B.'s poetic landscapes: see *Sordello* vi 779–85n. (I 763).

15. *weft*: 'The woof of cloth' (*J.*).

16. *orange cup*: of the flower (or 'weed') in question.

18. *honey-meal*: Not in *J.* as a compound; formed by analogy with the usual sense of 'meal', '[the] flower or edible part of corn' (*J.*).

21–30. Cp. Matthew Arnold's 'Lines Written in Kensington Gardens' (1852): 'Here at my feet what wonders pass, / What endless active life is here! / What blowing daisies, fragrant grass! / An air-stirr'd forest, fresh and clear' (ll. 13–16).

21. *champaign*: B.'s choice of this term is clearly influenced by its proximity to the Italian 'campagna', but it had come into English from Old French and

Silence and passion, joy and peace,
        An everlasting wash of air—
25   Rome's ghost since her decease.

6

Such life there, through such lengths of hours,
        Such miracles performed in play,
Such primal naked forms of flowers,
        Such letting Nature have her way
30   While Heaven looks from its towers.

7

How say you? Let us, O my dove,
        Let us be unashamed of soul,
As earth lies bare to heaven above.
        How is it under our control
35   To love or not to love?

---

had been in use since at least the fifteenth century in the sense of 'a flat open country' (J.); its pronunciation was originally a hard 'ch' (as in 'chalk') with the accent on the first syllable; by B.'s day the hard 'ch' had become soft ('sh') but the stress remained on the first syllable until late in the 19th century (*OED*). B. would have known of many literary precedents, from Shakespeare (*King Lear* I i 64) and Milton (*Paradise Regained* iii 257) to Wordsworth (*The Prelude* [1850] viii 212) and Keats (*Endymion* 386, *Isabella* 347); cp. esp. Christopher Smart's *Song to David* (1763), one of B.'s favourite poems: 'The world—the clustring spheres he made, / The glorious light, the soothing shade, / Dale, champaign, grove, and hill' (st. xxi, ll. 121–3).

24. wash of air: see headnote, *Sources*, for the echo of Shelley's *Epipsychidion* in this phrase. *OED* cites this as an example of the metaphorical use of the term 'wash' meaning '[the] washing of the waves upon the shore'; there might also be an allusion to the painter's 'wash', '[a] broad thin layer of colour laid on by a continuous movement of the brush'. Cp. also *Old Pictures* 7n. (p. 410).

25. The Campagna was depopulated as early as 300 BC; its relics belong to the earlier, Etruscan civilization (see headnote to *Love Among the Ruins*, p. 530).

26. life there] life here (*1868–88*).   *such lengths*] such length (*1863²*).

28. primal: primitive or pristine; see headnote, *Sources*.

30. For this Shelleyan image, see headnote, *Sources*.

31–5. The speaker tries to respond to the prompting of the landscape to spontaneous, all-encompassing passion by proposing a similar fusion between himself and his beloved, but immediately recognizes that human love falls short of this ideal.

31. O my dove: cp. (noting 'brickwork's cleft' in l. 13) *Song of Solomon* ii 14: 'O my dove, that art in the clefts of the rock . . . let me see thy countenance, let me hear thy voice'.

32. I.e. 'let our souls be as unashamed as the earth which "lies bare" to heaven here in the Campagna'.

8

I would that you were all to me,
   You that are just so much, no more—
Nor yours, nor mine,—nor slave nor free!
   Where does the fault lie? what the core
40 Of the wound, since wound must be?

9

I would I could adopt your will,
   See with your eyes, and set my heart
Beating by yours, and drink my fill
   At your soul's springs,—your part, my part
45 In life, for good and ill.

10

No. I yearn upward—touch you close,
   Then stand away. I kiss your cheek,
Catch your soul's warmth,—I pluck the rose

36–8. Fanny Kemble (see headnote, *Composition*) married Pierce Butler, one of
the largest slave-owners in Georgia, and her experiences of plantation life led her
to publish a robust condemnation of the slave trade in Georgia (*Journal of a Residence
on a Georgia Plantation* 1838–39) which made her famous in the anti-slavery movement. She underwent an acrimonious divorce from her husband in 1848–49, partly
caused by their irreconcilable differences over slavery, and she subsequently went
under the honorary title of 'Mrs Kemble' rather than Mrs Butler. On the motif
of slavery in B.'s poetry see Rowena Fowler, 'Browning and Slavery', *VP* xxxvii
(1999) 59–69.

39–40. Cp. *Aurora Leigh* iv 125–8: 'Let us lean / And strain together rather, each
to each, / Compress the red lips of this gaping wound / As far as two souls can.'
Cp. also *By the Fire-Side* 228–30 (p. 474).

40. Of the wound] O' the wound (*1870–88*).

41–5. On the desire for a perfect communion of souls which would avoid the
pain of the 'wound' and 'scar' left by mere proximity, see headnote. Several passages in B.'s letters to EBB. during their courtship express his yearning to be
subject to her will: 'I should like to breathe and move and live by your allowance
and pleasure' (23 April 1846; *Correspondence* xii 272); 'I wish your will to be mine,
to originate mine, your pleasure to be only mine' (4 June 1846; *Correspondence*
xiii 22).

46. I yearn upward: either because his beloved is above him, or as part of the movement towards the communion of souls described in the previous stanza.

48. I pluck the rose: implying that this deprives it of life; cp. *Othello* v ii 13–15:
'When I have pluck'd thy rose, / I cannot give it vital growth again; / It needs
must wither.'

And love it more than tongue can speak—
50   Then the good minute goes.

11

Already how am I so far
    Out of that minute? Must I go
Still like the thistle-ball, no bar,
    Onward, whenever light winds blow,
55   Fixed by no friendly star?

12

Just when I seemed about to learn!
    Where is the thread now? Off again!
The old trick! Only I discern—
    Infinite passion and the pain
60   Of finite hearts that yearn.

50. *the good minute*: cp., among many such images in B., *By the Fire-Side* 181 (p. 471).

53. *thistle ball*: 'the globular head of feathery seeds on the thistle' (*OED*).

55. *Fixed*: set on a particular course; cp. *Easter Day* 552 (III 123). The idea of the beloved as a 'friendly star' governing the poet's fate can also be seen in *My Star* (III 386).

56–60. Cp. J. E. Taylor's *Michel Angelo considered as A Philosophic Poet, with Translations* (*Collections* A2261), presented to B. in 1840, esp. this passage: 'Love, or desire, has been termed the motion of the soul: it originates in, and is a mark of, imperfection; prompted by a desire to attain something which is not possessed, it ceases when its object is attained; and the unconscious actions of the infant, and the highest aspirations of the sage, indicate alike a requirement unsatisfied. How admirable is the law of Providence, which constitutes these very proofs of imperfection the highest prerogative of our nature; rendering the finite power of the mind capable of an infinite longing after and pursuit of perfection!' (p. 43). We are grateful to Dr Robert Renton for drawing our attention to this work.

57. *the thread*: cp. the metaphor of the spider's web with which the poem began (ll. 8–9).

59–60. The difficulty of '[thrusting] in time eternity's concern' (*Sordello* i 566; I 432) is a recurring topic in B.'s poetry; cp. B.'s letter to Ruskin (Appendix B, p. 881): 'I *know* that I don't make out my conception by my language—all poetry being a putting the infinite within the finite.'

37 Cleon

Text, publication, and revision

First publ. *M & W*, 10 Nov. 1855; repr. *1863*, *1863²*, *1868*, *1872*, *1888*. Our text is *1855*. The poem was very lightly revised after *1855*, the least so of the long poems in *M & W*.

Composition and date

There are a number of circumstances linking the poem to the Brownings' period of residence in Rome during the winter of 1853–54. In Nov. 1853 the Brownings met and became friendly with the American artist William Page; he offered to paint B.'s portrait, and the poet sat for him 'above *fifty times*' (*EBB to Arabella* ii 81). The picture was finished in May 1854. It must have been at this time that Page communicated his 'discovery' about the proportions of the human body to the Brownings, as he later recalled: 'Subsequently [B.] advised me to publish it in some English periodical, and assisted me in recollecting the date of my first observations by saying: "I put it in *Cleon*, and my wife in *Aurora Leigh*"' (*Scribner's Monthly* xvii [Apr. 1879] 894–8). Page then quotes *Aurora Leigh* i 864–9, and *Cleon* 55–6 (for the 'discovery' itself see ll. 55–6n.). Page's recollection is corroborated by a letter of 28 May 1855 from B. in which he asks the painter whether or not he has 'completed [his] studies and discoveries of the proportions of the figure' (MS in Smithsonian Institution; cited in Julia Markus, ' "Andrea del Sarto" and William Page', *BIS* ii [1974] 2). A date of 1853–54 is also suggested by possible allusions to Matthew Arnold's *Empedocles on Etna* and *Poems* (1853); see next section.

Sources and influences

A. W. Crawford first suggested in 1927 that 'the real occasion of the poem was the publication of Arnold's *Empedocles on Etna*, and that B. was endeavoring to present a picture somewhat complementary to that sketched by Arnold' ('Browning's "Cleon", *JEGP* xxvi [1927] 485–90). Some of Crawford's assertions are, however, unsupported by convincing evidence. He states, for instance, that B. procured a copy of *Empedocles on Etna* on first publication, but the copy of the relevant volume in B.'s library seems to have come from Isa Blagden (*Collections* A101). Again, Crawford's statement that B. 'read [*Empedocles*] with interest and discernment, and is reported to have greatly favored the poem' derives (via Elisabeth L. Cary's *Browning: Poet and Man* [New York 1899] 127) from Arnold's dedication of the reprint of the poem to B. in 1867 (see below); it does not decisively establish that B. read the poem as soon as it appeared in 1853.

There is, however, evidence in favour of the possibility of a connection between the two poems in a letter of 2 May 1853 from EBB. to her brother George: 'Have you heard a volume of poems by Dr. Arnold's son ("by A") spoken of in London? There is a great deal of thought in them & considerable beauty. Mr. Lytton lent them to us the other day' (*George Barrett* 184). Since EBB. had read Arnold's *The Strayed Reveller, and Other Poems* on its first publication in 1849 (see *EBB to MRM* iii 283–7), this is almost certainly a reference to *Empedocles on Etna, and Other Poems*, publ. in Oct. 1852. Both *Cleon* and the title poem of Arnold's 1852 volume examine the adequacy of Pagan philosophies as a response to human life. Arnold's Empedocles bears little detailed resemblance to the

Pre-Socratic philosopher on whom he is supposedly based, although Arnold, like B., probably had some knowledge of the extant fragments of Empedocles (see ll. 99–111n.). Empedocles was seen by his contemporaries as something of a messianic figure, perhaps because of his advanced knowledge of the natural world; he is reputed to have brought a woman back to life from a 'trance', and his own death was shrouded in mystery and stories of apotheosis. Arnold transforms this shadowy figure into a precursor of his own brand of Stoicism who recognizes the human desire for 'joy' but cannot find any grounds for it in the beliefs available to him. (Specific resemblances to moments in Arnold's poem are noted below; see ll. 21n., 73–94n., 112–27n., 225–6n., 309–17n., 323–35n.) B.'s Cleon, in contrast, is a fictional figure living around the time when St Paul was attempting to spread the message of Christianity to the Pagan world, with limited success. He too realizes that the 'joy-hunger' of humanity is not satisfied by Pagan philosophy (although his is Epicurean or Hedonistic rather than Stoical), yet rejects out of hand the doctrine put forward by the 'barbarian Jew' Paul which might provide the answer to his difficulty by positing the existence of a future state. On the question of the dialogue between the two poems see Antony H. Harrison, 'Cleon's Joy-Hunger and the Empedoclean Context' (*SBC* ix.2 [1981] 57–68). It is possible that B. may have followed Arnold in consulting the surviving fragments of Empedocles' works; see esp. ll. 199–202n. It may be this philosophical dimension which led Ruskin to regard it as 'harder than most' of the poems in *M & W* in his letter to B. of 2 Dec 1855 (Appendix B, p. 878).

There may be a wider indebtedness to Arnold in the poem. Certain sections seem to echo the Stoicism of 'Resignation' (see ll. 235–72n., 271n.); see also headnote to *By the Fire-Side* (p. 456). There may also be a response to the arguments put forward in Arnold's famous 'Preface' to his *Poems. A New Edition*, publ. in Nov. 1853. In this Preface Arnold 'unmasks' himself as the author of *Empedocles*, but goes on to explain why he has excluded the poem from the current collection. It is, he argues, unhelpful to the modern age because 'the calm, the cheerfulness, the disinterested objectivity' of the 'early Greek genius' have been replaced in it by 'the dialogue of the mind with itself': 'modern problems have presented themselves; we hear already the doubts, we witness the discouragement, of Hamlet and of Faust' (R. H. Super [ed.], *The Complete Prose Works of Matthew Arnold* [Ann Arbor, 1960–] i 1). It is not therefore 'dedicated to Joy', as the highest forms of art should be. Arnold goes on to call for a return to antique norms in the construction of works of art; unlike modern writers, the ancients placed the representation of noble actions above the quality of expression: 'They regarded the whole; we regard the parts' (*ibid.* i 5). This neo-classical manifesto elicited a strong response from the literary journals, sparking a debate on the nature of the 'modern' subject in art which Arnold responded to in his inaugural lecture as Professor of Poetry at Oxford, 'On the Modern Element in Literature' (1857). The implicit antagonism in *Cleon* to the idea that Hellenic culture and philosophy are superior to Christianity might then be a rejoinder to Arnold's ideas (see also *Parallels*). B. later quoted an extract from this Preface in his own Preface to *The Agamemnon of Aeschylus* (1877).

Arnold eventually decided to reprint *Empedocles on Etna*—'I cannot say *republish*, for it was withdrawn from circulation before fifty copies were sold'—in 1867 'at the request of a man of genius, whom it had the honour and good fortune to interest,—Mr. Robert Browning.'

An influence closer to home may well have been that of the themes and characters which EBB. was beginning, in the period of the poem's composition, to develop in *Aurora Leigh*. As already noted, Page's 'discovery' of the proportions of the human body found its way into both poems (see above, *Composition*); Cleon resembles Aurora in the high value he places on his own art (see ll. 23–5n.) and in confronting the predicament of the 'latecomer' in culture.

Parallels in B.

The poem has often been seen as complementing *An Epistle* (DeVane *Handbook* 263; see headnote, pp. 509–10), examining the way in which the claims of Christianity might have been viewed by a representative of Hellenistic culture; they are also the only two epistolary poems in B.'s published work. Cp. also *Saul* (III 491) and the late poem *Imperante Augusto Natus Est—(Asolando*, 1889). Harrison (see above) suggests that *Rabbi Ben Ezra* (p. 649) can be seen as a counterpart in a different sense; the Rabbi's joyful old age, enlivened by his faith in God, contrasts with the futile hedonism of Cleon's search for 'joy' (see ll. 323–35n.). The limitations of the world-view implied by the 'perfection' of Pagan art are also examined in *Old Pictures* 81–160 (pp. 415–21), and this theme is taken up again (as DeVane notes) in *Gerard de Lairesse* (*Parleyings*, 1887).

"As certain also of your own poets have said"—

Cleon the poet, (from the sprinkled isles,
Lily on lily, that o'erlace the sea,

Epigraph. The quotation is from *Acts* xvii 28. In AD 51 Paul, having been driven to Athens from Thessalonika by the hostility of the Jews, meets 'certain philosophers of the Epicureans, and of the Stoicks', who invite him to expound his new philosophy on the Areopagus. Paul attempts to persuade the philosophers that they worship the Christian God without being aware of it: 'God that made the world and all things therein, seeing that he is Lord of heaven and earth, dwelleth not in temples made with hands . . . For in him we live, and move, and have our being; as certain also of your own poets have said, For we are also his offspring' (xvii 24–8). The last phrase comes from the *Phaenomena* of the Hellenistic poet Aratus, which opens with the lines: 'Let us begin with Zeus, whom *we* mortals never leave unspoken. / For every street, every market-place is full of Zeus. / Even the sea and the harbour are full of this deity. / Everywhere everyone is indebted to Zeus. / For we are indeed his offspring'. In 'The Apostle and the Poet: Paul and Aratus', R. Faber suggests that Paul might have known Aratus' work through the work of Aristobulus, a Jewish writer of the second century BC (*Clarion* xlii [1993] 291–304). Paul's was the first of many attempts to find corroboration for the Christian revelation in classical Greek literature and philosophy. A notable example is Clement of Alexandria, whose *Stromateis* ransacks the Hellenic corpus for anticipations of and parallels to Christian doctrine, including some of the fragments of Empedocles. (On the significance of Empedocles for the poem as a whole, see above.) Note that the poem begins with a quotation from the 'mere barbarian Jew' whom Cleon disparages at the end (see ll. 343–5). *1–4.* Cleon and Protos are fictional. *Turner* notes that 'Lemprière's *Classical Dictionary* (first published 1788) lists Cleons of many professions, including a general, a sculptor, an orator, a commentator, and a tyrant' (p. 373); and *Ohio* adds that 'Byron, in "Childish Recollections," gave the name Cleon to a college

And laugh their pride when the light wave lisps
    "Greece")—
To Protos in his Tyranny: much health!

5   They give thy letter to me, even now:
I read and seem as if I heard thee speak.
The master of thy galley still unlades
Gift after gift; they block my court at last
And pile themselves along its portico
10   Royal with sunset, like a thought of thee:
And one white she-slave from the group dispersed
Of black and white slaves, (like the chequer-work
Pavement, at once my nation's work and gift,
Now covered with this settle-down of doves)
15   One lyric woman, in her crocus vest
Woven of sea-wools, with her two white hands

---

friend of noble character (ll. 325–40)'. Cp. *Aristophanes' Apology* (1875) 3302.
sprinkled isles: cp. Ovid, *Metamorphoses*, bk 2: 'the scattered islands of the Cyclades'
(tr. A. D. Melville, OUP [1986], p. 32). Both *Ohio* and *Turner* suggest, almost
certainly rightly, that 'sprinkled isles' is simply a translation of *Sporades*. B. may
also be recalling Byron's famous song 'The isles of Greece' from canto II of
Don Juan.
4. *Protos*] Protus (*1865–88*). The revision brings the name closer to the Protus
who gives his name to another of the *M & W* poems (see III 635), although he
is a weakling from a later period of the eastern Empire at Constantinople.   *Tyranny*:
'Absolute monarchy imperiously administered' (*J.*). The Greek 'tyrannos',
although it underlies modern 'tyrant', means only a non-hereditary ruler, such as
Oedipus, although B. would have been conscious of Shelley's rendition of
Oedipus Tyrannos as *Swellfoot the Tyrant*, with reference to King George III as a
tyrant in the modern sense.
7. *unlades*: 'To discharge (a cargo, etc.) from a ship' (*OED*).
10. *Royal*: crimson-coloured.
13. *at once my nation's work and gift*: either 'the work of my countrymen, who
gave it to me as a gift' or 'a craft native to my country, which is also a "gift" or
talent'.
15. *lyric woman*: a woman given to singing; cp. *Grammarian* 34 (p. 591), the address
to EBB. ('O lyric love!') in *Ring* i 1391, and *Balaustion's Adventure* (1871) 186:
'Strangers, greet the lyric girl!'   *crocus vest*: a garment decorated or embroidered
with crocus-flowers. Crocus is a name for saffron, but the vest cannot be
saffron-coloured (see next note); it is also the name for a coarse cloth, but this
seems equally inappropriate since the context suggests Protos' lavish generosity.
16. *sea-wools*: 'wools dyed with sea-purple (Greek haliporphuros, from the
murex)'; Turner's gloss is esp. plausible in view of the extended allusion to the
murex in *Popularity* (p. 446).

Commends to me the strainer and the cup
Thy lip hath bettered ere it blesses mine.

Well-counselled, king, in thy munificence!
20 For so shall men remark, in such an act
Of love for him whose song gives life its joy,
Thy recognition of the use of life;
Nor call thy spirit barely adequate
To help on life in straight ways, broad enough
25 For vulgar souls, by ruling and the rest.
Thou, in the daily building of thy tower,
Whether in fierce and sudden spasms of toil,
Or through dim lulls of unapparent growth,
Or when the general work 'mid good acclaim
30 Climbed with the eye to cheer the architect,
Didst ne'er engage in work for mere work's sake—
Hadst ever in thy heart the luring hope
Of some eventual rest a-top of it,
Whence, all the tumult of the building hushed,
35 Thou first of men mightst look out to the east.

17. the strainer: a reference to the 'small cup-like utensils of silver or bronze' used for removing the dregs from good-quality wines in classical antiquity; see 'Vinum' in William Smith, *Dictionary of Greek and Roman Antiquities* (2 vols., 1870). *18. bettered*: improved, made of even higher quality.
21. joy: a key term in Arnold's *Empedocles on Etna* and his 1853 *Preface*; see head-note. See also the extensive use of the word in *Sordello*: e.g. vi 259–324 (I 732–6).
23–5. Cp. the defence of poetry in bk. i of EBB.'s *Aurora Leigh*: 'while common men / Lay telegraphs, gauge railroads, reign, reap, dine, / And dust the flaunty carpets of the world / For kings to walk on, or our president, / The poet suddenly will catch them up / With his voice like thunder' (ll. 869–74). See headnote, *Sources*.
26–36. Cleon praises Protos for realizing that sovereignty is not an end in itself, but that 'the use of life' is to acquire knowledge. He illustrates this by means of an extended metaphor, the building of a tower: through all the difficulties of its construction, the 'architect' (Protos) has kept in mind not just the material accomplishment of his design but its ultimate purpose, which is to enable him to 'look out to the east' (the traditional source of wisdom). B. may have intended a dramatic irony in Cleon's emphasis on 'the sun' (l. 36): as so often in the poem, Cleon puts his hand without realizing it on the key which would unlock his despair (belief in Christ as the *son* of God). Cleon's choice of metaphor has ominous associations: in the Bible the building of the tower of Babel (*Genesis* xi 1–9) is an image of overweening human pride; it is the incompleteness of Giotto's bell-tower in *Old Pictures* (see headnote, p. 408) which saves it from this judgement. Cleon returns to the tower metaphor in ll. 231 ff. in a passage which suggests that the view from its top is not so enticing after all.

The vulgar saw thy tower; thou sawest the sun.
For this, I promise on thy festival
To pour libation, looking o'er the sea,
Making this slave narrate thy fortunes, speak
40   Thy great words, and describe thy royal face—
Wishing thee wholly where Zeus lives the most
Within the eventual element of calm.

Thy letter's first requirement meets me here.
It is as thou hast heard: in one short life
45   I, Cleon, have effected all those things
Thou wonderingly dost enumerate.
That epos on thy hundred plates of gold

37–8. on thy festival / To pour libation: Cleon comes close here to saying that he will worship Protos as a god; cp. *Protus* 8–9 (III 637). See also next note.
41–2. Cleon's phrasing is equivocal at this point in the poem; since he does not in fact believe in the possibility of a life after death, he finds a way of wishing Protos a godlike fate which may, or may not, involve the survival of his personal consciousness. The 'element of calm' might suggest the happiness of the abode of the Greek gods on Mount Olympus, untroubled by human cares (*Turner* [p. 373] cites *Iliad* xxiv 526 and Lucretius, *De rerum natura* v 82); but an '*eventual* element of calm' rather suggests the peace of oblivion. Zeus 'lives the most, / Within the eventual element of calm' because he, as king of the gods, is supremely carefree; B. may have been aware of Empedocles' comment that the wise 'arise as gods highest in honour, sharing with other immortals their hearth and their table, without part in human sorrows or weariness' (Clement of Alexandria, *Stromateis* V, 122, 3, in G. S. Kirk, J. E. Raven and M. Schofield [eds.], *The Pre-Socratic Philosophers* [Cambridge 1983] 317). Out of courtesy (mixed with condescension) Cleon allows Protos to believe that he might one day share this state, but once he decides to tell Protos the whole truth of human life as he perceives it (see l. 181) he makes clear that for him this is an illusory hope.
44–61. Cp. *Ring* x 1702–4: 'But I, of body as of soul complete, / A gymnast at the games, philosopher / I' the schools, who painted, and made music . . .' The speaker is Euripides, as imagined by the Pope. B. had intended, at the beginning of his career, to work in all the arts: see the unpublished 'preface' he wrote for *Pauline* (p. 2).
47–50. Cp. Wordsworth, *The Prelude* (1850) v 201–8: 'That in the name of all inspirèd souls, / From Homer the great Thunderer, from the voice / That roars along the bed of Jewish song . . . from those loftiest notes / Down to the low and wren-like warblings, made / For cottagers and spinners at the wheel', noting its source in *Twelfth Night*: the 'old and plain song' which 'The spinsters and the knitters in the sun . . . Do use to chant' (IV ii 42–5).
47. epos: an epic poem; cp. *Aurora Leigh* v 155, and *Imperante Augusto Natus Est* (*Asolando*, 1889) 12.   *plates of gold*: the 'plates' would be thin tablets, incised with text; such (small) tablets have been found in tombs, but no parallel can be found in antiquity for this extravagant method of preserving a literary work, including that of Homer. The phrase 'plates of gold' in fact suggests a more modern source,

Is mine,—and also mine the little chaunt,
So sure to rise from every fishing-bark
50 When, lights at prow, the seamen haul their nets.
The image of the sun-god on the phare
Men turn from the sun's self to see, is mine;
The Poecile, o'er-storied its whole length,
As thou didst hear, with painting, is mine too.

---

the 'golden plates' on which Joseph Smith claimed to have received the Book of Mormon in 1827. According to Smith (in the so-called 'Wentworth Letter', publ. 1842), 'In this important and interesting book the history of ancient America is unfolded, from its first settlement by a colony that came from the Tower of Babel, at the confusion of languages to the beginning of the fifth century of the Christian Era . . . This book also tells us that our Savior made His appearance unto this continent after His resurrection; that He planted the Gospel here in all its fulness, and richness, and power, and blessing.' Smith's claim that these plates had been inscribed in antiquity was ridiculed on historical grounds. Knowledge of the Mormons could have come to B. from books and journal articles, or from American acquaintances in Florence and Rome; during the Brownings' lengthy stay in Rome in the winter of 1853–54, EBB. 'expressed a desire "to read about the Mormons"' to her friend Mary Brotherton (*EBB to Arabella* ii 183).

48. the little chaunt] the little chant (*1863–88*, except *1863²*, which agrees with *1855*). Both spellings were current in the first half of the 19th century.

50. haul their nets] haul their net (*1865–88*).

51. phare: lighthouse; this spelling, as distinct from 'Pharos', was uncommon by B.'s time: all *OED* examples for the nineteenth century are his. B. has 'snowy phares' at *Paracelsus* v 367 (I 286), and he also uses the word in his letter to EBB. of 11 Feb. 1845: 'like the light in those crazy Mediterranean phares I have watched at sea' (*Correspondence* x 70).

53. Poecile: B. wrote to Amelia Edwards on 14 Jan. 1879: '*Poecile* . . . means a "variegated place" *anywhere*—primarily at Athens where a gallery was so called from the paintings it was adorned with,—and afterwards, any such gallery—applicable therefore to one in Cleon's island—wherever *that* may have been' (Somerville College Oxford MS). He was responding to the erroneous gloss in her notes to *Cleon* in *A Poetry-Book of Modern Poets, consisting of Songs & Sonnets, Odes & Lyrics* (Leipzig 1878) 326. The original gallery was the Stoa Poecile in Athens, painted by Polygnotus of Thasos (5th century BC) and others; as Thomas points out, it was from this 'porch or covered colonnade' that the 'Stoics' took their name (*Thomas* 64). Cp. *Balaustion's Adventure* (1871) 2697, where the spelling 'Poikilé' conforms to a (supposedly) more correct system of transliterating Greek names; B.'s spelling here is rec. by *OED* from 1819. *o'er-storied*: decorated all over with scenes from history or legend. Given that mortality is a principal theme of the poem, there may be an echo of Gray's 'Elegy Written in a Country Churchyard': 'Can storied urn or animated bust / Back to its mansion call the fleeting breath?' (ll. 41–2). B. uses the word in *Luria* ii 75–6: 'their triumphal arch / Or storied pillar' (II 399) and *Ring* x 468–9: 'unwary folk / Who gaze at storied portal, statued spire'.

55   I know the true proportions of a man
      And woman also, not observed before;
      And I have written three books on the soul,
      Proving absurd all written hitherto,
      And putting us to ignorance again.
60   For music,—why, I have combined the moods,
      Inventing one. In brief, all arts are mine;
      Thus much the people know and recognise,
      Throughout our seventeen islands. Marvel not.
      We of these latter days, with greater mind
65   Than our forerunners, since more composite,
      Look not so great (beside their simple way)
      To a judge who only sees one way at once,
      One mind-point, and no other at a time,—
      Compares the small part of a man of us
70   With some whole man of the heroic age,
      Great in his way—not ours, nor meant for ours,
      And ours is greater, had we skill to know.

55–6. See headnote, *Composition and date*. Page's theory of human proportion, first put forward in his *New Geometrical Mode of Measuring the Proportions of the Human Body* (1860), was based on *Revelation* xxi 17: 'And he measured the wall thereof, an hundred and forty and four cubits, according to the measure of a man, that is, of the angel.' Page derived from this the rule that '*the figure in height and breadth is divided by twelve*' (*Scribner's Monthly* [April 1879] 895), and that the human figure with arms outstretched could therefore be contained within a grid of 144 squares. If Cleon's theory of human proportion coincides with this it would represent another unrecognized anticipation of the Christian revelation on his part. See also B.'s letter to Harriet Hosmer of 16 Nov. 1854: 'I carry in my mind all I can of his doctrine about the true proportions of the human figure, and test it by whatever strikes me as beautiful, or the reverse' (*Harriet Hosmer*, ed. Cornelia Carr [1913] 45).

57–9. The most important classical work on the soul is Aristotle's *De Anima*. In ch. ii, Aristotle lists previous definitions (incl. Empedocles'), and uses the word 'absurd' of most of them.

60. *moods*: more usually 'modes': the various musical scales which originated with the Greeks and survived until the 16th century in European music. In what sense the modes could be 'combined' is not clear: one sense might be, 'drawn together, systematised', or, anachronistically, 'made into a single scale', which is what took place in the tonal system which succeeded the modal.

63. *our seventeen islands*: cp. l. 1n. There is no group of Greek islands numbering seventeen; the Cyclades are 39 in number, the Sporades 11 and the Dodecanese 12.

64–72. Cp. Arnold's 'Preface' to his 1853 *Poems*: 'Achilles, Prometheus, Clytemnestra, Dido,—what modern poem presents personages as interesting, even to us moderns, as these personages of an "exhausted past"?' See next note, and headnote, *Sources*, pp. 557–8.

Yet, what we call this life of men on earth,
This sequence of the soul's achievements here,
75 Being, as I find much reason to conceive,
Intended to be viewed eventually
As a great whole, not analysed to parts,
But each part having reference to all,—
How shall a certain part, pronounced complete,
80 Endure effacement by another part?
Was the thing done?—Then what's to do again?
See, in the chequered pavement opposite,
Suppose the artist made a perfect rhomb,
And next a lozenge, then a trapezoid—
85 He did not overlay them, superimpose
The new upon the old and blot it out,
But laid them on a level in his work,
Making at last a picture; there it lies.
So, first the perfect separate forms were made,

73–94. The sense is that in both the individual life and the life of humankind as a whole no achievement or individual 'effaces' a predecessor; rather they all lie separately, as on a plane surface, and contribute towards the overall pattern. The phrasing recalls Arnold's *Empedocles*, where the human soul 'A thousand glimpses wins, / And never sees a whole' (I ii 84–5), and also the 1853 Preface, in which Arnold argues that Greek poetry is superior to modern poetry because it regards 'the whole' rather than 'the parts'. Cp. also Arnold's sonnet 'To a Friend', in which he describes Sophocles as an 'even-balanced soul' who 'saw life steadily, and saw it whole' (ll. 9, 12).

73. Yet] For (*1863–88*).

74. With 'this sequence', Oxford compares B.'s comments on evolution (mentioning *Cleon*) in the letter to Furnivall discussed at l. 202n.

76–8. A familiar sentiment in B.: *Turner* (p. 374) compares *By The Fire-Side* 246–50 (p. 475).

82. chequered pavement: cp. ll. 12–13; Adrienne Munich suggests a possible allusion here to George Herbert's 'The Church-floor': 'Mark you the floor? that square and speckled stone, / Which looks so firm and strong, / Is Patience: // And th'other black and grave, wherewith each one / Is checkered all along, / Humility' (ll. 1–6; 'Temporality in "Cleon"', *BIS* vi [1978] 130).

83. rhomb: 'A plane figure having four equal sides and the opposite angles equal (two being acute and two obtuse). Also, a lozenge-shaped object or formation' (*OED*). Cp. Milton, *Paradise Regained* iii 309: 'See how in warlike muster they appear, / In Rhombs and wedges, and half moons, and wings'.

84. lozenge: 'A plane rectilineal figure, having four equal sides and two acute and two obtuse angles; a rhomb, "diamond"' (*OED*). *trapezoid*: 'A quadrilateral figure no two of whose sides are parallel' (*OED*).

89–92. Referring to the idea of 'combination' which B. had found in Dante's *De Monarchia* (see headnote to *Sordello* I 366), and possibly also influenced by Empedoclean cosmogony, which supposed that first the separate limbs of the human

90   The portions of mankind—and after, so,
      Occurred the combination of the same.
      Or where had been a progress, otherwise?
      Mankind, made up of all the single men,—
      In such a synthesis the labour ends.
95   Now, mark me—those divine men of old time
      Have reached, thou sayest well, each at one point
      The outside verge that rounds our faculty;
      And where they reached, who can do more than reach?
      It takes but little water just to touch
100   At some one point the inside of a sphere,
      And, as we turn the sphere, touch all the rest
      In due succession; but the finer air
      Which not so palpably nor obviously,
      Though no less universally, can touch
105   The whole circumference of that emptied sphere,
      Fills it more fully than the water did;
      Holds thrice the weight of water in itself
      Resolved into a subtler element.

and animal creation appeared, only later being joined into composite forms (see e.g. Simplicius, *in De Caelo* 586.7). These lines, and ll. 126–37, evidently refer to contemporary discussions of evolution in the decade before the publication of Darwin's *Origin of Species* (1859); some ambiguous passages in Empedocles' own work have led modern commentators to perceive him as a proto-Darwinian.

92. Or where] For where (*1868– 88*).

99–111. The simile here is based on the Greek discovery that air, although invisible, has the properties of a substance, and might again specifically derive from Empedocles, who was the first to distinguish air from void in an experiment using a water-vessel; see Aristotle, *De Respiro* [*Loeb* ed.] 473a15: '[Respiration is] just as when a maid plays with a water-clock of gleaming bronze. When placing on her shapely hand the channel of the tube she dips it into the delicate body of water silver white, not then does the shower flow into the vessel, but the mass of air pressing from within on the crowded holes checks it, until she sets free the dense stream. Then the air gives way and the water duly enters. So in the same way, when the water lies in the depths of the bronze vessel, the passage and channel being blocked by the human hand, the air outside craving entrance keeps the water back about the gates of the resounding channel, holding fast its surface, until the maid lets go with her hand; then back again in the reverse way, as the air rushes in, the water duly flows away.'

100. a sphere: Cleon refers to a spherical vessel, but the sphere is also a prime image of perfection in Greek thought: B. may have had in mind Parmenides' resolution of the general order of things into the form of a sphere (see Simplicius *in Physica* 146.5). Cp. *Old Pictures* 133–6n. (pp. 419–20).

And yet the vulgar call the sphere first full
110 Up to the visible height—and after, void;
Not knowing air's more hidden properties.
And thus our soul, misknown, cries out to Zeus
To vindicate his purpose in its life—
Why stay we on the earth unless to grow?
115 Long since, I imaged, wrote the fiction out,
That he or other God, descended here
And, once for all, showed simultaneously
What, in its nature, never can he shown
Piecemeal or in succession;—showed, I say,
120 The worth both absolute and relative
Of all His children from the birth of time,
His instruments for all appointed work.
I now go on to image,—might we hear
The judgment which should give the due to each,
125 Shew where the labour lay and where the ease,
And prove Zeus' self, the latent, everywhere!
This is a dream. But no dream, let us hope,
That years and days, the summers and the springs

109–111. Cp. Empedocles: 'There is no part of the whole that is empty or over-full' (quoted Aetius, *Doxographia Graeci* 1.18.2). Empedocles accepted Parmenides' conclusion that there are no gaps in Nature, and that 'emptiness' is therefore impossible, but allows for change, which Parmenides excludes.

112–27. And thus . . . a dream: cp. Arnold, *Empedocles* I ii 377–86: ' "Changeful till now, we still / Look'd on to something new; / Let us, with changeless will, / Henceforth look on to you, / To find with you the joy we in vain here require!" // Fools! That so often here / Happiness mock'd our prayer, / I think, might make us fear / A like event elsewhere; / Make us, not fly to dreams, but moderate desire'.

113. in its life] in our life (*1863–88*).

115–22. Cleon's 'fiction' is of course invented, but some of its themes resemble those of B.'s own *Sordello*, esp. the problem of representing 'the Simultaneous and the Sole' by means of 'the Successive and the Many' (ii 594–5, I 500).

115. imaged: three senses are possible: 'imagined, conceived'; 'represented, projected in images'; 'represented in writing'. B. uses the word again in *A Grammarian* 69 (p. 593) where the sense is more straightforward: 'Image the whole, then execute the parts'. In EBB.'s *A Drama of Exile* (1844) the reverence shown by each angel who greets a redeemed human soul stems from the fact that 'upon your hands and feet / He images his Master's wounds' (ll. 2098–9).

126–7. And prove . . . a dream: this seems to rule out the pantheist implications of the passage from Aratus quoted in the note to the Epigraph (p. 565). For passages in which B. seems to support this possibility, see *Paracelsus* v 627–66 (I 296–8) and *Epilogue* (*DP*, 1864) 66–101 (esp. ll. 99–101).

126. the latent, everywhere] the latent everywhere (*1868–88*).

Follow each other with unwaning powers—
130   The grapes which dye thy wine, are richer far
      Through culture, than the wild wealth of the rock;
      The suave plum than the savage-tasted drupe;
      The pastured honey-bee drops choicer sweet;
      The flowers turn double, and the leaves turn flowers;
135   That young and tender crescent-moon, thy slave,
      Sleeping upon her robe as if on clouds,
      Refines upon the women of my youth.
      What, and the soul alone deteriorates?
      I have not chanted verse like Homer's, no—
140   Nor swept string like Terpander, no—nor carved
      And painted men like Phidias and his friend:
      I am not great as they are, point by point:
      But I have entered into sympathy
      With these four, running these into one soul,

131. culture: cultivation.

132. savage-tasted: combining the senses of 'primitive, crude to the taste' and 'the food of primitive people'.   *drupe*: in the letter to Amelia Edwards (see l. 53n.), B. responds to her gloss—'an over-ripe, wrinkled olive'—by suggesting that he might have been mistaken about the meaning of the word: '"drupe",—in accordance with certain paragraphs about horticulture I have happened to read,—I meant for the rude original fruit whence, by cultivation, the improved and refined fruit is obtained—as the apple from the crab, the plum from the sloe—But certainly the original word, both in Greek and Latin, is only used for a "mouldy olive:" its derivation is uncertain,—and I should hardly think it refers to the olive only: I must see farther—if it be worth while!' (Somerville College Oxford MS). B.'s etymology is correct, but the word in English simply designates 'a fleshy or pulpy fruit enclosing a stone or nut' (*OED*).

134. 'The flowers become double [in form, size or beauty] through cultivation, and the leaves themselves become flowers'.

136–7.] Refines upon the women of my youth— / Sleeping upon her robe as if on clouds. (*H proof*).

136.] Sleeping above her robe as buoyed by clouds, (*1888*).

139. verse like Homer's] verse like Homer (*1863²*, *1868–88*). It is rare for *1868–88* to contain a substantive variant which originates in *1863²*.

140. Terpander: 'a lyric poet and musician of Lesbos, 675 BC. It is said that he appeased a tumult at Sparta by the melody and sweetness of his notes. He added three strings to the lyre, which before his time had only four' (*Lemprière*). Cp. *Christmas-Eve* 674 (III 74).

141. Phidias: the most famous of Greek sculptors (*c.* 490–*c.* 430 BC). The syntax implies that his friend was a painter; candidates include Polygnotus of Thasos, who was according to *EB* '[the] contemporary, and perhaps the teacher, of Pheidias', and who 'painted . . . in the time of Cimon a picture of the taking of Ilium on the walls of the Stoa Poecile' (see above l. 53n.).

145   Who, separate, ignored each others' arts.
       Say, is it nothing that I know them all?
       The wild flower was the larger—I have dashed
       Rose-blood upon its petals, pricked its cup's
       Honey with wine, and driven its seed to fruit,
150   And show a better flower if not so large.
       I stand, myself. Refer this to the gods
       Whose gift alone it is! which, shall I dare
       (All pride apart) upon the absurd pretext
       That such a gift by chance lay in my hand,
155   Discourse of lightly or depreciate?
       It might have fallen to another's hand—what then?
       I pass too surely—let at least truth stay!

           And next, of what thou followest on to ask.
           This being with me as I declare, O king,
160   My works, in all these varicoloured kinds,
       So done by me, accepted so by men—
       Thou askest if (my soul thus in men's hearts)
       I must not be accounted to attain
       The very crown and proper end of life.
165   Inquiring thence how, now life closeth up,
       I face death with success in my right hand:

145. ignored each others' arts: either B. or Cleon is misinformed here: Phidias was renowned not only for his skill as a sculptor but as a painter and engraver, and according to Pliny opened up new possibilities in metalwork (*Oxford Classical Dictionary*). *each others' arts*] each other's arts (*1884*); each other's art (*1888*; 'each other's' is evidently a misprint, but was not corrected in *1889*).

147–50. Cp. ll. 130–4 above. The statement that 'the wild flower was the larger' is puzzling; primitive varieties are almost always smaller than those bred for show. The sense presumably is that the 'natural' flower was superior in vigour to its 'civilized' successor. Cleon 'anticipates' Rousseau's primitivism, and his contention that civilization is a degenerative force, although Cleon argues for the superiority of modern complex artistry over the 'primitive' single-mindedness of antiquity.

151–2. Refer . . . it is! this may be the line B. had in mind when he replied to John Kenyon's observations on the proofs of *M & W* in a letter of 1 Oct. 1855 with the comment: ' "The whole is with the Gods" as Cleon sums it up in one of the things I send you' (*SBC* iii [1975] 28–9, and see Appendix C, p. 892).

152–5. which, shall I dare . . . depreciate: 'which' refers back to 'gift' and '(All pride apart)' means 'leaving aside any personal feelings of pride I may have in my art'; Cleon argues that it would show disrespect to the gods for him to undervalue their gift simply on the basis of that gift having come to him by chance.

Whether I fear death less than dost thyself
The fortunate of men. "For" (writest thou)
"Thou leavest much behind, while I leave nought:
170   Thy life stays in the poems men shall sing,
The pictures men shall study; while my life,
Complete and whole now in its power and joy,
Dies altogether with my brain and arm,
Is lost indeed; since,—what survives myself?
175   The brazen statue that o'erlooks my grave,
Set on the promontory which I named.
And that—some supple courtier of my heir
Shall use its robed and sceptred arm, perhaps,
To fix the rope to, which best drags it down.
180   I go, then: triumph thou, who dost not go!"

Nay, thou art worthy of hearing my whole mind.
Is this apparent, when thou turn'st to muse
Upon the scheme of earth and man in chief,
That admiration grows as knowledge grows?
185   That imperfection means perfection hid,
Reserved in part, to grace the after-time?

---

167. than dost] even than (*H proof*, but not *H proof²*).
175–9. Cp. Shakespeare, Sonnet lv ('Not marble, nor the gilded monuments / Of princes shall outlive this pow'rful rhyme') and, noting 'brazen' in l. 175 and the fact that Protos is a 'tyrant' (l. 4), the closing lines of Sonnet cvii: 'And thou in this shall find thy monument, / When tyrants' crests and tombs of brass are spent'. The image of the tyrant's ruined statue also recalls that of Shelley's 'Ozymandias'. The most famous statue standing on a promontory in the ancient world was the Colossus of Rhodes, a statue of the sun-god Helios, destroyed by an earthquake in 226 BC; but B. may have had in mind a famous ode by Horace (I xxviii, 'Te maris et terrae'), a dramatic monologue addressed by an unnamed speaker (who turns out to be himself a ghost) to the dead philosopher, astronomer and statesman Archytas: 'Measurer of earth and ocean and number-less sand, / Archytas, you are now confined / near the Matine shore, by a little handful of dust duly sprinkled, / and it profits you nothing to have probed / the dwellings of air and traversed the round vault of heaven / with a mind that was to die' (ll. 1–6, transl. David West, *Horace: The Complete Odes and Epodes*, Oxford 1997). Besides being a philosopher and astronomer, Archytas was also (elected) ruler of Tarentum; although the position of his grave links him to Protos, the fate of the philosopher whose transcendent achievements are negated by his ineluctable mortality is applied by Cleon to himself, notably at ll. 308–23.
175. brazen: both 'made of brass' and 'hardened in effrontery'.   *that o'erlooks*] to o'erlook (*1868–88*).

If, in the morning of philosophy,
Ere aught had been recorded, aught perceived,
Thou, with the light now in thee, couldst have looked
190 On all earth's tenantry, from worm to bird,
Ere man had yet appeared upon the stage—
Thou wouldst have seen them perfect, and deduced
The perfectness of others yet unseen.
Conceding which,—had Zeus then questioned thee
195 "Wilt thou go on a step, improve on this,

187–214. If, in . . . be happy: the idea that in compensation for his lack of animal powers man was given reason is a commonplace in antiquity: cp. Plutarch, *Moralia* 98d.: 'Certainly, in so far as chance and Nature's endowment at birth are concerned, the great majority of brute animals are better off than man. For some are armed with horns, or teeth, or stings, and Empedocles says: "But as for hedgehogs / Growing upon their backs sharp darts of spines stand bristling," and still others are shod and clad with scales or hair, with claws or horny hoofs. Man alone, as Plato says, "naked, unarmed, with feet unshod, and with no bed to lie in," has been abandoned by Nature. Yet by one gift all this she mitigates, the gift of reasoning, diligence, and forethought.' The Christian tradition took up this idea but emphasized man's pre-eminence over the perfection of the natural world; cp. Milton's account of the sixth day of creation, in which, after the establishment of the animal kingdom, 'There wanted yet the master work, the end / Of all yet done; a creature who not prone / And brute as other creatures, but endued / With sanctity of reason, might erect / His stature, and upright with front serene / Govern the rest, self-knowing' (*PL* vii 505–10; see also ll. 199–202n.). Milton's phrase 'self-knowing' may refer to the Socratic precept 'Know thyself', but also implies self-consciousness, which is not identical to reason, and which seems to be Cleon's meaning here. The idea that self-consciousness defines and distinguishes the human goes back to Plato, but was most fully developed in Cartesian and Romantic philosophy; as Coleridge puts it, through self-consciousness 'we at once identify our being with that of the world without us, and yet place ourselves in contra-distinction to that world' (*The Friend* ed. B. E. Rooke [1969] Essay x: i 497). Cp. also Arnold, *Empedocles*, II 345–54: 'But mind, but thought— / If these have been the master part of us— / Where will *they* find their parent element? / What will receive *them*, who will call *them* home? / But we shall still be in them, and they in us, / And we shall be the strangers of the world, / And they will be our lords, as they are now; / And keep us prisoners of our consciousness, / And never let us clasp and feel the All / But through their forms, and modes, and stifling veils.'

187–92. If, in the morning . . . seen them perfect: Cleon (unwittingly) 'quotes' the first chapter of *Genesis*, in which God views his successive acts of creation and approves of his own handiwork; see e.g. v. 25, the final act of creation before that of man: 'And God made the beast of the earth after his kind, and cattle after their kind, and every thing that creepeth upon the earth after his kind: and God saw that it was good.' See also ll. 199–202n.

188. recorded, aught perceived] recorded, nay perceived (*1865–88*).

191. Ere man had yet] Ere man, her last, (*1865–88*).

195. "Wilt thou] "Shall I (*1863–88*).

Do more for visible creatures than is done?"
Thou wouldst have answered, "Ay, by making each
Grow conscious in himself—by that alone.
All's perfect else: the shell sucks fast the rock,
200   The fish strikes through the sea, the snake both swims
And slides; the birds take flight, forth range the beasts,
Till life's mechanics can no further go—
And all this joy in natural life, is put,
Like fire from off thy finger into each,
205   So exquisitely perfect is the same.
But 'tis pure fire—and they mere matter are;
It has them, not they it: and so I choose,
For man, Thy last premeditated work
(If I might add a glory to this scheme)
210   That a third thing should stand apart from both,
A quality arise within the soul,
Which, intro-active, made to supervise
And feel the force it has, may view itself,
And so be happy." Man might live at first

199–202. Cp. Milton, *PL* vii 501–4: 'earth in her rich attire / Consummate lovely smiled; air, water, earth, / By fowl, fish, beast, was flown, was swam, was walked / Frequent'. These lines come just before the creation of man, the 'master work': see ll. 187–214n. This view of nature refers to an original state of perfection; both Christian and classical accounts of the vicissitudes of physical life emphasize pain as well as pleasure, e.g. Empedocles: 'at one time, in the maturity of a vigorous life, all the limbs that are the body's portion come into one under love; at another time again, torn asunder by evil strifes, they wander, each apart, on the shore of life. So it is too for plants, and for fish that live in the water, and for wild animals who have their lairs in the hills, and for the wing-sped gulls' (Simplicius *in Physica* 1124.7). Note that Empedocles here conflates man with the animals, where Cleon is distinguishing them; and cp. ll. 309–23 below.
201.] And slides, forth range the beasts, the birds take flight, (*1870, 1872, 1888*).
202. life's mechanics: the process by which individual animals are adapted to their environments. B. cites this phrase in a letter to F. J. Furnivall commenting on his attitude towards Darwinism: '[All] that seems *proved* in Darwin's scheme was a conception familiar to me from the beginning: see in *Paracelsus* the progressive development from senseless matter to organized, until man's appearance (*Part* v). Also in *Cleon*, see the order of "life's mechanics,"—and I daresay in many passages of my poetry: for how can one look at Nature as a whole and doubt that, wherever there is a gap, a "link" must be "missing"—through the limited power and opportunity of the looker?' (11 Oct. 1881, *Trumpeter* 34).
209. to this scheme] to the scheme (*1863–88*).
211. within the soul] within his soul (*1865–88*).
212. intro-active: 'having the property of acting within, internally active' (*OED*, for which this is the first citation).

215   The animal life: but is there nothing more?
       In due time, let him critically learn
       How he lives; and, the more he gets to know
       Of his own life's adaptabilities,
       The more joy-giving will his life become.
220   The man who hath this quality, is best.

           But thou, king, hadst more reasonably said:
       "Let progress end at once,—man make no step
       Beyond the natural man, the better beast,
       Using his senses, not the sense of sense."
225   In man there's failure, only since he left
       The lower and inconscious forms of life.
       We called it an advance, the rendering plain
       A spirit might grow conscious of that life,
       And, by new lore so added to the old,
230   Take each step higher over the brute's head.
       This grew the only life, the pleasure-house,

---

220. The man] Thus man (*1865–88*).

223. natural man: again Cleon unwittingly agrees with St Paul in making God the origin of self-consciousness: 'But the natural man receiveth not the things of the Spirit of God: for they are foolishness unto him: neither can he know them, because they are spiritually discerned' (*1 Corinthians* ii 14).

224. the sense of sense: i.e. self-consciousness. *of sense.*"] of sense!" (*1872*).

225–6. The escape from human knowledge into primitive animal being is the subject of Callicles' song in Arnold's *Empedocles* ii 427–60, where Cadmus and Harmonia are transformed into snakes and '[w]holly forget their first sad life . . . and stray / For ever through the glens, placid and dumb' (ll. 458, 459–60). The idea of 'two bright and aged snakes' basking in the sunshine became a motif of B.'s correspondence with Isa Blagden.

225.] There's failure in man, only since he left (*H proof*, but not *H proof²*).

226. inconscious: alternative spelling of 'unconscious': very rare by B.'s time, but used by him nine times, as against 18 for 'unconscious'. From these instances, it would appear that B. uses 'unconscious' to mean simply 'unaware', 'inconscious' to mean 'ideationally blank, nescient', but the distinction is not invariable.

228. A spirit . . . that life] Man's spirit . . . man's life (*1865–88*).

231–4. Cp. the opening of Tennyson's 'The Palace of Art' (1842 text): 'I built my soul a lordly pleasure-house, / Wherein at ease for aye to dwell . . . A huge crag-platform, smooth as burnish'd brass / I chose. The rangèd ramparts bright / From level meadow-bases of deep grass / Suddenly scaled the light'. The soul is later described as 'Joying to feel herself alive, / Lord over nature, Lord of the visible earth, / Lord of the senses five; / Communing with herself' (ll. 178–81) and, in her 'God-like isolation', despising 'the darkening droves of swine / That range on yonder plain' (ll. 199, 201–2). Tennyson's 'pleasure-house' is itself indebted to the 'stately pleasure-dome' in Coleridge's 'Kubla Khan'. The 'Watch-tower'

Watch-tower and treasure-fortress of the soul,
Which whole surrounding flats of natural life
Seemed only fit to yield subsistence to;
235   A tower that crowns a country. But alas!
The soul now climbs it just to perish there,
For thence we have discovered ('tis no dream—
We know this, which we had not else perceived)
That there's a world of capability
240   For joy, spread round about us, meant for us,
Inviting us; and still the soul craves all,
And still the flesh replies, "Take no jot more
Than ere you climbed the tower to look abroad!
Nay, so much less, as that fatigue has brought
245   Deduction to it." We struggle—fain to enlarge
Our bounded physical recipiency,
Increase our power, supply fresh oil to life,
Repair the waste of age and sickness. No,
It skills not: life's inadequate to joy,
250   As the soul sees joy, tempting life to take.
They raise a fountain in my garden here
Wherein a Naiad sends the water-spurt
Thin from her tube; she smiles to see it rise.

---

evokes several biblical passages, notably *Isaiah* xxi 4–5: 'My heart panted, fear-fulness affrighted me: the night of my pleasure hath he turned into fear unto me. Prepare the table, watch in the watch-tower'; the 'treasure-fortress' may allude to Jesus's injunction in the Sermon on the Mount: 'Lay not up for yourselves treasures upon earth . . . But lay up for yourselves treasures in heaven' (*Matthew* vi 19–20).

235–72. Cp. the Stoical philosophy outlined in Arnold's *Resignation: To Fausta* (see headnote, *Sources*) 215–22: 'The World in which we live and move / Outlasts aversion, outlasts love: / Outlasts each effort, interest, hope, / Remorse, grief, joy:—and were the scope / Of these affections wider made, / Man still would see, and see dismay'd, / Beyond his passion's widest range / Far regions of eternal change.'

239–42. there's . . . abroad: cp. *Pauline* 268–80n. (p. 25).

243. you climbed] thou climbedst (*1863–68*); thou clombst (*1870–88*).

249. It skills not:] It skills not! (*1868–88*).

251–60. For an analogous use of this image of the fountain, cp. *Mr. Sludge* 1367–71 (p. 843): 'Young, you've force / Wasted like well-streams: old,—oh, then indeed, / Behold a labyrinth of hydraulic pipes / Through which you'd play off wondrous water-work; / Only, no water left to feed their play!'

252. Naiad: a statue in the form of a nymph; in Greek religion, Naiads were 'in-ferior deities who presided over rivers, springs, wells, and fountains' (*Lemprière*). *the water-spurt]* the water-bow (*1863–88*).

What if I told her, it is just a thread
255 From that great river which the hills shut up,
And mock her with my leave to take the same?
The artificer has given her one small tube
Past power to widen or exchange—what boots
To know she might spout oceans if she could?
260 She cannot lift beyond her first straight thread.
And so a man can use but a man's joy
While he sees God's. Is it, for Zeus to boast
"See, man, how happy I live, and despair—
That I may be still happier—for thy use!"
265 If this were so, we could not thank our Lord,
As hearts beat on to doing: 'tis not so—
Malice it is not. Is it carelessness?
Still, no. If care—where is the sign, I ask—
And get no answer: and agree in sum,
270 O king, with thy profound discouragement,
Who seest the wider but to sigh the more.
Most progress is most failure! thou sayest well.

The last point now:—thou dost except a case—
Holding joy not impossible to one
275 With artist-gifts—to such a man as I—
Who leave behind me living works indeed;
For, such a poem, such a painting lives.
What? dost thou verily trip upon a word,

---

260. straight thread] thin thread (*1863–88*).
262–4. Cp. *Old Pictures* 89–104 (pp. 416–17) and l. 288n.
268. where is the sign, I ask—] where is the sign? I ask, (*1865–88*). The desire for a 'sign' is repeatedly condemned by Jesus, e.g. *Mark* viii 11–12: 'And the Pharisees came forth, and began to question with him, seeking of him a sign from heaven, tempting him. And he sighed deeply in his spirit, and saith, Why doth this generation seek after a sign? verily I say unto you, There shall no sign be given unto this generation'; cp. also *Matthew* xii 39: 'An evil and adulterous generation seeketh after a sign'.
271. Cp. Arnold, 'Resignation', l. 214: '*Not deep the Poet sees, but wide*'; and see headnote.
273–300. Cp. *Aurora Leigh* v 434–501, esp. ll. 474–6: 'To have our books / Appraised by love, associated with love, / While *we* sit loveless!'. Cp. also *Last Ride* 67–89 (III 289–90) and *Grammarian* (p. 586).
278. B. continues to put biblical phrases in Cleon's mouth: 'verily' is esp. associated with Jesus's formulaic phrase 'verily I say unto you'; 'trip upon a word' recalls *1 Peter* ii 8: 'a stone of stumbling . . . even to them that stumble at the word'.

Confound the accurate view of what joy is
280 (Caught somewhat clearer by my eyes than thine)
With feeling joy? confound the knowing how
And showing how to live (my faculty)
With actually living?—Otherwise
Where is the artist's vantage o'er the king?
285 Because in my great epos I display
How divers men young, strong, fair, wise, can act—
Is this as though I acted? if I paint,
Carve the young Phoebus, am I therefore young?
Methinks I'm older that I bowed myself
290 The many years of pain that taught me art!
Indeed, to know is something, and to prove
How all this beauty might be enjoyed, is more:
But, knowing nought, to enjoy is something too.
Yon rower with the moulded muscles there
295 Lowering the sail, is nearer it than I.
I can write love-odes—thy fair slave's an ode.
I get to sing of love, when grown too grey
For being beloved: she turns to that young man
The muscles all a-ripple on his back.
300 I know the joy of kingship: well—thou art king!

"But," sayest thou—(and I marvel, I repeat,
To find thee tripping on a mere word) "what
Thou writest, paintest, stays: that does not die:
Sappho survives, because we sing her songs,
305 And Æschylus, because we read his plays!"

280. by my eyes] with my eyes (*H proof*).
288. carve the young Phoebus: 'Phoebus' is Phoebus Apollo, god of the sun and of
poetry, and the type of male beauty; B. may have in mind the famous statue of
the 'Apollo Belvedere' in the Vatican, long believed to be a pre-eminent example of ancient sculpture. In *Old Pictures* the perfection of Greek art is seen as
oppressive because it sets an unattainable standard for human beings (see ll. 89–104,
pp. 416–17); here the contrast has a Platonic inflection, since the work of art,
no matter how perfect, is at one remove from the real, so that no true
identification between it and its creator is possible.
304. Sappho: a famous female poet of the late 7th to early 6th century BC. In her
case especially, and to a certain extent that of Aeschylus in the following line,
Protos' statement has an element of dramatic irony: few of Sappho's poems
actually survive except as fragments, and nearly all of Aeschylus's plays are lost.
305. Æschylus: the earliest of the major Greek tragedians (525–456 BC).

Why, if they live still, let them come and take
Thy slave in my despite—drink from thy cup—
Speak in my place. Thou diest while I survive?
Say rather that my fate is deadlier still,—

310 In this, that every day my sense of joy
Grows more acute, my soul (intensified
In power and insight) more enlarged, more keen;
While every day my hairs fall more and more,
My hand shakes, and the heavy years increase—

315 The horror quickening still from year to year,
The consummation coming past escape
When I shall know most, and yet least enjoy—
When all my works wherein I prove my worth,
Being present still to mock in men's mouths,

320 Alive still, in the phrase of such as thou,
I, I, the feeling, thinking, acting man,
The man who loved his life so over much,
Shall sleep in my urn. It is so horrible,
I dare at times imagine to my need

325 Some future state revealed to us by Zeus,
Unlimited in capability
For joy, as this is in desire for joy,
To seek which, the joy-hunger forces us,
That, stung by straitness of our life, made strait

309–17. Cp. Arnold, *Empedocles* I ii 332–6: 'But still, as we proceed / The mass swells more and more / Of volumes yet to read, / Of secrets yet to explore. / Our hair grows grey, our eyes are dimm'd, our heat is tamed'.

309. Say rather] Say wiselier (*H proof*).

312. In power] By power (*1863–88*).

313. my hairs fall] my hair falls (*1872*), a rare example of a substantive variant unique to this ed.

320. in the phrase] in the praise (*1888*).

323–35. With this section cp. *Empedocles on Etna*, I ii 367–81; and contrast *Rabbi Ben Ezra* 19–24 (pp. 653–4).

323. sleep in my urn: cp. Tennyson, 'The Lotos-Eaters', l. 113, where the speakers refer to 'those old faces of our infancy' as 'Two handfuls of white dust, shut in an urn of brass!' Note that in using the image of death as sleep, Cleon flinches from affirming the certainty of his annihilation. Cp. also Byron, *Don Juan* iii 88: 'to what straits old Time reduces / Frail man, when paper—even a rag like this, / Survives himself, his tomb, and all that's his!' *Shall sleep*] Sleep (*H proof, 1888*), a very rare example of agreement between these two texts.

325–8. Harrison (see headnote, *Sources*) compares Keats's 'favourite speculation' that 'we shall enjoy ourselves here after by having what we called happiness on Earth repeated in a finer tone and so repeated' (letter to Bailey of 22 Nov. 1817).

328. forces us,] emended from 'forces us.' in *1855* in agreement with all other eds.

330   On purpose to make sweet the life at large—
       Freed by the throbbing impulse we call death
       We burst there as the worm into the fly,
       Who, while a worm still, wants his wings. But, no!
       Zeus has not yet revealed it; and, alas!
335   He must have done so—were it possible!

           Live long and happy, and in that thought die,
       Glad for what was. Farewell. And for the rest,
       I cannot tell thy messenger aright
       Where to deliver what he bears of thine
340   To one called Paulus—we have heard his fame
       Indeed, if Christus be not one with him—
       I know not, nor am troubled much to know,
       Thou canst not think a mere barbarian Jew,
       As Paulus proves to be, one circumcised,
345   Hath access to a secret shut from us?
       Thou wrongest our philosophy, O king,
       In stooping to inquire of such an one,

330. to make sweet] to make prized (*1868–88*).

337–53. And, for the rest . . . no sane man: Protos, who is anxious about the after-life, is evidently prepared to consult not just the famous and respectable Cleon but the lowly representatives of a new religion of which he has heard rumours. Cleon himself is hazy about the details of this obscure Jewish sect: his doubt as to whether Paul is identical to Christ (ll. 340–1) stems, as Adam Roberts remarks in his edition (*Robert Browning* [Oxford 1997] 766), from the fact that 'Christus' is not strictly speaking a proper name, but a title ('the Anointed One'). The fact that the new religion is spread by Jews and 'slaves' (l. 350) would increase Cleon's distaste (these slaves contrast with those at the beginning of the poem); but he is mistaken in calling Paul a 'barbarian' (l. 343), since he was in fact a Roman citizen and made great play with this status (see e.g. *Acts* xvi 37–9, xxii 25–9).

340. one called Paulus] him called Paulus (marked as a change in *H proof*, and included in the lists of errata which B. sent to his American publisher James T. Fields (*B to Fields* 194) and to D. G. Rossetti (*LH* 42), but not carried out in *1855* or any subsequent ed.).   *Paulus*: i.e. St Paul.

341. 'If Christ be not the same person [as Paul]'. Once again, Cleon is made to speak more than he knows; ironically he is 'quoting' Paul himself, in a passage which also recalls the poem's epigraph: 'For ye are all the children of God by faith in Christ Jesus. For as many of you as have been baptized into Christ have put on Christ. There is neither Jew nor Greek, there is neither bond nor free, there is neither male nor female: for ye are all one in Christ Jesus' (*Galatians* iii 26–8).

344. one circumcised] and circumcised (marked as a change in *H proof*, and included in the lists cited in l. 340n., but not carried out in *1855* or any subsequent ed.).

347. such an one] such a one (*H proof*).

As if his answer could impose at all.
He writeth, doth he? well, and he may write.
350   Oh, the Jew findeth scholars! certain slaves
Who touched on this same isle, preached him and Christ;
And (as I gathered from a bystander)
Their doctrines could be held by no sane man.

348. *impose*: 'take us in, hoodwink us'.

38 A Grammarian's Funeral
[*Time*—Shortly after the revival of learning in Europe]

Text and publication
First publ. *M & W*, 10 Nov. 1855; repr. *1863*, *1865²*, *1868*, *1872*, *1888*. Our text is *1855*. B.'s fair copy of ll. 137–48 (the last twelve lines of the poem) is in *Berg*. It is written on the first leaf of a four-sided sheet of notepaper, with B.'s crest; to the right of the crest is the heading 'In memoriam | Johannis Conington'; at the bottom is a note: '(From "A Grammarian's Funeral.")', followed by B.'s signature and the date, 1 Nov. 1869 (shortly after Conington's funeral, according to the Berg catalogue entry). Conington (1825–1869) was an Oxford classical scholar whom B. may have met through his friendship with Benjamin Jowett, the Master of Balliol College; B. received an honorary degree from Oxford in 1868. *Collections* (E153) mistakenly records the extract as beginning at l. 135. B. probably copied the lines from *1863*, not its revised reissue *1865*: see ll. 137n., 143n.

Composition
DeVane (*Handbook*, 270) speculates that the poem may be the product of the Brownings' period of residence in Rome during the winter of 1853–54; it is not, however, one of the poems identified by *Sharp* as belonging to this period.

Sources and contexts

(i) *Time and place*
The subtitle refers to 'the revival of learning', a phrase widely used in the early nineteenth century, but not with any exact chronological boundaries; see for instance Peacock's *Four Ages of Poetry* (1820) and Shelley's 'Essay on the literature, the arts, and the manners of the Athenians', publ. 1840. In James Montgomery's *A View of Modern English Literature* (1843) the 'revival of classic learning' is linked to phenomena of the late 15th and early 16th centuries (the Reformation, the discovery of the New World and the invention of the printing press) as one of the harbingers of what later came to be called the Renaissance; on the nineteenth-century elaboration of this concept see headnote to *Andrea* (pp. 386–7). B. had described an earlier phase of this 'revival' in *Sordello*, that of the early 13th century (i 569–83, I 434), but the period of the Grammarian's activity seems to belong to the 14th or 15th century, when the systematic study of Greek was taking hold in Italy and Germany. The nationality of the Grammarian is left deliberately unclear, as is the location of the city where he is buried, other than that it is in 'Europe'. The hilltop location fits Tuscany or Lombardy, but might equally refer to the Rhineland. The contrast in the opening lines between the 'common crofts, the vulgar thorpes' and the 'tall mountain, citied to the top' does, however, suggest a positive revaluation of the dominance of mountain over plain which B. associates with Italy: in *Sordello* Ecelin's tyranny is marked by castle-building in the

Title and subtitle.] A Grammarian's Funeral, | shortly after the revival of learning in Europe. (*1865–88*). On the time and place of the poem, see above.

mountains (i 257–68, I 412), and in *England in Italy* the mountains themselves are symbols of oppression (ll. 181–96, p. 264).

(ii) *The character of the Grammarian*
The jealousy, small-mindedness and ill-health of grammarians seem to have been proverbial; in *Praise of Folly* (1509; transl. John Wilson, 1668), Erasmus uses grammarians to illustrate the follies of the learned:

> I knew in my time . . . one of many Arts, a *Grecian*, a *Latinist*, a *Mathematician*, a *Philosopher*, a *Physitian* . . . a Man master of 'em all, and sixty years of age, who laying by all the rest, perplext and tormented himself for above twenty years, in the study of Grammar, fully reckoning himself a Prince, if he might but live so long, till he could certainly determine, how the Eight parts of Speech were to be distinguisht, which none of the *Greeks* or *Latines*, had yet fully clear'd; as if it were a matter to be decided by the Sword, if a man made an Adverb of a Conjunction; and for this cause is it, that we have as many Grammars, as Grammarians; nay more, forasmuch as my friend *Aldus*, has giv'n us above five, not passing by any kind of Grammar, how barbarously, or tediously soever compil'd, which he has not turn'd over, and examin'd; envying every mans [sic] attempts in this kind, how foolish so ever, and desperately concern'd, for fear another should forestal him of his glory, and the labours of so many years perish . . . they that write learnedly, to the understanding of a few Scholers . . . seem to me, rather to be pitied, than happy, as persons that are ever tormenting themselves; Adding, Changing, Putting in, Blotting out, Revising, Reprinting, showing 't to friends . . . and nine years in correcting, yet never fully satisfied; at so great a rate, do they purchase this vain reward, to wit Praise, and that too, of a very few, with so many watchings, so much sweat, so much vexation, and loss of sleep, the most pretious of all things: Add to this, the waste of health, spoil of complexion, weakness of eyes, or rather blindness, poverty, envie, abstinence from pleasure, over-hasty Old-age, untimely death, and the like; So highly does this Wise man value the approbation of one or two blear-ey'd fellows[.] (pp. 88–91)

Various suggestions have been made about the identity of the poem's 'grammarian', including Erasmus's contemporary Thomas Linacre (1460–1524) and Isaac Casaubon (1559–1614), but as DeVane puts it '[the] probability is that B. had several scholars of the early Renaissance in mind, and drew a composite figure' (*Handbook* 270). James F. Loucks ('Browning's Grammarian and "Herr Buttmann"', *SBC* ii.3 [1974] 79–83) has noted some similarities between the poem's portrait and the description of the German grammarian Philip Charles Buttman (1764–1829) in Edward Robinson's 1839 translation of his work. Buttman was, according to Robinson, 'embittered by severe physical suffering' during his final years:

> His body was racked by rheumatic affections [sic], which deprived him in great measure of the use of his limbs, and finally terminated his days, Jan. 21, 1829. For several preceding winters he had been confined to his house. The writer of these lines had the pleasure of an interview with him about a year before his death. He was seated before a table in a large armed chair, bolstered up with cushions, and with his feet on pillows; before him was a book, the leaves of which his swollen and torpid hands were just able to turn over; while a member of his family acted as amanuensis. That book was his earliest work, the intermediate Grammar.

(cited Loucks, pp. 81–2)

As Loucks points out, B. mentions Buttman by name in the late poem *Development* (*Asolando*, 1889), and cites him as an authority when defending his account of the 'doctrine of the enclitic *De*' (see ll. 131–2n.). B. was questioned on this matter by Tennyson, as a letter of 2 July 1863 (first publ. by Christopher Ricks, *TLS*, 3 June 1965, p. 464) makes clear:

> My dear Tennyson,
> There are tritons among minnows, even—and so I wanted the grammarian 'dead from the waist down'—(or 'feeling middling,' as you said last night)— to spend his last breath on the biggest of the littlenesses: such an one is the 'enclitic δε,' the 'inseparable,' just because it may be confounded with δέ, 'but', which keeps its accent . . . See Buttman on these points. It was just this pinpoint of a puzzle that gave 'de' its worth rather than the heaps of obvious rhymes to 'he'—in all the oblique cases, for instance, of personal pronouns . . . to which I beg you to add, in a guffaw, 'he-he-he!' Only, you *would* have it!

Erasmus's view of the grammarian is echoed by EBB. in *The Greek Christian Poets* (1842; rpt. *Poetical Works* [1907] 613):

> How many are there from Psellus to Bayle, bound hand and foot intellectually with the rolls of their own papyrus—men whose erudition has grown stronger than their souls! How many whom we would gladly see washed in the clean waters of a little ignorance, and take our own part in their refreshment! Not that knowledge is bad, but that wisdom is better; and that it is better and wiser in the sight of the angels of knowledge to think out one true thought with a thrush's song and a green light for all lexicon (or to think it without the light and without the song—because truth is beautiful, where they are not seen or heard)—than to mummy our benumbed soul with the circumvolutions of twenty thousand books. And so Michael Psellus was a learned man.

Similarly, Emerson in 'Intellect' (*Essays* [1841] 187–8) argues that when a man '[fastens] his attention on a single aspect of truth, and [applies] himself to that alone for a long time, the truth becomes distorted and not itself, but falsehood . . . How wearisome the grammarian, the phrenologist, the political or religious fanatic, or indeed any possessed mortal, whose balance is lost by the exaggeration of a single topic. It is incipient insanity'.

Form and metre

DeVane (*Handbook* 270) describes the poem as 'alternating five-measure iambic and two-measure dactylic'. This is clearly wrong: each line of the poem begins with a stressed syllable, and the shorter lines always contain five syllables rather than six. The metre can be better understood as an imitation of the classical hexameter, divided into two parts (eg ll. 21–2):

```
 /    ^  ^ |/  ^  ^ | /   / | /   ^   /   | /   ^  ^| /  /
Leave we the unlettered plain its herd and crop / Seek we sepulture
```

Cp. the transformation of short lines into long ones in the completed *Saul* (see headnote, III 491), and in the versions of *Cristina* and *England in Italy* published in the 1872 *Selections*, for which see I 774 and II 341 respectively. The dactylic quality of the shorter lines is more immediately apparent because a dactyl is obligatory in the fifth foot of a hexameter, but can be substituted by a spondee (or more usually in English a trochee) in any of the other feet. In addition, the metre is emphasized by the use of alliteration as a marker of accent in the shorter lines. B. makes one significant departure from the usual accentual hexameter;

the line break after the fourth foot leads him to make it a 'cretic' (/ ^ /) rather than a dactyl. This imparts an awkward rising intonation to the end of the long lines which may be intended to imitate the mourners' laborious procession up the mountain.

The use of an English equivalent to the metre of classical Greek poetry has an obvious relevance to the subject of the poem, a point reinforced by the use of terms such as 'measures' and 'feet' (l. 39) and 'accents' (l. 54) even where the primary sense is not that of metrical language. The question of the English hexameter was, moreover, topical during the late 1840s and early 1850s. Some of B.'s contemporaries, most notably Henry Wadsworth Longfellow (in *Evangeline*, 1847) and Arthur Hugh Clough (in *The Bothie of Toper-na-Fuosich*, 1848) wrote narrative poems in English hexameters, in part to refute the idea that the metre was not suited to the English language. The Brownings read Clough's poem on first publication, with EBB. noting in a letter of 1 Dec. 1849 to Mary Russell Mitford that the poem is 'written in loose & more-than-need-be unmusical hexameters, but full of vigour & freshness, & with passages & indeed whole scenes of great beauty & eloquence' (*EBB to MRM* iii 286). For the background to the hexameter debate, see J. Phelan, 'Radical Metre: The English Hexameter in Clough's *Bothie of Toper-na-Fuosich*', *RES* n.s. 1 (1999) 166–87.

Criticism and parallels in B.

The main precursor for the Grammarian in B.'s work is 'Sibrandus Schafnaburgensis', the pedant who gives his name to the second section of *Garden Fancies* (see p. 216). As *Oxford* suggests, EBB.'s admiration for the poem was expressed in a phrase which may have stuck in B.'s memory: 'I like your burial of the pedant *so* much!' (21 July 1845, *Correspondence* x 315). Debate on the poem has centred on whether or not it is a satire on the Grammarian. Is he a hero of obscure but valuable labour, or someone who has lost sight of the ends of life? There are a number of poems in which B. seems to criticize the attitude represented by the Grammarian; see Martin J. Svaglic, *VP* v (1967) 93–104, in which contrasts with *Paracelsus* are highlighted. Festus warns Paracelsus of the consequences of making the acquisition of knowledge the main aim of human life: 'How can that course be safe which from the first / Produces carelessness to human love?' (i 626–7, I 142); and Paracelsus himself recognizes that 'men have oft grown old among their books / And died, case-harden'd in their ignorance, / Whose careless youth had promised what long years / Of unremitted labour ne'er perform'd' (i 757–60, I 147). Svaglic also notes the relevance of a passage in *Cleon* (ll. 225–50, pp. 579–80); and it might be added that the Grammarian's painful and laborious old age contrasts with the joyful old age depicted in some of B.'s other poems, most notably *Rabbi Ben Ezra* (p. 649).

Another perennial question examined in this poem concerns the relation between this life and the next. The Grammarian's attitude derives from his certainty that the 'heavenly period' will '[perfect] the earthen' (ll. 103–4); cp. the choice of the speaker in *ED*, who makes the opposite decision to ignore the possibility of the life to come and focus exclusively on this life (III 123). In this sense the Grammarian's 'sacred thirst' for knowledge (l. 95) makes him into a kind of holy fool, since although he is searching for human wisdom he is doing so in a way which points beyond 'the world' (l. 121), in conformity with, e.g., *1 Corinthians* iii 18–19: 'If any man among you seemeth to be wise in this world, let him become a fool, that he may be wise. For the wisdom of this world is foolishness with God.' B. himself suggests this in a letter to James Kenward of 11 March 1867 in which he praises the 'self-denying zeal' of 'your Ap Ithel', adding that 'Purely disinterested scholarship always seemed to me to have far more important bearings, moral and intellectual, than are commonly recognized' (*Checklist* 67:33); see also *Sordello* iv 573–89n. (I 628). The balance between 'The petty Done [and] the Undone vast', and between 'bliss here' and 'life beyond' is the central theme of *Last Ride Together* (III 291), where, however, the lover fantasizes that heaven may lie not in a compensatory future but in infinite prolongation of the present moment.

> Let us begin and carry up this corpse,
>> Singing together.
> Leave we the common crofts, the vulgar thorpes,
>> Each in its tether
> 5 Sleeping safe on the bosom of the plain,
>> Cared-for till cock-crow.
> Look out if yonder's not the day again
>> Rimming the rock-row!
> That's the appropriate country—there, man's thought,
> 10 Rarer, intenser,
> Self-gathered for an outbreak, as it ought,
>> Chafes in the censer!
> Leave we the unlettered plain its herd and crop;
>> Seek we sepulture
> 15 On a tall mountain, citied to the top,

1–2. The poem is either a collective chant by the students, or the utterance of one of them speaking on behalf of all.

3. crofts: a croft is '[a] little close joining to a house that is used for corn or pasture' (*J.*). *thorpes*: *J.* lists various spellings (although not this one), and glosses as 'a village'. B.'s spelling occurs in a footnote to Thomas Warton's summary of Lydgate's *Storie of Thebes* (1561); see *The History of English Poetry* (1774–81) ii 74.

5. on the bosom] i' the bosom (*1872*).

7. yonder's not the day] yonder be not day (*1863–88*).

8. Rimming: bordering; *OED* cites Tennyson, 'The Gardener's Daughter' (1842) 177: 'A length of bright horizon rimm'd the dark'. *the rock-row!* the line of mountain peaks in the distance.

9–12. man's thought . . . censer. 'Thought requires concentration, when it is enclosed in the brain, like incense in a censer; but as it takes fire, it must break out (be expressed) in words' (*Turner* 381).

12. the censer. 'The pan or vessel in which incense is burned' (*J.*)

13–16. A. D. Nuttall suggests that the elevated burial place to which the 'grammarian' is taken 'entails a deft allusion to humanist values. Lucan's words *Caelo tegitur qui non habet urnam*, "He is covered by the sky, who has no funeral urn" (*De Bello Civili*, vii 819) was the favourite proverb of humanist [Sir Thomas] More's traveller, Hythloday' ('Browning's Grammarian: Accents Uncertain?', *Essays in Criticism* li [2001] 88).

14. sepulture: 'Interment; burial' (*J.*).

Crowded with culture!
All the peaks soar, but one the rest excels;
  Clouds overcome it;
No, yonder sparkle is the citadel's
20   Circling its summit!
Thither our path lies—wind we up the heights—
  Wait ye the warning?
Our low life was the level's and the night's;
  He's for the morning!
25 Step to a tune, square chests, erect the head,
  'Ware the beholders!
This is our master, famous, calm, and dead,
  Borne on our shoulders.

Sleep, crop and herd! sleep, darkling thorpe and croft,
30   Safe from the weather!
He, whom we convey to his grave aloft,
  Singing together,
He was a man born with thy face and throat,
  Lyric Apollo!
35 Long he lived nameless: how should spring take note
  Winter would follow?
Till lo, the little touch, and youth was gone!

---

16. *culture*: punning on the etymology of the word: the students leave the 'herd' on the 'unlettered plain' behind in their search for intellectual 'culture'.

19. *No, yonder*: contradicting the first impression that the clouds 'overcome' the summit of the mountain (and so obscure the citadel).   *citadel's*: the fortress which crowns the city, as the city the mountain: the highest and innermost structure.

22. 'Are you waiting for the signal?' Cp. Robert Southey, *A Vision of Judgement* (1821): 'Thus as I stood, the bell which awhile from its warning had rested, / Sent forth its note again, toll, toll, through the silence of evening' (i 22–3).

25. *the head*] each head (*1865–88*).

26. *'Ware*: 'Be aware of'.

33–4. Apollo is the god both of male beauty and of poetry: the Grammarian in his youth possesses both physical beauty ('face') and poetic power ('throat' is itself a poeticism for 'voice'). In *Sordello* Apollo is the type of perfection in life and art, the 'antique bliss' that Sordello covets but cannot in fact attain: see i 893–7 (I 454).

35–6. Inverting the sequence in the last line of Shelley's *Ode to the West Wind*: 'If Winter comes, can Spring be far behind?'

35. *nameless*: unknown to the wider world.

      Cramped and diminished,
      Moaned he, "New measures, other feet anon!
40   My dance is finished?"
      No, that's the world's way! (keep the mountain-side,
        Make for the city.)
      He knew the signal, and stepped on with pride
        Over men's pity;
45   Left play for work, and grappled with the world
        Bent on escaping:
      "What's in the scroll," quoth he, "thou keepest furled?
        Shew me their shaping,
      Theirs, who most studied man, the bard and sage,—
50   Give!"—So he gowned him,
      Straight got by heart that book to its last page:
        Learned, we found him!
      Yea, but we found him bald too—eyes like lead,
        Accents uncertain:
55   "Time to taste life," another would have said,
        "Up with the curtain!"
      This man said rather, "Actual life comes next?
        Patience a moment!
      Grant I have mastered learning's crabbed text,
60   Still, there's the comment.

38–40. 'When he found himself cramped and diminished, did he accept that his youth had gone and that he had to make way for others?'

39. measures . . . feet: the primary sense refers to the 'dance' of life, but there is a 'submerged' allusion to the poem's own prosody: see headnote. *anon!* soon.

47. scroll: a roll of paper or parchment, often associated with sacred texts: cp. *Revelation* vi 14: 'And the heaven departed as a scroll when it is rolled together; and every mountain and island were moved out of their places.' Nuttall (see ll. 13–16n.) suggests both Dickens's *A Christmas Carol* and *The Merchant of Venice*, II vii 63–4 as possible sources for this image.

48. their shaping: 'what they made', 'their accomplishments'. 'Shape' as a verb originally meant 'to create, to give form', and until the 16th century was applied to God as creator; it retained strong associations with both physical and imaginative creation. *OED* cites Tennyson, 'Lady Godiva': 'And there I shaped / The city's ancient legend into this' (ll. 3–4).

49. the bard and sage: generic terms for poet and philosopher.

50. gowned him: enrolled as a student (from the academic gowns worn at ancient universities).

54. Accents: the primary sense is the 'accent' of the voice, but its use here evokes the marks used to indicate stress in Greek prosody; see headnote.

60. comment: commentary.

Let me know all. Prate not of most or least,
    Painful or easy:
Even to the crumbs I'd fain eat up the feast,
    Ay, nor feel queasy!"
65 Oh, such a life as he resolved to live,
    When he had learned it,
When he had gathered all books had to give;
    Sooner, he spurned it!
Image the whole, then execute the parts—
70   Fancy the fabric
Quite, ere you build, ere steel strike fire from quartz,
    Ere mortar dab brick!

(Here's the town-gate reached: there's the market-place
    Gaping before us.)
75 Yea, this in him was the peculiar grace
    (Hearten our chorus)
Still before living he'd learn how to live—
    No end to learning.
Earn the means first—God surely will contrive

---

61. *know all*: cp. the 'principle of restlessness / Which would be all, have, see, know, taste, feel, all' which characterizes the speaker of *Pauline* (ll. 277–8, p. 26); see also l. 65n.

63–4. Cp. Karshish's description of himself as 'the picker-up of learning's crumbs' (*An Epistle* 1, p. 511).

65. Cp. *Pauline* 426–7: 'And I—ah! what a life was mine to be, / My whole soul rose to meet it' (p. 35).

68. 'He spurned the possibility of living his life before he had completed his training for it.' *spurned it!*] spurned it. (*1863–88*).

71. *ere steel . . . quartz*: the image is of dressing sandstone, which is composed of quartz, for use in building. In a letter to EBB. of 13 July 1845, B. used the image of a building site for work in progress, breaking down the absolute distinction between planning and execution which he maintains here: 'when I try and build a great building I shall want you to come with me and judge it and counsel me before the scaffolding is taken down, and while you have to make your way over hods of mortar & heaps of lime, and trembling tubs of size, and those thin broad whitewashing brushes I always had a desire to take up and bespatter with' (*Correspondence* x 306).

72. *mortar*: with a possible pun on the 'mortar board' hats worn by academics.

75. *peculiar grace*: a term drawn from Protestant theology describing the quality which sets the 'elect' apart; cp. Isaac Watts's version of Psalm cxlviii: 'God is our sun and shield, / Our light and our defence; / With gifts his hands are filled, / We draw our blessings thence; / He shall bestow / On Jacob's race / Peculiar grace / And glory too.'

77. *Still before*] That before (*1863–88*).

80   Use for our earning.
        Others mistrust and say—"But time escapes,—
        Live now or never!"
        He said, "What's Time? leave Now for dogs and apes!
        Man has For ever."
85   Back to his book then: deeper dropped his head;
            Calculus racked him:
        Leaden before, his eyes grew dross of lead;
            Tussis attacked him.
        "Now, Master, take a little rest"—not he!
90   (Caution redoubled!
        Step two a-breast, the way winds narrowly.)
            Not a whit troubled,
        Back to his studies, fresher than at first,
            Fierce as a dragon
95   He, (soul-hydroptic with a sacred thirst)

---

81. time escapes,—] escapes! (*1863–65, 1872*); escapes: (*1868, 1888*). This is a rare example of B. changing his mind three times in the course of successive editions.
83. dogs and apes: cp. Milton's sonnet on *Tetrachordon*: 'owls and cuckoos, asses, apes and dogs' (l. 4). B. could have found the exact phrase in a satirical topographical poem by Charles Cotton, *The Wonders of the Peake* (1681), in which the ascent up a mountain is described as anything but civilized: 'Propt round with Peasants, on you trembling go, / Whilst, every step you take, your Guides do show / In the uneven Rock the uncouth shapes / Of Men, of Lions, Horses, Dogs, and Apes: / But so resembling each the fancied shape, / The Man might be the Horse, the Dog the Ape' (ll. 109–14). 'Dogs and apes' also appear in 'The Ass and Brock', a fable by Allan Ramsay (1686–1758): 'The Ass . . . Pour'd out a Deluge of dull Phrases, / While Dogs and Apes leugh [i.e. laughed], and made Faces' (ll. 33, 37–8).
86. Calculus: 'The stone in the bladder' (*J.*); J. M. Ariail (*PMLA* xlviii [1933] 955) suggests an allusion to the other meaning of mathematical computation.
87. dross of lead: technically the scum of the metal left after boiling; the term 'dross' also connotes 'dregs', 'impurity', 'worthlessness'. *OED* cites Milton, *Paradise Regained* iii 23: 'All treasures and all gain esteem as dross'.
88. Tussis: a cough; Ariail (see l. 85n.) notes that 'tussis' is the paradigm of 'disyllabic i-stems of the third declension in Latin', with the suggestion that it therefore represents a particularly significant example of this class of noun.
95. soul-hydroptic: 'hydroptic' is an incorrect popular form of 'hydropic' (*J.* has 'hydropick'), from the medical condition known as 'dropsy', the morbid accumulation of fluid in the body; *OED* cites a suggestive use by Donne (*Letters* [1651] 51): 'An hydroptique immoderate desire of humane learning and languages'. The term 'soul-hydroptic' is B.'s coinage, and his positive valuation of a 'sacred thirst' is unusual; most instances of dropsy as an image of excessive thirst are negative (*OED* cites Shenstone, 1763: 'Thy voice, hydropic fancy! calls aloud / For costly draughts').

   Sucked at the flagon.
  Oh, if we draw a circle premature,
   Heedless of far gain,
  Greedy for quick returns of profit, sure,
100 Bad is our bargain!
  Was it not great? did not he throw on God,
   (He loves the burthen)—
  God's task to make the heavenly period
   Perfect the earthen?
105 Did not he magnify the mind, shew clear
   Just what it all meant?
  He would not discount life, as fools do here,
   Paid by instalment!
  He ventured neck or nothing—heaven's success
110 Found, or earth's failure:
  "Wilt thou trust death or not?" he answered "Yes.
   Hence with life's pale lure!"
  That low man seeks a little thing to do,
   Sees it and does it:
115 This high man, with a great thing to pursue,
   Dies ere he knows it.

97–100. Cp. the mistrust of material rewards in *Pictor Ignotus* (ll. 46–56, p. 230), and the circle metaphor in *Old Pictures* 133–6 (pp. 419–20).

101–4. 'Did he not give God the chance to show that the life to come supersedes and perfects this life?' See headnote, *Criticism*.

103–4. The primary sense is that the next life represents the completion, or consummation, of this life. B. plays on the fact that 'period' can mean both a course of time, and the point of completion or consummation of such a course; he almost certainly had in mind other connotations of the word, esp. in grammar and rhetoric ('a complete sentence', usually made up of several clauses), and ancient prosody ('a metrical group or series of verses'), as well as more specialized uses such as those belonging to artistic or geological 'periods'. Cp. *Abt Vogler* 72 (p. 768): 'On the earth the broken arcs; in the heaven, a perfect round'.

104. Perfect] Complete (*H proof,* but not *H proof²*). The accent falls on the first syllable: Pérfect.

105. magnify the mind] make the most of mind (*H proof,* but not *H proof²*).

107–8. This metaphor is drawn from the world of finance, and so continues the mercantile analogy of ll. 99–100. The comparison is with a bond or promissory note which can be 'discounted' or sold for its present worth before the full sum becomes payable; 'fools' who opt for this arrangement receive their payment 'by instalment' rather than all at once.

109. neck or nothing: a proverbial expression deriving from horse-riding and meaning 'all or nothing'; cp. Byron, *Don Juan* viii 355.

112. pale: paltry, inadequate.

116. knows: 'achieves'.

That low man goes on adding one to one,
　　His hundred's soon hit:
This high man, aiming at a million,
120　　Misses an unit.
That, has the world here—should he need the next,
　　Let the world mind him!
This, throws himself on God, and unperplext
　　Seeking shall find Him.
125　So, with the throttling hands of Death at strife,
　　Ground he at grammar;
Still, thro' the rattle, parts of speech were rife.
　　While he could stammer
He settled *Hoti's* business—let it be!—
130　　Properly based *Oun*—
Gave us the doctrine of the enclitic *De*,

117–20. Cp. *Bishop Blougram* 544–54 n. (p. 315); and cp. B.'s letter to EBB. (cited in headnote to *Popularity*, p. 446) on the subject of the painter Benjamin Haydon's inconsistent response to critical neglect: 'now with the high aim in view, now with the low aim'.

120. Misses an unit: either 'falls short by one' or 'fails to accomplish anything at all'; the latter reading is more consistent with the general sense of the passage.

121–2. 'Let the world (which he has chosen) take care of him.' Cp. *Matthew* vi 2, 5, 16, where those who do things for worldly reasons are said to 'have their reward' in this life (i.e. they have sacrificed their chance of salvation).

121. That: 'That one' (i.e. the 'low man').

123. This: 'This one' (i.e. the 'high man').

124. Cp. *Matthew* vii 7: 'Ask, and it shall be given you; seek, and ye shall find; knock, and it shall be opened unto you.'

127. rattle: the 'death-rattle', the sound caused by laborious or obstructed breathing in a dying person's throat. *parts of speech:* both 'incomplete utterances' and grammatical particles of the kind described in the next few lines.

129. Hoti's business] Oti's business (*H proof*). Nuttall (see ll. 13–16n.) states that 'hoti' is not a particle, but most commentators agree that it is a conjunction meaning 'that'.

130. Oun: a conjunction denoting inference, like 'therefore'.

131–2. The 'enclitic *De*' required several attempts at explanation by B.; see the letter to Tennyson (headnote, *Sources*) and another published in the *Daily News* on 21 November 1874: 'In a clever article this morning you speak of "the doctrine of the enclitic De"—"which, with all deference to Mr. Browning, in point of fact does not exist." No, not to Mr. Browning: but pray defer to Herr Buttmann, whose fifth list of "enclitics" ends "with the inseparable De"—or to Curtius, whose fifth list ends also with "De (meaning *towards*, and as a demonstrative appendage)". That this is not to be confounded with the accentuated "*De*, meaning *but*", was the "doctrine" which the Grammarian bequeathed to those capable of receiving it.' *Maynard* (p. 271) notes that T. H. Key, one of B.'s tutors at the University of London, introduced the term 'enclitic' into his Latin Grammar.

Dead from the waist down.
Well, here's the platform, here's the proper place.
Hail to your purlieus
135 All ye highfliers of the feathered race,
    Swallows and curlews!
Here's the top-peak! the multitude below
    Live, for they can there.
This man decided not to Live but Know—
140 Bury this man there?
Here—here's his place, where meteors shoot, clouds form,
    Lightnings are loosened,
Stars come and go! let joy break with the storm—
    Peace let the dew send!
145 Lofty designs must close in like effects:
    Loftily lying,
Leave him—still loftier than the world suspects,
    Living and dying.

134. purlieus: used here in the general sense of 'a place where one has the right to range at large; a place where one is free to come and go, or which one habitually frequents; a haunt' (*OED* 2); since the location is at the highest and most central point of the city, B. may have been aware of, and deliberately reversed, the sense of 'purlieu' as an outlying district or suburb, esp. 'a mean, squalid, or disreputable street or quarter' (*OED* 4).

139. Cp. *Paracelsus* ii 578–81 (I 187).

141–4. Cp. the opening of Shelley's 'Fragment: Supposed to be an Epithalamium of Francis Ravaillac and Charlotte Corday': "Tis midnight now—athwart the murky air, / Dank lurid meteors shoot a livid gleam; / From the dark storm-clouds flashes a fearful glare, / It shows the bending oak, the roaring stream'.

142. loosened: freed from restraint (*J.*).

143. let] Let (*1865–88*). *storm—*] storm, (*1863–88*). We record these minor variants because they bear on the text of *Berg MS* (see headnote); this extract does not have the first reading, but does have the second, making it almost certain that B. was copying it from *1863*.

145. Either 'The grandeur of his conceptions must be matched by the setting for his burial', or 'The grandeur of his conceptions must have an outcome as spectacular as the "effects" of weather just described'.

148–9. still loftier . . . dying: either 'He was loftier than the world knew, both in his life and in his death', or 'He is loftier than the world realizes, in that he is perpetually presenting us with a supreme example of human aspiration'.

39 One Word More

TO E. B. B.

Text and publication

First publ. *M & W*, 10 Nov. 1855, the concluding poem; repr. *1863* (see below, note to title), *1865²* (considerably shortened, and with no section numbers), *1868*, *1888*. Our text is *1855*. The fair-copy MS (5 pp.) used by the printer is in *Morgan* (MA 930); the MS title is 'A Last Word. | To E. B. B.' but the change must have been made at an early stage, since it is not rec. in *H proof*. *Texas* has a marked-up copy of *1865* intended for *1865²*, together with a proof of *1865²*, with no significant variants. We give a complete collation of all MS variants, including del. readings where recoverable. The poem posed B. particular problems, both with regard to its inclusion in a volume of selections, and more generally with regard to revision carried out after EBB.'s death.

Composition and revision

The poem was written as B. was completing the proof sheets of *M & W*; the MS is dated at the end: 'London, Sept 22. 1855'. EBB. wrote that the volume was to be dedicated to her in a letter of 3 October 1855, the date on which the last of the *M & W* proofs was despatched to the printer (*EBB to Arabella* ii 178).

The change in the title from 'A Last Word' was perhaps made in order to avoid too direct an echo of *Woman's Last Word* (III 273); the phrase 'one word more' also plays a part in the courtship correspondence, notably EBB.'s letter to B. of 31 August 1845 (*Correspondence* xi 54), entreating him not to renew his declaration of love for her: 'Therefore we must leave this subject—& I must trust you to leave it without one word more', and B.'s last letter to EBB. before their departure to Italy: 'Write to me one word more' (18 Sept. 1846, *Correspondence* xiii 379). The phrase 'one word more' is common in Shakespeare, notably being used several times in *The Tempest* I ii, as when Miranda is attempting to intercede with Prospero on behalf of Ferdinand: 'Silence! One word more / Shall make me chide thee, if not hate thee. What / An advocate for an impostor! Hush!' (ll. 475–7). It seems, however, to have been in common use in the mid-nineteenth century; see (e.g.) Anne Brontë's preface to the second edition of *The Tenant of Wildfell Hall* (1848): 'One word more, and I have done'.

Title.] A Last Word / To E. B. B. (*MS*) One Word More.★ / TO E.B.B. / *London, September,* 1855. (*1863, 1865, 1868,* except that there is no full stop after 'More' in *1868*); ADAPTED FROM "One Word More. / To E.B.B. / London, September, 1855." (*1865²*); One Word More.★ / TO E.B.B. / 1855. (*1888*). The asterisk in *1863, 1865,* and *1868–88* refers to a footnote: 'Originally appended to the collection of Poems called "Men and Women," the greater portion of which has now been, more correctly, distributed under the other titles of this volume [*1868–88*: edition].' As the opening lines state, the first edition of *M & W* consisted of fifty poems; for details of their redistribution, see Appendix D, III 747.

Sources and contexts

(i) Raphael's sonnets

The tradition that Raphael addressed a 'century of sonnets' to his mistress 'La Fornarina' is alluded to in one of B.'s habitual sources, *Baldinucci* (see headnote to *Andrea del Sarto*, pp. 388–9); Baldinucci states that when Guido Reni died certain items of value disappeared from his house: 'Persesi però, con una collana d'oro, ed alcune argenterie, il famoso libro de' cento sonetti di mano di Raffaello, che Guido aveva comperati [sic] in Roma, e ciò non senza qualche sussurro, quantunque poco fondato, che il tutto fosse stato rapito da un suo domestico' [Along with a gold necklace and various items of silverware, the famous book of one hundred sonnets from the hand of Raphael went missing, not without some (albeit ill-founded) murmurs that these things had been stolen by one of his [i.e. Guido's] domestic servants]. See Frederick Page, *TLS* xxxix (25 May 1940) 255. *Thomas* states: 'Of Raphael's "century of sonnets" only four are claimed by Browning scholars to be extant . . . One of these sonnets is written on some sketches for Raphael's fresco of the *Disputa*, in the Vatican' (p. 204).

The association of the sonnet form with intimate self-revelation became increasingly marked throughout the first half of the nineteenth century. In 'Scorn not the Sonnet' Wordsworth calls it the 'key' with which 'Shakespeare unlocked his heart' (ll. 2–3); and in his 1825 essay Thomas Babington Macaulay describes Milton's sonnets as 'simple but majestic records of the feelings of the poet; as little tricked out for the public eye as his diary would have been' (*Critical and Historical Essays* [London 1859] i 14). EBB. had of course contributed to this link with her *Sonnets from the Portuguese* (1850), widely recognized as an autobiographical account of her relationship with B. For B.'s ambivalence towards the sonnet in general, and the autobiographical uses of the form in particular, see *House* (*Pacchiarotto*, 1876): 'Shall I sonnet-sing you about myself? / Do I live in a house you would like to see? . . . No, thanking the public, I must decline. / A peep through my window, if folk prefer; / But, please you, no foot over threshold of mine!' (ll. 1–2, 10–12).

Along with Michelangelo, Raphael was the type for B., as for many other Victorians, of the undisputed genius of Renaissance painting: see, in this volume, *Andrea* 103 ff. (p. 395 ff), and *Fifine* (1872) 512–77 (sects. 35–36).

(ii) Dante's angel

In *La Vita Nuova*, section xxxiv, Dante tells how he drew a picture of an angel to commemorate the first anniversary of Beatrice's death (on 9 June 1291):

> In quello giorno nel quale si compiea l'anno che questa donna era fatta de li cittadini di vita eterna, io mi sedea in parte ne la quale, ricordandomi di lei, disegnava uno angelo sopra certe tavolette; e mentre io lo disegnava, volsi li occhi, e vidi lungo me uomini a li quali si convenia di fare onore. E' riguardavano quello che io facea; e secondo che me fu detto poi, elli erano stati già alquanto anzi che io me ne accorgesse. Quando li vidi, mi levai, e salutando loro dissi: 'Altri era testé meco, però pensava'. Onde partiti costoro, ritornaimi a la mia opera, cioè del disegnare figure d'angeli[.]

> [On that day which fulfilled the year since my lady had been made of the citizens of eternal life, remembering me of her as I sat alone, I betook myself to draw the resemblance of an angel upon certain tablets. And while I did thus, chancing to turn my head, I perceived that some were standing beside me to whom I should have given courteous welcome, and that they were observing what I did: also I learned afterwards that they had been there a while before I perceived them. Perceiving whom, I arose for salutation, and said: 'Another was with me.'

Afterwards, when they had left me, I set myself again to mine occupation,
to wit, to the drawing figures of angels(.)]

> (Transl. D. G. Rossetti, 'The New Life', in *The Early Italian Poets*,
> ed. Sally Purcell [1981], p. 200. Rossetti relegates the second part of
> Dante's reply—'però pensava' [And therefore was I in thought]—to a
> footnote on the grounds that 'the shorter speech is perhaps the more
> forcible and pathetic.')

B.'s partial translation of this passage (ll. 46–9) implies that the 'people of importance' prevent Dante from finishing the drawing; but the passage makes clear that
Dante returns to his work after they have left. B.'s alteration of the passage brings
it closer to the story of the 'person from Porlock' who interrupted Coleridge
during the composition of *Kubla Khan*, an idea which haunted B. as an emblem
of the inevitable discrepancy between conception and performance; see headnotes
to *Artemis Prologuizes* (II 106) and *Transcendentalism* (III 641). The title of B.'s
late collection *Parleyings with Certain People of Importance in their Day* (1887) is taken
from his translation of this passage.

B.'s admiration for Dante was of long standing: see headnote to *Sordello* (I 363–6).
In the 1850s this predilection would have been strengthened by that of the Pre-
Raphaelite group of younger writers and painters with whom he became friendly,
esp. Dante Gabriel Rossetti, for whom the *Vita Nuova* was a seminal work.

The link between the stories of Raphael and Dante is that both are attempting to express their deepest feelings by using an art form with which they are
unfamiliar. Such attempts are presented as proof of the absolute sincerity of the
artist's desire to articulate his own feelings for once; see below ll. 58–72.
Paradoxically, of course, B. is using his 'art familiar' in this poem, but claiming
to do so in a subtly different (because personal) way; see ll. 117–18n., and note
that the metre, too, is unique in his work (see below). B. seems to have enjoyed
drawing and making music, contrasting his own lack of pleasure in the physical
act of writing with what he imagined to be EBB.'s enjoyment of it: 'But I think
you like the operation of writing as I should like that of painting, or making
music, do you not?' (B. to EBB. 11 March 1845, *Correspondence* x 121).

(iii) *Poetics*

The link between poetry and prophecy which is affirmed by the parallel with
Moses in ll. 73–108 forms part of a strongly Carlylean image of the artist as hero
or 'great man', divinely inspired and battling against the ignorance or ill will of
those who should follow him. The pessimism of the poem, however, and its apparent retreat into a personal relationship whose ecstatic privacy compensates for
public rejection, may owe more to the influence of a younger contemporary,
Matthew Arnold, whose *Empedocles on Etna* (1852) B. admired: see headnote to
Cleon (pp. 563–4). Arnold's Empedocles resembles B.'s poet-prophet who 'bears
an ancient wrong about him' (l. 90); B. implies that EBB. has rescued him from
the isolation and despair which afflict the artist who is alienated from his contemporaries. See also headnote to *By the Fire-Side* (p. 458) for the possible influence
of Arnold's 'Resignation: to Fausta' on another *M & W* poem connected with
B.'s love for EBB. The poem stands in striking contrast to statements in which
B. affirms the *necessary* alienation, or at least detachment, of the artist, as he does
in *How It Strikes* (p. 435) and in his letter to Ruskin (Appendix B, pp. 881–2).

Metre

The poem is unique in B.'s work in its employment of trochaic pentameter.
This metre is rarely used in English poetry, although there is a strikingly similar

example in W. E. Aytoun's translation of Goethe's 'The Doleful Lay of the Wife of Asan Aga', first published in *Blackwood's Magazine* in July 1844:

> What is yon so white beside the greenwood?
> Is it snow or flight of cygnets resting?
> Were it snow, ere now it had been melted;
> Were it swans, ere now the flock had left us.

Like B., Aytoun makes extensive use of repetition and syntactic parallelism: 'And they halted by the once-loved dwelling, / And she gave the weeping children presents, / Gave each boy a cap with gold embroider'd, / Gave each girl a gay and costly garment' (ll. 76–9).

Parallels in B.

Although the poem claims to be unique as a first-person utterance, there are in fact many other poems by B. which are clearly autobiographical, including a number in *M & W* itself, e.g. *Guardian-Angel* (which refers directly to EBB. at l. 46: see III 19) and *Old Pictures* (p. 404). It may be claimed that the first person of these poems is a dramatic character, but the same might apply to *One Word More*, esp. since the imagery of the poem is shared with other fictional or dramatized lovers (esp. the moon imagery which dominates the poem from sect. 16 onwards: see notes). Similarly, the ideas of the poem (about poetry, and about what it means to be a poet), although here expressed in the poet's own voice, are not unique in B.'s work; in particular the fraught relationship between the artist-prophet and his ungrateful audience outlined in ll. 73–95 is a staple theme: see, in this volume, *Popularity* (p. 446). The *Epilogue* ('The poets pour us wine') to *Pacchiarotto* (1876) is an esp. significant example because B. uses a line from one of EBB.'s poems as the starting point for a ferocious attack on the stupidity and laziness of the reading public.

In personal terms, the most significant parallels come in poems and passages of poems written after EBB.'s death, often taking the form of prologues and epilogues: the invocation 'O lyric Love' in bk. i of *Ring* (ll. 1391–416), the *Prologue* (*Amphibian*) and *Epilogue* (*The Householder*) to *Fifine at the Fair* (1872), the *Prologue* ('O the old wall here!') to *Pacchiarotto*, 1876), *Never the Time and the Place* (*Jocoseria*, 1883), the *Epilogue* ('Oh, Love, no, Love') to *Ferishtah's Fancies* (1884), and *Dubiety* and *Speculative* (*Asolando*, 1889).

I

> There they are, my fifty men and women
> Naming me the fifty poems finished!
> Take them, Love, the book and me together.
> Where the heart lies, let the brain lie also.

1–2.] not *1865²*.
2. finished!] finished: (*MS, H proof*).
3. Love] love (*1868–88*). See ll. 116, 187.   *and me together.*] and me together— (*MS*); and me together: (*1863–88*).
4. the heart lies] the heart is (*MS, H proof*). The original reading strengthens the resemblance (noted by *Oxford*) to *Matthew* vi 21: 'For where your treasure is, there will your heart be also'; cp. l. 142 below.

2

5   Rafael made a century of sonnets,
      Made and wrote them in a certain volume
      Dinted with the silver-pointed pencil
      Else he only used to draw Madonnas:
      These, the world might view—but One, the volume.
10   Who that one, you ask? Your heart instructs you.
      Did she live and love it all her life-time?
      Did she drop, his lady of the sonnets,
      Die, and let it drop beside her pillow
      Where it lay in place of Rafael's glory,
15   Rafael's cheek so duteous and so loving—
      Cheek, the world was wont to hail a painter's,
      Rafael's cheek, her love had turned a poet's?

3

You and I would rather read that volume,
(Taken to his beating bosom by it)

5–31. For the story of Raphael's missing sonnets, see headnote, *Sources*.

5. *century of sonnets*: a collection of a hundred sonnets.

6. *made*: composed (as distinct from 'wrote': see next line).

7. *silver-pointed pencil*: silver-point is a technique in which a silver pencil is used on specially prepared paper (*OED*).

9. *but One*] one eye, (*MS first reading*, corr. to 'but one', the reading of *H proof*; see also next line). 'But' here means 'only'. *the volume.*] the volume: (*MS*).

10. *Who that one*] Whose that eye (*MS first reading*).

11. *her life-time?*] her life-time—(*MS*).

12–17. B. imagines that the lady outlives Raphael (who died young): on her deathbed she lets the volume 'drop beside her pillow', where it 'lay' (= had lain) as a token of her exceptional relationship with him. The book has been a substitute for Raphael's 'cheek' which would have rested on the pillow; the image (delicately but unequivocally) implies sexual love, but B. goes on to make the point that the lady has been, so to speak, sleeping with the private Raphael, the poet not the painter; to most people, a work by Raphael on one's pillow would signify the presence of his 'glory', whereas for her it signifies his 'duteous and loving' devotion to her.

12. *lady of the sonnets*: Raphael painted a number of likenesses of the lady who is supposed to have inspired his sonnets, including 'La Velata' in the Palazzo Pitti in Florence, and 'La Fornarina' in the Palazzo Barberini in Rome.

19. To read the sonnets would be to gain access to Raphael's 'heart', to his innermost feelings of love: see headnote, *Sources* on the link between such intimate knowledge and the sonnet form. The syntax of *taken to his beating bosom by it* suggests that we, the readers, would be conveyed by means of the book to (or into) Raphael's bosom; but B. may also want to evoke the idiom 'to take someone to one's bosom' as though, in reading his poems, we were embraced by Raphael himself.

20 Lean and list the bosom-beats of Rafael,
  Would we not? than wonder at Madonnas—
  Her, San Sisto names, and Her, Foligno,
  Her, that visits Florence in a vision,
  Her, that's left with lilies in the Louvre—
25 Seen by us and all the world in circle.

                    4

  You and I will never read that volume.
  Guido Reni, like his own eye's apple
  Guarded long the treasure-book and loved it.
  Guido Reni dying, all Bologna
30 Cried, and the world with it, "Ours—the treasure!"
  Suddenly, as rare things will, it vanished.

                    5

  Dante once prepared to paint an angel:
  Whom to please? You whisper "Beatrice."
  While he mused and traced it and retraced it,
35 (Peradventure with a pen corroded

20. list: listen to.
22–5. The first two Madonnas are the Sistine Madonna, now in Dresden, and the Madonna di Foligno in the Vatican Museum. The last two were identified by B. in a letter to William Rolfe, one of his earliest American editors: 'The Madonna at Florence is that called del Granduca, which represents her "as appearing to a votary in a vision"—so say the describers; it is in the earlier manner and very beautiful . . . about the one in the Louvre I think I meant La Belle Jardinière—but am not sure—from the picture in the Louvre' (Rolfe and Hersey eds., *Select Poems of Robert Browning* [New York 1886] 196; cited *Thomas* 206).
27. Guido Reni: Bolognese painter (1575–1642): the tradition that he owned the book containing Raphael's 'century of sonnets' comes from Baldinucci (see headnote, *Sources*).
30. with it,] cried too, (*1863–88*); B. noted this reading in his letter to D. G. Rossetti about the 'blunders' in *1855* (*LH* 42), and in the list of 'Errata' he sent to his American publisher James T. Fields (*B to Fields* 194); but it is clearly a revision, not a correction, and we have not emended *1855*.
32–49. See headnote. Dante Gabriel Rossetti produced a pen-and-ink drawing of 'The First Anniversary of the Death of Beatrice' in 1849, but it is not known if B. was aware of it.
33. Beatrice: four syllables, with the Italian pronunciation ('Bay-a-tree-chay').
35–41. Dante's practice of placing living citizens of Florence in Hell in the *Inferno* is imaged as a physical branding; the gesture of l. 37 comes from *Inferno* xxxii 97–9 when Dante seizes the traitor Bocca degli Abati by the hair in order to make him reveal his name: 'Allor lo presi per la cuticagna / e dissi: "El converrà che tu ti nomi, / O che capel qui su non ti rimagna"' [Then I seized him by

Still by drops of that hot ink he dipped for,
When, his left hand i' the hair o' the wicked,
Back he held the brow and pricked its stigma,
Bit into the live man's flesh for parchment,
40   Loosed him, laughed to see the writing rankle,
Let the wretch go festering thro' Florence)—
Dante, who loved well because he hated,
Hated wickedness that hinders loving,
Dante standing, studying his angel,—
45   In there broke the folk of his Inferno.
Says he—"Certain people of importance"
(Such he gave his daily, dreadful line to)
Entered and would seize, forsooth, the poet.
Says the poet—"Then I stopped my painting."

---

the hair at the nape of his neck, and said: 'You had better name yourself, or you won't have a single hair left here']. The action of placing a 'stigma' in the brow of the guilty person recalls *Genesis* iv 15 where God 'set[s] a mark upon Cain'.

35. (Peradventure] Peradventure (*MS, H proof*). See also l. 41.

41. Florence)—] Florence—(*MS, H proof*).

42–3. The concept of righteous hatred has biblical authority: cp., e.g., *Psalms* cxxxix 22: 'Do not I hate them, O Lord, that hate thee? . . . I hate them with perfect hatred'; the link with love is made in *Psalms* xcvii 10 ('Ye that love the Lord, hate evil') and *Amos* v 15 ('Hate the evil, and love the good'). In turn B. repeats this sentiment many times in his work, e.g. *Fifine at the Fair* (1872) 1513–14: 'Life means—learning to abhor / The false, and love the true' and *La Saisiaz* (1877) 285: 'life's lesson, hate of evil, love of good'.

42. Dante, who loved well] Dante then, who loved (*MS*); Dante, then, who loved (*H proof; H proof²* does not rec. a comma after 'then').

44. standing, studying] stood and studied thus (*MS first reading*).

46. "Certain people of importance": B.'s translation of 'uomini a li quali si convenia di fare onore'. *"Certain people]* "certain people (*MS first reading*); see headnote, *Sources*.

48. seize, forsooth,] see, forsooth, (*MS first reading*, corr. to 'sieze'); seize forsooth, (*1865²*). *the poet.]* the poet: (*MS*).

49.] no quotation marks in *MS*. The words in quotation marks are not in fact a translation of the relevant passage in *Vita Nuova*; on B.'s transformation of this passage, see headnote, *Sources*.

49^50.] there was originally no line space in *MS*. B. drew a line across the page between the two lines and wrote 'N.P.6' in the left margin; either he decided to do this in copying ll. 50–2, since the section number, '7' (at ll. 52^53) is perfectly clear, or it represents a slip in copying from the rough draft. See also below, ll. 95^96 and 156^157.

6

50 You and I would rather see that angel,
   Painted by the tenderness of Dante,
   Would we not?—than read a fresh Inferno.

7

   You and I will never see that picture.
   While he mused on love and Beatrice,
55 While he softened o'er his outlined angel,
   In they broke, those "people of importance:"
   We and Bice bear the loss forever.

8

   What of Rafael's sonnets, Dante's picture?

9

   This: no artist lives and loves that longs not
60 Once, and only once, and for One only,
   (Ah, the prize!) to find his love a language
   Fit and fair and simple and sufficient—
   Using nature that's an art to others,
   Not, this one time, art that's turned his nature.
65 Ay, of all the artists living, loving,
   None but would forego his proper dowry—
   Does he paint? he fain would write a poem,—
   Does he write? he fain would paint a picture,

53. *that picture*] the picture (*MS first reading*).
54. *love and Beatrice*] heaven and on Bice (*MS first reading*).
57. *Bice*: 'Bee-chay'; diminutive of Beatrice; cp. *Beatrice Signorini* (*Asolando*, 1889) 145 ff., where the same contraction is used.
58–64. See headnote for the idea of the artist turning to a different medium to express himself more intimately and personally than usual.
58–9.] In *1863–88* line 58 does not form a separate section; line 59 is the second line of section VIII, with no line space between them, and from this point on the section numbers in *1863–88* are one behind those of *1855*. (In *1865²*, which has no section numbers, there is no line space and line 58 begins a new verse paragraph.)
60. *for One only*] but once only (*MS*); for one only (*1868–88*); see also l. 70.
64. *Not, this one time, art*] Not, this time, an art (*MS*).
65. *Ay, of all*] Out of all (*MS*).
66. *proper dowry,—*] proper dowry, (*MS*), i.e. his own gift or endowment (for one particular art).
67. *Does he*]—Does he (*MS*). *a poem,—*] a poem, (*MS*).
68. *Does he*]—Does he (*MS*).

Put to proof art alien to the artist's,
70   Once, and only once, and for One only,
So to be the man and leave the artist,
Save the man's joy, miss the artist's sorrow.

                    10

Wherefore? Heaven's gift takes earth's abatement!
He who smites the rock and spreads the water,
75   Bidding drink and live a crowd beneath him,
Even he, the minute makes immortal,
Proves, perchance, his mortal in the minute,
Desecrates, belike, the deed in doing.
While he smites, how can he but remember,
80   So he smote before, in such a peril,
When they stood and mocked—"Shall smiting help us?"

70. for One only] for one only (*MS, 1868–88*).

72. Save] Gain (*1863–88*).

73–108.] not *1865²*. The poet attempts to explain why he (like Raphael and Dante) would prefer to use an 'alien' art form to address his beloved. He uses an extended comparison between the artist and Moses; cp. *Sordello* iii 800–4 and notes (I 580–2). The biblical allusion is to *Exodus* xvii, in which Moses is 'chided' by the people for having led them into the desert, whereupon God says to him: 'Behold, I will stand before thee there upon the rock in Horeb; and thou shalt smite the rock, and there shall come water out of it, that the people may drink' (v. 6). Cp. *Aurora Leigh* ii 168–72, where Romney Leigh identifies Moses not with the artist (who merely celebrates great deeds) but with the doer of those deeds: 'Who has time . . . to sit upon a bank / And hear the cymbal tinkle in white hands? / When Egypt's slain, I say, let Miriam sing!— / Before—where's Moses?' It is impossible to know whether or not this was written before *One Word More*. B.'s identification of the poet with Moses is anticipated in Hazlitt's discussion of Wordsworth in *The Spirit of the Age* (1825): 'He gathers manna in the wilderness; he strikes the barren rock for the gushing moisture' (*Collected Works*, ed. A. R. Waller and A. Glover [1902] iv 272).

73.] Ah,—for heaven's gift takes earth's abatement. (*MS*). 'Heaven's gift is limited or reduced in value by earthly conditions'; cp. the last line of *Pictor Ignotus* (p. 231): 'Tastes sweet the water with such specks of earth?'

75. beneath him,] beneath him (*MS*).

76. Even he]—Even he (*MS*).   *he, the minute*: 'he, whom the minute'.

77. Proves, perchance, his mortal] Brings, perchance, his mortal (*MS*); Proves, perchance, but mortal (*1865–88*). This is the only verbal revision to originate in *1865*. The phrase 'his mortal' means 'his state of being mortal, his mortality'.

78. belike: 'in all likelihood' (becoming archaic in the period; cp. the use of 'like' in l. 94).

79. but remember,] but remember (*MS*).

80. So he smote] So I smote (*MS first reading*). See also l. 84.

81–2.] single quotation marks in *MS*.

When they drank and sneered—"A stroke is easy!"
When they wiped their mouths and went their journey,
Throwing him for thanks—"But drought was pleasant."
85   Thus old memories mar the actual triumph;
Thus the doing savours of disrelish;
Thus achievement lacks a gracious somewhat;
O'er importuned brows becloud the mandate,
Carelessness or consciousness, the gesture.
90   For he bears an ancient wrong about him,
Sees and knows again those phalanxed faces,
Hears, yet one time more, the 'customed prelude—
"How should'st thou, of all men, smite, and save us?"
Guesses what is like to prove the sequel—
95   "Egypt's flesh-pots—nay, the drought was better."

82. *When they drank*] Then they drank (*MS first reading*).   *and sneered*] and smiled (*MS*).

83. *When they wiped*] Last they wiped (*MS*).

84.] single quotation marks in *MS*.   *Throwing him*] Throwing me (*MS first reading*).

85. *Thus old memories*] So past memories (*MS first reading*).

86. *Thus the doing*] So the doing (*MS first reading*).   *disrelish;*] disrelish, (*MS*). Cp. Milton's description of the punishment of the rebel angels after the Fall, as fruit turns to ashes in their mouths: 'With hatefulest disrelish writhed their jaws / With soot and cinders filled' (*PL* x 569–70).

87. *Thus achievement*] So achievement (*MS first reading*).

88. The prophet, beset by anxiety, struggles to discern his own divine mission; presumably the 'importuning' comes from the prophet's followers, otherwise the implication would be that God was 'beclouding' his own 'mandate'.   *importuned*: three syllables, with the stress falling on the second.

89. *consciousness*: self-consciousness, embarrassment.   *the gesture.*] the gesture—(*MS*); the dash goes with the deleted line which follows in *MS*.

89^90.] Make precipitate or mar retarding, (*MS first reading*). See also ll. 192^193.

90. *an ancient wrong*] an ancient grudge (*MS*), i.e. his awareness of the people's former ingratitude.

91. *phalanxed faces*] faces phalanxed (*MS first reading*), in the sense of a compact group of people, resembling the 'phalanx' of ancient military organization: *OED* cites Byron, *Childe Harold* I lxxx: 'Though now one phalanxed host should meet the foe'. B. uses 'phalanx' in *Sordello* iv 197 (I 604), *Ring* ix 389, and *Echetlos* (*DI²*, 1880) 16.

92.] Hears yet one time more the customed prelude—(*MS*); ''customed' is a contraction of 'accustomed'.

93. *should'st thou*] shouldst thou (*MS, 1863–88*).   *smite,*] smite (*MS*).

94. *like*: likely.

95. The ungrateful people are so unwilling to acknowledge their benefactor that they claim to have preferred slavery ('Egypt's flesh-pots') and drought: cp. *Exodus* xvi 3: 'Would to God we had died by the hand of the Lord in the land of Egypt, when we sat by the flesh pots, and when we did eat bread to the full; for ye

11

Oh, the crowd must have emphatic warrant!
Theirs, the Sinai-forehead's cloven brilliance,
Right-arm's rod-sweep, tongue's imperial fiat.
Never dares the man put off the prophet.

12

100   Did he love one face from out the thousands,
       (Were she Jethro's daughter, white and wifely,

---

have brought us forth into this wilderness, to kill this whole assembly with hunger.'
95^96.] there was originally no line space in *MS*. B. drew a line across the page
between the two lines and wrote 'N.P.11' in the left margin. As with the previous instance at ll. 49^50, B. may have made the decision to introduce a new
section here while copying the following lines, since the next section number,
'12' (at ll. 99^100) is clearly written, or it may represent a slip in copying from
the rough draft. See also ll. 156^157.
97. *Sinai-forehead's*] prophet-forehead's (*MS first reading*). This change was probably made after the insertion of line 99 (see below). W. H. French suggests that
the phrase 'Sinai-forehead's cloven brilliance' may recall the Vulgate's use of the
word 'cornuta' ('horned') to describe Moses' face in *Exodus* xxxiv 29, mistrans-
lating the Hebrew for 'shone': see *MLN* lvi (March 1946) 188, and note B.'s
translation of a sonnet by Giovanni Zappi, *Moses of Michael Angelo* (III 150).
98.] Right arm's rod-sweep and tongue's regal fiat. (*MS*; the full stop was corrected to a dash after the insertion of line 99). The 'right-arm's rod-sweep' refers
to the smiting of the rock; the 'tongue's imperial fiat' refers to Moses' status as
lawgiver and transmitter of God's commandments. A 'fiat' (noun) is a formal command, derived from the imperative form of the Latin irregular verb 'esse' (to be),
as in *Genesis* i 3, 'fiat lux', 'let there be light'. The noun 'fiat' does not appear
in the Latin translation of the Bible (the 'Vulgate') and would remind most educated Victorian readers of ancient Rome rather than the Bible; this association
would have been strengthened by the revision of 'regal' to 'imperial'. But 'regal'
was an awkward choice for a different reason, namely that the Israelites had no
kings until Saul, long after Moses, and to God's express displeasure.
99.] this line is written in a smaller hand and cramped at the bottom of the page
in *MS*, suggesting that it was added late, triggering the revision in l. 97 above.
The sense is: 'A man must claim supernatural powers in order to get his message
across to the crowd.' In B.'s play *Return of the Druses* (1843), the hero Djabal
colludes in his followers' belief that he is a divine figure; but his assumption
that the people must have such an 'emphatic warrant' is undercut by the play's
outcome, in which his pretence is exposed and he himself is killed.
100–8. If the artist were in love, he would prefer to be a 'dumb patient camel'
sacrificing its own meagre stock of water and its own life to save its mistress than
the benefactor who brings plentiful supplies of water to an ungrateful humanity.
100. *Did he love*: conditional: 'if he loved'.
101–2. *(Were she . . . bondslave,)*] no brackets in *MS*.
101. *Jethro's daughter*: Moses' wife Zipporah; *Exodus* ii 16, 21.

Were she but the Æthiopian bondslave,)
He would envy yon dumb patient camel,
Keeping a reserve of scanty water
105 Meant to save his own life in the desert;
Ready in the desert to deliver
(Kneeling down to let his breast be opened)
Hoard and life together for his mistress.

13

I shall never, in the years remaining,
110 Paint you pictures, no, nor carve you statues,
Make you music that should all-express me;
So it seems: I stand on my attainment.
This of verse alone, one life allows me;
Verse and nothing else have I to give you.
115 Other heights in other lives, God willing—
All the gifts from all the heights, your own, Love!

14

Yet a semblance of resource avails us—
Shade so finely touched, love's sense must seize it.

---

102. Aethiopian bondslave: Moses' 'Ethiopian' wife; see *Numbers* xii 1. Cp. also Brabantio's comment on Othello's elopement with Desdemona in *Othello* I ii 98–9: 'For if such actions may have passage free, / Bond-slaves and pagans shall our statesmen be'.

103. He would envy] Why, he'd envy (*MS*). The words 'He would' are in italic in *H proof*, a misprint probably resulting from the printer misunderstanding B.'s indication of this revision. *patient camel,*] patient camel (*MS*).

104. Keeping a reserve] Dowered with his reserve (*MS first reading*); Gifted a reserve (*MS second reading*). *scanty water*] scanty drinking (*MS first reading*).

105. the desert;] the desert, (*MS*).

106.] Ready in the desert—might he yield it—(*MS first reading*); Ready in the desert to be yielded, (*MS*).

107.] the parentheses were an afterthought in *MS*, replacing a dash at the end of the line.

108. for his mistress] to his mistress (*MS first reading*).

111. all-express me;] all-express me. (*MS*).

112. my attainment.] my attainment: (*MS*).

113. verse alone,] the desert (*MS*).

114. give you.] give you, (*MS*); give you; (*H proof*).

115. God willing—] God willing: (*1865–88*).

116. your own, Love!] your own, love! (*1868–75*); see ll. 3, 187.

117–18. The sense is that although B. cannot work in another medium, his modification of his own medium is his only 'resource'; and this modification is so subtle that it requires 'love's sense' to apprehend it.

Take these lines, look lovingly and nearly,
120 Lines I write the first time and the last time.
He who works in fresco, steals a hair-brush.
Curbs the liberal hand, subservient proudly,
Cramps his spirit, crowds its all in little,
Makes a strange art of an art familiar,
125 Fills his lady's missal-marge with flowerets.
He who blows thro' bronze, may breathe thro' silver,
Fitly serenade a slumbrous princess.
He who writes, may write for once as I do.

15

Love, you saw me gather men and women,
130 Live or dead or fashioned by my fancy,
Enter each and all, and use their service,

119. Take these lines] Take this verse (*MS*).

120. Lines I write] Verse I write (*MS*).

121–5. This poem is the equivalent of a fresco artist used to working on a large scale using a 'hair-brush' to produce tiny elegant drawings for his mistress.

121. a hair-brush] a paint-brush (*MS first reading*); an oil-brush (*MS*).

122. the liberal hand] the callous hand (*MS first reading*).

125. missal-marge: an irreverent gloss is supplied by Byron, *Don Juan* I xlvi: 'The Missal too (it was the family Missal) / Was ornamented in a sort of way / Which ancient mass-books often are, and this all / Kinds of grotesques illumined; and how they, / Who saw those figures on the margins kiss all, / Could turn their optics to the text and pray / Is more than I know . . .' Cp. also the young Lippo drawing faces 'within the antiphonary's marge' (*Fra Lippo* 130, p. 492).

126. Contrasting the music of brass instruments, e.g. trumpets, traditionally associated with public or ceremonial occasions with the intimacy of silver, i.e. woodwind instruments, and esp. the flute, often manufactured from silver. Cp. the late poem *Flute-Music, with an Accompaniment* (*Asolando*, 1889), a dialogue which begins with one speaker's assumption that the music comes from 'some heart which purely / Secretes globuled passion' (ll. 7–8).

127. A more positive image than in *Serenade at the Villa* (III 487); and the fairy-tale 'slumbrous princess' contrasts with the 'novice-queen' who is entertained by the poet in the guise of an 'archimage' in *Sordello* iii 580–91 (I 562–4).

128. for once as I do] emended in agreement with *MS* and *1865–88* from 'for once, as I do' in *1855* and *1863*; in *MS* the comma was originally present, then del.; its reappearance in proof may be a misprint.

128^129.] in *1865²* line 128 ends a page, and since there are no section numbers the division between verse paragraphs is not evident.

130. I.e. real people, either living or dead; or imaginary ones. Examples of the former would include Bishop Blougram (modelled on Cardinal Wiseman) and historical figures such as Andrea del Sarto or Fra Lippo Lippi; examples of the latter would include Karshish, Cleon and Childe Roland.

131. use their service] claim their service (*MS first reading*).

Speak from every mouth,—the speech, a poem.
Hardly shall I tell my joys and sorrows,
Hopes and fears, belief and disbelieving:
135 I am mine and yours—the rest be all men's,
Karshook, Cleon, Norbert and the fifty.
Let me speak this once in my true person,
Not as Lippo, Roland or Andrea,
Though the fruit of speech be just this sentence—
140 Pray you, look on these my men and women,
Take and keep my fifty poems finished;
Where my heart lies, let my brain lie also!
Poor the speech; be how I speak, for all things.

16

Not but that you know me! Lo, the moon's self!
145 Here in London, yonder late in Florence,
Still we find her face, the thrice-transfigured.
Curving on a sky imbrued with colour,

---

135. all men's,] all men's. (*1865²*; the reason for this change is the deletion of the next line).

136.] not *1865²*. *Karshook*] Karshish (*1870–88*). We have not emended *1855* because, although 'Karshook' is clearly an error for 'Karshish', it is an authorial mistake rather than a misprint; for B.'s comment on the mistake when it was pointed out to him by F. J. Furnivall, see headnote to *Ben Karshook* (III 659). Karshish is the 'author' of *An Epistle* (p. 507); Cleon the 'author' of the eponymous poem (p. 563); Norbert is one of the characters in *In a Balcony* (III 401). These figures, together with those in l. 138, form a group of the most substantial poems in *M & W*.

138.] not *1865²*.

139–40. this sentence— / Pray you,] this sentence / —Pray you, (*MS*). 'Sentence' here means 'a pithy or pointed saying' (*OED*); consciously ironic, since the speaker is simply repeating his own plain words from the start of the poem.

140–1.] Pray you, take and keep my men and women, (*1865²*).

142. my heart lies] my heart is (*MS, H proof*).

143. 'Let the fact that I am addressing you in my own person compensate for the deficiencies of my art.'

143^144.] in *1865²* line 143 ends a page, and since there are no section numbers the division between verse paragraphs is not evident.

145. The Brownings left Florence in June 1855, and arrived in London on 12 July. They spent most of the following year in Paris, only returning to Florence in late 1856. *Florence,*] Florence—(*MS*).

146. thrice-transfigured: a reference to the three states of the moon: new, full and old.

147. imbrued: soaked or drenched. *with colour,*] with colours (*MS, H proof*).

Drifted over Fiesole by twilight,
Came she, our new crescent of a hair's-breadth.
150 Full she flared it, lamping Samminiato,
Rounder 'twixt the cypresses and rounder,
Perfect till the nightingales applauded.
Now, a piece of her old self, impoverished,
Hard to greet, she traverses the houseroofs,
155 Hurries with unhandsome thrift of silver,
Goes dispiritedly,—glad to finish.

17
What, there's nothing in the moon note-worthy?
Nay—for if that moon could love a mortal,
Use, to charm him (so to fit a fancy)
160 All her magic ('tis the old sweet mythos)

148. Drifted over] Drifted us o'er (*MS first reading*).   *Fiesole*: A hilltop village to the north of Florence, situated in mountains said to resemble a crescent moon; see *Andrea* 15n. (p. 391).
150. she flared it: the construction is akin to 'flaunted it'; B.'s use of the word 'flare' is almost always pejorative, even sinister: cp. *Fra Lippo* 172 (p. 495), *Bishop Blougram* 573 (p. 316), *Heretic's Tragedy* 88 (III 226), and *Respectability* 23 (p. 347, noting 'lampions'). *lamping*: illuminating. *Samminiato*: the hilltop church of San Miniato al Monte, just outside the city wall of Florence; the moon which is 'over' Fiesole is seen as illuminating this church to the south of the city.
151. Rounder 'twixt the cypresses] Round a-top the cypress-walk (*MS first reading*); Rounded 'twixt the cypresses (*MS*).
156.] All dispirited and glad to finish. (*MS*).
156^157.] there was originally no line space in *MS*. B. drew a line across the page between the two lines and wrote 'N.P.17' in the left margin. It is difficult to tell when he decided to make this change, because the next section number, at ll. 179^180, is wrongly written '16', i.e. repeating the number at ll. 143^144, and the section number after that, at ll. 186^187, is written '17'. We suggest that B. made the change here instantaneously but that, in copying from his draft, he forgot to alter the subsequent section numbers, which would in any case have been one behind the correct order because of the added section number at ll. 95^96.
158–65. The 'old sweet mythos' (myth) is the story of Diana (the moon) and Endymion, the young shepherd with whom she falls in love; B.'s mention of Keats suggests that he is thinking of *Endymion* (1818), esp. since the word 'sweet' is a crucial Keatsian word. B.'s variation on the myth is to imagine that the goddess's gift to her beloved would be a sight no other mortal could have, namely the side of the moon invisible from earth.
159. Use, to charm him] Have to grace him (*MS first reading*); Use to charm him (*MS*).
160. All her magic] All her pleasure (*MS first reading*).

She would turn a new side to her mortal,
Side unseen of herdsman, huntsman, steersman—
Blank to Zoroaster on his terrace,
Blind to Galileo on his turret,
165 Dumb to Homer, dumb to Keats—him, even!
Think, the wonder of the moonstruck mortal—
When she turns round, comes again in heaven,
Opens out anew for worse or better?
Proves she like some portent of an ice-berg
170 Swimming full upon the ship it founders,
Hungry with huge teeth of splintered chrystals?
Proves she as the paved-work of a sapphire
Seen by Moses when he climbed the mountain?

162. herdsman, huntsman, steersman: people who routinely work by moonlight or use the moon to calculate their position. *herdsman, hunstman*] shepherd, huntsman (*MS first reading*).

163. Zoroaster: the founder (589–513 BC) of the Persian religion of Zoroastrianism, associated with astronomical observation; cp. one of the lines added to *Paracelsus* in *Poems* (1849): 'Oh Persic Zoroaster, lord of stars!' (v 174–5n., I 280).

164. Galileo: Galileo Galilei (1564–1642), astronomer, inventor of the telescope, and native of Tuscany (born in Pisa); he is associated with observation of the moon, and with the landscape around Florence, in *PL* i 287–91, where Satan's shield is compared to 'the moon, whose orb / Through optic glass the Tuscan artist views / At evening from the top of Fesole, / Or in Valdarno, to descry new lands, / Rivers or mountains in her spotty globe'. Cp. also EBB.'s *Casa Guidi Windows* i 1178–82, which alludes to the sights she and B. have seen at 'Tuscan Bellosguardo . . . standing on the actual blessed sward / Where Galileo stood at nights to take / The vision of the stars'.

165. A 'Hymn to the Moon', believed to be by Homer at the time, was translated by Shelley; for Keats see ll. 158–65n.

167.] What turns round and comes again in heaven, (*MS first reading*).

169.] Proves it some white portent of an ice-berg (*MS*).

170. founders: a verb, 'causes to founder'.

171. splintered chrystals] splintered crystals (*1863–88*). B. requested the singular 'chrystal' in the list of 'Errata' he sent to his American publisher James T. Fields (*B to Fields* 194), but the change was not made in any edition.

172–9. Cp. *Exodus* xxiv 9–11: 'Then went up Moses, and Aaron, Nadab, and Abihu, and seventy of the elders of Israel: And they saw the God of Israel: and there was under his feet as it were a paved work of a sapphire stone, and as it were the body of heaven in his clearness. And upon the nobles of the children of Israel he laid not his hand: also they saw God, and did eat and drink.'

172–3.] Proves she as when Moses climbed the mountain, / Saw the paved-work of a stone, a sapphire, (*MS*, which has 'it' for 'she' as a first reading). Line 173 in *MS* looks like an afterthought—it is squeezed between ll. 172 and 174.

173. the mountain?] the mountain—(*H proof*).

Moses, Aaron, Nadab and Abihu
175 Climbed and saw the very God, the Highest,
    Stand upon the paved-work of a sapphire.
    Like the bodied heaven in his clearness
    Shone the stone, the sapphire of that paved-work,
    When they ate and drank and saw God also!

                        18

180 What were seen? None knows, none ever shall know.
    Only this is sure—the sight were other,
    Not the moon's same side, born late in Florence,
    Dying now impoverished here in London.
    God be thanked, the meanest of his creatures
185 Boasts two soul-sides, one to face the world with,
    One to show a woman when he loves her.

                        19

    This I say of me, but think of you, Love!
    This to you—yourself my moon of poets!
    Ah, but that's the world's side—there's the wonder—
190 Thus they see you, praise you, think they know you.
    There, in turn I stand with them and praise you,

174. Moses]—Moses (*MS*).   *Abihu*] Abihu, (*MS*).
176. a sapphire.] a sapphire: (*MS*).
177. his clearness] his clearness—(*MS first reading*).
178.] this line was added as an afterthought in *MS*, squeezed between ll. 177 and
179.   that paved-work,] that paved work,—(*MS first reading*).
179. When] There (*MS first reading*).
180. What were seen? 'What would be seen (if we could see the dark side of the
moon)?'   *What*] Which (*MS first reading*).
182–3. Alluding to the composition in London of the final poem of a collection
'born late in Florence'. Cp. the conclusion to *Red Cotton Night-Cap Country* (1873):
'Can what Saint-Rambert flashed me in a thought, / Good gloomy London make
a poem of?' (ll. 4239–40); also *La Saisiaz* (1878) 629–30: 'So the poor smile played,
that evening: pallid smile long since extinct / Here in London's mid-November!'
186. when he loves her.] if he loves her. (*MS first reading*).
187. you, Love!] you, love! (*1868* only). See ll. 3, 116.
188–98. Reversing the negative image of the beloved as 'my everybody's moon'
in *Andrea* 29–32 (p. 392).
189.] Ah, but that's the world's side, there's the wonder, (*1863–88*).

Out of my own self, I dare to phrase it.
But the best is when I glide from out them,
Cross a step or two of dubious twilight,
195 Come out on the other side, the novel
Silent silver lights and darks undreamed of,
Where I hush and bless myself with silence.

20

Oh, their Rafael of the dear Madonnas,
Oh, their Dante of the dread Inferno,
200 Wrote one song—and in my brain I sing it,
Drew one angel—borne, see, on my bosom!

192. Out of my own self: the poet places himself in the position of the world, temporarily denying himself his more intimate knowledge of the 'hidden' side of EBB.
self, I dare to phrase it.] self—I dare to phrase it, *(MS first reading)*; self (I dare to
phrase it) *(MS)*. The full stop in *1855* is explained by the del. line in *MS* which
follows.
192^193.] Seeing—mine with all the eyes—our wonder. *(MS)*. Unlike the del.
line at ll. 89^90, this line was not removed until the poem was in proof (at an
earlier stage than that represented by *H proof*).
197. with silence] with beauty *(MS)*.
197^198.] there is no line space in *MS* and no section number '20'.
201. Drew] Made *(MS conjectural first reading)*. In *1863–88* the poem is signed
'R. B.', aligned right. In *1855* the poem is followed by 'The End', centred below
l. 201; *1863–65*: 'End of Vol. I.' *1868*: 'End of Vol. V.' *1888*: 'End of the Fourth
Volume.'

40 Caliban Upon Setebos;
or
Natural Theology in the Island

"Thou thoughtest that I was altogether such an one as thyself."

Text and Publication

First publ. *DP*, 28 May 1864; repr. *1864²*, *1865*, *1868*, *1872*, *1888*. Our text is *1864*.

The MS, part of the printer's copy for *DP*, is at *Morgan*. It is generally a clean copy, but reveals that B. had some difficulty with the initial apostrophes before Caliban's verbs: many may have been added in *MS* (at ll. 1, 25, 26, 31, 44, 98, 100, 104, 106, 112, 117, 138, 149, 171, 179, 205, 211, 225, 226, 229, 239, 240, 241), and they were subject to retention, omission or restoration through subsequent editions. On the last three pages of *MS* (l. 244 to end), B. has remembered to include apostrophes for verbs within the line but forgotten to include them at the beginning of the lines. This would suggest that the apostrophes were part of the plan from the outset, but that B. either did not originally feel they were necessary where the verb in question began the line, or forgot to include them at the beginnings of lines when drafting, and had to add them later. In 'A Note on Browning' (*MLN* xxiii [Mar. 1908] 93–4), Fred Newton Scott drew attention to these discrepancies, stating that there were only two other uses of this form by B., in *Fra Lippo* 43 (p. 487) and *Inn Album* (1875) 186; however, see also *An Epistle* 101, 205 (pp. 517, 522). In *Caliban* the rule seems to be that the first use of the verb in any sentence has the apostrophe, but subsequent ones do not (e.g. ''groans, curses' at l. 269, but note the exception at l. 192, ''Falls . . . 'piled'). In l. 257 the opening verb, 'Sees', does not have an apostrophe. This was, however, rectified in the 2nd edition and in all subsequent editions, and we have emended accordingly.

Composition and date

If we accept Richard Henry Stoddard's 'The Witch's Whelp' (publ. 1852) as a source for the poem (see below, *Sources*), then it might have its origins in the early 1850s. There is possible corroboration of this suggestion in a letter of 1 Apr. 1856 to B. from Dante Gabriel Rossetti, in which Rossetti asks: 'And now, how looks Sycorax?' On the strength of this, Doughty and Wahl conjecture that B. 'may have been contemplating a poem on Sycorax (if not one on her son) as early as 1856' (*Letters of Dante Gabriel Rossetti*, [Oxford 1965] i 297). This is possible, though unlikely; the reference and meaning of Rossetti's question are

Title] in *1888*, title and subtitle run on in the same font-size.   *Setebos*: Setebos is mentioned twice in *The Tempest* by Caliban, first as 'my dam's god, Setebos' (I ii 373), secondly in an invocation: 'O Setebos' (V i 261). No other character mentions him.

Subtitle] MS adds, 'Ps. 50'. Not *1868–75*.   *Such an one*] such a one (*1872*, *1888*).

Epigraph. Quoting *Psalms* l. 21: 'These things hast thou done, and I kept silence; thou thoughtest that I was altogether such an one as thyself: but I will reprove thee, and set them in order before thine eyes.' The 'things' comprise a prior list of iniquities.

impossible to reconstruct exactly. Some phrases used in *Caliban* are anticipated in the surviving redrafted version of *Sordello* (*Syracuse*), on which B. was working from the mid-1850s to the early 1860s: see headnote to our edition, I 354–9, and below, l. 5n., l. 46n., ll. 48–50n. These cannot be precisely dated, but they would fit with a date in the winter of 1859–60, when we know from EBB. that B. was working on a long poem (see Appendix C, p. 895). This date also fits the suggestion that the poem was a response to the publication, in 1859, of Charles Darwin's *Origin of Species*, though whether it directly engages with Darwin's ideas is debatable (see below). Even if the poem was begun in 1859–60, we do not know whether it was completed then, or whether, and to what extent, B. continued to work on it; it may have been finished by the autumn of 1862, when B. was confident that he had enough material for publication of a volume in the spring of 1863.

Sources and influences

(1) Literary

The principal source is Shakespeare's late play *The Tempest* (1611), in which Caliban appears, and refers to his 'dam' (mother, called 'Sycorax' by Shakespeare) and 'my dam's god, Setebos'; there too, Caliban is represented as a slave to Prospero and Prospero's daughter Miranda (see ll. 20–1 below).

In April 1884 F. J. Furnivall wrote to B. 'accusing [him] of not having done justice to Shakspere's Caliban & having left out all the signs of improvement that Sh. has put into Caliban'; Furnivall had raised these objections during a discussion at the Browning Society of a paper on the poem. B. replied on 25 April:

> Then, as to the divergence from Shakespeare's Caliban,—is it so decided? There is no "forgetfulness of his love for music"—since he makes a song and sings it,—nor of his "visions of Heaven," for he speculates on what goes on there,—nor of his resolve to "learn wisdom and seek grace"—seeing that he falls flat and loveth Setebos, and was a fool to gibe at a Power he had miscalculated. True, "he was a very different being at the end of the Play from what he was at its beginning"—but my Caliban indulges his fancies long before even that beginning. (*Trumpeter* 95–6 and 96n.)

B.'s responses to Furnivall's criticism are not always to be taken at face value: he would have known full well that his Caliban's 'song' (at ll. 276–8) is a far cry from the lyrical description given by Shakespeare's Caliban of the 'sounds and sweet airs' on the island (*Tempest* III ii 135–43). The final sentence appears to rule out the notion that the storm which concludes the poem is the same one that begins *The Tempest*, though B. may have been principally concerned to deflect Furnivall's attack.

It is possible that B.'s conception of Caliban was influenced by stage productions of *The Tempest*, in particular his then friend and patron William Charles Macready's celebrated one of 1838; Macready recorded in his diary giving B. dinner on 11 Nov., during the run (William Toynbee, ed., *The Diaries of William Charles Macready, 1833–1851* [London: Chapman & Hall 1912] i 475). From the Restoration to this point, *The Tempest* had normally been performed in the version of the play produced by Dryden and Davenant (1667), in which various supernumerary characters were introduced (such as a sister for Caliban, also, confusingly, called 'Sycorax', another for Miranda called 'Dorinda', and, complementarily to Miranda, a man, Hippolito, who has never seen a woman; even Ariel has an amorous entanglement), and in the midst of these dilutions Caliban's part was severely truncated. Macready restored Shakespeare's text, and with it the importance of Caliban's role; the actor playing Caliban, George Bennett, achieved a great success, and seems to have substituted a sympathetic portrayal for the traditional buffoonery of the part.

B. may also have drawn on some of the prototypes that have been identified for Shakespeare's Caliban, notably the figures of the Wild Man, Green Man or 'wodewose' in English tradition, Pulcinella or Harlequin in the *commedia dell'arte*, Polyphemus in the classical tradition, Jacobean antimasque characters and so on: see Alden T. Vaughan and Virginia Mason Vaughan, *Shakespeare's Caliban: a Cultural History* (Cambridge 1991). This book usefully traces the post-Shakespearean vicissitudes of Caliban's representation, though its discussion of B.'s poem is cursory and unsatisfactory. The authors establish that Caliban was already changing by the time the poem appeared from comic monster to human ancestor, whether of amphibian or simian type.

Alongside *The Tempest*, B. may have consulted any of the various Elizabethan and Jacobean redactions of Antonio Pigafetta's account of Magellan's circumnavigation of the globe, in which appears an account of the Patagonians, whose major god is called Setebos: 'when they dye there appere x or xii deuyls leapynge and daunsynge about the bodye of the deade and seeme to haue theyr boddyes paynted with dyuers colours. And that amonge other, there is one seene bygger then the residue, who maketh great mirth and reioysynge. This greate deuyll they caule *Setebos* . . . One of these giantes which they to[o]ke, declared by signes that he had seene deuyls with two hornes aboue theyr heades, with longe heare downe to theyr feete: And that they cast furth fyre at theyr throtes both before and behynde' (Pietro Martire d'Anghiera, *The decades of the newe worlde or west India conteynyng the nauigations and conquestes of the Spanyardes*, tr. Richard Eden [1555], p. 219, slightly modernized). The antagonism of 'Setebism' and Christianity may have been suggested by another passage from Pigafetta: 'On a tyme, as one made a crosse before him and kyssed it, shewynge it vnto hym, he suddeynely cryed **Setebos**, and declared by signes that if they made any more crosses, **Setebos** wold enter into his body and make him brust' (p. 220; Pigafetta goes on to narrate the conversion of this particular Setebist). *Berdoe* (p. 91) suggests that B., like Shakespeare, may have imported other legendary creatures from, e.g., *Purchas, his Pilgrimage* into his conception of Caliban. John Maynard suggests influence from one of B.'s favourite early books, Bernard de Mandeville's *Fable of the Bees*: '[Caliban] seems an ideal illustration of Mandeville's theory that primitive man's thinking is an outward projection of inner states of emotion, especially fear' (*Maynard* 333).

Joseph Phelan has recently suggested a possible intermediate source, the American poet R. H. Stoddard's 'The Witch's Whelp', first publ. in *Graham's Magazine* xxxix (1851) 74–5, and reprinted in Stoddard's *Poems* (1852: there is an advertisement for B.'s 1849 *Poems* at the front of this volume). The Brownings had many American friends in Florence, who could have drawn their attention to it or lent or had it sent to them. There are a number of other connections— EBB.'s friend Mary Russell Mitford knew and admired Stoddard's work, Bayard Taylor, Stoddard's best friend (and the poet whose 'Ariel in the Cloven Pine' [1849] prompted Stoddard's poem) knew and visited the Brownings, and all three (Taylor, Stoddard and B.) shared the same American publisher. For more detail on possible links between B. and Stoddard, see Joseph Phelan, 'Richard Henry Stoddard and the Brownings' (*BSN* xxxiii 58–68). The poem is, like B.'s, a blank verse dramatic monologue spoken by Caliban (it is 67 lines long); stylistically it owes more to Tennyson than to B. It is primarily concerned, like *Caliban*, with the landscape and zoology of the island, and expresses some similarly aggressive sentiments: Stoddard's Caliban squeezes adders to death and attacks 'monsters' with rocks and his spear; Sycorax is mentioned, as is also 'The Dragon of the Sea, my mother's god, / Enormous Setebos' (10–11), more specifically a sea-deity than B.'s Caliban's. A passage anticipatory of *Caliban* is the following:

> Hard by are swamps and marshes, reedy fens
> Knee-deep in water; monsters wade therein
> Thick-set with plated scales; sometimes in troops
> They crawl on slippery banks; sometimes they lash
> The sluggish waves, among themselves at war;
> Often I heave great rocks from off the crags,
> And crush their bones; often I push my spear
> Deep in their drowsy eyes, at which they howl
> And chase me inland; then I mount their humps
> And prick them back again, unwieldy, slow:
> At night the wolves are howling round the place,
> And bats sail there athwart the silver light,
> Flapping their wings; by day in hollow trees
> They hide, and slink into the gloom of dens. (ll. 45–58)

This prefigures the marsh habitat of ll. 1–23 and Caliban's vicious, capriciously playful attitude to the other denizens of the island. But Stoddard's Caliban is declaredly the reverse of speculative, as he reveals in the poem's ending:

> We live, my mother Sycorax and I,
> In caves with bloated toads and crested snakes;
> She can make charms, and philters, and brew storms,
> And call the great Sea Dragon from his deeps:
> Nothing of this know I, nor care to know;
> Give me the milk of goats in gourds or shells,
> The flesh of birds and fish, berries, and fruit,
> Nor want I more, save all day long to lie,
> And hear, as now, the voices of the sea. (ll. 59–67)

Note that the mention of Sycorax as living, with other details, indicates that the poem is set not only before the action of *The Tempest*, as B. claimed was the case for *Caliban* (see above), but before the arrival of Prospero and Miranda on the island, which takes place after Sycorax's death. 'The Witch's Whelp' was inspired by Stoddard's friend Bayard Taylor's 'Ariel in the Cloven Pine' (1849), and at ll. 32–6 Stoddard's Caliban refers to '[something] imprisoned' in the 'wrinkled bark' of a pine tree.

Although B. does not seem to have acknowledged any indebtedness to Stoddard, the American poet recognized the similarities between the two poems, referring late in his life to 'The Witch's Whelp' as an attempt at 'a magnificent subject, to which Browning did full justice a few years later in his "Caliban upon Setebos"' (from Stoddard's 'Prologue' to Bayard Taylor's *The Echo Club* [New York and London 1895], p. xi).

(2) *Religion and science*
(i) *'Natural theology' and metaphysics*
The best-known exponent of the 'natural theology' referred to in the subtitle before B.'s time, and still of current relevance in it, was William Paley, a famous

eighteenth-century philosopher-theologian (his works were set books in Oxford and Cambridge). Natural theology was an attempt to derive an account of the existence and character of God from observation of the natural order alone, without recourse to dogma or revelation, as the full title of Paley's best-known and most influential work indicates: *Natural Theology; or, Evidences of the Existence and Attributes of the Deity, Collected from the Appearances of Nature* (1802). The essential argument of this work is contained in the following passage: 'Contrivance proves design: and the predominant tendency of the contrivance indicates the disposition of the designer. The world abounds with contrivances: and all the contrivances which we are acquainted with, are directed to beneficial purposes. Evil, no doubt, exists; but is never, that we can perceive, the object of contrivance. Teeth are contrived to eat, not to ache; their aching now and then is incidental to the contrivance, perhaps inseparable from it; or even, if you will, let it be called, a defect in the contrivance: but it is not the object of it' (1857 edn, p. 258). In other words, the visible world establishes and represents not just the existence but also the goodness of God. Stuart Peterfreund ('Robert Browning's Decoding of Natural Theology in "Caliban upon Setebos"', *VP* xliii, no. 3 [2005] 317–31) disputes the contention that the poem refers directly to Paley's *Natural Theology*, pointing out that the phrase dates back to Raymond of Sebunda's fifteenth-century treatise *Theologia Naturalis*, transl. by Montaigne as *Théologie Naturelle* (1569); he also discounts Paley's influence in favour of that of Robert Chambers's *Vestiges of the Natural History of Creation* (1844) and its sequel, *Explanations* (1846). He draws attention to the fact that EBB. read (and disliked) Chambers's book at the same period as she began corresponding with B. However, there is no evidence that she and B. discussed the *Vestiges*, and there is in fact no evidence that B. himself read Chambers at all; by contrast B.'s library contained two works of Paley's, *Horae Paulinae. Clergyman's Companion* (*Collections*, p. 153; A1794) and *A View of the Evidences of Christianity* (ibid., A1795). Peterfreund cites a number of passages from Darwin's *Voyage of the Beagle* and *Origin of Species* as possible sources for the zoology of *Caliban*: see below, section (iv).

In the course of his monologue Caliban rehearses, first, the 'argument from design', that is, the claim that the perceived harmony of the natural order mirrors the qualities of its maker, and, second, a related position, the deduction of God from the sublime, that is, the claim that tremendous and terrible natural phenomena such as thunder, earthquake, whirlwind, fire, etc., reflect and express the overwhelming power of God. The idea that the divine presence is manifest through thunder and other manifestations is common in the Old Testament (see ll. 287–9n., 289–91n.); the association of this concept with that of the Sublime emerged strongly in the eighteenth century: 'The *Sublime* dilates and elevates the Soul, *Fear* sinks and contracts it; yet *both* are felt upon viewing what is great and awful. And we cannot conceive a *Deity* armed with *Thunder* without being struck with a sublime *Terror*; but if we regard him as the infinite *Source of Happiness*, the benign *Dispenser of Benefits*, it is not then the *dreadful*, but the *joyous Sublime* we feel' (John Baillie, *An Essay on the Sublime* [1747], p. 32). But Ruskin for one rejects this argument in terms which may have influenced B., especially for the ending of the poem: 'fear, mortal and extreme, may be felt respecting things ignoble, as the falling from a window, and without any conception of terribleness or majesty in the thing, or the accident dreaded; and even when fear is felt respecting things sublime, as thunder, or storm of battle, the tendency of it is to destroy all power of contemplation of their majesty, and to freeze and contract all the intellect into a shaking heap of clay; for absolute acute fear is of the same unworthiness and contempt from whatever source it arise, and degrades the mind and the outward bearing of the body alike, even though it be among hail of heaven and fire running along the ground' (Ruskin, *Modern Painters* ii, *Works*, ed. E. T. Cook and Alexander Wedderburn [1903–1912] iv 199).

Caliban's theology posits (at least) two metaphysical beings, Setebos himself and 'the Quiet'. Of these, Setebos is the lesser, and corresponds to the Platonic notion of the 'demiurge', or even the Gnostic/Manichaean concept of Satan as an inferior deity responsible for the creation of (corrupt) matter, as against God as creator of the non-sensory (including the human soul), who corresponds to Caliban's 'Quiet'. As Cooke suggests, this cosmology reflects ancient Greek specu-ation. A further link to Plato is suggested by Setebos as an imitative creator, producing a 'bauble-world to ape yon real' (l. 147): this evokes Plato's idealist notion of the 'Forms', the abstract entities which are real because immortal and absolute, in contrast to material beings which are mortal and contingent. The theory of the 'Forms' also underpins Plato's critique of art as doubly 'unreal', since it is the imitation of an imitation.

For B.'s comment on Caliban's metaphysics in relation to his own in *La Saisiaz* (1878), see below, *Parallels*.

(ii) *Darwin and evolution*

B. read *Origin of Species* soon after it appeared in 1859, and seems to have known Darwin's earlier *Journal of Researches into the Geology and Natural History of the vari-ous countries visited by H.M.S. Beagle* (popularly known as *The Voyage of the Beagle*), probably in the second edition of 1844; both of these may have influenced *Caliban*, as Peterfreund suggests (see above, section i); and like Darwin Caliban is a minutely attentive observer of the natural world, who reasons from his observations to gen-eral conclusions. But the status of the poem as a response to Darwin's central idea of 'natural selection' as the engine of evolution is more problematic. Judging from the letter he wrote to F. J. Furnivall on 11 Oct. 1881, B. seems not to have grasped the fundamental principle of natural selection, believing it to be analo-gous to his own ideas about a graduated scale of creation:

> In reality, all that seems *proved* in Darwin's scheme was a conception familiar to me from the beginning: see in *Paracelsus* the progressive development from senseless matter to organized, until man's appearance (*Part* v). Also in *Cleon*, see the order of 'life's mechanics,'—and I daresay in many passages of my poetry: for how can one look at Nature as a whole and doubt that, wherever there is a gap, a 'link' must be 'missing'—through the limited power and opportunity of the looker? (*Trumpeter* 34)

For the allusion to *Paracelsus* see v 638–70 (I 298–9); for *Cleon* see ll. 199–214 (p. 578). For a further citation from this letter, see *Mr Sludge* 891–6n. (p. 822). The poem does not, in fact, address the issue of evolution, and neither supports nor denies the transmutation of species—unlike St John in *A Death in the Desert* (see ll. 580–9n., p. 753). In '"He Hourly Humanises": Transformations and Appropriations of Shakespeare's Caliban' (*Sederi* vii [1996] 269–72) Sofia Muñoz Valdivieso claims that B.'s is a 'Darwinian Caliban' who reflects the view that human beings 'developed from some type of aquatic creature' (p. 295). But the dates do not fit: B.'s composition of the poem took place at most four or five years after the publication of *Origin of Species*, and before *The Descent of Man* (1872), the work in which Darwin made plain his views that mankind had evolved from lower organisms. There is no direct evidence in the poem to support the theory that Caliban is meant to represent a 'missing link' in the evolution of the human species, as opposed to a primitive stage in the evolution of human ideas about God, though the poem's subtitle may allude to the controversy about the common origins of the human race which developed in the immediate aftermath of the publication of *Origin of Species*. In 1863 the Anthropological Society of London was established by dissident members of the Ethnological Society who could no longer accept the older body's liberal and humanitarian insistence on the common humanity of all people, and who instead argued for a 'polygenist' view of multiple human origins. B.'s subtitle raises the question of whether or not all human beings are (in the words of the Aborigines' Protection Society's motto) 'ab uno sanguine' [from one blood].

Many if not all of the creatures Caliban observes, whether actually or for the purposes of comparison, are mentioned by Darwin, either in *Voyage of the Beagle* or *Origin of Species*, among them ants, auks, crabs, dung-beetles, finches, moles, otters, quails, sloths, squirrels and tortoises (see, e.g., ll. 100–11n., 206–7n.). This (incomplete) list in itself suggests that Caliban's island does not correspond to any identifiable geographical location: its flora and fauna come from diverse and incompatible habitats, some Northern, some tropical, some South American. (This miscellany is also Shakespearean: *The Tempest* has wolves, bears, urchins, ravens, toads, beetles, bats, apes, adders, crabs, jays, marmosets . . .). Similarly, the time of the poem has no historical markers: B. avoids Shakespearean pastiche and Caliban refers to no human artefacts that would denote a particular period. In one sense this allows B. to treat the island as a microcosm of the world, so that Caliban's speculations on the nature of God are not limited by particular conditions; but in another sense the fact of it being an *island* makes it an experimental space, with its own peculiar features. B. might have been influenced here by Darwin's observations on the particular characteristics of species on the different islands in the Galapagos archipelago, one of the building blocks of the theory of evolution.

The tone of some of Darwin's observations, linked to his own behaviour as a naturalist, may also have influenced B.'s representation of both Caliban and Caliban's idea of Setebos. Cp., e.g., this passage from *The Voyage of the Beagle* (ch. ix): 'One day I observed a cormorant playing with a fish which it had caught. Eight times successively the bird let its prey go, then dived after it, and although in deep water, brought it each time to the surface. In the Zoological Gardens I have seen the otter treat a fish in the same manner, much as a cat does a mouse: I do not know of any other instance where dame Nature appears so wilfully cruel.'

(iii) *Theories of language*

Caliban's practice of deleting the personal pronoun and substituting the third-person form of the verb (''Will sprawl', ''Thinketh', and so on) has been seen as an expression of awakening, but as yet incomplete, apperception (self-consciousness), commonly regarded, in the nineteenth century, as a precondition for language itself: 'No animal thinks, and no animal speaks, except man. Language and thought are inseparable. Words without thought are dead sounds; thoughts without words are nothing' (Friedrich Max Müller, *Lectures on the Science of Language* [1861] p. 427: note that the date makes it possible that B. could have known this text when writing *Caliban*). Orr puts it that 'he speaks, as children do, in the third person' (*Handbook*, p. 195), but the matter seems more complex, closely involved as it is with the question of whether Caliban 'talks to his own self' (l. 15) or to another. There is a striking resemblance between some aspects of the poem's language and documentary reportage of the period, such as that of Henry Mayhew of a street boy: 'Yes, he had heer'd of God, who made the world. Couldn't exactly recollec' where he had heer'd on him, but he had, most sartenly. Didn't know when the world was made or how anybody could do it. It must have taken a long time. It was afore his time, "or yourn either, sir". Knew there was a book called the Bible; didn't know what it was about; didn't mind to know . . . Had heer'd on another world; wouldn't mind if he was there hisself, if he could do better, for things was often queer here' (*London Labour and the London Poor* i [1861] 474; ll. 26–7n.). Note the deletion of the personal pronoun in the sentence initial position, and that the character's third-person self-reference is to be understood as a convention of reportage: in fact, the passage is written in a form of *style indirect libre*, as arguably *Caliban* also is. Given this similarity, it is worth noting that the first issue of the *Anthropological Review* (the journal of the Anthropological Society) also contains an article by E. Burnet Tylor entitled 'Wild Men and Beast Children' (pp. 21–32) which looks at mythological and more recent stories of children brought up away from other human beings for evidence of what 'primitive humanity' must have been like, and concludes: 'The inquirer who seeks to find out the beginnings of man's civilisation must deduce general principles by reasoning downward from the civilised European to the savage, and then descend to still lower possible levels of human existence, with such assistance as he can gain from the study of the undeveloped human mind in children' (p. 32).

A different understanding of the poem's language is put forward by E. K. Brown in 'The First Person in Caliban upon Setebos' (*MLN* lxvi [1951], 392–5). As Brown points out, Caliban does not refer to himself exclusively in the third person, but reverts on occasion to the more usual first-person form; see, e.g., ll. 68–9, 74–6, and especially Caliban's 'song' at ll. 276–8. This suggests a degree of self-consciousness about the use of these forms, which Brown relates to Caliban's fear that he will be overheard by the listening Setebos. At moments of excitement or indignation, or when he recognizes affinities between his own behaviour and that of Setebos, Caliban slips into the first person; at moments when he is acutely aware of the danger of being overheard, such as the opening and closing sections in square brackets, he uses his idiosyncratic third-person form.

Parallels in B.

In 'Browning's "Karshish" and St Paul' (*MLN* lxxii [Nov 1957] 494–6), Richard Altick specifies *Caliban* as one of 'five poems which, though there is no evidence that Browning intended them to form a sequence, in effect trace the history of man's groping progress towards a realization of the Christian God' (p. 494). Those poems are (in Altick's order): *Caliban, Saul, An Epistle, Cleon* and *A Death*. Evidence that B. did indeed intend some at least of these poems to be read as a sequence emerges from his grouping together of four of them in the concluding poems of *1872*: *Cleon, Instans Tyrannus, An Epistle, Caliban, Saul, Rabbi ben Ezra* and *Epilogue* (*DP*). In his prefatory note to this selection, B. claimed 'by simply stringing together certain pieces in the thread of an imaginary personality, I present them in succession . . . as the natural development of a particular experience'.

The letter Furnivall wrote to B. about the poem (see above, *Sources* 1 i) drew attention to the parallel with B.'s philosophical elegy, *La Saisiaz*, accusing B. of 'Calibaniz[ing]' by attempting to argue for the existence of the soul and the reality of the afterlife from the perspective of his own individual consciousness. B. replied on 25 April 1884: 'I don't see that, because a clown's conception of the laws of the Heavenly bodies is grotesque and impossible, that of Newton must be necessarily as absurd,—or that the writer of "La Saisiaz" must see through such horny eyes as those of Caliban: besides, in each case, there is a faculty of reason which should be employed in correcting and adjusting the first impressions of the senses—and, I hope, the two make a very different use of their respective faculties; one doubts and the other has no doubts at all, "—sayeth" so and so, as if Prospero could say no otherwise' (*Trumpeter* 95).

As with many other writers of the period, B.'s work engages with Shakespeare at many levels, from casual allusion to sustained engagement with Shakespearean characters, themes and dramatic situations: *Caliban* is the longest and most prominent example in a list which would run from B.'s first major work, *Pauline* (inspired by a performance of *Richard III*: see headnote, p. 2, and l. 1029n., p. 69), through plays and poems such as *Luria* (1846), whose subtitle might well have been 'The Moor of Florence', *Childe Roland* (p. 348), *Bishop Blougram's Apology* (see esp. ll. 485–554, pp. 311–16), *At the Mermaid* (*Pacchiarotto*, 1876), in which Shakespeare himself is the speaker, and the uncollected sonnet *The Names* (1884, *Penguin* ii 964). In other respects, however, *Caliban* is something of an anomaly in B.'s work. It is very unusual for B. to use another literary text as the starting point for his own imaginative creation; *Childe Roland* is an imaginative fantasy based on a single line of *King Lear* rather than (as here) an attempt to fill in some of the 'past' of one of Shakespeare's plays, and *Pan and Luna* (*Jocoseria*, 1883) similarly amplifies a brief narrative from Virgil's *Georgics*. Nor does the poem include the kind of commentary and reflection which characterizes B.'s later reworkings of Euripides in *Balaustion's Adventure* (1871) and *Aristophanes' Apology* (1875). *Caliban* is also the only poem in which B. attempts to represent mimetically a 'primitive' form of language.

Reception
Walter Bagehot's review-essay on *DP* and Tennyson's *Enoch Arden* volume has become celebrated as a seminal study of what Chesterton termed 'the serious grotesque'. Entitled 'Wordsworth, Tennyson, and Browning; or, Pure, Ornate, and Grotesque Art in English Poetry', it defines B. as 'a prolific master' of grotesque art, and comments:

> Mr. Browning has undertaken to describe what may be called *mind in difficulties* —mind set to make out the universe under the worst and harshest circumstances. He takes 'Caliban,' not perhaps exactly Shakespeare's Caliban, but an analogous and worse creature; a strong thinking power, but a nasty creature— a gross animal, uncontrolled and unelevated by any feeling of religion or duty . . . Whoever will work hard at such poems will find much mind in them: they are a sort of quarry of ideas, but who ever goes there will find these ideas in such a jagged, ugly, useless shape that he can hardly bear them. (*Literary Studies* [1911] ii 339, 341)

As such phrasing implies, Bagehot (unlike his predecessor Ruskin) has little or no sympathy with what he terms 'grotesque art', but his account has nevertheless played an important part in the evolution of its modern definitions, and may have influenced B.'s own theory of comedy: see *Aristophanes' Apology* (1875) 1352–79. B. himself had a higher opinion of *Caliban*, nominating it to represent the 'Dramatic' aspect of his art in a letter of 15 March 1885 to Edmund Gosse, who had requested 'four Poems, of moderate length, which represent their writer fairly' (*LH* 235). The poem has subsequently become one of B.'s most popular, highly regarded and widely discussed: according to Eliza Fitzgerald it was 'greatly praised by Lord Tennyson' (*Learned Lady* 11: Hallam Tennyson confirms this). Ernest Renan, whose *Vie de Jésus* B. criticized in a letter to Isa Blagden (see headnote to *A Death*, p. 721), also wrote a work on Caliban, in the form of a drama of 1878, though there is no evidence that he knew B.'s poem.

['Will sprawl, now that the heat of day is best,
Flat on his belly in the pit's much mire,
With elbows wide, fists clenched to prop his chin;
And, while he kicks both feet in the cool slush,
5   And feels about his spine small eft-things course,
Run in and out each arm, and make him laugh;
And while above his head a pompion-plant,
Coating the cave-top as a brow its eye,
Creeps down to touch and tickle hair and beard,
10 And now a flower drops with a bee inside,
And now a fruit to snap at, catch and crunch:
He looks out o'er yon sea which sunbeams cross
And recross till they weave a spider-web,
(Meshes of fire, some great fish breaks at times)
15 And talks to his own self, howe'er he please,
Touching that other, whom his dam called God.
Because to talk about Him, vexes—ha,
Could He but know! and time to vex is now,
When talk is safer than in winter-time.

1–23.] not in square brackets in *MS*. The only other example in B. of the use of square brackets to surround an introductory passage is another *DP* poem, *A Death* (see p. 725); in that poem the brackets indicate commentary on a written text, whereas here they cannot be intended by Caliban as graphic signs, and suggest, somewhat oddly, that he is 'introducing' himself as speaker. His concluding 'remarks' as the storm interrupts his speculations are also in square brackets: see ll. 284–95n.

5.] And feels small eft-things course about his spine, (*MS*). *eft-things*: cp. *Syracuse*, the text of *Sordello* on which B. drafted various revisions, some of which were implemented in *1863*, which at *Sordello* ii 302 (a page-end in the original text) inserts 'A cloud of birds, / The snake & eft' (I 481). An eft is a newt.

7. pompion-plant: not a water-lily (as in *Sordello* ii 775 [I 512]), but a pumpkin; Caliban's description of it '[coating] the cave-top as a brow its eye' (l. 8) draws attention to the fact that it is the fruit of a thin-stemmed trailing plant. Cp. l. 259.

10. a flower . . . with a bee inside: a favourite image: cp. *Porphyria* 43 (p. 73), *Christmas-Eve* 1274 (III 96), *Women and Roses* 29 (III 238), *Jochanan Hakkadosh* (*Jocoseria*, 1883) 670–5, *Gerard de Lairesse* (*Parleyings*, 1887) 127–8.

16. dam: mother (i.e. Sycorax). In *The Tempest* Prospero addresses Caliban: 'Thou poisonous slave, got by the devil himself / Upon thy wicked dam' (I ii 319–20), and later Caliban says of Prospero's magic: 'his art is of such power, / It would control my dam's god, Setebos, / And make a vassal of him' (*ibid.*, ll. 372–3).

19. In winter Setebos, whom Caliban imagines like himself, would have fewer distractions and would be likelier to overhear Caliban's subversive remarks.

20   Moreover Prosper and Miranda sleep
      In confidence he drudges at their task,
      And it is good to cheat the pair, and gibe,
      Letting the rank tongue blossom into speech.]

      Setebos, Setebos, and Setebos!
25   'Thinketh, He dwelleth i' the cold o' the moon.

      'Thinketh He made it, with the sun to match,
      But not the stars; the stars came otherwise;
      Only made clouds, winds, meteors, such as that:
      Also this isle, what lives and grows thereon,
30   And snaky sea which rounds and ends the same.

20–21. In *The Tempest*, Caliban is Prospero's slave; Prospero says to Miranda: 'he does make our fire, / Fetch in our wood, and serves in offices / That profit us' (I ii 311–13). See also ll. 150–1n.

20. Prosper: this abbreviation is used three times in *The Tempest*, twice by Caliban.

22. gibe: pronounced 'jibe' (a variant spelling): 'to utter taunts; to jeer, flout, scoff' (*OED*). Cp. *Mr. Sludge* 319–20 (p. 795) where the word is associated with 'undeveloped' spirits.

23. rank: filthy, offensive; the metaphor of the tongue blossoming links the word with its senses of 'over-luxuriant' and 'grossly rich, heavy or fertile' (*OED* 5, 11).

24. This triple invocation has biblical authority, from *Numbers* vi 24–6: 'The LORD bless thee and keep thee: The Lord make his face shine upon thee, and be gracious unto thee: The LORD lift up his countenance upon thee, and give thee peace' and *Isaiah* vi 3: 'Holy, holy, holy is the LORD of hosts'. These texts were also interpreted as anticipations of the Christian Trinity.

25. moon: in *The Tempest* Stephano, the drunken butler, tells Caliban that he has come 'Out o' th' moon, I do assure thee: I was the Man i' th' Moon when time was' (II ii 138–9); Caliban responds: 'I have seen thee in her, and I do adore thee. / My mistress show'd me thee, and thy dog, and thy bush' (ll. 140–1), and is ridiculed by Stephano's companion Trinculo for his credulity.

25^26.] no paragraph in *MS*.

26–7. Contradicting the narrative in *Genesis* i 16: 'And God made two great lights; the greater light to rule the day, and the lesser light to rule the night: he made the stars also.' An analogous opinion is found in Henry Mayhew's *London Labour and the London Poor* (1861), 'Of the uneducated state of costermongers': 'O, yes, I've heard of God; he made heaven and earth; I never heard of his making the sea; that's another thing, and you can best learn about that at Billingsgate. (He seemed to think that the sea was an appurtenance of Billingsgate.)' (p. 22). See also headnote, *Sources* 2 (iii). In *The Tempest* Prospero's fate 'doth depend upon / A most auspicious star, whose influence / If now I court not but omit, my fortunes / Will ever after droop' (I ii 181–4).

28. made] the (*MS*).

30. In Norse mythology, the ocean serpent Jörmungandr encircles Midgard (the world) and bites his own tail; the 'ouroboros', the serpent that bites its tail, is an ancient emblem of infinity.

'Thinketh, it came of being ill at ease:
He hated that He cannot change His cold,
Nor cure its ache. 'Hath spied an icy fish
That longed to 'scape the rock-stream where she lived,
35   And thaw herself within the lukewarm brine
O' the lazy sea her stream thrusts far amid,
A crystal spike 'twixt two warm walls of wave;
Only she ever sickened, found repulse
At the other kind of water, not her life,
40   (Green-dense and dim-delicious, bred o' the sun)
Flounced back from bliss she was not born to breathe,
And in her old bounds buried her despair,
Hating and loving warmth alike: so He.

'Thinketh, He made thereat the sun, this isle,
45   Trees and the fowls here, beast and creeping thing.
Yon otter, sleek-wet, black, lithe as a leech;
Yon auk, one fire-eye in a ball of foam,

33–43. Similar phenomena are noted by Darwin; see, e.g., ch. 3 of *The Voyage of the Beagle*, in which he observes 'how slowly the waters of the sea and river mixed. The latter, muddy and discoloured, from its less specific gravity, floated on the surface of the salt water. This was curiously exhibited in the wake of the vessel, where a line of blue water was seen mingling in little eddies with the adjoining fluid'. In ch. 12 of *Origin of Species*, Darwin notes that fresh-water fish might in theory move significant distances under such circumstances, 'so that we may imagine that a marine member of a fresh-water group might travel far along the shores of the sea, and subsequently become modified and adapted to the fresh waters of a distant land'. Caliban's example, in contrast, emphasizes the inability of living organisms to adapt to new environments.

36. amid] into (*MS*).

41. Flounced: physically, in the sense of 'plunge, flounder, struggle', often associated with aquatic animals (*OED* 2); with the added sense of 'flouncing off', i.e. leaving in a huff.

43^44.] Line 43 ends a page in *MS*: it is not clear that a paragraph was intended. Likewise *1868*.

45. Again, the language echoes *Genesis*: the creation of the trees in i 12, of 'fowl that may fly above the earth' in i 20, and of 'cattle, and creeping thing, and beast of the earth after his kind' in i 24; but the motive that Caliban attributes to Setebos is the opposite of that attributed to the Old Testament God, who blesses what he creates. See also l. 61n.

46. Syracuse inserts below *Sordello* ii 40 (the end of a page; see I 463): 'Sleek wet black & lithe as a leech—'.

47. auk: 'a diving bird, of the family *Alcidae*, e.g. guillemots, puffins, and razor-bills; they are mainly found in the cold northern oceans' (*OED*). B. may have been thinking of the Great Auk, a flightless species which became extinct in the 1840s: this bird had a distinctive white spot between the eye and the bill.

That floats and feeds; a certain badger brown
He hath watched hunt with that slant white-wedge eye
50   By moonlight; and the pie with the long tongue
That pricks deep into oakwarts for a worm,
And says a plain word when she finds her prize,
But will not eat the ants; the ants themselves
That build a wall of seeds and settled stalks
55   About their hole—He made all these and more,
Made all we see, and us, in spite: how else?
He could not, Himself, make a second self
To be His mate; as well have made Himself.
He would not make what He mislikes or slights,
60   An eyesore to Him, or not worth His pains:
But did, in envy, listlessness or sport,
Make what Himself would fain, in a manner, be—
Weaker in most points, stronger in a few,
Worthy, and yet mere playthings all the while,
65   Things He admires and mocks too,—that is it.
Because, so brave, so better though they be,
It nothing skills if He begin to plague.

48–50. *a certain . . . moonlight*: cp. *Syracuse*, at *Sordello* ii 954 (I 521–3): 'There was the Badger feeding with his slant white wedge eye by moonlight.'

50. *pie*: magpie: an archaism by B.'s time, from Shakespeare, 'maggot-pies' (*Macbeth* III iv 124).

51. *oakwarts*: another name for oak-gall, '[an] excrescence produced on trees, especially the oak, by the action of insects' (*OED*); cp. *Soliloquy of the Spanish Cloister* 14 (p. 201).

52. *she . . . her*] he . . . his (*MS*).

57–8. Cp. Milton, *PL* viii 403–11, where God teases Adam for asking for a companion: 'What thinkst thou then of me, and this my state . . . Who am alone / From all eternity, for none I know / Second to me or like, equal much less. / How have I then with whom to hold converse / Save with the creatures which I made, and those / To me inferior, infinite descents / Beneath what other creatures are to thee?'

61. *envy, listlessness or sport*: Wendell V. Harris (*SBC* iii.2 [1975], 95–103) contrasts Plato, *Timaeus*: 'Let us therefore state the reason why the framer of this universe of change framed it at all. He was good, and what is good has no particle of envy in it; being therefore without envy he wished all things to be as like himself as possible'. *or sport*] and sport (*MS*).

65.] He could admire and mock, too,—that is it: (*MS*).

67. *It nothing skills*: 'it doesn't help', 'it makes no difference'; cp. *Childe Roland* 64 (p. 357). This form of the phrase seems to be B.'s invention; the phrase 'it skills not' is common in Elizabethan and Jacobean literature, including Shakespeare, e.g. *Twelfth Night* V i 287–8: 'as a madman's epistles are no gospels, so it skills not much when they are deliver'd'.

Look now, I melt a gourd-fruit into mash,
Add honeycomb and pods, I have perceived,
70   Which bite like finches when they bill and kiss,—
Then, when froth rises bladdery, drink up all,
Quick, quick, till maggots scamper through my brain;
And throw me on my back i' the seeded thyme,
And wanton, wishing I were born a bird.
75   Put case, unable to be what I wish,
I yet could make a live bird out of clay:
Would not I take clay, pinch my Caliban
Able to fly?—for, there, see, he hath wings,
And great comb like the hoopoe's to admire,

68. I melt a gourd-fruit: the first of several occasions in the poem where Caliban refers to himself in the first person, rather than the third. For the possible significance of these moments, see headnote, *Sources* 2 (iii).

68–9. mash . . . pods: 'mash' is a term used in brewing for the mixture of ground malt and hot water which ferments to produce alcohol; Caliban is making a similar compound for himself out of the materials available to him.

70. Which bite] That bite (*MS*); the relative pronoun refers to the 'pods'.

71. Then] And (*MS*, which has 'Then', canc.; a rare example of *1864* reverting to a reading cancelled in *MS*).   *bladdery*: full of bubbles; not strictly speaking a correct usage, but B. repeats it in *Pan and Luna* (*Jocoseria*, 1883) 60: 'bladdery wave-worked yeast'.

72. I.e. he gets drunk. A 'maggot' in this sense is a 'whimsical, eccentric, strange, or perverse notion or idea' (*OED* 2a, citing. e.g., John Fletcher, *Women Pleased* (*c.* 1625): 'Are you not mad my Friend? . . . Have not you Maggots in your braines?' Caliban gets drunk in *The Tempest*, not on home-brew but on Stephano's 'celestial liquor' (II ii 117); see also below, ll. 276–8n.

73. And] Then (*MS*); Last, (*1872, 1888*). This is one of a number of revisions introduced in *1872*, most of them punctuation variants but some, as here, verbal: cp. l. 183n.

74. wanton: in the sense of 'to frolic unrestrainedly'; *OED* cites Charles Lamb, 'Christ's Hospital Five-and-Thirty Years Ago' (*Essays of Elia*, 1823): 'How merrily we would sally forth into the fields . . . and wanton like young dace in the streams.'

75–97. Referring to various myths of the creation of man, esp. the Greek version in which Prometheus creates humanity from clay, and to the Judaeo-Christian account of the Creation in *Genesis*. Cp. Empedocles: 'And so, at that time, when Kypris was busily producing forms, she moistened earth in water and gave it to swift fire to harden' (Simplicius, *in De Caelo* 530.5); and see also Frankenstein's creation of a human being in Mary Shelley's *Frankenstein* (1818), and B.'s echo of that in *Ring* i 742–59.

75. put case: 'put the case', 'let it be premised that . . .'; the first occurrence in B. of a phrase frequently used in subsequent works (nine examples).

79. And great] And a great (*MS*).   *the hoopoe's*: the hoopoe is an exotic bird with variegated plumage, a long curved beak and a large crest ('a great comb'), found in tropical climates but also in the north.

80   And there, a sting to do his foes offence,
      There, and I will that he begin to live,
      Fly to yon rock-top, nip me off the horns
      Of grigs high up that make the merry din,
      Saucy through their veined wings, and mind me not.
85   In which feat, if his leg snapped, brittle clay,
      And he lay stupid-like,—why, I should laugh;
      And if he, spying me, should fall to weep,
      Beseech me to be good, repair his wrong,
      Bid his poor leg smart less or grow again,—
90   Well, as the chance were, this might take or else
      Not take my fancy: I might hear his cry,
      And give the manikin three legs for his one,
      Or pluck the other off, leave him like an egg,
      And lessoned he was mine and merely clay.
95   Were this no pleasure, lying in the thyme,
      Drinking the mash, with brain become alive,
      Making and marring clay at will? So He.

      'Thinketh, such shows nor right nor wrong in Him,
      Nor kind, nor cruel: He is strong and Lord.
100   'Am strong myself compared to yonder crabs

81. live] walk (*MS*).
83. grigs] flies (*MS*). Caliban means a cricket or grasshopper, a commonly accepted term in the period; *OED* cites Tennyson, *The Brook* 54: 'High-elbow'd grigs that leap in summer grass'. Cp. also *Pippa* ii 244 (p. 139).
84. their veined] great veined (*MS*).
85. if] say (*MS*, canc.).
85–97. For parallels to this section, see *Rabbi Ben Ezra* 151–92n. (pp. 660–1).
88. repair] redress (*MS*, canc.).
91. cry] prayer (*MS*).
92. manikin] mankin (*MS, 1888*). The word can mean both a small representation or statue of a human figure, and a (living) dwarf; often used pejoratively, as in *Twelfth Night* III ii 51; cp. also Charlotte Brontë in *Villette*, ch. xiv: ' "The Colonel-Count!" I echoed. "The doll—the puppet—the manikin—the poor inferior creature!" ' *three legs*] three sound legs (*1888*). *for his one*] for one (*1868–88*).
93. the other] that one (*MS*).
94. lessoned: [having been] taught.
97. making and marring: cp. *Childe Roland* 148 (p. 362).
98–108. These lines have been seen by some commentators as a parody of the Calvinist doctrine of 'election'; see C. R. Tracy, 'Caliban upon Setebos', *SP* xxxv (1938) 489–90, and headnote to *Johannes Agricola* (p. 74).
98. such shows nor] such is nor (*MS*); this is not (*MS*, canc.).
100.] 'Am strong myself to yonder crawling crabs—(*MS*).
100–101. yonder crabs . . . the sea: Peterfreund (see headnote) cites Darwin, *Voyage of the Beagle*, ch. xx, on the cocoanut crab, *Birgos latro*: 'The Birgos is diurnal in

That march now from the mountain to the sea;
'Let twenty pass, and stone the twenty-first,
Loving not, hating not, just choosing so.
'Say, the first straggler that boasts purple spots
105 Shall join the file, one pincer twisted off;
'Say, this bruised fellow shall receive a worm,
And two worms he whose nippers end in red;
As it likes me each time, I do: so He.

Well then, 'supposeth He is good i' the main,
110 Placable if His mind and ways were guessed,
But rougher than His handiwork, be sure!
Oh, He hath made things worthier than Himself,
And envieth that, so helped, such things do more
Than He who made them! What consoles but this?
115 That they, unless through Him, do nought at all,
And must submit: what other use in things?
'Hath cut a pipe of pithless elder-joint
That, blown through, gives exact the scream o' the jay
When from her wing you twitch the feathers blue:
120 Sound this, and little birds that hate the jay
Flock within stone's throw, glad their foe is hurt:
Put case such pipe could prattle and boast forsooth
"I catch the birds, I am the crafty thing,
I make the cry my maker cannot make

its habits; but every night it is said to pay a visit to the sea, no doubt for the
purpose of moistening its branchiae.'
103. choosing so.] willing so: (*MS*).
108. As it likes me: 'as I like'.
110. Cp. *Romans* xi 33–4: 'O the depth of the riches both of the wisdom
and knowledge of God! how unsearchable are his judgments, and his ways past
finding out! For who hath known the mind of the Lord? or who hath been his
counsellor?'
111. rougher: 'Not polished; not finished by art' (*J.*).   *His handiwork*: Cp. *Psalms*
xix 1: 'The heavens declare the glory of God; and the firmament sheweth his
handywork.'
112. Oh, He hath] Oh, yes!
116. things] them (*MS*).
117. cut] made (*MS*, canc.).   *elder-joint*] elder-tree (*MS*).
118. That] Which (*MS*).
119. twitch the feathers blue: to 'twitch' is 'to pluck with a quick motion' (*J.*); cp.
Milton, *Lycidas* 192: 'Anon he rose and twitched his mantle blue'.
122. forsooth] and say (*MS*).

125   With his great round mouth; he must blow
                 through mine!"
       Would not I smash it with my foot? So He.

       But wherefore rough, why cold and ill at ease?
       Aha, that is a question! Ask, for that,
       What knows,—the something over Setebos
130   That made Him, or He, may be, found and fought,
       Worsted, drove off and did to nothing, perchance.
       There may be something quiet o'er His head,
       Out of His reach, that feels nor joy nor grief,
       Since both derive from weakness in some way.
135   I joy because the quails come; would not joy
       Could I bring quails here when I have a mind:
       This Quiet, all it hath a mind to, doth.
       'Esteemeth stars the outposts of its couch,
       But never spends much thought nor care that way.
140   It may look up, work up,—the worse for those
       It works on! 'Careth but for Setebos
       The many-handed as a cuttle-fish,

125. *mine*] me (*MS*).
126. *I . . . my*] he . . . his (*MS*).
129. *What knows*: cp. the 'glossa of Theotypas' in *A Death* (ll. 82–104, pp. 729–30), and see also l. 143.
130.] That made, or maybe He found out and fought (*MS*, which has 'found him out' for 'He found out', canc.).
131. *perchance*.] mayhap: (*MS*).
132–9. With the introduction of the 'Quiet' it becomes clear that in Caliban's theology Setebos has the status of a demiurge, i.e. a secondary creative principle, subordinate to the first (the 'Quiet') but not necessarily under its control. The concept of a deity that 'feels nor joy nor grief' is akin to the Epicurean concept of the gods as existing apart from, and indifferent to, human concerns; cp. *Cleon* 41–2 (p. 568).
132. *something quiet*] some live Quiet (*MS*, which has 'quiet', canc.).
134. *both derive*] each derives (*MS*).
135. *I joy because the quails come*: cp. *England in Italy* 16–21 (p. 257).
137. *Quiet*] other (*MS*).
139.] But never spends much thought, nor cares that way, (*MS*, which has 'a thought', canc.). Note the syntactical change introduced by the *1864* revision. Possibly echoing Stoddard, *Witch's Whelp*, l. 63: 'Nothing of this know I, nor care to know'.
141. *'Careth but*] Careth all (*MS*).
142. Perhaps a hint that this Setebos is, like Stoddard's, a marine god. *cuttle-fish*: used by Darwin as a synonym for 'octopus': 'I was much interested, on several occasions, by watching the habits of an Octopus, or cuttle-fish' (*Voyage of the Beagle*, ch. i).

Who, making Himself feared through what He does,
Looks up, first, and perceives He cannot soar
145 To what is quiet and hath happy life;
Next looks down here, and out of very spite
Makes this a bauble-world to ape yon real,
These good things to match those as hips do grapes.
'Tis solace making baubles, ay, and sport.
150 Himself peeped late, eyed Prosper at his books
Careless and lofty, lord now of the isle:
Vexed, 'stitched a book of broad leaves, arrow-shaped,
Wrote thereon, he knows what, prodigious words;
Has peeled a wand and called it by a name;
155 Weareth at whiles for an enchanter's robe
The eyed skin of a supple oncelot;
And hath an ounce sleeker than youngling mole,

143.] That makes Himself be feared through what He does, (*MS*).

145. and hath happy life;] and a happy life, (*MS*).

146. Next] So (*MS*).

147. Makes this a] Made this the (*MS*).   *to ape yon real*: 'to imitate the real world' [to which Setebos has no access]; for the evocation of Plato here, see headnote, *Sources* 2 (i).

148.] Our good things matching those as hips do grapes. (*MS*); Our good things matching these as hips do grapes, (*1872*).   *hips*: rose-hips.

149. On the pleasure and profit of mimesis, cp. *Fra Lippo* 296–306 (pp. 500–1).

150–1. Based on Caliban's resentment at Prospero's usurpation of the island in *The Tempest* (see I ii 331–2: 'This island's mine by Sycorax my mother, / Which thou tak'st from me') and his awe of Prospero's books (see III ii 91–3: 'Remember / First to possess his books; for without them / He's but a sot, as I am').

152. 'stitched] stitched (*MS*).

153. Wrote] Writes (*MS*).

156. eyed: dappled, spotted; more usually applied to peacocks or butterflies, and so used by B. in *Two Poets of Croisic* (1878) 435 ('the eyed wing').   *oncelot*] ocelot (*1872*). 'Oncelot', which appears in *MS*, is not recorded as a variant spelling in *OED*; the correct spelling in a single text (a volume of selections) may, oddly enough, be a misprint. 'A wild cat, *Felis pardalis*, having a tawny coat marked with numerous black rings, spots, and streaks, and found in forests and scrub from southern Texas to Argentina' (*OED*).

157. ounce: 'A medium-sized member of the cat family, as a lynx, puma, or cheetah. Now *arch.*' (*OED*). The other sense, 'the snow leopard', is excluded by the context. Cp. *A Midsummer Night's Dream*: 'Be it ounce, or cat, or bear, / Pard, or boar with bristled hair'.   *youngling mole*: 'youngling' (the young or offspring of an animal) was still current in B.'s day though becoming archaic; precedents for B.'s quasi-adjectival use of the term include William Cowper, 'youngling sparrows' (transl. *Iliad* ii 396, 1791) and Sara Coleridge, 'youngling heifer' ('Full oft before some gorgeous fane', *Phantasmion*, 1837). The mole is mentioned by Caliban in *The Tempest*: 'Pray you tread softly, that the blind mole may not / Hear a foot fall; we now are near his cell' (IV i 194–5).

    A four-legged serpent he makes cower and couch,
    Now snarl, now hold its breath and mind his eye,
160 And saith she is Miranda and my wife:
    'Keeps for his Ariel a tall pouch-bill crane
    He bids go wade for fish and straight disgorge;
    Also a sea-beast, lumpish, which he snared,
    Blinded the eyes of, and brought somewhat tame,
165 And split its toe-webs, and now pens the drudge
    In a hole o' the rock and calls him Caliban;
    A bitter heart, that bides its time and bites.
    'Plays thus at being Prosper in a way,
    Taketh his mirth with make-believes: so He.

170 His dam held that the Quiet made all things
    Which Setebos vexed only: 'holds not so.
    Who made them weak, meant weakness He might vex.

160. In *The Tempest* Caliban attempted to rape Miranda (before the action of the play begins: see I ii 345–51) and praises her beauty to Stephano and Trinculo (III ii 98–105).

161–2. Mimicking Prospero's commands to Ariel in *The Tempest*: cp., e.g. I ii 189–93: 'I come / To answer thy best pleasure; be't to fly, / To swim, to dive into the fire, to ride / On the curl'd clouds. To thy strong bidding, task / Ariel, and all his quality'.

161. *'Keeps*] Keeps (*MS*). *tall pouch-bill crane*: no species of crane has a feeding pouch, but B. may have been thinking of the adjutant-crane (*Ciconia Argala*) which is actually a species of stork, is tall, and has such a pouch. The compound 'pouch-bill' is B.'s coinage; the closest phrase in *OED* is 'pouch'd-lipp'd' (John Clare, *The Village Minstrel* (1821) i 137).

162. *bids go*] biddeth (*MS*).

163–7. In *The Tempest*, when Trinculo meets Caliban he takes him for a kind of 'sea-beast': 'What have we here? a man or a fish? dead or alive? A fish, he smells like a fish; a very ancient and fish-like smell; a kind of, not-of-the-newest poor-John. A strange fish! . . . Legged like a man; and his fins like arms!' (II ii 24–7, 33–4) For Caliban's hatred of Prospero, see above, ll. 150–1n.

163–4. Cp. Stoddard, *Witch's Whelp*, 51–4: 'often I push my spear / Deep in their drowsy eyes, at which they howl / And chase me inland; then I mount their humps / And prick them back again, unwieldy, slow'.

164. *brought*] made (*MS*).

168. *'Plays*] Plays (*MS*).

170. *Quiet*] quiet (*MS*).

171. *Which*] While (*MS*, canc.). *vexed*] vexes (*MS*).

172. *He might vex*] should be vexed (*MS*).

172–8. Caliban here takes up one of the objections to the argument that God's design of the natural world is beneficent, namely that this design is in many instances imperfect, and that a beneficent God ought surely to have made his creatures

Had He meant other, while His hand was in,
Why not make horny eyes no thorn could prick,
175   Or plate my scalp with bone against the snow,
Or overscale my flesh 'neath joint and joint,
Like an orc's armour? Ay,—so spoil His sport!
He is the One now: only He doth all.

'Saith, He may like, perchance, what profits Him.
180   Ay, himself loves what does him good; but why?
'Gets good no otherwise. This blinded beast
Loves whoso places flesh-meat on his nose,
But, had he eyes, would want no help, but hate
Or love, just as it liked him: He hath eyes.
185   Also it pleaseth Setebos to work,
Use all His hands, and exercise much craft,
By no means for the love of what is worked.
'Tasteth, himself, no finer good i' the world
When all goes right, in this safe summer time,
190   And he wants little, hungers, aches not much,
Than trying what to do with wit and strength.

---

stronger, better equipped to resist their enemies, etc. 'Natural theology' had to answer this objection without recourse to the traditional explanation that original sin had warped God's originally perfect creation (a variant of this view is found in ll. 170–1); the most common response was that the strengths and weaknesses of different creatures had to be seen as part of an overall design whose stability was maintained by a constant, divinely ordained balance of forces. Caliban, on the other hand, speculates that God creates his creatures weak in order to ensure their dependence on him.

174. could prick] pricks through (*MS*).

175. my scalp] the scalp (*MS*).

176. my flesh] soft flesh (*MS*, which has 'the soft flesh', canc.).

177. orc's armour: originally 'orc' designated 'any of various ferocious sea creatures', and though in B.'s time it was usually applied to the killer whale, *Orcinus orca*, his usage seems to favour the older meaning, perhaps influenced also by the other (etymologically unrelated) sense of 'devouring monster, ogre': see below, l. 274, and *Ring* ix 972: 'near and nearer comes the snorting orc'.

181. 'Gets] Gets (*MS*).

182. whoso] whom (*MS*, canc.).

183. but hate] would hate (*1872*).

184. He: i.e. Setebos.

188. 'Tasteth] Tastes (*MS*, canc.).

190.] Wanting for little, hungering, aching not, (*MS*).

'Falls to make something: 'piled yon pile of turfs,
And squared and stuck there squares of soft white chalk,
And, with a fish-tooth, scratched a moon on each,
195 And set up endwise certain spikes of tree,
And crowned the whole with a sloth's skull a-top,
Found dead i' the woods, too hard for one to kill.
No use at all i' the work, for work's sole sake;
'Shall some day knock it down again: so He.

200 'Saith He is terrible: watch His feats in proof!
One hurricane will spoil six good months' hope.
He hath a spite against me, that I know,
Just as He favours Prosper, who knows why?
So it is, all the same, as well I find.
205 'Wove wattles half the winter, fenced them firm
With stone and stake to stop she-tortoises
Crawling to lay their eggs here: well, one wave,
Feeling the foot of Him upon its neck,
Gaped as a snake does, lolled out its large tongue,
210 And licked the whole labour flat: so much for spite.
'Saw a ball flame down late (yonder it lies)
Where, half an hour before, I slept i' the shade:
Often they scatter sparkles: there is force!

192–9. Stoddard's Caliban similarly engages in pointless work: 'One day I thrust my spear within a cleft / No wider than its point, and something shrieked, / And falling cones did pelt me sharp as hail: / I picked the seeds that grew between their plates, / And strung them round my neck, with sea-mew eggs' (ll. 40–44). (The 'something' is Ariel, whom Sycorax has imprisoned in the pine tree.)

192. 'Falls . . . 'piled] Falls . . . piled (*MS*).

199. 'Shall] Shall (*MS*).

199^200]. Line 199 ends a page in *MS*: it is not clear that a paragraph was intended.

201. six good months'] the six months' (*MS*).

204. find] know (*MS*).

205. wattles: 'rods or stakes, interlaced with twigs or branches of trees, used to form fences and the walls and roofs of buildings' (*OED*).

206–7. she-tortoises . . . here: Peterfreund (see headnote) cites Darwin, *The Voyage of the Beagle* ch. xvii: 'the female, where the soil is sandy, deposits [the eggs] together and covers them up with sand; but where the ground is rocky she drops them indiscriminately in any hole'.

209. large] long (*MS*).

211. Probably referring to a meteorite. *late*] once (*MS*).

212. slept] ate (*MS*).

'Dug up a newt He may have envied once
215 And turned to stone, shut up inside a stone.
Please Him and hinder this?—What Prosper does?
Aha, if He would tell me how! Not He!
There is the sport: discover how or die!
All need not die, for of the things o' the isle
220 Some flee afar, some dive, some run up trees;
Those at His mercy, why, they please Him most
When . . . when . . . well, never try the same way twice!
Repeat what act has pleased, He may grow wroth.
You must not know His ways, and play Him off,
225 Sure of the issue. 'Doth the like himself:
'Spareth a squirrel that it nothing fears
But steals the nut from underneath my thumb,
And when I threat, bites stoutly in defence:
'Spareth an urchin that, contrariwise,
230 Curls up into a ball, pretending death
For fright at my approach: the two ways please.
But what would move my choler more than this,
That either creature counted on its life
To-morrow and next day and all days to come,
235 Saying forsooth in the inmost of its heart,

214–15. Caliban is referring to a fossil; his explanation of what it signifies is possibly B.'s joke at the expense of Christians who tried to account for the fossil record without having to admit that the earth was millions of years old.
214. 'Dug] Dug (*MS*).
215. And] All (*MS*).
217. me] you (*MS*).
220. flee] fly (*MS*).
221.] Those at His mercy,—why, it pleases Him (*MS*).
223–5. Another possible allusion to the Calvinist doctrine that grace and salvation are unmerited free gifts of God which cannot be 'earned' by human beings.
227. my thumb] his thumb (*MS*).
228. I threat] he threats (*MS*).
229. urchin: a hedgehog. Urchins are mentioned twice in *The Tempest* (I ii 328–8, II ii 4–7), but in the sense (obsolete by B.'s day) of 'a goblin or elf' in hedgehog form (*OED* 1c), and it is they who frighten Caliban.
231. my approach] his approach (*MS*).
232–40. Cp., among many instances in the Bible, the boast of 'the wicked' in *Psalms* x 6: 'He hath said in his heart, I shall not be moved; for I shall never be in adversity', followed by God's retribution and the triumphant affirmation of his power: 'Break thou the arm of the wicked and evil man . . . The LORD is King for ever and ever' (vv. 15–16).
232. my choler] his choler (*MS*). Choler is anger.

"Because he did so yesterday with me,
And otherwise with such another brute,
So must he do henceforth and always."—Ay?
'Would teach the reasoning couple what "must" means!
240   'Doth as he likes, or wherefore Lord? So He.

'Conceiveth all things will continue thus,
And we shall have to live in fear of Him
So long as He lives, keeps His strength: no change,
If He have done His best, make no new world
245   To please Him more, so leave off watching this,—
If He surprise not even the Quiet's self
Some strange day,—or, suppose, grow into it
As grubs grow butterflies: else, here are we,
And there is He, and nowhere help at all.

250   'Believeth with the life, the pain shall stop.
His dam held different, that after death
He both plagued enemies and feasted friends:
Idly! He doth His worst in this our life,
Giving just respite lest we die through pain,
255   Saving last pain for worst,—with which, an end.
Meanwhile, the best way to escape His ire
Is, not to seem too happy. 'Sees, himself,

236–8.] inverted commas added in MS.
237. *such another brute*,] such an other one (MS).
238. *must*] will (MS, canc.).
243. *keeps*] holds (MS, canc.).
246. *Quiet's*] quiet's (MS).
248. *As grubs grow butterflies*: cp. *Coriolanus* V iv 8–9: 'There is differency between a grub and a butterfly; yet your butterfly was a grub.'
249. *nowhere*] never (MS).
250–5. Caliban's denial of an afterlife of rewards and punishments, like other aspects of his doctrine, has affinities with Epicurean materialism, and its poetic embodiment in Lucretius' *De Rerum Natura*, which welcomed the idea of death as an end to suffering.
250. *'Believeth*] Believeth (MS).
251. *different, that*] different, held that (*1872*).
252. *both plagued*] plagued his (MS).
253. *doth His*] does his (MS).
254. *we die*] it stop (MS).
255. *last pain*] the last (MS).
257. *'Sees,*] emended, in line with *1864²–88* from *1864*, which has no initial apostrophe, the only instance in *1864* where B. omits an apostrophe before the main verb of a sentence.

Yonder two flies, with purple films and pink,
Bask on the pompion-bell above: kills both.
260   'Sees two black painful beetles roll their ball
On head and tail as if to save their lives:
Moves them the stick away they strive to clear.

Even so, 'would have Him misconceive, suppose
This Caliban strives hard and ails no less,
265   And always, above all else, envies Him.
Wherefore he mainly dances on dark nights,
Moans in the sun, gets under holes to laugh,
And never speaks his mind save housed as now:
Outside, 'groans, curses. If He caught me here,
270   O'erheard this speech, and asked "What chucklest at?"
'Would, to appease Him, cut a finger off,
Or of my three kid yearlings burn the best,
Or let the toothsome apples rot on tree,
Or push my tame beast for the orc to taste:
275   While myself lit a fire, and made a song

---

258. pink] brown (*MS*).

259. pompion-bell: this compound is not in *OED*; presumably the flower of the pumpkin plant: see l. 7n.

260. 'Sees] Sees (*MS*).

262. Moves] 'Moves (*1872*).

262^263.] no paragraph break in *MS*.

266–9. Wherefore . . . curses: contrast *Psalms* l 23: 'Whoso offereth praise glorifieth me: and to him that ordereth his conversation aright will I shew the salvation of God.'

267. under] into (*MS*).

268. housed] caved (*MS*).

269. me here] him now (*MS*).

270. at?"] emended in agreement with *MS* from at?' in *1864*, an error repeated in *1864²* and corrected in *1868–88*.

271–4. Disregarding God's injunction in *Psalms* l 9–10: 'I will take no bullock out of thy house, nor he goats out of thy folds. / For every beast of the forest is mine, and the cattle upon a thousand hills.' The psalm as a whole launches an attack on primitive sacrificial religion.

271. 'Would] Would (*MS*).

272. my] his (*MS*).

273.] Or let the toothsome apples rot on the tree, (*MS*); And let the apples rot upon four trees, (*MS*, canc.).

274. my] his (*MS*).

275. myself] himself (*MS*).

And sung it, *"What I hate, be consecrate*
To celebrate Thee and Thy state, no mate
For Thee; what see for envy in poor me?"
Hoping the while, since evils sometimes mend,
280   Warts rub away, and sores are cured with slime,
That some strange day, will either the Quiet catch
And conquer Setebos, or likelier He
Decrepit may doze, doze, as good as die.

·

[What, what? A curtain o'er the world at once!
285   Crickets stop hissing; not a bird—or, yes,

276–8. "What . . . me?"] not in italics in *MS*. The clumsiness of Caliban's song
here echoes not his praise of the island's music in *The Tempest* (III ii 135–43)
but his earlier drunken impromptu at II ii 180–7: 'No more dams I'll make for
fish, / Nor fetch in firing / At requiring, / Nor scrape trenchering, nor wash
dish. / 'Ban, 'Ban, Ca-Caliban / Has a new master, get a new man. / Freedom,
high-day! high-day, freedom! freedom, high-day, freedom!' Note that this song
is one of emancipation (however deluded) as opposed to the song of B.'s Caliban
which reaffirms his subservience.
280. rub] die (*MS*).
281.] That some strange way, or else the quiet catch (*MS*). Both formulations are
syntactically convoluted: the meaning is, 'that some time (way) or other, the Quiet
will catch (Setebos)'.
283. may] will (*MS*).   *as good as die*] wholly die (*MS*).
283^284.] no rule in *MS*.
284–95.] not in square brackets in *MS*. Brown (headnote, *Sources*) suggests that
this section 'abounds in third personal speech' as Caliban seeks to 'hide' from the
presence of Setebos, announced by the storm. The storm itself has both
Shakespearean and biblical associations: cp. *The Tempest* I ii 201–3: 'Jove's lightning, the precursors / O' th' dreadful thunder-claps, more momentary / And
sight-outrunning were not', and II ii 22–3, 37: 'If it should thunder as it did
before, I know not where to hide my head . . . Alas, the storm is come again!'
In the Bible, cp. *Exodus* ix 23: 'And Moses stretched forth his rod toward heaven:
and the Lord sent thunder and hail, and the fire ran along upon the ground; and
the Lord rained hail upon the land of Egypt' and *Psalms* lxxvii 17–18: 'The skies
poured out water: the skies sent out a sound: thine arrows also went abroad. /
The voice of thy thunder was in heaven: the lightnings lightened the world: the
earth trembled and shook'; see also *Exodus* xiii 21, *Psalms* i 3). Cp. also Stoddard,
The Witch's Whelp: 'The thunder breaks o'erhead, and in their lairs / The panthers roar; from out the stormy clouds / With hearts of fire, sharp lightnings rain
around / And split the oaks' (ll. 20–23). In B., cp. *Pippa* i 190–1 (p. 109): 'then
broke / The thunder like a whole sea overhead'.
284. What, what?] There, see! (*MS*).
285–6. Cp. Caliban in *The Tempest*: 'His spirits hear me, / And yet I needs must
curse'.

There scuds His raven that hath told Him all!
It was fool's play, this prattling! Ha! The wind
Shoulders the pillared dust, death's house o' the move,
And fast invading fires begin! White blaze—
290 A tree's head snaps—and there, there, there, there, there,
His thunder follows! Fool to gibe at Him!
Lo! 'Lieth flat and loveth Setebos!
'Maketh his teeth meet through his upper lip,
Will let those quails fly, will not eat this month
295 One little mess of whelks, so he may 'scape!]

286. Cp. bk. ii of Ovid's *Metamorphoses*, where the raven tells Apollo the news of Coronis' infidelity (and is turned black as a result). In *Macbeth*, the raven 'croaks the fatal entrance of Duncan' to Macbeth's castle (I v 39).   *that hath told*] having told (*MS*); that has told (*1888*).

287. Ha!] See! (*MS*).

289. fast] the (*MS*).

290–1. A tree's head . . . follows! Peterfreund (see headnote) compares *Psalms* i 22: 'Now consider this, ye that forget God, lest I tear you in pieces, and there be none to deliver.'

292. Lo] See (*MS*).

293. 'Maketh] Maketh (*MS*).

294–5. Cp. *Exodus* xvi and *Numbers* xi. In the former the Israelites are hankering for 'the flesh pots of Egypt', and God tells them he will send them 'manna' from heaven in the morning, and quails in the evening. In the latter the people are again yearning for Egypt and the varied diet they remember enjoying there (they forget the slavery they endured), and asking Moses for meat. In response to their murmurings against him, the Lord sends them a veritable tempest of quails from the sea; while they are still eating he smites them with a plague, and many die. A positive gloss is put on these episodes in *Psalms* cv 40: 'The people asked, and he brought quails, and satisfied them with the bread of heaven.'

295. mess: portion, dish (a biblical term, as in *2 Samuel* xi 8, 'a mess of meat').

41 A Likeness

Text and publication

First publ. *DP*, 28 May 1864; repr. *1864²*, *1868*, *1880*, *1888*. Our text is *1864*. The MS, part of the printer's copy for *DP*, is at *Morgan*. It is a very clean copy, with few instances of re-drafting; line 47 of the published poem is missing, but this was probably a transcription error, since otherwise line 50 would be unrhymed. There are few other verbal variants between *MS* and *1864*, and none in subsequent editions.

Composition and date

Some elements of the poem derive from B.'s early life. His father owned a large number of prints, including a print of an Andromeda by Polidoro da Caravaggio which B. kept above his desk in his parents' house before his marriage (see *Pauline* 656n; p. 49). Both *Maynard* (pp. 150–1) and *Thomas* (pp. 224–6) suggest that the print in question was by Giovanni Volpato (see l. 61); B. describes rescuing this print from his father's collection, in a passage with obvious relevance to the poem, in a letter to EBB. of 26 Feb. 1845:

> I have no little insight to the feelings of furniture, and treat books and prints with a reasonable consideration—how some people use their pictures, for instance, is a mystery to me—very revolting all the same: portraits obliged to face each other forever,—prints put together in portfolios, . . . my Polidoro's perfect Andromeda along with "Boors Carousing by Ostade,"—where I found her,— my own father's doing, or I would say more. (*Correspondence* x 99)

(Cp. 'Fifty in one portfolio', l. 43.) B. also, around this time, mentions seeing some prints by Marcantonio Raimondi (see l. 54n.), as he indicates in a letter to EBB. written the following year: 'I have this moment come from Town & Mrs Jameson .. the Marc Antonio Prints kept us all the morning' (11 May 1846; *Correspondence* xii 317).

Most of the poem's specific cultural allusions relate to the mid- to late 1850s. Tom Sayers (see l. 23n.) was one of the most famous boxers of the mid-nineteenth century; on 16 June 1857 he defeated William Perry ('the Tipton Slasher': see l. 18n.), and in April 1860 he fought the American John C. Heenan ('the Benicia Boy'); cp. *Mr Sludge*, l. 1269n. (p. 839). John Solomon Rarey's taming of Lord Dorchester's horse Cruiser (see l. 22n.) took place in April 1858, as did his publication of a book on horse-taming, which B. possessed. A new edition of Rabelais (l. 24) was published in Paris in 1857–8 (eds. J. H. Burgaud des Marets and E. J. B. Rathery). The establishment of a National Portrait Gallery (l. 50) was approved by Parliament in 1856, but it did not acquire permanent premises until much later; articles about its acquisitions, and speculation concerning its permanent home, appeared regularly in the press throughout the 1850s and 1860s.

The allusions to the late 1850s mean that the poem cannot have assumed its current form before the middle of 1858, and it is, therefore, possible that it was one of the poems shown to Isa Blagden in Siena in 1860 (see Appendix C, pp. 895–6).

Sources and influences

1 *Literary*

The principal source for the main motif of the poem is, we suggest, Byron's *Beppo* (1818) 81–104, esp. ll. 97–104:

Love in full life and length, not love ideal,
  No, nor ideal beauty, that fine name,
But something better still, so very real,
  That the sweet Model must have been the same;
A thing that you would purchase, beg, or steal,
  Wer't not impossible, besides a shame:
The face recalls some face, as 'twere with pain,
You once have seen, but ne'er will see again[.]

There is a similar notion in Coleridge's *Literary Remains*: 'a good portrait is an abstract of the personal; it is not the likeness for actual comparison, but for recollection. This explains why the likeness of a very good portrait is not always recognized; because some persons never abstract, and amongst these are to be numbered the near relations and friends of the subject, in consequence of the constant pressure and check exercised on their minds by the actual presence of the original' (vol. i, 1836, p. 225).

The list of bachelor items at ll. 11–24 recalls a number of mid-nineteenth-century novels, in particular Flaubert's *Madame Bovary*; see, e.g., ch. vi: 'He furnished in his head an apartment. He would lead an artist's life there! He would take lessons on the guitar! He would have a dressing-gown, a Basque cap, blue velvet slippers! He even already was admiring two crossed foils over his chimney-piece, with a death's head on the guitar above them'. B. had read *Madame Bovary* by Jan. 1859 (see *EBB to Arabella* ii 391), and professed a continuing 'passion' for it to Isa Blagden four years later (*Dearest Isa* 173).

2 Drawings, photographs and prints
EBB. wrote to Anna Jameson, on 2 May 1856: 'He just now has taken to drawing, and after thirteen days' application has produced some quite startling copies of heads' (*Letters of EBB* ii 230). *Collections* records many photographs dating from the years of the Brownings' marriage, during which time B. and EBB. frequently had portrait photographs of themselves and of their son Penini taken by Italian photographers, some of which they kept, others being sent to friends and relatives in England. That some at least of these photographs were made into prints is revealed by B.'s letter to his sister Sarianna of 9–10 May 1859: 'I got yesterday the engravings of Ba's portrait—a poor thing, metamorphosed into hardly any likeness at all from what was a very good one—but such as it is, it must do for the present: there is some little air of Ba in it that makes it bearable' (*New Letters* 118–19).

After EBB.'s death, the last photographs taken of her clearly took on a special status as final relics of her personal appearance. The most important was a group taken in Rome in 1861, a few months before her death, by a photographer called Alessandri. B. had copies made in Paris after EBB.'s death for family and friends. To Mrs Ogilvy he wrote, 'I will give you a photograph—perfect, the one likeness that exists, taken just before we left Rome' (29 July 1861, *B to Ogilvy* 174; the photograph is reproduced as plate V). He himself kept a copy in his study.

Parallels in B.
In its contemporary setting and predominantly jaunty tone, *A Likeness* goes with other *DP* lyrics, particularly *Confessions*, *Youth and Art* and *Dîs Aliter Visum*. Its focus on the representation of a woman's face has affinities with *A Face* (III 230), with which it was (perhaps significantly, given the poem's emphasis on the importance of placing items correctly) juxtaposed in *DP*. B.'s interest in portraiture reaches back to *My Last Duchess* (p. 197).

Some people hang portraits up
In a room where they dine or sup:
And the wife clinks tea-things under,
And her cousin, he stirs his cup,
5   Asks, "Who was the lady, I wonder?"
" 'Tis a daub John bought at a sale,"
Quoth the wife,—looks black as thunder:
"What a shade beneath her nose!
Snuff-taking, I suppose,—"
10 Adds the cousin, while John's corns ail.

Or else, there's no wife in the case,
But the portrait's queen of the place,
Alone mid the other spoils
Of youth,—masks, gloves and foils,
15 And pipe-sticks, rose, cherry-tree, jasmine,
And the long whip, the tandem-lasher,
And the cast from a fist ("not, alas! mine,

---

3. clinks] spreads (*MS*, canc.).

4. cousin: in *Andrea* 219 (p. 401) the 'cousin' is a euphemism for Lucrezia's lover; it is unlikely that this is the suggestion here, but cousins generally, male and female, do not fare well in B.: see, e.g., *Count Gismond* (II 161) and *Ring* ii 1540–7.

6. daub: a poorly executed painting.   *a sale*: i.e. an auction.

9. This is a joke: it was very unusual for women, and esp. young women, to take snuff at this period.

10. John's corns ail: presumably metaphorically, from pain at the turn of the conversation: we still say that 'someone has trodden on my corns'.

11–24. For this list of bachelor items, see headnote, *Sources*. The incongruous juxtaposition of sporting (and especially boxing) memorabilia with items of high cultural value recalls B.'s letter of 23 March 1840 commenting on the review of *Sordello* in a contemporary popular newspaper: 'Bell's Life in London, of yesterday-week, after exposing the malice of a report "that the long and earnestly expected set-to between Snuffy Seedsman and Bermondsey George was *off*—and setting an anxious correspondent ("Aliquis") right on "Grab the black tan crop-eared dog's mother's pedigree,["] assured its readers "Browning" was "a lofty poet"—somebody must have vouched to the Editor for my being seven feet high' (*Correspondence* iv 262; we read 'Aliquis' for 'Alligris'). The editors of *Correspondence* suggest that the references to 'Snuffy Seedsman', etc. are B.'s invention, parodying the paper's style (p. 263n.9).

15. pipe-sticks: pipe-stems; B. uses the word again in *Mihrab Shah* (*Ferishtah's Fancies*, 1884) 64.

16. tandem-lasher: a tandem is a two-horse carriage with the horses harnessed one in front of the other; a tandem whip therefore had to be extra long. *OED* does not record 'tandem-lasher' but has 'tandem whip' from 1835.

But my master's, the Tipton Slasher")
And the cards where pistol-balls mark ace,
20 And a satin shoe used for cigar-case,
And the chamois-horns ("shot in the Chablais")
And prints—Rarey drumming on Cruiser,
And Sayers, our champion, the bruiser,
And the little edition of Rabelais:
25 Where a friend, with both hands in his pockets,
May saunter up close to examine it,
And remark a good deal of Jane Lamb in it,
"But the eyes are half out of their sockets;
That hair's not so bad, where the gloss is,

18. *the Tipton Slasher*: William ('Bill') Perry (1819–1881) was known by this soubriquet. He was twice heavyweight champion of England (1850 and 1856), and was finally defeated by Tom Sayers in 1857 (see l. 23n., and headnote, *Composition*). Perry is the speaker's 'master' in the sense that he is employed as his trainer.
19. *And the cards*] And cards (*MS*).
21. *Chablais*: a region split between Switzerland and France. It is situated in the northern Alps, including Mont Blanc, and is one of the habitats of the 'chamois' or wild antelope, the horns of which adorn the room.
22. John S. Rarey (1827–66) was an American horse tamer who gave a number of demonstrations of his skill during 1858. The most celebrated of these was his taming of Lord Dorchester's notoriously ferocious horse Cruiser; see *The Times* (9 Apr. 1858) for Lord Dorchester's description of the event. Rarey is depicted 'drumming' on Cruiser; this was one of the ways in which he demonstrated that the horse in question had been completely subjugated. *The Times* for 25 Jan. 1858 describes another of Rarey's demonstrations in which he used this technique: 'bidding the horse rise . . . Mr. Rarey jumped upon his back and held by turns an umbrella over his head and beat a tattoo on a drum, the hitherto proud, restless animal, now owning subjection to a new master, remaining the while almost as motionless as a statue.' There is also a cartoon in *Punch* for 27 Mar. 1858 which shows a man emerging from a stable with a drum after having made an unsuccessful attempt to tame a horse using Rarey's methods. Prints of Rarey's taming of Cruiser began to appear almost instantly; in the *Daily News* for 24 May 1858, there is an account of an exhibition staged by the Photographic Society in Piccadilly which includes a picture of 'Mr. Rarey and Cruiser'. In a letter to Edward Chapman of 13 July 1858, B. added in a postscript, 'Please send by post Rarey's Horse-taming book pub. by Routledge' (*NL* 107). The book in question, *The Modern Art of Taming Wild Horses* (1858), was probably acquired (as DeVane and Knickerbocker point out) in connection with B.'s gift to Pen of a Sardinian pony.   *drumming*] a-drumming (*MS*).
23. *Sayers*: For Tom Sayers (1826–65), see headnote. It is very unlikely that B. saw him fight, since he was out of England during almost the whole period of Sayers's career, and prize-fighting was illegal at this time.
24. *little*] handy (*MS*, canc.).   *Rabelais*: François Rabelais (*c.* 1483–1553), the medieval French writer. At this period, his writings were a byword for obscenity: see *Garden-Fancies*, headnote and ii 32n. (pp. 213, 217–18). For the possible link between the 'little edition' and the date of composition, see headnote.
25. *Where*] And (*MS*).

30 But they've made the girl's nose a proboscis:
    Jane Lamb, that we danced with at Vichy!
    What, is not she Jane? Then, who is she?"

    All that I own is a print,
    An etching, a mezzotint;
35 'Tis a study, a fancy, a fiction,
    Yet a fact (take my conviction)
    Because it has more than a hint
    Of a certain face, I never
    Saw elsewhere touch or trace of
40 In women I've seen the face of:
    Just an etching, and, so far, clever.

    I keep my prints, an imbroglio,

---

30. proboscis: 'An elephant's trunk; the elongated mobile snout of some other mammals, such as tapirs and elephant seals . . . also *humorous*. A person's nose. Also *fig.*' (*OED*). The word appears frequently in the works of Samuel Butler; Coleridge uses it in a burlesque poem, 'The Nose', ll. 37–8 ('I vitrify thy torrid zone beneath, / Proboscis fierce! I am calcined! I die!'); B. uses it only here.

31. Vichy: a fashionable spa-town in France; mentioned in Thackeray's *The Newcomes* (1854), ch. x.

33–4. a print, / An etching, a mezzotint: three different ways of copying or reproducing an image. A print is '[a] picture or design made from an inked impression of an engraved metal plate, wooden block, lithographic stone'; an etching is '[a] copy or representation produced by the process of etching; an impression from an etched plate'; and a mezzotint is '[a] method of engraving copper and steel plates for printing, in which the surface of the plate is roughened uniformly and then partially scraped away in order to produce the tones and half-tones of the picture, while the untouched parts of the plate give the deepest tones' (*OED*). 'Mezzotint' is also used to refer to the print produced by this process.

35–6. The doublet 'fancy . . . fact' was to become a staple of B.'s aesthetic vocabulary from this period onwards: see, e.g., *Ring* i 464: 'Fancy with fact is just one fact the more'.

36.] Yet a fact—that's my conviction—(*MS*).

37–40. It remains unclear whether the portrait represents a real woman or an unattainable ideal.

42. imbroglio: 'A confused heap' (*OED*). *OED's* first citation is from Thomas Gray's skit 'A Long Story' (1750), a passage describing three ladies' search for a 'poet' suspected to be on the premises: 'Each hole and cupboard they explore, / Each creek and cranny of his chamber . . . Into the drawers and china pry, / Papers and books, a huge imbroglio! / Under a tea-cup he might lie, / Or creased, like dogs-ears, in a folio' (ll. 61–2, 65–8). This is one of only two occurrences of the word in a poem before B.'s; the other is R. W. Emerson's 'Illusions' (in *The Conduct of Life*, 1860), in a quite different context: 'endless imbroglio / Is law and the world' (ll. 31–2). B.'s own unfamiliarity with the word is perhaps reflected in *MS* where he first wrote 'embroglio'.

Fifty in one portfolio.
When somebody tries my claret,
45 We turn round chairs to the fire,
Chirp over days in a garret,
Chuckle o'er increase of salary,
Taste the good fruits of our leisure,
Talk about pencil and lyre,
50 And the National Portrait Gallery:
Then I exhibit my treasure.
After we've turned over twenty,
And the debt of wonder my crony owes
Is paid to my Marc Antonios,
55 He stops me—"*Festina lentè!*
What's that sweet thing there, the etching?"
How my waistcoat-strings want stretching,
How my cheeks grow red as tomatos,
How my heart leaps! But hearts, after leaps, ache.

60 "By the by, you must take, for a keepsake,
That other, you praised, of Volpato's."

43. portfolio] portfoglio (*MS*, probably a transcription error influenced by 'imbroglio' in the prec. line).
46. For Thackeray's translation of a song by Béranger, 'The Garret', see headnote to *Youth and Art* (p. 701); 'chirped' occurs in l. 10 of B.'s poem (p. 703).
47.] not *MS*: see headnote.
49. pencil and lyre: metonymies for, respectively, painting and poetry. Cp. Pope, 'Epistle to Mr Jervas', 69–70: 'The kindred Arts shall in their praise conspire, / One dip the pencil, and one string the lyre'; and Cowper, 'Charity', 106: 'The painter's pencil, and the poet's lyre'.
50. See headnote, *Composition*.
52. After] When (*MS*, canc.).
54.] He pays to my Marcantonios (*MS*, which has 'Is', erased, with 'He' written over; the original reading was probably 'Is paid', to which B. reverted in *1864*).
   Marc Antonios: Marcantonio Raimondi (*c.*1480–*c.*1534) was a Roman print-maker, closely associated with Raphael. He was responsible for several significant advances in the craft of engraving. For B.'s familiarity with his work, see headnote, *Composition*.
55. Festina lentè! literally, 'hasten slowly!', here, with the sense, 'hold on a minute!' B. uses this expression in a letter to EBB. of 6 May 1846 (*Correspondence* xii 305).
57. How] And (*MS*).
58. How] For (*MS*).
61. Volpato's: Giovanni Volpato (1735–1803) was an Italian engraver, who made prints of many celebrated Renaissance paintings. His primary field of activity was Rome, where he prepared a well-known set of coloured prints of the works of Raphael in the Vatican (see l. 54n.). For B.'s familiarity with his work, see headnote, *Composition*.

The fool! would he try a flight further and say
He never saw, never before to-day,
What was able to take his breath away,
65 A face to lose youth for, to occupy age
With the dream of, meet death with,—why,
   I'll not engage
But that, half in a rapture and half in a rage,
I should toss him the thing's self—"'Tis only a duplicate,
A thing of no value! Take it, I supplicate!"

63. He] That he (*MS*).
65. occupy] wile away (*MS*).
68–9. For the echo of Byron's *Beppo* here, see headnote, *Sources*. The speaker's words disguise a metaphysical and emotional response in a technical observation. On the surface he means that the portrait is merely a copy of the original, or one of an identical series of reproductions of it, and so has 'no (commercial) value'; but his real meaning is that, were his 'crony' to recognize the true meaning of the portrait, it would no longer be uniquely meaningful to *him*, and would therefore lose its value.
68. a duplicate: B.'s only other use of this word is in his play *Luria*, where it pleasingly occurs twice (i 377, ii 192; II 395, 404), but not with the metaphysical implication it carries here.

42 Rabbi Ben Ezra

Text and publication

First publ. *DP*. 28 May 1864; repr. *1864²*, *1865*, *1868*, *1872*, *1888*. Our text is *1864*. The MS, part of the printer's copy for *DP*, is at *Morgan*. It is a very clean copy, with few cancellations. Preserved with *MS* is a loose slip of semi-transparent paper with pencil readings not in B.'s hand (*MS slip*): these refer to six of the lines revised from *MS* in *1864* and are noted where they occur. Verbal variants between *MS* and *1864* are relatively numerous in comparison with other *DP* poems, though mostly minor; only one verbal variant was introduced in subsequent editions.

Composition and date

No precise date can be assigned to the poem, beyond the *terminus a quo* of 1852 if, as has been suggested, the poem 'replies' to Matthew Arnold's *Empedocles on Etna*, or 1859 if it is linked to Edward FitzGerald's *Rubáiyát of Omar Khayyam* (see below); but it is unlikely to have been composed before the publication of *M & W*, in which it would surely have been included, and B. almost certainly encountered the *Rubáiyát* not on its first publication but when it was 'discovered' by D. G. Rossetti and other members of the Pre-Raphaelite circle in 1861. This coincides with B.'s return to London, at a time when his friendship with Rossetti was at its closest, and Rossetti, as DeVane notes (*Handbook* 293), might well have drawn the work to B.'s attention. Moreover, as Edward C. McAleer notes, B.'s letters to Isa Blagden are filled with allusions to Arnold's *Empedocles*, beginning with his letter of 25 March 1862 (*Dearest Isa* 105n.5), and these allusions are all to a passage of Arnold's poem which refers to extreme old age; B. also met Arnold in this period (*ibid.* 138). We suggest dating the poem to 1862.

Sources and influences

B.'s knowledge of Judaism and especially of rabbinical legend, which was exceptional for a non-Jew of his time, came to him from his father, whose library contained a number of Hebrew texts and translations, though none by the original of the Rabbi here. The historical Abraham ben Meir ibn Ezra, also known as Abenezra, was a major Jewish scholar of the Middle Ages (1092/3–1167). Born in Spain, he later went into voluntary exile, spending much of his life wandering across Europe and the Near East. He is best known for his commentaries on the Bible, though he also composed poetry. He wrote in Hebrew, which B. probably could not read in 1864, though he had studied it in his youth and was to take it up again in old age; however, a number of his works were translated into Latin in the sixteenth and seventeenth centuries, and B. might have encountered them in that form. Many of Ibn Ezra's MSS were held in the British Museum, which B. used extensively during his early career; others were in the Bibliothèque Impériale (later Nationale) in Paris and the Vatican Library in Rome, both accessible to B. at different times. The body–soul relation in the poem appears contradictory, but in fact resembles that described by the historical Ibn Ezra. Michael Friedländer notes that in his writings '[s]ensuality, if allowed to grow, becomes the source of bodily and mental ruin' but that '[o]n the other hand, celibacy, being in opposition to the will of God as revealed in nature, is likewise objected to' (*Essays on the Writings of Abraham Ibn Ezra* [London 1877] 39). Ibn Ezra himself gives the following account in his commentary on *Ecclesiastes* vii 3: 'It is known that as long as the bodily desires are strong, the soul is weak and powerless against them, because they are supported by the body and all its powers; hence those who think only of eating and drinking, will never be wise. By the alliance of the intellect with the animal soul (sensibility) the desires are subordinated, and the eyes of the soul are opened a little; but the soul is not yet prepared for pure knowledge, on account of the animal soul which seeks dominion, and produces all kinds of passion; therefore after the victory, gained with the help of the animal soul over the desires, it is necessary that the soul should devote itself to wisdom.' Ben Ezra's commitment to the full span of human life seems to be based on principles put forward by Ibn Ezra, who prizes 'the knowledge acquired by the soul during its connection with the body': 'The soul is to Ibn Ezra a treasure of truth, founded both on impressions made by the outer world upon our senses, and on the action of certain intellectual faculties within us' (Friedländer, pp. 44, 44−5).

The two major contemporary poetic influences are Matthew Arnold's *Empedocles on Etna* (1852) and Edward FitzGerald's *Rubáiyát of Omar Khayyám* (1859). B.'s poem responds in general to the Stoic pessimism advanced by Empedocles at I ii 77−426: there are also verbal echoes. B. greatly admired Arnold's poem and told Isa Blagden he was 'really flattered' when Arnold, who had omitted the poem from collections after 1852, reprinted it in his 1867 *Poems* at B.'s solicitation (*Dearest Isa* 274). For other examples of Arnold's influence on B., see *Old Pictures* (p. 404) and *Cleon* (p. 563).

Arnold's *Empedocles* appears to deny significant afterlife; the historical Empedocles ambiguously seems to affirm it in several passages, seeing it as the conclusion of a cycle of reincarnation in which having been 'boy and girl, bush, bird, and a mute fish in the sea', enlightened souls 'come forth among men on earth as prophets, minstrels, physicians and leaders, and from these they arise as gods, highest in honour' and '[w]ith other immortals . . . share hearth and table, having no part in human sorrows, unwearied' (transl. M. R. Wright, *Empedocles: the Extant Fragments* [1981] 275, 291, 292). This proto-evolutionary scheme may have influenced the model of human existence put forward in B.'s poem.

Lines 151−92 seem to develop (and contradict) the imagery of the divine potter shaping human clay in FitzGerald's *Rubáiyát*, which itself alludes to passages in the Bible on this theme; in more general terms, Ben Ezra attacks the epicurean pessimism of the *Rubáiyát*. In 1909 F. L. Sargent published a parallel text comparing the two poems, as *Omar and the Rabbi*. On B.'s view of FitzGerald himself, see 'To Edward FitzGerald' (1889), which expresses his outrage over the posthumous publication of a letter in which FitzGerald had disparaged EBB. A letter to Anne Thackeray Ritchie of 20 July 1889 spoke however of FitzGerald as also 'a man of genius I was desirous of knowing more closely than through his brilliant Omar translation' (H. T. Fuller and V. Hammersley, *Thackeray's Daughter* [Dublin 1951] p. 166). B.'s library contained a copy of the third edition of FitzGerald's poem, inscribed 'R. B. from L. L. T. Sept. 1874' (*Collections* A0966).

The stanza-form has a metrical pattern of iambic trimeter in ll. 1−2, 4−5, with an iambic pentameter in line 3 and a hexameter in line 6, rhyming aabccb. It is anticipated in Christina Rossetti, *The Martyr*, which was privately printed in 1847 and again may well have been shown to B. by D. G. Rossetti. Like many of the poems in this early volume, *The Martyr* expresses longing for early death; B.'s poem may be an inversion of this. B.'s library contained an advance proof copy of Christina Rossetti's *Goblin Market and Other Poems* (1862: *Collections* A1968), presented by Gabriel: see ll. 175−80n.

B. may also have been responding to Tennyson's pessimistic poems on old age, esp. 'Ulysses' (1842) and 'Tithonus' (1860): 'Tithonus' first appeared in the *Cornhill* (Feb. 1860), and then in Tennyson's 1864 collection *Enoch Arden and Other Poems*. Tithonus, a figure from classical mythology, was given immortal life by Aurora, goddess of the dawn, but not immortal youth: like the Struldbrugs in pt. iii of Swift's *Gulliver's Travels*. he grows perpetually older without being able to die.

Other possible literary influences include Victor Hugo's *Boöz Endormi* [Boaz Asleep], published in his *La Légende des Siècles* (1859), a collection which B. read in that year with strong, though strongly qualified, admiration (*Dearest Isa* 48–9; his copy is extant, *Collections* A1266). With the poem's opening, cp. Isaac Williams's 'Elegiac Fragment' (1849): 'While lovely flowers of youth remain / Many designs man hath in vain; / Ne'er thinks he shall grow old and die' (ll. 7–9); also Thomas Moore, 'My Birth-day'. O. P. Rhyne ('Browning and Goethe', *MLN* xliv [1929] 327) compares a passage from Goethe's *Zahme Xenien* (1820).

Parallels in B.

A 'Rabbi ben Ezra' also appears in *Holy-Cross Day* as the author of a 'Song of Death' (ll. 69–120, pp. 549–52); as we point out, B.'s use of the name in the earlier poem may have been influenced by the name given to the fictional Jewish convert to Christianity in Manuel Lacunza's *The Coming of Messiah in Glory and Majesty* (1827); see headnote, pp. 541–2. *Ferishtah's Fancies* (1884) similarly presents the thought of another sage-like figure (this time Persian, like Omar Khayyám, but imaginary), who projects a predominantly optimistic view of human life, again in contrast to FitzGerald and Arnold. B.'s affirmative view of old age had been expressed in *Pauline* 617–19 (p. 46). In a note to *Sordello* i 965 (I 458–8) B. wrote: 'The soul endures but the body *changes*—even if for the better.' In *DP*, *A Death* (p. 714) provides another positive study of old age; cp. also the Pope in bk. x of *Ring* and the figure of the village Pope in *Iván Ivànovitch* (*DI* 1879), esp. ll. 309–321. With the pessimistic epicurean attitude Ben Ezra attacks in ll. 154–80, cp. *Cleon* (p. 563). Ben Ezra's emphasis on judging inner motives and impulses as well as external actions belongs to B.'s philosophy of human life as necessarily partial and imperfect, since the perfect conjunction of 'Power' with 'Love' (see ll. 55–7) belongs only to God; man can (and indeed must) aspire to this perfection, but cannot hope to attain it in earthly life; his progress therefore follows an evolutionary path, both from youth to age and from mortal to immortal life. This philosophy is present from B.'s earliest work (e.g. *Paracelsus* and *Sordello*), and shapes the visionary poetics of *Saul*: ''tis not what man Does which exalts him, but what man Would do' (l. 295, III 518); it is re-stated in late works such as *Apollo and the Fates* (*Parleyings*, 1887): 'Manhood—the actual? Nay, praise the potential! . . . What *is*? No, what *may* be—sing! that's Man's essential!' (ll. 211, 213). In this scheme age and death are ineluctable, yet relative to the larger design of which they form part: as the Fates put it, 'Our shuttles fly fast, / Weave living, not life sole and whole: as age—youth, / So death completes living, shows life in its truth. / Man learningly lives: till death help him—no lore! / It is doom and must be' (ll. 243–7).

Criticism

Matthew Arnold's 'Growing Old' (1867) is usually taken to be Arnold's response to a poem which responds to one of his own: it is deeply pessimistic, absolutely reversing B.'s attitude. It consists of a series of answers to the question: 'What is it to grow old?', concluding:

It is—last stage of all—
When we are frozen up within, and quite
The phantom of ourselves,
To hear the world applaud the hollow ghost
Which blamed the living man.

For a discussion of these two poems, and a possible joint source in
Wordsworth, see Robert E. Lovelace, 'A Note on Arnold's "Growing Old"',
MLN lxvii.1 (Jan. 1953) 21–23.

I

Grow old along with me!
The best is yet to be,
The last of life, for which the first was made:
Our times are in His hand
5   Who saith "A whole I planned,
Youth shows but half; trust God: see all, nor be afraid!"

2

Not that, amassing flowers,
Youth sighed "Which rose make ours,

1. Cp., here and *passim*, Wordsworth, *The Excursion* ix 50–92, which speaks of
old age as 'a final EMINENCE', or 'superior height', which can 'confer / Fresh
power to commune with the invisible world'. O. P. Rhyne (see headnote) compares the last line of Goethe's poem, 'Komm, ältele du mit mir', commenting
that B.'s line 'could very easily be considered a direct translation' of it.
4. Cp. *Psalms* xxxi 15: 'My times are in thy hand: deliver me from the hand of
mine enemies, and from them that persecute me.' Ben Ezra cites the verse again
at the end of the poem (l. 190).
5. A whole I planned: cp. l. 56. Probably reflecting Arnold's *Empedocles* I ii 82–5:
'Hither and thither spins / The wind-born, mirroring soul, / A thousand
glimpses wins / And never sees a whole'; also the source of this passage in the
writings of Empedocles: 'After observing a small part of life in their lifetime,
subject to a swift death they are borne up and waft away like smoke; they are
convinced only of that which each has experienced as they are driven in all
directions, yet all boast of finding the whole' (Sextus Empiricus *adversus mathe-
maticos* 7.122, transl. M. R. Wright, *Empedocles: the Extant Fragments* [1981] 155).
Cp. also Pope, *Essay on Man* (1732–44) i 60: ''Tis but a part we see, and not
a whole', and ll. 56–9.
6. Cp. *Isaiah* xii 2: 'Behold, God is my salvation; I will trust, and not be afraid'.
7–18. The sense is that Ben Ezra does not blame ('remonstrate' with) youth for
its experiential greed, however destructive its appetites may be; instead he prizes
what these things lead to, 'doubt', in contrast with the torpid animal acquiescence involved in certainty. Doubt is illustrated by both of the exclamations ascribed
to youth: inability to decide between different flowers, desire for some absolute,
transcendent star beyond those actually visible. With this ethic, cp. ll. 109–11;
also *Dis Aliter Visum* 116–30 (p. 697). See also *Pauline* 268–80n., esp. 277–8n.
(p. 26).

Which lily leave and then as best recall?"
10 Not that, admiring stars,
     It yearned "Nor Jove, nor Mars;
     Mine be some figured flame which blends,
          transcends them all!"

3
Not for such hopes and fears
Annulling youth's brief years,
15 Do I remonstrate: folly wide the mark!
     Rather I prize the doubt
     Low kinds exist without,
     Finished and finite clods, untroubled by a spark.

4
Poor vaunt of life indeed,
20 Were man but formed to feed
     On joy, to solely seek and find and feast:
     Such feasting ended, then
     As sure an end to men;

7–12. Based on Arnold's *Empedocles* I ii 352–70; cp. esp. ll. 356–7, a passage about the period of youth: 'Pleasure, to our hot grasp / Gives flowers after flowers'.
12. Cp. Hugo, *Booz Endormi*:
  Le vieillard, qui revient vers la source première,
  Entre aux jours éternels et sort des jours changeants;
  Et l'on voit de la flamme aux yeux des jeunes gens,
  Mais dans l'oeil du vieillard on voit de la lumière. (p. 36)
[The old man, returning to the primal source, enters the days of eternity and leaves behind the days of change; and while one sees flame in the eyes of young people, in the eye of the old man one sees light.]
Note that B.'s 'flame' is to be understood as a metonymy for 'star'.
15. *remonstrate*: the scansion dictates the pronunciation 're-món-strate'. *folly wide the mark*: i.e. it would be folly to blame 'youth' for 'such hopes and fears' (not that 'youth' itself exemplifies 'folly').
16–18. The praise of 'doubt' here does not refer to religious doubt (as in *Bishop Blougram* 600–5, p. 318) but to the discontent created in man by his unique attribute, self-consciousness: Ben Ezra directly counters the argument of the Greek poet-philosopher Cleon who sees in this faculty man's ultimate cause for despair (see esp. ll. 181–271, pp. 576–81).
20–21. *to feed / On joy*: cp. Dryden, *Aureng-Zebe* V 574–5: 'Reason's nice taste does our delights destroy: / Brutes are more bless'd, who gros[s]ly feed on joy'.
22–3. The historical Ben Ezra argued that 'In the absence of further development, the soul necessarily ceases to exist at the death of the body; this is the lot of the wicked' (Friedländer, p. 44).

Irks care the crop-full bird? Frets doubt the
     maw-crammed beast?

                          5
25 Rejoice we are allied
    To That which doth provide
    And not partake, effect and not receive!
    A spark disturbs our clod;
    Nearer we hold of God
30 Who gives, than of His tribes that take, I must believe.

                          6
    Then, welcome each rebuff
    That turns earth's smoothness rough,
    Each sting that bids nor sit nor stand but go!
    Be our joys three-parts pain!
35 Strive, and hold cheap the strain;
    Learn, nor account the pang; dare, never grudge
          the throe!

                          7
    For thence,—a paradox
    Which comforts while it mocks,—
    Shall life succeed in that it seems to fail:
40 What I aspired to be,
    And was not, comforts me:
    A brute I might have been, but would not sink i' the
          scale.

24. This line swiftly became notorious as an illustration of B.'s supposedly harsh
and clotted style, though it can of course be defended on mimetic grounds. Cp.
Pope, *Essay on Man* i 81–4: 'The lamb thy riot dooms to bleed to-day, / Had
he thy Reason, would he skip and play? / Pleas'd to the last, he crops the flow'ry
food, / And licks the hand just rais'd to shed his blood.' *crop-full*: this word
appears in Milton, *L'Allegro* 113. *maw-crammed*: apparently B.'s coinage; but
Shakespeare associates 'maw' with 'cram' in several passages: 'Do thou but think
/ What 'tis to cram a maw or clothe a back / From such a filthy vice' (*Measure
for Measure* III ii 21–3; see also *Romeo and Juliet* V iii 45, 48).
42–8. The concept of a 'scale' of life in which human beings are situated between
the animal (or physical) and the divine (or spiritual) has both classical and
Christian antecedents. Ben Ezra's argument is that each person can choose the
direction of their life: if you accept that the life of the body is primary, with the
soul at its service, you will 'sink i' the scale'; if you believe that the body's mission is to 'project [the] soul on its lone way', you will rise towards a higher form
of life. The contrast between 'bestial' appetite and the primacy of 'soul' is very
differently treated by other speakers in B., e.g. Fra Lippo Lippi (see e.g. ll. 258–70,
pp. 499–500). See also ll. 22–3n.

8

What is he but a brute
Whose flesh hath soul to suit,
45 Whose spirit works lest arms and legs want play?
To man, propose this test—
Thy body at its best,
How far can that project thy soul on its lone way?

9

Yet gifts should prove their use:
50 I own the Past profuse
Of power each side, perfection every turn:
Eyes, ears took in their dole,
Brain treasured up the whole;
Should not the heart beat once "How good to live and
learn?"

10

55 Not once beat "Praise be Thine!
I see the whole design,
I, who saw Power, see now Love perfect too:
Perfect I call Thy plan:
Thanks that I was a man!
60 Maker, remake, complete,—I trust what Thou shalt do!"

45. A soul in thrall to the body will exercise itself only on the body's behalf, neglecting its own, higher aims.

48. its lone way: According to Ibn Ezra, in his commentary on Psalms xxii 22, 'The soul of every man is called "lonely" . . . because it is separated, during its union with the human body, from the universal soul, into which it is again received when it departs from its earthly companion' (Friedländer, pp. 28–29).

52. their dole] the dole (*MS*, canc.). 'Dole' means 'portion' or 'lot', a sense still current in the period though now archaic; *OED*'s last citation is a poem by Tennyson publ. in 1871.

53. See l. 5n.

55–7. Cp. *56–9*. Cp. Empedocles: 'there was . . . a man [Empedocles himself, or possibly Parmenides or Pythagoras] knowing an immense amount, who had acquired a treasure of thoughts . . . for whenever he reached out with all his thoughts, easily he saw each of the things that there are, in ten and even twenty generations of men' (in Porphyry, *Vita Pythagorae* 30).

57. On the conjunction of 'Power' and 'Love' see headnote, *Parallels*. *see now*] shall see (*MS*); one of B.'s handwritten corrections to *1864 proof* (see Appendix C, p. 895).

58–9. Cp. Pope, *An Essay on Man* i 5–6: '[Let us] Expatiate free o'er all this scene of Man; / A mighty maze! but not without a plan'.

11

For pleasant is this flesh;
Our soul, in its rose-mesh
Pulled ever to the earth, still yearns for rest:
Would we some prize might hold
65   To match those manifold
Possessions of the brute,—gain most, as we did best!

12

Let us not always say
"Spite of this flesh to-day
I strove, made head, gained ground upon the whole!"
70   As the bird wings and sings,
Let us cry "All good things
Are ours, nor soul helps flesh more, now, than flesh helps
soul!"

13

Therefore I summon age
To grant youth's heritage,

---

62. *rose-mesh*: apparently B.'s coinage; cp. *Instans Tyrannus* 20 (III 261).

67–72. Reflecting the historical Ibn Ezra's belief that the soul's 'victory . . . over the desires' is obtained 'with the help of the animal soul', not against its resistance.

68. *this flesh*] the flesh (*MS*).

70. Cp. Shelley, 'To a Skylark' 9–10: 'The blue deep thou wingest, / And singing still dost soar, and soaring ever singest'. Cp. also Pippa's first song, in which 'The lark's on the wing' (i 219, p. 111).

71. *good things*: a common phrase in the Bible, as in *Joshua* xxiii 14: 'And, behold, this day I am going the way of all the earth: and ye know in all your hearts and in all your souls, that not one thing hath failed of all the good things which the Lord your God spake concerning you; all are come to pass unto you, and not one thing hath failed thereof', and *Hebrews* xl 7: 'If ye then, being evil, know how to give good gifts unto your children, how much more shall your Father which is in heaven give good things to them that ask him?'

72.] Are ours, nor soul helps flesh, more than flesh helps the soul!" (*MS*).

73–8. Contrast *Sordello* iii 950–57 (I 592) where Sordello is said to belong to the class of those who 'find our common nature . . . Cling when they would discard it; craving strength / To leap from the allotted world, at length / 'Tis left—they floundering without a term, / Each a God's germ, but doomed remain a germ / In unexpanded infancy'. The revised text for the *Poetical Works* of 1863 signposts the fact that this 'doom' may be avoided: 'Each a god's germ, doomed to remain a germ / In unexpanded infancy, unless ... / But that's the story!'—i.e. Sordello will be saved at the end by a vision of the necessary imperfection of human existence.

75 Life's struggle having so far reached its term:
   Thence shall I pass, approved
   A man, for aye removed
   From the developed brute; a God though in the germ.

14

   And I shall thereupon
80 Take rest, ere I be gone
   Once more on my adventure brave and new:
   Fearless and unperplexed,
   When I wage battle next,
   What weapons to select, what armour to indue.

15

85 Youth ended, I shall try
   My gain or loss thereby;
   Be the fire ashes, what survives is gold:
   And I shall weigh the same,
   Give life its praise or blame:
90 Young, all lay in dispute; I shall know, being old.

16

   For note, when evening shuts,
   A certain moment cuts
   The deed off, calls the glory from the grey:
   A whisper from the west
95 Shoots—"Add this to the rest,
   Take it and try its worth: here dies another day."

17

   So, still within this life,
   Though lifted o'er its strife,

76–8. The contrast between 'man' and 'the developed brute' could be read as anti-Darwinian.
79–84. A more ambivalent attitude to this prospect of a future existence of renewed struggle is expressed in *Old Pictures* 161–76 (p. 422). The image of life as a battle is common in B., most famously articulated in the *Epilogue* to his final volume, *Asolando* (1889).
82. *unperplexed*: used also of the 'high man' in *A Grammarian* (l. 123, p. 596).
84. *indue*: 'To put on as a garment; to clothe or cover' (*OED*).
87. Cp. *A Death* 105–6 (p. 730). *Be*] Leave (1868–88), the only verbal variant in eds. after 1864.
91–6. Cp. *Childe Roland* 45–8n. (p. 356).

Let me discern, compare, pronounce at last,
100 "This rage was right i' the main,
That acquiescence vain:
The Future I may face now I have proved the Past."

18

For more is not reserved
To man, with soul just nerved
105 To act to-morrow what he learns to-day:
Here, work enough to watch
The Master work, and catch
Hints of the proper craft, tricks of the tool's true play.

19

As it was better, youth
110 Should strive, through acts uncouth,
Toward making, than repose on aught found made;
So, better, age, exempt
From strife, should know, than tempt
Further. Thou waitedst age; wait death nor be afraid!

20

115 Enough now, if the Right
And Good and Infinite
Be named here, as thou callest thy hand thine own,

102. proved: using *OED* sense 6a of 'prove': 'To put (a person or thing) to the test; to test the genuineness or qualities of'.
104. To] For (*MS* canc.). *with soul just*] whose soul is (*MS*; the *1864* reading is noted on *MS slip*).
105. Cp. FitzGerald, *Rubáiyát*, st. xx: '*To-morrow?*—Why, To-morrow I may be / My self with Yesterday's Sev'n Thousand Years'. FitzGerald's Preface describes Khayyám as one who 'after vainly endeavouring to unshackle his Steps from Destiny, and to catch some authentic glimpse of Tomorrow, falls back upon Today (which has outlasted so many Tomorrows!) as the only Ground he got to stand on, however momentarily slipping from under his Feet' (p. xiii). *he learns*] it learns (*MS*; the *1864* reading is noted on *MS slip*).
111. aught found made;] what was made,— (*MS*; the *1864* reading is noted on *MS slip*).
113. know, than tempt] know,—attempt (*MS* canc.), indicating the sense in which 'tempt' is being used; cp. 'tempter' in *Sordello* iii 655 (I 570).
115. if] that (*MS*; the *1864* reading is noted on *MS slip*).
117. Be named] Are named (*MS*; the *1864* reading is noted on *MS slip*).

With knowledge absolute,
Subject to no dispute
120 From fools that crowded youth, nor let thee feel alone.

                              21

Be there, for once and all,
Severed great minds from small,
Announced to each his station in the Past!
Was I, the world arraigned,
125 Were they, my soul disdained,
Right? Let age speak the truth and give us peace at last!

                              22

Now, who shall arbitrate?
Ten men love what I hate,
Shun what I follow, slight what I receive;
130 Ten, who in ears and eyes
Match me: we all surmise,
They, this thing, and I, that: whom shall my soul
      believe?

                              23

Not on the vulgar mass
Called "work," must sentence pass,

---

120. Cp. *Empedocles* II: 220–9: 'Where shall thy votary fly then? back to men?—
/ But they will gladly welcome him once more, / And help him to unbend his
too tense thought, / And rid him of the presence of himself, / And keep their
friendly chatter at his ear, / And haunt him, till the absence from himself, / That
other torment, grow unbearable; / And he will fly to solitude again'. Ben Ezra
transforms this unproductive dialectic into an evolutionary progression. See also
l. 48n.   *From fools that crowded*] From that crowd round (*MS*; probably a copying error, with 'fools' omitted after 'From'; the *1864* reading is noted on *MS slip*).
121–3. Cp. *Master Hugues* 49–50 (III 393): 'Masters being lauded and sciolists shent,
/ Parted the sheep from the goats!' and *Cleon* 115–22 (p. 573).
124–5. 'whom' must be supplied between 'I', and 'the world' and 'they' and 'my
soul'. Edward Nolan's attempt to interpret the structures as absolute is uncon-
vincing ('Browning's "Rabbi Ben Ezra", Lines 124–125'. *Explicator* li [Jan. 1993] 90).
125. *my soul disdained*: cp. Shelley, *Rosalind and Helen* 566–7: 'in this erring world
to live / My soul disdained not'.
127–32. Cp. *La Saisiaz* (1878) 297–302.
132. *my soul*] a man (*MS*).
133–50. On the value of potential as opposed to actual achievement in B., see
headnote, *Parallels*. There are striking analogies here with *A Grammarian* (p. 586).
134. *must sentence*] will sentence (*MS*).

135   Things done, that took the eye and had the price;
       O'er which, from level stand,
       The low world laid its hand,
       Found straightway to its mind, could value in a trice:

                         24
       But all, the world's coarse thumb
140   And finger failed to plumb,
       So passed in making up the main account;
       All instincts immature,
       All purposes unsure,
       That weighed not as his work, yet swelled
              the man's amount:

                         25
145   Thoughts hardly to be packed
       Into a narrow act,
       Fancies that broke through language and escaped;
       All I could never be,
       All, men ignored in me,
150   This, I was worth to God, whose wheel the pitcher
              shaped.

                         26
       Ay, note that Potter's wheel,
       That metaphor! and feel

136. O'er which] Whereon (*MS*).
138. could value] and valued (*MS*).
141. passed in] passed by, (*MS*).
142. All] The (*MS*).
143. All] The (*MS*).
144. weighed . . . swelled] weigh . . . swell (*MS*; 'swell' is written over 'made').
145–6. Cp. *Sordello* v 547 (I 692): 'Thought is the soul of act', and *CE* 1035–8 (III 87).
145. hardly] never (*MS,* canc.).
150. This] All (*MS*).   *whose wheel the pitcher shaped*: inverted syntax: 'whose wheel shaped the pitcher'.
151–92. The metaphor of the divine potter is found in sts. lix–lxiii of FitzGerald's *Rubáiyát*, where it raises questions about the purpose of existence (e.g. st. lxi where one of the 'pots' states: 'Surely not in vain / My Substance from the common Earth was ta'en, / That He who subtly wrought me into Shape / Should stamp me back to common Earth again' and about God's justice, as in st. lxiii where another pot asks: 'They sneer at me for leaning all awry; / What! did the Hand

Why time spins fast, why passive lies our clay,—
Thou, to whom fools propound,
155 When the wine makes its round,
"Since life fleets, all is change; the Past gone, seize
to-day!"

27

Fool! All that is, at all,
Lasts ever, past recall;
Earth changes, but thy soul and God stand sure:
160 What entered into thee,
That was, is, and shall be:
Time's wheel runs back or stops; Potter and clay endure.

---

then of the Potter shake?' These images are found in the original Persian texts, but FitzGerald would have had in mind the extensive biblical sources for the divine potter, e.g. *Isaiah* xlv 9: 'Shall the clay say to him that fashioneth it, What makest thou? or thy work, He hath no hands?' and *Romans* ix 20–21: 'Shall the thing formed say to him that formed it, Why hast thou made me thus? Hath not the potter power over the clay, of the same lump to make one vessel unto honour, and another unto dishonour?'

153. spins fast] turns round (*MS*).

154–6. A general paraphrase of the dominant motif of FitzGerald's *Rubáiyát*, e.g. sts. iii–iv: 'I heard a Voice within the Tavern cry, / "Awake, my Little ones, and fill the Cup / Before Life's Liquor in its Cup be dry." // And, as the Cock crew, those who stood before / The Tavern shouted—"Open then the Door! / You know how little while we have to stay, / And, once departed, may return no more."', and st. xx: 'Ah, my Belovéd, fill the Cup that clears / To-day of past Regrets and future Fears'.

156. all] earth (*MS*). *seize to-day!* a literal translation of the Latin tag 'carpe diem' (Horace, *Odes* I xi 8).

157–8. Derived from Empedocles, who argues in many places that once the contents of the universe were constituted, 'nothing ever comes to birth later in addition to these, and there is no passing away, for if they were continually perishing they would no longer exist . . . Fools . . . who suppose that what formerly did not exist comes into existence, or that something dies and is completely destroyed' (transl. M. R. Wright, *Empedocles: the Extant Fragments* [1981] 167, 268). The 'atomic' theory of Epicurus was founded on this principle of the perpetual dissolution and reconstitution of matter, and was given poetic form in Lucretius' *De Rerum Natura*; the historical Ibn Ezra also endorsed this principle, though not the theological consequences that classical philosophy deduced from it: the indifference of the gods to human life and the finality of death.

159. changes, but thy soul] passes, but the soul (*MS*).

28
He fixed thee mid this dance
Of plastic circumstance,
165 This Present, thou, forsooth, wouldst fain arrest:
Machinery just meant
To give thy soul its bent,
Try thee and turn thee forth, sufficiently impressed.

29
What though the earlier grooves
170 Which ran the laughing loves
Around thy base, no longer pause and press?
What though, about thy rim,
Scull-things in order grim
Grow out, in graver mood, obey the sterner stress?

30
175 Look not thou down but up!
To uses of a cup,

163–74. The imagery here may be indebted to the historical Ibn Ezra's argument
that 'it is not so much *the soul* of the righteous that is to be everlasting as . . . *the
divine writing inscribed thereon,* that is, the knowledge acquired by the soul during
its connection with the body' (Friedländer, p. 44: Friedländer's italics).

163. this dance] that dance (*MS*).

164. plastic circumstance: cp. Charles Mackay, *Egeria* (1850) III 120–1: 'Him would
the Earth receive as king and lord, / Him would each plastic circumstance obey'.
'Plastic' here has the passive sense given in *OED* 6a: 'Capable of being moulded,
fashioned, or impressed'. (Cp. l. 168.) The word in its active sense was associated with pottery: *OED* 1a cites Ben Jonson, *The Magnetic Lady* (1632): 'a meere
Plastick, or Potters ambition'.

165. This Present] That Present (*MS*).

166. With this concept, cp. in *Sordello* iii 811–35 (I 582) the extended metaphor
of life as the construction of an 'engine', which at death will be 'Dismounted
wheel by wheel'. See also ll. 175–80n.

167. its bent] the bent (*MS*).

170. Which] That (*MS*). *laughing loves*: cp. Samuel Boyse, 'To Mr. William
Cumming going to France, in August 1735' 28–30: 'For *there* fair Venus keeps
her sov'reign Court, / There all her laughing *Loves* in Crowds resort, / And in
a thousand Shapes surprize the Heart!' As this context suggests, 'loves' are to be
understood here as cupids or cherubs (*OED* love: sense 7a), forming part of the
decoration of the 'cup'; cp. 'loves and doves' in *Dís Aliter Visum* 63 (p. 694).

173. scull-things: B.'s usual spelling at this date, as in *Dís Aliter Visum* 25 (p. 691).

175–80. Based on a number of Biblical texts, e.g. *Isaiah* xxiv 5–11 and lxv 8 and
(principally) *Matthew* xxvi 28–9: 'For this is my blood of the new testament, which
is shed for many for the remission of sins. But I say unto you, I will not drink

The festal board, lamp's flash and trumpet's peal,
The new wine's foaming flow,
The Master's lips a-glow!
180 Thou, heaven's consummate cup, what needst thou with
earth's wheel?

31

But I need, now as then,
Thee, God, who mouldest men;
And since, not even while the whirl was worst,
Did I,—to the wheel of life
185 With shapes and colours rife,
Bound dizzily,—mistake my end, to slake Thy thirst:

henceforth of this fruit of the vine, until that day when I drink it new with you in my Father's kingdom.' Cp. also Christina Rossetti, 'The Three Enemies' (1862): 'When Christ would sup / He drained the dregs from out my cup' (ll. 34–5), and her 'Christian and Jew' (1862), where believers in heaven are described: 'Boughs of the Living Vine . . . Sap of the Royal Vine it stirs like wine / In all' (ll. 33, 36–7). With the image of the feast and the 'feast-master', which evokes another New Testament text, cp. *Popularity* 16–20n. (pp. 451–2). With the contrast between the finished product and the process of its manufacture, cp. the passage from *Sordello* cited at l. 166 above, esp. ll. 814–16: '[we] watch construct , / In short, an engine: with a finished one / What it can do is all, nought how 'tis done'.
177. lamp's . . . trumpet's] lamps' . . . trumpets' (*MS*; B.'s positioning of the apostrophe is often ambiguous, but the one after 'trumpets' is decisively outside the 's'). *183–6.* For the source of this language in Arnold's *Empedocles*, see l. 5n. The historical Empedocles, unlike Arnold's character, speaks in some passages of an afterlife as the culmination of a progressive cycle of reincarnations: 'And at the end they come forth among men on earth as prophets, minstrels, physicians and leaders, and from these they arise as gods, highest in power' when '[w]ith other immortals they share hearth and table, having no part in human sorrows, unwearied' (Clement, *Stromateis* 4.150.1, 5.122.3: Clement uses Empedocles' idea as a Christian harbinger). Arnold himself alludes to the second of these passages in *The Strayed Reveller* 130–281, but reinforcing the distinction between the indifferent gods and the 'human sorrows' of anguished mortal poets: in *Empedocles*, Callicles' songs restate the contrast. The imagery recalls the myth of Ixion, who was punished by Zeus (for wooing Zeus' wife Hera) by being bound to a continually revolving wheel. B. dramatized the story in *Ixion* (*Jocoseria* 1883). The phrasing also recalls *King Lear*. 'I am bound / Upon a wheel of fire' (IV vii 45–7).

32

So, take and use Thy work!
Amend what flaws may lurk,
What strain o' the stuff, what warpings past the aim!
190   My times be in Thy hand!
Perfect the cup as planned!
Let age approve of youth, and death complete the same!

---

188. what] written over 'the' or 'those' in *MS*.
189. What strain . . . what warpings] The strain . . . the warpings (*MS*).
191. Perfect: the imperative verb ('Make the cup perfect'), so the accent falls
on the second syllable, though readers may also 'hear' the word as an adjective,
anticipating God's work: 'The cup is perfect'.   *the cup*] Thy work (*MS*).

43 James Lee

Text and publication

First publ. *DP*, 28 May 1864; repr. *1864²*, *1868* (when the title was changed to 'James Lee's Wife'), *1880*, *1888*. Our text is *1864*.

The MS, part of the printer's copy for *DP*, is at *Morgan*. Section vi was published as a separate poem in the *Atlantic Monthly* xiii (June 1864) 737–8, the third of three poems printed from advance proofs supplied by B. to his American publishers Ticknor and Fields. B. later claimed that he, personally, 'never contributed a line to the "Atlantic Monthly"', since James Fields 'chose to dispose of the poems . . . as he pleased, without reference to me' (2 Oct 1881, *Trumpeter* 29), yet his agreement with Fields specifically allowed for magazine publication (see Appendix C, p. 894). The first six stanzas of section vi had themselves been published years earlier in the *Monthly Repository* n.s. x (1836), under the title *Lines* (I 338). B. told Furnivall: 'The lines about the wind are somewhere in the "Repository": I retained no copy of them, and when, many years afterward, I wanted to include them in "James Lee", I applied to Mrs Fox,—who copied and sent the poem—possessing as she did the series of magazines' (2 Oct. 1881: *Trumpeter* 28). Only substantive variants from this early version are recorded here (*1836*). Five sections were reprinted in *1865*: i ('Song from "James Lee"') forms a separate item; ii, iii, and v are printed in the *DP* sequence (with the titles 'From "James Lee"', 'From the Same' and 'From the Same'); vii ('From "James Lee"') is a separate piece. Section vii appeared again in *1872* under the title 'Song from "James Lee"'. A version of section viii, under the title 'Study of a Hand, by Lionardo', was sent in 1857 for publication in *The Keepsake*, but did not appear (see III 700). Only substantive variants from this text are recorded here (*1857*).

The Houghton Library at Harvard has a copy of *1864* presented to George Eliot; its main interest lies in the MS stanzas added to *Gold Hair* which anticipate *1864²* (see Appendix C, p. 895), but it is noteworthy that *James Lee* is the only other poem where B. recorded readings in advance of the second edition; one of these (to the title of section i) is a unique variant.

The textual history of the poem is an anthology of exceptions to B.'s usual practices of composition and publication. It was very rare for him to incorporate material written or published earlier in a new context, yet in this poem he did it twice; he disliked being published in magazines; parts of the poem appear in two volumes of selections, and the whole poem in another. The addition of 61 lines to section viii of the poem in *1868* is also very unusual: they constitute the longest passage to be added to a poem since the revisions B. made for the *Poems* of 1849.

Composition and date

The setting of the poem on 'this bitter coast of France' (l. 27) suggests that it was begun during, or shortly after, one of the periods that B. spent in Brittany following EBB.'s death. He was there in the late summer of 1861, 1862, and 1863; 1862 is a plausible guess (*Gridley* 214 following DeVane, *Handbook* 285).

Title] *James Lee's Wife* (*1868–88*). The parts of the poem repr. in *1872* (see headnote) appear as 'from "James Lee"' even though the title had been changed in *1868*.

On 18 Aug. 1862 he described Sainte Marie, the 'wild little place in Brittany' where he was staying with his father, his sister Sarianna and his son Pen: 'a hamlet of a dozen houses, perfectly lonely—one may walk on the edge of the low rocks by the sea for miles—or go into the country at the back . . . The place is much to my mind; I have brought books, & write: I wanted a change' (*Dearest Isa* 116). In the same letter the phrase 'at the window', the title of the first section of the poem, occurs in a significant context: 'I feel out of the very earth sometimes, as I sit here at the window—with the little church, a field, a few houses, and the sea . . . Such a soft sea & such a mournful wind! I wrote a poem yesterday of 120 lines—& mean to keep writing, whether I like it or no' (p. 119). The 120 lines may belong to *James Lee*, though B.'s phrasing suggests a complete poem; if so, *Gold Hair* (135 lines) is a likelier candidate (DeVane *Handbook* 285). But in any case the landscape and mood evoked by B. are close to those of the poem. See also ll. 54–5n.

Sources and influences

Although B.'s feelings of loss and dissociation in the aftermath of EBB.'s death clearly shaped the poem, it does not straightforwardly present these feelings; they are transposed into a different emotional register and a different gender. The (unnamed) female speaker, who speaks throughout, is lamenting not her beloved's death but their separation, caused by his ceasing to love her; as B. wrote to Julia Wedgwood, they are 'people newly-married, trying to realize a dream of being sufficient to each other, in a foreign land (where you can try such an experiment) and finding it break up—the man being tired *first*,—and tired precisely of the love' (*RB & JW* 123). Elements of this situation can be aligned with that of B. and EBB., and specifically with Betty Miller's theory that B. had, indeed, tired of EBB. before her death (*Miller* 213–16, and on the poem, 225–6); but B.'s 'newly-married' does not fit this reading, nor does his significant (and generally overlooked) emphasis on 'the man being tired *first*', which implies that the woman, too, would have tired of the 'experiment' in time.

B.'s memories of his past life with EBB., and his involvement in the publication of her *Last Poems* (1862), suggest several lines of influence: from *Sonnets from the Portuguese*, whose speaker resembles the speaker of *James Lee* in her physical debility and self-conscious analysis of feeling; from the renunciation-poem 'Change upon Change' (*Poems*, 1850), which links the change in a man's feelings with the change from summer to winter; and from the poems of exhaustion and disenchantment that mark *Last Poems* ('My Heart and I', 'De Profundis'). The incorporation of two of his own uncollected pieces in sections vi and viii, and the re-use of the title 'By the Fireside' in section ii (see p. 456), imply that B.'s backward glance included his own career.

Besides *Sonnets from the Portuguese*, another and more recent sonnet-sequence, George Meredith's *Modern Love*, may have influenced both the form and subject-matter of B.'s poem: Meredith presented a copy to B. on publication in 1862 (see *Collections* A1588). But note that the theme of (double) sexual infidelity in Meredith's poem is not obviously present in *James Lee*, and bears more strongly on other poems in *DP* such as *The Worst of It*. The narrative technique, in which events take place in the intervals of a monologue (e.g. the couple's relationship deteriorates between i and ii, autumn has made a further advance between ii and iii, etc.) recalls Tennyson's *Maud* (1855), one section of which (II ii) is set in Brittany, and Arthur Hugh Clough's *Amours de Voyage*, which first appeared in the *Atlantic Monthly* between Feb. and May 1858; cp. *Dîs Aliter Visum* (p. 688).

Parallels in B.

James Lee is B.'s only sequence poem, and he was doubtful about its success: in the letter to Julia Wedgwood quoted above (*Sources* [1]), he remarked: 'I have expressed it all insufficiently, and will break the chain up, one day, and leave so many separate little round rings to roll each its way, if it can.' This may account for the dispersal of the poem in successive volumes of selections, though it was retained as a whole in collected editions (see above, *Text*). Thematically, the poem belongs to a series of studies of erotic failure and disillusion, which goes back through *M & W* (*In a Year* [p. 270], *Lovers' Quarrel* [p. 376], *Two in the Campagna* [p. 556], *Woman's Last Word* [III 273]) to early works such as *Earth's Immortalities* (II 250) or *The Lost Mistress* (II 293). The cluster of such poems in *DP* (*Too Late*, *The Worst of It*, *Dîs Aliter Visum* [p. 688]) is not in itself unusual; *M & W* has a striking imbalance between poems of happy and unhappy love. The short lines of the first section recall two poems of *M & W* with female speakers: *In a Year* and *Woman's Last Word*. Besides *Balaustion's Adventure* (1871) and *Aristophanes* (1875), each of which occupies an entire volume, and Pompilia's monologue in bk ix of *Ring*, *James Lee* is B.'s longest poem in a female voice.

I

AT THE WINDOW

I

Ah, love, but a day,
    And the world has changed!
The sun's away,
    And the bird's estranged;
5   The wind has dropped,
    And the sky's deranged:
Summer has stopped.

I Title] not *MS*; in the Houghton copy of *1864*, B. inserted 'James Lee's Wife' before 'At the Window'; JAMES LEE'S WIFE SPEAKS AT THE WINDOW (*1864²–1888*): Milsand's copy (ABL/JMA) also has 'James Lee's wife speaks at the window'. For the echo of a letter B. wrote while in Brittany, see headnote, *Sources*. The scene recalls Andrea del Sarto's plea to Lucrezia: 'let me sit / Here by the window with your hand in mine / And look a half hour forth on Fiesole, / Both of one mind, as married people use' (ll. 13–16, p. 391), and, by contrast, the invitation in Matthew Arnold's 'Dover Beach': 'Come to the window, sweet is the night-air!' (l. 6).

4. the bird's estranged: it is unusual to find 'estrange' collocated with a non-human subject in the period. It normally refers to estrangement between lovers or relations, or of a person from an abstraction such as heaven, home, or country. *bird's*] bird (*1868–88*).

6. deranged: 'disarranged, disturbed', with the implied sense of 'mad'; cp. *Pietro of Abano* (*DI²*, 1880) 192: 'Opium sets the brain to rights—by cark and care deranged'.

2

Look in my eyes!
　　Wilt thou change too?
10　Should I fear surprise?
　　Shall I find aught new
In the old and dear,
　　In the good and true,
With the changing year?

3

15　Thou art a man,
　　But I am thy love!
For the lake, its swan;
　　For the dell, its dove;
And for thee—(oh, haste!)
20　Me, to bend above,
Me, to hold embraced!

II

BY THE FIRESIDE

1

Is all our fire of shipwreck wood,
　　Oak and pine?
Oh, for the ills half-understood,

8–14. Cp. the opening stanza of EBB.'s 'Change upon Change', which recalls an idyllic landscape now altered by the change of season, and connects it to the lover's change of feeling: 'For if I do not hear thy foot, / The frozen river is as mute, / The flowers have dried down to the root: / And why, since these be changed since May, / Shouldst *thou* change less than *they*?' (ll. 7–11). See also headnote, *Sources*.

15–18. The speaker argues that man is to woman as the lake is to the swan and the 'dell' (wooded hollow) to the dove, i.e. her natural (and enclosing) element and refuge; but the image also suggests that man is incomplete without woman's love. Both swan and dove are traditional images of female beauty and purity; EBB. uses the latter in sonnet xxxv of *Sonnets from the Portuguese*: 'Yet love me— wilt thou? Open thine heart wide, / And fold within the wet wings of thy dove' (ll. 13–14). Cp. also *Woman's Last Word* 23–4: 'Be a man and fold me / With thine arm!' (III 275).

ii. Title] not *MS*. The echo of *By the Fire-Side*, a poem of triumphant love in *M & W* (p. 456), is almost certainly a deliberate irony. The 'conceit' comparing the married couple in their house to the crew of a ship, suggested initially by the fact that their fire is made from shipwreck wood, is maintained and developed throughout this section.

23. Oak for the hull of the traditional sailing-ship, pine for the masts.

25   The dim, dead woe
            Long ago
      Befallen this bitter coast of France!
      Well, poor sailors took their chance;
            I take mine.

                        2

30   A ruddy shaft our fire must shoot
            O'er the sea:
      Do sailors eye the casement—mute,
            Drenched and stark,
            From their bark—
35   And envy, gnash their teeth for hate
      O' the warm safe house and happy freight
            —Thee and me?

                        3

      God help you, sailors, at your need!
            Spare the curse!
40   For some ships, safe in port indeed,
            Rot and rust,
            Run to dust,
      All through worms i' the wood, which crept,
      Gnawed our hearts out while we slept:
45   That is worse!

                        4

      Who lived here before us two?
            Old-world pairs!

33. stark: stiff (with cold).
36. O' the] Of the (*MS*).   *freight*: playing on the nautical theme: the house is like
a ship, 'loaded' with the (supposedly) happy couple.
40–5. The couple's ship, though 'safe in port', might, the speaker suggests,
be destroyed from within, just as a ship in dock may rust and be attacked by
woodworm. The confusion between vehicle and tenor at ll. 43–4, in which the
woodworm is imagined gnawing the lovers' hearts out, may be a symptom of
the speaker's disturbed feelings.
41. Cp. *Job* xiii 28: 'And he, as a rotten thing, consumeth, as a garment that is
moth eaten', and *Matthew* vi 19: 'Lay not up for yourselves treasures upon earth,
where moth and rust doth corrupt'.
42. B. may recall George Herbert's 'Faith', ll. 41–2: 'What though my bodie runne
to dust? / Faith cleaves unto it'.
47. Old-world: old-fashioned; the implication is that marriage in previous generations was more solidly established, but the speaker is prompted to wonder if this
was really the case.

Did a woman ever—would I knew!—
   Watch the man
50 With whom began
Love's voyage full-sail,—(now, gnash your teeth!)
When planks start, open hell beneath
   Unawares?

III

IN THE DOORWAY

1

The swallow has set her six young on the rail,
55   And looks sea-ward:
The water's in stripes like a snake, olive-pale
   To the leeward,—
On the weather-side, black, spotted white with the wind:
"Good fortune departs, and disaster's behind,"—
60 Hark, the wind with its wants and its infinite wail!

2

Our fig-tree, that leaned for the saltness, has furled
   Her five fingers,
Each leaf like a hand opened wide to the world
   Where there lingers

48–53. The metaphor shifts again: the 'ship' of happiness no longer rots in port, but founders in mid-ocean while sailing on 'Love's voyage'. Remembering the 'old-world couple', the speaker asks: 'Did a woman [like me] ever [before me] watch the man with whom her "voyage" of love began, [only to see] the planks of their "ship" open up to reveal hell beneath?' The aside at l. 51 — '(now, gnash your teeth!)' — is directed at the imaginary sailors mentioned in l. 35 who 'gnash [their] teeth' with envy of the couple's supposed domestic contentment.
52. *start*: come apart. *open*: reveal.
iii. Title] not MS.
54–5. On 19 Sept. 1862 B. wrote to Isa Blagden from Brittany (see headnote, *Sources*) of his 'yearning' for Florence: 'Just now, at the approach of Autumn, I feel exactly like a swallow in a cage,—as if I *must* go there, have no business anywhere else, with the year drawing in' (*Dearest Isa* 122).
56–60. 'The sea resembles a striped snake, an omen of ill luck; and this is confirmed by the sound of the wind.' The look and behaviour of a snake are traditional features of augury, as are weather-signs.
60. Anticipating section vi, though there the speaker criticizes the young poet's facile assumption that nature reflects his moods. *wants*: either 'desires', or 'needs', or both.
61. Contrast (noting 'sea-ward' in l. 55) 'dark rosemary, ever a-dying, / Which, 'spite the wind's wrath, / So loves the salt rock's face to seaward', in the Mediterranean landscape of *England in Italy* (ll. 159–61, p. 263).

65   No glint of the gold, Summer sent for her sake:
     How the vines writhe in rows, each impaled on its stake!
     My heart shrivels up, and my spirit shrinks curled.

                                  3
     Yet here are we two; we have love, house enough,
          With the field there,
70   This house of four rooms, that field red and rough,
          Though it yield there,
     For the rabbit that robs, scarce a blade or a bent;
     If a magpie alight now, it seems an event;
     And they both will be gone at November's rebuff.

                                  4
75   But why must cold spread? but wherefore bring change
          To the spirit,
     God meant should mate His with an infinite range,
          And inherit

---

66. The image of torment here, together with the dearth in ll. 70–4, recalls the
landscape of *Childe Roland* (p. 348).

67. Cp. EBB., 'My Heart and I': 'How tired we feel, my heart and I! / We seem
of no use in the world; / Our fancies hang grey and uncurled / About men's
eyes indifferently' (ll. 15–18). See headnote, *Sources*.

72. *For the rabbit that robs*] For rabbits that rob (*MS*, canc.).   *bent*: stalk, blade of
grass; cp. *Childe Roland* 67–69: 'If there pushed any ragged thistle-stalk / Above
its mates, the head was chopped—the bents / Were jealous else' (p. 358).

73–4. Cp. *Lovers' Quarrel* 127–30: 'Could but November come, / Were the noisy
birds struck dumb / At the warning slash / Of his driver's-lash' (p. 383); but
note that the speaker of the earlier poem would welcome the chance to defy the
bleak weather.

75–81. The speaker argues that although the natural world will change with the
coming of winter, this should not affect the 'spirit', which ought to partake of
divine creativity; in other words, the love she and her husband have for each
other should survive the period of estrangement they are going through. The last
two lines are contrastive: 'We should practise a higher form of love than that
which depends on favourable circumstances (summer), and which breaks down
when those circumstances change (winter).'

75. *But*] Oh (*MS*, canc.).   *but*] And (*MS*).

76–7. *the spirit . . . infinite range*: the final section of *A Death* (ll. 666–88, pp. 757–8)
stages a theological debate about this concept of Christ as 'Groom for each bride',
but the speaker here is concerned with its existential meaning: supreme self-
fulfilment, in which the spirit becomes divine and acquires godlike creative power.
The image of Christ as the bridegroom of each individual soul derives from
biblical texts such as *2 Corinthians* xi 2: 'I have espoused you to one husband,
that I may present you as a chaste virgin to Christ', and *Revelation* xxii 17: 'And
the Spirit and the bride say, Come'.

His power to put life in the darkness and cold?
80   Oh, live and love worthily, bear and be bold!
Whom Summer made friends of, let Winter estrange!

IV
ALONG THE BEACH

1

I will be quiet and talk with you,
    And reason why you are wrong:
You wanted my love—is that much true?
85   And so I did love, so I do:
    What has come of it all along?

2

I took you—how could I otherwise?
    For a world to me, and more;
For all, love greatens and glorifies
90   Till God's a-glow, to the loving eyes,
    In what was mere earth before.

3

Yes, earth—yes, mere ignoble earth!
    Now do I mis-state, mistake?
Do I wrong your weakness and call it worth?
95   Expect all harvest, dread no dearth,
    Seal my sense up for your sake?

4

Oh, love, love, no, love! not so, indeed!
    You were just weak earth, I knew:

79. *in the*] into (*MS*).
iv. Title] not *MS*.
82. *And reason*] Will reason (*MS*).
87–8. A variant of Byron's famous lines in *Don Juan* I cxciv: 'Man's love is of man's life a thing apart, / 'Tis woman's whole existence'.
90. *a-glow*: first used in *Mesmerism* 105 (III 484), where it suggests occult erotic power; in another *DP* poem, 'The Worst of It', it marks the memory of happy love: 'My very name made great by your lip, / And my heart a-glow with the good I know / Of a perfect year when we both were young, / And I tasted the angels' fellowship' (ll. 63–6).
92. *yes, mere*] just mere (*MS*).
95. *all harvest*] all beauty (*MS*).

With much in you waste, with many a weed,
100 And plenty of passions run to seed,
    But a little good grain too.

5

And such as you were, I took you for mine:
    Did not you find me yours,
To watch the olive and wait the vine,
105 And wonder when rivers of oil and wine
    Would flow, as the Book assures?

6

Well, and if none of these good things came,
    What did the failure prove?
The man was my whole world, all the same,
110 With his flowers to praise, or his weeds to blame,
    And, either or both, to love.

7

Yet this turns now to a fault—there! there!
    That I do love, watch too long,
And wait too well, and weary and wear;
115 And 'tis all an old story, and my despair
    Fit subject for some new song:

104–6. Olive and vine are both emblems of prosperity and peace in the Bible ('the Book'); there are no rivers of wine, but *Job* xxix 6 has 'rivers of oil'. Cp. also *Psalms* iv 7: 'Thou hast put gladness in my heart, more than in the time that their corn and their wine increased'. The possibility that childlessness is one cause of the couple's discontent is supported by *Psalms* cxxviii 3: 'Thy wife shall be as a fruitful vine by the sides of thine house: thy children like olive plants round about thy table.'

111. And, either] —But, either (*MS*).

112–14. Cp. B.'s remark to Isa Blagden about how the man becomes 'tired precisely of the love' (headnote, *Sources*).

112. Yet this] And this (*MS*).

115. an old story: the subtitle of *Patriot* (p. 340), where it denotes, as here, a familiar pattern of human behaviour, in which self-devotion (whether in politics or love) is met initially with enthusiasm, and then with fickleness and ingratitude.

116–18. Ironically, the 'new song' (l. 116) is an old song, as is clear from the echo in ll. 117–18 of Pope's *Eloisa to Abelard* (1717) 75–6: 'Love, free as air, at sight of human ties, / Spreads his light wings, and in a moment flies'.

8

How the light, light love, he has wings to fly
    At suspicion of a bond:
How my wisdom has bidden your pleasure good-bye,
120 Which will turn up next in a laughing eye,
    And why should you look beyond?

V

ON THE CLIFF

1

I leaned on the turf,
I looked at a rock
Left dry by the surf;
125 For the turf, to call it grass were to mock:
Dead to the roots, so deep was done
The work of the summer sun.

2

And the rock lay flat
As an anvil's face:
130 No iron like that!
Baked dry; of a weed, of a shell, no trace:
Sunshine outside, but ice at the core,
Death's altar by the lone shore.

3

On the turf, sprang gay
135 With his films of blue,
No cricket, I'll say,

117–21.] in quotation marks, *1868–88*, making it clear that this is her song.
119. *How my wisdom*] And the wisdom (*MS*); My wisdom (*1868–88*).   *your pleasure*] the pleasure (*MS*).
120. *Which will turn*] Which turns (*MS*).   *laughing eye*: a cliché in descriptions of female beauty since the seventeenth century: nineteenth-century examples include Barbauld, Coleridge, Hood and Scott. This is the only indication of possible infidelity as a cause of the breakdown of the marriage.
121. *you look*] love look (*MS*).
v. Title] not *MS*.
123. *I looked*] And looked (*MS*).
126. *Dead*] Red (*MS*).
135. *films*: membranes.

But a warhorse, barded and chanfroned too,
The gift of a quixote-mage to his knight,
Real fairy, with wings all right.

4

140 On the rock, they scorch
Like a drop of fire
From a brandished torch,
Fell two red fans of a butterfly:
No turf, no rock, in their ugly stead,
145 See, wonderful blue and red!

5

Is it not so
With the minds of men?
The level and low,
The burnt and bare, in themselves; but then
150 With such a blue and red grace, not theirs,
Love settling unawares!

VI

UNDER THE CLIFF

1

"Still ailing, Wind? Wilt be appeased or no?
  Which needs the other's office, thou or I?
Dost want to be disburthened of a woe,

137. *barded and chanfroned*: a 'bard' was a breastplate, a 'chanfron' (or 'chamfron')
a frontlet protecting the horse's forehead; *J.* records 'chanfrin' as an old French
term for 'the forepart of the head of a horse'. These terms are authentically medieval,
but also feature in Romantic medievalism, e.g. 'barded' in Scott's *Lay of the Last
Minstrel* (1805) I xxix and Southey's *Joan of Arc* (1796) vi 300, x 273, 'chanfron'
in Sir James Bland Burges, *Richard the First* (1801) IV ii.
138. *quixote-mage*: 'a magician such as might be found in the pages of *Don Quixote*'.
For 'quixote' see *Sordello* i 5–7n. (I 395); 'mage' is a favourite term (occurring
in ten poems); see headnote to *Transcendentalism* (III 643).
140–3. The syntax is inverted: 'Two red fans of a butterfly fell on the rock [which]
they scorch like a drop of fire from a brandished torch.'
143. *Fell two*] The two (*MS*); Fall two (*1868–88*). *fans*: wings.
vi. Title] not *MS*; READING A BOOK, UNDER THE CLIFF (*1864²–1888*, a reading also
inserted by B. in the Houghton copy of *1864*, and in the copy of *DP* he presented to Milsand [*ABL/JMA*]).
152–81. B.'s own poem, first published in 1836: see headnote, *Text*.

155   And can, in truth, my voice untie
        Its links, and let it go?

                                    2
        "Art thou a dumb, wronged thing that would be righted,
            Entrusting thus thy cause to me? Forbear.
        No tongue can mend such pleadings; faith, requited
160   With falsehood,—love, at last aware
        Of scorn,—hopes, early blighted,—

                                    3
        "We have them; but I know not any tone
            So fit as thine to falter forth a sorrow:
        Dost think men would go mad without a moan,
165   If they knew any way to borrow
        A pathos like thy own?

                                    4
        "Which sigh wouldst mock, of all the sighs? The one
            So long escaping from lips starved and blue,
        That lasts while on her pallet-bed the nun
170   Stretches her length; her foot comes through
        The straw she shivers on;

                                    5
        "You had not thought she was so tall: and spent,
            Her shrunk lids open, her lean fingers shut
        Close, close, their sharp and livid nails indent
175   The clammy palm; then all is mute:
        That way, the spirit went.

                                    6
        "Or wouldst thou rather that I understand
            Thy will to help me?—like the dog I found

159. such pleadings] thy pleadings (*1836*).
166. thy] thine (*1836*).
167. mock: in the archaic sense of 'imitate', but the modern sense of 'ridicule' is
also present.   *The*] that (*1836, MS*).
169. pallet-bed: variant of 'pallet' in the sense of a straw bed, or a 'small, poor, or
mean bed or couch' (*OED*).
173. open, her] ope, and her (*1836*).
174. Close, close] So close (*1836, MS*).
178. me?—] me— (*1836, MS*, where the question ends at l. 181).

Once, pacing sad this solitary strand,
180   Who would not take my food, poor hound,
But whined and licked my hand."

———————————

7

All this, and more, comes from some young man's pride
    Of power to see,—in failure and mistake,
Relinquishment, disgrace, on every side,—
185   Merely examples for his sake,
Helps to his path untried:

8

Instances he must—simply recognize?
    Oh, more than so!—must, with a learner's zeal,
Make doubly prominent, twice emphasize,
190   By added touches that reveal
The god in babe's disguise.

9

Oh, he knows what defeat means, and the rest!
    Himself the undefeated that shall be:
Failure, disgrace, he flings them you to test,—
195   His triumph, in eternity
Too plainly manifest!

10

Whence, judge if he learn forthwith what the wind
    Means in its moaning—by the happy, prompt,
Instinctive way of youth, I mean; for kind
200   Calm years, exacting their accompt
Of pain, mature the mind:

179. Once, pacing] Once pacing (*1836*, MS). The revision makes it clear that it is the speaker, not the dog, who is 'pacing' the 'strand'. *this*] the (*1836*).
180. Who] That (*1836*).
181. hand.] hand? (*1836*). See l. 178n.
191. The] A (*MS*, canc.). 'A god' would have come less close to being an allusion to Jesus; that allusion is not explicit even so, but is allowed by the definite article.
196. Too] So (*MS*).
198. happy: 'lucky', as in 'happy tact' (*Bishop Blougram* 413, p. 307) but implying also 'facile, unthinking'.
200. Calm years] Long years (*MS*). *accompt*: variant of 'account' (in *J.*, but archaic by B.'s day).

11

And some midsummer morning, at the lull
    Just about daybreak, as he looks across
A sparkling foreign country, wonderful
205   To the sea's edge for gloom and gloss,
    Next minute must annul,—

12

Then, when the wind begins among the vines,
    So low, so low, what shall it mean but this?
"Here is the change beginning, here the lines
210   Circumscribe beauty, set to bliss
    The limit time assigns."

13

Nothing can be as it has been before;
    Better, so call it, only not the same.
To draw one beauty into our hearts' core,
215   And keep it changeless! such our claim;
    So answered,—Never more!

14

Simple? Why this is the old woe o' the world;
    Tune, to whose rise and fall we live and die.
Rise with it, then! Rejoice that man is hurled
220   From change to change unceasingly,
    His soul's wings never furled!

15

That's a new question; still replies the fact,
    Nothing endures: the wind moans, saying so;
We moan in acquiescence: there's life's pact,

203. Just about] Just before (*MS*).
208. mean] say (*1868–88*).
209–11.] not in inverted commas, *MS*.
212–21. B. may be glancing at Arnold's *The Scholar-Gipsy*: 'For what wears out
the life of mortal men? / 'Tis that from change to change their being rolls . . .
Thou hast not lived, why should'st thou perish, so? / Thou hadst *one* aim, *one*
business, *one* desire' (ll. 142–3, 151–2). Cp. *An Epistle* 15n. (p. 512). 'Never more'
in l. 216 may recall Edgar Allan Poe's 'The Raven' (1845).
215. changeless!] changelessly, (*MS*, canc.).
219. Rise with] Rise through (*MS*).
222. replies] remains (*MS*).

225   Perhaps probation—do *I* know?
       God does: endure His act!

16

       Only, for man, how bitter not to grave
           On his soul's hands' palms one fair, good, wise thing
       Just as he grasped it! For himself, death's wave;
230   While time first washes—ah, the sting!—
       O'er all he'd sink to save.

VII

AMONG THE ROCKS

I

Oh, good gigantic smile o' the brown old earth,
    This autumn morning! How he sets his bones
To bask i' the sun, and thrusts out knees and feet

227–9. Only, for man . . . grasped it! the image is of an impression left on the soul as indelible as the lines on the palms of the hand; if it were possible to record such an impression, it would then be legible by a kind of spiritual palmistry. *Ohio* notes a similarity to *Isaiah* xlix 16: 'Behold, I have graven thee upon the palms of my hands; thy walls are continually before me.'

228. his soul's] our soul's (*MS*).

229–31. For himself . . . to save: these are the consequences of *not* achieving the kind of permanence envisaged in ll. 227–9.

229. he] we (*MS*).   *himself*] ourselves (*MS*).

230. first washes] o'er ripples (*MS*, canc.); first ripples (*MS*).

231. O'er] First (*MS*, canc.).   *he'd sink*] we'd sink (*MS*).

vii. Title] not *MS*.

232–43. Both the laughing 'ripple' of the waves and the song of the 'sea-lark' are images of love lavished on a 'low nature': the speaker imagines the 'good old earth' as both the emblem of this 'low nature' and as voicing the 'doctrine' of compensation, perennial in B., according to which it is better to seek for 'gain above': God's reward surpasses fulfilment in this life, and to desire such fulfilment (let alone attain it) would mean abjuring heaven. See *Patriot* 26–30n. (p. 344).

232–4. This passage comes as close as B. ever does to endorsing the Romantic pantheism of Wordsworth in, for example, 'Tintern Abbey', but see also the *Epilogue* to *DP*, ll. 96–101. Nothing elsewhere in B.'s work quite matches this image of the earth itself as a giant form, but cp. *Paracelsus* v 749–52 (I 303), where the human race is compared to a 'glorious creature' that, 'when arous'd—each giant-limb awake', will 'start up, and stand on his own earth', and *Sordello* vi 852–5 (I 768) where a ruined castle wall is compared to 'the chine of some fossil animal / Half turned to earth and flowers'. The bones of the giant Og are (humorously) treated as a landscape feature in two of the three sonnets which B. included in the note he appended to *Jochanan Hakkadosh* (*Jocoseria*, 1883).

234. knees] arms (*MS*).

235   For the ripple to run over in its mirth;
            Listening the while, where on the heap of stones
        The white breast of the sea-lark twitters sweet.

2

        That is the doctrine, simple, ancient, true;
            Such is life's trial, as old earth smiles and knows.
240   If you loved only what were worth your love,
        Love were clear gain, and wholly well for you:
            Make the low nature better by your throes!
        Give earth yourself, go up for gain above!

VIII

BESIDE THE DRAWING-BOARD

I

        "As like as a Hand to another Hand:"
245   Whoever said that foolish thing,
        Could not have studied to understand
            The counsels of God in fashioning,
        Out of the infinite love of His heart,
        This Hand, whose beauty I praise, apart

---

237. sea-lark: a name applied to several small shore-birds, esp. the ringed plover and sandpiper. Cp. John Keble, 'Languor' (*Lyra Innocentium*, 1846), a poem which begins by the sea-shore, whose beauty prompts the question 'Say, can this earth a loving trance / Of deeper bliss reveal?' (ll. 17–18), to which the answer is the sight of a child recovering from illness: 'Our little sister, late as gay / As sea-lark drench'd in ocean spray, / Now from her couch of languor freed / One hour upon soft air to feed' (ll. 27–30).

238. ancient, true] old and true (*MS*).

239. as old] the old (*MS*).

242–3] Give the low nature comfort by your throes! / Leave it yourself, go up for gain above! (*MS*).

viii. Title] not MS.

244–69. These lines formed a separate poem with the title *Study of a Hand, by Lionardo*, written in 1857: see III 701–2, and headnote. In the earlier version Leonardo da Vinci is the speaker, whereas here the speaker is James Lee's wife; she projects Leonardo's voice in the revised and expanded second section, and the new third section, which B. added in *1868*: see below.

244.] "As like as a hand is to a hand!" (*1857*). The phrase sounds proverbial, though we have not located a prior example; the sense is akin to 'as like as two peas'. The speaker goes on to object that each 'hand' (and by extension person) is a unique product of God's fashioning.

245. said] says (*1857, MS*).

246. Could not] Cannot (*1857, MS*).

250 From the world of wonder left to praise,
    If I tried to learn the other ways
    Of love, in its skill, or love, in its power.
    "As like as a Hand to another Hand:"
    Who said that, never took his stand,
255 Found and followed, like me, an hour,
    The beauty in this,—how free, how fine
    To fear, almost,—of the limit-line!
    As I looked at this, and learned and drew,
    Drew and learned, and looked again,
260 While fast the happy minutes flew,
    Its beauty mounted into my brain,
    And a fancy seized me; I was fain
    To efface my work, begin anew,
    Kiss what before I only drew;
265 Ay, laying the red chalk 'twixt my lips,
    With soul to help if the mere lips failed,

250. the world] a world (*1857*).
251. If I tried to] Should one try and (*1857*).
252.] Of that love in the Skill, that love in the Power. (*1857*).
253.] not *1857*, MS.
254–5.] Oh, never he followed, a single hour, (*1857*).
254. said] says (*MS*). *took his stand*: cp. the use of 'take my stand' in *Toccata* 31 (p. 373).
256.] The Beauty alone, so free, so fine, (*1857*).
257. limit-line: the line that limits (i.e. articulates or circumscribes) the shape in question. Apparently B.'s coinage: *OED* cites only this use and it is the earliest example in *English Poetry*. B. also uses it in *Red Cotton Night-Cap Country* (1873) i 36 and *Plot-Culture* (*Fersishtah's Fancies*, 1886) 33–6: 'Did no limit-line / Round thee about, apportion thee thy place / Clean-cut from out and off the illimitable,— / Minuteness severed from immensity'.
258–9. In *1857* these lines, spoken by Leonardo da Vinci, may refer to his obsessive search for perfection as a painter; in their new context they allude to the speaker's painstaking effort as an amateur artist. These two readings are brought together in the lines added to the poem in *1868*: see below.
258. this] it (*1857*).
259. Drew] And drew, (*1857*).
261. Its beauty] The beauty (*1857*).
263. B. was preoccupied throughout his career with this idea: cp. Jules's breaking of his statues in *Pippa Passes*: 'I do but break these paltry models up / To begin art afresh' (ii 232–3, p. 138). *work,*] work and (*1857*).
264. only drew;] simply drew— (*1857*, MS).
266.] With my soul close by, if the weak lips ailed, (*1857*).

> I kissed all right where the drawing ailed,
> Kissed fast the grace that somehow slips
> Still from one's soulless finger-tips.

267–9. By holding the chalk between her lips, the speaker produces a botched drawing which, however, comes closer to the truth of her subject, since it better expresses the passion of her 'soul'. This is an extreme version of the contrast between technical perfection and imperfect aspiration in *Andrea* 79–82 (p. 395); see also *Pippa Passes* iv 33–56 (pp. 159–61). Note that in *1857* the speaker, Leonardo, does not act on his 'fancy': see l. 267n.

267. kissed all right] would kiss all safe (*1857*).   *ailed,*] failed (*1857*).

268. Kissed fast] —Kiss down (*1857*).

269^270] there is no division in MS. In *1868* a new second section was interpolated here, followed by a third section which concludes with ll. 270–1 of our text (i.e. what is now the whole of section 2 in *1864*). *1888* has one verbal variant at l. [46]; the transposed quotation marks in l. [61] also alter the sense. Note that in *1868–88* the sections or stanzas within the individual poems of the sequence are numbered in roman, as is standard in these editions:

II

'Tis a clay cast, the perfect thing,
  From Hand live once, dead long ago:
Princess-like it wears the ring
  To fancy's eye, by which we know
[5]   That here at length a master found
His match, a proud lone soul its mate,
As soaring genius sank to ground
  And pencil could not emulate
The beauty in this,—how free, how fine
[10] To fear almost!—of the limit-line.
Long ago the god, like me
The worm, learned, each in our degree:
Looked and loved, learned and drew,
  Drew and learned and loved again,
[15] While fast the happy minutes flew,
Till beauty mounted into his brain
And on the finger that outvied
  His art he placed the ring that's there,
Still by fancy's eye descried,
[20]   In token of a marriage rare:
For him on earth, his art's despair:
For him in heaven, his soul's fit bride.

III

Little girl with the poor coarse hand
  I turned from to a cold clay cast—
[25] I have my lesson, understand
  The worth of flesh and blood at last!
Nothing but beauty in a Hand?
  Because he could not change the hue,
  Mend the lines and make them true

[30] To this which met his soul's demand,—
    Would Da Vinci turn from you?
    I hear him laugh my woes to scorn—
    "The fool forsooth is all forlorn
    Because the beauty, she thinks best,
[35] Lived long ago or was never born,—
    Because no beauty bears the test
    In this rough peasant Hand! Confessed
    'Art is null and study void!'
    So sayest thou? So said not I,
[40] Who threw the faulty pencil by,
    And years instead of hours employed,
    Learning the veritable use
    Of flesh and bone and nerve beneath
    Lines and hue of the outer sheath,
[45] If haply I might reproduce
    One motive of the mechanism, [*1888*: powers profuse,]
    Flesh and bone and nerve that make
    The poorest coarsest human hand
    An object worthy to be scanned
[50] A whole life long for their sole sake.
    Shall earth and the cramped moment-space
    Yield the heavenly crowning grace?
    Now the parts and then the whole?
    Who art thou, with stinted soul
[55] And stunted body, thus to cry
    'I love,—shall that be life's strait dole?
    I must live beloved or die!'
    This peasant hand that spins the wool
    And bakes the bread, why lives it on,
[60] Poor and coarse with beauty gone,—
    What use survives the beauty? Fool!" [*1888*: beauty?" Fool!]
    Go, little girl, with the poor coarse hand!
    I have my lesson, shall understand.

In this revised scheme, it becomes clear that the speaker has been drawing from a clay cast of a woman's hand, whose supreme beauty the great artist Leonardo had long ago failed to capture in his own drawing. (It seems odd that she should own such an object, and to imagine it as a reproduction introduces an unwanted twist into the argument.) On one of the fingers of the hand the speaker 'sees' a visionary ring, placed there by the artist as a token of his acceptance of earthly failure, which will be redeemed by fulfilment in heaven. (Cp. *Abt Vogler* 72, p. 768.) The speaker imagines Leonardo going through the same process of trial and error as she has done, differing not in kind but in degree (he 'the god', she 'the worm'), but having a deeper understanding of the meaning of his failure. In the dialogue she imagines holding with him in section III, Leonardo rebukes her for turning away from a peasant-girl because her 'poor coarse hand' does not match the beauty of the clay cast: he himself abandoned art for the study of anatomy because he wanted to 'reproduce' not the 'outer sheath' but the 'motive of the mechanism'. The critique of art here echoes Plato's scorn of painting as an imitation of a 'reality' which is itself at one remove from the truth of the 'Forms',

2

270   Go, little girl, with the poor coarse hand!
       I have my lesson, shall understand.

IX

ON DECK

I

       There is nothing to remember in me,
           Nothing I ever said with a grace,
           Nothing I did that you cared to see,
275   Nothing I was that deserves a place
       In your mind, now I leave you, set you free.

---

but it does so in the context of an anti-elitism that goes back to B.'s partisanship of the 'warped souls and bodies' of the common people in *Sordello* (see iii 676–757, I 572–8, and note 'stinted soul / And stunted body', ll. [54–5]). B. may also have recalled EBB.'s *Aurora Leigh* vii 761–826, esp. 785–89: 'Look long enough / On any peasant's face here, coarse and lined, / You'll catch Antinous somewhere in that clay, / As perfect featured as he yearns at Rome / From marble pale with beauty'. The speaker's self-pitying insistence that her love must be reciprocated is a form of false consciousness, akin to despising a peasant-girl's hand for not being 'beautiful': value lies not in 'love' or 'beauty' but in productive 'use'. Although this argument embodies ideas which B. expresses elsewhere, it does so with an absolutism that belongs to its dramatic context; note also that the next (and final) section of the poem concludes with the speaker uttering, with undiminished intensity, her yearning for James Lee to return her love.
  The statement given to Leonardo that he 'threw the faulty pencil by' in favour of anatomical study is not historically accurate, and is probably the speaker's exaggeration rather than B.'s error. The 'clay cast' of a hand may have been suggested to B. by the cast of his and EBB.'s clasped hands made by Harriet Hosmer in Rome in 1853 (*Collections* H538; the original plaster cast is at Radcliffe College). B. himself had spent time modelling in clay in his friend William Wetmore Story's studio in Rome; EBB. wrote to Fanny Haworth in the autumn of 1860 that he was 'making extraordinary progress, turning to account his studies on anatomy' and that he was 'enchanted with his new trade' (*Letters of EBB* ii 411, and see also the long passage on this subject in her letter to Sarianna Browning written towards the end of March 1861, *ibid.* 434–6).
  270–71. The 'little girl' is the model.
  ix. Title] not *MS.* The speaker's departure by sea may recall Christina Rossetti's 'Wife to Husband', recently publ. in *Goblin Market and Other Poems* (1862), and itself a reply to B.'s *Any Wife to Any Husband* (III 647); the poem opens: 'Pardon the faults in me, / For the love of years ago: / Good bye. / I must drift across the sea, / I must sink into the snow, / I must die'.
  272–311. Unusually, the first line of each stanza ends with the same word, 'me', to which the third and fifth lines produce a different rhyme, 'free', 'plea', etc.
  272–6. When EBB. finally agreed to allow B. to visit her in Wimpole Street, she wrote to him: 'There is nothing to see in me,—nor to hear in me' (15 May 1845, *Correspondence* x 216).
  274. cared] care (*1868–88*).

2

Conceded! In turn, concede to me,
    Such things have been as a mutual flame.
Your soul's locked fast; but, love for a key,
280   You might let it loose, till I grew the same
In your eyes, as in mine you stand: strange plea!

3

For then, then, what would it matter to me
    That I was the harsh, ill-favoured one?
We both should be like as pea and pea;
285   It was ever so since the world begun:
So, let me proceed with my reverie.

4

How strange it were if you had all me,
    As I have all you in my heart and brain,

---

277. The phrase 'mutual flame' originates in Shakespeare's 'The Phoenix and Turtle'
('fled / In a mutual flame from hence', ll. 23–4), but in the eighteenth century
became a poetic commonplace, often used with knowing humour; it virtually
disappears after the 1820s, and B.'s speaker seems to deploy it here with a trace
of self-consciousness. In the lines that follow she recalls by inversion the metaphysical triumph of Shakespeare's (mythical) pair: 'So they loved as love in twain
/ Had the essence but in one . . . Hearts remote, yet not asunder; / Distance and
no space was seen / 'Twixt this Turtle and his queen . . . Either was the other's
mine' (ll. 25–6, 29–31, 36).
279.] My soul's locked fast, but, love for your key, (*MS*).   *but, love for a key*: 'but
with love for a key . . .'
280. *let it loose*] let loose (*MS*, canc.); let mine loose (*MS*).
283. *ill-favoured*: ugly. Possibly influenced by occurrences related to courtship and
marriage in *As You Like It*: Rosalind, scorning the shepherdess Phebe for her
supposed ugliness ('inky brows . . . black silk hair . . . bugle eyeballs'), turns to Phebe's
rejected suitor Silvius and says: 'You are a thousand times a properer man / Than
she a woman. 'Tis such fools as you / That makes the world full of ill-favour'd
children' (III v 46–7, 51–3). The phrase recurs in the final scene where
Touchstone refers to Audrey as 'an ill-favour'd thing, sir, but mine own' (V iv 58).
284. *should be*] should turn (*MS*).   *like as pea and pea*: B. uses this phrase to denote
artistic realism in *Fra Lippo* 178 (p. 495).
287–9. The language is close to that of the love-letters, e.g. B. to EBB., 16 Nov.
1845: 'my whole life is wound up and down and over you . . . I feel you stir
everywhere: I am not conscious of thinking or feeling but *about* you'
(*Correspondence* xi 174). The collocation 'heart and brain' is rare before the eighteenth century (though notable in George Herbert's 'Love. I', where 'mortall love'
is seen as 'possessing heart and brain' to the detriment of divine love) but used
with increasing frequency thereafter; its most famous occurrence in the period is
'the unquiet heart and brain' of Tennyson's *In Memoriam* v. B.'s work has 12
occurrences, e.g. *Sordello* ii 963 (I 522).

You, whose least word brought gloom or glee,
290   Who never lifted the hand in vain
Will hold mine yet, from over the sea!

5

Strange, if a face, when you thought of me,
    Rose like your own face present now,
With eyes as dear in their due degree,
295   Much such a mouth, and as bright a brow,
Till you saw yourself, while you cried "'Tis She!"

6

Well, you may, or you must, set down to me
    Love that was life, life that was love;
A tenure of breath at your lips' decree,
300   A passion to stand as your thoughts approve,
A rapture to fall where your foot might be.

7

But did one touch of such love for me
    Come in a word or a look of yours,
Whose words and looks will, circling, flee
305   Round me and round while life endures,—
Could I fancy "As I feel, thus feels He;"

289–91. Cp. *Sonnets from the Portuguese* vi, which begins with the speaker renouncing her lover (for his own sake) but declaring: 'Nevermore . . . I shall command / The uses of my soul, nor lift my hand / Serenely in the sunshine as before, / Without the sense of that which I forbore— / Thy touch upon the palm. The widest land / Doom takes to part us, leaves thy heart in mine / With pulses that beat double' (ll. 2, 4–10).

291.] Which still will hold me—from over the sea. (*MS*, canc.); Which still holds mine—from over the sea. (*MS*). The *1864* reading, which elides the relative pronoun, was introduced at the proof stage, and shows clearly the process by which B. created what Ruskin called his 'unconscionable ellipses' (see Appendix B, p. 880 for Ruskin's criticism, and p. 881 for B.'s reply).

297. or] canc. in *MS*; not *1868–88*.

298. Cp. the titles of the paired poems in *Men and Women*, 'Love in a Life' and 'Life in a Love' (III 1–3).

301. Cp. the closing lines of bk i of *Ring*, in which B. invokes EBB.'s blessing from 'that heaven thy home' and imagines himself 'blessing back . . . Some whiteness which, I judge, thy face makes proud, / Some wanness where, I think, thy foot may fall!'

304. and looks] and whose looks (*MS*, canc.).   *flee*] free (*MS*: presumably B.'s trancription error, since it does not make grammatical sense).

8

Why, fade you might to a thing like me,
　　And your hair grow these coarse hanks of hair,
　　And your skin, this bark of a gnarled tree,—
310　　You might turn myself; should I know or care,
　　When I should be dead of joy, James Lee?

310–11.] You might turn myself, I should know nor care / For I should be dead
of joy, James Lee! (*MS*).

44 Dîs Aliter Visum;

or,

Le Byron de nos Jours

Text and publication

First publ. *DP*, 28 May 1864; repr. *1864²*, *1868, 1880, 1888*. Our text is *1864*. The MS, part of the printer's copy for *DP*, is at *Morgan*. It is a very clean copy, with few cancelled readings. There is only a handful of verbal variants between *MS* and *1864* (mostly towards the end of the poem) and none in subsequent editions; all are minor, and the only significant textual change is in the speech-punctuation of ll. 99–100, where the re-positioning of quotation marks changes the way in which the speaker brings to a close her speculative 'voicing' of her companion's thoughts when they met ten years before.

Composition and date

The main action of the poem (the speaker's narrative) is almost certainly set in Pornic, a seaside resort on the Atlantic coast of Brittany, which B. began visiting after the death of EBB. Other poems reflecting this locale in *DP* include *James Lee* (p. 665) and *Gold Hair*; cp. also *Fifine at the Fair* (1872). As with *A Likeness* (p. 642), some details belong to the mid-1850s: Heine (l. 40) and Schumann (l. 36) both died in 1856. DeVane suggests that 'it is possible that the poem was the product of Browning's summer of 1858, spent at Le Havre with his wife and his father' (*Handbook* 288). But it must be remembered that, as with *Youth and Art* (p. 700), the speaker is alluding to events that have taken place years earlier, and that the 'now' of l. 36 ('Schumann's our music-maker now') belongs to a train of thought which is imagined to have taken place a decade before the present time of the poem. This complex poem may of course have been conceived and/or drafted over a long period and have a shifting frame of reference; but the Pornic setting establishes 1862–3 as the main period of composition, though note that B. also stayed at Sainte-Marie (also in Brittany, near Pornic) in 1862, and wrote poetry there (see headnote to *James Lee*, p. 666).

Setting

The situation is that at a public gathering – probably a ball, possibly in Paris – a woman has met a man she last met ten years before; before the poem's beginning he has told her that when they last met, at a seaside resort, he came near to suggesting that they marry or become lovers (see below), but decided against; the poem picks up the 'conversation' (i.e. the woman's monologue) at that point. We never quite fully learn what the man has said to her, beyond an admission

Title: Virgil, *Aeneid* ii 428. B. himself made what is evidently a translation of this tag in a letter to Lawrence Barrett of 3 Feb 1885: '"It has seemed otherwise to the Divinities" as the Poet says' (*LH* 235).
Subtitle: French: 'the Byron of our time', 'the latterday Byron'. No original for this phrase has been identified. It may possibly have been influenced by the title of B.'s friend Joseph Milsand's 1851 essay 'La Poésie Anglaise Depuis Byron' [English Poetry Since Byron]. For the 'Byronic' aspect of the poem, see headnote, *Sources*.

that he had decided not to declare his love for her. Clearly, a good deal of what she says represents a paraphrase of what he must be imagined as having just said to her. She reproaches him for what she takes to have been a combination of laziness, cowardice and needless pessimism on his part, and indicates that their liaison would have been superior to the relationships they now separately endure.

One issue concerns the nature of the proposal that the man is expected but fails to make to the woman. Orr assumes that he was 'on the point of offering her his hand' (*Handbook* 217), that is, of proposing marriage, and a number of critics have adopted this interpretation. It has been suggested that he might be considering asking her to consent to become his mistress: he is, after all, 'Famous . . . for verse and worse' and 'one whose love-freaks pass unblamed' (l. 60); the term 'my friend' (l. 76) fits this interpretation, since 'friend' appears elsewhere in B. as a euphemism for 'lover' (see, e.g., *Ring* v 198). On the other hand the phrases 'Thus were a *match* made' (l. 51, repeated with 'for best or worst' at l. 100), and the allusion to her 'money in the Three per cents' (l. 64) which would form part of a marriage settlement, point the other way.

Sources and influences

The subtitle has prompted a search for specific precedents in Byron's life and work, but none are fully convincing. It must be remembered that the allusion is to a 'latterday Byron', either a come-down from the authentic original (would the 'real' Byron have behaved with the timid calculation of his successor?) or that original grown older, in whom rational self-interest has outlived romance. There is no real foundation in the poem for, e.g., DeVane's suggestion that B. 'has in mind Byron's poem *The Dream* [1816], where he protests to Mary Chaworth that his life and hers would not have been ruined if she had accepted his love when he had offered it years before' (*Handbook* 289); for one thing, Byron was only 28 when he wrote it. The poem's sardonic tone, and its exaggeration of 'poetic' effect to the point of travesty, point to Byron's comic poems *Beppo* and *Don Juan*; and, further back, Samuel Butler's *Hudibras* (1660–80). Arthur Hugh Clough's recently published *Amours de Voyage* (1858) is a probable influence: it appeared in the *Atlantic Monthly*, the American journal in which several poems of *DP* were also published, and it contains a similar theme of a man fatally hesitating about his attitude to a woman, and losing his chance with her. The style is similarly racy and (self-)mocking. The Brownings had read Clough's *The Bothie* years earlier, with interest and approval; see headnote to *A Grammarian* (p. 589). Another possible source is Arnold's 'Marguerite' lyrics, publ. (mainly) 1852 and subsequent collections to 1857: see esp. 'To Marguerite—Continued', l. 21: 'A God, a God their severance ruled!'

The poem is unusual, probably unique, in that the second line of each stanza is internally and not externally rhymed, and the internal rhyme occurs at the end of the line: 'I say, the day', etc. This produces some striking phrases which sound like quotations, though few of them are.

Parallels in B.

The failure to take advantage of a supreme moment of opportunity contrasts with the denouement of *By the Fire-Side* (p. 456), to which this poem forms a bitter pendant. Its critique of amorous procrastination recalls *The Statue and the Bust* (III 342) and *Youth and Art* (p. 700), with which it shares its bohemian atmosphere; in both these poems the outcome is not conventionally 'tragic' but one of spiritual desiccation and a defeated acceptance of social conventions. Cp. also, in B.'s later work, *Inapprehensiveness* (*Asolando* 1889). The contemporary setting recalls *Respectability* (III 227) and *Fifine at the Fair* (1872), both set in France. The contrast between a life dominated by, respectively, art and love (ll. 31–40) is anticipated in *Last Ride* (III 285) and *Cleon* (p. 563). But its jarring cynicism of tone and moody jocularity link it with other poems in *DP*, notably *James Lee* (p. 665), *Confessions* and *A Likeness* (p. 642). The centrality of a poet in the poem's plot reflects a broader concern in *DP*, most notable in *Too Late*. The speaker's argument in the poem—that she and the man ought to have dared to bridge the gulf in age and experience between them, since the attempt itself would have affirmed their faith in transcendence, and thereby saved their souls—is underpinned by the 'doctrine of imperfection' which is central to B.'s metaphysics: see esp. ll. 116–20n., 141–2n.

The system of 'nested' voices within a dramatic monologue reaches its climax at ll. 81–5, in which the speaker 'voices' her interlocutor's thoughts when they met ten years previously, thoughts which involve *his* voicing of *her* thoughts if they were to marry. B. had not attempted this level of complexity since *Sordello*, which had recently been reprinted in the *Poetical Works* of 1863; many of B.'s revisions to the poem during the 1850s had involved him in wrestling with this kind of difficulty (see, e.g., iii 599n., I 565). As with *Sordello*, the printers of *1864* failed to cope: see l. 85n. B. returned to the charge in *Fifine at the Fair* (1872) where the situation is reversed: the male speaker (Don Juan) often 'voices' the thoughts of his wife, Elvire.

I

Stop, let me have the truth of that!
    Is that all true? I say, the day
Ten years ago when both of us
    Met on a morning, friends—as thus
5 We meet this evening, friends or what?—

2

Did you—because I took your arm
    And sillily smiled, "A mass of brass
That sea looks, blazing underneath!"
    While up the cliff-road edged with heath,
10 We took the turns nor came to harm—

3

Did you consider "Now makes twice
    That I have seen her, walked and talked
With this poor pretty thoughtful thing,
    Whose worth I weigh: she tries to sing;
15 Draws, hopes in time the eye grows nice;

1. One of three poems by B. beginning with the word 'Stop'; the others are *Transcendentalism* (III 641) and *Ponte dell' Angelo, Venice* (*Asolando*, 1889).
15. *nice*: 'That requires or involves great precision or accuracy' (*OED*).

4

"Reads verse and thinks she understands;
  Loves all, at any rate, that's great,
Good, beautiful; but much as we
  Down at the Bath-house love the sea,
20 Who breathe its salt and bruise its sands:

5

"While . . . do but follow the fishing-gull
  That flaps and floats from wave to cave!
There's the sea-lover, fair my friend!
  What then? Be patient, mark and mend!
25 Had you the making of your scull?"

6

And did you, when we faced the church
  With spire and sad slate roof, aloof
From human fellowship so far,
  Where a few graveyard crosses are,
30 And garlands for the swallows' perch,—

7

Did you determine, as we stepped
  O'er the lone stone fence, "Let me get
Her for myself, and what's the earth
  With all its art, verse, music, worth—
35 Compared with love, found, gained, and kept?

18–23. but much as we . . . fair my friend! The speaker is imagining what the man
might have been thinking when they met ten years ago, and suggests that he
would have seen her as naïve and inexperienced; the metaphor compares her love
for art and poetry to the 'love' of the sea claimed by a bather who merely 'bruise[s]
the sands' of the shore, and contrasts it with the genuine love of the sea felt by
the 'fishing-gull', a creature native to that element.

19. Bath-house: 'a building equipped with facilities for bathing, occas. public baths;
U.S., a place where one may change into beach clothes at the seaside, etc.' (*OED*).
B.'s usage here seems closer to the American sense than to the British one.

25. scull] skull (*1880*); cp. *Rabbi Ben Ezra* 173 (p. 662).

26–7. the church / With spire and sad slate roof: for the suggestion that B. might
have the church at Pornic in mind here, see headnote, *Composition*.

31–40. Cp. *Last Ride Together* 67–88 (III 289–90). In a letter to EBB. of 26 Feb.
1846, B. related an anecdote of the Baptist divine Robert Hall (1764–1831),
who 'when a friend admired that one with so high an estimate of the value of
intellectuality in women should yet marry some kind of cook[-]maid-animal, as
did the said Robert,—wisely answered—"you can't kiss Mind!"' (*Correspondence*
xii 105).

8

"Schumann's our music-maker now;
    Has his march-movement youth and mouth?
Ingres's the modern man that paints;
    Which will lean on me, of his saints?
40   Heine for songs; for kisses, how?"

9

And did you, when we entered, reached
    The votive frigate, soft aloft

36–7. The German composer Robert Schumann (1810–1856) wrote a number
of marches for piano; there may be a specific reference to his *Carnaval*
(1834–1835), which concludes with a 'march of the Davidsbündler against the
Philistines': B. refers in detail to *Carnaval* in *Fifine* (1872) at l. 588ff. *Ohio* notes
that in Nov. 1861 B. purchased *Boosey's Musical Cabinet*, containing piano works
by Schumann among others (*Collections* A1699); the date suggests that the purchase was made for Pen's education.

38–9. B. (or his speaker) may be engaging in deliberate paradox here: Jean Baptiste
Dominique Ingres (1780–1867), although he was at the height of his fame in the
1850s and 1860s, was regarded not as a 'modern' but as an upholder of classical
values in art; he was over 80 when the poem was published; nor was he
primarily a religious painter, and though his *Virgin Adoring the Host* (1852,
Metropolitan Museum of Art) and *Joan of Arc at the Coronation of Charles VII* (1854,
Louvre) were well-known works, he was more famous as a painter of the voluptuous female nude, epitomized in *The Turkish Bath* (1862, Louvre). *Ohio* notes
that Ingres exhibited his work at the Paris International Exposition of 1855, when
the Brownings were in Paris; see Rossetti's letter to Allingham of 25 November
1855, and EBB's to Julia Martin of 19 Dec. 1855, in which she notes that Ingres
has been made a Senator. Several of his paintings were also shown at the London
International Exhibition which ran from May to November 1862 and which B.
almost certainly attended.

40. Heine for songs: Heinrich Heine (1797–1856) was an immensely celebrated German
author. The word 'songs' may point to his *Buch der Lieder* ('Book of Songs', 1827),
which was translated into English by J. E. Wallis in 1856 and enjoyed a popular
vogue in England; this work would have held a special poignancy for B. because
EBB.'s versions of six of these songs formed the concluding item in her *Last Poems*,
which he edited in 1862. See John Woolford, *Browning the Revisionary* (1988) 91–2.
See also Matthew Arnold's essay 'Heinrich Heine' (1863). B. had mentioned
Heine in *Christmas-Eve* 1116 (III 90–1). In a letter to B. of 23 July 1864 Julia
Wedgwood quoted a couple of lines from the *Buch der Lieder*.

42. votive frigate: referring to a folk custom in Brittany whereby fishermen or other
seafarers who had survived a shipwreck would make a votive offering of a model
vessel to the Virgin Mary or the saint whose intercession had saved them, to be
placed in a niche or (as here) hung above the altar of their local church; these
models range from small-scale, primitive constructions to large and finely detailed
carvings offered by an entire community. B. could have seen examples in numerous churches and chapels in Brittany.

Riding on air this hundred years,
    Safe-smiling at old hopes and fears,—
45 Did you draw profit while she preached?

10

Resolving "Fools we wise men grow!
    Yes, I could easily blurt out curt
Some question that might find reply
    As prompt in her stopped lips, dropped eye,
50 And rush of red to cheek and brow:

11

"Thus were a match made, sure and fast,
    'Mid the blue weed-flowers round the mound
Where, issuing, we shall stand and stay
    For one more look at Baths and bay,
55 Sands, sea-gulls, and the old church last—

12

"A match 'twixt me, bent, wigged, and lamed,
    Famous, however, for verse and worse,
Sure of the Fortieth spare Arm-chair
    When gout and glory seat me there,
60 So, one whose love-freaks pass unblamed,—

13

"And this young beauty, round and sound

45. *she*: i.e. the 'votive frigate'.
51. *Thus*] So (*MS*).
57. *for verse*] through verse (*MS*). *verse and worse*: cp. Thomas Hood, 'Literary and Literal' (1830?) 23—4: 'Think of your prose and verse, and worse—delivered in / Hog's Norton!—'. Hood was a friend of B.'s in the 1840s.
58. Sure of election to the Académie Française, whose membership is restricted to forty; when an academician dies his (or, rarely, her) 'chair' (*fauteuil*) is declared vacant and a new occupant is nominated. Each chair is numbered, so the new occupant inherits it from a line of predecessors. The Académie was founded originally in the seventeenth century to purify the French language; B. may have known Matthew Arnold's essay 'The Literary Influence of Academies' (1864), which bestowed very high praise on the Académie's civilizing influence, though it appears here as a bastion of cultural orthodoxy: cp. *Respectability* (p. 345).
61. *round and sound*: the phrase occurs in Robert Lytton's 'An Evening in Tuscany' (1855) 81—2: 'And the grapes are green: this season / They'll be round and sound and true'. Lytton was a close friend of the Brownings in the 1850s. It was clearly a hawker's cry (so specified in Samuel Jackson's 'To Mr George Mavor' [1805] 1—4: 'And what to you, dear blithsome boy, / Compos'd of ease

As a mountain-apple, youth and truth
  With loves and doves, at all events
    With money in the Three per Cents;
65 Whose choice of me would seem profound:—

14

"She might take me as I take her.
  Perfect the hour would pass, alas!
Climb high, love high, what matter? Still,
  Feet, feelings, must descend the hill:
70 An hour's perfection can't recur.

15

"Then follows Paris and full time
  For both to reason: 'Thus with us!'
She'll sigh, 'Thus girls give body and soul
  At first word, think they gain the goal,
75 When 'tis the starting-place they climb!

16

"'My friend makes verse and gets renown;
  Have they all fifty years, his peers?

---

and health and joy, / Fair round and sound, as hawkers cry / Their early cherries, —"Buy, come buy?"').

62. *youth and truth*: cp. Philip James Bailey, *Festus* (1852): 'With the bright unworldly hearts of youth and truth, / And the maiden bosoms of the beautiful' (p. 43). Also Dickens, *Dombey and Son* (1848) ch. xxx: '"It is enough," said Edith, steadily, "that we are what we are. I will have no youth and truth dragged down to my level"' (p. 307).

63. *With loves and doves*: cp. *Too Late* 89. The phrase is frequently used to mock the clichés of romance, as in Walter Harte's 'Eulogius' (1767) 427–8: 'Where *limpid* streams are *clear*, and *sun-shine bright*; / Where *woos* and *coos*, and *loves* and *doves* unite.'

64. *Three per Cents*: government bonds yielding low but guaranteed interest, used here as an emblem of a safe, respectable social and financial situation.

72. *Thus with us*: cp. *Exodus* xiv 11: 'wherefore hast thou dealt thus with us, to carry us forth out of Egypt?' The phrase is not uncommon in prose works, particularly of the Renaissance.

73. Cp. EBB., 'Amy's Cruelty' 23–4: 'He wants my world, my sun, my heaven, / Soul, body, whole existence'. This would reinforce the connection with the mid-1850s (see headnote), as 'Amy's Cruelty' was probably given to Marguerite Power in Paris in 1856 (see headnote to *Mock Epitaph*, III 700). *'Thus*] "So (*MS*).

76. *friend*: see headnote.

He knows the world, firm, quiet, and gay;
   Boys will become as much one day:
80 They're fools; he cheats, with beard less brown.

17

" 'For boys say, *Love me or I die!*
   He did not say, *The truth is, youth*
I want, who am old and know too much;
   I'd catch youth: lend me sight and touch!
85 *Drop heart's blood where life's wheels grate dry!* '

18

"While I should make rejoinder"—(then
   It was, no doubt, you ceased that least
Light pressure of my arm in yours)
   " 'I can conceive of cheaper cures
90 For a yawning-fit o'er books and men.

19

" 'What? All I am, was, and might be,
   All, books taught, art brought, life's whole strife,
Painful results since precious, just
   Were fitly exchanged in wise disgust
95 For two cheeks freshened by youth and sea?

20

" 'All for a nosegay!—what came first;
   With fields on flower, untried each side;
I rally, need my books and men,

81–5. The speaker is, at this point, imagining how the man she is addressing would have imagined her response to him had they stayed together; part of this response consists of her attempt to exonerate him from the charge of having misled her with the language of romantic love (the passage in italics at ll. 82–5 consists of statements the speaker in this imagined past did not make). For the 'nesting' of voices within the speaker's monologue, see headnote, *Parallels*.

85. life's wheels] my wheels (*MS*, canc.). *dry!']* *1864* lacks the required closing quotation mark; we emend in agreement with *MS*, *1868*, and *1880*. *1888*, oddly enough, agrees with *1864*, a very rare instance of this text reverting to a misprint in an earlier edition.

94. fitly exchanged] a fit exchange (*MS*).

98. Cp. *Morning* [*Parting at Morning*] 4 (II 359): 'the need of a world of men for me'.

And find a nosegay: drop it, then,
100 No match yet made for best or worst!'"

21

That ended me. You judged the porch
    We left by, Norman; took our look
At sea and sky; wondered so few
    Find out the place for air and view;
105 Remarked the sun began to scorch;

22

Descended, soon regained the Baths,
    And then, good bye! Years ten since then:
Ten years! We meet: you tell me, now,
    By a window-seat for that cliff-brow,
110 On carpet-stripes for those sand-paths.

23

Now I may speak: you fool, for all
    Your lore! WHO made things plain in vain?
What was the sea for? What, the grey
    Sad church, that solitary day,
115 Crosses and graves and swallows' call?

99–100. nosegay: drop it . . . best or worst!'"] nosegay:' drop it . . . best or worst!"
(*1868–88*). The change in speech-punctuation in *1868–88* effects a small but
significant shift in the emotional balance of the poem: the man's speech (which
the woman is 'voicing') ends at 'nosegay', and the remaining, scornful words are
hers. Cp. the closing lines of *Pretty Woman* (III 24).

100. for best or worst: the phrase recalls, but is not from, the marriage service, which
has 'for better or for worse'.

101. That ended me: 'that finished my chance of securing your proposal'.

102–6. took . . . wondered . . . Remarked . . . Descended: 'we' must be understood as
the subject of all these verbs, though it appears nowhere: the effect is to incorporate the speaker's point of view in that of her companion ('you took our look',
etc.).

104. Find] Found (*MS*, written over 'Find', canc.); this is a rare instance of *1864*
returning to a reading cancelled in *MS*.

107–10. Years ten . . . sand-paths: the woman refers to the setting in which the man's
revelation of his earlier intentions ('you tell me, now') takes place, contrasting it
with that of the events she narrates.

107. And then] And so (*MS*).

24

Was there nought better than to enjoy?
   No feat which, done, would make time break,
And let us pent-up creatures through
   Into eternity, our due?
120   No forcing earth teach Heaven's employ?

25

No wise beginning, here and now,
   What cannot grow complete (earth's feat)
And Heaven must finish, there and then?
   No tasting earth's true food for men,
125   Its sweet in sad, its sad in sweet?

26

No grasping at love, gaining a share
   O' the sole spark from God's life at strife
With death, so, sure of range above
   The limits here? For us and love,
130   Failure; but, when God fails, despair.

.

116–20. The vocabulary here echoes many such moments of metaphysical stress in B., in which the yearning for transcendence is thwarted by the temporality of human life. Sordello's ruin is foreshadowed as the consequence of 'Thrusting in time eternity's concern' (i 566, I 432), and 'forcing earth teach Heaven's employ' also brings about the downfall of the poet Thamuris in the lyric 'Thamuris marching' (see headnote to *Abt Vogler*, p. 761), yet in another perspective these failures are gloriously superior to conventional triumph. The same might be said of the limitless ambition and tiny actual achievement of the Grammarian (p. 586). The dual application of this principle to both art and love is exemplified in Andrea del Sarto's famous cry: 'Ah, but a man's reach should exceed his grasp / Or what's a Heaven for?' (ll. 96–7, p. 395).

121–5. This is the only stanza in which the rhyme-scheme is varied (abccb, not abcca).

123. And] So (*MS*). *there and then*: revitalising the cliché: the 'wise beginning' of love between the speaker and the man would have been completed 'there' (in heaven) and 'then' (after death).

125. Cp. Crashaw, 'Sainte Mary Magdelene or The Weeper' (1636) 36: 'sweetnesse so sad, sadnesse so sweet'. *Its . . . its*] Her . . . her (*MS*).

127. O' the] Of the (*MS*).

128–9: so . . . here? I.e. 'in this way [by declaring your love for me], with confidence that there was a higher existence beyond this one'.

129. here? For] now: for (*MS*).

130. when God fails: 'when the idea of God fails' (as it did for the man, who failed to grasp the opportunity presented to him).

27

This you call wisdom? Thus you add
   Good unto good again, in vain?
You loved, with body worn and weak;
   I loved, with faculties to seek:
135   Were both loves worthless since ill-clad?

28

Let the mere star-fish in his vault
   Crawl in a wash of weed, indeed,
Rose-jacynth to the finger-tips:
   He, whole in body and soul, outstrips
140   Man, found with either in default.

29

But what's whole, can increase no more,
   Is dwarfed and dies, since here's its sphere.
The devil laughed at you in his sleeve!
   You knew not? That, I well believe;
145   Or you had saved two souls: nay, four.

131. wisdom] progress (*MS*).
134. with faculties to seek: 'with powers not yet developed'.
135.] Both loves worth nothing since ill-clad! (*MS*).
136–40. The identity of the starfish is in perfect harmony with its functions, but
this image of wholeness and completeness is paradoxically of less value than human
imperfection: cp. *A Death* 577–81 (pp. 752–3). See also l. 138n. and ll. 140–1n.
138. Rose-jacynth: the compound is B.'s coinage; 'jacynth' (more usually 'jacinth')
is a reddish-orange colour, from the gemstone of that name (*OED*). B. may have
known the (obsolete) sense of 'rose' as a starfish (*OED* 16a., citing an example
from 1688).
141–2. A common argument in B., reflecting the 'doctrine of imperfection': what
appears complete can be so only in the material world, and must hence be subject to mortality, diminution and dissolution, whereas incompleteness demands or
appears to demand completion in a spiritual world. See *Old Pictures* 130n. (p. 419),
and cp. *Wanting Is—What?* (*Jocoseria* 1884), esp. ll. 9–10: 'Come then, complete
incompletion, O comer, / Pant through the blueness, perfect the summer!' Cp. also
Rephan (*Asolando*, 1889).
141. But what's whole] What's whole now (*MS*).
142.] Dies or is dwarfed, since here's its sphere: (*MS*).
144–5. Samuel Butler's quip that the Carlyles' marriage ensured that only two
people were made miserable, not four, dates from 1884; but the jest was probably
ancient, and B. here characteristically inverts it.

30

For Stephanie sprained last night her wrist,
   Ancle, or something. "Pooh," cry you?
At any rate she danced, all say,
   Vilely: her vogue has had its day.
150 Here comes my husband from his whist.

---

146. Stephanie: the context suggests that this is the man's current wife or mistress,
who is a dancer. Cp. *Too Late* (*DP*, 1864) 79–80: 'so and so / Married a dancer'.
147. Ancle] Ankle (*1868–88*). 'Ancle' was a possible spelling in the period, and
generally preferred by B., as in a letter in which he remarks, 'I unluckily sprained
my ancle yesterday' (to Monckton Milnes, 23 May 1862: *NL* 145); but contrast
Youth and Art 44, p. 705.
150. whist: on the association of card-playing with immorality in B., cp. *Bishop
Blougram* 48n. (p. 288).

45 Youth and Art

Text and publication

First publ. *DP*, 28 May 1864; repr. *1864²*, *1865*, *1872*, *1888*. The MS, part of the printer's copy for *DP*, is at *Morgan*. It is a very clean copy, though in a somewhat larger and looser hand than usual with B. There are few copying errors and cancelled readings, and two verbal variants with *1864*; only two minor changes in wording were made in subsequent editions.

Composition and date

DeVane (*Handbook* 304) suggests that the poem was written before the death of EBB., due to its mention of John Gibson (1790–1866), the sculptor, who had a studio in Rome. The Brownings met Gibson at Bagni di Lucca in June 1849 (23 June 1849; *EBB to Arabella* i 257–8), and visited his studio during their period of residence in Rome in the winter of 1853–4. EBB. wrote to Mrs Jameson on 21 Dec. 1853:

> We got to Gibson's studio, which is close by, and saw his coloured Venus. I dont like her. She has come out of her cloud of the ideal, and to my eyes is not too decent. Then in the long slender throat, in the turn of it, and the setting on of the head, you have rather a grisette than a goddess. 'Tis over pretty and *petite*, the colour adding, of course, to this effect. Crawford's studio (the American sculptor) was far more interesting to me than Gibson's. (*Letters of EBB* ii 148; see also letter to Mary Russell Mitford of 18 Jan. 1854, *EBB to MRM* 402)

Miller, in contrast, links the poem to a later visit to Rome during 1859–60, and more specifically to Browning's 'brief friendship with Val Prinsep, who, with an unnamed French artist, introduced the poet that winter to the more unconventional aspects of Rome's artistic colony' (p. 211). Some of Prinsep's reminiscences of this period are reproduced in Orr *Life* 224–7. However, there is nothing specifically Roman about the atmosphere of the poem; by contrast, the London setting, which includes possible allusions to English artists whom B. knew (e.g. John Everett Millais: see l. 60n.) would link it rather to the early 1860s.

Although the poem might have been one of those shown to Isa Blagden in Siena in 1860 (see Appendix C, p. 896), there is not enough evidence available to verify this conjecture. For the reasons given above, and the poem's thematic similarity to *DP*'s other poem of missed opportunity, *Dîs Aliter Visum* (see headnote, p. 688) we prefer a date of 1862–3.

Sources and influences

B.'s interest in sculpture was life-long (e.g. Jules in *Pippa Passes* ii; see headnote, pp. 86–9), but was stimulated during the 1850s by his own initiation into clay-modelling through his American friend in Florence, William Wetmore Story. Cp. *Study of a Hand, by Lionardo*, III 701, later incorporated into *James Lee* viii (p. 680). The speaker of the poem is the only singer (of opera or classical *lieder*) in B.'s work, and indeed the only female artist who is also the speaker of a dramatic monologue. In her youthful ambition she invites comparison with Aurora in EBB.'s *Aurora Leigh* (1856), who begins her literary career on her own in London in 'a chamber up three flights of stairs' in unfashionable Kensington (iii 158). Aurora is kept free from any taint of Bohemianism, but EBB.'s comparison between

Gibson's tinted Venus and a 'grisette' (literally a milliner's assistant, so-called for her grey dress, but also used for the female members of the artistic colony) shows that she well understood the popular association between art and the 'vie de bohème' in both France and Britain. B.'s friendship with Dante Gabriel Rossetti, which began in the 1850s and was close in the years following B.'s return to London in 1861, suggests another source of personal knowledge of this way of life. This theme is explored in a number of British and French literary texts, but perhaps the closest parallels to B.'s poem come from two poems by Pierre-Jean de Béranger (1780–1857; for B.'s admiration of him see headnote to *Respectability*, p. 345). In the first, 'Maudit Printemps!' ['Cursed Spring!'], a young man humorously curses spring for restoring the leaves to the trees and depriving him of the sight of a pretty girl:

Je la voyais de ma fenêtre
   À la sienne tout cet hiver:
Nous nous aimions sans nous connaître;
   Nos baisers se croisaient dans l'air.
Entre ces tilleuls sans feuillage
   Nous regarder comblait nos jours.
Aux arbres tu rends leur ombrage;
   Maudit printemps! Reviendras-tu toujours?

[I used to see her from my window at hers all that winter: we loved each other without knowing each other; our kisses crossed in the air. To gaze at each other through these leafless limes was the high point of our days. You are giving the trees back their shade; cursed spring! Will you always return?]

B. made a serious use of the last line, which forms the refrain of the song: see headnote to *May and Death* (III 362). The second poem is 'Le Grenier' ['The Garret'], in which the speaker looks back fondly on his unrespectable youth: B. is the more likely to have known this song because it was translated by Thackeray in his *Paris Sketch-Book* (1840):

With pensive eyes the little room I view,
Where, in my youth, I weathered it so long;
With a wild mistress, a stanch friend or two,
And a light heart still breaking into song:
Making a mock of life, and all its cares,
Rich in the glory of my rising sun,
Lightly I vaulted up four pair of stairs,
In the brave days when I was twenty-one.

Yes; 'tis a garret—let him know't who will—
There was my bed—full hard it was and small.
My table there—and I decipher still
Half a lame couplet charcoaled on the wall.
Ye joys, that Time hath swept with him away,
Come to mine eyes, ye dreams of love and fun;
For you I pawned my watch how many a day,
In the brave days when I was twenty-one.

And see my little Jessy, first of all;
She comes with pouting lips and sparkling eyes:
Behold, how roguishly she pins her shawl
Across the narrow casement, curtain-wise;

Now by the bed her petticoat glides down,
And when did woman look the worse in none?
I have heard since who paid for many a gown,
In the brave days when I was twenty-one.

B. characteristically changes the gender of the speaker, so that the carefree celebration of youthful poverty and sexual licence takes on a different meaning, as
does the transposition of the action of the poem from Paris to London (e.g. the
reversal of the girl's gesture: in Béranger's poem she pins her shawl across the
window to conceal her lovemaking, whereas in B.'s poem [ll. 27–8] she puts up
a blind as a gesture of modesty). Nor does Béranger take seriously the connection between sexuality and artistic ambition in both men and women which is
at the heart of B.'s treatment of the subject. Note also the mention of 'days in
a garret' in *A Likeness* 46 (p. 647).

Parallels in B.

With the representation of Bohemian life, cp. *Respectability* (p. 345); with the
denouement of the poem, in which it becomes clear that the failure to take
the opportunity offered by life has resulted in personal and artistic decline, cp.
Dîs Aliter Visum (p. 688). As with *Dîs Aliter Visum* it is unclear whether the
relationship not undertaken would have been marriage or a liaison: the latter seems
likelier, giving this poem likewise a strong affinity with *The Statue and the Bust*
(III 342).

I

It once might have been, once only:
    We lodged in a street together,
You, a sparrow on the housetop lonely,
    I, a lone she-bird of his feather.

2

5   Your trade was with sticks and clay,
        You thumbed, thrust, patted and polished,

3. *sparrow*: the sparrow has traditionally been associated with urban life (as in the
expression 'cockney sparrow' for a Londoner). The allusion to the mating of
the (literal) sparrows in l. 33 suggests that B. also had in mind the sparrow's equally
traditional association with sex: it is one of Venus's birds, and became a byword
for lust, as in Chaucer's description of the Summoner in the *General Prologue*:
'As hoot he was and lecherous as a sparwe', a passage cited in Hazlitt's lecture
on Chaucer and Spenser (*Lectures on the English Poets*, 1818). Cp. *Pippa* iv 220
(p. 167).   *housetop*: attic rooms formed the traditional accommodation of aspiring artists (because they were the cheapest available); see headnote.
4. *of his feather*: 'of the same species, or of the same type or character': cp. the
proverbial expression 'birds of a feather flock together'.
5. *sticks and clay*: as is made clear in l. 15, the impoverished 'Smith' cannot afford
marble; the tools mentioned are used to make plaster 'sketches' of his projected
works. Note also the continuation of the metaphor begun in the previous stanza;
'sticks and clay' are nest-building materials.

Then laughed "They will see some day
    Smith made, and Gibson demolished."

3

    My business was song, song, song;
10   I chirped, cheeped, trilled and twittered,
    "Kate Brown's on the boards ere long,
      And Grisi's existence embittered!"

4

I earned no more by a warble
    Than you by a sketch in plaster;
15 You wanted a piece of marble,
    I needed a music-master.

5

We studied hard in our styles,
    Chipped each at a crust like Hindoos,
For air, looked out on the tiles,
20   For fun, watched each other's windows.

6

You lounged, like a boy of the South,
    Cap and blouse—nay, a bit of beard too;
Or you got it, rubbing your mouth
    With fingers the clay adhered to.

---

7. some day] one day (*MS*).
8. Gibson: the sculptor John Gibson (1790–1866); see headnote, *Composition*.
11. on the boards: 'on the stage'.
12. Grisi's: the singer Giulia Grisi (1810?–1869), the leading female opera singer of her day; she is mentioned in a number of mid-nineteenth-century novels, e.g. Disraeli, *Coningsby* (1844), ch. xv, and Thackeray, *The History of Pendennis* (1849), ch. xxx. She retired from the stage for the second and final time on 24 July 1861.
15. wanted: lacked, needed; see l. 5n.
18. Chipped each at a crust: 'survived on meagre rations of food', continuing the comparison with sparrows introduced in the first stanza. *Hindoos*: B.'s spelling was beginning to be superseded by 'Hindu' around this time; the word is not used elsewhere in his poetry. Hinduism was routinely represented in nineteenth-century Britain as an ascetic religion.
22. blouse: not in *J*.; imported into English to denote 'a light loose upper garment of linen or cotton' (*OED*) from French in the early nineteenth century. Along with the cap and the hint of a beard, it forms part of the typical appearance of the French or Italian artists whom 'Smith' is imitating.

7

25   And I—soon managed to find
      Weak points in the flower-fence facing,
    Was forced to put up a blind
      And be safe in my corset-lacing.

8

    No harm! It was not my fault
30   If you never turned your eyes' tail up,
    As I shook upon E *in alt.*,
      Or ran the chromatic scale up:

9

    For spring bade the sparrows pair,
      And the boys and girls gave guesses,
35   And stalls in our street looked rare
      With bulrush and watercresses.

10

    Why did not you pinch a flower
      In a pellet of clay and fling it?
    Why did not I put a power
40   Of thanks in a look, or sing it?

---

26. flower-fence: 'the plant *Poinciana pulcherrima*' (*OED*), planted in hedges to provide a screen between houses. The suggestion is that 'Kate Brown's' room is overlooked by the artist's garret.

28. corset-lacing: the corset was a standard item of underwear for Victorian women; it was pulled tight with laces.

30. turned your eyes' tail up: a slightly obscure formulation for 'looked up at me while I was singing'. *eyes'*] eye's (*1872, 1888*).

31. shook: i.e. executed a 'shake' or trill. E *in alt.*: i.e. 'in the octave above the treble stave beginning with G' (*OED*); B.'s poem is cited to illustrate this definition. Cp. *Aurora Leigh* v 905–6: 'Or Baldinacci, when her F in alt / Had touched the silver tops of heaven itself'.

34. The allusion is to a children's guessing game, possibly a make-believe courtship or kissing game, but we have not been able to identify it.

35. rare: fine, splendid (*OED* 6b).

36. bulrush: *Typha latifolia*, the Cat's-tail or Reed-mace; it is not clear for what purpose it is being sold, since the practice of strewing rushes on the floor was no longer current in nineteenth-century London. *watercresses*: a staple of London street-selling, usually by itinerant hawkers who bought their stock from the big wholesale markets at Covent Garden or Farringdon. The watercress 'season' begins in May, so they are a sign of spring. Their cheapness made them attractive to working people (and impoverished art students).

11

I did look, sharp as a lynx,
    (And yet the memory rankles)
When models arrived, some minx
    Tripped up-stairs, she and her ankles.

12

45 But I think I gave you as good!
        "That foreign fellow,—who can know
    How she pays, in a playful mood,
        For his tuning her that piano?"

13

    Could you say so, and never say
50   "Suppose we join hands and fortunes,
    And I fetch her from over the way,
        Her, piano, and long tunes and short tunes?"

14

    No, no: you would not be rash,
        Nor I rasher and something over:
55 You've to settle yet Gibson's hash,
        And Grisi yet lives in clover.

15

    But you meet the Prince at the Board,
        I'm queen myself at *bals-paré*,

---

44. ankles] ances (*MS*); the printers seem to have corrected B.'s preferred spelling here (still allowable in the period), though they left it alone in *Dîs Aliter Visum* 147 (p. 699).

49. and] yet (*MS* canc.)

50, 54. join hands and fortunes . . . rasher and something over: the first phrase implies marriage; the second an unmarried liaison (in which the speaker, as a woman, would risk more). On this uncertainty see headnote.

55. to settle yet Gibson's hash: 'to settle someone's hash' was 'to reduce to order; to silence, subdue; to make an end of, "do for"'(*OED*); the artist had unrealized ambitions to go beyond Gibson (for whom see headnote).

57. the Prince at the Board: possibly Prince Albert, and the Board of the Royal Academy (see below l. 60 n.), though no specific reference may be intended; the point being made is that 'Smith' now moves in the highest social circles. *Ohio* points out that B. was invited to meet the (18-year-old) Prince of Wales in Rome in 1859, to EBB.'s evident pleasure (*Letters of EBB* ii 309).

58. bals-paré: a 'bal paré' is a formal full-dress ball.

I've married a rich old lord,
60   And you're dubbed knight and an R. A.

16

Each life's unfulfilled, you see;
    It hangs still, patchy and scrappy:
We have not sighed deep, laughed free,
    Starved, feasted, despaired,—been happy.

17

65 And nobody calls you a dunce,
        And people suppose me clever:
    This could but have happened once,
        And we missed it, lost it for ever.

59. *lord*] Lord (*MS*, written over 'lord'); a rare example of *1864* reverting to a canc. reading in *MS*.

60. *dubbed knight*: awarded a knighthood by the Queen. A number of artists were honoured in this way during the nineteenth century, including Sir Charles Eastlake, President of the Royal Academy at the time of the poem's publication and a personal acquaintance of the Brownings.   *an R.A.*: a member of the Royal Academy of Arts, founded in the eighteenth century by Sir Joshua Reynolds, and the organ of official recognition in art, and, for that very reason, despised by artistic radicals such as the Pre-Raphaelite Brotherhood. John Everett Millais, one of the original Pre-Raphaelites, was elected to a membership of the Royal Academy on 18 Dec. 1863 (he was later given a baronetcy, though not until 1885).

61. *Each life's*] Each life (*1868–88*, except *1872*, which agrees with *1864*).

62. *hangs still*] hangs here (*MS*).

46 Apparent Failure

Text and publication

First publ. *DP*, 28 May 1864; repr. *1864²*, *1865*, *1868*, *1872*, *1888*, the penultimate poem in the volume. The MS, part of the printer's copy for *DP*, is at *Morgan*. The pages of the bound MS, from the title page of this poem to the end of the *Epilogue*, are numbered 1–11 in ink, and lack the pencil numbering of the rest of the MS, which suggests that they were added at a late stage. The MS is a very clean copy, with only two cancelled readings, and one variant from *1864*. With just one punctuation variant in subsequent editions, this is the least-revised poem in the *DP* volume.

Composition and date

The visit to the Morgue commemorated in the poem is said to have taken place 'Seven years since' (l. 1), during a visit to Paris which coincided with the 'baptism of your Prince' (l. 3). This is a reference to the baptism of Napoleon III's son, Napoléon Eugène Louis Jean Joseph (usually referred to as the Prince Imperial), which took place on 14 June 1856. EBB. witnessed the public celebrations, but did not herself participate in the festivities: 'The cortège was magnificent—but not a carriage is permitted—so I stay at home' (Fitzwilliam Museum MS). This date of 1856 is confirmed by the reference in ll. 7–8 to the Paris Congress, the meeting of Europe's great powers which brought the Crimean War to a formal end (see also ll. 7–8n.). The chronology of B.'s poem is, however, slightly confused, as the Congress ended on 16 Apr. 1856, nearly two months before the baptism of the Prince Imperial; the speaker may be confusing his memory of the baptism with his recollection of the public celebrations for the Prince's birth, which happened during the Congress on 16 Mar. 1856.

These allusions would, therefore, suggest a date of 1863 for the composition of the poem. DeVane speculates that the poem might have been written at Pornic in Brittany, where B. spent part of the summer of 1863 between late July and early September, but there is no direct evidence for this.

Setting

The Morgue mentioned in the poem stood in 1856 on the quai du Marché-Neuf on the Île de la Cité in Paris. There were already at this stage plans for its demolition as part of the rebuilding of Paris by Baron Haussmann; see, e.g., A.-J. Meindre, *Histoire de Paris et de son influence en Europe* (Paris 1855), p. 405. It was not, however, demolished until 1867, by which time a new and larger Morgue had been constructed behind Notre Dame (see *The Times* Thursday, 14 Jan. 1864, p. 10). Both DeVane (*Handbook* 313) and *Thomas* (pp. 32–3) mistakenly identify this later Morgue as the one referred to in the poem; the picture which accompanies *Thomas's* entry on the poem is in fact of the earlier Morgue.

Sources and influences

The function of the Morgue is succinctly described by Mrs Gore in her *Paris in 1841* (London 1842): 'On the Quai du Marché Neuf, adjoining the Parvis de Notre Dame, rising from the bed of the river, stands a small stone mansion of simple form, yet never viewed without awe—La Morgue,—in which are deposited the bodies of all persons found dead in the city or river, till claimed by their relatives. The bodies thus found are stripped and placed in a current of air on leaden trays, with a small jet of water trickling over them,—the clothes of each individual being suspended above, to facilitate recognition. The public is admitted to view them through a grating; and if not claimed, the bodies are subjected to anatomical purposes, and buried at the cost of government. It will readily be imagined that scenes of the most heartrending nature are constantly occurring at the Morgue' (pp. 125–6). As Firmin Maillard noted in 1860, the Morgue became a source of fascination to British visitors in particular: 'Les étrangers la visitent, particulièrement les Anglais: ceux-ci ne se contentent pas de la *Salle d'Exposition*, et, si on les y autorisait, ils visiteraient l'intérieur jusque dans ses moindres détails' [Foreigners visit it, the English in particular: these last do not content themselves with the 'Salle d'Exposition', and, if they were permitted to do so, would undertake a minute examination of the interior.] (Cited in Paul Veyriras, 'Visiteurs Britanniques à la Morgue de Paris au Dix-Neuvième Siècle', *Cahiers Victoriens et Edouardiennes* 15 (April 1982), 52.) One such visitor was Charles Dickens; in *The Uncommercial Traveller* (1861), he writes that he is 'dragged by invisible force into the Morgue' whenever he is in Paris:

> I never want to go there, but am always pulled there. One Christmas Day, when I would rather have been anywhere else, I was attracted in, to see an old grey man lying all alone on his cold bed, with a tap of water turned on over his grey hair, and running, drip, drip, drip, down his wretched face until it got to the corner of his mouth, where it took a turn, and made him look sly. One New Year's Morning (by the same token, the sun was shining outside, and there was a mountebank balancing a feather on his nose, within a yard of the gate), I was pulled in again to look at a flaxen-haired boy of eighteen, with a heart hanging on his breast—'from his mother,' was engraven on it—who had come into the net across the river, with a bullet wound in his fair forehead and his hands cut with a knife, but whence or how was a blank mystery. This time, I was forced into the same dread place, to see a large dark man whose disfigurement by water was in a frightful manner comic, and whose expression was that of a prize-fighter who had closed his eyelids under a heavy blow, but was going immediately to open them, shake his head, and 'come up smiling.' Oh what this large dark man cost me in that bright city! (pp. 94–5)

The Morgue also appeared in a number of nineteenth-century French and English literary texts. B. referred to its popularity with the French 'Convulsive School' as early as 1834 in a letter to Monclar: 'While on the subject of abortions let me observe, that your Convulsive School at Paris seems to be pretty nearly "done up"—Balzac, Sue &c. Our Journals assure us that Horrors are at a discount, & Puppyism "*no go*"—that you may see, here a dramatist ey[e]ing longingly the Slaughter-house & La Morgue, his quondam Academus' (5–7 Dec. 1834, *Correspondence* iii 110). One of its most famous appearances in English literature is the closing scene of Wilkie Collins's *The Woman in White* (1860), in which Count Fosco's body is exposed at the Morgue after being pulled out of the Seine.

In 1856 the Brownings' friend Eliza Ogilvy, an American whom they met in Florence, published *Poems of Ten Years*, a copy of which she presented to EBB. (*EBB to Ogilvy* 135n.). One of the poems is called 'La Morgue'; it contrasts the beauty of the Seine and the sights of Paris with the sights to be seen at the Morgue, where the drowned lie on 'brassy beds where living men ne'er lay', their identities almost completely erased:

> Ah who had known them as they were? not sister, no, nor wife,
> Not child who might have clomb their knees, not friend who shared their life,
> The seething waves had worked their will upon each senseless weft,
> A dim resemblance of our race was all that they had left.

Athwart a grated aperture the light upon them streamed
Revealing strangest lineaments such as were never dreamed,
And from the crowd of passengers a few turned back to gaze
And shuddering looked and crossed themselves and hastened on their ways.

The loneness of abandonment for grief was like a claim,
Yet no one knew their parentage, their history, or their name;
None guessed what once had been those forms so purpled by decay,
Or generous lovers of their kind or savage beasts of prey. (ll. 17–32)

With the second stanza, contrast B.'s boast in ll. 15–18; the last stanza may have
prompted his speculative treatment of the three men's life-stories in ll. 37–54.

In a letter of 18 Oct. 1849 from Dante Gabriel Rossetti to his brother William
Michael, headed 'Proem at the Paris Station', Rossetti claims to have come across
the Morgue 'In passing by'; he sees the corpse of a man 'Who had been stabbed
and tumbled in the Seine / Where he had stayed some days'. Rossetti's speculation focuses not on the identity of the victim but of the murderer:

> Now very likely, he who did the job
> Was standing among those who stood with us
> To look upon the corpse. You fancy him—
> Smoking an early pipe, and watching, as
> An artist, the effect of his last work.

Although the poem was not published until 1886, when it appeared as 'The Paris
Railway-Station', B. may have known it; he had become friendly with Rossetti
during the early 1850s, and the two men spent time together in London and Paris
during 1855–6 and again in the period following B.'s return to London in 1861.

Parallels in B.
The poem forms part of a group in *DP* set in France (*James Lee* [p. 665], *Gold
Hair, Dîs Aliter Visum* [p. 688]), though its specific mention of a public building in Paris looks back to *Respectability* in *M & W* (p. 345). Anecdotal poems
founded on events in B.'s personal life (whether or not we take the speaker
to be a self-portrait) are exceptionally rare: cp. *Guardian Angel* (III 13) and *Memorabilia*
(p. 553). Like *Guardian Angel*, the poem contains poignant allusions to EBB., though
here presented obliquely (as in the reference to Italian politics in ll. 6–7, and to
Vaucluse in l. 12). If the speaker is identified with B., ll. 37–54 would represent
an unusually direct and concrete statement of his political and ethical opinions;
his only unequivocally personal testimony of political affiliation, the sonnet 'Why
I Am a Liberal' (1885), is couched in much more abstract terms. The poem's
rejection of the doctrine of eternal punishment was reiterated in the late poem
Ixion (*Jocoseria*, 1883).

> "We shall soon lose a celebrated building."
> *Paris Newspaper.*

I

No, for I'll save it! Seven years since,
    I passed through Paris, stopped a day
To see the baptism of your Prince;

Epigraph: the 'Paris newspaper' in question has not been identified.
1–3. Seven years since . . . the baptism of your Prince: see headnote, *Composition*.

Saw, made my bow, and went my way:
5   Walking the heat and headache off,
    I took the Seine-side, you surmise,
Thought of the Congress, Gortschakoff,
    Cavour's appeal and Buol's replies,
So sauntered till—what met my eyes?

2

10 Only the Doric little Morgue!
    The dead-house where you show your drowned:
Petrarch's Vaucluse makes proud the Sorgue,
    Your Morgue has made the Seine renowned.
    One pays one's debt in such a case;
15   I plucked up heart and entered,—stalked,
Keeping a tolerable face
    Compared with some whose cheeks were chalked:
Let them! No Briton's to be baulked!

7–8. The Paris Congress, which took place between 25 Feb. and 16 Apr. 1856, brought the Crimean War to a formal conclusion. Prince Gortschakoff (1789–1866) was the Russian delegate, while Count Camillo Benso di Cavour (1810–61) represented the Kingdom of Piedmont at the Congress. He used the occasion to raise awareness of the 'Italian question', a strategy which brought him into conflict with Karl Ferdinand Graf von Buol-Schauenstein (1797–1865), the Austrian foreign minister. B. dined with Cavour at Lady Monson's on 1 April 1856, according to EBB. (*EBB to Arabella* ii 221). EBB. was a passionate supporter of Italian independence, and the shock of Cavour's death in 1861 may have hastened her own.

10. Doric little Morgue: the Morgue is described as 'a plain Doric building' in *Galignani's New Paris Guide for 1855* (Paris and London 1855), p. 324.

12. Shortly after their marriage, B. and EBB. 'made a pilgrimage to Vaucluse as became poets' in the course of their journey to Pisa, and, EBB. wrote in a letter to her sister Arabella, 'my spirits rose & the enjoyment of the hour spent at the sacred fountain was complete. It stands deep & still & green against a majestic wall of rock, & then falls, boils, breaks[,] foams over the stones, down into the channel of the little river winding away greenly, greenly' ([16–19 Oct 1846], *Correspondence* xiv 23–4).

13. has made] 'tis, makes (*MS*, canc.).

15. stalked: to stalk is 'To walk with high and superb steps', and is 'used commonly in a sense of dislike' (*J.*).

17. whose cheeks were chalked: 'whose cheeks were as white as if they had been rubbed with chalk'; *OED* 2b cites Tennyson, *The Princess* (1847) iv 357–8: 'Fear / Stared in her eyes, and chalked her face'. *were chalked*] grew chalked (*MS*).

18. baulked: 'Checked, foiled; disappointed' (*OED*).

3

First came the silent gazers; next,
20   A screen of glass, we're thankful for;
Last, the sight's self, the sermon's text,
    The three men who did most abhor
    Their life in Paris yesterday,
    So killed themselves: and now, enthroned
25 Each on his copper couch, they lay
    Fronting me, waiting to be owned.
I thought, and think, their sin's atoned.

4

Poor men, God made, and all for that!
    The reverence struck me; o'er each head
30 Religiously was hung its hat,
    Each coat dripped by the owner's bed,
    Sacred from touch: each had his berth,

21. the sight's self: 'the sight itself', 'what people come to see'.

22–4. The three men . . . killed themselves: Rowena Fowler ('Blougram's Wager, Guido's Odds: Browning, Chance, and Probability', *VP* 41.1 [Spring 2003]) argues that these lines relate to 'those most quoted of all nineteenth-century statistics: the suicide figures' and to the individual's anxiety about becoming a 'statistical subject': 'Two hundred and forty people, in an average year, drowned in the Seine, most of them apparently suicides . . . Although Browning's poem suggests that the three people had killed themselves "yesterday," the law of averages suggests that three bodies would typically represent three or four days' drownings' (pp. 13–14 and p. 26n.18).

25. copper couch: Mrs Gore describes the inclined slabs on which the bodies were placed as 'leaden'; Eliza Ogilvy has 'brassy' (see headnote); no other source identifies them as 'copper'.

26. Fronting: facing; with the sense of 'confronting', 'presenting a bold front to' (*OED* 3a).

27. their sin's atoned: in Christian, and esp. Catholic, doctrine, suicide was a mortal sin, whose punishment was eternal damnation; the 'wood of suicides' is one of the locations in Dante's *Inferno* (canto xiii). Suicides were refused burial in consecrated ground in Britain until 1823 (the act itself remained illegal until 1961); socially it carried a terrible stigma. B. does not deny the sinfulness of suicide, but claims that this sin, like others, can be 'atoned' (implicitly by Christ's sacrifice); in the last stanza he explicitly attacks the concept of eternal punishment itself.
    their] these (*MS* canc.).

29–32. The display of the person's clothes, which the poet here converts into an act of reverence, was designed to help identify the body.

His bounds, his proper place of rest,
Who last night tenanted on earth
35   Some arch, where twelve such slept abreast,—
Unless the plain asphalte seemed best.

5

How did it happen, my poor boy?
    You wanted to be Buonaparte
And have the Tuileries for toy,
40   And could not, so it broke your heart?
You, old one by his side, I judge,
    Were, red as blood, a socialist,
A leveller! Does the Empire grudge
    You've gained what no Republic missed?
45   Be quiet, and unclench your fist!

---

33. bounds: limits or boundaries; the poet's point is that the deceased have the dignity of their own designated space in death, something which was not afforded to them in life.   *proper place of rest*: combining the archaic sense 'one's own' (*J.*) with the later meaning of 'decent, decorous, respectable, seemly' (*OED*).
36. I.e. unless it seemed best simply to sleep on the pavement, rather than under the arch of a bridge.   *asphalte*: B.'s use of the French spelling highlights this material's association with Paris; EBB. frequently mentions the 'asphalte' in her descriptions of Parisian life.
38. Buonaparte: France was ruled at this time by the Emperor Louis Napoleon, nephew of Napoleon Buonaparte, whose claims to be the legitimate hereditary ruler of France had been disputed by most until the *coup d'état* of Dec. 1851 which brought him to power. Cp. *Bishop Blougram* 436 ff. (p. 308).
39. Tuileries: the royal palace in the heart of Paris adopted by Napoleon Buonaparte as his official residence; Napoleon III moved the seat of government back there after becoming Emperor in 1852.
42–3. red as blood, a socialist, / A leveller! The terms 'socialist' and 'socialism' seem to have originated in Owenite circles in Britain during the 1820s, but were quickly adopted in France, and came to be associated with the revolutionary disturbances that punctuated French history throughout the nineteenth century. The earliest citation in *OED* linking the colour red with Socialism comes from 1851, but the association is already present in a letter from EBB. to her sister Henrietta, dated to 4–5 May 1849, in which she playfully refers to some of Pen's 'red republican and socialist pretensions' (*Correspondence* xv 281). The French Socialists fiercely opposed Louis Napoleon's *coup d'état*, and were violently repressed as a result. The speaker places socialists in apposition to 'levellers', the English Civil War grouping associated with John Lilburne, which argued in favour of greater equality and popular participation in government. B. refers twice to the pillorying of Lilburne in letters to Alfred Domett in 1844–5, with admiration for Lilburne's behaviour (*Correspondence* ix 69, xi 193).
44. what no Republic missed: i.e. avoided; namely, the 'equality' of death.
45. quiet, and] quiet then (*MS*, canc.).

6

And this—why, he was red in vain,
   Or black,—poor fellow that is blue!
What fancy was it, turned your brain?
   Oh, women were the prize for you!
50 Money gets women, cards and dice
   Get money, and ill-luck gets just
The copper couch and one clear nice
   Cool squirt of water o'er your bust,
The right thing to extinguish lust!

7

55 It's wiser being good than bad;
   It's safer being meek than fierce:
It's fitter being sane than mad.
   My own hope is, a sun will pierce
The thickest cloud earth ever stretched;
60   That, after Last, returns the First,
Though a wide compass round be fetched;
   That what began best, can't end worst,
Nor what God blessed once, prove accurst.

46–7. red in vain, / Or black: as the remainder of the stanza makes clear, the primary reference here is to gambling, and more specifically to the red and black suits that make up a deck of cards. For B.'s puritanical dislike of card-playing, see *Bishop Blougram* 48n. (p. 288).

52–3. The jets of water sprayed onto the corpses are mentioned in most accounts of the Morgue.

58–9. Cp. the description of the Day of Judgement in *ED* 501–46 (III 123–5).

60. Cp. *Revelation* xxii 13: 'I am Alpha and Omega, the beginning and the end, the first and the last.'

61. The expression 'to fetch a compass' means 'to take a circular or circuitous course' and occurs several times in the Bible, e.g. *2 Samuel* v 23, *Acts* xxviii 13. *OED* cites one of Archbishop John Tillotson's *Sermons* (1693): 'What a compass do many men fetch to go to heaven, by innumerable devices.' The fame of Tillotson's sermons makes it plausible that B. had come across this text in his father's library, which had rich holdings in the religious literature of the seventeenth century.

63. accurst: 'That which is cursed or doomed to misery' (*J.*). This archaic spelling is used on a number of occasions by B.; cp., e.g., *Bad Dreams III* (*Asolando* 1889) 36.

47 A Death in the Desert

Text and publication

First publ. *DP*, 28 May 1864; repr. *DP²*, *1868*, *1880*, *1888*. The MS, part of the printer's copy for *DP*, is at *Morgan*. It is a fairly clean copy, with some denser patches of re-drafting. The title page is misbound, coming between pp. 6 and 7 of the MS of the poem itself. There are very few variants between *1864* and subsequent editions, and none are of major significance except the omission of l. 213.

Composition and date

Critics have generally assumed that *A Death* represents a response to the views on the origins and authorship of the gospel of John put forward by Ernest Renan in his controversial and hugely influential *Vie de Jésus* (publ. 23 June 1863). This would place the composition of the poem in the period between early Nov. 1863, when B. told Isa Blagden that he had 'just read' Renan's book (19 Nov. 1863; *Dearest Isa* 180), and 26 Apr. 1864, when he sent the proofs of *DP* to Moncure Conway (*New Letters* 160). (B.'s letter to Isa Blagden is discussed in more detail below; see *Sources and influences*.) In an influential discussion of the relation between the *Vie de Jésus* and *A Death*, Elinor Shaffer suggests that there is also 'internal evidence' in the poem itself which 'points conclusively to the use of Renan'; but the evidence in question is in fact less than conclusive (see *Sources and influences*: (2) Contemporary religious history and controversy). The assumption that Renan prompted or influenced the poem was, moreover, directly contradicted by the Reverend J. Llewellyn Davies at a meeting of the Browning Society on 25 Feb. 1887, when he asserted that Browning 'wrote the poem long prior to the publication of Renan's work . . . [as] an answer to Strauss' (cited in W.O. Raymond, *The Infinite Moment* (Toronto, 1950), p. 33). B. had been aware of Strauss's *Life of Jesus* (1835) since the 1840s, if not earlier; it forms part of the background to *CE & ED* (see headnote to *CE*, III 43–4), and the German critic is mentioned by name in *Bishop Blougram* 577 (p. 317; see also *Sources and influences* below). If Llewellyn Davies is right – and, as Raymond notes, 'one could wish that Mr. Davies had stated the source of his information' (p. 34) – then the poem might have been written at any time during the 1850s or early 1860s. We know that some of the poems included in *DP* were written, or at least drafted, by the summer of 1860, and that B. had been working on a 'long poem' in the winter of 1859–60 (see Appendix C, p. 895). Moreover, *A Death* has affinities of theme and technique with a number of *M & W* poems, most notably *An Epistle* (p. 507) and *Cleon* (p. 563). Other evidence for a date in the 1850s is provided by the similarities between the poem and the episode in *Sordello* in which 'John the Beloved' says farewell to his 'flock' in Antioch at the house of Xanthus, a fictional follower (iii 963–94; I 592); B. was actively revising *Sordello* during 1855–6, and eventually published his revised version in the *Poetical Works* of 1863 (see headnote, I 354–55).

There are, however, other elements which link the poem to the early 1860s. In 1862 the German scholar Konstantin von Tischendorf published a facsimile of a Greek manuscript he had discovered in St. Catherine's monastery on Mount Sinai. This *Codex Sinaiticus*, as it came to be known, contained very early texts of many books of the Old and New Testaments, as well as various annotations and commentaries from successive generations of interpreters. Some of these shed light on the process of the transmission of ancient texts, and attest to the culture of 'prison scholarship' amongst Christian martyrs: 'A text of the Book of Esther cites its remarkable origin: "Copied and corrected against the Hexapla of Origen," runs its subscription, "as corrected by Origen himself. The confessor Antoninus collated. I, Pamphilus, corrected the roll in prison"' (Robin Lane Fox, *Pagans and Christians* [Harmondsworth 1986] 471; Pamphilus was martyred in 309 at Caesarea). The *Codex Sinaiticus* also provides a good deal of information about the form of manuscripts in the ancient world; it is written on parchment, but each page contains four narrow columns which are believed to have been copied from earlier texts written on 'rolls' (see l. 2n.). Although there is no direct evidence that B. saw the *Codex Sinaiticus*, the poem's account of the origins and transmission of the fictional document it contains might well have been influenced by von Tischendorf's discoveries. Additional evidence linking the poem to the 1860s has recently been put forward by Robert Inglesfield, who highlights an apparent reference to Herbert Spencer's philosophical treatise *First Principles* (1862) in the poem (*VP* 41.3 [2003] 333−47; see ll. 393−401n.). If Inglesfield is correct, the poem must have been written, or at least redrafted, after 1862, which would make the suggestion of direct influence by Renan more plausible.

In the light of this evidence, we suggest that, though the poem may have been begun in the late 1850s, it was substantially revised and completed in 1862−3.

Setting
According to Revd G. U. Pope, who knew B. towards the end of the poet's life, '[the] idea of the piece . . . is briefly this: − some Christian, whose name is not given (9, 10), is supposed to be examining his library − looking up and classifying his choice treasures. One imagines that he was an Ephesian (or perhaps an Alexandrian); that he may have lived in the beginning of the third century; that it was a time of hot persecution, when he was in daily peril of death; and that he is looking over a few of the more ancient Christian records to strengthen himself for coming trial, by the contemplation of the struggles of those that had gone before. He finds among others a parchment scroll attributed to Pamphylax of Antioch, who had died a martyr in Ephesus, just after the death of St John the Apostle. This MS. is described in a very minute and realistic way. It is No. 5 in his library; consists of three skins of parchment glued together; is in the Greek language; and is incomplete, since it ranges from Epsilon to Mu, so that four sections − pages we may call them − are missing in the beginning, and perhaps some at the end. This precious MS. is kept in a "select chest", an ark containing the most precious part of his literary treasures' (*St. John in the Desert. An Introduction and Notes to Browning's 'A Death in the Desert'* [1897] 39−40). Pope adds that the first twelve lines of the poem − the 'prologue' − are 'supposed to be written by this anonymous owner on the outer side of the parchment', and that this prologue is followed by 'the MS. itself of Pamphylax' (p. 40).

There is some speculation and unsupported assertion in Pope's account. The location of the document's current owner is not specified in the poem, and nor is the place of martyrdom of Pamphylax. Pope's assertion about the 'prologue' implies that the other sections in square brackets (ll. 82−104 and 666−88) are additions to the document by other hands, whereas it is equally possible to read them all as editorial insertions by the current owner, especially if lines 1−12 are read not as an annotation on the parchment itself, but as an introduction to a *transcript* of it being made by its owner for a third party. Pope's account, however, does highlight the poem's emphasis on the fragility of such early Christian documents, and on the dangers attending those who produced, owned or transmitted them; on this topic, see below, *Sources*.

Pamphylax's narrative recounts the deathbed testimony of the Apostle John. The cave in which John, Pamphylax and the others are hiding from persecution must be just outside Ephesus, as the narrator returns to Ephesus after John's death (l. 647). In placing John and his entourage in Ephesus, a city in modern-day Turkey, B. is following the tradition of the early church. Numerous sources place John in Ephesus at the end of his life; according to Irenaeus, Bishop of Lyons at the end of the second century, 'John, the disciple of the Lord, who also leaned on his breast . . . produced his gospel, while he was living at Ephesus in Asia' (*Adversus haereses* III i 1; for Irenaeus' story of John's encounter at Ephesus with the heretic Cerinthus, see below, *Sources*). Perhaps the most striking parallel to the poem is provided by the so-called 'Monarchian Prologue' to John's gospel, which dates from the fourth century. This Prologue is found in many of the MS versions of the Vulgate, and attempts to counteract speculation about its authenticity by providing information about the circumstances of its composition:

> [John] wrote this gospel in Asia, after he had written the Apocalypse in the island of Patmos, in order that to whom the incorruptible beginning was ascribed in Genesis, to Him might also be ascribed the incorruptible end by a virgin in the Apocalypse, wherein Christ says: 'I am Alpha and Omega.' And it is this John, who knowing that the day of his retirement had come, having called together his disciples at Ephesus, and having proved Christ to them by many signs, descended into the place which had been dug for his sepulture, and after praying was gathered to his fathers, as free from the pain of death as he was from corruption of the flesh. (transl. John Chapman, *Notes on the Early History of the Vulgate Gospels* [1908] 228–9)

(For another possible allusion to the Monarchian Prologues, see l. 1n.) The precise date of John's death is, however, rather less easy to pinpoint. B. adopts the tradition that John lived to a very old age; at l. 643 John speculates what might happen should he 'tarry a new hundred years'. This would place the poem at the end of the first century of the Christian era. The narrator refers to 'the decree' (l. 23) and 'the persecution' (l. 41); this might, at first sight, appear to refer to the 'second persecution' of Christians during the reign of the Emperor Domitian (81–96 AD), but tradition links this persecution with John's exile in Patmos and the composition of *Revelation* (see l. 140n.). There was, however, a widely held belief that the Emperor Trajan (AD 98–117) inaugurated a new persecution; Foxe's *Book of Martyrs*, for instance, speaks of the 'third persecution' of Christians under Trajan, during which 'many thousands of them [were] daily put to death, of which none did any thing contrary to the Roman laws worthy of persecution' (ch. ii). The evidence for this persecution is a letter from Pliny the Younger to the Emperor, written in 112, asking for advice on how to deal with Christians. Trajan's reply makes it clear that Christians are not to be actively 'sought out', and that anonymous denunciation is not acceptable, perhaps implying that these practices were widespread (*Bettenson* 6). The most likely explanation is that B. has inferred the existence of an 'edict' authorizing renewed persecution of Christians from this evidence and dated it to early in the reign of Trajan, around AD 98–100.

Sources and influences

(1) Biblical and patristic texts
Daniel Karlin ('A Life in the Desert: Browning, Moses and St. John', *SBC* xxv [Sept. 2003] 49–71) suggests that B. modelled the poem on the Old Testament

book of *Deuteronomy*, in which Moses, like B.'s St John in extreme old age, though unlike him in that 'his eye was not dim, nor his natural force abated' (xxxiv 7), delivers a deathbed speech which sums up a lifetime's service to God, admonishes the living, and forecasts the backsliding of future generations; like John he dies in the wilderness and 'no man knoweth of his sepulchre unto this day' (xxxiv 6). For B.'s interest in the figure of Moses as a type of the prophet-poet, see below, *Parallels in B.*

The words attributed to St John in the poem are imagined as reaching us through a complex and unstable process of textual transmission, analogous to that found in early 'witnesses' to the existence of John's gospel. The *Ecclesiastical History* of Eusebius (*c.* AD 260–341), for instance, makes reference to a five-volume work by Papias, Bishop of Hierapolis, entitled *Expositions of the Oracles of the Lord*, written around 130: 'Now Papias himself in the introduction to his writings makes no claim to be a hearer and eye-witness of the holy Apostles, but to have received the contents of the faith from those that were known to them. He tells us this in his own words: "I shall not hesitate to set down for you, along with my interpretations, all things which I learnt from the elders with care and recorded with care, being well assured of their truth."' According to Eusebius, Papias goes on to record some of the observations of 'John the Elder' on the gospel of Mark: 'He says: "The Elder used to say this also: Mark became the interpreter of Peter and he wrote down accurately, but not in order, as much as he remembered of the sayings and doings of Christ. For he was not a hearer or a follower of the Lord, but afterwards, as I said, of Peter, who adapted his teachings to the needs of the moment and did not make an ordered exposition of the sayings of the Lord"' (*Bettenson* 38, 39). The sayings of 'John the Elder' are, then, given at third hand by Eusebius, in a process with obvious analogies to the poem's own procedures. The doubts introduced by this unstable process of transmission are underlined by the fact that the 'John the Elder' cited by Papias has been seen by many commentators as a different person from the Apostle John (on the controversy over the authenticity of the writings attributed to John, see below). B.'s fictional document is, therefore, intended to imitate the form of many lost early Christian documents, like Papias's *Expositions*, and indeed like the *Life of Pamphilus* also written by Eusebius (see *Composition and date*). B. objects to Renan's interpretation of the testimony of Papias in his letter to Isa Blagden; see below.

A Death also makes reference to the tradition that John's gospel was written in response to the emerging Gnostic theology, later characterized by the church as heretical; see esp. ll. 327–33. John mentions two antagonists by name – Ebion and Cerinthus – and the anonymous commentator who adds the closing lines to the poem also mentions Cerinthus. Both are known about exclusively through the writings of the Church Fathers; the first mention of Cerinthus, for example, occurs in the writings of Irenaeus (*c.* AD 170). According to Irenaeus, Cerinthus was a contemporary of John; he tells the story of how 'John, the disciple of the Lord, going to bathe at Ephesus, and perceiving Cerinthus within, rushed out of the bath-house without bathing, exclaiming, "Let us fly, lest even the bath-house fall down, because Cerinthus, the enemy of the truth, is within"' (*Adversus haereses* III iii 4). Both the Ebionites and Cerinthus attempted to separate the human and divine natures of Christ. The Ebionites 'revered Jesus as the greatest of the prophets, endowed with supernatural virtue and power' but 'obstinately rejected the preceding existence and divine perfections of the Logos, or Son of God, which are so clearly defined in the Gospel of St. John' (Gibbon, *Decline and Fall*, ch. xxi). Cerinthus too 'distinguished between Jesus and Christ':

Jesus was mere man, though eminent in holiness. He suffered and died and was raised from the dead, or, as some say Cerinthus taught, He will be raised from the dead at the Last Day and all men will rise with Him. At the moment of baptism, Christ or the Holy Ghost was sent by the Highest God, and dwelt in Jesus teaching Him, what not even the angels knew, the Unknown God. This union between Jesus and Christ continues till the Passion, when Jesus suffers alone and Christ returns to heaven. (*Catholic Encyclopaedia*)

The first Epistle of John, written against the 'many false prophets' who have 'gone out into the world' has often been seen as an attempt to counteract these specific 'heresies': 'Hereby know ye the Spirit of God; Every spirit that confesseth that Jesus Christ is come in the flesh is of God: And every spirit that confesseth not that Jesus Christ is come in the flesh is not of God; and this is that spirit of antichrist, whereof ye have heard that it should come; and even now already is it in the world' (*1 John* iv 2–3).

B.'s other main source in the poem is the writing attributed to John himself. In addition to the gospel, B.'s John alludes to the Epistles which bear his name (e.g. ll. 131–2n.) and to *Revelation* (e.g. l. 141n.). There are also quotations from the other gospels, most notably in John's discussion of his demeanour during the arrest and crucifixion of Jesus, when he uses an expression found in both *Matthew* and *Mark*.

(2) *Contemporary religious history and controversy*
(i) *The background to the debate*
The poem's fidelity to the traditions surrounding the life of St John, and its frequent use of the words of the five books attributed to John in the New Testament, constitute an implicit rejoinder to some of the scepticism about the authenticity of John's gospel expressed by biblical critics during the nineteenth century. By the time of the poem's publication the so-called Higher Criticism of the Bible, which subjected it to rigorous textual and historical scrutiny, had placed the gospel of John under suspicion for a number of reasons. (On the Higher Criticism see headnote to *CE & ED*, III 43–4). The account of the life of Jesus given in *John* differs markedly from that contained in the other three ('synoptic') gospels; as Philip Harwood puts it in his lectures on Strauss, the New Testament contains 'two versions of Christ and Christianity . . . one in the first three gospels taken collectively, and the other in the fourth gospel' (*German Anti-Supernaturalism* [1841] 35). A number of incidents – most famously, the resurrection of Lazarus – occur only in John's gospel (see headnote to *An Epistle*, pp. 507–9); and many of the incidents narrated by the synoptics are absent from *John*. The language of the fourth gospel is, moreover, very different from that of the other three gospels, and seems to anticipate, or to have been influenced by, the theological debates and heresies of the second century; the Jesus of John's gospel 'is a mystic, a theologian of the Alexandrine school, discoursing of his divine sonship, his coming down from heaven, the need of eating his flesh and drinking his blood, and other things of that kind . . . We have got far away from the old gospel of the kingdom, to a new gospel of the Logos and the Paraclete' (Harwood, *German Anti-Supernaturalism* 35–36). In addition, the five books of the New Testament which carry the name of John (the gospel, *Revelation* and the three epistles) contain little or no internal evidence of his authorship: 'Only the Apocalypse [*Revelation*] mentions the name "John" in the text, and it does not say that this John was one of the sons of Zebedee and an Apostle; the Fourth Gospel and the First Epistle claim to be by people who knew Jesus intimately, but neither actually claims to

be written by John' (J.C. O'Neill, 'The Study of the New Testament', in *Nineteenth Century Religious Thought in the West*, 3 vols [Cambridge, 1988], vol. iii, p. 153). There are also significant differences of style and tone between these various books, leading to speculation that they might not in fact have been written by the same author. Finally, the references to and quotations from John's gospel in the work of his immediate contemporaries and successors are relatively few in number, and date from the latter part of the second century; this would imply that the gospel was not written (as it claims to be) by an intimate associate of Jesus who witnessed the events depicted, but by someone writing during the second century of the Christian era.

(ii) *Strauss's* Life of Jesus

In 1820 Karl Gottlieb Bretschneider's *Probabilia de evangelii et epistolarum Ioannis apostoli indole et origine* (1820) amassed the evidence against the traditional ascription of authorship of the fourth gospel to the Apostle; Bretschneider published his book in Latin to shield the public from his findings, but still, according to a modern historian of the period, managed to '[stir] up a storm of attention over the authorship of John' (Sean P. Kealy, *John's Gospel and the History of Biblical Interpretation* [Lewiston 2002] 379). It was, however, David Friedrich Strauss who first confronted the public, not just of Germany but of Europe as a whole, with an analysis which cast considerable doubt on the authenticity of John's gospel and indeed of all the gospel narratives. Strauss's approach was to see the gospels not as historical accounts of the life of Jesus written by eye-witnesses, but as poetic or mythological expressions of the beliefs and ideas about the Messiah prevalent amongst Jews and early Christians. His reading of John's gospel convinced him that it was the least historical and the most overtly mythological of the four gospels. In his examination of the fifth chapter of *John*, for instance, concerning a cure wrought by Jesus on the Sabbath, Strauss notes the differences between 'the practical spirit' of Jesus' discourse in the synoptics and the metaphysical quality of his teaching in *John*:

> The fourth Evangelist . . . makes him argue from the uninterrupted activity of God, and reminds us by the expression which he puts into the mouth of Jesus, My Father worketh hitherto . . . of a principle in the Alexandrian metaphysics, viz. God never ceases to act . . . a metaphysical proposition more likely to be familiar to the author of the fourth gospel than to Jesus. (*Life of Jesus*, tr. Marian Evans [George Eliot], 1846, rpt. 1892, p. 372)

Such infiltrations of 'Alexandrian metaphysics' are to be found everywhere in *John*, and lead Strauss to conclude that most of the speeches attributed to Jesus in this book are 'free compositions of the Evangelist written in the spirit of Alexandrian or Hellenic philosophy' (O'Neill, 'Study', p. 157). External evidence – '[the] earliest quotation expressly stated to be from the Gospel of John is found in Theophilus of Antioch, about the year 172' (*Life of Jesus* 73) – also leads to the conclusion that the gospel is a product of the latter part of that century, and has no genuine connection with the Apostle John.

Earlier writers who had arrived at a similar conclusion (most notably Lessing in the *Wölfenbuttel Fragments*) had suggested that the gospels, which take the form of first-hand accounts of the life of Jesus, were a deliberate attempt to deceive the public, but Strauss sees them as the result of an inevitable and entirely natural process:

> According to all the rules of probability, the Apostles were all dead before the close of the first century; not excepting John, who is said to have lived till

A.D. 100; concerning whose age and death, however, many fables were invented. What an ample scope for attributing to the Apostles manuscripts they never wrote! The Apostles, dispersed abroad, had died in the latter half of the first century; the Gospel became more widely preached throughout the Roman Empire, and by degrees acquired a fixed form . . . It was doubtless from this orally circulated Gospel that the many passages agreeing accurately with passages in our Gospels, which occur without any indication of their source in the earliest ecclesiastical writers, were actually derived. Before long this oral traditionary Gospel became deposited in different manuscripts; this person or that, possibly an apostle, furnishing the principal features of the history . . . It appears that these manuscripts did not originally bear the names of their compilers . . . Nothing however was more natural than the supposition which arose among the early Christians, that the histories concerning Jesus which were circulated and used by the churches had been written by his immediate disciples. (*Life of Jesus* 73–4)

Although Strauss denies the historical accuracy and authenticity of John's gospel, he does not impute dishonesty either to the Apostle or to the anonymous gospel writer. The former is innocent of things that were later done in his name; and the latter is merely setting down what he and others like him believe the Messiah must have done, according to canons of evidence and verisimilitude very different from those prevailing in the nineteenth century.

Strauss's work was translated into English by Marian Evans (the future George Eliot) in 1846; but there is extensive evidence of its circulation in what Timothy Larsen calls 'plebeian, infidel circles' before this date (*Contested Christianity: The Political and Social Contexts of Victorian Theology* [Waco, TX 2004] 44). Although it was neither plebeian nor infidel, the Unitarian South Place Chapel in London was open to radical new ideas emanating from Germany; and in 1841 Philip Harwood published his series of six lectures given there on Strauss's *Life of Jesus* under the title *German Anti-Supernaturalism*. B. knew South Place Chapel well; it was set up by his early mentor W. J. Fox, and his childhood friend Eliza Flower was choirmaster there (*Maynard* 183). It is, under these circumstances, possible that he might have heard Harwood's elegant and lucid exposition of Strauss's doctrines; but, even if he did not, Harwood's lectures indicate the way in which Strauss was received and understood in the advanced and liberal dissenting circles to which B. belonged.

At the end of his first lecture, in which he describes the principal features of Strauss's 'mythological' approach to the gospels, Harwood offers his own opinion that such a view is not 'antecedently improbable':

[The gospels] are not, in any sense, the beginning, the cause of Christianity, but an effect of it. Christianity, in its beginning, was traditionary; communicated orally from the living heart to the living heart, in words that were spirit and life. It was not at all a thing of books. It did not grow up among a writing and reading people, but among a speaking and hearing people. Men would not begin with writing about Christ; they would leave that till they found themselves beginning to forget him, and would then take pen and parchment as helps to feeble and fading memories. [. . .] It seems altogether a likely thing . . . that [Christianity's] gospels should be of this mixed, indefinite, second-hand sort; half poetry and half tradition; mere offshoots and collateral results and expressions of the Gospel . . . a growth from the roots, not of facts scrupulously collected, rigidly tested and carefully arranged, and discourses taken down in shorthand as from the lips of a theological lecturer – but of ideas, impulses, memories and hopes, to which past, present and future, things visible and things invisible, furnished their several contributions, in proportions which neither they who wrote nor we who read can scientifically analyse. (*German Anti-Supernaturalism* 13–14)

The idea of taking 'pen and parchment as helps to feeble and fading memories' anticipates the poem's description both of the fictional document itself and of the gospel of John (which is already in semi-permanent form at the time of John's death, according to the poem; see l. 60n.). Harwood also emphasizes the way in which the perception of Jesus changed as the prospects of the Second Coming receded, leading to a greater willingness to impute messianic miracles (such as the raising of Lazarus from the dead) to Jesus: 'as the Second Coming went further and further off into the remoteness of uncertainty, the church would make more and more of the First Coming; would turn to the past rather than the future, and incorporate the Messianic idea *there*, with growing distinctness and fulness. See a suggestion to this effect in Schnitzer's Review of the German translation of Mr. Hennell's "Inquiry;" *Allgemeine Litteratur-Zeitung*, May 1840' (*German Anti-Supernaturalism* 68n.). The supreme miracle – the resurrection of Jesus himself – would have had the strongest effect, gradually transforming Christians' understanding of the life of Jesus through a natural process of growth and 'accretion': 'And, this faith [in the resurrection] once gained, we may think how it would react on all their recollections of the past; how the whole history of Jesus would shape itself more and more into poetry and mythus . . . Every text would have a new interpretation; every recollected fact would take a new shape and meaning; tradition would grow fast and freely, accumulating ever fresh and varied supernaturalism . . . And so it would go on, gaining fresh accretions day by day, till the time came for fixing the whole in writing' (pp. 88–9; cp. esp. ll. 168–75; and for another parallel with Harwood, see ll. 393–401n.)

(iii) *Renan's* Vie de Jésus

B.'s longstanding interest in questions connected with the Higher Criticism of the Bible, attested to by both *CE & ED* and *Bishop Blougram*, seems to have been revived by the publication of Ernest Renan's *Vie de Jésus*. Renan's novelistic rewriting of the life of Jesus attracted a great deal of interest throughout Europe, and particularly in Britain. Along with controversial publications such as *Essays and Reviews* (1860), a volume of essays by various authors who held liberal theological views, and Bishop John Colenso's *The Pentateuch and Book of Joshua Critically Examined* (1862), Renan's book helped to prompt what was felt by many British intellectuals to be a long overdue discussion of the status of the foundations of Christianity; see, for instance, James Anthony Froude's 'Plea for the Free Discussion of Theological Difficulties' (1863). B. himself, in another of the *DP* poems, *Gold Hair*, alluded to this climate of opinion:

> The candid incline to surmise of late
>   That the Christian faith may be false, I find;
> For our Essays-and-Reviews debate
>   Begins to tell on the public mind,
> And Colenso's words have weight . . . (ll. 126–30)

In his letter to Isa Blagden (see *Composition and date*), B. focuses on Renan's interpretation of the evidence for the authenticity of the gospel narratives:

> I have just read Renan's book, and find it weaker and less honest than I was led to expect. I am glad it is written: if he thinks he can prove what he says,

he has fewer doubts on the subject than I—but mine are none of his. As to
the Strauss school, I don't understand their complacency about the book—he
admits many points they have thought it essential to dispute—and substitutes
his explanation, which I think impossible. The want of candour is remarkable:
you could no more deduce the character of his text from the substance of his
notes, than rewrite a novel from simply reading the mottoes at the head of
each chapter: they often mean quite another thing,—unless he cuts away the
awkward part—as in the parable of the Rich Man & Lazarus. His admissions
& criticisms on St John are curious. I make no doubt he imagines *himself* stating a fact, with the inevitable license—so must John have done. His argument
against the genuineness of Matthew—from the reference to what Papias says
of the λογία—is altogether too gross a blunder to be believed in a Scholar,—
and is yet repeated half a dozen times throughout the book . . . [miracles] were
cheats, and their author a cheat! What do you think of the figure *he* cuts who
makes his hero participate in the wretched affair with Lazarus, and then calls
him all the pretty names that follow? Take away every claim to man's respect
from Christ and then give him a wreath of gum-roses and calico-lilies—or as
Constance says to Arthur in King John—"Give Grannam kingdom, and it
grannam will Give it a plum, an apple and a fig". (*Dearest Isa* 180)

Renan differs from Strauss, at least in the earlier editions of the *Vie de Jésus*, in
attempting to argue that all four of the gospels have a basis in historical fact: 'En
somme, j'admets comme authentiques les quatre évangiles canoniques. Tous, selon
moi, remontent au premier siècle, et ils sont à peu près des auteurs à qui on
les attribue; mais leur valeur historique est fort diverse' [To sum up, I accept
the four canonical gospels as authentic. For me, all of them have their origins
in the first century, and are more or less by the authors to whom they have
been attributed; but their historical value differs considerably.] Renan admits the
'serious problems' caused by this assumption in the case of John, and goes on to
offer the following explanation:

On est tenté de croire que Jean, dans sa vieillesse, ayant lu les récits
évangéliques qui circulaient, d'une part, y remarqua diverses inexactitudes, de
l'autre, fut froissé de voir qu'on ne lui accordait pas dans l'histoire du Christ
une assez grande place; qu'alors il commença à dicter une foule de choses qu'il
savait mieux que les autres, avec l'intention de montrer que, dans beaucoup
de cas où on ne parlait que de Pierre, il avait figuré avec et avant lui. Déjà,
du vivant de Jésus, ces légers sentiments de jalousie s'étaient trahis entre les fils
de Zébédée et les autres disciples. Depuis la mort de Jacques, son frère, Jean
restait seul héritier des souvenirs intimes dont ces deux apôtres, de l'aveu de
tous, étaient dépositaires. De là sa perpétuelle attention à rappeler qu'il est le
dernier survivant des témoins oculaires, et le plaisir qu'il prend à raconter des
circonstances que lui seul pouvait connaître. De là, tant de petits traits de pré-
cision qui semblent comme des scolies d'un annotateur: «Il était six heures;»
«il était nuit;» «cet homme s'appelait Malchus;» «ils avaient allumé un réchaud,
car il faisait froid;» «cette tunique était sans couture.» De là, enfin, le désordre
de la rédaction, l'irrégularité de la marche, le décousu des premiers chapitres;
autant de traits inexplicables dans la supposition où notre évangile ne serait qu'une
thèse de théologie sans valeur historique, et qui, au contraire, se comprennent
parfaitement, si l'on y voit, conformément à la tradition, des souvenirs de vieillard, tantôt d'une prodigieuse fraîcheur, tantôt ayant subi d'étranges altérations.
(*Vie de Jésus* [Paris, 1863], pp. xxvii–xxix).

[It is tempting to believe that John, in his old age, having read the evangelical stories in circulation, on the one hand noticed various inaccuracies, and on the other was offended to see that he had not been accorded a sufficiently important place in the story of Christ; that he then began to dictate a mass of things he knew better than the others, with the intention of showing that, in numerous instances where Peter alone was spoken of, he had figured alongside and ahead of him. Already, during Jesus' lifetime, these small traces of jealousy between the sons of Zebedee and the other disciples had manifested themselves. Since the death of his brother James, John was the sole inheritor of intimate memories of which these two Apostles were, according to the testimony of all, the beneficiaries. Hence his habit of continually drawing attention to the fact that he is the last surviving eye-witness, and the pleasure he takes in recounting circumstances only he could have known: 'It was six o'clock'; 'it was night'; 'this man was called Malchus'; 'they had lit a brazier, because it was cold'; 'this tunic was seamless'. Hence, finally, the lack of order in the redaction, the irregularity of the movement, the disjointedness of the early chapters; all are inexplicable features on the assumption that our gospel is a theological treatise without historical value, but are perfectly comprehensible if one sees in it (in accordance with tradition) the memories of an old man, at times of an astounding freshness, at times having undergone strange alterations.]

Like Harwood, then, Renan rejects the Straussian understanding of the fourth gospel as 'a theological treatise', and prefers to see it as the result of a natural process; John's memories, varying in precision and accuracy, form the basis of the narrative constructed by his followers. This is, presumably, one of the points B. was referring to in his comments on the 'complacency' of the Straussians.

As B.'s letter to Isa Blagden indicates, he had doubts about the intellectual honesty of Renan's procedure in the *Vie de Jésus*. Some of Renan's difficulties arise from his attempt to see John and the other evangelists as sources of genuine historical information about the life of Jesus, while citing in support of this view the work of Strauss and the Tübingen School which, as we have seen, represents the gospels as more or less devoid of factual content. (Renan in fact resolved this difficulty in later editions of the *Vie de Jésus* by removing the claim that the gospels were written by the first-century followers of Jesus whose names they bear.) This means, as Elinor Shaffer points out in *'Kubla Khan' and The Fall of Jerusalem* (Cambridge 1980), that he was forced to find psychological explanations where Strauss and his followers had offered textual or mythological ones. Thus, for instance, what B. calls 'the wretched affair with Lazarus' is explained by Strauss as a later projection of messianic attributes onto Jesus, but by Renan as a demonstration of Jesus' power thought up by Lazarus's family at Bethany and half-willingly participated in by Jesus. Shaffer is, however, guilty of overstating the extent to which Renan '[attacks] John as dishonest and Jesus as duplicitous' (p. 194). One of the key differences between *John* and the Synoptics concerns the crucifixion; *John* represents 'the disciple . . . whom [Jesus] loved' as standing alongside Mary at the foot of the cross, while the other gospels fail to mention this fact. Shaffer suggests that this episode epitomizes for Renan the self-aggrandisement apparent throughout John's gospel, citing in evidence one of Renan's footnotes on the passage in question (*John* xix 25–27):

This is, in my opinion, one of those features in which John betrays his personality and the desire he has of giving himself importance[.] John, after the death of Jesus, appears in fact to have received the mother of his master into

his house, and to have adopted her . . . The great consideration which Mary
enjoyed in the early church, doubtless led John to pretend that Jesus, whose
favourite disciple he wished to be regarded [sic], had, when dying, recommended
to his care all that was dearest to him. ('*Kubla Khan*' 196–7)

Shaffer, however, mistranslates the French word 'prétendre' (it does not mean
'pretend' but 'claim'); there is no suggestion of deception in the original.
Moreover, there is no warrant in the poem or elsewhere for Shaffer's assertion
that 'Browning fully accepted the basic position of the Tübingen school as to the
lateness and philosophical gnosticism of the Fourth Gospel' (p. 209); B.'s poem,
with its dependence on tradition and the words attributed to John in the New
Testament, in fact implies a more conservative position than either Strauss's or
Renan's on the question of apostolic authorship of the fourth gospel.

3 Literary and artistic sources

The modern (post-medieval) tradition of writing narrative or dramatic poems set
in biblical times reaches back to Milton's *Samson Agonistes* (publ. 1671), which
like *A Death* relates the last hours of its protagonist, but there is almost no precedent for a poem which claims to reproduce the voice of one of Jesus' disciples,
but in which what is spoken goes beyond a paraphrase of the biblical text. B.
will have known works by Romantic writers such as Byron's *Cain* (1821) and
Coleridge's 'The Wanderings of Cain' (publ. 1828), as well as EBB.'s *The
Seraphim* (1837) and *A Drama of Exile* (1844); note that EBB. herself had turned
in the 1850s to contemporary political and social settings. Painting may also be
of importance in the poem's conception, not just the long tradition of religious
genre painting depicting the deathbed of a saint surrounded by disciples, or saints
who famously lived and died in deserts (e.g. St Paul the Hermit, often represented in the cave where he lived and died) but the more modern work of the
Pre-Raphaelite school whose treatment of biblical subjects emphasized the symbolic function of realistic, 'historical' detail, as in John Everett Millais's *Christ in
the House of His Parents* (1849–50) or William Holman Hunt's *The Scapegoat* (1856).

Parallels in B.

As has been mentioned in *Composition*, the poem forms a kind of trilogy, with
An Epistle and *Cleon*, of works set in the years immediately following Jesus' death;
the late poem *Imperante Augusto Natus Est* (*Asolando*, 1889) is set just before Jesus'
birth. Like *A Death*, *An Epistle* and *Cleon* are primarily concerned, in terms of
their religious thought, with the Christian doctrine of the Incarnation, the transcendent 'event' which, whether 'historically' true or not, B. believed offered
mankind the perfect conjunction of absolute power with absolute love: the clearest statement of this belief is in another poem with a biblical subject, *Saul* (III 491).

St John makes an appearance at the end of bk iii of *Sordello* (see *Composition
and date*). The figure of the prophet in the wilderness is principally associated
with Moses, again in *Sordello* (iii 790–804, I 580–2) and in *One Word More* (see
ll. 73–108, pp. 606–9). Deathbed utterances in B. include *Tomb at St. Praxed's*
(p. 232), Rabbi Ben Ezra's 'Song of Death' in *Holy-Cross Day* (p. 549), and Guido's
second monologue in bk. xi of *Ring*; the Pope's monologue in bk. x comes close
to being a deathbed speech, and the Pope resembles St John in being old, wise
and full of foreboding about the future of the Christian faith. *Ring* is the poem's
most significant parallel for another reason, namely its preoccupation with the
transmission of stories, both orally and by writing, and with the problem of determining 'truth' by reference to a document, however 'authentic' it may appear.

[Supposed of Pamphylax the Antiochene:
It is a parchment, of my rolls the fifth,
Hath three skins glued together, is all Greek,
And goeth from *Epsilon* down to *Mu:*
5   Lies second in the surnamed Chosen Chest,
Stained and conserved with juice of terebinth,
Covered with cloth of hair, and lettered *Xi,*
From Xanthus, my wife's uncle, now at peace:
Mu and *Epsilon* stand for my own name,
10   I may not write it, but I make a cross

1–12. A description of the ensuing manuscript by an unnamed commentator: see headnote, *Setting*. With the use of square brackets to distinguish comment from utterance, cp. *Caliban* (p. 625), though in that poem commentator and speaker are one and the same.

1. Pamphylax the Antiochene: The name Pamphylax seems to be B.'s invention; a lost *Life of Pamphilus*, detailing the life of a martyr who died in 309, was written by the early church historian Eusebius (see headnote, *Composition and date* and *Setting*). The Greek-speaking city of Antioch in Syria plays an important part in the early history of Christianity; it was there that 'the disciples were called Christians first' (*Acts* xi 26), and Luke is described as 'Antiochensis' (from Antioch) in both the Anti-Marcionite and Monarchian Prologues (see headnote, *Sources and influneces*).

2. parchment: an animal skin prepared for writing.   *rolls:* the normal form in which books were kept in antiquity; the roll usually consisted of a number of sheets of papyrus glued together and wound around a stick, but this 'roll' is made from three pieces of parchment (see l. 3).

3. all Greek: the four gospels were written in Greek, the common language of intellectual life throughout the Eastern portion of the Roman Empire. The commentator's statement implies that some of his other 'rolls' contain a mixture of languages; Jesus and his disciples spoke Aramaic, and one theory of the synoptic gospels suggested that they emerged from a set of 'logia' or sayings of Jesus in Aramaic.

4. Epsilon . . . Mu: Letters were used for numbers in ancient Greece: 'Epsilon' is five, and 'Mu' forty. As Pope (headnote, *Setting*) points out, this indicates that the text is incomplete, as sections 1–4 are missing.

5. surnamed: 'designated, known by the name of' (it does not mean 'marked with the owner's surname': see ll. 9–10). This chest is clearly a repository for the commentator's most treasured documents, implying that he is the keeper of an archive of sacred texts in an early Christian community: see ll. 9–10n.

6. juice of terebinth: the resin of the terebinth or turpentine tree (*Pistacia Terebinthus*), used here to protect the parchment from insects.

7. Xi: the fourteenth letter of the Greek alphabet.

8. Xanthus: see headnote, *Composition and date*. It is unclear whether or not this 'Xanthus' is the one mentioned by 'Pamphylax' as present at John's death (see ll. 29–30).

9–10. The commentator conceals his identity beneath a cipher, suggesting that he is living during one of the periods of persecution of the early church; see headnote, *Setting*. It was not until the edict of the Emperor Decius in 249 that

To show I wait His coming, with the rest,
And leave off here: beginneth Pamphylax.]

I said, "If one should wet his lips with wine,
And slip the broadest plantain-leaf we find,
15   Or else the lappet of a linen robe,
Into the water-vessel, lay it right,
And cool his forehead just above the eyes,
The while a brother, kneeling either side,
Should chafe each hand and try to make it warm,—
20   He is not so far gone but he might speak."

This did not happen in the outer cave,
Nor in the secret chamber of the rock,
Where, sixty days since the decree was out,
We had him, bedded on a camel-skin,

---

persecution of Christians became widespread and received official sanction; see
Fox (headnote, *Setting*), ch. 9.

11. His coming: i.e. the Second Coming of Christ. An active belief in the imminence of the Second Coming is apparent in a number of early Christian
writings; see, e.g., *Matthew* xxiv 34: 'Verily I say unto you, This generation shall
not pass, till all these things be fulfilled'. John's Epistles make frequent reference
to the 'Antichrist', whose arrival heralds the Second Coming (e.g. *1 John* iv 3);
and *Revelation*, traditionally attributed to John, contains a vision of the event itself.
On the relation between the disappointment of these hopes and the form of John's
gospel, see headnote, *Sources and influences*. The commentator's reference to the
Second Coming indicates the persistence of the literal form of this belief well
beyond the lifetime of the first Christians.

13. 'I' is the person believed by the commentator to be Pamphylax. For the other
(equally fictional) members of John's entourage, see ll. 29–30.

14. plantain-leaf: the Greater Plantain, *Plantago major*, 'a low herb with broad flat
leaves spread out close to the ground, and close spikes of inconspicuous flowers';
its medicinal properties are recorded in English literature since medieval times.
'Plantain' is also a term for the plane-tree (*Platanus orientalis*), a native of the Middle
East which was also thought to have healing properties (*OED* 1, quot. 1398).

15. lappet: 'A loose or overlapping part of a garment, forming a flap or fold' (*OED*).

21–8. John and his followers are hiding in a group of caves to escape persecution (see l. 23n.); the action of the poem takes place not in the 'outer cave' (too
risky) nor the 'secret chamber' (too dark), but in the 'midmost' cave which admits
some light and therefore allows his followers to see his face. Cp. the allegory of
the cave in book vii of Plato's *Republic*, and the mysterious Empedoclean fragment, 'We have come under this roofed cave' (transl. M. R. Wright, *Empedocles:
the Extant Fragments* [1981] 280), usually taken as an allegory of human, as opposed
to divine existence.

23. the decree: the supposed persecution inaugurated by the Emperor Trajan; on
the evidence for this see headnote, *Setting*.

25   And waited for his dying all the while;
But in the midmost grotto: since noon's light
Reached there a little, and we would not lose
The last of what might happen on his face.

     I at the head, and Xanthus at the feet,
30   With Valens and the Boy, had lifted him,
And brought him from the chamber in the depths,
And laid him in the light where we might see:
For certain smiles began about his mouth,
And his lids moved, presageful of the end.

35   Beyond, and half way up the mouth o' the cave,
The Bactrian convert, having his desire,
Kept watch, and made pretence to graze a goat
That gave us milk, on rags of various herb,
Plantain and quitch, the rocks' shade keeps alive:
40   So that if any thief or soldier passed,
(Because the persecution was aware)
Yielding the goat up promptly with his life,
Such man might pass on, joyful at a prize,
Nor care to pry into the cool o' the cave.
45   Outside was all noon and the burning blue.

     "Here is wine," answered Xanthus,—dropped a drop;
I stooped and placed the lap of cloth aright,
Then chafed his right hand, and the Boy his left:
But Valens had bethought him, and produced

---

27. *we would not*: 'we did not wish to'.

29–30. Xanthus . . . Valens . . . the Boy: fictional members of John's entourage. Pope (headnote, *Setting*) suggests that Pamphylax (Greek), Valens (Roman), and the Bactrian (barbarian) (see l. 36n.) symbolize 'the world-wide diffusion of Christianity'.

36. Bactrian: an inhabitant of an area of what is now eastern Iran which was for a time a Greek colony; the 'convert' might well therefore have been Greek-speaking.

39. quitch: another name for couch-grass; see *Sordello* iv 23n. (I 595). *the rocks' shade keeps alive*: '[which] the rocks' shade keeps alive'.

41. persecution: see l. 23 above and note. *aware*: in the obsolete sense of 'Watchful, vigilant, cautious, on one's guard' (*OED*).

42. promptly with his life: although the syntax is ambiguous, this probably means that the Bactrian is willing to give both the goat and his own life, as the 'prize' of the goat (l. 43) will prevent any thieves or soldiers from probing further.

50   And broke a ball of nard, and made perfume.
      Only, he did—not so much wake, as—turn
      And smile a little, as a sleeper does
      If any dear one call him, touch his face—
      And smiles and loves, but will not be disturbed.

55   Then Xanthus said a prayer, but still he slept:
      It is the Xanthus that escaped to Rome,
      Was burned, and could not write the chronicle.

      Then the Boy sprang up from his knees, and ran,
      Stung by the splendour of a sudden thought,
60   And fetched the seventh plate of graven lead
      Out of the secret chamber, found a place,
      Pressing with finger on the deeper dints,
      And spoke, as 'twere his mouth proclaiming first,
      "I am the Resurrection and the Life."

65   Whereat he opened his eyes wide at once,
      And sat up of himself, and looked at us;
      And thenceforth nobody pronounced a word:
      Only, outside, the Bactrian cried his cry

50. nard: 'A fragrant ointment or perfume prepared from the rhizome of the plant of the same name . . . and much prized by the ancients' (*OED*); referred to as 'spikenard' in *John* xii 3: 'Then took Mary a pound of ointment of spikenard, very costly, and anointed the feet of Jesus, and wiped his feet with her hair; and the house was filled with the odour of the ointment.'

56–7. An imaginary martyrology; burning to death was a typical method of execution for persecuted Christians; see, e.g., the account of the martyrdom of Polycarp, Bishop of Smyrna, in 155 in *Bettenson* 12–16.

57. the chronicle: perhaps suggesting that Xanthus was originally supposed to write the document.

59. Cp. Keats, *Eve of St Agnes* 136–7: 'Sudden a thought came like a full-blown rose, / Flushing his brow'.

60. plate of graven lead: lead tablets were used for writing instead of papyrus on occasion in the ancient world; the strong suggestion here is that John or one of his entourage has already written down all or part of his life of Jesus. Cp. *Cleon* 47n. (pp. 568–9).

63. as 'twere his mouth proclaiming first: 'as if he were Jesus saying [these words] for the first time'.

64. Jesus' words as recorded in *John* xi 25, but not in any of the other gospels; the implication is that this is one of the sayings of Jesus that John has shared with his followers; see headnote, *Sources*.

66. of himself: by himself.

Like the lone desert-bird that wears the ruff,
70   As signal we were safe, from time to time.

First he said, "If a friend declared to me,
This my son Valens, this my other son,
Were James and Peter,—nay, declared as well
This lad was very John,—I could believe!
75   —Could, for a moment, doubtlessly believe:
So is myself withdrawn into my depths,
The soul retreated from the perished brain
Whence it was wont to feel and use the world
Through these dull members, done with long ago.
80   Yet I myself remain; I feel myself:
And there is nothing lost. Let be, awhile!"

[This is the doctrine he was wont to teach,
How divers persons witness in each man,
Three souls which make up one soul: first, to wit,
85   A soul of each and all the bodily parts,
Seated therein, which works, and is what Does,
And has the use of earth, and ends the man
Downward: but, tending upward for advice,
Grows into, and again is grown into
90   By the next soul, which, seated in the brain,
Useth the first with its collected use,
And feeleth, thinketh, willeth,—is what Knows:

69. *lone desert-bird that wears the ruff*: according to Thomas P. Harrison, this is either the Egyptian Vulture or the Hermit Ibis; Harrison adds: 'It is unlikely that Browning knew either' ('Birds in the Poetry of Browning', *RES* vii 28 (1956), 393–405). But B.'s knowledge of wildlife was wide and eclectic, and included other desert creatures such as the jerboa (*Saul* 45, III 499).

70.] From time to time, as signal we were safe. (*MS* original reading, marked for transposition).

82–104. The 'glossa [commentary] of Theotypas' (a fictitious commentator) illustrates the ways in which the original impulse of Christianity is already turning into dogma. Pope (headnote, *Setting*) suggests that this section might be a commentary on a passage in one of St John's epistles: 'For there are three that bear record in heaven, the Father, the Word, and the Holy Ghost; and these three are one. And there are three that bear witness in earth, the Spirit, and the water, and the blood: and these three agree in one' (*1 John* v 7–8), and also points out the trilogy of terms 'spirit and soul and body' in *1 Thessalonians* v 23. Cp. also *John* i 13, where the 'sons of God' are said to be 'born, not of blood, nor of the will of the flesh, nor of the will of man, but of God'.

83. *witness*: '[bear] witness [to the presence of]'.

Which, duly tending upward in its turn,
Grows into, and again is grown into
95   By the last soul, that uses both the first,
Subsisting whether they assist or no,
And, constituting man's self, is what Is—
And leans upon the former, makes it play,
As that played off the first: and, tending up,
100 Holds, is upheld by, God, and ends the man
Upward in that dread point of intercourse,
Nor needs a place, for it returns to Him.
What Does, what Knows, what Is; three souls, one man.
I give the glossa of Theotypas.]

105 And then, "A stick, once fire from end to end;
Now, ashes save the tip that holds a spark!
Yet, blow the spark, it runs back, spreads itself
A little where the fire was: thus I urge
The soul that served me, till it task once more
110 What ashes of my brain have kept their shape,
And these make effort on the last o' the flesh,
Trying to taste again the truth of things—"
(He smiled)—"their very superficial truth;
As that ye are my sons, that it is long
115 Since James and Peter had release by death,
And I am only he, your brother John,
Who saw and heard, and could remember all.
Remember all! It is not much to say.
What if the truth broke on me from above
120 As once and oft-times? Such might hap again:
Doubtlessly He might stand in presence here,
With head wool-white, eyes flame, and feet like brass,
The sword and the seven stars, as I have seen—

115. James and Peter had release by death: there are several uses of the name James in the New Testament; John is here referring to his brother, also known as St James the Greater (to distinguish him from St James the Less, the brother of Jesus), martyred in AD 44 by Herod Agrippa I (*Acts* xii 1–2). St Peter was martyred in Rome towards the end of the reign of the Emperor Nero (*c*. AD 67); there is an implicit anticipation of his death in John's gospel (xxi 18–19).

116. your brother John: Pope (headnote, *Setting*) compares *Revelation* i 9: 'I, John, who also am your brother'. For the significance of such references in the context of nineteenth-century biblical criticism, see headnote, *Sources*.

122–3. Cp. the description of the 'Son of man' in *Revelation* i 14–16: 'His head and his hairs were white like wool, as white as snow; and his eyes were as

I who now shudder only and surmise
125 'How did your brother bear that sight and live?'

"If I live yet, it is for good, more love
Through me to men: be nought but ashes here
That keep awhile my semblance, who was John,—
Still, when they scatter, there is left on earth
130 No one alive who knew (consider this!)
—Saw with his eyes and handled with his hands
That which was from the first, the Word of Life.
How will it be when none more saith 'I saw?'

"Such ever was love's way: to rise, it stoops.
135 Since I, whom Christ's mouth taught, was bidden teach,
I went, for many years, about the world,
Saying 'It was so; so I heard and saw,'
Speaking as the case asked: and men believed.
Afterward came the message to myself
140 In Patmos isle; I was not bidden teach,
But simply listen, take a book and write,
Nor set down other than the given word,
With nothing left to my arbitrament
To choose or change: I wrote, and men believed.
145 Then, for my time grew brief, no message more,
No call to write again, I found a way,

a flame of fire; And his feet like unto fine brass, as if they burned in a furnace;
and his voice as the sound of many waters. And he had in his right hand seven
stars: and out of his mouth went a sharp twoedged sword: and his countenance
was as the sun shineth in his strength.'
125. Pope (headnote, *Setting*) compares *Revelation* i 17: 'And when I saw him,
I fell at his feet as dead.'
127–8. Continuing the metaphor begun at ll. 105–8 above.
129. when they scatter. i.e. 'when these ashes scatter'.
131–2. Cp. *1 John* i 1: 'That which was from the beginning, which we have heard,
which we have seen with our eyes, which we have looked upon, and our hands
have handled, of the Word of life.'
139–44. The fictional John's account of the composition of the Book of
Revelation.
140. Patmos: the island in the Aegean Sea where John claims to have had the
vision recorded in *Revelation* (see i 9).
141. Cp. *Revelation* i 11: 'What thou seest, write in a book, and send it unto the
seven churches which are in Asia.'
143. arbitrament: 'Will; determination; choice' (*J.*).
145–62. 'His epistles. Antichrists.' (Pope; headnote, *Setting*).

And, reasoning from my knowledge, merely taught
Men should, for love's sake, in love's strength, believe;
Or I would pen a letter to a friend
150   And urge the same as friend, nor less nor more:
Friends said I reasoned rightly, and believed.
But at the last, why, I seemed left alive
Like a sea-jelly weak on Patmos strand,
To tell dry sea-beach gazers how I fared
155   When there was mid-sea, and the mighty things;
Left to repeat, 'I saw, I heard, I knew,'
And go all over the old ground again,
With Antichrist already in the world,
And many Antichrists, who answered prompt
160   'Am I not Jasper as thyself art John?
Nay, young, whereas through age thou mayest forget:
Wherefore, explain, or how shall we believe?'
I never thought to call down fire on such,
Or, as in wonderful and early days,
165   Pick up the scorpion, tread the serpent dumb;
But patient stated much of the Lord's life

149–51. The three epistles attributed to John are brief, and the third is addressed to a named individual (Gaius). It is described by the *Catholic Encyclopaedia* as 'entirely a personal affair'.

152–5. For a different treatment of the contrast between those who keep to the shore and those who have knowledge of the deep ocean, cp. *Dís Aliter Visum* 18–23 (p. 691).

153. sea-jelly: jellyfish.

158–9. Antichrist: John's first and second Epistles introduce the term 'antichrist', and imply that the proliferation of 'antichrists' is one of the signs of the impending Apocalypse: see, e.g., *1 John* ii 18 – 'Little children, it is the last time: and as ye have heard that antichrist shall come, even now are there many antichrists; whereby we know that it is the last time' – and cp. *1 John* iv 2–3 and *2 John* vii.

160. Echoing *Matthew* xiv 55, in which the Nazarenes express scepticism that Jesus, whose family they know, can be the Messiah: 'Is not this the carpenter's son? is not his mother called Mary? and his brethren, James, and Joses, and Simon, and Judas?' *Jasper*: a fictitious figure; the name does not appear in the Bible, though the variant 'Gaspar' was the traditional name of one of the Magi; as a precious stone it is mentioned in *Revelation* (e.g. iv 3; xxi 11).

162. Wherefore] Therefore (*MS*).

163. to call down fire: in *Luke* ix 54–6 John and his brother James (see l. 115n.) ask Jesus if he wants them to 'command fire to come down from heaven, and consume' a Samaritan village which would not receive him; Jesus replied that 'the Son of man is not come to destroy lives, but to save them'.

165. Cp. *Luke* x 19: 'Behold, I give unto you power to tread on serpents and scorpions, and over all the power of the enemy: and nothing shall by any means hurt you.'

Forgotten or misdelivered, and let it work:
Since much that at the first, in deed and word,
Lay simply and sufficiently exposed,
170 Had grown (or else my soul was grown to match,
Fed through such years, familiar with such light,
Guarded and guided still to see and speak)
Of new significance and fresh result;
What first were guessed as points, I now knew stars,
175 And named them in the Gospel I have writ.
For men said, 'It is getting long ago:'
'Where is the promise of His coming?'—asked
These young ones in their strength, as loth to wait,
Of me who, when their sires were born, was old.
180 I, for I loved them, answered, joyfully,
Since I was there, and helpful in my age;
And, in the main, I think such men believed.
Finally, thus endeavouring, I fell sick,
Ye brought me here, and I supposed the end,
185 And went to sleep with one thought that, at least,
Though the whole earth should lie in wickedness,
We had the truth, might leave the rest to God.
Yet now I wake in such decrepitude
As I had slidden down and fallen afar,

167. forgotten or misdelivered: alerting his auditors to the possibility that his account of events might, at this distance of time, contain errors; see headnote, *Sources and influences*.

168–75. An attempt to explain the differences between John and the synoptic gospels; although the passage of time has made John's memories less reliable, it has enabled certain features of Jesus' life and sayings to acquire 'new significance and fresh result'; see headnote, *Sources*.

169. simply and sufficiently: cp. *One Word More* 62 (p. 605).

172. guided still] guided on (*MS* canc.).

175. named them] named so (*MS* canc.). *the Gospel I have writ*: an emphatic implicit rejection of Strauss's position that the Gospel of John was written after the Apostle's death; see l. 60 above, and headnote.

176. For] Since (*MS* canc.).

177. "Where is the promise of His coming?": the words of the 'scoffers' who doubt the second coming of the Lord in *2 Peter* iii 4.

181. Since] That (*MS*).

183. thus] so (*MS*, written over 'thus'; a rare example of *1864* reverting to a reading cancelled in *MS*).

186. Cp. *1 John* v 19: 'And we know that we are of God, and the whole world lieth in wickedness.'

189–92. The image of a man falling and grasping desperately for a 'foothold' recurs in Caponsacchi's prediction of Guido's fate in *Ring* vi 1913–18: 'left o' the very ledge of things, / I seem to see him catch convulsively / One by one

190   Past even the presence of my former self,
       Grasping the while for stay at facts which snap,
       Till I am found away from my own world,
       Feeling for foot-hold through a blank profound,
       Along with unborn people in strange lands,
195   Who say—I hear said or conceive they say—
       'Was John at all, and did he say he saw?
       Assure us, ere we ask what he might see!'

       "And how shall I assure them? Can they share
       —They, who have flesh, a veil of youth and strength
200   About each spirit, that needs must bide its time,
       Living and learning still as years assist
       which wear the thickness thin, and let man see—
       With me who hardly am withheld at all,
       But shudderingly, scarce a shred between,
205   Lie bare to the universal prick of light?
       Is it for nothing we grow old and weak,
       We whom God loves? When pain ends, gain ends too.
       To me, that story—ay, that Life and Death
       Of which I wrote 'it was'—to me, it is;
210   —Is, here and now: I apprehend nought else.
       Is not God now i' the world His power first made?

---

at all honest forms of life, / At reason, order, decency and use— / To cramp
him and get foothold by at least; / And still they disengage them from his clutch';
Guido slides down to 'the horizontal line, creation's verge, / From what just is
to absolute nothingness' (ll. 1930–1) where he meets his soul-mate, Judas.
193. a blank] the blank (*MS*).
196–7. Another anticipation of John's nineteenth-century critics; see headnote,
Sources (2).
199. who have flesh, a veil] with the flesh, the veil (*MS*).   *a veil of youth and strength*:
in 2 *Corinthians* iii 13–18 Paul speaks of the 'veil' between human beings and
God under the old law, 'which veil is done away in Christ'; however, John's
metaphor here refers not to this distinction between Judaism and Christianity but
to a theory of human development by which we become more conscious of the
spiritual world as we grow older. B. expounds this theory in several other poems;
cp., e.g., *Rabbi Ben Ezra* (p. 649).
200. that needs must] that must (*MS*).
203. withheld: i.e. from the divine presence.
207. we] men (*MS canc.*).
209. it is] still is (*MS, canc.*).
211–21. A concise statement of John's theology: God's presence in the world is
not limited to the historical moment of the Incarnation, but manifests itself in
the continuing struggle between Sin and Love. On the significance of the
Incarnation in B. see headnote, *Parallels*.
211.] Is not God in the world His power once made? (*MS*, altering an earlier
draft of the first part of the line: 'For is not God i' this world').

Is not His love at issue still with sin,
Closed with and cast and conquered, crucified
Visibly when a wrong is done on earth?
215 Love, wrong, and pain, what see I else around?
Yea, and the Resurrection and Uprise
To the right hand of the throne—what is it beside,
When such truth, breaking bounds, o'erfloods my soul,
And, as I saw the sin and death, even so
220 See I the need yet transiency of both,
The good and glory consummated thence?
I saw the Power; I see the Love, once weak,
Resume the Power: and in this word 'I see,'
Lo, there is recognized the Spirit of both
225 That, moving o'er the spirit of man, unblinds
His eye and bids him look. These are, I see;
But ye, the children, His beloved ones too,
Ye need,—as I should use an optic glass
I wondered at erewhile, somewhere i' the world,

212. *at issue still*] at struggle here (*MS*).

213.] not *1868–88*. It is rare for whole lines to be either added or deleted in editions after *1864*. B. may have thought twice about giving the impression that God's
love could be defeated, even if temporarily.

214. *on earth*] on it (*MS*, written over 'earth'). *1864* rarely reverts to a cancelled
MS reading; B. may have thought on reflection that the antecedent of 'it', namely
'world' in l. 211, was too distant.

216–17. *Resurrection and Uprise / To the right hand of the throne*: Cp. *Mark* xvi 19:
'So then after the Lord had spoken unto them, he was received up into heaven,
and sat on the right hand of God.'

223. *Resume*: 're-assume', 'take back'; *OED* records a special sense of this word
(1b) in relation to 'strength, power, influence, etc.', citing, e.g., Hooker's
Ecclesiastical Polity (1597): 'They which have once received this power may not
think . . . to take it, reject, and resume it as often as they themselves list'. *in this
word 'I see'*: in answering his imaginary future critics, John emphasizes the visionary dimension of 'seeing' (which enables him to perceive Christ's death and
resurrection as an ongoing spiritual reality) rather than his physical presence at
the events in question.

224. *there is*] I have (*MS* canc.).

226. *look. These are*] look: this is (*MS*, canc.; B. omitted to change the colon after
'look' to a full stop in *MS*; this was done in proof).

227. *beloved ones too*] beloved too (*MS*).

228–35. The instrument John describes, with its 'tube', seems more akin to a reverse
telescope than a microscope. The telescope was unknown in antiquity, but primitive magnifying lenses were known to have been used by Near Eastern civiliza-
tions: in 1853 Sir Austen Layard brought back to England lenses made of rock
crystal found during the excavation of Nimrud in ancient Assyria (modern Iraq).

228. *an*] the (*MS* canc.).

230   It had been given a crafty smith to make;
       A tube, he turned on objects brought too close,
       Lying confusedly insubordinate
       For the unassisted eye to master once:
       Look through his tube, at distance now they lay,
235   Become succinct, distinct, so small, so clear!
       Just thus, ye needs must apprehend what truth
       I see, reduced to plain historic fact,
       Diminished into clearness, proved a point
       And far away: ye would withdraw your sense
240   From out eternity, strain it upon time,
       Then stand before that fact, that Life and Death,
       Stay there at gaze, till it dispart, dispread,
       As though a star should open out, all sides,
       And grow the world on you, as it is my world.

245   "For life, with all it yields of joy and woe,
       And hope and fear,—believe the aged friend,—

233. to master once:] to master thus: (*MS*).
234. at distance now they lay] they lay at distance now (*MS* original reading, marked for transposition).
236–44. Cp. *Epilogue* (*DP*, *1864*), in which the 'Second Speaker', identified in *1864²* as Renan, laments the loss of faith in Christianity: 'Gone now! All gone across the dark so far, / Sharpening fast, shuddering ever, shutting still, / Dwindling into the distance, dies that star / Which came, stood, opened once! / We gazed our fill / With upturned faces on as real a Face . . .' (ll. 22–6). He is answered by the 'Third Speaker' (B. himself): 'That one Face, far from vanish, rather grows, / Or decomposes but to recompose, / Becomes my universe that feels and knows' (ll. 99–101). Contrast also *My Star* 12–13 (III 387): 'What matter to me if their star is a world? / Mine has opened its soul to me; therefore I love it.'
236. Just thus] Just so (*MS*).   *ye needs must*] ye need to (*MS*, canc.).
237. Pope (headnote, *Setting*) compares Tennyson, *In Memoriam*, xxv: 'The past will always win / A glory from its being far; / And orb into the perfect star / We saw not, when we moved therein.'
238. proved a point: cp. l. 174 above, and ll. 243–4 below; John accuses those who doubt him of attempting to reverse the process of 'growth' set in motion by the original revelation.
242. dispart, dispread: cp. *Sordello* i 881–3 (I 452): 'songs go up exulting, then dispread, dispart, disperse, lingering overhead / Like an escape of angels'. *J.* defines 'dispart' as 'To divide in two; to separate; to break; to burst; to rive'. Cp. also *Abt Vogler* 11 (p. 763).
244. And grow] Grow (*1870* [rev. ed. of *1868*]–*1888*)   *on you, as it is*] on you: it is (*MS*; 'on' is written over 'to').
244^245.] no line-space in *MS*; B. wrote 'New par.' in the l. margin and added quotation marks at the start of l. 246.

Is just our chance o' the prize of learning love,
How love might be, hath been indeed, and is;
And that we hold thenceforth to the uttermost
250 Such prize despite the envy of the world,
And, having gained truth, keep truth: that is all.
But see the double way wherein we are led,
How the soul learns diversely from the flesh!
With flesh, that hath so little time to stay,
255 And yields mere basement for the soul's emprise,
Expect prompt teaching. Helpful was the light,
And warmth was cherishing and food was choice
To every man's flesh, thousand years ago,
As now to yours and mine; the body sprang
260 At once to the height, and stayed: but the soul,—no!
Since sages who, this noontide, meditate
In Rome or Athens, may descry some point
Of the eternal power, hid yestereve;
And as thereby the power's whole mass extends,
265 So much extends the æther floating o'er,
The love that tops the might, the Christ in God.

248. *How love*] How it (*MS*).
251.] Having gained truth, dare keep truth—that is all. (*MS*).
252–99. The argument is that, if we were able to acquire knowledge of spiritual reality with the same certainty that we acquire knowledge about the physical world, faith would cease to have any value; in metaphysical terms, the human condition is defined by a constant struggle against doubt, and by the affirmation of belief against, not with, the tide of the 'world's' opinion. The necessity of doubt is a defining principle of B.'s religious philosophy: major treatments of the theme include *Bishop Blougram* (see esp. ll. 599–605, p. 318) and, in *DP*, *Mr Sludge*; spiritualism's claim to *prove* the existence of a spiritual world and an afterlife was one of the reasons B. was so hostile to it: see headnote, p. 779.
253. *diversely*: differently.
254. *With*] From (*MS*, canc.).
255. *basement*: groundwork; *OED* 2 cites Isaac Taylor, *Natural History of Enthusiasm* (1829): 'This belief [in God as creator and sustainer of all life] constitutes the basement-principle of all religion' (p. 64). *emprise*: 'Attempt of danger; undertaking of hazard; enterprise' (*J.*).
261. *sages who, this*] men who, this same (*MS*, canc.).
262. *In Rome or Athens, may descry*] In Rome, in Athens, shall descry] (*MS*, canc.). *descry*: 'To detect; to find out any thing concealed' (*J.*).
263. *yestereve*] yesterday (*MS* canc.).
265. *extends*] hath waxed (*MS*). *æther floating o'er*] fiery floating sea (*MS* canc.). 'Æther' (more usually 'ether') has a range of meanings: literally it is a poeticism for 'the clear upper sky' (Pope's transl. of *Iliad* xvi 361: 'All the unmeasured æther flames with light'); it has associations with the 'diviner air' breathed by the classical gods, as in Arthur Hugh Clough's description of Italy as 'a land wherein

Then, as new lessons shall be learned in these
Till earth's work stop and useless time run out,
So duly, daily, needs provision be
270   For keeping the soul's prowess possible,
Building new barriers as the old decay,
Saving us from evasion of life's proof,
Putting the question ever, 'Does God love,
And will ye hold that truth against the world?'
275   Ye know there needs no second proof with good
Gained for our flesh from any earthly source:
We might go freezing, ages,—give us fire,
Thereafter we judge fire at its full worth,
And guard it safe through every chance, ye know!
280   That fable of Prometheus and his theft,

---

gods of the old time wandered, / Where every breath even now changes to ether
divine' (*Amours de Voyage* i 3–4); in ancient cosmology it was conceived of as 'an
element filling all space beyond the sphere of the moon, and as the constituent
substance of the stars and planets'; from this sense it passed into seventeenth-
and eighteenth-century physics as a substance 'believed to permeate the whole
of planetary and stellar space, not only filling the interplanetary spaces, but also
the interstices between the particles of air and other matter on earth; the medium
through which the waves of light are propagated'. This theory was still maintained in B.'s day (*OED* cites Huxley, 1872); its figurative sense is illustrated by
Carlyle, *Sartor Resartus* (1831): 'We are—we know not what;—light-sparkles floating in the æther of Deity!'
267. Then, as] And as (*MS*).
272. proof: test.
276. our flesh] man's flesh (*MS*).
277. We . . . us] He . . . him (*MS*).
278. we . . . its full worth] he will . . . worth (*MS*).
280–7. The value of fire is apparent even to those who no longer believe in the
literal truth of the myth of Prometheus, who is reputed to have been punished
by Zeus (or Jove) for stealing fire and giving it to humanity. The 'myth of Aeschylus'
(l. 285) alludes to the first part of his Prometheus trilogy, *Prometheus Firebearer*, now
lost, but which was still extant at the time the poem is set. In one of his early letters
to EBB., who had translated the only surviving part of the trilogy, *Prometheus
Bound*, B. urged her to 'restore' this lost play, thus making a new trilogy along
with Shelley's *Prometheus Unbound* (11 March 1845: *Correspondence* x 119–20). The
satyrs, however, come not from the tragic drama but from the comic piece which
traditionally followed the performance of a tragic trilogy: this piece is also lost,
but as Pope (headnote, *Setting*) points out, B. would have found the detail he
records in a fragment cited by Plutarch: 'The Satyr would have kissed and embraced
the fire the first time he saw it; but Prometheus bids him take heed, else he might
have cause to lament the loss of his beard if he came too near that which burns
all it touches' ('How a Man May Receive Advantage and Profit from His Enemies',
Moralia, transl. William W. Goodwin [Boston 1878], §555).
280. That . . . the theft] The . . . his theft (*MS*).

How mortals gained Jove's fiery flower, grows old
(I have been used to hear the pagans own)
And out of mind; but fire, howe'er its birth,
Here is it, precious to the sophist now
285   Who laughs the myth of Æschylus to scorn,
As precious to those satyrs of his play,
Who touched it in gay wonder at the thing.
While were it so with the soul,—this gift of truth
Once grasped, were this our soul's gain safe, and sure
290   To prosper as the body's gain is wont,—
Why, man's probation would conclude, his earth
Crumble; for he both reasons and decides,
Weighs first, then chooses: will he give up fire
For gold or purple once he knows its worth?
295   Could he give Christ up were His worth as plain?
Therefore, I say, to test man, shift the proofs,
Nor may he grasp that fact like other fact,
And straightway in his life acknowledge it,
As, say, the indubitable bliss of fire.
300   Sigh ye, 'It had been easier once than now?'
To give you answer I am left alive;
Look at me who was present from the first!
Ye know what things I saw; then came a test,

281. Pope (headnote, *Setting*) compares *Prometheus Bound*, l. 7: 'thine own bright flower' (EBB.'s transl.). Cp. also ll. 280–7n. *Jove's*] the (*MS*, canc.).

282. own: admit.

283. out of mind: 'no longer active in people's minds'.

284. sophist: originally 'A professor of philosophy', but John's use also glances at its later meaning of 'an artful but insidious logician' (*J.*).

285. myth] tale (*MS*).

286. those satyrs of] the satyrs in (*MS*, canc). *his play*] your bard (*MS*).

288. While] But (*MS*).

291. probation: 'Trial; examination' (*J.*).

293. Weighs first, then] Weighs worth, and (*MS*).

294. gold or purple: money or power; 'purple' is the traditional colour of royalty: cp. *Protus* 10n., III 637.

295. Could] Would (*MS*, canc.).

296. shift the proofs] the proofs shift (*1868–88*); the revision indicates more clearly that John is describing an objective (and providential) process.

299. As, say, the] As the (*MS* first draft).

300. "It had been easier": 'would it have been easier' (i.e. when Christ was still present on the earth).

301. give you answer] give that answer (*MS*).

My first, befitting me who so had seen:
305   'Forsake the Christ thou sawest transfigured, Him
Who trod the sea and brought the dead to life?
What should wring this from thee?'—ye laugh and ask.
What wrung it? Even a torchlight and a noise,
The sudden Roman faces, violent hands,
310   And fear of what the Jews might do! Just that,
And, it is written, 'I forsook and fled':
There was my trial, and it ended thus.
Ay, but my soul had gained its truth, could grow:
Another year or two,—what little child,
315   What tender woman that had seen no least
Of all my sights, but barely heard them told,
Who did not clasp the cross with a light laugh,
Or wrap the burning robe round, thanking God?
Well, was truth safe for ever, then? Not so.
320   Already had begun the silent work
Whereby truth, deadened of its absolute blaze,

304. My . . . me] The . . . him (*MS*).
305–6. The three incidents mentioned by John include one narrated only in his gospel, one narrated by the synoptics only, and one shared by John and the synoptics (see below).
305. transfigured: Christ took three of his disciples – Peter, James and John – with him to a 'high mountain' where he was 'transfigured': 'his raiment became shining exceeding white as snow . . . And there appeared unto them Elias with Moses; and they were talking with Jesus' (*Mark* ix 2–4). The incident figures in the other synoptic gospels (*Matthew* xvii 2; *Luke* ix 28–30) but is not mentioned in *John*.
306. trod the sea: John vi 19–20; cp. *Matthew* xiv 26; *Mark* vi 49.   *brought the dead to life*: the story of the resurrection of Lazarus occurs only in John's gospel (xi 1–45); see headnote to *Karshish* (p. 507).
307–8. wring this from thee? . . . wrung it?] do this with thee? . . . did it? (*MS*).
308–10. Describing Jesus' arrest in the Garden of Gethsemane; cp. *John* xviii 3: 'Judas, then, having received a band of men and officers from the chief priests and Pharisees, cometh thither with lanterns and torches and weapons.'
311. Cp. *Matthew* xxvi 56: 'Then all the disciples forsook him, and fled'; see also *Mark* xiv 50. John's statement implies that the other gospels were already in existence during his lifetime. There is no suggestion in John's gospel that John and the other disciples forsook Jesus and fled.
312. ended thus] issued thus (*MS*, with 'thus' written over 'so').
313. my soul] the soul (*MS*).
314–18. what little child . . . thanking God? cp. the description of St John's flock in *Sordello* iii 967–77 (I 592).
315. woman that] woman who (*MS*).
316. heard them told] heard of them (*MS*, canc.).
318. wrap the burning robe round: i.e. embrace being burned alive.

Might need love's eye to pierce the o'erstretched doubt:
Teachers were busy, whispering 'All is true
As the aged ones report; but youth can reach
325   Where age gropes dimly, weak with stir and strain,
And the full doctrine slumbers till to-day.'
Thus, what the Roman's lowered spear was found,
A bar to me who touched and handled truth,
Now proved the glozing of some new shrewd tongue,
330   This Ebion, this Cerinthus or their mates,
Till imminent was the outcry 'Save us Christ!'
Whereon I stated much of the Lord's life
Forgotten or misdelivered, and let it work.
Such work done, as it will be, what comes next?
335   What do I hear say, or conceive men say,
'Was John at all, and did he say he saw?
Assure us, ere we ask what he might see!'

"Is this indeed a burthen for late days,
And may I help to bear it with you all,

322. Might need] Should need (*MS*).
323. whispering] saying (*MS*).
325. gropes] feels (*MS*, canc.).   *weak with stir*] through its stir (*MS*).
326.] So the full doctrine slumbered until now (*MS* canc.).   *the full doctrine*: the ideas advanced by Ebion, Cerinthus and others; see l. 330n.
327. Roman's lowered spear: John compares the physical impediment which led him to forsake Jesus with the intellectual impediments placed in the way of truth by false teachers of the younger generation of Christians.
329. glozing] comment (*MS*). To 'gloze' combines the senses 'To flatter; to wheedle; to insinuate; to fawn' and the (erroneous) use 'to gloss' (both *J.*) to suggest that the new 'teachers' offer versions of Christ's message designed to appeal to their audience. Cp. Milton, *PL* ix 549–50: 'So glozed the tempter . . . Into the heart of Eve his words made way'.
330. For the doctrines of Ebion and Cerinthus see headnote, *Sources and influences*.
331. Till imminent was the outcry] Till the outcry was imminent (*MS*, replacing the original reading: 'And so the cry came to me').
332–3. John claims to have given his account of the life and teachings of Jesus as a way of countering the spread of false doctrine; this tallies with the traditional notion that John's gospel was written to counter the heresies of Cerinthus. See headnote, *Sources and influences*.
334. Such work done] This done with (*MS* canc.).
335. do . . . men say] did . . . men said (*MS*).
336–7. The clearest anticipation of John's nineteenth-century critics in the poem; cp. ll. 196–7n.

340   Using my weakness which becomes your strength?
       For if a babe were born inside this grot,
       Grew to a boy here, heard us praise the sun,
       Yet had but yon sole glimmer in light's place,—
       One loving him and wishful he should learn,
345   Would much rejoice himself was blinded first
       Month by month here, so made to understand
       How eyes, born darkling, apprehend amiss:
       I think I could explain to such a child
       There was more glow outside than gleams he caught,
350   Ay, nor need urge 'I saw it, so believe!'
       It is a heavy burthen you shall bear
       In latter days, new lands, or old grown strange,
       Left without me, which must be very soon.
       What is the doubt, my brothers? Quick with it!
355   I see you stand conversing, each new face,
       Either in fields, of yellow summer eves,
       On islets yet unnamed amid the sea;
       Or pace for shelter 'neath a portico
       Out of the crowd in some enormous town
360   Where now the larks sing in a solitude;
       Or muse upon blank heaps of stone and sand
       Idly conjectured to be Ephesus:

341–8. Another version of Plato's parable of the Cave in the seventh book of the Republic; see headnote, *Sources and influences*.

341. *grot*: grotto or cave.

346. *so made*] and made (*MS*); 'so' was the original reading; it is rare for *1864* to revert to a reading cancelled in *MS*.

347. *darkling*: 'Being in the dark; being without light' (*J.*).

354. John's question is addressed not just to his immediate audience, but to all future Christians.

355. *each new face*] you new men (*MS* canc.).

361–2. Cp. Macaulay's image of the 'New Zealander' sketching the ruins of St Paul's, made famous by Doré's engraving; imagining one's own civilization as a ruin is a variant on the 'fallen empire' topos so popular in this period: see headnote to *Love Among the Ruins*, p. 528. Ephesus was one of the great cities of antiquity, located in modern-day Turkey; its population in the second century BC has been estimated at 150,000 (Robin Lane Fox, *Pagans and Christians*, p. 46). For the tradition of John's residence and death there, see headnote, *Setting*. As *Ohio* notes, the archaeologist J. T. Wood, sponsored by the British Museum, began excavating the ruins of Ephesus in 1863. He was searching for traces not of the Christian community but of the Temple of Diana, one of the Seven Wonders of the ancient world.

362. *Idly*] Barely (*MS*).

And no one asks his fellow any more
'Where is the promise of His coming?' but
365   'Was He revealed in any of His lives,
As Power, as Love, as Influencing Soul?'

"Quick, for time presses, tell the whole mind out,
And let us ask and answer and be saved!
My book speaks on, because it cannot pass;
370   One listens quietly, nor scoffs but pleads
'Here is a tale of things done ages since;
What truth was ever told the second day?
Wonders, that would prove doctrine, go for nought.
Remains the doctrine, love; well, we must love,
375   And what we love most, power and love in one,
Let us acknowledge on the record here,
Accepting these in Christ: must Christ then be?
Has He been? Did not we ourselves make Him?
Our mind receives but what it holds, no more.
380   First of the love, then; we acknowledge Christ—
A proof we comprehend His love, a proof
We had such love already in ourselves,
Knew first what else we should not recognize.
'Tis mere projection from man's inmost mind,

364. Cp. l. 177n.

365. His lives: the different 'lives' of Jesus in circulation (including John's own).

366^367.] no line-space in *MS*; B. wrote 'New par.' in the l. margin and added quotation marks at the start of l. 367.

367–422. For the resemblance between the ideas of this imaginary future critic and some of the strands of the 'Higher Criticism' of the nineteenth century see headnote, *Sources and influences* (2).

370. One listens] One reads it (*MS* canc.).

373. Wonders: miraculous occurrences; in saying that these 'go for nought' John's imaginary critic suggests that they are no longer a stable basis for religious belief. Both Renan and Strauss (see headnote, *Sources* 2) rejected the authenticity of miracles; cp. earlier attacks on supernaturalism, e.g. Hume's 'Essay on Miracles' (1748).
   Wonders, that] Then, wonders that (*MS*).

374–5. we must love . . . we love] man must love . . . he loves (*MS* canc.).

379. Cp. Coleridge, *Dejection: an Ode* 47–8: 'O Lady! we receive but what we give, / And in our life alone does Nature live'. Coleridge goes on to state that perception of 'higher worth . . . from the soul itself must issue forth' (ll. 50–3). The sceptic whom St John imagines extends this argument from 'Nature' to the spiritual world. *what it holds*: 'what it is capable of holding'.

384. projection: 'a mental figure or image visualized and regarded as an objective reality' (*OED*); the earliest examples given are from Emerson.

385   And, what he loves, thus falls reflected back,
        Becomes accounted somewhat out of him;
        He throws it up in air, it drops down earth's,
        With shape, name, story added, man's old way.
        How prove you Christ came otherwise at least?
390   Next try the power: He made and rules the world:
        Certes there is a world once made, now ruled,
        Unless things have been ever as we see.
        Our sires declared a charioteer's yoked steeds
        Brought the sun up the east and down the west,
395   Which only of itself now rises, sets,
        As if a hand impelled it and a will,—
        Thus they long thought, they who had will and hands:
        But the new question's whisper is distinct,
        'Wherefore must all force needs be like ourselves?
400   We have the hands, the will; what made and drives
        The sun is force, is law, is named, not known,

---

385. thus falls] so falls (*MS*).

389. 'How can you prove that this is not how the idea of Christ was developed by humanity?'

391. Certes: 'It is certain that' (obs.).

392. as we see] as you see (*MS* canc.).

393–401. In Greek mythology, Phaeton drove the sun in a chariot. As Robert Inglesfield (see headnote, *Composition and date*) points out, Herbert Spencer uses a remarkably similar example to illustrate the mental progress of humanity in his *First Principles* (1862; rpt. 1867, p. 103): 'Of old the Sun was regarded as the chariot of a god, drawn by horses. How far the idea thus grossly expressed, was idealized, we need not inquire. It suffices to remark that this accounting for the apparent motion of the Sun by an agency like certain visible terrestrial agencies, reduced a daily wonder to the level of the commonest intellect. When, many centuries after, Kepler discovered that the planets moved round the Sun in ellipses and described equal areas in equal times, he concluded that in each planet there must exist a spirit to guide its movements. Here we see that with the progress of Science, there had disappeared the idea of a gross mechanical traction, such as was first assigned in the case of the Sun; but that while for this there was substituted an indefinite and less-easily conceivable force, it was still thought needful to assume a special personal agent as a cause of the regular irregularity of motion. When, finally, it was proved that these planetary revolutions with all their variations and disturbances, conformed to one universal law — when the presiding spirits which Kepler conceived were set aside, and the force of gravitation put in their place; the change was really the abolition of an imaginable agency, and the substitution of an unimaginable one.'

393. Our sires: 'our forefathers'.

397. they . . . they who had] we . . . we who have (*MS*).

While will and love we do know; marks of these,
Eye-witnesses attest, so books declare—
As that, to punish or reward our race,
405 The sun at undue times arose or set
Or else stood still: what do not men affirm?
But earth requires as urgently reward
Or punishment to-day as years ago,
And none expects the sun will interpose:
410 Therefore it was mere passion and mistake,
Or erring zeal for right, which changed the truth.
Go back, far, farther, to the birth of things;
Ever the will, the intelligence, the love,
Man's!—which he gives, supposing he but finds,
415 As late he gave head, body, hands and feet,
To help these in what forms he called his gods.
First, Jove's brow, Juno's eyes were swept away,
But Jove's wrath, Juno's pride continued long;
As last, will, power, and love discarded these,
420 So law in turn discards power, love, and will.
What proveth God is otherwise at least?
All else, projection from the mind of man!'

"Nay, do not give me wine, for I am strong,

402–11. The critic's point is that, since we now reject miraculous and anthropo-
morphic stories about the sun as being mere projections of human desire and
agency, we ought logically to do the same in the case of Christ.

403.] Eye-witnesses, it is affirmed, attest (*MS*).

404–6. There are numerous examples of the sun moving erratically at someone's
behest in the Bible; see, e.g., *Joshua* x 12, *Isaiah* xxxviii 8, *Amos* viii 9 and *Luke*
xxiii 45.

405.] The sun arose or set at undue times (*MS*, marked for transposition).

416. what forms the forms (*MS* canc.).

417–20. Pagan religion incarnates emotions such as 'wrath' or 'pride' in the
physical attributes of the gods ('Jove's brow, Juno's eyes'); a more advanced
philosophy conceives of the gods as representing or symbolizing 'wrath' or
'pride' in the abstract; this way of thinking is superseded by Christianity (with
'power' as the Father, 'love' as the Son, and 'will' as the Holy Spirit); this in turn
is finally displaced by the concept of 'law', i.e. universal, impersonal forces that
determine the nature of existence, and thus our own human nature.

417. First . . . were swept] Now . . . are swept (*MS*).

418. continued] lingered (*MS*).

419. As last] At last (*MS* canc.).

420.] Power shall in turn discard Power, Love and Will. (*MS*).

422. All else,] All is (*MS* canc.).

423–4. John asks to feel the 'plates' containing his gospel again; see l. 60n.

But place my gospel where I put my hands.

425   "I say that man was made to grow, not stop;
       That help, he needed once, and needs no more,
       Having grown up but an inch by, is withdrawn:
       For he hath new needs, and new helps to these.
       This imports solely, man should mount on each
430   New height in view; the help whereby he mounts,
       The ladder-rung his foot has left, may fall,
       Since all things suffer change save God the Truth.
       Man apprehends Him newly at each stage
       Whereat earth's ladder drops, its service done;
435   And nothing shall prove twice what once was proved.
       You stick a garden-plot with ordered twigs
       To show inside lie germs of herbs unborn,
       And check the careless step would spoil their birth;
       But when herbs wave, the guardian twigs may go,
440   Since should ye doubt of virtues, question kinds,
       It is no longer for old twigs ye look,
       Which proved once underneath lay store of seed,
       But to the herb's self, by what light ye boast,
       For what fruit's signs are. This book's fruit is plain,

424. I put] I rest (*MS* canc.).

427. grown up but] grown but (*1870* [rev. edn of *1868*]–*1888*).

429–32: Cp. Tennyson, *In Memoriam* (1850): 'I held it truth, with him who sings / To one clear harp in divers tones, / That men may rise on stepping-stones / Of their dead selves to higher things' (ll. 1–4). See also l. 602. For B.'s knowledge of and admiration for *In Memoriam*, see headnote to *"De Gustibus—"* (III 25). With the general sentiment of this passage, cp. *Christmas-Eve* 313–17 (III 60).

429. imports: matters.

431. The] What (*MS*, written over 'The'; one of the rare instances in which *1864* reverts to a reading cancelled in *MS*).

435. 'It is impossible to prove the same thing twice' (because the original circumstances in which it was first proved have changed). This bears some resemblance to the paradox put forward by the Pre-Socratic philosopher Heraclitus, who argued that it is impossible to step into the same river twice; see also l. 452 and l. 479. John is clearly familiar with some of the canons of philosophical debate in the Hellenistic world.

437. germs of herbs] herbs as yet (*MS*).

440. virtues . . . kinds] virtue . . . kind (*MS*); healing or other medicinal properties.

442. proved once] proved that (*MS*).   *underneath lay store of seed*] there lay store of seed to save (*MS* canc.).

444. Cp. *Matthew* vii 15–20: 'Beware of false prophets, which come to you in sheep's clothing, but inwardly they are ravening wolves. Ye shall know them by their fruits. Do men gather grapes of thorns, or figs of thistles? Even so every good tree bringeth forth good fruit; but a corrupt tree bringeth forth evil fruit. A good tree cannot bring forth evil fruit, neither can a corrupt tree bring forth good fruit. Every tree that bringeth not forth good fruit is hewn down, and cast into the fire. Wherefore by their fruits ye shall know them.'

445   Nor miracles need prove it any more.
Doth the fruit show? Then miracles bade 'ware
At first of root and stem, saved both till now
From trampling ox, rough boar and wanton goat.
What? Was man made a wheelwork to wind up,
450   And be discharged, and straight wound up anew?
No!—grown, his growth lasts; taught, he ne'er forgets:
May learn a thousand things, not twice the same.

"This might be pagan teaching: now hear mine.

"I say, that as the babe, you feed awhile,
455   Becomes a boy and fit to feed himself,
So, minds at first must be spoon-fed with truth:
When they can eat, babe's nurture is withdrawn.
I fed the babe whether it would or no:
I bid the boy or feed himself or starve.
460   I cried once, 'That ye may believe in Christ,
Behold this blind man shall receive his sight!'
I cry now, 'Urgest thou, *for I am shrewd*

445. *need prove it*] shall prove it (*MS*).
446–8. Working out the analogy with the herb garden: Christ's miracles are the 'ordered twigs' which identified and protected the seed of his teaching until it could bear fruit and make itself known.
449–50. *a wheelwork to wind up*: cp. Carlyle's rejection of the analogy between human beings and machines in 'Signs of the Times' (1829); B. had, however, used the image of human civilization as an engine with 'strange wheelwork' in *Sordello* iii 810–35 (I 582).
451–2. Pope (headnote, *Setting*) notes a similarity to *Fifine at the Fair* (1872) 817–22: 'I search but cannot see / What purpose serves the soul that strives, or world it tries / Conclusions with, unless the fruit of victories / Stay, one and all, stored up and guaranteed its own / For ever, by some mode whereby shall be made known / The gain of every life'.
452^453.] no line-space in *MS*.
453. *This might be pagan teaching*: 'This could just as well be pagan teaching'. *"This might be*] This is a (*MS*).
453^454.] no line-space in *MS*; B. wrote 'New par.' in the l. margin and added quotation marks at the start of l. 454.
456. *So, minds*] The mind (*MS canc.*).
457. *When they*] When he (*MS*).
459. *or . . . or*: a Gallicism for 'either . . . or', also common in early modern writers (e.g. Dryden).
460–1. John seems to imply that he was able to perform miracles in the period immediately following the death of Christ; *Acts* contains a number of references to apostolic miracles (e.g. vi 8; viii 6).
462–4. 'Do you urge me (since you are too shrewd to believe in mere stories of miracles) to repeat my miracles in order to procure your faith?'

And smile at stories how John's word could cure—
Repeat that miracle and take my faith?'

465   I say, that miracle was duly wrought
      When, save for it, no faith was possible.
      Whether a change were wrought i' the shows o' the
            world,
      Whether the change came from our minds which see
      Of the shows o' the world so much as and no more

470   Than God wills for His purpose,—(what do I
      See now, suppose you, there where you see rock
      Round us?)—I know not; such was the effect,
      So faith grew, making void more miracles
      Because too much: they would compel, not help.

475   I say, the acknowledgment of God in Christ
      Accepted by thy reason, solves for thee
      All questions in the earth and out of it,
      And has so far advanced thee to be wise.
      Wouldst thou unprove this to re-prove the proved?

480   In life's mere minute, with power to use that proof,
      Leave knowledge and revert to how it sprung?
      Thou hast it; use it and forthwith, or die!

      "For I say, this is death and the sole death,
      When a man's loss comes to him from his gain,

485   Darkness from light, from knowledge ignorance,
      And lack of love from love made manifest;
      A lamp's death when, replete with oil, it chokes;
      A stomach's when, surcharged with food, it starves.
      With ignorance was surety of a cure.

---

464. *faith?'*] emended in agreement with all other eds; *1864* lacks the necessary closing quotation mark.

467. *were wrought*] was wrought (*MS*).   *shows*: appearances.

469–70. *so much as . . . Than*] just so much . . . As (*MS*).

473. *So*: And (*MS* canc.).   *void*: either 'empty and pointless', 'impossible', or 'unnecessary'.

474. Pope (headnote, *Setting*) compares *Easter-Day* 71–2 (III 50).

479. *this to re-prove*] just to re-prove (*MS* canc.).

481. *sprung*] grew (*MS* canc.). 'Sprung' may be a synonym of 'grew', but the likelihood is that B. preferred the sense of 'began, originated'.

489. 'The state of ignorance made it possible to provide a cure' (by contrast with those who regress from knowledge to ignorance).

490 When man, appalled at nature, questioned first
'What if there lurk a might behind this might?'
He needed satisfaction God could give,
And did give, as ye have the written word:
But when he finds might still redouble might,
495 Yet asks, 'Since all is might, what use of will?'
—Will, the one source of might,—he being man
With a man's will and a man's might, to teach
In little how the two combine in large,—
That man has turned round on himself and stands,
500 Which in the course of nature is, to die.

"And when man questioned, 'What if there be love
Behind the will and might, as real as they?'—
He needed satisfaction God could give,
And did give, as ye have the written word:
505 But when, beholding that love everywhere,
He reasons, 'Since such love is everywhere,
And since ourselves can love and would be loved,
We ourselves make the love, and Christ was not,'—
How shall ye help this man who knows himself,
510 That he must love and would be loved again,
Yet, owning his own love that proveth Christ,
Rejecteth Christ through very need of Him?

490–500. We begin by asking whether there is a power greater than that of Nature, and the answer is that God has revealed that there is such a power (the 'written word' of l. 493 probably refers to the Old Testament, specifically to Genesis). We must not however make the mistake of discarding the concept of a personal God as the source of this power over Nature. We ought to know from our own experience that 'power' has no agency in itself, but is the instrument of our 'will', our conscious purpose; if this is true of us, it must also be true of God, and the concept of a universe governed only by 'natural laws' is meaningless; to believe in such a universe is a form of spiritual death.
490–3. Contrast Caliban's speculations about Setebos and the 'Quiet' (ll. 127–34, p. 632).
490. appalled: 'To fright; to strike with sudden fear; to depress; to discourage' (*J.*).
491. might: power.
495. Yet] And (*MS canc.*).
499. stands: comes to a standstill.
501–14. The argument is similar to that in ll. 490–500: God has revealed the transcendent power of love (the 'written word' of l. 504 is here the New Testament), and we should not make the mistake of interpreting that love as a projection of our own nature.

The lamp o'erswims with oil, the stomach flags
Loaded with nurture, and that man's soul dies.

515   "If he rejoin, 'But this was all the while
A trick; the fault was, first of all, in thee,
Thy story of the places, names and dates,
Where, when and how the ultimate truth had rise,
—Thy prior truth, at last discovered none,
520   Whence now the second suffers detriment.
What good of giving knowledge if, because
Of the manner of the gift, its profit fail?
And why refuse what modicum of help
Had stopped the after-doubt, impossible
525   I' the face of truth—truth absolute, uniform?
Why must I hit of this and miss of that,
Distinguish just as I be weak or strong,
And not ask of thee and have answer prompt,
Was this once, was it not once?—then and now
530   And evermore, plain truth from man to man.
Is John's procedure just the heathen bard's?
Put question of his famous play again
How for the ephemerals' sake, Jove's fire was filched,
And carried in a cane and brought to earth:

513–14. Recurring to the metaphors in ll. 487–8.

515–40. Pope (headnote, *Setting*) suggests a reference to Strauss in this passage; Strauss, however, does not characterize John's errors as a 'trick' to induce belief, but as the outcome of the dominant beliefs of the time; see headnote, *Sources and influences.*

517. Thy story] That story (*MS* canc.).

522. Of the] O' the (*1870* [rev. edn of *1868*]–*1888*)   *its profit fail?*] its profit pass,— (*MS*).

524. after-doubt: not in *OED*; the expression is also used by Wilkie Collins in *Armadale* (1866). Perhaps coined by analogy with 'Aberglaube' or 'after-belief', the German term for superstition.

526. and miss] and fail (*MS*).

528. have answer] be answered (*MS* canc.).

531. just] but (*MS* canc.).   *heathen bard's*: Aeschylus' (see l. 285 above).

532. play] tale (*MS*).

533: for the ephemerals' sake] for ephemerals' sake (*MS*), i.e. 'for the sake of (ephemeral) human beings'; both Pope and Inglesfield (see headnote, *Setting*) note that the Chorus in *Prometheus Bound* refers to human beings as ἐφήμεροι (*ephemeroi*), which EBB. translates as 'creatures of a day' in her second version of the play (l. 299).

534. carried in a cane: 'Because I stole / The secret fount of fire, whose bubbles went / Over the ferule's brim' (*Prometheus Bound*, tr. EBB., ll. 122–4).

535   *The fact is in the fable*, cry the wise,
      Mortals obtained the boon, so much is fact,
      Though fire be spirit and produced on earth.
      As with the Titan's, so now with thy tale:
      Why breed in us perplexity, mistake,
540   Nor tell the whole truth in the proper words?'

      "I answer, Have ye yet to argue out
      The very primal thesis, plainest law,
      —Man is not God but hath God's end to serve,
      A master to obey, a course to take,
545   Somewhat to cast off, somewhat to become?
      Grant this, then man must pass from old to new,
      From vain to real, from mistake to fact,
      From what once seemed good, to what now proves best.
      How could man have progression otherwise?
550   Before the point was mooted 'What is God?'
      No savage man inquired 'What am myself?'
      Much less replied, 'First, last, and best of things.'
      Man takes that title now if he believes
      Might can exist with neither will nor love,
555   In God's case—what he names now Nature's Law—
      While in himself he recognizes love

535. The fact is in the fable: cp. *Christmas-Eve* 873 (III 81). *cry the wise*] cry his friends (*MS* canc.).

538. the Titan's: Prometheus was one of the Titans, the race of gods overthrown by the Olympians in Greek myth. *the Titan's*] the Titan (*MS*).

546–50. Pope (headnote, *Setting*) cites *Fifine at the Fair* (1872) 2182–3: 'Truth inside, and outside, truth also; and between / Each, falsehood that is change, as truth is permanence.'

546. then man] and man (*MS*).

550–1. Cp. *Caliban* (p. 616), which explores the link between the idea of a deity and self-consciousness through the medium of a 'savage' or primitive being.

550. mooted: debated.

551. 'What am] 'What is (*MS*).

552. First, last, and best] first and last and best (*MS*, revising an earlier draft: 'Man, first and last'. The revised *MS* line is unmetrical, an error which survived into *1864 proof*; B. corrected it by hand in the two sets of proof he gave to his sister Sarianna and Moncure D. Conway: see headnote, *Text*. Cp. *Revelation* xxii 13: 'I am Alpha and Omega, the beginning and the end, the first and the last'; and Wordsworth's description of the Alps in *The Prelude* (1850) vi 638–40: 'Characters of the great Apocalypse, / The types and symbols of Eternity, / Of first, and last, and midst, and without end', itself quoting Milton, *PL* v 165.

553. that title: i.e. 'First, last and best of things'. *now*] soon (*MS* canc.).

No less than might and will: and rightly takes.
Since if man prove the sole existent thing
Where these combine, whatever their degree,
560   However weak the might or will or love,
So they be found there, put in evidence,—
He is as surely higher in the scale
Than any might with neither love nor will,
As life, apparent in the poorest midge,
565   When the faint dust-speck flits, ye guess its wing,
Is marvellous beyond dead Atlas' self:
I give such to the midge for resting-place!
Thus, man proves best and highest—God, in fine,
And thus the victory leads but to defeat,
570   The gain to loss, best rise to the worst fall,
His life becomes impossible, which is death.

"But if, appealing thence, he cower, avouch
He is mere man, and in humility
Neither may know God nor mistake himself;
575   I point to the immediate consequence
And say, by such confession straight he falls
Into man's place, a thing nor God nor beast,

---

557. and rightly takes: 'and rightly takes it' (i.e. the title referred to at l. 553) if human beings exceed God by their capacity for love, which is otherwise absent from 'Nature's Law'.

565. faint] poor (*MS*). *flits*] soars (*MS* canc.).

566. dead Atlas' self: the primary reference is to the Atlas mountain range, which is 'dead' because it is inanimate matter, and is thus, for all its gigantic size, lower in the scale of creation than the tiniest and most ephemeral living creature; but B. probably also intends an allusion to the Titan after whom the mountain is named, and who was given the task of holding up the heavens as a punishment for his rebellion against Zeus. As a pagan deity, he is 'dead' in another sense.

566–7. self: / I give such to the midge] self— / Given to the nobler midge (*1870* [rev. ed. of *1868*]–*1888*).

568–71. The predicament John describes is close to that of the philosopher Cleon: see ll. 214-172, pp. 578–81.

568. Thus, man proves best] Man proves the best (*MS*).

570. best rise] most rise (*MS*).

572. avouch] confess (*MS*).

573. He is] Himself (*MS* canc.).

574. Neither may know God: cp. *Job* xi 7–8: 'Canst thou by searching find out God? canst thou find out the Almighty unto perfection? It is as high as heaven; what canst thou do? deeper than hell; what canst thou know?' *mistake himself*: i.e. make the mistake of believing himself to be godlike.

Made to know that he can know and not more:
Lower than God who knows all and can all,
580 Higher than beasts which know and can so far
As each beast's limit, perfect to an end,
Nor conscious that they know, nor craving more;
While man knows partly but conceives beside,
Creeps ever on from fancies to the fact,
585 And in this striving, this converting air
Into a solid he may grasp and use,
Finds progress, man's distinctive mark alone,
Not God's, and not the beasts': God is, they are,
Man partly is and wholly hopes to be.
590 Such progress could no more attend his soul
Were all it struggles after found at first
And guesses changed to knowledge absolute,
Than motion wait his body, were all else
Than it the solid earth on every side,
595 Where now through space he moves from rest to rest.
Man, therefore, thus conditioned, must expect

578. A variant of the famous story in Plato's *Apology*: the oracle at Delphi proclaimed Socrates the wisest of men; Socrates argued that this was because he was
the only man who knew that he knew nothing.
579. can all: is capable of all.
580–9. Although B.'s St John is able to anticipate and counter the arguments of
the 'Higher Criticism', he is not concerned with scientific arguments against religion: he takes for granted here the immutability of species which Darwin had
recently challenged. On the question of B.'s knowledge of Darwin in this period,
see headnote to *Caliban*, p. 621. B. evokes the 'perfection' of the creation before
the advent of mankind in a number of other poems, e.g. *Paracelsus* v 638–70
(I 298–9) and *Cleon* 199–205 (p. 578).
580. beasts] brutes (*MS canc.*).
584. fancies to the fact: see *A Likeness* 35–6n. (p. 646). *fancies*] fancy (*MS*).
585. air: i.e. the 'fancies'.
587. Man's distinctive mark alone,] only Man's distinctive mark (*MS canc.*).
590. attend his soul] be for his soul (*MS*).
591. at first: 'immediately', 'at the first attempt'.
593–5. The physics of this argument are those of Epicurus, who postulated that
the cosmos was made up of atoms of matter moving through the void; the example given by John, of the impossibility of movement were the universe made up
of matter alone, is found in bk. i of Lucretius' *De Rerum Natura*.
593. wait his body] for his body (*MS*).
594. the solid] made solid (*MS*).
595. Where now] Whereas (*MS*).
596. conditioned: 'situated', 'subject to these conditions'.

He could not, what he knows now, know at first;
What he considers that he knows to-day,
Come but to-morrow, he will find misknown;
600   Getting increase of knowledge, since he learns
Because he lives, which is to be a man,
Set to instruct himself by his past self:
First, like the brute, obliged by facts to learn,
Next, as man may, obliged by his own mind,
605   Bent, habit, nature, knowledge turned to law.
God's gift was that man should conceive of truth
And yearn to gain it, catching at mistake,
As midway help till he reach fact indeed.
The statuary ere he mould a shape
610   Boasts a like gift, the shape's idea, and next
The aspiration to produce the same;
So, taking clay, he calls his shape thereout,
Cries ever 'Now I have the thing I see':
Yet all the while goes changing what was wrought,
615   From falsehood like the truth, to truth itself.
How were it had he cried 'I see no face,
No breast, no feet i' the ineffectual clay?'
Rather commend him that he clapped his hands,
And laughed 'It is my shape and lives again!'
620   Enjoyed the falsehood, touched it on to truth,
Until yourselves applaud the flesh indeed
In what is still flesh-imitating clay.
Right in you, right in him, such way be man's!

597.] What he knows now, he could not know at first; (MS).
598. considers] conceits him (MS canc.).
599. misknown: B.'s only other use of this word occurs in Cleon 112 (p. 573).
600. Getting] Bringing (MS canc.).
604. his own mind] his own soul (MS).
605. Bent: natural tendency. turned to law] grown his law (MS canc.).
609–22. B.'s use of sculpture as a means of thinking about human creativity in general goes back to the Jules-Phene episode of Pippa: see headnote (pp. 86–9), noting esp. the praise of the sculptor Canova for the life-likeness of his figures. Cp. also Fifine at the Fair (1872) 756–93.
609. statuary: sculptor.
613. Cries] Says (MS canc.).
617. i' the] in the (MS canc.).
619. my shape] thy shape (MS canc.).
623. Right in you, right in him: 'You are right to applaud the sculptor, just as he was right, for having realized his "idea" in clay.' be man's] is man's (MS).

God only makes the live shape at a jet.
625 Will ye renounce this pact of creatureship?
The pattern on the Mount subsists no more,
Seemed awhile, then returned to nothingness;
But copies, Moses strove to make thereby,
Serve still and are replaced as time requires:
630 By these, make newest vessels, reach the type!
If ye demur, this judgment on your head,
Never to reach the ultimate, angels' law,
Indulging every instinct of the soul
There where law, life, joy, impulse are one thing!

635 "Such is the burthen of the latest time.
I have survived to hear it with my ears,
Answer it with my lips: does this suffice?

624. *at a jet*: more usually 'at a single jet', meaning 'at a single effort of the mind'; unlike human beings, which have (like the sculptor) to struggle to embody their conceptions in material form, God is capable of instantaneous creation. Cp. (noting ll. 633–4 below) *ED* 799–807 (III 133–4) where Michelangelo is imagined creating perfect works of art in heaven.

626–30. God summons Moses to Mount Sinai in *Exodus* xix, and in the following chapters (xx–xxii) instructs him as to the mode of worship and ethical code the Israelites are to follow. The word 'pattern' occurs in ch. xxv: 'According to all that I shew thee, after the pattern of the tabernacle, and the pattern of all the instruments thereof, even so shall ye make it . . . And look that thou make them [the 'vessels'] after their pattern, which was shewed thee in the mount' (vv. 9, 40). B. may also have been thinking of the stone tablets on which God himself originally wrote the Ten Commandments, and which Moses broke in anger when he descended from Mount Sinai to discover the Israelites worshipping the Golden Calf (xxxii 15–19). Moses subsequently made a copy of these tables in his own hand (xxxiv 1–4, 27–9).

630. *type*: in the sense both of the 'pattern or model after which something is made' and 'a perfect example or specimen of something' (*OED* 5a, 7a): to 'reach the type' is therefore simultaneously a return to the divine original and the attainment of perfection in the future. There is also an allusion to the habit of reading the Old Testament 'typologically' as a symbolic anticipation of events in the New Testament. On B.'s knowledge of biblical typology see headnote to *Saul* (III 491).

632. *to reach*] to have (*MS* canc.).

633. *instinct*] impulse (*MS* canc.).

635. *burthen*: leading idea or sentiment, with a possible reference to the sense of a musical undersong or accompaniment.

637. *my lips*] my tongue (*MS* canc.).

For if there be a further woe than such,
Wherein my brothers struggling need a hand,
640   So long as any pulse is left in mine,
May I be absent even longer yet,
Plucking the blind ones back from the abyss,
Though I should tarry a new hundred years!"

But he was dead: 'twas about noon, the day
645   Somewhat declining: we five buried him
That eve, and then, dividing, went five ways,
And I, disguised, returned to Ephesus.

By this, the cave's mouth must be filled with sand.
Valens is lost, I know not of his trace;
650   The Bactrian was but a wild, childish man,
And could not write nor speak, but only loved:
So, lest the memory of this go quite,
Seeing that I to-morrow fight the beasts,

638–43. In a letter to Julia Wedgwood of 19 Aug. 1864, B. transcribed from a book he was reading an anecdote about the superhuman patience of Rabbi Perida, who would 'read and explain the same thing four hundred times over'; on one occasion he did this twice running, 'At which, a voice was heard from heaven, to the following purpose, "Perida, either live four hundred years, or obtain innocence and eternal life for thee and thy posterity!" Perida without hesitation chose the latter: but his scholars, out of cruel kindness, cried "No no no—but four hundred years for Perida!"' (*RB & JW* 61–2). B. goes on to compare himself to Perida: 'I keep trying to be quite intelligible, next poem: what if the Saturday Review should get me four hundred years more of rendering-intelligible, by general outcry to heaven?' On the *Saturday Review*, see Appendix C, pp. 892–3.
638. than such] than this (*MS* canc.).
640. is left] be left (*MS* canc.).
641. absent: i.e. from heaven.
643. a new hundred years: for the tradition that John lived to extreme old age, see headnote, *Setting*.
645. we five: Pamphylax, Xanthus, Valens, the Boy and the Bactrian convert who kept guard outside the cave.
647. Ephesus: see above ll. 361–2n.
652. So, lest] I—lest (*MS* canc.).
653. I to-morrow fight the beasts: 'In the early church, martyrdoms were exceptionally public events, because Christians coincided with a particular phase in the history of public entertainment: they were pitched into the cities' arenas for unarmed combat with gladiators or bulls, leopards and the dreaded bears' (Robin Lane Fox, *Pagans and Christians*, p. 420). Cp. Paul's insistence on the truth of the resurrection in *1 Corinthians* xv 32: 'If after the manner of men I have fought with beasts at Ephesus, what advantageth it me, if the dead rise not? Let us eat and drink; for tomorrow we die.'

I tell the same to Phœbas, whom believe!
655 For many look again to find that face,
Beloved John's to whom I ministered,
Somewhere in life about the world; they err:
Either mistaking what was darkly spoke
At ending of his book, as he relates,
660 Or misconceiving somewhat of this speech
Scattered from mouth to mouth, as I suppose.
Believe ye will not see him any more
About the world with his divine regard!
For all was as I say, and now the man
665 Lies as he lay once, breast to breast with God.

[Cerinthus read and mused; one added this:

"If Christ, as thou affirmest, be of men
Mere man, the first and best but nothing more,—
Account Him, for reward of what He was,
670 Now and for ever, wretchedest of all.

656–9. Cp., noting l. 665 below, John's description of himself at the Last Supper: 'Now there was leaning on Jesus' bosom one of the disciples, whom Jesus loved' (*John* xiii 23). The detail of his 'lying on Jesus' breast' is repeated in v. 25, and again at the very end of the gospel, in the context of a rumour that John himself would be spared death: Peter asks the risen Christ what will happen to 'the disciple whom Jesus loved . . . which also leaned on his breast at supper', and receives an apparently ambiguous reply: 'If I will that he tarry till I come, what is that to thee?' John, however, denies that Jesus meant 'that that disciple should not die' (xxi 20–23).

658. *spoke*] said (*MS*, replacing 'writ').

665. See ll. 656–9n.

665^666.] no line-space in *MS*, where l. 665 ends the page and there is no indication of a new paragraph.

666–88. Cerinthus's 'musings' on the document are not recorded, but it is implied that he continued to 'affirm' that Christ was 'Mere man'; another commentator attempts to rebut him in ll. 667–88. The last comment in the poem is either by the owner of the document, or another annotator: see headnote, *Setting*.

666^667.] no line-space in *MS*; B. wrote 'New par.' in the l. margin and added quotation marks at the start of l. 667.

666. *Cerinthus*: on Cerinthus and his doctrines, see headnote. The argument used by the commentator to combat his doctrines in the following lines does not derive from John, and may itself be the subject of B.'s satire as over-literal and pedantic (e.g. l. 679).

For see; Himself conceived of life as love,
Conceived of love as what must enter in,
Fill up, make one with His each soul He loved:
Thus much for man's joy, all men's joy for Him.
675 Well, He is gone, thou sayest, to fit reward.
But by this time are many souls set free,
And very many still retained alive:
Nay, should His coming be delayed awhile,
Say, ten years longer (twelve years, some compute)
680 See if, for every finger of thy hands,
There be not found, that day the world shall end,
Hundreds of souls, each holding by Christ's word
That He will grow incorporate with all,
With me as Pamphylax, with him as John,
685 Groom for each bride! Can a mere man do this?
Yet Christ saith, this He lived and died to do.
Call Christ, then, the illimitable God,
Or lost!"

But 'twas Cerinthus that is lost.]

671–4. Cp. 1 John iv 8: 'God is love', and the first question in the Westminster
Shorter Catechism: 'Q. What is the chief end of man? A. Man's chief end is to glorify God, and to enjoy him forever'.
674. Him] His (MS).
676.] By this time there be many souls set free, (MS).   set free: i.e. released by
death; cp. Paracelsus i 775 (I 148).
678–9. Another reference to the belief in the imminence of the Second Coming
in some sections of the early church.
683. Cp. PL iii 341: 'God shall be all in all'; and 1 Corinthians xv 28.
685. Groom for each bride: Jesus uses the metaphor of a wedding for the kingdom
of heaven in several parables (e.g. Matthew xxv 1–13), and is named as the 'bridegroom' by John the Baptist (John iii 19–20); the New Jerusalem is 'prepared as
a bride adorned for her husband' in Revelation xxi 2. But Jesus himself nowhere
claims that he will be the bridegroom of each saved soul; this image seems to
derive from St Paul in 2 Corinthians xi 2: 'I have espoused you [the Corinthians]
to one husband, that I may present you as a chaste virgin to Christ', itself recalling Isaiah liv 5: 'thy Maker is thy husband'.
688. The odd sequence of tenses here implies that Cerinthus is lost for ever, or
still lost.

48 Abt Vogler
(after he has been extemporizing upon the musical instrument of his invention)

Text and publication

First publ. *DP*, 28 May 1864; repr. *1864²*, *1865*, *1868*, *1872*, *1888*. Our text is *1864*.

The MS, part of the printer's copy for *DP*, is at *Morgan*. It has a good deal of overwriting and some deletions and re-drafting, but is clearly a fair copy of an earlier draft. There are few variants between its text and that of *1864*; the text is virtually unchanged in subsequent editions, with only a handful of changes in punctuation and the change (standard in *1868*) to lower-case for the divine pronoun ('He', 'Thee', Thou', etc.; note however that the 'ineffable Name' of ll. 7 and 65 remained in upper-case).

Composition and date

There is no direct evidence for the date of composition of the poem. The *Musical World* (18 Apr. 1863, p. 252) reported on a concert at Leipsic [Leipzig]: 'The programme of the Eighteenth Subscription Concert, on the 19th of February, was a peculiar one. First part:—Symphony in C major, by the Abbé Vogler . . .' See ll. 95–6n. and next section.

Sources and influences

B. prided himself on his musical knowledge and musicianship, which he refers to early in his correspondence with EBB.: 'I know, I have always been jealous of my own musical faculty (I can write music.)' (14 June 1845, *Correspondence* x 264). His own musical education was rooted in theory and practice current at the turn of the eighteenth century, including that of Abt [Abbot] Georg Joseph Vogler (1749–1814), more usually referred to as Abbé Vogler (as in B.'s letter to Furnivall of 22 Jan 1889: *Trumpeter* 153). Vogler's system of harmony was certainly known to John Relfe, one of B.'s early music teachers; according to François-Joseph Fétis, who met Relfe in London in 1829, Relfe's system 'was taken from the books of . . . Vogler and Schicht' (*Biographie universelle des musiciens et bibliographie générale de la musique*, 8 vols [Paris 1860–8] vii 225). Vogler performed several concerts in London between Jan. and Aug. 1790. The suggestion (DeVane *Handbook* 290) that Relfe studied under Vogler seems, however, to be without foundation. Some indication of B.'s knowledge of Vogler's work is given in Frederick Wedmore's account of a letter he received from B. shortly after the publication of the poem: 'He answered [my question about Vogler] . . . very courteously and fully; saying, amongst other things, that Abt Vogler had taught Meyerbeer counterpoint' (*Memories* [1912] 52). Performances of Vogler's music were rare in England in the mid-nineteenth century, though they featured

---

Subtitle. *after he has been extemporizing*] after extemporizing (*MS*): the 'musical instrument of his invention' is the 'orchestrion'; see below, *Sources*. As with *Caliban*, the subtitle appears on the separate title page which precedes each poem in *1864*, but not on the first page of the text itself, which has the title *Abt Vogler* on its own.

in the annual series of Concerts of Ancient Music; one account of such a
concert in March 1846 has a suggestive ring: commenting on Vogler's *Graduale*,
'De Profundis', the reviewer states that it 'aims at more than it can reach. The
author had some effect in view which he had not the power to attain' (*The Examiner*,
no. 1989, 14 Mar. 1846, p. 166). Cp. *Andrea* 96–7 (p. 395) and below, *Parallels
in B*.

Vogler was famous in his lifetime as a composer and performer, and as a
theorist and teacher of music. His interest in the technicalities of sound production led to a number of experiments with existing organs, and finally led him to
develop his own simplified organ, or 'orchestrion', which he worked on during
his time as Kappelmeister to the King of Sweden, and demonstrated in public in
1789. It consisted of four 'manuals' or keyboards, each containing several octaves,
and a pedalboard of thirty-nine notes. According to contemporary testimony, the
resulting instrument was 'extraordinarily effective, as you are brought to believe
that in it you hear all the instruments of a complete orchestra' (cited Schweiger,
p. 161). There are numerous testimonies to his brilliance as a virtuoso organ player:
'Tempestuous power and an almost magical conquest of difficulties is a characteristic of Vogler's playing' (cited in Hertha Schweiger, 'Abt Vogler', *The Musical
Quarterly* xxv [1939] 162). His contemporaries also agreed that he excelled above
all in improvisation rather than composition, which allowed him to make use of
'[his] vivid imagination, his stormy temperament, his willingness to experiment
with sound, dynamics, rhythm, and his exact knowledge of musical effects'
(Schweiger, p. 162). Vogler frequently attempted descriptive compositions, in which
he would claim to depict a particular event or landscape in music; one of his
concert programmes, for example, lists a piece entitled 'A pleasure trip on the
Rhine, interrupted by a thunderstorm' (*ibid.* 164). As a musical theorist, Vogler's
most significant achievement was his work on the theory of harmony (see ll. 91–6n.),
which greatly influenced his two most illustrious pupils, Weber and Meyerbeer.
Vogler was often mentioned in reviews of the work of Meyerbeer in particular,
and usually characterized as the originator of a dry, pedantic style of composition which Meyerbeer ultimately rejected.

Like Fra Lippo Lippi (see headnote, p. 478), Vogler remained a clergyman
throughout his career, having been ordained as a Jesuit priest in Rome during
the early 1770s. According to one of the authorities cited by *Cooke*, Vogler liked
to array himself in his ecclesiastical finery for his recitals, and was not above
ostentatious displays of piety: 'He would take his prayer-book with him into
society, and often keep his visitors waiting while he finished his devotions'
(p. 3). Vogler's religion features in accounts of him current in the 1860s: see,
e.g., the report of a London concert in *The Era* (3 May 1863, p. 16), in which
Vogler's name is linked with that of two other composers who were also
Catholic priests, Martini and Stadler, as 'among the most dry and unrefreshing
composers there have ever been. They clung to the rules with great pertinacity,
and were so devoid of anything like freedom of ideas, that they could almost
seem to have desired the introduction of dogmas into music with all the strict-
ness of unyielding orthodoxy.' Some aspects of the theory of music developed
by B.'s Vogler, such as his comparison between his composition and a religious
edifice, and his desire to transform a necessarily transient and time-bound art-
form into a permanent structure, have been seen as typically Catholic: Berdoe
(*Cyclopedia* 6) cites a passage on music in John Henry Newman's sermon on
'The Theory of Developments in Religious Doctrine' (1843), preached while
Newman was contemplating the possibility of converting to the Roman Catholic
church:

There are seven notes in the scale; make them thirteen; yet what a slender outfit for so vast an enterprise! What science brings so much out of so little? Out of what poor elements does some great master in it create his new world! Shall we say that all this exuberant inventiveness is a mere ingenuity or trick of art, like some game or fashion of the day, without reality, without meaning? [. . .] Can it be that those mysterious stirrings of heart, and keen emotions, and strange yearnings after we know not what, and awful impressions from we know not whence, should be wrought in us by what is unsubstantial, and comes and goes, and begins and ends in itself? It is not so; it cannot be. No; they have escaped from some higher sphere; they are the outpourings of eternal harmony in the medium of created sound; they are echoes from our Home; they are the voice of Angels, or the Magnificat of Saints, or the living laws of Divine Governance, or the Divine Attributes; something are they besides themselves, which we cannot compass, which we cannot utter,—though mortal man, and he perhaps not otherwise distinguished above his fellows, has the gift of elicit-ing them. (Newman, *Sermons, Chiefly on the Theory of Religious Belief*, 2nd edn [Oxford 1844], pp. 348–50)

The significance of Vogler's Catholicism is also suggested by the allusion to 'Rome's dome' (St Peter's); see l. 23. According to Rebecca W. Smith (*MP* xxix.2 [1931] 187–98) this building may have served as the prototype for Milton's Pandæmonium, the palace constructed in hell by the fallen angels (*PL* i 692–717); Pandæmonium has in turn been seen as one of the sources for Vogler's 'palace of music' (see ll. 13–16n.). Vogler's attempt to reach up to heaven recalls (just as Milton's Pandæmonium anticipates) the story of Babel; see l. 28n. For the iconography of the imagined 'palace', cp. the account of the construction of the New Jerusalem in *Revelation* xxi 10–21 (see l. 19n.). Gal Manor gives an account of B.'s use of Talmudic and Kabbalistic sources in 'The Allure of Supernatural Language: The Ineffable Name in Robert Browning's Poems', *BSN* xxv (Dec. 1998) 6–18.

Vogler's insistence on the providential mechanism whereby evil only gives rise to 'so much good more' (l. 71) has a more orthodox lineage, going back to Augustine and Plato; its most famous literary exponent in English is Milton in *PL*. However, Vogler's analogy of evil as 'silence implying sound' (l. 70) may have a more contemporary point, as a rebuttal of Carlyle's well-known (and paradoxical) praise of silence as a supreme spiritual and aesthetic value: 'Under all speech that is good for anything there lies a silence that is better. Silence is deep as Eternity; speech is shallow as Time' ('Sir Walter Scott', *Critical and Miscellaneous Essays* [1838]). Vogler's praise of music as peculiarly close to divine creativity, and privileged above painting and poetry (ll. 43–50), belongs to a long tradition of debate between the different arts; cp. B.'s mischievous 'hope' that the great Renaissance painters have all 'attained to be poets' in heaven, where they 'see God face to face' (*Old Pictures* 49–55, p. 413).

Parallels in B.
Abt Vogler takes its place alongside other poems in which B. represents or reflects on the act of musical creation: see esp. *Master Hugues* (III 388), *A Toccata* (p. 367), *Charles Avison* (*Parleyings*, 1887) and the episode of *Fifine at the Fair* (1872) 1588ff., in which Don Juan plays Schumann's 'Carnaval' and conjures up a vision of Venice. The biblical imagery of the poem, and the trajectory from ecstatic vision to a more sober ending, suggest an analogy with David's song in *Saul* (III 491), confirmed by B.'s pairing of the two poems (see below); cp. also the song 'Thamuris

marching', originally composed as a separate piece and then incorporated into *Aristophanes' Apology* (1875) 5182–258. Thamuris' song brings heaven and earth together in the same way that Vogler describes; note, however, that his story is a tragedy, since he challenges the Muses and is blinded for his presumption, whereas Vogler, at ll. 87–8, claims an intimate commission from God. Manor (see above) notes other poems in which B. invokes the figure of Solomon as one of glory and power, e.g. *Popularity* 41–50 (pp. 453–4) and the late poem *Solomon and Balkis* (*Jocoseria*, 1883). Vogler's religious aesthetics has many parallels: line 72, for example, sums up the 'doctrine of imperfection' which is one of B.'s most constant principles: cp., e.g., *Old Pictures*, esp. ll. 113–36 (pp. 418–20), and *Dîs Aliter Visum* 116–42 (pp. 697–8); with line 76, cp. Sordello's misguided ambition to '[thrust] in time eternity's concern' (i 566, I 432) and B.'s statement to Ruskin that poetry represents an impossible 'putting the infinite within the finite' (Appendix B, p. 881); contrast the 'moment, one and infinite' of the lovers in *By the Fire-Side* 181 (p. 471), in which the attainment of perfect bliss bears fruit in an earthly marriage.

Reception

When asked by Edmund Gosse in 1885 to nominate 'Four poems, of moderate length, which represent their writer fairly', B. selected *Abt Vogler* (alongside *Saul*) in the 'Lyrical' category (*LH* 235). Besides the thematic link between the two poems (see above) he may have been responding to the fact that, like *Saul*, *Abt Vogler* had become one of his most popular poems.

I

Would that the structure brave, the manifold music
   I build,
    Bidding my organ obey, calling its keys to their work,
Claiming each slave of the sound, at a touch, as when
   Solomon willed

1–10. The first sentence appears to finish at l. 8 and to have no main verb; the main clause ('Would that the structure brave') is interrupted by a series of subordinate clauses, then resumed and eventually 'resolved' in ll. 9–10.

1. brave: 'magnificent, grand' (*J.*); cp. *Bishop Blougram* 426 (p. 308). *manifold*: see *An Epistle* 294n. (p. 527).

3–8. Another illustration of B.'s detailed knowledge of Jewish tradition: 'A well-known passage in *Gittin* 68a (part of the Talmud) tells of King Solomon that he ruled not only over men but also over demons. He was desirous of obtaining the mythical *shamir*, that by its aid the stones for the building of the Temple might be cut without the employment of iron. So he ordered Ashmedai, the king of the Demons, to be brought before him' (Armand Kaminka, 'The Origin of the Ashmedai Legend in the Babylonian Talmud', *Jewish Quarterly Review*, n.s. xiii [1922], 221).

3. slave of the sound: cp. Ruskin's category of 'Servile Ornament' in 'The Nature of Gothic' (1853), in which he argues that the workman, forced to subordinate his individuality entirely to the overall plan of the building, was 'a slave' in both the Greek and the Assyrian traditions of architecture.

Armies of angels that soar, legions of demons that lurk,
5   Man, brute, reptile, fly,—alien of end and of aim,
     Adverse, each from the other heaven-high, hell-deep
         removed,—
     Should rush into sight at once as he named the ineffable
         Name,
     And pile him a palace straight, to pleasure the princess
         he loved!

                                      2

     Would it might tarry like his, the beautiful building of
         mine,
10   This which my keys in a crowd pressed and
         importuned to raise!
     Ah, one and all, how they helped, would dispart now and
         now combine,
     Zealous to hasten the work, heighten their master his
         praise!
     And one would bury his brow with a blind plunge down
         to hell,
     Burrow awhile and build, broad on the roots of things,

5. *Man, brute, reptile, fly*: another Rabbinical tradition claimed that King Solomon had the power to talk to animals.

7. *ineffable Name*: King Solomon was reputed to have possessed a magical ring with the name of God ('the ineffable name') engraved on it, which he used in conjuring spirits. See *Mr. Sludge* 1074n. (p. 830). Cp. also *Aurora Leigh* ii 1149–51.

8. *pleasure*: this verb did not necessarily have sexual connotations in the mid-nineteenth century, but B.'s usage does not exclude this possibility. *the princess he loved*: cp. *1 Kings* iii 1: 'And Solomon made affinity with Pharaoh king of Egypt, and took Pharaoh's daughter, and brought her into the city of David, until he had made an end of building his own house, and the house of the LORD, and the wall of Jerusalem round about.'

10. *my keys*] the keys (*MS*). See also l. 41n.

11. *dispart*: see *A Death* 242n. (p. 736), noting the musical context of the *Sordello* quotation.

12. *heighten their master his praise!* 'Enhance the praise which their master received.'

13–16. Continuing the comparison between the notes with which Vogler raises his 'palace' of sound, and the demons employed by King Solomon. *Thomas* (20–1) suggests a possible reminiscence of the description of Pandæmonium in *PL* i 705–13: 'A third as soon had formed within the ground / A various mould, and from the boiling cells / By strange conveyance filled each hollow nook, / As in an organ from one blast of wind / To many a row of pipes the sound-board breathes. / Anon out of the earth a fabric huge / Rose like an exhalation, with the sound / Of dulcet symphonies and voices sweet, / Built like a temple[.]'

15   Then up again swim into sight, having based me my
         palace well,
         Founded it, fearless of flame, flat on the nether springs.

                              3

      And another would mount and march, like the excellent
         minion he was,
         Ay, another and yet another, one crowd but with many
            a crest,
      Raising my rampired walls of gold as transparent as glass,
20   Eager to do and die, yield each his place to the rest:
      For higher still and higher (as a runner tips with fire,
         When a great illumination surprises a festal night—
      Outlining round and round Rome's dome from space to
         spire)
         Up, the pinnacled glory reached, and the pride of my
            soul was in sight.

                              4

25   In sight? Not half! for it seemed, it was certain, to match
         man's birth,

16. *the nether springs*: cp. *Judges* i 15: 'And she said unto him, Give me a blessing:
for thou hast given me a south land; give me also springs of water. And Caleb
gave her the upper springs and the nether springs.'
17. *minion*: 'A favourite; a darling; a low dependant' (*J*). See *Love Among the
Ruins* 47n. (p. 536).
19. *rampired*: J. defines 'to rampire' as 'to fortify with ramparts'; first of three uses
by B. of this archaism; cp., e.g., *Red Cotton Night-Cap Country* 1381.   *transparent
as glass*: cp. the description of the New Jerusalem in *Revelation* xxi 21: 'the street
of the city was pure gold, as it were transparent glass'.
20. *to do and die*: cp. the stock phrase 'to do or die'; Vogler's modification emphasizes the temporal dimension of the art of music (in which the notes 'die'
after having performed their task).
21–3. The Brownings spent the winter of 1853–4 in Rome; they themselves
witnessed an evening event at St Peter's on Easter Day 1854, which involved
'torch-lighted sculpture' (EBB. to Anne Braun, 16 Apr. 1854 [ABL MS]). On
the significance of St Peter's in the poem, see headnote, *Sources and influences*.
24. *pinnacled glory*: the adjective 'pinnacled' was usually associated with Gothic or
'pointed' architecture; on the possible influence of Ruskin's aesthetics on the poem,
see l. 3n.   *the pride of my soul was in sight*: either 'I was close to what my soul
desired', or 'I had made the pride of my soul apparent to everyone'.
25. *Not half!* 'A long way from the due amount' (*OED*), rather than the demotic
sense 'certainly!' The poet's efforts are to be 'matched' by those of heaven (see
next note).   *to match man's birth*: 'to match that which a man had given birth
to', i.e. Vogler's music.

Nature in turn conceived, obeying an impulse as I;
And the emulous heaven yearned down, made effort to
　　reach the earth,
　　As the earth had done her best, in my passion, to scale
　　　　the sky:
Novel splendours burst forth, grew familiar and dwelt
　　with mine,
30　　Not a point nor peak but found and fixed its
　　　　wandering star;
Meteor-moons, balls of blaze: and they did not pale nor pine,
　　For earth had attained to heaven, there was no more
　　　　near nor far.

5

Nay more; for there wanted not who walked in the glare
　　and glow,
　　Presences plain in the place; or, fresh from the Protoplast,
35　Furnished for ages to come, when a kindlier wind should
　　　　blow,
　　　　Lured now to begin and live, in a house to their liking
　　　　　　at last;
Or else the wonderful Dead who have passed through the
　　body and gone,
　　But were back once more to breathe in an old world
　　　　worth their new:

27–8. Vogler's benign vision of earth and heaven reciprocally reaching towards
each other inverts the story of the Tower of Babel (*Genesis* xi 1–9) in which the
builders aspired to build 'a city and a tower, whose top may reach unto heaven'
in order to 'make us a name', and in which God 'came down to see the city and
the tower' only to prevent its accomplishment.
30. *fixed its wandering star*. cp. *Jude* i 13: 'wandering stars, to whom is reserved
the blackness of darkness for ever'. Cp. also *Two in the Campagna* 55n. (p. 562).
31. *they*: i.e. the 'meteor moons' fixed to earth by Vogler's music.
32. Cp. 'Thamuris marching', the song B. incorporated into *Aristophanes' Apology*
(see headnote, *Parallels in B.*): 'Such earth's community of purpose, such / The
ease of earth's fulfilled imaginings,—/ So did the near and far appear to touch /
I' the moment's transport,—that an interchange / Of function, far with near, seemed
scarce too much . . .' (ll. 5224–6).
33–8. Vogler imagines his music as conjuring up 'presences', who are either the
spirits of the as-yet-unborn, or those of the 'wonderful Dead' returned to their
'old world'. The sense is a little obscured by B.'s use of the Gallicism 'or . . . or'
for 'either . . . or'.
33. *wanted*: 'lacked'.
34. *Protoplast*: 'The first creator or shaper of a thing' (*OED*); usually (as here) God.
35. *Furnished for ages to come*: provided for future ages.

What never had been, was now; what was, as it shall be
    anon;
40   And what is,—shall I say, matched both? for I was
    made perfect too.

6

All through my keys that gave their sounds to a wish of
    my soul,
    All through my soul that praised as its wish flowed
        visibly forth,
All through music and me! For think, had I painted the
    whole,
    Why, there it had stood, to see, nor the process so
        wonder-worth:
45   Had I written the same, made verse—still, effect proceeds
    from cause,
    Ye know why the forms are fair, ye hear how the tale
        is told;
It is all triumphant art, but art in obedience to laws,
    Painter and poet are proud in the artist-list enrolled:—

7

But here is the finger of God, a flash of the will that can,
50   Existent behind all laws, that made them and, lo, they are!

39–40. what was . . . what is] what is . . . what was (*MS*, canc.).

40. I was made perfect too: the question of perfection is debated in a number of Paul's Epistles; the most relevant parallel is probably provided by *Galatians* iii 3: 'Are ye so foolish? having begun in the Spirit, are ye now made perfect by the flesh?'

41. my keys] these keys (*MS*).

42. All through my soul that praised] And through my soul that praised (*MS*, redrafting an earlier version: 'And my soul that praised the while').

44. to see: 'to be seen'.

45–6. still . . . told: 'The pleasure you experience is directly traceable to its origins in the things the painter shows you, or the things you are told by the poet.'

48. Painter] Poet (*MS*, canc.); perhaps the draft from which B. was copying originally read 'Poet and painter' and he changed his mind in the course of transcribing.

49. the finger of God: cp. *Exodus* xxxi 18; bearing in mind the earlier reference to St Peter's in the poem, see ll. 21–3n; Vogler may also have in mind Michelangelo's famous depiction of the moment of creation in the Sistine Chapel, in which God imparts life to Adam through his outstretched finger. *the will that can*: it is very unusual to find 'can' without an object; the sense is an absolute one, and suitable to omnipotence. Cp. the supremacy of the 'Quiet' in *Caliban* 137 (p. 632).

50. and, lo, they are!] and there they are! (*MS*, canc.).

And I know not if, save in this, such gift be allowed to
    man,
    That out of three sounds he frame, not a fourth sound,
      but a star.
Consider it well: each tone of our scale in itself is nought;
    It is everywhere in the world—loud, soft, and all is said:
55 Give it to me to use! I mix it with two in my thought;
    And, there! Ye have heard and seen: consider and bow
      the head!

8

Well, it is gone at last, the palace of music I reared;
    Gone! and the good tears start, the praises that come
      too slow;
For one is assured at first, one scarce can say that he
    feared,
60   That he even gave it a thought, the gone thing was to go.
Never to be again! But many more of the kind
    As good, nay, better perchance: is this your comfort to
      me?
To me, who must be saved because I cling with my mind
    To the same, same self, same love, same God: ay, what
      was, shall be.

9

65 Therefore to whom turn I but to Thee, the ineffable
    Name?
    Builder and maker, Thou, of houses not made with
      hands!

---

52. frame] frames (*MS*, written over a word which may be 'forms').   *three sounds*:
the three notes which make up a chord; see l. 91n.   *a star*: the association of
music with heavenly bodies goes back to Pythagorean and Neo-Platonic speculation in antiquity. B. characteristically inverts the usual image of the 'harmony
of the spheres' (e.g. *The Merchant of Venice* V i 60–1: 'There's not the smallest
orb which thou behold'st / But in his motion like an angel sings'); here, the
effect of musical creation is itself figured as a star.

60.] That he even gave it thought that the gone thing was to go: (*MS*).

61. Never to be again! As Vogler's music is improvised, there is no lasting record
of the 'palace of music'.

63. must] shall (*MS*, written above 'hope to', canc.)

64. ay, what was] for what was (*MS*, revising an earlier draft: 'what was once').

65. the ineffable Name: see l. 7n.

66. houses not made with hands: 2 Corinthians v 1; cp. *By the Fire-Side* 135 (p. 468).

What, have fear of change from Thee who art ever the
    same?
    Doubt that Thy power can fill the heart that Thy
        power expands?
There shall never be one lost good! What was, shall live
    as before;
70   The evil is null, is nought, is silence implying sound;
What was good, shall be good, with, for evil, so much
    good more;
    On the earth the broken arcs; in the heaven, a perfect
      round.

10

All we have willed or hoped or dreamed of good, shall
    exist;
    Not its semblance, but itself; no beauty, nor good, nor
      power
75 Whose voice has gone forth, but each survives for the
    melodist
    When eternity affirms the conception of an hour.
The high that proved too high, the heroic for earth too
    hard,
    The passion that left the ground to lose itself in the sky,
Are music sent up to God by the lover and the bard;
80   Enough that He heard it once: we shall hear it by-and-by.

---

69. shall live] shall (*MS*).
70.] The evil is nought—defect—the silence implying sound (*MS*, canc.). For a possible allusion to Carlyle's praise of silence, see headnote, *Sources and influences*.
71. for evil: 'in place of evil'.
72. Cp. Tennyson, 'Will Waterproof's Lyrical Monologue' (1842) 65–72: 'This earth is rich in man and maid; / With fair horizons bound: / This whole wide earth of light and shade / Comes out a perfect round. / High over roaring Temple-bar, / And set in Heaven's third story, / I look at all things as they are, / But through a kind of glory.' EBB. quoted a phrase from this poem in a letter she wrote marking the anniversary of B.'s first visit to Wimpole Street: 'And now as the year has rounded itself to "the perfect round" . . .' (19 May 1846, *Correspondence* xii 340).
73. willed or hoped] hoped or willed (*MS*).
74. semblance] likeness (*MS*); this reading does not appear in *1864 proof* and was therefore a very late change. *nor power*] emended in agreement with *MS* and all other eds from 'power' in *1864*.
75. each survives] still survives (*MS*, altering earlier draft: 'still shall survive').
77. for earth] on earth (*MS*, canc.).
79. Are music] Are the music (*MS*, canc.).
80. it . . . it] them . . . them (*MS*, canc.).

11

And what is our failure here but a triumph's evidence
    For the fulness of the days? Have we withered or
        agonized?
    Why else was the pause prolonged but that singing might
        issue thence?
        Why rushed the discords in, but that harmony should
            be prized?
85 Sorrow is hard to bear, and doubt is slow to clear,
        Each sufferer says his say, his scheme of the weal and
            woe:
    But God has a few of us whom He whispers in the ear;
        The rest may reason and welcome: 'tis we musicians
            know.

12

Well, it is earth with me; silence resumes her reign:
90   I will be patient and proud, and soberly acquiesce.
    Give me the keys. I feel for the common chord again,

81. a triumph's evidence: i.e. the evidence of a (future) triumph.

82. For] In (*MS*). *the fulness of the days*: this expression is not used in the King James version of the Bible, but appears five times in Robert Young's *The Holy Bible . . . literally and idiomatically translated out of the original languages* (usually known as *Young's Literal Translation*), Edinburgh, 1863. There are no uses of it in B. before *Abt Vogler*, but the expression appears frequently in his work thereafter; see, e.g., *Ring* viii 716; *Prince Hohenstiel-Schwangau* (1871) 349. *agonized*: intransitively (as here), the verb means 'To feel agonies; to be in excessive pain' (*J.*).

83. Why else was] Well, why was (*MS*, canc.).

86. says] has (*MS*, canc.). *weal and woe*: prosperity and misfortune.

88. 'tis we musicians know: cp. *Charles Avison* (*Parleyings*, 1887) 138–9: 'There is no truer truth obtainable / By Man than comes of music'.

91–6. A number of critics have questioned this description of a chromatic cadence resolving to C major; Charles Stanford suggests that '[sliding] by semitones till I sink to the minor' is 'the refuge of the destitute amateur improviser', while W. Wright Roberts asks whether 'any musician [has] made sense of it' (both cited in Nachum Schoffman, *There is no Truer Truth: The Musical Aspect of Browning's Poetry* [New York, 1991] 78–9). Schoffman himself, however, defends B.'s description as a technically accurate account: 'The description of the cadence is not only poetically and dramatically valid but musically valid as well. There is nothing awkward or amateurish about sliding down by semitones. The conclusion of Bach's *Chromatic Fantasy* provides a masterful example of such a cadence, sliding down by semitones and pausing on a minor ninth chord before resolving to the tonic' (p. 79).

91. the common chord: 'the basic triad made up of the first, third, and fifth notes of the scale, probably in the key of C major'; James E. Neufeld, 'Some Notes on Browning's Musical Poems', *SBC* vi.1 (1978) 51.

Sliding by semitones, till I sink to the minor,—yes,
And I blunt it into a ninth, and I stand on alien ground,
Surveying a while the heights I rolled from into the
deep;
95 Which, hark, I have dared and done, for my resting-place
is found,
The C Major of this life: so, now I will try to sleep.

92. Sliding] Striking (*MS*, canc.).

93. I blunt it into a ninth: Neufeld (see l. 91n.) points out that the 'fundamental principle' of Vogler's system of harmony was 'that not only the triad (common chord), but also the discords of the seventh, ninth and eleventh could be introduced on any degree of the scale without involving modulation'. Vogler's use of a ninth in the poem is not, therefore, 'purely capricious', but indicates B.'s knowledge of his subject: 'It is an interval Vogler might have used in such circumstances and for which he might have gained some notoriety' ('Some Notes', p. 52).

94. a while] awhile (*MS, 1868–88*), a rare example of printed eds. returning to a reading in *MS*.

95–6. Nachum Schoffman (see ll. 91–6n.) notes that 'the key of C major, devoid of sharps and flats, is Browning's symbol for the ultimate simplicity, the ultimate truth' (p. 75), and compares *Charles Avison* (*Parleyings*, 1887) 361–4. For a contemporary performance of Vogler's symphony in C major, see headnote, *Composition and date*.

95. Which, hark] Which, see (*MS*). *dared and done*: a favourite phrase of B.'s, deriving from the final line of Christopher Smart's *Song to David* (1765): 'And now the matchless deed's achiev'd, / DETERMIN'D, DAR'D, and DONE!' B. uses it in many different contexts: cp., e.g., *Ring* i 801–2, where it alludes to Guido's murder of Pompilia, and the opening line of B.'s elegy *La Saisiaz* (1872): 'Dared and done: at last I stand upon the summit, Dear and True!'

49 Mr. Sludge, "the Medium"

Text and publication

First publ. *DP*, 28 May 1864; repr. *1864²*, *1868*, *1880*, *1888*. The MS, part of the printer's copy for *DP*, is at *Morgan*. It is much less clean than other MSS in the volume, with numerous cancelled readings and evidence of drafting; nevertheless it is not the first draft, since there is clear evidence that it was copied from an earlier version (e.g. B. originally wrote l. 69 immediately after l. 67, then interpolated l. 68; this does not make sense except as a copying error). There are, moreover, some indications in the MS that the poem might have been revised by B. at a very late stage. The title page has been pasted onto another page; the bottom right-hand corner of the original page is visible, with the words '2000 to follow' written in pencil. (There are 1689 lines in the last three poems in the volume.) There are numbers at top right and bottom right of alternate pages; the numbers at bottom right, beginning with '92', indicate the position of the page in the MS volume, and those at top right its position within *Mr. Sludge*. For the most part these sequences coincide, but there are some pages of the MS where they are out of phase. The page with '95' at bottom right, for instance (ll. 111–34) comes where there should be a page without numbers, and some indecipherable writing is visible near the binding, suggesting that it might have been taken from a different draft. There are similar disruptions of the sequences at '104' (ll. 481–502) and '113' (ll. 845–68). On the first of these pages, someone – presumably the compositor – has written '193' and drawn a line to the space between ll. 481 and 482; on the second, there are similar markings, with the number '209'. In both cases, these marginal numbers correspond to the page numbers in *1864*. Finally, most of the paragraph breaks are indicated in the poem by means of a single line drawn across the page, but in some sections – such as '105' – B. has indicated a new paragraph by leaving a space on the page. Taken as a whole, these features suggest that B. removed *Mr. Sludge* from the MS volume and substituted a revised version while *DP* was in production. Revision after publication was very light; an unusual number of new readings appear in *1875* (a revised re-issue of *1868*), almost all converting 'of the' to 'o' the', 'in the' to 'i' the', etc.

Composition and date

B. and EBB. had argued about spiritualism since the 1850s, and B. quarrelled with the American medium Daniel Dunglas Home (the original of Sludge) in 1855: see below. But though B. may have conceived the poem before EBB.'s death in 1861, its tone makes it unlikely that he wrote it while she was alive (compare *Mesmerism* in *M & W*, III 475). Home was in the news in 1860 following a sympathetic article by Robert Bell, 'Stranger than Fiction', in the *Cornhill Magazine* (vol. ii, pp. 211–24), which both B. and EBB. saw (*EBB to Arabella* ii 485); the same year saw the founding in London of the *Spiritual Magazine*, which was forwarded to EBB. in Florence, and in which Home is frequently mentioned (see, e.g., 'Two Evenings with Mr. Home', June 1860, 266–9). Home also contributed articles of his own to the *Spiritual Magazine*; see below, *Sources and influences*. B.'s letters of 1862 and 1863 contain scathing comments about Home's deceit and cowardice, showing that B. kept track of his bugbear. Home's autobiography, *Incidents in My Life*, appeared in March 1863, in time to influence the poem's setting and details of Sludge's character. In a letter of 19 April 1863 B. told Isa Blagden: 'I never read Hume's book,—avoid looking at an extract from it' (*Dearest Isa 160*). The present tense of this denial is perhaps significant, though B. may be referring primarily to extracts in reviews; the evidence of the poem, however, strongly suggests that B. did consult the book, perhaps after realizing that neither he nor EBB. was named in it. We date the main period of composition to the spring and summer of 1863.

Sources and influences

(1) *Nineteenth-century spiritualism*
In 1848, in Hydesville (near Rochester, New York) two sisters, Kate and Margaret Fox, aged 12 and 10 respectively, claimed to be in communication with a spirit who replied to their questions in coded 'raps'. The 'Rochester rappers' became famous as mediums, and did not confess their imposture until 1888 (the confession itself is repudiated by believers in spiritualism). The range of phenomena manifested by the spirits grew rapidly, as did the numbers of people claiming to be mediums: séances became both a social craze and a commercial activity. The terms 'spiritualism' and 'spiritualist', which had formerly denoted tendencies within religious philosophy, came into use in the early 1850s to denote belief in the reality of communication either with supernatural beings or, more usually, the spirits of the dead. (The *OED*'s earliest citation for 'spiritualist' in this sense is from EBB.'s letter of 13–14 May 1852 to her brother George [*George Barrett* 181], and there is in fact an even earlier example: see below.) The movement spread from America to Europe, helped by the increasing numbers of American visitors in the period, including those whom the Brownings met in Florence. American spiritualism was initially associated with progressive social and religious tendencies (the first patrons of the Fox sisters were Quakers) though its social reach widened as the century progressed. By the same token, opponents of the movement, especially in Britain, often stigmatized it as 'vulgar' and 'canting' in the same way as the more extreme forms of Dissent (see headnote to *CE & ED*, III 41, and note EBB.'s comment on Home's 'trance', below). At the time B. published *Mr. Sludge*, spiritualism had attained its peak of popularity and credibility, but it never formed a coherent movement or gained a permanent foothold in any established religious denomination.

Spiritualism was linked with other paranormal phenomena, esp. mesmerism (or 'magnetism'), which had been popular since the turn of the century; the connection can be seen clearly in EBB.'s letter to Arabella of 21 Dec. 1852 which moves from a discussion of the authenticity of the 'Rapping spirits' to an account of a 'magnetizing' session that she and B. witnessed (*EBB to Arabella* i 525–6); see also headnote to *Mesmerism*, III 475–6. Advocates of spiritualism claimed that its manifestations heralded a new age of religious, specifically Christian revelation; EBB., for example, had friends who thought that the manifestations were those of evil spirits, and that 'the access to this world permitted lately with affluence to these spirits, is one of the great signs of the [Second] Coming' (*EBB to Arabella* i 485). She herself came to believe that spiritualism afforded '*scientific proof* that what we call death is a mere change of circumstances' (to Madame Braun, 10 Aug. 1858, *Letters of EBB* ii 289), that 'the whole theory of spiritualism, all the phenomena, are strikingly *confirmatory* of revelation', and that 'our reigning philosophy will modify itself . . . the materialism which stifles the higher instincts of men will be dislodged' (to Fanny Haworth, *c*. Jan. 1861, *ibid*. ii 422).

(2) *The Brownings and spiritualism*
Spiritualism was well established in the expatriate community in Florence by the early 1850s, and some of its most fervent supporters were close friends and associates of the Brownings. According to EBB., they first heard of the phenomena,

probably in 1851, from two American artists: the sculptor Hiram Powers in Florence, and the poet and painter Thomas Buchanan Read in London (*EBB to Arabella* i 485 and 489n.13). The American connection continued to be strong: EBB. wrote to Arabella on 15–17 Jan. 1853: 'Meanwhile the thing is spreading in America to a degree which wd be scarcely credible to you, as we hear from every American "within hail" of us' (*ibid.* 531). EBB.'s attitude, to start with, was cautious. She told Arabella that she had 'a great deal of (peradventure unlawful) curiosity as to all these things—in which I hold what may be called a *potential* belief . . . that is, I *could* believe anything of the sort upon sufficient evidence. The evidence is not however sufficient yet' (*ibid.* 485). In the same letter she shows some humorous scepticism about the prospect of 'daily intercourse between families & their deceased kindred': 'Napoleon & Franklin, & various others, have been kind enough to give their autographs lately in confirmation of the same' (cp. l. 35n.). However, by mid-1853 she had become a firm believer in the reality of the manifestations, and her letters on the subject are filled with the kind of 'rational' arguments that Sludge cites with relish as evidence of the credulity of his dupes: the attested truth of the phenomena, the 'impossibility' of trickery in the face of so many witnesses, the unimpeachable character, hard-headedness and social status of the witnesses themselves, together with an insistence that the exposure of some mediums as cheats did not invalidate the authenticity of others: see ll. 321–3n., 471–81n., 555–73n.

EBB. records disagreement with B. about spiritualism from the spring of 1853 onwards, noting his scepticism in the face not just of her own conviction but that of their friends in Florence. She wrote to Eliza Ogilvy on 2 June 1853: 'I am up to the throat in all manner of superstitions, so called . . . swimming in spiritualisms. There has been a continued stream of Americans through the Casa Guidi this winter—and if you could hear us talking in this room, Mr. Powers, Mr. [Frederick] Tennyson, Mr. Lytton, & me, . . while poor Robert overwhelmed . . . by the majority against him, declares with his last breath that until he sees & hears with his own eyes & ears, he will give credence to nothing . . . you would set us down as mad' (*EBB to Ogilvy* 97). B.'s attitude in this early period seems to have alternated between defensive scepticism and a more subversive mockery. As EBB. told John Kenyon in a letter of 16 May 1853: 'We tried the table experiment in this room [in Casa Guidi] a few days since, by-the-bye, and failed; but we were impatient, and Robert was playing Mephistopheles, as Mr. Lytton said, and there was little chance of success under the circumstances' (*Letters of EBB* ii 116–17). On another occasion, at Bagni di Lucca in October 1853, their friend William Wetmore Story 'tried the "tables" for some twenty minutes—Under such disadvantages though.—for Robert just laughs & jokes—we had to turn him away after five minutes' (*George Barrett* 200–1). That B. was not (or not yet) angry or alarmed by EBB.'s credulity, and prepared to think of spiritualism as a relatively harmless pastime, seems confirmed by the playful allusion in ll. 43–9 of *Lovers' Quarrel* (p. 379) a poem that probably dates from early 1853. However, in her letter to Arabella of 28–29 Nov. 1853 EBB registers a change of tone: 'I say calmly . . . the disbelief of men is more wonderful to me than the access of spirits! I *never* discuss the subject now with Robert—I never will again—He said to me suddenly the other day—"If those are spirits, Ba, they are *evil* spirits." That remains to be proved. It is not proved to *me*' (*EBB to Arabella* ii 48). EBB. hoped that B. would, one day, receive the convincing personal manifestation he required, and she may have counted on the séance they attended in England in the summer of 1855, conducted by the famous American medium Daniel Dunglas Home, to secure this; but the result was to bring B.'s feelings to a head, and bring the quarrel between him and EBB. into the open.

(3) *Daniel Dunglas Home*
(i) *Home's life and character*
Daniel Dunglas Home (pronounced 'Hume' and so-spelt by both B. and EBB.)
was born in Scotland in 1833 and adopted by an aunt who took him when he
was nine years old to America. He began his public career as a medium in 1851,
with extraordinary success; by the time of his first journey to England, in 1855,
he was the most famous medium of the time, whose repertoire included every
variety of 'manifestation': rapping, trances, the appearance of 'spirit-hands', automatic writing, even levitation. EBB. had heard of Home in Florence from American
friends and correspondents and wrote to her sister that she looked forward to
meeting 'the great medium' in London (*Letters to Arabella* ii 115, 138). In June
1855 she and B. attended a séance at the house of friends of theirs in Ealing (see
below); B.'s conviction that Home was a fake stems from this encounter, and
persisted for the remainder of his life.

    However, although B.'s animus against Home undoubtedly shaped the poem
(notably in the choice of Sludge's nationality and the depiction of his temperament), Sludge's career, as B. describes it, does not directly match that of Home.
Sludge is a servant boy in a wealthy household, who begins by pretending to
have seen a ghost, and is taken up by his gullible and self-serving employers. He
mentions no family and speaks (metaphorically) of his 'gorge / On offal in the
gutter' (cp. *Fra Lippo Lippi* 112–23, p. 491). None of this applies to Home, whose
family, though not wealthy, was well established in Connecticut; he lived with
his aunt until the age of eighteen, when, according to Home's account, she threw
him out of the house because she believed his 'manifestations' came from the
devil. Sludge is caught during a séance he is conducting for a single patron, but
Home almost never agreed to such 'private' consultations, at any rate at the outset of his career; he preferred small groups. It is not clear whether Hiram H.
Horsefall is actually paying Sludge a fee, as opposed to giving him presents of
money and jewellery; Home and his supporters made much of the fact that he did
not accept direct payment for his performances. Sludge leaves America to avoid
exposure; Home travelled to Europe in part at least for health reasons. Finally,
Home was never exposed as a fraud; indeed, in one of his last works, *Lights and
Shadows of Spiritualism* (New York: G. W. Carleton & Co. 1877), he gave a detailed
account of the means used by fraudulent mediums to cheat their public, including
many of the tricks described in B.'s poem, while disclaiming their application to
himself, and regretting the damage done to 'a cause in the service of which my
life has been passed, and with which such foulnesses have nothing in common'
(p. 217). B. himself, in a conversation with F. H. Myers late in life, admitted
that 'he had never detected Home cheating, and that the only definite evidence
which he could show for his opinion that Home was an impostor was based upon
a second-hand rumour that Home was once caught in Italy experimenting with
Phosphorus' (Frank Podmore, *Modern Spiritualism: A History and a Criticism*; rpt.
R. A. Gilbert ed., *The Rise of Victorian Spiritualism*, 8 vols (London 2000), vii 230).

    The outline of Sludge's career therefore does not correspond exactly to Home's;
this might support B.'s contention that he had not read Home's autobiography,
Incidents in My Life (1863; see above, *Date*). Yet some features of Sludge's temperament match Home's self-portrait, and some of Home's anecdotes seem to
have been bent to make them fit Sludge's exposé of his methods. For example,
Home describes himself as being 'very delicate as a child, and of a highly nervous temperament . . . I was, from my delicate health, unable to join the sports
of other boys of my own age' (*Incidents* 1–2); cp. ll. 387–400. Again, Home refers
repeatedly to séances in which the spirit of a dead child appears to its parents

(*Incidents* 38, 152, 178); Sludge cites this as an effective means of shaking people's ability to think clearly during a séance (ll. 466–94). Parts of the long passage on Providence and the question of whether God takes a direct hand in the lives of individuals (ll. 927–55) are close to Home's discussion of this subject (*Incidents* 167). Like Sludge, Home repeatedly claimed that his 'manifestations' had promoted religious belief, both in *Incidents* and in his other writings: see ll. 664–93n.

B. may also have seen some of Home's articles in the *Spiritual Magazine*. One in particular, on the subject of 'Our Public Teachers and the Study of Spiritual Laws' (Feb. 1860; 66–69), anticipates Sludge's mixture of mockery and defiance in the face of those who deny the reality of spiritual phenomena: 'The very idea of there being any new thing under the sun, without the aid of A. B. and C. being called in, is of course preposterous, and ought at once to be assailed, and its originators sneered at, and without more ado, stigmatised as either impostors or madmen' (p. 66). Home adds that 'the finer religious feelings are but too often regarded as effeminate', and offers the following characterization of his opponents' views of his conduct: 'Some there may be that will have the kind-heartedness to consider him as being the dupe of his senses, or of his imagination, or of designing persons; but the generality will brand him as an impostor or a madman, and will soon bring their intercourse with him to an end. The man that is in advance of his time has ever been the leper of society, and as such has been shunned.'

(ii) *The Ealing séance and its aftermath*

The Brownings spent the summer of 1855 in Paris and London. On 23 July they attended a séance held by Home at the Ealing residence of the Rymer family, to whom they had been introduced by their friend Anna Jameson. Two days later B. wrote a lengthy account of the occasion to his friend Mrs Kinney (MS at Yale; repr. in Karlin, *Browning's Hatreds*, pp. 49–53). He stated that though he could not account for some of the phenomena he witnessed, which included rapping, movement of the table, the appearance of 'spirit-hands' and the playing of an accordion, he did not believe they were of supernatural origin (from remarks later reported by EBB. we know that he thought the 'hands' were made of gutta-percha: see *EBB to Arabella* ii 185). One action reported by B., the placing of a wreath by the 'spirit-hand' on EBB.'s head, was later to be used by Home in his own account: see below. B. poured scorn on the ignorance and vulgarity of the speech Home delivered 'in the character of the spirits collectively'; he implied that Home exploited the Rymers' belief that they were in communication with the spirit of their dead child (though he acknowledged that Home had not initiated this belief); and he made clear his personal revulsion at Home's behaviour: '[he] affects the manners, endearments and other peculiarities of a very little child indeed—speaking of Mr. & Mrs. Rymer as his "Papa & Mama" & kissing the family abundantly—he professes timorousness, "a love of love"—and is unpleasant enough in it all—being a well-grown young man, over the average height, and, I should say, of quite the ordinary bodily strength—his face is rather handsome & prepossessing, and indicative of intelligence,—and I observed nothing offensive or pretentious in his demeanour beyond the unmanlinesses I mention, which are in the worst taste'. B. made no claim in this letter to have detected Home in the act of cheating, and indeed stressed his reluctance to make any attempt to do so, out of consideration for the Rymers: 'one could no more presume to catch at the hands (for instance) of what they believed the spirit of their child, than one could have committed any other outrage on their feelings'. For the same reason he did not express his scepticism at the séance itself: 'I treated "the spirit" with the forms & courtesies observed by the others, and in no respect impeded the "developments" by expressing the least symptom of unbelief.' Cp. ll. 346–57 below.

EBB. wrote to her sister Henrietta on 17 Aug., giving an account of the séance 'on the condition though, that when you write to me you don't say a word on the subject—because it's a *tabooed* subject in this house—Robert and I taking completely different views, and he being a good deal irritated by any discussion of it' (*EBB to Henrietta* 219). She described the manifestations: 'we were touched by the invisible, heard the music and raps, saw the table moved, and had sight of the hands. Also, at the request of the medium, the spiritual hands took from the table a garland which lay there, and placed it upon my head' (*ibid.* 220). EBB. conceded that during the 'trance at the conclusion . . . the medium talked a great deal of much such twaddle as may be heard in any fifth rate conventicle', but argued that 'this does not militate at all against the general facts . . . if these are spirits, many among them talk prodigious nonsense, or rather most ordinary commonplace. For my own part I am confirmed in all my opinions. To me it was wonderful and conclusive; and I believe that the medium present was no more *responsible* for the things said and done, than I myself was' (*ibid.* 220–1). She re-affirmed her belief in Home's integrity in a letter of 29 Aug. to Miss M. A. de Gaudrion (publ. *TLS*, 28 Nov. 1902, p. 356); Miss de Gaudrion had attended a séance at Ealing with her fiancé, who was convinced that Home was an impostor, and she wrote to ask EBB.'s opinion. With her letter EBB. enclosed a note from B. written in the formal third person, in which he declared his view that 'the whole display of "hands," "spirit-utterances," &c., were a cheat and imposture', and that 'the best and rarest of natures may begin by the proper mistrust of the more ordinary results of reasoning when employed in such investigations as these, go on to an abnegation of the regular tests of truth and rationality in favour of those particular experiments, and end in a voluntary prostration of the whole intelligence before what is assumed to transcend all intelligence'. The medium's dupes will then do his work for him: 'Once arrived at this point, no trick is too gross—absurdities are referred to "low spirits," falsehoods to "personating spirits"—and the one terribly apparent spirit, the Father of Lies, has it all his own way.'

Home describes some of his Ealing séances in *Incidents*, without mentioning the Brownings by name, but did not give his own account of the episode involving the Brownings until nine years later, in the aftermath of the publication of the poem, as part of an article in *The Spiritual Magazine* ('Mr. Robert Browning on Spiritualism', July 1864, pp. 310–17, repr. in Home's *Incidents in My Life, Second Series* [1872] 99–108). The first part of the article (pp. 310–15), written by an anonymous correspondent, attacks B. as a conceited mediocrity, accuses him of irreligion and concludes by stating that the poem was 'a shocking libel on his wife and her dearest beliefs', in which he had 'desecrate[d] her memory and her sweet muse by this ribald nonsense'. Home's account of the séance follows (pp. 315–17): he claims that 'Mr. Browning was requested to investigate everything as it occurred, and he availed himself freely of the invitation' and that 'Several times during the evening he voluntarily and earnestly declared that anything like imposture was out of the question'. Home's credibility is weakened by the ill-advised reason he gives for B.'s animosity, namely that a wreath of clematis, which was 'raised from the table by supernatural power in the presence of us all', was placed on EBB.'s head and not on his own. We know that B. saw this article: he refers to it in a letter of 6 Jan. 1871 to Mrs Kinney, who requested permission to publish B.'s letter to her about the Ealing séance. B. refused: 'I should thereby give the unmitigated scoundrel in question a right as well as opportunity to retaliate, after his natural fashion, by a fresh vomit of lies such as he printed five years ago in a *Spiritual Magazine*—wherein, referring to this very "séance," he attributed all my unbelief to my "ludicrous jealousy of my wife,—whom the

Spirits crowned as 'The Poet,' passing over—me!" If I ever cross the fellow's path I shall probably be silly enough to soil my shoe by kicking him,—but I should prefer keeping that disgrace from myself as long as possible' (*New Letters* 199).

However, Home is on more convincing ground in his account of what happened next. In his letter to Miss de Gaudrion, B. stated: 'Mr. Browning had some difficulty in keeping from an offensive expression of his feelings at the [Rymers]; he has since seen Mr Hume and relieved himself.' This remark refers to an encounter with Home a week or so after the Ealing séance, when Home, in company with Mrs Rymer and her eldest son, called at the Brownings' lodgings in Dorset Street. As Home relates it, B. refused to shake hands with him (see l. 1280 of the poem), told Mrs Rymer that he was 'exceedingly dissatisfied' with what he had seen during the séance and ignored Home when he attempted to speak. B.'s 'face was pallid with rage, and his movements, as he swayed backwards and forwards on his chair, were like those of a maniac'. EBB., by contrast, shook hands with Home and showed distress at her husband's behaviour, saying as he left 'Dear Mr. Home, I am not to blame. Oh, dear! oh, dear!' B. himself gave William Allingham a more highly coloured account, also in the aftermath of the publication of the poem. Allingham reports him as saying, of the séance, that he 'was openly called upon to give his frank opinion on what had passed, in presence of Home and the company, upon which he declared with emphasis that so impudent a piece of imposture he never saw before in all his life, and so took his leave'—a statement that looks suspiciously like the mirror-image of Home's claim that B. 'voluntarily and earnestly declared that anything like imposture was out of the question'. Allingham goes on to report that when Home came to visit B. and offered his hand, 'Browning looked sternly at him (as he is very capable of doing) and pointing to the open door, not far from which is rather a steep staircase, said—"If you are not out of that door in half a minute I'll fling you down the stairs." Home attempted some expostulation, but B. moved towards him, and the Medium disappeared with as much grace as he could manage' (*Allingham* 101–2, entry for 30 June 1864). Note that in Allingham's account EBB. is absent from both the séance and the subsequent confrontation. It was not long before the rumour spread that B. had actually thrown Home down the stairs, or out of the house. In later years, Pen Browning remembered his father 'repeatedly' stating that he 'caught hold of his [Home's] foot under the table' (*TLS*, loc. cit.), a direct contradiction of what he told Mrs Kinney.

EBB. wrote of the occasion as an 'explosion', and was surprised when, at Paris in Oct. 1855, B. had sufficient command of his feelings to discuss 'Home and the Ealing manifestations' with friends without losing his temper (*EBB to Arabella* ii 185); even so, she told Arabella, she did not mention Home in her letters to Florence: 'The ground is dangerous and should be trodden lightly' (*ibid.* ii 185, 187). She herself remained sensitive on the subject: in a letter of 11 Sept. 1856 she told Arabella that she was 'horribly vexed with Robert yesterday for disproving & laughing at all my convictions' (*ibid.* 250). Home's name 'still means gunpowder', she wrote on 27 Nov. 1857 (*ibid.* 329), and when Home visited Florence in March 1858 she made a half-joking 'compact' with B.: 'If he meets Hume in the street, he shant kick him; and I, for my part, will not go anywhere where he can be met' (*ibid.* 340). Yet she referred to Home in a letter of 27 March as her 'protégé prophet' (*Letters of EBB* ii 280), and she continued to the end of her life to affirm her belief in spiritualist phenomena. It seems likely that, as her health declined in the late 1850s, B. became more tender of her feelings; in a letter of 16 June 1860 to Fanny Haworth, she wrote: 'Here is Robert, whose heart softens to the point of letting me have the "Spiritual Magazine" from England'

(*Letters of EBB* ii 395). In the period between EBB.'s death and the composition of *Mr. Sludge*, B. mentions Home several times in his letters: he told the Storys that he had heard that Home was trying to pretend he was not 'the Mr. Hume Mr B. insulted' but 'quite another man' (19 Mar. 1862, *American Friends* 103), and he wrote to Isa Blagden that when he unexpectedly came across Home at a London evening party the medium hurriedly left: 'I can't help flattering myself, that the announcement of my name did him no good' (19 Apr. 1863, *Dearest Isa* 160).

(4) *The American background*
Mr. Sludge is B.'s only poem set in America. Neither he nor EBB. ever visited the United States, but they had many American friends in Florence and 'a continued stream of Americans', as EBB. put it (see above), passed through Casa Guidi in the 1850s, bringing news of the 'rapping spirits' and helping to familiarize B. with American social customs, literary and cultural references, and speech. B.'s representation of America, however, is also influenced by images which circulated in recent British writing about America, both fiction and non-fiction.

The poem is set in Boston, the acknowledged centre of American progressive intellectual culture, with which spiritualism had close connections. However, New York is indicated as the setting by some of the poem's details (such as the reference to Horace Greeley, the editor of the *New York Tribune*) and by some of the *MS* readings (e.g. l. 940, l. 1299). It is possible that B. might have moved the action from New York to Boston at a late stage of composition in order to distance Sludge slightly from Home. Both B. and EBB. greatly admired the writings of Ralph Waldo Emerson, the leading figure of the 'Transcendentalist' movement, and had been friends of Margaret Fuller (Countess Ossoli), whom they met in Florence in 1849–50; Nathaniel Hawthorne and James Russell Lowell also became personal friends (see ll. 1439–41). However, Sludge's patron, Hiram H. Horsefall, is not cast as an intellectual or artist; his profession is not stated, but his wealth, material possessions, social circle and character (as it comes across through Sludge's satirical 'portrait' of him) suggest a businessman or lawyer, vain of his hard-headed 'Yankee' shrewdness, and all the more liable to be taken in by a charlatan. His last name implies that his pride takes a fall, and may also allude to what falls from a horse (cp. Carlyle's Professor Teufelsdröck, i.e. Devil's-dung). In this light, B.'s depiction of American provincial society, with its dollar-worship, its bluster and boastfulness, and its social and personal hypocrisy, is close to that of Dickens in *American Notes* (1842) and *Martin Chuzzlewit* (1843–4). B. is likely to have known other books by English visitors, such as Fanny Trollope's *Domestic Manners of the Americans* (1832), Harriet Martineau's *Society in America* (1837) and Anthony Trollope's *North America* (1862). Despite this, it would be a mistake to conclude that his prevailing view of America was hostile or contemptuous; the reverse is the case.

Although the poem was published during the American Civil War, the date of the action seems to be a little earlier, perhaps around the time of Home's departure for England in 1855. There is no mention of the Civil War (whereas the Mexican War of 1846–8 is mentioned at l. 233). Boston's pre-eminence as the bastion of abolitionism does not feature in the poem, and Sludge's only racial allusion (l. 32) is pejorative; see also the cancelled line 1513^1514. B. himself was a passionate supporter of the Unionist cause; in Dec. 1861, when the 'Trent' affair brought Britain and the United States close to war, he wrote to his American friends the Storys: 'Come what will, *I*—insignificant unit here—make no "war" in my soul with my truest brothers & friends: noone ever had cause to love a country better than I, who have so long been only not an American because people can hardly experience such generosity except as strangers' (*American Friends* 90).

The accuracy of B.'s representation of American speech has been questioned, notably by DeVane: 'As for the curious Americanisms which Sludge uses in his speech, it is to be hoped that they never existed outside the poet's imagination' (*Handbook* 312). John Vincent Fleming ('Browning's Yankee Medium', *American Speech* xxxix [1964] 26–32) offers a partial defence, pointing out that some of the idioms which B. was assumed to have invented or got wrong, such as 'V-note' (see l. 100n.), are in fact plausible, and listing instances of American vocabulary, usage and syntax which establish that B. had done his homework. Fleming notes that the poem's first American reviewer complained not of inaccuracy as such, but of unconvincingness: 'a few Yankee phrases are pasted into Mr Sludge's talk . . . there is no character in them at all' (*Atlantic Monthly* xiv [1864] 647, cited Fleming, p. 27). B.'s worst blunder concerned the ferocity of the 'prairie-dog' (see l. 576n.).

Parallels in B.

(1) *Religious and philosophical contexts*
The claims that spiritualism was, on the one hand, a biblical 'sign of the times', or, on the other hand, a 'scientific' proof of the reality of the spirit-world, would have been equally obnoxious to B. The former was characteristic of the extreme Protestantism against which he had rebelled in his youth, and satirized in *CE & ED* (see headnote, III 38, 42–3); the latter was even more suspect, not because B. was himself a materialist and rationalist, but because he believed that the search for 'proof' of the existence of God or the reality of life after death undermined the need for faith; if such 'proof' were forthcoming, it would substitute a sterile certainty for the struggle against doubt from which everything good in human life (including art) derived. This view is stated in *Bishop Blougram* (see ll. 693–712, pp. 324–5) and in *A Death in the Desert* 252–337 (pp. 737–41). Moreover, since B. believed that such proof was by its very nature impossible, any person or system of ideas that claimed to have it must be either deluded or fraudulent. In a letter to Julia Wedgwood of 27 June 1864 he rejected Cardinal Newman's claim to be as certain of the existence of God as of his own: 'I believe he deceives himself and that no sane man has ever had, with mathematical exactness, equal conviction on these two points' (*RB & JW* 33–4). B.'s language here establishes a hierarchy in which the only philosophical certainty we have is of our own existence; this position enables faith in a spiritual world, but it may also lead to a lack of belief in the reality of other people, and thus enable us to treat them as objects and instruments of our own desires: this is the philosophy proclaimed by Sludge in ll. 905–11, whose edge comes from its closeness to what B. himself believed. In this sense Sludge is a precursor of Guido in *Ring* (on which B. was already working at the time he published *DP*), but also of B.'s own persona in his philosophical elegy *La Saisiaz* (1877).

(2) *The occult*
B. had a long-standing interest in magic, the occult and the paranormal, nourished by his father's library which gave him an unusual knowledge of Hermetic and Neoplatonic traditions (see Curtis Dahl and J. L. Brewer, 'Browning's "Saul" and the Fourfold Vision: a Neoplatonic-Hermetic Approach', *BIS* iii [1975] 101–18). The analogy (benign or sinister) which might be suggested between the art of magic and that of poetry is implied by the epigraph to his first published poem, *Pauline*, from the Renaissance mage Cornelius Agrippa (I 26–8); *Paracelsus* is based on another Renaissance alchemist and occultist, who like Sludge is 'exposed' as a quack; magic features in *Sordello* in relation both to the characters of the poem

(e.g. Ecelin's wife Adelaide: see i 396, 751–6; I 420, 446), and the poet himself, who convenes a 'ghostly' audience of dead poets to hear his story (i 31 ff., I 396), and compares himself to an 'archimage' putting on a dazzling but delusory show (i 579–91, I 562–4); parallels in *M & W*, the volume preceding *DP*, include *An Epistle* in which Karshish recalls the occult master who taught him in his youth (ll. 167–73, p. 520) and, most significantly, *Mesmerism* (III 475), whose topic, like that of *Mr. Sludge*, was also a subject of disagreement between B. and EBB. Examples after *DP* include the 'mage' in bk i of *Ring*, whose ambiguous power to raise the dead is contrasted with that which derives directly from God (ll. 741–59), and a poem about another Renaissance figure, *Pietro of Abano* (*DI²*, 1880).

(3) *Dramatic monologue as 'apologia'*
Sludge belongs to a group of speakers who justify their behaviour and way of life to sceptical or indifferent listeners. Prototypes from the 1840s include *My Last Duchess* (p. 197) and *Tomb at St. Praxed's* (p. 232), but the form really comes into its own with the much longer monologues of *M & W* (*Fra Lippo Lippi*, *Bishop Blougram*, *Andrea del Sarto*) which give the speakers the room they need in order to deal with a whole life. *Fra Lippo Lippi* is especially notable because it, too, begins with someone clutching the speaker by the throat. In *DP*, Sludge is 'answered' by the most 'spiritual' of the gospel-writers, St John, in *A Death in the Desert*. The 'apologetic' monologue figures as legal deposition in *Ring*: bks v–vii are spoken by the three main characters in the case, Guido, Caponsacchi and Pompilia, and Guido gets a second opportunity, in his death-cell, in bk xi; the Pope's judgment, in bk x, doubles as a self-justification. Later 'apologetic' monologues include *Prince Hohenstiel-Schwangau* (1871), *Fifine at the Fair* (1872) and *Aristophanes' Apology* (1875); the first of these is, like Sludge, a 'transparent' portrait of a contemporary public figure, Napoleon III.

> Now, don't sir! Don't expose me! Just this once!
> This was the first and only time, I'll swear,—
> Look at me,—see, I kneel,—the only time,
> I swear, I ever cheated,—yes, by the soul
> 5 Of Her who hears—(your sainted mother, sir!)
> All, except this last accident, was truth—
> This little kind of slip!—and even this,
> It was your own wine, sir, the good champagne,
> (I took it for Catawba,—you're so kind)
> 10 Which put the folly in my head!

1. Now, don't sir! Don't] Now don't, Sir! don't (*MS*). 'Sir' is consistently upper case in *MS*.
9. Catawba: A 'light sparkling rich-flavoured wine' (*OED*) made from the American grape *Vitis Labrusca*. In his *Autobiography*, Moncure Conway remarked that B. 'enjoyed some of our American writers, admired our women, and liked our sparkling Catawba, to which I had the pleasure of introducing him' (ii 23).
10. Which] That (*MS*, canc.).

"Get up?"
You still inflict on me that terrible face?
You show no mercy?—Not for Her dear sake,
The sainted spirit's, whose soft breath even now
Blows on my cheek—(don't you feel something, sir?)
15   You'll tell?

              Go tell, then! Who the devil cares
What such a rowdy chooses to . . .

                              Aie—aie—aie!
Please, sir! your thumbs are through my windpipe, sir!
Ch—ch!

              Well, sir, I hope you've done it now!
Oh Lord! I little thought, sir, yesterday,
20   When your departed mother spoke those words
Of peace through me, and moved you, sir, so much,
You gave me—(very kind it was of you)
These shirt-studs—(better take them back again,
Please, sir!)—yes, little did I think so soon
25   A trifle of trick, all through a glass too much
Of his own champagne, would change my best of friends
Into an angry gentleman!

                       Though, 'twas wrong.
I don't contest the point; your anger's just:
Whatever put such folly in my head,

11.] You'll still inflict on me that terrible face (*MS*); You'll still inflict that terrible face on me? (*MS*, canc.).
12. You] You'll (*MS*).
13. spirit's] spirit (*MS*, canc.).
16. rowdy: at this time, a distinctively American term for 'a rough, disorderly person'; one of several examples of American idiom in the poem (see *Headnote*).
     Aie—aie—aie! Sludge's cries of pain; cp. Guido's first appearance before his judges in *Ring* v 9.
18. Ch—ch!: choking noises made by Sludge as he recovers from the assault.
22–3. You gave . . . shirt-studs: in a letter of 24 March 1858 to her sister Arabella, EBB., speaking of Home, mentioned 'the splendid presents presented to him by the kings & queens of the earth—among these, a most magnificent set of studs in black pearls & diamonds, by the Empress Eugenie' (*EBB to Arabella* ii 340).
24. so soon] that soon (*MS*, canc.).
29. such folly] this folly (*MS*, canc.).

30   I know 'twas wicked of me. There's a thick,
       Dusk, undeveloped spirit (I've observed)
       Owes me a grudge—a negro's, I should say,
       Or else an Irish emigrant's; yourself
       Explained the case so well last Sunday, sir,
35   When we had summoned Franklin to clear up
       A point about those shares in the telegraph:
       Ay, and he swore . . or might it be Tom Paine? . .
       Thumping the table close by where I crouched,
       He'd do me soon a mischief: that's come true!

40   Why, now your face clears! I was sure it would!
       Then, this one time . . don't take your hand away,
       Through yours I surely kiss your mother's hand . .
       You'll promise to forgive me?—or, at least,
       Tell nobody of this? Consider, sir!
45   What harm can mercy do? Would but the shade
       Of the venerable dead-one just vouchsafe
       A rap or tip! What bit of paper's here?
       Suppose we take a pencil, let her write,

31. Dusk] dark, *(MS).*

35. Franklin: Benjamin Franklin (1706–1790), US scientist and statesman, served as Postmaster-General during the colonial period, and would therefore have been the right spirit to ask about 'shares in the telegraph' (l. 35). He seems to have been a favourite of the spiritualists; see *EBB to Arabella* i 485 (28 Apr. 1852); and see also Podmore (headnote), vi 268: 'Of all the august names which figure in the "inspirational" literature of the period, none . . . occurs more frequently, or is made sponsor for more outrageous nonsense, than that of Franklin.'

36. those] your *(MS, canc.).*

37. Tom Paine: Thomas Paine (1737–1809) was an English pamphleteer and controversialist who spent much time in America, supporting the American Revolution of 1776; later he became a supporter of the French Revolution, but returned to America in 1802 after being imprisoned in France. His best-known work was *The Rights of Man* (1791), which was banned in England; his attack on religion in *The Age of Reason* (1794) cost him much of his popularity in America. Paine was another favourite of the mediums; one of the earliest books of 'automatic writing' was *The Pilgrimage of Thomas Paine and others to the Seventh Circle*, by the Rev. C. Hammond (New York 1852).

38.] added in *MS.*

44. Consider, sir!] Consider it—*(MS, canc.).*

47. a rap or tip: an allusion to the Spirits' usual methods of communication, either by 'rapping' on tables or 'tipping' (i.e. tilting) them in a certain direction. *here?]* this? *(MS).*

48. we] I *(MS, canc.).*

48–50. Suppose we take a pencil . . . Forgiveness? Another common form of communication by the Spirits; EBB.'s letters contain numerous anecdotes about 'automatic

Make the least sign, she urges on her child
50 Forgiveness? There now! Eh? Oh! 'Twas your foot,
And not a natural creak, sir?

Answer, then!
Once, twice, thrice . . . see, I'm waiting to say "thrice!"
All to no use? No sort of hope for me?
It's all to post to Greely's newspaper?

55 What? If I told you all about the tricks?
Upon my soul!—the whole truth, and nought else,
And how there's been some falsehood—for your part,
Will you engage to pay my passage out,
And hold your tongue until I'm safe on board?
60 England's the place, not Boston—no offence!
I see what makes you hesitate: don't fear!
I mean to change my trade and cheat no more,

---

writing' of this kind, which often assumed the form of a language unknown to the writer.

49. the least] just a (*MS*)   *child*] son (*MS*, canc.).

50. 'Twas your foot: the suggestion that the apparently supernatural noises heard during séances are attributable to the 'cracking of toe-joints' was put forward at an early stage of the investigations into spiritualism by three doctors from Buffalo, New York, who had observed a séance involving the Fox girls: 'we have heard of several cases in which movements of the bones entering into other articulations are produced by muscular effort, giving rise to sounds. We have heard of a person who can develop knockings from the ankle, of several who can produce noises with the joints of the toes and fingers, of one who can render loudly audible the shoulder, and another the hip-joint' (cited in Podmore [headnote, *Sources and influences*], vi 185). EBB. also mentions this possibility in a letter to Mary Russell Mitford of Feb. 1853 in connection with a recent article by Dickens which makes fun of a visiting American medium: 'I understand that Dickens has caught a wandering spirit in London & shown him up victoriously in Household Words as neither more nor less than the "cracking of toe-joints"—but it is absurd to try to adapt such an explanation to cases in general' (*EBB to MRM* iii 377; the article was 'The Ghost of the Cock-Lane Ghost', publ. in the issue of 10 Nov. 1852).

52. "thrice!"] "thrice"—(*MS*).

54. Greely's newspaper: Horace Greeley [*sic*: B. corrected the spelling in later eds.] (1811–72) was the editor of the *New York Tribune* newspaper, and a famous liberal campaigning journalist. B. would have been told of him by American friends in Florence. His newspaper gave extensive publicity (and credibility) to the 'spiritualist' movement during its early years; see Podmore (headnote, *Sources and influences*) vi 183.

55. told] tell (*MS*, canc.).

Yes, this time really it's upon my soul!
Be my salvation!—under Heaven, of course.
65   I'll tell some queer things. Sixty Vs must do.
A trifle, though, to start with! We'll refer
The question to this table?

                                    How you're changed!
Then split the difference; thirty more, we'll say.
Ay, but you leave my presents! Else I'll swear
70   'Twas all through those: you wanted yours again,
So, picked a quarrel with me, to get them back!
Tread on a worm, it turns, sir! If I turn,
Your fault! 'Tis you'll have forced me! Who's obliged
To give up life yet try no self-defence?
75   At all events, I'll run the risk. Eh?

                                    Done!
May I sit, sir? This dear old table, now!
Please, sir, a parting egg-nogg and cigar!
I've been so happy with you! Nice stuffed chairs,
And sympathetic sideboards; what an end
80   To all the instructive evenings! (It's alight.)
Well, nothing lasts, as Bacon came and said!

---

64. Heaven, of course.] Providence! (*MS*, canc.).

65. Vs: i.e. 'V-notes', five-dollar bills: the earliest *OED* example is 1837. B. is the only English writer to use the word, and he uses it only in this poem. See also ll. 100, 105, 1493, 1524.

67. How you're changed! Horsefall has clearly rejected Sludge's disingenuous attempt to allow 'the table' to decide the exact amount he has to pay.

68.] added in *MS*.

70. those:] that— (*MS*, canc.).

73–4. Who's obliged . . . self-defence? Cp. *Ring* i 1273–4: 'Satan's old saw being apt here—skin for skin, / All a man hath that will he give for life.' See *Job* ii 4 for 'Satan's old saw'.

73. you'll have forced me!] you that force me! (*MS*, canc.).

74. try] use (*MS*, canc.).

77. egg-nogg: 'A drink in which the white and yolk of eggs are stirred up with hot beer, cider, wine, or spirits' (*OED*); earliest entry 1825. This seems to be another attempt to provide an American flavour to Sludge's monologue, as most of the *OED*'s examples are American.

79. sympathetic sideboards: the primary reference here is to Horsefall's generosity as Sludge's host, but there is also perhaps a mischievous allusion on Sludge's part to his habit of using items of furniture to communicate with the spirits.

81. Bacon: referring to Francis Bacon, Lord Verulam, Viscount St Albans (1561–1626), philosopher, scientist, statesman: see also ll. 309–10n. In spite of his

Here goes,—but keep your temper, or I'll scream!

Fol-lol-the-rido-liddle-iddle-ol!
You see, sir, it's your own fault more than mine;
85   It's all your fault, you curious gentlefolk!
You're prigs,—excuse me,—like to look so spry,
So clever, while you cling by half a claw
To the perch whereon you puff yourselves at roost,
Such piece of self-conceit as serves for perch
90   Because you chose it, so it must be safe.
Oh, otherwise you're sharp enough! You spy
Who slips, who slides, who holds by help of wing,
Wanting real foothold,—who can't keep upright
On the other perch, your neighbour chose, not you:
95   There's no outwitting you respecting him!
For instance, men love money—that, you know—

---

reputation as a pioneer of scientific method and empirical rationalism, Bacon seems
to have been an important figure to the spiritualist movement. Podmore (see headnote, *Sources and influences*) reprints part of Bacon's 'spirit message' given in Edmonds
and Dexter's *Spiritualism* (New York 1853), and the February issue of *The
Spiritual Magazine* for 1860 concludes with a motto from Bacon: 'Read not to
contradict and confute, nor to believe and take for granted, nor to find talk and
discourse, but to weigh and consider' (p. 96). The following month's issue contains an article entitled 'Lord Bacon and spiritualism' (pp. 113–116), in which it
is claimed that Bacon's work, if understood properly, is not incompatible with
belief in the reality of spiritual 'phenomena'.
83. This is the first and longest example of Sludge's tendency to burst out into
periodic fits of nonsense song: see also l. 284.
86–182. The extended metaphor here compares Sludge's patrons to birds observing each others' behaviour: they instinctively sense when one of their number is
losing his footing (by engaging in deception, or other unsound practice) when
this involves a subject (such as finance) in which they are expert; but taken off
their own ground onto a ground on which they feel a misplaced confidence,
they are easy to deceive. Specifically: if a servant-boy claimed to own money
they would assume he obtained it dishonestly, but if he claimed to have seen a
ghost they would give him credit. The 'perch' represents belief in some bizarre
idea (such as 'that ghosts may be', l. 140) that distorts people's judgment.
87. while you cling] you can cling (*MS*).
88. puff: Birds (e.g. pigeons) puff themselves up (*OED* 4a), but the word also
means to 'swell with vanity' (5a) and to praise something or someone 'in inflated
or extravagant terms, usually from interested motives' (6a): Horsefall and his friends
boast about their acumen and the steadiness and reliability of their position ('at
roost').
89.] Each piece of self-conceit that serves for perch (*MS*); The special self-
conceit that serves for perch (*MS*, canc.).
95. him!] his! (*MS*); that! (*MS*, canc.).

And what men do to gain it: well, suppose
A poor lad, say a help's son in your house,
Listening at keyholes, hears the company
100 Talk grand of dollars, V-notes, and so forth,
How hard they are to get, how good to hold,
How much they buy,—if, suddenly, in pops he—
"*I*'ve got a V-note!"—what do you say to him?
What's your first word which follows your last kick?
105 "Where did you steal it, rascal?" That's because
He finds you, fain would fool you, off your perch,
Not on the special piece of nonsense, sir,
Elected your parade-ground: let him try
Lies to the end of the list,—"He picked it up,
110 His cousin died and left it him by will,
The President flung it to him, riding by,
An actress trucked it for a curl of his hair,
He dreamed of luck and found his shoe enriched,
He dug up clay, and out of clay made gold"—
115 How would you treat such possibilities?
Would not you, prompt, investigate the case
With cow-hide? "Lies, lies, lies," you'd shout: and why?
Which of the stories might not prove mere truth?
This last, perhaps, that clay was turned to coin!
120 Let's see, now, give him me to speak for him!
How many of your rare philosophers,

---

98. help's: a 'help' is an Americanism for a servant.
99. hears the company] heard the company (*MS*); hearing company (*MS*, canc.).
100. V-notes: see l. 65n.
102. How much they] How much they'll (*MS*); What things they'll (*MS*, canc.).
104. which] that (*MS*).
106. finds you, fain would] finds you, tries to (*MS*); finds, and tries to (*MS*, canc.).
107. the special] your favourite (*MS*, canc.).
111. flung] threw (*MS*, canc.).
112. trucked] gave (*MS*, canc.).
113. enriched,] held this (*MS*, canc.).
115. would] is it (*MS*); do (*MS*, canc.).
116. Would] Do (*MS*, which has 'Would', canc.). *1864* returns to *MS* canc. reading.
117. cow-hide: a whip; another Americanism (*OED* 3). *you'd*] you (*MS*, which has 'you'd', canc.). *1864* returns to *MS* canc. reading.
118. mere] the (*MS*, canc.).
120. give him me] had he me (*MS*, canc.).
121. of your rare philosophers,] rare philosophers of old (*MS*, canc.). *rare philosophers*: alchemists, believers in the 'philosopher's stone', supposedly able to transmute base metals into gold. B. had consulted many of their 'plaguy books' for *Paracelsus* (1835: I 98).

In plaguy books I've had to dip into,
Believed gold could be made thus, saw it made
And made it? Oh, with such philosophers
125 You're on your best behaviour! While the lad—
With him, in a trice, you settle likelihoods,
Nor doubt a moment how he got his prize:
In his case, you hear, judge and execute,
All in a breath: so would most men of sense.

130 But let the same lad hear you talk as grand
At the same keyhole, you and company,
Of signs and wonders, the invisible world;
How wisdom scouts our vulgar unbelief
More than our vulgarest incredulity;
135 How good men have desired to see a ghost,
What Johnson used to say, what Wesley did,
Mother Goose thought, and fiddle-diddle-dee:—
If he then break in with, "Sir, *I* saw a ghost!"
Ah, the ways change! He finds you perched and prim;
140 It's a conceit of yours that ghosts may be:
There's no talk now of cow-hide. "Tell it out!

123. Believed] Had faith (*MS*, canc.).
125. behaviour! While] behaviour—while (*MS*); behaviour—but (*MS*, canc.).
128. his] this (*MS*, canc.).
129. most] all (*MS*).
130. grand] fine (*MS*).
131.] added in *MS*.
132. signs and wonders: this expression is used on many occasions in the Bible, perhaps most relevantly in *Mark* xiii 22: 'For false Christs and false prophets shall rise, and shall shew signs and wonders, to seduce, if it were possible, even the elect.'
133. scouts our vulgar unbelief] our vulgar disbelief (*MS*). To 'scout' is to 'reject with scorn' (*OED*).
134. incredulity] credulity (*1875–88*). There is a case for emending *1864*, but is unusual for B. to miss an error in several printings.
136. Johnson: Many early spiritualist writings cited Dr Samuel Johnson's half-belief in the possibility of ghosts, as expressed by Imlac in *Rasselas*: 'There is no people, rude or learned, among whom apparitions of the dead are not related and believed. This opinion, which, perhaps, prevails as far as human nature is diffused, could become universal only by its truth' (London, 1759: p. 41). Johnson was famously involved in the investigation of the 'Cock Lane Ghost', which proved to be fraudulent.   *what Wesley*] and Wesley (*MS*, canc.). Samuel Wesley, father of the founder of Methodism. There were several records of the supposed haunting of his household in 1716–17, and it became a *cause célèbre*, discussed in print by, for example, Joseph Priestley, Coleridge and Southey.
140. a conceit] your conceit (*MS*, canc.). Either B. changed his mind, or found he was mistranscribing.
141. out] all— (*MS*, canc.).

Don't fear us! Take your time and recollect!
Sit down first: try a glass of wine, my boy!
And, David, (is not that your Christian name?)
145   Of all things, should this happen twice—it may—
Be sure, while fresh in mind, you let us know!"
Does the boy blunder, blurt out this, blab that,
Break down in the other, as beginners will?
All's candour, all's considerateness—"No haste!
150   Pause and collect yourself! We understand!
That's the bad memory, or the natural shock,
Or the unexplained *phenomena*!"

Egad,
The boy takes heart of grace; finds, never fear,
The readiest way to ope your own heart wide,
155   Show—what I call your peacock-perch, pet post
To strut, and spread the tail, and squawk upon!
"Just as you thought, much as you might expect!
There be more things in heaven and earth, Horatio," . .

144.] And, David—is not that your Christian name? (*MS*). Many commentators assume that 'David' is Sludge's own first name, but this is never unequivocally established: Horsefall is represented as addressing him as 'Sludge' at l. 1471; it could just be an exemplary name, though it is the poem's premise that 'David's' experiences parallel Sludge's. In either case, there is an ironic parallel with the David whose visionary singing comforts a different kind of patron in *Saul* (III 491). See ll. 591–2n.

145. should this happen twice—it may—] should it happen yet again (*MS*, canc.).

148. in the other] in lying (*MS*, canc.).

152. phenomena!] phenomena. (*MS*: not italic). Sense 4 of 'phenomenon' in *OED* is 'A very notable or extraordinary thing; a highly exceptional or unaccountable fact or occurrence; (*colloq.*) a thing, person, or animal remarkable for some unusual quality; a prodigy'. The mocking italics are interesting when it is noted that this was the term routinely used by believers in spiritualism, including EBB., to refer to the apparitions and manifestations of the 'Spirits'; see, e.g., her letter to Arabella of 28 April 1852: 'these phenomena are spreading throughout America to an extent quite extraordinary' (*EBB to Arabella* ii 485).

152–3. Egad . . . heart of grace: to take 'heart of grace' means to take courage. Sludge's archaic idiom here recalls some lines from Thomas Chatterton's *The Revenge: A Burletta* (1795): 'Zounds, I'll take heart of grace, and brave her clapper; / And, if my courage holds, egad, I'll strap her'.

154.] The readiest way to set your heart ope wide (*MS*, canc.).

155. post] place (*MS*, canc.).

155–6. The comparison now extends to birds' mating rituals.

156. the tail] your tail (*MS*).

158. Cp. *Hamlet* I v 166–7. Home, in *Incidents*, remarks: 'there are more strange things in Heaven and earth than are dreamt of, even in my philosophy' (p. 131).

And so on. Shall not David take the hint,
160   Grow bolder, stroke you down at quickened rate?
If he ruffle a feather, it's "Gently, patiently!
Manifestations are so weak at first!
Doubting, moreover, kills them, cuts all short,
Cures with a vengeance!"

                                   There, sir, that's your style!
165   You and your boy—such pains bestowed on him,
Or any headpiece of the average worth,
To teach, say, Greek, would perfect him apace,
Make him a Person ("Porson?" thank you, sir!)
Much more, proficient in the art of lies.
170   You never leave the lesson! Fire alight,
Catch you permitting it to die! You've friends;
There's no withholding knowledge, least from those
Apt to look elsewhere for their souls' supply:
Why should not you parade your lawful prize?
175   Who finds a picture, digs a medal up,
Hits on a first edition,—he henceforth
Gives it his name, grows notable: how much more,
Who ferrets out a "medium?" "David's yours,
You highly-favoured man? Then, pity souls
180   Less privileged! Allow us share your luck!"
So, David holds the circle, rules the roast,
Narrates the vision, peeps in the glass ball,

---

160. rate] pace (*MS*, canc.).

162. manifestations: another word for Spiritualist 'phenomena'; see *EBB to Arabella*
15–17 Jan. 1853: 'the manifestations are spreading like a fire' (i 532).

167. apace] in Greek (*MS*, canc.).

168. Porson: referring to Richard Porson (1759–1808), the son of a country parish
clerk, Huggin Person (note, in respect of Sludge's error), who after an education
at Eton and King's, Cambridge became the foremost classical scholar of his day.

169. the art] this art (*MS*, canc.).

170. Fire] Fire's (*MS*, canc.).

172. least from those: 'least [of all] from those'.

173.] Not apt to look for their supply to you (*MS*, canc.). Not apt to look to
you for their supply (MS, canc., first reading); 'soul's' may have been inserted at
any stage.

176. a first] a rare (*MS*, canc.).

177. notable:] famous (*MS*, canc.).

181.] So David holds his circle, rules his roast, (*MS*).   *rules the roast*: 'to have full
sway or authority' (*OED*).

182. in the glass ball] in his glass ball (*MS*); into his ball (*MS*, canc.).

Sets to the spirit-writing, hears the raps,
As the case may be.

Now mark! To be precise—
185 Though I say, "lies" all these, at this first stage,
'Tis just for science' sake: I call such grubs
By the name of what they'll turn to, dragonflies.
Strictly, it's what good people style untruth;
But yet, so far, not quite the full-grown thing:
190 It's fancying, fable-making, nonsense-work—
What never meant to be so very bad—
The knack of story-telling, brightening up
Each dull old bit of fact that drops its shine.
One does see somewhat when one shuts one's eyes,
195 If only spots and streaks; tables do tip
In the oddest way of themselves: and pens, good Lord,
Who knows if you drive them or they drive you?
'Tis but a foot in the water and out again;
Not that duck-under which decides your dive.
200 Note this, for it's important: listen why.

I'll prove, you push on David till he dives
And ends the shivering. Here's your circle, now:
Two-thirds of them, with heads like you their host,
Turn up their eyes, and cry, as you expect,
205 "Lord, who'd have thought it!" But there's always one
Looks wise, compassionately smiles, submits
"Of your veracity no kind of doubt,
But—do you feel so certain of that boy's?
Really, I wonder! I confess myself

---

183. Sets to the] Sets to his (*MS*); Begins his (*MS*, canc.).   *the raps*] his raps (*MS*).
187. to, dragonflies] to—butterflies (*MS*).
188. style] call (*MS*).
189. But] And (*MS*, canc.).   *not quite*] it's scarce (*MS*, canc.).   *full-grown thing:*]
full-blown thing—(*MS*).
192.] But as one tells a story, brightening up (*MS*, canc.).
193. Each] The (*MS*).
195. spots] sparks (*MS*).   *tables do tip*] and tables tip (*MS*, canc.).
197.] Who knows when you drive them and they drive you? (*MS*, canc.).
199. duck-under: seemingly B.'s coinage; not in *OED*.   *that*] a (*MS*, canc.).
200. important; listen why.] important,—this is why: (*MS*, canc.).
201. I'll prove,] This way (*MS*).
203.] Two thirds of them have heads like you their host (*MS*).

210 More chary of my faith!" That's galling, sir!
    What, he the investigator, he the sage,
    When all's done? Then, you just have shut your eyes,
    Opened your mouth, and gulped down David whole,
    You! Terrible were such catastrophe!
215 So, evidence is redoubled, doubled again,
    And doubled besides; once more, "He heard, we heard,
    You and they heard, your mother and your wife,
    Your children and the stranger in your gates:
    Did they or did they not?" So much for him,
220 The black sheep, guest without the wedding-garb,
    And doubting Thomas! Now's your turn to crow:
    "He's kind to think you such a fool: Sludge cheats?
    Leave you alone to take precautions!"

                                    Straight
    The rest join chorus. Thomas stands abashed,
225 Sips silent some such beverage as this,
    Considers if it be harder, shutting eyes
    And gulping David in good fellowship,
    Than going elsewhere, getting, in exchange,
    With no egg-nogg to lubricate the food,

212. Then,] Why, (*MS*); Then (*MS*, canc.). *1864* returns to *MS* canc. reading.
213. down David] this David (*MS*).
214. Terrible were] Anything but (*MS*, canc.).
215. So,] The (*MS*).   *redoubled, doubled*] redoubled, and doubled (*MS*, canc.).
216. He heard, we heard] I heard, you heard (*MS*, canc.).
217. You] We (*MS*, canc.).
218. the stranger in your gates: cp. *Exodus* xx 10: 'thy stranger that is within thy gates.'
220.] added in *MS*. See next note. *guest without the wedding-garb*: the interpolated line reinforces the sequence of biblical allusions; see *Matthew* xxii 1–14, in which Jesus tells the story of a stranger invited to a wedding feast by a king; the guest's failure to wear a 'wedding garment' leads to his being 'cast . . . into outer darkness'.
221–3.] The doubting Thomas: now's your turn to crow: / "He's kind to think you such a fool: Sludge cheats? (*MS*); The doubter: now's your turn to crow: "he's kind / To think you such a fool: David a cheat? (*MS*, canc.). See l. 144n.
221. doubting Thomas! See *John* xx 24–29.
226. it be harder, shutting] it's harder shutting (*MS*).
227. good fellowship] good company (*MS*); such company (*MS*, canc.).
228. Than] Or (*MS*, canc.).
229.] added in *MS*.

230   Some just as tough a morsel. Over the way,
      Holds Captain Sparks his court: is it better there?
      Have not you hunting-stories, scalping-scenes,
      And Mexican War exploits to swallow plump
      If you'd be free of the stove-side, rocking-chair,
235   And trio of affable daughters?

                              Doubt succumbs!
      Victory! All your circle's yours again!
      Out of the clubbing of submissive wits,
      David's performance rounds, each chink gets patched,
      Every protrusion of a point's filed fine,
240   All's fit to set a-rolling round the world,
      And then return to David finally,
      Lies seven-feet-thick about his first half-inch.
      Here's a choice birth of the supernatural,
      Poor David's pledged to! You've employed no tool
245   That laws exclaim at, save the devil's own,
      Yet screwed him into henceforth gulling you
      To the top of your bent,—all out of one half-lie!

      You hold, if there's one half or a hundredth part
      Of a lie, that's his fault,—his be the penalty!
250   I dare say! You'd prove firmer in his place?

231.] Our Captain holds his court—is it better there? (*MS*, with 'The', canc.).
233.] Mexican exploits to be swallowed plump (*MS*). *Mexican War*: the war began in Apr. 1846 and ended when the United States occupied Mexico City in Sept. 1847.
234. free of the] free o' the (*1875–88*). To be 'free of' in this sense means to 'have free access to'. *rocking-chair*: said to have been 'introduced by the Americans' (*OED* 1, citation of 1855).
235. trio] brace (*MS*, canc.). *Doubt succumbs!*] He succumbs (*MS*, canc.).
239. 'Every aspect of David's tales that sticks out awkwardly is smoothed down'. *point's*] point (*MS*, canc.).
240. set] go (*MS*, canc.).
244. Poor] That (*MS*, canc.). *tool*] tools (*MS*).
245. That laws exclaim] The law exclaims (*MS*).
246. screwed: forced, constrained; B. may have known that in American college slang 'screw' meant 'to press with an excessive and unnecessarily minute examination' (*OED* 6c, citation of 1851).
246–7. gulling you / To the top of your bent: cp. *Hamlet* III ii 373–4. *MS* has 'fooling' for 'gulling'; the *1864* reading slightly masks the allusion.
247. of your bent] o' your bent (*1875–88*).
248.] You hold, if there be half or a hundredth part (*MS*, which has 'say' for 'hold', canc.).
249. his] *his be the*] his the (*MS*, canc.).

You'd find the courage,—that first flurry over,
That mild bit of romancing-work at end,—
To interpose with "It gets serious, this;
Must stop here. Sir, I saw no ghost at all.
255 Inform your friends I made . . . well, fools of them,
And found you ready made. I've lived in clover
These three weeks: take it out in kicks of me!"
I doubt it! Ask your conscience! Let me know,
Twelve months hence, with how few embellishments
260 You've told almighty Boston of this passage
Of arms between us, your first taste of the foil
From Sludge who could not fence, sir! Sludge, your boy!
I lied, sir,—there! I got up from my gorge
On offal in the gutter, and preferred
265 Your canvass-backs: I took their carver's size,
Measured his modicum of intelligence,
Tickled him on the cockles of his heart
With a raven feather, and next week found myself
Sweet and clean, dining daintily, dizened smart,
270 Set on a stool buttressed by ladies' knees,
Every soft smiler calling me her pet,
Encouraging my story to uncoil
And creep out from its hole, inch after inch,
"How last night, I no sooner snug in bed,

252.] That mild bit of romancing at an end,— (*MS*); That mild bit of romancing
—in good time (*MS*, canc.).
253. *To interpose with "It gets*] To interpose – " 'Tis getting (*MS*, canc).
254. *stop*] end (*MS*, canc.). B. presumably noticed the proximity of 'end' in l. 252.
260. *of this passage*] this short passage (*MS*).
262. *your boy*] the boy (*MS*, canc.).
263. *I lied*] They lied (*MS*, canc.; presumably a mistranscription).
265. *canvass-backs*: the canvas-back is 'A North American duck . . . so called from
the colour of the back feathers' (*OED*, which cites from 1832: 'the man who
has feasted on canvass-back ducks cannot be said to have lived in vain'). *their*]
the (*MS*, canc.).
266–7. *his . . . him . . . his*] your . . . you . . . your (*MS*, canc.).
267–8. *Tickled . . . raven feather*: ravens have traditionally been associated with
witchcraft and divination.
268. *week*] day (*MS*).
269. *dining daintily*] stuffed with dainties (*MS*).   *dizened*] dressed out (*MS*, canc.).
270. *buttressed*] fenced round (*MS*, canc.).
271. *soft*] sweet (*MS*).
273. *its hole*] this was B.'s original reading in *MS*, which he altered to 'its dark
hole' and then altered back again.
274. "Of how last night, no sooner snug in bed, (*MS*).

275   Tucked up, just as they left me,—than came raps!
       While a light whisked" . . "Shaped somewhat like
           a star?"
       "Well, like some sort of stars, ma'am."—"So we
           thought!
       And any voice? Not yet? Try hard, next time,
       If you can't hear a voice; we think you may:
280   At least, the Pennsylvanian 'mediums' did."
       Oh, next time comes the voice! "Just as we hoped!"
       Are not the hopers proud now, pleased, profuse
       Of the natural acknowledgment?

                                        Of course!
       So, off we push, illy-oh-yo, trim the boat,
285   On we sweep with a cataract ahead,
       We're midway to the Horse-shoe: stop, who can,
       The dance of bubbles gay about our prow!
       Experiences become worth waiting for,
       Spirits now speak up, tell their inmost mind,
290   And compliment the "medium" properly,
       Concern themselves about his Sunday coat,
       See rings on his hand with pleasure. Ask yourself
       How you'd receive a course of treats like these!
       Why, take the quietest hack and stall him up,
295   Cram him with corn a month, then out with him
       Among his mates on a bright April morn,
       With the turf to tread; see if you find or no
       A caper in him, if he bucks or bolts!
       Much more a youth whose fancies sprout as rank
300   As toadstool-clump from melon-bed. 'Tis soon,
       "Sirrah, you spirit, come, go, fetch and carry,

275. than came raps!] than the raps! (*MS*); quick the raps! (*MS*, canc.).
276. While] Then (*MS*).
280. 'mediums'] mediums (*MS*).
281. we hoped] they hoped (*MS*).
282. Are] Is (*MS*, canc.).   *hopers*] top fool (*MS*, canc.).   *pleased, profuse*] pleased
and profuse (*MS*, canc.).
283. Of the] O' the (*1875–88*).
286. the Horse-shoe: the waterfall on the Canadian side of Niagara Falls.
289. now] that (*MS*, canc.).
293. treats] things (*MS*, canc.).
296. his mates on a bright] the females on an (*MS*, canc.).
299. more a youth] more in a youth (*MS*); more a man (*MS*, canc.).
300.] As a toadstool clump on a melon-bed. 'Tis soon (*MS*).

   Read, write, rap, rub-a-dub, and hang yourself!"
   I'm spared all further trouble; all's arranged;
   Your circle does my business; I may rave
305 Like an epileptic dervish in the books,
   Foam, fling myself flat, rend my clothes to shreds;
   No matter: lovers, friends and countrymen
   Will lay down spiritual laws, read wrong things right
   By the rule of reverse. If Francis Verulam
310 Styles himself Bacon, spells the name beside
   With a *y* and a *k*, says he drew breath in York,
   Gave up the ghost in Wales when Cromwell reigned,
   (As, sir, we somewhat fear he was apt to say,
   Before I found the useful book that knows)
315 Why, what harm's done? The circle smiles apace,
   "It was not Bacon, after all, do you see!
   We understand; the trick's but natural:
   Such spirits' individuality
   Is hard to put in evidence: they incline
320 To gibe and jeer, these undeveloped sorts.
   You see, their world's much like a jail broke loose,
   While this of ours remains shut, bolted, barred,

302. and hang yourself!] and then be hanged! (*MS*, canc.).

304. may] might (*MS*, canc.).

305. Like an epileptic] Like epileptic (*MS*, canc.).

307. lovers, friends and countrymen: a jumble of quotations from *Henry V*: 'And calls them brothers, friends, and countrymen' (IV [Chorus] 34) and *Julius Caesar*: 'Friends, Romans, countrymen, lend me your ears!' (III ii 73).

308.] Lay down the spiritual laws, read wrong things right (*MS*).

309–10. If Francis . . . Bacon: Francis Bacon became Lord Verulam, but it could never be proper to call him 'Francis Verulam': 'Francis, Lord Verulam' would be correct. Despite his claim to later enlightenment, Sludge remains ignorant of English titles of nobility. See ll. 694–5n.

310. Styles] Calls (*MS*, canc.).

310–11. spells . . . a k: presumably meaning 'Francys Bakon'.

311–12. says he . . . reigned: both, of course, obvious errors.

311. says he drew breath] and he was born (*MS*, canc.).

312.] And died in Wales when Oliver Cromwell reigned (*MS*, canc.).

315. smiles apace] smiles, that's all (*MS*, canc.).

317. but natural:] a common one— (*MS*, canc.).

318. Such] These (*MS*).

321–3. Cp. EBB.'s defence of the 'phenomena' of spiritualism in a letter to Thomas Westwood of 2 Feb. 1854: 'if you are in a dungeon and a friend knocks through the outer wall, spelling out by knocks the words you comprehend—you don't think the worse of the friend standing in the sun who remembers you' (*Letters of EBB* ii 158).

322. shut, bolted, barred,] barred, bolted fast, (*MS*, canc.).

With a single window to it. Sludge, our friend,
Serves as this window, whether thin or thick,
325   Or stained or stainless; he's the medium-pane
Through which, to see us and be seen, they peep:
They crowd each other, hustle for a chance,
Tread on their neighbour's kibes, play tricks enough!
Does Bacon, tired of waiting, swerve aside?
330   Up in his place jumps Barnum—'I'm your man,
I'll answer you for Bacon!' Try once more!"

Or else it's—"What's a 'medium'? He's a means,
Good, bad, indifferent, still the only means
Spirits can speak by; he may misconceive,
335   Stutter and stammer,—he's their Sludge and drudge,
Take him or leave him; they must hold their peace,
Or else, put up with having knowledge strained
To half-expression through his ignorance.

324.] Serves as this window,—whether thin or thick (*MS*); Serves as its pane of glass, whether thin or thick (*MS*, canc., which has 'or', canc., above 'whether').
326.] Through which they peep to see us and be seen: (*MS*, canc.). B has also indicated the final version of the line by writing '2' over the words 'they peep' and an arrow indicating the position to which this expression is to be moved.
328. kibes: a 'kibe' is literally 'A chapped or ulcerated chilblain, esp. one on the heel' (*OED*), but here *OED* sense b is involved: 'fig. in phrases, as: to gall or tread on (one's) kibes, to press upon closely so as to irritate or annoy, to hurt one's feelings'. Cp. *Hamlet* V i 139–41: 'the age is grown so pick'd that the toe of the peasant comes so near the heel of the courtier, he galls his kibe.'
329. swerve aside?] duck his head— (*MS*).
330. Barnum: Phineas Taylor Barnum (1810–1891) was an American showman, sometimes called 'the Prince of humbugs', who ran a number of enterprises (including two visits to England to show the dwarf 'General Tom Thumb'); ironically, in this context, he was neither a supporter of spiritualism (in *The Humbugs of the World* [1865] he defied any 'medium' to prove contact with the dead), nor dead in 1864.
331. Try once more!"] It's too clear!" (*MS*, canc.).
332–46. EBB. offers a similar defence of apparently garbled or incoherent messages from the 'Spirits': 'What is wanted is a persistent assembling together of intelligent & devout minds— Then we should have intenser responses, I think. The mediumship of insulated individuals seems as if it could not bear the *strain* of continuous & logical communication— The sentences break into fragments, . . . the thought does not cohere: the medium gives back short breathings from the spirit-world . . . gasps of half-articulated significances, . . . & fails in anything beyond— It's an imperfect echo repeating faintly the last syllable of a full utterance. We have not learnt how to deal with this power; & it's our business to learn . . . that's certain' (EBB. to Mary Brotherton, *c.* March 1854; Univ. of Texas MS).
335. and drudge] the same (*MS*, canc.).
337.] Or, wiselier, put up with their knowledge strained (*MS*).

Suppose, the spirit Beethoven wants to shed
340   New music he's brimfull of; why, he turns
The handle of this organ, grinds with Sludge,
And what he poured in at the mouth o' the mill
As a Thirty-third Sonata, (fancy now!)
Comes from the hopper as bran-new Sludge, nought else,
345   The Shakers' Hymn in G, with a natural F,
Or the 'Stars and Stripes' set to consecutive fourths."

Sir, where's the scrape you did not help me through,
You that are wise? And for the fools, the folk
Who came to see,—the guests, (observe that word!)
350   Pray do you find guests criticize your wine,
Your furniture, your grammar, or your nose?
Then, why your "medium?" What's the difference?
Prove your madeira red-ink and gamboge,—
Your Sludge, a cheat—then, somebody's a goose
355   For vaunting both as genuine. "Guests!" Don't fear!
They'll make a wry face, nor too much of that,
And leave you in your glory.

"No, sometimes

339. the spirit] a spirit (*MS*, canc.).   *shed*] spill (*MS*, canc.).
340. New music] The music (*MS*).
342. he] was (*MS*, which has 'he', canc.).
343.] As the Thirty third Sonata .. fancy now! .. (*MS*).   *Thirty-third Sonata*:
Beethoven did indeed publish thirty-two sonatas.
344.] Comes from the hopper—bran-new Sludge, nought else, (*MS*); Comes from
the hopper – as a treat for Sludge— (*MS*, canc.).
345. Shaker's hymn . . . natural F: 'Simple Gifts', also known as 'Lord of the Dance'.
The key signature of G major requires F sharp rather than F natural.
346. Stars and Stripes . . . consecutive fourths: one of the names for the American
national anthem. Consecutive fourths are discordant. Both this and the example
in the previous line suggest that Sludge's knowledge of music is very limited.
349–57. B. attributed his own reluctance to 'expose' Home during the Ealing
séance to similar feelings; see headnote, *Sources and influences.*
349.] That came to see,—the guests,—observe that word! (*MS*).
350. Pray] Say (*MS*, canc.).
352. Then, why] Why then, (*MS*, canc.).
353. Prove your madeira] If your madeira's (*MS*, canc.).   *gamboge*: a brightly
coloured gum-resin, used as a pigment in painting.
354. then,] why, (*MS*).
356. They'll] Just (*MS*, canc.).
357. And] Then (*MS*, which has 'And', canc.).   *"No, sometimes*] "Oh, sometimes,
(*MS*).

They doubt and say as much!" Ay, doubt they do!
And what's the consequence? "Of course they doubt"—
360   (You triumph) "that explains the hitch at once!
Doubt posed our 'medium,' puddled his pure mind;
He gave them back their rubbish: pitch chaff in,
Could flour come out o' the honest mill?" So, prompt
Applaud the faithful: cases flock in point,
365   "How, when a mocker willed a 'medium' once
Should name a spirit James whose name was George,
'James' cried the 'medium,'—'twas the test of truth!"
In short, a hit proves much, a miss proves more.
Does this convince? The better: does it fail?
370   Time for the double-shotted broadside, then—
The grand means, last resource. Look black and big!
"You style us idiots, therefore—why stop short?
Accomplices in rascality: this we hear
In our own house, from our invited guest
375   Found brave enough to outrage a poor boy
Exposed by our good faith! Have you been heard?

358. doubt they do!] that they do—(*MS*).
359. they do] you do (*MS*, canc., written over an erased identical reading). See
l. 360n.
360. You] We (*MS*, canc., written over 'You', canc.). See l. 359n.   *that*] which
(*MS*, canc.).
361. Doubt] That (*MS*, canc.).   *puddled*] puzzled (*MS*, canc.).   To 'puddle'
means 'to muddle, confuse, or corrupt (a person or his or her outlook, imagination, understanding, etc.)' (*OED*).
362. them . . . their] you . . . your (*MS*, canc.).
363. Could] Does (*MS*).
364. faithful: cases flock in point,] faithful: every case in point, (*MS*, canc.).
366. name] call (*MS*, canc.).
367–8.] *MS* lacks l. 368 and introduces a line-space at l. 369.
370. the double-shotted broadside: to 'double-shot' is defined in *OED* as 'To load
(a cannon) with a double quantity of shot'. *OED* cites an earlier example, Frederick
Marryat's *The King's Own* (1830), ch. xvi: 'The enemy, who, in his disabled state,
was not in a situation to choose whether he would be boarded or not, poured
in a double-shotted and destructive broadside.'
371. The grand] The time (*MS*, canc.). Presumably an error, carried down from
the prec. line.
373. rascality:] cheatery (*MS*); crime—and (*MS*, canc.).
375. Found] Who's (*MS*).   *a poor boy*] innocense (*MS*, canc.).
376. our] mere (*MS*, which has 'its own', canc., and 'our', canc.).   *Have you been
heard?*] May this suffice? (*MS*, canc.).

Now, then, hear us; one man's not quite worth twelve.
You see a cheat? Here's some twelve see an ass:
Excuse me if I calculate: good day!"
380   Out slinks the sceptic, all the laughs explode,
Sludge waves his hat in triumph!

                               Or—he don't.
There's something in real truth (explain who can!)
One casts a wistful eye at, like the horse
Who mopes beneath stuffed hay-racks and won't munch
385   Because he spies a corn-bag: hang that truth,
It spoils all dainties proffered in its place!
I've felt at times when, cockered, cossetted
And coddled by the aforesaid company,
Bidden enjoy their bullying,—never fear,
390   But o'er their shoulders spit at the flying man,—
I've felt a child; only, a fractious child
That, dandled soft by nurse, aunt, grandmother,
Who keep him from the kennel, sun and wind,
Good fun and wholesome mud,—enjoined be sweet,
395   And comely and superior,—eyes askance
The ragged sons of the gutter at their game,
Fain would be down with them i' the thick of the filth,

---

377. us;] me— (*MS*). Cp. *Bishop Blougram* 368–73 (pp. 303–4). B. may have known Thoreau's dictum in *Resistance to Civil Government* (1849): 'any man more right than his neighbours constitutes a majority of one already'.

378.] You see a cheat? Here's twelve that see an ass: (*MS*, canc.).

381. Or—] Well, (*MS*, canc.).

382.] There's something in real truth; explain who can, (*MS*).

383. One casts a wistful eye] That one casts wistful eyes (*MS*); One casts a wistful eye (*MS*, canc.).   *the horse*] a horse (*MS*).

384. Who] That (*MS*, canc.).   *beneath stuffed hay-racks*] 'neath a stuffed hay-rack (*MS*, canc., which has an earlier canc. reading, 'crammed' for 'stuffed').

385. a corn-bag] the corn-bag (*MS*).   *that*] the (*MS*).

387. cockered: to 'cocker' is 'To indulge or pamper (a child, favourite, etc.)' (*OED*, citing *Ecclesiasticus* xxx 9: 'Cocker thy child, and he shall make thee afraid').

389. their] your (*MS*).

390. their shoulders] your shoulder (*MS*, which has 'shoulders', canc.).   *spit at the flying man*: 'flying' means retreating, referring to the sceptic expelled in the lines above.

391. child; only,] child—but then, (*MS*).

392. dandled soft] chorussed round (*MS*, canc.).

393. kennel: 'The surface drain of a street; the gutter' (*OED*).

394. mud] dirt (*MS*, canc.).   *sweet*] clean (*MS*, canc.).

396. sons] ones (*MS*, canc.).

396–7. of the gutter . . . of the filth] o' the gutter . . . o' the filth (*1875–88*).

Making dirt-pies, laughing free, speaking plain,
And calling granny the grey old cat she is.
400   I've felt a spite, I say, at you, at them,
Huggings and humbug—gnashed my teeth to mark
A decent dog pass! It's too bad, I say,
Ruining a soul so!

                   But what's "so," what's fixed,
Where may one stop? Nowhere! The cheating's nursed
405   Out of the lying, softly and surely spun
To just your length, sir! I'd stop soon enough:
But you're for progress. "All old, nothing new?
Only the usual talking through the mouth,
Or writing by the hand? I own, I thought
410   This would develop, grow demonstrable,
Make doubt absurd, give figures we might see,
Flowers we might touch. There's no one doubts you,
    Sludge!
You dream the dreams, you see the spiritual sights,
The speeches come in your head, beyond dispute.
415   Still, for the sceptics' sake, to stop all mouths,
We want some outward manifestation!—well,
The Pennsylvanians gained such; why not Sludge?
He may improve with time!"

                        Ay, that he may!
He sees his lot: there's no avoiding fate.
420   'Tis a trifle at first. "Eh, David? Did you hear?

---

399. the grey old] the grey (*MS*).
400. you, at] you and (*MS*).
401. Huggings] Your huggings (*MS*, canc.).   *mark*] see (*MS*, canc.).
403. Ruining] Fooling (*MS*).   *But*] "So?" (*MS*, canc.).
408. the mouth] your mouth (*MS*, canc.).
409. the hand?] your hand: (*MS*, canc.).   *thought*] hoped (*MS*, canc.).
411. give] show (*MS*, canc.).
412. you, Sludge!] your faith: (*MS*, canc.).
413. you see] and see (*MS*, canc.).
414. into] in (*MS*, canc.).   *beyond dispute.*] no doubt—(*MS*, canc.).
416. Some outward manifestation! Don't despair—well (*MS*, canc.). B. altered
the line by adding 'We want' at the beginning and erasing 'Don't despair'.
417. such;] them, (*MS*, canc.).
419. fate] now (*MS*, canc.).
420. "Eh] "Sure (*MS*, canc.).

You jogged the table, your foot caused the squeak,
This time you're . . . joking, are you not, my boy?"
"N-n-no!"—and I'm done for, bought and sold
    henceforth.
The old good easy jog-trot way, the . . . eh?
425   The . . . not so very false, as falsehood goes,
The spinning out and drawing fine, you know,—
Really mere novel-writing of a sort,
Acting, or improvising, make-believe,
Surely not downright cheatery! Any how,
430   'Tis done with and my lot cast; Cheat's my name:
The fatal dash of brandy in your tea
Has settled what you'll have the souchong's smack:
The caddy gives way to the dram-bottle.

Then, it's so cruel easy! Oh, those tricks
435   That can't be tricks, those feats by sleight of hand,
Clearly no common conjuror's!—no, indeed!
A conjuror? Choose me any craft in the world
A man puts hand to; and with six months' pains,
I'll play you twenty tricks miraculous
440   To people untaught the trade: have you seen glass blown,
Pipes pierced? Why, just this biscuit that I chip,
Did you ever watch a baker toss one flat
To the oven? Try and do it! Take my word,
Practise but half as much, while limbs are lithe,

422. This time] And now (*MS*, canc.).
424. The old good easy patient partial way, (*MS*, first reading).
425. falsehood] lying (*MS*).
427. mere] 'twas (*MS*).
431–3. Once they have acquired a taste for his lies, Sludge's patrons will demand more (and more elaborate) fictions; in turn he will become addicted to lying.
432. what . . . souchong's smack] how . . . souchong smack (*1880*). 'Souchong' is 'one of the finer varieties of black tea' (*OED*); 'smack' in the sense of 'taste', whether noun or verb, occurs in several other poems, e.g. *Red Cotton Night-Cap Country* (1873) where a drink is spiced 'Till beverage obtained the fancied smack' (iv 431).
436. Clearly no common conjuror's!] So clearly not a conjuror's! (*MS*).
437. A conjuror?] Conjuror? (*MS*). *Choose me any craft*] Take any honest craft (*MS*, canc.). *in the world*] i' the world (*1875–88*).
438. hand to;] will to, (*MS*).
439. I'll] We'll (*MS*, canc.). *you twenty tricks miraculous*] a dozen tricks extravagant (*MS*, with 'impossible' canc.).
440. people] hands (*MS*).
441. biscuit] cracker (*MS*, canc.). *chip*: cp. *Youth and Art* l. 18n. (p. 703).
444. while limbs are lithe] with pliant limbs (*MS*; 'with limbs like these', canc.).

445   To turn, shove, tilt a table, crack your joints,
       Manage your feet, dispose your hands aright,
       Work wires that twitch the curtains, play the glove
       At end of your slipper,—then put out the lights
       And . . . there, there, all you want you'll get, I hope!
450   I found it slip, easy as an old shoe.

       Now, lights on table again! I've done my part,
       You take my place while I give thanks and rest.
       "Well, Judge Humgruffin, what's your verdict, sir?
       You, hardest head in the United States,—
455   Did you detect a cheat here? Wait! Let's see!
       Just an experiment first, for candour's sake!
       I'll try and cheat you, Judge! The table tilts:
       Is it I that move it? Write! I'll press your hand:
       Cry when I push, or guide your pencil, Judge!"
460   Sludge still triumphant! "That a rap, indeed?
       That, the real writing? Very like a whale!
       Then, if, sir, you—a most distinguished man,
       And, were the Judge not here, I'd say, . . no matter!
       Well, sir, if you fail, you can't take us in,—
465   There's little fear that Sludge will!"

                                   Won't he, ma'am?

447. gloves hands (MS, canc.).

448. of your slipper] o' your slipper (*1875–88*).

449. you'll] you've (*MS*, canc.; MS reads 'you'll got', presumably because B. forgot to amend the verb in line with the new reading).

452. take my place] may succeed (*MS*, canc.).

453. Well] Now, (*MS*, canc.). *Judge Humgruffin*: probably based on Judge John Worth Edmonds (1799–1874), who was Judge of the first New York Circuit and later of the New York Supreme Court: in 1853 he published *Spiritualism*, in which he declared his belief in the reality of spiritualist manifestations. EBB. calls Edmonds 'one of the most distinguished judges of the United States', and cites his 'mediumship' as evidence of the reality of the phenomenon of spiritualism in a letter of 1–2 Apr. 1853 (*EBB to Arabella* i 552). *your*] the (*MS*, canc.).

454. hardest] the best (*MS*, canc.).

459. Judge] Sir (*MS*, which has 'Judge', canc.).

460. That a] A (*MS*, canc.).

461. That, the] The (*MS*, canc.). *Very like a whale! Hamlet* III ii 372, from a passage in which Hamlet makes fun of Polonius's gullibility.

462. Then,] And (*MS*, canc.).

464. fail, you can't] fail thus to (*MS*, canc.).

465. that Sludge] a Sludge (*MS*, which has 'that Sludge', canc.). *Won't he, ma'am?* Sludge addresses a female member of his audience at the imaginary séance.

But what if our distinguished host, like Sludge,
Bade God bear witness that he played no trick,
While you believed that what produced the raps
Was just a certain child who died, you know,
470 And whose last breath you thought your lips had felt?
Eh? That's a capital point, ma'am: Sludge begins
At your entreaty with your dearest dead,
The little voice set lisping once again,
The tiny hand made feel for yours once more,
475 The poor lost image brought back, plain as dreams,
Which image, if a word had chanced recall,
The customary cloud would cross your eyes,
Your heart return the old tick, pay its pang!
A right mood for investigation, this!
480 One's at one's ease with Saul and Jonathan,
Pompey and Cæsar: but one's own lost child . . .
I wonder, when you heard the first clod drop
From the spadeful at the grave-side, felt you free
To investigate who twitched your funeral scarf
485 Or brushed your flounces? Then, it came of course,
You should be stunned and stupid; then, (how else?)

468. While] And (*MS*).
469. who died, you know] that died last year (*MS*, canc.).
471–81. People who believe the medium has put them in touch with a dead child are much less likely to investigate his claims than those who are told they are hearing the voices of famous biblical or historical characters. B. thought that Home used this tactic of exploiting people's feelings of loss, especially in relation to children: see headnote, *Sources and influences*. In a letter to John Kenyon of 16 May [1853], EBB. spoke of meeting 'a cultivated woman with truthful, tearful eyes, whose sister is a medium, and whose mother believes herself to be in daily communion with her eldest daughter, dead years ago' (*Letters of EBB.* ii 117).
470. And whose last] Whose latest (*MS*, canc.).
473. lisping once again] stammering once more (*MS*, canc.).
474. once more] again (*MS*, canc.).
476.] Which, if a careless word had chanced recall, (*MS*).
477.] The usual cloud would cross your eyes, I think, (*MS*); The usual cloud would cross your brow, you know, (*MS*, canc.).
478.] Your heart return the old tick, give the pang! (*MS*); And your heart sound the old tick, one pang more! (*MS*, canc.).
481. own lost] little (*MS*, canc.).
483. felt] were (*MS*). *grave-side, felt you*] grave, did you feel (*1880*).
484. scarf] cloak (*MS*).
485. flounces] hat-band (*MS*). Clearly B. altered the figure from male to female.
486. You should be] That you were (*MS*, canc.).

Your breath stopped with your blood, your brain struck
    work.
But now, such causes fail of such effects,
All's changed,—the little voice begins afresh,
490   Yet you, calm, consequent, can test and try
And touch the truth. "Tests? Didn't the creature tell
Its nurse's name, and say it lived six years,
And rode a rocking-horse? Enough of tests!
Sludge never could learn that!"

                                      He could not, eh?
495   You compliment him. "Could not?" Speak for yourself!
I'd like to know the man I ever saw
Once,—never mind where, how, why, when,—once saw,
Of whom I do not keep some matter in mind
He'd swear I "could not" know, sagacious soul!
500   What? Do you live in this world's blow of blacks,
Palaver, gossipry, a single hour
Nor find one smut has settled on your nose,
Of a smut's worth, no more, no less?—one fact
Out of the drift of facts, whereby you learn
505   What some one was, somewhere, somewhen, somewhy?
You don't tell folk—"See what has stuck to me!
Judge Humgruffin, our most distinguished man,
Your uncle was a tailor, and your wife
Thought to have married Miggs, missed him, hit
    you!"—

487. *struck work*: to 'strike work' means 'to go on strike': here, metaphorically.
488. *such causes*] these causes (*MS*, canc.).
489. *afresh,*] again (*MS*, canc.).
490. *Yet*] And (*MS*)   *can test and try*] have tested, tried (*MS*, canc.).
491. *touch*] touched (*MS*, canc.).
493. *rode*] had (*MS*, canc.).
498. *in mind*] treasured (*1880*).
499. *soul*] sir! (*MS*, which has 'friend', canc.).
500. *blow of blacks*: air in which 'blacks' (small particles of soot) are blowing about.
501. *Palaver*: 'Unnecessary, profuse, or idle talk; chatter' (*OED*).
502. *one*] some (*MS*, canc.).   *your*] my (*MS*, canc.).
503. *less?—one*] less, one (*MS*, which has 'some' for 'one', canc.).
504. *you*] I (*MS*, canc.).
505. The last half of this line was extensively redrafted in MS.
506. *You*] I (*MS*, canc.).   *folk*] folks (*MS*).
509. *Miggs*: a Miss Miggs appears in Dickens's *Barnaby Rudge* (1841).

510   Do you, sir, though you see him twice a-week?
      "No," you reply, "what use retailing it?
      Why should I?" But, you see, one day you *should*,
      Because one day there's much use,—when this fact
      Brings you the Judge upon both gouty knees
515   Before the supernatural; proves that Sludge
      Knows, as you say, a thing he "could not" know:
      Will not Sludge thenceforth keep an outstretched face,
      The way the wind drives?

                              "Could not!" Look you now,
      I'll tell you a story! There's a whiskered chap,
520   A foreigner, that teaches music here
      And gets his bread,—knowing no better way:
      He says, the fellow who informed of him
      And made him fly his country and fall West,
      Was a hunchback cobbler, sat, stitched soles and sang,
525   In some outlandish place, the city Rome,
      In a cellar by their Broadway, all day long;
      Never asked questions, stopped to listen or look,
      Nor lifted nose from lapstone; let the world
      Roll round his three-legged stool, and news run in
530   The ears he hardly seemed to keep pricked up.
      Well, that man went on Sundays, touched his pay,
      And took his praise from government, you see;

---

510. Do] Would (*MS*, canc.).

511. No] Now (*MS*, canc.).   *it*] this (*MS*).

512. I] you (*MS*, canc.).

514. both gouty knees] his gouty knees (*MS*, which has 'bended' for 'gouty', canc.).

516. as you say] sure enough (*MS*, canc.).

516^517.] And once begin the traffic, never fear (*MS*, canc.). This is the first deletion of an entire line in the *MS*.

517. Will not Sludge] But Sludge will (*MS*, canc.).   *thenceforth*] henceforth (*MS*).

518. drives?] blows (*MS*, canc.).   *now*] sir (*MS*, canc.).

518–43. you now . . . not Sludge!": with this 'detective' figure, cp. *How It Strikes*
(p. 435).

519. a story! There's] something: there's (*MS*, canc.).

524. cobbler, sat, stitched] cobbler that stitched (*MS*).

526. by their Broadway] by the highway (*MS*, canc.). The parochial nature of the
comparison with Broadway would have been much more apparent in 1864.

527. or look] once (*MS*, canc.).

528. lapstone: 'a stone that shoemakers lay in their laps to beat their leather upon'
(*OED*).

531. touched his pay: 'To take in the hand, take, receive, draw (money)' (*OED*).

For something like two dollars every week,
He'd engage tell you some one little thing
535   Of some one man, which led to many more,
(Because one truth leads right to the world's end,)
And make you that man's master—when he dined
And on what dish, where walked to keep his health
And to what street. His trade was, throwing thus
540   His sense out, like an anteater's long tongue,
Soft, innocent, warm, moist, impassible,
And when 't was crusted o'er with creatures—slick,
Their juice enriched his palate. "Could not Sludge!"

I'll go yet a step further, and maintain,
545   Once the imposture plunged its proper depth
In the rotten of your natures, all of you,—
(If one's not mad nor drunk, and hardly then)
It's impossible to cheat—that's, be found out!
Go tell your brotherhood this first slip of mine,
550   All to-day's tale, how you detected Sludge,
Behaved unpleasantly, till he was fain confess,
And so has come to grief! You'll find, I think,
Why Sludge still snaps his fingers in your face.
There now, you've told them! What's their prompt
    reply?
555   "Sir, did that youth confess he had cheated me,

534.] He'd engage answer questions—some one thing (*MS*).

535.] Of some one man; leading to some few more, (*MS*, which has 'very many' for 'some few', canc.).

537. And make you that man's master] And so become his master (*MS*).   *When*] where (*MS*).

538. where] when (*MS*, canc.)

541. moist,] and (*MS*, canc.).   *impassible*: 'Incapable of feeling or emotion; impassive, insensible, unimpressible' (*OED*).

545. imposture plunged] foundation sunk (*MS*).

546. In the] I' the (*1875–88*).   *rotten*] weakness (*MS*).

547. drunk, and hardly then)] drunk—nor hardly then—(*MS*, canc.).

550. tale] story (*MS*, canc.).

551. unpleasantly] unfriendly (MS, canc.; conj. reading).   *till*] and (*MS*, canc.).

554. There] They (*MS*, canc.).   *you've*] you (*MS*, canc.).   *their*] the (*MS*, canc.). It is difficult to determine the sequence of these alterations, so we record them separately.

555–73. With this defence of Sludge on the grounds of his ' "medium"-nature', cp. EBB.'s reaction to reports of Home's trickery in a letter to Anna Jameson of Jan. 1856: 'Since I spoke to you a little of the medium now at Florence, I should tell you that his moral character has failed lately, & that there has been a tremendous

I'd disbelieve him. He may cheat at times;
That's in the 'medium'-nature, thus they're made,
Vain and vindictive, cowards, prone to scratch.
And so all cats are; still, a cat's the beast
560   You coax the strange electric sparks from out,
By rubbing back its fur; not so a dog,
Nor lion, nor lamb: 'tis the cat's nature, sir!
Why not the dog's? Ask God, who made them beasts!
D' ye think the sound, the nicely-balanced man
565   (Like me"—aside)—"like you yourself,"—(aloud)
"—He's stuff to make a 'medium?' Bless your soul,
'Tis these hysteric, hybrid half-and-halfs,
Equivocal, worthless vermin yield the fire!
We must take such as we find them, 'ware their tricks,
570   Wanting their service. Sir, Sludge took in you—
How, I can't say, not being there to watch:
He was tried, was tempted by your easiness,—
He did not take in me!"

---

explosion in Florence about him, everybody quarrelling with everybody. Powers
who believed in him entirely, writes to me that he suspects him of partial trickery—but as this opinion is plainly an *après coup* . . . I mean the consequence of
irritated feeling upon other grounds, *subsequent* to the holding of seánces, . . .
I do not give much weight to it—Other persons equally vexed with Hume as
a man, consider his medium-ship as real as possible. He is said to be doing the
most extraordinary things just now . . . more wonderful than ever—The failure
of moral character seems to refer to some intrigue . . . but I have'nt had it specifically
described to me. Young Rymer, they say, had quarrelled with him in consequence & had returned home to his father. Perhaps I ought'nt to write of this,
I know so little—However it is,—the faculty of the medium being a physical
peculiarity (according to all the theories) it need surprise nobody that he has proved
himself incapable of resisting a temptation of the senses—My impression of him
always was that he was weak & vain .. commonplace to the most ordinary level.
Robert is loud in triumph of course. Still, he admits that in the evidence *against*,
which has reached us, there's an evident mixture of personal feeling' (Berg Collection
MS).
556.] I'd disbelieve him: true, he cheats at times— (*MS*).
557. *thus*] so (*MS*).
559.] Why, so all cats are,—still a cat's the beast (*MS*).
561. *its*] his (*MS, canc.*).
562. *cat's*] beast's (*MS, canc.*).
563. *the dog's*] theirs too (*MS, canc.*).   *beasts!*] all. (*MS, canc.*).
569. *We must take*] We take (*1888*).
571. *watch:*] see— (*MS, canc.*). B. was evidently bothered by the near-rhyme of
'say . . . see'; he initially obliterated 'say', changed his mind, restored 'say', and
altered 'see' instead.

Thank you for Sludge!
I'm to be grateful to such patrons, eh,
575 When what you hear's my best word? 'Tis a challenge;
"Snap at all strangers, you half-tamed prairie-dog,
So you cower duly at your keeper's nod!
Cat, show what claws were made for, muffling them
Only to me! Cheat others if you can,
580 Me, if you dare!" And, my wise sir, I dared—
Did cheat you first, made you cheat others next,
And had the help of your vaunted manliness
To bully the incredulous. You used me?
Have not I used you, taken full revenge,
585 Persuaded folk they knew not their own name,
And straight they'd own the error! Who was the fool
When, to an awe-struck, wide-eyed, open-mouthed
Circle of sages, Sludge would introduce
Milton composing baby-rhymes, and Locke
590 Reasoning in gibberish, Homer writing Greek
In noughts and crosses, Asaph setting psalms
To crotchet and quaver? I've made a spirit squeak
In sham voice for a minute, then outbroke
Bold in my own, defying the imbeciles—

575. 'Tis] 'Twas (*MS*, canc.).
576. you] not *1868–88.   prairie-dog*] wild brute (*MS*), with 'beast' for 'brute', canc.
B. must have heard the term 'prairie-dog' without realizing that it refers not to
an American wild dog but to a harmless burrowing rodent.
577. nod] foot (*MS*, canc.); beck (*1888*).
578. Cat, show what] Show what those (*MS*).
580. dared] could (*MS*).
582. of your] o' your (*1875–88*).
583.] To bully the doubters. You made use of me? (*MS*, canc.).
584. taken] had my (*MS*, canc.).
585. name] names (*MS*).
586–96. Who was . . . undisguised: in this list of Sludge's scornful self-exposures,
Milton of course is the poet, Locke the philosopher (B. owned a copy of his
Essay of Humane Understanding, 1695: *Collections* A1468), Homer the Greek epic
poet, Asaph King David's principal musician in *1 Chronicles*.
586. they'd own] they owned (*MS*, canc.).
589. baby-rhymes] 'baby-verse' (*MS*, canc.).
591–2. Asaph . . . quaver? i.e. committing the anachronism of attributing a knowledge of modern musical notation to a composer of archaic times. Cp. ll. 345–6n.
   Asaph] The MS suggests that B. started to write 'David' and then changed his
mind, possibly having remembered that Sludge had already used this name.
594. the imbeciles] the set of fools (*MS*); such a set of fools (*MS*, canc.).

595 Have copied some ghost's pothooks, half a page,
    Then ended with my own scrawl undisguised.
    "All right! The ghost was merely using Sludge,
    Suiting itself from his imperfect stock!"
    Don't talk of gratitude to me! For what?
600 For being treated as a showman's ape,
    Encouraged to be wicked and make sport,
    Fret or sulk, grin or whimper, any mood
    So long as the ape be in it and no man—
    Because a nut pays every mood alike.
605 Curse your superior, superintending sort,
    Who, since you hate smoke, send up boys that climb
    To cure your chimney, bid a "medium" lie
    To sweep you truth down! Curse your women too,
    Your insolent wives and daughters, that fire up
610 Or faint away if a male hand squeeze theirs,
    Yet, to encourage Sludge, may play with Sludge
    As only a "medium," only the kind of thing
    They must humour, fondle . . . oh, to misconceive
    Were too preposterous! But I've paid them out!
615 They've had their wish—called for the naked truth,
    And in she tripped, sat down and bade them stare:
    They had to blush a little and forgive!
    "The fact is, children talk so; in next world
    All our conventions are reversed,—perhaps
620 Made light of: something like old prints, my dear!

595. pothooks: 'A curved or hooked stroke made with the pen, esp. as a component of an unfamiliar or unintelligible script or when learning to write; (also) a crooked character, a scrawl' (*OED*).
598. his] an (*MS*).
603. be] was (*MS*, canc.).
604. pays] paid (*MS*, canc.).
605. sort] souls (*MS*).
606. you] they (*MS*). *that climb*] like me (*MS*, canc.).
608. sweep you truth down! Curse] find their truth out: curse (*MS*).
611. play with Sludge] fondle him (*MS*, canc.).
612. only the] that mere (*MS*); just that (*MS*, canc.).
613.] They humoured, fondled . . . oh, to misconceive (*MS*, canc.); To be man never? oh, to misconceive (*MS*, canc.). There is further canc. drafting at the beginning of the line, which might be 'You must flirt with'.
614. Were too preposterous!] —That were too foolish! (*MS*).
620–28. The judge's print resembles a number of Renaissance paintings; see, e.g., Giorgione's *Le Concert Champêtre* (*c.*1510).
620. prints, my dear!] pictures, this— (*MS*, canc.).

The Judge has one, he brought from Italy,
A metropolis in the background,—o'er a bridge,
A team of trotting roadsters,—cheerful groups
Of wayside travellers, peasants at their work
625 And, full in front, quite unconcerned, why not?
Three nymphs conversing with a cavalier,
And never a rag among them: 'fine,' folk cry—
And heavenly manners seem not much unlike!
Let Sludge go on; we'll fancy it's in print!"
630 If such as came for wool, sir, went home shorn,
Where is the wrong I did them? 'Twas their choice;
They tried the adventure, ran the risk, tossed up
And lost, as some one's sure to do in games;
They fancied I was made to lose,—smoked glass
635 Useful to spy the sun through, spare their eyes:
And had I proved a red-hot iron plate
They thought to pierce, and, for their pains, grew blind,
Whose were the fault but theirs? While, as things go,
Their loss amounts to gain, the more's the shame!
640 They've had their peep into the spirit-world,
And all this world may know it! They've fed fat
Their self-conceit which else had starved: what chance
Save this, of cackling o'er a golden egg
And compassing distinction from the flock,
645 Friends of a feather? Well, they paid for it,

622. *metropolis*] city (*MS*, canc.).
623. *roadsters,*—] horses— (*MS*, canc.).
625. *quite*] all (*MS*).
627.] B. tried 'And not a rag among them' and 'And not a rag upon them' at
the beginning of the line.   *them: 'fine,' folk*] them—"fine," folks (*MS*).
628. *seem*] are (*MS*).   And heavenly manner may be unlike! (*MS*, canc.).
629.] not in *MS*, which has a line-space between ll. 628 and 630.
630.] If some, that came for wool, went home thus shorn, (*MS*, canc.). The proverbial expression 'to go out for wool and come home shorn' is of Spanish origin;
it occurs in Smollett's transl. of *Don Quixote* (I vii), which W. S. Landor presented to Pen Browning in July 1863 (*Collections* A604).
634. *I*] Sludge (*MS*).
635. *Useful to*] Of use to (*MS*).
636. *I*] he (*MS*).
637. *thought*] hoped (*MS*, which has 'thought', canc.).   *grew*] grown (*MS*, canc.).
642. *Their*] The (*MS*).
642–3. *starved: what chance / Save this*] starved—what way / Like this (*MS*).
643. *a golden*] their golden (*MS*).
645. *Friends*] The friends (*MS*, canc.).

And not prodigiously; the price o' the play,
Not counting certain pleasant interludes,
Was scarce a vulgar play's worth. When you buy
The actor's talent, do you dare propose
650　For his soul beside? Whereas, my soul you buy!
Sludge acts Macbeth, obliged to be Macbeth,
Or you will not hear his first word! Just go through
That slight formality, swear himself's the Thane,
And thenceforth he may strut and fret his hour,
655　Spout, spawl, or spin his target, no one cares!
Why hadn't I leave to play tricks, Sludge as Sludge?
Enough of it all! I've wiped out scores with you—
Vented your fustian, let myself be streaked
Like a tom-fool with your ochre and carmine,
660　Worn patchwork your respectable fingers sewed
To metamorphose somebody,—yes, I've earned
My wages, swallowed down my bread of shame,

648. *worth. When*] worth,— where (*MS*, canc.).

649. *do you*] never (*MS*, canc.).

652. *you will*] you'll (*1868–88*).

653. *That*] The (*MS*). *himself's*] he's (*MS*, canc.). The revision reduces 'formality' from four syllables to three. *Thane*: traditional Scottish aristocratic title, 'ranking with the son of an earl' (*OED*). Macbeth is successively Thane of Glamis and Thane of Cawdor.

654. *strut and fret his hour*: adapting *Macbeth* V v 24–5: 'Life's but a walking shadow, a poor player / That struts and frets his hour upon the stage'.

655. *Spout*: 'To engage in declamation or recitation; to make a speech or speeches, esp. at great length or without much matter' (*OED*). *spawl*: 'To spit copiously or coarsely; to expectorate' (*OED*). In context, drawing on the transitive sense, 'To utter in a coarse manner'. *spin his target*: a 'target' is a shield; there seems to be no precedent for the whole phrase, which in context must mean, 'twirl his shield around', i.e. perform a meaningless, showy action.

656.] not in *MS*, which has a line-space after l. 655.

658. *fustian*: 'Inflated, turgid, or inappropriately lofty language [. . .] bombast, rant; in early use also jargon, made-up language, gibberish' (*OED*).

659. *tom-fool*: 'One who enacts the part of a fool in the drama . . . a buffoon' (*OED*).
　ochre: 'Any of various natural earthy materials or clays which are rich in iron oxides and vary in colour from light yellow to deep orange-red or brown; a pigment made from such a material'. *your ochre*] ochre (*MS*, canc.). The revision reduces 'ochre' from two syllables to one. *carmine*: 'A beautiful red or crimson pigment obtained from cochineal' (*OED*).

660.] And worn the patchwork your clean fingers sewed (*MS*). *patchwork*: the 'motley' or multi-coloured clothing of the licensed fool.

662. *bread of shame*: an undeserved gift that brings no enjoyment; the expression is of Jewish rabbinical origin. *wages, swallowed*] pay and swallowed (*MS*).

And shake the crumbs off—where but in your face?

As for religion—why, I served it, sir!
665 I'll stick to that! With my *phenomena*
I laid the atheist sprawling on his back,
And propped Saint Paul up, or, at least, Swedenborg!
In fact, it's just the proper way to baulk
These troublesome fellows—liars, one and all,
670 Are not these sceptics? Well, to baffle them,
No use in being squeamish: lie yourself!
Erect your buttress just as wide o' the line,
Your side, as they've built up the wall on theirs;
Where both meet, midway in a point, is truth,
675 High overhead: so, take your room, pile bricks,
Lie! Oh, there's titillation in all shame!
What snow may lose in white, it gains in rose:
Miss Stokes turns—Rahab,—nor a bad exchange!
Glory be on her, for the good she wrought,
680 Breeding belief anew 'neath ribs of death,

664–93. Cp. Home's description of the effect of one of his Ealing séances on T. A. Trollope: 'When at length the light did beam upon his soul, and the chords of his spirit vibrated in unison with the celestial harmonies that ushered in the birth of faith through the shadows of his old unbelief, the result was too much for his stoicism, and the tears of holy joy coursed down his manly cheeks . . . It was an impressive scene, and an occasion of deep interest. There are many such in the life of a spirit medium' (letter from Home to the *Hartford Times*, rpt. in the *Yorkshire Spiritual Telegraph* for Oct. 1855; cited in Podmore [headnote, *Sources and influences*], vii 229).
665.] A capital point! Doing these pretty tricks (*MS*). This is a rare example of the complete substitution of one line for another between *MS* and *1864*.
667. *And propped Saint Paul up*] I propped Saint Paul up (*MS*, which has 'helped Saint Paul' canc.); Propped up Saint Paul, (*1868–88*). *Swedenborg*: Emanuel Swedenborg (1688–1772) was a Swedish philosopher, scientist, theologian and visionary, whose work was extensively studied by the Brownings, and esp. by EBB., during the 1850s: see headnote to *Evelyn Hope* (p. 274).
668. *proper way*] only way (*MS*). *baulk*] stop (*MS*, canc.).
673. *they've built*] they run (*MS*). *wall*] works (*MS*, canc.).
675.] High o'er our heads: so, take your room and build— (*MS*).
676. *all shame!*] the shame,— (*MS*).
677. *What snow*] The snow (*MS*, canc.).
678. *Rahab*: a prostitute in *Joshua* ii–vi who sheltered two spies of the Israelites in Jericho, in return for safety for herself and her family.
679–83. *Glory be . . . the altar!* Sludge compares the fictitious 'Miss Stokes' to Rahab; like the biblical figure, she has compromised her purity, but in the process succeeded in imparting something of the 'live coal' of true belief to those who were spiritually dead before.
679.] Blessings be on her, for the good she did, (*MS*, canc.).

Brow-beating now the unabashed before,
Ridding us of their whole life's gathered straws
By a live coal from the altar! Why, of old,
Great men spent years and years in writing books
685   To prove we've souls, and hardly proved it then:
Miss Stokes with her live coal, for you and me!
Surely, to this good issue, all was fair—
Not only fondling Sludge, but, even suppose
He let escape some spice of knavery,—well,
690   In wisely being blind to it! Don't you praise
Nelson for setting spy-glass to blind eye
And saying . . what was it—that he could not see
The signal he was bothered? Ay, indeed!

I'll go beyond: there's a real love of a lie,
695   Liars find ready-made for lies they make,
As hand for glove, or tongue for sugar-plum.
At best, 'tis never pure and full belief;
Those furthest in the quagmire,—don't suppose
They strayed there with no warning, got no chance

681.] Bringing the shameless sceptic unabashed (*MS, canc.*).
682. gathered] piled-up (*MS*).   Disposing of a whole life's hoarded straws (*MS,* canc.*).
684. years and years] all their lives (*MS, canc.*).
685. hardly proved it then:] hardly did it, then! (*MS*); did not do it, then (*MS,* canc.*).
686. live coal: cp. *Isaiah* vi 6–7: 'Then flew one of the seraphims unto me, having a live coal in his hand, which he had taken with the tongs from off the altar: And he laid it upon my mouth, and said, Lo, this hath touched thy lips; and thine iniquity is taken away, and thy sin purged.'
689. knavery,—well,] cheatery, (*MS*).
690–93. Don't you . . . bothered? During the Battle of Copenhagen (1801), an order to discontinue the engagement was flown as a signal; Nelson responded: ' "Leave off action? Now, damn me if I do! You know, Foley," turning to the captain, "I have only one eye,—I have a right to be blind sometimes:"—and then putting the glass to his blind eye, in that mood of mind which sports with bitterness, he exclaimed, "I really do not see the signal!" Presently he exclaimed, "Damn the signal! Keep mine for closer battle flying!" ' (Southey, *Life of Nelson* [1813], ch. vii). Cp. *Here's to Nelson's Memory* (II 248).
691. eye] brow (*MS*, which has 'eye', canc.).
692. it—that he] it? . . . he (*MS, canc.*). The revision changes the stress from 'whát was ít' to 'what wás it'.
693. bothered] beaten (*MS*); bothered with (*1888*).
694–5. Cp. Bacon's famous discussion, in 'Of Truth', of the 'natural, though corrupt, love of the lie itself', which meant that 'A mixture of a lie doth ever add pleasure' (*Essays,* 1625). See ll. 309–10n.

700   Of a filth-speck in their face, which they clenched teeth,
       Bent brow against! Be sure they had their doubts,
       And fears, and fairest challenges to try
       The floor o' the seeming solid sand! But no!
       Their faith was pledged, acquaintance too apprised,
705   All but the last step ventured, kerchiefs waved,
       And Sludge called "pet:" 'twas easier marching on
       To the promised land; join those who, Thursday next
       Meant to meet Shakespeare; better follow Sludge—
       Prudent, oh sure—on the alert, how else?
710   But making for the mid-bog, all the same!
       To hear your outcries, one would think I caught
       Miss Stokes by the scuff o' the neck, and pitched her
           flat,
       Foolish-face-foremost! Hear these simpletons,
       That's all I beg, before my work's begun,
715   Before I've touched them with my finger-tip!
       Thus they await me (do but listen, now!
       It's reasoning, this is,—I can't imitate
       The baby voice, though) "In so many tales
       Must be some truth, truth though a pin-point big,
720   Yet, some: a single man's deceived, perhaps—
       Hardly, a thousand: to suppose one cheat
       Can gull all these, were more miraculous far

700. *face, which they clenched*] face, they clenched the (*MS*, canc.).
701.] And beat the brow on: oh, they had their doubts, (*MS*, canc.).
704. *acquaintance too*] acquaintances (*MS*).
706. *"pet:"*] "dear"— (*MS*, canc.).
707.] To the crowning-party—for next Thursday night (*MS*, canc.).
708.] Join company with Shakespeare,—follow Sludge (*MS*); When Shakespeare was expected: follow Sludge (*MS*, canc.).
710. *making*] make we (*MS*)
713. *simpletons*] people talk (*MS*).
714. *work's begun*] work begins (*MS*).
715. *I've touched*] I touch (*MS*).
718–23. "In so many . . . miracle": similar to one of the arguments for the authenticity of the gospel narratives developed by Paley in *Evidences of Christianity* (a book in B.'s library: see headnote to *Caliban*, p. 620); he suggests that the number of witnesses to Jesus' miracles and resurrection, and the hardships they were willing to undergo, constitute a proof of the reliability of their testimony.
720. *Yet*] Still (*MS*). *a single . . . perhaps*—] a single man may be deceived, (*MS*, canc.).
722. *Can gull all*] Gulls all of (*MS*). The line originally read 'Gulls all these, that were more miraculous far'.

Than aught we should confess a miracle"—
And so on. Then the Judge sums up—(it's rare)—
725   Bids you respect the authorities that leap
To the judgment-seat at once,—why, don't you note
The limpid nature, the unblemished life,
The spotless honour, indisputable sense
Of the first upstart with his story? What—
730   Outrage a boy on whom you ne'er till now
Set eyes, because he finds raps trouble him?

Fools, these are: ay, and how of their opposites
Who never did, at bottom of their hearts,
Believe for a moment?—Men emasculate,
735   Blank of belief, who played, as eunuchs use,
With superstition safely,—cold of blood,
Who saw what made for them in the mystery,
Took their occasion, and supported Sludge
—As proselytes? No, thank you, far too shrewd!
740   —But promisers of fair play, encouragers
Of the claimant; who in candour needs must hoist
Sludge up on Mars' Hill, get speech out of Sludge
To carry off, criticize, and cant about!
Didn't Athens treat Saint Paul so?—at any rate,

723. we should confess] that constitutes (*MS*); what would confess (*MS*, canc.). The canc. line is ungrammatical, suggesting either a copying error (in view of B.'s later return to a similar form of words), or a change of mind while drafting.
724. sums up] begins (*MS*).
725. Bids you respect] He bids you mark (*MS*).
726. why, don't you] why don't you (*1868, 1888*).   *note*] see (*MS*, canc.).
731. finds] says (*MS*, canc.).
732.] But fools, these: ay, but how of their opposites (*MS*, canc.).
734–5. emasculate, / Blank of belief] emasculate / Of all belief (*MS*).
735. played] play (*MS*, canc.).
737. Who saw] Saw prompt (*MS*).   *in the mystery*] i' the mystery (*1880, 1888*).
738. occasion] B. started to write 'advantage', but changed his mind.
741. Of the claimant] O' the claimant (*1875–88*).
742. Mars' Hill: in *Acts* xvii 22 St Paul 'stood in the midst of Mars' hill' to address the Athenians; see next notes, and see also the note to the epigraph of *Cleon* (p. 565).   *get speech*] get a speech (*MS*, canc.).   *Sludge*] him (*MS*).
744–5. Cp. *Acts* xvii, 19–21, where the philosophers of Athens say to Paul: 'May we know what this new doctrine, whereof thou speakest, is? For thou bringest certain strange things to our ears. (For all the Athenians and strangers which were there spent their time in nothing else, but either to tell, or to hear some new thing.)'
744. at any rate] and meantime (*MS*, canc.).

745 It's "a new thing," philosophy fumbles at.
     Then there's the other picker out of pearl
     From dung heaps,—ay, your literary man,
     Who draws on his kid gloves to deal with Sludge
     Daintily and discreetly,—shakes a dust
750 Of the doctrine, flavours thence, he well knows how,
     The narrative or the novel,—half-believes,
     All for the book's sake, and the public's stare,
     And the cash that's God's sole solid in this world!
     Look at him! Try to be too bold, too gross
755 For the master! Not you! He's the man for muck;
     Shovel it forth, full-splash, he'll smooth your brown
     Into artistic richness, never fear!
     Find him the crude stuff; when you recognize
     Your lie again, you'll doff your hat to it,
760 Dressed out for company! "For company,"
     I say, since there's the relish of success:
     Let all pay due respect, call the lie truth,
     Save the soft silent smirking gentleman
     Who ushered in the stranger: you must sigh
765 "How melancholy, he, the only one,
     Fails to perceive the bearing of the truth
     Himself gave birth to!"—There's the triumph's smack!

745^746.] a new paragraph was indicated here as usual in MS (see headnote, *Text and publication*) but there is no visible line-space in *1864*, where l. 745 ends the page.

746.] Then there's the picker of the other pearl (*MS*, canc.).

747. literary man] poet, novelist (*MS*, canc.).

748.] Your literary man who deals in Sludge (*MS*, canc.).   *draws on*] takes off (*MS*).   *with*] in (*MS*).

749. dust] spice (*MS*, canc.).

750. Of the doctrine] O' the doctrine (*1875–88*).   *thence*] just (*MS*).

751. narrative or the] narrative, the (*MS*).

753. God's sole solid] God's real solid (*MS*); all God's solid (*MS*, canc.).

756. your brown] the brown (*MS*).

759. again, you'll] once, you'll (*MS*, canc.). The canc. reading makes little sense in context, and leaves the line unmetrical: probably B. began to transcribe 'once more' from his draft, changed his mind, erased 'once' and wrote 'again' over the erasure.

761.] Observe,—for there's the relish of success (*MS*, canc.).   *I say,*] Observe, (*MS*).

762. Let] When (*MS*).   *due respect*] due respects (*MS*); their respects (*MS*, canc.).

763. Save the soft] Save him, the (*MS*).

764. Who] That (*MS*).

767. gave] gives (*MS*).   *smack*: 'relish' (as in l. 761); cp. l. 432n.

That man would choose to see the whole world roll
I' the slime o' the slough, so he might touch the tip
770   Of his brush with what I call the best of browns—
Tint ghost-tales, spirit-stories, past the power
Of the outworn umber and bistre!

Yet I think
There's a more hateful form of foolery—
The social sage's, Solomon of saloons
775   And philosophic diner-out, the fribble
Who wants a doctrine for a chopping-block
To try the edge of his faculty upon,
Prove how much common sense he'll hack and hew
In the critical minute 'twixt the soup and fish!
780   These were my patrons: these, and the like of them
Who, rising in my soul now, sicken it,—
These I have injured! Gratitude to these?
The gratitude, forsooth, of a prostitute
To the greenhorn and the bully—friends of hers,
785   From the wag that wants the queer jokes for his club,
To the snuff-box-decorator, honest man,
Who just was at his wits' end where to find

---

768. That man] The man (*MS*, with 'That' canc.); i.e. the 'literary man' (l. 747).
roll] wallow (*MS*).
769. so] if (*MS*, canc.).
771. spirit-stories] phantom-stories (*MS*); Spirit-stories (*MS*, canc.).
772. umber and bistre: brown pigments.
772. Yet I think] B. wrote 'Yet one' and then changed his mind.
774. sage's] sage, the (*MS*).
775. And] The (MS). *fribble*: 'A trifling, frivolous person' (*OED*). In *Ring* vi 87,
Caponsacchi refers to his reputation as 'fribble . . . coxcomb, fool'.
776. Who wants a] That wants the (*MS*).
778. he'll hack and hew] is hewn and hacked (*MS*); is hacked and hewn (*MS*, canc.);
may be hacked and hewn (*MS*, canc.: first reading).
779. In the] I' the (*1875–88*).
780. these . . . them] them . . . these (MS, canc.).
781. sicken it] sicken me (*MS*).
783–90. For the parallel between Sludge and a prostitute, cp. ll. 678n., 1330–33n.
784. greenhorn: a novice; (here, the prostitute's young, inexperienced client); though
English in origin, by B.'s day a recognized Americanism. *bully*: 'the "gallant"
or protector of a prostitute' (*OED* 4a).
785. From] And (*MS*, canc.). *for*] at (*MS*, canc.).
786. To] And (*MS*. canc.). *snuff-box-decorator*: collecting snuff boxes exemplifies
devotion to a frivolous pastime in *Easter-Day* 155–60 (III 106).

So genial a Pasiphae! All and each
Pay, compliment, protect from the police,
790 And how she hates them for their pains, like me!
So much for my remorse at thanklessness
Toward a deserving public!

But, for God?
Ay, that's a question! Well, sir, since you press—
(How you do teaze the whole thing out of me!
795 I don't mean you, you know, when I say "them:"
Hate you, indeed! But that Miss Stokes, that Judge!
Enough, enough—with sugar: thank you, sir!)
Now for it, then! Will you believe me, though?
You've heard what I confess; I don't unsay
800 A single word: I cheated when I could,
Rapped with my toe-joints, set sham hands at work,
Wrote down names weak in sympathetic ink,
Rubbed odic lights with ends of phosphor-match,
And all the rest; believe that: believe this,
805 By the same token, though it seem to set
The crooked straight again, unsay the said,

---

788. So genial a Pasiphae!] A model for a Pasiphae! (*MS*, canc.). In Greek myth, the wife of King Minos of Crete lusted after a white bull; famous re-tellings of the story include Virgil, *Eclogues* vi 45–60 and Ovid, *Ars Amatoria* i 295–326. *All and each*] All these pay, (*MS*).

789. Pay, compliment,] And compliment, (*MS*, with 'Their compliments' canc.).

789^790.] Allow her privilege, try pet names on her— (*MS*, canc.).

790.] And how she hates them all, as I hate you! (*MS*).

791–2. at thanklessness / Toward] at having sinned / Against (*MS*).

792. deserving] respectable (*MS*).

794. teaze] get (*MS*, canc.).

796. that Judge] you know (*MS*, canc.).

797. with sugar: thank you, sir! Horsefall's offer of a drink indicates that Sludge is beginning to gain his confidence again, not least because of Sludge's tendency to 'sweeten' his criticism of his other patrons with praise of Horsefall.

798. though?] Sir? (*MS*).

800. A single word] A word of it (*MS*, canc.).

802. sympathetic ink: in writing indistinct enough to bear a number of different interpretations; with this use of 'sympathetic' cp. l. 79n. *down names*] the names (*MS*).

803. Rubbed odic lights] Made odic spots (*MS*); Drew odic streaks (*MS*, canc.). 'Odic lights' were alleged to derive from the 'od-force', a form of mystical energy associated with mesmerism in the period: see *Mesmerism* 57–65n. (III 481–2).

805–6. set / The crooked straight again: cp. *Isaiah* xl 4: 'Every valley shall be exalted, and every mountain and hill shall be made low; and the crooked shall be made straight, and the rough places plain'.

Stick up what I've thrown down; I can't help that:
It's truth! I somehow vomit truth to-day.
This trade of mine—I don't know, can't be sure
810   But there was something in it, tricks and all!
Really, I want to light up my own mind.
They were tricks,—true, but what I mean to add
Is also true. First,—don't it strike you, sir?
Go back to the beginning,—the first fact
815   We're taught is, there's a world beside this world,
With spirits, not mankind, for tenantry;
That much within that world once sojourned here,
That all upon this world will travel there,
And therefore that we, bodily here below,
820   Must have exactly such an interest
In learning what may be the ways o' the world
Above us, as the disembodied folk
Have (by all analogic likelihood)
In watching how things go in the old world
825   With us, their sons, successors, and what not.
Oh, yes, with added powers probably,
Fit for the novel state,—old loves grown pure,
Old interests understood aright,—they watch!
Eyes to see, ears to hear, and hands to help,
830   Proportionate to advancement: they're ahead,
That's all—do what we do, but noblier done—
Use plate, whereas we eat our meals off delf,
(To use a figure.)

Concede that, and I ask
Next, what may be the mode of intercourse

810. *there was*] there's been (*MS*, canc.).
811. *Really, I want*] I really want (*MS*, canc.).
812. *mean*] want (*MS*, canc.).
813. *sir?*—] now?— (*MS*).
817. *That*] And (*MS*, canc.).
818.] And all on this our world will soon pass there, (*MS*, canc.).   *travel*] visit (*1868–88*).
822. *the disembodied*] the same embodied (*MS*); the above embodied (*MS*, canc.).
826. *Oh, yes*] Watching (*MS*).
829. *hear, and hands*] hear, hands (*MS*, canc.).
830. *to advancement*] to the advancement (*MS*).
831. *but noblier*] are noble (*MS*, canc.).
832. *plate . . . delf:* china and everyday crockery (more usually 'delft').
833. *Concede that, and I*] Concede me that, I (*MS*).

835   Between us men here, and those once-men there?
       First comes the Bible's speech; then, history
       With the supernatural element,—you know—
       All that we sucked in with our mothers' milk,
       Grew up with, got inside of us at last,
840   Till it's found bone of bone and flesh of flesh.
       See now, we start with the miraculous,
       And know it used to be, at all events:
       What's the first step we take, and can't but take,
       In arguing from the known to the obscure?
845   Why this: "What was before, may be to-day.
       Since Samuel's ghost appeared to Saul,—of course
       My brother's spirit may appear to me."
       Go tell your teacher that! What's his reply?
       What brings a shade of doubt for the first time
850   O'er his brow late so luminous with faith?
       "Such things have been," says he, "and there's no doubt
       Such things may be: but I advise mistrust
       Of eyes, ears, stomach, and, more than all, your brain,
       Unless it be of your great-grandmother,
855   Whenever they propose a ghost to you!"
       The end is, there's a composition struck;
       'Tis settled, we've some way of intercourse
       Just as in Saul's time; only, different:
       How, when and where, precisely,—find it out!
860   I want to know, then, what's so natural
       As that a person born into this world
       And seized on by such teaching, should begin

---

835. us] the (*MS*).   *those*] the (*MS*).
836. Bible's speech;] Bible in— (*MS*).
839. Grew] Grow (MS, canc.).   *got*] get (*MS*, canc.).   *of us*] in us (*MS*, canc.).
840. it's found] it's our (*MS*); it is our (*MS*, canc.).   *bone of bone and flesh of flesh*:
Sludge proves his point by quoting Adam's words on first seeing Eve: 'This is
now bone of my bones, and flesh of my flesh' (*Genesis* ii 23).
842. And know it] Knowing what (*MS*, canc.).
846. Samuel's ghost appeared to Saul: see 1 *Samuel* xxviii 3–20.
850. his] the (*MS*).
851.] interpolated in *MS*. Speech marks were deleted from the beginning of the
next line in *MS* to accommodate this change.
853.] Of your eyes, ears, stomach, and most of all, your brain, (*MS*, with 'brain
most of all' canc.); Of eyes, ears, stomach,—more than all, of brain, (*1880*).
856. composition: in the sense of 'compromise' (*OED* 24).
859. How] What (*MS*).
862. such] this (*MS*).

With firm expectancy and a frank look-out
For his own allotment, his especial share
865 In the secret,—his particular ghost, in fine?
I mean, a person born to look that way,
Since natures differ: take the painter-sort,
One man lives fifty years in ignorance
Whether grass be green or red,—"No kind of eye
870 For colour," say you; while another picks
And puts away even pebbles, when a child,
Because of bluish spots and pinky veins—
"Give him forthwith a paint-box!" Just the same
Was I born . . . "medium," you won't let me say,—
875 Well, seer of the supernatural
Everywhen, everyhow and everywhere,—
Will that do?

            I and all such boys of course
Started with the same stock of bible-truth;
Only,—what in the rest you style their sense,
880 Instinct, blind reasoning but imperative,
This, betimes, taught them the old world had one law
And ours another: "New world, new laws," cried they:
"None but old laws, seen everywhere at work,"
Cried I, and by their help explained my life
885 The Jews' way, still a working way to me.

---

863. expectancy] assurance (*MS*, canc.).
864. allotment,] endowment (*MS*, canc.).
865. In the secret] I' the secret (*1875–88*).
867. Since] For (*MS*, canc.).   *take*] there's (*MS*).
869. grass] the grass (*MS*).   *red*] written over what may be the beginning of 'yellow' or 'grey' in *MS*.
871. even] the (*MS*, canc.).   *when*] while (*MS*).
872. spots] eyes (*MS*, canc.).
876.] Every where, every how and every when (*MS*, canc.).
877. all such boys of course] all the other boys (*MS*).
878. Started] The MS suggests that B. started to write 'Began', then changed his mind.
879.] Ghost-stories,—only, what you style their sense, (*MS*, canc.).
881. This, betimes, taught them] Taught them, betimes, (*MS*).
882.] And this of ours another: "new laws" cried they (*MS*).
883. "None but old laws,] –"None but the old, (*MS*).
884. my life] the world (*MS*).
885. Jews' way: as in the Old Testament, in which God intervenes directly in human affairs.

Ghosts made the noises, fairies waved the lights,
Or Santaclaus slid down on New Year's Eve
And stuffed with cakes the stocking at my bed,
Changed the worn shoes, rubbed clean the fingered slate
890 Of the sum that came to grief the day before.

This could not last long: soon enough I found
Who had worked wonders thus, and to what end:
But did I find all easy, like my mates?
Henceforth no supernatural any more?
895 Not a whit: what projects the billiard-balls?
"A cue," you answer: "Yes, a cue," said I;
"But what hand, off the cushion, moved the cue?
What unseen agency, outside the world,
Prompted its puppets to do this and that,
900 Put cakes and shoes and slates into their mind,
These mothers and aunts, nay even schoolmasters?"
Thus high I sprang, and there have settled since.
Just so I reason, in sober earnest still,
About the greater godsends, what you call
905 The serious gains and losses of my life.
What do I know or care about your world

887. Or Santaclaus slid] Old Santaclaus came (*MS*); Old Santa Claus came (*1888*). The spelling 'Santaclaus' is common in early nineteenth-century American texts. Santa Claus is of American origin; we do not know where B. got the idea that he came on New Year's Eve, since the association with Christmas Eve was well established, and the only alternative is 6 Dec., the feast day of St Nicholas (see e.g. Washington Irving's *History of New York* [*1809*], ch. ix). On the other hand the custom of gift-giving in Britain, as in other European countries, had long been associated with New Year rather than Christmas, so B. may have conflated the two traditions.

890. Of the sum] O' the sum (*1875–88*).

892. worked wonders thus] done all these things (*MS*, canc.).

895–7. Cp. B.'s letter to F. J. Furnivall of 11 Oct. 1884, in which he discusses his attitude to Darwin: 'But go back and back, as you please, *at* the back, as Mr. Sludge is made to insist, you find (*my* faith is constant) creative intelligence, acting as matter but not resulting from it. Once set the balls rolling, and ball may hit ball and send any number in any direction over the table; but I believe in the cue pushed by the hand' (*Trumpeter* 34). See also headnote to *Caliban*, p. 621.

896. you answer:] they answered— (*MS*, canc.).

897.] "But what hand, off the table's edge, moved that? (*MS*, canc.).

898. the] this (*MS*, canc.).

899. its] the (*MS*).

901.] not *MS*, which has a new paragraph instead; no paragraph in *1864*.

902. Thus] So (*MS*, canc.).   *have*] I've (*MS*, canc.).

905. my] this (*MS*, canc.).

Which either is or seems to be? This snap
Of my fingers, sir! My care is for myself;
Myself am whole and sole reality
910 Inside a raree-show and a market-mob
Gathered about it: that's the use of things.
'Tis easy saying they serve vast purposes,
Advantage their grand selves: be it true or false,
Each thing may have two uses. What's a star?
915 A world, or a world's sun: doesn't it serve
As taper also, time-piece, weather-glass,
And almanac? Are stars not set for signs
When we should shear our sheep, sow corn, prune
trees?
The Bible says so.

Well, I add one use
920 To all the acknowledged uses, and declare
If I spy Charles's Wain at twelve to-night,
It warns me, "Go, nor lose another day,
And have your hair cut, Sludge!" You laugh: and why?
Were such a sign too hard for God to give?
925 No: but Sludge seems too little for such grace:
Thank you, sir! So you think, so does not Sludge!

907. Which] That (*MS*).
908. Of my fingers] O' my fingers (*1875–88*).
909.] Myself, the whole and sole reality. (*MS*). See *Bishop Blougram* 58n. (p. 289).
910. Inside] I see (*MS*, canc.).   *raree-show*: originally a small portable peep-show;
later extended to mean to any kind of spectacular display.   *a market-mob*] the
market-mob (*MS*). Sludge compares himself to a showman entertaining crowds
at a market.
911.] Gathered about it to advantage me— (*MS*, with 'just to profit me' canc.).
913.] Live for their own grand selves: that's true or false— (*MS*).
914–15. What's . . . world's sun: cp. *My Star* (III 386).
914. Each thing] Still, a thing (*MS*).
915.] A world, or a world's sun,—but none the less (*MS*).
916. As taper] Our taper (*MS*); 'Tis man's clock (*MS*, canc.).
918. shear our sheep] shear sheep (*MS*).   *corn, prune*] corn, or prune (*MS*).
919. The Bible says so: in *Genesis* i 14 God creates 'lights in the firmament of the heaven'
and declares: 'let them be for signs, and for seasons, and for days, and for years.'
919. I] I'll (*MS*).
920. all the] these (*MS*).
921. spy] see (*MS*, canc.).   *Charles's Wain*: now more usually the Plough, in the
constellation Ursa Major; a 'wain' is a wagon.   *twelve to-night*] nine to night (*MS*).
923. and why?] but why? (*MS*).
924. Were] Is (*MS*).
925.] Sludge is found too little for the grace: (*MS*, canc.).

When you and good men gape at Providence,
Go into history and bid us mark
Not merely powder-plots prevented, crowns
930   Kept on kings' heads by miracle enough,
But private mercies—oh, you've told me, sir,
Of such interpositions! How yourself
Once, missing on a memorable day
Your handkerchief—just setting out, you know,—
935   You must return to fetch it, lost the train,
And saved your precious self from what befell
The thirty-three whom Providence forgot.
You tell, and ask me what I think of this?
Well, sir, I think then, since you needs must know,
940   What matter had you and Boston city to boot
Sailed skyward, like burnt onion-peelings? Much
To you, no doubt: for me—undoubtedly
The cutting of my hair concerns me more,
Because, however sad the truth may seem,
945   Sludge is of all-importance to himself.
You set apart that day in every year
For special thanksgiving, were a heathen else:
Well, I who cannot boast the like escape,
Suppose I said "I don't thank Providence

929. powder-plots: conspiracies against government, like the 'gunpowder plot' of 1605 led by Guy Fawkes against James I, which was uncovered on the eve of its execution.

931–7. B. had had a similar experience in 1861. On arrival at the station to catch a train from Paris to Boulogne, he was informed that he would not be able to take his son's pony on board, but after a long dispute prevailed: 'Had they persisted, I should have been forced to go by the 8. p.m. train, arriving at 12: and, as you see by the papers, at 11 there was the dreadful accident & loss of life on the line at Amiens' (30 Sept. 1861, *George Barrett* 274–5).

932. such] plain (*MS*); such (*MS*, canc.).   *How yourself*] You, yourself (*MS*).

933. Once, missing] How, missing, (*MS*).

935. lost] lose (*MS*, canc.).

937. forgot.] o'erlooked— (*MS*, which has 'forgot', canc.).

938. this?] that? (*MS*).

939. you needs must know] you want the truth (*MS*, canc.).

940. Boston city] all New York (*MS*).

941. like burnt] Sir, like (*MS*, canc.).

945. all-importance] most importance (*MS*, canc.).

948. cannot boast] never had (*MS*).

949. said] say (*MS*, which has 'said', canc.).   *don't*] can't (*MS*).

950 For my part, owing it no gratitude?"
  "Nay, but you owe as much"—you'd tutor me,
  "You, every man alive, for blessings gained
  In every hour of the day, could you but know!
  I saw my crowning mercy: all have such,
955 Could they but see!" Well, sir, why don't they see?
  "Because they won't look,—or perhaps, they can't."
  Then, sir, suppose I can, and will, and do
  Look, microscopically as is right,
  Into each hour with its infinitude
960 Of influences at work to profit Sludge?
  For that's the case: I've sharpened up my sight
  To spy a providence in the fire's going out,
  The kettle's boiling, the dime's sticking fast
  Despite the hole i' the pocket. Call such facts
965 Fancies, too petty a work for Providence,
  And those same thanks which you exact from me,
  Prove too prodigious payment: thanks for what,
  If nothing guards and guides us little men?
  No, no, sir! You must put away your pride,
970 Resolve to let Sludge into partnership!
  I live by signs and omens: looked at the roof
  Where the pigeons settle—"If the further bird,
  The white, takes wing first, I'll confess when thrashed;
  Not, if the blue does"—so I said to myself
975 Last week, lest you should take me by surprise:
  Off flapped the white,—and I'm confessing, sir!
  Perhaps 'tis Providence's whim and way

---

951. owe as much"—] do owe much" (*MS*).
953. of the day] o' the day (*1875–88*).
955. sir,] then, (*MS*).
957. Then] But (*MS*).
958. is right,] you bid, (*MS*, canc.).
961. For that's] That's just (*MS*). *sharpened*] trained (*MS*, canc.); B. changed this word to 'sharpened' before completing the line. *sight*] eyes (*MS*).
962. spy] see (*MS*, canc.).
964. such facts] these facts, (*MS*).
965.] Fancies—too petty, in short, for Providence, (*MS*).
967. Prove] Were (*MS*).
968.] not MS, which inserts a line-space instead.
971. looked] look (*1880*).
972. further bird] farther bird (*1880*).
973. when thrashed;] the trick— (*MS*); the tricks— (*MS*, canc.).
975.] When you grew angry, took me by surprise— (*MS*).

With only me, in the world: how can you tell?
"Because unlikely!" Was it likelier, now,
980   That this our one out of all worlds beside,
The what-d'you-call-'em millions, should be just
Precisely chosen to make Adam for,
And the rest o' the tale? Yet the tale's true, you know:
Such undeserving clod was graced so once;
985   Why not graced likewise undeserving Sludge?
Are we merit-mongers, flaunt we filthy rags?
All you can bring against my privilege
Is, that another way was taken with you,—
Which I don't question. It's pure grace, my luck.
990   I'm broken to the way of nods and winks,
And need no formal summoning. You've a help;
Holloa his name or whistle, clap your hands,
Stamp with your foot or pull the bell: all's one,
He understands you want him, here he comes.
995   Just so, I come at the knocking: you, sir, wait
The tongue of the bell, nor stir before you catch
Reason's clear tingle, nature's clapper brisk,
Or that traditional peal was wont to cheer

978. in the world] i' the world (*1875–88*).

982. chosen] that chosen (*MS*).

984. Clod was graced so once;] clod, if graced so, once, (*MS*, canc.).

985–9. Sludge uses Calvinist theological terms here: salvation comes by God's grace, not man's merit. See l. 986n.

985. graced] grace (*MS*).

986.] not *MS*, which inserts a line-space instead between pages.   *Merit-mongers*: people 'who [seek] to merit salvation or eternal reward by good works' (*OED*).
    flaunt we filthy rags: cp. *Isaiah* lxiv 6: 'But we are all as an unclean thing, and all our righteousnesses are as filthy rags'.

988. was] is (*MS*).

990. I'm broken] I've got used (*MS*).

991. need] want (*MS*, canc.).

992. Holloa] Hallo (*MS*); Call out (*MS*, canc.).

993. pull] ring (*MS*, canc.).

994. comes.] stands: (*MS*).

995–1000. Sludge contrasts his own readiness to come at the first 'knocking' of his master with Horsefall's unwillingness to respond until the appeal is backed by reason, nature, or the 'traditional peal' (l. 998) of organized religion.

995. knocking] whistle (*MS*).

996. of the bell] o' the bell (*1875–88*).   *catch*] hear (*MS*, canc.).

997. clapper] summons (*MS*).

998. that] the (*MS*, canc.).   *peal*] voice (*MS*, canc.).

Your mother's face turned heavenward: short of these
1000   There's no authentic intimation, eh?
Well, when you hear, you'll answer them, start up
And stride into the presence, top of toe,
And there find Sludge beforehand, Sludge that sprung
At noise o' the knuckle on the partition-wall!
1005   I think myself the more religious man.
Religion's all or nothing; it's no mere smile
Of contentment, sigh of aspiration, sir—
No quality of the finelier-tempered clay
Like its whiteness or its lightness; rather, stuff
1010   Of the very stuff, life of life, self of self.
I tell you, men won't notice; when they do,
They'll understand. I notice nothing else,
I'm eyes, ears, mouth of me, one gaze and gape,
Nothing eludes me, everything's a hint,
1015   Handle and help. It's all absurd, and yet
There's something in it all, I know: how much?
No answer! What does that prove? Man's still man,
Still meant for a poor blundering piece of work
When all's done; but, if somewhat's done, like this,
1020   Or not done, is the case the same? Suppose
I blunder in my guess at the true sense

999. *Short*] of (*MS*, canc.).
1001. *them*] then (*MS*, canc.).
1003. *sprung*] knew (*MS*); sprang (*1888*).
1004. *on the partition wall!* Cp. ll. 321–3n.   *At*] The (*MS*).
1005.] not *MS*, which inserts instead a line-space between ll. 1004 and 1006.
1006. *no mere smile*] no smile (*MS*).
1007. *Of contentment*] Of content, or (*MS*, canc.); O' contentment, or (*1875–88*).
    sir] merely (*MS*).
1008. *of the*] o' the (*1875–88*).
1009.] Like whiteness or lightness; Sir, it's very stuff (*MS*, which has the *1864* reading, canc., except 'Sir, it's' for 'rather,').
1010. *Of the very stuff*, life of our life itself (*MS*); O' the very stuff, life of life, and self of self. (*1875–88*).
1010^*1011.*] Everywhere, whether recognized or no. (*MS*, canc.).
1011. *won't*] don't (*MS*, canc.).   *do*] will (*MS*, canc.).
1012. *I notice nothing else*] for I do: nothing else (*MS*, canc.).
1013.] Eyes, and ears, and mouth, one gaze and gape, (*MS*, canc.).
1014. *eludes*] escapes (*MS*, canc.).
1017. *No answer*] No telling (*MS*, canc.).
1018. *a poor*] just a (*MS*, which has the *1864* reading, canc.).
1021. *guess at the true sense*] guesses at the sense (*MS*).

Of the knuckle-summons, nine times out of ten,—
What if the tenth guess happen to be right?
If the tenth shovel-load of powdered quartz
1025 Yield me the nugget? I gather, crush, sift all,
Pass o'er the failure, pounce on the success.
To give you a notion, now—(let who wins, laugh!)
When first I see a man, what do I first?
Why, count the letters which make up his name,
1030 And as their number chances, even or odd,
Arrive at my conclusion, trim my course:
Hiram H. Horsefall is your honoured name,
And haven't I found a patron, sir, in you?
"Shall I cheat this stranger?" I take apple-pips,
1035 Stick one in either *canthus* of my eye,
And if the left drops first—(your left, sir, stuck)
I'm warned, I let the trick alone this time.
You, sir, who smile, superior to such trash,
You judge of character by other rules:
1040 Don't your rules sometimes fail you? Pray, what rule
Have you judged Sludge by hitherto?

                                        Oh, be sure,
You, everybody blunders, just as I,
In simpler things than these by far! For see:
I knew two farmers,—one, a wiseacre,
1045 Who studied seasons, rummaged almanacs,
Quoted the dew-point, registered the frost,
And then declared, for outcome of his pains,

1023. happen to be right] happens to be true (*MS*, canc.).
1024–5. For another allusion to the 1849 'gold rush', see ll. 1207–10.
1025. Yield] Yields (*MS*, canc.)   *gather*] save (*MS*, canc.).
1027] not *MS*, which instead inserts a line-space between ll. 1026 and 1028.
1029. which] that (*MS*, canc.).
1032. Hiram H. Horsefall: see headnote, *Sources and influences* (iv).
1034. stranger?" I take] man?" I take two (*MS*).
1035. one] each (*MS*, canc.).   *canthus*] corner (*MS*).
1037. I'm warned, I] I lie by, (*MS*, canc.).
1041. Have you judged] Did you judge (*MS*).   *hitherto*] added in *MS*.
1043. In] The (*MS*, canc.).
1045. rummaged] searched in (*MS*).
1046. Quoted the dew-point,] Measured the rain and (*MS*).
1047. for] as (*MS*).

Next summer must be dampish: 't was a drought.
His neighbour prophesied such drought would fall,
1050　Saved hay and corn, made cent. per cent. thereby,
And proved a sage indeed: how came his lore?
Because one brindled heifer, late in March,
Stiffened her tail of evenings, and somehow
He got into his head that drought was meant!
1055　I don't expect all men can do as much:
Such kissing goes by favour. You must take
A certain turn of mind for this,—a twist
I' the flesh, as well. Be lazily alive,
Open-mouthed, like my friend the anteater,
1060　Letting all nature's loosely-guarded motes
Settle and, slick, be swallowed! Think yourself
The one i' the world, the one for whom the world
Was made, expect it tickling at your mouth!
Then will the swarm of busy buzzing flies,
1065　Clouds of coincidence, break egg-shell, thrive,
Breed, multiply, and bring you food enough.

I can't pretend to mind your smiling, sir!
Oh, what you mean is this! Such intimate way,
Close converse, frank exchange of offices,
1070　Strict sympathy of the immeasurably great
With the infinitely small, betokened here
By a course of signs and omens, raps and sparks,
How does it suit the dread traditional text

1048. *Next summer must*] That summer would (*MS*, canc.).
1049. *fall*] be (*MS*, canc.).
1050. *made cent. per cent.*: i.e. made a hundred for every hundred invested.　*cent. per cent.*] money, a mint, (*MS*, canc.).
1051. *a sage*] the sage (*MS*).　*came his lore*] came his guess (*MS*); grew his guess (*MS*, canc.).
1052. *one*] a (*MS*).　*brindled*: 'Streaked, tabby, marked with streaks' (*J.*).　*March*] Spring (*MS*).
1055.] not *MS*, which instead inserts a line-space between ll. 1054 and 1056. There is, however, no new paragraph in *1864*.
1061.] Settle and so be swallowed: think yourself (*MS*).
1064. *buzzing*] little (*MS*).
1065.] Coïncidences, break their egg-shell, thrive (*MS*, which has 'chip' for 'break', canc.).
1066.] Multiply, and prove irresistible! (*MS*); They multiply, they are irresistible (*MS*, canc., which has 'And' for 'They', also canc.).
1068. *this! Such*] this—the (*MS*).

Of the "Great and Terrible Name?" Shall the Heaven of
    Heavens
1075   Stoop to such child's-play?

                           Please sir, go with me
A moment, and I'll try to answer you.
The "*Magnum et terribile*" (is that right?)
Well, folk began with this in the early day;
And all the acts they recognized in proof
1080   Were thunders, lightnings, earthquakes, whirlwinds, dealt
Indisputably on men whose death they caused.
There, and there only, folk saw Providence
At work,—and seeing it, 'twas right enough
All heads should tremble, hands wring hands amain,
1085   And knees knock hard together at the breath
Of the Name's first letter; why, the Jews, I'm told,
Won't write it down, no, to this very hour,
Nor speak aloud: you know best if 't be so.
Each ague-fit of fear at end, they crept
1090   (Because somehow people once born must live)
Out of the sound, sight, swing and sway of the Name,
Into a corner, the dark rest of the world,
And safe space where as yet no fear had reached;

1074. Of the] O' the (*1875–88*).   *"Great and Terrible Name?"*: Psalms xcix 3.   *Heaven of Heavens*: biblical phrase (e.g. *1 Kings* viii 27); here a metonymy for God.
1077. "Magnum et terribile" (is that right?): not quite; the Latin text of the Psalm in question (number 110 in the Vulgate) has 'sanctum et terribile' for 'great and terrible'.
1078. folk] folks (*MS*).   *this*] that (*MS*).
1079. And all the acts they] The only acts men (*MS*).
1082. There, and there] Here, and here (*MS*, canc.).   *folk*] they (*MS*).
1083. seeing it,] seeing thus (*MS*).
1085. hard] fast (*MS*, canc.).
1086. Of the] O' the (*1875–88*).   *why,*] and (*MS*, canc.).
1087. hour,] day, (*MS*, canc.).
1088.] Nor speak it aloud—you know, Sir, if 'tis so. (*MS*).
1089–95. Cp. the storm in *Caliban* 284–95 (pp. 640–1).
1089. Each] Such (*MS*).   *crept*] crawled (*MS*, canc.).
1090. people once born must live] a man once born must live (*MS*); a man is born to live (*MS*, canc.).
1091. of the] o' the (*1875–88*).
1092. corner, the dark rest] corner—called the rest (*MS*, with 'say, the rest' canc.).
1093. And] The (*MS*, which has 'And', canc.).   *reached;*] come (*MS*, canc.).

'T was there they looked about them, breathed again,
1095 And felt indeed at home, as we might say.
The current of common things, the daily life,
This had their due contempt; no Name pursued
Man from the mountain-top where fires abide,
To his particular mouse-hole at its foot
1100 Where he ate, drank, digested, lived in short:
Such was man's vulgar business, far too small
To be worth thunder: "small," folk kept on, "small,"
With much complacency in those great days!
A mote of sand, you know, a blade of grass—
1105 What was so despicable as mere grass,
Except perhaps the life of the worm or fly
Which fed there? These were "small" and men were
     great.
Well, sir, the old way's altered somewhat since,
And the world wears another aspect now:
1110 Somebody turns our spyglass round, or else
Puts a new lens in it: grass, worm, fly grow big:

1094. 'T was] And (MS).   *again*] at length (MS, canc.).
1095. felt indeed at home] felt at home again (MS, canc.).
1096. of] o' (*1875–88*).   *things, the daily life*] things which make up life (MS, with 'that' canc.).
1098. the mountain-top where fires abide: Cp. *Exodus* xxiv 17: 'the glory of the LORD was like devouring fire on the top of the mount'.
1099. at] in (MS, canc.).
1101. Such was man's vulgar business] That was man's proper business (MS).   *far*] and (MS, canc.).
1102. "small," folk kept on, "small,"] men repeated "small" (MS); men said "small" (MS, canc.: leaving the line unmetrical).
1103. great days!] same days— (MS).
1105. despicable as mere grass] despicable, now, as grass (MS); despicable, too, as grass (MS, canc.).   *sir*] now (MS, canc.).
1106. of the] o' the (*1875–88*).
1107. Which] That (MS).   *These*] They (MS, canc.).
1109. wears another aspect] looks quite differently (MS, canc.).
1110–23. This apparent reversal of the principles of the Sublime is in fact antici-pated in Burke's celebrated treatise *On the Sublime and Beautiful* (1759): 'as the great extreme of dimension is sublime, so the last extreme of littleness is in some measure sublime likewise; when we attend to the infinite divisibility of matter, when we pursue animal life into these excessively small, and yet organised beings, that escape the nicest inquisition of the sense, when we push our discoveries yet downward, and consider those creatures so many degrees yet smaller, and the still diminishing scale of existence, in tracing which the imagination is lost as well as the sense, we become amazed and confounded at the wonders of minuteness' (pp. 128–9).
1111. grass, worm, fly] little things (MS).

We find great things are made of little things,
And little things go lessening till at last
Comes God behind them. Talk of mountains now?
1115   We talk of mould that heaps the mountain, mites
That throng the mould, and God that makes the mites.
The Name comes close behind a stomach-cyst,
The simplest of creations, just a sac
That's mouth, heart, legs and belly at once, yet lives
1120   And feels, and could do neither, we conclude,
If simplified still further one degree:
The small becomes the dreadful and immense!
Lightning, forsooth? No word more upon that!
A tin-foil bottle, a strip of greasy silk,
1125   With a bit of wire and knob of brass, and there's
Your dollar's-worth of lightning! But the cyst—
The life of the least of the little things?

                                            No, no!
Preachers and teachers try another tack,
Come near the truth this time: they put aside
1130   Thunder and lightning: "That's mistake," they cry,
"Thunderbolts fall for neither fright nor sport,
But do appreciable good, like tides,
Changes of the wind, and other natural facts—
'Good' meaning good to man, his body or soul.

1117. Name comes close behind] "Nomen" close behind (*MS*, with 'just behind' canc.).   *stomach-cyst*: this compound is not in *OED*; Sludge clearly intends (as he indicates in the lines that follow) to describe the simplest organism imaginable.
1119. legs] wings (*MS*, canc.).
1120. conclude] suppose (*MS*, canc.).
1122.] The Small's become the dreadful and the great! (*MS*).
1124–7. It is, Sludge suggests, possible to simulate or manufacture a 'dollar's-worth of lightning', but impossible to understand how life is transmitted to minute organisms.
1124.] A tin-foil bottle and a bit of silk, (*MS*, canc.).
1125. With a] And (*MS*, canc.).
1126. cyst] sac (*MS*, canc.).
1130. Thunder and lightning] whirlwind and earthquake (*MS*, canc.).   *mistake,*] mere stuff (*MS*, canc.).
1131. for neither] neither for (*MS*, canc.).
1132. But] They (*MS*).
1133. of the] o' the (*1875–88*).   *wind*] moon (*MS*, canc.).
1134. 'Good' meaning] And good means (*MS*).

1135   Mediate, immediate, all things minister
       To man,—that's settled: be our future text
       'We are His children!' " So, they now harangue
       About the intention, the contrivance, all
       That keeps up an incessant play of love,—
1140   See the Bridgewater book.

                                 Amen to it!
       Well, sir, I put this question: I'm a child?
       I lose no time, but take you at your word:
       How shall I act a child's part properly?
       Your sainted mother, sir,—used you to live
1145   With such a thought as this a-worrying you?
       "She has it in her power to throttle me,
       Or stab or poison: she may turn me out,
       Or lock me in,—nor stop at this, to-day,
       But cut me off to-morrow from the estate
1150   I look for"—(long may you enjoy it, sir!)
       "In brief she may unchild the child I am."
       You never had such crotchets? Nor have I!
       Who, frank confessing childship from the first,
       Cannot both fear and take my ease at once,
1155   So, don't fear,—know what might be, well enough,
       But know too, child-like, that it will not be,

1137.] "We are His children"—so they're preaching now (*MS*, which has 'and' for 'so', canc.). Cp. *1 John* iii 1, in which Christians are referred to as children of God.

1140. The Bridgewater book: *The Bridgewater Treatises on the Power Wisdom and Goodness of God as Manifested in the Creation* (1833–6) was a series of eight essays on various aspects of the natural world paid for by a bequest from Francis Henry Egerton, eighth Earl of Bridgewater; EBB. records having read some of them in a letter to Lady Margaret Cocks of November 1835 (*Correspondence* iii 152–3).

1141. Well] Then (*MS*).

1142.] added in *MS*.

1151.]—"In brief, she may unchild the child I am"? (*MS*); —"In brief, unchild the child of hers I am"? (*MS*, canc.). 'unchild' is defined as 'To deprive of the status of a child or of the qualities peculiar to childhood'; this is one of only two usages cited in *OED*.

1153. from] at (*MS*, canc.).

1154. Cannot] Could not (*MS*, canc.).

1156. will not] cannot (*MS*, canc.).

At least in my case, mine, the son and heir
Of the kingdom, as yourself proclaim my style.
But do you fancy I stop short at this?
1160 Wonder if suit and service, sons and heirs
Needs must expect, I dare pretend to find?
If, looking for signs proper to such an one,
I straight perceive them irresistible?
Concede that homage is a son's plain right,
1165 And, never mind the nods and raps and winks,
'Tis the pure obvious supernatural
Steps forward, does its duty: why, of course!
I have presentiments; my dreams come true:
I fancy a friend stands whistling all in white
1170 Blithe as a boblink, and he's dead I learn.
I take dislike to a dog my favourite long,
And sell him; he goes mad next week and snaps.
I guess that stranger will turn up to-day
I have not seen these three years; there's his knock.
1175 I wager "sixty peaches on that tree!"—
That I pick up a dollar in my walk,
That your wife's brother's cousin's name was George—
And win on all points. Oh, you wince at this?
You'd fain distinguish between gift and gift,

1157. *mine*] me, (*MS*, canc.).
1157–8. *the son and heir / Of the kingdom*: cp. *James* ii 5: 'Hearken, my beloved brethren, Hath not God chosen the poor of this world rich in faith, and heirs of the kingdom which he hath promised to them that love him?' The expression 'heir of the kingdom' is used in evangelical Christianity to refer to the faithful.
1158. *Of the*] O' the (*1875–88*)
1159–83. Sludge argues that if he is a true 'son and heir of the kingdom', then he has a right to expect 'suit and service' (l. 1160) from the supernatural realm— hence the fact that supernatural events seem to happen at his request.
1159.] not *MS*, which has a line-space instead.
1160.] And yet you wonder that what sons and heirs (*MS*).   *sons and heirs*] son and heir (*1888*).
1162. *If, looking*] That looking (*MS*); I looked (*MS*, canc.).
1163. And may not say they are irresistible? (*MS*, canc.).   *straight*] should dare (*MS*).
1164.] Concede, on the other hand, these signs my right (*MS*).
1166. *obvious supernatural*] naked Supernatural (*MS*).
1167. *forward, does its duty:*] forward to instruct me: (*MS*).
1170. *boblink*: or bobolink, American songbird, 'the happiest bird of our spring' (*OED* cit. 1840).   *dead I learn*] dead, I find (*MS*).
1171. *long,*] now, (*MS*).

1180   Washington's oracle and Sludge's itch
        O' the elbow when at whist he ought to trump?
        With Sludge it's too absurd? *Fine, draw the line*
        Somewhere, but, sir, your somewhere is not mine!

        Bless us, I'm turning poet! It's time to end.
1185   How you have drawn me out, sir! All I ask
        Is—am I heir or not heir? If I'm he,
        Then, sir, remember, that same personage
        (To judge by what we read in the newspaper)
        Requires, beside one nobleman in gold
1190   To carry up and down his coronet,
        Another servant, probably a duke,
        To hold egg-nogg in readiness: why want
        Attendance, sir, when helps in his father's house
        Abound, I'd like to know?

                                        Enough of talk!
1195   My fault is that I tell too plain a truth.
        Why, which of those who say they disbelieve,
        Your clever people, but has dreamed his dream,
        Caught his coincidence, stumbled on his fact
        He can't explain, (he'll tell you smilingly)

1180. Washington's oracle: i.e. the wisdom Sludge pronounces when visited by the spirit of George Washington.

1183^1184.] paragraph added in *MS*.

1184. I'm turning poet! Because of the accidental rhymes in ll. 1182–3 ('fine . . . line . . . mine').

1186. heir or not heir? I.e. 'of the kingdom'; see ll. 1157–8n.

1186–94. Sludge continues the metaphor by comparing himself to the heir to the throne of a (worldly) kingdom, who is able to call on the service of noblemen for menial offices.

1187. Then] Please (*MS*).

1188. in the] i' the (*1875–88*). *the newspaper*] newspapers (*MS*).

1189. nobleman] gentleman (*MS*, canc.).

1192. egg-nogg] cigars (*MS*).

1192–3. why want / Attendance: 'Why (should I) lack service of this kind?'

1193. Attendance] Service (*MS*). *helps*] servants (*MS*). *his father's house*: Jesus refers to the Temple in Jerusalem as 'my Father's house'; see *John* ii 16.

1195.] It's [sic] fault is that it's far too plain a truth. (*MS*).

1196.] Why, which one out of those who disbelieve, (*MS*, canc.).

1197. Your] The (*MS*).

1199. he'll tell] he tells (*MS*, canc.).

1200   Which he's too much of a philosopher
        To count as supernatural, indeed,
        So calls a puzzle and problem, proud of it:
        Bidding you still be on your guard, you know,
        Because one fact don't make a system stand,
1205   Nor prove this an occasional escape
        Of spirit beneath the matter: that's the way!
        Just so wild Indians picked up, piece by piece,
        The fact in California, the fine gold
        That underlay the gravel—hoarded these,
1210   But never made a system stand, nor dug!
        So wise men hold out in each hollowed palm
        A handful of experience, sparkling fact
        They can't explain; and since their rest of life
        Is all explainable, what proof in this?
1215   Whereas I take the fact, the grain of gold,
        And fling away the dirty rest of life,
        And add this grain to the grain each fool has found
        Of the million other such philosophers,—
        Till I see gold, all gold and only gold,

1200. Which] But (*MS*, which has 'Which', canc.).
1202. So] But (*MS*, canc.). *puzzle and problem,*] puzzle, a problem— (*MS*, canc.).
1205–6. an occasional escape / Of spirit: with this use of 'escape' to mean the emergence of something previously hidden into visible form, cp. *Sordello* iii 312n. (I 545).
1205. Nor prove this an] Or prove this the (*MS*); Prove possible (*MS*, canc.).
1206. Of spirit] Of the spirit (*MS*, canc.).
1207–10. See ll. 1024–5n. Sludge compares the 'philosophers' who refuse to generalize from a single fact to the 'wild Indians' who pick up pieces of gold but never think to investigate its source or dig for more.
1207. wild] poor (*MS*).
1209. gravel] granite (*MS*, canc.).
1210. nor] or (*MS*, canc.).
1211.] Such wise man holds out in his hollowed palm (*MS*).   *out*] you (*MS*, canc.).
1212. A handful] His handsel (*MS*).   *sparkling*] his sparkling (*MS*, canc.).
1213. They] He (*MS*).   *their*] his (*MS*).   *their rest of life*: i.e. the rest of their lives.
1214. proof in this?] proves the fact? (*MS*, canc.).
1215. the fact, the] his fact, his (*MS*).
1216. the] his (*MS*).
1217. this] his (*MS*, canc.).   *to the grain*] to grain (*MS*, canc.).
1218. Of the] O' the (*1875–88*).   *other such*] other (*MS*); such (*MS*, canc.). The *MS* line is unmetrical, perhaps indicating hasty redrafting.
1219. Till] Why (*MS*, canc.).

1220 Truth questionless though unexplainable,
     And the miraculous proved the commonplace!
     The other fools believed in mud, no doubt—
     Failed to know gold they saw: was that so strange?
     Are all men born to play Bach's fiddle-fugues,
1225 "Time" with the foil in carte, jump their own height,
     Cut the mutton with the broadsword, skate a five,
     Make the red hazard with the cue, clip nails
     While swimming, in five minutes row a mile,
     Pull themselves three feet up with the left arm,
1230 Do sums of fifty figures in their head,
     And so on, by the scores of instances?
     The Sludge with luck, who sees the spiritual facts,
     His fellows strive and fail to see, may rank
     With these, and share the advantage!

1221. *commonplace,*] daily thing. (*MS*, canc.).

1223. *was*] is (*MS*, canc.).

1224. *Bach's fiddle-fugues*: Sludge's homely way of referring to Bach's violin compositions; the first of a series of miscellaneous examples of physical and mental dexterity.

1224^1225.] at billiards, put a pistol ball in the black (*MS*, canc.: there is a considerable space before the beginning of this draft, suggesting that B. intended to interpolate material before 'at billiards', but abandoned the attempt). See also next note.

1225–31.] "Time" with the foil in carte, I'd like to know,
        Cut the leg of mutton with the broadsword, skate,
        Make the red hazard with the cue, do sums
        Of fifty figures in their brains, swim, row,
        Pull themselves up, over head, with the left arm,
        Trip on a tight-rope stretched across the Falls
        And so on, by the scores of instances? (*MS*, with the following canc.
readings: 'foil' after 'know', 'fence' before 'skate', 'Learn to speak French in six weeks' for 'Make the red hazard with the cue', 'do a sum' for 'do sums', and 'Cross' for 'Trip'; 'stretched' was added to the sixth line). The feat of crossing the Niagara Falls on a tightrope was achieved by the French acrobat Blondin, in 1859.

1225. *"Time" with the foil in carte*: 'carte' is 'one of the eight parries and two usual guards of the small-sword' in fencing (*OED*); to 'time' is to execute a manoeuvre (see *OED* sense 8).

1226. *Cut the mutton with the broadsword*: i.e. carve a joint of meat with a large and unwieldy implement.   *skate a five*: leave the impression of the number 5 on the ice.

1227. *Make the red hazard with the cue*: to 'hazard' in this context is to pocket the red ball in billiards.

1232. *who sees the spiritual facts*] that sees the golden facts (*MS*).

1233. *fail*] strain (*MS*).

1234. *and share*] you see (*MS*, canc.).

                                                           Ay, but share
1235   The drawback! Think it over by yourself;
        I have not heart, sir, and the fire's gone grey.
        Defect somewhere compensates for success,
        Everyone knows that! Oh, we're equals, sir!
        The big-legged fellow has a little arm
1240   And a less brain, though big legs win the race:
        Do you suppose I 'scape the common lot?
        Say, I was born with flesh so sensitive,
        Soul so alert, that, practice helping both,
        I guess what's going on outside the veil,
1245   Just as a prisoned crane feels pairing-time
        In the islands where his kind are, so must fall
        To capering by himself some shiny night,
        As if your back-yard were a plot of spice—
        Thus am I 'ware of the spirit-world: while you,
1250   Blind as a beetle that way,—for amends,
        Why, you can double fist and floor me, sir!
        Ride that hot, hardmouthed, horrid horse of yours,
        Laugh while it lightens, play with the great dog,
        Speak your mind though it vex some friend to hear,
1255   Never brag, never bluster, never blush,—
        In short, you've pluck, when I'm a coward—there!
        I know it, I can't help it,—folly or no,
        I'm paralyzed, my hand's no more a hand,
        Nor my head, a head, in danger: you can smile
1260   And change the pipe in your cheek. Your gift's not
           mine.

1236. heart] time (*MS*).   *grey*] out (*MS*).
1237. somewhere] added in *MS*.
1240. the race] a race (*MS*).
1242. Say,] Yes, (*MS*).
1243. alert, that,] alert—my (*MS*, canc.).
1244. guess] know (*MS*).
1245. pairing-time: the mating season. Cp. *Youth and Art* 33 (p. 704).
1246. so] needs (*MS*).
1249. Thus] So (*MS*).   *Of the*] O' the (*1875–88*).
1251. double fist: 'clench [your] fist' (*OED* 8a).
1254. Speak your mind] Tell the truth (*MS*, canc.).
1255. blush,—] lie,— (*MS*).
1256. when] while (*MS*).
1257. folly] fool (*MS*, canc.).
1259. smile] laugh (*MS*).
1260. cheek. Your gift's not mine.] cheek—your gift, you see. (*MS*); gift, this time.
(*MS*, canc.).

Would you swap for mine? No! but you'd add my gift
To yours: I dare say! I too sigh at times,
Wish I were stouter, could tell truth nor flinch,
Kept cool when threatened, did not mind so much
1265 Being dressed gaily, making strangers stare,
Eating nice things; when I'd amuse myself,
I shut my eyes and fancy in my brain
I'm—now the President, now, Jenny Lind,
Now, Emerson, now, the Benicia Boy—
1270 With all the civilized world a-wondering
And worshipping! I know it's folly and worse:
I feel such tricks sap, honeycomb the soul,
But I can't cure myself,—despond, despair,
And then, hey, presto, there's a turn of the wheel,
1275 Under comes uppermost, fate makes full amends;
Sludge knows and sees and hears a hundred things
You all are blind to,—I've my taste of truth,
Likewise my touch of falsehood,—vice no doubt,
But you've your vices also: I'm content.

1280 What, sir? You won't shake hands? "Because I cheat!
You've found me out in cheating!" That's enough
To make an apostle swear! Why, when I cheat,
Mean to cheat, do cheat, and am caught in the act,
Are you, or rather, am I sure of the fact?
1285 (There's verse again, but I'm inspired somehow.)
Well then, I'm not sure! I may be, perhaps,
Free as a babe from cheating: how it began,
My gift, no matter; what 'tis got to be
In the end now, that's the question: answer that!

1263. *stouter, could tell*] stout, could tell the (*MS*).
1264. *Kept*] Were (*MS*).
1265. *gaily, making strangers stare,*] fine, making strangers stare at me, (*MS*).
strangers stare at me] folks envy me (*MS*, canc.).
1266. *I'd amuse myself*] I amuse myself (*MS*).
1268. *Jenny Lind*: famous opera singer, nicknamed the 'Swedish nightingale'.
1269. *the Benicia Boy*: see headnote to *A Likeness* (p. 642).
1272.] These same tricks that emasculate the soul, (*MS*); These vile tricks that emasculate the soul (*MS*, canc., which also has 'This vile trick', canc.).
1273. *myself,—despond, despair,*] myself, all but despair, (*MS*, canc.).
1274. *of the*] o' the (*1875–88*).
1275. *Under comes*] And under's (*MS*).
1278. *Likewise my*] And just my (*MS*); And just the (*MS*, canc.).
1281. *You've found*] You found (*MS*); You caught (*MS*, canc.).
1284. *of the*] o' the (*1875–88*).

1290   Had I seen, perhaps, what hand was holding mine,
        Leading me whither, I had died of fright,
        So, I was made believe I led myself.
        If I should lay a six-inch plank from roof
        To roof, you would not cross the street, one step,
1295   Even at your mother's summons: but, being shrewd,
        If I paste paper on each side of the plank
        And swear 'tis solid pavement, why, you'll cross
        Humming a tune the while, in ignorance
        Beacon Street stretches a hundred feet below:
1300   I walked thus, took the paper-cheat for stone.
        Some impulse made me set a thing on the move
        Which, started once, ran really by itself;
        Beer flows thus, suck the siphon; toss the kite,
        It takes the wind and floats of its own force.
1305   Don't let truth's lump rot stagnant for the lack
        Of a timely helpful lie to leaven it!
        Put a chalk-egg beneath the clucking hen,
        She'll lay a real one, laudably deceived,
        Daily for weeks to come. I've told my lie,
1310   And seen truth follow, marvels none of mine;
        All was not cheating, sir, I'm positive!
        I don't know if I move your hand sometimes
        When the spontaneous writing spreads so far,
        If my knee lifts the table all that height,

1295. but] if (*MS*).
1296. If I paste] I paste first (*MS*).   paste] put (*MS*, canc.).   *each side of*] each side (*1875–88*).
1297.] And swore 'twas solid pavement, why, you'd cross (*MS*, canc.).
1298. Humming] Whistling (*MS*).
1299. Beacon Street stretches] The broadway stretches (*MS*, with 'stretched' canc.). Beacon Street is one of the principal thoroughfares of Boston.
1300. thus,] and (*MS*).
1301. Some] An (*MS*); The (*MS*, canc.).   *a thing*] the thing (*MS*).   *on the*] o' the (*1875–88*).
1303. flows] runs (*MS*, canc.).
1304. of] on (*MS*, canc.).
1305–6. Cp. *Galatians* v 9: 'A little leaven leaveneth the whole lump.'
1305. rot] lie (*MS*, canc.).
1306. a timely] the timely (*MS*).
1307. beneath] underneath (*MS*); beneath (*MS*, canc.).
1309. I've] I (*MS*).
1310. seen] saw (*MS*).
1313. so far] itself (*MS*).

1315 Why the inkstand don't fall off the desk a-tilt,
      Why the accordion plays a prettier waltz
      Than I can pick out on the piano-forte,
      Why I speak so much more than I first intend,
      Describe so many things I never saw.
1320 I tell you, sir, in one sense, I believe
      Nothing at all,—that everybody can,
      Will, and does cheat: but in another sense
      I'm ready to believe my very self—
      That every cheat's inspired, and every lie
1325 Quick with a germ of truth.

                                        You ask perhaps
      Why I should condescend to trick at all
      If I know a way without it? This is why!
      There's a strange secret sweet self-sacrifice
      In any desecration of one's soul
1330 To a worthy end,—isn't it Herodotus
      (I wish I could read Latin!) who describes
      The single gift of the land's virginity,

1315. fall] run (*MS*, canc.).
1316. the accordion plays a prettier waltz: accordions are mentioned in several
accounts of Home's séances, including the Ealing séance attended by the
Brownings: see headnote, *Sources and influences*. Cp. also the letter from 'J. G. C.'
to the editor of *The Spiritual Magazine* (Feb. 1860; 88–90): 'Mr. Home . . . said
that he held the accordion under the table by one hand only, when it played our
beautiful English tune, "Home, Sweet Home", in a most finished style' (i 89),
and 'Two Evenings with Mr. Home', *The Spiritual Magazine*, June 1860 (i 266):
'The spirit of Albert then took the accordion and played a beautiful air of unearthly
harmony'. *waltz*] tune (*MS*).
1317. can pick] pick (*MS*).
1318. first intend] intend (*MS*).
1319. never saw] never see (*MS*); do not see (*MS*, canc.).
1324. and every] every (*MS*).
1325. Quick] Is quick (*MS*). *You*] You'll (*MS*).
1326. trick] cheat (*MS*, canc.).
1327. If] Since (*MS*).
1328–37. Sludge misrepresents the Greek (not Roman) historian Herodotus'
account of ritual prostitution at Babylon (not Egypt). Herodotus is disapproving:
'The most disgraceful of the Babylonian customs is the following: every native
woman is obliged, once in her life, to sit in the temple of Venus and have intercourse with some stranger' (*Histories* i 199. transl. Henry Cary, 1848).
1330–33.] To a worthy end,—self-prostitution, say, / The single gift of one's
virginity, / Religious in the old Egyptian rite (*MS*, canc., with 'Venus's' written
over 'one's' in the second line, and 'rites', canc., in the third line.)
1332. of the] o' the (*1875–88*).

Demanded in those old Egyptian rites,
(I've but a hazy notion—help me, sir!)
1335   For one purpose in the world, one day in a life,
One hour in the day—thereafter, purity,
And a veil thrown o'er the past for evermore!
Well now, they understood a many things
Down by Nile city, or wherever it was!
1340   I've always vowed, after the minute's lie,
And the good end's gain,—truth should be mine
        henceforth.
This goes to the root of the matter, sir,—this plain
Plump fact: accept it and unlock with it
The wards of many a puzzle!

                                        Or, finally,
1345   Why should I set so fine a gloss on things?
What need I care? I cheat in self-defence,
And there's my answer to a world of cheats!
Cheat? To be sure, sir! What's the world worth else?
Who takes it as he finds, and thanks his stars?
1350   Don't it want trimming, turning, furbishing up
And polishing over? Your so-styled great men,
Do they accept one truth as truth is found,
Or try their skill at tinkering? What's your world?
Here are you born, who are, I'll say at once,

1334.] probably interpolated in MS; it is written in the margin at the top of the page.
1336. the] that (*MS*).
1337.] Forgetfulness of the past for evermore! (*MS*); And forgetfulness of the past for evermore! (*MS*, canc.).
1338–9.] interpolated in *MS*.
1341. the good end's] the end's (*1875–88*). *should*] shall (*MS*, canc.).
1342. This goes] I go (*MS*). *of the*] o' the (*1875–88*) *this*] the (*MS*).
1343. unlock with it] detect, with mine, (*MS*, canc.).
1344. The wards] The play (*MS*, canc.). Wards are 'the ridges projecting from the inside plate of a lock, serving to prevent the passage of any key the bit of which is not provided with incisions of corresponding form and size' (*OED*).
1345. gloss on things?] point on it? (*MS*).
1347. a] your (*MS*, which has 'a', canc.).
1351. And polishing] Polishing (*MS*).
1352. is found,] they found (*MS*, canc.).
1353^1354.] As you open eyes to it? I'll tell you, Sir. (*MS*, canc.; B. has drawn a line joining 1353 and 1354 in *MS*).

1355 One of the luckiest whether in head and heart,
      Body and soul, or all that helps the same.
      Well, now, look back: what faculty of yours
      Came to its full, had ample justice done
      By growing when rain fell, biding its time,
1360 Solidifying growth when earth was dead,
      Spiring up, broadening wide, in seasons due?
      Never! You shot up and frost nipped you off,
      Settled to sleep when sunshine bade you sprout;
      One faculty thwarted its fellow: at the end,
1365 All you boast is, "I had proved a topping tree
      In other climes"—yet this was the right clime
      Had you foreknown the seasons. Young, you've force
      Wasted like well-streams: old,—oh, then indeed,
      Behold a labyrinth of hydraulic pipes
1370 Through which you'd play off wondrous waterwork;
      Only, no water left to feed their play!
      Young,—you've a hope, an aim, a love; it's tossed
      And crossed and lost: you struggle on, some spark
      Shut in your heart against the puffs around,
1375 Through cold and pain; these in due time subside,
      Now then for age's triumph, the hoarded light
      You mean to loose on the altered face of things,—

1355.] Of the luckiest whether as to head and heart (*1880*); Of the luckiest kind, whether in head and heart, (*1888*).   *whether*] ones (*MS*).
1356. *or*] and (*MS*).   *the same*] them both (*1888*).
1357–67. *Well, now . . . the seasons*: cp. Hazlitt's essay 'On Personal Character' (*The Plain Speaker*, 1826): 'The accession of knowledge, the pressure of circumstances, favourable or unfavourable, does little more than minister occasion to the first predisposing bias—than assist, like the dews of heaven, or retard like the nipping north, the growth of the seed originally sown in our constitution.'
1364. *thwarted*] thwarts (*MS*).
1365–6.] All you can boast is, "I had proved a tree / In other climes—" and yet this *was* the clime (*MS*).
1368. *well-streams*: 'a stream flowing from a spring'; *OED*'s last citation is 1390, and B.'s is the only instance after this date recorded in *English Poetry*.   *well-streams: old*,] well-stream water old (*MS*, canc.).
1371. *no water left*] no water's left (*1888*).
1372–3.] Young,—you've a hope, an aim, a love, suppose: / It's crossed and tost: you struggle on, the spark (*MS*).
1374. *your*] the (*MS*, canc.).
1375. *due time subside*] due subside (*MS* [error]); due season die (*MS*, canc.; B. also tried 'due season die').
1376. *Now then for age's triumph*] And now then for your triumph (*MS*, with 'pain's fruit' canc.).
1377. *You mean to loose*] To let loose (*MS*).

Up with it on the tripod! It's extinct.
Spend your life's remnant asking, which was best,
1380 Light smothered up that never peeped forth once,
Or the cold cresset with full leave to shine?
Well, accept this too,—seek the fruit of it
Not in enjoyment, proved a dream on earth,
But knowledge, useful for a second chance,
1385 Another life,—you've lost this world—you've gained
Its knowledge for the next.—What knowledge, sir,
Except that you know nothing? Nay, you doubt
Whether 'twere better have made you man or brute,
If aught be true, if good and evil clash.
1390 No foul, no fair, no inside, no outside,
There's your world!

               Give it me! I slap it brisk
With harlequin's pasteboard sceptre: what's it now?
Changed like a rock-flat, rough with rusty weed,
At first wash-over of the returning wave!
1395 All the dry, dead, impracticable stuff
Starts into life and light again; this world
Pervaded by the influx from the next.
I cheat, and what's the happy consequence?
You find full justice straightway dealt you out,
1400 Each want supplied, each ignorance set at ease,
Each folly fooled. No life-long labour now

1378. Up with it on the] High on triumphant (*MS*, canc.). *tripod*: a three-legged support; B. may have had in mind the tripod at Delphi from which the priestess of Apollo delivered her oracles (*OED* 2).
1379. your] the (*MS*, canc.).
1380. that] nor (*MS*, canc.).
1381.] Or the cold altar-lamp with leave to shine! (*MS*, canc.). *cresset*: torch.
1383. a dream on earth] impossible (*MS*, canc.).
1386. Its] This (*MS*).
1388.] Whether twere better you were man or brute, (*MS*); Whether twere better you had been a brute, (*MS*, canc.). *have made you*] have been made (*1880*).
1389. true] real (*MS*, canc.).
1390. foul] real (*MS*).
1393.] Changed like a rock-flat with its rusty weed (*MS*).
1394. of the] o' the (*1875–88*).
1398. cheat, and] cheat you,— (*MS*).
1399–1400.] Each man finds justice straightway dealt to him, / Each want of his supplied, each ignorance cured, (*MS*).
1401. folly fooled. No] folly further fooled; no (*MS*, canc.).

As the price of worse than nothing! No mere film
Holding you chained in iron, as it seems,
Against the outstretch of your very arms
1405   And legs in the sunshine moralists forbid!
What would you have? Just speak and, there, you see!
You're supplemented, made a whole at last,
Bacon advises, Shakespeare writes you songs,
And Mary Queen of Scots embraces you.
1410   Thus it goes on, not quite like life perhaps,
But so near, that the very difference piques,
Shows that e'en better than this best will be—
This passing entertainment in a hut
Whose bare walls take your taste since, one stage more,
1415   And you arrive at the palace: all half real,
And you, to suit it, less than real beside,
In a dream, lethargic kind of death in life,
That helps the interchange of natures, flesh
Transfused by souls, and such souls! Oh, 'tis choice!
1420   And if at whiles the bubble, blown too thin,
Seem nigh on bursting,—if you nearly see
The real world through the false,—what *do* you see?
Is the old so ruined? You find you're in a flock
Of the youthful, earnest, passionate—genius, beauty,

1402–5. No mere film . . . moralists forbid! Sludge seems to be suggesting that his lies make the spiritual realm seem more tangible, and so prevent the feeling that natural impulses—'the outstretch of your very arms / And legs in the sunshine'— have been thwarted by 'moralists' for nothing.
1403. chained] captive (*MS*, canc.).
1405. in the] i' the (*1875–88*).
1406. and, there,] and here, (*MS*, canc.).
1408. Shakespeare advises you, and Bacon warns (*MS*, canc.).   *writes*] sings (*MS*).
1410. Thus] So (*MS*).
1412. this] the (*MS*, canc.).
1414. your] our (*MS*).   *stage*] day (*MS*, canc.).
1415. half] is (*MS*).
1416.] And we, to suit it, grown unreal besides (*MS*).
1417. lethargic] half-lethargy, (*MS*).
1419. choice] rare! (*MS*).
1420. bubble, blown too thin,] bubble be blown too thin (*MS*, which has 'thin,' canc.).
1421. nearly] come to (*MS*).
1422. the false] this false (*MS*).
1423. you're] yourself (*MS*).
1424. Of the] O' the (*1875–88*).   *beauty,*] Sir, (*MS*).

1425 Rank and wealth also, if you care for these,
   And all depose their natural rights, hail you,
   (That's me, sir) as their mate and yoke-fellow,
   Participate in Sludgehood—nay, grow mine,
   I veritably possess them—banish doubt,
1430 And reticence and modesty alike!
   Why, here's the Golden Age, old Paradise
   Or new Eutopia! Here is life indeed,
   And the world well won now, yours for the first time!

   And all this might be, may be, and with good help
1435 Of a little lying shall be: so, Sludge lies!
   Why, he's at worst your poet who sings how Greeks
   That never were, in Troy which never was,
   Did this or the other impossible great thing!
   He's Lowell—it's a world, you smile and say,
1440 Of his own invention—wondrous Longfellow,
   Surprising Hawthorne! Sludge does more than they,
   And acts the books they write: the more's his praise!

   But why do I mount to poets? Take plain prose—
   Dealers in common sense, set these at work,
1445 What can they do without their helpful lies?

1425. these] them (*MS*, canc.).

1427. (That's me, sir): in referring to himself in the second person for the purpose of his argument, Sludge has blurred the distinction between himself and his addressee.

1428. grow mine,] grow yours, (*MS*).

1429. I] You (*MS*).

1432. Eutopia: 'a region of ideal happiness or good order'; not synonymous with 'Utopia' though the two terms were sometimes confused (*OED*, whose last citation is 1638). *Here is*] This is (*MS*); Here is (*1888*).

1433. the world well won: contrast the title of Dryden's 1678 adaptation of *Antony and Cleopatra*: *All for Love Or, the World well Lost. now, yours for*] now, for (*MS*).

1436–8. Alluding to the controversy over the authorship of Homer's epic poems prompted by F.A. Wolf's *Prolegomena to Homer* (1795). Cp. B.'s late poem on this subject, *Development* (*Asolando*, 1889).

1436. how] that (*MS*); how (*MS*, canc.).

1437. That] Who (*MS*).

1439–41. Luminaries of contemporary American literature: James Russell Lowell (1819–91), Henry Wadsworth Longfellow (1807–82) and Nathaniel Hawthorne (1804–64). Lowell and Hawthorne were acquaintances of the Brownings.

1439. Lowell] Homer (*MS*). *world, you smile and say,*] (you smile applause) (*1888*).

1442. the more's] the more (*1868–88*).

1444. these] each (*MS*).

1445. they . . . their] he . . . his (*MS*).

Each states the law and fact and face of the thing
Just as he'd have them, finds what he thinks fit,
Is blind to what missuits him, just records
What makes his case out, quite ignores the rest.
1450 It's a History of the World, the Lizard Age,
The Early Indians, the Old Country War,
Jerome Napoleon, whatsoever you please,
All as the author wants it. Such a scribe
You pay and praise for putting life in stones,
1455 Fire into fog, making the past your world.
There's plenty of "How did you contrive to grasp
The thread which led you through this labyrinth?
How build such solid fabric out of air?
How on so slight foundation found this tale,
1460 Biography, narrative?" or, in other words,
"How many lies did it require to make
The portly truth you here present us with?"
"Oh," quoth the penman, purring at your praise,
"'Tis fancy all; no particle of fact:
1465 I was poor and threadbare when I wrote that book
'Bliss in the Golden City.' I, at Thebes?

1446. of the] o' the (*1875–88*).
1447. them,] these— (*MS*).
1449. quite] and (*MS*).
1450.] Its a history of the world, the lizard age, (*MS*).   *the Lizard Age*: the age of the dinosaurs.
1451. the Old Country War: presumably the War of Independence from Britain, though we have not found other uses of this phrase.
1452. Jerome Napoleon: 1784–1860, brother of Napoleon Bonaparte; his first wife, Elizabeth Patterson, was American.
1453. All] Just (*MS*, canc.).   *wants*] would have (*MS*).
1454. pay] thank (*MS*).
1457. In Greek myth, Theseus unwinds a ball of thread in the Cretan labyrinth as he searches for the Minotaur, enabling him to find his way back out after killing the monster.   *this*] the (*MS*).
1458. such] this (*MS*).
1459. so] such (*MS*).
1460. narrative?" or] "description?"— (*MS*).
1461. make] tell (*MS*).
1464.] 'Twas fancy all—no particle of fact— (*MS*, which lacks quotation marks).
1466. 'Bliss in the Golden City': an imaginary title. The Brownings' American friend, William Ware, wrote books set in the cities of antiquity; see headnote to *Love Among the Ruins* (pp. 531–2).   *Thebes*: the ancient capital of Upper Egypt.
    'Bliss] "Life (*MS*).

We writers paint out of our heads, you see!"
"Ah, the more wonderful the gift in you,
The more creativeness and godlike craft!"
1470   But I, do I present you with my piece,
It's "What, Sludge? When my sainted mother spoke
The verses Lady Jane Grey last composed
About the rosy bower in the seventh heaven
Where she and Queen Elizabeth keep house,—
1475   You made the raps? 'T was your invention that?
Cur, slave and devil"—eight fingers and two thumbs
Stuck in my throat!

                 Well, if the marks seem gone,
'Tis because stiffish cock-tail, taken in time,
Is better for a bruise than arnica.

1480   There, sir! I bear no malice: 'tisn't in me.
I know I acted wrongly: still, I've tried
What I could say in my excuse,—to show
The devil's not all devil . . . I don't pretend,
An angel, much less such a gentleman
1485   As you, sir! And I've lost you, lost myself,
Lost all, l-l-l- . . . .

                No—are you in earnest, sir?
O, yours, sir, is an angel's part! I know

1467. writers] poets (*MS*).

1472–4. Lady Jane Grey was proclaimed Queen at the age of sixteen after the death of Edward VI in 1553; she reigned for nine days before being taken prisoner by her rival Mary Tudor; she was beheaded the following year. As a popular Protestant heroine, her story was often depicted on stage and in romances; Sludge places her in heaven with Queen Mary's other Protestant rival, Elizabeth I. The phrase 'rosy bower' is a poetical commonplace, but cp. *Waring* 152^153n. (p. 192).

1474.] written in the margin at the bottom of the page in *MS*; prob. a copying error on what are some of the cleanest pages of the *MS*.

1475. 'Twas] All (*MS*).

1476. Cur] Beast (*MS*). *slave*] swine (*MS*, canc.).

1477. seem] are (*MS*).

1478. stiffish: 'rather strong (in alcohol content)'. *cock-tail*: an Americanism; often so-spelt in the period (*OED* 3a).

1479. arnica: a medicine prepared from mountain tobacco.

1484. An] He's an (*MS*, canc.).

1485–6. And I've . . . all, l-l-l. . . .] not *MS*.

1486. are you in earnest, sir? Horsefall has agreed not to expose Sludge.

What prejudice must be, what the common course
Men take to soothe their ruffled self-conceit:
1490 Only you rise superior to it all!
No, sir, it don't hurt much; it's speaking long
That makes me choke a little: the marks will go!
What? Twenty V-notes more, and outfit too,
And not a word to Greely? One—one kiss
1495 Of the hand that saves me! You'll not let me speak,
I well know, and I've lost the right, too true!
But I must say, sir, if She hears (she does)
Your sainted . . . Well, sir, be it so! That's, I think,
My bed-room candle. Good night! Bl-l-less you, sir!

────────────

1500 R-r-r, you brute-beast and blackguard! Cowardly scamp!
I only wish I dared burn down the house
And spoil your sniggering! Oh, what, you're the man?
You're satisfied at last? You've found out Sludge?
We'll see that presently: my turn, sir, next!
1505 I too can tell my story: brute,—do you hear?—
You throttled your sainted mother, that old hag,
In just such a fit of passion: no, it was . . .
To get this house of hers, and many a note
Like these . . . I'll pocket them, however . . . five,
1510 Ten, fifteen . . . ay, you gave her throat the twist,
Or else you poisoned her! Confound the cuss!

1488. *must be, what*] is, and what (*MS*); prompts, and what's (*1875–88*).
1489. *self-conceit:*] vanity— (*MS*).
1493. *V-notes*: see l. 65n.   *and*] for (*MS*, canc., which also has 'and', canc.).
1494. *Greely*] Greeley (*1868–88*); see l. 54n.
1495. *Of the hand*] O' the hand (*1875–88*).
1496. *I've*] I know (*MS*, canc.).
1498. *be it*] best (*MS*); better (*MS*, canc.).
1499.] My bed-room candle—Good night, —bless you, Sir! (*MS*).   *night; —bless*] night; and bless (*MS*, canc.).
1500–25. With Sludge's concluding outburst, delivered after Horsefall leaves the room, cp. the endings of *Caliban* (p. 640) and *A Death* (p. 757), and the narrative coda to *Bishop Blougram* (p. 336).
1500. *R-r-r*] Aie (*MS*).
1502. *sniggering*] smirking (*MS*, canc.).
1505. For Home's autobiography, *Incidents in My Life*, see headnote.
1510. *fifteen*] fifty (*MS*, canc.).   *the twist*] a twist (*MS*, canc.).
1511. *cuss*: an Americanism; 'a sneaking, ill-natured fellow' (*OED* citation 1866).

Where was my head? I ought to have prophesied
He'll die in a year and join her: that's the way.

I don't know where my head is: what had I done?
1515   How did it all go? I said he poisoned her,
And hoped he'd have grace given him to repent,
Whereon he picked this quarrel, bullied me
And called me cheat: I thrashed him,—who could help?
He howled for mercy, prayed me on his knees
1520   To cut and run and save him from disgrace:
I do so, and once off, he slanders me.
An end of him! Begin elsewhere anew!
Boston's a hole, the herring-pond is wide,
V-notes are something, liberty still more.
1525   Beside, is he the only fool in the world?

1513^1514.] Sure to succeed, the niggers say—who knows? (*MS,* canc.); B. indicates a new paragraph in the margin.
1517. this] his (*MS,* canc.).   *quarrel, bullied*] quarrel .. and bullied (*MS,* canc.).
1520. from] sure (*MS,* canc.).
1522. An] And (*MS,* canc.).   *him! Begin*] him, we'll begin (MS).
1523. the herring-pond: the Atlantic Ocean; like Home, Sludge has decided to leave
America for Europe.
1524. something] B. started to write 'somewhat' in *MS,* then altered the word.
   still] is (*MS,* canc.).
MS has what looks like 'L.D.I.E.' written after the end of the poem. B. placed
this tag, which presumably stands for 'Laus Deo in excelsis' (Praise God in the
highest), at the end of a number of his later MSS; it also appears, for example,
in *Prince Hohenstiel-Schwangau* (1871) and *Fifine at the Fair* (1872).

Appendix A
ESSAY ON SHELLEY

Text and publication

First publ. in *Letters of Percy Bysshe Shelley. With an introductory essay, by Robert Browning* (Moxon, 1852); the volume appeared on 14 Feb. B.'s essay occupies pp. 1–44; the twenty-five letters occupy pp. 47–165. No MS is extant. The volume was withdrawn soon after publication when it was discovered that the letters were forgeries (see below). Repr. 1881, with B.'s permission but not under his supervision, as the first issue of *Browning Society's Papers* by the Browning Society's chairman Frederick Furnivall, under Furnivall's title: *On the Poet Objective and Subjective: On the Latter's Aim: On Shelley as Man and Poet* (Furnivall also added running titles). In 1888 it was repr., again with B.'s consent, ed. by W. T. Harden, for the Shelley Society. Our text is *1852*.

Composition and date

The letters themselves are not annotated, and T. J. Wise claimed that 'In reply to a question I asked him when reprinting his Introductory Essay for the Browning Society in 1888, Browning told me distinctly that he never saw the originals of the supposed Shelley Letters, but wrote his Essay after reading a set of transcripts which had been supplied to him by Moxon' (*A Browning Library* [1929] 19). Since he was in London when the proposition was originally made to him, this seems surprising, although he may have meant that he worked from copies later when in Paris, where most if not all of the writing took place: the *Essay* makes in fact very little reference to the letters, quoting them nowhere.

EBB.'s letters provide a fairly complete account of the process of composition of the *Essay on Shelley*. To Eliza Ogilvy she wrote on 20 Aug. 1851: 'Robert has agreed to a proposition about editing some new ms. letters of Shelley's, for which he is to be well paid' (*EBB to Ogilvy* 51). In her letter dated 12–14 Oct. 1851, EBB. wrote to her sister Arabella: 'Now, we are always together again, except when he writes about Shelley in the next room' (*EBB to Arabella* i 416). In a letter to Carlyle of 22 Oct. 1851 B. himself commented: 'I have just done the little thing I told you of—a mere Preface to some new letters of Shelley; not admitting of much workmanship of any kind, if I had it to give. But I have put down a few thoughts that presented themselves—one or two, in respect of opinions of your own (I mean, that I was thinking of those opinions while I wrote). However it be done, it is what I was "up to", just now, and will soon be off my mind' (*LH* 36). (Carlyle had recently travelled with the Brownings to Paris, so they had seen a good deal of each other.) In her letter of 31 Oct–2 Nov., EBB. remarked: 'Robert has done his Shelley, except something of the writing out part' (*EBB to Arabella* i 420–1); this suggests that B.'s claim to have 'done' the work meant that he had fully conceived it and had a working draft, not that he had finished it. On 18 Nov. EBB. added: 'Robert was interrupted in Shelley by the arrival of his father & sister, & could not touch it while they were here' [i.e. to the end of November] (*ibid.* i 426). To Henrietta she wrote on 1 Dec: 'Robert has finished and is sending off his Shelley' (*EBB to Henrietta* 149). In a letter to her brother George of 4–5 Dec. she wrote: 'He has been absorbed between his father & sister . . . & the Shelley edition,—which is off his hands today' (*George Barrett* 159). (Since the essay is datemarked 'Paris, Dec. 4th, 1851' this is probably accurate.) Her final comment comes in a letter of 18 Feb. 1852 to Arabella, where she remarks 'I want to say particularly that Robert has directed his Shelley to be sent with his best love to George. We have only six copies to give away, or you should have one for yourself—but you will read George's .. & I dont think you will care a bit about the "Letters," which in truth are by no means interesting, & Robert's part is a mere preface, as you will see. He thinks very lightly of it himself—but the occasion admitted of nothing more' (*EBB to Arabella* i 462). EBB. mentions the discovery of the forgery in a letter of 18 Mar. 1852 to Eliza Ogilvy: 'Carlyle says that Robert's essay is "the first human voice he had heard for ever so long"—but you see what a scrape we are all in about the forgery-conviction. Still, Robert is not implicated any wise' (*EBB to Ogilvy* 74). Richard Hengist Horne wrote a letter on the subject exonerating B. and Moxon to the *Literary Gazette* on 11 Mar. 1852, for which B. wrote to thank him on 15 Mar. (unpubl. MS at *ABL*). In a letter to Furnivall of 15 Sept 1881, B. promised that 'When I get home and have a copy before me, I will give you in a few words the true account of the whole transaction—and *perhaps* some remarks on the Essay by a very distinguished personage indeed' (*Trumpeter* 25). There is, however, no sign of either of these elements in Furnivall's edition; Hood speculates, almost certainly rightly, that the 'remarks' were Carlyle's (see below).

The discovery of the forgery

On 23 Feb. 1852 Moxon received a letter from Sir Francis Palgrave stating: 'It is a duty I owe both to you and myself to inform you that in the letters just brought out by you and ascribed to Mr. Shelley there is one, viz. that dated Florence, which is cribbed from an article by me on that city published in the Q[uarterly] R[eview]' (Theodore G. Ehrsam, *Major Byron: the Incredible Career of a Literary Forger* [New York and London 1951] 88–9). Moxon immediately withdrew the volume from sale. The *Athenaeum* of 6 Mar. 1852 has a detailed circumstantial account of the whole transaction (pp. 278–9; see also the issue of 20 Mar., pp. 325–6). The forger was a man claiming to be the son of Byron, calling himself 'Major [or Captain, or Colonel] George Gordon Byron'; T. J. Wise (p. 19; see above) identifies him as 'de Gibler', but Ehrsam cites this only as one of several aliases. He also perpetrated forgeries of Byron and Keats: according to Monckton Milnes they constituted 'a monument of criminal ingenuity' (*Athenaeum*, 17 Apr. 1852, p. 431). The *Literary Gazette* of 6 Mar. 1852 claimed that 'the letters submitted to him [B.] by Mr. Moxon were printed mainly on his judgment' (presumably Moxon made this defensive claim), magnanimously adding that this 'is no disparagement to the acumen of Mr. Browning' (p. 230).

Despite the volume's withdrawal, B. presented a 'M. Van Der Weyer' with a signed copy on 7 Aug. 1852 (*Collections* C637; the two other surviving copies he presented bear no date). He presented three copies of the Shelley Society reprint to friends in 1889.

Sources and contexts

(i) *B. and Shelley*

B.'s admiration of Shelley (both man and poet) was of long standing: see *Pauline* 141–229 (pp. 19–24) and *Sordello* (I 367–71n.); see also, in this volume, *Memorabilia* (p. 553). His knowledge of Shelley's work was (for the time) comprehensive; when he wrote his essay, he would have known Shelley's *Posthumous*

Poems and the *Defence of Poetry*, both published (by Moxon) in 1840. The essay makes clear B.'s partisanship in the face of continuing hostility towards Shelley's political and religious opinions, culminating in the claim that 'had Shelley lived he would have finally ranged himself with the Christians' (ll. 523–4). (B. was not alone in this belief: cp. De Quincey's comment that 'Infidel by his intellect, Shelley was a Christian in the tendencies of his heart': 'Percy Bysshe Shelley', *Essays on the Poets* [Boston 1853] 50–1.) B. was also aware of attacks on Shelley's personal conduct, but the essay vigorously defends his 'moral constitution' (l. 264). This attitude continued until Thomas Hookham, some time between 1856 and 1858, showed B. letters establishing that Shelley had deserted Harriet, his first wife, and their child, leading to her suicide (see *Trumpeter* 78–9). B.'s poem *Cenciaja* (*Pacchiarotto*, 1876), a pendant to Shelley's *The Cenci*, publicly maintained the tone of admiration (see note to l. 622 below), but his private comments were scathing: 'I painfully contrast my notions of Shelley the man and Shelley—well, even the poet,—with what they were sixty years ago, when I only had his works, for a certainty, and took his character on trust' (to Furnivall, 8 Dec 1885, *Trumpeter* 127). A striking instance of B.'s changed attitude is provided by Mary Campbell, the wife of James Dykes Campbell, in her unpublished reminiscences of the poet:

> On only two occasions was I ever privileged to see Mr. Browning deeply moved. One was at a dinner-party at the house of Mrs. Matthews—the younger of Lord Leighton's sisters—when I was taken in by Mr. Alfred Hunt the water-colour painter and we sat directly opposite to Mr. Browning and his partner with only a somewhat narrow table dividing us. It came just after the bringing to light of a series of letters from Shelley to Harriet, his first wife, which proved the dastardly way in which he treated her and the falseness of his accusations against her made to his new father-in-law Godwin. Literary London was much excited over these Letters at the time and fierce were the arguments in favour of and against Shelley and his conduct. Mr. Browning's partner thinking I have no doubt that she would please him—who had been such an admirer of the young Shelley and his poetry—was upholding the Poet and making all sorts of excuses for him [and his conduct] when Mr. Browning, who had been silent for some minutes, turned upon her full of wrathful indignation. How could any-one stand up for a man who did such mean and contemptible actions? & How could she think that because a man was a Poet he was to be excused for behaving like a cad? &c &c & ending up by saying & that you, a Woman, should say such things! It is unbelievable. He spoke in a low voice but one full of righteous indignation[.]

> (BL Add. MS. 49525B fos. 105–6)

(ii) *'Objective' and 'subjective'*

As B.'s slightly self-conscious phrasing indicates ('as the phrase now goes', l. 12, 'of modern classification', l. 82), the modern opposition between these terms, around which the essay is structured, was of relatively recent date in English philosophy and aesthetics. *OED* (sense 2b) defines 'objective' as

> Opposed to *subjective* in the modern sense: That is or belongs to what is presented to consciousness, as opposed to the consciousness itself; that is the object of perception or thought, as distinct from the perceiving or thinking subject; hence, that is, or has the character of being, a 'thing' external to the mind; real. This sense is occasional in writers of the later 17th and early 18th *c.* (the early examples being more or less transitional); but its current use appears to

be derived from Kant, and to appear in English subsequently to 1790, and chiefly after 1817 (see quot. from Coleridge).

The Coleridge quotation is from *Biographia Literaria* (1817): 'The very words *objective* and *subjective* of such constant recurrence in the schools of yore, I have ventured to re-introduce' (bk. I, sect. x). An important precedent for B.'s usage comes in EBB.'s second letter to him (15 Jan. 1845, *Correspondence* x 26): 'You have in your vision two worlds—or to use the language of the schools of the day, you are both subjective & objective in the habits of your mind—You can deal both with abstract thought, & with human passion in the most passionate sense. Thus, you have an immense grasp in Art'. (Note that EBB., too, uses the terms self-consciously.) Cp. B.'s insistence in the essay that the same poet may produce perfect works in both 'objective' and 'subjective' modes, although he situates this possibility in the future (ll. 155–9, and see below, *Parallels*).

(iii) *Biographical criticism*
Shelley makes a claim on behalf of biography which goes directly against B.'s beliefs in respect of his own work. He admits the desire for more knowledge of 'objective poets' such as Shakespeare ('Doubtless, with respect to such a poet, we covet his biography', ll. 45–6), even though he argues that such knowledge is not strictly necessary to an understanding of the work; with regard to the 'subjective poet', however, biography is not just desirable but essential: 'in our approach to the poetry, we necessarily approach the personality of the poet . . . as readers of his poetry [we] must be readers of his biography also' (ll. 107–12). B.'s position here develops that of Samuel Johnson in the eighteenth century, and Carlyle and Emerson in the nineteenth, all of whom emphasized the importance of biography; note B.'s statement that he wrote the essay with some of Carlyle's ideas in mind (see above), among which the notion of the poet as 'hero' or prophet was almost certainly prominent (see *On Heroes and Hero-worship*, 1840). Carlyle in turn associated B.'s essay with a work of Emerson's which he had recently read (see below, *Reception*); this was probably Emerson's volume of biographical essays, *Representative Men*, publ. in 1850. B. offers a special justification for biography where the work of a 'seer' is 'the very radiance and aroma of his personality' (l. 106), and extends this justification to the publication of private letters, something he had resolutely opposed in his correspondence with EBB. and which he went to great lengths to forestall in his own case; he also refused to cooperate with any biographer of EBB. after her death.

Contemporary reception
Eight reviews of the volume appeared, incl. one in the *Athenaeum* by its editor, B.'s friend H. F. Chorley, and one by G. H. Lewes which appeared after the volume's withdrawal (*Westminster Review* n.s. i [1 April 1852] 502–11). Lewes defended B.'s intention, but not his execution:

we are struck with the unseemly merriment excited by Mr. Browning's Introduction. The critics, now the letters are known to be forgeries, make merry with Mr. Browning for having written an elaborate preface to them; but if any one will read the preface with candid attention, he will see that it is not specifically an introduction to these few letters, but to the whole mass of Shelley's authentic correspondence. Considered, indeed, as a preface to the new letters it is little less incongruous than the façade of the Parthenon would be to a wayside cottage. But it is quite evident that Browning wanted to say something about Shelley, and seized this occasion for saying it. We will not quarrel with the occasion, nor indeed with the style. The one has proved unhappy; the other is misty and metaphorical, as the prose style of poets is apt to be. A poet is out of his element in prose . . . But if the manner of this preface be open to criticism, the matter is acceptable.

(p. 504)

The response which meant most to B. (see above, *Composition*) came in a private letter from Carlyle of 8 March 1852 (before news of the forgery had reached him). Carlyle's letter also illustrates the difficulties B. had to contend with at this period in arguing for Shelley's personal and poetic supremacy:

> I liked the Essay extremely well indeed: a solid, well-wrought massive manful bit of discourse; and interesting to me, over and above, as the first bit of *prose* I had ever seen from you—I hope only the first of very many . . . This Essay of yours, and another little word by Emerson are the only new things I have read with real pleasure for a great while past. I agree with what you say of Shelley's moralities and spiritual position; I honour and respect the weighty estimate you have formed of the Poetic Art; and I admire very much the grave expressiveness of style (a *little* too elaborate here and there), and the dignified tone, in which you manage to deliver yourself on all that.
>
> The Letters themselves are very innocent and clear; and deserve printing, with such a name attached to them; but it is not they that I care for on the present occasion. In fact I am not sure but you would excommunicate me,— at least lay me under the 'lesser sentence,' for a time,—if I told you all I thought of Shelley! Poor soul, he has always seemed to me an extremely weak creature, and lamentable much more than admirable. Weak in genius, weak in character (for these two always go together); a poor, thin, spasmodic, hectic, shrill and pallid being;—one of those unfortunates, of whom I often speak, to whom the 'talent of *silence*,' first of all, has been denied. The speech of such is never good for much. Poor Shelley, there is something void and Hades-like in the whole inner world of him; his universe is all vacant azure, hung with a few frosty mournful if beautiful stars; the very voice of him (his style &c), shrill, shrieky, to my ear has too much of the *ghost*!—In a word, it is not with Shelley, but with Shelley's Commentator that I take up my quarters at all: and to this latter I will say with emphasis, Give us some more of *your* writing, my friend: we decidedly need a man or two like you, if we could get them! Seriously, dear Browning, you must at last gird up your loins again; and give us a right stroke of work:—I do not wish to hurry you . . . Nor do I restrict you to Prose, in spite of all I have said and still say: Prose or Poetry, either of them you can master; and we will wait for you with welcome in whatever form your own *Daimon* bids.
>
> (*The Collected Letters of Thomas and Jane Welsh Carlyle*, ed. Charles A.
> Sanders et al., xxvii [Durham, NC, and London 1999] 64–6).

Parallels in B.

Like B.'s only other piece of published criticism, *Chatterton* (Appendix C, II 475), *Shelley* is an elaborate defence of a predecessor whose character was under attack; note the allusion to Chatterton at l. 567. (*Chatterton*, by coincidence, was a defence of a literary forger; 'Major Byron' was compared to Chatterton in the *Athenaeum* article of 6 Mar. [p. 279; see above]). *Shelley* also has affinities to some of B.'s 'dramatic apologies', e.g. *Bishop Blougram* (p. 279), where Blougram's 'objective' worldliness contrasts with the 'subjective' idealism of Gigadibs; and *Mr. Sludge* (p. 771); cp., in later work, *Prince Hohenstiel-Schwangau* (1871), *Fifine at the Fair* (1872) and *Aristophanes' Apology* (1875). In the latter poem the opposition between Aristophanes and Euripides, and between their respective genres of comedy and tragedy, strongly resembles that between the 'objective' and 'subjective' poet.

> An opportunity having presented itself for the acquisition
> of a series of unedited letters by Shelley, all more or less directly
> supplementary to and illustrative of the collection already
> published by Mr. Moxon, that gentleman has decided on
> 5 securing them. They will prove an acceptable addition to a
> body of correspondence, the value of which towards a right
> understanding of its author's purpose and work, may be said
> to exceed that of any similar contribution exhibiting the
> worldly relations of a poet whose genius has operated by a
> 10 different law.
>   Doubtless we accept gladly the biography of an objective
> poet, as the phrase now goes; one whose endeavour has been
> to reproduce things external (whether the phenomena of
> the scenic universe, or the manifested action of the human
> 15 heart and brain) with an immediate reference, in every case,
> to the common eye and apprehension of his fellow men,
> assumed capable of receiving and profiting by this repro-
> duction. It has been obtained through the poet's double
> faculty of seeing external objects more clearly, widely, and
> 20 deeply, than is possible to the average mind, at the same time
> that he is so acquainted and in sympathy with its narrower
> comprehension as to be careful to supply it with no other
> materials than it can combine into an intelligible whole.
> The auditory of such a poet will include, not only the

3–4. the collection already published by Mr. Moxon: Mary Shelley's edition of *Essays, Letters from Abroad, Translations and Fragments*, 2 vols., 1840. Edward Moxon had published B.'s work of the 1840s, from *Sordello* (1840) to *Bells and Pomegranates* (1841–46: see Appendix C, p. 883). B. had recently switched to Chapman and Hall for *CE & ED* (1850), but he remained on good terms with Moxon, as the preface to *1865²* confirms.

11–12. an objective poet, as the phrase now goes: for this term, and the term 'sub-jective poet' to which it is opposed (l. 82), see headnote.

19–20. seeing external objects more clearly, widely, and deeply, than is possible to the average mind. Cp. Wordsworth, *Preface* to *Lyrical Ballads* (1802): 'What is a Poet? To whom does he address himself? And what language is to be expected from him? He is a man speaking to men: a man, it is true, endued with more lively sensibility, more enthusiasm and tenderness, who has a greater knowledge of human nature, and a more comprehensive soul, than are supposed to be common among mankind' (*Lyrical Ballads*, ed. M. Mason [1992], pp. 70–1).

25 intelligences which, save for such assistance, would have missed
the deeper meaning and enjoyment of the original objects,
but also the spirits of a like endowment with his own, who,
by means of his abstract, can forthwith pass to the reality it
was made from, and either corroborate their impressions of
30 things known already, or supply themselves with new from
whatever shows in the inexhaustible variety of existence may
have hitherto escaped their knowledge. Such a poet is properly the ποιητης, the fashioner; and the thing fashioned,
his poetry, will of necessity be substantive, projected from
35 himself and distinct. We are ignorant what the inventor of
"Othello" conceived of that fact as he beheld it in completeness, how he accounted for it, under what known law
he registered its nature, or to what unknown law he traced
its coincidence. We learn only what he intended we should
40 learn by that particular exercise of his power,—the fact itself,—
which, with its infinite significances, each of us receives for
the first time as a creation, and is hereafter left to deal with,
as, in proportion to his own intelligence, he best may. We
are ignorant, and would fain be otherwise.
45   Doubtless, with respect to such a poet, we covet his biography. We desire to look back upon the process of gathering together in a lifetime, the materials of the work we behold
entire; of elaborating, perhaps under difficulty and with hin-
drance, all that is familiar to our admiration in the apparent
50 facility of success. And the inner impulse of this effort and
operation, what induced it? Did a soul's delight in its own
extended sphere of vision set it, for the gratification of an
insuppressible power, on labour, as other men are set on rest?
Or did a sense of duty or of love lead it to communicate
55 its own sensations to mankind? Did an irresistible sympathy
with men compel it to bring down and suit its own provision of knowledge and beauty to their narrow scope?
Did the personality of such an one stand like an open watch-
tower in the midst of the territory it is erected to gaze on,

---

33. ποιητης: the correct form is ποιητής; Oxford emends on the grounds that
this is a printer's error, but without the MS we cannot be sure that the error was
not made by B. The Greek 'poietes', meaning 'maker', is the root of the English
word 'poet'.

35–6. the inventor of "Othello": cp. Bishop Blougram 487–8 (pp. 311–12).

58–9. Did the personality . . . erected to gaze on: cp. the image of the watch-tower
in Cleon 231 ff. (pp. 579–80).

60   and were the storms and calms, the stars and meteors, its
      watchman was wont to report of, the habitual variegation
      of his every-day life, as they glanced across its open roof
      or lay reflected on its four-square parapet? Or did some sunken
      and darkened chamber of imagery witness, in the artificial
65   illumination of every storied compartment we are permitted
      to contemplate, how rare and precious were the outlooks
      through here and there an embrasure upon a world beyond,
      and how blankly would have pressed on the artificer the
      boundary of his daily life, except for the amorous diligence
70   with which he had rendered permanent by art whatever came
      to diversify the gloom? Still, fraught with instruction and
      interest as such details undoubtedly are, we can, if needs be,
      dispense with them. The man passes, the work remains. The
      work speaks for itself, as we say: and the biography of the
75   worker is no more necessary to an understanding or enjoy-
      ment of it, than is a model or anatomy of some tropical
      tree, to the right tasting of the fruit we are familiar with on
      the market-stall,—or a geologist's map and stratification,
      to the prompt recognition of the hill-top, our land-mark of
80   every day.
          We turn with stronger needs to the genius of an opposite
      tendency—the subjective poet of modern classification.
      He, gifted like the objective poet with the fuller perception
      of nature and man, is impelled to embody the thing he
85   perceives, not so much with reference to the many below
      as to the one above him, the supreme Intelligence which
      apprehends all things in their absolute truth,—an ultimate
      view ever aspired to, if but partially attained, by the poet's
      own soul. Not what man sees, but what God sees—the *Ideas*
90   of Plato, seeds of creation lying burningly on the Divine
      Hand—it is toward these that he struggles. Not with the

63–4. some sunken and darkened chamber of imagery: cp. the image of Eglamor as a
'poor gnome' in his 'rock-chamber', *Sordello* ii 215 ff. (I 476), an image B. took
up again in *Chatterton* (II 502–3).
85–6. not so much with reference to the many below as to the one above him: cp. *How
It Strikes* 67–8 (p. 442).
91. it is toward these that he struggles: cp. Shelley, *Defence of Poetry*: 'Poets,
according to the circumstances of the age and nation in which they appeared,
were called, in the earlier epochs of the world, legislators or prophets: a poet
essentially comprises and unites both these characters. For he not only beholds
intensely the present as it is, and discovers those laws according to which
present things ought to be ordered, but he beholds the future in the present,

combination of humanity in action, but with the primal
elements of humanity he has to do; and he digs where
he stands,—preferring to seek them in his own soul as the
95   nearest reflex of that absolute Mind, according to the intu-
itions of which he desires to perceive and speak. Such a poet
does not deal habitually with the picturesque groupings and
tempestuous tossings of the forest-trees, but with their roots
and fibres naked to the chalk and stone. He does not paint
100 pictures and hang them on the walls, but rather carries them
on the retina of his own eyes: we must look deep into his
human eyes, to see those pictures on them. He is rather a
seer, accordingly, than a fashioner, and what he produces will
be less a work than an effluence. That effluence cannot be
105 easily considered in abstraction from his personality,—being
indeed the very radiance and aroma of his personality, projected from it but not separated. Therefore, in our approach
to the poetry, we necessarily approach the personality of the
poet; in apprehending it we apprehend him, and certainly
110 we cannot love it without loving him. Both for love's and for
understanding's sake we desire to know him, and as readers
of his poetry must be readers of his biography also.

    I shall observe, in passing, that it seems not so much from
any essential distinction in the faculty of the two poets or
115 in the nature of the objects contemplated by either, as in
the more immediate adaptability of these objects to the distinct purpose of each, that the objective poet, in his appeal
to the aggregate human mind, chooses to deal with the doings
of men, (the result of which dealing, in its pure form, when
120 even description, as suggesting a describer, is dispensed
with, is what we call dramatic poetry), while the subjective
poet, whose study has been himself, appealing through
himself to the absolute Divine mind, prefers to dwell upon
those external scenic appearances which strike out most

---

and his thoughts are the germs of the flower and the fruit of latest time' (*Peacock's
Four Ages of Poetry, Shelley's Defence of Poetry, Browning's Essay on Shelley*, ed.
H. F. B. Brett-Smith [1921; repr. 1972], p. 27).

111–12. as readers of his poetry must be readers of his biography also: see headnote,
Sources.

119–21. the result of which dealing . . . is what we call dramatic poetry: cp. *Sordello* i
14–17 (I 394): 'A story I could body forth so well / By making speak, myself
kept out of view, / The very man as he was wont to do, / And leaving you to
say the rest for him'.

125   abundantly and uninterruptedly his inner light and power, selects that silence of the earth and sea in which he can best hear the beating of his individual heart, and leaves the noisy, complex, yet imperfect exhibitions of nature in the manifold experience of man around him, which serve only to

130   distract and suppress the working of his brain. These opposite tendencies of genius will be more readily descried in their artistic effect than in their moral spring and cause. Pushed to an extreme and manifested as a deformity, they will be seen plainest of all in the fault of either artist, when sub

135   sidiarily to the human interest of his work his occasional illustrations from scenic nature are introduced as in the earlier works of the originative painters—men and women filling the foreground with consummate mastery, while mountain, grove and rivulet show like an anticipatory revenge on that

140   succeeding race of landscape-painters whose "figures" disturb the perfection of their earth and sky. It would be idle to inquire, of these two kinds of poetic faculty in operation, which is the higher or even rarer endowment. If the subjective might seem to be the ultimate requirement of every

145   age, the objective, in the strictest state, must still retain its original value. For it is with this world, as starting point and basis alike, that we shall always have to concern ourselves: the world is not to be learned and thrown aside, but reverted to and relearned. The spiritual comprehension may be

150   infinitely subtilised, but the raw material it operates upon, must remain. There may be no end of the poets who communicate to us what they see in an object with reference to their own individuality; what it was before they saw it, in reference to the aggregate human mind, will be as desirable

155   to know as ever. Nor is there any reason why these two modes

---

136–7. *the earlier works of the originative painters*: the painters of the early Renaissance whom B. was to celebrate in *Old Pictures* (p. 404).

146–9. *For it is with this world . . . reverted to and relearned*: Oxford rightly compares *Fra Lippo* 313–15 (p. 501); cp. also Wordsworth, *The Prelude* (recently publ. in 1850 after Wordsworth's death): 'the very world, which is the world / Of all of us,—the place where, in the end, / We find our happiness, or not at all!' (xi 142–4); the context of these lines is Wordsworth's evocation of the period of the French Revolution and the opportunities it afforded both to 'play-fellows of fancy . . . who in lordly wise had stirred / Among the grandest objects of the sense', and to 'schemers more mild / And in the region of their peaceful selves', a pairing which foreshadows B.'s 'objective' and 'subjective' types.

of poetic faculty may not issue hereafter from the same poet
in successive perfect works, examples of which, according
to what are now considered the exigences of art, we have
hitherto possessed in distinct individuals only. A mere
160 running-in of the one faculty upon the other, is, of course,
the ordinary circumstance. Far more rarely it happens that
either is found so decidedly prominent and superior, as to
be pronounced comparatively pure: while of the perfect shield,
with the gold and the silver side set up for all comers to
165 challenge, there has yet been no instance. Either faculty in
its eminent state is doubtless conceded by Providence as a
best gift to men, according to their especial want. There is
a time when the general eye has, so to speak, absorbed its
fill of the phenomena around it, whether spiritual or mater-
170 ial, and desires rather to learn the exacter significance of
what it possesses, than to receive any augmentation of what
is possessed. Then is the opportunity for the poet of loftier
vision, to lift his fellows, with their half-apprehensions, up
to his own sphere, by intensifying the import of details and
175 rounding the universal meaning. The influence of such an
achievement will not soon die out. A tribe of successors
(Homerides) working more or less in the same spirit, dwell
on his discoveries and reinforce his doctrine; till, at
unawares, the world is found to be subsisting wholly on the
180 shadow of a reality, on sentiments diluted from passions,
on the tradition of a fact, the convention of a moral, the
straw of last year's harvest. Then is the imperative call for
the appearance of another sort of poet, who shall at once
replace this intellectual rumination of food swallowed long
185 ago, by a supply of the fresh and living swathe; getting at
new substance by breaking up the assumed wholes into parts

177. Homerides: i.e. derivative followers of an original genius; from the Latin *Homeridæ*,
'a guild of poets in Chios who claimed descent from Homer and a hereditary
property in the Homeric poems, which they recited publicly' (*OED*). Cp. the
activities of 'Hobbs, Nobbs, Stokes and Nokes' in *Popularity* (ll. 56–65, pp. 454–5).
181–2. the straw of last year's harvest: cp. Shelley, *Defence of Poetry*: 'Their language
is vitally metaphorical; that is, it marks the before unapprehended relations of
things and perpetuates their apprehension, until the words which represent them,
become, through time, signs for portions or classes of thoughts instead of pictures of integral thoughts; and then if no new poets should arise to create afresh
the associations which have been thus disorganized, language will be dead to all
the nobler purposes of human intercourse.'

of independent and unclassed value, careless of the unknown
laws for recombining them (it will be the business of yet
another poet to suggest those hereafter), prodigal of objects
190   for men's outer and not inner sight, shaping for their uses
a new and different creation from the last, which it displaces
by the right of life over death,—to endure until, in the
inevitable process, its very sufficiency to itself shall require,
at length, an exposition of its affinity to something higher,
195   —when the positive yet conflicting facts shall again precipitate themselves under a harmonising law, and one more
degree will be apparent for a poet to climb in that mighty
ladder, of which, however cloud-involved and undefined may
glimmer the topmost step, the world dares no longer doubt
200   that its gradations ascend.

Such being the two kinds of artists, it is naturally, as
I have shown, with the biography of the subjective poet
that we have the deeper concern. Apart from his recorded
life altogether, we might fail to determine with satisfactory
205   precision to what class his productions belong, and what
amount of praise is assignable to the producer. Certainly, in
the face of any conspicuous achievement of genius, philosophy, no less than sympathetic instinct, warrants our belief
in a great moral purpose having mainly inspired even where
210   it does not visibly look out of the same. Greatness in a work
suggests an adequate instrumentality; and none of the lower
incitements, however they may avail to initiate or even effect
many considerable displays of power, simulating the nobler
inspiration to which they are mistakenly referred, have been
215   found able, under the ordinary conditions of humanity, to
task themselves to the end of so exacting a performance as
a poet's complete work. As soon will the galvanism that pro-
vokes to violent action the muscles of a corpse, induce it to
cross the chamber steadily: sooner. The love of displaying
220   power for the display's sake, the love of riches, of distinction,
of notoriety,—the desire of a triumph over rivals, and the
vanity in the applause of friends,—each and all of such
whetted appetites grow intenser by exercise and increasingly sagacious as to the best and readiest means of self-
225   appeasement,—while for any of their ends, whether the
money or the pointed finger of the crowd, or the flattery

217. *galvanism*: cp. *Ring* i 740: 'Mimic creation, galvanism for life'.

and hate to heart's content, there are cheaper prices to pay,
they will all find soon enough, than the bestowment of a
life upon a labour, hard, slow, and not sure. Also, assuming
230   the proper moral aim to have produced a work, there are
many and various states of an aim: it may be more intense
than clear-sighted, or too easily satisfied with a lower field
of activity than a steadier aspiration would reach. All the
bad poetry in the world (accounted poetry, that is, by its
235   affinities) will be found to result from some one of the infinite
degrees of discrepancy between the attributes of the poet's
soul, occasioning a want of correspondency between his
work and the verities of nature,—issuing in poetry, false under
whatever form, which shows a thing not as it is to mankind
240   generally, nor as it is to the particular describer, but as it is
supposed to be for some unreal neutral mood, midway
between both and of value to neither, and living its brief
minute simply through the indolence of whoever accepts
it or his incapacity to denounce a cheat. Although of such
245   depths of failure there can be no question here we must in
every case betake ourselves to the review of a poet's life ere
we determine some of the nicer questions concerning
his poetry,—more especially if the performance we seek to
estimate aright, has been obstructed and cut short of com-
250   pletion by circumstances,—a disastrous youth or a premature death. We may learn from the biography whether his
spirit invariably saw and spoke from the last height to which
it had attained. An absolute vision is not for this world, but
we are permitted a continual approximation to it, every degree
255   of which in the individual, provided it exceed the attainment of the masses, must procure him a clear advantage.
Did the poet ever attain to a higher platform than where
he rested and exhibited a result? Did he know more than
he spoke of?
260   I concede however, in respect to the subject of our study
as well as some few other illustrious examples, that the un-
mistakeable quality of the verse would be evidence enough,
under usual circumstances, not only of the kind and degree
of the intellectual but of the moral constitution of Shelley:
265   the whole personality of the poet shining forward from the

255–6. *the attainment of the masses*: on the resonance in the period of the term
'masses' and 'the mass of men', see headnote to *In a Balcony* (III 402–3).

poems, without much need of going further to seek it.
The "Remains"—produced within a period of ten years, and
at a season of life when other men of at all comparable genius
have hardly done more than prepare the eye for future sight
270   and the tongue for speech—present us with the complete
enginery of a poet, as signal in the excellence of its several
adaptitudes as transcendent in the combination of effects,
examples, in fact, of the whole poet's function of beholding
with an understanding keenness the universe, nature and
275   man, in their actual state of perfection in imperfection,—
of the whole poet's virtue of being untempted by the
manifold partial developments of beauty and good on every
side, into leaving them the ultimates he found them,—induced
by the facility of the gratification of his own sense of those
280   qualities, or by the pleasure of acquiescence in the shortcomings of his predecessors in art, and the pain of disturb-
ing their conventionalisms,—the whole poet's virtue, I
repeat, of looking higher than any manifestation yet made
of both beauty and good, in order to suggest from the utmost
285   actual realisation of the one a corresponding capability in
the other, and out of the calm, purity and energy of nature,
to reconstitute and store up for the forthcoming stage of man's
being, a gift in repayment of that former gift, in which man's
own thought and passion had been lavished by the poet on
290   the else-incompleted magnificence of the sunrise, the else-
uninterpreted mystery of the lake,—so drawing out, lifting
up, and assimilating this ideal of a future man, thus descried
as possible, to the present reality of the poet's soul already
arrived at the higher state of development, and still aspirant to
295   elevate and extend itself in conformity with its still-improving
perceptions of, no longer the eventual Human, but the actual
Divine. In conjunction with which noble and rare powers,
came the subordinate power of delivering these attained

267. *The "Remains"*: as *Oxford* points out, not a reference to posthumous publication of Shelley's work, but to the whole corpus of his writings: 'what he left
behind'.
272. *adaptitudes*: 'Adaptedness; aptitude specially produced'; the first (and only other)
instance of this word rec. by *OED* comes in EBB.'s critical essay *The Greek Christian
Poets*, which had appeared in the *Athenaeum* in 1842. B. uses it again at l. 570
below.

results to the world in an embodiment of verse more closely
300 answering to and indicative of the process of the informing
spirit, (failing as it occasionally does, in art, only to succeed
in highest art),—with a diction more adequate to the task
in its natural and acquired richness, its material colour and
spiritual transparency,—the whole being moved by and
305 suffused with a music at once of the soul and the sense,
expressive both of an external might of sincere passion and
an internal fitness and consonancy,—than can be attributed
to any other writer whose record is among us. Such was
the spheric poetical faculty of Shelley, as its own self-
310 sufficing central light, radiating equally through immaturity
and accomplishment, through many fragments and occasional
completion, reveals it to a competent judgment.

But the acceptance of this truth by the public, has been
retarded by certain objections which cast us back on the
315 evidence of biography, even with Shelley's poetry in our hands.
Except for the particular character of these objections,
indeed, the non-appreciation of his contemporaries would
simply class, now that it is over, with a series of experiences
which have necessarily happened and needlessly been
320 wondered at, ever since the world began, and concerning
which any present anger may well be moderated, no less in
justice to our forerunners than in policy to ourselves. For the
misapprehensiveness of his age is exactly what a poet is sent
to remedy; and the interval between his operation and the
325 generally perceptible effect of it, is no greater, less indeed,
than in many other departments of the great human effort.
The "E pur si muove" of the astronomer was as bitter a word
as any uttered before or since by a poet over his rejected
living work, in that depth of conviction which is so like despair.

299–302. an embodiment of verse . . . succeed in highest art): cp. the description of
Raphael's painting in *Andrea* 103–13 (pp. 395–6). The vocabulary, although not
quite the thought, recalls an early letter of B.'s to EBB. (13 Jan. 1845) in which,
pressed to say what he thought the defects of her poetry, he wrote: 'What "struck
me as faults," were not matters on the removal of which, one was to have—
poetry, or high poetry,—but the very highest poetry, so I thought,—and that,
to universal recognition' (*Correspondence* x 21–2).
318–20. a series of experiences . . . ever since the world began: for this concept of the
necessary neglect of the 'true poet', see headnote to *Popularity*, p. 449.
327. The "E pur si muove" of the astronomer: Galileo's famous (apocryphal)
statement ('And yet, it does move') after his enforced retraction, in 1634, of his
theory that the earth moves around the sun.

330   But in this respect was the experience of Shelley peculiarly unfortunate—that the disbelief in him as a man, even
preceded the disbelief in him as a writer; the misconstruc-
tion of his moral nature preparing the way for the mis-
appreciation of his intellectual labours. There existed from
335   the beginning,—simultaneous with, indeed anterior to his
earliest noticeable works, and not brought forward to
counteract any impression they had succeeded in making,—
certain charges against his private character and life, which,
if substantiated to their whole breadth, would materially
340   disturb, I do not attempt to deny, our reception and enjoyment of his works, however wonderful the artistic qualities
of these. For we are not sufficiently supplied with instances
of genius of his order, to be able to pronounce certainly how
many of its constituent parts have been tasked and strained
345   to the production of a given lie, and how high and pure a
mood of the creative mind may be dramatically simulated
as the poet's habitual and exclusive one. The doubts, therefore, rising from such a question, required to be set at rest,
as they were effectually, by those early authentic notices
350   of Shelley's career and the corroborative accompaniment of
his letters, in which not only the main tenor and principal
result of his life, but the purity and beauty of many of the
processes which had conduced to them, were made apparent enough for the general reader's purpose,—whoever
355   lightly condemned Shelley first, on the evidence of reviews
and gossip, as lightly acquitting him now, on that of
memoirs and correspondence. Still, it is advisable to lose
no opportunity of strengthening and completing the chain
of biographical testimony; much more, of course, for the sake
360   of the poet's original lovers, whose volunteered sacrifice
of particular principle in favour of absorbing sympathy we
might desire to dispense with, than for the sake of his foolish
haters, who have long since diverted upon other objects
their obtuseness or malignancy. A full life of Shelley should
365   be written at once, while the materials for it continue
in reach; not to minister to the curiosity of the public, but
to obliterate the last stain of that false life which was forced
on the public's attention before it had any curiosity on
the matter,—a biography, composed in harmony with the
370   present general disposition to have faith in him, yet not
shrinking from a candid statement of all ambiguous passages,
through a reasonable confidence that the most doubtful of

them will be found consistent with a belief in the eventual
perfection of his character, according to the poor limits of
375   our humanity. Nor will men persist in confounding, any more
than God confounds, with genuine infidelity and an atheism
of the heart, those passionate, impatient struggles of a boy
towards distant truth and love, made in the dark, and
ended by one sweep of the natural seas before the full moral
380   sunrise could shine out on him. Crude convictions of boyhood, conveyed in imperfect and inapt forms of speech,
—for such things all boys have been pardoned. There are
growing-pains, accompanied by temporary distortion, of
the soul also. And it would be hard indeed upon this young
385   Titan of genius, murmuring in divine music his human
ignorances, through his very thirst for knowledge, and his
rebellion, in mere aspiration to law, if the melody itself
substantiated the error, and the tragic cutting short of life
perpetuated into sins, such faults as, under happier circum-
390   stances, would have been left behind by the consent of the
most arrogant moralist, forgotten on the lowest steps of youth.

    The responsibility of presenting to the public a biog-
raphy of Shelley, does not, however lie with me: I have only
to make it a little easier by arranging these few supplemen-
395   tary letters, with a recognition of the value of the whole
collection. This value I take to consist in a most truthful
conformity of the Correspondence, in its limited degree, with
the moral and intellectual character of the writer as displayed
in the highest manifestations of this genius. Letters and poems
400   are obviously an act of the same mind, produced by the same
law, only differing in the application to the individual or
collective understanding. Letters and poems may be used
indifferently as the basement of our opinion upon the
writer's character; the finished expression of a sentiment in
405   the poems, giving light and significance to the rudiments of
the same in the letters, and these, again, in their incipiency
and unripeness, authenticating the exalted mood and re-
attaching it to the personality of the writer. The musician speaks
on the note he sings with; there is no change in the scale,
410   as he diminishes the volume into familiar intercourse. There
is nothing of that jarring between the man and the author,
which has been found so amusing or so melancholy; no
dropping of the tragic mask, as the crowd melts away; no
mean discovery of the real motives of a life's achievement,
415   often, in other lives, laid bare as pitifully as when, at the

close of a holiday, we catch sight of the internal lead-pipes
and wood-valves, to which, and not to the ostensible conch
and dominant Triton of the fountain, we have owed our
admired waterwork. No breaking out, in household privacy,
420 of hatred anger and scorn, incongruous with the higher mood
and suppressed artistically in the book: no brutal return to
self-delighting, when the audience of philanthropic schemes
is out of hearing: no indecent stripping off the grander feeling and rule of life as too costly and cumbrous for every-
425 day wear. Whatever Shelley was, he was with an admirable
sincerity. It was not always truth that he thought and spoke;
but in the purity of truth he spoke and thought always.
Everywhere is apparent his belief in the existence of Good,
to which Evil is an accident; his faithful holding by what
430 he assumed to be the former, going everywhere in company with the tenderest pity for those acting or suffering on
the opposite hypothesis. For he was tender, though tenderness is not always the characteristic of very sincere natures;
he was eminently both tender and sincere. And not only do
435 the same affection and yearning after the well-being of his
kind, appear in the letters as in the poems, but they express
themselves by the same theories and plans, however crude
and unsound. There is no reservation of a subtler, less costly,
more serviceable remedy for his own ill, than he had pro-
440 posed for the general one; nor does he ever contemplate
an object on his own account, from a less elevation than
he uses in exhibiting it to the world. How shall we help
believing Shelley to have been, in his ultimate attainment,
the splendid spirit of his own best poetry, when we find even
445 his carnal speech to agree faithfully, at faintest as at strongest,
with the tone and rhythm of his most oracular utterances?
     For the rest, these new letters are not offered as pre-
senting any new feature of the poet's character. Regarded
in themselves, and as the substantive productions of a man,
450 their importance would be slight. But they possess interest
beyond their limits, in confirming the evidence just
dwelt on, of the poetical mood of Shelley being only
the intensification of his habitual mood; the same tongue
only speaking, for want of the special excitement to sing.

417–18. the ostensible conch and dominant Triton of the fountain: cp. *Up at a Villa*
26–30 (III 145–6).

455 The very first letter, as one instance for all, strikes the key-
      note of the predominating sentiment of Shelley throughout
      his whole life—his sympathy with the oppressed. And
      when we see him at so early an age, casting out, under the
      influence of such a sympathy, letters and pamphlets on
460 every side, we accept it as the simple exemplification of the
      sincerity, with which, at the close of his life, he spoke of
      himself, as—

      "One whose heart a stranger's tear might wear
      As water-drops the sandy fountain stone;
465 Who loved and pitied all things, and could moan
      For woes which others hear not, and could see
      The absent with the glass of phantasy,
      And near the poor and trampled sit and weep,
      Following the captive to his dungeon deep—
470 One who was as a nerve o'er which do creep
      The else-unfelt oppressions of this earth."

      Such sympathy with his kind was evidently developed in
      him to an extraordinary and even morbid degree, at a period
      when the general intellectual powers it was impatient to put
475 in motion, were immature or deficient.
      I conjecture, from a review of the various publications of
      Shelley's youth, that one of the causes of his failure at the
      outset, was the peculiar *practicalness* of his mind, which was not
      without a determinate effect on his progress in theorising.
480 An ordinary youth, who turns his attention to similar
      subjects, discovers falsities, incongruities, and various points
      for amendment, and, in the natural advance of the purely
      critical spirit unchecked by considerations of remedy, keeps

---

455. The very first letter: letter 1 purports to be addressed to the editor of the *Statesman*,
and is dated 22 Feb. 1811; portions had been taken from a genuine Shelley
letter of 2 Mar. 1811. The letter as B. knew it is about government repression
of freedom of speech and writing.
461–2. he spoke of himself: the lines which B. goes on to quote are from *Julian
and Maddalo*, written in 1818 but first publ. posthumously in 1824, hence B.'s
assumption that they date from 'the close of [Shelley's] life'. They are spoken
by the madman whose long speech Count Maddalo (Byron) quotes to Julian
(Shelley), and are not a direct self-description; but B. is probably justified in thinking that Shelley had himself in mind. The passage begins 'But *me*—whose heart';
in l. 6 B. has 'And near' for 'And with'; in l. 8, 'One who was' for '*Me*—who am'.

up before his young eyes so many instances of the same error
485   and wrong, that he finds himself unawares arrived at the
startling conclusion, that all must be changed—or nothing:
in the face of which plainly impossible achievement, he is
apt (looking perhaps a little more serious by the time he
touches at the decisive issue), to feel, either carelessly or con-
490   siderately, that his own attempting a single piece of service
would be worse than useless even, and to refer the whole
task to another age and person—safe in proportion to his incapacity. Wanting words to speak, he has never made a fool
of himself by speaking. But, in Shelley's case, the early
495   fervour and power to *see*, was accompanied by as precocious
a fertility to *contrive*: he endeavoured to realise as he went
on idealising; every wrong had simultaneously its remedy,
and, out of the strength of his hatred for the former, he took
the strength of his confidence in the latter—till suddenly
500   he stood pledged to the defence of a set of miserable little
expedients, just as if they represented great principles, and
to an attack upon various great principles, really so, without leaving himself time to examine whether, because they
were antagonistical to the remedy he had suggested, they
505   must therefore be identical or even essentially connected with
the wrong he sought to cure,—playing with blind passion
into the hands of his enemies, and dashing at whatever red
cloak was held forth to him, as the cause of the fireball
he had last been stung with—mistaking Churchdom for
510   Christianity, and for marriage, "the sale of love" and the law
of sexual oppression.

Gradually, however, he was leaving behind him this low
practical dexterity, unable to keep up with his widening intellectual, perception; and, in exact proportion as he did so,
515   his true power strengthened and proved itself. Gradually he

---

*509–11. mistaking Churchdom for Christianity, and for marriage, "the sale of love" and
the law of sexual oppression.* Both these topics are dealt with in the spurious
letters. Letter iv (pp. 59–63), dated 8 March 1811, criticises organized religion as
'the bond of aristocracy, monopoly, and despotism' (p. 61). Letters v and vi
(pp. 64–70) praise James Lawrence for attacking the institution of marriage in his
novel *The Empire of the Nairs* (1812): 'Your "Empire of the Nairs," which I read
this spring, succeeded in making me a perfect convert to its doctrines. I then
retained no doubt of the evils of marriage,—Mrs. Wollstonecraft reasons too well
for that; but I had been dull enough not to perceive the greatest argument against
it, until developed in the "Nairs," viz. prostitution both *legal* and *illegal*' (pp. 64–5).

was raised above the contemplation of spots and the attempt
at effacing them, to the great Abstract Light, and, through
the discrepancy of the creation, to the sufficiency of the
First Cause. Gradually he was learning that the best way
520   of removing abuses is to stand fast by truth. Truth is one,
as they are manifold; and innumerable negative effects are
produced by the upholding of one positive principle. I shall
say what I think,—had Shelley lived he would have finally
ranged himself with the Christians; his very instinct for help-
525   ing the weaker side (if numbers make strength), his very "hate
of hate," which at first mistranslated itself into delirious Queen
Mab notes and the like, would have got clearer-sighted
by exercise. The preliminary step to following Christ, is the
leaving the dead to bury their dead—not clamouring on His
530   doctrine for an especial solution of difficulties which are
referable to the general problem of the universe. Already he
had attained to a profession of "a worship to the Spirit of
good within, which requires (before it sends that inspiration
forth, which impresses its likeness upon all it creates)

525–6. his very "hate of hate,": B. is quoting Tennyson's 'The Poet' (l. 3), first
publ. in *Poems, Chiefly Lyrical* (1830).
526–7. delirious Queen Mab notes: Shelley's early radical, visionary poem *Queen Mab*
(1813) has seventeen prose notes at the back, 'many of them substantial essays,
"against Jesus Christ, & God the Father, & the King, & the Bishops, & Marriage,
& the Devil knows what', as Shelley himself put it' (*Oxford Companion to English
Literature*). B.'s tone of disparagement here disguises the evident influence this
work had on his own early poetry and politics.
529. leaving the dead to bury their dead: from *Luke* ix 59–60: 'And he [Jesus] said
unto another, Follow me. But he said, Lord, suffer me first to go and bury my
father. Jesus said unto him, Let the dead bury their dead: but go thou and preach
the kingdom of God.'
532–5. a worship . . . as Coleridge says: a rearrangement, as *Oxford* points out (with
acknowledgment to Professor Timothy Webb) of a passage in one of Shelley's
letters (to Maria Gisborne, 13 to 14 Oct. 1819). In rearranging the passage B.
has, however, altered the sense by omitting the opening part of Shelley's statement. Shelley attributes to Coleridge the idea that 'Hope . . . is a solemn duty
which we owe alike to ourselves & to the world' (*Letters of P.B. Shelley*, ed. Frederick
L. Jones, 2 vols. [Oxford, 1964] vol. ii, p. 125). In an earlier letter to Byron, of
8 Sept. 1816, Shelley had quoted Coleridge as saying that 'Hope is a most awful
duty, the nurse of all other duties' (*Letters*, ed. Jones, vol. I, p. 504). Neither
statement has yet been convincingly identified with any passage in Coleridge's
writings; Joseph Raben suggests that Shelley may have received a version of one
of them 'from oral report' (*RES* n.s. xvii, 67 [1966], 284).

535   devoted and disinterested homage, *as Coleridge says*,"—and
       Paul likewise. And we find in one of his last exquisite frag-
       ments, avowedly a record of one of his own mornings and
       its experience, as it dawned on him at his soul and body's
       best in his boat on the Serchio—that as surely as

540   "The stars burnt out in the pale blue air,
       And the thin white moon lay withering there—
       Day had kindled the dewy woods,
       And the rocks above, and the stream below,
       And the vapours in their multitudes,
545   And the Apennine's shroud of summer snow—
       Day had awakened all things that be;"

       just so surely, he tells us (stepping forward from this deli-
       cious dance-music, choragus-like, into the grander measure
       befitting the final enunciation),

550   "All rose to do the task He set to each,
       Who shaped us to his ends and not our own;
       The million rose to learn, and One to teach
       What none yet ever knew or can be known."

       No more difference than this, from David's pregnant
555   conclusion so long ago!
       Meantime, as I call Shelley a moral man, because he was
       true, simple-hearted, and brave, and because what he acted
       corresponded to what he knew, so I call him a man of
       religious mind, because every audacious negative cast up by
560   him against the Divine, was interpenetrated with a mood of

535–6. and Paul likewise: there are many references to the 'spirit' in St Paul's Epistles;
the conjunction with 'worship' suggests *Philippians* iii 3, 'worship God in the Spirit';
cp. also *2 Timothy* i 14: 'the Holy Ghost which dwelleth in us'.
536–7. one of his last exquisite fragments: the lines which B. goes on to quote come
from another posthumously published poem, 'The Boat on the Serchio', written
in 1821. B. quotes ll. 7–8, 11–14, and 17, followed by ll. 30–3.
548. choragus-like: 'like the leader of the chorus (in a Greek play)'.
554–5. David's pregnant conclusion: *Oxford* suggests that this 'pregnant conclusion'
is found 'throughout the Psalms', but B.'s analogy seems to us more hopeful than
accurate; there is nothing in *Psalms* about God as a taskmaster, nor do they speak
of a teacher who teaches in riddles.

reverence and adoration,—and because I find him everywhere
taking for granted some of the capital dogmas of Christianity,
while most vehemently denying their historical basement.
There is such a thing as an efficacious knowledge of and
565   belief in the politics of Junius, or the poetry of Rowley, though
a man should at the same time dispute the title of
Chatterton to the one, and consider the author of the
other, as Byron wittily did, "really, truly, nobody at all."★
There is even such a thing, we come to learn wonderingly
570   in these very letters, as a profound sensibility and adaptitude
for art, while the science of the percipient is so little

★ Or, to take our illustrations from the writings of Shelley himself, there
is such a thing as admirably appreciating a work by Andrea Verocchio,—
and fancifully characterising the Pisan Torre Guelfa by the Ponte a Mare,
black against the sunsets,—and consummately painting the islet of San
Clemente with its penitentiary for rebellious priests, to the west between
Venice and the Lido—while you believe the first to be a fragment of an
antique sarcophagus,—the second, Ugolino's Tower of Famine (the vestiges of which should be sought for in the Piazza de' Cavalieri)—and the
third (as I convinced myself last summer at Venice), San Servolo with its
madhouse—which, far from being "windowless," is as full of windows as
a barrack. [B.'s footnote]

565. the politics of Junius, or the poetry of Rowley: 'Junius' was the pseudonym of an
eighteenth-century Whig pamphleteer, who castigated corruption in government;
the controversy over his real identity was still active in the period (B.'s father
owned several books on the subject). 'Rowley' was the name of the medieval
monk to whom Thomas Chatterton ascribed his forgeries (see headnote,
Parallels). B. had paired Junius with Rowley in *Waring* 188–91 (p. 193).
568. as Byron wittily did: in 'The Vision of Judgment'; the shade of Junius appears
in all his baffling impenetrability, whereupon Byron offers his own 'hypothesis',
that 'what Junius we are wont to call / Was *really—truly*—nobody at all' (st. lxxx,
ll. 7–8).
[B.'s footnote] *to take our illustrations from the writings of Shelley himself*: the point is
that Shelley's genuine artistry shines through the inaccurate information on which
it was based, just as his spiritual qualities are evident despite the wrong-headedness
of their expression. B.'s examples are drawn from passages of Shelley's prose and
poetry in which he reveals his ignorance of Italian art and literary topography:
mistaking a bas-relief by the Florentine sculptor and painter Andrea Verrochio
(*c.*1435–88) for 'the sides of a sarcophagus' (B. would have found this error in
'Remarks on some of the Statues in the Gallery of Florence', in the volume he
mentions at the beginning of the essay: see ll. 3–4n.); misidentifying the Pisan
'Tower of Famine' (where Ugolino and his children perished: Dante, *Inferno* xxxiii)
in a note to the poem of that title; and mistaking the Venetian location of the
madhouse in *Julian and Maddalo*. B. emphasizes his own insider's knowledge of
the three Italian cities.

advanced as to admit of his stronger admiration for Guido
(and Carlo Dolce!) than for Michael Angelo. A Divine Being
has Himself said, that "a word against the Son of man shall
575   be forgiven to a man," while "a word against the Spirit of
God" (implying a general deliberate preference of perceived
evil to perceived good) "shall not be forgiven to a man."
Also, in religion, one earnest and unextorted assertion of belief
should outweigh, as a matter of testimony, many assertions
580   of unbelief. The fact that there is a gold-region is established
by the finding of one lump, though you miss the vein never
so often.

He died before his youth ended. In taking the measure
of him as a man, he must be considered on the whole and
585   at his ultimate spiritual stature, and not be judged of at the
immaturity and by the mistakes of ten years before: that,
indeed, would be to judge of the author of "Julian and
Maddalo" by "Zastrozzi." Let the whole truth be told of his
worst mistake. I believe, for my own part, that if anything
590   could now shame or grieve Shelley, it would be an attempt
to vindicate him at the expense of another.

In forming a judgment, I would, however, press on the
reader the simple justice of considering tenderly his constitution of body as well as mind, and how unfavourable it
595   was to the steady symmetries of conventional life; the body,
in the torture of incurable disease, refusing to give repose to
the bewildered soul, tossing in its hot fever of the fancy,—
and the laudanum-bottle making but a perilous and pitiful
truce between these two. He was constantly subject to "that

572–3. Guido (and Carlo Dolce!) than for Michael Angelo: Guido Reni (1575–1642),
greatly admired in Britain in the eighteenth and early nineteenth centuries; Carlo
Dolci (*sic*; 1616–87), Florentine painter also much patronized by British aristo-
crats on the Grand Tour; both suffered from Ruskin's comprehensive disparagement of seventeenth-century painting in favour of the religious art of earlier periods,
a taste B. shared and helped to propagate: see headnote to *Old Pictures*, p. 407,
and l. 232n. (p. 428). For Michelangelo as one of the unquestionable masters of
the Renaissance, see headnote to *Andrea* (p. 386).
573–4. A Divine Being has Himself said: *Luke* xii 10: 'And whosoever shall speak
a word against the Son of man, it shall be forgiven him: but unto him that
blasphemeth against the Holy Ghost it shall not be forgiven.' B.'s biblical
quotation is unusually 'free'; note esp. the avoidance of the word 'blasphemeth'.
588. "Zastrozzi": Shelley's Gothic romance, publ. in 1810 when its author was
eighteen.

600   state of mind" (I quote his own note to "Hellas") "in which
       ideas may be supposed to assume the force of sensation,
       through the confusion of thought with the objects of
       thought, and excess of passion animating the creations of the
       imagination": in other words, he was liable to remarkable
605   delusions and hallucinations. The nocturnal attack in Wales,
       for instance, was assuredly a delusion; and I venture to express
       my own conviction, derived from a little attention to the
       circumstances of either story, that the idea of the enamoured
       lady following him to Naples, and of the "man in the cloak"
610   who struck him at the Pisan post-office, were equally illu-
       sory,—the mere projection, in fact, from himself, of the image
       of his own love and hate.

       "To thirst and find no fill—to wail and wander
       With short unsteady steps—to pause and ponder—
615   To feel the blood run through the veins and tingle
       When busy thought and blind sensation mingle,—
       To nurse the image of *unfelt caresses*
       Till dim imagination just possesses
       The half-created shadow"—

620   of unfelt caresses,—and of unfelt blows as well: to such
       conditions was his genius subject. It was not at Rome only
       (where he heard a mystic voice exclaiming, "Cenci, Cenci,"
       in reference to the tragic theme which occupied him at the
       time),—it was not at Rome only that he mistook the cry

600. his own note to "Hellas": in a note to l. 815 of *Hellas: a Lyrical Drama* (1822),
Shelley defends his decision to make Mahmud's vision of the fall of Constantinople
in 1453 a product of psychological suggestion, not a supernatural event. B. slightly
misquotes: 'and the excess of passion animating the creations of imagination'.
605. The nocturnal attack in Wales: an incident which took place on 26 Feb. 1813
at Tremadoc; shots were fired in the night, and Shelley claimed an attempt had
been made to kill him.
613. "To thirst and find no fill: a fragment first publ. in Shelley's *Poetical Works*
(1839), ed. by Mary Shelley; after 'shadow;' B. omits 'then all the night / Sick'
which is where the fragment breaks off. The italics are his.
622. a mystic voice exclaiming, "Cenci, Cenci,": while working in Rome on his drama,
The Cenci (1819), Shelley heard this cry in the street; it was not, however, a
'mystic voice' but a street-seller, since 'cenci' means 'old rags'. *Oxford* points out
that B. returned to this pun with the title of his poem *Cenciaja* (*Pacchiarotto*, 1876),
which means 'a trifle' (lit. a bundle of rags); the poem professes itself to be no
more than a pendant to Shelley's work.

625 of "old rags." The habit of somnambulism is said to have
extended to the very last days of his life.

  Let me conclude with a thought of Shelley as a poet.
In the hierarchy of creative minds, it is the presence of the
highest faculty that gives first rank, in virtue of its kind,
630 not degree; no pretension of a lower nature, whatever the
completeness of development or variety of effect, impeding the
precedency of the rarer endowment though only in the germ.
The contrary is sometimes maintained; it is attempted to make
the lower gifts (which are potentially included in the higher
635 faculty) of independent value, and equal to some exercise
of the special function. For instance, should not a poet
possess common sense? Then the possession of abundant
common sense implies a step towards becoming a poet. Yes;
such a step as the lapidary's, when, strong in the fact of
640 carbon entering largely into the composition of the diamond,
he heaps up a sack of charcoal in order to compete with
the Koh-i-noor. I pass at once, therefore, from Shelley's minor
excellencies to his noblest and predominating characteristic.
  This I call his simultaneous perception of Power and Love
645 in the absolute, and of Beauty and Good in the concrete,
while he throws, from his poet's station between both,
swifter, subtler, and more numerous films for the connexion
of each with each, than have been thrown by any modern
artificer of whom I have knowledge; proving how, as he says,

650 "The spirit of the worm within the sod,
  In love and worship blends itself with God."

628–30. *it is the presence . . . not degree*: this idea is satirically treated by Bishop
Blougram (see ll. 78–85, p. 290), who spends the rest of his speech attempting
to rebut it; it is restated with exalted (although also grotesque) fervour by the
student chorus of *A Grammarian* (ll. 113–24, pp. 595–6).

636–7. *should not a poet possess common sense?*: Naddo, the epitome of the fatuous
critic in *Sordello*, expresses the view that poetry must be 'Based upon common
sense; there's nothing like / Appealing to our nature!' (ii 792–3, I 512).

642. *the Koh-i-noor*: one of the diamonds in the Crown Jewels; B. mentions it
again in *Old Pictures* 245 (p. 429).

647. *swifter, subtler, and more numerous films*: with this (positive) image of the artist-
spider, cp. *Sordello* i 665–71n. (I 440–1).

650. *"The spirit of the worm*: *Epipsychidion* (1821) 128–9; B. has 'within' for 'beneath'.
Cp. *Christmas-Eve* 285 (III 59).

I would rather consider Shelley's poetry as a sublime fragmentary essay towards a presentment of the correspondency
of the universe to Deity, of the natural to the spiritual, and
655 of the actual to the ideal, than I would isolate and separately
appraise the worth of many detachable portions which
might be acknowledged as utterly perfect in a lower moral
point of view, under the mere conditions of art. It would
be easy to take my stand on successful instances of object-
660 ivity in Shelley: there is the unrivalled "Cenci;" there is the
"Julian and Maddalo" too; there is the magnificent "Ode to
Naples:" why not regard, it may be said, the less organised
matter as the radiant elemental foam and solution, out of
which would have been evolved, eventually, creations as
665 perfect even as those? But I prefer to look for the highest
attainment, not simply the high,—and, seeing it, I hold by
it. There is surely enough of the work "Shelley" to be known
enduringly among men, and, I believe, to be accepted of
God, as human work may; and around the imperfect
670 proportions of such, the most elaborated productions of
ordinary art must arrange themselves as inferior illustrations.
It is because I have long held these opinions in assurance
and gratitude, that I catch at the opportunity offered to me
of expressing them here; knowing that the alacrity to fulfil
675 an humble office conveys more love than the acceptance of
the honour of a higher one, and that better, therefore, than
the signal service it was the dream of my boyhood to
render to his fame and memory, may be the saying of a
few, inadequate words upon these scarcely more important
680 supplementary letters of SHELLEY.

PARIS, *Dec. 4th*, 1851.

Appendix B
RUSKIN'S LETTER TO BROWNING
ABOUT *MEN AND WOMEN*,
AND BROWNING'S REPLY

(a) *John Ruskin to Robert Browning, 2 Dec. 1855*

Source: D. DeLaura (ed.), 'Ruskin and the Brownings: Twenty-five Unpublished Letters', *BJRL* liv (1972) 314–56.

Dear Mr Browning

I know you have been wondering that I did not write, but I could not till now—and hardly can, now: not because I am busy—nor careless, but because I cannot at all make up my mind about these poems of yours: and so far as my mind *is* made up, I am not sure whether it is in the least right. Of their power there can of course be no question—nor do you need to be told of it; for everyone who *has* power of this kind, knows it—*must* know it. But as to the Presentation of the Power, I am in great doubt. Being hard worked at present, & not being able to give the cream of the day to poetry—when I take up these poems in the evening I find them absolutely and literally a set of the most amazing Conundrums that ever were proposed to me. I try at them, for—say twenty minutes—in which time I make out about twenty lines, always having to miss two, for every one that I make out. I enjoy the twenty, each separately, very much, but the puzzlement about the intermediate ones increases in comfortlessness till I get a headache, & give in.

Now that you may exactly understand the way I feel about them—I will read, with you, one poem—as I read it to myself, with all my comments and questions. I open at random—Cleon?—no—that's not a fair example being harder than most. The Twins?—no—I have made out that—(except the fifth stanza)—so it is not a fair example on the other side being easier than most. Popularity?—yes, that touches the matter in hand.

> Stand still, true poet that you are
> I know you;—let me try and draw you:

(Does this mean: literally—stand still? or where was the poet figuratively going —and why couldn't he be drawn as he went?) "Some night you'll fail us?" (Why some *night*?—rather than some day?—"Fail us." How? Die?) "When afar you Rise"—(Where?—How?) "remember &c." (very good—I understand.) "My star, God's glowworm." (Very fine. I understand and like that.) "Why ^ extend that loving hand." (Grammatically, this applies to the Poet. The ellipsis of "Should He" at ^ throws one quite out—like a step in a floor which one doesn't expect.

"Yet locks you safe." How does God's hand lock him; do you mean—keeps him from being seen?—and how does it make him safe. Why is a poet safer or more locked up than anybody else. I go on—in hope. "His clenched hand ——beauty"—very good—but I don't understand why the hand should have held close so long—which is just the point I wanted to be explained. Why the poet *had to be* locked up.

"My poet holds the future fast." How? Do you mean he anticipates it in his mind—trusts in it—I *don't* know if you mean that, because I don't know if poets *do* that. If you mean that—I wish you had said so plainly.

"That day the earth's feastmaster's brow." Who is the earth's F.? An Angel?—an Everybody?

"The chalice *raising*." This, grammatically, agrees with "*brow*," and makes me uncomfortable. "Others, &c.", very pretty, I like that. "Meantime I'll draw you." Do you mean—his Cork?—we have not had anything about painting for ever so long—very well. *Do* draw him then: I should like to have him drawn very much.

"I'll say—a fisher—&c." Now, where *are* you going to—this is, I believe, pure malice against *me*, for having said that painters should always grind their own colours.

"Who has not heard——merchant sells." Do you mean—the silk that the merchant sells Raw—or what do you want with the merchant at all.

"And each bystander." Who are these bystanders—I didn't hear of any before—Are they people who have gone to see the fishing?

"Could criticise, & quote tradition." Criticise what? the fishing?—and why should they—what was wrong in it?—"Quote tradition." Do you mean about purple? But if they made purple at the time, it wasn't tradition merely—but experience.—You might as well tell me you heard the colourmen in Long-Acre, quote tradition touching their next cargo of Indigo, or cochineal.

"Depths—sublimed." I don't know what you mean by "sublimed." Made sublime?—if so—it is not English.[1] To sublime means to evaporate dryly, I believe, and has participle "Sublimated."

"Worth scepter, crown and ball"—Indeed. Was there ever such a fool of a King?—You ought to have put a note saying who.

"Yet there's, &c." Well. I understand that, & it's very pretty.

"Enough to furnish Solomon, &c." I don't think Solomon's spouse swore—at least not about blue-bells. I understand this bit, but fear most people won't. How many have noticed a blue-bell's stamen?

"Bee to her groom" I don't understand. I thought there was only one Queen-bee and *she* never was out o'nights—nor came home drunk or disorderly. Besides if she does, unless you had told me what o'clock in the morning she comes home at, the simile is of no use to me.

"Mere conchs." Well, but what has this to do with the Poet. Who "pounds" *him*? I don't understand—

"World stands aloof—" yes—from the purple manufactory, but from Pounding of Poets?—does it?—and if so—who distils—or fines, & bottles them.

"Flasked & fine." Now *is* that what you call painting a poet. Under the whole & sole image of a bottle of Blue, with a bladder over the cork? The Arabian fisherman with his genie was nothing to this.

"Hobbs, Nobbs, &c. paint the future." Why the future. Do you mean *in* the future.

"Blue into their line?" I don't understand;—do you mean Quote the Poet, or write articles upon him—or in his style? And if so—was this what God kept him *safe* for? to feed Nobbs with Turtle. Is this what you call Accepting the future ages' duty.—I don't understand.

"What porridge?" Porridge is a Scotch dish, I believe; typical of bad fare. Do you mean that Keats had bad fare? But if he had—how was he kept safe to the world's end? I don't understand at all!!!!!!!

Now, that is the way I read, as well as I can, poem after poem, picking up a little here & there & enjoying it, but wholly unable to put anything together. I can't say I have really made out any yet, except the epistle from the Arabian physician, whch I like immensely, and I am only a stanza or so out with one or two others—in "By the Fireside" for instance I am only *dead* beat by the 41–43, and in "Fra Lippo"—I am only fast at the grated orris-root, which I looked for in the Encyclopaedia and couldn't find; and at the "There's for you"[2]—give me six months—because I don't know *What's* for you.

Well, how far all this is as it should be, I really know not. There is a stuff and fancy in your work which assuredly is in no other living writer's, and how far this purple of it *must* be within this terrible shell, and only to be fished for among threshing of foam & slippery rocks, I don't know. There are truths & depths in it, far beyond anything I have read except Shakespeare—and truly, if you had just written Hamlet, I believe I should have written to you, precisely this kind of letter—merely quoting your own Rosencrantz against you—"I understand you not, my Lord." I cannot write in enthusiasic praise, because I look at you every day as a monkey does at a cocoanut, having great faith in the milk—hearing it rattle indeed—inside—but quite beside myself for the Fibres. Still less can I write in blame. When a man has real power, God only knows how he *can* bring it out, or ought to bring it out. But, I would pray you, faith, heartily, to consider with yourself, how far you can amend matters, & make the real virtue of your work acceptable & profitable to more people.

For one thing, I entirely deny & refuse the right of any poet to require me to pronounce words short and long, exactly as he likes—to require me to read a plain & harsh & straightforward piece of prose. "Till I felt where the foldskirts (*fly*, redundant) open. Then once more I prayed;" as a dactylic verse, with skirts! for a short syllable.[3] "Foldskïrts flÿ"—as tremendous a long monosyllable as any in the language, and to say, "Wunce-mur-y" prayed, instead of "once more I."

And in the second place, I entirely deny that a poet of your real dramatic power ought to let *himself* come up, as you constantly do, through all manner of characters, so that every now and then poor Pippa herself shall speak a long piece of Robert Browning.

And in the third place, your ellipses are quite unconscionable: before one can get through ten lines, one has to patch you up in twenty places, wrong or right, and if one hasn't much stuff of one's own to spare to patch with! You are worse than the worst Alpine glacier I ever crossed. Bright, & deep enough truly, but so full of clefts that half the journey has to be done with ladder and hatchet.

However, I have found some great things in you already, and I think you must be a wonderful mine, when I have real time & strength to set to work properly. That bit about the Bishop & St Praxed, in the older poems, is very glorious. Rossetti showed it me. In fact, I oughtn't to write to you yet, at all, but such is my state of mind at present and it may perhaps be well that you should know it, even though it may soon change to a more acceptant one, because it most certainly represents the feelings of a good many more, besides myself, who ought to admire you & learn from you, but can't because you are so difficult.

Well—there's a specimen for you of my art of saying pleasant things to my friends.

I have no time left, now, for any unpleasant ones—so I must just say goodbye and beg you to accept, with my dear Mrs Browning, the assurance of my exceeding regard & respect.

Ever most faithfully Yours,

J Ruskin.

(b) *Browning to Ruskin, 10 Dec. 1855*

Source: W. G. Collingwood, *Life and Work of John Ruskin*, 2 vols. (1893), i 199–202.

My dear Ruskin,—for so you let me begin, with the honest friendliness that befits,—you were never more in the wrong than when you professed to say "your unpleasant things" to me. This is pleasant and proper at all points, over-liberal of praise here and there, kindly and sympathetic everywhere, and with enough of yourself in even—what I fancy—the misjudging, to make the whole letter precious indeed. I wanted to thank you thus much at once,—that is, when the letter reached me; but the strife of lodging-hunting was too sore, and only now that I can sit down for a minute without self-reproach do I allow my thoughts to let go south-aspects, warm bedrooms and the like, and begin as you see. For the deepnesses you think you discern,—may they be more than mere blacknesses! For the hopes you entertain of what may come of subsequent readngs,—all success to them! For your bewilderment more especially noted—how shall I help *that*? We don't read poetry the same way, by the same law; it is too clear. I cannot begin writing poetry till my imaginary reader has conceded licences to me which you demur at altogether. I *know* that I don't make out my conception by my language; all poetry being a putting the infinite within the finite. You would have me paint it all plain out, which can't be; but by various artifices I try to make shift with touches and bits of outlines which *succeed* if they bear the conception from me to you. You ought, I think, to keep pace with the thought tripping from ledge to ledge of my "glaciers," as you call them; not stand poking your alpenstock into the holes, and demonstrating that no foot could have stood there;—suppose it sprang over there? In *prose* you may criticise so—because that is the absolute representation of portions of truth, what chronicling is to history—but in asking for more *ultimates* you must accept less *mediates*, nor expect that a Druid stone-circle will be traced for you with as few breaks to the eye as the North Crescent and South Crescent that go together so cleverly in many a suburb. Why, you look at my little song as if it were Hobbs' or Nobbs' lease of his house, or testament of his devisings, wherein, I grant you, not a "then and there," "to him and his heirs," "to have and to hold," and so on, would be superfluous; and so you begin:—"Stand still,—why?" For the reason indicated in the verse, to be sure—*to let me draw him*—and because he is at present going his way, and fancying nobody notices him,—and moreover, "going on" (as we say) against the injustice of that,—and lastly, inasmuch as one night he'll fail us, as a star is apt to drop out of heaven, in authentic astronomic records, and I want to make the most of my time. So much may be in "stand still." And how much more was (for instance) in that "stay!" of Samuel's (I. xv. 16).[4] So could I twit you through the whole series of your objurgations, but the declaring my own notion of the law on the subject will do. And why,—I prithee, friend and fellow-student,—why, having told the Poet what you read,—may I not turn to the bystanders, and tell them a bit of my own mind about their own stupid thanklessness and mistaking? Is the jump too much there? The whole is all but a simultaneous feeling with me.

The other hard measure you deal me I won't bear—about my requiring you to pronounce words short and long, exactly as I like. Nay, but exactly as the language likes, in this case. *Foldskirts* not a trochee? A spondee possible in English? Two of the "longest monosyllables" continuing to be each of the old length when in junction? Sentence: let the delinquent be forced to supply the stone-cutter with a thousand companions to "Affliction sore—long time he bore," after the fashion of "He lost his life—by a pen-knife"—"He turned to clay—last Good Friday," "Departed hence—nor owed six-pence," and so on—so would pronounce a jury accustomed from the nipple to say lord and landlord, bridge and Cambridge, Gog and Magog, man and woman, house and work-house, skirts and fold-skirts, more and once more,—in short! Once *more* I prayed!—is the confession of a self-searching professor![5] "I stand here for law!"[6]

The last charge I cannot answer, for you may be right in preferring it, how-ever unwitting I am of the fact. I *may* put Robert Browning into Pippa and other men and maids. If so, *peccavi*:[7] but I don't see myself in them, at all events.

Do you think poetry was ever generally understood—or can be? Is the busi-ness of it to tell people what they know already, as they know it, and so pre-cisely that they shall be able to cry out—"Here you should supply *this*—*that*, you evidently pass over, and I'll help you from my own stock"? It is all teach-ing, on the contrary, and the people hate to be taught. They say otherwise,—make foolish fables about Orpheus enchanting stocks and stones, poets standing up and being worshipped,—all nonsense and impossible dreaming. A poet's affair is with God, to whom he is accountable, and of whom is his reward: look elsewhere, and you find misery enough. Do you believe people under-stand *Hamlet*? The last time I saw it acted, the heartiest applause went to a little by-play of the actor's own—who, to simulate madness in a hurry, plucked forth his handkerchief and flourished it hither and thither: certainly a third of the play, with no end of noble things, had been (as from time immemorial) suppressed, with the auditory's amplest acquiescence and benediction. Are these wasted, therefore? No—they act upon a very few, who react upon the rest: as Goldsmith says, "some lords, my acquaintance, that settle the nation, are pleased to be kind."

Don't let me lose *my* lord by any seeming self-sufficiency or petulance: I look on my own shortcomings too sorrowfully, try to remedy them too earnestly: but I shall never change my point of sight, or feel other than disconcerted and apprehensive when the public, critics and all, begin to understand and approve me. But what right have *you* to disconcert me in the other way? Why won't you ask the next perfumer for a packet of *orris*-root? Don't everybody know 'tis a corruption of *iris*-root—the Florentine lily, the *giaggolo*, of world-wide fame as a good savour? And because "iris" means so many objects already, and I use the old word, you blame me! But I write in the blind-dark and bitter cold, and past post-time as I fear. Take my truest thanks, and understand at least this rough writing, and, at all events, the real affection with which I venture to regard you. And "I" means my wife as well as

Yours ever faithfully,
Robert Browning.

---

[1] *Made sublime?—if so—it is not English*: Ruskin's challenge is incorrect: the *OED* records 'sublime' as a verb meaning 'to make sublime' from the 17th century, and many of the examples are of the past participle 'sublimed'.

[2] *the grated orris-root, which I looked for in the Encyclopaedia and couldn't find and at the "There's for you"*: see *Fra Lippo* 351n. and 345n. (pp. 504, 503).

[3] *a short syllable*: See *Saul* 20n. (III 496).

[4] *that "stay!" of Samuel's (I. xv. 16)*: cp. *Saul* 213–4n. (III 513).

[5] *a self-searching professor*. A 'self-searching professor' means someone who professes, or claims, to engage in soul-searching: the sense is that if you put the accent on *more* rather than *once* in the phrase 'Once more I prayed' you imply that the speaker is boasting about the number of times he prayed, rather than emphasising a renewed effort.

[6] *"I stand here for law!"*: Shylock's words in *The Merchant of Venice* IV i 142.

[7] *peccavi*: Latin, 'I have sinned'.

Appendix C

BELLS AND POMEGRANATES, MEN AND
WOMEN AND DRAMATIS PERSONAE

(1) Bells and Pomegranates

Between 1841 and 1846 B. published his poems and plays in a series of cheap paper-bound pamphlets, published by Edward Moxon, with the general title *Bells and Pomegranates*. There were eight numbers of *B & P*:

(i)   *Pippa Passes* (1841)
(ii)   *King Victor and King Charles* (1842)
(iii) *Dramatic Lyrics* (1842)
(iv) *The Return of the Druses* (1843)
(v)   *A Blot in the 'Scutcheon* (1843)
(vi) *Colombe's Birthday* (1844)
(vii) *Dramatic Romances and Lyrics* (1845)
(viii) *Luria* and *A Soul's Tragedy* (1846)

No. i was priced at 6*d*.; nos. ii–vi at 1*s*.; no. vii at 2*s*.; and no. viii at 2*s*. 6*d*.

Numbers iii and vii are collections of verse; the remaining numbers comprise seven plays, of which four (nos. ii, iv, v and vi) were written for the stage; one of these (no. v) was actually performed (11 Feb. 1843); for the circumstances, and consequences, of this disastrous episode, see *Oxford* iii 357–64. *Pippa Passes* and *Luria* were 'closet dramas'; there is some doubt about *A Soul's Tragedy*, which may have been intended for the stage when B. first conceived it, but was completed and published after B. had abandoned his theatrical ambitions.

None of the numbers went into a commercial second edition; for the technical 'second' edition of *A Blot in the 'Scutcheon* (no. v), see DeVane *Handbook* 136–7. After 1846 the remainder of the separate numbers were bound together and sold as a single volume. The *B & P* title was dropped in the two-volume *Poems* of 1849, and in subsequent collected editions.

Composition

The germ of the series first appears in a letter from B. to the publisher William Smith (7 April 1840, *Correspondence* iv 267):

> Sir,
>
>   Mr Moxon has just published a long Poem of mine, "Sordello", meant for a limited class of readers—and I am on the point of following it up by three new Dramas, written in a more popular style, and addressed to the Public at large:—a friend has called my notice to your handsome Reprints and suggested the proposal I am about to make. Would it answer your purpose to try the experiment of coming out with a *new* work as part of your series?—As in that case I will give you the 1ˢᵗ· Edition for nothing—for the sake of your large circulation among a body to which my works have little access at present. Of course I mean that these Dramas should form one publication, of the same size and at the same low price as your other pamphlets.

With this letter B. enclosed a torn-off leaf from *Sordello* containing the advertisement for the 'three new Dramas' he mentions, which were announced as 'nearly ready': *Pippa Pases, King Victor and King Charles* and *Mansoor the Hierophant* (later renamed *The Return of the Druses*). Note that at this stage B. is not thinking of a series but of a single volume; the emphasis is on the cheap format. The implication may be that Moxon, though he had advertised the works, was having second thoughts about publishing them, and that B. was looking elsewhere. On the other hand it is possible that Moxon himself recommended Smith, and this would partially confirm the traditional account of the genesis of the series, given, before B.'s letter to Smith was known, by Edmund Gosse (*Robert Browning: Personalia* [1890] 52–3, repr. Orr *Life* 112–13):

> One day, as the poet was discussing the matter with Mr. Edward Moxon, the publisher, the latter remarked that at that time he was bringing out some editions of the old Elizabethan dramatists in a comparatively cheap form, and that if Mr. Browning would consent to print his poems as pamphlets, using this cheap type, the expense would be very inconsiderable. The poet jumped at the idea, and it was agreed that each poem should form a separate brochure of just one sheet,—sixteen pages, in double columns,—the entire cost of which should not exceed twelve or fifteen pounds. In this fashion began the celebrated series of *Bells and Pomegranates . . . Pippa Passes* led the way, and was priced first at sixpence; then, the sale being inconsiderable, at a shilling, which greatly encouraged the sale; and so, slowly, up to half a crown, at which the price of each number finally rested.

If Moxon was indeed the 'friend' to whom B. attributes the proposal in his letter to Smith, then Gosse's account (based on conversations with B. in the year before his death) may conflate the two publishers; but it should be stressed that the 'friend' may be someone else, or an imaginary figure. Presumably Smith turned down the proposal, and B. eventually came to an agreement with Moxon himself, with the crucial added element of a *series* of pamphlets; Gosse's phrasing does not make clear whose idea this was. Moxon's list at this period includes reprints of editions of Ben Jonson (1838, price 16*s*.), Massinger and Ford (1840, 16*s*.) and Beaumont and Fletcher (2 vols, 1840, 32*s*.)—large volumes, which were indeed 'comparatively cheap', all in double columns, and using the same type and layout as for the pamphlets of *B & P*. Moxon's similar edition of Samuel Rogers's popular poem *Italy*, a work comparable in length to the early numbers of *B & P* and priced at 1*s. 6d.*, may also have contributed to the idea. The price of the later numbers of the series went up not just for the reason Gosse gives, but because the pamphlets themselves became longer: the final number was twice the length of the first. B.'s father paid for the publication of the whole series.

In the 'Advertisement' in *Pippa Passes*, which was intended as a preface to the whole series, B. wrote:

> Two or three years ago I wrote a play [*Strafford*, 1837], about which the chief matter I much care to recollect at present is, that a Pit-full of goodnatured people applauded it:—ever since, I have been desirous of doing something in the same way that should better reward their attention. What follows I mean for the first of a series of Dramatical Pieces, to come out at intervals, and I amuse myself by fancying that the cheap mode in which they appear will for once help me to a sort of Pit-audience again. Of course such a work must go on no longer than it is liked . . .

This makes it clear that B. had no definite plan for the series' length or contents, other than that it would consist of 'Dramatical Pieces'; he planned at one time to include a revised version of *Strafford* itself (letter to Alfred Domett of 22 May

1842, *Correspondence* v 357). Initially he seems to have interpreted the term 'Dramatical Pieces' to mean plays, whether written for the stage or not, and it was Moxon who persuaded him to stretch the phrase to cover the shorter poems of *Dramatic Lyrics*; B. agreed to this 'for popularity's sake', as he told Domett (*ibid.* 356), but felt the need to justify it by a brief 'Advertisement' at the start of the number:

> Such Poems as the following come properly enough, I suppose, under the head of "Dramatic Pieces;" being, though for the most part Lyric in expression, always Dramatic in principle, and so many utterances of so many imaginary persons, not mine.

It may seem odd that the impulse to publish a collection of shorter poems should come not from B. himself but from a third party, but the same thing happened some years later in the case of *Men and Women* (see below).

Reception

DeVane (*Handbook* 89–90) points out that all the pamphlets were published as 'By Robert Browning, Author of *Paracelsus*', and comments that 'the *Bells* show Browning beginning anew in his attempt to rebuild his literary reputation after the havoc which *Sordello* had made of his old one'. However, the title of the series itself caused general bewilderment and was felt to be entirely in keeping with B.'s esoteric difficulty. 'Mr. Browning's conundrums begin with his very title-page', wrote the reviewer of *Pippa Passes* in the *Athenaeum* (11 Dec. 1841, p. 952; repr. *Correspondence* v 399–400): '"Bells and Pomegranates" is the general title given (it is reasonable to suppose Mr. Browning knows why, but certainly we have not yet found out—indeed we "give it up")'. The title derives from *Exodus* xxviii 33–5, and concerns the making of the 'ephod' (tunic) of Aaron the High Priest:

> And beneath upon the hem of it thou shalt make pomegranates of blue, and of purple, and of scarlet, round about the hem thereof; and bells of gold between them round about: a golden bell and a pomegranate, a golden bell and a pomegranate, upon the hem of the robe round about. And it shall be upon Aaron to minister: and his sound shall be heard when he goeth in unto the holy place before the Lord, and when he cometh out, that he die not.

B. wrote to EBB. on 18 Oct. 1845: 'The Rabbis make Bells & Pomegranates symbolical of Pleasure and Profit, the Gay & the Grave, the Poetry & the Prose, Singing and Sermonising—Such a mixture of effects as in the original hour (that is quarter of an hour) of confidence & creation, I meant the whole should prove at last' (*Correspondence* xi 131). EBB. urged him, against his inclination, to make this explanation public:

> Dearest, I persist in thinking that you ought not to be too disdainful to explain your meaning in the Pomegranates. Surely you might say in a word or two that, your title having been doubted about (to your surprise, you *might* say!), you refer the doubters to the Jewish priest's robe, & the Rabbinical gloss . . . Consider that Mr. Kenyon & I may fairly represent the average intelligence of your readers,—& that *he* was altogether in the clouds as to your meaning . . . had not the most distant notion of it—while I, taking hold of the priest's garment, missed the Rabbins & the distinctive significance, as completely as he did. Then for Vasari, it is not the handbook of the whole world . . . Now why should you be too proud to teach such persons as only desire to be taught? I persist—I shall teaze you. (24 March 1846, *Correspondence* xii 173).

For the allusion to Vasari's *Lives of the Painters*, a favourite book of B.'s, see below; B. had presumably mentioned it in conversation with EBB. He deferred to her in a letter of 25 March 1846: 'I will at Ba's bidding amuse and instruct the world at large, and make them know all to be known—for my purposes—about Bells & Pomegranates—yes, it will be better' (*ibid.* 178). He placed a note between *Luria* and *A Soul's Tragedy* in the last number of the series:

> Here ends my first series of "Bells and Pomegranates:" and I take the opportunity of explaining, in reply to inquiries, that I only meant by that title to indicate an endeavour towards something like an alternation, or mixture, of music with discoursing, sound with sense, poetry with thought; which looks too ambitious, thus expressed, so the symbol was preferred. It is little to the purpose, that such is actually one of the most familiar of the many Rabbinical (and Patristic) acceptations of the phrase; because I confess that, letting authority alone, I supposed the bare words, in such juxtaposition, would sufficiently convey the desired meaning. "Faith and good works" is another fancy, for instance, and perhaps no easier to arrive at: yet Giotto placed a pomegranate fruit in the hand of Dante, and Raffaelle crowned his Theology (in the *Camera della Segnatura*) with blossoms of the same; as if the Bellari and Vasari would be sure to come after, and explain that it was merely "*simbolo delle buone opere—il qualo Pomo granato fu però usato nelle vesti del Pontefice appresso gli Ebrei*" [a symbol of good works—for this reason the pomegranate was used in the vestment of the High Priest among the Hebrews; our transl.].

B.'s intense reluctance to 'amuse and instruct the world at large' may account for his omitting to identify the actual biblical text from which the phrase comes, and for his concluding his forced explanation with an untranslated Italian quotation from Giovanni Pietro Bellori's [sic] *Descrizione delle immagini depinte de Raffaello d'Urbino* (1695); see Eleanor Cook, 'Browning's "Bellari"', *N & Q* xvii.9 (1970), pp. 334–5. Cp. his exasperated response to Ruskin's queries about the meanings of particular words or phrases in the poems of *M & W* (Appendix B, pp. 881–2). Even the placing of the note caused confusion: EBB. at first thought that it was meant to exclude *A Soul's Tragedy* from the series (13 April 1846, *Correspondence* xii 243), but B. denied this (14 April, *ibid.* 246).

Eventually *B & P* became part of the legend of B.'s early literary career, and the pamphlets themselves collectors' items; but its demise in collected editions went unremarked, and of its contents only *Pippa Passes* and the two collections of shorter poem have a secure place in the 'canon' of B.'s work. The juxtaposition of 'music with discoursing, sound with sense, poetry with thought' was replaced by the single, all-embracing opposition between 'fancy' and 'fact' in B.'s later work (see *A Likeness* 35–6n., p. 646). The impulse towards constructing larger structures of meaning for individual works can be seen in the 'structured collections' of the 1860s and beyond: on this subject see John Woolford, *Browning the Revisionary* (1988), chs 4–6.

(2) *Men and Women*[1]

Publication

M & W was published in two volumes by Chapman and Hall on 10 Nov. 1855, priced at 12 shillings (a little over a third of the price of a new three-volume

---

[1] Our tracing of the history of composition and publication of *M & W* has been greatly helped by William S. Peterson's article 'The Proofs of Browning's *Men and Women*' (*SBC* iii, no. 2 [Fall 1975], pp. 23–39), the first scholarly study of the document we refer to as *H proof*.

novel). The first American edition, printed from advance proofs, was published in one volume by Ticknor and Fields, Boston, on 8 Dec. 1855, but dated 1856 on the title page. The contents of the English edition were as follows:

Volume 1
Love Among the Ruins
A Lovers' Quarrel
Evelyn Hope
Up at a Villa—Down in the City
A Woman's Last Word
Fra Lippo Lippi
A Toccata of Galuppi's
By the Fire-Side
Any Wife to Any Husband
An Epistle containing the Strange Medical Experience of Karshish, the Arab Physician
Mesmerism
A Serenade at the Villa
My Star
Instans Tyrannus
A Pretty Woman
"Childe Roland to the Dark Tower came"
Respectability
A Light Woman
The Statue and the Bust
Love in a Life
Life in a Love
How It Strikes a Contemporary
The Last Ride Together
The Patriot
Master Hugues of Saxe-Gotha
Bishop Blougram's Apology
Memorabilia

Volume 2
Andrea del Sarto
Before
After
In Three Days
In a Year
Old Pictures in Florence
In a Balcony
Saul
"De Gustibus—"
Women and Roses
Protus
Holy-Cross Day
The Guardian-Angel
Cleon
The Twins
Popularity
The Heretic's Tragedy
Two in the Campagna
A Grammarian's Funeral

One Way of Love
Another Way of Love
"Transcendentalism:" A Poem in Twelve Books
Misconceptions
One Word More

In the *Poetical Works* of 1863, and subsequent collected editions, B. undertook a comprehensive re-ordering of the contents of his three collections of shorter poems, *Dramatic Lyrics* (1842), *Dramatic Romances and Lyrics* (1845) and *M & W*. The latter was reduced to 13 poems, not all of them from the original volume. For details of this re-ordering, see Appendix D, III 747–50.

The manuscripts
Only a few MSS survive from the period in which B. composed the poems of *M & W*, along with a few MSS from later periods, written as album contributions, or as dedications, or as printer's copy for volumes of selections. Some of the printer's copy for *M & W* would have been in the hand of the Brownings' close friend Isa Blagden, who acted as B.'s amanuensis in the spring and early summer of 1855 (see Appendix C, III 739). The most important surviving pre-publication MSS are those of *Love Among the Ruins*, *The Twins*, *One Word More* and *A Woman's Last Word*; there are also MSS for two poems written in the early 1850s but not published in *M & W*, *A Face* and *May and Death*. The status of the MS of *Love Among the Ruins* is a mystery: it is a fair copy, but not made for the printer; it has an alternative title, *Sicilian Pastoral*, but few other variants; and it carries no indication of date or of the occasion for which it was written. The MSS of *The Twins* and *One Word More* are printers' copies (*One Word More* has an alternative title, *A Last Word. To E. B. B.*); both were probably preserved by B. because of their association with EBB. The MS of *A Woman's Last Word* is in some ways the rarest of the four, since it represents, as Michael Meredith argues ('Foot Over the Threshold: Browning at Work', *BSN* xxvi [May 2000] 48–54) a genuine working draft. The MS is on a leaf torn from a notebook, and presented to Mrs Mary Ford on 18 March 1866. The draft of the poem is on the recto, 'neatly copied in two columns, presumably from RB's original rough working. This has been further worked on and a number of minor changes made' (Meredith, p. 49). The poem is untitled, and dated at the bottom 'Feb. 18'. The whole of the draft has subsequently been crossed through. As Meredith remarks, the MS 'provides evidence that RB used to copy out completed poems in a notebook, rework them at leisure, and then copy them out again for the printer . . . Once recopied, he would cross through the drafts in the notebook' (p. 51).

The proofs
The Huntington Library has two documents which record pre-publication readings. One is a set of bound proof-sheets (*H proof*) which B. presented to the painter Frederic Leighton, probably in late Oct. 1855, when he sent lists of corrections and revisions to the first edition to D. G. Rossetti in England and to Fields in America (Peterson, p. 33; see below, *Errata*). Several handwritten corrections in *H proof*, mainly in *Old Pictures in Florence*, correspond to the readings in these lists. The second document (*H proof²*) is a copy of the first edition of *M & W* (1855), with proof-readings written in by hand. The readings in *H proof²* may have been transcribed from *H proof*, but the evidence allows the possibility that they were transcribed from a different set of proofs, and we therefore record

variants from *H proof²* on the same basis as those from *H proof*. For a detailed discussion of the evidence, see Appendix C, III 742–3.

B.'s lists of 'errata'

The Brownings left for Paris on 17 Oct., before the final printing of *M & W*. B. was sent a final set of proofs (or something more in the nature of an advance copy), and noticed several errors, which he listed in letters to his American publisher James T. Fields and to Dante Gabriel Rossetti. These lists contain revisions as well as corrections, and we have emended our text only with regard to the latter. For details, see Appendix C, III 743–4.

Composition and date

B.'s first new publication after his marriage in September 1846 was *CE & ED*, begun in Nov. 1849 (though probably conceived earlier: see headnote, III 35–6) and published in April 1850. Up to this point he had written (at most) only a handful of shorter poems, and of these only *Guardian-Angel* (III 13) can be dated with certainty. His main effort had been backward-looking, namely the major revision of his earlier work which he undertook for the two-volume *Poems* of 1849. The intellectual and emotional ferment of *CE & ED* may be attributed to the influence of EBB., and may also have been a reaction to the death of B.'s mother in March 1849, which took place barely a week after the birth of his son. But after the burst of energy represented by *CE & ED*, B. seems to have written only sporadically for the next two years; we conjecture that the longest poem in *M & W*, *Bishop Blougram*, was begun in 1850–1 (again as the result of a strong stimulus, B.'s anger at the so-called 'Papal Aggression' of 1850: see headnote, pp. 279–81) but not completed until 1853–4. It seems clear that B. had, at this time, no plans to compile a volume of shorter poems along the lines of *Dramatic Lyrics* (1842) and *Dramatic Romances and Lyrics* (1845). Modern readers are used to thinking of these two volumes as containing some of B.'s most popular and enduring works (*My Last Duchess*, *The Pied Piper of Hamelin*, *Home-Thoughts, from Abroad*, *The Lost Leader*) and as having established B. as the master of a central Victorian poetic genre, the dramatic monologue; but contemporary criticism did not endorse this view. B.'s best-known, and still best-liked, work was *Paracelsus* (1835), followed by *Pippa Passes* (1841), and both works, though in different modes, were dramas rather than collections of dramatic monologues.

Encouragement to publish a volume of shorter poems came to B. from his friend Bryan Waller Procter (the poet 'Barry Cornwall'). In an unpublished letter of 5 Nov. 1851 (now at University of Iowa), Procter wrote to B., who was then in Paris:

> I should like to see a book of your lyrics—any book of yours indeed;—but lyrics (like your others) indicative of your different moods of thought & feeling—would draw less upon your time than any long elaborate poems—& might be quite as popular perhaps. They might be dotted down at once as the easy expression of your mood—one at a time. Twould amount to a book before you would be aware of it. (Here Mʳˢ. Browning joins me I know in urging you to this pleasant little task.)—How many things you will see where you are—how many things you *are* seeing now—how many dreams—everyone of which will suggest a poem to you.

Procter's idea of lyric poetry as 'the easy expression of [one's] mood' is almost comically alien to B., who satirized it in the late poem 'Touch him ne'er so lightly, into song he burst', the epilogue to *DI²* (1880), but the mention of 'popularity' may well have struck a chord. B. suffered from recurring fits of optimism about his chances of reaching a wider public; cp., e.g., his remarks about *Sordello* (see headnote, I 350) and in this volume see his preface to the *Bells and Pomegranates* series (p. 884), and headnote to *Popularity* (p. 446). To this motive may be added that of self-reproach for not being as productive as he had anticipated in his courtship of EBB., during which he had repeatedly declared that marriage would lead to a regeneration of his art: 'I look forward to a real life's work for us both: *I* shall do all,—under your eyes and with your hand in mine,—all I was intended to do' (6 Feb. 1846, *Correspondence* xii 45).

According to accounts which he gave late in life, B. decided in January 1853 that he had been 'rather lazy' and 'resolved [he] would write something every day'; he duly wrote *Women and Roses* (see headnote, III 235) and *Childe Roland* (p. 348), but then 'relapsed into [his] old desultory way'. But this latter statement seems not to correspond with an increasing rate of production in the winter and spring of 1853, which can be traced in a series of letters from EBB. In a letter of 15–17 Jan. she wrote to her sister Arabella: 'Robert & I are doing a little writing, & passing a happy tranquil time' (*EBB to Arabella* i 539); on 2 March: 'Robert's work is a collection of Lyrics in which he will assert himself as an original writer I dare say—there will be in them a good deal of Italian art . . . pictures, music. Both he & I mean to make a success if we can' (i 542); on 15 March she wrote to Mary Russell Mitford that B. was 'busy with another book' (*EBB to MRM* iii 381); on 30 April–1 May, to Arabella: 'Robert & I are very busy with our new books, & he has nearly enough lyrics to print he announced to me the other day' (i 575). On 11 June she anticipated publication in 1854: 'Depend on it Arabel, if we are alive & God suffers it, we shall be with you early in next year's summer. . . . We shall be in England as soon as the weather is mild enough, print-ing our books . . . that will be a business-necessity' (i 583). This last prediction was too optimistic: the Brownings did not in fact travel to England until the summer of 1855, and a considerable portion of *M & W* had not yet been written.

EBB.'s wording, especially in the letter of 2 March, confirms that B. had begun to think along the lines suggested by Procter, substituting for Procter's 'moods of thought & feeling' the dramatic representation of 'Italian art . . . pictures, music'. In a letter of 24 Feb. 1853 to his friend and admirer, the French critic Joseph Milsand, B. wrote: 'I am writing a sort of first step towards popularity—(for me!)— 'Lyrics,' with more music & painting than before, so as to get people to hear & see . . . something to follow, if I can compass it!' (first publ. in *Revue Germanique* xii [1921] 253; corr. text from *EBB to Arabella* i 542 n.34). As Scott Lewis points out, *A Toccata* (p. 367) and *Woman's Last Word* (III 273) date from this period; the latter poem reminds us that B.'s concentration on 'music & painting' was not exclusive, and indeed such poems make up a small, though important, part of the finished *M & W*. B.'s desire for commercial success is evident in a letter of 5 March 1853 to his publisher Edward Chapman, in which he mentions Helen Faucit's forthcoming production of his 1844 play *Colombe's Birthday* and adds: 'if there were to be any sort of success, it would help the poems to fetch up their lee-way, I suppose. Hadn't you better advertise? . . . Meantime, I shall give you something saleable one of these days—see if I don't' (*New Letters* 59).

Several poems can be assigned to the summer and early autumn of 1853, e.g. *In a Balcony* and *By the Fire-Side*, both associated with the Brownings' stay at Bagni di Lucca. On 10 Aug. EBB. wrote to H. F. Chorley: 'Robert is working at a volume of lyrics, of which I have seen but a few, and those seemed to me as fine as anything he has done' (*Letters of EBB* ii 131); the last phrase suggests that some of the longer poems in the volume had already been drafted. On 7 Oct. EBB. wrote to her brother George: 'We have been very happy here, & not idle either. Robert especially has done a great deal of work, & will have his volume ready for the spring without failure, he says' (*George Barrett* 200). The autumn of 1853 in Florence was 'disturbed' by 'too much coming and going even with agreeable people', EBB. wrote to B.'s sister Sarianna. 'There has been no time for work. In Rome it must be different, or we shall get on poorly with our books, I think. Robert seems, however, by his account, to be in an advanced state already' (*Letters of EBB* ii 144). The next major phase of productivity seems accordingly to have come in the winter of 1853–4, during the Brownings' stay in Rome: *An Epistle, Love Among the Ruins, Holy-Cross Day, Two in the Campagna* and *Cleon* are among the poems likely to date from this period, at least in their conception; B. wrote to William Wetmore Story on 11 June 1854, after his return to Florence: 'I am trying to make up for wasted time in Rome and setting my poetical house in order' (cited in Henry James, *William Wetmore Story and His Friends* [Boston 1903] i 288). A week earlier he had written to John Forster in terms which strongly suggest that this process was already well under way: 'I must be in London, or Paris at farthest, to print my poems. . . . This is what I have written—only a number of poems of all sorts and sizes and styles and subjects— not written before last year, but the beginning of an expressing the spirit of all the fruits of the years since I last turned the winch of the wine press. The manner will be newer than the matter. I hope to be listened to, this time, and I am glad I have been made to wait this not very long while' (*New Letters* 77). By late summer of 1854 the collection had grown sufficiently for B. to write to the American publisher James T. Fields: 'I expect to bring out in London, next season, a collection of new Poems, containing about 5000 lines' (24 Aug. 1854, publ. *Century Illustrated Monthly Magazine* lxxxiv [May–Oct. 1912] 130). Since *M & W* contains a little over 7,000 lines, the implication is that more poems were added between this date and the spring of 1855, when the contents of *M & W* were more or less finalized. On 10 Jan. 1855 EBB. wrote to Arabella: 'Robert & I do work every day—he has a large volume of short poems which will be completed by the spring' (*EBB to Arabella* ii 125), and on 15 May: 'Robert has six thousand lines written out clear, & the rest nearly ready' (ii 143). The phrase 'written out clear' suggests that B. was by now engaged in making fair copies from his drafts, not writing new poems, though this process probably involved a good deal of revising. The Brownings arrived in England in July 1855, and *M & W* was in proof by 6 Sept., when B. wrote to Fields: 'I find that my poems are grown so considerably as to fill *two* books, *not* one. The first is before me, in the same type & form as [Tennyson's] "Maud" [publ. July 1855], but with 260 pages instead of 154: and two thirds of the second volume are printed—(it will extend to the same number of pages.) [. . .] These poems, too are *all new entirely*—unpublished I mean. They are the best of me, hitherto and for some time to come probably—and I have given my whole mind to the correcting & facilitating' (*B to Fields* 28). A letter from EBB. to Arabella of 10 Sept. 1855 makes it clear that she helped B. with the proofreading of the volume (*EBB to Arabella* ii 170). The whole of *M & W* had been set up in type by 1 Oct., when B. sent proofs of 'the last of the second volume' to his and EBB.'s close friend and financial supporter John Kenyon (MS at Harvard University). In this letter B. repeated that he had 'gone over the preceding portion of the two volumes perhaps half a dozen times or more very carefully, making minute improvements which "tell" on the general effect'. He told Kenyon that he had adopted several of his suggestions with regard to *Saul* (see l. 37n., III 498), and it is likely that other readers made suggestions which affected the text: proofs were sent to Forster, to B.'s 'literary father' W. J. Fox (for whom see *Correspondence* iii 313–14), to a more recent friend, the young

Robert Bulwer Lytton, and to Milsand. On 3 Oct. EBB. wrote to Arabella:
'We have just despatched Robert's last proof. I am most sanguine about the
work, believing in it, I for one' (*EBB to Arabella* ii 178). *M & W* was published
on 10 Nov.

Reception
B. had high hopes of *M & W*; he was buoyed up not just by EBB.'s praise but
by the all-but-unanimous opinion of those friends to whom he showed the
collection in proof (see above, *Composition*). The one dissenting voice was that
of Kenyon, who, while greatly admiring *Saul*, regretted the preponderance of
'dramatic' poetry in the volume (Kenyon's reverence for Wordsworth, who had
been a friend of his for many years, may have played a part in this reaction).
B.'s respect and affection for Kenyon did not prevent him from rebutting his
criticism and from expressing optimism about the prospects for *M & W*:

> In your remarks on the little or no pleasure you derive from dramatic—in
> comparison with lyric—poetry (understanding the vulgar or more obvious form
> of drama,—scene & dialogue,—for lyrics may be dramatic also in the highest
> sense)—I partake your feeling to a great degree: lyric is the oldest, most natural,
> most *poetical* of poetry, and I would always get it if I could: but I find in these
> latter days that one has a great deal to say, and try and get attended to, which
> is out of the lyrical element and capability—and I am forced to take the nearest
> way to it: and then it is undeniable that the common reader is susceptible to
> plot, story, and the simplest form of putting a matter "Said I," "Said He" &
> so on. "The whole is with the Gods" as Cleon sums up in one of the things
> I send you. Well, dear Mr Kenyon, of this you are sure, I hope and believe,—
> that I have done my very best, with whatever effect and acceptance: and
> I really believed, like a goose, that this time I should get your white ball in my
> urn,—it was not to be! But why should not I tell you, what will give you the
> pleasure you would give me were it in your power—that Fox and Forster,—
> and I will associate with them Lytton, young as he is,—these three and your-
> self being my sole referees hitherto, with one exception,—well, these three
> take one's breath away with their—not sympathy merely—but anticipations of
> success—of "a sale" in short: and Chapman, shrewd as he is, makes no scruple
> of declaring that he expects the same. My exception—my fourth critic is the
> fine fellow of the Revue des Deux Mondes—who writes of the first volume
> (to me) "il y a là du colossal!". I put all this down impudently on paper to
> please you, as I say—for I know whether you will grieve or no to find your
> dark auguries met by some blue bits in various parts of my poor horizon. So
> I leave it till another month [to] justify one or the other prophecy. (Harvard
> MS; the 'fine fellow of the Revue des Deux Mondes' is Joseph Milsand, whose
> opinion may be translated as 'there's tremendous stuff in there!')

In the light of this and other such expressions of confidence, it is not hard to see
how dismayed B. must have been by the reception of *M & W* in England. He
saw the English newspapers and magazines at Galignani's Reading Room in Paris;
on 5 Dec. he wrote to Chapman that he had seen a few, 'the *Examiner* being
the best,—as for the worst, there's no saying *that*. The serious notices are to come,
it is to be hoped. How this style of thing helps or hinders the *sale*, is what you
must counsel me about' (*New Letters* 84). By 'this style of thing' B. presumably
meant reviews such as the one in *The Saturday Review* (24 Nov. 1855, i 69–70):
'It is really high time that this sort of thing should, if possible, be stopped. Here
is another book of madness and mysticism—another melancholy specimen of power

wantonly wasted, and talent deliberately perverted—another act of self-prostration before that demon of bad taste who now seems to hold in absolute possession the fashionable masters of our ideal literature' (repr. *Critical Heritage* 158; the conjectural attribution of this review to B.'s friend Joseph Arnould may be confidently dismissed). The review in *The Athenæum* (17 Nov., pp. 1327–8), with one of whose editors, H. F. Chorley, both B. and EBB. had been on friendly terms in the 1840s, takes a similar line, a little less intemperately: 'Who will not grieve over energy wasted and power misspent,—over fancies chaste and noble, so overhung by the "seven veils" of obscurity, that we can oftentimes be only sure that fancies exist?' (*Critical Heritage* 155). EBB. was indignant: 'The Athenaeum has treated us very shabbily, and, if M^r. Chorley wrote that article—shame on him for it!' (22 Nov. 1855, *EBB to Arabella* ii 190; the review was indeed by Chorley). On 17 Dec. B. wrote again to Chapman: 'don't take to heart the zoological utterances I have stopped my ears against at Galignani's of late. "Whoo-oo-oo-oo" mouths the big monkey—"Whee-ee-ee-ee" squeaks the little monkey and such a dig with the end of my umbrella as I should give the brutes if I couldn't keep my temper, and consider how they miss their nut[s] and gingerbread!' (*New Letters* 85). Further 'zoological utterances' arrived in January 1856 in the shape of *Fraser's Magazine* (liii 105–6): 'genius unfaithful to its trust . . . what might have been a beautiful garden is but a wilderness overgrown with a rank and riotous vegetation . . . strong natural powers weakened by self-indulgence, by caprice, by hankering after originality, by all the mental vices which are but so many names of vanity and self-seeking' (*Critical Heritage* 165). January also brought more thoughtful and discriminating judgments by George Eliot in *The Westminster Review* (lxv 290–6) and by David Masson in *The British Quarterly Review* (xxiii 151–80), but they were not sufficient to stem the tide. Sales of the book, initially promising, rapidly tailed off. In America reviews and sales were both more positive, but B. earned nothing in royalties from the sales and it is clear that popularity abroad could not console him for rejection at home. He wrote nothing of substance for several years, and EBB. became alarmed at his apparent indifference to poetry; only towards the end of the 1850s (and the end of EBB.'s life) are there signs of a creative revival. Several of the major long poems of *Dramatis Personae* (1864) have their roots in this latter period, notably *Caliban upon Setebos*.

One particular response to *M & W* in the months after its publication deserves special mention, both because it provoked B. to an articulate and sustained defence of his poetics, and because it exposed the extent of his frustration and anger at the incomprehension of his readers, even those who professed to admire him. In Dec. 1855 he received a long letter from Ruskin, criticizing *M & W* wholesale and in detail; the centrepiece was a sustained (and sharply satirical) close reading of *Popularity* (p. 446 in this volume), a poem which, as Ruskin put it, 'touches the matter in hand'. Ruskin's letter, and B.'s equally eloquent reply to it, are printed in Appendix B.

By the spring of 1856 B. had turned his attention to negotiating terms for a new edition of EBB.'s collected poems, and her forthcoming 'novel-poem' *Aurora Leigh*; at the end of a long letter to Chapman on this subject he remarked: 'As to my own Poems—they must be left to Providence and that fine sense of discrimination which I never cease to meditate upon and admire in the public: they cry out for new things and when you furnish them with what they cried for, "it's *so* new," they grunt. The half-dozen people who know and could impose their opinions on the whole sty of grunters say nothing to *them* (I don't wonder) and speak so low in my own ear that it's lost to all intents and purposes' (*New Letters* 92–3). B. implies that influential friends such as D. G. Rossetti, Ruskin and Carlyle might have been more active in their public support; his sense of being an exile from literary London is at its sharpest in such comments. He could not, of course, appreciate that the tide of his reputation had begun to turn, and that the passionate enthusiasm of Rossetti and his circle, though it could not yet affect his wider public image, or increase his sales to match those of his wife, foretold the fame he achieved in the 1860s. B. was never to reach the popularity of Tennyson, and remained in many ways an acquired taste for the 'British Public, ye who like me not', as he addressed them in *Ring* (i 410); but as his reputation grew, the poems of *M & W* became, and have continued to be, its cornerstone.

(3) *Dramatis Personae*

Publication

DP was published on Saturday 28 May 1864 in London by Chapman and Hall, and simultaneously in Boston by Ticknor & Fields (from advance proofs supplied by B.). There are minimal differences between the 1st British and American editions. The volume had no dedication or preface and consisted of the following poems:

James Lee
    i   At the Window
    ii   By the Fireside
    iii In the Doorway
    iv Along the Beach
    v   On the Cliff
    vi Under the Cliff
    vii Among the Rocks
    viii Beside the Drawing-Board
    ix On Deck
Gold Hair
The Worst of It
Dîs Aliter Visum; or, Le Byron de nos Jours
Too Late
Abt Vogler
Rabbi Ben Ezra
A Death in the Desert
Caliban upon Setebos: or, Natural Theology in the Island
Confessions
May and Death
Prospice
Youth and Art
A Face
A Likeness
Mr. Sludge, "the Medium"
Apparent Failure
Epilogue

B., against his usual practice, gave Ticknor & Fields permission to publish some of the poems in their journal the *Atlantic Monthly*; in a letter to James T. Fields of 16 Oct. 1863, he wrote: 'With respect to your offer of "£60 for the sheets of my new volume, one month in advance of publication,—or £100 for the additional right of printing one or two of the pieces (not printed elsewhere) in your magazine"—I accept it' (Houghton Library MS; cited in Gertrude Reece Hudson, *Robert Browning's Literary Life* [Austin, Tx: 1982], p. 413). *Gold Hair* appeared in the issue for May 1864 (vol. xiii, pp. 596–8), and *Prospice* and *Under the Cliff* (section vi of *James Lee*) in the June issue (xiii 694, 737). There is no evidence to suggest that B. had any say in which poems were chosen. *James Lee* incorporates two previously-written poems, one of which had been published many years earlier: see headnote, p. 665.

A second (British) edition was issued in September 1864, the first time this had happened in B.'s career. The copy of the first edition used by B. in preparing this second edition is now in the Tinker Library at Yale. The only notable change was the addition of three stanzas to *Gold Hair*, in response to a comment by George Eliot. In the *Poetical Works* of 1868, *DP* was included in vol. VI, following *In a Balcony*, and contained two additional short poems, inserted on either side of *Prospice*: *Deaf and Dumb; a Group by Woolner* and *Eurydice to Orpheus; a Picture by Leighton*. The title of *James Lee* was altered to *James Lee's Wife*. In the *Poetical Works* of 1888 *DP* was included in vol. VII, again following *In a Balcony*.

Manuscript and proofs

DP marks a watershed in the textual history of B.'s poems, since from this point on we have all the printer's-copy manuscripts for his individual volumes. Moreover, unlike the MS of *CE & ED* and the (lost) MSS of *M & W*, the *DP* MS is all in B.'s hand. The MS, consisting of bound pages written on one side only, is at *Morgan* (M.A.33). With some notable exceptions, it is a fairly clean fair copy of the poems in the order they appeared in the volume. Up to the end of *Mr. Sludge, "the Medium"*, the pages of the MS are numbered in pencil and the poems are also numbered in order of appearance; the last eleven pages, containing *Apparent Failure* and *Epilogue*, are separately numbered in ink and the poems themselves carry no number, suggesting that they were added to the volume at a late stage. Two poems contain substantial evidence of drafting and revision, *Caliban upon Setebos* and *Mr. Sludge*: the state of the latter in particular suggests that it may have undergone some redrafting while the volume was in press (see headnote, p. 771).

B. gave his sister Sarianna a set of proofs with some corrections in his hand, now in the Tinker Library at Yale, and another set to Moncure D. Conway, also with a few corrections, for use in preparing a review, now in the Berg Collection at the New York Public Library. As *Ohio* notes, these proofs are identical except that the Yale set bears the date 'London, April 12, 1864' at the end, and they represent a very late stage of the text: there are no significant variants with *1864*. We cite only B.'s autograph corrections in our notes (*1864 proof*).

Composition and date

The critical and commercial failure of *M & W* plunged B. into a depression from which he began to recover only towards the end of the 1850s. He told Isa Blagden in a letter of 1 Aug. 1857—after perpetrating a three-line skit on her name—that he had 'begun to write poetry again' (*Dearest Isa* 3; see also our edition, III 703), but the one serious poem that can be dated to this period, *Study of a Hand, by Lionardo*, is a by-product of activities (drawing and clay-modelling) which B. took up as alternatives to writing (see headnote, III 701). It was not until the winter of 1859–60 that he engaged in a sustained bout of composition: in a letter of 18 May 1860 to Fanny Haworth, EBB. reported that during the winter he had been 'working at a long poem which I have not seen a line of, and producing short lyrics which I *have* seen, and may declare worthy of him' (*Letters of EBB* ii 388).

B. showed some of these shorter poems to Isa Blagden at Siena in the late summer of 1860 (*Dearest Isa* 176, 180) but we have not been able to identify them with any certainty. We can discount *A Face* (an album-poem from 1852: see headnote, III 230), *May and Death* (publ. in *The Keepsake* for 1857; see headnote, III 361), and the three poems inspired by B.'s trips to Brittany after EBB.'s death: *James Lee*, *Gold Hair* and *Dîs Aliter Visum*. For the rest, conjecture may point in different directions. DeVane, for example, mentions 'such pieces as *Confessions*, *Youth and Art*, *Too Late*, *A Likeness* and *The Worst of It*' (*Handbook* 281), but the first two are just as likely to have been the product of B.'s return to England and his renewed contact with British social and intellectual life, and the third, which concerns the death of a woman married to a poet who is accused of 'tagging [her] epitaph', hardly seems a tactful choice of subject for B. in 1860. Nor is there any indication as to how far he got with the 'long poem'. He seems to have made little or no progress in the months that followed: writing from Rome in March 1861 to B.'s sister Sarianna, EBB. attempted to explain this lack of productivity. B. was 'peculiar in his ways of work as a poet' and would not (unlike Tennyson, she noted) put in regular hours of work; he 'waits for an inclination—works by fits and starts—he can't do otherwise he says. . . . I wanted his poems done this winter very much—and here was a bright room with three windows consecrated to use. But he had a room all last summer, and did nothing. Then, he worked himself out by riding for three or four hours together—there has been little done since last winter, when he did much. He was not inclined to write this winter. . . . He has the material for a volume, and will work at it this summer, he says' (*Letters of EBB* ii 434–6). But B. was not able to fulfil this pledge.

EBB. died in Florence on 29 June 1861. B.'s decision to leave Italy was immediate: he announced it to his sister in the letter he wrote to her the following day (*LH* 62). He arrived in London on 27 September. His immediate concern was with his son Pen's education; his first professional business was the preparation of EBB.'s *Last Poems*, published in March 1862. As far as his own work was concerned, his friends John Forster and B. W. Procter were compiling a volume of *Selections from the Poetical Works* published by Chapman and Hall in November 1862 (with the date 1863), and though the choice of poems was theirs, he made some revisions and corrections to the text; he also carried out more extensive revisions for the three-volume *Poetical Works* of 1863. He probably wrote *James Lee* in Brittany in August 1862 (see headnote, p. 665), and possibly also *Gold Hair*, and these would have joined the group of shorter poems he had already drafted in 1860; but the date of composition of the longer poems in *DP*—*Caliban upon Setebos*, *A Death in the Desert*, and *Mr. Sludge*, *'the Medium'*—is uncertain. One of these must be the 'long poem' he was working on in the winter of 1859–60 and which EBB. had not seen; the likeliest candidate, in our view, is *Caliban*, but it is not known when B. completed it. He probably continued to work on the volume in London in the autumn of 1862; he told Isa Blagden on 19 Dec. 1862 that it would be published in the spring of 1863 (*Dearest Isa* 142). In a letter to the Storys of 5 March 1863, however, he announced a delay, which he attributed to the slow progress being made with the printing of the *Poetical Works*: 'I shall not be able to bring out the new book till Autumn: wanting to draw a distinct line between past & present' (*American Friends* 118). Then, in a letter to Isa Blagden of 19 November 1863, he gave a different reason for delay: he wrote that he would soon 'go to press' with the new poems (i.e. have them set up in type) but that publication would be deferred to the spring of 1864: 'we wait, because there is some success attending the complete edition, and we let it work' (*Dearest Isa* 180); he told Mrs Story the same thing a week later (*American Friends* 136).

This commercial tactic seems to have been suggested by Frederick Chapman, B.'s publisher. On the whole we think it unlikely that the volume as it stands was ready to appear in the spring of 1863 (in particular, there are strong indications that *Mr. Sludge* was written, or substantially revised, in the spring and summer of that year: see headnote, p. 771). However, it seems probable that with the exception of the *Epilogue*, the volume was ready by November 1863. This does not mean, of course, that B. made no changes between then and the date of publication: he thought of the first typesetting of his work as a necessary stage of composition (see Karlin and Woolford, *Robert Browning*, p. 27).

In a letter to Isa Blagden of 18 Oct. 1862, B. referred to the volume as 'a new book of "Men and Women" (or . . . some such name)' (*Dearest Isa* 128). To the Storys he specified that the reason for choosing an alternative title would be 'to please the publisher' (5 Sept. 1863, *American Friends* 130).

Reception

The fact that a second edition of *DP* appeared in the same year as the first suggests that the tide of B.'s popularity had turned. DeVane (*Handbook* 283) argues that *M & W* 'had been slowly making an impression upon the British public', and that both the *Poetical Works* of 1863 and the *Selections* edited by Forster and Procter helped B. 'to be recognized for the force he was'. In this light, Chapman's tactic of delaying the appearance of *DP* until these editions had made their way seems shrewd, though B. was angered by an article (by William Stigand) in the *Edinburgh Review* in October 1864 (repr. *CH* 230–60) which subsumed its critique of *DP* in a hostile survey of his whole career: as he put it to Julia Wedgwood: 'The clever creature rummages over my wardrobe of thirty years' accumulation, strips every old coat of its queer button or odd tag and tassel, then holds them out, "So Mr. B. goes dressed now!"—of the cut of the coats, not a word' (*RB & JW* 103). However, this article was not a sign of the times; in January 1865 the *Edinburgh* was itself attacked in the *Saturday Review* (repr. *CH* 262–70) not just for criticizing B., but for doing so in a dated tone of captious sarcasm. John Woolford ('Periodicals and the Practice of Literary Criticism, 1855–64', in *The Victorian Periodical Press: Samplings and Soundings*, ed. J. Shattock and M. Wolff, Leicester University Press 1982) suggests that this controversy signalled a sea-change in the style of periodical literary criticism from which B. was to benefit for the remainder of his career.

B.'s return to England, and his greater visibility in the social and intellectual life of the capital, undoubtedly contributed to his rehabilitation, *pace* his own view of the matter, expressed in a letter to Isa Blagden of 19 Aug. 1865:

I suppose that what you call "my fame within these four years" comes from a little of this gossiping and going out, and showing myself to be alive: and so indeed some folks say—but I hardly think it: for remember I was uninterruptedly (almost) in London from the time I published Paracelsus—till I ended that string of plays with Luria: and I used to go out then, and see far more of merely literary people, critics &c—than I do now,—but what came of it? There were always a few people who had a certain opinion of my poems, but nobody cared to speak what he thought, or the things printed twenty five years ago would not have waited so long for a good word—but at last a new set of men arrive who don't mind the conventionalities of ignoring one and seeing everything in another: Chapman says, "The orders come from Oxford and Cambridge", and all my new cultivators are young men: more than that, I observe that some of my old friends don't like at all the irruption of *outsiders* who rescue me from their sober and private approval and take those words out of their mouths "which they always meant to say", and never *did*. When there gets to be a general feeling of this kind, that there must be *something* in the works of an author, the reviews are obliged to notice him, such notice as it is: but what poor work, even when doing its best! (*Dearest Isa* 219–20)

The phrase 'ignoring one and seeing everything in another' almost certainly alludes to Tennyson, whose *Enoch Arden and Other Poems* was published in the same year as *DP*. B.'s acknowledgment of success is still marked by a sense of injury and resentment, vividly conveyed in his sardonic dig at his 'old friends'.

Index of Titles and First Lines